Cowan Microbiology
A SYSTEMS APPROACH
THIRD EDITION

LearnSmart

McGraw-Hill LearnSmart™ is an adaptive diagnostic tool, powered by Connect Microbiology. LearnSmart is based on artificial intelligence and constantly assesses a student's knowledge of the course material. Sophisticated diagnostics adapt to each student's individual knowledge base in order to match and improve what they know. Students actively learn the required concepts more easily and efficiently.

Learn more at www.mhlearnsmart.com.

McGraw-Hill Higher Education and Blackboard® have teamed up! What does this mean for you?

Do More

Your life, simplified. Now you and your students can access McGraw-Hill's Connect and Create™ right from within your Blackboard course—all with one single sign-on! Say goodbye to the days of logging in to multiple applications.

Deep integration of content and tools. Not only do you get single sign-on with Connect and Create, you also get deep integration of McGraw-Hill content and content engines right in Blackboard. Whether you're choosing a book for your course or building Connect assignments, all the tools you need are right where you want them—inside of Blackboard.

Seamless gradebooks. Are you tired of keeping multiple gradebooks and manually synchronizing grades into Blackboard? We thought so. When a student completes an integrated Connect assignment, the grade for that assignment automatically (and instantly) feeds your Blackboard grade center.

A solution for everyone. Whether your institution is already using Blackboard or you just want to try Blackboard on your own, we have a solution for you. McGraw-Hill and Blackboard can now offer you easy access to industry leading technology and content, whether your campus hosts it, or we do. Be sure to ask your local McGraw-Hill representative for details.

THIRD EDITION

Microbiology

A SYSTEMS APPROACH

Marjorie Kelly Cowan

Miami University

McGraw Hill

Connect
Learn
Succeed™

MICROBIOLOGY: A SYSTEMS APPROACH, THIRD EDITION

Published by McGraw-Hill, a business unit of The McGraw-Hill Companies, Inc., 1221 Avenue of the Americas, New York, NY 10020. Copyright © 2012 by The McGraw-Hill Companies, Inc. All rights reserved. Previous editions © 2009 and 2006. No part of this publication may be reproduced or distributed in any form or by any means, or stored in a database or retrieval system, without the prior written consent of The McGraw-Hill Companies, Inc., including, but not limited to, in any network or other electronic storage or transmission, or broadcast for distance learning.

Some ancillaries, including electronic and print components, may not be available to customers outside the United States.

This book is printed on acid-free paper.

Printed in the United States of America.

2 3 4 5 6 7 8 9 0 QDB/QDB 1 0 9 8 7 6 5 4 3 2

ISBN 978–0–07–352252–4
MHID 0–07–352252–X

Vice President, Editor-in-Chief: *Marty Lange*
Vice President, EDP: *Kimberly Meriwether David*
Senior Director of Development: *Kristine Tibbetts*
Sponsoring Editor: *Lynn M. Breithaupt*
Senior Developmental Editor: *Kathleen R. Loewenberg*
Marketing Manager: *Amy L. Reed*
Lead Project Manager: *Sheila M. Frank*
Senior Buyer: *Laura Fuller*
Senior Media Project Manager: *Jodi K. Banowetz*
Senior Designer: *Laurie B. Janssen*
Cover Image: *Dr. Volker Brinkmann/Visuals Unlimited, Inc.*
Senior Photo Research Coordinator: *John C. Leland*
Photo Research: *Emily Tietz/Editorial Image, LLC*
Compositor: *Electronic Publishing Services Inc., NYC*
Typeface: *10/12 Palatino LT Std*
Printer: *Quad/Graphics*

All credits appearing on page or at the end of the book are considered to be an extension of the copyright page.

Library of Congress Cataloging-in-Publication Data

Cowan, M. Kelly.
    Microbiology : a systems approach / Marjorie Kelly Cowan. — 3rd ed.
        p.   cm.
    Includes index.
    ISBN 978–0–07–352252–4 — ISBN 0–07–352252–X (hard copy : alk. paper)   1. Microbiology.   I. Title.
    QR41.2.C69 2012
    616.9′041 — dc22
                                        2010037851

Brief Contents

About the Authors

Kelly Cowan has been a microbiologist at Miami University since 1993. She received her Ph.D. at the University of Louisville, and later worked at the University of Maryland Center of Marine Biotechnology and the University of Groningen in The Netherlands. Kelly has published (with her students) twenty-four research articles stemming from her work on bacterial adhesion mechanisms and plant-derived antimicrobial compounds. But her first love is teaching—both doing it and studying how to do it better. She is chair of the Undergraduate Education Committee of the American Society for Microbiology (ASM). When she is not teaching or writing, Kelly hikes, reads, takes scuba lessons, and still tries to (s)mother her three grown kids.

The addition of a *proven* educator as a digital author makes a *proven* learning system even better.

Writing a textbook takes an enormous amount of time and effort. No textbook author has the time to write a great textbook and also write an entire book's worth of accompanying digital learning tools—at least not with any amount of success or accuracy. In the past this material has often been built after the text publishes, but hopefully in time for classes to start! With the new digital era upon us, it is time to begin thinking of digital tools differently. In classrooms across the country thousands of students who are visual learners and have been using computers, video games, smartphones, music players, and a variety of other gadgets since they could talk are begging for an interactive way to learn their course material. Enter the digital author. With this third edition, we are so excited to add professor **Jennifer Herzog** from Herkimer County Community College to the team. Jen has worked hand-in-hand with the textbook author, creating online tools that truly complement and enhance the book's content. She ensured that all key topics in the book have interactive, engaging activities spanning levels of Bloom's taxonomy, and tied to Learning Outcomes in the book. Instructors can now assign material based on what they cover in class, assess their students on the Learning Outcomes, and run reports indicating individual and/or class performance on a variety of data. Because of Jen, we can now offer you a robust digital learning program, tied to Learning Outcomes, to enhance your lecture and lab, whether you run a traditional, hybrid, or fully online course.

Students:

Welcome to the microbial world! I think you will find it fascinating to understand how microbes interact with us, and with our environment. The interesting thing is that each of you has already had a lot of experience with microbiology. For one thing, you are thoroughly populated with microbes right now, and much of your own genetic material actually came from viruses and other microbes. And while you have probably had some bad experiences with quite a few microbes, in the form of diseases, you have certainly been greatly benefited by them as well.

This book is suited for all kinds of students and doesn't require any prerequisite knowledge of biology or chemistry. If you are interested in entering the health care profession in some way, this book will give you a strong background in the biology of microorganisms, without overwhelming you with unnecessary details. Don't worry if you're not in the health professions. A grasp of this topic is important for everyone—and can be attained with this book.

This has been called the Age of Biology. The 20th century was often thought of as the Age of Physics, with the development of quantum theories and the theory of relativity. The Human Genome Project is just the most visible sign of the Biology Age; in the 21st century we have an unprecedented understanding of genes and DNA, and a new respect for the beauty and power of microorganisms. This book can give you the tools you'll need to read about and interpret new biological discoveries in the years ahead.

—Kelly Cowan

I dedicate this book to all public health workers who devote their lives to bringing the advances and medicines enjoyed by the industrialized world to *all* humans.

Connecting Instructors to Students

McGraw-Hill Higher Education and Blackboard® have teamed up! What does this mean for you?

Do More

Your life, simplified.   Now you and your students can access McGraw-Hill Connect™ and Create™ right from within your Blackboard course—all with one single sign on! Say goodbye to the days of logging in to multiple applications.

Deep integration of content and tools.   Not only do you get single sign on with Connect and Create, you also get deep integration of McGraw-Hill content and content engines right in Blackboard. Whether you're choosing a book for your course or building Connect assignments, all the tools you need are right where you want them—inside of Blackboard.

Seamless gradebooks.   Are you tired of keeping multiple gradebooks and manually synchronizing grades into Blackboard? We thought so. When a student completes an integrated Connect assignment, the grade for that assignment automatically (and instantly) feeds your Blackboard grade center.

A solution for everyone.   Whether your institution is already using Blackboard or you just want to try Blackboard on your own, we have a solution for you. McGraw-Hill and Blackboard can now offer you easy access to industry leading technology and content, whether your campus hosts it, or we do. Be sure to ask your local McGraw-Hill representative for details.

Author Kelly Cowan is now on Twitter!   She shares interesting facts, breaking news in microbiology, teaching hints and tips, and more. If you have a Twitter account, follow her: **@CowanMicro**. To set up a Twitter account, go to twitter.com.

Introducing McGraw-Hill ConnectPlus™ Microbiology

McGraw-Hill ConnectPlus™ Microbiology integrated learning platform provides auto-graded assessments; a customizable, assignable eBook; an adaptive diagnostic tool; and powerful reporting against Learning Outcomes and level of difficulty—all in an easy-to-use interface. Connect Microbiology is specific to your book and can be completely customized to your course and specific Learning Outcomes, so you help your students connect to just the material they need to know.

Save time with auto-graded assessments and tutorials.

Fully editable, customizable, auto-graded interactive assignments using high-quality art from the textbook, animations, and videos from a variety of sources take you way beyond multiple choice. Assignable content is available for every Learning Outcome in the book. Extremely high-quality content, created by digital author Jennifer Herzog, includes case study modules, concept mapping activities, animated learning modules, and more!

"... I and my adjuncts have reduced the time we spend on grading by 90 percent and student test scores have risen, on average, 10 points since we began using Connect!"

—William Hoover, Bunker Hill Community College

Gather assessment information

Generate powerful data related to student performance against Learning Outcomes, specific topics, level of difficulty, and more.

INSTRUCTORS
Connect *via Customization*

Presentation Tools
allow you to customize your lectures.

Enhanced Lecture Presentations contain lecture outlines, Flex Art, art, photos, tables, and animations embedded where appropriate. Fully customizable, but complete and ready to use, these presentations will enable you to spend less time preparing for lecture!

Flex Art   Fully editable (labels and leaders) line art from the text, with key figures that can be manipulated. Take the images apart and put them back together again during lecture so students can understand one step at a time.

Animations   Over 100 animations bringing key concepts to life, available for instructors and students.

Animation PPTs   Animations are truly embedded in PowerPoint® for ultimate ease of use! Just copy and paste into your custom slideshow and you're done!

Take your course online—*easily*—
with one-click Digital Lecture Capture.

McGraw-Hill Tegrity Campus™ records and distributes your lectures with just a click of a button. Students can view them anytime/anywhere via computer, iPod, or mobile device. Tegrity Campus indexes as it records your slideshow presentations, and anything shown on your computer, so **students can use keywords to find exactly what they want to study.**

Connect *24/7 with Personalized Learning Plans*

Access content anywhere, any time, with a customizable, interactive eBook.

McGraw-Hill ConnectPlus eBook takes digital texts beyond a simple PDF. With the same content as the printed book, but optimized for the screen, ConnectPlus has embedded media, including animations and videos, which bring concepts to life and provide "just in time" learning for students. Additionally, fully integrated, self-study questions and in-line assessments allow students to interact with the questions in the text and determine if they're gaining mastery of the content. These questions can also be assigned by the instructor.

> "Use of technology, especially LEARNSMART, assisted greatly in keeping on track and keeping up with the material."
>
> —student, Triton College

McGraw-Hill LearnSmart™ A Diagnostic, Adaptive Learning System

McGraw-Hill LearnSmart is an adaptive diagnostic tool, powered by Connect Microbiology, which is based on artificial intelligence and constantly assesses a student's knowledge of the course material.

Sophisticated diagnostics adapt to each student's individual knowledge base in order to match and improve what they know. Students actively learn the required concepts more easily and efficiently.

> "I love LearnSmart. Without it, I would not be doing as well."
>
> —student, Triton College

Self-study resources are also available at www.mhhe.com/cowan3.

Making Connections

Connecting Students to Their Future Careers

Many students taking this course will be entering the health care field in some way, and it is absolutely critical that they have a good background in the biology of microorganisms. Author Kelly Cowan has made it her goal to help all students make the connections between microbiology and the world they see around them. She does this through the features that this textbook has become known for: its engaging writing style, instructional art program, and focus on active learning. The "building blocks" approach establishes the big picture first and then gradually layers concepts onto this foundation. This logical structure helps students build knowledge and ***connect*** important concepts.

"Diagnosing Infections" Chapter

Chapter 17 brings together in one place the current methods used to diagnose infectious diseases. The chapter starts with collecting samples from the patient and details the biochemical, serological, and molecular methods used to identify causative microbes.

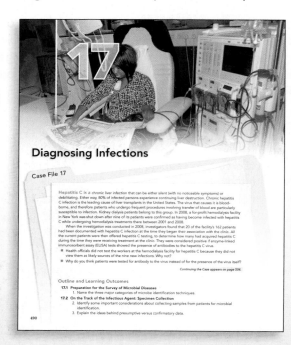

Unequaled Level of Organization in the Infectious Disease Material

Microbiology: A Systems Approach takes a unique approach to diseases by consistently covering multiple causative agents of a particular disease in the same section and summarizing this information in tables. The causative agents are categorized in a logical manner based on the presenting symptoms in the patient. Through this approach, students study how diseases affect patients—the way future health care professionals will encounter them in their jobs. A summary table follows the textual discussion of each disease and summarizes the characteristics of agents that can cause that disease.

This approach is refreshingly logical, systematic, and intuitive, as it encourages clinical and critical thinking in students—the type of thinking they will be using if their eventual careers are in health care. Students learn to examine multiple possibilities for a given condition and grow accustomed to looking for commonalities and differences among the various organisms that cause a given condition.

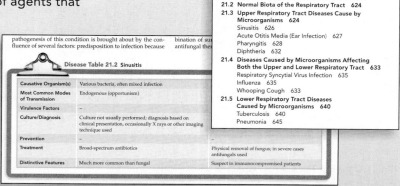

Chapter Opening Case Files!

Each chapter opens with a Case File, which helps the students understand how microbiology impacts their lives and grasp the relevance of the material they're about to learn. The questions that directly follow the Case File challenge students to begin to think critically about what they are about to read, expecting that they'll be able to answer them once they've worked through the chapter. A new Continuing the Case feature now appears within the chapter to help students follow the real-world application of the case. The Case File Wrap-Up summarizes the case at the end of the chapter, pulling together the applicable content and the chapter's topics. Nearly all case files are new in the third edition, including hot microbiological topics that are making news headlines today.

"The organization is well planned so that the topics are presented logically, allowing the student to understand basic information before more advanced material is introduced."

—Terri J. Lindsey, Ph.D., Tarrant County College

Making Connections

Connecting Students to the Content with a Truly Instructional Art Program

An instructional art program not only looks pretty, but helps students visualize complex concepts and processes and paints a conceptual picture for them. The art combines vivid colors, multidimensionality, and self-contained narrative to help students study the challenging concepts of microbiology from a visual perspective. Art is often paired with photographs or micrographs to enhance comprehension.

> *"The figures and tables found in this book are detailed enough to provide valuable information without being too overwhelming. Another strength of this book are the animations that accompany it."*
>
> —Jedidiah Lobos, Antelope Valley College

Figure 8.11 A simplified model of energy production. The central events of cell energetics include the release of energy during the systematic dismantling of a fuel such as glucose. This is achieved by the shuttling of hydrogens and electrons to sites in the cell where their energy can be transferred to ATP. In aerobic metabolism, the final products are CO_2 and H_2O molecules.

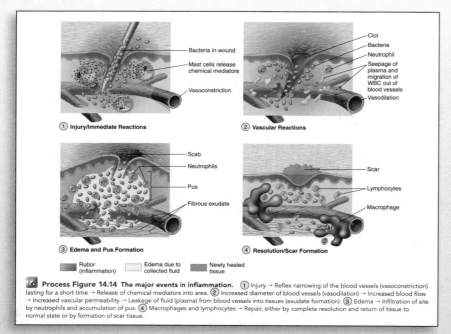

Process Figure 14.14 The major events in inflammation. ① Injury → Reflex narrowing of the blood vessels (vasoconstriction) lasting for a short time → Release of chemical mediators into area. ② Increased diameter of blood vessels (vasodilation) → Increased blood flow → Increased vascular permeability → Leakage of fluid (plasma) from blood vessels into tissues (exudate formation). ③ Edema → Infiltration of site by neutrophils and accumulation of pus. ④ Macrophages and lymphocytes → Repair, either by complete resolution and return of tissue to normal state or by formation of scar tissue.

Process Figures

Many difficult microbiological concepts are best portrayed by breaking them down into stages that students will find easy to follow. These process figures show each step clearly marked with a yellow, numbered circle and correlated to accompanying narrative to benefit all types of learners. Process figures are clearly marked next to the figure number. The accompanying legend provides additional explanation.

Connecting Students to Microbiology with Relevant Examples

Real Clinical Photos Help Students Visualize Diseases

Clinical Photos

Color photos of individuals affected by disease provide students with a real-life, clinical view of how microorganisms manifest themselves in the human body.

Figure 5.17 Nutritional sources (substrates) for fungi. **(a)** A fungal mycelium growing on raspberries. The fine hyphal filaments and black sporangia are typical of *Rhizopus*. **(b)** The skin of the foot infected by a soil fungus, *Fonsecaea pedrosoi*.

Figure 18.3 Impetigo lesions on the face.

Combination Figures

Line drawings combined with photos give students two perspectives: the realism of photos and the explanatory clarity of illustrations. The authors chose this method of presentation often to help students comprehend difficult concepts.

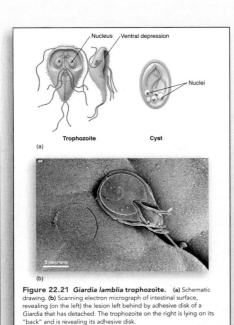

Figure 22.21 *Giardia lamblia* trophozoite. **(a)** Schematic drawing. **(b)** Scanning electron micrograph of intestinal surface, revealing (on the left) the lesion left behind by adhesive disk of a *Giardia* that has detached. The trophozoite on the right is lying on its "back" and is revealing its adhesive disk.

Figure 22.8 The effects of paramyxoviruses. **(a)** When they infect a host cell, paramyxoviruses induce the cell membranes of adjacent cells to fuse into large multinucleate giant cells, or syncytia. **(b)** This fusion allows direct passage of viruses from an infected cell to uninfected cells by communicating membranes. Through this means, the virus evades antibodies.

Making Connections

Connecting Students to Microbiology Through Student-Centered Pedagogy

Pedagogy Created to Promote Active Learning

New Learning Outcomes and *"Can You?"* Assessment Questions

Every chapter in the book now opens with an Outline and a list of Learning Outcomes. "Can You?" questions conclude each major section of the text. The Learning Outcomes are tightly correlated to digital material. Instructors can easily measure student learning in relation to the specific Learning Outcomes used in their course. You can also assign "Can You?" questions to students through the eBook with McGraw-Hill ConnectPlus Microbiology.

New Animated Learning Modules

Certain topics in microbiology need help to come to life off the page. Animations, video, audio, and text all combine to help students understand complex processes. Many figures in the text have a corresponding animation available online for students and instructors. Key topics now have an Animated Learning Module assignable through Connect. A new icon in the text indicates when these learning modules are available.

Notes

Notes appear, where appropriate, throughout the text. They give students helpful information about various terminologies, exceptions to the rule, or provide clarification and further explanation of the prior subject.

A Note About Clones

Like so many words in biology, the word "clone" has two different, although related, meanings. In this chapter we will discuss genetic clones created within microorganisms. What we are cloning is *genes*. We use microorganisms to allow us to manipulate and replicate genes outside of the original host of that gene. You are much more likely to be familiar with the other type of cloning—which we will call [...] is also known as reproductive cloning [...] creating an identical organism using [...] Dolly the sheep was the first cloned [...] others followed in her wake. These [...] scope of this book.

Figure 5.7 Changes in the cell and nucleus that accompany mitosis in a eukaryotic cell such as a yeast. (a) Before mitosis (at interphase), chromosomes are visible only as chromatin. As mitosis proceeds (early prophase), chromosomes take on a fine, threadlike appearance as they condense, and the nuclear membrane and nucleolus are temporarily disrupted. (b) By metaphase, the chromosomes are fully visible as X-shaped structures. The shape is due to duplicated chromosomes attached at a central point, the centromere. Spindle fibers attach to these and facilitate the separation of individual chromosomes during metaphase. Later phases serve in the completion of chromosomal separation and division of the cell proper into daughter cells.

Tables

This edition contains numerous illustrated tables. Horizontal contrasting lines set off each entry, making it easy to read.

Table 7.3 Nutritional Categories of Microbes by Energy and Carbon Source

Category/Carbon Source	Energy Source	Example
Autotroph/CO₂	**Nonliving Environment**	
Photoautotroph	Sunlight	Photosynthetic organisms, such as algae, plants, cyanobacteria
Chemoautotroph	Simple inorganic chemicals	Only certain bacteria, such as methanogens, deep-sea vent bacteria
Heterotroph/Organic	**Other Organisms or Sunlight**	
Chemoheterotroph	Metabolic conversion of the nutrients from other organisms	Protozoa, fungi, many animals
Saprobe	Metabolizing the organic matter of dead organisms	Fungi, bacteria (decomposers)
Parasite	Utilizing the tissues, fluids of a live host	Various parasites and pathogens; can be bacteria, fungi, protozoa, animals
Photoheterotroph	Sunlight	Purple and green photosynthetic bacteria

Insight Readings

Found throughout each chapter, current, real-world readings allow students to see an interesting application of the concepts they're studying.

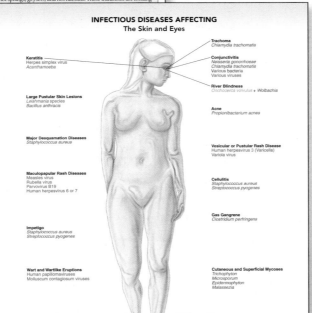

INFECTIOUS DISEASES AFFECTING
The Skin and Eyes

System Summary Figures

"Glass body" figures at the end of each disease chapter highlight the affected organs and list the diseases that were presented in the chapter. In addition, the microbes that could cause the diseases are color coded by type of microorganism.

▶ Summing Up

Taxonomic Organization Microorganisms Causing Diseases of the Skin and Eyes

Microorganism	Disease	Chapter Location
Gram-positive bacteria		
Propionibacterium acnes	Acne	Acne, p. 515
Staphylococcus aureus	Impetigo, cellulitis, scalded skin syndrome, folliculitis, abscesses (furuncles and carbuncles), necrotizing fasciitis	Impetigo, p. 516; Cellulitis, p. 521; Scalded skin syndrome, p. 522, Insight 18.1, p. 518, Note on p. 521
Streptococcus pyogenes	Impetigo, cellulitis, erysipelas, necrotizing fasciitis, scarlet fever	Impetigo, p. 520; Cellulitis, p. 521, Insight 18.1, p. 518
Clostridium perfringens	Gas gangrene	Gas gangrene, p. 523
Bacillus anthracis	Cutaneous anthrax	Large pustular skin lesions, p. 543
Gram-negative bacteria		
Neisseria gonorrhoeae	Neonatal conjunctivitis	Conjunctivitis, p. 540
Chlamydia trachomatis	Neonatal conjunctivitis, trachoma	Conjunctivitis, p. 540; Trachoma, p. 541
Wolbachia (in combination with *Onchocerca*)	River blindness	River blindness, p. 543
DNA viruses		
Human herpesvirus 3 (varicella) virus	Chickenpox	Vesicular or pustular rash diseases, p. 525
Variola virus	Smallpox	Vesicular or pustular rash diseases, p. 527
Parvovirus B19	Fifth disease	Maculopapular rash diseases, p. 532
Human herpesvirus 6 and 7	Roseola	Maculopapular rash diseases, p. 532
Human papillomavirus	Warts	Warts and wartlike eruptions, p. 534
Molluscum contagiosum virus	Molluscum contagiosum	Warts and wartlike eruptions, p. 534
Herpes simplex virus	Keratitis	Keratitis, p. 542
RNA viruses		
Measles virus	Measles	Maculopapular rash diseases, p. 530
Rubella virus	Rubella	Maculopapular rash diseases, p. 531
Fungi		
Trichophyton	Ringworm	Ringworm, p. 536
Microsporum	Ringworm	Ringworm, p. 536
Epidermophyton	Ringworm	Ringworm, p. 536
Malassezia species	Superficial mycoses	Superficial mycoses, p. 538
Protozoa		
Leishmania spp.	Leishmaniasis	Large pustular skin lesions, p. 535
Acanthamoeba		
Helminths		
Onchocerca volvulus (in combination with *Wolbachia*)	River blindness	River blindness, p. 543

Taxonomic List of Organisms

A taxonomic list of organisms is presented at the end of each disease chapter so students can see the diversity of microbes causing diseases in that body system.

Making Connections

Connecting to
Different Learning Styles with Active Learning

The end-of-chapter material for the third edition is now linked to Bloom's taxonomy. It has been carefully planned to promote active learning and provide review for different learning styles and levels of difficulty. Multiple-Choice and True-False questions (Knowledge and Comprehension) precede the synthesis-level Visual Connections questions and Concept Mapping exercises. The consistent layout of each chapter allows students to develop a learning strategy and gain confidence in their ability to master the concepts, leading to success in the class!

Chapter Summary

A brief outline of the main chapter concepts is provided for students with important terms highlighted. Key terms are also included in the glossary at the end of the book.

Multiple-Choice Questions

Students can assess their knowledge of basic concepts by answering these questions. Other types of questions and activities that follow build on this foundational knowledge. The ConnectPlus eBook allows students to quiz themselves interactively using these questions!

Critical Thinking Questions

Using the facts and concepts they just studied, students must reason and problem solve to answer these specially developed questions. Questions do not have just a single correct answer and thus open doors to discussion and application.

Chapter Summary

4.1 Prokaryotic Form and Function
- Prokaryotes are the oldest form of cellular life. They are also the most widely dispersed, occupying every conceivable microclimate on the planet.

4.2 External Structures
- The external structures of bacteria include appendages (flagella, fimbriae, and pili) and the glycocalyx.
- Flagella vary in number and arrangement as well as in the type and rate of motion they produce.

4.3 The Cell Envelope: The Boundary Layer of Bacteria
- The cell envelope is the complex boundary structure surrounding a bacterial cell. In gram-negative bacteria, the envelope consists of an outer membrane, the cell wall, and the cell membrane. Gram-positive bacteria have only the cell wall and cell membrane.
- In a Gram stain, gram-positive bacteria retain the crystal

4.4 Bacterial Internal Structure
- The cytoplasm of bacterial cells serves as a solvent for materials used in all cell functions.
- The genetic material of bacteria is DNA. Genes are arranged on large, circular chromosomes. Additional genes are carried on plasmids.
- Bacterial ribosomes are dispersed in the cytoplasm in chains (polysomes) and are also embedded in the cell membrane.
- Bacteria may store nutrients in their cytoplasm in structures called inclusions. Inclusions vary in structure and the materials that are stored.
- Some bacteria manufacture long actin filaments that help determine their cellular shape.
- A few families of bacteria produce dormant bodies called endospores, which are the hardiest of all life forms, surviving for hundreds or thousands of years.
- The genera *Bacillus* and *Clostridium* are sporeformers, and

Multiple-Choice and True-False Questions   Knowledge and Comprehension

Multiple-Choice Questions. Select the correct answer from the answers provided.

1. Which of the following is not found in all bacterial cells?
   a. cell membrane   c. ribosomes
   b. a nucleoid   d. actin cytoskeleton
2. Pili are tubular shafts in _____ bacteria that serve as a means of _____.
   a. gram-positive, genetic exchange
   b. gram-positive, attachment
   c. gram-negative, genetic exchange
   d. gram-negative, protection
3. An example of a glycocalyx is
   a. a capsule.   c. an outer membrane.
   b. a pilus.   d. a cell wall.
4. Which of the following is a primary bacterial cell wall function?
   a. transport   c. support
   b. motility   d. adhesion
5. Which of the following is present in both gram-positive and gram-negative cell walls?
   a. an outer membrane   c. teichoic acid
   b. peptidoglycan   d. lipopolysaccharides
6. Darkly stained granules are concentrated crystals of _____ that are found in _____.
   a. fat, *Mycobacterium*   c. sulfur, *Thiobacillus*
   b.

7. B
   a.
   b.

8. A bacterial arrangement in packets of eight cells is described as a _____.
   a. micrococcus   c. tetrad
   b. diplococcus   d. sarcina
9. To which division of bacteria do cyanobacteria belong?
   a. Tenericutes   c. Firmicutes
   b. Gracilicutes   d. Mendosicutes
10. Which stain is used to distinguish differences between the cell walls of medically important bacteria?
   a. simple stain   c. Gram stain
   b. acridine orange stain   d. negative stain

True-False Questions. If the statement is true, leave as is. If it is false, correct it by rewriting the sentence.

11. One major difference in the envelope structure between gram-positive bacteria and gram-negative bacteria is the presence or absence of a cytoplasmic membrane.
12. A research microbiologist looking at evolutionary relatedness between two bacterial species is more likely to use *Bergey's Manual of Determinative Bacteriology* than *Bergey's Manual of Systematic Bacteriology*.
13. Nanobes may or may not actually be bacteria.
14. Both bacteria and archaea are prokaryotes.

Critical Thinking Questions   Application and Analysis

These questions are suggested as a *writing-to-learn* experience. For each question, compose a one- or two-paragraph answer that includes the factual information needed to completely address the question.

1. a. Name several general characteristics that could be used to define the prokaryotes.
   b. Do any other microbial groups besides bacteria have prokaryotic cells?
   c. What does it mean to say that prokaryotes are ubiquitous? In what habitats are they found? Give some general means by which bacteria derive nutrients.

2. a. Describe the structure of a flagellum and how it operates. What are the four main types of flagellar arrangement?
   b. How does the flagellum dictate the behavior of a motile bacterium? Differentiate between flagella and periplasmic flagella.

3. Differentiate between pili and fimbriae.

Concept Mapping Exercises

Three different types of concept mapping activities are used throughout the text in the end-of-chapter material to help students learn and retain what they've read. Concept Mapping exercises are now made interactive on ConnectPlus Microbiology!

Concept Mapping Synthesis

Appendix D provides guidance for working with concept maps.

1. Construct your own concept map using the following words as the *concepts*. Supply the linking words between each pair of concepts.

genus   species
serotype   domain
Borrelia   *burgdorferi*
spirochete

Visual Connections

Visual Connections questions, renamed from the 2nd edition, take images and concepts learned in previous chapters and ask students to apply that knowledge to concepts newly learned in the current chapter.

Visual Connections Synthesis

These questions use visual images or previous content to make connections to this chapter's concepts.

1. **From chapter 3, figure 3.10.** Do you believe that the bacteria spelling "*Klebsiella*" or the bacteria spelling "*S. aureus*" possess the larger capsule? Defend your answer.

2. **From chapter 1, figure 1.14.** Study this figure. How would it be drawn differently if the archaea were more closely related to bacteria than to eukaryotes?

Making Connections

New to *Microbiology, A Systems Approach*

Global changes:

Case Files

The Case Files are now more integrated into the chapter, with the chapter-opening "Case File," a "Continuing the Case" box, and a final "Case Wrap-Up." All but two of these chapter case files are new to this edition.

The Case Files are linked to the second edition of *Laboratory Applications in Microbiology, A Case Study Approach,* by Barry Chess.

Learning Outcomes and "Can You. . ." Assessment Questions

- The chapter overviews now include Learning Outcomes, which help focus the student's attention on key concepts in the chapter. All Connect online content is directly correlated to these same Learning Outcomes.
- Each section of a chapter ends with assessment questions that tie directly to the Learning Outcomes. Additional online Connect questions will also help analyze performance against the Learning Outcomes.

Improved End-of-Chapter Material

- Each Chapter Summary is now bulleted and easier to read.
- All review questions are now linked to Bloom's taxonomy.
- Answers for *all* multiple-choice, true-false, and matching questions are available in Appendix C for student self-practice.
- Corresponding interactive Concept Maps in Connect reinforce the key terms and concepts in the chapter mapping exercises.

Chapter changes:

Chapter 1

- A new discussion about the subject of evolution has been added.
- The tree of life was expanded to a "web of life" based on new findings.

Chapter 2

- A new Insight reading on the periodic table is now included.
- The chapter has been updated with a new emphasis on the regulatory RNAs.

Chapter 3

- The presentation on magnification, resolution, and contrast has been improved.
- The different types of microscopes are more clearly illustrated and compared side-by-side in a new table (table 3.5).

Chapter 4

- Sixteen pieces of art in this chapter have been updated or improved.
- The use of the terms *bacterium* versus *prokaryote* has been clarified.

Chapter 5

- The concept of Last Common Ancestor is introduced, based on the newest research on the evolutionary history of prokaryotes and eukaryotes.

- Information about the cytoskeleton has been revised from two fiber types to three (actin filaments, microtubules, and intermediate filaments).
- The figure illustrating the eukaryotic cell now includes the prokaryotic cell for comparison.
- The discussion on the taxonomy of protists has been updated.

Chapter 6

- The ubiquity of viruses and their role in the biosphere and evolution receives significant attention.
- The discussion of different viral replication strategies has been greatly improved.
- The discussion of cancer and viruses has been expanded.
- The bacteriophage life cycle illustration now includes the lysogenic and lytic phases in one illustration.

Chapter 7

- The order of presenting diffusion versus osmosis has been switched for better presentation.
- The facilitated diffusion figure has been improved.
- A large section of text and accompanying figures about biofilms and quorum sensing has been added.
- The binary fission figure has been updated to reflect current research findings.

Chapter 8

- An illustration about activation energy has been added to this chapter.
- A new visual icon based on the first overview figure in the chapter has been included with several later figures to help students better understand where each of the later figures fits in "the big picture."
- The Krebs Cycle illustration has been moved out of a boxed reading and into the main text.
- The illustrations of the electron transport system have been greatly improved, and prokaryotes are now emphasized over eukaryotes.

Chapter 9

- The phrase *horizontal gene transfer* is now used to describe transformation, transduction, and conjugation, and the significance of this phenomenon for eukaryotic development is discussed.
- Content on phase variation and pathogenicity islands has been added.
- A new Insight reading about the virulence of *Salmonella* in space and how it relates to earth infections has been added.

Chapter 10

- More emphasis has been put on automated versus manual sequencing.
- A new section on synthetic biology has been added.

- More information on siRNAs and gene silencing techniques as therapeutic interventions is now included.
- Information on single nucleotide polymorphisms (SNPs) in the human genome was added.
- The discussion on microarray analysis has been improved.
- The section on ethical issues has been expanded.

Chapter 11
- Osmotic pressure as a control measure has been included in this chapter.

Chapter 12
- Information on the fifth generation of cephalosporins is now included.
- More information about the efficacy of antibiotics in biofilm infections has been added.
- A new table (Table 12.3) about the spectrum of activity of various antibacterials has been added.
- The possibility of phage therapy is now included in this chapter.
- The role of bystander microbes in harboring antibiotic resistance has been added.

Chapter 13
- This chapter was updated with a discussion of the Human Microbiome Project, which is revolutionizing the idea of normal biota.
- A new discussion of the role of stress hormones on the expression of pathogenicity genes in bacteria is now in this chapter.
- A new figure summarizing the path to disease (Figure 13.8) has been added.
- The section on epidemiology has been improved.

Chapter 14
- The chapter now addresses the difference between non-self antigens that are pathogenic and non-self antigens that are commensal, and how that trains the immune response.
- Content on pattern recognition receptors (PRRs) has been added to the discussion of pathogen-associated molecular patterns (PAMPs).
- The nonspecific immune system has been reorganized into four sections: inflammation, phagocytosis, fever, and antimicrobial proteins.

Chapter 15
- The content has been restructured so it is easier to follow (sections were renamed after the flowchart that appears at the beginning of the chapter).
- New information on T_H17 cells and T regulatory cells has been included.
- New information on CD3 molecules as part of the T-cell receptor has been added.
- The "types of vaccines" have been reordered to a much more logical format.
- An Insight reading about the antivaccination movement has been added.

Chapter 16
- The first illustration in this chapter and the organization of disorders have been rearranged and improved for better clarity.
- It has been made more apparent that autoimmune diseases fit into multiple "Types of Hypersensitivities" sections by the reorganization of content in these sections.

Chapter 17
- The section on genotyping has been updated. For example, the PNA FISH technique is now included.
- The discussion of specificity and sensitivity has been improved.
- Information about *imaging* in microbial diagnosis has been added.

Chapter 18
- New, paradigm-shifting data from the Human Microbiome Project about normal biota have been added to this chapter.
- A discussion regarding the current thought that antimicrobial peptides are a major skin defense has also been included.

Chapter 20
- CMV has been removed as a cause of infectious mononucleosis, reflecting new data; similarly, HTLV-II has been removed as a cause of hairy cell leukemia.
- A section on Chikungunya virus hemorrhagic fever has been added.
- Important new data on vaccine failure and also success for HIV, including a new approach that some say could eliminate HIV, have been included.

Chapter 21
- More emphasis has been put on polymicrobial diseases in the respiratory tract.
- A section on an important new cause of pharyngitis has been added.
- A separate note about "emerging pneumonias" has been added; the information on SARS has been moved out of the main pneumonia table and included with this category, along with the new adenovirus pneumonias, reflecting the relative importance of these infections.
- A new Insight reading linking the timeline of influenza pandemics with historical events has been added.

Chapter 22
- New material on normal biota in the stomach has been added.
- A discussion regarding the link between oral biota and heart disease has been included.
- A new Insight reading on the possible microbial cause of Crohn's disease appears.

Chapter 23
- New information about the different biota (and infection consequences) of circumcised versus uncircumcised men is now included.
- A "Note" box explaining the confusing world of STD statistics has been added.
- A discussion on parents' fears about the HPV vaccine has been included.

Chapter 24
- This chapter was significantly rewritten to incorporate genomic findings of new microbes in the environment.
- New findings about viruses and genes in the ocean are also included.

Chapter 25
- The section on water contamination has been moved from chapter 24 to this chapter.
- Chapter headings were changed to be more logical to the reader.
- Information about algal biofuels has been added.

Making Connections

Customize your course materials to your learning outcomes!

Create what you've only imagined.

Introducing McGraw-Hill Create™—a new, self-service website that allows you to create custom course materials—print and eBooks—by drawing upon McGraw-Hill's comprehensive, cross-disciplinary content. Add your own content quickly and easily. Tap into other rights-secured third-party sources as well. Then, arrange the content in a way that makes the most sense for your course. Even personalize your book with your course name and information! Choose the best format for your course: color print, black-and-white print, or eBook. The eBook is now even viewable on an iPad! And, when you are done, you will receive a free PDF review copy in just minutes!

Finally, a way to quickly and easily create the course materials you've always wanted.

Imagine that.

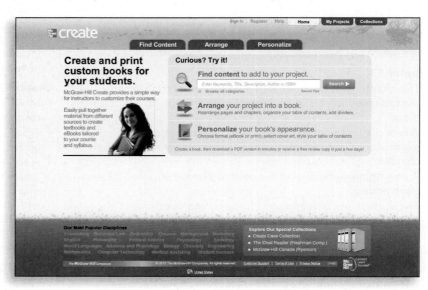

Need a lab manual for your microbiology course? Customize any of these manuals—add your text material—and *Create* your perfect solution!

McGraw-Hill offers several lab manuals for the microbiology course. Contact your McGraw-Hill representative for packaging options with any of our lab manuals.

Brown: *Benson's Microbiological Applications: Laboratory Manual in General Microbiology*, 12th edition
   Short Version (978-0-07-337527-4)
   Complete Version (978-0-07-730213-9)

Chess: *Laboratory Applications in Microbiology: A Case Study Approach*, 2nd edition (978-0-07340237-6)

Chess: *Photographic Atlas for Laboratory Applications in Microbiology*, 1st edition (978-0-07-737159-3)

Harley: *Laboratory Exercises in Microbiology*, 8th edition
   (978-0-07-729281-2)

Kleyn: *Microbiology Experiments*, 6th edition
   (978-0-07-299549-7)

Morello: *Lab Manual and Workbook in Microbiology: Applications to Patient Care*, 10th edition
   (978-0-07-352253-1)

Visit McGraw-Hill Create—www.mcgrawhillcreate.com—today and begin building your perfect book.

Acknowledgments

I am most grateful to my patient students who have tried to teach me how to more effectively communicate a subject I love. The professors who reviewed manuscript for me were my close allies, especially when they were liberal in their criticism! Kathy Loewenberg at McGraw-Hill was polite enough not to point out how often she had to fix things for me and for that I thank her. Lynn Breithaupt, Amy Reed, Marty Lange, Michael Lange, and Sheila Frank were indispensable members of the team that helped this edition come together. In the end, it is not possible to write and rewrite an 800+ page book without impacting the way you live with people around you. So I thank my family: Ted, Taylor, Sam, Suzanne, and new son-in-law Aaron for their patience and understanding. I promise to learn how to use that stove this year!

—Kelly Cowan

Reviewers

Michelle L. Badon, *University of Texas at Arlington*
Suzanne Butler, *Miami Dade College*
Chantae M. Calhoun, *Lawson State Community College*
Sujata Chiplunkar, *Cypress College*
James K. Collins, *University of Arizona*
Robin L. Cotter, *Phoenix College*
Ana L. Dowey, *Palomar College*
Melissa Elliott, *Butler Community College*
Elizabeth Emmert, *Salisbury University*
Luti Erbeznik, *Oakland Community College*
Clifton Franklund, *Ferris State University*
Susan Finazzo, *Georgia Perimeter College*
Christina A. Gan, *Highline Community College*
Elmer K. Godeny, *Baton Rouge Community College*
Jenny Hardison, *Saddleback College*
Julie Harless, *Lone Star College–Montgomery*
Jennifer A. Herzog, *Herkimer County Community College*
Dena Johnson, *Tarrant County College NW*
Richard D. Karp, *University of Cincinnati*
Judy Kaufman, *Monroe Community College*
Janardan Kumar, *Becker College*
Terri J. Lindsey, *Tarrant County College District–South Campus*
Jedidiah Lobos, *Antelope Valley College*
Melanie Lowder, *University of North Carolina at Charlotte*
Elizabeth F. McPherson, *The University of Tennessee*
Steven Obenauf, *Broward College*
Gregory Paquette, *University of Rhode Island*
Marcia M. Pierce, *Eastern Kentucky University*
Teri Reiger, *University of Wisconsin–Oshkosh*

Brenden Rickards, *Gloucester County College*
Seth Ririe, *Brigham Young University–Idaho*
Benjamin Rowley, *University of Central Arkansas*
Mark A. Schneegurt, *Wichita State University*
Denise L. Signorelli, *College Southern Nevada*
Heidi R. Smith, *Front Range Community College*
Steven J. Thurlow, *Jackson Community College*
Sanjay Tiwary, *Hinds Community College*
Liana Tsenova, *NYC College of Technology*
Winfred Watkins, *McLennan Community College*
Valerie A. Watson, *West Virginia University*
Suzi Welch, *Howard College, San Angelo*

Symposium Participants

Linda Allen, *Lon Morris College*
Michelle Badon, *University of Texas–Arlington*
Carroll Bottoms, *Collin College*
Nancy Boury, *Iowa State University*
William Boyko, *Sinclair Community College*
Chad Brooks, *Austin Peay State University*
Terri Canaris, *Brookhaven College*
Liz Carrington, *Tarrant County College*
Erin Christensen, *Middlesex Community College*
Deborah Crawford, *Trinity Valley Community College*
Paula Curbo, *Hill College*
John Dahl, *Washington State University*
David Daniel, *Weatherford College*
Alison Davis, *East Los Angeles College*
Ana Dowey, *Palomar College*

Susan Finazzo, *Georgia Perimeter College*
Clifton Franklund, *Ferris State University*
Edwin Gines-Candalaria, *Miami–Dade College*
Amy Goode, *Illinois Central College*
Todd Gordon, *Kansas City Kansas Community College*
Gabriel Guzman, *Triton College*
Judy Haber, *California State University–Fresno*
Julie Harless, *Lone Star College*
Jennifer Herzog, *Herkimer County Community College*
Dena Johnson, *Tarrant County College*
Eunice Kamunge, *Essex County College*
Amine Kidane, *Columbus State Community College*
Terri Lindsey, *Tarrant County College*
Peggy Mason, *Brookhaven College*
Caroline McNutt, *Schoolcraft College*
Elizabeth McPherson, *University of Tennessee–Knoxville*
Tracey Mills, *Ivy Tech CC–Lawrence Campus*
Bethanye Morgan, *Tarrant County College*
Steven Obenauf, *Broward College*
Tammy Oliver, *Eastfield College*
Janis Pace, *Southwestern University*

Marcia Pierce, *Eastern Kentucky University*
Madhura Pradhan, *The Ohio State University*
Todd Primm, *Sam Houston State University*
Jackie Reynolds, *Richland College*
Beverly Roe, *Erie Community College*
Silvia Rossbach, *Western Michigan University*
Benjamin Rowley, *University of Central Arkansas*
Mark Schneegurt, *Wichita State University*
Teri Shors, *University of Wisconsin*
Margaret Silva, *Mountain View College*
Heidi Smith, *Front Range Community College*
Sherry Stewart, *Navarro College*
Debby Sutton, *Mountain View College*
Louise Thai, *University of Missouri–Columbia*
Steven Thurlow, *Jackson Community College*
Sanjay Tiwary, *Hinds Community College*
Stephen Wagner, *Stephen F Austin State University*
Delon Washo-Krupps, *Arizona State University*
Winifred Watkins, *McLennan Community College*
Samia Williams, *Santa Fe Community College*

Table of Contents

CHAPTER **10**

Genetic Engineering and Recombinant DNA   268

CHAPTER **11**

Physical and Chemical Control of Microbes   297

CHAPTER **12**

Drugs, Microbes, Host—The Elements of Chemotherapy   327

CHAPTER **13**

Microbe-Human Interactions: Infection and Disease   362

CHAPTER **14**

Host Defenses I: Overview and Nonspecific Defenses   397

The Main Themes of Microbiology

Case File 1

In 2000, genomic researcher J. Craig Venter stood with physician and geneticist Francis Collins and U.S. President Bill Clinton to announce that the Human Genome Project, a worldwide effort to identify all the genes in a human being, was essentially complete. Two years later, Venter was aboard his 95-foot sailboat, the *Sorcerer II*, "fishing" for new genomes to map—those of microorganisms living in the ocean.

As the *Sorcerer II* sailed the Sargasso Sea, Venter and his assistants collected 200-liter samples of seawater and filtered them so that only organisms 1 to 3 μm in size were retained. They then froze these life forms onto filter paper and sent them to Venter's facility in Rockville, Maryland, for analysis. Using molecular biology techniques first developed for the Human Genome Project, Venter hoped to classify the new life forms by identifying novel genes without having to coax organisms to grow in the lab. Venter's efforts were so successful that many people compared his voyage to that of the British naturalist Charles Darwin, which had occurred over 170 years earlier and led to Darwin's theory of evolution, a premise that underlies nearly every aspect of biology today.

- What are some possible benefits of discovering new microbial species?
- What does the theory of evolution state?

Continuing the Case appears on page 15.

Outline and Learning Outcomes

1.1 The Scope of Microbiology
1. List the various types of microorganisms.
2. Identify multiple types of professions using microbiology.

1.2 The Impact of Microbes on Earth: Small Organisms with a Giant Effect
3. Describe the role and impact of microbes on earth.
4. Explain the theory of evolution and why it is called a theory.

1.1 The Scope of Microbiology

Microbiology is a specialized area of biology that deals with living things ordinarily too small to be seen without magnification. Such **microscopic** organisms are collectively referred to as **microorganisms** (my"-kroh-or'-gun-izms), **microbes,** or several other terms depending on the kind of microbe or the purpose. In the context of infection and disease, some people call them germs, viruses, or agents; others even call them "bugs"; but none of these terms are clear. In addition, some of these terms place undue emphasis on the disagreeable reputation of microorganisms. But, as we will learn throughout the course of this book, only a small minority of microorganisms are implicated in causing harm to other living beings. There are several major groups of microorganisms that we'll be studying. They are **bacteria, algae, protozoa, helminths** (parasitic invertebrate animals such as worms), and **fungi.** All of these microbes—just like plants and animals—can be infected by **viruses,** which are noncellular, **parasitic,** protein-coated genetic elements, dependent on their infected host. They can cause harm to the host they infect. Although viruses are not strictly speaking microorganisms—namely, cellular beings—their evolutionary history and impact are intimately connected with the evolution of microbes and their study is thus integrated in the science of microbiology. As we will see in subsequent chapters, each group of microbes exhibits a distinct collection of biological characteristics.

The nature of microorganisms makes them both very easy and very difficult to study—easy because they reproduce so rapidly and we can quickly grow large populations in the laboratory and difficult because we can't see them directly. We rely on a variety of indirect means of analyzing them in addition to using microscopes.

Microbiology is one of the largest and most complex of the biological sciences because it includes many diverse biological disciplines. Microbiologists study every aspect of microbes—their cell structure and function, their growth and physiology, their genetics, their taxonomy and evolutionary history, and their interactions with the living and nonliving environment. The latter includes their uses in industry and agriculture and the way they interact with mammalian hosts, in particular, their properties that may cause disease or lead to benefits.

Some descriptions of different branches of study appear in **table 1.1.** Studies in microbiology have led to greater understanding of many general biological principles. For example, the study of microorganisms established universal concepts concerning the chemistry of life (see chapters 2 and 8); systems of inheritance (see chapter 9); and the global cycles of nutrients, minerals, and gases (see chapter 24).

1.1 Learning Outcomes—Can You . . .

1. . . . list the various types of microorganisms?
2. . . . identify multiple types of professions using microbiology?

1.2 The Impact of Microbes on Earth: Small Organisms with a Giant Effect

The most important knowledge that should emerge from a microbiology course is the profound influence microorganisms have on all aspects of the earth and its residents. For billions of years, microbes have extensively shaped the development of the earth's habitats and the evolution of other life forms. It is understandable that scientists searching for life on other planets first look for signs of microorganisms.

Bacterial-type organisms have been on this planet for about 3.5 billion years, according to the fossil record. It appears that they were the only living inhabitants on earth for almost 2 billion years. At that time (about 1.8 billion years ago), a more complex type of single-celled organism arose, of a **eukaryotic** (yoo"-kar-ee-ah'-tik) cell type. Eu-kary means *true nucleus,* which gives you a hint that those first inhabitants, the bacteria, had no true nucleus. For that reason they are called **prokaryotes** (proh"-kar'-ee-otes) (prenucleus).

A Note About "-Karyote" Versus "-Caryote"

You will see the terms *prokaryote* and *eukaryote* spelled with *c* (*procaryote* and *eucaryote*) as well as *k*. Both spellings are accurate. This book uses the *k* spelling.

The early eukaryotes were the precursors of the cell type that eventually formed multicellular animals, including humans. But you can see from **figure 1.1** how long that took! On the scale pictured in the figure, humans seem to have just appeared. The prokaryotes preceded even the earliest animals by about 3 billion years. This is a good indication that humans are not likely to—nor should we try to—eliminate bacteria from our environment. They've survived and adapted to many catastrophic changes over the course of their geologic history.

Another indication of the huge influence bacteria exert is how **ubiquitous** they are. Microbes can be found nearly everywhere, from deep in the earth's crust, to the polar ice caps and oceans, to the bodies of plants and animals. Being mostly invisible, the actions of microorganisms are usually not as obvious or familiar as those of larger plants and animals. They make up for their small size by occurring in large numbers and living in places that many other organisms cannot survive. Above all, they play central roles in the earth's landscape that are essential to life.

When we point out that prokaryotes have adapted to a wide range of conditions over the 3.8 billion years of their presence on this planet, we are talking about evolution. The presence of life in its present form would not be possible if the earliest life forms had not changed constantly, adapting to their environment and circumstances. Getting from the far left in figure 1.1 to the far right, where humans appeared, involved billions and billions of tiny changes, starting with the first cell that appeared about a billion years after the planet itself was formed.

You have no doubt heard this concept described as the "theory of evolution." Let's clarify some terms. **Evolution** is the accumulation of changes that occur in organisms as they adapt to their environments. It is documented every day in all corners of the planet, an observable phenomenon testable by science. It is often referred to as the **theory of evolution.** This has led to great confusion among the public. As we will explain in section 1.6, scientists use the term "theory" in a different way than the general public does. By the time a principle has been labeled a theory in science, it has undergone years and years of testing and not been disproven. This is much different than the common usage, as in "My theory is that he overslept and that's why he was late." The theory of evolution, like the germ theory and many other scientific theories, are labels for well-studied and well-established natural phenomena.

Microbial Involvement in Shaping Our Planet

Microbes are deeply involved in the flow of energy and food through the earth's ecosystems.[1] Most people are aware that plants carry out **photosynthesis,** which is the light-fueled conversion of carbon dioxide to organic material, accompanied by the formation of oxygen (called oxygenic photosynthesis). However, bacteria invented photosynthesis long before first plants appeared, first as a

1. Ecosystems are communities of living organisms and their surrounding environment.

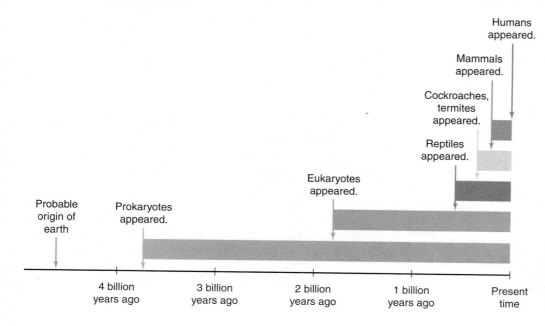

Humans appeared.

Mammals appeared.

Cockroaches, termites appeared.

Reptiles appeared.

Eukaryotes appeared.

Probable origin of earth

Prokaryotes appeared.

| 4 billion years ago | 3 billion years ago | 2 billion years ago | 1 billion years ago | Present time |

Figure 1.1 Evolutionary time line. The first bacteria appeared approximately 3.5 billion years ago. They were the only form of life for half of the earth's history.

Table 1.1 Microbiology—A Sampler

A. Medical Microbiology

This branch deals with microbes that cause diseases in humans and animals. Researchers examine factors that make the microbes virulent and mechanisms for inhibiting them.

Figure A. A staff microbiologist at the Centers for Disease Control and Prevention (CDC) examines a culture of influenza virus identical to one that circulated in 1918. The lab is researching why this form of the virus was so deadly and how to develop vaccines and other treatments. Handling such deadly pathogens requires a high level of protection with special headgear and hoods.

B. Public Health Microbiology and Epidemiology

These branches monitor and control the spread of diseases in communities. Institutions involved in this concern are the U.S. Public Health Service (USPHS) with its main agency, the Centers for Disease Control and Prevention (CDC) located in Atlanta, Georgia, and the World Health Organization (WHO), the medical limb of the United Nations.

Figure B. Epidemiologists from the CDC employ an unusual method for microbial sampling. They are collecting grass clippings to find the source of an outbreak of tularemia in Massachusetts.

C. Immunology

This branch studies the complex web of protective substances and cells produced in response to infection. It includes such diverse areas as vaccination, blood testing, and allergy (see chapters 15, 16, and 17).

Figure C. An immunologist harvests chicken antibodies from egg yolks.

D. Industrial Microbiology

This branch safeguards our food and water, and also includes biotechnology, the use of microbial metabolism to arrive at a desired product, ranging from bread making to gene therapy. Microbes can be used to create large quantities of substances such as amino acids, beer, drugs, enzymes, and vitamins.

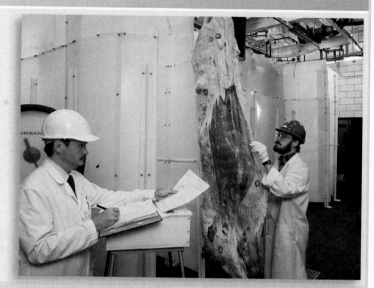

Figure D. Food inspectors sample a beef carcass for potential infectious agents. The safety of the food supply has wide-ranging importance.

E. Agricultural Microbiology

This branch is concerned with the relationships between microbes and domesticated plants and animals.

Plant specialists focus on plant diseases, soil fertility, and nutritional interactions.

Animal specialists work with infectious diseases and other associations animals have with microorganisms.

Figure E. Plant microbiologists examine images of alfalfa sprouts to see how microbial growth affects plant roots.

F. Environmental Microbiology

These microbiologists study the effect of microbes on the earth's diverse habitats. Whether the microbes are in freshwater or saltwater, topsoil or the earth's crust, they have profound effects on our planet. Subdisciplines of environmental microbiology are

Aquatic microbiology—the study of microbes in the earth's surface water

Soil microbiology—the study of microbes in terrestrial parts of the planet

Geomicrobiology—the study of microbes in the earth's crust and

Astrobiology (also known as exobiology)—the search for/study of microbial and other life in places off of our planet (see Insight 1.3)

Figure F. Researchers collect samples and data in Lake Erie.

(a)   (b)

Figure 1.2 Examples of microbial habitats. **(a)** Summer pond with a thick mat of algae—a rich photosynthetic community.
(b) Microbes play a large role in decomposing dead animal and plant matter.

process that did not produce oxygen (*anoxygenic photosynthesis*). This anoxygenic photosynthesis later evolved into oxygenic photosynthesis, which not only produced oxygen but also was much more efficient in extracting energy from sunlight. Hence, bacteria were responsible for changing the atmosphere of the earth from one without oxygen to one with oxygen. The production of oxygen also led to the use of oxygen for aerobic respiration and the formation of ozone, both of which set off an explosion in species diversification. Today, photosynthetic microorganisms (bacteria and algae) account for more than 70% of the earth's photosynthesis, contributing the majority of the oxygen to the atmosphere **(figure 1.2*a*).**

Another process that helps keep the earth in balance is the process of biological **decomposition** and nutrient recycling. Decomposition involves the breakdown of dead matter and wastes into simple compounds that can be directed back into the natural cycles of living things **(figure 1.2*b*).** If it were not for multitudes of bacteria and fungi, many chemical elements would become locked up and unavailable to organisms; we humans would drown in our own industrial and personal wastes! In the long-term scheme of things, microorganisms are the main forces that drive the structure and content of the soil, water, and atmosphere. For example:

- The very temperature of the earth is regulated by gases, such as carbon dioxide, nitrous oxide, and methane, which create an insulation layer in the atmosphere and help retain heat. Many of these gases are produced by microbes living in the environment and the digestive tracts of animals.

- Recent estimates propose that, based on weight and numbers, up to 50% of all organisms exist within and beneath the earth's crust in sediments, rocks, and even volcanoes. It is increasingly evident that this enormous underground community of microbes is a significant influence on weathering, mineral extraction, and soil formation.
- Bacteria and fungi live in complex associations with plants that assist the plants in obtaining nutrients and water and may protect them against disease. Microbes form similar interrelationships with animals, notably, in the stomach of cattle, where a rich assortment of bacteria digest the complex carbohydrates of the animals' diets.

1.2 Learning Outcomes—Can You …

3. … describe the role and impact of microbes on the earth?
4. … explain the theory of evolution and why it is called a theory?

1.3 Human Use of Microorganisms

Microorganisms clearly have monumental importance to the earth's operation. It is this very same diversity and versatility that also makes them excellent candidates for solving human problems. By accident or choice, humans have been using microorganisms for thousands of years to improve life and even to shape civilizations. Baker's and brewer's yeast, types of single-celled fungi, cause bread to rise and ferment sugar into alcohol to make wine and beers. Other fungi are used to make special cheeses such as Roquefort or Camembert. These and other "home" uses of microbes have been in use for thousands of years. For example, historical records show that households in ancient Egypt kept moldy loaves of bread to apply directly to wounds and lesions. When humans manipulate microorganisms to make products in an industrial setting, it is called biotechnology. For example, some specialized bacteria have unique capacities to mine precious metals or to clean up human-created contamination **(figure 1.3).**

Genetic engineering is an area of biotechnology that manipulates the genetics of microbes, plants, and animals for the purpose of creating new products and genetically modified organisms (GMOs). One powerful technique for designing GMOs is termed **recombinant DNA technology.** This technology makes it possible to transfer genetic material from one organism to another and to deliberately alter DNA.[2] Bacteria and fungi were some of the first organisms to be genetically engineered. This was possible because they are single-celled organisms and they are so adaptable to changes in their genetic makeup. Recombinant DNA technology has unlimited potential in terms of medical, industrial, and agricultural uses. Microbes can be engineered to synthesize desirable products such as drugs, hormones, and enzymes.

Among the genetically unique organisms that have been designed by bioengineers are bacteria that mass produce antibiotic-like substances, yeasts that produce human insulin, pigs that produce human hemoglobin, and plants that contain natural pesticides or fruits that do not ripen too rapidly. The techniques also pave the way for characterizing human genetic material and diseases.

Another way of tapping into the unlimited potential of microorganisms is the science of **bioremediation** (by'-oh-ree-mee-dee-ay"-shun). This process involves the introduction of microbes into the environment to restore stability or to clean up toxic pollutants. Microbes have a surprising capacity to break down chemicals that would be harmful to other organisms. This includes even manmade chemicals that scientists have developed and for which there are no natural counterparts.

Agencies and companies have developed microbes to handle oil spills and detoxify sites contaminated with heavy metals, pesticides, and other chemical wastes **(figure 1.3c).** The solid waste disposal industry is interested in developing methods for degrading the tons of garbage in landfills, especially human-made plastics and paper products. One form of bioremediation that has been in use for some time is the treatment of water and sewage. Because clean freshwater supplies are dwindling worldwide, it will become even more important to find ways to reclaim polluted water.

1.3 Learning Outcomes—Can You . . .

5. . . . explain the ways that humans manipulate organisms for their own uses?

2. DNA, or deoxyribonucleic acid, is the chemical substance that comprises the genetic material of organisms.

(a)

(b)

(c)

Figure 1.3 Microbes at work. (a) An aerial view of a copper mine looks like a giant quilt pattern. The colored patches are bacteria in various stages of extracting metals from the ore. **(b)** Microbes as synthesizers. Fermenting tanks at a winery. **(c)** Members of a biohazard team from the National Oceanic and Atmospheric Agency (NOAA) participate in the removal and detoxification of 63,000 tons of crude oil released by a wrecked oil tanker on the coast of Spain. The bioremediation of this massive spill made use of naturally occurring soil and water microbes as well as commercially prepared oil-eating species of bacteria and fungi.

1.4 Infectious Diseases and the Human Condition

One of the most fascinating aspects of the microorganisms with which we share the earth is that, despite all of the benefits they provide, they also contribute significantly to human misery as **pathogens** (path'-oh-jenz). The vast majority of microorganisms that associate with humans cause no harm. In fact, they provide many benefits to their human hosts. There is little doubt that a diverse microbial biota living in and on humans is an important part of human well-being. However, humankind is also plagued by nearly 2,000 different microbes that can cause various types of disease. Infectious diseases still devastate human populations worldwide, despite significant strides in understanding and treating them. The World Health Organization (WHO) estimates there are a total of 10 billion new infections across the world every year. Infectious diseases are also among the most common causes of death in much of humankind, and they still kill a significant percentage of the U.S. population. **Table 1.2** depicts the 10 top causes of death per year (by all causes, infectious and noninfectious) in the United States and worldwide. The worldwide death toll from infections is about 13 million people per year. For example, the CDC reports that every 30 seconds a child dies from malaria.

In **figure 1.4,** you can see that high-income countries like ours see many more deaths caused by chronic, noninfectious, diseases (heart disease, cancer, stroke) than those caused by infections. Low-income countries (on the left on the graph) suffer high rates of death from these diseases but even higher rates of deaths from infections. Economics is closely tied to survival in these countries.

Malaria, which kills more than a million people every year worldwide, is caused by a microorganism transmitted by mosquitoes (see chapter 20). Currently, the most effective way for citizens of developing countries to avoid infection with the causal agent of malaria is to sleep under a bed net, because the mosquitoes are most active in the evening. Yet even this inexpensive

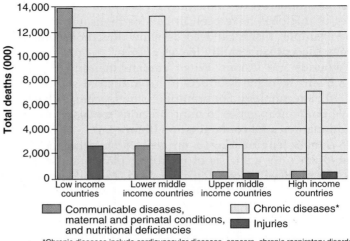

*Chronic diseases include cardiovascular diseases, cancers, chronic respiratory disorders, diabetes, neuropsychiatric and sense organ disorders, musculoskeletal and oral disorders, digestive diseases, genitourinary diseases, congenital abnormalities, and skin diseases.

Figure 1.4 The role of infectious diseases vs. other causes of death in countries of varying income.

solution is beyond the reach of many. Mothers in Southeast Asia and elsewhere have to make nightly decisions about which of their children will sleep under the single family bed net, because a second one, priced at about $3 to $5, is too expensive for them.

Adding to the overload of infectious diseases, we are also witnessing an increase in the number of new (emerging) and older (reemerging) diseases. AIDS, hepatitis C, and viral encephalitis are examples of diseases that cause severe mortality and morbidity. To somewhat balance this trend, there have also been some advances in eradication of diseases such as polio, measles, and leprosy and diseases caused by certain parasitic worms.

One of the most eye-opening discoveries in recent years is that many diseases that used to be considered noninfectious probably do involve microbial infection. The most famous of these is gastric ulcers, now known to be caused by a bacterium called *Helicobacter*. But there are more. An association has been established between certain cancers and bacteria and

Table 1.2 Top Causes of Death—All Diseases			
United States	**No. of Deaths**	**Worldwide**	**No. of Deaths**
1. Heart disease	652,000	1. Heart disease	12.2 million
2. Cancer	559,000	2. Stroke	5.7 million
3. Stroke	144,000	3. Cancer	5.7 million
4. Chronic lower-respiratory disease	131,000	4. Respiratory infections*	3.9 million
5. Unintentional injury (accidents)	118,000	5. Chronic lower-respiratory disease	3.6 million
6. Diabetes	75,000	6. Accidents	3.5 million
7. Alzheimer's disease	72,000	7. HIV/AIDS	2.9 million
8. Influenza and pneumonia	63,000	8. Perinatal conditions	2.5 million
9. Kidney problems	44,000	9. Diarrheal diseases	2.0 million
10. Septicemia (bloodstream infection)	34,000	10. Tuberculosis	1.6 million

*Diseases in red are those most clearly caused by microorganisms.
Source: Data from the World Health Organization, 2008.

viruses, between diabetes and the Coxsackie virus, and between schizophrenia and a virus called the Borna agent. Diseases as different as multiple sclerosis, obsessive compulsive disorder, coronary artery disease, and even obesity have been linked to chronic infections with microbes or viruses. It seems that the golden age of microbiological discovery, during which all of the "obvious" diseases were characterized and cures or preventions were devised for them, should more accurately be referred to as the *first* golden age. We're now discovering the subtler side of microorganisms. Their roles in quiet but slowly destructive diseases are now well known. These include female infertility caused by *Chlamydia* infection, and malignancies such as liver cancer (hepatitis viruses) and cervical cancer (human papillomavirus). Here again, low-income countries differ from high-income countries. It seems that up to 26% of cancers in low-income countries are caused by viruses or bacteria, while less than 7% of malignancies in the developed world are microbially induced.

As mentioned earlier, another important development in infectious disease trends is the increasing number of patients with weakened defenses that are kept alive for extended periods. They are subject to infections by common microbes that are not pathogenic to healthy people. There is also an increase in microbes that are resistant to drugs. It appears that even with the most modern technology available to us, microbes still have the "last word," as the great French scientist Louis Pasteur observed **(Insight 1.1).**

1.4 Learning Outcomes—Can You . . .

6. . . . summarize the relative burden of human disease caused by microbes?

INSIGHT 1.1   The More Things Change . . .

In 1964, the surgeon general of the United States delivered a speech to Congress: "It is time to close the book on infectious diseases," he said. "The war against pestilence is over."

In 1998, Surgeon General David Satcher had a different message. The *Miami Herald* reported his speech with this headline: "Infectious Diseases a Rising Peril; Death Rates in U.S. Up 58% Since 1980."

The middle of the last century was a time of great confidence in science and medicine. With the introduction of antibiotics in the 1940s, and a lengthening list of vaccines that prevented the most frightening diseases, Americans felt that it was only a matter of time before diseases caused by microorganisms (i.e., infectious diseases) would be completely manageable. The nation's attention turned to the so-called chronic diseases, such as heart disease, cancer, and stroke.

So what happened to change the optimism of the 1960s to the warning expressed in the speech from 1998? Dr. Satcher explained it this way: "Organisms changed and people changed." First, we are becoming more susceptible to infectious disease precisely because of advances in medicine. People are living longer. Sicker people are staying alive much longer than in the past. Older and sicker people have heightened susceptibility to what we might call garden-variety microbes. Second, the population has become more mobile. Travelers can crisscross the globe in a matter of hours, taking their microbes with them and

United States Surgeon General David Satcher in 1998.

introducing them into new "naive" populations. Third, there are growing numbers of microbes that truly are new (or at least, new to us). The conditions they cause are called **emerging diseases.** Changes in agricultural practices and encroachment of humans on wild habitats are just two probable causes of emerging diseases. The mass production and packing of food increases the opportunity for large outbreaks, especially if foods are grown in fecally contaminated soils or are eaten raw or poorly cooked. In the past several years, dozens of food-borne outbreaks have been associated with the bacterium *Escherichia coli* O157:H7 in fresh vegetables, fruits, and meats. Fourth, microorganisms have demonstrated their formidable capacity to respond and adapt to our attempts to control them, most spectacularly by becoming resistant to the effects of our miracle drugs.

And there's one more thing: Evidence is mounting that many conditions formerly thought to be caused by genetics or lifestyle, such as heart disease and cancer, can often be at least partially caused by microorganisms.

Microbes never stop surprising us—in their ability not only to harm but also to help us. The best way to keep up is to learn as much as you can about them. This book is a good place to start.

United States Surgeon General Luther Terry addressing a press conference in 1964.

1.5 The General Characteristics of Microorganisms

Cellular Organization

As discussed earlier, two basic cell lines appeared during evolutionary history. These lines, termed **prokaryotic cells** and eukaryotic cells, differ not only in the complexity of their cell structure **(figure 1.5a)** but also in contents and function.

In general, prokaryotic cells are about 10 times smaller than eukaryotic cells, and they lack many of the eukaryotic cell structures such as **organelles.** Organelles are small, double-membrane-bound structures in the eukaryotic cell that perform specific functions and include the nucleus, mitochondria, and chloroplasts. The microorganisms that consist of these two different cell types (called prokaryotes and eukaryotes) are covered in more detail in chapters 4 and 5.

All prokaryotes are microorganisms, but only some eukaryotes are microorganisms. The majority of microorganisms are single-celled (all prokaryotes and some eukaryotes), but some consist of a few cells **(figure 1.6).** Certain invertebrate animals—such as helminths (worms), many of which can be seen with the naked eye, are also included in the study of infectious diseases because of the way they are transmitted and the way the body responds to them, though they are not microorganisms.

Lifestyles of Microorganisms

The majority of microorganisms live a free existence in habitats such as soil and water, where they are relatively harmless and often beneficial. A free-living organism can derive all required foods and other factors directly from the nonliving environment. Some microorganisms require interactions with other organisms. Sometimes these microbes are termed **parasites.** They are harbored and nourished by other living organisms called **hosts.** A parasite's actions cause damage to its host through infection and disease. Although parasites cause important diseases, they make up only a small proportion of microbes.

A Note on Viruses

Viruses are subject to intense study by microbiologists. As mentioned before, they are not independently living cellular organisms. Instead, they are small particles that exist at the level of complexity somewhere between large molecules and cells **(figure 1.5b).** Viruses are much simpler than cells; outside their host, they are composed essentially of a small amount of hereditary material (either DNA or RNA but never both) wrapped up in a protein covering that is sometimes enveloped by a protein-containing lipid membrane. In this extracellular state, they are individually referred to as a **virus particle** or **virion.** When inside their host organism, in the intracellular state, viruses usually exist only in the form of genetic material that confers a partial genetic program on the host organisms. That is why many microbiologists refer to viruses as parasitic particles; however, a few consider them to be very primitive organisms. Nevertheless, all biologists agree that viruses are completely dependent on an infected host cell's machinery for their multiplication and dispersal.

1.5 Learning Outcomes—Can You ...

7. ... differentiate between prokaryotic and eukaryotic microorganisms?
8. ... identify a third type of microorganism?
9. ... compare and contrast the relative sizes of the different microbes?

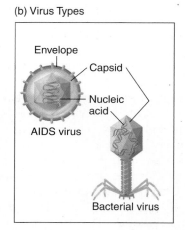

(a) Cell Types

Prokaryotic — Chromosome, Ribosomes, Cell wall, Cell membrane, Flagellum

Eukaryotic — Ribosomes, Nucleus, Mitochondria, Flagellum, Cell membrane

(b) Virus Types

Envelope, Capsid, Nucleic acid, AIDS virus, Bacterial virus

Figure 1.5 Cell structure. **(a)** Comparison of a prokaryotic cell and a eukaryotic cell (not to scale). **(b)** Two examples of viruses. These cell types and viruses are discussed in more detail in chapters 4, 5, and 6.

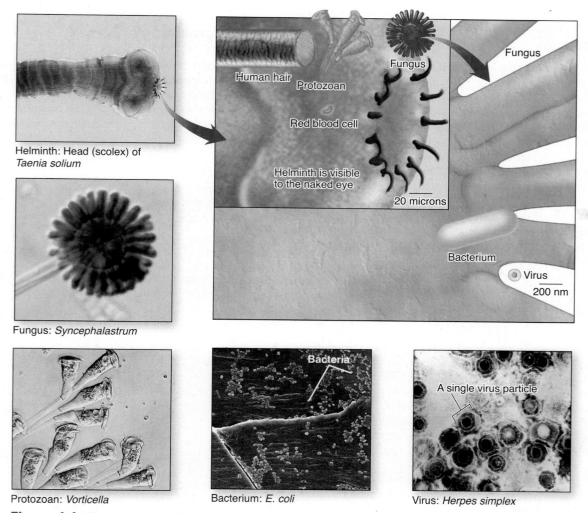

Helminth: Head (scolex) of *Taenia solium*

Human hair

Protozoan

Red blood cell

Helminth is visible to the naked eye

Fungus

Fungus

20 microns

Bacterium

Virus

200 nm

Fungus: *Syncephalastrum*

Protozoan: *Vorticella*

Bacteria

Bacterium: *E. coli*

A single virus particle

Virus: *Herpes simplex*

Figure 1.6 Five types of microorganisms. The drawing at top right shows relative size differences. The photos of organisms around the drawing are pictured at different magnifications in order to show their details.

1.6 The Historical Foundations of Microbiology

If not for the extensive interest, curiosity, and devotion of thousands of microbiologists over the last 300 years, we would know little about the microscopic realm that surrounds us. Many of the discoveries in this science have resulted from the prior work of men and women who toiled long hours in dimly lit laboratories with the crudest of tools. Each additional insight, whether large or small, has added to our current knowledge of living things and processes. This section summarizes the prominent discoveries made in the past 300 years: microscopy; the rise of the scientific method; and the development of medical microbiology, including the germ theory and the origins of modern microbiological techniques. Table B.1 in appendix B summarizes some of the pivotal events in microbiology, from its earliest beginnings to the present.

The Development of the Microscope: "Seeing Is Believing"

From very earliest history, humans noticed that when certain foods spoiled they became inedible or caused illness, and yet other "spoiled" foods did no harm and even had enhanced flavor. Indeed, several centuries ago, there was already a sense that diseases such as the black plague and smallpox were caused by some sort of transmissible matter. But the causes of such phenomena were vague and obscure because the technology to study them was lacking. Consequently, they remained cloaked in mystery and regarded with superstition—a trend that led even well-educated scientists to believe in spontaneous generation **(Insight 1.2).**

True awareness of the widespread distribution of microorganisms and some of their characteristics was finally made possible by the development of the first microscopes. These devices revealed microbes as discrete entities sharing many of the characteristics of larger, visible plants and

INSIGHT 1.2   The Fall of Superstition and the Rise of Microbiology

For thousands of years, people believed that certain living things arose from vital forces present in nonliving or decomposing matter. This ancient belief, known as **spontaneous generation,** was continually reinforced as people observed that meat left out in the open soon "produced" maggots, that mushrooms appeared on rotting wood, that rats and mice emerged from piles of litter, and other similar phenomena. Though some of these early ideas seem quaint and ridiculous in light of modern knowledge, we must remember that, at the time, mysteries in life were accepted, and the scientific method was not widely practiced.

Even after single-celled organisms were discovered during the mid-1600s, the idea of spontaneous generation continued to exist. Some scientists assumed that microscopic beings were an early stage in the development of more complex ones.

Over the subsequent 200 years, scientists waged an experimental battle over the two hypotheses that could explain the origin of simple life forms. Some tenaciously clung to the idea of **abiogenesis** (a = without, bio = life, genesis = beginning—*beginning in absence of life*), which embraced spontaneous generation. On the other side were advocates of **biogenesis** (*beginning with life*) saying that living things arise only from others of their same kind. There were serious proponents on both sides, and each side put forth what appeared on the surface to be plausible explanations of why their evidence was more correct. Gradually, the abiogenesis hypothesis was abandoned, as convincing evidence for biogenesis continued to mount. The following series of experiments were among the most important in finally tipping the balance.

One of the first people to test the spontaneous generation theory was Francesco Redi of Italy. He conducted a simple experiment in which he placed meat in a jar and covered it with fine gauze. Flies gathering at the jar were blocked from entering and thus laid their eggs on the outside of the gauze. The maggots subsequently developed without access to the meat, indicating that maggots were the offspring of flies and did not arise from some "vital force" in the meat. This and related experiments laid to rest the idea that more complex animals such as insects and mice developed through abiogenesis, but it did not convince many scientists of the day that simpler organisms could not arise in that way.

Redi's Experiment

Closed — Meat with no maggots
Open — Maggots hatching into flies

The Frenchman Louis Jablot reasoned that even microscopic organisms must have parents, and his experiments with hay infusions (dried hay steeped in water) supported that hypothesis. He divided into two containers an infusion that had been boiled to destroy any living things: a heated container that was closed to the air and a heated container that was freely open to

Jablot's Experiment

Infusions

Covered — Dust
Uncovered — Dust

Remains clear; no growth
Heavy microbial growth

animals. Several early scientists fashioned magnifying lenses, but their microscopes lacked the optical clarity needed for examining bacteria and other small, single-celled organisms. The likely earliest record of microbes is in the works of Englishman Robert Hooke. In the 1660s, Hooke studied a great diversity of material from household objects, plants, and trees; described for the first time cellular structures in tree bark; and drew sketches of "little structures" that seemed to be alive. Using a single-lens microscope he made himself, Hooke described spots of mold he found on the sheepskin cover of a book:

> These spots appear'd, through a good Microscope, to be a very pretty shap'd vegetative body, which, from almost the same part of the Leather, shot out multitudes of small long cylindrical and transparent stalks, not exactly straight, but a little bended with the weight of a round and white knob that grew on the top of each of them. . . .

Figure 1.7a is a reproduction of the drawing he made to accompany his written observations. Hooke paved the way for even more exacting observations of microbes by Antonie van Leeuwenhoek, a Dutch linen merchant and self-made microbiologist.

Imagine a dusty linen shop in Holland in the late 1600s. Ladies in traditional Dutch garb came in and out, choosing among the bolts of linens for their draperies and upholstery. Between customers, Leeuwenhoek retired to the workbench in the back of his shop, grinding glass lenses to ever-finer specifications so he could see with increasing clarity the threads in his fabrics. Eventually, he became interested in things other than thread counts. He took rainwater from a clay pot, smeared it on his specimen holder, and peered at it through his finest lens. He found "animals appearing to me ten thousand times less than those which may be perceived in the water with the naked eye."

the air. Only the open vessel developed microorganisms, which he presumed had entered in air laden with dust.

Additional experiments further defended biogenesis. Franz Shultze and Theodor Schwann of Germany felt sure that air was the source of microbes and sought to prove this by passing air through strong chemicals or hot glass tubes into heat-treated infusions in flasks. When the infusions again remained devoid of living things, the supporters of abiogenesis claimed that the treatment of the air had made it incapable of the spontaneous development of life.

part of the necks. He heated the flasks to sterilize the broth and then incubated them. As long as the flask remained intact, the broth remained sterile; but if the neck was broken off so that dust fell directly down into the container, microbial growth immediately commenced.

Pasteur summed up his findings, "For I have kept from them, and am still keeping from them, that one thing which is above the power of man to make; I have kept from them the germs that float in the air, I have kept from them life."

Shultze and Schwann's Test

Air inlet

Flame heats air.

Previously sterilized infusion remains sterile.

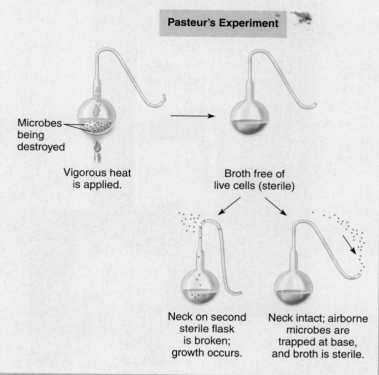

Pasteur's Experiment

Microbes being destroyed

Vigorous heat is applied.

Broth free of live cells (sterile)

Neck on second sterile flask is broken; growth occurs.

Neck intact; airborne microbes are trapped at base, and broth is sterile.

Then, in the mid-1800s, the acclaimed chemist and microbiologist Louis Pasteur entered the arena. He had recently been studying the roles of microorganisms in the fermentation of beer and wine, and it was clear to him that these processes were brought about by the activities of microbes introduced into the beverage from air, fruits, and grains. The methods he used to discount abiogenesis were simple yet brilliant.

To further clarify that air and dust were the source of microbes, Pasteur filled flasks with broth and fashioned their openings into long, swan-neck-shaped tubes. The flasks' openings were freely open to the air but were curved so that gravity would cause any airborne dust particles to deposit in the lower

He didn't stop there. He scraped the plaque from his teeth, and from the teeth of some volunteers who had never cleaned their teeth in their lives, and took a good close look at that. He recorded: "In the said matter there were many very little living animalcules, very prettily a-moving. . . . Moreover, the other animalcules were in such enormous numbers, that all the water . . . seemed to be alive." Leeuwenhoek started sending his observations to the Royal Society of London, and eventually he was recognized as a scientist of great merit.

Leeuwenhoek constructed more than 250 small, powerful microscopes that could magnify up to 300 times

Figure 1.7 The first depiction of microorganisms.
(a) Drawing of "hairy mould" colony made by Robert Hooke in 1665.
(b) Photomicrograph of the fungus probably depicted by Hooke. It is a species of *Mucor*, a common indoor mold.

(a)

(b)

(figure 1.8). Considering that he had no formal training in science, his descriptions of bacteria and protozoa (which he called "animalcules") were astute and precise. Because of Leeuwenhoek's extraordinary contributions to microbiology, he is known as the father of bacteriology and protozoology.

From the time of Hooke and Leeuwenhoek, microscopes became more complex and improved with the addi-

Lens

Specimen holder

Focus screw

Handle

(a)

(b)

Figure 1.8 Leeuwenhoek's microscope. **(a)** A brass replica of a Leeuwenhoek microscope and how it is held. **(b)** Examples of bacteria drawn by Leeuwenhoek.

tion of refined lenses, a condenser, finer focusing devices, and built-in light sources. The prototype of the modern compound microscope, in use from about the mid-1800s, was capable of magnifications of 1,000 times or more. Even our modern laboratory microscopes are not greatly different in basic structure and function from those early microscopes. The technical characteristics of microscopes and microscopy are a major focus of chapter 3.

These events marked the beginning of our understanding of microbes and the diseases they can cause. Discoveries continue at a breakneck pace, however. In fact, the 2000s are being widely called the Century of Biology, fueled by our new abilities to study genomes and harness biological processes. Microbes have led the way in these discoveries and continue to play a large role in the new research.

Of course, between the "Golden Age of Microbiology" and the "Century of Biology" there have been thousands of important discoveries. But to give you a feel for what has happened most recently, let's take a glimpse of some very recent discoveries that have had huge impacts on our understanding of microbiology.

Discovery of restriction enzymes—1970s. Three scientists, Daniel Nathans, Werner Arber, and Hamilton Smith, discovered these little molecular "scissors" inside prokaryotes. They chop up DNA in specific ways. Their job in the prokaryotes is to destroy invading (viral) DNA. The reason their discovery was such a major event in biology is that these enzymes can be harvested from the bacteria and then utilized in research labs to cut up DNA in a controlled way that then allows us to splice the DNA pieces into vehicles that can carry them into other cells. This opened the floodgates to genetic engineering—and all that has meant for the treatment of diseases, the investigation into biological processes, and the biological "revolution" of the 21st century.

The invention of the PCR technique—1980s. The polymerase chain reaction (PCR) was a breakthrough in our ability to detect tiny amounts of DNA and then amplify them into quantities sufficient for studying. It has provided a new and powerful method for discovering new organisms and diagnosing infectious diseases and for forensic work such as crime scene investigation. Its inventor is Kary Mullis, a scientist working at a company in California at the time. He won the Nobel Prize for this invention in 1993.

The importance of biofilms in infectious diseases— 1980s, 1990s, and 2000s. Biofilms are accumulations of bacteria and other microbes on surfaces. Often there are multiple species in a single biofilm and often they are several layers thick **(figure 1.9).** They have been recognized in environmental microbiology for a long time. Biofilms on rocks, biofilms on ship hulls, even biofilms on ancient paintings have been well studied. We now understand that biofilms are relatively common in the human body (dental plaque is a great example) and may be responsible for infections that are tough to conquer, such as some ear infections and recalcitrant infections of the prostate. Biofilms are also a big danger to the

Channel

Biofilm
material

Figure 1.9 A biofilm made of three different bacterial species.   This biofilm was artificially grown in the lab by adding three bacterial species to a flowing chamber. The film is several bacterial layers thick and mimics the kinds of biofilms found in industrial settings, such as in water lines, and also in human infections.

success of any foreign body implanted in the body. Artificial hips, hearts, and even IUDs (intrauterine devices) have all been seen to fail due to biofilm colonization.

The importance of small RNAs—2000s.   Once we were able to sequence entire genomes (another big move forward), scientists discovered something that turned a concept we literally used to call "dogma" on its head. You will learn in chapter 9 that DNA leads to the creation of proteins, the workhorses of all cells. The previously held "Central Dogma of Biology" was that RNA (a molecule related to DNA) was the go-between molecule. DNA was made into RNA, which dictated the creation of proteins. Genome sequencing has revealed that perhaps only 2% of DNA leads to a resulting protein. There is a lot of RNA that is being made that doesn't end up with a protein counterpart. These pieces of RNA are usually small. It now appears that they have absolutely critical roles in regulating what happens in the cell. This is important not just to correct scientific assumptions but there are important practical uses as well. It has led to new approaches to how diseases are treated. For example, if the small RNAs are in bacteria infecting humans, they can be new targets for antimicrobial therapy.

The preceding example highlights a feature of biology—and all of science—that is perhaps underappreciated. Because we have thick textbooks containing all kinds of assertions and "facts," many people think science is an iron-clad collection of facts. Wrong! Science is an ever-evolving collection of new information, gleaned from observable phenomena and synthesized with old information to come up with the cur-

rent understandings of nature. Some of these observations have been confirmed so many times over such a long period of time that they are, if not "fact," very close to fact. Many other observations will be altered over and over again as new findings emerge. And that is the beauty of science.

The Establishment of the Scientific Method

A serious impediment to the development of true scientific reasoning and testing was the tendency of early scientists to explain natural phenomena by a mixture of belief, superstition, and argument. The development of an experimental system that answered questions objectively and was not based on prejudice marked the beginning of true scientific thinking. These ideas gradually crept into the consciousness of the scientific community during the 1600s. The general approach taken by scientists to explain a certain natural phenomenon is called the **scientific method.** A primary aim of this method is to formulate a **hypothesis,** a tentative explanation to account for what has been observed or measured. A good hypothesis should be in the form of a statement. It must be capable of being either supported or discredited by careful observation or experimentation. For example, the statement that "microorganisms cause diseases" can be experimentally determined by the tools of science, but the statement "diseases are caused by evil spirits" cannot.

Case File 1   *Continuing the Case*

In 1831, Charles Darwin embarked on a 5-year voyage around the globe on a ship called the *HMS Beagle.* While on this journey, Darwin identified many never-before-seen plant and animal species. Eventually his studies of these organisms led to the development of his theory of evolution by natural selection, which states, in part, that as the genetic material of living beings changes over time, new life forms with unique structures and functions are produced. Traits that favor the survival of an organism, such as the ability to metabolize a new food source, are retained and passed on to the organism's descendents.

J. Craig Venter's initial efforts led to the discovery of 1.2 million new genes and 1,800 new species. He heads an organization called the Institute for Biological Energy Alternatives. One of the institute's goals is to create synthetic organisms tailor-made for a specific purpose, such as synthesizing chemicals, degrading waste products, or producing energy. It stands to reason that Venter's discovery of new species will increase the potential for even more useful products, both naturally occurring and manmade.

Deductive and Inductive Reasoning

Science is a process of investigation, using observation, experimentation, and reasoning. In some investigations, you make individual decisions by using accepted general principles as a guide. This is called deductive reasoning. Deductive reasoning, using general principles to explain specific observations, is the reasoning of mathematics, philosophy, politics, and ethics; deductive reasoning is also the way a computer works. All of us rely on deductive reasoning as a way to make everyday decisions—like whether you should open attachments in e-mails from unknown senders **(figure 1.10).** We use general principles as the basis for examining and evaluating these decisions.

Inductive Reasoning

Where do general principles come from? Religious and ethical principles often have a religious foundation; political principles reflect social systems. Some general principles, however, such as those behind the deductive reasoning example above, are not derived from religion or politics but from observation of the physical world around us. If you drop an apple, it will fall whether or not you wish it to and despite any laws you may pass that forbid it to do so. Science is devoted to discovering the general principles that govern the operation of the physical world.

How do scientists discover such general principles? Scientists are, above all, observers: They look at the world to understand how it works. It is from observations that scientists determine the principles that govern our physical world.

The process of discovering general principles by careful examination of specific cases is termed inductive reasoning. This way of thought first became popular about 400 years ago, when Isaac Newton, Francis Bacon, and others began to conduct experiments and from the results infer general principles about how the world operates. Their experiments were sometimes quite simple. Newton's consisted simply of releasing an apple from his hand and watching it fall to the ground. From a host of particular observations, each no more complicated than the falling of an apple, Newton inferred a general principle—that all objects fall toward the center of the earth. This principle was a possible explanation, or hypothesis, about how the world works. You also make observations and formulate general principles based on your observations, like forming a general principle about the reliability of unknown e-mail attachments in figure 1.10. Like Newton, scientists work by forming and testing hypotheses, and observations are the materials on which they build them.

As you can see, the deductive process is used when a general principle has already been established; induction is a discovery process, and leads to the creation of a general principle.

A lengthy process of experimentation, analysis, and testing eventually leads to conclusions that either support or refute the hypothesis. If experiments do not uphold the hypothesis—that is, if it is found to be flawed—the hypothesis or some part of it is rejected; it is either discarded or modified to fit the results of the experiment. If the hypothesis is supported by the results from the experiment, it is not (or should not be) immediately accepted as fact. It then must be tested and retested. Indeed, this is an important guideline in the acceptance of a hypothesis. The results of the experiment must be published and then repeated by other investigators.

In time, as each hypothesis is supported by a growing body of data and survives rigorous scrutiny, it moves to the next level of acceptance—the **theory.** A theory is a collection of statements, propositions, or concepts that explains or accounts for a natural event. A theory is not the result of a single experiment repeated over and over again but is an entire body of ideas that expresses or explains many aspects of a phenomenon. It is not a fuzzy or weak speculation, as is sometimes the popular notion, but a viable declaration that has stood the test of time and has yet to be disproved by serious scientific endeavors. Often, theories develop and progress through decades of research and are added to and modified by new findings. At some point, evidence of the accuracy and predictability of a theory is so compelling that the next level of confidence is reached and the theory becomes a law, or principle. For example, although we still refer to the germ *theory* of disease, so little question remains that microbes can cause disease that it has clearly passed into the realm of law. The theory of evolution falls in this category as well.

Science and its hypotheses and theories must progress along with technology. As advances in instrumentation allow new, more detailed views of living phenomena, old theories may be reexamined and altered and new ones proposed. But scientists do not take the stance that theories or even "laws" are ever absolutely proved.

The characteristics that make scientists most effective in their work are curiosity, open-mindedness, skepticism, creativity, cooperation, and readiness to revise their views of natural processes as new discoveries are made. The events described in Insight 1.2 provide important examples.

Deductive reasoning

Knowing that opening attachments from unknown senders can introduce viruses or other bad things to your computer, you chose the specific action of not opening the attachment.

General principle

Inductive reasoning

You have performed the specific action of clicking on unknown attachments three different times and each time your computer crashed This leads you to conclude that opening unknown attachments can be damaging to your computer.

Figure 1.10 Deductive and inductive reasoning.

The Development of Medical Microbiology

Early experiments on the sources of microorganisms led to the profound realization that microbes are everywhere: Not only are air and dust full of them, but the entire surface of the earth, its waters, and all objects are inhabited by them. This discovery led to immediate applications in medicine. Thus, the seeds of medical microbiology were sown in the mid to latter half of the 19th century with the introduction of the germ theory of disease and the resulting use of sterile, aseptic, and pure culture techniques.

The Discovery of Spores and Sterilization

Following Pasteur's inventive work with infusions (see Insight 1.2), it was not long before English physicist John Tyndall provided the initial evidence that some of the microbes in dust and air have very high heat resistance and that particularly vigorous treatment is required to destroy them. Later, the discovery and detailed description of heat-resistant bacterial endospores by Ferdinand Cohn, a German botanist, clarified the reason that heat would sometimes fail to completely eliminate all microorganisms. The modern sense of the word **sterile,** meaning completely free of all life forms (including spores) and virus particles, was established from that point on (see chapter 11). The capacity to sterilize objects and materials is an absolutely essential part of microbiology, medicine, dentistry, and some industries.

The Development of Aseptic Techniques

From earliest history, humans experienced a vague sense that "unseen forces" or "poisonous vapors" emanating from decomposing matter could cause disease. As the study of microbiology became more scientific and the invisible was made visible, the fear of such mysterious vapors was replaced by the knowledge and sometimes even the fear of "germs." About 125 years ago, the first studies by Robert Koch clearly linked a microscopic organism with a specific disease. Since that time, microbiologists have conducted a continuous search for disease-causing agents.

At the same time that abiogenesis was being hotly debated, a few physicians began to suspect that microorganisms could cause not only spoilage and decay but also infectious diseases. It occurred to these rugged individualists that even the human body itself was a source of infection. Dr. Oliver Wendell Holmes, an American physician, observed that mothers who gave birth at home experienced fewer infections than did mothers who gave birth in the hospital; and the Hungarian Dr. Ignaz Semmelweis showed quite clearly that women became infected in the maternity ward after examinations by physicians coming directly from the autopsy room.

The English surgeon Joseph Lister took notice of these observations and was the first to introduce **aseptic** (ay-sep'-tik) **techniques** aimed at reducing microbes in a medical setting and preventing wound infections. Lister's concept of asep-

sis was much more limited than our modern precautions. It mainly involved disinfecting the hands and the air with strong antiseptic chemicals, such as phenol, prior to surgery. It is hard for us to believe, but as recently as the late 1800s surgeons wore street clothes in the operating room and had little idea that hand washing was important. Lister's techniques and the application of heat for sterilization became the foundations for microbial control by physical and chemical methods, which are still in use today.

The Discovery of Pathogens and the Germ Theory of Disease

Louis Pasteur of France **(figure 1.11)** introduced techniques that are still used today. Pasteur made enormous contributions to our understanding of the microbial role in wine and beer formation. He invented pasteurization and completed some of the first studies showing that human diseases could arise from infection. These studies, supported by the work of other scientists, became known as the **germ theory of disease.** Pasteur's contemporary, Robert Koch, established *Koch's postulates,* a series of proofs that verified the germ theory and could establish whether an organism was pathogenic and which disease it caused (see chapter 13). About 1875, Koch used this experimental system to show that anthrax was caused by a bacterium called *Bacillus anthracis.* So useful were his postulates that the causative agents of 20 other diseases were discovered between 1875 and 1900, and even today, they are the standard for identifying pathogens of plants and animals.

Numerous exciting technologies emerged from Koch's prolific and probing laboratory work. During this golden age

Figure 1.11 Louis Pasteur (1822–1895), one of the founders of microbiology. Few microbiologists can match the scope and impact of his contributions to the science of microbiology.

of the 1880s, he realized that study of the microbial world would require separating microbes from each other and growing them in culture. It is not an overstatement to say that he and his colleagues invented most of the techniques that are described in chapter 3: inoculation, isolation, media, maintenance of pure cultures, and preparation of specimens for microscopic examination. Other highlights in this era of discovery are presented in later chapters on microbial control (see chapter 11) and vaccination (see chapter 15).

1.6 Learning Outcomes—Can You . . .

10. . . . make a time line of the development of microbiology from the 1600s to today?

11. . . . list some recent microbiology discoveries of great impact?

12. . . . explain what is important about the scientific method?

1.7 Naming, Classifying, and Identifying Microorganisms

Students just beginning their microbiology studies are often dismayed by the seemingly endless array of new, unusual, and sometimes confusing names for microorganisms. Learning microbial **nomenclature** is very much like learning a new language, and occasionally its demands may be a bit overwhelming. But paying attention to proper microbial names is just like following a baseball game or a theater production: you cannot tell the players apart without a program! Your understanding and appreciation of microorganisms will be greatly improved by learning a few general rules about how they are named.

The science of classifying living beings is **taxonomy.** It originated more than 250 years ago when Carl von Linné (also known as Linnaeus; 1701–1778), a Swedish botanist, laid down the basic rules for *classification* and established taxonomic categories, or **taxa** (singular: taxon).

Von Linné realized early on that a system for recognizing and defining the properties of living beings would prevent chaos in scientific studies by providing each organism with a unique name and an exact "slot" in which to catalog it. This classification would then serve as a means for future identification of that same organism and permit workers in many biological fields to know if they were indeed discussing the same organism. The von Linné system has served well in categorizing the 2 million or more different kinds of organisms that have been discovered since that time, including organisms that have gone extinct.

The primary concerns of modern taxonomy are still naming, classifying, and identifying. These three areas are interrelated and play a vital role in keeping a dynamic inventory of the extensive array of living and extinct beings. In general,

Nomenclature is the assignment of scientific names to the various taxonomic categories and individual organisms.
Classification attempts the orderly arrangement of organisms into a hierarchy of taxa.

Identification is the process of discovering and recording the traits or organisms so that they may be recognized or named and placed in an overall taxonomic scheme.

With the rapid increase in knowledge largely due to the mind-boggling pace of improvement in scientific instrumentation and analysis, taxonomy has never stood still. Instead, it has evolved from a science that artificially classified organisms from a viewpoint of the organism's usefulness, danger, or esthetic appeal to humans to a science that devised a system of natural relationships between organisms. A survey of some general methods of identification appears in chapter 3. Discovery of present or extinct life forms in space would certainly provide an ultimate test for our existing taxonomy and shed light on the origins of life on our planet earth **(Insight 1.3).**

Assigning Specific Names

Many macroorganisms are known by a common name suggested by certain dominant features. For example, a bird species might be called a red-headed blackbird or a flowering plant species a black-eyed Susan. Some species of microorganisms (especially those that directly or indirectly affect our well-being) are also called by informal names, including human pathogens such as "gonococcus" (*Neisseria gonorrhoeae*) or fermenters such as "brewer's yeast" (*Saccharomyces cerevisiae*), or the recent "Iraqabacter" (*Acinetobacter baumannii*), but this is not the usual practice. If we were to adopt common names such as the "little yellow coccus" the terminology would become even more cumbersome and challenging than scientific names. Even worse, common names are notorious for varying from region to region, even within the same country. A decided advantage of standardized nomenclature is that it provides a universal language, thereby enabling scientists from all countries to accurately exchange information.

The method of assigning a scientific or specific name is called the **binomial** (two-name) **system of nomenclature.** The scientific name is always a combination of the generic (genus) name followed by the species name. The generic part of the scientific name is capitalized, and the species part begins with a lowercase letter. Both should be italicized (or underlined if using handwriting), as follows:

<u>Staphylococcus aureus</u>

The two-part name of an organism is sometimes abbreviated to save space, as in *S. aureus,* but only if the genus name has already been stated. The source for nomenclature is usually Latin or Greek. If other languages such as English or French are used, the endings of these words are revised to have Latin endings. An international group oversees the naming of every new organism discovered, making sure that standard procedures have been followed and that there is not already an earlier name for the organism or another organism with that same name. The inspiration for names is extremely varied and often rather imaginative. Some species have been named in honor of a microbiologist who originally

INSIGHT 1.3   Martian Microbes and Astrobiology

Professional and amateur scientists have long been intrigued by the possible existence of life on other planets and in the surrounding universe. This curiosity has given rise to a new discipline—astrobiology—that applies principles from biology, chemistry, geology, and physics to investigate extraterrestrial life. One of the few accessible places to begin this search is the planet Mars. It is relatively close to the earth and the only planet in the solar system besides earth that is not extremely hot, cold, or bathed in toxic gases.

The possibility that it could support at least simple life forms has been an important focus of NASA space projects stretching over 30 years. Several Mars explorations have included experiments and collection devices to gather evidence for certain life signatures or characteristics. One of the first experiments launched with the *Viking Explorer* was an attempt to culture microbes from Martian soil. Another used a gas chromatograph to check for complex carbon-containing (organic) compounds in the soil samples. No signs of life or organic matter were detected. But in scientific research, a single experiment is not sufficient to completely rule out a hypothesis, especially one as attractive as this one. Many astrobiologists reason that the nature of the "life forms" may be so different that they require a different experimental design.

In 1996, another finding brought considerable excitement and controversy to the astrobiology community. Scientists doing electron microscopic analyses of an ancient Martian meteorite from the Antarctic discovered tiny rodlike structures that resembled earth bacteria. Though the idea was appealing, many scientists argued that the rods did not contain the correct form of carbon and that geologic substances often contain crystals that mimic other objects. Another team of NASA researchers later discovered chains of magnetite crystals (tiny iron oxide magnets) in another Martian meteorite. These crystals bear a distinct resemblance to forms found in certain modern bacteria on earth and are generally thought to be formed only by living processes.

Growing blobs of water on leg of a Mars lander (2009).

Obviously, these findings have added much fodder for speculation and further research. There has been a great deal of evidence that the planet harbored water at one time, considered to be a prerequisite for life of any kind. Channels resembling rivers have been documented by the multiple Mars landers NASA has deployed. Some scientists believe that there is still liquid water on Mars, perhaps in subsurface aquifers that bubble to the surface from time to time.

In 2009, a group of scientists reported on photographs that were taken of the legs of the Phoenix lander. The photographs appeared to show large droplets of water (see photo). The "droplets" grew larger over time, leading scientists to conclude that the (salty) water was absorbing more moisture from water vapor in the atmosphere. Whether this turns out to be true or not, the evidence for life-sustaining water on Mars seems to be accumulating.

Astrobiologists long ago put aside the quaint idea of meeting "little green men" when they got to the red planet, but they have not yet given up the possibility of finding "little green microbes." One hypothesis proposes that microbes hitchhiking on meteors and asteroids have seeded the solar system and perhaps universe with simple life forms. Certainly, of all organisms on earth, hardy prokaryotes are the ones most likely to survive the rigors of such travel. Recently scientists have tested this hypothesis and found that the bacteria in the experiment survived conditions that mimicked an asteroid hit. This raises the possibility that microbes could have traveled from a planet with life forms on it to other planets and possibly seeded a new beginning of life there. It also makes us wonder whether microbes could have blasted off of the surface of the earth only to return thousands of years later in asteroid hits, thereby confusing our sense of how organisms here evolved. As Benjamin Weiss of the Massachusetts Institute of Technology said in response to this study, "It's becoming more apparent that the planets are unlikely to have been biologically isolated from one another."

Martian microbes or mere molecules? Internal view of a section of a 4.5-billion-year-old Martian meteor shows an intriguing tiny cylinder (50,000×).

For more information on this subject, use a search engine to access the NASA Astrobiology Institute, NASA Mission to Mars, or NASA Exploration Program websites.

discovered the microbe or who has made outstanding contributions to the field. Other names may designate a characteristic of the microbe (shape, color), a location where it was found, or a disease it causes. Some examples of specific names, their pronunciations, and their origins are:

- *Staphylococcus aureus* (staf'-i-lo-kok'-us ah'-ree-us) Gr. *staphule,* bunch of grapes, *kokkus,* berry, and Gr. *aureus,* golden. A common bacterial pathogen of humans.
- *Campylobacter jejuni* (cam'-peh-loh-bak-ter jee-joo'-neye) Gr. *kampylos,* curved, *bakterion,* little rod, and *jejunum,* a section of intestine. One of the most important causes of intestinal infection worldwide.
- *Lactobacillus sanfrancisco* (lak'-toh-bass-ill'-us san-fran-siss'-koh) L. *lacto,* milk, and *bacillus,* little rod. A bacterial species used to make sourdough bread.
- *Vampirovibrio chlorellavorus* (vam-py'-roh-vib-ree-oh klor-ell-ah'-vor-us) F. *vampire;* L. *vibrio,* curved cell; *Chlorella,* a genus of green algae; and *vorus,* to devour. A small, curved bacterium that sucks out the cell juices of *Chlorella.*
- *Giardia lamblia* (jee-ar'-dee-uh lam'-blee-uh) for Alfred Giard, a French microbiologist, and Vilem Lambl, a Bohemian physician, both of whom worked on the organism, a protozoan that causes a severe intestinal infection.

Here's a helpful hint: These names may seem difficult to pronounce and the temptation is to simply "slur over them." But when you encounter the names of microorganisms in the chapters ahead, it will be extremely useful to take the time to sound them out and repeat them until they seem familiar. You are much more likely to remember them that way—and they are less likely to end up in a tangled heap with all of the new language you will be learning.

The Levels of Classification

The main units of a classification scheme are organized into several descending ranks, beginning with a most general all-inclusive taxonomic category as a common denominator for organisms to exclude all others, and ending with the smallest and most specific category. This means that all members of the highest category share only one or a few general characteristics, whereas members of the lowest category are essentially the same kind of organism—that is, they share the majority of their characteristics. The taxonomic categories from top to bottom are: **domain, kingdom, phylum** or **division,**[3] **class, order, family, genus,** and **species.** Thus, each kingdom can be subdivided into a series of phyla or divisions, each phylum is made up of several classes, each class contains several orders, and so on. Because taxonomic schemes are to some extent artificial, certain groups of organisms may not exactly fit into the main categories. In such a case, additional taxonomic levels can be

imposed above (super) or below (sub) a taxon, giving us such categories as "superphylum" and "subclass."

Let's compare the taxonomic breakdowns of a human and a protozoan (proh'-tuh-zoh'-uhn) to illustrate the fine points of this system **(figure 1.12).** Humans and protozoa are both organisms with nucleated cells (eukaryotes); therefore, they are in the same domain but they are in different kingdoms. Humans are multicellular animals (Kingdom Animalia) whereas protozoa are single-cellular organisms that, together with algae, belong to the Kingdom Protista. To emphasize just how broad the category "kingdom" is, ponder the fact that we humans belong to the same kingdom as jellyfish. Of the several phyla within this kingdom, humans belong to the Phylum Chordata, but even a phylum is rather all-inclusive, considering that humans share it with other vertebrates as well as with creatures called sea squirts. The next level, Class Mammalia, narrows the field considerably by grouping only those vertebrates that have hair and suckle their young. Humans belong to the Order Primates, a group that also includes apes, monkeys, and lemurs. Next comes the Family Hominoidea, containing only humans and apes. The final levels are our genus, *Homo* (all races of modern and ancient humans), and our species, *sapiens* (meaning wise). Notice that for the human as well as the protozoan, the taxonomic categories in descending order become less inclusive and the individual members more closely related. We need to remember that all taxonomic **hierarchies** are based on the judgment of scientists with certain expertise in a particular group of organisms and that not all other experts may agree with the system being used. Consequently, no taxa are permanent to any degree; they are constantly being revised and refined as new information becomes available or new viewpoints become prevalent. In this text, we are usually concerned with only the most general (kingdom, phylum) and specific (genus, species) taxonomic levels.

The Origin and Evolution of Microorganisms

As we indicated earlier, *taxonomy,* the science of classification of biological species, is used to organize all of the forms of modern and extinct life. In biology today, there are different methods for deciding on taxonomic categories, but they all rely on the degree of relatedness among organisms. The scheme that represents the natural relatedness (relation by descent) between groups of living beings is called their *phylogeny* (Gr. *phylon,* race or class; L. *genesis,* origin or beginning), and—when unraveled—biologists use phylogenetic relationships to refine the system of taxonomy.

To understand the natural history of and the relatedness among organisms, we must understand some fundamentals of the process of evolution. Evolution is an important theme that underlies all of biology, including the biology of microorganisms. As we said earlier, evolution states that the hereditary information in living beings changes gradually through time (usually hundreds of millions of years) and that these changes result in various structural and functional

---

3. The term *phylum* is used for bacteria, protozoa, and animals; the term *division* is used for algae, plants, and fungi.

Domain: Eukarya (All eukaryotic organisms)

Domain: Eukarya (All eukaryotic organisms)

Kingdom: Animalia

Lemur

Sea squirt

Sea star

Phylum: Chordata

Class: Mammalia

Order: Primates

Family: Hominoidea

Genus: *Homo*

Species: *sapiens*

(a)

Kingdom: Protista
Includes protozoa and algae

Phylum: Ciliophora
Only protozoa with cilia

Class: Hymenostomea
Single cells with regular rows of cilia; rapid swimmers

Order: Hymenostomatida
Elongated oval cells with cilia in the oral cavity

Family: Parameciidae
Cells rotate while swimming and have oral grooves.

Genus: *Paramecium*
Pointed, cigar-shaped cells with macronuclei and micronuclei

Species: *caudatum*
Cells cylindrical, long, and pointed at one end

(b)

Figure 1.12 Sample taxonomy. Two organisms belonging to the Eukarya domain, traced through their taxonomic series. **(a)** Modern humans, *Homo sapiens*. **(b)** A common protozoan, *Paramecium caudatum*.

changes through many generations. The process of evolution is selective in that those changes that most favor the survival of a particular organism or group of organisms tend to be retained whereas those that are less beneficial to survival tend to be lost. Charles Darwin called this process *natural selection.*

Evolution is founded on the two preconceptions that (1) all new species originate from preexisting species and (2) closely related organisms have similar features because they evolved from a common ancestor; hence, difference emerged by divergence. Usually, evolution progresses toward greater complexity but there are many examples of evolution toward lesser complexity (reductive evolution). This is

because individual organisms never evolve in isolation but as populations of organisms in their specific environments, which exert the functional pressures of selection. Because of the divergent nature of the evolutionary process, the phylogeny, or relatedness by descent, of organisms is often represented by a diagram of a tree. The trunk of the tree represents the origin of ancestral lines, and the branches show offshoots into specialized groups (clades) of organisms. This sort of arrangement places taxonomic groups with less divergence (less change in the heritable information) from the common ancestor closer to the root of the tree and taxa with lots of divergence closer to the top **(figures 1.13 and 1.14).**

Systems of Presenting a Universal Tree of Life

The first trees of life were constructed a long time ago on the basis of just two kingdoms, plants and animals, by Charles Darwin and Ernst Haeckel. These trees were chiefly based on visible morphological characteristics. It became clear that certain (micro)organisms such as algae and protozoa, which only existed as single cells, did not truly fit either of those categories, so a third kingdom was recognized by Haeckel for these simpler organisms. It was named Protista. Eventually, when significant differences became evident among even the unicellular organisms, a fourth kingdom was established in the 1870s by Haeckel and named Monera. Almost a century passed before Robert Whittaker extended this work and added a fifth kingdom for fungi during the period of 1959 to 1969. The relationships that were used in Whittaker's tree were those based on structural similarities and differences, such as prokaryotic and eukaryotic cellular organization, and the way these organisms obtained their nutrition. These criteria indicated that there were five major taxonomic units, or kingdoms: the monera, protists, plants, fungi, and animals, all of which consisted of one of the two cell types, the prokaryotic and eukaryotic. Whittaker's five-kingdom system quickly became the standard (see figure 1.13).

With the rise of genetics as a molecular science, newer methods for determining phylogeny have led to the development of a differently shaped tree—with important implications for our understanding of evolutionary relatedness. Molecular genetics allowed an in-depth study of the structure and function of the genetic material at the molecular level. These studies have revealed that two of the four macromolecules that contribute to cellular structure and function, the proteins and nucleic acids, are very well suited to study how organisms differ from one another because their sequences can be aligned and compared. In 1975, Carl Woese discovered that one particular macromolecule, the ribonucleic acid in the small subunit of the ribosome (ssu rRNA), was highly conserved—meaning that it was nearly identical in organisms within the smallest taxonomic category, the species. Based on a vast amount of experimental data and the knowledge that protein synthesis proceeds in

Figure 1.13 Traditional Whittaker system of classification.   In this system, kingdoms are based on cell structure and type, the nature of body organization, and nutritional type. Bacteria and Archaea (monerans) are made of prokaryotic cells and are unicellular. Protists are made of eukaryotic cells and are mostly unicellular. They can be photosynthetic (algae), or they can feed on other organisms (protozoa). Fungi are eukaryotic cells and are unicellular or multicellular; they have cell walls and are not photosynthetic. Plants have eukaryotic cells, are multicellular, have cell walls, and are photosynthetic. Animals have eukaryotic cells, are multicellular, do not have cell walls, and derive nutrients from other organisms. Source: After Dolphin, *Biology Lab Manual*, 4th ed., Fig. 14.1, p. 177, McGraw-Hill.

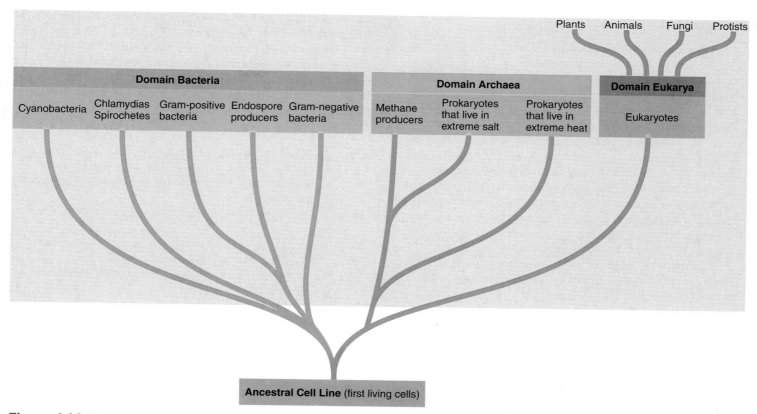

Figure 1.14 Woese-Fox system.   A system for representing the origins of cell lines and major taxonomic groups as proposed by Carl Woese and colleagues. They propose three distinct cell lines placed in superkingdoms called domains. The first primitive cells, called progenotes, were ancestors of both lines of prokaryotes (Domain Bacteria and Archaea), and the Archaea emerged from the same cell line as eukaryotes (Domain Eukarya). Some of the traditional kingdoms are still present with this system (see figure 1.13).

all organisms facilitated by the ribosome, Woese hypothesized that ssu rRNA provides a "biological chronometer" or a "living record" of the evolutionary history of a given organism. Extended analysis of this molecule in prokaryotic and eukaryotic cells indicated that all members in a certain group of bacteria, then known as archaeobacteria, had ssu rRNA with a sequence that was significantly different from the ssu rRNA found in other bacteria and in eukaryotes. This discovery led Carl Woese and collaborator George Fox to propose a separate taxonomic unit for the archaeobacteria, which they named **Archaea.** Under the microscope, they resembled the prokaryotic structure of bacteria, but molecular biology has revealed that the archaea, though prokaryotic in nature, were actually more closely related to eukaryotic cells than to bacterial cells (see table 4.6). To reflect these relationships, Carl Woese and George Fox proposed an entirely new system that assigned all known organisms to one of the three major taxonomic units, the **domains,** each being a different type of cell (see figure 1.14).

The domains are the highest level in hierarchy and can contain many kingdoms and superkingdoms. The prokaryotic cell types are represented by the domains Archaea and **Bacteria,** whereas eukaryotes are all placed in the domain **Eukarya.** Analysis of the ssu rRNAs from all organisms in these three domains suggests that all modern and extinct organisms on earth arose from a common ancestor. Therefore, eukaryotes did not emerge from prokaryotes. Both types of cells emerged separately from a different, now extinct, cell type.

To add another level of complexity, the most current data suggests that "trees" of life do not truly represent the relatedness—and evolution—of organisms at all. It has become obvious that genes travel horizontally—meaning from one species to another in nonreproductive ways—and that the neat generation-to-generation changes are combined with neighbor-to-neighbor exchanges of DNA. For example, it is estimated that 40% to 50% of human DNA has been carried to humans from other species (by viruses). Another example: The genome of the cow contains a piece of snake DNA. For these reasons, most scientists like to think of a *web* as the proper representation of life these days. The three-domain system somewhat complicates the presentation of organisms in the original Kingdom Protista, which is now a collection of protozoa and algae that exist in several separate kingdoms (discussed in chapter 5). Nevertheless, this new scheme does not greatly affect our presentation of most microbes, because we will discuss them at the genus or species level. But be aware that biological taxonomy and, more important, our view of how organisms evolved on earth are in a period of transition. Keep in mind that our methods of classification or evolutionary schemes reflect our current

Case File 1 *Wrap-Up*

Based on the extraordinary success of the first *Sorcerer II* voyage, a more extensive second voyage visited many different locations around the world, including the Galápagos Islands, where Darwin made many of his observations. J. Craig Venter's second voyage led to the discovery of 20 million new genes and thousands of new protein families. Of particular interest to Venter were a group of genes called *rhodopsins*, which help bacteria capture energy from the sun. Venter hopes these bacteria may one day be used as an alternative energy source. He articulated this hope in a 2007 interview when he said, "We really need to find an alternative to taking carbon out of the ground, burning it, and putting it into the atmosphere. That is the single biggest contribution I could make."

On March 19, 2009, the *Sorcerer II* left her home port of San Diego for a third voyage. Further exciting discoveries seem likely.

See: 2007. *PLoS Biol.* 2007 Mar 13; 5(3): 16.

understanding and will change as new information is uncovered.

Please note that viruses are not included in any of the classification or evolutionary schemes, because they are not cells or organisms and their position in a "tree of life" cannot be determined. The special taxonomy of viruses is discussed in chapter 6.

1.7 Learning Outcomes—Can You ...

13. ... differentiate between the terms nomenclature, taxonomy, and classification?

14. ... create a mnemonic device for remembering the taxonomic categories?

15. ... correctly write the binomial name for a microorganism?

16. ... draw a diagram of the three major domains?

17. ... explain the difference between traditional and molecular approaches to taxonomy?

Chapter Summary

1.1 The Scope of Microbiology
- Microorganisms are defined as "living organisms too small to be seen with the naked eye." Among the members of this huge group of organisms are bacteria, algae, protozoa, fungi, parasitic worms (helminths), and viruses.
- Microorganisms live nearly everywhere and influence many biological and physical activities on earth.
- There are many kinds of relationships between microorganisms and humans; most are beneficial, but some are harmful.

1.2 The Impact of Microbes on Earth: Small Organisms with a Giant Effect
- Groups of organisms are constantly evolving to produce new forms of life.
- Microbes are crucial to the cycling of nutrients and energy that are necessary for all life on earth.

1.3 Human Use of Microorganisms
- Humans have learned how to manipulate microbes to do important work for them in industry, medicine, and in caring for the environment.

1.4 Infectious Diseases and the Human Condition
- In the last 120 years, microbiologists have identified the causative agents for many infectious diseases. In addition, they have discovered distinct connections between microorganisms and diseases whose causes were previously unknown.
- While microbial diseases continue to cause disease worldwide, low-income countries are much harder hit by them directly and indirectly.

1.5 The General Characteristics of Microorganisms
- Excluding the viruses, there are two types of microorganisms: prokaryotes, which are small and lack a nucleus and organelles, and eukaryotes, which are larger and have both a nucleus and organelles.

- Viruses are not cellular and are therefore sometimes called particles rather than organisms. They are included in microbiology because of their small size and close relationship with cells.

1.6 The Historical Foundations of Microbiology
- The microscope made it possible to see microorganisms and thus to identify their widespread presence, particularly as agents of disease.
- The theory of spontaneous generation of living organisms from "vital forces" in the air was disproved once and for all by Louis Pasteur.
- The scientific method is a process by which scientists seek to explain natural phenomena. It is characterized by specific procedures that either support or discredit an initial hypothesis.
- Knowledge acquired through the scientific method is rigorously tested by repeated experiments by many scientists to verify its validity. A collection of valid hypotheses is called a theory. A theory supported by much data collected over time is called a law.
- Scientific dogma or theory changes through time as new research brings new information.
- Medical microbiologists developed the germ theory of disease and introduced the critically important concept of aseptic technique to control the spread of disease agents.

1.7 Naming, Classifying, and Identifying Microorganisms
- The taxonomic system has three primary functions: naming, classifying, and identifying species.
- The major groups in the most advanced taxonomic system are (in descending order): domain, kingdom, phylum or division, class, order, family, genus, and species.
- Evolutionary patterns show a treelike or weblike branching thereby describing the diverging evolution of all life forms from the gene pool of a common ancestor.
- The Woese-Fox classification system places all eukaryotes in the domain Eukarya and subdivides the prokaryotes into the two domains Archaea and Bacteria.

Multiple-Choice and True-False Questions   Knowledge and Comprehension

Multiple-Choice Questions. Select the correct answer from the answers provided.

1. Which of the following is not considered a microorganism?
   a. alga
   b. bacterium
   c. protozoan
   d. mushroom

2. Which process involves the deliberate alteration of an organism's genetic material?
   a. bioremediation
   b. biotechnology
   c. decomposition
   d. recombinant DNA technology

3. Which of the following parts was absent from Leeuwenhoek's microscopes?
   a. focusing screw
   b. lens
   c. specimen holder
   d. condenser

4. Abiogenesis refers to the
   a. spontaneous generation of organisms from nonliving matter.
   b. development of life forms from preexisting life forms.
   c. development of aseptic technique.
   d. germ theory of disease.

5. A hypothesis can be defined as
   a. a belief based on knowledge.
   b. knowledge based on belief.
   c. a scientific explanation that is subject to testing.
   d. a theory that has been thoroughly tested.

6. When a hypothesis has been thoroughly supported by long-term study and data, it is considered
   a. a law.
   b. a speculation.
   c. a theory.
   d. proved.

7. Which is the correct order of the taxonomic categories, going from most specific to most general?
   a. domain, kingdom, phylum, class, order, family, genus, species
   b. division, domain, kingdom, class, family, genus, species
   c. species, genus, family, order, class, phylum, kingdom, domain
   d. species, family, class, order, phylum, kingdom

8. Which of the following are prokaryotic?
   a. bacteria
   b. archaea
   c. protists
   d. both a and b

9. Order the following items by size, using numbers: 1 = smallest through 8 = largest.
   _____ AIDS virus _____ worm
   _____ amoeba _____ coccus-shaped bacterium
   _____ rickettsia _____ white blood cell
   _____ protein _____ atom

10. How would you classify a virus?
    a. prokaryotic
    b. eukaryotic
    c. neither a nor b

True-False Questions. If the statement is true, leave as is. If it is false, correct it by rewriting the sentence.

11. Organisms in the same order are more closely related than those in the same family.

12. Eukaryotes evolved from prokaryotes.

13. Prokaryotes have no nucleus.

14. In order to be called a theory, a scientific idea has to undergo a great deal of testing.

15. Microbes are ubiquitous.

Critical Thinking Questions   Application and Analysis

These questions are suggested as a *writing-to-learn* experience. For each question, compose a one- or two-paragraph answer that includes the factual information needed to completely address the question.

1. Explain the important contributions microorganisms make in the earth's ecosystems.

2. Why was the abandonment of the spontaneous generation theory so significant? Using the scientific method, describe the steps you would take to test the theory of spontaneous generation.

3. a. Differentiate between a hypothesis and a theory.
   b. Is the germ theory of disease really a law? Why or why not?

4. What is a binomial system of nomenclature, and why is it used?

5. Compare the new domain system with the five-kingdom system. Does the newer system change the basic idea of prokaryotes and eukaryotes? What is the third cell type?

6. Evolution accounts for the millions of different species on the earth and their adaptation to its many and diverse habitats. Explain this. Cite examples in your answer.

7. Where do you suppose the "new" infectious diseases come from?

8. Can you develop a scientific hypothesis and means of testing the cause of stomach ulcers? (Is it caused by an infection? By too much acid? By a genetic disorder?)

9. Where do you suppose viruses came from? Why do they require the host's cellular machinery?

10. Archaea are often found in hot, sulfuric, acidic, salty habitats, much like the early earth's conditions. Speculate on the origin of life, especially as it relates to the archaea.

Concept Mapping   Synthesis

Appendix D provides guidance for working with concept maps.

1. Supply your own linking words or phrases in this concept map, and provide the missing concepts in the empty boxes.

Visual Connections   Synthesis

These questions use visual images or previous content to make connections to this chapter's concepts.

1. **Figure 1.1.** Look at the blue bar (the time that prokaryotes have been on earth) and at the pink arrow (the time that humans appeared). Speculate on the probability that we will be able to completely disinfect our planet or prevent all microbial diseases.

www.connect.microbiology.com

Enhance your study of this chapter with study tools and practice tests. Also ask your instructor about the resources available through ConnectPlus, including the media-rich eBook, interactive learning tools, and animations.

The Chemistry of Biology

Case File 2

A group of scientists at the Centers for Disease Control (CDC) noted 13 cases of *Salmonella enterica* infection in sick people in a dozen states during November 2008. The typical symptoms of salmonellosis (infection with salmonella) include vomiting and diarrhea, and may result from ingesting any of more than 1,500 different *strains*, or unique subspecies, of *S. enterica*. Two weeks later, a similar outbreak of 27 cases of the disease, spread across 14 states, was found to be caused by the same strain of the organism seen in the first outbreak. By February 2009, 682 people from 46 states and Canada had become infected, nine had died, a large corporation had filed for bankruptcy, and several criminal investigations had begun.

PulseNet is a branch of the CDC that seeks to identify food-borne disease clusters by carefully studying the bacterial isolates thought to be the source of an outbreak. Usually this means obtaining DNA profiles, called *fingerprints*, of each bacterium and using that information to compare *isolates* (isolated strains of bacteria) from different outbreaks. Because the fingerprints from the two outbreak strains in this case were similar to one another—but also different from any fingerprint within the PulseNet database—CDC scientists initiated an epidemiological investigation.

S. enterica was identified in unopened 5-pound containers of King Nut peanut butter in Minnesota and Connecticut, in the peanut butter factory, and in bacteria isolated from the patients. At the time, King Nut peanut butter was manufactured by the Peanut Corporation of America (PCA) in Blakely, Georgia, and sold to schools, hospitals, restaurants, cafeterias, and other large institutions rather than directly to consumers. Examination of the bacteria revealed several different *S. enterica* strains, but only a few of them were linked to the illnesses.

- ■ What chemicals make up DNA?
- ■ Without knowing the specific details of DNA fingerprinting, how do you think these profiles could be used to show that a particular bacterial strain is *not* part of an outbreak?

Continuing the Case appears on page 34.

Outline and Learning Outcomes

2.1 Atoms, Bonds, and Molecules: Fundamental Building Blocks

The universe is composed of an infinite variety of substances existing in the gaseous, liquid, and solid states. All such tangible materials that occupy space and have mass are called **matter.** The organization of matter—whether air, rocks, or bacteria—begins with individual building blocks called atoms. An **atom** is defined as a tiny particle that cannot be subdivided into smaller substances without losing its properties. Even in a science dealing with very small things, an atom's minute size is striking; for example, an oxygen atom is only 0.0000000013 mm (0.0013 nm) in diameter, and 1 million of them in a cluster would barely be visible to the naked eye.

The exact composition of atoms has been well established by extensive physical analysis using sophisticated instruments. In general, an atom derives its properties from a combination of subatomic particles called **protons** (p^+), which are positively charged; **neutrons** (n^0), which have no charge (are neutral); and **electrons** (e^-), which are negatively charged. The relatively larger protons and neutrons make up a central

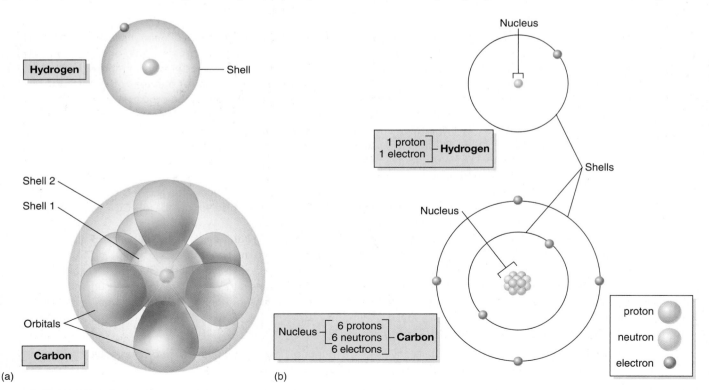

Figure 2.1 Models of atomic structure. **(a)** Three-dimensional models of hydrogen and carbon that approximate their actual structure. The nucleus is surrounded by electrons in orbitals that occur in levels called shells. Hydrogen has just one shell and one orbital. Carbon has two shells and four orbitals; the shape of the outermost orbitals is paired lobes rather than circles or spheres. **(b)** Simple models of the same atoms make it easier to show the numbers and arrangements of shells and electrons and the numbers of protons and neutrons in the nucleus. (Not to accurate scale.)

core, or *nucleus*,[1] that is surrounded by one or more electrons **(figure 2.1)**. The nucleus makes up the larger mass (weight) of the atom, whereas the electron region accounts for the greater volume. To get a perspective on proportions, consider this: If an atom were the size of a baseball stadium, the nucleus would be about the size of a marble! The stability of atomic structure is largely maintained by (1) the mutual attraction of the protons and electrons (opposite charges attract each other) and (2) the exact balance of proton number and electron number, which causes the opposing charges to cancel each other out. At least in theory, then, isolated intact atoms do not carry a charge.

---

1. Be careful not to confuse the nucleus of an atom with the nucleus of a cell (discussed later).

Different Types of Atoms: Elements and Their Properties

All atoms share the same fundamental structure. All protons are identical, all neutrons are identical, and all electrons are identical. But when these subatomic particles come together in specific, varied combinations, unique types of atoms called **elements** result. Each element has a characteristic atomic structure and predictable chemical behavior. To date, about 118 elements, both naturally occurring and artificially produced by physicists, have been described. By convention, an element is assigned a distinctive name with an abbreviated shorthand symbol. The elements are often depicted in a periodic table. **Table 2.1** lists some of the elements common

Table 2.1 The Major Elements of Life and Their Primary Characteristics

Element	Atomic Symbol*	Atomic Mass**	Examples of Ionized Forms	Significance in Microbiology
Calcium	Ca	40.1	Ca^{2+}	Part of outer covering of certain shelled amoebas; stored within bacterial spores
Carbon	C	12.0	CO_3^{-2}	Principal structural component of biological molecules
Carbon•	C-14	14.0		Radioactive isotope used in dating fossils
Chlorine	Cl	35.5	Cl^-	Component of disinfectants, used in water purification
Cobalt	Co	58.9	Co^{2+}, Co^{3+}	Trace element needed by some bacteria to synthesize vitamins
Cobalt•	Co-60	60		An emitter of gamma rays; used in food sterilization; used to treat cancer
Copper	Cu	63.5	Cu^+, Cu^{2+}	Necessary to the function of some enzymes; Cu salts are used to treat fungal and worm infections
Hydrogen	H	1	H^+	Necessary component of water and many organic molecules; H_2 gas released by bacterial metabolism
Hydrogen•	H3	3		Has 2 neutrons; radioactive; used in clinical laboratory procedures
Iodine	I	126.9	I^-	A component of antiseptics and disinfectants; used in the Gram stain
Iodine•	I-131, I-125	131, 125		Radioactive isotopes for diagnosis and treatment of cancers
Iron	Fe	55.8	Fe^{2+}, Fe^{3+}	Necessary component of respiratory enzymes; required by some microbes to produce toxin
Magnesium	Mg	24.3	Mg^{2+}	A trace element needed for some enzymes; component of chlorophyll pigment
Manganese	Mn	54.9	Mn^{2+}, Mn^{3+}	Trace element for certain respiratory enzymes
Nitrogen	N	14.0	NO_3^-	Component of all proteins and nucleic acids; the major atmospheric gas
Oxygen	O	16.0		An essential component of many organic molecules; molecule used in metabolism by many organisms
Phosphorus	P	31	PO_4^{3-}	A component of ATP, nucleic acids, cell membranes; stored in granules in cells
Phosphorus•	P-32	32		Radioactive isotope used as a diagnostic and therapeutic agent
Potassium	K	39.1	K^+	Required for normal ribosome function and protein synthesis; essential for cell membrane permeability
Sodium	Na	23.0	Na^+	Necessary for transport; maintains osmotic pressure; used in food preservation
Sulfur	S	32.1	SO_4^{-2}	Important component of proteins; makes disulfide bonds; storage element in many bacteria
Zinc	Zn	65.4	Zn^{++}	An enzyme cofactor; required for protein synthesis and cell division; important in regulating DNA

*Based on the Latin name of the element. The first letter is always capitalized; if there is a second letter, it is always lowercased.
**The atomic mass or weight is equal to the average mass number for the isotopes of that element.

to biological systems, their atomic characteristics, and some of the natural and applied roles they play.

The Major Elements of Life and Their Primary Characteristics

The unique properties of each element result from the numbers of protons, neutrons, and electrons it contains, and each element can be identified by certain physical measurements.

Isotopes are variant forms of the same element that differ in the number of neutrons. These multiple forms occur naturally in certain proportions. Carbon, for example, exists primarily as carbon 12 with 6 neutrons; but a small amount (about 1%) is carbon 13 with 7 neutrons and carbon 14 with 8 neutrons. Although isotopes have virtually the same chemical properties, some of them have unstable nuclei that spontaneously release energy in the form of radiation. Such *radioactive isotopes* play a role in a number of research and medical applications. Because they emit detectable signs, they can be used to trace the position of key atoms or molecules in chemical reactions, they are tools in diagnosis and treatment, and they are even applied in sterilization procedures (see ionizing radiation in chapter 11). Another application of isotopes is in dating fossils and other ancient materials.

Electron Orbitals and Shells

The structure of an atom can be envisioned as a central nucleus surrounded by a "cloud" of electrons that constantly rotate about the nucleus in pathways (see figure 2.1). The pathways, called **orbitals,** are not actual objects or exact locations but represent volumes of space in which an electron is likely to be found. Electrons occupy energy shells, proceeding from the lower-level energy electrons nearest the nucleus to the higher-level energy electrons in the farthest orbitals.

Electrons fill the orbitals and shells in *pairs,* starting with the shell nearest the nucleus. The first shell contains one orbital and a maximum of 2 electrons; the second shell has four orbitals and up to 8 electrons; the third shell with nine orbitals can hold up to 18 electrons; and the fourth shell with 16 orbitals contains up to 32 electrons. The number of orbitals and shells and how completely they are filled depend on the numbers of electrons, so that each element will have a unique pattern. For example, helium has only a filled first shell of 2 electrons; oxygen has a filled first shell and a partially filled second shell of 6 electrons; and magnesium has a filled first shell, a filled second one, and a third shell that fills only one orbital, so is nearly empty. As we will see, the chemical properties of an element are controlled mainly by the distribution of electrons in the outermost shell. Figure 2.1 and **figure 2.2** present various

Figure 2.2 Examples of biologically important atoms. Simple models show how the shells are filled by electrons as the atomic numbers increase. Notice that these elements have incompletely filled outer shells since they have less than 8 electrons.

INSIGHT 2.1   The Periodic Table: Not as Concrete as You Think

Most of us have seen images of the periodic table like the one in figure 2.3 over and over again as we progressed through school. Like many things in science, it seems easy to view the periodic table as "set in stone," with only an occasional addition to the end of it as new elements are found. But since the time it was proposed, there have been legitimate arguments about how it should be represented. These arguments continue today.

The first periodic table, the work of Russian chemist Dimitri Mendeleev, was published in 1869. It is called the periodic table because it lays out the pattern of chemicals based on certain properties in them that repeat. Repeating patterns = periodicity. When you realize that the rows indicate increasing atomic number and each column represents a group in which the elements have related valences, which confers on them similar chemical properties, the current table seems elegant and, well, right. However, current scientists have been questioning whether the two-dimensional way of representing the elements is the best. The table leads to some minor inaccuracies that not all chemists are comfortable with. Two 3-D representations have been proposed and are pictured here. Also, you see here a unique walk-up version of the traditional periodic table. Another example of how science—even the most familiar "facts" and ideas—is an ever-evolving entity.

A Note About Mass, Weight, and Related Terms

Mass refers to the quantity of matter that an atomic particle contains. The proton and neutron have almost exactly the same mass, which is about 1.66×10^{-24} grams, a unit of mass known as a Dalton (Da) or unified atomic mass unit (U). All elements can be measured in these units. The terms mass and weight are often used interchangeably in biology, even though they apply to two different but related aspects of matter. Weight is a measurement of the gravitational pull on the mass of a particle, atom, or object. Consequently, it is possible for something with the same mass to have different weights. For example, an astronaut on the earth (normal gravity) would weigh more than the same astronaut on the moon (weak gravity). Atomic weight has been the traditional usage for biologists, because most chemical reactions and biological activities occur within the normal gravitational conditions on earth. This permits use of the atomic weight as a standard of comparison. You will also see the terms formula weight and molecular weight used interchangeably, and they are indeed synonyms. They both mean the sum of atomic weights of all atoms in a molecule.

simplified models of atomic structure and electron maps. **Figure 2.3** presents all the elements in the familiar periodic table. (Although 118 have been described, only 112 have been officially sanctioned to date.) To see how the periodic table might look different, see **Insight 2.1.**

Bonds and Molecules

Most elements do not exist naturally in pure, uncombined form but are bound together as molecules and compounds. A **molecule** is a distinct chemical substance that results from the combination of two or more atoms. Some molecules such as oxygen (O_2) and nitrogen gas (N_2) consist of atoms of the same element. Molecules that are combinations of two or more *different* elements are termed **compounds.** Compounds such as water (H_2O) and biological molecules (proteins, sugars, fats) are the predominant substances in living systems. When atoms bind together in molecules, they lose the properties of the atom and take on the properties of the combined substance.

The **chemical bonds** of molecules and compounds result when two or more atoms share, donate (lose), or accept (gain) electrons **(figure 2.4).** The number of electrons in the outermost shell of an element is known as its **valence.** The valence determines the degree of reactivity and the types of bonds an element can make. Elements with a filled outer orbital are relatively stable because they have no extra electrons to share with or donate to other atoms. For example, helium has one filled shell, with no tendency either to give

up electrons or to take them from other elements, making it a stable, inert (nonreactive) gas. Elements with partially filled outer orbitals are less stable and are more apt to form some sort of bond. Many chemical reactions are based on the tendency of atoms with unfilled outer shells to gain greater stability by achieving, or at least approximating, a filled outer shell. For example, an atom such as oxygen that can accept 2 additional electrons will bond readily with atoms (such as hydrogen) that can share or donate electrons. We explore some additional examples of the basic types of bonding in the following section.

In addition to reactivity, the number of electrons in the outer shell also dictates the number of chemical bonds an atom can make. For instance, hydrogen can bind with one other atom, oxygen can bind with up to two other atoms, and carbon can bind with four.

Covalent Bonds and Polarity: Molecules with Shared Electrons

Covalent (cooperative valence) **bonds** form between atoms that share electrons rather than donating or receiving them. A simple example is hydrogen gas (H_2), which consists of two hydrogen atoms. A hydrogen atom has only a single electron, but when two of them combine, each will bring its electron to orbit about both nuclei, thereby approaching a filled orbital (2 electrons) for both atoms and thus creating a single covalent bond **(figure 2.5a).** Covalent bonding also occurs in

Figure 2.3 The periodic table. The 1–18 group designation has been recommended by the International Union of Pure and Applied Chemistry (IUPAC) but is not yet in wide use.

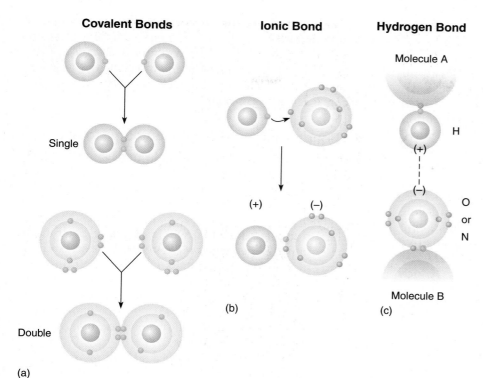

Figure 2.4 General representation of three types of bonding. **(a)** Covalent bonds, both single and double. **(b)** Ionic bond. **(c)** Hydrogen bond. Note that hydrogen bonds are represented in models and formulas by dotted lines, as shown in (c).

oxygen gas (O_2) but with a difference. Because each atom has 2 electrons to share in this molecule, the combination creates two pairs of shared electrons, also known as a double covalent bond **(figure 2.5b).** The majority of the molecules associated with living things are composed of single and double covalent bonds between the most common biological ele-

ments (carbon, hydrogen, oxygen, nitrogen, sulfur, and phosphorus), which are discussed in more depth in chapter 7. Double bonds in molecules and compounds introduce more rigidity than single bonds. A slightly more complex pattern of covalent bonding is shown for methane gas (CH_4) in **figure 2.5c.**

Figure 2.5 Examples of molecules with covalent bonding. **(a)** A hydrogen molecule is formed when two hydrogen atoms share their electrons and form a single bond. **(b)** In a double bond, the outer orbitals of two oxygen atoms overlap and permit the sharing of 4 electrons (one pair from each) and the saturation of the outer orbital for both. **(c)** Simple, three-dimensional, and working models of methane. Note that carbon has 4 electrons to share and hydrogens each have one, thereby completing the shells for all atoms in the compound, and creating 4 single bonds.

Other effects of bonding result in differences in polarity. When atoms of different electronegativity[2] form covalent bonds, the electrons are not shared equally and may be pulled more toward one atom than another. This pull causes one end of a molecule to assume a partial negative charge and the other end to assume a partial positive charge. A molecule with such an asymmetrical distribution of charges is termed **polar** and has positive and negative poles. Observe the water molecule shown in **figure 2.6** and note that, because the oxygen atom is larger and has more protons than the hydrogen atoms, it will tend to draw the shared electrons with greater force toward its nucleus. This unequal force causes the oxygen part of the molecule to express a negative charge (due to the electrons being attracted there) and the hydrogens to express a positive charge (due to the protons). The polar nature of water plays an extensive role in a number of biological reactions, which are discussed later. Polarity is a significant property of many large molecules in living systems and greatly influences both their reactivity and their structure.

A Note About Diatomic Elements

You will notice that hydrogen, oxygen, nitrogen, chlorine, and iodine are often shown in notation with a 2 subscript—H_2 or O_2. These elements are diatomic (two atoms), meaning that in their pure elemental state, they exist in pairs, rather than as a single atom. The reason for this phenomenon has to do with their valences. The electrons in the outer shell are configured so as to complete a full outer shell for both atoms when they bind. You can see this for yourself in figures 2.3 and 2.5. Most of the diatomic elements are gases.

2. Electronegativity—the ability to attract electrons.

When covalent bonds are formed between atoms that have the same or similar electronegativity, the electrons are shared equally between the two atoms. Because of this balanced distribution, no part of the molecule has a greater attraction for the electrons. This sort of electrically neutral molecule is termed **nonpolar.**

Ionic Bonds: Electron Transfer Among Atoms

In reactions that form **ionic bonds**, electrons are transferred completely from one atom to another and are not shared. These reactions invariably occur between atoms with valences that complement each other, meaning that one atom has an unfilled shell that will readily accept electrons and the other atom has an unfilled shell that will readily lose electrons. A striking example is the reaction that occurs between sodium (Na) and chlorine (Cl). Elemental sodium is a soft, lustrous metal so reactive that it can burn flesh, and molecular chlorine is a very poisonous yellow gas. But when the two are combined, they form sodium chloride[3] (NaCl)—the familiar nontoxic table salt—a compound with properties quite different from either parent element **(figure 2.7).**

How does this transformation occur? Sodium has 11 electrons (2 in shell one, 8 in shell two, and only 1 in shell three), so it is 7 short of having a complete outer shell. Chlorine has 17 electrons (2 in shell one, 8 in shell two, and 7 in shell three), making it 1 short of a complete outer shell. These two atoms are very reactive with one another, because a sodium atom will readily donate its single electron and a chlorine atom will avidly receive it. (The reaction is slightly more involved than a single sodium atom's combining with a single chloride atom **(Insight 2.2)**, but this complexity does not detract from

3. In general, when a salt is formed, the ending of the name of the negatively charged ion is changed to -ide.

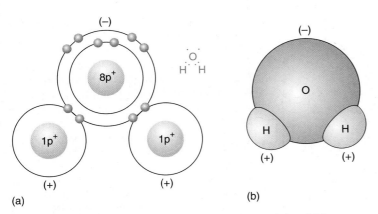

Figure 2.6 Polar molecule.   (a) A simple model and **(b)** a three-dimensional model of a water molecule indicate the polarity, or unequal distribution, of electrical charge, which is caused by the pull of the shared electrons toward the oxygen side of the molecule.

Case File 2   *Continuing the Case*

DNA is a long molecule made up of repeating units called nucleotides. The identity and order in which the four nucleotides (adenine, guanine, thymine, and cytosine) occur are the basis for the genetic information held by a particular stretch of DNA. The eventual expression of this information by the cell results in the production of physical features that can be used to distinguish one cell from another. Also, because DNA is used to transfer genetic information from one generation to the next, all cells descended from a single original cell have similar or identical DNA sequences, while the DNA from strains that are not closely related is less alike. The DNA differences that exist between the various types of *Salmonella* have led to *S. enterica* being subdivided into many strains, or *serotypes*, based on differences in the major surface components. In fact, *Salmonella* strains are often identified by their genus, species, *and* serotype, such as *S. enterica* Typhimurium or *S. enterica* serotype Tennessee.

(a) Sodium atom (Na)   Chlorine atom (Cl)

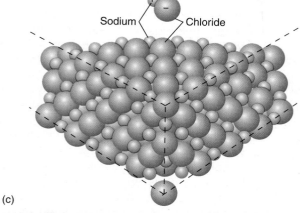

(b) Na : C̈l· ⟶ [Na]⁺ [Cl]⁻

Sodium   Chloride

(c)

(d)

Figure 2.7 Ionic bonding between sodium and chlorine.
(a) When the two elements are placed together, sodium loses its single outer orbital electron to chlorine, thereby filling chlorine's outer shell. **(b)** Simple model of ionic bonding. **(c)** Sodium and chloride ions form large molecules, or crystals, in which the two atoms alternate in a definite, regular, geometric pattern. **(d)** Note the cubic nature of NaCl crystals at the macroscopic level.

the fundamental reaction as described here.) The outcome of this reaction is not many single, isolated molecules of NaCl but rather a solid crystal complex that interlinks millions of sodium and chloride ions **(figure 2.7c,d).**

Ionization: Formation of Charged Particles   Molecules with intact ionic bonds are electrically neutral, but they can produce charged particles when dissolved in a liquid called a solvent. This phenomenon, called **ionization,** occurs when the ionic bond is broken and the atoms dissociate (separate)

The metabolic work of cells, such as synthesis, movement, and digestion, revolves around energy exchanges and transfers. The management of energy in cells is almost exclusively dependent on chemical rather than physical reactions because most cells are far too delicate to operate with heat, radiation, and other more potent forms of energy. The outer-shell electrons are readily portable and easily manipulated sources of energy. It is in fact the movement of electrons from molecule to molecule that accounts for most energy exchanges in cells. Fundamentally, then, a cell must have a supply of atoms that can gain or lose electrons if they are to carry out life processes.

The phenomenon in which electrons are transferred from one atom or molecule to another is termed an **oxidation** and **reduction** (shortened to **redox**) reaction. The term *oxidation* was originally adopted for reactions involving the addition of oxygen. In current usage, the term oxidation can include any reaction causing electron loss, regardless of the involvement of oxygen. By comparison, *reduction* is any reaction that causes an atom to receive electrons, because all redox reactions occur in pairs.

To analyze the phenomenon, let us again review the production of NaCl but from a different standpoint.

When these two atoms react to form sodium chloride, a sodium atom gives up an electron to a chlorine atom. During this reaction, sodium is oxidized because it loses an electron, and chlorine is reduced because it gains an electron (figure 2.7). With this system, an atom such as sodium that can donate electrons and thereby reduce another atom is a **reducing agent.** An atom that can receive extra electrons and thereby oxidize another molecule is an **oxidizing agent.** You may find this concept easier to keep straight if you think of redox agents as partners: The reducing partner gives its electrons away and is oxidized; the oxidizing partner receives the electrons and is reduced. A mnemonic device to keep track of this is "LEO says GER" (Lose Electrons Oxidized; Gain Electrons Reduced).

Redox reactions are essential to many of the biochemical processes discussed in chapter 8. In cellular metabolism, electrons are frequently transferred from one molecule to another as described here. In other reactions, oxidation and reduction occur with the transfer of a hydrogen atom (a proton and an electron) from one compound to another.

e^- → ▢ → ⬡ → ⬡

Reducing agent   Oxidizing agent   Oxidized product   Reduced product

Simplified diagram of the exchange of electrons during an oxidation-reduction reaction.

into unattached, charged particles called **ions (figure 2.8).** To illustrate what gives a charge to ions, let us look again at the reaction between sodium and chlorine. When a sodium atom reacts with chlorine and loses 1 electron, the sodium is left with one more proton than electrons. This imbalance produces a positively charged sodium ion (Na^+). Chlorine, on the other hand, has gained 1 electron and now has 1 more electron than protons, producing a negatively charged ion (Cl^-). Positively charged ions are termed **cations,** and negatively charged ions are termed **anions.** (A good mnemonic device is to think of the "t" in cation as a plus (+) sign and the first "n" in anion as a negative (−) sign.) Substances such as salts, acids, and bases that release ions when dissolved in water are termed **electrolytes** because their charges enable them to conduct an electrical current. Owing to the general rule that particles of like charge repel each other and those of opposite charge attract each other, we can expect ions to interact electrostatically with other ions and polar molecules. Such interactions are important in many cellular chemical reactions, in the formation of solutions, and in the

reactions microorganisms have with dyes. The transfer of electrons from one molecule to another constitutes a significant mechanism by which biological systems store and release energy.

Hydrogen Bonding   Some types of bonding do not involve sharing, losing, or gaining electrons but instead are due to attractive forces between nearby molecules or atoms. One such bond is a **hydrogen bond,** a weak type of bond that forms between a hydrogen covalently bonded to one molecule and an oxygen or nitrogen atom on the same molecule or on a different molecule. Because hydrogen in a covalent bond tends to be positively charged, it will attract a nearby negatively charged atom and form an easily disrupted bridge with it. This type of bonding is usually represented in molecular models with a dotted line. A simple example of hydrogen bonding occurs between water molecules **(figure 2.9).** More extensive hydrogen bonding is partly responsible for the structure and stability of proteins and nucleic acids, as you will see later on.

Other similar noncovalent associations between molecules are the **van der Waals forces.** These weak attractions occur between molecules that demonstrate low levels of polarity. Neighboring groups with slight attractions will interact and remain associated. These forces are an essential factor in maintaining the cohesiveness of large molecules with many packed atoms.

It is safe to say that though each of these two types of bonds, hydrogen bonds and van der Waals forces, are relatively weak on their own, they provide great stability to molecules because there are often many of them in one area. The weakness of each individual bond also provides flexibility, allowing molecules to change their shapes and also to bind and unbind to other objects relatively easily. The fundamental processes of life involve bonding and unbond-

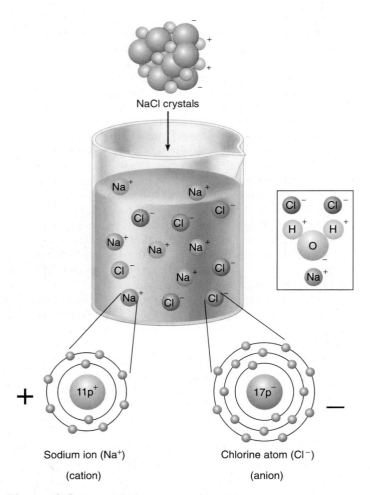

Figure 2.8 Ionization. When NaCl in the crystalline form is added to water, the ions are released from the crystal as separate charged particles (cations and anions) into solution. (See also figure 2.12.) In this solution, Cl^- ions are attracted to the hydrogen component of water, and Na^+ ions are attracted to the oxygen (box).

Figure 2.9 Hydrogen bonding in water. Because of the polarity of water molecules, the negatively charged oxygen end of one water molecule is weakly attracted to the positively charged hydrogen end of an adjacent water molecule.

ing (for example, the DNA helix has to "unbond" or unwind in order for replication to occur, enzymatic reactions require proteins to bind to other molecules and then be released), and hydrogen bonds and van der Waals forces are custom made for doing just that.

Chemical Shorthand: Formulas, Models, and Equations

The atomic content of molecules can be represented by a few convenient formulas. We have already been using the molecular formula, which concisely gives the atomic symbols and the number of the elements involved in subscript (CO_2, H_2O). More complex molecules such as glucose ($C_6H_{12}O_6$) can also be symbolized this way, but this formula is not unique, because fructose and galactose also share it. Molecular formulas are useful, but they only summarize the atoms in a compound; they do not show the position of bonds between atoms. For this purpose, chemists use structural formulas illustrating the relationships of the atoms and the number and types of bonds **(figure 2.10)**. Other structural models present the three-dimensional appearance of a molecule, illustrating the orientation of atoms (differentiated by color) and the molecule's overall shape **(figure 2.11)**. These are often called space-filling models, as you can get an idea of how the molecule actually occupies its space. The spheres surrounding each atom indicate how far the atom's influence can be felt, let's say. Sometimes it is also referred to as the atom's volume.

The printed page tends to make molecules appear static, but this picture is far from correct, because molecules are capable of changing through chemical reactions. For ease in tracing chemical exchanges between atoms or molecules, and to provide some sense of the dynamic character of reactions, chemists use shorthand equations containing symbols, numbers, and arrows to simplify or summarize the major characteristics of a reaction. Molecules entering or starting a reaction are called **reactants**, and substances left by a reaction are called **products**. In most instances, summary chemical reactions do not give the details of the exchange, in order to keep the expression simple and to save space.

In a *synthesis reaction*, the reactants bond together in a manner that produces an entirely new molecule (reactant A plus reactant B yields product AB). An example is the production of sulfur dioxide, a by-product of burning sulfur fuels and an important component of smog:

$$S + O_2 \rightarrow SO_2$$

Some synthesis reactions are not such simple combinations. When water is synthesized, for example, the reaction does not really involve one oxygen atom combining with two hydrogen atoms, because elemental oxygen exists as O_2 and elemental hydrogen exists as H_2. A more accurate equation for this reaction is:

$$2H_2 + O_2 \rightarrow H_2O$$

The equation for reactions must be balanced—that is, the number of atoms on one side of the arrow must equal the

Figure 2.10 Comparison of molecular and structural formulas. **(a)** Molecular formulas provide a brief summary of the elements in a compound. **(b)** Structural formulas clarify the exact relationships of the atoms in the molecule, depicting single bonds by a single line and double bonds by two lines. **(c)** In structural formulas of organic compounds, cyclic or ringed compounds may be completely labeled, or **(d)** they may be presented in a shorthand form in which carbons are assumed to be at the angles and attached to hydrogens. See figure 2.15 for structural formulas of three sugars with the same molecular formula, $C_6H_{12}O_6$.

Figure 2.11 Three-dimensional, or space-filling, models of (a) water, (b) carbon dioxide, and (c) glucose. The red atoms are oxygen, the white ones hydrogen, and the black ones carbon.

number on the other side to reflect all of the participants in the reaction. To arrive at the total number of atoms in the reaction, multiply the prefix number by the subscript number; if no number is given, it is assumed to be 1.

In *decomposition reactions,* the bonds on a single reactant molecule are permanently broken to release two or more product molecules. One example is the resulting molecules when large nutrient molecules are digested into smaller units; a simpler example can be shown for the common chemical hydrogen peroxide:

$$2H_2O_2 \rightarrow 2H_2O + O_2$$

During *exchange reactions,* the reactants trade portions between each other and release products that are combinations of the two. This type of reaction occurs between acids and bases when they form water and a salt:

$$AB + XY \rightleftharpoons AX + BY$$

The reactions in biological systems can be reversible, meaning that reactants and products can be converted back and forth. These reversible reactions are symbolized with a double arrow, each pointing in opposite directions, as in the preceding exchange reaction. Whether a reaction is reversible depends on the proportions of these compounds, the difference in energy state of the reactants and products, and the presence of **catalysts** (substances that increase the rate of a reaction). Additional reactants coming from another reaction can also be indicated by arrows that enter or leave at the main arrow:

$$\begin{array}{c} CD\ C \\ \curvearrowright \\ X + XY \longrightarrow XYD \end{array}$$

Solutions: Homogeneous Mixtures of Molecules

A **solution** is a mixture of one or more substances called **solutes** uniformly dispersed in a dissolving medium called a **solvent.** An important characteristic of a solution is that the solute cannot be separated by filtration or ordinary settling. The solute can be gaseous, liquid, or solid, and the solvent is usually a liquid. Examples of solutions are salt or sugar dissolved in water and iodine dissolved in alcohol. In general, a solvent will dissolve a solute only if it has similar electrical characteristics as indicated by the rule of solubility, expressed simply as "like dissolves like." For example, water is a polar molecule and will readily dissolve an ionic solute such as NaCl, yet a nonpolar solvent such as benzene will not dissolve NaCl.

Water is the most common solvent in natural systems, having several characteristics that suit it to this role. The polarity of the water molecule causes it to form hydrogen bonds with other water molecules, but it can also interact readily with charged or polar molecules. When an ionic solute such as NaCl crystals is added to water, it is dissolved, thereby releasing Na^+ and Cl^- into solution. Dissolution occurs because Na^+ is attracted to the negative pole of the water molecule and Cl^- is attracted to the positive pole; in this way, they are drawn away from the crystal separately into solution. As it leaves, each ion becomes **hydrated,** which means that it is surrounded by a sphere of water molecules **(figure 2.12).** Molecules such as salt or sugar that attract water to their surface are termed **hydrophilic.** Nonpolar molecules, such as benzene, that repel water are considered **hydrophobic.** A third class of molecules, such as the phospholipids in cell membranes, are considered **amphipathic** because they have both hydrophilic and hydrophobic properties.

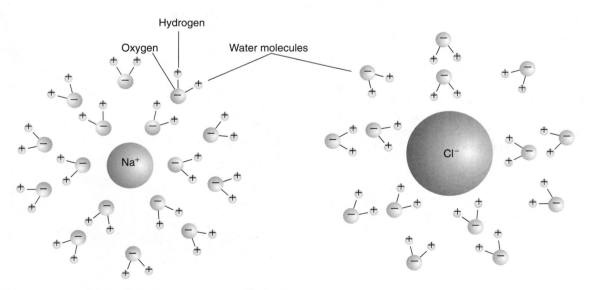

Figure 2.12 Hydration spheres formed around ions in solution.   In this example, a sodium cation attracts the negatively charged region of water molecules, and a chloride anion attracts the positively charged region of water molecules. In both cases, the ions become covered with spherical layers of specific numbers and arrangements of water molecules.

Because most biological activities take place in aqueous (water-based) solutions, the concentration of these solutions can be very important (see chapter 7). The **concentration** of a solution expresses the amount of solute dissolved in a certain amount of solvent. It can be calculated by weight, volume, or percentage. A common way to calculate percentage of concentration is to use the weight of the solute, measured in grams (g), dissolved in a specified volume of solvent, measured in milliliters (ml). For example, dissolving 3 g of NaCl in 100 ml of water produces a 3% solution; dissolving 30 g in 100 ml produces a 30% solution; and dissolving 3 g in 1,000 ml (1 liter) produces a 0.3% solution.

A common way to express concentration of biological solutions is by its molar concentration, or *molarity* (M). A standard molar solution is obtained by dissolving one *mole*, defined as the molecular weight of the compound in grams, in 1 liter (1,000 ml) of solution. To make a 1 mole solution of sodium chloride, we would dissolve 58 grams of NaCl to give 1 liter of solution; a 0.1 mole solution would require 5.8 grams of NaCl in 1 liter of solution.

Acidity, Alkalinity, and the pH Scale

Another factor with far-reaching impact on living things is the concentration of acidic or basic solutions in their environment. To understand how solutions develop acidity or basicity, we must look again at the behavior of water molecules. Hydrogens and oxygen tend to remain bonded by covalent bonds, but in certain instances, a single hydrogen can break away as the ionic form (H^+), leaving the remainder of the molecule in the form of an OH^- ion. The H^+ ion is positively charged because it is essentially a hydrogen ion that has lost its electron; the OH^- is negatively charged because it remains in possession of that electron. Ionization of water is constantly occurring, but in pure water containing no other ions, H^+ and OH^- are produced in equal amounts, and the solution remains neutral. By one definition, a solution is considered **acidic** when a component dissolved in water (acid) releases excess hydrogen ions[4] (H^+); a solution is **basic** when a component releases excess hydroxyl ions (OH^-), so that there is no longer a balance between the two ions.

To measure the acid and base concentrations of solutions, scientists use the **pH scale,** a graduated numerical scale that ranges from 0 (the most acidic) to 14 (the most basic). This scale is a useful standard for rating relative acidity and basicity; use **figure 2.13** to familiarize yourself with the pH readings of some common substances. Because the pH scale is a logarithmic scale, each increment (from pH 2.0 to pH 3.0) represents a tenfold change in concentration of ions. (Take a moment to glance at Appendix A to review logarithms and exponents.)

More precisely, the pH is based on the negative logarithm of the concentration of H^+ ions (symbolized as [H^+]) in a solution, represented as:

$$pH = -\log[H^+]$$

The quantity is expressed in moles per liter. Recall that a mole is simply a standard unit of measurement and refers to the amount of substance containing 6×10^{23} atoms.

Acidic solutions have a greater concentration of H^+ than OH^-, starting with pH 0, which contains 1.0 mole H^+/liter.

---

4. Actually, it forms a hydronium ion (H_3O^+), but for simplicity's sake, we will use the notation of H^+.

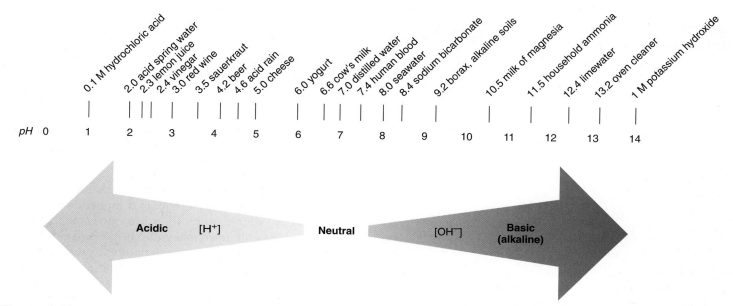

Figure 2.13 The pH scale.   Shown are the relative degrees of acidity and basicity and the approximate pH readings for various substances.

Each of the subsequent whole-number readings in the scale changes in $[H^+]$ by a tenfold reduction, so that pH 1 contains [0.1 mole H^+/liter], pH 2 contains [0.01 mole H^+/liter], and so on, continuing in the same manner up to pH 14, which contains [0.00000000000001 mole H^+/liter]. These same concentrations can be represented more manageably by exponents: pH 2 has an $[H^+]$ of 10^{-2} mole, and pH 14 has an $[H^+]$ of 10^{-14} mole **(table 2.2)**. It is evident that the pH units are derived from the exponent itself. Even though the basis for the pH scale is $[H^+]$, it is important to note that, as the $[H^+]$ in a solution decreases, the $[OH^-]$ increases in direct proportion. At midpoint—pH 7, or neutrality—the concentrations are exactly equal and neither predominates, this being the pH of pure water previously mentioned.

In summary, the pH scale can be used to rate or determine the degree of acidity or basicity (also called alkalinity) of a solution. On this scale, a pH below 7 is acidic, and the lower the pH, the greater the acidity. A pH above 7 is basic, and the higher the pH, the greater the basicity. Incidentally, although pHs are given here in even whole numbers, more often, a pH reading exists in decimal form, for example, pH 4.5 or 6.8 (acidic) and pH 7.4 or 10.2 (basic). Because of the damaging effects of very concentrated acids or bases, most cells operate best under neutral, weakly acidic, or weakly basic conditions (see chapter 7).

Aqueous solutions containing both acids and bases may be involved in **neutralization** reactions, which give rise to water and other neutral by-products. For example, when equal molar solutions of hydrochloric acid (HCl) and sodium hydroxide (NaOH, a base) are mixed, the reaction proceeds as follows:

$$HCl + NaOH \rightarrow H_2O + NaCl$$

Table 2.2	Hydrogen Ion and Hydroxide Ion Concentrations at a Given pH		
Moles/Liter of Hydrogen Ions	**Logarithm**	**pH**	**Moles/Liter of OH⁻**
1.0	10^{-0}	0	10^{-14}
0.1	10^{-1}	1	10^{-13}
0.01	10^{-2}	2	10^{-12}
0.001	10^{-3}	3	10^{-11}
0.0001	10^{-4}	4	10^{-10}
0.00001	10^{-5}	5	10^{-9}
0.000001	10^{-6}	6	10^{-8}
0.0000001	10^{-7}	7	10^{-7}
0.00000001	10^{-8}	8	10^{-6}
0.000000001	10^{-9}	9	10^{-5}
0.0000000001	10^{-10}	10	10^{-4}
0.00000000001	10^{-11}	11	10^{-3}
0.000000000001	10^{-12}	12	10^{-2}
0.0000000000001	10^{-13}	13	10^{-1}
0.00000000000001	10^{-14}	14	10^{-0}

Here the acid and base ionize to H^+ and OH^- ions, which form water, and other ions, Na^+ and Cl^-, which form sodium chloride. Any product other than water that arises when acids and bases react is called a salt. Many of the organic acids (such as lactic and succinic acids) that function in **metabolism** are available as the acid and the salt form (such as lactate, succinate), depending on the conditions in the cell (see chapter 8).

The Chemistry of Carbon and Organic Compounds

So far, our main focus has been on the characteristics of atoms, ions, and small, simple substances that play diverse roles in the structure and function of living things. These substances are often lumped together in a category called **inorganic chemicals.** A chemical is usually inorganic if it does not contain both carbon and hydrogen. Examples of inorganic chemicals include NaCl (sodium chloride), $Mg_3(PO_4)_2$ (magnesium phosphate), $CaCO_3$ (calcium carbonate), and CO_2 (carbon dioxide). In reality, however, most of the chemical reactions and structures of living things involve more complex molecules, termed **organic chemicals.** These are carbon compounds with a basic framework of the element carbon bonded to other atoms. Organic molecules vary in complexity from the simplest, methane (CH_4; see figure 2.5c), which has a molecular weight of 16, to certain antibody molecules (part of our immune systems) that have a molecular weight of nearly 1,000,000 and are among the most complex molecules on earth.

The role of carbon as the fundamental element of life can best be understood if we look at its chemistry and bonding patterns. The valence of carbon makes it an ideal atomic building block to form the backbone of organic molecules; it has 4 electrons in its outer orbital to be shared with other atoms (including other carbons) through covalent bonding. As a result, it can form stable chains containing thousands of carbon atoms and still has bonding sites available for forming covalent bonds with numerous other atoms. The bonds that carbon forms are linear, branched, or ringed, and it can form four single bonds, two double bonds, or one triple bond **(figure 2.14).** The atoms with which carbon is most often associated in organic compounds are hydrogen, oxygen, nitrogen, sulfur, and phosphorus.

Functional Groups of Organic Compounds

One important advantage of carbon's serving as the molecular skeleton for living things is that it is free to bind with an unending array of other molecules. These special molecular groups or accessory molecules that bind to organic compounds are called **functional groups.** Functional groups help define the chemical class of certain groups of organic compounds and confer unique reactive properties on the whole molecule **(table 2.3).** Because each type of functional group behaves in a distinctive manner, reactions of an organic compound can be predicted by knowing the kind of functional group or groups it carries. Many reactions rely upon functional groups such as R—OH or R—NH_2. The —R designation on a molecule is shorthand for residue, and its placement in a formula indicates that the residue (functional group) varies from one compound to another.

Figure 2.14 The versatility of bonding in carbon.
In most compounds, each carbon makes a total of four bonds.
(a) Both single and double bonds can be made with other carbons, oxygen, and nitrogen; single bonds are made with hydrogen. Simple electron models show how the electrons are shared in these bonds. **(b)** Multiple bonding of carbons can give rise to long chains, branched compounds, and ringed compounds, many of which are extraordinarily large and complex.

2.1 Learning Outcomes—Can You ...

1. ... explain the relationship between atoms and elements?
2. ... list and define four types of chemical bonds?
3. ... differentiate between a solute and a solvent?
4. ... give a brief defintion of pH?

Table 2.3 Representative Functional Groups and Classes of Organic Compounds

Formula of Functional Group	Name	Class of Compounds
R* — O — H	Hydroxyl	Alcohols, carbohydrates
(R—C(=O)—OH)	Carboxyl	Fatty acids, proteins, organic acids
(R—C(H)(H)—NH₂)	Amino	Proteins, nucleic acids
(R—C(=O)—O—R)	Ester	Lipids
(R—C(H)(H)—SH)	Sulfhydryl	Cysteine (amino acid), proteins
(R—C(=O)—H)	Carbonyl, terminal end	Aldehydes, polysaccharides
(R—C(=O)—C—)	Carbonyl, internal	Ketones, polysaccharides
(R—O—P(=O)(OH)—OH)	Phosphate	DNA, RNA, ATP

*The R designation on a molecule is shorthand for residue, and it indicates that what is attached at that site varies from one compound to another.

2.2 Macromolecules: Superstructures of Life

The compounds of life fall into the realm of **biochemistry.** Biochemicals are organic compounds produced by (or components of) living things, and they include four main families: carbohydrates, lipids, proteins, and nucleic acids **(table 2.4).** The compounds in these groups are assembled from smaller molecular subunits, or building blocks, and because they are often very large compounds, they are termed **macromolecules.** All macromolecules except lipids are formed by polymerization, a process in which repeating subunits termed **monomers** are bound into chains of various lengths termed **polymers.** For

Table 2.4 Macromolecules and Their Functions

Macromolecule	Description/Basic Structure	Examples	Notes About the Examples
Carbohydrates			
Monosaccharides	3- to 7-carbon sugars	Glucose, fructose	Sugars involved in metabolic reactions; building block of disaccharides and polysaccharides
Disaccharides	Two monosaccharides	Maltose (malt sugar)	Composed of two glucoses; an important breakdown product of starch
		Lactose (milk sugar)	Composed of glucose and galactose
		Sucrose (table sugar)	Composed of glucose and fructose
Polysaccharides	Chains of monosaccharides	Starch, cellulose, glycogen	Cell wall, food storage
Lipids			
Triglycerides	Fatty acids + glycerol	Fats, oils	Major component of cell membranes; storage
Phospholipids	Fatty acids + glycerol + phosphate	Membrane components	
Waxes	Fatty acids, alcohols	Mycolic acid	Cell wall of mycobacteria
Steroids	Ringed structure	Cholesterol, ergosterol	In membranes of eukaryotes and some bacteria
Proteins			
	Amino acids	Enzymes; part of cell membrane, cell wall, ribosomes, antibodies	Serve as structural components and perform metabolic reactions
Nucleic acids			
	Pentose sugar + phosphate + nitrogenous base Purines: adenine, guanine Pyrimidines: cytosine, thymine, uracil		
Deoxyribonucleic acid (DNA)	Contains deoxyribose sugar and thymine, not uracil	Chromosomes; genetic material of viruses	Mediate inheritance
Ribonucleic acid (RNA)	Contains ribose sugar and uracil, not thymine	Ribosomes; mRNA, tRNA	Facilitate expression of genetic traits

example, proteins (polymers) are composed of a chain of amino acids (monomers). The large size and complex, three-dimensional shape of macromolecules enables them to function as structural components, molecular messengers, energy sources, enzymes (biochemical catalysts), nutrient stores, and sources of genetic information. In the following section and in later chapters, we consider numerous concepts relating to the roles of macromolecules in cells. Table 2.4 will also be a useful reference when you study metabolism in chapter 8.

Carbohydrates: Sugars and Polysaccharides

The term **carbohydrate** originates from the composition of members of this class: they are combinations of carbon (carbo-) and water (-hydrate). Although carbohydrates can be generally represented by the formula $(CH_2O)_n$, in which n indicates the number of units of this combination of atoms **(figure 2.15a)**, some carbohydrates contain additional atoms of sulfur or nitrogen.

Carbohydrates exist in a great variety of configurations. The common term sugar **(saccharide)** refers to a simple carbohy-

drate such as a monosaccharide or a disaccharide. A **monosaccharide** is a simple sugar containing from 3 to 7 carbons; a **disaccharide** is a combination of two monosaccharides; and a **polysaccharide** is a polymer of five or more monosaccharides bound in linear or branched chain patterns **(figure 2.15b)**. Monosaccharides and disaccharides are specified by combining a prefix that describes some characteristic of the sugar with the suffix *-ose*. For example, **hexoses** are composed of 6 carbons, and **pentoses** contain 5 carbons. **Glucose** (Gr. sweet) is the most common and universally important hexose; **fructose** is named for fruit (one place where it is found); and xylose, a pentose, derives its name from the Greek word for wood. Disaccharides are named similarly: **lactose** (L. milk) is an important component of milk; **maltose** means malt sugar; and **sucrose** (Fr. sugar) is common table sugar or cane sugar.

The Nature of Carbohydrate Bonds

The subunits of disaccharides and polysaccharides are linked by means of **glycosidic bonds,** in which carbons (each is assigned a number) on adjacent sugar units are bonded to the

Figure 2.15 Common classes of carbohydrates. (a) Three hexoses with the same molecular formula and different structural formulas. Both linear and ring models are given. The linear form emphasizes aldehyde and ketone groups, although in solution the sugars exist in the ring form. Note that the carbons are numbered so as to keep track of reactions within and between monosaccharides. (b) Major saccharide groups, named for the number of sugar units each contains.

same oxygen atom like links in a chain **(figure 2.16).** For example, maltose is formed when the number 1 carbon on a glucose bonds to the oxygen on the number 4 carbon on a second glucose; sucrose is formed when glucose and fructose bind oxygen between their number 1 and number 2 carbons; and lactose is formed when glucose and galactose connect by their number 1 and number 4 carbons. In order to form this bond, 1 carbon gives up its OH group and the other (the one contributing the oxygen to the bond) loses the H from its OH group. Because a water molecule is produced, this reaction is

Figure 2.16 Glycosidic bond in a common disaccharide. (a) General scheme in the formation of a glycosidic bond by dehydration synthesis. (b) A 1,4 bond between a galactose and glucose produces lactose.

known as **dehydration synthesis,** a process common to most polymerization reactions (see proteins, page 47). Three polysaccharides (starch, cellulose, and glycogen) are structurally and biochemically distinct, even though all are polymers of the same monosaccharide—glucose. The basis for their differences lies primarily in the exact way the glucoses are bound together, which greatly affects the characteristics of the end product **(figure 2.17).** The synthesis and breakage of each type of bond requires a specialized catalyst called an enzyme (see chapter 8).

The Functions of Polysaccharides

Polysaccharides typically contribute to structural support and protection and serve as nutrient and energy stores. The cell walls in plants and many microscopic algae derive their strength and rigidity from **cellulose,** a long, fibrous polymer **(figure 2.17a).** Because of this role, cellulose is probably one of the most common organic substances on the earth, yet it is digestible only by certain bacteria, fungi, and protozoa. These microbes, called decomposers, play an essential role in breaking down and recycling plant materials (see figure 7.2). Some bacteria secrete slime layers of a glucose polymer called *dextran.* This substance causes a sticky layer to develop on teeth that leads to plaque, described later in chapter 22.

Other structural polysaccharides can be conjugated (chemically bonded) to amino acids, nitrogen bases, lipids, or proteins. **Agar,** an indispensable polysaccharide in preparing solid culture media, is a natural component of certain seaweeds. It is a complex polymer of galactose and sulfur-containing carbohydrates. The exoskeletons of certain fungi contain **chitin** (ky-tun), a polymer of glucosamine (a sugar with an amino functional group). **Peptidoglycan** (pep-tih-doh-gly'-kan) is one special class of compounds in which polysaccharides (glycans) are linked to peptide fragments (a short chain of amino acids). This molecule provides the main source of structural support to the bacterial cell wall. The cell wall of gram-negative bacteria also contains **lipopolysaccharide,** a complex of lipid and polysaccharide responsible for symptoms such as fever and shock (see chapters 4 and 13).

The outer surface of many cells has a "sugar coating" composed of polysaccharides bound in various ways to proteins (the combination is a glycoprotein). This structure, called the **glycocalyx,** functions in attachment to other cells or as a site for *receptors*—surface molecules that receive external stimuli or act as binding sites. Small sugar molecules account for the differences in human blood types, and carbohydrates are a component of large protein molecules called antibodies. Viruses also have glycoproteins on their surface with which they bind to and invade their host cells.

Polysaccharides are usually stored by cells in the form of glucose polymers such as starch **(figure 2.17b)** or **glycogen,** but only organisms with the appropriate digestive enzymes can break them down and use them as a nutrient source. Because a water molecule is required for breaking the bond between two glucose molecules, digestion is also termed **hydrolysis.** Starch is the primary storage food of green plants, microscopic algae, and some fungi; glycogen (ani-

(a) **Cellulose**   (b) **Starch**

Figure 2.17 Polysaccharides.   **(a)** Cellulose is composed of β glucose bonded in 1,4 bonds that produce linear, lengthy chains of polysaccharides that are H-bonded along their length. This is the typical structure of wood and cotton fibers. **(b)** Starch is also composed of glucose polymers, in this case α glucose. The main structure is amylose bonded in a 1,4 pattern, with side branches of amylopectin bonded by 1,6 bonds. The entire molecule is compact and granular.

mal starch) is a stored carbohydrate for animals and certain groups of bacteria and protozoa.

Lipids: Fats, Phospholipids, and Waxes

The term **lipid,** derived from the Greek word *lipos,* meaning fat, is not a chemical designation but an operational term for a variety of substances that are not soluble in polar solvents such as water (recall that oil and water do not mix) but will dissolve in nonpolar solvents such as benzene and chloroform. This property occurs because the substances we call lipids contain relatively long or complex C—H (hydrocarbon) chains that are nonpolar and thus hydrophobic. The main groups of compounds classified as lipids are triglycerides, phospholipids, steroids, and waxes.

Important storage lipids are the **triglycerides,** a category that includes fats and oils. Triglycerides are composed of a single molecule of glycerol bound to three fatty acids **(figure 2.18). Glycerol** is a 3-carbon alcohol[5] with three OH groups that serve as binding sites, and fatty acids are long-chain hydrocarbon molecules with a carboxyl group (COOH) at one end that is free to bind to the glycerol. The hydrocarbon portion of a fatty acid can vary in length from 4 to 24 carbons; and, depending on the fat, it may be saturated or unsaturated. If all carbons in the chain are single-bonded to 2 other carbons and 2 hydrogens, the fat is saturated; if there is at least one C=C double bond in the chain, it is unsaturated. The structure of fatty acids is what gives fats and oils (liquid fats) their greasy, insoluble nature. In general, solid fats (such as butter) are more saturated, and liquid fats (such as oils) are more unsaturated. In recent

5. Alcohols are carbon compounds containing OH groups.

Figure 2.18 Synthesis and structure of a triglyceride. **(a)** Because a water molecule is released at each ester bond, this is another form of dehydration synthesis. The jagged lines and R symbol represent the hydrocarbon chains of the fatty acids, which are commonly very long. **(b)** Structural and three-dimensional models of fatty acids and triglycerides. (1) A saturated fatty acid has long, straight chains that readily pack together and form solid fats. (2) An unsaturated fatty acid—here a polyunsaturated one with 3 double bonds—has bends in the chain that prevent packing and produce oils (right).

INSIGHT 2.3	**Membranes: Cellular Skins**

(a) Extreme magnification of a cross section of a cell membrane, which appears as double tracks. **(b)** A generalized version of the fluid mosaic model of a cell membrane indicates a bilayer of lipids with globular proteins embedded to some degree in the lipid matrix. This structure explains many characteristics of membranes, including flexibility, solubility, permeability, and transport.

years there has been a realization that a type of triglyceride, called popularly "trans fat" is harmful to the health of those who consume it. A trans fat is an unsaturated triglyceride with one or more of its fatty acids in a position (trans) that is not often found in nature, but is a common occurrence in processed foods.

In most cells, triglycerides are stored in long-term concentrated form as droplets or globules. When they are acted on by digestive enzymes called lipases, the fatty acids and glycerol are freed to be used in metabolism. Fatty acids are a superior source of energy, yielding twice as much per gram as other storage molecules (starch). Soaps are K^+ or Na^+ salts of fatty acids whose qualities make them excellent grease removers and cleaners (see chapter 11).

Membrane Lipids

A class of lipids that serves as a major structural component of cell membranes is the **phospholipids.** Although phospholipids also contain glycerol and fatty acids, they have some significant differences from triglycerides. Phospholipids contain only two fatty acids attached to the glycerol, and the third glycerol binding site holds a phosphate group. The phosphate is in turn bonded to an alcohol, which varies from one phospholipid to another **(figure 2.19a).** These lipids have a hydrophilic region from the charge on the phosphoric acid–alcohol "head" of the molecule and a hydrophobic region that corresponds to the long, uncharged "tail" (formed by the fatty acids). When exposed to an aqueous solution, the charged heads are attracted to the water phase, and the nonpolar tails are repelled from the water phase **(figure 2.19b).** This property causes lipids to naturally assume single and double layers (bilayers), which contribute to their biological significance

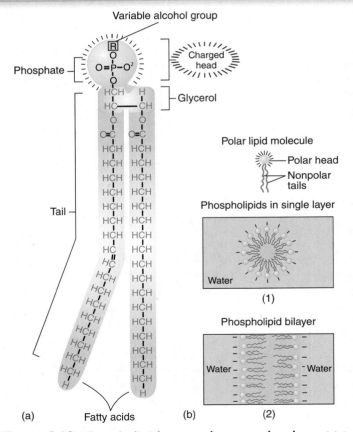

Figure 2.19 Phospholipids—membrane molecules.   **(a)** A model of a single molecule of a phospholipid. The phosphate-alcohol head lends a charge to one end of the molecule; its long, trailing hydrocarbon chain is uncharged. **(b)** The behavior of phospholipids in water-based solutions causes them to become arranged (1) in single layers called micelles, with the charged head oriented toward the water phase and the hydrophobic nonpolar tail buried away from the water phase, or (2) in double-layered phospholipid systems with the hydrophobic tails sandwiched between two hydrophilic layers.

The word **membrane** appears frequently in descriptions of cells in this chapter and in chapters 4 and 5. The word itself describes any lining or covering, including such multicellular structures as the mucous membranes of the body. From the perspective of a single cell, however, a membrane is a thin, double-layered sheet composed of lipids such as phospholipids and sterols (averaging about 40% of membrane content) and protein molecules (averaging about 60%). The primary role of membranes is as a cell membrane that completely encases the cytoplasm. Membranes are also components of eukaryotic organelles such as nuclei, mitochondria, and chloroplasts, and they appear in internal pockets of certain prokaryotic cells. Even some viruses, which are not cells at all, can have a membranous protective covering.

Cell membranes are so thin—on the average, just 0.0070 µm (7 nm) thick—that they cannot actually be seen with an optical microscope. Even at magnifications made possible by electron microscopy (500,000×), very little of the precise architecture can be visualized, and a cross-sectional view has the appearance of railroad tracks. Following detailed microscopic and chemical analysis, S. J. Singer and C. K. Nicholson proposed a simple and elegant theory for membrane structure called the **fluid mosaic model**. According to this theory, a membrane is a continuous bilayer formed by lipids that are oriented with the polar lipid heads toward the outside and the nonpolar tails toward the center of the membrane. Embedded at numerous sites in this bilayer are various-size globular proteins. Some proteins are situated only at the surface; others extend fully through the entire membrane. The configuration of the inner and outer sides of the membrane can be quite different because of the variations in protein shape and position.

Membranes are dynamic and constantly changing because the lipid phase is in motion and many proteins can migrate freely about, somewhat as icebergs do in the ocean. This fluidity is essential to such activities as engulfment of food and discharge or secretion by cells. The structure of the lipid phase provides an impenetrable barrier to many substances. This property accounts for the selective permeability and capacity to regulate transport of molecules. It also serves to segregate activities within the cell's cytoplasm. Membrane proteins function in receiving molecular signals (receptors), in binding and transporting nutrients, and in acting as enzymes, topics to be discussed in chapters 7 and 8.

in membranes. When two single layers of polar lipids come together to form a double layer, the outer hydrophilic face of each single layer will orient itself toward the solution, and the hydrophobic portions will become immersed in the core of the bilayer. The structure of lipid bilayers confers characteristics on membranes such as selective permeability and fluid nature **(Insight 2.3)**.

Steroids and Waxes

Steroids are complex ringed compounds commonly found in cell membranes and animal hormones. The best known of these is the sterol (meaning a steroid with an OH group) called **cholesterol (figure 2.20)**. Cholesterol reinforces the structure of the cell membrane in animal cells and in an unusual group of cell-wall-deficient bacteria called the mycoplasmas (see chapter 4). The cell membranes of fungi also contain a sterol, called ergosterol.

Chemically, a *wax* is an ester formed between a long-chain alcohol and a saturated fatty acid. The resulting material is typically pliable and soft when warmed but hard and water resistant when cold (paraffin, for example). Among living things, fur, feathers, fruits, leaves, human skin, and insect exoskeletons are naturally waterproofed with a coating of wax. Bacteria that cause tuberculosis and leprosy produce a wax that repels ordinary laboratory stains and contributes to their pathogenicity.

Proteins: Shapers of Life

The predominant organic molecules in cells are **proteins**, a fitting term adopted from the Greek word *proteios*, meaning first or prime. To a large extent, the structure, behavior, and unique qualities of each living thing are a consequence of the

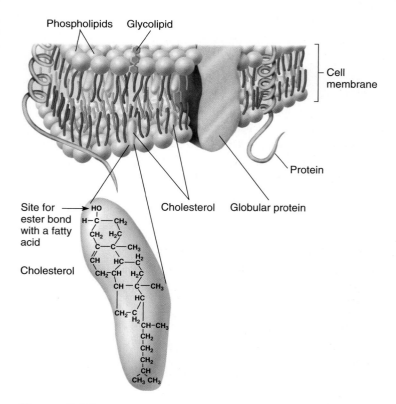

Figure 2.20 Cutaway view of a membrane with its bilayer of lipids. The primary lipid is phospholipid—however, cholesterol is inserted in some membranes. Other structures are protein and glycolipid molecules. Cholesterol can become esterified with fatty acids at its OH⁻ group, imparting a polar quality similar to that of phospholipids.

proteins they contain. To best explain the origin of the special properties and versatility of proteins, we must examine their general structure. The building blocks of proteins are **amino acids,** which exist in 20 different naturally occurring forms **(table 2.5).** Various combinations of these amino acids account for the nearly infinite variety of proteins. Amino acids have a basic skeleton consisting of a carbon (called the α carbon) linked to an amino group (NH_2), a carboxyl group (COOH), a hydrogen atom (H), and a variable R group. The variations among the amino acids occur at the R group, which is different in each amino acid and imparts the unique characteristics to the molecule and to the proteins that contain it **(figure 2.21).** A covalent bond called a **peptide bond** forms between the amino group on one amino acid and the carboxyl group on another amino acid. As a result of peptide bond formation, it is possible to produce molecules varying in length from two amino acids to chains containing thousands of them.

Various terms are used to denote the nature of proteins. **Peptide** usually refers to a molecule composed of short chains of amino acids, such as a dipeptide (two amino acids), a tripeptide (three), and a tetrapeptide (four). A **polypeptide** contains an unspecified number of amino acids but usually has more than 20 and is often a smaller subunit of a protein. A protein is the largest of this class of compounds and usually contains a minimum of 50 amino acids. It is common for the term *protein* to be used to describe all of these molecules; we

used it in its general sense in the first sentence of this paragraph. But not all polypeptides are large enough to be considered proteins. In chapter 9, we see that protein synthesis is not just a random connection of amino acids; it is directed by information provided in DNA.

Protein Structure and Diversity

The reason that proteins are so varied and specific is that they do not function in the form of a simple straight chain of amino acids (called the primary structure). A protein has a natural

Table 2.5 Twenty Amino Acids and Their Abbreviations

Acid	Abbreviation	Characteristic of R Groups
Alanine	Ala	nonpolar
Arginine	Arg	+
Asparagine	Asn	polar
Aspartic acid	Asp	−
Cysteine	Cys	polar
Glutamic acid	Glu	−
Glutamine	Gln	polar
Glycine	Gly	polar
Histidine	His	+
Isoleucine	Ile	nonpolar
Leucine	Leu	nonpolar
Lysine	Lys	+
Methionine	Met	nonpolar
Phenylalanine	Phe	nonpolar
Proline	Pro	nonpolar
Serine	Ser	polar
Threonine	Thr	polar
Tryptophan	Trp	nonpolar
Tyrosine	Tyr	polar
Valine	Val	nonpolar

+ = positively charged; − = negatively charged.

Figure 2.21 Structural formulas of selected amino acids.   The basic structure common to all amino acids is shown in blue type; and the variable group, or R group, is placed in a colored box. Note the variations in structure of this reactive component.

tendency to assume more complex levels of organization, called the secondary, tertiary, and quaternary structures **(figure 2.22)**. The **primary (1°) structure** is the type, number, and order of amino acids in the chain, which varies extensively from protein to protein. The **secondary (2°) structure** arises when various functional groups exposed on the outer surface of the molecule interact by forming hydrogen bonds. This interaction causes the amino acid chain to twist into a coiled configuration called the α *helix* or to fold into an accordion pattern called a β-*pleated sheet*. Many proteins contain both types of secondary configurations. Proteins at the secondary level undergo a third degree of torsion called the **tertiary (3°) structure** created by additional bonds between functional groups **(figure 2.22c)**. In proteins with the sulfur-containing amino acid **cysteine,** considerable tertiary stability is achieved through covalent disulfide bonds between sulfur atoms on two different parts of the molecule. Some complex proteins assume a **quaternary (4°) structure,** in which more than one polypeptide forms a large, multiunit protein. This is typical of antibodies (see chapter 15) and some enzymes that act in cell synthesis.

The most important outcome of the various forms of bonding and folding is that each different type of protein develops a unique shape, and its surface displays a distinctive pattern of pockets and bulges. As a result, a protein can react only with molecules that complement or fit its particular surface features like a lock and key. Such a degree of specificity can provide the functional diversity required for many thousands of different cellular activities. **Enzymes** serve as the catalysts for all chemical reactions in cells, and nearly every reaction requires a different enzyme (see chapter 8). This specificity comes from the architecture of the binding site which determines which molecules fit it. The same is true of antibodies; **antibodies** are complex glycoproteins with specific regions of attachment for bacteria, viruses, and other microorganisms. Certain bacterial toxins (poisonous products) react with only one specific organ or tissue; and proteins embedded in the cell membrane have reactive sites restricted to a certain nutrient. The functional three-dimensional form of a protein is termed the *native state,* and if it is disrupted by some means, the protein is said to be *denatured.* Such agents as heat, acid, alcohol, and some disinfectants disrupt (and thus denature) the stabilizing intrachain bonds and cause the molecule to become nonfunctional, as described in chapter 11.

The Nucleic Acids: A Cell Computer and Its Programs

The nucleic acids, **deoxyribonucleic acid (DNA)** and **ribonucleic acid (RNA),** were originally isolated from the cell nucleus. Shortly thereafter, they were also found in other parts of nucleated cells, in cells with no nuclei (bacteria), and in viruses. The universal occurrence of nucleic acids in all known cells and viruses emphasizes their important roles as informational molecules. DNA, the master computer of cells, contains a special coded genetic program with detailed and specific instructions for each organism's heredity. It transfers

the details of its program to RNA, "helper" molecules responsible for carrying out DNA's instructions and translating the DNA program into proteins that can perform life functions. For now, let us briefly consider the structure and some functions of DNA, RNA, and a close relative, adenosine triphosphate (ATP).

Both DNA and RNA are polymers of repeating units called **nucleotides,** each of which is composed of three smaller units: a **nitrogen base,** a **pentose** (5-carbon) sugar, and a

(a) Amino acid sequence

Gly Asp Trp Gln Leu His Val Phe Ala Lys Glu

(b) Beta-pleated sheet

Alpha helix   Random coil

(c) Folded polypeptide chain

(d) Two or more polypeptide chains

Figure 2.22 Stages in the formation of a functioning protein. **(a)** Its primary structure is a series of amino acids bound in a chain. **(b)** Its secondary structure develops when the chain forms hydrogen bonds that fold it into one of several configurations such as an α helix or β-pleated sheet. Some proteins have several configurations in the same molecule. **(c)** A protein's tertiary structure is due to further folding of the molecule into a three-dimensional mass that is stabilized by hydrogen, ionic, and disulfide bonds between functional groups. **(d)** The quaternary structure exists only in proteins that consist of more than one polypeptide chain. The chains in this protein each have a different color.

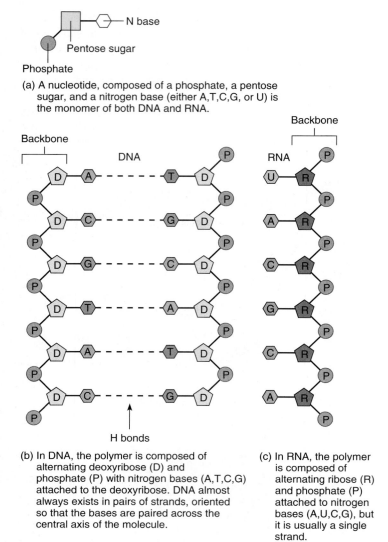

(a) A nucleotide, composed of a phosphate, a pentose sugar, and a nitrogen base (either A,T,C,G, or U) is the monomer of both DNA and RNA.

(b) In DNA, the polymer is composed of alternating deoxyribose (D) and phosphate (P) with nitrogen bases (A,T,C,G) attached to the deoxyribose. DNA almost always exists in pairs of strands, oriented so that the bases are paired across the central axis of the molecule.

(c) In RNA, the polymer is composed of alternating ribose (R) and phosphate (P) attached to nitrogen bases (A,U,C,G), but it is usually a single strand.

Figure 2.23 The general structure of nucleic acids.

(a) **Pentose sugars**

(b) **Purine bases**

(c) **Pyrimidine bases**

Figure 2.24 The sugars and nitrogen bases that make up DNA and RNA. **(a)** DNA contains deoxyribose, and RNA contains ribose. **(b)** A and G purine bases are found in both DNA and RNA. **(c)** Pyrimidine bases are found in both DNA and RNA, but T is found only in DNA, and U is found only in RNA.

phosphate **(figure 2.23a).**[6] The nitrogen base is a cyclic compound that comes in two forms: *purines* (two rings) and *pyrimidines* (one ring). There are two types of purines—**adenine (A)** and **guanine (G)**—and three types of pyrimidines—**thymine (T), cytosine (C),** and **uracil (U) (figure 2.24).** A characteristic that differentiates DNA from RNA is that DNA contains all of the nitrogen bases except uracil, and RNA contains all of the nitrogen bases except thymine. The nitrogen base is covalently bonded to the sugar *ribose* in RNA and *deoxyribose* (because it has one less oxygen than ribose) in DNA. Phosphate provides the final covalent bridge that connects sugars in series. Thus, the backbone of a nucleic acid strand is a chain of alternating phosphate-sugar-phosphate-sugar molecules, and the nitrogen bases branch off the side of this backbone **(figure 2.23b,c).**

The Double Helix of DNA

DNA is a huge molecule formed by two very long polynucleotide strands linked along their length by hydrogen bonds between complementary pairs of nitrogen bases. The pairing

6. The nitrogen base plus the pentose is called a *nucleoside*.

of the nitrogen bases occurs according to a predictable pattern: Adenine always pairs with thymine, and cytosine with guanine. The bases are attracted in this way because each pair shares oxygen, nitrogen, and hydrogen atoms exactly positioned to align perfectly for hydrogen bonds **(figure 2.25).**

For ease in understanding the structure of DNA, it is sometimes compared to a ladder, with the sugar-phosphate backbone representing the rails and the paired nitrogen bases representing the steps. Owing to the manner of nucleotide pairing and stacking of the bases, the actual configuration of DNA is a *double helix* that looks somewhat like a spiral staircase. As is true of protein, the structure of DNA is intimately related to its function. DNA molecules are usually extremely long. The hydrogen bonds between pairs break apart when DNA is being copied, and the fixed complementary base pairing is essential to maintain the genetic code.

RNA: Organizers of Protein Synthesis

Like DNA, RNA consists of a long chain of nucleotides. However, RNA is often a single strand, except in some viruses.

Figure 2.26 An ATP molecule. **(a)** The structural formula. Wavy lines connecting the phosphates represent bonds that release large amounts of energy. **(b)** A ball and stick model.

Figure 2.25 A structural representation of the double helix of DNA. Shown are the details of hydrogen bonds between the nitrogen bases of the two strands.

It contains ribose sugar instead of deoxyribose and uracil instead of thymine (see figure 2.23). Several functional types of RNA are formed using the DNA template through a replicationlike process. Three major types of RNA are important for protein synthesis. Messenger RNA (mRNA) is a copy of a gene (a single functional part of the DNA) that provides the order and type of amino acids in a protein; transfer RNA (tRNA) is a carrier that delivers the correct amino acids for protein assembly; and ribosomal RNA (rRNA) is a major component of ribosomes (described in chapter 4). A fourth type of RNA is the RNA that acts to regulate the genes and gene expression. More information on these important processes is presented in chapter 9.

ATP: The Energy Molecule of Cells

A relative of RNA involved in an entirely different cell activity is **adenosine triphosphate (ATP).** ATP is a nucleotide containing adenine, ribose, and three phosphates rather than just one **(figure 2.26).** It belongs to a category of high-energy compounds (also including guanosine triphosphate [GTP]) that give off energy when the bond is broken between the second and third (outermost) phosphate. The presence of these high-energy bonds makes it possible for ATP to release and store energy for cellular chemical reactions. Breakage of the bond of the terminal phosphate releases energy to do cellular work and also gener-

ates adenosine diphosphate (ADP). ADP can be converted back to ATP when the third phosphate is restored, thereby serving as an energy depot. Carriers for oxidation-reduction activities (nicotinamide adenine dinucleotide [NAD], for instance) are also derivatives of nucleotides (see chapter 8).

2.2 Learning Outcomes—Can You ...

5. ... name the four main families of biochemicals?
6. ... provide examples of cell components made from each of the families of biochemicals?
7. ... explain primary, secondary, tertiary, and quaternary structure as seen in proteins?
8. ... list the three components of nucleic acids?
9. ... name the nucleotides of DNA? RNA?
10. ... list the three components of ATP?

2.3 Cells: Where Chemicals Come to Life

As we proceed in this chemical survey from the level of simple molecules to increasingly complex levels of macromolecules, at some point we cross a line from the realm of lifeless molecules and arrive at the fundamental unit of life called a **cell.**[7] A cell is indeed a huge aggregate of carbon, hydrogen,

7. The word *cell* was originally coined from an Old English term meaning "small room" because of the way plant cells looked to early microscopists.

oxygen, nitrogen, and many other atoms, and it follows the basic laws of chemistry and physics, but it is much more. The combination of these atoms produces characteristics, reactions, and products that can only be described as *living*.

Fundamental Characteristics of Cells

The bodies of living things such as bacteria and protozoa consist of only a single cell, whereas those of animals and plants contain trillions of cells. Regardless of the organism, all cells have a few common characteristics. They tend to be spherical, polygonal, cubical, or cylindrical, and their protoplasm (internal cell contents) is encased in a cell or cytoplasmic membrane (see Insight 2.3). They have chromosomes containing DNA and ribosomes for protein synthesis, and they are exceedingly complex in function. Aside from these few similarities, most cell types fall into one of three fundamentally different lines (discussed in chapter 1): the small, seemingly simple bacterial and archaeal cells and the larger, structurally more complicated eukaryotic cells.

Eukaryotic cells are found in animals, plants, fungi, and protists. They contain a number of complex internal parts called organelles that perform useful functions for the cell involving growth, nutrition, or metabolism. By convention, organelles are defined as cell components that perform specific functions and are enclosed by membranes. Organelles also partition the eukaryotic cell into smaller compartments. The most visible organelle is the nucleus, a roughly ball-shaped mass surrounded by a double membrane that contains the DNA of the cell. Other organelles include the Golgi apparatus, endoplasmic reticulum, vacuoles, and mitochondria.

Bacterial and archaeal cells may seem to be the cellular "have nots" because, for the sake of comparison, they are described by what they lack. They have no nucleus and generally no other organelles. This apparent simplicity is misleading, however, because the fine structure of

prokaryotes is complex. Overall, prokaryotic cells can engage in nearly every activity that eukaryotic cells can, and many can function in ways that eukaryotes cannot. Chapters 4 and 5 delve deeply into the properties of prokaryotic and eukaryotic cells.

2.3 Learning Outcome—Can You . . .

11. . . . point out three characteristics all cells share?

Chapter Summary

2.1 Atoms, Bonds, and Molecules: Fundamental Building Blocks

- Protons (p^+) and neutrons (n^0) make up the nucleus of an atom. Electrons (e^-) orbit the nucleus.
- All elements are composed of atoms but differ in the numbers of protons, neutrons, and electrons they possess.
- Isotopes are varieties of one element that contain the same number of protons but different numbers of neutrons.
- The number of electrons in an element's outermost orbital (compared with the total number possible) determines the element's chemical properties and reactivity.
- Covalent bonds are chemical bonds in which electrons are shared between atoms. Equally distributed electrons form nonpolar covalent bonds, whereas unequally distributed electrons form polar covalent bonds.
- Ionic bonds are chemical bonds resulting from opposite charges. The outer electron shell either donates or receives electrons from another atom so that the outer shell of each atom is completely filled.

- Hydrogen bonds are weak chemical attractions that form between covalently bonded hydrogens and either oxygens or nitrogens on different molecules. These as well as van der Waals forces are critically important in biological processes.
- Chemical equations express the chemical exchanges between atoms or molecules.
- Solutions are mixtures of solutes and solvents that cannot be separated by filtration or settling.
- The pH, ranging from a highly *acidic* solution to a highly *basic* solution, refers to the concentration of hydrogen ions. It is expressed as a number from 0 to 14.
- Biologists define organic molecules as those containing both carbon and hydrogen.
- Carbon is the backbone of biological compounds because of its ability to form single, double, or triple covalent bonds with itself and many different elements.

- Functional (R) groups are specific arrangements of organic molecules that confer distinct properties, including chemical reactivity, to organic compounds.

2.2 Macromolecules: Superstructures of Life

- Macromolecules are very large organic molecules (polymers) built up by polymerization of smaller molecular subunits (monomers).
- Carbohydrates are biological molecules whose polymers are monomers linked together by glycosidic bonds. Their main functions are protection and support (in organisms with cell walls) and also nutrient and energy stores.
- Lipids are biological molecules such as fats that are insoluble in water. Their main functions are as cell components, cell secretions, and nutrient and energy stores.
- Proteins are biological molecules whose polymers are chains of amino acid monomers linked together by peptide bonds.

- Proteins are called the "shapers of life" because of the many biological roles they play in cell structure and cell metabolism.
- Protein structure determines protein function. Structure and shape are dictated by amino acid composition and by the pH and temperature of the protein's immediate environment.
- Nucleic acids are biological molecules whose polymers are chains of nucleotide monomers linked together by phosphate–pentose sugar covalent bonds. Double-stranded nucleic acids are linked together by hydrogen bonds. Nucleic acids are information molecules that direct cell metabolism and reproduction. Nucleotides such as ATP also serve as energy transfer molecules in cells.

2.3 Cells: Where Chemicals Come to Life

- As the atom is the fundamental unit of matter, so is the cell the fundamental unit of life.

Multiple-Choice and True-False Questions   Knowledge and Comprehension

Multiple-Choice Questions. Select the correct answer from the answers provided.

1. The smallest unit of matter with unique characteristics is
   a. an electron.   c. an atom.
   b. a molecule.   d. a proton.

2. The ____ charge of a proton is exactly balanced by the ____ charge of a (an) ____.
   a. negative, positive, electron
   b. positive, neutral, neutron
   c. positive, negative, electron
   d. neutral, negative, electron

3. Electrons move around the nucleus of an atom in pathways called
   a. shells.   c. circles.
   b. orbitals.   d. rings.

4. Bonds in which atoms share electrons are defined as ____ bonds.
   a. hydrogen   c. double
   b. ionic   d. covalent

5. Hydrogen bonds can form between ____ adjacent to each other.
   a. two hydrogen atoms
   b. two oxygen atoms
   c. a hydrogen atom and an oxygen atom
   d. negative charges

6. An atom that can donate electrons during a reaction is called
   a. an oxidizing agent.   c. an ionic agent.
   b. a reducing agent.   d. an electrolyte.

7. A solution with a pH of 2 ____ than a solution with a pH of 8.
   a. has less H^+ c. has more OH^-
   b. has more H^+ d. is less concentrated

8. Proteins are synthesized by linking amino acids with ____ bonds.
   a. disulfide   c. peptide
   b. glycosidic   d. ester

9. DNA is a hereditary molecule that is composed of
   a. deoxyribose, phosphate, and nitrogen bases.
   b. deoxyribose, a pentose, and nucleic acids.
   c. sugar, proteins, and thymine.
   d. adenine, phosphate, and ribose.

10. RNA plays an important role in what biological process?
    a. replication   c. lipid metabolism
    b. protein synthesis   d. water transport

True-False Questions. If the statement is true, leave as is. If it is false, correct it by rewriting the sentence.

11. Elements have varying numbers of protons, neutrons, and electrons.

12. Covalent bonds are those that are made between two different elements.

13. A compound is called "organic" if it is made of all-natural elements.

14. Cysteine is the amino acid that participates in disulfide bonds in proteins.

15. Membranes are mainly composed of macromolecules called carbohydrates.

Critical Thinking Questions   Application and Analysis

These questions are suggested as a *writing-to-learn* experience. For each question, compose a one- or two-paragraph answer that includes the factual information needed to completely address the question.

1. Which kinds of elements tend to make covalent bonds?
2. Distinguish between a single and a double bond.

3. Why are hydrogen bonds relatively weak?
4. What determines whether a substance is an acid or a base?

5. What atoms must be present in a molecule for it to be considered organic?

6. What characteristics of carbon make it ideal for the formation of organic compounds?

7. The "octet rule" in chemistry helps predict the tendency of atoms to acquire or donate electrons from the outer shell. It says that those with fewer than 4 tend to donate electrons and those with more than 4 tend to accept additional electrons; those with exactly 4 can do both. Using this rule, determine what category each of the following elements falls into: N, S, C, P, O, H, Ca, Fe, and Mg. (You will need to work out the valence of the atoms.)

8. Draw the following molecules and determine which are polar: Cl_2, NH_3, CH_4.

9. Distinguish between polar and ionic compounds, using your own words.

10. Looking at figure 2.25, can you see why adenine forms hydrogen bonds with thymine and why cytosine forms them with guanine?

Concept Mapping   Synthesis

Appendix D provides guidance for working with concept maps.

1. Supply your own linking words or phrases in this concept map, and provide the missing concepts in the empty boxes.

Visual Connections   Synthesis

These questions use visual images or previous content to make connections to this chapter's concepts.

1. **Figure 2.19a** and **Figure 2.20.** Speculate on why sterols like cholesterol can add "stiffness" to membranes that contain them.

www.connect.microbiology.com

Enhance your study of this chapter with study tools and practice tests. Also ask your instructor about the resources available through ConnectPlus, including the media-rich eBook, interactive learning tools, and animations.

Tools of the Laboratory
The Methods for Studying Microorganisms

Case File 3

One August morning in 2008, a large proportion of the inmates at a Wisconsin county jail awoke complaining of nausea, vomiting, and diarrhea. The local health department suspected an outbreak of food-borne illness, and along with the Wisconsin Division of Public Health, initiated an investigation.

Because of the strict routine and controlled environment of prison life, it was relatively easy to find out what the inmates had eaten in the past 24 hours and how their food had been prepared. A written questionnaire distributed to the inmates revealed 194 probable cases of food intoxication. Four respondents commented on the unusual taste of the casserole they had eaten the night before, which contained macaroni, ground beef, ground turkey, frozen vegetables, and gravy. Stool samples were obtained from six symptomatic inmates and cultured for the presence of pathogenic bacteria.

- What five basic techniques are used to identify a microorganism in the laboratory?
- What types of media might a lab technician use to differentiate bacteria from one another?

Continuing the Case appears on page 66.

Outline and Learning Outcomes

3.1 Methods of Culturing Microorganisms: The Five I's
  1. Explain what the five I's mean and what each step entails.
  2. Name and define the three ways to categorize media.
  3. Provide examples for each of the three categories of media.

3.2 The Microscope: Window on an Invisible Realm
  4. Convert among different lengths within the metric system.
  5. Describe the earliest microscopes.
  6. List and describe the three elements of good microscopy.
  7. Differentiate between the principles of light and electron microscopy.
  8. Name the two main categories of stains.
  9. Give examples of a simple, differential, and special stain.

An Overview of Major Techniques Performed by Microbiologists to Locate, Grow, Observe, and Characterize Microorganisms

Specimen Collection:
Nearly any object or material can serve as a source of microbes. Common ones are body fluids and tissues, foods, water, or soil. Specimens are removed by some form of sampling device: a swab, syringe, or a special transport system that holds, maintains, and preserves the microbes in the sample.

A GUIDE TO THE FIVE I's: How the Sample Is Processed and Profiled

Streak plate

Syringe

Blood bottle

Bird embryo

Incubator

1. Inoculation:
The sample is placed into a container of sterile **medium** containing appropriate nutrients to sustain growth. Inoculation involves spreading the sample on the surface of a solid medium or introducing the sample into a flask or tube. Selection of media with specialized functions can improve later steps of isolation and identification. Some microbes may require a live organism (animal, egg) as the growth medium.

2. Incubation:
An incubator creates the proper growth temperature and other conditions. This promotes multiplication of the microbes over a period of hours, days, and even weeks. Incubation produces a culture—the visible growth of the microbe in or on the medium.

Subculture

Isolation

3. Isolation:
One result of inoculation and incubation is **isolation** of the microbe. Isolated microbes may take the form of separate colonies (discrete mounds of cells) on solid media, or turbidity (free-floating cells) in broths. Further isolation by subculturing involves taking a bit of growth from an isolated colony and inoculating a separate medium. This is one way to make a pure culture that contains only a single species of microbe.

4. Inspection:
The colonies or broth cultures are observed macroscopically for growth characteristics (color, texture, size) that could be useful in analyzing the specimen contents. Slides are made to assess microscopic details such as cell shape, size, and motility. Staining techniques may be used to gather specific information on microscopic morphology.

Microscopic morphology: shape, staining reactions

Biochemical tests

Immunologic tests

DNA analysis

5. Identification:
A major purpose of the Five I's is to determine the type of microbe, usually to the level of species. Information used in identification can include relevant data already taken during initial inspection and additional tests that further describe and differentiate the microbes. Specialized tests include biochemical tests to determine metabolic activities specific to the microbe, immunologic tests, and genetic analysis.

Figure 3.1 A summary of the general laboratory techniques carried out by microbiologists.   It is not necessary to perform all the steps shown or to perform them exactly in this order, but all microbiologists participate in at least some of these activities. In some cases, one may proceed right from the sample to inspection, and in others, only inoculation and incubation on special media are required.

3.1 Methods of Culturing Microorganisms: The Five I's

Biologists studying large organisms such as animals and plants can, for the most part, immediately see and differentiate their experimental subjects from the surrounding environment and from one another. In fact, they can use their senses of sight, smell, hearing, and even touch to detect and evaluate identifying characteristics and to keep track of growth and developmental changes. Microbiologists, however, are confronted by some unique problems. First, most habitats (such as the soil and the human mouth) harbor microbes in complex associations, so it is often necessary to separate the species from one another. Second, to maintain and keep track of such small research subjects, microbiologists usually have to grow them under artificial (and thus distorting) conditions. A third difficulty in working with microbes is that they are invisible and widely distributed, and undesirable ones can be introduced into an experiment and cause misleading results.

Microbiologists use five basic techniques to manipulate, grow, examine, and characterize microorganisms in the laboratory: inoculation, incubation, isolation, inspection, and identification (the Five I's; **figure 3.1**). Some or all of these procedures are performed by microbiologists, whether beginning laboratory students, researchers attempting to isolate drug-producing bacteria from soil, or clinical microbiologists working with a specimen from a patient's infection. These procedures make it possible to handle and maintain microorganisms as discrete entities whose detailed biology can be studied and recorded. Keep in mind as we move through this chapter: It is not necessary to cultivate a microorganism to identify it anymore, though it still remains a very common method. You will read about noncultivation methods of identifying microbes in chapter 17.

Inoculation: Producing a Culture

To cultivate, or **culture,** microorganisms, one introduces a tiny sample (the inoculum) into a container of nutrient **medium** (pl. media), which provides an environment in which they multiply. This process is called **inoculation.** Any instrument used for sampling and inoculation must initially be **sterile.** The observable growth that appears in or on the medium after **incubation** is known as a culture. The nature of the sample being cultured depends on the objectives of the analysis. Clinical specimens for determining the cause of an infectious disease are obtained from body fluids (blood, cerebrospinal fluid), discharges (sputum, urine, feces), or diseased tissue. Other samples subject to microbiological analysis are soil, water, sewage, foods, air, and inanimate objects. Procedures for proper specimen collection are discussed in chapter 17.

Isolation: Separating One Species from Another

Certain **isolation** techniques are based on the concept that if an individual bacterial cell is separated from other cells and provided adequate space on a nutrient surface, it will grow into a discrete mound of cells called a **colony (figure 3.2).** If it was formed from a single cell, a colony consists of just that one species and no other. Proper isolation requires that a small number of cells be inoculated into a relatively large volume or over an expansive area of medium. It generally requires the following materials: a medium that has a relatively firm surface (see agar in "Physical States of Media," page 60), a Petri dish (a clear, flat dish with a cover), and inoculating tools. In the streak plate method, a small droplet of culture or sample is spread over the surface of the medium with an **inoculating loop** according to a pattern that gradually thins out the sample and separates the cells spatially over several sections of the plate **(figure 3.3a,b).** Because of its ease and effectiveness, the streak plate is the method of choice for most applications.

In the loop dilution, or pour plate, technique, the sample is inoculated serially into a series of cooled but still liquid agar tubes so as to dilute the number of cells in each successive tube in the series **(figure 3.3c,d).** Inoculated tubes are then plated out (poured) into sterile Petri dishes and are allowed to solidify (harden). The end result (usually in the second or third plate) is that the number of cells per volume is so decreased that cells

Figure 3.2 Isolation technique. Stages in the formation of an isolated colony, showing the microscopic events and the macroscopic result. Separation techniques such as streaking can be used to isolate single cells. After numerous cell divisions, a macroscopic mound of cells, or a colony, will be formed. This is a relatively simple yet successful way to separate different types of bacteria in a mixed sample.

Mixture of cells in sample

Parent cells

Separation of cells by spreading or dilution on agar medium

Incubation

Growth increases the number of cells.

Microbes become visible as isolated colonies containing millions of cells.

Microscopic view

Macroscopic view

have ample space to grow into separate colonies. One difference between this and the streak plate method is that in this technique some of the colonies will develop deep in the medium itself and not just on the surface.

With the spread plate technique, a small volume of liquid, diluted sample is pipetted onto the surface of the medium and spread around evenly by a sterile spreading tool (sometimes called a "hockey stick"). Like the streak plate, cells are pushed onto separate areas on the surface so that they can form individual colonies **(figure 3.3e,f).**

Before we continue to cover information on the Five I's, we will take a side trip to look at media in more detail.

Media: Providing Nutrients in the Laboratory

A major stimulus to the rise of microbiology in the late 1800s was the development of techniques for growing microbes out of their natural habitats and in pure form in the laboratory. This milestone enabled the close examination of a microbe and its morphology, physiology, and genetics. It was evident from the very first that for successful cultivation, each microorganism had to be provided with all of its required nutrients in an artificial medium.

Some microbes require only a very few simple inorganic compounds for growth; others need a complex list of specific

Figure 3.3 Methods for isolating bacteria. (a) Steps in a quadrant streak plate and (b) resulting isolated colonies of bacteria. (c) Steps in the loop dilution method and (d) the appearance of plate 3. (e) Spread plate and (f) its result.

Note: This method only works if the spreading tool (usually an inoculating loop) is resterilized after each of steps 1–4.

(a) Steps In a Streak Plate

(b)

(c) Steps In Loop Dilution

(d)

"Hockey stick"

(e) Steps In a Spread Plate

(f)

INSIGHT 3.1   Animal Inoculation: "Living Media"

A great deal of attention has been focused on the uses of animals in biology and medicine. Animal rights activists are vocal about practically any experimentation with animals and have expressed their outrage quite forcefully. Certain kinds of animal testing may seem trivial and unnecessary, but many times it is absolutely necessary to use animals bred for experimental purposes, such as guinea pigs, mice, chickens, and even armadillos. Such animals can be an indispensable aid for studying, growing, and identifying microorganisms. One special use of animals involves inoculation of the early life stages (embryos) of birds. Vaccines for influenza are currently produced in chicken embryos. The major rationales for live animal inoculation can be summarized as follows:

1. Animal inoculation is an essential step in testing the effects of drugs and the effectiveness of vaccines before they are administered to humans. It makes progress toward prevention, treatment, and cure possible without risking the lives of humans.

2. Researchers develop animal models for evaluating new diseases or for studying the cause or process of a disease. Koch's postulates are a series of proofs to determine the causative agent of a disease and require a controlled experiment with an animal that can develop a typical case of the disease.

3. Animals are an important source of antibodies, antisera, antitoxins, and other immune products that can be used in therapy or testing.

4. Animals are sometimes required to determine the pathogenicity or toxicity of certain bacteria. One such test is the mouse neutralization test for the presence of botulism toxin in food. This test can help identify even very tiny amounts of toxin and thereby can avert outbreaks of this disease. Occasionally, it is necessary to inoculate an animal to distinguish between pathogenic or nonpathogenic strains of *Listeria* or *Candida* (a yeast).

5. Some microbes will not grow on artificial media but will grow in a suitable animal and can be recovered in a more or less pure form. These include animal viruses, the spirochete of syphilis, and the leprosy bacillus (grown in armadillos).

The nude or athymic mouse has genetic defects in hair formation and thymus development. It is widely used to study cancer, immune function, and infectious diseases.

---

inorganic and organic compounds. This tremendous diversity is evident in the types of media that can be prepared. More than 500 different types of media are used in culturing and identifying microorganisms. Culture media are contained in test tubes, flasks, or Petri dishes, and they are inoculated by such tools as loops, needles, pipettes, and swabs. Media are extremely varied in nutrient content and consistency and can be specially formulated for a particular purpose. Culturing microbes that cannot grow on artificial media (all viruses and certain bacteria) requires cell cultures or host animals **(Insight 3.1).**

For an experiment to be properly controlled, sterile technique is necessary. This means that the inoculation must start with a sterile medium and inoculating tools with sterile tips must be used. Measures must be taken to prevent introduction of nonsterile materials, such as room air and fingers, directly into the media.

Types of Media

Media can be classified according to three properties **(table 3.1):**

1. physical state,
2. chemical composition, and
3. purpose, functional type.

Most media discussed here are designed for bacteria and fungi, though algae and some protozoa can be propagated in media.

Table 3.1 Three Categories of Media Classification

Physical State*	Chemical Composition	Functional Type	
1. Liquid	1. Synthetic (chemically defined)	1. General purpose	5. Anaerobic growth
2. Semisolid	2. Nonsynthetic (complex; not chemically defined)	2. Enriched	6. Specimen transport
3. Solid (can be converted to liquid)		3. Selective	7. Assay
4. Solid (cannot be liquefied)		4. Differential	8. Enumeration

*Some media can serve more than one function. For example, a medium such as brain-heart infusion is general purpose and enriched; mannitol salt agar is both selective and differential; and blood agar is both enriched and differential.

Physical States of Media

Liquid media are water-based solutions that do not solidify at temperatures above freezing and that tend to flow freely when the container is tilted **(figure 3.4)**. These media, termed broths, milks, or infusions, are made by dissolving various solutes in distilled water. Growth occurs throughout the container and can then present a dispersed, cloudy, or particulate appearance. A common laboratory medium, *nutrient broth*, contains beef extract and peptone dissolved in water. Methylene blue milk and litmus milk are opaque liquids containing whole milk and dyes. Fluid thioglycollate is a slightly viscous broth used for determining patterns of growth in oxygen.

At ordinary room temperature, **semisolid media** exhibit a clotlike consistency **(figure 3.5)** because they contain an amount of solidifying agent (agar or gelatin) that thickens them but does not produce a firm substrate. Semisolid media are used to determine the motility of bacteria and to localize a reaction at a specific site.

Solid media provide a firm surface on which cells can form discrete colonies **(figure 3.6)** and are advantageous for isolating and culturing bacteria and fungi. They come in two forms: liquefiable and nonliquefiable. Liquefiable solid media, sometimes called reversible solid media, contain a solidifying agent that changes their physical properties in response to temperature. By far the most widely used and effective of these agents is **agar,** a complex polysaccharide isolated from the red alga *Gelidium.* The benefits of agar are numerous. It is solid at room temperature, and it melts (liquefies) at the boiling temperature of water (100°C). Once liquefied, agar does not resolidify until it cools to 42°C, so it can be inoculated and poured in liquid form at temperatures (45° to 50°C) that will not harm the microbes or the handler. Agar is flexible and moldable, and it provides a basic framework to hold moisture and nutrients, though it is not itself a digestible nutrient for most microorganisms.

Any medium containing 1% to 5% agar usually has the word **agar** in its name. **Nutrient agar** is a common one. Like nutrient broth, it contains beef extract and peptone, as well as 1.5% agar by weight. Many of the examples covered in the section on functional categories of media contain agar. Although gelatin is not nearly as satisfactory as agar, it will create a reasonably solid surface in concentrations of 10% to 15%. Agar medium is illustrated in figure 3.7 and figure 3.9.

Nonliquefiable solid media have less versatile applications than agar media because they do not melt. They include materials such as rice grains (used to grow fungi), cooked meat media (good for anaerobes), and potato slices; all of these media start out solid and remain solid after heat sterilization. Other solid media containing egg and serum start out liquid and are permanently coagulated or hardened by moist heat.

Figure 3.4 Sample liquid media. **(a)** Liquid media tend to flow freely when the container is tilted. **(b)** Urea broth is used to show a biochemical reaction in which the enzyme urease digests urea and releases ammonium. This raises the pH of the solution and causes the dye to become increasingly pink. Left: uninoculated broth, pH 7; middle: weak positive, pH 7.5; right: strong positive, pH 8.0.

Figure 3.5 Sample semisolid media. **(a)** Semisolid media have more body than liquid media but less body than solid media. They do not flow freely and have a soft, clotlike consistency. **(b)** Sulfur indole motility medium (SIM). The **(1)** medium is stabbed with an inoculum and incubated. Location of growth indicates nonmotility **(2)** or motility **(3)**. If H_2S gas is released, a black precipitate forms **(4)**.

Figure 3.6 Solid media that are reversible to liquids. **(a)** Media containing 1%–5% agar are solid enough to remain in place when containers are tilted or inverted. They are reversibly solid and can be liquefied with heat, poured into a different container, and resolidified. **(b)** Nutrient gelatin contains enough gelatin (12%) to take on a solid consistency. The top tube shows it as a solid. The bottom tube indicates what happens when it is warmed or when microbial enzymes digest the gelatin and liquefy it.

Chemical Content of Media

Media whose compositions are precisely chemically defined are termed **synthetic** (also known as *defined*). Such media contain pure organic and inorganic compounds that vary little from one source to another and have a molecular content specified by means of an exact formula. Synthetic media come in many forms. Some media, such as minimal media for fungi, contain nothing more than a few essential compounds such as salts and amino acids dissolved in water. Others contain a variety of defined organic and inorganic chemicals **(table 3.2)**. Such standardized and reproducible media are most useful in research and cell culture when the exact nutritional needs of the test organisms are known. If even one component of a given medium is not chemically definable, the medium belongs in the *complex* category.

Complex, or nonsynthetic, media contain at least one ingredient that is *not* chemically definable—not a simple, pure compound and not representable by an exact chemical formula. Most of these substances are extracts of animals, plants, or yeasts, including such materials as ground-up cells, tissues, and secretions. Examples are blood, serum, and meat extracts or infusions. Other nonsynthetic ingredients are milk, yeast extract, soybean digests, and peptone. Peptone is a partially degraded protein, rich in amino acids, that is often used as a carbon and nitrogen source. Nutrient broth, blood agar, and MacConkey agar, though different in function and appearance, are all complex nonsynthetic media. They present a rich mixture of nutrients for microbes that have complex nutritional needs.

Table 3.2 provides a practical comparison of the two categories, using a *Staphylococcus* medium. Every substance in medium A is known to a very precise degree. The substances in medium B are mostly macromolecules that contain dozens of unknown (but required) nutrients. Both A and B will satisfactorily grow the bacterium.

Media for Different Purposes

Microbiologists have many types of media at their disposal, with new ones being devised all the time. Depending on what is added, a microbiologist can fine-tune a medium for nearly any purpose. Until recently, microbiologists knew of only a few species of bacteria or fungi that could not be cultivated artificially. Newer DNA detection technologies have shown us just how wrong we were; it is now thought that there are many times more microbes that we don't know how to cultivate in the lab than those that we do. Previous discovery and identification of microorganisms relied on our ability to grow them. Now we can detect a single bacterium in its natural habitat.

General-purpose media are designed to grow as broad a spectrum of microbes as possible. As a rule, they are nonsynthetic and contain a mixture of nutrients that could support the growth of a variety of microbial life. Examples include nutrient agar and broth, brain-heart infusion, and trypticase soy agar (TSA). An **enriched medium** contains complex organic substances such as blood, serum, hemoglobin, or special **growth factors** (specific vitamins, amino acids) that certain species must have in order to grow. Bacteria that require growth factors and complex nutrients are termed **fastidious.** Blood agar, which is made by adding sterile sheep, horse, or rabbit blood to a sterile agar base

Table 3.2A	Chemically Defined Synthetic Medium for Growth and Maintenance of Pathogenic *Staphylococcus aureus*	
0.25 Grams Each of These Amino Acids	**0.5 Grams Each of These Amino Acids**	**0.12 Grams Each of These Amino Acids**
Cystine	Arginine	Aspartic acid
Histidine	Glycine	Glutamic acid
Leucine	Isoleucine	
Phenylalanine	Lysine	
Proline	Methionine	
Tryptophan	Serine	
Tyrosine	Threonine	
	Valine	

Additional ingredients

0.005 mole nicotinamide ⎤
0.005 mole thiamine ⎥
0.005 mole pyridoxine ⎥ — Vitamins
0.5 micrograms biotin ⎦
1.25 grams magnesium sulfate ⎤
1.25 grams dipotassium hydrogen phosphate ⎥
1.25 grams sodium chloride ⎥ — Salts
0.125 grams iron chloride ⎦

Ingredients dissolved in 1,000 milliliters of distilled water and buffered to a final pH of 7.0.

Table 3.2B	Brain-Heart Infusion Broth: A Complex, Nonsynthetic Medium for Growth and Maintenance of Pathogenic *Staphylococcus aureus*

27.5	grams brain, heart extract, peptone extract
2	grams glucose
5	grams sodium chloride
2.5	grams di-sodium hydrogen phosphate

Ingredients dissolved in 1,000 milliliters of distilled water and buffered to a final pH of 7.0.

(figure 3.7a) is widely employed to grow fastidious streptococci and other pathogens. Pathogenic *Neisseria* (one species causes gonorrhea) are grown on Thayer-Martin medium or "chocolate" agar, which is made by heating blood agar **(figure 3.7b)**.

Selective and Differential Media Some of the most inventive media recipes belong to the categories of selective and differential media **(figure 3.8)**. These media are designed for special microbial groups, and they have extensive applications in isolation and identification. They can permit, in a single step, the preliminary identification of a genus or even a species.

A **selective medium (table 3.3)** contains one or more agents that inhibit the growth of a certain microbe or microbes (call them A, B, and C) but not others (D) and thereby encourages, or *selects*, microbe D and allows it to grow. Selective media are very important in primary isolation of a specific type of microorganism from samples containing dozens of different species—for example, feces, saliva, skin, water, and soil. They speed up isolation by suppressing the unwanted background organisms and favoring growth of the desired ones.

(a)

(b)

Figure 3.7 Examples of enriched media. **(a)** Blood agar plate growing bacteria from the human throat. Note that this medium also differentiates among colonies by the zones of hemolysis (clear areas) they may show. **(b)** Culture of *Neisseria* sp. on chocolate agar. Chocolate agar gets its brownish color from cooked blood (not chocolate) and does not produce hemolysis.

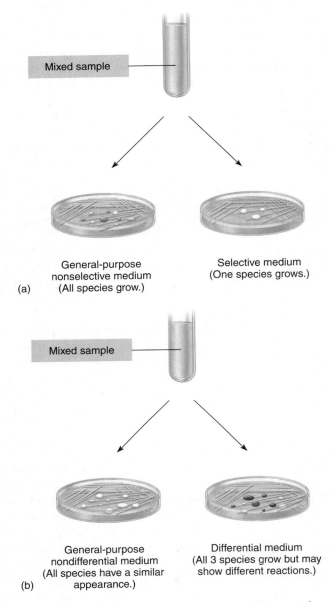

Figure 3.8 Comparison of selective and differential media with general-purpose media. **(a)** A mixed sample containing three different species is streaked onto plates of general-purpose nonselective medium and selective medium. Note the results. **(b)** Another mixed sample containing three different species is streaked onto plates of general-purpose nondifferential medium and differential medium. Note the results.

Table 3.3 Selective Media, Agents, and Functions

Medium	Selective Agent	Used For
Mueller tellurite	Potassium tellurite	Isolation of *Corynebacterium diphtheriae*
Enterococcus faecalis broth	Sodium azide, tetrazolium	Isolation of fecal enterococci
Phenylethanol agar	Phenylethanol chloride	Isolation of staphylococci and streptococci
Tomato juice agar	Tomato juice, acid	Isolation of lactobacilli from saliva
MacConkey agar	Bile, crystal violet	Isolation of gram-negative enterics
Salmonella/Shigella (SS) agar	Bile, citrate, brilliant green	Isolation of *Salmonella* and *Shigella*
Lowenstein-Jensen	Malachite green dye	Isolation and maintenance of *Mycobacterium*
Sabouraud's agar	pH of 5.6 (acid)	Isolation of fungi—inhibits bacteria

Mannitol salt agar (MSA) **(figure 3.9a)** contains a high concentration of NaCl (7.5%) that is quite inhibitory to most human pathogens. One exception is the genus *Staphylococcus,* which grows well in this medium and consequently can be amplified in mixed samples. Bile salts, a component of feces, inhibit most gram-positive bacteria while permitting many gram-negative rods to grow. Media for isolating intestinal pathogens (Mac-Conkey agar, Hektoen enteric [HE] agar) contain bile salts as a selective agent **(figure 3.9b).** Dyes such as methylene blue and crystal violet also inhibit certain gram-positive bacteria. Other agents that have selective properties are antimicrobial drugs and acid. Some selective media contain strongly inhibitory agents to favor the growth of a pathogen that would otherwise be overlooked because of its low numbers

in a specimen. Selenite and brilliant green dye are used in media to isolate *Salmonella* from feces, and sodium azide is used to isolate enterococci from water and food.

Differential media allow multiple types of microorganisms to grow but are designed to display visible differences among those microorganisms. Differentiation shows up as variations in colony size or color, in media color changes, or in the formation of gas bubbles and precipitates **(table 3.4).** These variations come from the type of chemicals these media contain and the ways that microbes react to them. For example, when microbe X metabolizes a certain substance not used by organism Y, then X will cause a visible change in the medium and Y will not. The simplest differential media show two reaction types such as the use or nonuse of a particular nutrient or a color change in some colonies but not in others. Some media are

(a)

(b)

Figure 3.9 Examples of media that are both selective and differential. **(a)** Mannitol salt agar is used to isolate members of the genus *Staphylococcus*. It is selective because *Staphylococcus* can grow in the presence of 7.5% sodium chloride, whereas many other species are inhibited by this high concentration. It contains a dye that also differentiates those species of *Staphylococcus* that produce acid from mannitol and turn the phenol red dye to a bright yellow. **(b)** MacConkey agar selects against gram-positive bacteria. It also differentiates between lactose-fermenting bacteria (indicated by a pink-red reaction in the center of the colony) and lactose-negative bacteria (indicated by an off-white colony with no dye reaction).

Table 3.4 Differential Media

Medium	Substances That Facilitate Differentiation	Differentiates Between
Blood agar	Intact red blood cells	Types of hemolysis displayed by different species of *Streptococcus*
Mannitol salt agar	Mannitol, phenol red	Species of *Staphylococcus*
Hektoen enteric (HE) agar	Brom thymol blue, acid fuchsin, sucrose, salicin, thiosulfate, ferric ammonium citrate	*Salmonella, Shigella,* other lactose fermenters from nonfermenters
MacConkey agar	Lactose, neutral red	Bacteria that ferment lactose (lowering the pH) from those that do not
Urea broth	Urea, phenol red	Bacteria that hydrolyze urea to ammonia
Sulfur indole motility (SIM)	Thiosulfate, iron	H_2S gas producers from nonproducers
Triple-sugar iron agar (TSIA)	Triple sugars, iron, and phenol red dye	Fermentation of sugars, H_2S production
Birdseed agar	Seeds from thistle plant	*Cryptococcus neoformans* and other fungi

(a)

(b)

Figure 3.10 Media that differentiate characteristics.
(a) Triple-sugar iron agar (TSIA) in a slant tube. This medium contains three fermentable carbohydrates, phenol red to indicate pH changes, and a chemical (iron) that indicates H_2S gas production. Reactions (from left to right) are: no growth; growth with no acid production; acid production in the bottom (butt) only; acid production all through the medium; and acid production in the butt with H_2S gas formation (black). **(b)** A state-of-the-art medium developed for culturing and identifying the most common urinary pathogens. CHROMagar Orientation™ uses color-forming reactions to distinguish at least seven species and permits rapid identification and treatment. In the example, the bacteria were streaked so as to spell their own names.

sufficiently complex to show three or four different reactions **(figure 3.10).** A single medium can be both selective and differential, owing to different ingredients in its composition. MacConkey agar, for example, appears in table 3.3 (selective media) and table 3.4 (differential media).

Dyes can be used as differential agents because many of them are pH indicators that change color in response to the production of an acid or a base. For example, MacConkey agar contains neutral red, a dye that is yellow when neutral and pink or red when acidic. A common intestinal bacterium such as *Escherichia coli* that gives off acid when it metabolizes the lactose in the medium develops red to pink colonies, and one like *Salmonella* that does not give off acid remains its natural color (off-white).

Miscellaneous Media   A **reducing medium** contains a substance (thioglycollic acid or cystine) that absorbs oxygen or slows the penetration of oxygen in a medium, thus reducing its availability. Reducing media are important for growing anaerobic bacteria or for determining oxygen requirements of isolates (described in chapter 7). **Carbohydrate fermentation media** contain sugars that can be fermented (converted to acids) and a pH indicator to show this reaction (see

figure 3.9*a* and **figure 3.11**). Media for other biochemical reactions that provide the basis for identifying bacteria and fungi are presented in chapter 17.

Transport media are used to maintain and preserve specimens that have to be held for a period of time before clinical analysis or to sustain delicate species that die rapidly if not held under stable conditions. Transport media contain

Figure 3.11 Carbohydrate fermentation in broths. This medium is designed to show fermentation (acid production) and gas formation by means of a small, inverted Durham tube for collecting gas bubbles. The tube on the left is an uninoculated negative control; the center tube is positive for acid (yellow) and gas (open space); the tube on the right shows growth but neither acid nor gas.

salts, buffers, and absorbants to prevent cell destruction by enzymes, pH changes, and toxic substances but will not support growth. **Assay media** are used by technologists to test the effectiveness of antimicrobial drugs (see chapter 12) and by drug manufacturers to assess the effect of disinfectants, antiseptics, cosmetics, and preservatives on the growth of microorganisms. **Enumeration media** are used by industrial and environmental microbiologists to count the numbers of organisms in milk, water, food, soil, and other samples.

Back to the Five I's: Incubation, Inspection, and Identification

Once a container of medium has been inoculated, it is **incubated,** which means it is placed in a temperature-controlled chamber (incubator) to encourage multiplication. Although microbes have adapted to growth at temperatures ranging from freezing to boiling, the usual temperatures used in laboratory propagation fall between 20°C and 40°C. Incubators can also control the content of atmospheric gases such as oxygen and carbon dioxide that may be required for the growth of certain microbes. During the incubation period (ranging from a day to several weeks), the microbe multiplies and produces growth that is observable macroscopically. Microbial growth in a liquid medium materializes as cloudiness, sediment, scum, or color. A common manifestation of growth on solid media is the appear-

ance of colonies, especially in bacteria and fungi. Colonies are actually large masses of piled-up cells (see chapter 7).

In some ways, culturing microbes is analogous to gardening. Cultures are formed by "seeding" tiny plots (media) with microbial cells. Extreme care is taken to exclude weeds (contaminants). Once microbes have grown after incubation, the clinician must **inspect** the container (Petri dish, test tube, etc.). A **pure culture** is a container of medium that grows only a single known species or type of microorganism **(figure 3.12a).**

(a)

(b)

(c)

Figure 3.12 Various conditions of cultures. **(a)** Three tubes containing pure cultures of *Escherichia coli* (white), *Micrococcus luteus* (yellow), and *Serratia marcescens* (red). **(b)** A mixed culture of *M. luteus* (bright yellow colonies) and *E. coli* (faint white colonies). **(c)** This plate of *S. marcescens* was overexposed to room air, and it has developed a large, white colony. Because this intruder is not desirable and not identified, the culture is now contaminated.

This type of culture is most frequently used for laboratory study, because it allows the systematic examination and control of one microorganism by itself. Instead of the term **pure culture,** some microbiologists prefer the term **axenic,** meaning that the culture is free of other living things except for the one being studied. A standard method for preparing a pure culture is to **subculture,** or make a second-level culture from a well-isolated colony. A tiny bit of cells is transferred into a separate container of media and incubated (see figure 3.1, step 3).

A **mixed culture (figure 3.12***b***)** is a container that holds two or more **identified,** easily differentiated species of microorganisms, not unlike a garden plot containing both carrots and onions. A **contaminated culture (figure 3.12***c***)** was once pure or mixed (and thus a known entity) but has since had **contaminants** (unwanted microbes of uncertain identity) introduced into it, like weeds into a garden. Because contaminants have the potential for causing disruption, constant vigilance is required to exclude them from microbiology laboratories, as you will no doubt witness from your own experience. Contaminants get into cultures when the lids of tubes or Petri dishes are left off for too long, allowing airborne microbes to settle into the medium. They can also enter on an incompletely sterilized inoculating loop or on an instrument that you have inadvertently reused or touched to the table or your skin.

How does one determine (i.e., identify) what sorts of microorganisms have been isolated in cultures? Certainly, microscopic appearance can be valuable in differentiating the smaller, simpler prokaryotic cells from the larger, more complex eukaryotic cells. Appearance can be especially useful in identifying eukaryotic microorganisms to the level of genus or species because of their distinctive morphological features; however, bacteria are generally not identifiable by these methods because very different species may appear quite similar. For them, we must include other techniques, some of which characterize their cellular metabolism. These methods, called biochemical tests, can determine fundamental chemical characteristics such as nutrient requirements, products given off during growth, presence of enzymes, and mechanisms for deriving energy.

Several modern analytical and diagnostic tools that focus on genetic characteristics can detect microbes based on their DNA. Identification can also be accomplished by testing the isolate against known antibodies (immunologic testing). In the case of certain pathogens, further information on a microbe is obtained by inoculating a suitable laboratory animal. A profile is prepared by compiling physiological testing results with both macroscopic and microscopic traits. The profile then becomes the raw material used in final identification. In chapter 17, we present more detailed examples of identification methods.

Maintenance and Disposal of Cultures

In most medical laboratories, the cultures and specimens constitute a potential hazard and require prompt and proper disposal. Both steam sterilizing (see autoclave, chapter 11) and incineration (burning) are used to destroy microorganisms. On the other hand, many teaching and research laboratories maintain a line of **stock cultures** that represent "living catalogs" for study and experimentation. The largest culture collection can be found at the American Type Culture Collection in Manassas, Virginia, which maintains a voluminous array of frozen and freeze-dried fungal, bacterial, viral, and algal cultures.

3.1 Learning Outcomes—Can You . . .

1. . . . explain what the Five I's mean and what each step entails?
2. . . . name and define the three ways to categorize media?
3. . . . provide examples for each of the three categories of media?

3.2 The Microscope: Window on an Invisible Realm

Imagine Leeuwenhoek's excitement and wonder when he first viewed a drop of rainwater and glimpsed an amazing microscopic world teeming with unearthly creatures. Beginning

---

Case File 3 *Continuing the Case*

The process of identifying a microbial pathogen in the laboratory follows a customary path of inoculation, incubation, isolation, inspection, and identification, often referred to as the Five I's. These steps allow a laboratory technician to sample, grow, and isolate a microbe in order to determine its physical, biochemical, and physiological properties. Once characterization is complete, it is generally a simple matter to identify the unknown microbe.

Biochemical tests of the prisoners' stool samples were negative for *Salmonella, Shigella, Campylobacter,* and *Escherichia coli* O157:H7. However, *Clostridium perfringens* enterotoxin was present in all six samples. *C. perfringens* is found in soil and also commonly inhabits the intestinal tracts of mammals, including humans. In addition, it is a frequent contaminant of meats and gravies and is usually associated with inadequate heating and cooling during the cooking process. When food products contaminated with *C. perfringens* are allowed to remain at temperatures between 40°C and 50°C (104°F and 122°F), enterotoxin-producing vegetative cells are rapidly produced; illness results from the enterotoxin's action on the small intestine. *C. perfringens* is responsible for an estimated 250,000 cases of diarrhea annually in the United States.

microbiology students still experience this sensation, and even experienced microbiologists remember their first view. Before we examine microscopes, let's consider how small microbes actually are.

Microbial Dimensions: How Small Is Small?

When we say that microbes are too small to be seen with the unaided eye, what sorts of dimensions are we talking about? The concept of thinking small is best visualized by comparing microbes with the larger organisms of the macroscopic world and also with the atoms and molecules of the molecular world **(figure 3.13).** Whereas the dimensions of macroscopic organisms are usually given in centimeters (cm) and meters (m), those of microorganisms fall within the range of millimeters (mm) to micrometers (μm) to nanometers (nm). The size range of most microbes extends from the smallest bacteria, measuring around 200 nm, to protozoa and algae that measure 3 to 4 mm and are visible with the naked eye. Viruses, which can infect all organisms including microbes, measure between 20 nm and 800 nm, and some of them are thus not much bigger than large molecules, whereas others are just a tad larger than the smallest bacteria.

Figure 3.13 The size of things. Common measurements encountered in microbiology and a scale of comparison from the macroscopic to the microscopic, molecular, and atomic. Most microbes encountered in our studies will fall between 100 μm and 10 nm in overall dimensions. The microbes shown are more or less to scale within size zone but not *between* size zones.

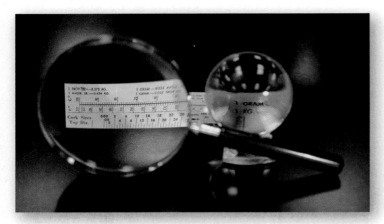

Figure 3.14 Effects of magnification.   Demonstration of the magnification and image-forming capacity of clear glass "lenses." Given a proper source of illumination, this magnifying glass and crystal ball magnify a ruler two to three times.

The microbial existence is indeed another world, but it would remain largely uncharted without an essential tool: the microscope. Your efforts in exploring microbes will be more meaningful if you understand some essentials of **microscopy** and specimen preparation.

Magnification and Microscope Design

A discovery by early microscopists that spurred the advancement of microbiology was that a clear, glass sphere could act as a lens to magnify small objects. Magnification in most microscopes results from a complex interaction between visible light waves and the curvature of the lens. When a beam or ray of light transmitted through air strikes and passes through the convex surface of glass, it experiences some degree of **refraction,** defined as the bending or change in the angle of the light ray as it passes through a medium such as a lens. The greater the difference in the composition of the two substances the light passes between, the more pronounced is the refraction. When an object is placed a certain distance from the spherical lens and illuminated with light, an optical replica, or image, of it is formed by the refracted light. Depending upon the size and curvature of the lens, the image appears enlarged to a particular degree, which is called its power of magnification and is usually identified with a number combined with × (read "times"). This behavior of light is evident if one looks through an everyday object such as a glass ball or a magnifying glass **(figure 3.14).** It is basic to the function of all optical, or light, microscopes, though many of them have additional features that define, refine, and increase the size of the image.

The first microscopes were simple, meaning they contained just a single magnifying lens and a few working parts. Examples of this type of microscope are a magnifying glass, a hand lens, and Leeuwenhoek's basic little tool shown earlier in figure 1.8*a*. Among the refinements that led to the development of today's compound microscope were the addition of a second magnifying lens system, a lamp in the base to give off visible light and illuminate the specimen, and a special lens called the condenser that converges or focuses the rays of light to a single point on the object. The fundamental parts of a modern compound light microscope are illustrated in **figure 3.15.**

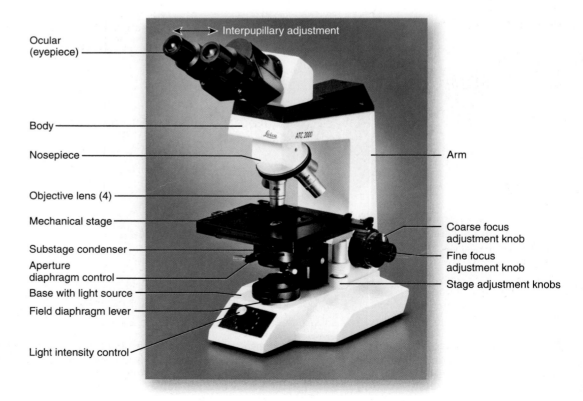

Ocular (eyepiece)
Interpupillary adjustment
Body
Nosepiece
Arm
Objective lens (4)
Mechanical stage
Coarse focus adjustment knob
Substage condenser
Fine focus adjustment knob
Aperture diaphragm control
Stage adjustment knobs
Base with light source
Field diaphragm lever
Light intensity control

Figure 3.15 The parts of a student laboratory microscope.   This microscope is a compound light microscope with two oculars (called binocular). It has four objective lenses, a mechanical stage to move the specimen, a condenser, an iris diaphragm, and a built-in lamp.

Principles of Light Microscopy

To be most effective, a microscope should provide adequate magnification, resolution, and good contrast. Magnification of the object or specimen by a compound microscope occurs in two phases. The first lens in this system (the one closest to the specimen) is the objective lens, and the second (the one closest to the eye) is the ocular lens, or eyepiece (figure 3.16). The objective forms the initial image of the specimen, called the **real image**. When this image is projected up through the microscope body to the plane of the eyepiece, the ocular lens forms a second image, the **virtual image**. The virtual image is the one that will be received by the eye and converted to a retinal and visual image. The magnifying power of the objective alone usually ranges from 4× to 100×, and the power of the ocular alone ranges from 10× to 20×. The total power of magnification of the final image formed by the combined lenses is a product of the separate powers of the two lenses:

Power of objective	×	Usual power of ocular	×	Total magnification
10× low power objective	×	10×	=	100×
40× high dry objective	×	10×	=	400×
100× oil immersion objective	×	10×	=	1,000×

Microscopes are equipped with a nosepiece holding three or more objectives that can be rotated into position as needed. The power of the ocular usually remains constant for a given microscope. Depending on the power of the ocular, the total magnification of standard light microscopes can vary from 40× with the lowest power objective (called the scanning objective) to 2,000× with the highest power objective (the oil immersion objective).

Resolution: Distinguishing Magnified Objects Clearly   As important as magnification is for visualizing tiny objects or cells, an additional optical property is essential for seeing clearly. That property is resolution, or **resolving power**. Resolution is the capacity of an optical system to distinguish or separate two adjacent objects or points from one another. For example, at a certain fixed distance, the lens in the human eye can resolve two small objects as separate points just as long as the two objects are no closer than 0.2 millimeters apart. The eye examination given by optometrists is in fact a test of the resolving power of the human eye for various-size letters read at a distance of 20 feet. Because microorganisms are extremely small and usually very close together, they will not be seen with clarity or any degree of detail unless the microscope's lenses can resolve them.

A simple equation in the form of a fraction expresses the main factors in resolution:

$$\text{Resolving power (RP)} = \frac{\text{Wavelength of light in nm}}{2 \times \text{Numerical aperture of objective lens}}$$

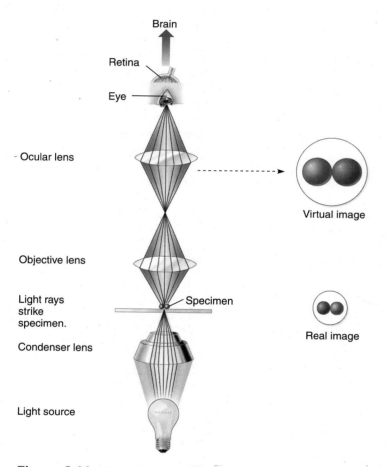

Figure 3.16 The pathway of light and the two stages in magnification of a compound microscope.   As light passes through the condenser, it forms a solid beam that is focused on the specimen. Light leaving the specimen that enters the objective lens is refracted so that an enlarged primary image, the real image, is formed. One does not see this image, but its degree of magnification is represented by the lower circle. The real image is projected through the ocular, and a second image, the virtual image, is formed by a similar process. The virtual image is the final magnified image that is received by the retina and perceived by the brain. Notice that the lens systems cause the image to be reversed.

This equation demonstrates that the resolving power is a function of the wavelength of light that forms the image, along with certain characteristics of the objective. The light source for optical microscopes consists of a band of colored wavelengths in the visible spectrum. The shortest visible wavelengths are in the violet-blue portion of the spectrum (400 nanometers), and the longest are in the red portion (750 nanometers). Because the wavelength must pass between the objects that are being resolved, shorter wavelengths (in the 400–500 nanometer range) will provide better resolution (figure 3.17). Some microscopes have a special blue filter

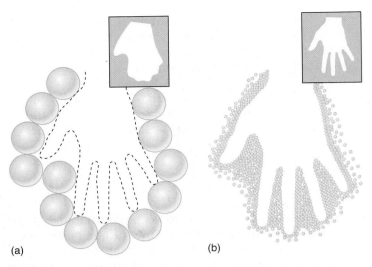

(a)   (b)

Figure 3.17 Effect of wavelength on resolution.   A simple model demonstrates how the wavelength influences the resolving power of a microscope. Here an outline of a hand represents the object being illuminated, and two different-size circles represent the wavelengths of light. In **(a)**, the longer waves are too large to penetrate between the finer spaces and produce a fuzzy, undetailed image. In **(b)**, shorter waves are small enough to enter small spaces and produce a much more detailed image that is recognizable as a hand.

placed over the lamp to limit the longer wavelengths of light from entering the specimen.

The other factor influencing resolution is the **numerical aperture,** a mathematical constant that describes the relative efficiency of a lens in bending light rays. Without going into the mathematical derivation of this constant, it is sufficient to say that each objective has a fixed numerical aperture reading that is determined by the microscope design and ranges from 0.1 in the lowest power lens to approximately 1.25 in the highest power (oil immersion) lens.

In practical terms, the oil immersion lens can resolve any cell or cell part as long as it is at least 0.2 micron in diameter, and it can resolve two adjacent objects as long as they are at least 0.2 micron apart **(figure 3.19).** In general, organisms that are 0.5 micron or more in diameter are readily seen. This includes fungi and protozoa, some of their internal structures, and most bacteria. However, a few bacteria and most viruses are far too small to be resolved by the optical microscope and require electron microscopy (discussed later in this chapter). In summary then, the factor that most limits the clarity of a microscope's image is its resolving power. Even if a light microscope were designed to magnify several thousand times, its resolving power could not be increased, and the image it produced would simply be enlarged and fuzzy.

A Note About Oil Immersion Lenses

The most important thing to remember is that a higher numerical aperture number will provide better resolution. In order for the oil immersion lens to arrive at its maximum resolving capacity, a drop of oil must be inserted between the tip of the lens and the specimen on the glass slide. Because oil has the same optical qualities as glass, it prevents refractive loss that normally occurs as peripheral light passes from the slide into the air; this property effectively increases the numerical aperture **(figure 3.18).**

Figure 3.18 Workings of an oil immersion lens.   Without oil, some of the peripheral light that passes through the specimen is scattered into the air or onto the glass slide; this scattering decreases resolution.

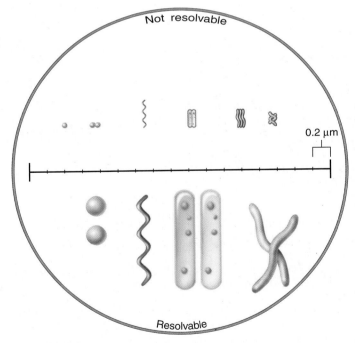

Figure 3.19 Effect of magnification.   Comparison of cells that would not be resolvable versus those that would be resolvable under oil immersion at 1,000× magnification. Note that in addition to differentiating two adjacent things, good resolution also means being able to observe an object clearly.

Contrast The third quality of a well-magnified image is its degree of contrast from its surroundings. The contrast is measured by a quality called the **refractive index.** Refractive index refers to the degree of bending that light undergoes as it passes from one medium (such as water or glass) to another medium, such as some bacterial cells. The higher the difference in refractive indexes (the more bending of light), the sharper the contrast that is registered by the microscope and the eye. Because too much light can reduce contrast and burn out the image, an adjustable iris diaphragm on most microscopes controls the amount of light entering the condenser. The lack of contrast in cell components is compensated for by using special lenses (the phase-contrast microscope) and by adding dyes.

Variations on the Light Microscope

Optical microscopes that use visible light can be described by the nature of their **field,** meaning the circular area viewed through the ocular lens. There are four types of visible-light microscopes: bright-field, dark-field, phase-contrast, and interference. A fifth type of optical microscope, the fluorescence microscope, uses ultraviolet radiation as the illuminating source; and another, the confocal microscope, uses a laser beam. Each of these microscopes is adapted for viewing specimens in a particular way, as described in **table 3.5.**

Preparing Specimens for Optical Microscopes

A specimen for optical microscopy is generally prepared by mounting a sample on a suitable glass slide that sits on the stage between the condenser and the objective lens. The manner in which a slide specimen, or mount, is prepared depends upon: (1) the condition of the specimen, either in a living or preserved state; (2) the aims of the examiner, whether to observe overall structure, identify the microorganisms, or see movement; and (3) the type of microscopy available, whether it is bright-field, dark-field, phase-contrast, or fluorescence.

Fresh, Living Preparations

Live samples of microorganisms are placed in wet mounts or in hanging drop mounts so that they can be observed as near to their natural state as possible. The cells are suspended in a suitable fluid (water, broth, saline) that temporarily maintains viability and provides space and a medium for locomotion. A wet mount consists of a drop or two of the culture placed on a slide and overlaid with a coverslip. Although this type of mount is quick and easy to prepare, it has certain disadvantages. The coverslip can damage larger cells, and the slide is very susceptible to drying and can contaminate the handler's fingers. A more satisfactory alternative is the hanging drop preparation made with a special concave (depres-

Figure 3.20 Hanging drop technique. Cross-section view of slide and coverslip. (Vaseline actually surrounds entire well of slide.)

sion) slide, a Vaseline adhesive or sealant, and a coverslip from which a tiny drop of sample is suspended **(figure 3.20).** These types of short-term mounts provide a true assessment of the size, shape, arrangement, color, and motility of cells. Greater cellular detail can be observed with phase-contrast or interference microscopy.

Fixed, Stained Smears

A more permanent mount for long-term study can be obtained by preparing fixed, stained specimens. The smear technique, developed by Robert Koch more than 100 years ago, consists of spreading a thin film made from a liquid suspension of cells on a slide and air-drying it. Next, the air-dried smear is usually heated gently by a process called heat fixation that simultaneously kills the specimen and secures it to the slide. Another important action of fixation is to preserve various cellular components in a natural state with minimal distortion. Sometimes fixation of microbial cells is performed with chemicals such as alcohol and formalin.

Like images on undeveloped photographic film, the unstained cells of a fixed smear are quite indistinct, no matter how great the magnification or how fine the resolving power of the microscope. The process of "developing" a smear to create contrast and make inconspicuous features stand out requires staining techniques. Staining is any procedure that applies colored chemicals called dyes to specimens. Dyes impart a color to cells or cell parts by becoming affixed to them through a chemical reaction. In general, they are classified as basic (cationic) dyes, which have a positive charge, or acidic (anionic) dyes, which have a negative charge. Because chemicals of opposite charge are attracted to each other, cell parts that are negatively charged will attract basic dyes and those that are positively charged will attract acidic dyes **(table 3.6).** Many cells, especially those of bacteria, have numerous negatively charged acidic substances and thus stain more readily with basic dyes. Acidic dyes, on the other hand, tend to be repelled by cells, so they are good for negative staining (discussed in the next section).

Negative Versus Positive Staining Two basic types of staining technique are used, depending upon how a dye reacts

Table 3.5 Comparison of Types of Microscopy

Microscope	Maximum Practical Magnification	Resolution	
Visible light as source of illumination			
Bright-field	2,000×	0.2 μm (200 nm)	The bright-field microscope in the most widely used type of light microscope. Although we ordinarily view objects like the words on this page with light reflected off the surface, a bright-field microscope forms its image when light is transmitted through the specimen. The specimen, being denser and more opaque than its surroundings, absorbs some of this light, and the rest of the light is transmitted directly up through the ocular into the field. As a result, the specimen will produce an image that is darker than the surrounding brightly illuminated field. The bright-field microscope is a multipurpose instrument that can be used for both live, unstained material and preserved, stained material.

Paramecium (400×)

Dark-field	2,000×	0.2 μm	A bright-field microscope can be adapted as a dark-field microscope by adding a special disc called a *stop* to the condenser. The stop blocks all light from entering the objective lens—except peripheral light that is reflected off the sides of the specimen itself. The resulting image is a particularly striking one: brightly illuminated specimens surrounded by a dark (black) field. The most effective use of dark-field microscopy is to visualize living cells that would be distorted by drying or heat or that cannot be stained with the usual methods. Dark-field microscopy can outline the organism's shape and permit rapid recognition of swimming cells that might appear in dental and other infections, but it does not reveal fine internal details.

Paramecium (400×)

Phase-contrast	2,000×	0.2 μm	If similar objects made of clear glass, ice, cellophane, or plastic are immersed in the same container of water, an observer would have difficulty telling them apart because they have similar optical properties. Internal components of a live, unstained cell also lack contrast and can be difficult to distinguish. But cell structures do differ slightly in density, enough that they can alter the light that passes through them in subtle ways. The phase-contrast microscope has been constructed to take advantage of this characteristic. This microscope contains devices that transform the subtle changes in light waves passing through the specimen into differences in light intensity. For example, denser cell parts such as organelles alter the pathway of light more than less dense regions (the cytoplasm). Light patterns coming from these regions will vary in contrast. The amount of internal detail visible by this method is greater than by either bright-field or dark-field methods. The phase-contrast microscope is most useful for observing intracellular structures such as bacterial spores, granules, and organelles, as well as the locomotor structures of eukaryotic cells such as cilia.

Paramecium (400×)

Differential interference	2,000×	0.2 μm	Like the phase-contrast microscope, the differential interference contrast (DIC) microscope provides a detailed view of unstained, live specimens by manipulating the light. But this microscope has additional refinements, including two prisms that add contrasting colors to the image and two beams of light rather than a single one. DIC microscopes produce extremely well-defined images that are vividly colored and appear three-dimensional.

Amoeba proteus (160×)

Ultraviolet rays as source of illumination			
Fluorescent	2,000×	0.2 μm	The fluorescent microscope is a specially modified compound microscope furnished with an ultraviolet (UV) radiation source and a filter that protects the viewer's eye from injury by these dangerous rays. The name of this type of microscopy originates from the use of certain dyes (acridine, fluorescein) and minerals that show **fluorescence.** The dyes emit visible light when bombarded by short ultraviolet rays. For an image to be formed, the specimen must first be coated or placed in contact with a source of fluorescence. Subsequent illumination by ultraviolet radiation causes the specimen to give off light that will form its own image, usually an intense yellow, orange, or red against a black field.

Fluorescence microscopy has its most useful applications in diagnosing infections caused by specific bacteria, protozoans, and viruses. |

Cheek epithelial cells (the larger unfocused green or red cells). Bacteria are the filamentous green and red rods and the green diplococci (400×).

Microscope	Maximum Practical Magnification	Resolution
Confocal	2,000×	0.2 µm

Myofibroblasts, cells involved in tissue repair (400×)

The scanning confocal microscope overcomes the problem of cells or structures being too thick, a problem resulting in other microscopes being unable to focus on all their levels. This microscope uses a laser beam of light to scan various depths in the specimen and deliver a sharp image focusing on just a single plane. It is thus able to capture a highly focused view at any level, ranging from the surface to the middle of the cell. It is most often used on fluorescently stained specimens but it can also be used to visualize live unstained cells and tissues.

Electron beam forms image of specimen

Transmission electron microscope (TEM)	100,000,000×	0.5 nm

Coronavirus, causative agent of many respiratory infections (100,000×)

Transmission electron microscopes are the method of choice for viewing the detailed structure of cells and viruses. This microscope produces its image by transmitting electrons through the specimen.

Because electrons cannot readily penetrate thick preparations, the specimen must be sectioned into extremely thin slices (20–100 nm thick) and stained or coated with metals that will increase image contrast. The darkest areas of TEM micrographs represent the thicker (denser) parts, and the lighter areas indicate the more transparent and less dense parts.

Scanning electron microscope (SEM)	100,000,000×	10 nm

An alga showing a cell wall made of calcium disks (10,000×)

The scanning electon microscope provides some of the most dramatic and realistic images in existence. This instrument is designed to create an extremely detailed three-dimensional view of all kinds of objects—from plaque on teeth to tapeworm heads. To produce its images, the SEM does not transmit electrons, it bombards the surface of a whole metal-coated specimen with electrons while scanning back and forth over it. A shower of electrons deflected from the surface is picked up with great fidelity by a sophisticated detector, and the electron pattern is displayed as an image on a television screen.

The contours of the specimen resolved with scanning electron microscopy are very revealing and often surprising. Areas that look smooth and flat with the light microscope display intriguing surface features with the SEM.

Atomically sharp tip probes surface of specimen

Atomic force microscope (AFM)	100,000,000×	0.01 Angstroms

Prion fibrils, which may only be 5 mm in diameter

In atomic force microscopy, a diamond or metal tip with a radius of 1–50 nanometers scans a specimen and moves up and down with contour of surface at the atomic level. The movement of the tip is measured with a laser and translated into an image.

Scanning tunneling microscope (STM)	100,000,000×	0.01 Angstroms

Strands of DNA (inset is a magnified view of the bare gold surface, verifying that it is clean).

In scanning tunneling microscopy, a tungsten tip hovers over specimen while electrical voltage is applied, generating a current that is dependent on the distance between the tip and surface. Image is produced from the electrical signal of the tip's pathway. See **Insight 3.2** for more information about probing microscopes.

with the specimen (summarized in table 3.6). Most procedures involve a **positive stain,** in which the dye actually sticks to the specimen and gives it color. A **negative stain,** on the other hand, is just the reverse (like a photographic negative). The dye does not stick to the specimen but settles around its outer boundary, forming a silhouette. In a sense, negative staining "stains" the glass slide to produce a dark background around the cells. Nigrosin (blue-black) and India ink (a black suspension of carbon particles) are the dyes most commonly used for negative staining. The cells themselves do not stain because these dyes are negatively charged and are repelled by the negatively charged surface of the cells. The value of negative staining is its relative simplicity and the reduced shrinkage or distortion of cells, as the smear is not heat fixed. A quick assessment can thus be made regarding cellular size, shape, and arrangement. Negative staining is also used to accentuate the capsule that surrounds certain bacteria and yeasts **(figure 3.21).**

Simple Versus Differential Staining   Positive staining methods are classified as simple, differential, or special (figure 3.21). Whereas **simple stains** require only a single dye and an uncomplicated procedure, **differential stains** use two differently colored dyes, called the **primary dye** and the **counterstain,** to distinguish between cell types or parts. These staining techniques tend to be more complex and sometimes require additional chemical reagents to produce the desired reaction.

Most simple staining techniques take advantage of the ready binding of bacterial cells to dyes like malachite green, crystal violet, basic fuchsin, and safranin. Simple stains cause all cells in a smear to appear more or less the same color, regardless of type, but they can still reveal bacterial characteristics such as shape, size, and arrangement.

Types of Differential Stains   A satisfactory differential stain uses differently colored dyes to clearly contrast two cell types or cell parts. Common combinations are red and purple, red and green, or pink and blue. Differential stains can also pinpoint other characteristics, such as the size, shape, and arrangement of cells. Typical examples include Gram, acid-fast, and endospore stains. Some staining techniques (spore, capsule) fall into more than one category.

Gram staining, a century-old method named for its developer, Hans Christian Gram, remains the most universal diagnostic staining technique for bacteria. It permits ready differentiation of major categories based upon the color reaction of the cells: **gram-positive,** which stain purple, and **gram-negative,** which stain pink (red). The Gram stain is the basis of several important bacteriological topics, including bacterial taxonomy, cell wall structure, and identification and diagnosis of infection; in some cases, it even guides the selection of the correct drug for an infection. Gram staining is discussed in greater detail in Insight 4.2.

The **acid-fast** stain, like the Gram stain, is an important diagnostic stain that differentiates acid-fast bacteria (pink) from non-acid-fast bacteria (blue). This stain originated as a specific method to detect *Mycobacterium tuberculosis* in specimens. It was determined that these bacterial cells have a particularly impervi-

Table 3.6   Comparison of Positive and Negative Stains

Medium	Positive Staining	Negative Staining
Appearance of cell	Colored by dye	Clear and colorless
Background	Not stained (generally white)	Stained (dark gray or black)
Dyes employed	Basic dyes: Crystal violet Methylene blue Safranin Malachite green	Acidic dyes: Nigrosin India ink
Subtypes of stains	Several types: Simple stain Differential stains Gram stain Acid-fast stain Spore stain Special stains Capsule Flagella Spore Granules Nucleic acid	Few types: Capsule Spore

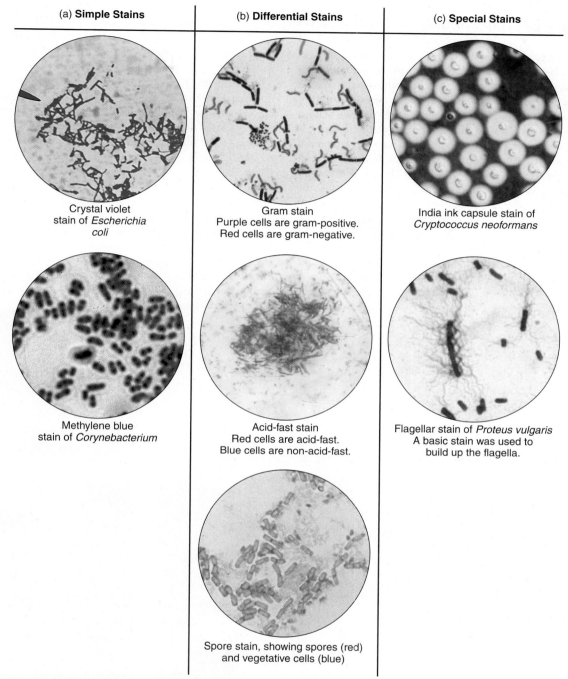

| (a) **Simple Stains** | (b) **Differential Stains** | (c) **Special Stains** |

Crystal violet
stain of *Escherichia
coli*

Gram stain
Purple cells are gram-positive.
Red cells are gram-negative.

India ink capsule stain of
Cryptococcus neoformans

Methylene blue
stain of *Corynebacterium*

Acid-fast stain
Red cells are acid-fast.
Blue cells are non-acid-fast.

Flagellar stain of *Proteus vulgaris*
A basic stain was used to
build up the flagella.

Spore stain, showing spores (red)
and vegetative cells (blue)

Figure 3.21 Types of microbiological stains.   **(a)** Simple stains. **(b)** Differential stains: Gram, acid-fast, and spore. **(c)** Special stains: capsule and flagellar.

ous outer wall that holds fast (tightly or tenaciously) to the dye (carbol fuchsin) even when washed with a solution containing acid or acid alcohol. This stain is used for other medically important mycobacteria such as the Hansen's disease (leprosy) bacillus and for *Nocardia*, an agent of lung or skin infections.

The endospore stain (spore stain) is similar to the acid-fast method in that a dye is forced by heat into resistant bodies called spores or endospores (their formation and significance are discussed in chapter 4). This stain is designed to distinguish between spores and the cells that they come from (so-called **vegetative** cells). Of significance in medical

microbiology are the gram-positive, spore-forming members of the genus *Bacillus* (the cause of anthrax) and *Clostridium* (the cause of botulism and tetanus)—dramatic diseases that we consider in later chapters.

Special stains are used to emphasize certain cell parts that are not revealed by conventional staining methods. **Capsule staining** is a method of observing the microbial capsule, an unstructured protective layer surrounding the cells of some bacteria and fungi. Because the capsule does not react with most stains, it is often negatively stained with India ink, or it may be demonstrated by special positive stains. The fact that

INSIGHT 3.2 The Evolution in Resolution: Probing Microscopes

In the past, chemists, physicists, and biologists had to rely on indirect methods to provide information on the structures of the smallest molecules. But technological advances have created a new generation of microscopes that "see" atomic structure by actually feeling it. *Scanning probe microscopes* operate with a minute needle tapered to a tip that can be as narrow as a single atom! This probe scans over the exposed surface of a material on the end of an arm and records an image of its outer texture. (Think of an old-fashioned record player. . . .) These revolutionary microscopes have such profound resolution that they have the potential to image single atoms (but not subatomic structure yet) and to magnify 100 million times. There are two types of scanning probe microscopes, the atomic force microscope (AFM) and the scanning tunneling microscope (STM). The STM uses a tungsten probe that hovers near the surface of an object and follows its topography while simultaneously giving off an electrical signal of its pathway, which is then imaged on a screen. The STM was used initially for detecting defects on the surfaces of electrical conductors and computer chips composed of silicon, but it has also provided the first incredible close-up views of DNA.

The atomic force microscope (AFM) gently forces a diamond and metal probe down onto the surface of a specimen like a needle on a record. As it moves along the surface, any deflection of the metal probe is detected by a sensitive device that relays the information to an imager. The AFM is very useful in viewing the detailed structures of biological molecules such as antibodies and enzymes.

These powerful new microscopes can also move and position atoms, spawning a field called *nanotechnology*—the science of the "small." When this ability to move atoms was first discovered, scientists had some fun (see illustration on the left). But it has opened up an entirely new way to manipulate atoms in chemical reactions (illustration on the right) and to create nanoscale devices for computers and other electronics. In the future, it may be possible to use microstructures to deliver drugs and treat disease.

Scanning tunneling microscopy. The figure on the left was created when scientists dragged iron atoms over a copper matrix to spell (in kanji, a Japanese written alphabet) "atom" (literally: "original child"). On the right you see a chemical reaction performed by an STM microscope. At the top (a), two iodobenzene molecules appear as two bumps on a copper surface. The STM tip emits a burst of electrons and causes the iodine groups to dissociate from each of the benzene groups (b). The tip then drags away the iodine groups (c), and the two carbon groups bind to one another (d and e).

Source: http://www.almaden.ibm.com/vis/stm/ atomo.html, page 80.

not all microbes exhibit capsules is a useful feature for identifying pathogens. One example is *Cryptococcus,* which causes a serious fungal meningitis in AIDS patients (see chapter 19).

Flagellar staining is a method of revealing flagella, the tiny, slender filaments used by bacteria for locomotion. Because the width of bacterial flagella lies beyond the resolving power of the light microscope, in order to be seen, they must be enlarged by depositing a coating on the outside of the filament and then staining it. Their presence, number, and arrangement on a cell are taxonomically useful.

3.2 Learning Outcomes—Can You . . .

4. . . . convert among different lengths within the metric system?

5. . . . describe the earliest microscopes?

6. . . . list and describe the three elements of good microscopy?

7. . . . differentiate between the principles of light and electron microscopy?

8. . . . name the two main categories of stains?

9. . . . give examples of a simple, differential, and special stain?

Chapter Summary

3.1 Methods of Culturing Microorganisms: The Five I's

- Many microorganisms can be cultured on artificial media, but some can be cultured only in living tissue or in cells.
- Artificial media are classified by their *physical state* as either liquid, semisolid, liquefiable solid, or nonliquefiable solid.
- Artificial media are classified by their *chemical composition* as either *synthetic* or *nonsynthetic,* depending on whether the exact chemical composition is known.
- Artificial media are classified by their *function* as either general-purpose media or media with one or more specific purposes. Enriched, selective, differential, transport, assay, and enumerating media are all examples of media designed for specific purposes.
- The Five I's—inoculation, incubation, isolation, inspection, and identification—summarize the kinds of laboratory procedures used in microbiology.
- Following *inoculation,* cultures are *incubated* at a specified temperature to encourage growth.
- *Isolated colonies* that originate from single cells are composed of large numbers of cells piled up together.
- A culture may exist in one of the following forms: A pure culture contains only one species or type of microorganism. A mixed culture contains two or more known species. A contaminated culture contains both known and unknown (unwanted) microorganisms.
- During inspection, the cultures are examined and evaluated macroscopically and microscopically.
- Microorganisms are identified in terms of their macroscopic or immunologic morphology; their microscopic morphology; their biochemical reactions; and their genetic characteristics.
- Microbial cultures are usually disposed of in two ways: steam sterilization or incineration.

3.2 The Microscope: Window on an Invisible Realm

- Magnification, resolving power, and contrast all influence the clarity of specimens viewed through the optical microscope.
- The maximum resolving power of the optical microscope is 200 nm, or 0.2 µm. This is sufficient to see the internal structures of eukaryotes and the morphology of most bacteria.
- There are six types of optical microscopes. Four types use visible light for illumination: bright-field, dark-field, phase-contrast, and interference microscopes. The fluorescence microscope uses UV light for illumination, but it has the same resolving power as the other optical microscopes. The confocal microscope can use UV light or visible light reflected from specimens.
- Electron microscopes (EM) use electrons, not light waves, as an illumination source to provide high magnification (5,000× to 1,000,000×) and high resolution (0.5 nm). Electron microscopes can visualize cell ultrastructure (transmission EM) and three-dimensional images of cell and virus surface features (scanning EM).
- The newest generation of microscope is called the scanning probe microscope and uses precision tips to image structures at the atomic level.
- Specimens viewed through optical microscopes can be either alive or dead, depending on the type of specimen preparation, but all EM specimens are dead because they must be viewed in a vacuum.
- Stains increase the contrast of specimens and they can be designed to differentiate cell shape, structure, and biochemical composition of the specimens being viewed.

Multiple-Choice and True-False Questions   Knowledge and Comprehension

Multiple-Choice Questions. Select the correct answer from the answers provided.

1. The term *culture* refers to the _____ growth of microorganisms in _____.
   a. rapid, an incubator
   b. macroscopic, media
   c. microscopic, the body
   d. artificial, colonies

2. A mixed culture is
   a. the same as a contaminated culture.
   b. one that has been adequately stirred.
   c. one that contains two or more known species.
   d. a pond sample containing algae and protozoa.

3. Resolution is _____ with a longer wavelength of light.
   a. improved
   b. worsened
   c. not changed
   d. not possible

4. A real image is produced by the
   a. ocular.
   b. objective.
   c. condenser.
   d. eye.

5. A microscope that has a total magnification of 1,500× when using the oil immersion objective has an ocular of what power?
   a. 150×
   b. 1.5×
   c. 15×
   d. 30×

6. The specimen for an electron microscope is always
   a. stained with dyes.
   b. sliced into thin sections.
   c. killed.
   d. viewed directly.

7. Motility is best observed with a
   a. hanging drop preparation.
   b. negative stain.
   c. streak plate.
   d. flagellar stain.

8. Bacteria tend to stain more readily with cationic (positively charged) dyes because bacteria
    a. contain large amounts of alkaline substances.
    b. contain large amounts of acidic substances.
    c. are neutral.
    d. have thick cell walls.

9. **Multiple Matching.** For each type of medium, select all descriptions that fit. For media that fit more than one description, briefly explain why this is the case.
    ____ mannitol salt agar
    ____ chocolate agar
    ____ MacConkey agar
    ____ nutrient broth
    ____ Sabouraud's agar
    ____ triple-sugar iron agar
    ____ *Euglena* agar
    ____ SIM medium

    a. selective medium
    b. differential medium
    c. chemically defined (synthetic) medium
    d. enriched medium
    e. general-purpose medium
    f. complex medium
    g. transport medium

10. A fastidious organism must be grown on what type of medium?
    a. general-purpose medium
    b. differential medium
    c. synthetic medium
    d. enriched medium

True-False Questions. If the statement is true, leave as is. If it is false, correct it by rewriting the sentence.

11. Agar has the disadvantage of being easily decomposed by microorganisms.

12. A subculture is a culture made from an isolated colony.

13. The factor that most limits the clarity of an image in a microscope is the *magnification.*

14. Living specimens can be examined either by light microscopy or electron microscopy.

15. The best stain to use to visualize a microorganism with a large capsule is a simple stain.

 ## Critical Thinking Questions   Application and Analysis

These questions are suggested as a *writing-to-learn* experience. For each question, compose a one- or two-paragraph answer that includes the factual information needed to completely address the question.

1. a. Describe briefly what is involved in the Five I's.
   b. Name three basic differences between inoculation and contamination.

2. a. Explain what is involved in isolating microorganisms and why it is necessary to do this.
   b. Compare and contrast three common laboratory techniques for separating bacteria in a mixed sample.
   c. Describe how an isolated colony forms.
   d. Explain why an isolated colony and a pure culture are not the same thing.

3. Differentiate between microscopic and macroscopic methods of observing microorganisms, citing a specific example of each method.

4. Trace the pathway of light from its source to the eye, explaining what happens as it passes through the major parts of the microscope.

5. Compare bright-field, dark-field, phase-contrast, and fluorescence microscopy as to field appearance, specimen appearance, light source, and uses.

6. a. Compare and contrast the optical compound microscope with the electron microscope.
   b. Why is the resolution so superior in the electron microscope?

   c. What will you never see in an unretouched electron micrograph?

7. a. Why are some bacteria difficult to grow in the laboratory? Relate this to what you know so far about metabolism.
   b. Why are viruses hard to cultivate in the laboratory?

8. Biotechnology companies have engineered hundreds of different types of mice, rats, pigs, goats, cattle, and rabbits to have genetic diseases similar to diseases of humans or to synthesize drugs and other biochemical products. They have patented these animals, and they sell them to researchers for study and experimentation.
   a. What do you think of creating new life forms just for experimentation?
   b. Comment on the benefits, safety, and ethics of this trend.

9. Some human pathogenic bacteria are resistant to most antibiotics. How would you prove a bacterium is resistant to antibiotics using laboratory culture techniques?

10. Some scientists speculate that the reason we can't grow some bacteria on artificial medium at this time is that they are found in polymicrobial communities in their natural settings. If that were true, how would you go about trying to cultivate them?

Concept Mapping   Synthesis

Appendix D provides guidance for working with concept maps.

1. Supply your own linking words or phrases in this concept map, and provide the missing concepts in the empty boxes.

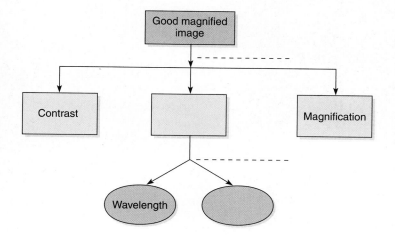

2. Construct your own concept map using the following words as the *concepts*. Supply the linking words between each pair of concepts.

inoculation

isolation

incubation

inspection

identification

medium

multiplication

staining

biochemical tests

subculturing

source of microbes

transport medium

streak plate

Visual Connections   Synthesis

These questions encourage active learning by connecting previously seen material to this chapter's concepts.

1. **Figure 3.3a and b.** If you were using the quadrant streak plate method to plate a very dilute broth culture (with many fewer bacteria than the broth used for 3b) would you expect to see single, isolated colonies in quadrant 4 or quadrant 3? Explain your answer.

(a) Steps in a Streak Plate   (b)

2. **From chapter 1, figure 1.6.** Which of these photos from chapter 1 is an SEM image? Which is a TEM image?

Bacterium: *E. coli*

Fungus: *Thamnidium*

Virus: *Herpes simplex*

Protozoan: *Vorticella*

www.connect.microbiology.com

Enhance your study of this chapter with study tools and practice tests. Also ask your instructor about the resources available through ConnectPlus, including the media-rich eBook, interactive learning tools, and animations.

4

Prokaryotic Profiles
The Bacteria and Archaea

Case File 4

A 15-year-old girl was admitted to the hospital after presenting at the emergency room (ER) in a semiconscious state. Feeling ill was nothing new for this patient—she had a 9-year history of systemic lupus erythematosus (SLE), a condition the ER physicians took into account as they examined her. SLE, sometimes called "lupus," is an autoimmune disease in which the body produces antibodies against many of its own tissues; some organs eventually become damaged or fail to function. The specific symptoms of SLE differ, depending on which organs are affected, but kidney failure, heart problems, lung inflammation, and blood abnormalities are common. The cause of SLE is unknown.

   The patient's initial workup revealed abnormally rapid breathing, fever, and low blood pressure. Additionally, her fingers and toes were cold, and she was producing no urine. The ER staff took samples of her blood and cerebrospinal fluid (CSF) and found bacteria in both. Because of the patient's history of SLE, magnetic resonance imaging (MRI) of the abdomen was performed to assess the condition of her organs. The MRI revealed that the lupus had led to the complete destruction of the patient's spleen, a complication called "autosplenectomy" that occurs in approximately 5% of SLE cases.

- ■ The presence of bacteria in the blood and the cerebrospinal fluid is considered a serious sign. Why?

Continuing the Case appears on page 88.

Outline and Learning Outcomes

4.1 Prokaryotic Form and Function
1. Name the structures all bacteria possess.
2. Name at least four structures that some, but not all, bacteria possess.

4.2 External Structures
3. Describe the structure and function of four different types of bacterial appendages.
4. Explain how a flagellum works in the presence of an attractant.

In chapter 1, we described prokaryotes as being cells with no true nucleus. (Eukaryotes have a membrane around their DNA, and this structure is called the nucleus.) Some microbiologists have recently been suggesting that we are not defining what a prokaryote is, only what it is *not*—and therefore we are not really defining it at all. This is one way scientists work. A previously accepted notion (i.e., what a prokaryote is) is questioned publicly, causing a variety of reactions ranging from surprise to dismissal. Usually other scientists begin discussing the question and the truth that might be behind the assertion is examined in a new way. But this whole chapter is about the type of cell we call a prokaryote. So how do we know whether a cell is prokaryotic or eukaryotic? A prokaryote can be distinguished from the other type of cell (a eukaryote) because of certain characteristics it possesses:

- *The way its DNA is packaged:* Prokaryotes have nuclear material that is not encased in a membrane (i.e., they do not have a nucleus). Eukaryotes have a membrane around their DNA (making up a nucleus). Prokaryotes don't wind their DNA around proteins called **histones;** eukaryotes do.
- *The makeup of its cell wall:* Prokaryotes (bacteria and archaea) generally have a wall structure that is unique compared to eukaryotes. Bacteria have sturdy walls made of a chemical called peptidoglycan. Archaeal walls are also tough and made of other chemicals, distinct from bacteria and distinct from eukaryotic cells.
- *Its internal structures:* Prokaryotes don't have complex, membrane-bounded organelles in their cytoplasm (eukaryotes do). A few prokaryotes have internal membranes, but they don't surround organelles.

Both prokaryotic and eukaryotic microbes are found throughout nature. Both can cause infectious diseases.

Examples of bacterial diseases include "strep" throat, Lyme disease, and ear infections. The medical response to them is informed by their "prokaryoteness." Eukaryotic infections (examples: histoplasmosis, malaria) often require a different approach. In this chapter and coming chapters, you'll discover why that is.

4.1 Prokaryotic Form and Function

The evolutionary history of prokaryotic cells extends back at least 3.8 billion years. It is now generally thought that the very first cells to appear on the earth were a type of prokaryote, possibly related to modern forms that live on sulfur compounds in geothermal ocean vents. The fact that these organisms have endured for so long in such a variety of habitats indicates a cellular structure and function that are amazingly versatile and adaptable.

The general cellular organization of a prokaryotic cell can be represented with this flowchart:

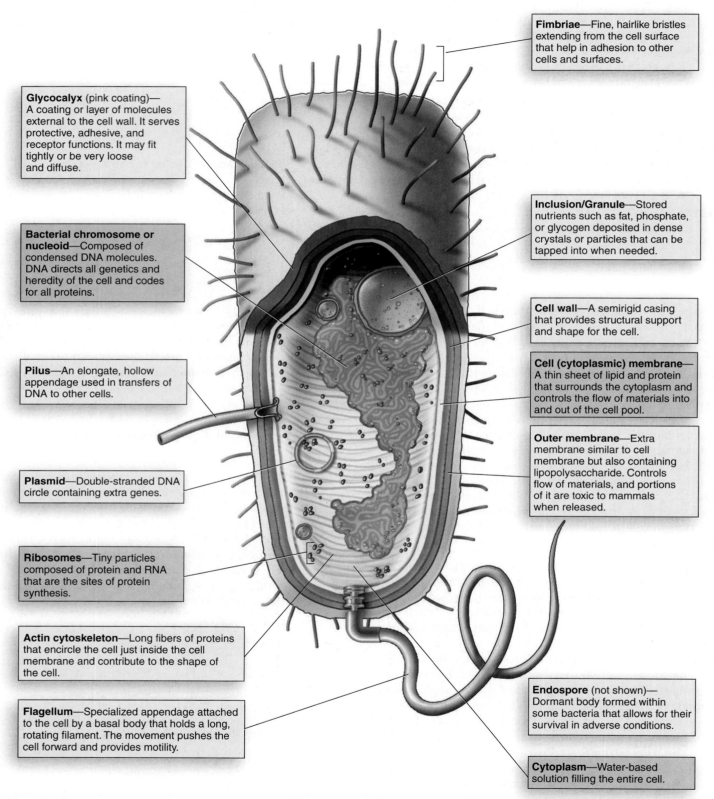

Fimbriae—Fine, hairlike bristles extending from the cell surface that help in adhesion to other cells and surfaces.

Glycocalyx (pink coating)—A coating or layer of molecules external to the cell wall. It serves protective, adhesive, and receptor functions. It may fit tightly or be very loose and diffuse.

Bacterial chromosome or nucleoid—Composed of condensed DNA molecules. DNA directs all genetics and heredity of the cell and codes for all proteins.

Pilus—An elongate, hollow appendage used in transfers of DNA to other cells.

Plasmid—Double-stranded DNA circle containing extra genes.

Ribosomes—Tiny particles composed of protein and RNA that are the sites of protein synthesis.

Actin cytoskeleton—Long fibers of proteins that encircle the cell just inside the cell membrane and contribute to the shape of the cell.

Flagellum—Specialized appendage attached to the cell by a basal body that holds a long, rotating filament. The movement pushes the cell forward and provides motility.

Inclusion/Granule—Stored nutrients such as fat, phosphate, or glycogen deposited in dense crystals or particles that can be tapped into when needed.

Cell wall—A semirigid casing that provides structural support and shape for the cell.

Cell (cytoplasmic) membrane—A thin sheet of lipid and protein that surrounds the cytoplasm and controls the flow of materials into and out of the cell pool.

Outer membrane—Extra membrane similar to cell membrane but also containing lipopolysaccharide. Controls flow of materials, and portions of it are toxic to mammals when released.

Endospore (not shown)—Dormant body formed within some bacteria that allows for their survival in adverse conditions.

Cytoplasm—Water-based solution filling the entire cell.

Figure 4.1 Structure of a bacterial cell. Cutaway view of a typical rod-shaped bacterium, showing major structural features. Note that not all components are found in all cells; dark-blue boxes indicate structures that all bacteria possess.

All bacterial cells invariably have a cell membrane, cytoplasm, ribosomes, and one (or a few) chromosome(s); the majority have a cell wall, a cytoskeleton, and some form of surface coating or glycocalyx. Specific structures that are found in some but not all prokaryotes are flagella, pili, fimbriae, inclusions, endospores, and intracellular membranes.

The Structure of a Generalized Bacterial Cell

Bacterial cells appear featureless and two-dimensional when viewed with an ordinary microscope. Not until they are subjected to the scrutiny of the electron microscope and biochemical studies does their intricate and functionally complex nature become evident. Note that in this chapter, the descriptions of prokaryotic structure, except where otherwise noted, refer to the **bacteria.** Later in the chapter we will describe the ways in which archaea differ from bacteria. Otherwise, we will be focusing on bacteria. **Figure 4.1** presents a three-dimensional anatomical view of a generalized, rod-shaped, bacterial cell. As we survey the principal anatomical features of this cell, we will perform a microscopic dissection of sorts, following a course that begins with the outer cell structures and proceeds to the internal contents.

4.1 Learning Outcomes—Can You ...

1. ... name the structures all bacteria possess?
2. ... name at least four structures that some, but not all, bacteria possess?

4.2 External Structures

Appendages: Cell Extensions

Several discrete types of accessory structures sprout from the surface of bacteria. These long **appendages** are common but are not present on all species. Appendages can be divided into two major groups: those that provide motility (flagella and axial filaments) and those that provide attachment points or channels (fimbriae and pili).

Flagella—Prokaryotic Propellers

The prokaryotic **flagellum** (flah-jel'-em), an appendage of truly amazing construction, is certainly unique in the biological world. The primary function of flagella is to confer **motility,** or self-propulsion—that is, the capacity of a cell to swim freely through an aqueous habitat. The extreme thinness of a bacterial flagellum necessitates high magnification to reveal its special architecture, which has three distinct parts: the filament, the hook (sheath), and the basal body **(figure 4.2).** The **filament,** a helical structure composed of proteins, is approximately 20 nanometers in diameter and varies from 1 to 70 microns in length. It is inserted into a curved, tubular hook. The hook is anchored to the cell by the basal body, a stack of rings firmly anchored

(a)

(b)

Figure 4.2 Details of the basal body of a flagellum in a gram-negative cell. **(a)** The hook, rings, and rod function together as a tiny device that rotates the filament 360°. **(b)** An electron micrograph of the basal body of a bacterial flagellum.

through the cell wall, to the cell membrane and the outer membrane. This arrangement permits the hook with its filament to rotate 360°, rather than undulating back and forth like a whip as was once thought.

One can generalize that all spirilla, about half of the bacilli, and a small number of cocci are flagellated (these bacterial shapes are shown in figure 4.23). Flagella vary both in number and arrangement according to two general patterns:

1. In a *polar* arrangement, the flagella are attached at one or both ends of the cell. Three subtypes of this pattern are: **monotrichous** (mah"-noh-trik'-us), with a single flagellum; **lophotrichous** (lo"-foh-), with small bunches or tufts of flagella emerging from the same site; and **amphitrichous** (am"-fee-), with flagella at both poles of the cell.
2. In a **peritrichous** (per"-ee-) arrangement, flagella are dispersed randomly over the surface of the cell **(figure 4.3)**.

The presence of motility is one piece of information used in the laboratory identification or diagnosis of pathogens. Flagella are hard to visualize in the laboratory, but often it is sufficient to know simply whether a bacterial species is motile. One way to detect motility is to stab a tiny mass of cells into a soft (semisolid) medium in a test tube. Growth spreading rapidly through the entire medium is indicative of motility. Alternatively, cells can be observed microscopically with a hanging drop slide. A truly motile cell will flit, dart, or wobble around the field, making some progress, whereas one that is nonmotile jiggles about in one place but makes no progress.

Fine Points of Flagellar Function Flagellated bacteria can perform some rather sophisticated feats. They can detect and move in response to chemical signals—a type of behavior called **chemotaxis** (ke"-moh-tak'-sis). Positive chemotaxis is movement of a cell in the direction of a favorable chemical stimulus (usually a nutrient); negative chemotaxis is movement away from a repellent (potentially harmful) compound.

The flagellum is effective in guiding bacteria through the environment primarily because the system for detecting chemicals is linked to the mechanisms that drive the flagellum. Located in the cell membrane are clusters of receptors[1] that bind specific molecules coming from the immediate environment. The attachment of sufficient numbers of these molecules transmits signals to the flagellum and sets it into rotary motion. The actual "fuel" for the flagellum to turn is a gradient of protons (hydrogen ions) that are generated by the metabolism of the bacterium and that bind to and detach from parts of the flagellar motor within the cell membrane, causing the filament to rotate. If several flagella are present, they become aligned and rotate as a group **(figure 4.4).** As a flagellum rotates counterclockwise, the cell itself swims in a smooth linear direction toward the stimulus; this action is called a **run**. Runs are interrupted at various intervals by **tumbles**, during which the flagellum

1. Cell surface molecules that bind specifically with other molecules.

(a)

(b)

(c)

(d)

Figure 4.3 Electron micrographs depicting types of flagellar arrangements. **(a)** Monotrichous flagellum on the bacterium *Bdellovibrio*. **(b)** Lophotrichous flagella on *Vibrio fischeri*, a common marine bacterium (23,000×). **(c)** Unusual flagella on *Aquaspirillum* are amphitrichous (and lophotrichous) in arrangement and coil up into tight loops. **(d)** An unidentified bacterium discovered inside *Paramecium* cells exhibits peritrichous flagella.
Source: (b) From Reichelt and Baumann, *Arch. Microbiol.* 94:283–330. © Springer-Verlag, 1973.

reverses direction and causes the cell to stop and change its course. It is believed that attractant molecules inhibit tumbles and permit progress toward the stimulus. Repellents cause numerous tumbles, allowing the bacterium to redirect itself away from the stimulus **(figure 4.5).** Some photosynthetic bacteria exhibit **phototaxis**, movement in response to light rather than chemicals.

Periplasmic Flagella

Corkscrew-shaped bacteria called **spirochetes** (spy'-roh-keets) show an unusual, wriggly mode of locomotion caused by two or more long, coiled threads, the periplasmic flagella or **axial filaments**. A periplasmic flagellum is a type of internal flagellum that is enclosed in the space between the cell wall and the cell membrane **(figure 4.6).** The filaments curl closely around the spirochete coils yet are free to contract and impart a twisting or flexing motion to the cell. This form of locomotion must be seen in live cells such as the spirochete of syphilis to be truly appreciated.

Appendages for Attachment and Mating

The structures termed **pilus** (pil-us) and **fimbria** (fim'-bree-ah) are both bacterial surface appendages that provide some type of adhesion, but not locomotion.

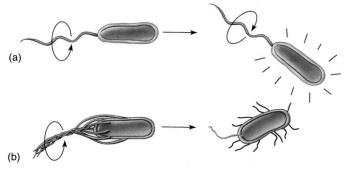

(a)

(b)

Figure 4.4 The operation of flagella and the mode of locomotion in bacteria with polar and peritrichous flagella. **(a)** In general, when a polar flagellum rotates in a counterclockwise direction, the cell swims forward. When the flagellum reverses direction and rotates clockwise, the cell stops and tumbles. **(b)** In peritrichous forms, all flagella sweep toward one end of the cell and rotate as a single group. During tumbles, the flagella lose coordination.

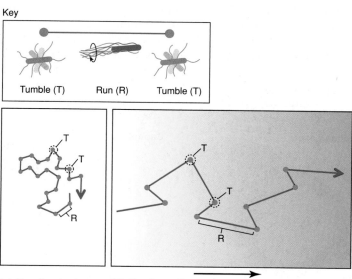

Key

Tumble (T)   Run (R)   Tumble (T)

(a) No attractant or repellent   **(b)** Gradient of attractant concentration

Figure 4.5 Chemotaxis in bacteria. **(a)** A bacterium moves via a random series of short runs and tumbles when there is no attractant or repellent. **(b)** The cell spends more time on runs as it gets closer to the attractant.

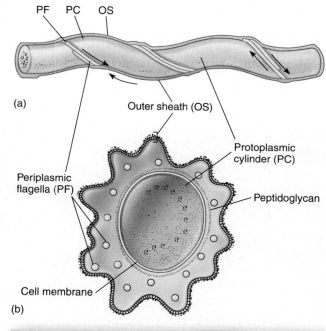

PF   PC   OS

(a)   Outer sheath (OS)

Periplasmic flagella (PF)   Protoplasmic cylinder (PC)

Peptidoglycan

Cell membrane

(b)

(c)

Figure 4.6 The orientation of periplasmic flagella on the spirochete cell. **(a)** Longitudinal section. **(b)** Cross section (end-on view). Contraction of the filaments imparts a spinning and undulating pattern of locomotion. **(c)** Electron micrograph captures the details of periplasmic flagella and their insertion points (arrows) in *Borrelia burgdorferi*, the cause of Lyme disease. One flagellum has escaped the outer sheath, probably during preparation for EM. (Bar = 0.2 microns)

Fimbriae are small, bristlelike fibers sprouting off the surface of many bacterial cells **(figure 4.7).** Their exact composition varies, but most of them contain protein. Fimbriae have an inherent tendency to stick to each other and to surfaces. They may be responsible for the mutual clinging of cells that leads to biofilms and other thick aggregates of cells on the surface of liquids and for the microbial colonization of inanimate solids such as rocks and glass **(Insight 4.1).** Some pathogens can colonize and infect host tissues because of a tight adhesion between their fimbriae and epithelial cells **(figure 4.7b).** For example, the gonococcus (agent of gonorrhea) colonizes the genitourinary tract, and *Escherichia coli* colonizes the intestine by this means. Mutant forms of these pathogens that lack fimbriae are unable to cause infections.

A pilus (also called a "**sex**" **pilus**) is an elongate, rigid tubular structure made of a special protein, **pilin.** So far, true pili have been found only on gram-negative bacteria, where they are utilized in a "mating" process between cells called **conjugation,**[2] which involves partial transfer of DNA from

---

2. Although the term *mating* is sometimes used for this process, it is not a form of sexual reproduction.

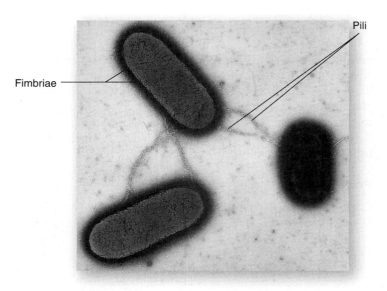

Figure 4.8 Three bacteria in the process of conjugating. Clearly evident are the sex pili forming mutual conjugation bridges between a donor (upper cell) and two recipients (two lower cells). (Fimbriae can also be seen on the donor cell.)

one cell to another **(figure 4.8).** A pilus from the donor cell unites with a recipient cell thereby providing a cytoplasmic connection for making the transfer. Production of pili is controlled genetically, and conjugation takes place only between compatible gram-negative cells. Conjugation in gram-positive bacteria does occur but involves aggregation proteins rather than "sex" pili. The roles of pili and conjugation are further explored in chapter 9.

The Bacterial Surface Coating, or Glycocalyx

The bacterial cell surface is frequently exposed to severe environmental conditions. The **glycocalyx** develops as a coating of repeating polysaccharide units, protein, or both. This protects the cell and, in some cases, helps it adhere to its environment. Glycocalyces differ among bacteria in thickness, organization, and chemical composition. Some bacteria are covered with a loose shield called a **slime layer** that evidently protects them from loss of water and nutrients **(figure 4.9a).** A glycocalyx is called a **capsule** when it is bound more tightly to the cell than

(a)

(b)

E. coli cells

Intestinal microvilli

Figure 4.7 Form and function of bacterial fimbriae. **(a)** Several cells of pathogenic *Escherichia coli* covered with numerous stiff fibers called fimbriae (30,000×). Note also the dark-blue granules, which are the chromosomes. **(b)** A row of *E. coli* cells tightly adheres by their fimbriae to the surface of intestinal cells (12,000×). This is how the bacterium clings to the body during an infection. (G = glycocalyx)

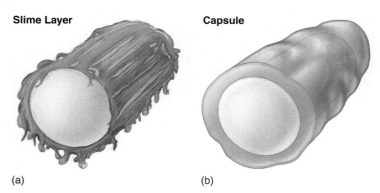

Slime Layer   Capsule

(a)   (b)

Figure 4.9 Drawing of sectioned bacterial cells to show the types of glycocalyces.   **(a)** The slime layer is a loose structure that is easily washed off. **(b)** The capsule is a thick, structured layer that is not readily removed.

INSIGHT 4.1   Biofilms—The Glue of Life

Being aware of the widespread existence of microorganisms on earth, we should not be surprised that, when left undisturbed, they gather in masses, cling to various surfaces, and capture available moisture and nutrients. The formation of these living layers, called **biofilms,** is actually a universal phenomenon that all of us have observed. Consider the scum that builds up in toilet bowls and shower stalls in a short time if they are not cleaned; or the algae that collect on the walls of swimming pools; and, more intimately, the constant deposition of plaque on teeth. Microbes making biofilms is a primeval tendency that has been occurring for billions of years as a way to create stable habitats with adequate access to food, water, atmosphere, and other essential factors. Biofilms are often cooperative associations among several microbial groups (bacteria—and archaea—fungi, algae, and protozoa) as well as plants and animals.

Substrates are most likely to accept a biofilm if they are moist and have developed a thin layer of organic material such as polysaccharides or glycoproteins on their exposed surface

First colonists

Organic surface coating

Surface

Cells stick to coating.

Glycocalyx

As cells divide, they form a dense mat bound together by sticky extracellular deposits.

Additional microbes are attracted to developing film and create a mature community with complex function.

3h

8h

11h

(see figure below). This depositing process occurs within a few minutes to hours, making a slightly sticky texture that attracts primary colonists, usually bacteria. These early cells attach and begin to multiply on the surface. As they grow, various substances (receptors, fimbriae, slime layers, capsules, and even DNA molecules) increase the binding of cells to the surface and thicken the biofilm. The extracellular matrix (the green material in our drawing is clearly visible. As the biofilm evolves, it undergoes specific adaptations to the habitat in which it forms. In many cases, the earliest colonists contribute nutrients and create microhabitats that serve as a matrix for other microbes to attach and grow into the film, forming complex communities. The biofilm varies in thickness and complexity, depending upon where it occurs and how long it keeps developing. Complexity ranges from single cell layers to thick microbial mats with dozens of dynamic interactive layers.

Biofilms are a profoundly important force in the development of terrestrial and aquatic environments. They dwell permanently in bedrock and the earth's sediments, where they play an essential role in recycling elements, leaching minerals, and forming soil. Biofilms associated with plant roots promote the mutual exchange of nutrients between the microbes and roots. Invasive biofilms can wreak havoc with human-made structures such as cooling towers, storage tanks, air conditioners, and even stone buildings.

Biofilms also have serious medical implications. Biofilms accumulate most easily on damaged tissues (such as rheumatic heart valves), hard tissues (teeth), and foreign materials (catheters, intrauterine devices [IUDs], artificial hip joints). But they also seem to grow on otherwise healthy tissues under certain conditions. Persistent ear infections and lung infections in patients with cystic fibrosis are due to biofilms. Microbes in a biofilm are extremely difficult to eradicate with antimicrobials. Previously it was assumed that the drugs had difficulty penetrating the viscous biofilm matrix. Now scientists have discovered that bacteria in biofilms turn on different genes when they are in a biofilm than when they are "free-floating." This altered gene expression gives the bacteria a different set of characteristics, often making them impervious to antibiotics. It is estimated that treating biofilm-related infections costs more than 1 billion dollars in the United States alone.

a slime layer is and it is denser and thicker **(figure 4.9b)**. Capsules can be viewed after a special staining technique **(figure 4.10a)**. They are also often visible due to a prominently sticky (mucoid) character to colonies on agar **(figure 4.10b)**.

Specialized Functions of the Glycocalyx Capsules are formed by many pathogenic bacteria, such as *Streptococcus pneumoniae* (a cause of pneumonia, an infection of the lung), *Haemophilus influenzae* (one cause of meningitis), and *Bacillus anthracis* (the cause of anthrax). Encapsulated bacterial cells generally have greater pathogenicity because capsules protect the bacteria against white blood cells called phagocytes. Phagocytes are a natural body defense that can engulf and destroy foreign cells through phagocytosis, thus preventing infection. A capsular coating blocks the mechanisms that phagocytes use to attach to and engulf bacteria. By escaping phagocytosis, the bacteria are free to multiply and infect body tissues. Encapsulated bacteria that mutate to nonencapsulated forms usually lose their ability to cause disease.

Other types of glycocalyces can be important in formation of biofilms. The thick, white plaque that forms on teeth

comes in part from the surface slimes produced by certain streptococci in the oral cavity. This slime protects them from being dislodged from the teeth and provides a niche for other oral bacteria that, in time, can lead to dental disease. The glycocalyx of some bacteria is so highly adherent that it is responsible for persistent colonization of nonliving materials such as plastic catheters, intrauterine devices, and metal pacemakers that are in common medical use **(figure 4.11)**.

Capsule

Cell body

(a)

(b)

Figure 4.10 Encapsulated bacteria.   **(a)** Negative staining reveals the microscopic appearance of a large, well-developed capsule. **(b)** Colony appearance of a nonencapsulated (left) and encapsulated (right) version of a soil bacterium called *Sinorhizobium*.

Glycocalyx slime

Catheter surface

Cell cluster

Figure 4.11 Biofilm.   Scanning electron micrograph of *Staphylococcus aureus* cells attached to a catheter by a slime secretion.

4.2 Learning Outcomes—Can You ...

3. ... describe the structure and function of four different types of bacterial appendages?

4. ... explain how a flagellum works in the presence of an attractant?

4.3 The Cell Envelope: The Boundary Layer of Bacteria

$$
\text{Cell envelope} - \begin{cases} \text{(Outer membrane)} \\ \text{Cell wall} \\ \text{Cell membrane} \end{cases}
$$

The majority of bacteria have a chemically complex external covering, termed the cell envelope, that lies outside of the cytoplasm. It is composed of two or three basic layers: the cell wall, the cell membrane, and in some bacteria, the outer membrane. The layers of the envelope are stacked one upon another and are often tightly bonded together like the outer husk and casings of a coconut. Although each envelope layer performs a distinct function, together they act as a single protective unit.

Differences in Cell Envelope Structure

More than a hundred years ago, long before the detailed anatomy of bacteria was even remotely known, a Danish physician named Hans Christian Gram developed a staining technique, the **Gram stain,** that delineates two generally different groups of bacteria **(Insight 4.2).** The two major groups shown by this technique are the **gram-positive** bacteria and the **gram-negative** bacteria.

The structural difference denoted by the designations gram-positive and gram-negative lie in the cell envelope **(figure 4.12).** In gram-positive cells, a microscopic section resembles an open-faced sandwich with two layers: the thick cell wall, composed primarily of peptidoglycan (defined in the next section), and the cytoplasmic membrane. A similar section of a gram-negative cell envelope shows a complete sandwich with three layers: an outer membrane, a thin cell wall, and the cytoplasmic membrane.

Moving from outside to in, the outer membrane (if present) lies just under the glycocalyx. Next comes the cell wall. Finally, the innermost layer is always the cytoplasmic membrane. Because only some bacteria have an outer membrane, we discuss the cell wall first.

Structure of the Cell Wall

The **cell wall** accounts for a number of important bacterial characteristics. In general, it helps determine the shape of a bacterium, and it also provides the kind of strong structural support necessary to keep a bacterium from bursting or collapsing because of changes in osmotic pressure. In this way, the cell wall functions like a bicycle tire that maintains the necessary shape and prevents the more delicate inner tube (the cytoplasmic membrane) from bursting when it is expanded.

The cell walls of most bacteria gain their relatively rigid quality from a unique macromolecule called **peptidoglycan (PG).** This compound is composed of a repeating framework of long **glycan (sugar)** chains cross-linked by short peptide (protein) fragments to provide a strong but flexible

Peptidoglycan

Cell membrane

Gram (+)

Cell membrane
Peptidoglycan

(a)

Cell membrane

Peptidoglycan

Outer membrane

Gram (−)

Cell membrane
Periplasmic space
Peptidoglycan
Outer membrane

(b)

Figure 4.12 A comparison of the envelopes of gram-positive and gram-negative cells. **(a)** A photomicrograph of a gram-positive cell wall/membrane and an artist's interpretation of its open-faced-sandwich-style layering with two layers. **(b)** A photomicrograph of a gram-negative cell wall/membrane and an artist's interpretation of its complete-sandwich-style layering with three distinct layers.

INSIGHT 4.2   The Gram Stain: A Grand Stain

In 1884, Hans Christian Gram discovered a staining technique that could be used to make bacteria in infectious specimens more visible. His technique consisted of timed, sequential applications of crystal violet (the primary dye), Gram's iodine (the mordant), an alcohol rinse (decolorizer), and a contrasting counterstain. The initial counterstain used was yellow or brown and was later replaced by the red dye safranin. Bacteria that stain purple are called gram-positive, and those that stain red are called gram-negative.

Although these staining reactions involve an attraction of the cell to a charged dye (see chapter 3), it is important to note that the terms **gram-positive** and **gram-negative** are not used to indicate the electrical charge of cells or dyes but whether or not a cell retains the primary dye-iodine complex after decolorization. There is nothing specific in the reaction of gram-positive cells to the primary dye or in the reaction of gram-negative cells to the counterstain. The different results in the Gram stain are due to differences in the structure of the cell wall and how it reacts to the series of reagents applied to the cells.

In the first step, crystal violet is added to the cells in a smear. It stains them all the same purple color. The second and key differentiating step is the addition of the mordant—Gram's iodine. The mordant is a stabilizer that causes the dye to form large complexes in the peptidoglycan meshwork of the cell wall. Because the peptidoglycan layer in gram-positive cells is thicker, the entrapment of the dye is far more extensive in them than in gram-negative cells. Application of alcohol in the third step dissolves lipids in the outer membrane and removes the dye from the peptidoglycan layer and the gram-negative cells. By contrast, the crystals of dye tightly embedded in the peptidoglycan of gram-positive bacteria are relatively inaccessible and resistant to removal. Because

gram-negative bacteria are colorless after decolorization, their presence is demonstrated by applying the counterstain safranin in the final step.

This century-old staining method remains the universal basis for bacterial classification and identification. It permits differentiation of four major categories based upon color reaction and shape: gram-positive rods, gram-positive cocci, gram-negative rods, and gram-negative cocci (see table 4.1). The Gram stain can also be a practical aid in diagnosing infection and in guiding drug treatment. For example, Gram staining a fresh urine or throat specimen can help pinpoint the possible cause of infection, and in some cases it is possible to begin drug therapy on the basis of this stain. Even in this day of elaborate and expensive medical technology, the Gram stain remains an important and unbeatable first tool in diagnosis.

Step	Microscopic Appearance of Cell		Chemical Reaction in Cell Wall (very magnified view)	
	Gram (+)	Gram (−)	Gram (+)	Gram (−)
1. Crystal violet			Both cell walls affix the dye	
2. Gram's iodine			Dye complex trapped in wall	No effect of iodine
3. Alcohol			Crystals remain in cell wall	Outer membrane weakened; wall loses dye
4. Safranin (red dye)			Red dye masked by violet	Red dye stains the colorless cell

support framework **(figure 4.13).** The amount and exact composition of peptidoglycan vary among the major bacterial groups.

Because many bacteria live in aqueous habitats with a low concentration of dissolved substances, they are constantly absorbing excess water by osmosis. Were it not for the strength and relative rigidity of the peptidoglycan in the cell wall, they would rupture from internal pressure. This function of the cell wall has been a tremendous boon to the drug industry. Several types of drugs used to treat

infection (penicillin, cephalosporins) are effective because they target the peptide cross-links in the peptidoglycan, thereby disrupting its integrity. With their cell walls incomplete or missing, such cells have very little protection from **lysis** (ly'-sis), which is the disintegration or rupture of the cell. Lysozyme, an enzyme contained in tears and saliva, provides a natural defense against certain bacteria by hydrolyzing the bonds in the glycan chains and causing the wall to break down. (Chapter 11 discusses the actions of antimicrobial chemical agents.)

(a) The peptidoglycan can be seen as a crisscross network pattern similar to a chainlink fence.

(b) An idealized view of the molecular pattern of peptidoglycan. It contains alternating glycans (G and M) bound together in long strands. The G stands for *N*-acetyl glucosamine, and the M stands for *N*-acetyl muramic acid. A muramic acid molecule binds to an adjoining muramic acid on a parallel chain by means of a cross-linkage of peptides.

Glycan chains

Peptide cross-links

(c) A detailed view of the links between the muramic acids. Tetrapeptide chains branching off the muramic acids connect by interbridges also composed of amino acids. The types of amino acids in the interbridge can vary and it may be lacking entirely (gram-negative cells). It is this linkage that provides rigid yet flexible support to the cell and that may be targeted by drugs like penicillin.

Tetrapeptide

L–alanine
D–glutamate
L–lysine —— glycine
D–alanine

L–alanine
D–glutamate
L–lysine
D–alanine

glycine
glycine
glycine
glycine

Interbridge

Figure 4.13 Structure of peptidoglycan in the cell wall.

The Gram-Positive Cell Wall

The bulk of the gram-positive cell wall is a thick, homogeneous sheath of peptidoglycan ranging from 20 to 80 nm in thickness. It also contains tightly bound acidic polysaccharides, including **teichoic acid** and **lipoteichoic acid (figure 4.14).** Teichoic acid is a polymer of ribitol or glycerol (alcohols) and phosphate that is embedded in the peptidoglycan sheath. Lipoteichoic acid is similar in structure but is attached to the lipids in the plasma membrane. These molecules appear to function in cell wall maintenance and enlargement during

Gram-Positive   **Gram-Negative**

Figure 4.14 A comparison of the detailed structure of gram-positive and gram-negative cell envelopes.

cell division, and they also contribute to the acidic charge on the cell surface.

The Gram-Negative Cell Wall

The gram-negative wall is a single, thin (1–3 nm) sheet of peptidoglycan. Although it acts as a somewhat rigid protective structure as previously described, its thinness gives gram-negative bacteria a relatively greater flexibility and sensitivity to lysis.

Nontypical Cell Walls

Several bacterial groups lack the cell wall structure of gram-positive or gram-negative bacteria, and some bacteria have no cell wall at all. Although these exceptional forms can stain positive or negative in the Gram stain, examination of their fine structure and chemistry shows that they do not really fit the descriptions for typical gram-negative or -positive cells. For example, the cells of *Mycobacterium* and *Nocardia* contain peptidoglycan and stain gram-positive, but the bulk of their cell wall is composed of unique types of lipids. One of these is a very-long-chain fatty acid called **mycolic acid**, or cord factor, that contributes to the pathogenicity of this group (see chapter 21). The thick, waxy nature imparted to the cell wall by these lipids is also responsible for a high degree of resistance to certain chemicals and dyes. Such resistance is the basis for the

acid-fast stain used to diagnose tuberculosis and leprosy. In this stain, hot carbol fuchsin dye becomes tenaciously attached (is held fast) to these cells so that an acid-alcohol solution will not remove the dye (see chapter 3).

Because they are from a more ancient and primitive line of prokaryotes, the archaea exhibit unusual and chemically distinct cell walls. In some, the walls are composed almost entirely of polysaccharides, and in others, the walls are pure protein; but as a group, they all lack the true peptidoglycan structure described previously. Because a few archaea and all mycoplasmas (next section) lack a cell wall entirely, their cell membrane must serve the dual functions of support and transport.

Mycoplasmas and Other Cell-Wall-Deficient Bacteria

Mycoplasmas are bacteria that naturally lack a cell wall. Although other bacteria require an intact cell wall to prevent the bursting of the cell, the mycoplasma cell membrane is stabilized by sterols and is resistant to lysis. These extremely tiny, **pleomorphic** cells are very small bacteria, ranging from 0.1 to 0.5 μm in size. They range in shape from filamentous to coccus or doughnut-shaped. They are *not* obligate parasites and can be grown on artificial media, although added sterols are required for the cell membranes of some species. Mycoplasmas are found in many habitats, including plants,

Figure 4.15 Scanning electron micrograph of
***Mycoplasma pneumoniae* (magnified 62,000×).**   Cells like
these that naturally lack a cell wall exhibit extreme variation in shape.

soil, and animals. The most important medical species is
Mycoplasma pneumoniae **(figure 4.15),** which adheres to the
epithelial cells in the lung and causes an atypical form of
pneumonia in humans (described in chapter 21).

Some bacteria that ordinarily have a cell wall can lose
it during part of their life cycle. These wall-deficient forms
are referred to as **L forms** or L-phase variants (for the Lister
Institute, where they were discovered). L forms arise naturally from a mutation in the wall-forming genes, or they
can be induced artificially by treatment with a chemical
such as lysozyme or penicillin that disrupts the cell wall.
When a gram-positive cell is exposed to either of these two
chemicals, it will lose the cell wall completely and become
a **protoplast,** a fragile cell bounded only by a membrane
that is highly susceptible to lysis **(figure 4.16a).** A gram-
negative cell exposed to these same substances loses its
peptidoglycan but retains at least part of its outer membrane, leaving a less fragile but nevertheless weakened

spheroplast **(figure 4.16b).** Evidence points to a role for L
forms in certain infections.

The Gram-Negative Outer Membrane

The **outer membrane** (OM) is somewhat similar in construction to the cell membrane, except that it contains specialized
types of polysaccharides and proteins. The uppermost layer
of the OM contains **lipopolysaccharide (LPS).** The polysaccharide chains extending off the surface function as antigens
and receptors. The lipid portion of LPS has been referred to
as **endotoxin** because it stimulates fever and shock reactions in gram-negative infections such as meningitis and
typhoid fever. The innermost layer of the OM is a phospholipid layer anchored by means of lipoproteins to the peptidoglycan layer below. The outer membrane serves as a partial
chemical sieve by allowing only relatively small molecules
to penetrate. Access is provided by special membrane channels formed by **porin proteins** that completely span the
outer membrane. The size of these porins can be altered
so as to block the entrance of harmful chemicals, making
them one defense of gram-negative bacteria against certain
antibiotics (see figure 4.14).

Cell Membrane Structure

Appearing just beneath the cell wall is the **cell,** or **cytoplasmic, membrane,** a very thin (5–10 nm), flexible sheet
molded completely around the cytoplasm. Its general composition was described in chapter 2 as a lipid bilayer with
proteins embedded to varying degrees (see Insight 2.3). Bacterial cell membranes have this typical structure, containing
primarily phospholipids (making up about 30%–40% of the
membrane mass) and proteins (contributing 60%–70%).
Major exceptions to this description are the membranes of
mycoplasmas, which contain high amounts of sterols—rigid
lipids that stabilize and reinforce the membrane—and the
membranes of archaea, which contain unique branched
hydrocarbons rather than fatty acids.

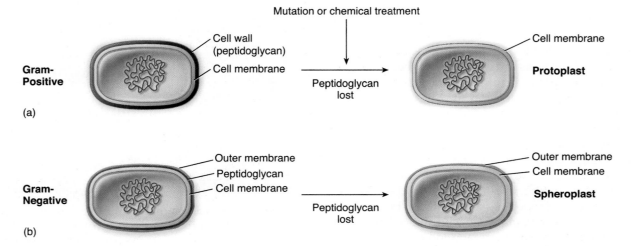

Figure 4.16 The conversion of walled bacterial cells to L forms.   **(a)** Gram-positive bacteria. **(b)** Gram-negative bacteria.

Some environmental bacteria, including photosynthesizers and ammonia oxidizers, contain dense stacks of internal membranes that are studded with enzymes or photosynthetic pigments. The inner membranes allow a higher concentration of these enzymes and pigments and also accomplish a compartmentalization that allows for higher energy production.

Functions of the Cell Membrane

Because prokaryotes have none of the eukaryotic organelles, the cell membrane provides a site for functions such as energy reactions, nutrient processing, and synthesis. A major action of the cell membrane is to regulate **transport,** that is, the passage of nutrients into the cell and the discharge of wastes. Although water and small uncharged molecules can diffuse across the membrane unaided, the membrane is a **selectively permeable** structure with special carrier mechanisms for passage of most molecules (see chapter 7). The glycocalyx and cell wall can bar the passage of large molecules, but they are not the primary transport apparatus. The cell membrane is also involved in **secretion,** or the discharge of a metabolic product into the extracellular environment.

The membranes of prokaryotes are an important site for a number of metabolic activities. Most enzymes of respiration and ATP synthesis reside in the cell membrane since prokaryotes lack mitochondria (see chapter 8). Enzyme structures located in the cell membrane also help synthesize structural macromolecules to be incorporated into the cell envelope and appendages. Other products (enzymes and toxins) are secreted by the membrane into the extracellular environment.

Practical Considerations of Differences in Cell Envelope Structure

Variations in cell envelope anatomy contribute to several other differences between the two cell types. The outer membrane contributes an extra barrier in gram-negative bacteria that makes them impervious to some antimicrobial chemicals such as dyes and disinfectants, so they are generally more difficult to inhibit or kill than are gram-positive bacteria. One exception is alcohol-based compounds, which can dissolve the lipids in the outer membrane and disturb its integrity. Treating infections caused by gram-negative bacteria often requires different drugs from gram-positive infections, especially drugs that can cross the outer membrane.

The cell envelope or its parts can interact with human tissues and contribute to disease. Proteins attached to the outer portion of the cell wall of several gram-positive species, including *Corynebacterium diphtheriae* (the agent of diphtheria) and *Streptococcus pyogenes* (the cause of strep throat), also have toxic properties. The lipids in the cell walls of certain *Mycobacterium* species are harmful to human cells as well. Because most macromolecules in the cell walls are foreign to humans, they stimulate antibody production by the immune system (see chapter 15).

4.3 Learning Outcomes—Can You ...

5. ... differentiate between the two main types of bacterial envelope structure?
6. ... discuss why gram-positive cell walls are stronger than gram-negative cell walls?
7. ... name a substance in the envelope structure of some bacteria that can cause severe symptoms in humans?

4.4 Bacterial Internal Structure

Internal — Cytoplasm
Ribosomes
Inclusions
Nucleoid/chromosome
Actin cytoskeleton
Endospore

Contents of the Cell Cytoplasm

Encased by the cell membrane is a gelatinous solution referred to as **cytoplasm,** which is another prominent site for many of the cell's biochemical and synthetic activities. Its major component is water (70%–80%), which serves as a solvent for the cell pool, a complex mixture of nutrients including sugars, amino acids, and salts. The components of this pool serve as building blocks for cell synthesis or as sources of energy. The cytoplasm also contains larger, discrete cell masses such as the chromatin body, ribosomes, granules, and actin/tubulin strands that act as a cytoskeleton in bacteria that have them.

Bacterial Chromosomes and Plasmids: The Sources of Genetic Information

The hereditary material of most bacteria exists in the form of a single circular strand of DNA designated as the **bacterial chromosome.** Some bacteria have multiple chromosomes. By definition, bacteria do not have a nucleus; that is, their DNA is not enclosed by a nuclear membrane but instead is aggregated in a dense area of the cell called the **nucleoid (figure 4.17).** The chromosome is actually an extremely long molecule of

Figure 4.17 Chromosome structure. Fluorescent staining highlights the chromosomes of the bacterial pathogen *Salmonella enteritidis.* The cytoplasm is orange, and the chromosome fluoresces bright yellow.

double-stranded DNA that is tightly coiled around special basic protein molecules so as to fit inside the cell compartment. Arranged along its length are genetic units (genes) that carry information required for bacterial maintenance and growth.

Although the chromosome is the minimal genetic requirement for bacterial survival, many bacteria contain other, nonessential pieces of DNA called **plasmids** (refer to figure 4.1 for a representation of the nuclear material). These tiny strands exist as separate double-stranded circles of DNA, although at times they can become integrated into the chromosome. During conjugation, they may be duplicated and passed on to related nearby bacteria. During bacterial reproduction, they are duplicated and passed on to offspring. They are not essential to bacterial growth and metabolism, but they often confer protective traits such as resisting drugs and producing toxins and enzymes (see chapter 9). Because they can be readily manipulated in the laboratory and transferred from one bacterial cell to another, plasmids are an important agent in genetic engineering techniques.

Ribosomes: Sites of Protein Synthesis

A prokaryotic cell contains thousands of tiny **ribosomes,** which are made of RNA and protein. When viewed even by very high magnification, ribosomes show up as fine, spherical specks dispersed throughout the cytoplasm that often occur in chains called polysomes. Many are also attached to the cell membrane. Chemically, a ribosome is a combination of a special type of RNA called ribosomal RNA, or rRNA (about 60%), and protein (40%). One method of characterizing ribosomes is by S, or Svedberg,[3] units, which rate the molecular sizes of various cell parts that have been spun down and separated by

---

3. Named in honor of T. Svedberg, the Swedish chemist who developed the ultracentrifuge in 1926.

Ribosome (70S)

Large subunit (50S)

Small subunit (30S)

Figure 4.18 **A model of a prokaryotic ribosome, showing the small (30S) and large (50S) subunits, both separate and joined.**

molecular weight and shape in a centrifuge. Heavier, more compact structures sediment faster and are assigned a higher S rating. Combining this method of analysis with high-resolution electron micrography has revealed that the prokaryotic ribosome, which has an overall rating of 70S, is actually composed of two smaller subunits **(figure 4.18).** They fit together to form a miniature platform upon which protein synthesis is performed. Note: eukaryotic ribosomes are 80S—and this will be very important in future chapters. We examine the more detailed functions of ribosomes in chapter 9.

Inclusions, or Granules: Storage Bodies

Most bacteria are exposed to severe shifts in the availability of food. During periods of nutrient abundance, some can compensate by laying down nutrients intracellularly in **inclusion bodies,** or **inclusions,** of varying size, number, and content. As the environmental source of these nutrients becomes depleted, the bacterial cell can mobilize its own storehouse as required. Some inclusion bodies carry condensed, energy-rich organic substances, such as glycogen and poly β-hydroxybutyrate (PHB), within special single-layered membranes **(figure 4.19).** A unique type of

(a)

MP

(b)

Figure 4.19 **Bacterial inclusion bodies.** **(a)** Large particles (pink) of polyhydroxybutyrate are deposited in a concentrated form that provides an ample long-term supply of that nutrient (32,500×). **(b)** A section through *Aquaspirillum* reveals a chain of tiny iron magnets (magnetosomes = MP). These unusual bacteria use these inclusions to orient themselves within their habitat (123,000×).

inclusion found in some aquatic bacteria is gas vesicles that provide buoyancy and flotation. Other inclusions, also called granules, are crystals of inorganic compounds and are not enclosed by membranes. Sulfur granules of photosynthetic bacteria and polyphosphate granules of *Corynebacterium* and *Mycobacterium*, described later, are of this type. The latter represent an important source of building blocks for nucleic acid and ATP synthesis. They have been termed **metachromatic granules** because they stain a contrasting color (red, purple) in the presence of methylene blue dye.

Perhaps the most unique cell granule is not involved in cell nutrition but rather in cell orientation. Magnetotactic bacteria contain crystalline particles of iron oxide (magnetosomes) that have magnetic properties. The bacteria use these granules to be pulled by the polar and gravitational fields into deeper habitats with a lower oxygen content.

The Cytoskeleton

Until very recently, scientists thought that the shape of all bacteria was completely determined by the peptidoglycan layer (cell wall). Although this is true of many bacteria, particularly the cocci, other bacteria produce long polymers of a protein called **actin and tubulin,** arranged in helical ribbons around the cell just under the cell membrane **(figure 4.20).** These fibers contribute to cell shape, perhaps by influencing the way peptidoglycan is manufactured, and also function in cell division. The fibers have been found in rod-shaped and spiral bacteria.

Figure 4.20 Bacterial cytoskeleton. The actin fibers in these rod-shaped bacteria are fluorescently stained.

A Note on Terminology

The word *spore* can have more than one usage in microbiology. It is a generic term that refers to any tiny compact cells that are produced by vegetative or reproductive structures of microorganisms. Spores can be quite variable in origin, form, and function. The bacterial type discussed here is called an **endospore,** because it is produced inside a cell. With the exception of the endospores of the bacterium *Metabacterium polyspora* mentioned in the text, they function in *survival*, not in reproduction, because no increase in cell numbers is involved in their formation. In contrast, the fungi produce many different types of spores for both survival and reproduction (see chapter 5).

Bacterial Endospores: An Extremely Resistant Stage

Ample evidence indicates that the anatomy of bacteria helps them adjust rather well to adverse habitats. But of all microbial structures, nothing can compare to the bacterial **endospore** (or simply spore) for withstanding hostile conditions and facilitating survival.

Endospores are dormant bodies produced by the bacteria *Bacillus*, *Clostridium*, and *Sporosarcina*. These bacteria have a two-phase life cycle—a vegetative cell and an endospore **(figure 4.21).** The vegetative cell is a metabolically active and growing entity that can be induced by environmental conditions to undergo spore formation, or **sporulation.** Once formed, the spore exists in an inert, resting condition that shows up prominently in a spore or Gram stain **(figure 4.22).** Features of spores, including size, shape, and position in the vegetative cell, are somewhat useful in identifying some species. Both gram-positive and gram-negative bacteria can form endospores, but the medically relevant ones are all gram-positive. Most bacteria form only one endospore and therefore this is not a reproductive function for them. One bacterium called *Metabacterium polyspora*, an inhabitant of the guinea pig intestine, produces as many as nine endospores.

Endospore Formation and Resistance

The depletion of nutrients, especially an adequate carbon or nitrogen source, is the stimulus for a vegetative cell to begin endospore formation. Once this stimulus has been received by the vegetative cell, it undergoes a conversion to become a sporulating cell called a **sporangium.** Complete transformation of a vegetative cell into a sporangium and then into an endospore requires 6 to 8 hours in most spore-forming species. Figure 4.21 illustrates some major physical and chemical events in this process. Bacterial endospores are the hardiest of all life forms, capable of withstanding extremes in heat, drying, freezing, radiation, and chemicals that would readily kill vegetative cells. Their survival under such harsh conditions is due to several factors. The heat resistance of spores has been

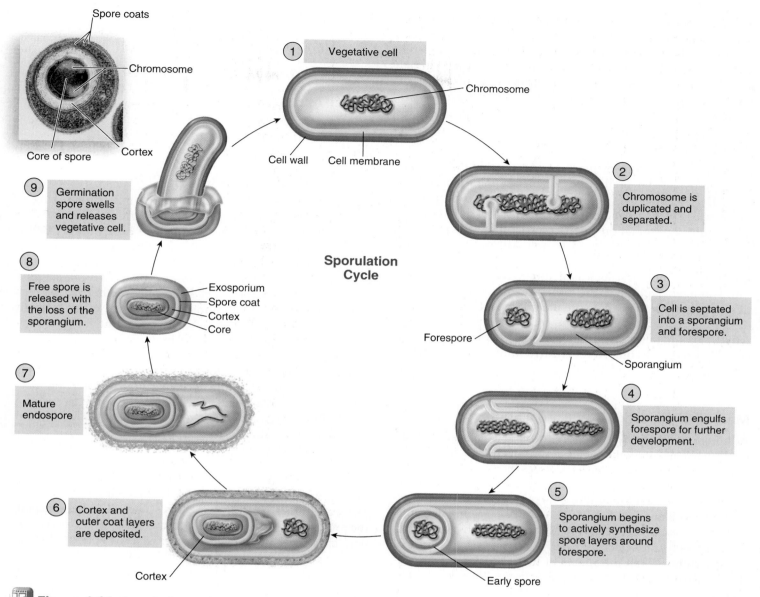

Figure 4.21 **A typical sporulation cycle in *Bacillus* species from the active vegetative cell to release and germination.** This process takes, on average, about 10 hours. Inset is a high-magnification (10,000×) cross section of a single spore showing the dense protective layers that surround the core with its chromosome.

The labels in the sporulation cycle diagram read:

1. Vegetative cell — Chromosome, Cell wall, Cell membrane
2. Chromosome is duplicated and separated.
3. Cell is septated into a sporangium and forespore. — Forespore, Sporangium
4. Sporangium engulfs forespore for further development.
5. Sporangium begins to actively synthesize spore layers around forespore. — Early spore
6. Cortex and outer coat layers are deposited. — Cortex
7. Mature endospore
8. Free spore is released with the loss of the sporangium. — Exosporium, Spore coat, Cortex, Core
9. Germination spore swells and releases vegetative cell.

Sporulation Cycle

Inset labels: Spore coats, Chromosome, Core of spore, Cortex

Figure 4.22 Endospore inside *Bacillus thuringiensis*.

The genus *Bacillus* forms endospores. *B. thuringiensis* additionally forms crystalline bodies (pink) that are used as insecticides.

endospore

linked to their high content of calcium and **dipicolinic acid**, although the exact role of these chemicals is not yet clear. We know, for instance, that heat destroys cells by inactivating proteins and DNA and that this process requires a certain amount of water in the protoplasm. Because the deposition of calcium dipicolinate in the endospore removes water and leaves the endospore very dehydrated, it is less vulnerable to the effects of heat. It is also metabolically inactive and highly resistant to damage from further drying. The thick, impervious cortex and spore coats also protect against radiation and chemicals. The longevity of bacterial spores verges on immortality. One record describes the isolation of viable endospores from a fossilized bee that was 25 million years old. More recently, microbiologists unearthed a viable endospore from a 250-million-year-old salt crystal. Initial analysis of this ancient microbe indicates it is a species of *Bacillus* that is genetically different from known species.

The Germination of Endospores

After lying in a state of inactivity for an indefinite time, endospores can be revitalized when favorable conditions arise. The breaking of dormancy, or germination, happens in the presence of water and a specific chemical or environmental stimulus (germination agent). Once initiated, it proceeds to completion quite rapidly ($1\frac{1}{2}$ hours). Although the specific germination agent varies among species, it is generally a small organic molecule such as an amino acid or an inorganic salt. This agent stimulates the formation of hydrolytic (digestive) enzymes by the endospore membranes. These enzymes digest the cortex and expose the core to water. As the core rehydrates and takes up nutrients, it begins to grow out of the endospore coats. In time, it reverts to a fully active vegetative cell, resuming the vegetative cycle.

Medical Significance of Bacterial Spores

Although the majority of spore-forming bacteria are relatively harmless, several bacterial pathogens are sporeformers. In fact, some aspects of the diseases they cause are related to the persistence and resistance of their spores. *Bacillus anthracis* is the agent of anthrax; its persistence in endospore form makes it an ideal candidate for bioterrorism. The genus *Clostridium* includes even more pathogens, such as *C. tetani,* the cause of tetanus (lockjaw), and *C. perfringens,* the cause of gas gangrene. When the spores of these species are embedded in a wound that contains dead tissue, they can germinate, grow, and release potent toxins. Another toxin-forming species, *C. botulinum,* is the agent of botulism, a deadly form of food poisoning. (Each of these disease conditions is discussed in the infectious disease chapters, according to the organ systems it affects.)

Because they inhabit the soil and dust, endospores are constant intruders where sterility and cleanliness are important. They resist ordinary cleaning methods that use boiling water, soaps, and disinfectants, and they frequently contaminate cultures and media. Hospitals and clinics must take precautions to guard against the potential harmful effects of endospores in wounds. Endospore destruction is a particular concern of the food-canning industry. Several endospore-forming species cause food spoilage or poisoning. Ordinary boiling (100°C) will usually not destroy such spores, so canning is carried out in pressurized steam at 120°C for 20 to 30 minutes. Such rigorous conditions ensure that the food is sterile and free from viable bacteria.

4.4 Learning Outcomes—Can You ...

8. ... identify five things that might be contained in bacterial cytoplasm?
9. ... detail the causes and mechanisms of sporogenesis and germination?

4.5 Prokaryotic Shapes, Arrangements, and Sizes

For the most part, prokaryotes function as independent single-celled, or unicellular, organisms. Each individual prokaryotic cell is fully capable of carrying out all necessary life activities, such as reproduction, metabolism, and nutrient processing, unlike the more specialized cells of a multicellular organism. It should be noted that sometimes prokaryotes *can* act as a group. When bacteria are close to one another in colonies or in biofilms, they communicate with each other through chemicals that cause them to behave differently than if they were living singly. More surprisingly, many bacteria seem to communicate with each other using structures called nanowires, which are appendages that can be many microns long that attach bacterium to bacterium, transferring electrons or other substances. This is not the same as being a multicellular organism but it represents new findings about microbial cooperation.

Prokaryotes exhibit considerable variety in shape, size, and colonial arrangement. See **Insight 4.3** for a discussion on size. It is convenient to describe most prokaryotes by one of three general shapes as dictated by the configuration of the cell wall **(figure 4.23)**. If the cell is spherical or ball-shaped, the prokaryote is described as a **coccus** (kok'-us). Cocci can be perfect spheres, but they also can exist as oval, bean-shaped, or even pointed variants. A cell that is cylindrical (longer than wide) is termed a rod, or **bacillus** (bah-sil'-lus). There is also a genus named *Bacillus*. As might be expected, rods are also quite varied in their actual form. Depending on the species, they can be blocky, spindle-shaped, round-ended, long and threadlike (filamentous), or even club-shaped or drumstick-shaped. When a rod is short and plump, it is called a **coccobacillus;** if it is gently curved, it is a **vibrio** (vib'-ree-oh). A bacterium having a slightly curled or spiral-shaped cylinder is called a **spirillum** (spy-ril'-em), a rigid helix, twisted twice or more along its axis (like a corkscrew). Another spiral cell mentioned earlier in conjunction with periplasmic flagella is the **spirochete,** a more flexible form that resembles a spring. Because prokaryotic cells look two-dimensional and flat with traditional staining and microscope techniques, they are seen to best advantage with a scanning electron microscope, which emphasizes their striking three-dimensional forms **(figure 4.23)**.

It is common for cells of a single species to vary to some extent in shape and size. This phenomenon, called

INSIGHT 4.3	Redefining Prokaryotic Size

Most microbiologists believe we are still far from having a complete assessment of the prokaryotic world, mostly because the world is so large and prokaryotes are so small. This fact becomes evident in the periodic discoveries of exceptional bacteria that are reported in newspaper headlines. Among the most remarkable are giant and dwarf bacteria.

Big Bacteria Break Records

In 1985, biologists discovered a new bacterium living in the intestine of surgeonfish that at the time was a candidate for the *Guinness Book of World Records.* The large cells, named *Epulopiscium fishelsoni* ("guest at a banquet of fish"), measure around 100 μm in length, although some specimens were as large as 300 μm. This record was recently broken when marine microbiologist Heide Schultz discovered an even larger species of bacteria living in ocean sediments near the African country of Namibia. These gigantic cocci are arranged in strands that look like pearls and contain hundreds of golden sulfur granules, inspiring their name, *Thiomargarita namibia* ("sulfur pearl of Namibia") (see photo). The size of the individual cells ranges from 100 up to 750 μm ($\frac{3}{4}$ mm), and many are large enough to see with the naked eye. By way of comparison, if the average bacterium were the size of a mouse, *Thiomargarita* would be as large as a blue whale!

Closer study revealed that they are indeed prokaryotic and have bacterial ribosomes and DNA, but that they also have some unusual adaptations to their life cycle. They live an attached existence embedded in sulfide sediments (H_2S) that are free of gaseous oxygen. They obtain energy through oxidizing these sulfides using dissolved nitrates (NO_3). Because the quantities of these substances can vary with the seasons, they must be stored in cellular depots. The sulfides are carried as granules in the cytoplasm, and the nitrates occupy a giant, liquid-filled vesicle that takes up a major proportion of cell volume. Due to their morphology and physiology, the cells can survive for up to 3 months without an external source of nutrients by tapping into their "storage tanks." These bacteria are found in such large numbers in the sediments that it is thought that they are essential to the ecological cycling of H_2S gas in this region, converting it to less toxic substances.

Miniature Microbes—The Smallest of the Small

At the other extreme, microbiologists are being asked to reevaluate the lower limits of bacterial size. Up until now it has been generally accepted that the smallest cells on the planet are some form of mycoplasma with dimensions of 0.2 to 0.3 μm, which is right at the limit of resolution with light microscopes. A new controversy is brewing over the discovery of tiny cells that look like dwarf bacteria but are 10 times smaller than mycoplasmas and a hundred times smaller

1 millimeter   1 millimeter

than the average bacterial cell. These minute cells have been given the name **nanobacteria** or **nanobes** (Gr. *nanos,* one-billionth).

Nanobacteria-like forms were first isolated from blood and serum samples. The tiny cells appear to grow in culture, have cell walls, and contain protein and nucleic acids, but their size range is only from 0.05 to 0.2 μm. Similar nanobes have been extracted by mineralogists studying sandstone rock deposits in the ocean at temperatures of 100°C to 170°C and deeply embedded in billion-year-old minerals. The minute filaments were able to grow and are capable of depositing minerals in a test tube. Many geologists are convinced that these nanobes are real, that they are probably similar to the first microbes on earth, and that they play a strategic role in the evolution of the earth's crust. Microbiologists tend to be more skeptical. It has been postulated that the minimum cell size to contain a functioning genome and reproductive and synthetic machinery is approximately 0.14 μm. They believe that the nanobes are really just artifacts or bits of larger cells that have broken free.

Nanobe "believers" have recently been bolstered by a series of findings indicating that nanobes can infect humans and have been linked to diseases such as kidney stones and ovarian cancer. These diseases are influenced in some way by calcification that is catalyzed by nanobes.

It seems the real question is not whether nanobes exist but whether we should classify them as bacteria. One of the early nanobe discoverers, Olavi Kajander, blames himself for getting scientists distracted by that question by first coining the name "nanobacteria." "Calcifying self-propagating nanoparticles would have been much better," he says now.* Additional studies are needed to test this curious question of nanobes, and possibly to answer some questions about the origins of life on earth and even other planets.

*Wired.com news story, March 14, 2005.

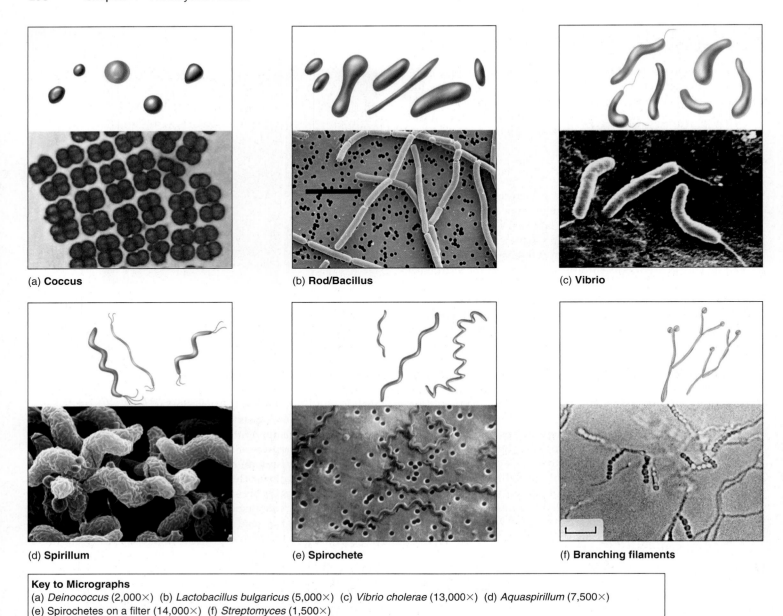

(a) **Coccus**

(b) **Rod/Bacillus**

(c) **Vibrio**

(d) **Spirillum**

(e) **Spirochete**

(f) **Branching filaments**

Key to Micrographs
(a) *Deinococcus* (2,000×) (b) *Lactobacillus bulgaricus* (5,000×) (c) *Vibrio cholerae* (13,000×) (d) *Aquaspirillum* (7,500×)
(e) Spirochetes on a filter (14,000×) (f) *Streptomyces* (1,500×)

Figure 4.23 Bacterial shapes and arrangements.   Drawings show examples of shape variations for cocci, rods, vibrios, spirilla, spirochetes, and branching filaments. Below each shape is a micrograph of a representative example.

pleomorphism **(figure 4.24),** is due to individual variations in cell wall structure caused by nutritional or slight genetic differences. For example, although the cells of *Corynebacterium diphtheriae* are generally considered rod-shaped, in culture they display variations such as club-shaped, swollen, curved, filamentous, and coccoid. Pleomorphism reaches an extreme in the mycoplasmas, which entirely lack cell walls and thus display extreme variations in shape (see figure 4.15).

The cells of prokaryotes can also be categorized according to arrangement, or style of grouping (see figure 4.23). The main factors influencing the arrangement of a particular

cell type are its pattern of division and how the cells remain attached afterward. The greatest variety in arrangement occurs in cocci, which can be single, in pairs (diplococci), in **tetrads** (groups of four), in irregular clusters (both staphylococci and micrococci), or in chains of a few to hundreds of cells (streptococci). An even more complex grouping is a cubical packet of eight, sixteen, or more cells called a **sarcina** (sar'-sih-nah). These different coccal groupings are the result of the division of a coccus in a single plane, in two perpendicular planes, or in several intersecting planes; after division, the resultant daughter cells remain attached.

Figure 4.24 Pleomorphic bacteria.   If you look closely at this micrograph of stained *Dermatophilus* bacteria, you will see some coccoid cells, some long filamentous cells, and some rod-shaped cells.

Bacilli are less varied in arrangement because they divide only in the transverse plane (perpendicular to the axis). They occur either as single cells, as a pair of cells with their ends attached (diplobacilli), or as a chain of several cells (streptobacilli). Spirilla are occasionally found in short chains, but spirochetes rarely remain attached after division.

4.5 Learning Outcomes—Can You . . .

10. . . . describe the three major shapes of prokaryotes?
11. . . . describe other more unusual shapes of prokaryotes?

4.6 Classification Systems in the Prokaryotae

Classification systems serve both practical and academic purposes. They aid in differentiating and identifying unknown species in medical and applied microbiology. They are also useful in organizing prokaryotes and as a means of studying their relationships and origins. Since classification was started around 200 years ago, several thousand species of bacteria and archaea have been identified, named, and cataloged.

For years scientists have had intense interest in tracing the origins of and evolutionary relationships among prokaryotes, but doing so has not been an easy task. One of the questions that has plagued taxonomists is, "What characteristics are the most indicative of closeness in ancestry?" Early bacteriologists found it convenient to classify bacteria according to shape, variations in arrangement, growth characteristics, and habitat. However, as more species were discovered and as techniques for studying their biochemistry were developed, it soon became clear that similarities in cell shape, arrangement, and staining reactions do not automatically indicate relatedness. Even though the gram-negative rods look alike, there are hundreds of different species, with highly significant differences in biochemistry and genetics. If we attempted to classify them on the basis of Gram stain and shape alone, we could not assign them to a more specific level than class. Increasingly, classification schemes are turning to genetic and molecular traits that cannot be visualized under a microscope or in culture.

One of the most viable indicators of evolutionary relatedness and affiliation is comparison of the sequence of nitrogen bases in ribosomal RNA, a major component of ribosomes. Ribosomes have the same function (protein synthesis) in all cells, and they tend to remain more or less stable in their nucleic acid content over long periods. Thus, any major differences in the sequence, or "signature," of the rRNA is likely to indicate some distance in ancestry. This technique is powerful at two levels: It is effective for differentiating general group differences (it was used to separate the three superkingdoms of life discussed in chapter 1), and it can be fine-tuned to identify at the species level (for example in *Mycobacterium* and *Legionella*). Elements of these and other identification methods are presented in more detail in chapter 17.

The definitive published source for prokaryotic classification, called *Bergey's Manual,* has been in print continuously since 1923. The basis for the early classification in *Bergey's* was the **phenotypic** traits of bacteria, such as their shape, cultural behavior, and biochemical reactions. These traits are still used extensively by clinical microbiologists or researchers who need to quickly identify unknown bacteria. As methods for RNA and DNA analysis became available, this information was used to supplement the phenotypic information. The current version of the publication, called *Bergey's Manual of Systematic Bacteriology,* presents a comprehensive view of prokaryotic relatedness, combining phenotypic information with rRNA sequencing information to classify prokaryotes; it is a huge, five-volume set. (We need to remember that all prokaryotic classification systems are in a state of constant flux; no system is ever finished.)

With the explosion of information about evolutionary relatedness among bacteria, the need for a *Bergey's Manual* that contained easily accessible information for identifying unknown bacteria became apparent. Now there is a separate book, called *Bergey's Manual of Determinative Bacteriology,* based entirely on phenotypic characteristics. It is utilitarian in focus, categorizing bacteria by traits commonly assayed in clinical, teaching, and research labs. It is widely used by microbiologists who need to identify bacteria but need not know their evolutionary backgrounds. This phenotypic classification is more useful for students of medical microbiology, as well.

Taxonomic Scheme

Bergey's Manual of Determinative Bacteriology organizes the prokaryotes into four major divisions. These somewhat natural divisions are based on the nature of the cell wall. The **Gracilicutes** (gras"-ih-lik'-yoo-teez) have gram-negative cell walls and thus are thin-skinned; the **Firmicutes** have gram-positive cell walls that are thick and strong; the **Tenericutes** (ten"-er-ik'-yoo-teez) lack a cell wall and thus are soft; and the **Mendosicutes** (men-doh-sik'-yoo-teez) are the archaea (also called archaebacteria), primitive prokaryotes with unusual cell walls and nutritional habits. The first two divisions contain the greatest number of species. The 200 or so species that are so-far known to cause human and animal diseases can be found in four classes: the Scotobacteria, Firmibacteria, Thallobacteria, and Mollicutes. The system used in *Bergey's Manual* further organizes prokaryotes into subcategories such as classes, orders, and families, but these are not available for all groups.

Diagnostic Scheme

As mentioned earlier, many medical microbiologists prefer an informal working system that outlines the major families and genera. **Table 4.1** is an example of an adaptation of the phenotypic method of classification that might be used in clinical microbiology. This system is more applicable for diagnosis because it is restricted to bacterial disease agents, depends less on nomenclature, and is based on readily accessible morphological and physiological tests rather than on phylogenetic relationships. It also divides the bacteria into gram-positive, gram-negative, and those without cell walls and then subgroups them according to cell shape, arrangement, and certain physiological traits such as oxygen usage: **Aerobic** bacteria use oxygen in metabolism; **anaerobic** bacteria do not use oxygen in metabolism; and *facultative* bacteria may or may not use oxygen. Further tests not listed in the table would be required to separate closely related genera and species. Many of these are included in later chapters on specific bacterial groups.

Species and Subspecies in Prokaryotes

Among most organisms, the species level is a distinct, readily defined, and natural taxonomic category. In animals, for instance, a species is a distinct type of organism that can produce viable offspring only when it mates with others of its own kind. This definition does not work for prokaryotes primarily because they do not exhibit a typical mode of sexual reproduction. They can accept genetic information from unrelated forms, and they can also alter their genetic makeup by a variety of mechanisms. Thus, it is necessary to hedge a bit when we define a bacterial species. Theoretically, it is a collection of bacterial cells, all of which share an overall similar pattern of traits, in contrast to other groups whose patterns differ significantly. Although

the boundaries that separate two closely related species in a genus are in some cases arbitrary, this definition still serves as a method to separate the bacteria into various kinds that can be cultured and studied. As additional information on prokaryotic genomes is discovered, it may be possible to define species according to specific combinations of genetic codes found only in a particular isolated culture.

Individual members of given species can show variations, as well. Therefore more categories within species exist, but they are not well defined. Microbiologists use terms like **subspecies**, **strain**, or **type** to designate bacteria of the same species that have differing characteristics. **Serotype** refers to representatives of a species that stimulate a distinct pattern of antibody (serum) responses in their hosts, because of distinct surface molecules.

4.6 Learning Outcomes—Can You ...

12. ... differentiate between *Bergey's Manual of Systematic Bacteriology* and *Bergey's Manual of Determinative Bacteriology*?
13. ... name four divisions ending in –cutes and describe their characteristics?
14. ... explain what a species is?

4.7 The Archaea

Archaea: The Other Prokaryotes

The discovery and characterization of novel prokaryotic cells that have unusual anatomy, physiology, and genetics changed our views of microbial taxonomy and classification (see chapter 1). These single-celled, simple organisms, called **archaea,** are now considered a third cell type in a separate superkingdom (the Domain Archaea). We include them in this chapter because they are prokaryotic in general structure and they do share many bacterial characteristics. But it has become clear that they are actually more closely related to Domain Eukarya than to bacteria. For example, archaea and eukaryotes share a number of ribosomal RNA sequences that are not found in bacteria, and their protein synthesis and ribosomal subunit structures are similar. **Table 4.2** outlines selected points of comparison of the three domains.

Among the ways that the archaea differ significantly from other cell types are that certain genetic sequences are found only in their rRNA, and that they have unique membrane lipids and cell wall construction. It is clear that the archaea are the most primitive of all life forms and are most closely related to the first cells that originated on the earth 4 billion years ago. The early earth is thought to have contained a hot, anaerobic "soup" with sulfuric gases and salts in abundance. The modern archaea still live in the remaining habitats on the earth that have these same ancient conditions—the most extreme habitats in nature. It is for this reason that they are

Table 4.1 Medically Important Families and Genera of Bacteria, with Notes on Some Diseases*

I. Bacteria with gram-positive cell wall structure

Cocci in clusters or packets
   Family Micrococcaceae: *Staphylococcus* (members cause boils, skin infections)

Cocci in pairs and chains
   Family Streptococcaceae: *Streptococcus* (species cause strep throat, dental caries)

Anaerobic cocci in pairs, tetrads, irregular clusters
   Family Peptococcaceae: *Peptococcus, Peptostreptococcus* (involved in wound infections)

Spore-forming rods
   Family Bacillaceae: *Bacillus* (anthrax), *Clostridium* (tetanus, gas gangrene, botulism)

Non-spore-forming rods
   Family Lactobacillaceae: *Lactobacillus, Listeria, Erysipelothrix* (erysipeloid)
   Family Propionibacteriaceae: *Propionibacterium* (involved in acne)

   Family Corynebacteriaceae: *Corynebacterium* (diphtheria)

   Family Mycobacteriaceae: *Mycobacterium* (tuberculosis, leprosy)

   Family Nocardiaceae: *Nocardia* (lung abscesses)

   Family Actinomycetaceae: *Actinomyces* (lumpy jaw), *Bifidobacterium*

   Family Streptomycetaceae: *Streptomyces* (important source of antibiotics)

II. Bacteria with gram-negative cell wall structure

Aerobic cocci
   Neisseria (gonorrhea, meningitis), *Branhamella*

Aerobic coccobacilli
   Moraxella, Acinetobacter

Anaerobic cocci
   Family Veillonellaceae
   Veillonella (dental disease)

Miscellaneous rods
   Brucella (undulant fever), *Bordetella* (whooping cough), *Francisella* (tularemia)

Aerobic rods
   Family Pseudomonadaceae: *Pseudomonas* (pneumonia, burn infections)
   Miscellaneous: *Legionella* (Legionnaires' disease)

Facultative or anaerobic rods and vibrios
   Family Enterobacteriaceae: *Escherichia, Edwardsiella, Citrobacter, Salmonella* (typhoid fever), *Shigella* (dysentery), *Klebsiella, Enterobacter, Serratia, Proteus, Yersinia* (one species causes plague)
   Family Vibronaceae: *Vibrio* (cholera, food infection), *Campylobacter, Aeromonas*

   Miscellaneous genera: *Chromobacterium, Flavobacterium, Haemophilus* (meningitis), *Pasteurella, Cardiobacterium, Streptobacillus*

Anaerobic rods
   Family Bacteroidaceae: *Bacteroides, Fusobacterium* (anaerobic wound and dental infections)

Helical and curviform bacteria
   Family Spirochaetaceae: *Treponema* (syphilis), *Borrelia* (Lyme disease), *Leptospira* (kidney infection)

Obligate intracellular bacteria
   Family Rickettsiaceae: *Rickettsia* (Rocky Mountain spotted fever), *Coxiella* (Q fever)
   Family Bartonellaceae: *Bartonella* (trench fever, cat scratch disease)
   Family Chlamydiaceae: *Chlamydia* (sexually transmitted infection)

III. Bacteria with no cell walls

Family Mycoplasmataceae: *Mycoplasma* (pneumonia), *Ureaplasma* (urinary infection)

*Details of pathogens and diseases appear in chapters 18 through 23.

Table 4.2 Comparison of Three Cellular Domains

Characteristic	Bacteria	Archaea	Eukarya
Cell type	Prokaryotic	Prokaryotic	Eukaryotic
Chromosomes	Single, or few, circular	Single, circular	Several, linear
Types of ribosomes	70S	70S but structure is similar to 80S	80S
Contains unique ribosomal RNA signature sequences	+	+	+
Number of sequences shared with Eukarya	1	3	(all)
Protein synthesis similar to Eukarya	−	+	
Presence of peptidoglycan in cell wall	+	−	−
Cell membrane lipids	Fatty acids with ester linkages	Long-chain, branched hydrocarbons with ether linkages	Fatty acids with ester linkages
Sterols in membrane	− (some exceptions)	−	+

often called extremophiles, meaning that they "love" extreme conditions in the environment.

Metabolically, the archaea exhibit incredible adaptations to what would be deadly conditions for other organisms. These hardy microbes have adapted to multiple combinations of heat, salt, acid, pH, pressure, and atmosphere. Included in this group are methane producers, hyperthermophiles, extreme halophiles, and sulfur reducers.

Members of the group called **methanogens** can convert CO_2 and H_2 into methane gas (CH_4) through unusual and complex pathways. These archaea are common inhabitants of anaerobic swamp mud, the bottom sediments of lakes and oceans, and even the digestive systems of animals. The gas they produce collects in swamps and may become a source of fuel. Methane may also contribute to the "greenhouse effect," which maintains the earth's temperature and can contribute to global warming (see chapter 24).

Other types of archaea—the extreme halophiles—require salt to grow, and some have such a high salt tolerance that they can multiply in sodium chloride solutions (36% NaCl) that would destroy most cells. They exist in the saltiest places on the earth—inland seas, salt lakes, salt mines, and salted fish. They are not particularly common in the ocean because the salt content is not high enough. Many of the "halobacteria" use a red pigment to synthesize ATP in the presence of light. These pigments are responsible for the color of the Red Sea, and the red color of salt ponds **(figure 4.25).**

(a)

5 μm

(b)

Figure 4.25 Halophiles around the world.   (a) A solar evaporation pond in Owens Lake, California, is extremely high in salt and mineral content. The archaea that dominate in this hot, saline habitat produce brilliant red pigments with which they absorb light to drive cell synthesis. **(b)** A sample taken from a saltern in Australia viewed by fluorescent microscopy (1,000×). Note the range of cell shapes (cocci, rods, and squares) found in this community.

Archaea adapted to growth at very low temperatures are called **psychrophilic** (loving cold temperatures); those growing at very high temperatures are **hyperthermophilic** (loving high temperatures). Hyperthermophiles flourish at temperatures between 80°C and 113°C and cannot grow at 50°C. They live in volcanic waters and soils and submarine vents and are also often salt- and acid-tolerant as well. One member, *Thermoplasma*, lives in hot, acidic habitats in the waste piles around coal mines that regularly sustain a pH of 1 and a temperature of nearly 60°C.

Archaea are not just environmental microbes. They have been isolated from human tissues such as the colon, the mouth, and the vagina. Recently, an association was found between the degree of severity of periodontal disease and the presence of archaeal RNA sequences in the gingiva, suggesting—but not proving—that archaea may be capable of causing human disease.

4.7 Learning Outcomes—Can You ...

15. ... List some differences between archaea and bacteria?

Case File 4   *Wrap-Up*

The opening of the case asked why the discovery of bacteria in cerebrospinal fluid and the blood is a serious sign. You will learn in later chapters that these two body compartments are generally off limits to bacteria and have little or no normal microbial inhabitants, unlike the digestive tract or the respiratory tract. It is more difficult for microbes to enter both of these compartments for several reasons, one being that antibodies can attach to bacteria and prevent them from crossing the boundaries into these areas. Apparently this patient was missing the antibodies that would have acted against the encapsulated bacteria. The patient was treated for septic shock and respiratory failure for 9 days. Physicians administered dopamine and epinephrine to stabilize her blood pressure, as well as antibiotics to treat the underlying bacterial infection. Artificial ventilation was necessary for the first 4 days of treatment. Prior to being discharged, the patient was injected with pneumococcal vaccine and placed on prophylactic (preventive) penicillin therapy. She recovered fully.

See: 2005. *Rheumatology* 44(12):1586–88.

Chapter Summary

4.1 Prokaryotic Form and Function
- Prokaryotes are the oldest form of cellular life. They are also the most widely dispersed, occupying every conceivable microclimate on the planet.

4.2 External Structures
- The external structures of bacteria include appendages (flagella, fimbriae, and pili) and the glycocalyx.
- Flagella vary in number and arrangement as well as in the type and rate of motion they produce.

4.3 The Cell Envelope: The Boundary Layer of Bacteria
- The cell envelope is the complex boundary structure surrounding a bacterial cell. In gram-negative bacteria, the envelope consists of an outer membrane, the cell wall, and the cell membrane. Gram-positive bacteria have only the cell wall and cell membrane.
- In a Gram stain, gram-positive bacteria retain the crystal violet and stain purple. Gram-negative bacteria lose the crystal violet and stain red from the safranin counterstain.
- Gram-positive bacteria have thick cell walls of peptidoglycan and acidic polysaccharides such as teichoic acid. The cell walls of gram-negative bacteria are thinner and have a wide periplasmic space.
- The outer membrane of gram-negative cells contains lipopolysaccharide (LPS). LPS is toxic to mammalian hosts.
- The bacterial cell membrane is typically composed of phospholipids and proteins, and it performs many metabolic functions as well as transport activities.

4.4 Bacterial Internal Structure
- The cytoplasm of bacterial cells serves as a solvent for materials used in all cell functions.
- The genetic material of bacteria is DNA. Genes are arranged on large, circular chromosomes. Additional genes are carried on plasmids.
- Bacterial ribosomes are dispersed in the cytoplasm in chains (polysomes) and are also embedded in the cell membrane.
- Bacteria may store nutrients in their cytoplasm in structures called inclusions. Inclusions vary in structure and the materials that are stored.
- Some bacteria manufacture long actin filaments that help determine their cellular shape.
- A few families of bacteria produce dormant bodies called endospores, which are the hardiest of all life forms, surviving for hundreds or thousands of years.
- The genera *Bacillus* and *Clostridium* are sporeformers, and both contain deadly pathogens.

4.5 Prokaryotic Shapes, Arrangements, and Sizes
- Most prokaryotes have one of three general shapes: coccus (round), bacillus (rod), or spiral, based on the configuration of the cell wall. Two types of spiral cells are spirochetes and spirilla.
- Shape and arrangement of cells are key means of describing prokaryotes. Arrangements of cells are based on the number of planes in which a given species divides.
- Cocci can divide in many planes to form pairs, chains, packets, or clusters. Bacilli divide only in the transverse plane. If they remain attached, they form chains or palisades.

4.6 Classification Systems in the Prokaryotae

- Prokaryotes are formally classified by phylogenetic relationships and phenotypic characteristics.
- Medical identification of pathogens uses an informal system of classification based on Gram stain, morphology, biochemical reactions, and metabolic requirements.
- A bacterial species is loosely defined as a collection of bacterial cells that shares an overall similar pattern of traits different from other groups of bacteria.

- Variant forms within a species (subspecies) include strains and types.

4.7 The Archaea

- Archaea are another type of prokaryotic cell that constitute the third domain of life. They exhibit unusual biochemistry and genetics that make them different from bacteria. Many members are adapted to extreme habitats with low or high temperature, salt, pressure, or acid.

Multiple-Choice and True-False Questions   Knowledge and Comprehension

Multiple-Choice Questions. Select the correct answer from the answers provided.

1. Which of the following is not found in all bacterial cells?
   a. cell membrane
   b. a nucleoid
   c. ribosomes
   d. actin cytoskeleton

2. Pili are tubular shafts in _____ bacteria that serve as a means of _____.
   a. gram-positive, genetic exchange
   b. gram-positive, attachment
   c. gram-negative, genetic exchange
   d. gram-negative, protection

3. An example of a glycocalyx is
   a. a capsule.
   b. a pilus.
   c. an outer membrane.
   d. a cell wall.

4. Which of the following is a primary bacterial cell wall function?
   a. transport
   b. motility
   c. support
   d. adhesion

5. Which of the following is present in both gram-positive and gram-negative cell walls?
   a. an outer membrane
   b. peptidoglycan
   c. teichoic acid
   d. lipopolysaccharides

6. Darkly stained granules are concentrated crystals of _____ that are found in _____.
   a. fat, *Mycobacterium*
   b. dipicolinic acid, *Bacillus*
   c. sulfur, *Thiobacillus*
   d. PO$_4$, *Corynebacterium*

7. Bacterial endospores usually function in
   a. reproduction.
   b. survival.
   c. protein synthesis.
   d. storage.

8. A bacterial arrangement in packets of eight cells is described as a _____.
   a. micrococcus
   b. diplococcus
   c. tetrad
   d. sarcina

9. To which division of bacteria do cyanobacteria belong?
   a. Tenericutes
   b. Gracilicutes
   c. Firmicutes
   d. Mendosicutes

10. Which stain is used to distinguish differences between the cell walls of medically important bacteria?
    a. simple stain
    b. acridine orange stain
    c. Gram stain
    d. negative stain

True-False Questions. If the statement is true, leave as is. If it is false, correct it by rewriting the sentence.

11. One major difference in the envelope structure between gram-positive bacteria and gram-negative bacteria is the presence or absence of a cytoplasmic membrane.

12. A research microbiologist looking at evolutionary relatedness between two bacterial species is more likely to use *Bergey's Manual of Determinative Bacteriology* than *Bergey's Manual of Systematic Bacteriology*.

13. Nanobes may or may not actually be bacteria.

14. Both bacteria and archaea are prokaryotes.

15. A collection of bacteria that share an overall similar pattern of traits is called a *species*.

Critical Thinking Questions   Application and Analysis

These questions are suggested as a *writing-to-learn* experience. For each question, compose a one- or two-paragraph answer that includes the factual information needed to completely address the question.

1. a. Name several general characteristics that could be used to define the prokaryotes.
   b. Do any other microbial groups besides bacteria have prokaryotic cells?
   c. What does it mean to say that prokaryotes are ubiquitous? In what habitats are they found? Give some general means by which bacteria derive nutrients.

2. a. Describe the structure of a flagellum and how it operates. What are the four main types of flagellar arrangement?
   b. How does the flagellum dictate the behavior of a motile bacterium? Differentiate between flagella and periplasmic flagella.

3. Differentiate between pili and fimbriae.

4. a. Compare the cell envelopes of gram-positive and gram-negative bacteria.
   b. What function does peptidoglycan serve?
   c. Give a simple description of its structure.
   d. What happens to a cell that has its peptidoglycan disrupted or removed?
   e. What functions does the LPS layer serve?

5. List five functions that the cell membrane performs in bacteria.

6. a. Describe the vegetative stage of a bacterial cell.
   b. Describe the structure of an endospore, and explain its function.
   c. Describe the endospore-forming cycle.
   d. Explain why an endospore is not considered a reproductive body.
   e. Why are endospores so difficult to destroy?

7. a. Explain the characteristics of archaea that indicate that they constitute a unique domain of living things that is neither bacterial nor eukaryotic.
   b. What leads microbiologists to believe the archaea are more closely related to eukaryotes than to bacteria?
   c. What is meant by the term *extremophile*? Describe some archaeal adaptations to extreme habitats.

8. a. Name a bacterium that has no cell walls.
   b. How is it protected from osmotic destruction?

9. a. What are some possible adaptations that the giant bacterium *Thiomargarita* has had to make because of its large size?
   b. If a regular bacterium were the size of an elephant, estimate the size of a nanobe at that scale.

10. Propose a hypothesis to explain how bacteria and archaea could have, together, given rise to eukaryotes.

Concept Mapping   Synthesis

Appendix D provides guidance for working with concept maps.

1. Construct your own concept map using the following words as the *concepts*. Supply the linking words between each pair of concepts.

genus	species
serotype	domain
Borrelia	*burgdorferi*
spirochete	

Visual Connections   Synthesis

These questions use visual images or previous content to make connections to this chapter's concepts.

1. **From chapter 3, figure 3.10.** Do you believe that the bacteria spelling "*Klebsiella*" or the bacteria spelling "*S. aureus*" possess the larger capsule? Defend your answer.

2. **From chapter 1, figure 1.14.** Study this figure. How would it be drawn differently if the archaea were more closely related to bacteria than to eukaryotes?

www.connect.microbiology.com

Enhance your study of this chapter with study tools and practice tests. Also ask your instructor about the resources available through ConnectPlus, including the media-rich eBook, interactive learning tools, and animations.

5

Eukaryotic Cells and Microorganisms

Case File 5

In June 2005, a ban on clamming was instituted along much of the Oregon coast after razor clams in that area were found to contain high levels of domoic acid, a naturally occurring toxin produced by algae in the genus *Pseudo-nitzschia*. Filter-feeding mollusks, such as clams and mussels, accumulate high levels of domoic acid during periods of robust algal growth known as blooms. Ingestion of domoic acid by humans causes amnesiac shellfish poisoning, which is marked by headache, dizziness, nausea, confusion, and potentially permanent loss of short-term memory. In severe cases, respiratory paralysis and death may occur within a day.

A different kind of shellfish illness, paralytic shellfish poisoning, results from ingesting saxitoxins, which are, like domoic acid, produced by certain species of algae. In this case, algae in the genus *Alexandrium* produce the toxin, which then accumulates in mussels, clams, scallops, oysters, crabs, and lobsters during periods of greater than usual algal growth. Ingestion of saxitoxin by humans can lead to numbness, paralysis, disorientation, and death due to respiratory failure. Neither domoic acid nor saxitoxin is affected by temperature, so cooking or freezing has no effect on the toxin.

- The number of cases of seafood poisoning is far greater in the summer months. Besides the fact that people are more likely to harvest seafood when the weather is warm, why else would illnesses due to ingestion of harmful algae be more prevalent in the summer?
- The number and size of harmful algal blooms seem correlated to an increased use of fertilizers. Speculate on a possible connection between these two events.

Continuing the Case appears on page 128.

Outline and Learning Outcomes

5.1 The History of Eukaryotes
1. Relate both prokaryotic and eukaryotic cells to the Last Common Ancestor.
2. List the types of eukaryotic microorganisms and denote which are unicellular and which are multicellular.

5.1 The History of Eukaryotes

Evidence from paleontology indicates that the first eukaryotic cells appeared on the earth approximately 2 billion years ago. Some fossilized cells that look remarkably like modern-day algae or protozoa appear in shale sediments from China, Russia, and Australia that date from 850 million to 950 million years ago (figure 5.1). While it used to be thought that eukaryotic cells evolved directly from prokaryotic cells, we now believe that both prokaryotes and eukaryotes evolved from a different kind of cell, a precursor to both prokaryotes and eukaryotes that biologists call the Last Common Ancestor. This ancestor was neither prokaryotic nor eukaryotic, but gave rise to both in different ways. It now seems clear that some of the **organelles** that distinguish eukaryotic cells originated from more primitive cells that became trapped inside them **(Insight 5.1)**. The structure of these first eukaryotic cells was so versatile that eukaryotic microorganisms soon spread out into available habitats and adopted greatly diverse styles of living.

The first primitive eukaryotes were probably single-celled and independent, but, over time, some forms began to aggregate, forming colonies. With further evolution, some of the cells within colonies became *specialized*, or adapted to perform a particular function advantageous to the whole colony, such as locomotion, feeding, or reproduction. Complex

(a)

(b)

Figure 5.1 Ancient eukaryotic protists caught up in fossilized rocks. **(a)** An alga-like cell found in Siberian shale deposits and dated from 850 million to 950 million years ago. **(b)** A large, disclike cell bearing a crown of spines is from Chinese rock dated 590 million to 610 million years ago.

INSIGHT 5.1   The Extraordinary Emergence of Eukaryotic Cells

For years, biologists have grappled with the problem of how a cell as complex as the modern eukaryotic cell originated. The explanation seems to be **endosymbiosis,** which suggests that eukaryotic cells arose when a very large prokaryote engulfed smaller prokaryotic cells that began to live and reproduce inside the large cell rather than being destroyed. As the smaller cells took up permanent residence, they came to perform specialized functions for the larger cell, from (perhaps) serving as a nucleus, to performing functions such as food synthesis and oxygen utilization. Many of these endosymbionts enhanced the cell's versatility and survival. Over time, the engulfed bacteria gave up their ability to live independently and transferred some of their genes to the host cell.

The biologist responsible for early consideration of the theory of endosymbiosis is Dr. Lynn Margulis. Using molecular techniques, she accumulated convincing evidence of the relationships between the organelles of modern eukaryotic cells and the structure of prokaryotes. In many ways, the mitochondrion of eukaryotic cells is something like a tiny cell within a cell. It is capable of independent division, contains a circular chromosome that has bacterial DNA sequences, and has ribosomes that are clearly prokaryotic. Mitochondria also have bacterial membranes and can be inhibited by drugs that affect only bacteria.

Chloroplasts likely arose when endosymbiotic cyanobacteria provided their host cells with a built-in feeding mechanism. Margulis also found convincing evidence that eukaryotic cilia are the consequence of endosymbiosis between spiral bacteria and the cell membrane of early eukaryotic cells.

As molecular techniques improve, more evidence accumulates for the endosymbiont "theory," which is now widely accepted among evolutionary scientists.

Larger Prokaryotic Cell

Smaller Prokaryotic Cell

Cell would have flexible membrane.

Cells are aerobic bacteria, similar to purple bacteria.

Early nucleus

Larger cell engulfs smaller one; smaller one survives and begins an endosymbiotic association.

Smaller bacterium becomes established in its host's cytoplasm and multiplies; it can utilize aerobic metabolism and increase energy availability for the host.

Early endoplasmic reticulum

Early mitochondria

Nuclear envelope

Ancestral eukaryotic cell develops extensive membrane pouches that become the endoplasmic reticulum and nuclear envelope.

Photosynthetic bacteria (cyanobacteria) are also engulfed; they develop into chloroplasts.

Ancestral cell

(a) Dr. Lynn Margulis

(b) Protozoa, fungi, animals

Chloroplast

Algae, higher plants

multicellular organisms evolved as individual cells in the organism lost the ability to survive apart from the intact colony. Although a multicellular organism is composed of many cells, it is more than just a disorganized assemblage of cells like a colony. Rather, it is composed of distinct groups of cells that cannot exist independently of the rest of the body. The cell groupings of multicellular organisms that have a specific function are termed *tissues*, and groups of tissues make up *organs*.

Looking at modern eukaryotic organisms, we find examples of many levels of cellular complexity **(table 5.1)**. All protozoa, as well as numerous algae and fungi, are unicellular. Truly multicellular organisms are found only among plants and animals and some of the fungi (mushrooms) and algae (seaweeds). Only certain eukaryotes are traditionally studied by microbiologists—primarily the protozoa, the microscopic algae and fungi, and animal parasites, or helminths.

5.1 Learning Outcomes—Can You . . .

1. . . . relate both prokaryotic and eukaryotic cells to the Last Common Ancestor?
2. . . . list the types of eukaryotic microorganisms and denote which are unicellular and which are multicellular?

Table 5.1 Eukaryotic Organisms Studied in Microbiology

Always Unicellular	May Be Unicellular or Multicellular	Always Multicellular
Protozoa	Fungi Algae	Helminths (have unicellular egg or larval forms)

5.2 Form and Function of the Eukaryotic Cell: External Structures

The cells of eukaryotic organisms are so varied that no one member can serve as a typical example. **Figure 5.2** presents the generalized structure of typical algal, fungal, and protozoan cells. The flowchart on the next page shows the organization of a eukaryotic cell, and compares it to the organization for prokaryotic cells that you already saw in chapter 4.

In general, eukaryotic microbial cells have a cytoplasmic membrane, nucleus, mitochondria, endoplasmic reticulum, Golgi apparatus, vacuoles, cytoskeleton, and glycocalyx. A cell wall, locomotor appendages, and chloroplasts are

*Structure not present in all cell types

Figure 5.2 Structure of a eukaryotic cell. The figure of a prokaryotic cell from chapter 4 is included here for comparison.

Structure Flowchart

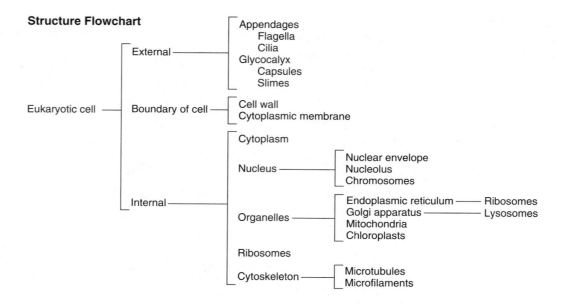

found only in some groups. In the following sections, we cover the microscopic structure and functions of the eukaryotic cell. As with the prokaryotes, we begin on the outside and proceed inward through the cell.

Locomotor Appendages: Cilia and Flagella

Motility allows a microorganism to locate nutrients and to migrate toward positive stimuli such as sunlight; it also permits them to avoid harmful substances and stimuli. Locomotion by means of flagella or cilia is common in protozoa, many algae, and a few fungal and animal cells.

Although they share the same name, eukaryotic flagella are much different from those of prokaryotes. The eukaryotic flagellum is thicker (by a factor of 10), structurally more complex, and covered by an extension of the cell membrane. A single flagellum is a long, sheathed cylinder containing regularly spaced hollow tubules—microtubules—that extend along its entire length **(figure 5.3a)**. A cross section reveals nine pairs of closely attached microtubules surrounding a single central pair. This scheme, called the 9 + 2 arrangement, is pattern of eukaryotic flagella and cilia **(figure 5.3b)**. During locomotion, the adjacent microtubules slide past each other, whipping the flagellum back and forth. Although details of this process are too complex to discuss here, it involves expenditure of energy and a coordinating mechanism in the cell membrane. The placement and number of flagella can be useful in identifying flagellated protozoa and certain algae.

Cilia are very similar in overall architecture to flagella, but they are shorter and more numerous (some cells have several thousand). They are found only on a single group of protozoa and certain animal cells. In the ciliated protozoa,

Figure 5.3 Microtubules in flagella.   **(a)** Longitudinal section through a flagellum, showing microtubules. **(b)** A cross section that reveals the typical 9 + 2 arrangement found in both flagella and cilia.

the cilia occur in rows over the cell surface, where they beat back and forth in regular oarlike strokes **(figure 5.4)**. Such protozoa are among the fastest of all motile cells. On some cells, cilia also function as feeding and filtering structures.

The Glycocalyx

Most eukaryotic cells have a **glycocalyx,** an outermost boundary that comes into direct contact with the environment (see figure 5.2). This structure, which is sometimes called an extracellular matrix, is usually composed of polysaccharides and appears as a network of fibers, a slime layer, or a capsule much like the glycocalyx of prokaryotes. Because of its positioning, the glycocalyx contributes to protection, adherence of cells to surfaces, and reception of signals from other cells and from the environment. The nature of the layer beneath the glycocalyx varies among the several eukaryotic groups. Fungi and most algae have a thick, rigid cell wall surrounding a cell membrane, whereas protozoa, a few algae, and all animal cells lack a cell wall and have only a cell membrane.

(a)

Form and Function of the Eukaryotic Cell: Boundary Structures

Boundary of cell — Cell wall / Cytoplasmic membrane

The Cell Wall

The cell walls of fungi and algae are rigid and provide structural support and shape, but they are different in chemical

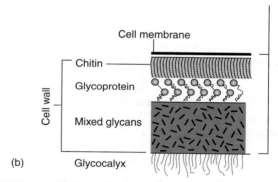
(b)

Figure 5.5 Cross-sectional views of fungal cell walls.

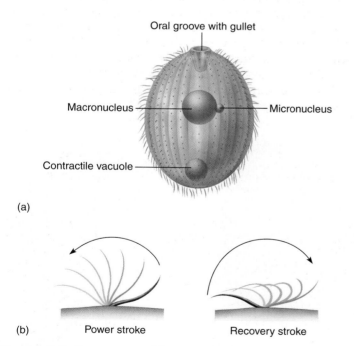

(a)

(b) Power stroke   Recovery stroke

Figure 5.4 Structure and locomotion in ciliates. **(a)** The structure of a simple representative, *Holophrya*, with a regular pattern of cilia in rows. **(b)** Cilia beat in coordinated waves, driving the cell forward and backward. View of a single cilium shows that it has a pattern of movement like a swimmer, with a power forward stroke and a repositioning stroke.

composition from prokaryotic cell walls. Fungal cell walls have a thick, inner layer of polysaccharide fibers composed of chitin or cellulose and a thin outer layer of mixed glycans **(figure 5.5)**. The cell walls of algae are quite varied in chemical composition. Substances commonly found among various algal groups are cellulose, pectin,[1] mannans,[2] and minerals such as silicon dioxide and calcium carbonate.

The Cytoplasmic Membrane

The cytoplasmic (cell) membrane of eukaryotic cells is a typical bilayer of phospholipids in which protein molecules are embedded. In addition to phospholipids, eukaryotic membranes also contain *sterols* of various kinds. Sterols are different from phospholipids in both structure and behavior, as you may recall from chapter 2. Their relative rigidity makes eukaryotic membranes more stable. This strengthening feature is extremely important in those cells that lack a cell wall. Cytoplasmic membranes of eukaryotes are functionally similar to those of prokaryotes, serving as

1. A polysaccharide composed of galacturonic acid subunits.
2. A polymer of the sugar known as mannose.

selectively permeable barriers. Membranes have extremely sophisticated mechanisms for transporting nutrients *in* and waste and other products *out*. You'll read about these transport systems in prokaryotic membranes in chapter 7, but the systems in prokaryotes and eukaryotes are very similar.

5.2 Learning Outcomes—Can You ...

3. ... differentiate between cilia and flagella in eukaryotes, and between flagella in prokaryotes and eukaryotes?
4. ... describe the important characteristics of a glycocalyx in eukaryotes?
5. ... list which eukaryotic microorganisms have a cell wall?
6. ... list similarities and differences between eukaryotic and prokaryotic cytoplasmic membranes?

5.3 Form and Function of the Eukaryotic Cell: Internal Structures

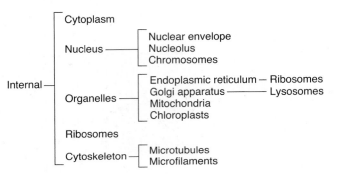

Unlike prokaryotes, eukaryotic cells contain a number of individual membrane-bound organelles that are extensive enough to account for 60% to 80% of their volume.

The Nucleus: The Control Center

The nucleus is a compact sphere that is the most prominent organelle of eukaryotic cells. It is separated from the cell cytoplasm by an external boundary called a nuclear envelope. The envelope has a unique architecture. It is composed of two parallel membranes separated by a narrow space, and it is perforated with small, regularly spaced openings, or pores, formed at sites where the two membranes unite **(figure 5.6)**. The nuclear pores are passageways through which macromolecules migrate from the nucleus to the cytoplasm and vice versa. The nucleus contains a matrix called the nucleoplasm and a granular mass, the **nucleolus,** that stains more intensely than the immediate surroundings because of its RNA content. The nucleolus is the site for ribosomal RNA synthesis and a collection area for ribosomal subunits. The subunits are transported through the nuclear pores into the cytoplasm for final assembly into ribosomes.

A prominent feature of the nucleoplasm in stained preparations is a network of dark fibers known as **chromatin.** Analysis has shown that chromatin actually comprises the eukaryotic **chromosomes,** large units of genetic information in the cell. The chromosomes in the nucleus of most cells are not readily visible because they are long, linear DNA molecules bound in varying degrees to **histone** proteins, and they are far too fine to be resolved as distinct structures without extremely high magnification. During **mitosis,** however, when the duplicated chromosomes are separated equally into daughter cells, the chromosomes themselves become readily visible as discrete bodies **(figure 5.7)**. This happens when the DNA becomes highly condensed by forming coils and supercoils around the histones to prevent the chromosomes from tangling as they are separated into new cells. This process is described in more detail in chapter 9.

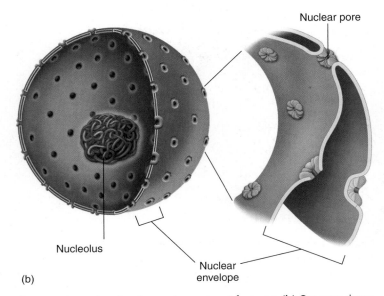

Figure 5.6 The nucleus.   **(a)** Electron micrograph section of an interphase nucleus, showing its most prominent features. **(b)** Cutaway three-dimensional view of the relationships of the nuclear envelope and pores.

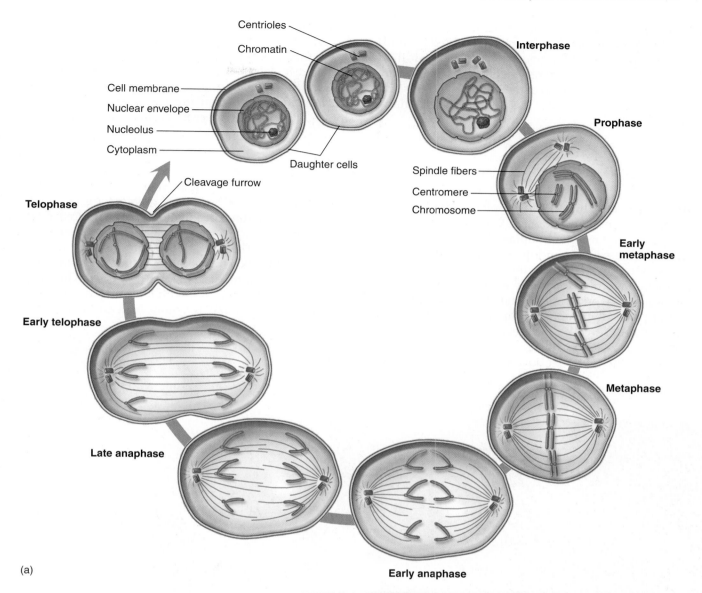

Centrioles

Chromatin

Cell membrane

Nuclear envelope

Nucleolus

Cytoplasm

Daughter cells

Cleavage furrow

Telophase

Early telophase

Late anaphase

Early anaphase

Interphase

Prophase

Spindle fibers

Centromere

Chromosome

Early metaphase

Metaphase

(a)

Figure 5.7 Changes in the cell and nucleus that accompany mitosis in a eukaryotic cell such as a yeast.   **(a)** Before mitosis (at interphase), chromosomes are visible only as chromatin. As mitosis proceeds (early prophase), chromosomes take on a fine, threadlike appearance as they condense, and the nuclear membrane and nucleolus are temporarily disrupted. **(b)** By metaphase, the chromosomes are fully visible as X-shaped structures. The shape is due to duplicated chromosomes attached at a central point, the centromere. Spindle fibers attach to these and facilitate the separation of individual chromosomes during metaphase. Later phases serve in the completion of chromosomal separation and division of the cell proper into daughter cells.

Centromere

(b)

The nucleus, as you've just seen, contains instructions in the form of DNA. Elaborate processes have evolved for transcription and duplication of this genetic material. In addition to mitosis, some cells also undergo **meiosis,** the process by which sex cells are created. Much of the protein synthesis and other work of the cell takes place outside the nucleus in the cell's other organelles.

Endoplasmic Reticulum: A Passageway in the Cell

The **endoplasmic reticulum (ER)** is a microscopic series of tunnels used in transport and storage. Two kinds of endoplasmic reticulum are the **rough endoplasmic reticulum (RER) (figure 5.8)** and the **smooth endoplasmic reticulum (SER).** Electron micrographs show that the RER originates from the outer membrane of the nuclear envelope and extends in a continuous network through the cytoplasm, even all the way out to the cell membrane. This architecture permits the spaces in the RER, called cisternae (singular = cistern), to transport materials from the nucleus to the cytoplasm and ultimately to the cell's exterior. The RER appears rough because of large numbers of ribosomes partly attached to its membrane surface. Proteins synthesized on the ribosomes are shunted into the inside space (the lumen) of the RER and held there for later packaging and transport. In contrast to the RER, the SER is a closed tubular network without ribosomes that functions in nutrient processing and in synthesis and storage of nonprotein macromolecules such as lipids.

Golgi Apparatus: A Packaging Machine

The **Golgi**[3] **apparatus,** also called the Golgi complex or body, is the site in the cell in which proteins are modified and then sent to their final destinations. It is a discrete organelle consisting of a stack of several flattened, disc-shaped sacs called cisternae. These sacs have outer limiting membranes and cavities like those of the endoplasmic reticulum, but they do not form a continuous network **(figure 5.9).** This organelle is always closely associated with the endoplasmic reticulum both in its location and function. At a site where it meets

---

3. Named for C. Golgi, an Italian histologist who first described the apparatus in 1898.

(a) (b) (c)

Nuclear envelope
Nuclear pore
Polyribosomes
Cistern
Small subunit
mRNA
Ribosome
Large subunit
RER membrane
Cistern
Protein being synthesized

Figure 5.8 The origin and detailed structure of the rough endoplasmic reticulum (RER).   **(a)** Schematic view of the origin of the RER from the outer membrane of the nuclear envelope. **(b)** Three-dimensional projection of the RER. **(c)** Detail of the orientation of a ribosome on the RER membrane.

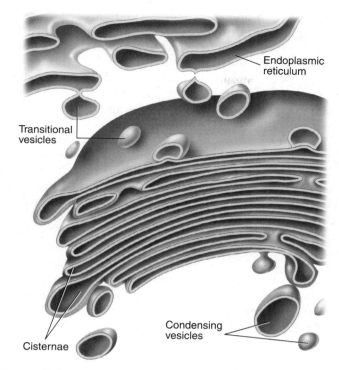

Figure 5.9 Detail of the Golgi apparatus. The flattened layers are cisternae. Vesicles enter the upper surface and leave the lower surface.

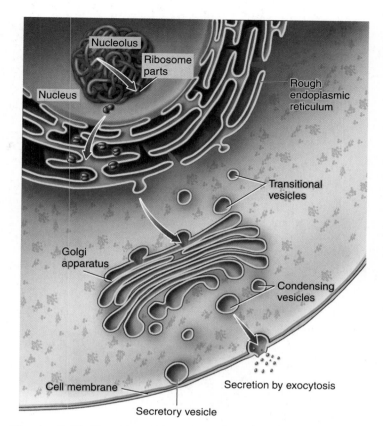

Figure 5.10 The transport process. The cooperation of organelles in protein synthesis and transport: nucleus → RER → Golgi apparatus → vesicles → secretion.

the Golgi apparatus, the endoplasmic reticulum buds off tiny membrane-bound packets of protein called *transitional vesicles* that are picked up by the forming face of the Golgi apparatus. Once in the complex itself, the proteins are often modified by the addition of polysaccharides and lipids. The final action of this apparatus is to pinch off finished *condensing vesicles* that will be conveyed to organelles such as lysosomes or transported outside the cell as secretory vesicles **(figure 5.10).**

Nucleus, Endoplasmic Reticulum, and Golgi Apparatus: Nature's Assembly Line

As the keeper of the eukaryotic genetic code, the nucleus ultimately governs and regulates all cell activities. But, because the nucleus remains fixed in a specific cellular site, it must direct these activities through a structural and chemical network (figure 5.10). This network includes ribosomes, which originate in the nucleus, and the rough endoplasmic reticulum, which is continuously connected with the nuclear envelope, as well as the smooth endoplasmic reticulum and the Golgi apparatus. Initially, a segment of the genetic code of DNA containing the instructions for producing a protein is copied into RNA and passed out through the nuclear pores directly to the ribosomes on the endoplasmic reticulum. Here, specific proteins are synthesized from the RNA

code and deposited in the lumen (space) of the endoplasmic reticulum. After being transported to the Golgi apparatus, the protein products are chemically modified and packaged into vesicles that can be used by the cell in a variety of ways. Some of the vesicles contain enzymes to digest food inside the cell; other vesicles are secreted to digest materials outside the cell, and yet others are important in the enlargement and repair of the cell wall and membrane.

A **lysosome** is one type of vesicle originating from the Golgi apparatus that contains a variety of enzymes. Lysosomes are involved in intracellular digestion of food particles and in protection against invading microorganisms. They also participate in digestion and removal of cell debris in damaged tissue. Other types of vesicles include **vacuoles** (vak'-yoo-ohlz), which are membrane-bound sacs containing fluids or solid particles to be digested, excreted, or stored. They are formed in phagocytic cells (certain white blood cells and protozoa) in response to food and other substances that have been engulfed. The contents of a food vacuole are digested through the merger of the vacuole with a lysosome. This merged structure is called a phagosome **(figure 5.11).** Other types of vacuoles are used in storing reserve food such as fats and glycogen. Protozoa living in freshwater habitats regulate osmotic pressure by means of

Food particle

Lysosomes

Cell membrane

Nucleus

Golgi apparatus

Engulfment of food

Food vacuole

Formation of food vacuole

Lysosome

Merger of lysosome and vacuole

Phagosome

Digestion

Digestive vacuole

Figure 5.11 The origin and action of lysosomes in phagocytosis.

contractile vacuoles, which regularly expel excess water that has diffused into the cell (described later).

Mitochondria: Energy Generators of the Cell

Although the nucleus is the cell's control center, none of the cellular activities it commands could proceed without a constant supply of energy, the bulk of which is generated in most eukaryotes by **mitochondria** (my"-toh-kon'-dree-uh). When viewed with light microscopy, mito-

chondria appear as round or elongated particles scattered throughout the cytoplasm. The internal ultrastructure reveals that a single mitochondrion consists of a smooth, continuous outer membrane that forms the external contour, and an inner, folded membrane nestled neatly within the outer membrane **(figure 5.12).** The folds on the inner membrane, called **cristae** (kris'-te), may be tubular, like fingers, or folded into shelflike bands.

The cristae membranes hold the enzymes and electron carriers of aerobic respiration. This is an oxygen-using process that extracts chemical energy contained in nutrient molecules and stores it in the form of high-energy molecules, or ATP. More detailed functions of mitochondria are covered in chapter 8. The spaces around the cristae are filled with a chemically complex fluid called the **matrix,** which holds ribosomes, DNA, and the pool of enzymes and other compounds involved in the metabolic cycle. Mitochondria (along with chloroplasts) are unique among organelles in that they divide independently of the cell, contain circular strands of DNA, and have prokaryotic-sized 70S ribosomes. These findings have prompted some intriguing speculations on their evolutionary origins (see Insight 5.1).

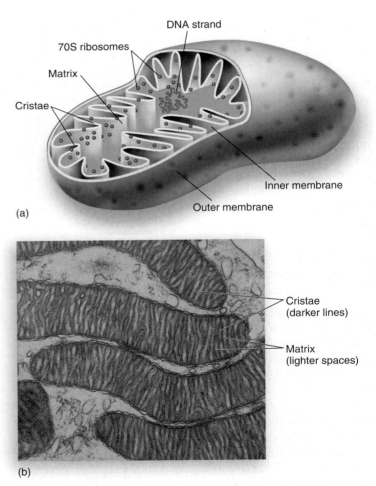

DNA strand

70S ribosomes

Matrix

Cristae

Inner membrane

Outer membrane

(a)

Cristae (darker lines)

Matrix (lighter spaces)

(b)

Figure 5.12 General structure of a mitochondrion. **(a)** A three-dimensional projection. **(b)** An electron micrograph. In most cells, mitochondria are elliptical or spherical, although in certain fungi, algae, and protozoa, they are long and filament-like.

Chloroplasts: Photosynthesis Machines

Chloroplasts are remarkable organelles found in algae and plant cells that are capable of converting the energy of sunlight into chemical energy through photosynthesis. The photosynthetic role of chloroplasts makes them the primary producers of organic nutrients upon which all other organisms (except certain bacteria) ultimately depend. Another important photosynthetic product of chloroplasts is oxygen gas. Although chloroplasts resemble mitochondria, chloroplasts are larger, contain special pigments, and are much more varied in shape.

There are differences among various algal chloroplasts, but most are generally composed of two membranes, one enclosing the other. There is a smooth, outer membrane in addition to an inner membrane. Inside the chloroplast is a third membrane folded into small, disclike sacs called **thylakoids** that are stacked upon one another into **grana.** These structures carry the green pigment chlorophyll and sometimes additional pigments as well. Surrounding the thylakoids is a ground substance called the **stroma (figure 5.13).** The role of the photosynthetic pigments is to absorb and transform solar energy into chemical energy, which is then used during reactions in the stroma to synthesize carbohydrates. We further explore some important aspects of photosynthesis in chapters 8 and 24.

Ribosomes: Protein Synthesizers

In an electron micrograph of a eukaryotic cell, ribosomes are numerous, tiny particles that give a "dotted" appearance to the cytoplasm. Ribosomes are distributed throughout the cell: Some are scattered freely in the cytoplasm and cytoskeleton; others are intimately associated with the rough endoplasmic reticulum as previously described. Still others appear inside the mitochondria and in chloroplasts. Multiple ribosomes are often found arranged in short chains called polyribosomes (polysomes). The basic structure of eukaryotic ribosomes is similar to that of prokaryotic ribosomes, described in chapter 4. Both are composed of large and small subunits of ribonucleoprotein (see figure 5.8). By contrast, however, the eukaryotic ribosome (except in the mitochondrion) is the larger 80S variety that is a combination of 60S and 40S subunits. As in the prokaryotes, eukaryotic ribosomes are the staging areas for protein synthesis.

The Cytoskeleton: A Support Network

The cytoplasm of a eukaryotic cell is crisscrossed by a flexible framework of molecules called the cytoskeleton **(figure 5.14).** This framework appears to have several functions, such as

Cell membrane
Actin filaments
Mitochondrion
Intermediate filaments
Endoplasmic reticulum
Microtubule

(a)

(b)

Figure 5.14 The cytoskeleton.   (a) Drawing of microtubules, actin filaments, and intermediate filaments. **(b)** Microtubules are dyed fluorescent green in this micrograph.

Chloroplast envelope (double membrane)
70S ribosomes
Stroma matrix
DNA strand
Granum
Thylakoids

Figure 5.13 Detail of an algal chloroplast.

anchoring organelles, moving RNA and vesicles, and permitting shape changes and movement in some cells. The three main types of cytoskeletal elements are *actin filaments, intermediate filaments,* and *microtubules.* **Actin filaments** are long thin protein strands about 7 nanometers in diameter. They are found throughout the cell but are most highly concentrated just inside the cell membrane. Actin filaments are responsible for cellular movements such as contraction, crawling, pinching during cell division, and formation of cellular extensions. **Microtubules** are long, hollow tubes that maintain the shape of eukaryotic cells without walls and transport substances from one part of a cell to another. The spindle fibers that play an essential role in mitosis are actually microtubules that attach to chromosomes and separate them into daughter cells. As indicated earlier, microtubules are also responsible for the movement of cilia and flagella. **Intermediate filaments** are ropelike structures that are about 10 nanometers in diameter. (Their name comes from their intermediate size, between actin filaments and microtubules.) Their main role is in structural reinforcement of the cell and of organelles. For example, they support the structure of the nuclear envelope.

Table 5.2 summarizes the differences between eukaryotic and prokaryotic cells. Viruses (discussed in chapter 6) are included as well.

Survey of Eukaryotic Microorganisms

With the general structure of the eukaryotic cell in mind, let us next examine the amazingly wide range of adaptations that this cell type has undergone. The following sections contain a general survey of the principal eukaryotic microorganisms—fungi, algae, protozoa, and parasitic worms—while also introducing elements of their structure, life history, classification, identification, and importance.

5.3 Learning Outcomes—Can You . . .

7. . . . describe the important component parts of a nucleus?
8. . . . diagram how the nucleus, endoplasmic reticulum, and Golgi apparatus, together with vesicles, act together?
9. . . . explain the function of the mitochondria?
10. . . . discuss the function of chloroplasts and explain which cells contain them and why?
11. . . . explain the importance of ribosomes and differentiate between eukaryotic and prokaryotic types?
12. . . . list and describe the three main fibers of the cytoskeleton?

Table 5.2 The Major Elements of Life and Their Primary Characteristics

Function or Structure	Characteristic*	Prokaryotic Cells	Eukaryotic Cells	Viruses**
Genetics	Nucleic acids	+	+	+
	Chromosomes	+	+	−
	True nucleus	−	+	−
	Nuclear envelope	−	+	−
Reproduction	Mitosis	−	+	−
	Production of sex cells	+/−	+	−
	Binary fission	+	+	−
Biosynthesis	Independent	+	+	−
	Golgi apparatus	−	+	−
	Endoplasmic reticulum	−	+	−
	Ribosomes	+***	+	−
Respiration	Mitochondria	−	+	−
Photosynthesis	Pigments	+/−	+/−	−
	Chloroplasts	−	+/−	−
Motility/locomotor structures	Flagella	+/−***	+/−	−
	Cilia	−	+/−	−
Shape/protection	Membrane	+	+	+/−
	Cell wall	+***	+/−	− (have capsids instead)
	Capsule	+/−	+/−	−
Complexity of function		+	+	+/−
Size (in general)		0.5–3 μm*****	2–100 μm	< 0.2 μm

*+ means most members of the group exhibit this characteristic; − means most lack it; +/− means some members have it and some do not.

**Viruses cannot participate in metabolic or genetic activity outside their host cells.

***The prokaryotic type is functionally similar to the eukaryotic, but structurally unique.

****Much smaller and much larger bacteria exist; see Insight 4.3.

A Note About the Taxonomy of Eukaryotic Cells

Exploring the origins of eukaryotic cells with molecular techniques has significantly clarified our understanding of relationships among the organisms in Domain Eukarya. The characteristics traditionally used for placing plants, animals, and fungi into separate kingdoms are general cell type, level of organization (body plan), and nutritional type. While it now appears that these criteria often do reflect accurate differences among these organisms and give rise to the same classifications as molecular techniques, in many cases the molecular data point to new and different classifications.

Because our understanding of the phylogenetic relationships is still in development, there is not yet a single official system of taxonomy for presenting all of the eukaryotes. This is especially true of the protists (which contain algae and protozoa). Genetic analysis has determined that this group, generally classified at the kingdom level, is far more diverse than previously appreciated and probably should instead be divided into several different kingdoms. Some organisms we call protists are more related to fungi than they are to other protists, for instance. For that reason, most scientists believe that the label "protist" is meaningless, taxonomically.

For the purposes of this book and your class, the term is still used as it refers to eukaryotes that are not plants, animals, or fungi. But be aware that the science is still developing.

5.4 The Kingdom of the Fungi

Although fungi were originally classified with the green plants (along with algae and bacteria), they were later separated from plants and placed in a group with algae and protozoa (the Protista). Even at that time, however, many microbiologists were struck by several unique qualities of fungi that warranted their being placed into their own separate kingdom, and eventually they were.

The Kingdom Fungi, or Myceteae, is large and filled with forms of great variety and complexity. For practical purposes, the approximately 100,000 species of fungi can be divided into two groups: the *macroscopic fungi* (mushrooms, puffballs, gill fungi) and the *microscopic fungi* (molds, yeasts). Although the majority of fungi are either unicellular or colonial, a few complex forms such as mushrooms and puffballs are considered multicellular. Cells of the microscopic fungi exist in two basic morphological types: yeasts and hyphae. A yeast cell is distinguished by its round to oval shape and by its mode of asexual reproduction. It grows swellings on its surface called buds, which then become separate cells. **Hyphae** (hy'-fee) are long, threadlike cells found in the bodies of filamentous fungi, or molds (**figure 5.15**). Some species form a **pseudohypha**, a chain of yeasts formed when buds remain attached in a row (**figure 5.16**). Because of its manner

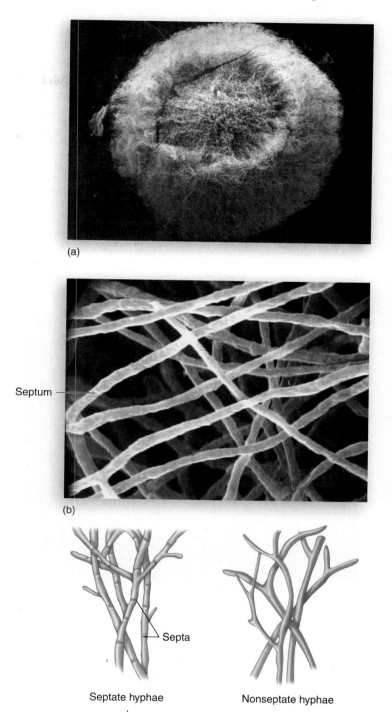

(a)

Septum

(b)

Septa

Septate hyphae — as in *Penicillium*

Nonseptate hyphae — as in *Rhizopus*

(c)

Figure 5.15 *Diplodia maydis*, **a pathogenic fungus of corn plants.** (a) Scanning electron micrograph of a single colony showing its filamentous texture (24×). (b) Close-up of hyphal structure (1,200×). (c) Basic structural types of hyphae.

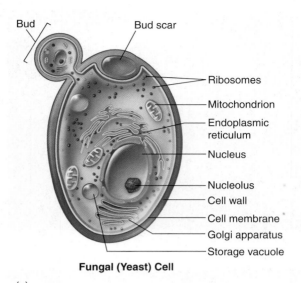

Bud — Bud scar

Ribosomes

Mitochondrion

Endoplasmic reticulum

Nucleus

Nucleolus

Cell wall

Cell membrane

Golgi apparatus

Storage vacuole

Fungal (Yeast) Cell

(a)

(b)

Bud

Nucleus

Bud scars

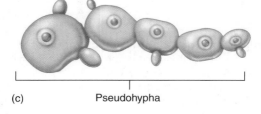

(c)   Pseudohypha

of formation, it is not a true hypha like that of molds. While some fungal cells exist only in a yeast form and others occur primarily as hyphae, a few, called **dimorphic,** can take either form, depending on growth conditions, such as changing temperature. This variability in growth form is particularly characteristic of some pathogenic molds.

Fungal Nutrition

All fungi are **heterotrophic.** They acquire nutrients from a wide variety of organic materials called **substrates (figure 5.17).** Most fungi are **saprobes,** meaning that they obtain these substrates from the remnants of dead plants and animals in soil or aquatic habitats. Fungi can also be **parasites** on the bodies of living animals or plants, although very few fungi absolutely require a living host. In general, the fungus penetrates the substrate and secretes enzymes that reduce it to small molecules that can be absorbed by the cells. Fungi have enzymes for digesting an incredible array of substances, including feathers, hair, cellulose, petroleum products, wood, and rubber. It has been said that every naturally occurring organic material on the earth can be attacked by some type of fungus. Fungi are often found in nutritionally poor or adverse environments. Various fungi thrive in substrates with high salt or sugar content, at relatively high temperatures, and even in snow and glaciers. Their medical and agricultural impact is extensive. A number of species cause **mycoses** (fungal infections) in animals, and thousands of species are important plant pathogens. Fungal toxins may cause disease in humans, and airborne fungi are a frequent cause of allergies and other medical conditions **(Insight 5.2).**

Organization of Microscopic Fungi

The cells of most microscopic fungi grow in loose associations or colonies. The colonies of yeasts are much like those of bacteria in that they have a soft, uniform texture and appearance. The colonies of filamentous fungi are noted for the striking cottony, hairy, or velvety textures that arise from their microscopic organization and morphology. The woven, intertwining mass of hyphae that makes up the body or colony of a mold is called a **mycelium.**

Although hyphae contain the usual eukaryotic organelles, they also have some unique organizational features. In most fungi, the hyphae are divided into segments by cross walls, or **septa,** a condition called septate (see figure 5.15c). The nature of the septa varies from solid partitions with no communication between the compartments to partial walls with small pores that allow the flow of organelles and nutrients

Figure 5.16 Microscopic morphology of yeasts. (a) General structure of a yeast cell, representing major organelles. Note the presence of a cell wall and lack of locomotor organelles. (b) Scanning electron micrograph of the brewer's, or baker's, yeast *Saccharomyces cerevisiae* (21,000×). (c) Formation and release of yeast buds and pseudohypha (a chain of budding yeast cells).

(a)

(b)

Figure 5.17 Nutritional sources (substrates) for fungi.   **(a)** A fungal mycelium growing on raspberries. The fine hyphal filaments and black sporangia are typical of *Rhizopus*. **(b)** The skin of the foot infected by a soil fungus, *Fonsecaea pedrosoi*.

between adjacent compartments. Nonseptate hyphae consist of one long, continuous cell *not* divided into individual compartments by cross walls. With this construction, the cytoplasm and organelles move freely from one region to another, and each hyphal element can have several nuclei.

Hyphae can also be classified according to their particular function. Vegetative hyphae (mycelia) are responsible for the visible mass of growth that appears on the surface of a substrate and penetrates it to digest and absorb nutrients. During the development of a fungal colony, the vegetative hyphae give rise to structures called reproductive, or fertile, hyphae, which branch off a vegetative mycelium. These hyphae are responsible for the production of fungal reproductive bodies called **spores.** Other specializations of hyphae are illustrated in **figure 5.18.**

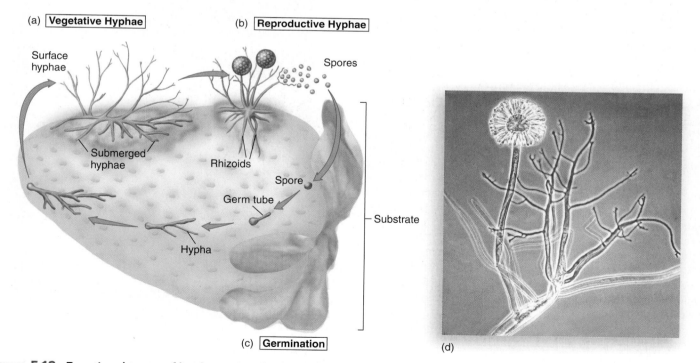

Figure 5.18 Functional types of hyphae using the mold *Rhizopus* as an example.   **(a)** Vegetative hyphae are those surface and submerged filaments that digest, absorb, and distribute nutrients from the substrate. This species also has special anchoring structures called rhizoids. **(b)** Later, as the mold matures, it sprouts reproductive hyphae that produce asexual spores. **(c)** During the asexual life cycle, the free mold spores settle on a substrate and send out germ tubes that elongate into hyphae. Through continued growth and branching, an extensive mycelium is produced. So prolific are the fungi that a single colony of mold can easily contain 5,000 spore-bearing structures. If each of these released 2,000 single spores and if every spore were able to germinate, we would soon find ourselves in a sea of mycelia. Most spores do not germinate, but enough are successful to keep the numbers of fungi and their spores very high in most habitats. **(d)** *Syncephalastrum* demonstrates all major stages in the life cycle of a zygomycota.

INSIGHT 5.2   Two Faces of Fungi

The importance of fungi in the ecological structure of the earth is well recognized. They are essential contributors to complex environments such as soil, and they play numerous beneficial roles as decomposers of organic debris and as partners to plants. Fungi also have great practical importance due to their metabolic versatility. They are productive sources of drugs (penicillin) to treat human infections and other diseases, and they are used in industry to ferment foods and synthesize organic chemicals.

The fact that fungi are so widespread also means that they frequently share human living quarters, especially in locations that provide ample moisture and nutrients. Often their presence is harmless and limited to a film of mildew on shower stalls or other moist environments. In some cases, depending on the amount of contamination and the type of mold, these indoor fungi can also give rise to various medical problems. Such common air contaminants as *Penicillium, Aspergillus, Cladosporium,* and *Stachybotrys* all have the capacity to give off airborne spores and toxins that, when inhaled, cause a whole spectrum of symptoms sometimes referred to as "sick building syndrome." (Sick building syndrome can also be caused by nonbiological factors, such as the formaldehyde in carpets and furniture.) The usual source of harmful fungi is the presence of chronically water-damaged walls, ceilings, and other building materials that have come to harbor these fungi. People exposed to these houses or buildings report symptoms that range from skin rash, flulike reactions, sore throat, and headaches to fatigue, diarrhea, allergies, and immune suppression. Recent reports of sick buildings have been on the rise, affecting thousands of people, and some deaths have been reported in small children. The control of indoor fungi requires correcting the moisture problem, removing the contaminated materials, and decontaminating the living spaces. Mycologists are currently studying the mechanisms of toxic effects with an aim to develop better diagnosis and treatment.

Fungal Law Enforcement?

Biologists are developing some rather imaginative uses for fungi as a way of controlling both the life and death of plants. Government biologists working for narcotic control agencies have unveiled a recent plan to use fungi to kill unwanted plants. The main targets would be plants grown to produce illegal drugs like cocaine and heroin in the hopes of cutting down on these drugs right at the source. A fungus infection (*Fusarium*) that wiped out 30% of the coca crop in Peru dramatically demonstrated how effective this might be. Since then, at least two other fungi that could destroy opium poppies and marijuana plants have been isolated.

Purposefully releasing plant pathogens such as *Fusarium* into the environment has stirred a great deal of controversy. Critics in South America emphasize that even if the fungus appears specific to a particular plant, there is too much potential for it to switch hosts to food and ornamental plants and wreak havoc with the ecosystem. United States biologists who support the plan of using fungal control agents say that it is not as dangerous as massive spraying with pesticides, and that extensive laboratory tests have

(a)

(b)

(a) *Stachybotrys chartarum* hyphae and spores. **(b)** Drywall and wallpaper that have been colonized by mold.

proved that the species of fungi being used will be very specific to the illegal drug plants and will not affect close relatives. Some call it biological warfare; others call it an innovative combination of science and law enforcement. What do you think?

Reproductive Strategies and Spore Formation

Fungi have many complex and successful reproductive strategies. Most can propagate by the simple outward growth of existing hyphae or by fragmentation, in which a separated piece of mycelium can generate a whole new colony. But the primary reproductive mode of fungi involves the production of various types of spores. (Do not confuse fungal spores with the more resistant, nonreproductive bacterial spores.) Fungal spores are responsible not only for multiplication but also for survival, producing genetic variation, and dissemination. Because of their compactness and relatively light weight, spores are dispersed widely through the environment by air, water, and living things. Upon encountering a favorable substrate, a spore will germinate and produce a new fungus colony in a very short time (see figure 5.18).

The fungi exhibit such a marked diversity in spores that they are largely classified and identified by their spores and spore-forming structures. There are elaborate systems for naming and classifying spores, but we won't cover them. The most general subdivision is based on the way the spores arise. Asexual spores are the products of mitotic division of a single parent cell, and sexual spores are formed through a process involving the fusing of two parental nuclei followed by meiosis.

Asexual Spore Formation

There are two subtypes of asexual spore, **sporangiospores** and **conidiospores,** also called conidia **(figure 5.19):**

1. Sporangiospores **(figure 5.19*a*)** are formed by successive cleavages within a saclike head called a **sporangium,** which is attached to a stalk, the sporangiophore. These spores are initially enclosed but are released when the sporangium ruptures.
2. Conidiospores, or **conidia,** are free spores not enclosed by a spore-bearing sac. They develop either by the pinching off of the tip of a special fertile hypha or by the segmentation of a preexisting vegetative hypha. There are many different forms of conidia, illustrated in **figure 5.19*b*.**

Sexual Spore Formation

Fungi can propagate themselves successfully with their millions of asexual spores. That being the case, what is the function of their sexual spores? The answer lies in important variations that occur when fungi of different genetic makeup combine their genetic material. Just as in plants and animals, this linking of genes from two parents creates offspring with

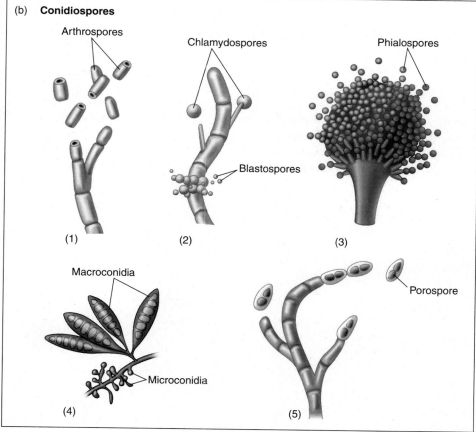

Figure 5.19 Types of asexual mold spores. **(a)** Sporangiospores: (1) *Absidia,* (2) *Syncephalastrum.* **(b)** Conidial variations: (1) arthrospores (e.g., *Coccidioides*), (2) chlamydospores and blastospores (e.g., *Candida albicans*), (3) phialospores (e.g., *Aspergillus*), (4) macroconidia and microconidia (e.g., *Microsporum*), and (5) porospores (e.g., *Alternaria*).

combinations of genes different from that of either parent. The offspring from such a union can have slight variations in form and function that are potentially advantageous in the adaptation and survival of their species.

The majority of fungi produce sexual spores at some point. The nature of this process varies from the simple fusion of fertile hyphae of two different strains to a complex union of differentiated male and female structures and the development of special fruiting structures. It may be a surprise to discover that the fleshy part of a mushroom is actually a fruiting body designed to protect and help disseminate its sexual spores.

Fungal Identification and Cultivation

Fungi are identified in medical specimens by first being isolated on special types of media and then being observed macroscopically and microscopically. Because the fungi are classified into general groups by the presence and type of sexual spores, it would seem logical to identify them in the same way, but sexual spores are rarely if ever detected in the laboratory setting. As a result, the asexual spore-forming structures and spores are usually used to identify organisms to the level of genus and species. Other characteristics that contribute to identification are hyphal type, colony texture and pigmentation, physiological characteristics, and genetic makeup. Even as bacterial and viral identification relies increasingly on molecular techniques, fungi are some of the most strikingly beautiful life forms, and their appearance under the microscope is still heavily relied on to identify them (figure 5.20a,b).

The Roles of Fungi in Nature and Industry

Nearly all fungi are free-living and do not require a host to complete their life cycles. Even among those fungi that are pathogenic, most human infection occurs through accidental contact with an environmental source such as soil, water, or dust. Humans are generally quite resistant to fungal infection, except for two main types of fungal pathogens: the primary pathogens, which can sicken even healthy persons, and the opportunistic pathogens, which attack persons who are already weakened in some way. So far, about 270 species of fungi have been found to be able to cause human disease.

Mycoses (fungal infections) vary in the way the agent enters the body and the degree of tissue involvement (table 5.3). The list of opportunistic fungal pathogens has been increasing in the past few years because of newer medical techniques that keep immunocompromised patients alive. Even so-called harmless species found in the air and dust around us may be able to cause opportunistic infections in patients who already have AIDS, cancer, or diabetes (see Insight 21.2 in chapter 21).

Fungi are involved in other medical conditions besides infections (see Insight 5.2). Fungal cell walls give off chemical substances that can cause allergies. The toxins produced by poisonous mushrooms can induce neurological disturbances and even death. The mold *Aspergillus flavus* synthesizes a potentially lethal poison called aflatoxin, which is the cause of a disease in domestic animals that have eaten grain contaminated with the mold and is also a cause of liver cancer in humans.

Fungi pose an ever-present economic hindrance to the agricultural industry. A number of species are pathogenic to field plants such as corn and grain, and fungi also rot fresh produce during shipping and storage. It has been estimated that as much as 40% of the yearly fruit crop is consumed not by humans but by fungi. On the beneficial side, however, fungi play an essential role in decomposing organic matter and returning essential minerals to the soil. They form stable associations with plant roots (mycorrhizae) that increase the ability of the roots to absorb water and nutrients. Industry has tapped the biochemical potential of fungi to produce large quantities of antibiotics, alcohol, organic acids, and vitamins. Some fungi are eaten or used to impart flavorings to food. The yeast *Saccharomyces* produces the alcohol in beer and wine and the gas that causes bread to rise. Blue cheese, soy sauce, and cured meats derive their unique flavors from the actions of fungi (see chapter 25).

(a)

(b)

Figure 5.20 Representative fungi. **(a)** *Circinella*, a fungus associated with soil and decaying nuts. **(b)** *Aspergillus*, a ubiquitous environmental fungus that can be associated with human disease.

Table 5.3 Major Fungal Infections of Humans

Degree of Tissue Involvement and Area Affected	Name of Infection	Name of Causative Fungus
Superficial (not deeply invasive)		
Outer epidermis	Tinea versicolor	*Malassezia furfur*
Epidermis, hair, and dermis can be attacked.	Dermatophytosis, also called tinea or ringworm of the scalp, body, feet (athlete's foot), toenails	*Microsporum, Trichophyton,* and *Epidermophyton*
Mucous membranes, skin, nails	Candidiasis, or yeast infection	*Candida albicans*
Systemic (deep; organism enters lungs; can invade other organs)		
Lung	Coccidioidomycosis (San Joaquin Valley fever)	*Coccidioides immitis dermatitidis*
	North American blastomycosis (Chicago disease)	*Blastomyces*
	Histoplasmosis (Ohio Valley fever)	*Histoplasma capsulatum*
	Cryptococcosis (torulosis)	*Cryptococcus neoformans*
Lung, skin	Paracoccidioidomycosis (South American blastomycosis)	*Paracoccidioides brasiliensis*

5.4 Learning Outcomes—Can You ...

13. ... list some general features of fungal anatomy?
14. ... differentiate among the terms heterotroph, saprobe, and parasite?
15. ... connect the concepts of fungal hyphae and a mycelium?
16. ... describe two ways in which fungal spores arise?
17. ... list two detrimental and two beneficial activities of fungi (from the viewpoint of humans)?

5.5 The Protists

The algae and protozoa have been traditionally combined into the Kingdom Protista. The two major taxonomic categories of this kingdom are Subkingdom Algae and Subkingdom Protozoa. Although these general types of microbes are now known to occupy several kingdoms, it is still useful to retain the concept of a protist as any unicellular or colonial organism that lacks true tissues. We will only briefly mention algae, as they do not cause human infections for the most part.

The Algae: Photosynthetic Protists

The **algae** are a group of photosynthetic organisms usually recognized by their larger members, such as seaweeds and kelps. In addition to being beautifully colored and diverse in appearance, they vary in length from a few micrometers to 100 meters. Algae occur in unicellular, colonial, and filamentous forms, and the larger forms can possess tissues and simple organs. **Figure 5.21** depicts various types of algae. Algal cells as a group exhibit all of the eukaryotic organelles. The most noticeable of these are the chloroplasts, which contain, in addition to the

(a)

(b)

(c)

Figure 5.21   Representative microscopic algae.   **(a)** *Spirogyra,* a colonial filamentous form with spiral chloroplasts. **(b)** A collection of beautiful algae called diatoms shows the intricate and varied structure of their silica cell walls. **(c)** *Pfiesteria piscicida.* Although it is free-living, it is known to parasitize fish and release potent toxins that kill fish and sicken humans.

green pigment chlorophyll, a number of other pigments that create the yellow, red, and brown coloration of some groups.

Algae are widespread inhabitants of fresh and marine waters. They are one of the main components of the large floating community of microscopic organisms called **plankton.** In this capacity, they play an essential role in the aquatic food web and produce most of the earth's oxygen. Other algal habitats include the surface of soil, rocks, and plants, and several species are even hardy enough to live in hot springs or snowbanks.

Animal tissues would be rather inhospitable to algae, so algae are rarely infectious. One exception is *Prototheca*, an unusual nonphotosynthetic alga, which has been associated with skin and subcutaneous infections in humans and animals.

The primary medical threat from algae is due to a type of food poisoning caused by the toxins of certain marine algae. During particular seasons of the year, the overgrowth of these motile algae imparts a brilliant red color to the water, which is referred to as a "red tide." When intertidal animals feed, their bodies accumulate toxins given off by the algae that can persist for several months. Paralytic shellfish poisoning is caused by eating exposed clams or other invertebrates. It is marked by severe neurological symptoms and can be fatal. Ciguatera is another serious intoxication caused by algal toxins that have accumulated in fish such as bass and mackerel. Cooking does not destroy the toxin, and there is no antidote.

Several episodes of a severe infection caused by *Pfiesteria piscicida*, a toxic algal form, have been reported over the past several years in the United States. The disease was first reported in fish and was later transmitted to humans. This newly identified species occurs in at least 20 forms, including spores, cysts, and amoebas (see figure 5.21*c*), that can release potent toxins. Both fish and humans develop neurological symptoms and bloody skin lesions. The cause of the epidemic has been traced to nutrient-rich agricultural runoff water that promoted the sudden "bloom" of *Pfiesteria*. These microbes first attacked and killed millions of fish and later people whose occupations exposed them to fish and contaminated water.

Biology of the Protozoa

If a poll were taken to choose the most engrossing and vivid group of microorganisms, many biologists would choose the protozoa. Although their name comes from the Greek for "first animals," they are far from being simple, primitive organisms. The protozoa constitute a very large group (about 65,000 species) of creatures that although single-celled, have startling properties when it comes to movement, feeding, and behavior. Although most members of this group are harmless, free-living inhabitants of water and soil, a few species are parasites collectively responsible for hundreds of millions of infections of humans each year. Before we consider a few examples of important pathogens, let us examine some general aspects of protozoan biology, remembering that the term "protozoan" is more of a convenience than an accurate taxonomic designation. As we describe them in the next paragraph, you will see why they are categorized together. It is because of their similar physical characteristics rather than their genetic relatedness, as it turns out.

Case File 5   *Continuing the Case*

Shortly after the 2005 shellfish harvesting closure, the Oregon Harmful Algal Bloom Monitoring Project was initiated. The project monitors water at five locations along the Oregon coast, retrieving samples every week or two (depending on the site) and examining each sample for the presence of algal species that produce domoic acid or saxitoxin. When sudden blooms lead to high levels of harmful algae, specific harvesting controls can be instituted. In Oregon, beaches are closed to clamming when domoic acid levels reach 20 parts per million (ppm) in randomly selected clams. Projects like this operate throughout the United States to ensure the safety of harvested seafood.

Officials try to keep harvest control measures as geographically limited and short-lived as possible. On June 21, 2006, due in part to ongoing water sampling by the Oregon Harmful Bloom Monitoring Project, the entire Oregon coast was opened to razor clamming for the first time in 4 years (although short stretches of beach were temporarily closed later in the summer).

- Several months after beaches are closed to clamming, the same beaches can be declared safe and reopened. Why are unsafe clams later deemed safe?

Protozoan Form and Function

Most protozoan cells are single cells containing the major eukaryotic organelles except chloroplasts. Their organelles can be highly specialized for feeding, reproduction, and locomotion. The cytoplasm is usually divided into a clear outer layer called the **ectoplasm** and a granular inner region called the **endoplasm.** Ectoplasm is involved in locomotion, feeding, and protection. Endoplasm houses the nucleus, mitochondria, and food and contractile vacuoles. Some ciliates and flagellates[4] even have organelles that work somewhat like a primitive nervous system to coordinate movement. Because protozoa lack a cell wall, they have a certain amount of flexibility. Their outer boundary is a cell membrane that regulates the movement of food, wastes, and secretions. Cell shape can remain constant (as in most ciliates) or can change constantly (as in amoebas). Certain amoebas (foraminiferans) encase themselves in hard shells made of calcium carbonate. The size of most protozoan cells falls within the range of 3 to 300 μm. Some notable exceptions are giant amoebas and ciliates that are large enough (3 to 4 mm in length) to be seen swimming in pond water.

Nutritional and Habitat Range   Protozoa are heterotrophic and usually require their food in a complex organic form. Free-living species scavenge dead plant or animal debris and even graze on live cells of bacteria and algae. Some species have special feeding structures such as oral grooves, which carry food particles into a passageway or gullet that packages

---

4. The terms *ciliate* and *flagellate* are common names of protozoan groups that move by means of cilia and flagella.

the captured food into vacuoles for digestion. Some protozoa absorb food directly through the cell membrane. Parasitic species live on the fluids of their host, such as plasma and digestive juices, or they can actively feed on tissues.

Although protozoa have adapted to a wide range of habitats, their main limiting factor is the availability of moisture. Their predominant habitats are fresh and marine water, soil, plants, and animals. Even extremes in temperature and pH are not a barrier to their existence; hardy species are found in hot springs, ice, and habitats with low or high pH. Many protozoa can convert to a resistant, dormant stage called a cyst.

Styles of Locomotion Except for one group (the Apicomplexa), protozoa can move through fluids by means of **pseudopods** ("false feet"), **flagella,** or **cilia.** A few species have both pseudopods (also called pseudopodia) and flagella. Some unusual protozoa move by a gliding or twisting movement that does not appear to involve any of these locomotor structures. Pseudopods are blunt, branched, or long and pointed, depending on the particular species. The flowing action of the pseudopods results in amoeboid motion, and pseudopods also serve as feeding structures in many amoebas. (The structure and behavior of flagella and cilia were discussed in the first section of this chapter.) Flagella vary in number from one to several, and in certain species they are attached along the length of the cell by an extension of the cytoplasmic membrane called the *undulating membrane* (**figure 5.22a**). In most ciliates, the cilia are distributed over the entire surface of the cell in characteristic patterns. Because of the tremendous variety in ciliary arrangements and functions, ciliates are among the most diverse and awesome cells in the biological world. In certain protozoa, cilia line the oral groove and function in feeding; in others, they fuse together to form stiff props that serve as primitive rows of walking legs.

Figure 5.22 Examples of the four types of locomotion in protozoa. (a) Mastigophora: *Trichomonas vaginalis,* displaying flagella. (b) Sarcodina: *Amoeba,* with pseudopods. (c) Ciliophora: *Stentor,* displaying cilia. (d) Sporozoan: *Cryptosporidium.* Sporozoa have no specialized locomotion organelles.

Life Cycles and Reproduction   Most protozoa can be recognized in their motile feeding stage called the **trophozoite.** This is a stage that requires ample food and moisture to remain active. A large number of species are also capable of entering into a dormant, resting stage called a **cyst** when conditions in the environment become unfavorable for growth and feeding. During *encystment,* the trophozoite cell rounds up into a sphere, and its ectoplasm secretes a tough, thick cuticle around the cell membrane **(figure 5.23).** Because cysts are more resistant than ordinary cells to heat, drying, and chemicals, they can survive adverse periods. They can be dispersed by air currents and may even be an important factor in the spread of diseases such as amoebic dysentery. If provided with moisture and nutrients, a cyst breaks open and releases the active trophozoite.

The life cycles of protozoans vary from simple to complex. Several protozoan groups exist only in the trophozoite state. Many alternate between a trophozoite and a cyst stage, depending on the conditions of the habitat. The life cycle of a parasitic protozoan dictates its mode of transmission to other hosts. For example, the flagellate *Trichomonas vaginalis* causes a common sexually transmitted disease. Because it does not form cysts, it is more delicate and must be transmitted by intimate contact between sexual partners. In contrast, intestinal pathogens such as *Entamoeba histolytica* and *Giardia lamblia* form cysts and are readily transmitted in contaminated water and foods.

All protozoa reproduce by relatively simple, asexual methods, usually mitotic cell division. Several parasitic species, including the agents of malaria and toxoplasmosis, reproduce asexually by multiple fission inside a host cell. Sexual reproduction also occurs during the life cycle of most protozoa. Ciliates participate in **conjugation,** a form of genetic exchange in which two cells fuse temporarily and exchange micronuclei. This process of sexual recombination yields new and different genetic combinations that can be advantageous in evolution.

Classification of Selected Important Protozoa

As has been stated, taxonomists have problems classifying protozoa. They are very diverse and frequently frustrate attempts to generalize or place them in neat groupings. We will use a common and simple system of four groups, based on method of motility, mode of reproduction, and stages in the life cycle, summarized here and in figure 5.22.

The Mastigophora (Also Called Zoomastigophora) Motility is primarily by flagella alone or by both flagellar and amoeboid motion. Single nucleus. Sexual reproduction, when present, by syngamy; division by longitudinal fission. Several parasitic forms lack mitochondria and Golgi apparatus. Most species form cysts and are free-living; the group also includes several parasites. Some species

Figure 5.23 The general life cycle exhibited by many protozoa.   All protozoa have a trophozoite form, but not all produce cysts.

Trophozoite
(active, feeding stage)

Trophozoite
is reactivated

Cell rounds up,
loses motility

Drying, lack
of nutrients

Cyst wall
breaks open

Moisture,
nutrients restored

Early cyst wall
formation

Mature cyst
(dormant, resting stage)

are found in loose aggregates or colonies, but most are solitary. Members include: *Trypanosoma* and *Leishmania*, important blood pathogens spread by insect vectors; *Giardia*, an intestinal parasite spread in water contaminated with feces; *Trichomonas*, a parasite of the reproductive tract of humans spread by sexual contact (figure 5.22*a*).

The Sarcodina (Amoebas)   Cell form is primarily an amoeba **(figure 5.22*b*)**. Major locomotor organelles are pseudopods, although some species have flagellated reproductive states. Asexual reproduction by fission. Two groups have an external shell; mostly uninucleate; usually encyst. Most amoebas are free-living and not infectious; *Entamoeba* is a pathogen or parasite of humans; shelled amoebas called foraminifera and radiolarians are responsible for chalk deposits in the ocean.

The Ciliophora (Ciliated)   Trophozoites are motile by cilia; some have cilia in tufts for feeding and attachment; most develop cysts; have both macronuclei and micronuclei; division by transverse fission; most have a definite mouth and feeding organelle; show relatively advanced behavior **(figure 5.22*c*)**. The majority of ciliates are free-living and harmless.

The Apicomplexa (Sporozoa)   Motility is absent in most cells except male gametes. Life cycles are complex, with well-developed asexual and sexual stages. Sporozoa produce special sporelike cells called **sporozoites (figure 5.22*d*)** following sexual reproduction, which are important in transmission of infections; most form thick-walled zygotes called oocysts; entire group is parasitic. *Plasmodium*, the most prevalent protozoan parasite, causes 100 million to 300 million cases of malaria each year worldwide. It is an intracellular parasite with a complex cycle alternating between humans and mosquitoes. *Toxoplasma gondii* causes an acute infection (toxoplasmosis) in humans, which is acquired from cats and other animals.

Just as with the prokaryotes and other eukaryotes, protozoans that cause disease produce symptoms in different organ systems. These diseases are covered in chapters 18 through 23.

Protozoan Identification and Cultivation

The unique appearance of most protozoa makes it possible for a knowledgeable person to identify them to the level of genus and often species by microscopic morphology alone. Characteristics to consider in identification include the shape and size of the cell; the type, number, and distribution of locomotor structures; the presence of special organelles or cysts; and the number of nuclei. Medical specimens taken from blood, sputum, cerebrospinal fluid, feces, or the vagina are smeared directly onto a slide and observed with or without special stains. Occasionally, protozoa are cultivated on artificial media or in laboratory animals for further identification or study.

Important Protozoan Pathogens

Although protozoan infections are very common, they are actually caused by only a small number of species often restricted geographically to the tropics and subtropics **(table 5.4)**. In this section, we look at an example of a very

Table 5.4   Major Pathogenic Protozoa

Protozoan	Disease	Reservoir/Source
Amoeboid Protozoa		
Entamoeba histolytica	Amoebiasis (intestinal and other symptoms)	Humans, water and food
Naegleria, Acanthamoeba	Brain infection	Free-living in water
Ciliated Protozoa		
Balantidium coli	Balantidiosis (intestinal and other symptoms)	Pigs, cattle
Flagellated Protozoa		
Giardia lamblia	Giardiasis (intestinal distress)	Animals, water and food
Trichomonas vaginalis	Trichomoniasis (vaginal symptoms)	Human
Trypanosoma brucei, T. cruzi	Trypanosomiasis (intestinal distress and widespread organ damage)	Animals, vector-borne
Leishmania donovani, L. tropica, L. brasiliensis	Leishmaniasis (either skin lesions or widespread involvement of internal organs)	Animals, vector-borne
Apicomplexan Protozoa		
Plasmodium vivax, P. falciparum, P. malariae	Malaria (cardiovascular and other symptoms)	Human, vector-borne
Toxoplasma gondii	Toxoplasmosis (flulike illness)	Animals, vector-borne
Cryptosporidium	Cryptosporidiosis (intestinal and other symptoms)	Free-living, water, food
Cyclospora cayetanensis	Cyclosporiasis (intestinal and other symptoms)	Water, fresh produce

common protozoan disease that illustrates some of the main features of protozoan diseases.

The study of protozoa and helminths is sometimes called *parasitology.* Although a parasite can technically be any organism that obtains food and other requirements at the expense of a host, the term *parasite* is most often used to denote protozoan and helminth pathogens.

Pathogenic Flagellate: Trypanosomes Trypanosomes are protozoa belonging to the genus *Trypanosoma* (try-pan"-oh-soh'-mah). The two most important representatives are *T. brucei* and *T. cruzi,* species that are closely related but geographically restricted. *Trypanosoma brucei* occurs in Africa, where it causes approximately 35,000 new cases of sleeping sickness each year (see chapter 19). *Trypanosoma cruzi,* the cause of Chagas disease,[5] is endemic to South and Central America, where it infects several million people a year. Both species have long, crescent-shaped cells with a single flagellum that is sometimes attached to the cell body by an undulating membrane. Both are found in the blood during infection and are transmitted by blood-sucking vectors. We use *T. cruzi* to illustrate the phases of a trypanosomal life cycle and to demonstrate the complexity of parasitic relationships.

The trypanosome of Chagas disease relies on the close relationship of a warm-blooded mammal and an insect that feeds on mammalian blood. The mammalian hosts are numerous, including dogs, cats, opossums, armadillos, and foxes. The vector is the *reduviid* (ree-doo'-vee-id) *bug,* an insect that is sometimes called the "kissing bug" because of its habit of biting its host at the corner of the mouth. Transmission occurs from bug to mammal and from mammal to bug, but usually not from mammal to mammal, except across the placenta during pregnancy. The general phases of this cycle are presented in **figure 5.24.**

The trypanosome trophozoite multiplies in the intestinal tract of the reduviid bug and is harbored in the feces. The bug seeks a host and bites the mucous membranes, usually of the eye, nose, or lips. As it fills with blood, the bug defecates on the bite site and contaminates it with feces containing the trypanosome. Ironically, the victims themselves inadvertently contribute to the entry of the microbe by scratching the bite wound. The trypanosomes ultimately become established and multiply in muscle and white blood cells. Periodically, these parasitized cells rupture, releasing large numbers of new trophozoites into the blood. Eventually, the trypanosome can spread to many systems, including the lymphoid organs, heart, liver, and brain. Manifestations of the resultant disease range from mild to very severe and include fever, inflammation, and heart and brain damage. In many cases, the disease has an extended course and can cause death.

5. Named for Carlos Chagas, the discoverer of *T. cruzi.*

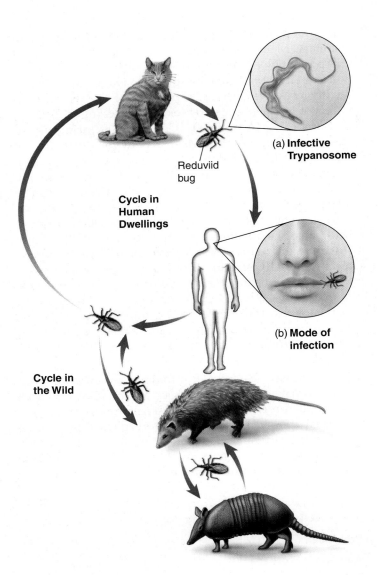

Figure 5.24 Cycle of transmission in Chagas disease.
Trypanosomes (inset *a*) are transmitted among mammalian hosts and human hosts by means of a bite from the kissing bug (inset *b*).

(a) Infective Trypanosome

Reduviid bug

Cycle in Human Dwellings

(b) Mode of infection

Cycle in the Wild

Infective Amoebas: *Entamoeba* Several species of amoebas cause disease in humans, but probably the most common disease is amoebiasis, or amoebic dysentery, caused by *Entamoeba histolytica* (see chapter 22). This microbe is widely distributed in the world, from northern zones to the tropics, and is nearly always associated with humans. Amoebic dysentery is the fourth most common protozoan infection in the world. This microbe has a life cycle quite different from the trypanosomes in that it does not involve multiple hosts and a blood-sucking vector. It lives part of its cycle as a trophozoite and part as a cyst. Because the cyst is the more resistant form and can survive in water and soil for several weeks, it is the more important stage for transmission. The primary way that people become infected is by ingesting food or water contaminated with human feces.

5.5 Learning Outcomes—Can You ...

18. ... use protozoan characteristics to explain why they are informally placed into a single group?

19. ... list three means of locomotion by protozoa?

20. ... explain why a cyst stage might be useful?

21. ... give an example of a disease caused by each of the four types of protozoa?

5.6 The Parasitic Helminths

Tapeworms, flukes, and roundworms are collectively called helminths, from the Greek word meaning worm. Adult animals are usually large enough to be seen with the naked eye, and they range from the longest tapeworms, measuring up to about 25 m in length, to roundworms less than 1 mm in length. Nevertheless, they are included among microorganisms because of their infective abilities and because the microscope is necessary to identify their eggs and larvae.

On the basis of body type, the two major groups of parasitic helminths are the flatworms (Phylum Platyhelminthes) and the roundworms (Phylum Aschelminthes, also called **nematodes**). Flatworms have a very thin, often segmented body plan **(figure 5.25)**, and roundworms have an elongate, cylindrical, unsegmented body **(figure 5.26)**. The flatworm group is subdivided into the **cestodes,** or tapeworms, named for their long, ribbonlike arrangement, and the **trematodes,** or flukes, characterized by flat, ovoid bodies. Not all flatworms and roundworms are parasites by nature; many live free in soil and water. Because most disease-causing helminths spend part of their lives in the gastrointestinal tract, they are discussed in chapter 22.

Figure 5.25 Parasitic flatworms. **(a)** A cestode (tapeworm), showing the scolex; long, tapelike body; and magnified views of immature and mature proglottids (body segments). **(b)** Actual tapeworm. **(c)** The structure of a trematode (liver fluke). Note the suckers that attach to host tissue and the dominance of reproductive and digestive organs. **(d)** Actual liver fluke.

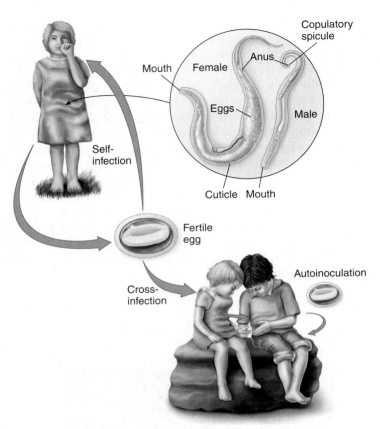

Figure 5.26 The life cycle of the pinworm, a roundworm. Eggs are the infective stage and are transmitted by unclean hands. Children frequently reinfect themselves and also pass the parasite on to others.

General Worm Morphology

All helminths are multicellular animals equipped to some degree with organs and organ systems. In parasitic helminths, the most developed organs are those of the reproductive tract, with some degree of reduction in the digestive, excretory, nervous, and muscular systems. In particular groups, such as the cestodes, reproduction is so dominant that the worms are reduced to little more than a series of flattened sacs filled with ovaries, testes, and eggs (see figure 5.25a,b). Not all worms have such extreme adaptations as cestodes, but most have a highly developed reproductive potential, thick cuticles for protection, and mouth glands for breaking down the host's tissue (figure 5.25c).

Life Cycles and Reproduction

The complete life cycle of helminths includes the fertilized egg (embryo), larval, and adult stages. In the majority of helminths, adults derive nutrients and reproduce sexually in a host's body. In nematodes, the sexes are separate and usually different in appearance; in trematodes, the sexes can be either separate or **hermaphroditic,** meaning that male and female sex organs are in the same worm; cestodes are generally hermaphroditic. For a parasite's continued survival as a species, it must complete the life cycle by transmitting an infective form, usually an egg or larva, to the body of another host, either of the same or a different species. The host in which larval development occurs is the intermediate (secondary) host, and adulthood and mating occur in the **definitive (final) host.** A transport host is an intermediate host that experiences no parasitic development but is an essential link in the completion of the cycle.

In general, sources for human infection are contaminated food, soil, and water or infected animals, and routes of infection are by oral intake or penetration of unbroken skin. Humans are the definitive hosts for many of the parasites listed in **table 5.5,** and in about half the diseases, they are also the sole biological reservoir. In other cases, animals or insect vectors serve as reservoirs or are required to complete worm development. In the majority of helminth infections, the worms must leave their host to complete the entire life cycle.

Fertilized eggs are usually released to the environment and are provided with a protective shell and extra food to aid their development into larvae. Even so, most eggs and larvae are vulnerable to heat, cold, drying, and predators and are destroyed or unable to reach a new host. To counteract this formidable mortality rate, certain worms have adapted a reproductive capacity that borders on the incredible: A single female *Ascaris*[6] can lay 200,000 eggs a day, and a large female can contain over 25 million eggs at varying stages of development! If only a tiny number of these eggs makes it to another host, the parasite will have been successful in completing its life cycle.

A Helminth Cycle: The Pinworm

To illustrate a helminth cycle in humans, we use the example of a roundworm, *Enterobius vermicularis,* the pinworm or seatworm. This worm causes a very common infestation of the large intestine. Worms range from 2 to 12 mm long and have a tapered, curved cylinder shape (see figure 5.26). The condition they cause, enterobiasis, is usually a simple, uncomplicated infection that does not spread beyond the intestine.

A cycle starts when a person swallows microscopic eggs picked up from another infected person by direct contact or by touching articles that person has touched. The eggs hatch in the intestine and then release larvae that mature into adult worms within about 1 month. Male and female worms mate, and the female migrates out to the anus to deposit eggs, which cause intense itchiness that is relieved by scratching. Herein lies a significant means of dispersal: Scratching contaminates the fingers, which, in turn, transfer eggs to bedclothes and other inanimate objects. This person becomes a host and a source of eggs and can spread them to others in addition to reinfesting himself. Enterobiasis occurs most often among families and in other close living situations. Its distribution is worldwide among all socioeconomic groups, but it seems to attack younger people more frequently than older ones.

---

6. *Ascaris* is a genus of parasitic intestinal roundworms.

Table 5.5 Examples of Helminths and Their Modes of Transmission

Classification	Common Name of Disease or Worm	Life Cycle Requirement	Spread to Humans By
Roundworms			
Nematodes			Ingestion
Intestinal Nematodes			
Infective in egg (embryo) stage			
Ascaris lumbricoides	Ascariasis	Humans	Fecal pollution of soil with eggs
Enterobius vermicularis	Pinworm	Humans	Close contact
Infective in larval stage			
Trichinella spiralis	Trichina worm	Pigs, wild mammals	Consumption of meat containing larvae
Tissue Nematodes			Burrowing of larva into tissue
Onchocerca volvulus	River blindness	Humans, black flies	Fly bite
Dracunculus medinensis	Guinea worm	Humans and *Cyclops* (an aquatic invertebrate)	Ingestion of water containing *Cyclops*
Flatworms			
Trematodes	Blood fluke	Humans and snails	Ingestion of fresh water containing larval stage
Schistosoma japonicum			
Cestodes			
Taenia solium	Pork tapeworm	Humans, swine	Consumption of undercooked or raw pork
Diphyllobothrium latum	Fish tapeworm	Humans, fish	Consumption of undercooked or raw fish

Helminth Classification and Identification

The helminths are classified according to their shape; their size; the degree of development of various organs; the presence of hooks, suckers, or other special structures; the mode of reproduction; the kinds of hosts; and the appearance of eggs and larvae. They are identified in the laboratory by microscopic detection of the adult worm or its larvae and eggs, which often have distinctive shapes or external and internal structures. Occasionally, they are cultured in order to verify all of the life stages.

Distribution and Importance of Parasitic Worms

About 50 species of helminths parasitize humans. They are distributed in all areas of the world that support human life. Some worms are restricted to a given geographic region, and many have a higher incidence in tropical areas. This knowledge must be tempered with the realization that jet-age travel, along with human migration, is gradually changing the patterns of worm infections, especially of those species that do not require alternate hosts or special climatic conditions for development. The yearly estimate of worldwide cases numbers in the billions, and these are not confined to developing countries. A conservative estimate places 50 million helminth infections in North America alone. The primary targets are malnourished children.

You have now learned about the variety of organisms that microbiologists study and classify. And as you've seen, many such organisms are capable of causing disease. In chapter 6, you'll learn about the "not-quite-organisms" that can cause disease, namely, viruses.

5.6 Learning Outcomes—Can You ...

22. ... list the two major groups of helminths and then the two subgroups of one of these groups?
23. ... describe a typical helminth lifestyle?

Case File 5 *Wrap-Up*

A primary reason for the increased number of cases of shellfish illness in the summer months is that algal growth is always greater when supported by warmer water temperatures. In addition, algal blooms often occur when phosphorus and nitrogen, which are common ingredients in fertilizers, accumulate in the water. Fertilizers used on land leach into the groundwater and eventually find their way to open bodies of water, where they induce abnormally robust growth of algal populations. When algal levels decrease, the toxins eventually leach out of the shellfish, but it can take weeks to months before a beach may be safely reopened.

See: Oregon Department of Fish and Wildlife. http://www.dfw.state.or.us/MRP/shellfish/razorclams/plankton.asp.

Chapter Summary

5.1 The History of Eukaryotes

- Eukaryotes are cells with a nucleus and organelles compartmentalized by membranes. They, like prokaryotes, originated from a primitive cell referred to as the Last Common Ancestor. Eukaryotic cell structure enabled eukaryotes to diversify from single cells into a huge variety of complex multicellular forms.
- The cell structures common to most eukaryotes are the cell membrane, nucleus, vacuoles, mitochondria, endoplasmic reticulum, Golgi apparatus, and a cytoskeleton. Cell walls, chloroplasts, and locomotor organs are present in some eukaryote groups.

5.2 Form and Function of the Eukaryotic Cell: External Structures

- Microscopic eukaryotes use locomotor organs such as flagella or cilia for moving themselves or their food.
- The glycocalyx is the outermost boundary of most eukaryotic cells. Its functions are protection, adherence, and reception of chemical signals from the environment or from other organisms. The glycocalyx is supported by either a cell wall or a cell membrane.
- The cytoplasmic (cell) membrane of eukaryotes is similar in function to that of prokaryotes, but it differs in composition, possessing sterols as additional stabilizing agents.

5.3 Form and Function of the Eukaryotic Cell: Internal Structures

- The genome of eukaryotes is located in the nucleus, a spherical structure surrounded by a double membrane. The nucleus contains the nucleolus, the site of ribosome synthesis. DNA is organized into chromosomes in the nucleus.
- The endoplasmic reticulum (ER) is an internal network of membranous passageways extending throughout the cell.
- The Golgi apparatus is a packaging center that receives materials from the ER and then forms vesicles around them for storage or for transport to the cell membrane for secretion.
- The mitochondria generate energy in the form of ATP to be used in numerous cellular activities.
- Chloroplasts, membranous packets found in plants and algae, are used in photosynthesis.

- Ribosomes are the sites for protein synthesis present in both eukaryotes and prokaryotes.
- The cytoskeleton maintains the shape of cells and produces movement of cytoplasm within the cell, movement of chromosomes at cell division, and, in some groups, movement of the cell as a unit.

5.4 The Kingdom of the Fungi

- The fungi are nonphotosynthetic haploid species with cell walls. They are either saprobes or parasites and may be unicellular, colonial, or multicellular.
- All fungi are heterotrophic.
- Fungi have many reproductive strategies, including both asexual and sexual.
- Fungi have asexual spores called sporangiospores and conidiospores.
- Fungal sexual spores enable the organisms to incorporate variations in form and function.
- Fungi are often identified on the basis of their microscopic appearance.
- There are two categories of fungi that cause human disease: the primary pathogens, which infect healthy persons, and the opportunistic pathogens, which cause disease only in compromised hosts.

5.5 The Protists

- The protists are mostly unicellular or colonial eukaryotes that lack specialized tissues. There are two major organism types: the algae and the protozoa.
- Algae are photosynthetic organisms that contain chloroplasts with chlorophyll and other pigments.
- Protozoa are heterotrophs that usually display some form of locomotion. Most are single-celled trophozoites, and many produce a resistant stage, or cyst.

5.6 The Parasitic Helminths

- The Kingdom Animalia has only one group that contains members that are (sometimes) microscopic. These are the helminths or worms. Parasitic members include flatworms and roundworms that are able to invade and reproduce in human tissues.

Multiple-Choice and True-False Questions   Knowledge and Comprehension

Multiple-Choice Questions. Select the correct answer from the answers provided.

1. Both flagella and cilia are found primarily in
   a. algae.
   c. fungi.
   b. protozoa.
   d. both b and c

2. Features of the nuclear envelope include
   a. ribosomes.
   b. a double membrane structure.
   c. pores that allow communication with the cytoplasm.
   d. b and c
   e. all of these

3. The cell wall is found in which eukaryotes?
   a. fungi
   c. protozoa
   b. algae
   d. a and b

4. Yeasts are _____ fungi, and molds are _____ fungi.
   a. macroscopic, microscopic
   b. unicellular, filamentous
   c. motile, nonmotile
   d. water, terrestrial

5. Algae generally contain some type of
   a. spore.
   c. locomotor organelle.
   b. chlorophyll.
   d. toxin.

6. Almost all protozoa have a
   a. locomotor organelle.
   c. pellicle.
   b. cyst stage.
   d. trophozoite stage.

7. All mature sporozoa are
   a. parasitic.
   c. carried by vectors.
   b. nonmotile.
   d. both a and b

8. Parasitic helminths reproduce with
   a. spores.
   c. mitosis.
   b. eggs and sperm.
   d. cysts.
   e. all of these

9. Mitochondria likely originated from
   a. archaea.
   b. invaginations of the cell membrane.
   c. bacteria.
   d. chloroplasts.

10. Most helminth infections
    a. are localized to one site in the body.
    b. spread through major systems of the body.
    c. develop within the spleen.
    d. develop within the liver.

True-False Questions. If the statement is true, leave as is. If it is false, correct it by rewriting the sentence.

11. Prokaryotes and eukaryotes arose from the same kind of primordial cell.

12. Hyphae that are divided into compartments by cross walls are called septate hyphae.

13. The infective stage of a protozoan is the trophozoite.

14. In humans, fungi can only infect the skin.

15. Fungi generally derive nutrients through photosynthesis.

Critical Thinking Questions   Application and Analysis

These questions are suggested as a *writing-to-learn* experience. For each question, compose a one- or two-paragraph answer that includes the factual information needed to completely address the question.

1. Construct a chart that reviews the major similarities and differences between prokaryotic and eukaryotic cells.

2. a. Describe the anatomy and functions of each of the major eukaryotic organelles.
   b. How are flagella and cilia similar? How are they different?
   c. Compare and contrast the smooth ER, the rough ER, and the Golgi apparatus in structure and function.

3. For what reasons would a cell need a "skeleton"?

4. a. Differentiate between the yeast and hypha types of fungal cell.
   b. What is a mold?
   c. What does it mean if a fungus is dimorphic?

5. What is a working definition of a "protist"?

6. a. Briefly outline the characteristics of the four protozoan groups.
   b. What is an important pathogen in each group?

7. Suggest some ways that one would go about determining if mitochondria and chloroplasts are modified prokaryotic cells.

8. Explain the general characteristics of the protozoan life cycle.

9. What general type of multicellular parasite is composed primarily of thin sacs of reproductive organs?

10. Can you think of a way to determine if a child is suffering from pinworms? Hint: Scotch tape is involved.

Concept Mapping   Synthesis

Appendix D provides guidance for working with concept maps.

1. Construct your own concept map using the following words as the *concepts*. Supply the linking words between each pair of concepts.

Golgi apparatus   ribosomes
chloroplasts   flagella
cytoplasm   nucleolus
endospore

Visual Connections   Synthesis

These questions use visual images or previous content to make connections to this chapter's concepts.

1. **From chapter 4, figure 4.25a.** You may have seen similar sites to this one. Can you think of two locations you encountered that have shown colorful evidence of microbial growth?

2. **From chapter 1, figure 1.13.** Which of the groups of organisms from this figure will contain a nucleus? Why?

www.connect.microbiology.com

Enhance your study of this chapter with study tools and practice tests. Also ask your instructor about the resources available through ConnectPlus, including the media-rich eBook, interactive learning tools, and animations.

An Introduction to the Viruses

Case File 6

Did you know that poultry farmers routinely use vaccines to keep their chickens from developing infectious diseases? This is especially true of larger farming operations. Here we describe an incident at a facility that produces vaccines for poultry. On November 25, 2006, a case of salmonellosis in an employee of such a facility was reported to the Maine Department of Health and Human Services (MDHHS). Because a similar case of salmonellosis had been reported 10 days earlier, the MDHHS began an outbreak investigation. Approximately one week prior to the first salmonellosis case, a spill had occurred in a fermentation room at the vaccine production facility, releasing 1 to 1.5 L of a highly concentrated culture of *Salmonella enterica* serotype Enteritidis (this bacterium is referred to as SE), that was being used in vaccine production. The room was unoccupied at the time of the spill, and afterward it was cleaned by a worker wearing a biohazard suit, hat, booties, mask, and gloves using 5% bleach and a commercial disinfectant effective against SE. That worker later reported the first case of salmonellosis.

Following the first two reported cases, the workers in the production area filled out a questionnaire asking about their work routines and whether they had experienced symptoms of salmonellosis (defined as three or more loose, watery stools in a 24-hour period) since November 1, 2006. Of a total of 26 employees who had been working in the room where the spill occurred, 18 reported illness. No illness was seen in the seven workers who had never entered the room. In addition to the cases from the vaccine facility, seven SE isolates from persons presumably unconnected to the plant were submitted to the MDHHS during that same time period.

- The employee who originally cleaned the culture spill reported having diarrhea for 1 day but taking no time off work. What is the importance of this fact?

- The CDC estimates that the 42,000 cases of salmonellosis reported yearly may be only 10% of the actual number of cases. Why do you think this may be true?

Continuing the Case appears on page 157.

Outline and Learning Outcomes

6.1 The Search for the Elusive Viruses

The discovery of the light microscope made it possible to see firsthand the agents of many bacterial, fungal, and protozoan diseases. But the techniques for observing and cultivating these relatively large microorganisms were useless for viruses. For many years, the cause of viral infections such as smallpox and polio was unknown, even though it was clear that the diseases were transmitted from person to person. The French scientist Louis Pasteur was certainly on the right track when he postulated that rabies was caused by a "living thing" smaller than bacteria, and in 1884 he was able to develop the first vaccine for rabies. Pasteur also proposed the term **virus** (L. poison) to denote this special group of infectious agents.

The first substantial revelations about the unique characteristics of viruses occurred in the 1890s. First, D. Ivanovski and M. Beijerinck showed that a disease in tobacco was caused by a virus (tobacco mosaic virus). Then, Friedrich Loeffler and Paul Frosch discovered an animal virus that causes foot-and-mouth disease in cattle. These early researchers found that when infectious fluids from host organisms were passed through porcelain filters designed to trap bacteria, the filtrate remained infectious. This result proved that an infection could be caused by a cell-free fluid containing agents smaller than bacteria and thus first introduced the concept of a *filterable virus.*

Over the succeeding decades, a remarkable picture of the physical, chemical, and biological nature of viruses began to take form. Years of experimentation were required to show that viruses were noncellular particles with a definite size, shape, and chemical composition. Using special techniques, they could be cultured in the laboratory. By the 1950s, virology had grown into a multifaceted discipline that promised to provide much information on disease, genetics, and even life itself **(Insight 6.1).**

6.1 Learning Outcomes—Can You . . .

1. . . . describe the significance of viruses being recognized as "filterable"?

INSIGHT 6.1   **A Positive View of Viruses**

Looking at this beautiful tulip, one would never guess that it derives its pleasing appearance from a viral infection. It contains tulip mosaic virus, which alters the development of the plant cells and causes complex patterns of colors in the petals. Aside from this, the virus does not cause severe harm to the plants. Despite the reputation of viruses as cell killers, there is another side of viruses—that of being harmless, and in some cases, even beneficial.

Although there is no agreement on the origins of viruses, it is very likely that they have been in existence for billions of years. Virologists are convinced that viruses have been an important force in the evolution of living things. This is based on the fact that they interact with the genetic material of their host cells and that they carry genes from one host to another (transduction). It is convincing to imagine that viruses arose early in the history of cells as loose pieces of genetic material that became dependent nomads, moving from cell to cell. Viruses are also a significant factor in the functioning of many ecosystems. For example, it is documented that seawater can contain 10 million viruses per milliliter. Because viruses are made of the same elements as living cells, it is estimated that the sum of viruses in the ocean represents 270 million metric tons of organic matter.

Over the past several years, biomedical experts have been looking at viruses as vehicles to treat infections and disease. Viruses are already essential for production of vaccines to treat viral infections such as influenza, polio, and measles. Vaccine experts have also engineered new types of viruses by combining a less harmful virus such as vaccinia or adenovirus with some genetic material from a pathogen such as herpes simplex. This technique creates a vaccine that provides immunity but does not expose the person to the intact pathogen. Several of these types of vaccines are currently in development.

Scientists have recently had important successes using a virus called vesicular stomatitis virus (VSV) to cure cancer. They alter a gene in VSV to make it completely safe for normal cells, and then inject it intravenously. VSV targets and kills tumor cells (in many different kinds of cancers, including brain, prostate, and ovarian cancers) and has even been shown to track down metastatic tumor cells in distant parts of the body. An older therapy getting a second chance involves use of bacteriophages to treat bacterial infections. This technique was tried in the past with mixed success but was abandoned for more efficient antimicrobial drugs. The basis behind the therapy is that bacterial viruses would seek out only their specific host bacteria and would cause complete destruction of the bacterial cell. Newer experiments with animals have demonstrated that this method can control infections as well as traditional drugs can. Some potential applications being considered are adding phage suspension to grafts to control skin infections and to intravenous fluids for blood infections.

6.2 The Position of Viruses in the Biological Spectrum

Viruses are a unique group of biological entities known to infect every type of cell, including bacteria, algae, fungi, protozoa, plants, and animals. Viruses are extremely abundant on our planet. Norwegian ocean waters have been found to contain 60,000 viruses in a single milliliter (less than a thimbleful) of water. Lake water contains many more—as many as 250 million viruses per milliliter. We are just beginning to understand the impact of these huge numbers of viruses in our environment. The exceptional and curious nature of viruses prompts numerous questions, including:

1. Are they organisms; that is, are they alive?
2. What role did viruses play in the evolution of life?
3. What are their distinctive biological characteristics?
4. How can particles so small, simple, and seemingly insignificant be capable of causing disease and death?
5. What is the connection between viruses and cancer?

In this chapter, we address these questions and many others.

The unusual structure and behavior of viruses have led to debates about their connection to the rest of the microbial world. One viewpoint holds that since viruses are unable to multiply independently from the host cell, they are not living things but are more akin to infectious molecules. Another viewpoint proposes that even though viruses do not exhibit most of the life processes of cells, they can direct them and thus are certainly more than inert and lifeless molecules. This view is the predominant one among scientists today. This debate has greater philosophical than practical importance when discussing disease because viruses are agents of disease and must be dealt with through control, therapy, and prevention, whether we regard them as living or not. In keeping with their special position in the biological spectrum, it is best to describe viruses as *infectious particles* (rather than organisms) and as either *active* or *inactive* (rather than alive or dead).

Viruses are not just agents of disease. They have many positive uses (Insight 6.1). More importantly than that, recent discoveries suggest that viruses have been absolutely vital in forming cells and other life forms as they are today. By infecting other cells, and sometimes influencing their genetic makeup, they have shaped the way cells, tissues, bacteria, plants, and animals have evolved to their present forms. For example, scientists think that anywhere from 35% to 90% of the human genome consists of sequences that come from viruses that have incorporated their genetic material permanently into human DNA. Bacterial DNA contains 10% to 20% viral sequences. As you learn more about how viruses work, you will see how this could happen.

Viruses are different from their host cells in size, structure, behavior, and physiology. They are a type of *obligate intracellular parasites* that cannot multiply unless they invade a specific host cell and instruct its genetic and metabolic machinery to make and release quantities of new viruses. Other unique properties of viruses are summarized in **table 6.1**.

6.2 Learning Outcomes—Can You ...

2. ... construct arguments on both sides of the "Are viruses living?" debate?

3. ... identify better terms for viruses than "alive" or "dead"?

Table 6.1 Properties of Viruses

- Are obligate intracellular parasites of bacteria, protozoa, fungi, algae, plants, and animals.
- Are ubiquitous in nature and have had major impact on development of biological life.
- Are ultramicroscopic in size, ranging from 20 nm up to 450 nm (diameter).
- Are not cells; structure is very compact and economical.
- Do not independently fulfill the characteristics of life.
- Are inactive macromolecules outside the host cell and active only inside host cells.
- Basic structure consists of protein shell (capsid) surrounding nucleic acid core.
- Nucleic acid can be either DNA or RNA but not both.
- Nucleic acid can be double-stranded DNA, single-stranded DNA, single-stranded RNA, or double-stranded RNA.
- Molecules on virus surface impart high specificity for attachment to host cell.
- Multiply by taking control of host cell's genetic material and regulating the synthesis and assembly of new viruses.
- Lack enzymes for most metabolic processes.
- Lack machinery for synthesizing proteins.

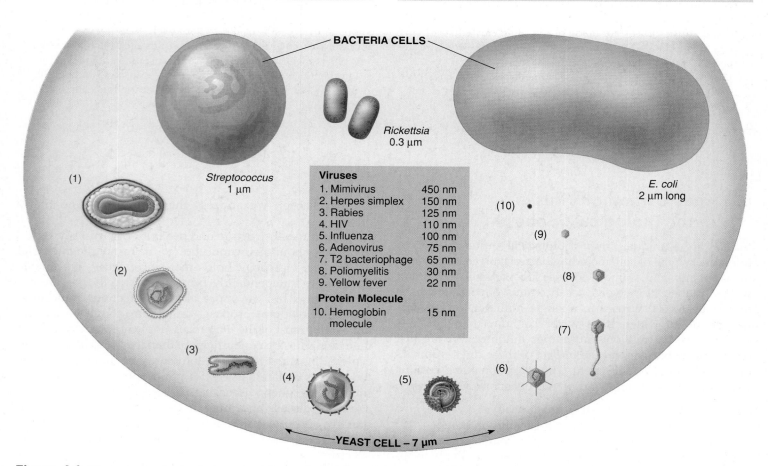

BACTERIA CELLS

Rickettsia
0.3 μm

(1)

Streptococcus
1 μm

Viruses
1. Mimivirus	450 nm
2. Herpes simplex	150 nm
3. Rabies	125 nm
4. HIV	110 nm
5. Influenza	100 nm
6. Adenovirus	75 nm
7. T2 bacteriophage	65 nm
8. Poliomyelitis	30 nm
9. Yellow fever	22 nm

Protein Molecule
10. Hemoglobin molecule	15 nm

(10)

(9)

E. coli
2 μm long

(8)

(7)

(6)

(5)

(4)

(3)

(2)

YEAST CELL – 7 μm

Figure 6.1 Size comparison of viruses with a eukaryotic cell (yeast) and bacteria.   Viruses range from largest (1) to smallest (9). A molecule of protein (10) is included to indicate proportion of macromolecules.

Figure 6.2 Methods of viewing viruses. **(a)** Negative staining of an orf virus (a type of poxvirus), revealing details of its outer coat. **(b)** Positive stain of the Ebola virus, a type of filovirus, so named because of its tendency to form long strands. Note the textured capsid. **(c)** Shadowcasting image of a vaccinia virus.

6.3 The General Structure of Viruses

Size Range

As a group, viruses represent the smallest infectious agents (with some unusual exceptions to be discussed later in this chapter). Their size relegates them to the realm of the ultramicroscopic. This term means that most of them are so minute (<0.2 μm) that an electron microscope is necessary to detect them or to examine their fine structure. They are dwarfed by their host cells: More than 2,000 bacterial viruses could fit into an average bacterial cell, and more than 50 million polioviruses could be accommodated by an average human cell. Animal viruses range in size from the small parvoviruses[1] (around 20 nm [0.02 μm] in diameter) to mimiviruses[2] that are larger than small bacteria (up to 450 nm [0.4 μm] in length) **(figure 6.1)**. Some cylindrical viruses are relatively long (800 nm [0.8 μm] in length) but so narrow in diameter (15 nm [0.015 μm]) that their visibility is still limited without the high magnification and resolution of an electron microscope. Figure 6.1 compares the sizes of several viruses with prokaryotic and eukaryotic cells and molecules.

Viral architecture is most readily observed through special stains in combination with electron microscopy **(figure 6.2)**.

Viral Components: Capsids, Nucleic Acids, and Envelopes

It is important to realize that viruses bear no real resemblance to cells and that they lack any of the protein-synthesizing machinery found in even the simplest cells. Their molecular structure is composed of regular, repeating subunits that give rise to their crystalline appearance. Indeed, many purified viruses can form large aggregates or crystals if subjected to special treatments **(figure 6.3)**. The general plan of virus organization is the utmost in simplicity and compactness.

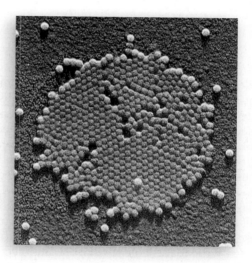

Figure 6.3 The crystalline nature of viruses. Highly magnified (150,000×) electron micrograph of purified poliovirus crystals, showing hundreds of individual viruses.

Viruses contain only those parts needed to invade and control a host cell: an external coating and a core containing one or more nucleic acid strands of either DNA or RNA, and sometimes one or two enzymes. This pattern of organization can be represented with a flowchart:

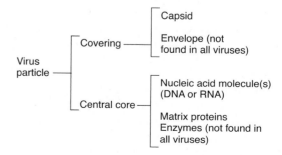

All viruses have a protein **capsid,** or shell, that surrounds the nucleic acid in the central core. Together the capsid and the

---

1. DNA viruses that cause respiratory infections in humans.
2. Mimivirus was just identified in 2003. Its name stands for "mimicking microbe."

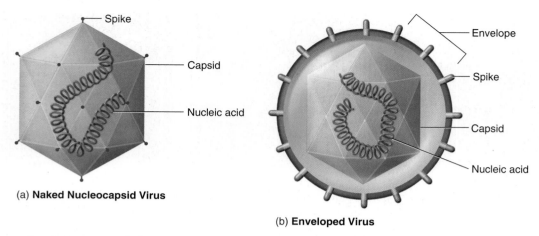

(a) **Naked Nucleocapsid Virus**

(b) **Enveloped Virus**

Figure 6.4 Generalized structure of viruses.   **(a)** The simplest virus is a naked virus (nucleocapsid) consisting of a geometric capsid assembled around a nucleic acid strand or strands. **(b)** An enveloped virus is composed of a nucleocapsid surrounded by a flexible membrane called an envelope.

nucleic acid are referred to as the **nucleocapsid (figure 6.4).** Members of 13 of the 20 families of animal viruses possess an additional covering external to the capsid called an envelope, which is usually a modified piece of the host's cell membrane **(figure 6.4b).** Viruses that consist of only a nucleocapsid are considered *naked viruses* **(figure 6.4a).** Both naked and enveloped viruses possess proteins on their outer surfaces that project from either the nucleocapsid or the envelope. They are the molecules that allow viruses to dock with their host cells. As we shall see later, the enveloped viruses differ from the naked viruses in the way that they enter and leave a host cell. A fully formed virus that is able to establish an infection in a host cell is often called a **virion.**

The Viral Capsid: The Protective Outer Shell

When a virus particle is magnified several hundred thousand times, the capsid appears as the most prominent geometric feature. In general, each capsid is constructed from identical subunits called **capsomers** that are constructed from protein molecules. The capsomers spontaneously self-assemble into the finished capsid. Depending on how the capsomers are shaped and arranged, this assembly results in two different types: helical and icosahedral.

The simpler **helical** capsids have rod-shaped capsomers that bond together to form a series of hollow discs resembling a bracelet. During the formation of the nucleocapsid, these discs link with other discs to form a continuous helix into which the nucleic acid strand is coiled **(figure 6.5).** In electron micrographs, the appearance of a helical capsid varies with the type of virus. The nucleocapsids of naked helical viruses are very rigid and tightly wound into a cylinder-shaped package **(figure 6.6a,b).** An example is the tobacco mosaic virus, which attacks tobacco leaves. Enveloped helical nucleocapsids are more flex-

ible and tend to be arranged as a looser helix within the envelope **(figure 6.6c,d).** This type of morphology is found in several enveloped human viruses, including influenza, measles, and rabies.

The capsids of a number of major virus families are arranged in an **icosahedron** (eye"-koh-suh-hee'-drun)—a

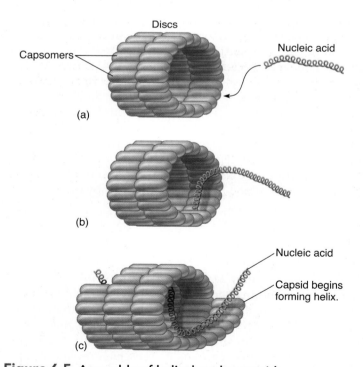

Figure 6.5 Assembly of helical nucleocapsids.
(a) Capsomers assemble into hollow discs. **(b)** The nucleic acid is inserted into the center of the disc. **(c)** Elongation of the nucleocapsid progresses from one or both ends, as the nucleic acid is wound "within" the lengthening helix.

(a)

(b)

(c)

Envelope

Nucleocapsid

(d)

Capsid

Nucleocapsid

Nucleic acid

Figure 6.6 Typical variations of viruses with helical nucleocapsids. Naked helical virus (tobacco mosaic virus): **(a)** a schematic view and **(b)** a greatly magnified micrograph. Note the overall cylindrical morphology. **Enveloped helical virus (influenza virus): (c)** a schematic view and **(d)** an electron micrograph of the same virus (350,000×).

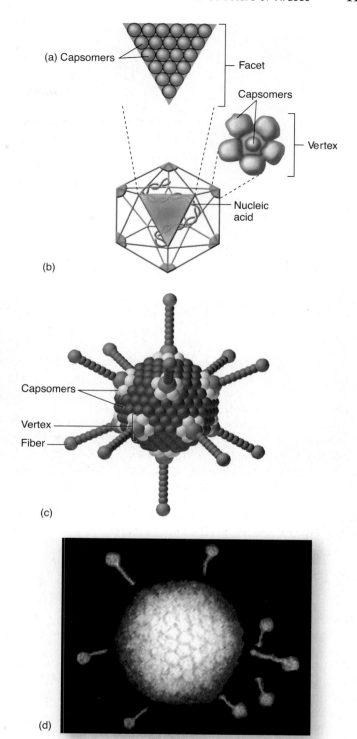

Figure 6.7 The structure and formation of an icosahedral virus (adenovirus is the model). **(a)** A facet or "face" of the capsid is composed of 21 identical capsomers arranged in a triangular shape. A vertex or "point" consists of a different type of capsomer with a single penton in the center. Other viruses can vary in the number, types, and arrangement of capsomers. **(b)** An assembled virus shows how the facets and vertices come together to form a shell around the nucleic acid. **(c)** A three-dimensional model (640,000×) of this virus shows fibers (spikes) attached to the pentons. **(d)** A negative stain of this virus highlights its texture and fibers that have fallen off.

three-dimensional, 20-sided figure with 12 evenly spaced corners. The arrangements of the capsomers vary from one virus to another. Some viruses construct the capsid from a single type of capsomer while others may contain several types of capsomers **(figure 6.7)**. Although the capsids of all icosahedral viruses have this sort of symmetry, they can have major variations in the number of capsomers; for example, a poliovirus has 32, and an adenovirus has 252 capsomers. Individual capsomers can look either ring- or dome-shaped, and the capsid itself can appear spherical or cubical **(figure 6.8)**. During assembly of the virus, the nucleic acid is packed into the center of this icosahedron, forming a nucleocapsid. While most viruses have capsids that are either icosahedral or helical, there is another category of capsid that is simply called "complex." Complex capsids, found in the viruses that infect bacteria, may have multiple types of proteins and take shapes that are not symmetrical. An example of a complex virus is shown in **figure 6.9**. Another factor

(a)

(a) Capsomers

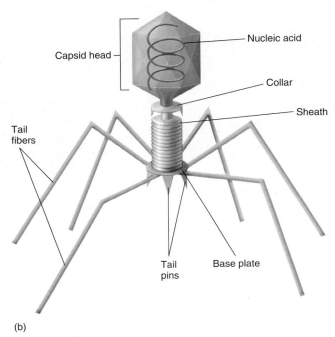

Capsid head

Nucleic acid

Collar

Sheath

Tail fibers

Tail pins

Base plate

(b)

Figure 6.9 Structure of complex viruses.
(a) Photomicrograph and **(b)** diagram of a T4 bacteriophage, a virus that infects bacteria.

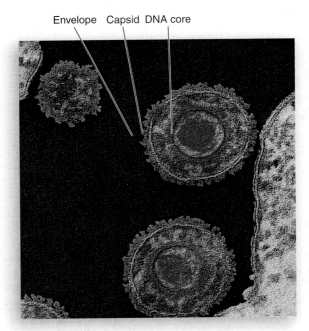

Envelope Capsid DNA core

(b)

Figure 6.8 Two types of icosahedral viruses, highly magnified.   **(a)** Upper view: A negative stain of rotaviruses with unusual capsomers that look like spokes on a wheel; lower view is a three-dimensional model of this virus. **(b)** Herpes simplex virus, a type of enveloped icosahedral virus (300,000×).

that alters the appearance of icosahedral viruses is whether or not they have an outer envelope; contrast a papillomavirus (causes warts) and its naked nucleocapsid with herpes simplex (causes cold sores) and its enveloped nucleocapsid **(figure 6.10).**

The Viral Envelope

When enveloped viruses (mostly animal) are released from the host cell, they take with them a bit of its membrane system in the form of an envelope, as described later on. Some viruses bud off the cell membrane; others leave via the nuclear envelope or the endoplasmic reticulum. Whichever

Figure 6.10 Enveloped and nonenveloped viruses.   **(a)** Micrograph of papillomaviruses with unusual, ring-shaped capsomers. **(b)** Herpesvirus, an enveloped icosahedron (300,000×). Both micrographs have been colorized.

avenue of escape, the viral envelope differs significantly from the host's membranes. In the envelope, some or all of the regular membrane proteins are replaced with special viral proteins. Some of the envelope proteins attach to the capsid of the virus, and glycoproteins (proteins bound to a carbohydrate) remain exposed on the outside of the envelope. These protruding molecules, called spikes when they are on enveloped viruses, are essential for the attachment of viruses to the next host cell. Because the envelope is more supple than the capsid, enveloped viruses are pleomorphic, and range from spherical to filamentous in shape.

Functions of the Viral Capsid/Envelope

The outermost covering of a virus is indispensable to viral function because it protects the nucleic acid from the effects of various enzymes and chemicals when the virus is outside the host cell. For example, the capsids of enteric (intestinal) viruses such as polio and hepatitis A are resistant to the acid- and protein-digesting enzymes of the gastrointestinal tract. Capsids and envelopes are also responsible for helping to introduce the viral DNA or RNA into a suitable host cell, first by binding to the cell surface using special binding proteins and then by assisting in penetration of the viral nucleic acid (to be discussed in more detail later in the chapter). In addition, parts of viral capsids and envelopes stimulate the immune system to produce antibodies that can neutralize viruses and protect the host's cells against future infections (see chapter 15).

Nucleic Acids: At the Core of a Virus

The sum total of the genetic information carried by an organism is known as its **genome.** So far, one biological

constant is that the genetic information of living cells is carried by nucleic acids (DNA, RNA). Viruses, although neither alive nor cells, are no exception to this rule, but there is a significant difference. Unlike cells, which contain both DNA and RNA, viruses contain either DNA or RNA *but not both.* Because viruses must pack into a tiny space all of the genes necessary to instruct the host cell to make new viruses, the number of viral genes is quite small compared with that of a cell. It varies from four genes in hepatitis B virus to hundreds of genes in some herpesviruses. Viruses possess only the genes needed to invade host cells and redirect their activity. By comparison, the bacterium *Escherichia coli* has approximately 4,000 genes, and a human cell has approximately 23,000 genes. These additional genes allow cells to carry out the complex metabolic activity necessary for independent life.

In chapter 2, you learned that DNA usually exists as a double-stranded molecule and that RNA is single-stranded. Although most viruses follow this same pattern, a few exhibit distinctive and exceptional forms. Notable examples are the parvoviruses, which contain single-stranded DNA, and reoviruses (a cause of respiratory and intestinal tract infections), which contain double-stranded RNA. In fact, viruses exhibit wide variety in how their RNA or DNA is configured. DNA viruses can have single-stranded (ss) or double-stranded (ds) DNA; the dsDNA can be arranged linearly or in ds circles. RNA viruses can be double-stranded but are more often single-stranded. You will learn in chapter 9 that all proteins are made by "translating" the nucleic acid code on a single strand of RNA into an amino acid sequence. Single-stranded RNA genomes that are ready for immediate translation into proteins are called **positive-sense RNA.** Other RNA genomes have to be converted into the proper form to

Table 6.2 Medically Relevant DNA Virus Groups

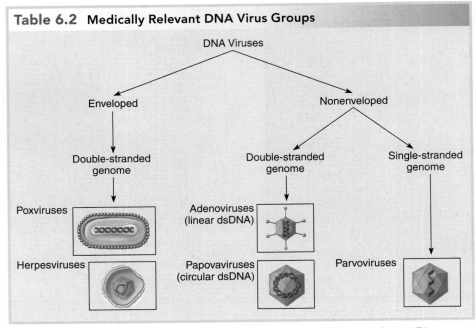

Source: Adapted from: *Poxviridae* from Buller et al., National Institute of Allergy & Infectious Disease, Department of Health & Human Services.

be made into proteins, and these are called **negative-sense RNA.** RNA genomes may also be *segmented*, meaning that the individual genes exist on separate pieces of RNA. The influenza virus (an orthomyxovirus) is an example of this. A special type of RNA virus is called a *retrovirus*. We'll discuss it later. **Tables 6.2** and **6.3** summarize the structures of some medically relevant DNA and RNA viruses.

In all cases, these tiny strands of genetic material carry the blueprint for viral structure and functions. In a very real sense, viruses are genetic parasites because they cannot multiply until their nucleic acid has reached the internal habitat of the host cell. At the minimum, they must carry genes for synthesizing the viral capsid and genetic material, for regulating the actions of the host, and for packaging the mature virus.

Table 6.3 Medically Relevant RNA Viruses

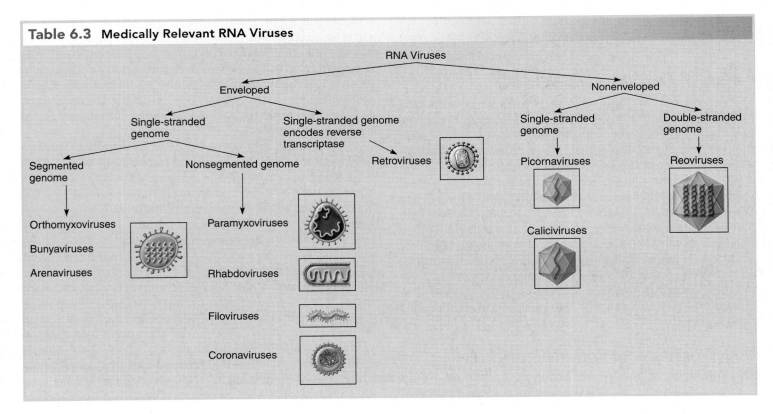

Other Substances in the Virus Particle

In addition to the protein of the capsid, the proteins and lipids of envelopes, and the nucleic acid of the core, viruses can contain enzymes for specific operations within their host cell. They may come with preformed enzymes that are required for viral replication. Examples include **polymerases** (pol-im'-ur-ace-uz) that synthesize DNA and RNA, and replicases that copy RNA. The AIDS virus comes equipped with **reverse transcriptase** for synthesizing DNA from RNA. However, viruses completely lack the genes for synthesis of metabolic enzymes. As we shall see, this deficiency has little consequence, because viruses have adapted to completely take over their hosts' metabolic resources. Some viruses can actually carry away substances from their host cell. For instance, arenaviruses pack along host ribosomes, and retroviruses "borrow" the host's tRNA molecules.

6.3 Learning Outcomes—Can You ...

4. ... discuss the size of viruses relative to other microorganisms?
5. ... describe the function and structure(s) of viral capsids?
6. ... distinguish between enveloped and naked viruses?
7. ... explain the importance of viral surface proteins, or spikes?
8. ... diagram the possible configurations of nucleic acid viruses may possess?

6.4 How Viruses Are Classified and Named

Although viruses are not classified as members of the kingdoms discussed in chapter 1, they are diverse enough to require their own classification scheme to aid in their study and identification. In an informal and general way, we have already begun classifying viruses—as animal, plant, or bacterial viruses; enveloped or naked viruses; DNA or RNA viruses; and helical or icosahedral viruses. These introductory categories are certainly useful in organization and description, but the study of specific viruses requires a more standardized method of nomenclature. For many years, the animal viruses were classified mainly on the basis of their hosts and the kind of diseases they caused. Newer systems for naming viruses

also take into account the actual nature of the virus particles themselves, with only partial emphasis on host and disease. The main criteria presently used to group viruses are structure, chemical composition, and similarities in genetic makeup.

In 2005, the International Committee on the Taxonomy of Viruses issued its latest report on the classification of viruses. The committee listed 3 orders, 73 families, and 287 genera of viruses. Previous to 2000, there had been only a single recognized order of viruses. Examples of each of the three orders of viruses are presented in **table 6.4**. Note the naming conventions—that is, virus families are written with "-viridae" on the end of the name, and genera end with "-virus."

Historically, some virologists had created an informal **species** naming system that mirrors the species names in higher organisms, using genus and species epithets such as *Measles morbillivirus*. This has not been an official designation, however. The species category has created a lot of controversy within the virology community, with many scientists arguing that nonorganisms such as viruses can never be speciated. Others argue that viruses are too changeable, and thus fine distinctions used for deciding on species classifications will quickly disappear. Over the past decade, virologists have largely accepted the concept of viral species, defining them as consisting of members that have a number of properties in common but have some variation in their properties. In other words, a virus is placed in a species on the basis of a collection of properties. For viruses that infect humans, species may be defined based on relatively minor differences in host range and how they affect their hosts. The important thing to remember is that viral species designations, in the words of one preeminent viral taxonomist, are "fuzzy sets with hazy boundaries."[3]

Because the use of standardized species names has not been widely accepted, the genus or common English vernacular names (for example, poliovirus and rabies virus) predominate in discussions of specific viruses in this text. **Table 6.5** illustrates the naming system for important viruses and the diseases they cause.

3. van Regenmortel, M. H. V., and Mahy, B. W. J. Emerging issues in virus taxonomy. *Emerg. Infect. Dis.* [serial online] 2004 Jan. Available from http://www.cdc.gov/ncidod/EID/vol10no1/03-0279.htm.

Table 6.4 Examples from the Three Orders of Viruses

Order	Family	Genus	Species	Host
Caudovirales	Myoviridae	SPO1-like virus	Bacillus phage	Bacterium
Mononegavirales	Paramyxoviridae	Morbillivirus	Measles virus	Animal
	Filoviridae	Ebola virus	Ebola virus	Animal
	Sequiviridae	Sequivirus	Parsnip yellow fleck virus	Plant
Nidovirales	Togaviridae	Rubivirus	Rubella virus	Animal
	Luteoviridae	Tobamovirus	Tobacco mosaic virus	Plant

Table 6.5 Important Human Virus Families, Genera, Common Names, and Types of Diseases

	Family	Genus of Virus	Common Name of Genus Members	Name of Disease
DNA Viruses				
ds	Poxviridae	*Orthopoxvirus*	Variola and vaccinia	Smallpox, cowpox
	Herpesviridae	*Simplexvirus*	Herpes simplex (HSV) 1 virus	Fever blister, cold sores
			Herpes simplex (HSV) 2 virus	Genital herpes
		Varicellovirus	Varicella zoster virus (VZV)	Chickenpox, shingles
		Cytomegalovirus	Human cytomegalovirus (CMV)	CMV infections
	Adenoviridae	*Mastadenovirus*	Human adenoviruses	Adenovirus infection
	Papillomaviridae	*Papillomavirus*	Human papillomavirus (HPV)	Several types of warts
		Polyomavirus	JC virus (JCV)	Progressive multifocal leukoencephalopathy (PML)
	Hepadnaviridae	*Hepadnavirus*	Hepatitis B virus (HBV or Dane particle)	Serum hepatitis
ss	Parvoviridae	*Erythrovirus*	Parvovirus B19	Erythema infectiosum
RNA Viruses				
+ polarity	Picornaviridae	*Enterovirus*	Poliovirus	Poliomyelitis
			Coxsackievirus	Hand-foot-mouth disease
		Hepatovirus	Hepatitis A virus (HAV)	Short-term hepatitis
		Rhinovirus	Human rhinovirus	Common cold, bronchitis
	Caliciviridae	*Calicivirus*	Norwalk virus	Viral diarrhea, Norwalk virus syndrome
	Togaviridae	*Alphavirus*	Eastern equine encephalitis virus	Eastern equine encephalitis (EEE)
			Western equine encephalitis virus	Western equine encephalitis (WEE)
			Yellow fever virus	Yellow fever
			St. Louis encephalitis virus	St. Louis encephalitis
		Rubivirus	Rubella virus	Rubella (German measles)
	Flaviviridae	*Flavivirus*	Dengue fever virus	Dengue fever
			West Nile fever virus	West Nile fever
	Coronaviridae	*Coronavirus*	Infectious bronchitis virus (IBV)	Bronchitis
			Enteric corona virus	Coronavirus enteritis
			SARS virus	Severe acute respiratory syndrome
– polarity	Filoviridae	*Filovirus*	Ebola, Marburg virus	Ebola fever
	Orthomyxoviridae	*Influenza virus*	Influenza virus, type A (Asian, Hong Kong, viruses)	Influenza or "flu" and swine influenza
	Paramyxoviridae	*Paramyxovirus*	Parainfluenza virus, types 1–5	Parainfluenza
			Mumps virus	Mumps
	Rhabdoviridae	*Lyssavirus*	Rabies virus	Rabies (hydrophobia)
	Bunyaviridae	*Bunyavirus*	Bunyamwera viruses	California encephalitis
		Hantavirus	Sin Nombre virus	Respiratory distress syndrome
		Phlebovirus	Rift Valley fever virus	Rift Valley fever

	Family	Genus of Virus	Common Name of Genus Members	Name of Disease
		Nairovirus	Crimean–Congo hemorrhagic fever virus (CCHF)	Crimean–Congo hemorrhagic fever
dsRNA	Reoviridae	*Coltivirus*	Colorado tick fever virus	Colorado tick fever
		Rotavirus	Human rotavirus	Rotavirus gastroenteritis
		Morbillivirus	Measles virus	Measles (red)
		Pneumovirus	Respiratory syncytial virus (RSV)	Common cold syndrome
special RNA	Retroviridae	*Oncornavirus*	Human T-cell leukemia virus (HTLV)	T-cell leukemia
		Lentivirus	HIV (human immunodeficiency viruses 1 and 2)	Acquired immunodeficiency syndrome (AIDS)
	Arenaviridae	*Arenavirus*	Lassa virus	Lassa fever

6.4 Learning Outcomes—Can You ...

9. … explain why some find it difficult to assign species names to viruses?

10. … demonstrate how family and genus names in viruses are written?

6.5 Modes of Viral Multiplication

Viruses are closely associated with their hosts. In addition to providing the viral habitat, the host cell is absolutely necessary for viral multiplication. The process of viral multiplication is an extraordinary biological phenomenon. Viruses are minute parasites that seize control of the synthetic and genetic machinery of cells. The nature of this cycle dictates the way the virus is transmitted and what it does to its host, the responses of the immune defenses, and human measures to control viral infections. From these perspectives, we cannot overemphasize the importance of a working knowledge of the relationship between viruses and their host cells.

Multiplication Cycles in Animal Viruses

The general phases in the life cycle of animal viruses are

- **adsorption,**
- **penetration,**
- **uncoating,**
- **synthesis,**
- **assembly,**
- and **release** from the host cell.

The length of the entire multiplication cycle varies from 8 hours in polioviruses to 36 hours in some herpesviruses. See **figures 6.11** and **6.13** for the major phases of the viral life cycle.

Adsorption and Host Range

Invasion begins when the virus encounters a susceptible host cell and adsorbs specifically to receptor sites on the cell membrane. The membrane receptors that viruses attach to are usually glycoproteins the cell requires for its normal function. For example, the rabies virus affixes to the acetylcholine receptor of nerve cells, and the human immunodeficiency virus (HIV) attaches to the CD4 protein on certain white blood cells. The mode of attachment varies between the two general types of viruses. In enveloped forms such as influenza virus and HIV, glycoprotein spikes bind to the cell membrane receptors. Viruses with naked nucleocapsids (adenovirus, for example) use molecules on their capsids that adhere to cell membrane receptors **(figure 6.12).** Because a virus can invade its host cell only through making an exact fit with a specific host molecule, the range of hosts it can infect in a natural setting is limited. This limitation, known as the **host range,** may be restricted as in the case of hepatitis B, which infects only liver cells of humans; intermediate like the poliovirus, which infects intestinal and nerve cells of primates (humans, apes, and monkeys); or as broad as the rabies virus, which can infect various cells of all mammals. Cells that lack compatible virus receptors are resistant to adsorption and invasion by that virus. This explains why, for example, human liver cells are not infected by the canine hepatitis virus and dog liver cells cannot host the human hepatitis A virus. It also explains why viruses usually have tissue specificities called *tropisms* (troh'-pizmz) for certain cells in the body. The hepatitis B virus targets the liver, and the mumps virus targets salivary glands.

Penetration/Uncoating of Animal Viruses

Animal viruses exhibit some impressive mechanisms for entering a host cell. The flexible cell membrane of the host is

Process Figure 6.11
General features in the multiplication cycle of RNA animal viruses. **(a)** The major events in the life cycle of an enveloped + strand RNA virus. **(b)** Differing modes of synthesis in other types of RNA viruses.

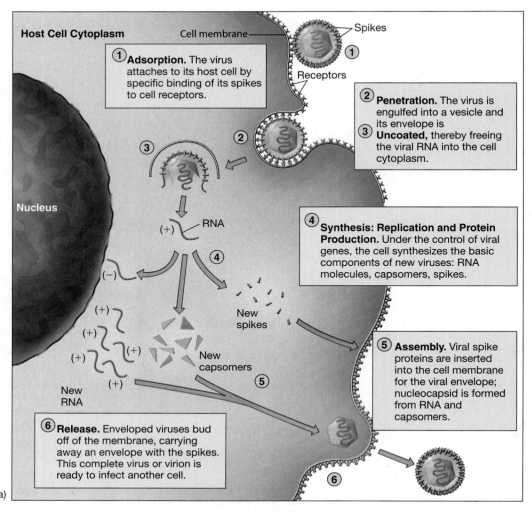

Host Cell Cytoplasm   Cell membrane   Spikes

① **Adsorption.** The virus attaches to its host cell by specific binding of its spikes to cell receptors.

Receptors

② **Penetration.** The virus is engulfed into a vesicle and its envelope is
③ **Uncoated,** thereby freeing the viral RNA into the cell cytoplasm.

Nucleus

(+) —— RNA

④ **Synthesis: Replication and Protein Production.** Under the control of viral genes, the cell synthesizes the basic components of new viruses: RNA molecules, capsomers, spikes.

(−)

New spikes

(+)
(+)
(+)   (+)
        New capsomers
(+)

⑤ **Assembly.** Viral spike proteins are inserted into the cell membrane for the viral envelope; nucleocapsid is formed from RNA and capsomers.

New RNA

⑥ **Release.** Enveloped viruses bud off of the membrane, carrying away an envelope with the spikes. This complete virus or virion is ready to infect another cell.

(a)

+RNA Genome
−RNA
Positive single-stranded RNA viruses (e.g., picornaviruses)

−RNA
+RNA   −RNA
Negative single-stranded RNA viruses (e.g., paramyxoviruses and orthomyxoviruses)

±RNA
±RNA
Double-stranded RNA viruses (e.g., reoviruses)

+RNA   −DNA   ±DNA
+RNA
Retroviruses (e.g., HIV)

(b)

penetrated by the whole virus or its nucleic acid **(figure 6.14).** In penetration by **endocytosis (figure 6.14a),** the entire virus is engulfed by the cell and enclosed in a vacuole or vesicle. When enzymes in the vacuole dissolve the envelope and capsid, the virus is said to be uncoated, a process that releases

the viral nucleic acid into the cytoplasm. The exact manner of uncoating varies, but in most cases, the virus fuses with the wall of the vesicle. Another means of entry involves direct fusion of the viral envelope with the host cell membrane (as in influenza and mumps viruses) **(figure 6.14b).** In this form

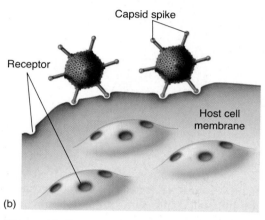

Figure 6.12 The mode by which animal viruses adsorb to the host cell membrane. **(a)** An enveloped coronavirus with prominent spikes. The configuration of the spike has a complementary fit for cell receptors. The process in which the virus lands on the cell and plugs into receptors is termed docking. **(b)** An adenovirus has a naked capsid that adheres to its host cell by nestling surface molecules on its capsid into the receptors on the host cell's membrane.

of penetration, the envelope merges directly with the cell membrane, thereby liberating the nucleocapsid into the cell's interior.

Synthesis: Replication and Protein Production

The synthetic and replicative phases of animal viruses are highly regulated and extremely complex at the molecular level. Free viral nucleic acid exerts control over the host's synthetic and metabolic machinery. How this control proceeds will vary, depending on whether the virus is a DNA or an RNA virus. In general, the DNA viruses (except poxviruses) enter the host cell's nucleus and are replicated and assembled there. With few exceptions (such as retroviruses), RNA viruses are replicated and assembled in the cytoplasm.

In figure 6.11 we provide an overview of the process, using a + strand RNA virus as a model. Rubella viruses

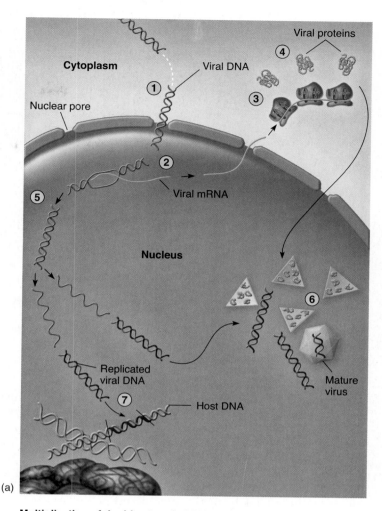

Multiplication of double-stranded DNA viruses.
The virus penetrates the host cell and releases DNA, which

① enters the nucleus and

② is transcribed in two phases. In the early phase viral DNA that codes for enzymes needed to replicate DNA is transcribed. In the late phase viral DNA that codes for structural proteins is transcribed.

③ The RNA transcripts move to the cytoplasm.

④ Viral mRNA is translated into structural proteins; proteins enter the nucleus.

⑤ Viral DNA is replicated repeatedly in the nucleus.

⑥ Viral DNA and proteins are assembled into a mature virus in the nucleus.

⑦ Because it is double-stranded, the viral DNA can insert itself into host DNA (latency).

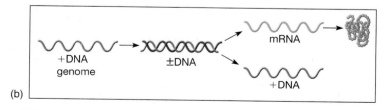

Process Figure 6.13 General features in the multiplication cycle of DNA animal viruses. **(a)** Synthesis in a dsDNA virus. **(b)** Synthesis in a + strand ssDNA virus.

Figure 6.14 Two principal means by which animal viruses penetrate.   **(a)** Endocytosis (engulfment) and uncoating of a herpesvirus. **(b)** Fusion of the cell membrane with the viral envelope (mumps virus).

are an example of this type of virus. Almost immediately upon entry, the viral nucleic acid begins to synthesize the building blocks for new viruses. First, the +ssRNA, which can serve immediately upon entry as mRNA, starts being translated into viral proteins, especially those useful for further viral replication (illustrated in figure 6.11a). The + strand is then replicated by host machinery into −ssRNA. This RNA becomes the template for the creation of many new +ssRNAs, used as the viral genomes for new viruses. Additional +ssRNAs are synthesized and used for late-stage mRNAs. Some viruses come equipped with the necessary enzymes for synthesis of viral components; others utilize those of the host. Proteins for the capsid, spikes, and viral enzymes are synthesized on the host's ribosomes using its amino acids. Figure 6.11b shows how the synthesis of new genomes and mRNAs for translation differs among the various types of RNA viruses. Note that the retroviruses turn their RNA genomes into DNA. This step is accomplished by a viral enzyme called reverse transcriptase and has important implications in infections with these viruses, one of which is HIV. The retroviral cycle is explained in more detail in chapter 20.

DNA viruses generally follow the same steps of adsorption, penetration, uncoating, synthesis, assembly, and release. The steps of the synthesis process vary. Figure 6.13 illustrates this. Replication of dsDNA viruses is divided into phases (figure 6.13a). During the early phase, viral DNA enters the nucleus, where several genes are transcribed into a messenger

RNA. The newly synthesized RNA transcript then moves into the cytoplasm to be translated into viral proteins (enzymes) needed to replicate the viral DNA; this replication occurs in the nucleus. The host cell's own DNA polymerase is often involved, though some viruses (herpes, for example) have their own polymerase. During the late phase, other parts of the viral genome are transcribed and translated into proteins

Figure 6.15 Nucleus of a cell, containing a crystalline mass of adenovirus (35,000×).

(a)

(b)

Figure 6.16 Maturation and release of enveloped viruses. **(a)** As parainfluenza virus is budded off the membrane, it simultaneously picks up an envelope and spikes. **(b)** AIDS viruses (HIV) leave their host T cell by budding off its surface.

required to form the capsid and other structures. The new viral genomes and capsids are assembled, and the mature viruses are released by budding or cell disintegration. Double-stranded DNA viruses interact directly with the DNA of their host cell. In some viruses, the viral DNA becomes silently *integrated* into the host's genome by insertion at a particular site on the host genome. This integration may later lead to the transformation of the host cell into a cancer cell and the production of a tumor.

A slightly different replication mechanism is used by ssDNA viruses; this is illustrated in figure 6.13*b*.

Assembly of Animal Viruses: Host Cell as Factory

Toward the end of the cycle, mature virus particles are constructed from the growing pool of parts. In most instances, the capsid is first laid down as an empty shell that will serve as a receptacle for the nucleic acid strand. Electron micrographs taken during this time show cells with masses of viruses, often in crystalline packets **(figure 6.15)**. One important event leading to the release of enveloped viruses is the insertion of viral spikes into the host's cell membrane so they can be picked up as the virus buds off with its envelope, as discussed earlier.

Release of Mature Viruses

To complete the cycle, assembled viruses leave their host in one of two ways. Nonenveloped and complex viruses that reach maturation in the cell nucleus or cytoplasm are released when the cell lyses or ruptures. Enveloped viruses are liberated by **budding** or **exocytosis**[4] from the membranes of the cytoplasm, nucleus, endoplasmic reticulum, or vesicles. During this process, the nucleocapsid binds to the membrane, which curves completely around it and forms a small pouch. Pinching off the pouch releases the virus with its envelope **(figure 6.16)**. Budding of enveloped viruses causes them to be shed gradually, without the sudden destruction of the cell. But regardless of how the virus leaves, most active viral infections are ultimately lethal to the cell because of accumulated damage. The number of viruses released by infected cells is variable, controlled by factors such as the size of the virus and the health of the host cell. About 3,000 to 4,000 virions are released from a single cell infected with poxviruses, whereas a poliovirus-infected cell can release over 100,000 virions. If even a small number of these virions happen to meet another susceptible cell and infect it, the potential for rapid viral proliferation is immense.

---

4. For enveloped viruses, these terms are interchangeable. They mean the release of a virus from an animal cell by enclosing it in a portion of membrane derived from the cell.

Damage to the Host Cell and Persistent Infections

The short- and long-term effects of viral infections on animal cells are well documented. **Cytopathic** (sy″-toh-path′-ik) **effects (CPEs)** are defined as virus-induced damage to the cell that alters its microscopic appearance. Individual cells can become disoriented, undergo gross changes in shape or size, or develop intracellular changes **(figure 6.17a).** It is common to find **inclusion bodies,** or compacted masses of viruses or damaged cell organelles, in the nucleus and cytoplasm **(figure 6.17b).** Examination of cells and tissues for cytopathic effects is an important part of the diagnosis of viral infections. **Table 6.6** summarizes some prominent cytopathic effects associated with specific viruses. One very common CPE is the fusion of multiple host cells into single large cells containing multiple nuclei. These **syncytia** are a result of some viruses' ability to fuse membranes. One virus (respiratory syncytial virus) is even named for this effect.

Although accumulated damage from a virus infection kills most host cells, some cells maintain a carrier relationship, in which the cell harbors the virus and is not immediately lysed. These so-called *persistent infections* can last from a few weeks to the remainder of the host's life. Viruses can remain latent in the cytoplasm of a host cell, or can incorporate into the DNA of the host. When viral DNA is incorporated into the DNA of the host, it is called a **provirus.** The virus that causes roseola has been found to be passed down from parent to infant in the provirus state, the first such instance of this form of transmission that can result in disease symptoms. One of the more serious complications occurs with the measles virus. It may remain hidden in brain cells for many years, causing progressive damage and loss of function. Several types of viruses remain in a *chronic latent state,*[5] periodically becoming

Table 6.6 Cytopathic Changes in Selected Virus-Infected Animal Cells

Virus	Response in Animal Cell
Smallpox virus	Cells round up; inclusions appear in cytoplasm
Herpes simplex	Cells fuse to form multinucleated syncytia; nuclear inclusions (see figure 6.17)
Adenovirus	Clumping of cells; nuclear inclusions
Poliovirus	Cell lysis; no inclusions
Reovirus	Cell enlargement; vacuoles and inclusions in cytoplasm
Influenza virus	Cells round up; no inclusions
Rabies virus	No change in cell shape; cytoplasmic inclusions (Negri bodies)
Measles virus	Syncytia form (multinucleate)

reactivated. Examples of this are herpes simplex viruses (cold sores and genital herpes) and herpes zoster virus (chickenpox and shingles). Both viruses can go into latency in nerve cells and later emerge under the influence of various stimuli to cause recurrent symptoms. Specific damage that occurs in viral diseases is covered more completely in chapters 18 through 23.

Viruses and Cancer

Some animal viruses enter their host cell and permanently alter its genetic material, leading to cancer. Experts estimate that up

5. Meaning that they exist in an inactive state over long periods.

Figure 6.17 Cytopathic changes in cells and cell cultures infected by viruses. **(a)** Human epithelial cells infected by herpes simplex virus demonstrate multinucleate giant cells. **(b)** Fluorescent-stained human cells infected with cytomegalovirus. Note the inclusion bodies. Note also that both viruses disrupt the cohesive junctions between cells, which would ordinarily be arranged side by side in neat patterns.

to 20% of human cancers are caused by viruses. These viruses are termed **oncogenic,** and their effect on the cell is called **transformation.** Viruses that cause cancer in animals act in several different ways, illustrated in **figure 6.18.** In some cases, the virus carries genes that directly cause the cancer. In other cases, the virus produces proteins that induce a loss of growth regulation in the cell, leading to cancer. Transformed cells have an increased rate of growth; alterations in chromosomes; changes in the cell's surface molecules; and the capacity to divide for an indefinite period, unlike normal animal cells. Mammalian viruses capable of initiating tumors are called **oncoviruses.** Some of these are DNA viruses such as papillomavirus (genital warts are associated with cervical cancer), herpesviruses (Epstein-Barr virus causes Burkitt's lymphoma), and hepatitis B virus (liver cancer). A virus related to HIV—HTLV I[6]—is also involved in human cancers. These findings have spurred a great deal of speculation on the possible involvement of viruses in cancers whose cause is still unknown.

Viruses That Infect Bacteria

We now turn to the life cycle of another type of virus called bacteriophage. When Frederick Twort and Felix d'Herelle discovered bacterial viruses in 1915, it first appeared that the bacterial host cells were being eaten by some unseen parasite, hence the name bacteriophage was used (**phage** coming from the Greek word for "eating"). Most bacteriophages (often shortened to **phage**) contain double-stranded DNA, although single-stranded DNA and RNA types exist as well. So far as is known, every bacterial species is parasitized by various specific bacteriophages. Bacteriophages are of great interest to medical microbiologists because they often make the bacteria

6. Human T-cell lymphotropic virus: causes type of leukemia.

Case File 6   *Continuing the Case*

Epidemiological investigations depend on being able to link a number of instances of an infection to a common source, whether an item of food, a shared experience, or a common sexual partner. Therefore, the fact that the worker who had cleaned up the spill later reported symptoms of salmonellosis could provide a clue to the origin of the infection. Officials suspect that salmonellosis is underreported because many conditions—both infectious and noninfectious—can cause a person to experience three loose stools in a 24-hour period. More often than not, the infection resolves itself, and the patient never seeks medical attention.

For infections such as those caused by *Salmonella,* for which 42,000 cases were reported in 2006, epidemiological studies must be able to differentiate between two organisms of the same species. One procedure routinely used for this purpose is called phage typing. For example, to determine whether the cases seen among the facility workers were connected to the seven community cases, phage typing of SE isolates was performed. Samples tested included four isolates from the facility workers, four stock cultures housed at the facility, and all seven isolates from community members infected with SE.

■ Based on what you have just read about how phages work, how do you think phages can be used to identify the species of a bacterium?

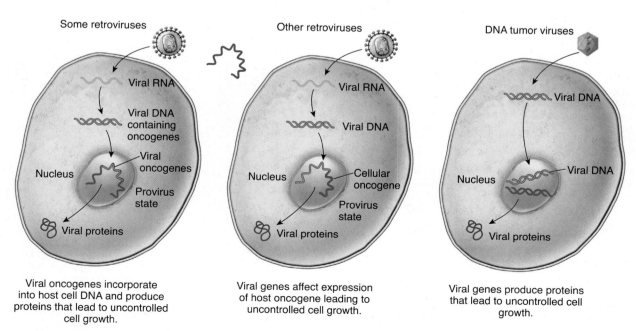

Figure 6.18 Three mechanisms for viral induction of cancer.

they infect more pathogenic for humans (more about this later). Probably the most widely studied bacteriophages are those of the intestinal bacterium *Escherichia coli*—especially the ones known as the T-even phages such as T2 and T4. They have an icosahedral capsid head containing DNA, a central tube (surrounded by a sheath), collar, base plate, tail pins, and fibers, which in combination make an efficient package for infecting a bacterial cell (see figure 6.9). Momentarily

setting aside a strictly scientific and objective tone, it is tempting to think of these extraordinary viruses as minute spacecrafts docking on an alien planet, ready to unload their genetic cargo.

T-even bacteriophages go through similar stages as the animal viruses described earlier **(figure 6.19).** They *adsorb* to host bacteria using specific receptors on the bacterial surface. Although the entire phage does not enter the host cell, the

The lysogenic state in bacteria.
The viral DNA molecule is inserted at specific sites on the bacterial chromosome. The viral DNA is duplicated along with the regular genome and can provide adaptive genes for the host bacterium.

Bacteriophage assembly line.
First the capsomers are synthesized by the host cell. A strand of viral nucleic acid is inserted during capsid formation. In final assembly, the prefabricated components fit together into whole parts and finally into the finished viruses.

Figure 6.19 Events in the lytic cycle of T-even bacteriophages. The lytic cycle (1–7) involves full completion of viral infection through lysis and release of virions. Occasionally the virus enters a reversible state of lysogeny (left) and is incorporated into the host's genetic material.

nucleic acid *penetrates* the host after being injected through a rigid tube the phage inserts through the bacterial membrane and wall **(figure 6.20).** This eliminates the need for *uncoating.* Entry of the nucleic acid causes the cessation of host cell DNA replication and protein synthesis. Soon the host cell machinery is used for viral *replication* and synthesis of viral proteins. As the host cell produces new phage parts, the parts spontaneously *assemble* into bacteriophages.

An average-size *E. coli* cell can contain up to 200 new phage units at the end of this period. Eventually, the host cell becomes so packed with viruses that it **lyses**—splits open—thereby releasing the mature virions **(figure 6.21).** This process is hastened by viral enzymes produced late in the infection cycle that digest the cell envelope, thereby

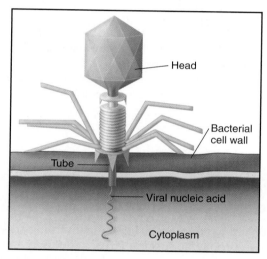

Figure 6.20 Penetration of a bacterial cell by a T-even bacteriophage. After adsorption, the phage plate becomes embedded in the cell wall and the sheath contracts, pushing the tube through the cell wall and releasing the nucleic acid into the interior of the cell.

Figure 6.21 A weakened bacterial cell, crowded with viruses. The cell has ruptured and released numerous virions that can then attack nearby susceptible host cells. Note the empty heads of "spent" phages lined up around the ruptured wall.

weakening it. Upon release, the virulent phages can spread to other susceptible bacterial cells and begin a new cycle of infection.

Bacteriophage infection may result in lysis of the cell, as described above. When this happens the phage is said to have been in the lytic phase or cycle. Alternatively, phages can be less obviously damaging, in a cycle called the lysogenic cycle.

Lysogeny: The Silent Virus Infection

Special DNA phages, called **temperate phages,** while they can participate in a lytic phase, also have the ability to undergo adsorption and penetration into the bacterial host and not undergo replication or release immediately. Instead, the viral DNA enters an inactive **prophage** state, during which it is inserted into the bacterial chromosome. This viral DNA will be retained by the bacterial cell and copied during its normal cell division so that the cell's progeny will also have the temperate phage DNA **(figure 6.22).** This condition, in which the host chromosome carries bacteriophage DNA, is termed **lysogeny** (ly-soj'-uhn-ee). Because viral particles are not produced, the bacterial cells carrying temperate phages do not lyse, and they appear entirely normal. (This will remind you, appropriately, of the provirus state of animal viruses.) On occasion, in a process called **induction,** the prophage in a lysogenic cell will be activated and progress directly into viral replication and the lytic cycle. Lysogeny is a less deadly form of parasitism than the full lytic cycle and is thought to be an advancement that allows the virus to spread without killing the host.

Bacteriophages are just now receiving their due as important shapers of biologic life. Scientists believe that there are more bacteriophages than all other forms of life in the biosphere combined. As we mentioned in the opening

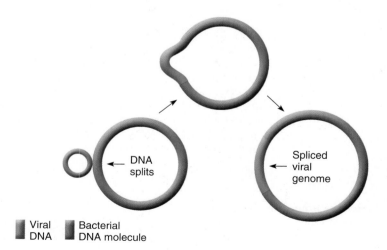

Figure 6.22 The lysogenic state in bacteria. A bacterial DNA molecule can accept and insert viral DNA molecules at specific sites on its genome. This additional viral DNA is duplicated along with the regular genome and can provide adaptive characteristics for the host bacterium.

paragraphs of this chapter, viral genes linger in human, animal, plant, and bacterial genomes in huge numbers. It is estimated that 10% to 20% of DNA in bacteria is actually prophage DNA. As such, viruses can contribute what are essentially permanent traits to the bacteria, so much so that it could be said that all bacteria—indeed all organisms—are really hybrids of themselves and the viruses that infect them.

The Danger of Lysogeny in Human Disease

Many bacteria that infect humans are lysogenized by phages. And sometimes that is very bad news for the human: Occasionally phage genes in the bacterial chromosome cause the production of toxins or enzymes that cause pathology in the human. When a bacterium acquires a new trait from its temperate phage, it is called **lysogenic conversion**. The phenomenon was first discovered in the 1950s in the bacterium that causes diphtheria, *Corynebacterium diphtheriae*. The diphtheria toxin responsible for the deadly nature of the disease is a bacteriophage product. *C. diphtheriae* without the phage are harmless. Other bacteria that are made virulent by their prophages are *Vibrio cholerae*, the agent of cholera, and *Clostridium botulinum*, the cause of botulism.

The life cycles of animal and bacterial viruses (see figure 6.11, figure 6.13, and figure 6.19) illustrate general features of viral multiplication in a very concrete way. The two cycles are compared in **table 6.7.** It is fascinating to realize that viruses are capable of lying "dormant" in their host cells, possibly becoming active at some later time. Because of the intimate association between the genetic material of the virus and host, phages occasionally serve as transporters of bacterial genes from one bacterium to another and consequently can play a profound role in bacterial genetics. This phenomenon, called transduction, is one way that genes for toxin production and drug resistance are transferred between bacteria (see chapters 9 and 12).

6.5 Learning Outcomes—Can You ...

11. ... diagram the five-step life cycle of animal viruses?
12. ... explain what cytopathic effects are?
13. ... discuss both persistent and transforming infections?
14. ... provide a thorough description of lysogenic and lytic bacteriophage infections?

Table 6.7 Comparison of Bacteriophage and Animal Virus Multiplication

	Bacteriophage	**Animal Virus**
Adsorption	Precise attachment of special tail fibers to cell wall	Attachment of capsid or envelope to cell surface receptors
Penetration	Injection of nucleic acid through cell wall; no uncoating of nucleic acid	Whole virus is engulfed and uncoated, or virus surface fuses with cell membrane, nucleic acid is released
Synthesis and Assembly	Occurs in cytoplasm Cessation of host synthesis Viral DNA or RNA is replicated and begins to function Viral components synthesized	Occurs in cytoplasm and nucleus Cessation of host synthesis Viral DNA or RNA is replicated and begins to function Viral components synthesized
Viral Persistence	Lysogeny	Latency, chronic infection, cancer
Release from Host Cell	Cell lyses when viral enzymes weaken it	Some cells lyse; enveloped viruses bud off host cell membrane
Cell Destruction	Immediate or delayed	Immediate or delayed

6.6 Techniques in Cultivating and Identifying Animal Viruses

One problem hampering earlier animal virologists was their inability to propagate specific viruses routinely in pure culture and in sufficient quantities for their studies. Virtually all of the pioneering attempts at cultivation had to be performed in an organism that was the usual host for the virus. But this method had its limitations. How could researchers have ever traced the stages of viral multiplication if they had been restricted to the natural host, especially in the case of human viruses? Fortunately, systems of cultivation with broader applications were developed, including *in vivo* (in vee'-voh) inoculation of laboratory-bred animals and embryonic bird tissues and *in vitro* (in vee'-troh) cell (or tissue) culture methods. Such use of substitute host systems permits greater control, uniformity, and wide-scale harvesting of viruses.

The primary purposes of viral cultivation are:

1. to isolate and identify viruses in clinical specimens;
2. to prepare viruses for vaccines; and
3. to do detailed research on viral structure, multiplication cycles, genetics, and effects on host cells.

Using Live Animal Inoculation

Specially bred strains of white mice, rats, hamsters, guinea pigs, and rabbits are the usual choices for animal cultivation of viruses. Invertebrates (insects) or nonhuman primates are occasionally used as well. Because viruses can exhibit some host specificity, certain animals can propagate a given virus more readily than others. The animal is exposed to the virus by injection of a viral preparation or specimen into the brain, blood, muscle, body cavity, skin, or footpads.

Using Bird Embryos

An embryo is an early developmental stage of animals marked by rapid differentiation of cells. Birds undergo their embryonic period within the closed protective case of an egg, which makes an incubating bird egg a nearly perfect system for viral propagation. It is an intact and self-supporting unit, complete with its own sterile environment and nourishment. Furthermore, it furnishes several embryonic tissues that readily support viral multiplication.

Chicken, duck, and turkey eggs are the most common choices for inoculation. The egg must be injected through the shell, usually by drilling a hole or making a small window. Rigorous sterile techniques must be used to prevent contamination by bacteria and fungi from the air and the outer surface of the shell. The exact part of the egg that is inoculated is guided by the type of virus being cultivated and the goals of the experiment (**figure 6.23**).

Viruses multiplying in embryos may or may not cause effects visible to the naked eye. The signs of viral growth include death of the embryo, defects in embryonic development, and localized areas of damage in the membranes, resulting in discrete, opaque spots called pocks (a variant of *pox*). If a virus does not produce overt changes in the developing embryonic tissue, virologists have other methods of detection. Embryonic fluids and tissues can be prepared for direct examination with an electron microscope. Certain viruses can also be detected by their ability to agglutinate red blood cells (form big clumps) or by their reaction with an antibody of known specificity that will affix to its corresponding virus, if it is present.

Using Cell (Tissue) Culture Techniques

The most important early discovery that led to easier cultivation of viruses in the laboratory was the development of a simple and effective way to grow populations of isolated animal cells in culture. These types of *in vitro* cultivation systems are termed cell culture or tissue culture. (Although these terms are used interchangeably, cell culture is probably a more accurate description.) So prominent is this method that most viruses are propagated in some sort of cell culture, and much of the virologist's work involves developing and maintaining these cultures. Animal cell cultures are grown in sterile chambers with special media that contain the correct nutrients required by animal cells to survive. The cultured cells grow in the form of a *monolayer,* a

(a)

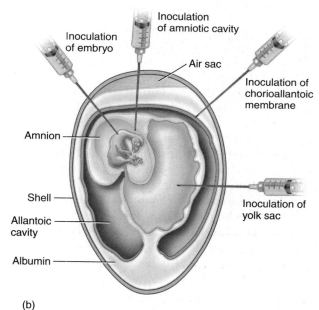

(b)

Figure 6.23 Cultivating animal viruses in a developing bird embryo. **(a)** A technician inoculates fertilized chicken eggs with viruses in the first stage of preparing vaccines. This process requires the highest levels of sterile and aseptic precautions. Most influenza vaccine is prepared this way. **(b)** The shell is perforated using sterile techniques, and a virus preparation is injected into a site selected to grow the viruses. Targets include the allantoic cavity, a fluid-filled sac that functions in embryonic waste removal; the amniotic cavity, a sac that cushions and protects the embryo itself; the chorioallantoic membrane, which functions in embryonic gas exchange; the yolk sac, a membrane that mobilizes yolk for the nourishment of the embryo; and the embryo itself.

single, confluent sheet of cells that supports viral multiplication and permits close inspection of the culture for signs of infection (**figure 6.24**).

Cultures of animal cells usually exist in the primary or continuous form. *Primary cell cultures* are prepared by placing freshly isolated animal tissue in a growth medium. The cells undergo a series of mitotic divisions to produce a monolayer. Embryonic, fetal, adult, and even cancerous tissues have served as sources of primary cultures. A primary culture retains several characteristics of the original tissue from which it was derived, but this original line generally has a limited existence. Eventually, it will die out or mutate into a line of cells that can grow continuously. Continuous cell lines tend to have altered chromosome numbers, grow rapidly, and show changes in morphology; and they can be continuously subcultured, provided they are routinely transferred to fresh nutrient medium. One very clear advantage of cell culture is that a specific cell line can be available for viruses with a very narrow host range.

The recent avian flu worries have prompted scientists to look for faster and more efficient ways to grow the vaccine strains of influenza virus, which has been grown in chicken eggs since the 1950s. Scientists have succeeded in propagating the viruses in a continuous cell line derived from dog kidney cells. There were plans to produce flu vaccine in cell culture beginning in 2009, but they were mostly thwarted. During the run-up to the fall 2009 flu season, only one company was manufacturing flu vaccine in cell culture; the rest were using chicken eggs.

One way to detect the growth of a virus in culture is to observe degeneration and lysis of infected cells in the monolayer of cells. The areas where virus-infected cells have been destroyed show up as clear, well-defined patches in the cell sheet called **plaques** (figure 6.24). Plaques are essentially the macroscopic manifestation of cytopathic effects (CPEs), discussed earlier. This same technique is used to detect and count bacteriophages, because they also produce plaques when grown in soft agar cultures of their host cells (bacteria). A plaque develops when the viruses released by an infected host cell radiate out to adjacent host cells (figure 6.24). As new cells become infected, they die and release more viruses, and so on. As this process continues, the infection spreads gradually and symmetrically from the original point of infection, causing the macroscopic appearance of round, clear spaces that correspond to areas of dead cells.

Even though growing viruses remains a challenge, scientists have recently succeeded in artificially creating viruses (**Insight 6.2**).

6.6 Learning Outcomes—Can You …

15. … list the three principal purposes of cultivating viruses?
16. … describe three ways in which viruses are cultivated?

(a)

(b)

(c)

Figure 6.24 Appearance of normal and infected cell cultures. **(a)** Microscopic view of an undisturbed layer of animal cells. **(b)** Plaques in the animal cell layer. These are open spaces where cells have been disrupted by viral infection. **(c)** Macroscopic view of a lawn of *E. coli* on agar. The clear, round spaces are plaques, points of infection by bacteriophages.

INSIGHT 6.2   Artificial Viruses Created!

Newspapers are filled with stories of the debate over the ethics of creating life through cloning techniques. Dolly the cloned sheep and the cattle, swine, and goats that have followed in her footsteps have raised ethical questions about scientists "playing God" when they harvest genetic material from an animal and create an identical organism from it, as is the case with cloning.

Meanwhile, in a much less publicized event in 2002, scientists at the State University of New York at Stony Brook succeeded in artificially creating a virus that is virtually identical to natural poliovirus. They used DNA nucleotides they bought "off the shelf" and put them together according to the published poliovirus sequence. They then added an enzyme that would transcribe the DNA sequence into the RNA genome used by poliovirus. They ended up with a virus that was nearly identical to poliovirus (see illustration), with a similar capsid as well as a similar ability to infect host cells and reproduce itself.

The creation of the virus was greeted with controversy, particularly because poliovirus is potentially devastating to human health. The scientists, who were working on a biowarfare defense

project funded by the Department of Defense, argued that they were demonstrating what could be accomplished if information and chemicals fell into the wrong hands.

In the fall of 2005, scientists at the Centers for Disease Control and Prevention and Mount Sinai School of Medicine reconstructed the strain of influenza that caused the worldwide flu pandemic of 1918. That pandemic killed 20–50 million people in the world and was noteworthy because of how deadly it was to otherwise healthy young adults. Scientists decided to recreate the virus so that they could determine the genetic basis of its extreme danger to human health, knowledge that could prove valuable as new influenza strains emerge. It was handled and stored in a very high security environment, and multiple safeguards were employed to make sure there was no possibility of an accidental release of the virus. But the prospect of harmful misuse of the new technology has prompted scientific experts to team with national security and bioethics experts to discuss the pros and cons of the new technology and ways to ensure its acceptable uses.

6.7 Medical Importance of Viruses

The number of viral infections that occur on a worldwide basis is nearly impossible to measure accurately. Certainly, viruses are the most common cause of acute infections that do not result in hospitalization, especially when one considers widespread diseases such as colds, hepatitis, chickenpox, influenza, herpes, and warts. If one also takes into account prominent viral infections found only in certain regions of the world, such as Dengue fever, Rift Valley fever, and yellow fever, the total could easily exceed several billion cases each year. Although most viral infections do not result in death, some, such as rabies, AIDS, and Ebola, have very high mortality rates, and others can lead to long-term debility (polio, neonatal rubella). Current research is focused on the possible connection of viruses to chronic afflictions of unknown cause, such as type I diabetes, multiple sclerosis, various cancers, and even obesity **(Insight 6.3)**. Additionally, as mentioned earlier, several cancers have their origins in viral infection.

Don't forget that despite the reputation viruses have for being highly detrimental, in some cases, they may actually show a beneficial side (see Insight 6.1).

6.7 Learning Outcomes—Can You . . .

17. . . . analyze the relative importance of viruses in human infection and disease?

6.8 Other Noncellular Infectious Agents

Not all noncellular infectious agents have typical viral morphology. One group of unusual forms, even smaller and simpler than viruses, is implicated in chronic, persistent diseases in humans and animals. These diseases are called spongiform encephalopathies because the brain tissue removed from affected animals resembles a sponge. The infection has a long period of latency (usually several years) before the first clinical signs appear. Signs range from mental derangement to loss of muscle control. The diseases are progressive and universally fatal.

A common feature of these conditions is the deposition of distinct protein fibrils in the brain tissue. Researchers have hypothesized that these fibrils are the agents of the disease and have named them **prions** (pree'-onz).

Creutzfeldt-Jakob disease afflicts the central nervous system of humans and causes gradual degeneration and death. Cases in which medical workers developed the disease after handling autopsy specimens seem to indicate that it is transmissible, but by an unknown mechanism. Several animals (sheep, mink, elk) are victims of similar transmissible diseases. Bovine spongiform encephalopathy (BSE), or "mad cow disease," was recently the subject of fears and a crisis in Europe when researchers found evidence that the disease could be acquired by humans who consumed contaminated beef. This was the first incidence of prion disease transmission

INSIGHT 6.3   A Vaccine for Obesity?

Could it be true? That it was not really the late-night brownies and lack of exercise that made you put on the 20 pounds? Researchers from several different labs are producing evidence that at least some types of obesity may be caused by viruses.

The evidence that viruses cause obesity in humans is somewhat indirect at this point, although animal models provide supporting evidence. So far, at least nine different viruses have been proven to cause obesity in animals, including dogs, rats, and birds. The viruses range from canine distemper virus, to the Borna virus (in rats), to several adenoviruses that cause obesity in multiple species.

Of course researchers cannot inject humans with these viruses just to see if they cause them to get fat. So they use more indirect methods. In 2007 one group, led by Nikhil Dhurnadhar at

Louisiana State University, tested stored blood from 500 people and found one particular adenovirus in 30% of obese people and in only 11% of nonobese people.

This group also studied 26 sets of twins and found that when one twin had evidence of the viral infection and the other did not, the infected twin always had a higher weight. In 2008 they discovered a single gene in the virus that is responsible for the creation of fat cells, raising the possibility of being able to treat obesity by altering the effect of that gene.

The researchers emphasize that obesity has many causes. Other factors considered to be important include a genetic predisposition and, yes, poor diet and exercise. But in the future, people may be offered a vaccine against these viruses to prevent at least some causes of obesity.

---

from animals to humans. Several hundred Europeans developed symptoms of a variant form of Creutzfeldt-Jakob disease, leading to strict governmental controls on exporting cattle and beef products. In 2003, isolated cows with BSE were found in Canada and in the United States. Extreme precautionary measures have been taken to protect North American consumers. As of 2009, only two BSE-positive cows have been found in the United States, compared to over 184,000 in the United Kingdom. (This disease is described in more detail in chapter 19.)

The exact mode of prion infection is currently being analyzed. The fact that prions are composed primarily of protein (no nucleic acid) has certainly revolutionized our ideas of what can constitute an infectious agent. One of the most compelling questions is just how a prion could be replicated, because all other infectious agents require some nucleic acid.

Other fascinating viruslike agents in human disease are defective forms called satellite viruses that are actually dependent on other viruses for replication. Two remarkable examples are the adeno-associated virus (AAV), so named because it was originally thought that it could only replicate in cells infected with adenovirus. But it can also infect cells that are infected with other viruses or which have had their DNA disrupted through other means. Another satellite virus, called the delta agent, is a naked circle of RNA that is expressed only in the presence of the hepatitis B virus and can worsen the severity of liver damage.

Plants are also parasitized by viruslike agents called **viroids** that differ from ordinary viruses by being very small (about one-tenth the size of an average virus) and being composed of only naked strands of RNA, lacking a capsid or any other type of coating. Viroids are significant pathogens in several economically important plants, including tomatoes, potatoes, cucumbers, citrus trees, and chrysanthemums.

6.8 Learning Outcomes—Can You . . .

18. . . . name at least three noncellular infectious agents besides viruses?

Case File 6   *Wrap-Up*

It is possible to classify different members of a bacterial species into phage types, or strains, based on their susceptibility to lysis. Each phage has a limited number of bacterial strains that are susceptible to infection by that phage, and these strains therefore constitute the specific host range of that phage.

In the lab, the bacterium to be tested is inoculated onto a solid medium in a Petri plate so that it will grow to completely cover the medium, forming a bacterial lawn. The plate is then marked off into squares, and each square is inoculated with a single drop of a suspension containing a different phage to be used in typing. The plate is allowed to incubate for 24 hours and is then examined for clear zones within the bacterial lawn. If a circumstantial connection exists between several isolates, and the phage types of the isolates are identical, the chances are great that they are epidemiologically related.

In this case, phage typing of samples revealed that the spilled *Salmonella enterica* Enteritidis culture was phage type 8 (as expected) and that all four employee isolates were also phage type 8. DNA fingerprinting showed no difference between the employee isolates and the community isolates, but phage typing revealed that all seven community isolates were phage type 13A. Based on this information, it was assumed that all of the employees who became ill did so as a result of exposure to a strain of *Salmonella enterica* Enteritidis that was used in vaccine production and that the illnesses seen in the community, despite being caused by the same bacterial species, were unrelated to the incident at the production facility.

Based on the results of this case, the Maine Department of Health and Human Services recommended that the facility implement new practices for handling spills and routinely disinfecting work areas. In addition, improved hand-washing practices and the use of personal protection equipment, including gloves, gowns, and face shields, were suggested.

See: 2007. *MMWR* 56:877–79.

6.9 Treatment of Animal Viral Infections

The nature of viruses has at times been a major impediment to effective therapy. Because viruses are not bacteria, antibiotics aimed at disrupting prokaryotic cells do not work on them. Out of necessity, many antiviral drugs block virus replication by targeting the function of host cells and can cause severe side effects. Almost all antiviral drugs are designed to target one of the steps in the viral life cycle you learned about earlier in this chapter. Azidothymidine (AZT), a drug used to treat AIDS, targets the synthesis stage. The integrase inhibitor class of HIV drugs interrupts the ability of HIV genetic information to incorporate into the host cell DNA. Another compound that is used with some success in treating and preventing viral infections is a naturally occurring human cell product called interferon (see chapters 12 and 14). Vaccines that stimulate immunity are an extremely valuable tool but are available for only a limited number of viral diseases (see chapter 15).

We have completed our survey of prokaryotes, eukaryotes, and viruses and have described characteristics of different representatives of these three groups. Chapters 7 and 8 explore how microorganisms maintain themselves, beginning with nutrition (chapter 7) and then looking into microbial metabolism (chapter 8).

6.9 Learning Outcomes—Can You ...

19. ... discuss the primary reason that antiviral drugs are more difficult to design than antibacterial drugs?

Chapter Summary

6.1 The Search for the Elusive Viruses

- Viruses are noncellular entities whose properties have been identified through technological advances in microscopy and tissue culture.

6.2 The Position of Viruses in the Biological Spectrum

- Viruses are infectious particles that invade every known type of cell. They are not alive, yet they are able to redirect the metabolism of living cells to reproduce virus particles.
- Viruses have a profound influence on the genetic makeup of the biosphere.
- Viral replication inside a cell usually causes death or loss of function of that cell

6.3 The General Structure of Viruses

- Virus size range is from 20 nm to 450 nm (diameter). Viruses are composed of an outer protein capsid enclosing either DNA or RNA plus a variety of enzymes. Some viruses also exhibit an envelope around the capsid.
- Spikes on the surface of the virus capsid or envelope are critical for their attachment to host cells.

6.4 How Viruses Are Classified and Named

- Viruses are grouped in various ways. This textbook uses their structure, genetic composition, and host range to categorize them.
- The International Committee on the Taxonomy of Viruses oversees naming and classification of viruses. Viruses are classified into orders, families, and genera.

6.5 Modes of Viral Multiplication

- Viruses go through a multiplication cycle that generally involves adsorption, penetration (sometimes followed by uncoating), viral synthesis and assembly, and viral release by lysis or budding.
- These events turn the host cell into a factory solely for making and shedding new viruses. This results in the ultimate destruction of the cell.
- Animal viruses can cause acute infections or can persist in host tissues as chronic latent infections that can reactivate periodically throughout the host's life. Some persistent animal viruses are oncogenic.
- Bacteriophages vary significantly from animal viruses in their methods of adsorption, penetration, site of replication, and method of exit from host cells.
- Lysogeny is a condition in which viral DNA is inserted into the bacterial chromosome and remains inactive for an extended period. It is replicated right along with the chromosome every time the bacterium divides.
- Some bacteria express virulence traits that are coded for by the bacteriophage DNA in their chromosomes. This phenomenon is called lysogenic conversion.

6.6 Techniques in Cultivating and Identifying Animal Viruses

- Animal viruses must be studied in some type of host cell environment such as laboratory animals, bird embryos, or tissue cultures.
- Cell and tissue cultures are cultures of host cells grown in special sterile chambers containing correct types and proportions of growth factors using aseptic techniques to exclude unwanted microorganisms.
- Virus growth in cell culture, and bacteriophage growth on bacterial lawns, is detected by the appearance of plaques.

6.7 Medical Importance of Viruses

- Viruses are easily responsible for several billion infections each year. It is conceivable that many chronic diseases of unknown cause will eventually be connected to viral agents.

6.8 Other Noncellular Infectious Agents

- Other noncellular agents of disease are the prions, which are not viruses at all but protein fibers; viroids, extremely small lengths of protein-coated nucleic acid; and satellite viruses, which require the presence of larger viruses to cause disease.

6.9 Treatment of Animal Viral Infections

- Viral infections are difficult to treat because the drugs that attack viral replication also cause side effects in the host.

Multiple-Choice and True-False Questions   Knowledge and Comprehension

Multiple-Choice Questions. Select the correct answer from the answers provided.

1. A virus is a tiny infectious
   a. cell.
   b. living thing.
   c. particle.
   d. nucleic acid.

2. Viruses are known to infect
   a. plants.
   b. bacteria.
   c. fungi.
   d. all organisms.

3. The nucleic acid of a virus is
   a. DNA only.
   b. RNA only.
   c. both DNA and RNA.
   d. either DNA or RNA.

4. The general steps in a viral multiplication cycle are
   a. adsorption, penetration, synthesis, assembly, and release.
   b. endocytosis, uncoating, replication, assembly, and budding.
   c. adsorption, uncoating, duplication, assembly, and lysis.
   d. endocytosis, penetration, replication, maturation, and exocytosis.

5. A prophage is an early stage in the development of a/an
   a. bacterial virus.
   b. poxvirus.
   c. lytic virus.
   d. enveloped virus.

6. In general, RNA viruses multiply in the cell ____, and DNA viruses multiply in the cell ____.
   a. nucleus, cytoplasm
   b. cytoplasm, nucleus
   c. vesicles, ribosomes
   d. endoplasmic reticulum, nucleolus

7. Viruses cannot be cultivated in
   a. tissue culture.
   b. bird embryos.
   c. live mammals.
   d. blood agar.

8. Clear patches in cell cultures that indicate sites of virus infection are called
   a. plaques.
   b. pocks.
   c. colonies.
   d. prions.

9. Label the parts of this virus. Identify the capsid, nucleic acid, and other features of this virus. Can you identify which virus it is?

10. Circle the viral infections from this list: cholera, rabies, plague, cold sores, whooping cough, tetanus, genital warts, gonorrhea, mumps, Rocky Mountain spotted fever, syphilis, rubella.

True-False Questions. If the statement is true, leave as is. If it is false, correct it by rewriting the sentence.

11. In lysogeny, viral DNA is inserted into the host chromosome.

12. A viral capsid is composed of subunits called virions.

13. The envelope of an animal virus is derived from the cell wall of its host cell.

14. The nucleic acid of animal viruses enters the cell through a process called translocation.

15. Viruses that persist in the (host) cell and cause recurrent disease are called latent.

Critical Thinking Questions   Application and Analysis

These questions are suggested as a *writing-to-learn* experience. For each question, compose a one- or two-paragraph answer that includes the factual information needed to completely address the question.

1. a. Since viruses lack metabolic enzymes, how can they synthesize necessary components?
   b. What are some enzymes with which the virus is equipped?

2. a. What characteristics of viruses could be used to characterize them as life forms?
   b. What makes them more similar to lifeless molecules?

3. a. If viruses that normally form envelopes were prevented from budding, would they still be infectious?
   b. If the RNA of an influenza virus were injected into a cell by itself, could it cause a lytic infection?

4. a. Given that DNA viruses can actually be carried in the DNA of the host cell's chromosomes, comment on what this phenomenon means in terms of inheritance in the offspring.
   b. Discuss the connection between viruses and cancers, giving possible mechanisms for viruses that cause cancer.

5. HIV attacks only specific types of human cells, such as certain white blood cells and nerve cells. Can you explain why a virus can enter some types of human cells but not others?

6. a. What is the principal effect of the agent of Creutzfeldt-Jakob disease?
   b. How is the proposed agent different from viruses?
   c. What are viroids?

7. Why are viral diseases more difficult to treat than bacterial diseases?

8. a. If you were involved in developing an antiviral drug, what would be some important considerations? (Can a drug "kill" a virus?)
   b. How could multiplication be blocked?

9. Is there such a thing as a "good virus"? Explain why or why not. Consider both bacteriophages and viruses of eukaryotic organisms.

10. Discuss some advantages and disadvantages of bacteriophage therapy in treating bacterial infections.

Concept Mapping   Synthesis

Appendix D provides guidance for working with concept maps.

1. Supply your own linking words or phrases in this concept map, and provide the missing concepts in the empty boxes.

Visual Connections   Synthesis

These questions use visual images or previous content to make connections to this chapter's concepts.

1. **From chapter 1, table 1.2 .** This chart from chapter 1 identified diseases most clearly caused by microorganisms. Considering what you have learned in this chapter, are there more deaths caused by microorganisms than might be accounted for by the red-labeled diseases? Can you make a rough guess of how many total deaths might be caused by viruses?

Table 1.2 Top Causes of Death—All Diseases

United States	No. of Deaths	Worldwide	No. of Deaths
1. Heart disease	652,000	1. Heart disease	12.2 million
2. Cancer	559,000	2. Stroke	5.7 million
3. Stroke	144,000	3. Cancer	5.7 million
4. Chronic lower-respiratory disease	131,000	4. Respiratory infections*	3.9 million
5. Unintentional injury (accidents)	118,000	5. Chronic lower-respiratory disease	3.6 million
6. Diabetes	75,000	6. Accidents	3.5 million
7. Alzheimer's disease	72,000	7. HIV/AIDS	2.9 million
8. Influenza and pneumonia	63,000	8. Perinatal conditions	2.5 million
9. Kidney problems	44,000	9. Diarrheal diseases	2.0 million
10. Septicemia (bloodstream infection)	34,000	10. Tuberculosis	1.6 million

*Diseases in red are those most clearly caused by microorganisms.
Source: Data from the World Health Organization, 2008.

www.connect.microbiology.com

Enhance your study of this chapter with study tools and practice tests. Also ask your instructor about the resources available through ConnectPlus, including the media-rich eBook, interactive learning tools, and animations.

Microbial Nutrition, Ecology, and Growth

Case File 7

A Nevada resident who had just returned home from a cruise on Prince William Sound in July 2007 was struck by gastrointestinal distress so severe that medical intervention was required. Laboratory tests for this patient indicated the presence of *Vibrio parahaemolyticus*, a pathogenic bacterium known to cause gastroenteritis. Infection usually occurs through consuming raw or undercooked shellfish, particularly oysters. In this case, the patient's illness began 3 days after eating raw oysters from Prince William Sound.

Further investigation by the epidemiology section of the Alaska Division of Public Health revealed that a total of 54 people had developed watery diarrhea, along with various other gastrointestinal symptoms, beginning within 2 days of consuming raw oysters collected from Alaskan waters. Stool samples provided by eight patients all contained *V. parahaemolyticus*. However, the discovery of this bacterium was puzzling because *V. parahaemolyticus* requires a minimum water temperature of 16.5°C to survive, and the waters of Prince William Sound have historically been colder than that.

- Into which of three temperature classifications for bacteria does *V. parahaemolyticus* fall?
- What could explain the change in the ability of *V. parahaemolyticus* to survive?

Continuing the Case appears on page 183.

Outline and Learning Outcomes

7.1 Microbial Nutrition

1. List the essential nutrients of a bacterial cell.
2. Differentiate between macronutrients and micronutrients.
3. Construct four different terms that describe an organism's sources of carbon and energy.
4. Define saprobe and parasite.
5. Discuss diffusion and osmosis.
6. Identify the effects on a cell of isotonic, hypotonic, and hypertonic conditions.
7. Name two types of passive transport and three types of active transport.

7.2 Environmental Factors That Influence Microbes
  8. Name five types of bacteria based on their temperature preferences.
  9. Explain how different organisms deal with oxygen.
  10. Name three other physical factors that microbes must contend with.
  11. List and describe the five types of associations microbes can have with their hosts.
  12. Discuss characteristics of biofilms that differentiate them from planktonic bacteria.

7.3 The Study of Microbial Growth
  13. Describe the major way that bacteria divide; name another way used by fewer bacteria.
  14. Define doubling time and how it relates to exponential growth.
  15. Compare and contrast the four phases of growth in a bacterial growth curve.
  16. Identify three methods besides a growth curve to count bacteria.

7.1 Microbial Nutrition

Nutrition is a process by which chemical substances called **nutrients** are acquired from the environment and used in cellular activities such as metabolism and growth. With respect to nutrition, microbes are not really so different from humans. Bacteria living in mud on a diet of inorganic sulfur or protozoa digesting wood in a termite's intestine seem to live radical lifestyles, but even these organisms require a constant influx of certain substances from their habitat. In general, all living things require a source of elements such as carbon, hydrogen, oxygen, phosphorus, potassium, nitrogen, sulfur, calcium, iron, sodium, chlorine, magnesium, and certain other elements. But the ultimate source of a particular element, its chemical form, and how much of it the microbe needs are all points of variation between different types of organisms. Any substance, whether in elemental or molecular form, that must be provided to an organism is called an **essential nutrient.** Once absorbed, nutrients are processed and transformed into the chemicals of the cell.

Two categories of essential nutrients are **macronutrients** and **micronutrients.** Macronutrients are required in relatively large quantities and play principal roles in cell structure and metabolism. Examples of macronutrients are carbon, hydrogen, and oxygen. Micronutrients, or **trace elements,** such as manganese, zinc, and nickel, are present in much smaller amounts and are involved in enzyme function and maintenance of protein structure. What constitutes a micronutrient can vary from one microbe to another.

Another way to categorize nutrients is according to their carbon content. An inorganic nutrient is an atom or simple molecule that contains a combination of atoms other than carbon and hydrogen. The natural reservoirs of inorganic compounds are mineral deposits in the crust of the earth, bodies of water, and the atmosphere. Examples include metals and their salts (magnesium sulfate, ferric nitrate, sodium phosphate), gases (oxygen, carbon dioxide), and water **(table 7.1).** In contrast, the molecules of organic nutrients contain carbon and hydrogen atoms and are usually the products of living things. They range from the simplest organic molecule, methane (CH_4), to large polymers (carbohydrates, lipids, proteins, and nucleic acids). The source of nutrients is extremely varied: Some microbes obtain their nutrients entirely from inorganic sources, and others require a combination of organic and inorganic sources. Parasites capable of invading and living on the human body derive all essential nutrients from host tissues, tissue fluids, secretions, and wastes.

Chemical Analysis of Microbial Cytoplasm

Examining the chemical composition of a bacterial cell can indicate its nutritional requirements. **Table 7.2** lists the major contents of the intestinal bacterium *Escherichia coli*. Some of these components are absorbed in a ready-to-use form, and others must be synthesized by the cell from simple nutrients. Several important features of cell composition can be summarized as follows:

- Water is the most abundant of all the components (70%).
- Proteins are the next most prevalent chemical.
- About 97% of the dry cell weight is composed of organic compounds.

Table 7.1 Principal Inorganic Reservoirs of Elements

Element	Inorganic Environmental Reservoir
Carbon	CO_2 in air; CO_3^{2-} in rocks and sediments
Oxygen	O_2 in air, certain oxides, water
Nitrogen	N_2 in air; NO_3^-, NO_2^-, NH_4^+ in soil and water
Hydrogen	Water, H_2 gas, mineral deposits
Phosphorus	Mineral deposits (PO_4^{3-}, H_3PO_4)
Sulfur	Mineral deposits, volcanic sediments (SO_4^{2-}, H_2S, S^0)
Potassium	Mineral deposits, the ocean (KCl, K_3PO_4)
Sodium	Mineral deposits, the ocean ($NaCl$, $NaSi$)
Calcium	Mineral deposits, the ocean ($CaCO_3$, $CaCl_2$)
Magnesium	Mineral deposits, geologic sediments ($MgSO_4$)
Chloride	The ocean ($NaCl$, NH_4Cl)
Iron	Mineral deposits, geologic sediments ($FeSO_4$)
Manganese, molybdenum, cobalt, nickel, zinc, copper, other micronutrients	Various geologic sediments

- About 96% of the cell is composed of six elements (represented by CHONPS).
- Chemical elements are needed in the overall scheme of cell growth, but most of them are available to the cell as compounds and not as pure elements (see table 7.2).
- A cell as "simple" as *E. coli* contains on the order of 5,000 different compounds, yet it needs to absorb only a few types of nutrients to synthesize this great diversity. These include $(NH_4)_2SO_4$, $FeCl_2$, NaCl, trace elements, glucose, KH_2PO_4, $MgSO_4$, $CaHPO_4$, and water.

Sources of Essential Nutrients

In their most basic form, elements that make up nutrients exist in environmental inorganic reservoirs. These reservoirs not only serve as a permanent, long-term source of these elements but also can be replenished by the activities of organisms. In fact, as we shall see in chapter 24, the ability of microbes to keep elements cycling is essential to all life on the earth.

For convenience, this section on nutrients is organized by element. You will no doubt notice that some categories overlap and that many of the compounds furnish more than one element.

Carbon Sources

It seems worthwhile to emphasize a point about the *extracellular source* of carbon as opposed to the *intracellular function* of carbon compounds. Although a distinction is made between the type of carbon compound cells absorb as nutrients (inorganic or organic), the majority of carbon compounds involved in the normal structure and metabolism of all cells are organic.

A **heterotroph** is an organism that must obtain its carbon in an organic form. Because organic carbon originates from the bodies of other organisms, heterotrophs are dependent on other life forms (*hetero-* is a Greek prefix meaning "other"). Among the common organic molecules that can satisfy this requirement are proteins, carbohydrates, lipids, and nucleic acids. In most cases, these nutrients provide several other elements as well. Some organic nutrients available to heterotrophs already exist in a form that is simple enough for absorption (for example, monosaccharides and amino acids), but many larger molecules must be digested by the cell before absorption. Moreover, heterotrophs vary in their capacities to use different organic carbon sources. Some are restricted to a few substrates, whereas others (certain *Pseudomonas* bacteria, for example) are so versatile that they can metabolize more than 100 different substrates.

An **autotroph** ("self-feeder") is an organism that uses inorganic CO_2 as its carbon source. Because autotrophs have the special capacity to convert CO_2 into organic compounds, they are not nutritionally dependent on other living things.

Nitrogen Sources

The main reservoir of nitrogen is nitrogen gas (N_2), which makes up 79% of the earth's atmosphere. This element is indispensable to the structure of proteins, DNA, RNA, and ATP. Such nitrogenous compounds are the primary nitrogen source for heterotrophs, but to be useful, they must first be degraded into their basic building blocks (proteins into amino acids; nucleic acids into nucleotides). Some bacteria and algae utilize inorganic nitrogenous nutrients (NO_3^-, NO_2^-, or NH_3). A small number of prokaryotes can transform N_2 into compounds usable by other organisms through the process of nitrogen fixation (see chapter 24). Regardless of the initial form in which the inorganic nitrogen enters the cell, it must first be converted to NH_3, the only form that can be directly combined with carbon to synthesize amino acids and other compounds.

Oxygen Sources

Because oxygen is a major component of organic compounds such as carbohydrates, lipids, nucleic acids, and proteins, it plays an important role in the structural and enzymatic functions of the cell. Oxygen is likewise a common component of inorganic salts such as sulfates, phosphates, nitrates, and water. Free gaseous oxygen (O_2) makes up 20% of the atmosphere. It is absolutely essential to the metabolism of many organisms, as we shall see later in this chapter and in chapter 8.

Hydrogen Sources

Hydrogen is a major element in all organic and several inorganic compounds, including water (H_2O), salts ($Ca[OH]_2$), and certain naturally occurring gases (H_2S, CH_4, and H_2). These gases are both used and produced by microbes. Hydrogen performs these overlapping roles in the biochemistry of cells:

1. maintaining **pH**,
2. forming **hydrogen bonds** between molecules, and
3. serving as the source of **free energy** in oxidation-reduction reactions of respiration (see chapter 8).

Table 7.2 Analysis of the Chemical Composition of an *Escherichia coli* Cell

	% Total Weight	% Dry Weight			% Dry Weight
Organic Compounds				**Elements**	
Proteins	15	50		Carbon (C)	50
Nucleic acids				Oxygen (O)	20
RNA	6	20		Nitrogen (N)	14
DNA	1	3		Hydrogen (H)	8
Carbohydrates	3	10		Phosphorus (P)	3
Lipids	2	10		Sulfur (S)	1
Miscellaneous	2	4		Potassium (K)	1
				Sodium (Na)	1
Inorganic Compounds				Calcium (Ca)	0.5
Water	70			Magnesium (Mg)	0.5
All others	1	3		Chlorine (Cl)	0.5
				Iron (Fe)	0.2
				Trace metals	0.3

Phosphorus (Phosphate) Sources

The main inorganic source of phosphorus is phosphate (PO_4^{3-}), derived from phosphoric acid (H_3PO_4) and found in rocks and oceanic mineral deposits. Phosphate is a key component of nucleic acids and is therefore essential to the genetics of cells and viruses. Because it is also found in ATP, it also serves in cellular energy transfers. Other phosphate-containing compounds are phospholipids in cell membranes and coenzymes such as NAD^+ (see chapter 8). Certain environments have very little available phosphate for use by organisms and therefore limit the ability of these organisms to grow. However, *Corynebacterium* is able to concentrate and store phosphate in metachromatic granules.

Sulfur Sources

Sulfur is widely distributed throughout the environment in mineral form. Rocks and sediments (such as gypsum) can contain sulfate (SO_4^{2-}), sulfides (FeS), hydrogen sulfide gas (H_2S), and elemental sulfur (S). Sulfur is an essential component of some vitamins (vitamin B_1) and the amino acids methionine and cysteine; the latter help determine shape and structural stability of proteins by forming unique linkages called disulfide bonds (described in chapter 2).

Other Nutrients Important in Microbial Metabolism

Other important elements in microbial metabolism include mineral ions. Potassium is essential to protein synthesis and membrane function. Sodium is important for certain types of cell transport. Calcium is a stabilizer of the cell wall and endospores of bacteria. Magnesium is a component of chlorophyll and a stabilizer of membranes and ribosomes. Iron is an important component of the cytochrome proteins of cell respiration. Zinc is an essential regulatory element for eukaryotic genetics. It is a major component of "zinc fingers"—binding factors that help enzymes adhere to specific sites on DNA. Cop-

per, cobalt, nickel, molybdenum, manganese, silicon, iodine, and boron are needed in small amounts by some microbes but not others. On the other hand, in chapter 11 you will see that metals can also be very toxic to microbes. The concentration of metal ions can even influence the diseases microbes cause. For example, the bacteria that cause gonorrhea and meningitis grow more rapidly in the presence of iron ions.

Growth Factors: Essential Organic Nutrients

Few microbes are as versatile as *Escherichia coli* in assembling molecules from scratch. Many fastidious bacteria lack the genetic and metabolic mechanisms to synthesize every organic compound they need for survival. An organic compound such as an amino acid, nitrogenous base, or vitamin that cannot be synthesized by an organism and must be provided as a nutrient is a **growth factor.** For example, although all cells require 20 different amino acids for proper assembly of proteins, many cells cannot synthesize all of them. Those that must be obtained from food are called essential amino acids.

How Microbes Feed: Nutritional Types

The earth's limitless habitats and microbial adaptations are matched by an elaborate menu of microbial nutritional schemes. Fortunately, most organisms show consistent trends and can be described by a few general categories **(table 7.3)** and a few selected terms (see "A Note on Terminology" on page 174). The main determinants of a microbe's nutritional type are its sources of carbon and energy. In a previous section, microbes were defined according to their carbon sources as autotrophs or heterotrophs. Now we will subdivide all bacteria according to their energy source as **phototrophs** or **chemotrophs.** Microbes that photosynthesize are phototrophs and those that gain energy from chemical compounds are chemotrophs. The terms for carbon and energy source are often merged into a single word

---

Table 7.3 Nutritional Categories of Microbes by Energy and Carbon Source

Category/Carbon Source	Energy Source	Example
Autotroph/CO₂	**Nonliving Environment**	
Photoautotroph	Sunlight	Photosynthetic organisms, such as algae, plants, cyanobacteria
Chemoautotroph	Simple inorganic chemicals	Only certain bacteria, such as methanogens, deep-sea vent bacteria
Heterotroph/Organic	**Other Organisms or Sunlight**	
Chemoheterotroph	Metabolic conversion of the nutrients from other organisms	Protozoa, fungi, many bacteria, animals
Saprobe	Metabolizing the organic matter of dead organisms	Fungi, bacteria (decomposers)
Parasite	Utilizing the tissues, fluids of a live host	Various parasites and pathogens; can be bacteria, fungi, protozoa, animals
Photoheterotroph	Sunlight	Purple and green photosynthetic bacteria

for convenience (see table 7.3). The categories described here are meant to describe only the major nutritional groups and do not include unusual exceptions.

Autotrophs and Their Energy Sources

Autotrophs derive energy from one of two possible non-living sources: sunlight (photoautotrophs) and chemical reactions involving simple chemicals (chemoautotrophs). **Photoautotrophs** are photosynthetic—that is, they capture the energy of light rays and transform it into chemical energy that can be used in cell metabolism. Because photosynthetic organisms (algae, plants, some bacteria) produce organic molecules that can be used by themselves and heterotrophs, they form the basis for most food webs. Their role as primary producers of organic matter is discussed in chapter 24.

Chemoautotrophs are of two types: one of these is the group called chemoorganic autotrophs. These use organic compounds for energy and inorganic compounds as a carbon source. The second type of chemoautotroph is a group called **lithoautotrophs,** which requires neither sunlight nor organic nutrients, relying totally on inorganic minerals. These bacteria derive energy in diverse and rather amazing ways. In very simple terms, they remove electrons from inorganic substrates such as hydrogen gas, hydrogen sulfide, sulfur, or iron and combine them with carbon dioxide and hydrogen. This reaction provides simple organic molecules and a modest amount of energy to drive the synthetic processes of the cell. Lithoautotrophic bacteria play an important part in recycling inorganic nutrients. For an example of lithoautotrophy and its importance to deep-sea communities, see Insight 7.3.

An interesting group of chemoautotrophs is **methanogens** (meth-an'-oh-gen), which produce methane (CH_4) from hydrogen gas and carbon dioxide **(figure 7.1).**

$$4H_2 + CO_2 \rightarrow CH_4 + 2H_2O$$

Methane, sometimes called "swamp gas" or "natural gas," is formed in anaerobic, hydrogen-containing microenvironments of soil, swamps, mud, and even in the intestines of some animals. Methanogens are archaea, some of which live in extreme habitats such as ocean vents and hot springs, where temperatures reach up to 125°C **(Insight 7.1).** Methane, which is used as a fuel in some homes, can also be produced in limited quantities using a type of generator primed with a mixed population of microbes (including methanogens) and fueled with various waste materials that can supply enough methane to drive a steam generator. Methane also plays a role as one of the greenhouse gases that is currently an environmental concern (see chapter 24).

Heterotrophs and Their Energy Sources

The majority of heterotrophic microorganisms are **chemoheterotrophs** that derive both carbon and energy from organic compounds. Processing these organic molecules by respiration or fermentation releases energy in the form of ATP. An example of chemoheterotrophy is **aerobic respiration,** the principal energy-yielding pathway in animals, most proto-

(a)

(b)

Figure 7.1 Methane-producing archaea.   Members of this group are primitive prokaryotes with unusual cell walls and membranes. **(a)** SEM of a small colony of *Methanosarcina*. **(b)** *Methanococcus jannaschii*, a motile archaea that inhabits hot vents in the seafloor and uses hydrogen gas as a source of energy.

zoa and fungi, and aerobic bacteria. It can be simply represented by the equation:

$$\text{Glucose } [(CH_2O)_n] + O_2 \rightarrow CO_2 + H_2O + \text{Energy (ATP)}$$

This reaction is complementary to photosynthesis. Here, glucose and oxygen are reactants, and carbon dioxide is given off. Indeed, the earth's balance of both energy and metabolic gases is greatly dependent on this relationship. Chemoheterotrophic microorganisms belong to one of two main categories that differ in how they obtain their organic nutrients: **Saprobes** are free-living microorganisms that feed primarily on organic detritus from dead organisms, and **parasites** ordinarily derive nutrients from the cells or tissues of a living host.

Saprobic Microorganisms   Saprobes occupy a niche as decomposers of plant litter, animal matter, and dead microbes. If not for the work of decomposers, the earth would gradually fill up with organic material, and the nutrients it contains would not be recycled. Most saprobes, notably bacteria and fungi, have a rigid cell wall and cannot

INSIGHT 7.1　Life in the Extremes

Any extreme habitat—whether hot, cold, salty, acidic, alkaline, high pressure, arid, oxygen-free, or toxic—is likely to harbor microorganisms that have made special adaptations to their conditions. Although in most instances the inhabitants are archaea and bacteria, certain fungi, protozoa, and algae are also capable of living in harsh habitats. Microbiologists have termed such remarkable organisms **extremophiles.**

Hot and Cold

Some of the most extreme habitats are hot springs, geysers, volcanoes, and ocean vents, all of which support flourishing microbial populations. Temperatures in these regions range from 50°C to well above the boiling point of water, with some ocean vents even approaching 350°C. Many heat-adapted microbes are archaea whose genetics and metabolism are extremely modified for this mode of existence. A unique ecosystem based on hydrogen sulfide–oxidizing bacteria exists in the hydrothermal vents lying along deep oceanic ridges (see Insight 7.3). Some recent evidence suggests that some of these bacteria actually survive through photosynthesis—even though they may be as far as a mile and a half from the surface (and sunlight). In these cases it is hypothesized that the bacteria scavenge the few photons of light that come from infrared radiation given off by the hydrothermal vent water. Heat-adapted bacteria even plague home water heaters and the heating towers of power and industrial plants.

A large part of the earth exists at cold temperatures. Microbes settle and grow throughout the Arctic and Antarctic, and in the deepest parts of the ocean, in temperatures that hover near the freezing point of water. Several species of algae and fungi thrive on the surfaces of snow and glacier ice (see figure 7.9). More surprising still is that some bacteria and algae are adapted to the sea ice of Antarctica. Although the ice appears to be completely solid, it is honeycombed by various-size pores and tunnels filled with liquid water. These frigid microhabitats harbor a microcosm of planktonic life, including predators (fish and shrimp) that live on these algae and bacteria. Scientists are particularly interested in bacteria that can live at extremely cold temperatures, since most of the planets in the solar system that could theoretically support life are very cold. Finding bacteria on this planet that can thrive at those temperatures suggests that life may exist on those planets as well.

Salt, Acidity, Alkalinity

The growth of most microbial cells is inhibited by high amounts of salt; for this reason, salt is a common food preservative. Yet whole communities of salt-dependent bacteria and algae occupy habitats in oceans, salt lakes, and inland seas, some of which are saturated with salt (30%—which is almost 10 times as salty as a normal ocean). Most of these microbes have demonstrable metabolic requirements for high levels of minerals such as sodium, potassium, magnesium, chlorides, or iodides. Because of their salt-loving nature, some species are pesky contaminants in salt-processing plants, pickling brine, and salted fish.

Other Frontiers to Conquer

It was once thought that the region far beneath the soil and upper crust of the earth's surface was sterile. However, work with deep core samples (from 330 m down) indicates a vast microbial population in these zones. Myriad bacteria, protozoa, and fungi exist in this moist clay, which is high in minerals and complex organic substrates. Even deep mining deposits 2 miles into the earth's crust harbor a rich assortment of bacteria. They thrive in mineral deposits that are hot (90°C) and radioactive. Many biologists believe these are very similar to the first ancient microbes to have existed on earth.

Numerous species have carved a niche for themselves in the depths of mud, swamps, and oceans, where oxygen gas and sunlight cannot penetrate. The predominant living things in the deepest part of the oceans (10,000 m or below) are pressure- and cold-loving microorganisms. Even parched zones in sand dunes and deserts harbor a hardy brand of microbes, and thriving bacterial populations can be found in petroleum, coal, and mineral deposits containing copper, zinc, gold, and uranium.

As a rule, a microbe that has adapted to an extreme habitat will die if placed in a moderate one. And, except for rare cases, none of the organisms living in these extremes are pathogens, because the human body is a hostile habitat for them.

(a)

(b)

(a) Cells of *Sulfolobus*, an archaean that lives in mineral deposits of hot springs and volcanoes. It can survive temperatures of about 90°C and acidity of pH 1.5. **(b)** Clumps of bacteria (dark matter) growing on crystals of ice deep in the Antarctic sediments.

A Note About Terminology

Much of the vocabulary for describing microbial adaptations is based on some common root words. These are combined in various ways that assist in discussing the types of nutritional or ecological adaptations, as shown in this partial list:

Root	Meaning	Example of Use
troph-	Food,	Trophozoite—the feeding stage of protozoa
-phile	To love	Extremophile—an organism that has adapted to ("loves") extreme environments
-obe	To live	Microbe—to live "small"
hetero-	Other	Heterotroph—an organism that requires nutrients from other organisms
auto-	Self	Autotroph—an organism that does not need other organisms for food (obtains nutrients from a nonliving source)
photo-	Light	Phototroph—an organism that uses light as an energy source
chemo-	Chemical	Chemotroph—an organism that uses chemicals for energy, rather than light
sapro-	Rotten	Saprobe—an organism that lives on dead organic matter
halo-	Salt	Halophile—an organism that can grow in high-salt environments
thermo-	Heat	Thermophile—an organism that grows best at high temperatures
psychro-	Cold	Psychrophile—an organism that grows best at cold temperatures
aero-	Air (O_2)	Aerobe—an organism that uses oxygen in metabolism

Modifier terms are also used to specify the nature of an organism's adaptations. **Obligate** or **strict** refers to being restricted to a narrow niche or habitat, such as an obligate thermophile that requires high temperatures to grow. By contrast, **facultative** means not being so restricted but being able to adapt to a wider range of metabolic conditions and habitats. A facultative halophile can grow with or without high salt concentration.

engulf large particles of food. To compensate, they release enzymes to the extracellular environment and digest the food particles into smaller molecules that can be transported into the cell **(figure 7.2)**. *Obligate saprobes* exist strictly on dead organic matter in soil and water and are unable to adapt to the body of a live host. This group includes many free-living protozoa, fungi, and bacteria. Apparently, there are fewer of these strict species than was once thought, and many supposedly nonpathogenic saprobes can infect a susceptible host. When a saprobe does infect a host, it is considered a *facultative parasite*. Such an infection usually occurs when the host is compromised, and the microbe is considered an *opportunistic pathogen*. For example, although its natural habitat is soil and water, *Pseudomonas aeruginosa* frequently causes infections in hospitalized patients. The yeast *Cryptococcus neoformans* causes a severe lung and brain infection in AIDS patients (see chapter 19), yet its natural habitat is the soil.

Parasitic Microorganisms   Parasites live in or on the body of a host, which they harm to some degree. Because parasites cause damage to tissues (disease) or even death, they are also called **pathogens.** Parasites range from viruses to helminths (worms) and they can live on the body (ectoparasites), in the organs and tissues (endoparasites), or even within cells (intracellular parasites, the most extreme type). *Obligate parasites* (for example, the leprosy bacillus and the syphilis spirochete) are unable to grow outside of a living host. Parasites that are less strict can be cultured artificially if provided with the correct nutrients and environmental conditions. Bacteria such as *Streptococcus pyogenes* (the cause

of strep throat) and *Staphylococcus aureus* can grow on artificial media.

Obligate intracellular parasitism is an extreme but relatively common mode of life. Microorganisms that spend all or part of their life cycle inside a host cell include the viruses, a few bacteria (rickettsias, chlamydias), and certain protozoa (apicomplexans). Contrary to what one might think, the cell interior is not completely without hazards, and microbes must overcome some difficult challenges. They must find a way into the cell, keep from being destroyed, not destroy the host cell too soon, multiply, and find a way to infect other cells. Intracellular parasites obtain different substances from the host cell, depending on the group. Viruses are extreme, parasitizing the host's genetic and metabolic machinery. Rickettsias are primarily energy parasites, and the malaria protozoan is a hemoglobin parasite.

Transport Mechanisms for Nutrient Absorption

A microorganism's habitat provides necessary nutrients—some abundant, others scarce—that must still be taken into the cell. Survival also requires that cells transport waste materials out of the cell (and into the environment). Whatever the direction, transport occurs across the cell membrane, the structure specialized for this role. This is true even in organisms with cell walls (bacteria, algae, and fungi), because the cell wall is usually too nonselective to screen the entrance or exit of molecules. Before we talk about transport mechanisms, let's examine the basic principles of diffusion.

Digestion in Bacteria and Fungi

(a)   Walled cell is a barrier.

Organic debris

(b)   Enzymes are transported outside the wall.

Enzymes

(c)   Enzymes hydrolyze the bonds on nutrients.

(d)   Smaller molecules are transported across the wall into the cytoplasm.

Figure 7.2 Extracellular digestion in a saprobe with a cell wall (bacterium or fungus). **(a)** A walled cell is inflexible and cannot engulf large pieces of organic debris. **(b)** In response to a usable substrate, the cell synthesizes enzymes that are transported across the wall into the extracellular environment. **(c)** The enzymes hydrolyze the bonds in the debris molecules. **(d)** Digestion produces molecules small enough to be transported into the cytoplasm.

The Movement of Molecules: Diffusion and Transport

The driving force of transport is atomic and molecular movement—the natural tendency of atoms and molecules to be in constant random motion. The existence of this motion is evident in Brownian movement of particles sus-pended in liquid. It can also be demonstrated by a variety of simple observations. A drop of perfume released into one part of a room is soon smelled in another part, or a lump of sugar in a cup of tea spreads through the whole cup without stirring. This phenomenon of molecular movement, in which atoms or molecules move in a gradient from an area of higher density or concentration to an area of lower density or con-centration, is **diffusion (figure 7.3).**

Diffusion

All molecules, regardless of being in a solid, liquid, or gas, are in continuous movement, and as the temperature increases, the molecular movement becomes faster. This is called "ther-mal" movement. In any solution, including cytoplasm, these moving molecules cannot travel very far without having col-lisions with other molecules and, therefore, will bounce off each other like millions of pool balls every second. As a result of each collision, the directions of the colliding molecules are altered and the direction of any one molecule is unpredict-able and is therefore "random." If we start with a solution in which the solute, or dissolved substance, is more concen-trated in one area than another, then the random thermal

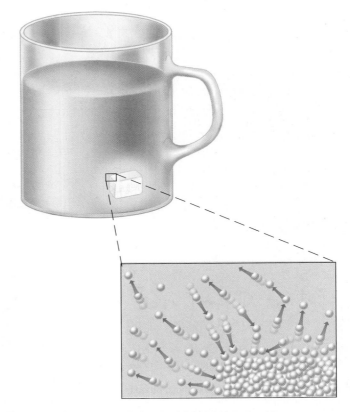

Figure 7.3 Diffusion of molecules in aqueous solutions.   A high concentration of sugar exists in the cube at the bottom of the liquid. An imaginary molecular view of this area shows that sugar molecules are in a constant state of motion. Those at the edge of the cube diffuse from the concentrated area into more dilute regions. As diffusion continues, the sugar will spread randomly throughout the aqueous phase, and eventually there will be no gradient. At that point, the system is said to be in equilibrium.

movement of molecules in this solution will eventually distribute the molecules from the area of higher concentration to the area of lower concentration, thus evenly distributing the molecules. This net movement of molecules down their concentration gradient by random thermal motion is known as diffusion. Diffusion of molecules across the cell membrane is largely determined by the concentration gradient and permeability of the substance. But before we talk about movement of nutrients (molecules, solutes) in and out of cells, we'll address the movement of water, or osmosis. You might want to take a moment to review solutes and solvents on page 38 in chapter 2.

The Movement of Water: Osmosis

Diffusion of water through a selectively permeable membrane, a process called **osmosis,** is also a physical phenomenon that is easily demonstrated in the laboratory with nonliving materials. It provides a model of how cells deal with various solute concentrations in aqueous solutions **(figure 7.4).** In an osmotic system, the membrane is *selectively,* or *differentially, permeable,* having passageways that allow free diffusion of water but can block certain

other dissolved molecules. When this membrane is placed between solutions of differing concentrations and the solute is not diffusible (protein, for example), then under the laws of diffusion, water will diffuse at a faster rate from the side that has more water to the side that has less water. As long as the concentrations of the solutions differ, one side will experience a net loss of water and the other a net gain of water, until equilibrium is reached and the rate of diffusion is equalized.

Osmosis in living systems is similar to the model shown in figure 7.4. Living membranes generally block the entrance and exit of larger molecules and permit free diffusion of water. Because most cells are surrounded by some free water, the amount of water entering or leaving has a far-reaching impact on cellular activities and survival. This osmotic relationship between cells and their environment is determined by the relative concentrations of the solutions on either side of the cell membrane **(figure 7.5).** Such systems can be compared using the terms **isotonic, hypotonic,** and **hypertonic.** (The root -*tonic* means "tension." *Iso-* means "the same," *hypo-* means "less," and *hyper-* means "over" or "more.")

Under **isotonic** conditions, the environment is equal in solute concentration to the cell's internal environment, and

Solute

Water

(a) Inset shows a close-up of the osmotic process. The gradient goes from the outer container (higher concentration of H_2O) to the sac (lower concentration of H_2O). Some water will diffuse in the opposite direction but the net gradient favors osmosis into the sac.

(b) As the H_2O diffuses into the sac, the volume increases and forces the excess solution into the tube, which will rise continually.

(c) Even as the solution becomes diluted, there will still be osmosis into the sac. Equilibrium will not occur because the solutions can never become equal. (Why?)

Figure 7.4 Model system to demonstrate osmosis.   Here we have a solution enclosed in a sack-shaped membrane and attached to a hollow tube. The membrane is permeable to water (solvent) but not to solute. The sack is immersed in a container of pure water and observed over time.

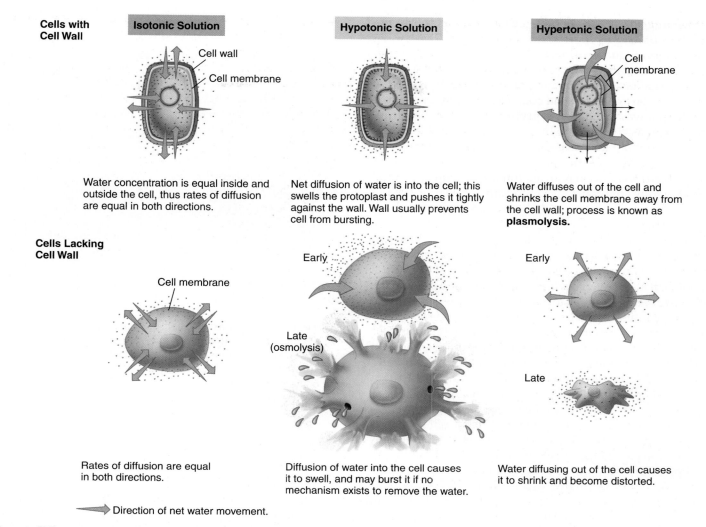

Figure 7.5 Cell responses to solutions of differing osmotic content.

because diffusion of water proceeds at the same rate in both directions, there is no net change in cell volume. Isotonic solutions are generally the most stable environments for cells, because they are already in an osmotic steady state with the cell. Parasites living in host tissues are most likely to be living in isotonic habitats.

Under **hypotonic** conditions, the solute concentration of the external environment is lower than that of the cell's internal environment. Pure water provides the most hypotonic environment for cells because it has no solute. The net direction of osmosis is from the hypotonic solution into the cell, and cells without walls swell and can burst.

A slightly hypotonic environment can be quite favorable for bacterial cells. The constant slight tendency for water to flow into the cell keeps the cell membrane fully extended and the cytoplasm full. This is the optimum condition for the many processes occurring in and on the membrane. Slight hypotonicity is tolerated quite well by most bacteria because of their rigid cell walls.

Hypertonic[1] conditions are also out of balance with the tonicity of the cell's cytoplasm, but in this case, the environment has a higher solute concentration than the cytoplasm. Because a hypertonic environment will force water to diffuse out of a cell, it is said to have high *osmotic pressure* or potential. The growth-limiting effect of hypertonic solutions on microbes is the principle behind using concentrated salt and sugar solutions as preservatives for food, such as in salted hams.

Adaptations to Osmotic Variations in the Environment

Let us now see how specific microbes have adapted osmotically to their environments. In general, isotonic conditions pose little stress on cells, so survival depends on

---

1. It will help you to recall these osmotic conditions if you remember that the prefixes iso-, hypo-, and hyper- refer to the environment *outside* of the cell.

counteracting the adverse effects of hypertonic and hypotonic environments.

A bacterium and an amoeba living in fresh pond water are examples of cells that live in constantly hypotonic conditions. The rate of water diffusing across the cell membrane into the cytoplasm is rapid and constant, and the cells would die without a way to adapt. As just mentioned, the majority of bacterial cells compensate by having a cell wall that protects them from bursting even as the cytoplasmic membrane becomes *turgid* (ter'-jid) from pressure. The amoeba's (without a cell wall) adaptation is an anatomical and physiological one that requires the constant expenditure of energy. It has a water, or contractile, vacuole that moves excess water back out into the habitat like a tiny pump.

A microbe living in a high-salt environment (hypertonic) has the opposite problem and must either restrict its loss of water to the environment or increase the salinity of its internal environment. Halobacteria living in the Great Salt Lake and the Dead Sea actually absorb salt to make their cells isotonic with the environment; thus, they have a physiological need for a high-salt concentration in their habitats (see halophiles on page 185).

So far, the discussion of passive or simple diffusion has not included the added complexity of membranes or cell walls, which hinder simple diffusion by adding a physical barrier. Therefore, simple diffusion is limited to small nonpolar molecules like oxygen or lipid-soluble molecules that may pass through the membranes. It is imperative that a cell be able to move polar molecules and ions across the plasma membrane, and given the greatly decreased permeability of these chemicals, simple diffusion will not allow this movement. Therefore the concept of **facilitated diffusion** must be introduced **(figure 7.6).** This type of mediated transport mechanism utilizes a carrier protein that will bind a specific substance. This binding changes the conformation of the carrier proteins so that the substance is moved across the membrane. Once the substance is transported, the carrier protein resumes its original shape and is ready to transport again. These carrier proteins exhibit **specificity,** which means that they bind and transport only one or a few types of molecules. For example, a carrier protein that transports sodium will not bind glucose.

A second characteristic exhibited by facilitated diffusion is **saturation.** The rate of transport of a substance is limited by the number of binding sites on the transport proteins. As the substance's concentration increases, so does the rate of transport until the concentration of the transported substance is such that all of the transporters' binding sites are occupied. Then the rate of transport reaches a steady state and cannot move faster despite further increases in the substance's concentration. A third characteristic of these carrier proteins is that they exhibit competition. This is when two molecules of similar shape can bind to the same binding site on a carrier protein. The chemical with the higher binding affinity, or the chemical in the higher concentration, will be transported at a greater rate.

Neither simple diffusion nor facilitated diffusion requires energy, because molecules are moving down a concentration gradient, from an area of higher concentration to an area of lower concentration.

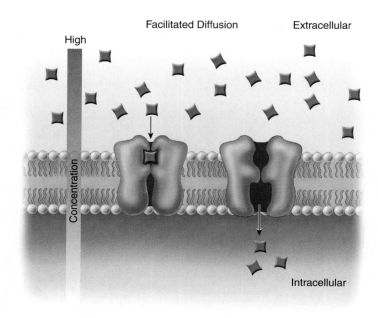

Figure 7.6 Facilitated diffusion. Facilitated diffusion involves the attachment of a molecule to a specific protein carrier. Bonding of the molecule causes a conformational change in the protein that facilitates the molecule's passage across the membrane. The membrane receptor opens into the cell and releases the molecule.

Active Transport: Bringing in Molecules Against a Gradient

Free-living microbes exist under relatively nutrient-starved conditions and cannot rely completely on slow and rather inefficient passive transport mechanisms. To ensure a constant supply of nutrients and other required substances, microbes must capture those that are in extremely short supply and actively transport them into the cell. Features inherent in **active transport** systems are:

1. the transport of nutrients against the diffusion gradient or in the same direction as the natural gradient but at a rate faster than by diffusion alone,
2. the presence of specific membrane proteins (permeases and pumps; **figure 7.7a**), and
3. the expenditure of energy. Examples of substances transported actively are monosaccharides, amino acids, organic acids, phosphates, and metal ions. Some freshwater algae have such efficient active transport systems that an essential nutrient can be found in intracellular concentrations 200 times that of the habitat.

An important type of active transport involves specialized pumps, which can rapidly carry ions such as K^+, Na^+, and H^+ across the membrane. This behavior is particularly important in membrane ATP formation and protein synthesis, as described in chapter 8. Another type of active transport, **group translocation,** couples the transport of a nutrient with its conversion to a substance that is immediately useful inside the cell **(figure 7.7b).** This method is used

Figure 7.7 Active transport. In active transport mechanisms, energy is expended to transport the molecule across the cell membrane. **(a)** Carrier-mediated active transport. The membrane proteins (permeases) have attachment sites for essential nutrient molecules. As these molecules bind to the permease, they are pumped into the cell's interior through special membrane protein channels. Microbes have these systems for transporting various ions (sodium, iron) and small organic molecules. **(b)** In group translocation, the molecule is actively captured, but along the route of transport, it is chemically altered. By coupling transport with synthesis, the cell conserves energy. **(c)** Endocytosis (phagocytosis and pinocytosis). Solid particles are phagocytosed by large cell extensions called pseudopods, and fluids and/or dissolved substances are pinocytosed into vesicles by very fine cell protrusions called microvilli. Oil droplets fuse with the membrane and are released directly into the cell.

by certain bacteria to transport sugars (glucose, fructose) while simultaneously adding molecules such as phosphate that prepare them for the next stage in metabolism.

Endocytosis: Eating and Drinking by Cells

Some eukaryotic cells transport large molecules, particles, liquids, or even other cells across the cell membrane. Because the cell usually expends energy to carry out this transport, it is also a form of active transport. The substances transported do not pass physically through the membrane but are carried into the cell by **endocytosis**. First the cell encloses the substance in its membrane, simultaneously forming a vacuole and engulfing it (**figure 7.7c**). Amoebas and certain white blood cells ingest whole cells or large solid matter by a type of endocytosis called **phagocytosis**. Liquids, such as oils or molecules in solution, enter the cell through **pinocytosis**. The mechanisms for transport of molecules into cells are summarized in **table 7.4**.

7.1 Learning Outcomes—Can You ...

1. ... list the essential nutrients of a bacterial cell?
2. ... differentiate between macronutrients and micronutrients?
3. ... construct four different terms that describe an organism's sources of carbon and energy?
4. ... define saprobe and parasite?
5. ... discuss diffusion and osmosis?
6. ... identify the effects on a cell of isotonic, hypotonic, and hypertonic conditions?
7. ... name two types of passive transport and three types of active transport?

7.2 Environmental Factors That Influence Microbes

Microbes are exposed to a wide variety of environmental factors in addition to nutrients. Microbial ecology focuses on ways that microorganisms deal with or adapt to such factors as heat, cold, gases, acid, radiation, osmotic and hydrostatic pressures, and even other microbes. Adaptation is a complex adjustment in biochemistry or genetics that enables long-term survival and growth. For most microbes, environmental factors fundamentally affect the function of metabolic enzymes. Thus, survival in a changing environment is largely a matter of whether the enzyme systems of microorganisms can adapt to alterations in their habitat. Incidentally, one must be careful to differentiate between growth in a given condition and tolerance, which implies survival without growth.

Temperature Adaptations

Microbial cells are unable to control their temperature and therefore assume the ambient temperature of their natural habitats. Their survival is dependent on adapting to whatever temperature variations are encountered in that habitat. The range of temperatures for the growth of a given microbial species can be expressed as three *cardinal temperatures*. The **minimum temperature** is the lowest temperature that permits a microbe's continued growth and metabolism; below this temperature, its activities are inhibited. The **maximum temperature** is the highest temperature at which growth and metabolism can proceed. If the temperature rises slightly above maximum, growth will stop, but if it contin-

Table 7.4 Summary of Transport Processes in Cells

General Process	Nature of Transport	Examples	Description	Qualities
Passive	Energy expenditure is not required. Substances exist in a gradient and move from areas of higher concentration toward areas of lower concentration in the gradient.	Diffusion	A fundamental property of atoms and molecules that exist in a state of random motion	Nonspecific Brownian movement
		Facilitated diffusion	Molecule binds to a receptor in membrane and is carried across to other side	Molecule specific; transports both ways
Active	Energy expenditure is required. Rate of transport is increased. Transport may occur against a concentration gradient.	Carrier-mediated active transport	Atoms or molecules are pumped into or out of the cell by specialized receptors. Driven by ATP or the proton motive force	Transports simple sugars, amino acids, inorganic ions (Na^+, K^+)
		Group translocation	Molecule is moved across membrane and simultaneously converted to a metabolically useful substance	Alternate system for transporting nutrients (sugars, amino acids)
		Bulk transport	Mass transport of large particles, cells, and liquids by engulfment and vesicle formation	Includes endocytosis, phagocytosis, pinocytosis

Figure 7.8 Ecological groups by temperature of adaptation. Psychrophiles can grow at or near 0°C and have an optimum below 15°C. Psychrotrophs have an optimum of from 15° to 30°C. As a group, mesophiles can grow between 10°C and 50°C, but their optima usually fall between 20°C and 40°C. Generally speaking, thermophiles require temperatures above 45°C and grow optimally between this temperature and 80°C. Extreme thermophiles have optima above 80°C. Note that the ranges can overlap to an extent.

ues to rise beyond that point, the enzymes and nucleic acids will eventually become permanently inactivated (otherwise known as denaturation) and the cell will die. This is why heat works so well as an agent in microbial control. The **optimum temperature** covers a small range, intermediate between the minimum and maximum, which promotes the fastest rate of growth and metabolism (rarely is the optimum a single point). Small chemical differences in bacterial membranes, which affect their fluidity, also allow them to thrive at different temperatures.

Depending on their natural habitats, some microbes have a narrow cardinal range, others a broad one. Some strict parasites will not grow if the temperature varies more than a few degrees below or above the host's body temperature. For instance, the typhus rickettsia multiplies only in the range of 32°C to 38°C, and rhinoviruses (one cause of the common cold) multiply most successfully in tissues that are slightly below normal body temperature (33°C to 35°C). Other organisms are not so limited. Strains of *Staphylococcus aureus* grow within the range of 6°C to 46°C, and the intestinal bacterium *Enterococcus faecalis* grows within the range of 0°C to 44°C.

Another way to express temperature adaptation is to describe whether an organism grows optimally in a cold, moderate, or hot temperature range. The terms used for these ecological groups are **psychrophile, mesophile,** and **thermophile** (figure 7.8), respectively.

A **psychrophile** (sy'-kroh-fyl) is a microorganism that has an optimum temperature below 15°C and is capable of growth at 0°C. It is obligate with respect to cold and generally cannot grow above 20°C. Laboratory work with true psychrophiles can be a real challenge. Inoculations have to be done in a cold room because room temperature can be lethal to the organisms. Unlike most laboratory cultures, storage in the refrigerator incubates, rather than inhibits, them. As one might predict, the habitats of psychrophilic bacteria, fungi, and algae are lakes and rivers, snowfields **(figure 7.9),** polar ice, and the deep ocean. Rarely, if ever, are they pathogenic. True psychrophiles must be distinguished from *psychrotrophs* or *facultative psychrophiles* that grow slowly in cold but have an optimum temperature between 15°C and 30°C. Bacteria such as *Staphylococcus aureus* and *Listeria monocytogenes* are a concern because they can grow in refrigerated food and cause food-borne illness.

(a)

(b)

Figure 7.9 Red snow. **(a)** An early summer snowbank provides a perfect habitat for psychrophilic photosynthetic organisms like *Chlamydomonas nivalis.* **(b)** Microscopic view of this snow alga (actually classified as a "green" alga although a red pigment dominates at this stage of its life cycle).

INSIGHT 7.2   Cashing In on "Hot" Microbes

The smoldering thermal springs in Yellowstone National Park are more than just one of the geologic wonders of the world. They are also a hotbed of some of the most unusual microorganisms in the world. The thermophiles thriving at temperatures near the boiling point are the focus of serious interest from the scientific community. For many years, biologists have been intrigued that any living organism could function at such high temperatures. Such questions as these come to mind: Why don't they melt and disintegrate, why don't their proteins coagulate, and how can their DNA possibly remain intact?

One of the earliest thermophiles to be isolated was *Thermus aquaticus*. It was discovered by Thomas Brock in Yellowstone's Mushroom Pool in 1965 and was registered with the American Type Culture Collection. Interested researchers studied this species and discovered that it has extremely heat-stable proteins and nucleic acids, and its cell membrane does not break down readily at high temperatures. Later, an extremely heat-stable DNA- replicating enzyme was isolated from the species.

What followed is a riveting example of how pure research for the sake of understanding and discovery also offered up a key ingredient in a multimillion-dollar process. Once an enzyme was discovered that was capable of copying DNA at very high temperatures (65°C to 72°C), researchers were able to improve upon a technique called the polymerase chain reaction (PCR), which could amplify a single piece of DNA into hundreds of thousands of identical copies. The process had been invented already, but the replication had to take place under high temperatures and all of the DNA polymerases available at the time were quickly denatured. The process was slow and cumbersome. The discovery of the heat-stable enzyme, called **Taq polymerase** (from *Thermus aquaticus*), revolutionized PCR, making it an indispensable tool for forensic science, microbial ecology, and medical diagnosis. (Kary Mullis, who recognized the utility of Taq and developed the PCR technique in 1983, won the Nobel Prize in Chemistry for it in 1993.)

Biotechnology researchers harvesting samples in Yellowstone National Park.

Spurred by this remarkable success story, biotechnology companies have descended on Yellowstone, which contains over 10,000 hot springs, geysers, and hot habitats. These industries are looking to unusual bacteria and archaea as a source of "extremozymes," enzymes that operate under high temperatures and acidity. Many other organisms with useful enzymes have been discovered. Some provide applications in the dairy, brewing, and baking industries for high-temperature processing and fermentations. Others are being considered for waste treatment and bioremediation.

This quest has also brought attention to questions such as: Who owns these microbes, and can their enzymes be patented? In the year 2000, the Park Service secured a legal ruling that allows it to share in the profits from companies and to add that money to its operating budget. The U.S. Supreme Court has also ruled that a microbe isolated from natural habitats cannot be patented. Only the technology that uses the microbe can be patented.

The majority of medically significant microorganisms are **mesophiles** (mez'-oh-fylz), organisms that grow at intermediate temperatures. Although an individual species can grow at the extremes of 10°C or 50°C, the optimum growth temperatures (optima) of most mesophiles fall into the range of 20°C to 40°C. Organisms in this group inhabit animals and plants as well as soil and water in temperate, subtropical, and tropical regions. Most human pathogens have optima somewhere between 30°C and 40°C (human body temperature is 37°C). *Thermoduric* microbes, which can survive short exposure to high temperatures but are normally mesophiles, are common contaminants of heated or pasteurized foods (see chapter 11). Examples include heat-resistant cysts such as *Giardia* or sporeformers such as *Bacillus* and *Clostridium*.

A **thermophile** (thur'-moh-fyl) is a microbe that grows optimally at temperatures greater than 45°C. Such heat-loving microbes live in soil and water associated with volcanic activity, in compost piles, and in habitats directly exposed to the sun. Thermophiles vary in heat requirements, with a general range of growth of 45°C to 80°C. Most eukaryotic forms cannot survive above 60°C, but a few thermophilic bacteria, called extreme thermophiles, grow between 80°C and 121°C (currently thought to be the temperature limit established by enzymes and cell structures). Strict thermophiles are so heat tolerant that researchers may use an autoclave to isolate them in culture. Currently, there is intense interest in thermal microorganisms on the part of biotechnology companies **(Insight 7.2).**

Case File 7   *Continuing the Case*

Inspectors from the U.S. Food and Drug Administration (FDA) investigated disinfection and food-handling practices aboard the cruise ship and obtained food and water samples for laboratory testing. They also assessed the oyster farm that had supplied the suspect oysters. When samples of oysters, water, and sediment were retrieved for analysis, two water samples, one sediment sample, and six oyster samples were culture-positive for *V. parahaemolyticus*. In addition, the inspectors measured the water temperature at several locations and depths; their findings are illustrated in the accompanying graph.

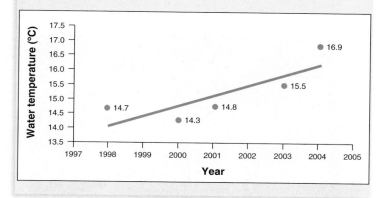

Gas Requirements

The atmospheric gases that most influence microbial growth are O_2 and CO_2. Of these, oxygen gas has the greatest impact on microbial growth. Not only is it an important respiratory gas, but it is also a powerful oxidizing agent that exists in many toxic forms. In general, microbes fall into one of three categories:

- those that use oxygen and can detoxify it;
- those that can neither use oxygen nor detoxify it and;
- those that do not use oxygen but can detoxify it.

How Microbes Process Oxygen

As oxygen enters into cellular reactions, it is transformed into several toxic products. Singlet oxygen written either as (O) or as $\overset{\bullet}{O}_2$ is an extremely reactive molecule produced by both living and nonliving processes. Notably, it is one of the substances produced by phagocytes to kill invading bacteria (see chapter 14). The buildup of singlet oxygen and the oxidation of membrane lipids and other molecules can damage and destroy a cell. The highly reactive superoxide ion (O_2^-), hydrogen peroxide (H_2O_2), and hydroxyl radicals (OH^-) are other destructive metabolic by-products of oxygen. To protect themselves against damage, most cells have developed enzymes that go about the business of scavenging and neutralizing these chemicals. The complete conversion of superoxide

ion into harmless oxygen requires a two-step process and at least two enzymes:

Step 1. $2O_2^- + 2H^+ \xrightarrow{\text{Superoxide dismutase}} H_2O_2 \text{ (hydrogen peroxide)} + O_2$

Step 2. $2H_2O_2 \xrightarrow{\text{Catalase}} 2H_2O + O_2$

In this series of reactions (essential for aerobic organisms), the superoxide ion is first converted to hydrogen peroxide and normal oxygen by the action of an enzyme called superoxide dismutase. Because hydrogen peroxide is also toxic to cells (it is used as a disinfectant and antiseptic), it must be degraded by the enzyme catalase into water and oxygen. If a microbe is not capable of dealing with toxic oxygen by these or similar mechanisms, it is forced to live in habitats free of oxygen.

With respect to oxygen requirements, several general categories are recognized. An **aerobe** (air'-ohb) (aerobic organism) can use gaseous oxygen in its metabolism and possesses the enzymes needed to process toxic oxygen products. An organism that cannot grow without oxygen is an **obligate** aerobe. Most fungi and protozoa, as well as many bacteria, have to have oxygen in their metabolism.

A **facultative anaerobe** is an aerobe that does not require oxygen for its metabolism and is capable of growth in the absence of it. This type of organism metabolizes by aerobic respiration when oxygen is present, but in its absence, it adopts an anaerobic mode of metabolism such as fermentation. Facultative anaerobes usually possess catalase and superoxide dismutase. A large number of bacterial pathogens fall into this group (for example, gram-negative intestinal bacteria and staphylococci). A **microaerophile** (myk"-roh-air'-oh-fyl) does not grow at normal atmospheric concentrations of oxygen but requires a small amount of it in metabolism. Most organisms in this category live in a habitat (soil, water, or the human body) that provides small amounts of oxygen but is not directly exposed to the atmosphere.

An **anaerobe** (anaerobic microorganism) lacks the metabolic enzyme systems for using oxygen in respiration. Because strict, or obligate, anaerobes also lack the enzymes for processing toxic oxygen, they cannot tolerate any free oxygen in the immediate environment and will die if exposed to it. Strict anaerobes live in highly reduced habitats, such as deep muds, lakes, oceans, and soil. Even though human cells use oxygen and oxygen is found in the blood and tissues, some body sites present anaerobic pockets or microhabitats where colonization or infection can occur. One region that is an important site for anaerobic infections is the oral cavity. Dental caries is partly due to the complex actions of aerobic and anaerobic bacteria, and most gingival infections consist of similar mixtures of oral bacteria that have invaded damaged gum tissues (see chapter 22). Another common site for anaerobic infections is the large intestine, a relatively oxygen-free habitat that harbors a rich assortment of strictly anaerobic bacteria. Anaerobic infections can occur following abdominal surgery and traumatic injuries (gas gangrene and tetanus).

(a)

Lockscrew

Outer lid | Inner lid

Catalyst chamber contains palladium pellets, which scavenge excess oxygen.

$2H_2 + O_2 \longrightarrow 2H_2O$
$CO_2 \longleftarrow \qquad H_2$

Rubber gasket provides airtight seal.

Gas Pack

Petri dishes

Gas generator envelope. Water is added to chemicals in envelope to generate H_2 and CO_2. H_2 combines with oxygen in chamber to produce H_2O, which is visible as condensation on the walls of the chamber.

Anaerobic indicator strip (Methylene blue becomes colorless in absence of O_2.)

(b)

Figure 7.10 Culturing techniques for anaerobes.
(a) A special anaerobic environmental chamber makes it possible to handle strict anaerobes without exposing them to air. It also has provisions for incubation and inspection in a completely O_2-free system. **(b)** A simpler anaerobic, or CO_2, incubator system. To create an anaerobic environment, a packet is activated to produce hydrogen gas and the chamber is sealed tightly. The gas reacts with available oxygen to produce water. Carbon dioxide can also be added to the system for growth of organisms needing high concentrations of it.

Growing anaerobic bacteria usually requires special media, methods of incubation, and handling chambers that exclude oxygen **(figure 7.10a).**

Aerotolerant anaerobes do not utilize oxygen but can survive and grow to a limited extent in its presence. These anaerobes are not harmed by oxygen, mainly because they possess alternate mechanisms for breaking down peroxides and superoxide. Certain lactobacilli and streptococci use manganese ions or peroxidases to perform this task.

Determining the oxygen requirements of a microbe from a biochemical standpoint can be a very time-consuming process. Often it is illuminating to perform culture tests with reducing media (those that contain an oxygen-absorbing chemical). One such technique demonstrates oxygen requirements by the location of growth in a tube of fluid thioglycollate **(figure 7.11).**

Figure 7.11 Use of thioglycollate broth to demonstrate four different oxygen requirements. Thioglycollate is a reducing agent that allows anaerobic bacteria to grow in tubes exposed to air. Oxygen concentration is highest at the top of the tube. When a series of tubes is inoculated with bacteria that differ in O_2 requirements, the relative position of growth provides some indication of their adaptations to oxygen use. Tube 1 (on the left): aerobic (*Pseudomonas aeruginosa*); Tube 2: facultative (*Staphylococcus aureus*); Tube 3: facultative (*Escherichia coli*); Tube 4: obligate anaerobe (*Clostridium butyricum*).

Although all microbes require some carbon dioxide in their metabolism, *capnophiles* grow best at a higher CO_2 tension than is normally present in the atmosphere. This becomes important in the initial isolation of some pathogens from clinical specimens, notably *Neisseria* (gonorrhea, meningitis), *Brucella* (undulant fever), and *Streptococcus pneumoniae*. Incubation is carried out in a CO_2 incubator that provides 3% to 10% CO_2 **(figure 7.10b).**

Effects of pH

Microbial growth and survival are also influenced by the pH of the habitat. The term pH was defined in chapter 2 as the degree of acidity or alkalinity (basicity) of a solution. It is expressed by the pH scale, a series of numbers ranging from 0 to 14. The pH of pure water (7.0) is neutral, neither acidic nor basic. As the pH value decreases toward 0, the acidity increases, and as the pH increases toward 14, the alkalinity increases. The majority of organisms live or grow in habitats between pH 6 and 8 because strong acids and bases can be highly damaging to enzymes and other cellular substances.

A few microorganisms live at pH extremes. Obligate *acidophiles* include *Euglena mutabilis*, an alga that grows in acid pools between 0 and 1.0 pH, and *Thermoplasma*, an archaea that lacks a cell wall, lives in hot coal piles at a pH of 1 to 2, and will lyse if exposed to pH 7. *Picrophilus* thrives at a pH of 0.7, and can grow at a pH of 0. Because many molds and yeasts tolerate moderate acid, they are the most common spoilage agents of pickled foods. Alkalinophiles, such as *Natronomonas* species, live in hot pools and soils that contain high levels of basic minerals (up to pH 12.0). Bacteria that decompose urine create alkaline conditions, because ammonium (NH_4^+) can be produced when urea (a component of urine) is digested. Metabolism of urea is one way that *Proteus* spp. can neutralize the acidity of the urine to colonize and infect the urinary system.

Osmotic Pressure

Although most microbes exist under hypotonic or isotonic conditions, a few, called **osmophiles,** live in habitats with a high solute concentration. One common type of osmophile prefers high concentrations of salt; these organisms are called **halophiles** (hay'-loh-fylz). Obligate halophiles such as *Halobacterium* and *Halococcus* inhabit salt lakes, ponds, and other hypersaline habitats. They grow optimally in solutions of 25% NaCl but require at least 9% NaCl (combined with other salts) for growth. These archaea have significant modifications in their cell walls and membranes and will lyse in hypotonic habitats. *Facultative halophiles* are remarkably resistant to salt, even though they do not normally reside in high-salt environments. For example, *Staphylococcus aureus* can grow on NaCl media ranging from 0.1% up to 20%. Although it is common to use high concentrations of salt and sugar to preserve food (jellies, syrups, and brines), many bacteria and fungi actually thrive under these conditions and are common spoilage agents.

Miscellaneous Environmental Factors

Various forms of electromagnetic radiation (ultraviolet, infrared, visible light) stream constantly onto the earth from the sun. Some microbes (phototrophs) can use visible light rays as an energy source, but nonphotosynthetic microbes tend to be damaged by the toxic oxygen products produced by contact with light. Some microbial species produce yellow carotenoid pigments to protect against the damaging effects of light by absorbing and dismantling toxic oxygen. Other types of radiation that can damage microbes are ultraviolet and ionizing rays (X rays and cosmic rays). In chapter 11, you will see just how these types of energy are applied in microbial control.

Descent into the ocean depths subjects organisms to increasing hydrostatic pressure. Deep-sea microbes called **barophiles** exist under pressures that range from a few times to over 1,000 times the pressure of the atmosphere. These bacteria are so strictly adapted to high pressures that they will rupture when exposed to normal atmospheric pressure.

Because of the high water content of cytoplasm, all cells require water from their environment to sustain growth and metabolism. Water is the solvent for cell chemicals, and it is needed for enzyme function and digestion of macromolecules. A certain amount of water on the external surface of the cell is required for the diffusion of nutrients and wastes. Even in apparently dry habitats, such as sand or dry soil, the particles retain a thin layer of water usable by microorganisms. Only dormant, dehydrated cell stages (for example, spores and cysts) tolerate extreme drying because of the inactivity of their enzymes.

Ecological Associations Among Microorganisms

Up to now, we have considered the importance of nonliving environmental influences on the growth of microorganisms. Another profound influence comes from other organisms that share (or sometimes are) their habitats. In all but the rarest instances, microbes live in shared habitats, which give rise to complex and fascinating associations. Some associations are between similar or dissimilar types of microbes; others involve multicellular organisms such as animals or plants. Interactions can have beneficial, harmful, or no particular effects on the organisms involved; they can be obligatory or nonobligatory to the members; and they often involve nutritional interactions. This outline provides an overview of the major types of microbial associations:

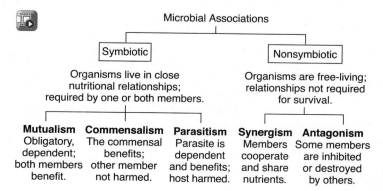

Microbial Associations

Symbiotic — Organisms live in close nutritional relationships; required by one or both members.

Nonsymbiotic — Organisms are free-living; relationships not required for survival.

Mutualism Obligatory, dependent; both members benefit.

Commensalism The commensal benefits; other member not harmed.

Parasitism Parasite is dependent and benefits; host harmed.

Synergism Members cooperate and share nutrients.

Antagonism Some members are inhibited or destroyed by others.

| **INSIGHT 7.3** | **Life Together: Mutualism** |

A tremendous variety of mutualistic partnerships occurs in nature. These associations gradually evolve over millions of years as the participating members come to rely on some critical substance or habitat that they share. One of the earliest such associations is thought to have resulted in eukaryotic cells (see Insight 5.1).

Protozoan cells often receive growth factors from symbiotic bacteria and algae that, in turn, are nurtured by the protozoan cell. One peculiar ciliate propels itself by affixing symbiotic bacteria to its cell membrane to act as "oars." These relationships become so obligatory that some amoebas and ciliates require mutualistic bacteria for survival. This kind of relationship is especially striking in the complex mutualism of termites, which harbor protozoa specialized to live only inside them. The protozoans, in turn, contain endosymbiotic bacteria. Wood eaten by the termite gets processed by the protozoan and bacterial enzymes, and all three organisms thrive.

Symbiosis Between Microbes and Animals

Microorganisms carry on symbiotic relationships with animals as diverse as sponges, worms, and mammals. Bacteria and protozoa are essential in the operation of the rumen (a complex, four-chambered stomach) of cud-chewing mammals. These mammals produce no enzymes of their own to break down the cellulose that is a major part of their diet, but the microbial population harbored in their rumens does. The complex food materials are digested through several stages, during which time the animal regurgitates and chews the partially digested plant matter (the cud) and occasionally burps methane produced by the microbial symbionts.

Thermal Vent Symbionts

Another fascinating symbiotic relationship has been found in the deep hydrothermal vents in the seafloor, where geologic forces spread the crustal plates and release heat and gas. These vents are a focus of tremendous biological and geologic activity. Giant six-foot long tube worms, pictured above, have no digestive system but instead are stuffed full of a bacterial species that combines hydrogen sulfide (the gas that smells like rotting eggs which is in great abundance on the seafloor) with oxygen (supplied by the tube worm) to make sulfur, water, and energy. The bacteria then use the energy to make carbon-based foods to nourish their host, the tube worm.

(a) A view of a vent community based on mutualism and chemoautotrophy. The giant tube worm *Riftia* houses bacteria in its specialized feeding organ, the trophosome. The trophosome (gray) is filled with bacteria.

(b) Termites are insects responsible for wood damage; however, it is the termite's endosymbiont (the protozoan pictured here) that provides the enzymes for digesting wood.

A general term used to denote a situation in which two organisms live together in a close partnership is **symbiosis,**[2] and the members are termed *symbionts*. Three main types of symbiosis occur. **Mutualism** exists when organisms live in an obligatory but mutually beneficial relationship. This association is rather common in nature because of the survival value it has for the members involved. **Insight 7.3** gives several examples to illustrate this concept. In other symbiotic relationships the relationship tends to be unequal, meaning it benefits one member and not the other, and it can be obligatory.

In a relationship known as **commensalism,** the member called the commensal receives benefits, while its coinhabitant

2. Note that **symbiosis** is a neutral term and does not by itself imply benefit or detriment.

Staphylococcus aureus
growth

Haemophilus satellite
colonies

Figure 7.12 Satellitism, a type of commensalism between two microbes. In this example, *Staphylococcus aureus* provides growth factors to *Haemophilus influenzae*, which grows as tiny satellite colonies near the streak of *Staphylococcus*. By itself, *Haemophilus* could not grow on blood agar. The *Staphylococcus* gives off several nutrients such as vitamins and amino acids that diffuse out to the *Haemophilus*, thereby promoting its growth.

is neither harmed nor benefited. A classic commensal interaction between microorganisms called **satellitism** arises when one member provides nutritional or protective factors needed by the other **(figure 7.12).** Some microbes can break down a substance that would be toxic or inhibitory to another

microbe. Relationships between humans and resident commensals that derive nutrients from the body are discussed in a later section.

In an earlier section, we introduced the concept of **parasitism** as a relationship in which the host organism provides the parasitic microbe with nutrients and a habitat. Multiplication of the parasite usually harms the host to some extent. As this relationship evolves, the host may even develop tolerance for or dependence on a parasite, at which point we call the relationship commensalism or mutualism.

Synergism is an interrelationship between two or more free-living organisms that benefits them but is not necessary for their survival. Together, the participants cooperate to produce a result that none of them could do alone. Biofilms are the best examples of synergism.

In synergistic infections, a combination of organisms can produce tissue damage that a single organism would not cause alone. Gum disease, dental caries, and gas gangrene involve mixed infections by bacteria interacting synergistically.

Biofilms

You have already heard about the importance of biofilms, both in chapter 1 and in chapter 4 (Insight 4.1). The National Institutes of Health estimates that 80% of chronic infections are caused by biofilms **(figure 7.13).** These include chronic ear infections, prostate infections, and lung infections in cystic fibrosis patients, and wound infections, as well as many others. Ordinary antibiotic treatment does not work against most biofilms (which is why the infections remain chronic). We'll learn more about that aspect of biofilms in chapter 12.

(a)

Process Figure 7.13 Biofilms. **(a)** SEM of a biofilm formed on a gauze bandage. The blue bacteria are methicillin-resistant *Staphylococcus aureus* (MRSA); the orange substance is the polymeric substance, and the green tubes are fibers of the gauze. This is probably a single-species biofilm. **(b)** Steps in the formation of a biofilm.

① Pioneer bacteria colonize a surface.

② Pioneers secrete extracellular material that helps keep them on the surface and serves as attachment point for later colonizers. Quorum sensing chemicals (red dots) are released by bacteria.

③ In many (but not all) biofilms, other species join and may contribute to the extracellular matrix and/or participate in quorum sensing with their own chemicals or the ones released by other species.

④ Mature biofilms may stop or minimize quorum sensing. Biofilms serve as a constant source of bacteria that can "escape" and become planktonic again.

(b)

A Note About Coevolution

Organisms that have close, ongoing relationships with each other participate in **coevolution**, the process whereby a change in one of the partners leads to a change in the other partner, which may in turn lead to another change in the first partner, and so on. This is another example of the interconnectedness of biological entities on this planet. There are many well-documented examples of the relationships between plants and insects. One of the earliest is the discovery by Charles Darwin of a plant that had a nectar tube that was 10 inches long. Knowing that the plant depended on insects for pollination, Darwin predicted the existence of an insect with a 10-inch tongue—and 41 years later one was discovered. The plant and the insect had influenced each other's evolution over time. Commensal gut bacteria are considered to have coevolved with their mammalian hosts, with the hosts evolving mechanisms to prevent the disease effects of their bacterial passengers, and the bacteria evolving mechanisms to be less pathogenic to their hosts.

Many, if not all, biofilms are mixed communities of different kinds of bacteria and other microbes. Usually there is a "pioneer" colonizer, a bacterium that initially attaches to a surface, such as a tooth or the lung tissue. Other microbes then attach either to those bacteria or to the polymeric sugar and protein substance that inevitably is secreted by microbial colonizers of surfaces. In many cases, once the cells are attached, they are stimulated to release chemicals that accumulate as the cell population grows. By this means, they can monitor the size of their own population. This is a process called **quorum sensing.** Bacteria can use quorum sensing to interact with other members of the same species as well as members of other species that are close by (in a biofilm, for example). Eventually large complex communities are formed, which have different physical and biological characteristics in different locations of the community. The very bottom of a biofilm may have very different pH and oxygen conditions than the surface of a biofilm, for example. It is now clearly established that microbes in a biofilm, as opposed to those in a planktonic (free-floating) state, behave and respond very differently to their environments. Different genes are even utilized in the two situations. The same chemicals cells secrete during quorum sensing are responsible for some of this change in gene expression. At any rate, a single biofilm is usually a partnership among multiple microbial inhabitants and thus cannot be eradicated by traditional methods targeting individual infections. This kind of synergism has led to the necessity of rethinking treatment of a great many different conditions.

Biofilms are so prevalent that they dominate the structure of most natural environments on earth. This tendency of microbes to form biofilm communities is an ancient and effective adaptive strategy. Not only do biofilms favor microbial persistence in habitats, but they also offer greater access to life-sustaining conditions for the microbes.

For many years, biologists regarded most single-celled microbes as simple individuals that do not work together other than to cling together in colonies as they multiply. But these assumptions have turned out to be incorrect. It is now evident that microbes show a well-developed capacity to communicate and cooperate in the formation and function of biofilms. This is especially true of bacteria, although fungi and other microorganisms can participate in these activities.

Biofilms are known to be a rich ground for genetic transfers among neighboring cells (see chapter 9). As our knowledge of biofilm patterns grows, it will likely lead to greater understanding of their involvement in infections and their contributions to disinfectant and drug resistance.

Antagonism is an association between free-living species that arises when members of a community compete. In this interaction, one microbe secretes chemical substances into the surrounding environment that inhibit or destroy another microbe in the same habitat. The first microbe may gain a competitive advantage by increasing the space and nutrients available to it. Interactions of this type are common in the soil, where mixed communities often compete for space and food. *Antibiosis*—the production of inhibitory compounds such as antibiotics—is actually a form of antagonism. Hundreds of naturally occurring antibiotics have been isolated from bacteria and fungi and used as drugs to control diseases (see chapter 12).

Interrelationships Between Microbes and Humans

The human body is a rich habitat for symbiotic bacteria, fungi, and a few protozoa. Microbes that normally live on the skin, in the alimentary tract, and in other sites are called the **normal microbiota** (see chapter 13). These residents participate in commensal, parasitic, and synergistic relationships with their human hosts. For example, *Escherichia coli* living symbiotically in the intestine produce vitamin K, and species of symbiotic *Lactobacillus* residing in the vagina help maintain an acidic environment that protects against infection by other microorganisms. Hundreds of commensal species "make a living" on the body without either harming or benefiting it. For example, many bacteria and yeasts reside in the outer dead regions of the skin; oral microbes feed on the constant flow of nutrients in the mouth; and billions of bacteria live on the wastes in the large intestine. Because the normal microbiota and the body are in a constant state of change, these relationships are not absolute, and a commensal can convert to a parasite by invading body tissues and causing disease.

7.2 Learning Outcomes—Can You ...

8. ... name five types of bacteria based on their temperature preferences?

9. ... explain how different organisms deal with oxygen?

10. ... name three other physical factors that microbes must contend with?

11. ... list and describe the five types of associations microbes can have with their hosts?

12. ... discuss characteristics of biofilms that differentiate them from planktonic bacteria?

7.3 The Study of Microbial Growth

When microbes are provided with nutrients and the required environmental factors, they become metabolically active and grow. Growth takes place on two levels. On one level, a cell synthesizes new cell components and increases its size; on the other level, the number of cells in the population increases. This capacity for multiplication, increasing the size of the population by cell division, has tremendous importance in microbial control, infectious disease, and biotechnology. In the following sections, we will focus primarily on the characteristics of bacterial growth that are generally representative of single-celled microorganisms.

The Basis of Population Growth: Binary Fission

The division of a bacterial cell occurs mainly through **binary fission;** *binary* means that one cell becomes two. During binary fission, the parent cell enlarges, duplicates its chromosome, and then starts to pull its cell envelope together in the center of the cell using a band of protein

A Note About Bacterial Reproduction—and the "Culture Bias"

By far most of the bacteria that have ever been studied reproduce via binary fission, as described in this chapter. But there are important exceptions. In recent years, researchers have discovered bacteria that produce multiple offspring within their cytoplasm and then split open to release multiple new bacteria (killing the mother cell). One example is *Epulopiscium*, a symbiont of surgeon fish. Most of these bacteria have never been cultured but have been studied by dissecting the animals they colonize. The long-standing belief that bacteria always multiply by binary fission is another by-product of the "culture bias"—meaning that we understand most about the bacteria that we were able to cultivate in the lab, even though there are many more bacteria that exist in the biosphere that have not yet been cultivated.

that is made up of proteins that resemble actin and tubulin—the protein component of microtubules in eukaryotic cells. The cell wall eventually forms a complete central septum. This process divides the cell into two daughter cells. This process is repeated at intervals by each new daughter cell in turn, and with each successive round of division, the population increases. The stages in this continuous process are shown in greater detail in **figure 7.14** and **figure 7.15.**

The Rate of Population Growth

The time required for a complete fission cycle—from parent cell to two new daughter cells—is called the **generation,** or **doubling, time.** The term *generation* has a similar meaning as

■ Cell wall
□ Cell membrane
○ Chromosome 1
○ Chromosome 2
• Ribosomes

① A young cell.

② Chromosome is replicated and new and old chromosomes move to different sides of cell.

③ Protein band forms in center of cell.

④ Septum formation begins.

⑤ When septum is complete, cells are considered divided. Some species will separate completely as shown here, while others remain attached, forming chains or doublets, for example.

Process Figure 7.14 Steps in binary fission of a rod-shaped bacterium. Note that even though the two chromosomes are colored differently, the new one is an exact copy of the old one (with some mistakes that you will learn about later).

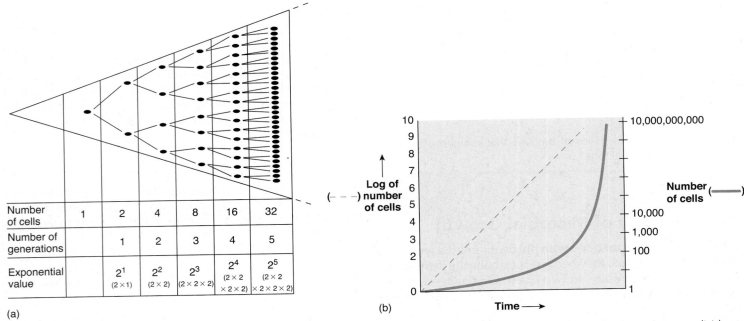

Number of cells	1	2	4	8	16	32
Number of generations		1	2	3	4	5
Exponential value		2^1 (2×1)	2^2 (2×2)	2^3 (2×2×2)	2^4 (2×2 ×2×2)	2^5 (2×2 ×2×2×2)

(a)

(b)

Figure 7.15 The mathematics of population growth. (a) Starting with a single cell, if each product of reproduction goes on to divide by binary fission, the population doubles with each new cell division or generation. This process can be represented by logarithms (2 raised to an exponent) or by simple numbers. **(b)** Plotting the logarithm of the cells produces a straight line indicative of exponential growth, whereas plotting the cell numbers arithmetically gives a curved slope.

it does in humans. It is the period between an individual's birth and the time of producing offspring. In bacteria, each new fission cycle or generation increases the population by a factor of 2, or doubles it. Thus, the initial parent stage consists of 1 cell, the first generation consists of 2 cells, the second 4, the third 8, then 16, 32, 64, and so on. As long as the environment remains favorable, this doubling effect can continue at a constant rate. With the passing of each generation, the population will double, over and over again.

The length of the generation time is a measure of the growth rate of an organism. Compared with the growth rates of most other living things, bacteria are notoriously rapid. The average generation time is 30 to 60 minutes under optimum conditions. The shortest generation times can be 10 to 12 minutes, and longer generation times require days. For example, *Mycobacterium leprae*, the cause of Hansen's disease, has a generation time of 10 to 30 days—as long as that of some animals. Environmental bacteria commonly have generation times measured in months. Most pathogens have relatively short doubling times. *Salmonella enteritidis* and *Staphylococcus aureus*, bacteria that cause food-borne illness, double in 20 to 30 minutes, which is why leaving food at room temperature even for a short period has caused many cases of food-borne disease. In a few hours, a population of these bacteria can easily grow from a small number of cells to several million.

Figure 7.15a shows several quantitative characteristics of growth: The cell population size can be represented by the number 2 with an exponent ($2^1, 2^2, 2^3, 2^4$); the exponent increases by one in each generation; and the number of the exponent

is also the number of the generation. This growth pattern is termed **exponential.** Because these populations often contain very large numbers of cells, it is useful to express them by means of exponents or logarithms (see appendix A). The data from a growing bacterial population are graphed by plotting the number of cells as a function of time (figure 7.15b). The cell number can be represented logarithmically or arithmetically. Plotting the logarithm number over time provides a straight line indicative of exponential growth. Plotting the data arithmetically gives a constantly curved slope. In general, logarithmic graphs are preferred because an accurate cell number is easier to read, especially during early growth phases.

Predicting the number of cells that will arise during a long growth period (yielding millions of cells) is based on a relatively simple concept. One could use the method of addition 2 + 2 = 4; 4 + 4 = 8; 8 + 8 = 16; 16 + 16 = 32, and so on, or a method of multiplication (for example, $2^5 = 2 × 2 × 2 × 2 × 2$), but it is easy to see that for 20 or 30 generations, this calculation could be very tedious. An easier way to calculate the size of a population over time is to use an equation such as:

$$N_f = (N_i)2^n$$

In this equation, N_f is the total number of cells in the population at some point in the growth phase, N_i is the starting number, the exponent n denotes the generation number, and 2^n represents the number of cells in that generation. If we know any two of the values, the other values can be calculated. Let us use the example of *Staphylococcus aureus* to calculate how many cells (N_f) will be present in an egg salad sandwich after it sits in a warm car for 4 hours. We will assume that N_i is 10 (number of cells deposited in the sandwich while it was being prepared). To derive n, we need to divide 4 hours (240 minutes) by the generation time (we will use 20 minutes). This calculation comes out to 12, so 2^n is equal to 2^{12}. Using a calculator, we find that 2^{12} is 4,096.

$$\text{Final number } (N_f) = 10 \times 4{,}096$$
$$= 40{,}960 \text{ bacterial cells in the sandwich}$$

This same equation, with modifications, is used to determine the generation time, a more complex calculation that requires knowing the number of cells at the beginning and end of a growth period. Such data are obtained through actual testing by a method discussed in the following section.

The Population Growth Curve

In reality, a population of bacteria does not maintain its potential growth rate and does not double endlessly, because in most systems numerous factors prevent the cells from continuously dividing at their maximum rate. Laboratory studies indicate that a population typically displays a predictable pattern, or **growth curve,** over time. The method traditionally used to observe the population growth pattern is a viable count technique, in which the total number of live cells is counted over a given time period. In brief, this method entails:

1. placing a tiny number of cells into a sterile liquid medium;
2. incubating this culture over a period of several hours;
3. sampling the broth at regular intervals during incubation;
4. plating each sample onto solid media; and
5. counting the number of colonies present after incubation.

Insight 7.4 gives the details of this process.

Stages in the Normal Growth Curve

The system of batch culturing described in Insight 7.4 is *closed,* meaning that nutrients and space are finite and there is no mechanism for the removal of waste products. Data from an entire growth period of 3 to 4 days typically produce a curve with a series of phases termed the lag phase, the exponential growth (log) phase, the stationary phase, and the death phase **(figure 7.16).**

The **lag phase** is a relatively "flat" period on the graph when the population appears not to be growing or is growing at less than the exponential rate. Growth lags primarily because

1. the newly inoculated cells require a period of adjustment, enlargement, and synthesis;
2. the cells are not yet multiplying at their maximum rate; and
3. the population of cells is so sparse or dilute that the sampling misses them.

The length of the lag period varies somewhat from one population to another. It is important to note that even though the population of cells is not increasing (growing), individual cells are metabolically active as they increase their contents and prepare to divide.

The cells reach the maximum rate of cell division during the **exponential growth (logarithmic or log) phase,** a period during which the curve increases geometrically. This phase will continue as long as cells have adequate nutrients and the environment is favorable.

At the **stationary growth phase,** the population enters a survival mode in which cells stop growing or grow slowly. The curve levels off because the rate of cell inhibition or

Figure 7.16 The growth curve in a bacterial culture. On this graph, the number of viable cells expressed as a logarithm (log) is plotted against time. See text for discussion of the various phases. Note that with a generation time of 30 minutes, the population has risen from 10 (10^1) cells to 1,000,000,000 (10^9) cells in only 16 hours.

INSIGHT 7.4   Steps in a Viable Plate Count—Batch Culture Method

A growing population is established by inoculating a flask containing a known quantity of sterile liquid medium with a few cells of a pure culture. The flask is incubated at that bacterium's optimum temperature and timed. The population size at any point in the growth cycle is quantified by removing a tiny measured sample of the culture from the growth chamber and plating it out on a solid medium to develop isolated colonies. This procedure is repeated at evenly spaced intervals (i.e., every hour for 24 hours).

Evaluating the samples involves a common and important principle in microbiology: One colony on the plate represents one cell or colony-forming unit (CFU) from the original sample. Because the CFU of some bacteria is actually composed of several cells (consider the clustered arrangement of *Staphylococcus*, for instance), using a colony count can underestimate

the exact population size to an extent. This is not a serious problem because, in such bacteria, the CFU is the smallest unit of colony formation and dispersal. Multiplication of the number of colonies in a single sample by the container's volume gives a fair estimate of the total population size (number of cells) at any given point. The growth curve is determined by graphing the number for each sample in sequence for the whole incubation period (see figure 7.16).

Because of the scarcity of cells in the early stages of growth, some samples can give a zero reading even if there are viable cells in the culture. Also, the sampling itself can remove enough viable cells to alter the tabulations, but since the purpose is to compare relative trends in growth, these factors do not significantly change the overall pattern.

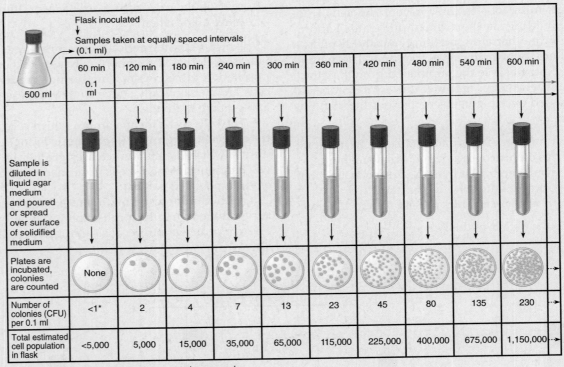

	60 min	120 min	180 min	240 min	300 min	360 min	420 min	480 min	540 min	600 min
Plates are incubated, colonies are counted	None									
Number of colonies (CFU) per 0.1 ml	<1*	2	4	7	13	23	45	80	135	230
Total estimated cell population in flask	<5,000	5,000	15,000	35,000	65,000	115,000	225,000	400,000	675,000	1,150,000

*Only means that too few cells are present to be assayed.

death balances out the rate of multiplication. The decline in the growth rate is caused by depleted nutrients and oxygen plus excretion of organic acids and other biochemical pollutants into the growth medium, due to the increased density of cells.

As the limiting factors intensify, cells begin to die at an exponential rate (literally perishing in their own wastes), and they are unable to multiply. The curve now dips downward as the **death phase** begins. The speed with which death occurs depends on the relative resistance of the species and

how toxic the conditions are, but it is usually slower than the exponential growth phase. Viable cells often remain many weeks and months after this phase has begun. In the laboratory, refrigeration is used to slow the progression of the death phase so that cultures will remain viable as long as possible.

Practical Importance of the Growth Curve

The tendency for populations to exhibit phases of rapid growth, slow growth, and death has important implications in microbial control, infection, food microbiology, and culture technology. Antimicrobial agents such as heat and disinfectants rapidly accelerate the death phase in all populations, but microbes in the exponential growth phase are more vulnerable to these agents than are those that have entered the stationary phase. In general, actively growing cells are more vulnerable to conditions that disrupt cell metabolism and binary fission.

Growth patterns in microorganisms can account for the stages of infection (see chapter 13). A person shedding bacteria in the early and middle stages of an infection is more likely to spread it to others than is a person in the late stages. The course of an infection is also influenced by the relatively faster rate of multiplication of the microbe, which can overwhelm the slower growth rate of the host's own cellular defenses.

Understanding the stages of cell growth is crucial for work with cultures. Sometimes a culture that has reached the stationary phase is incubated under the mistaken impression that enough nutrients are present for the culture to multiply. In most cases, it is unwise to continue incubating a culture beyond the stationary phase, because doing so will reduce the number of viable cells and the culture could die out completely. It is also preferable to use young cultures to do stains (an exception is the spore stain) and motility tests, because the cells will show their natural size and correct reaction and motile cells will have functioning flagella.

For certain research or industrial applications, closed batch culturing with its four phases is inefficient. The alternative is an automatic growth chamber called the **chemostat,** or continuous culture system. This device can admit a steady stream of new nutrients and siphon off used media and old bacterial cells, thereby stabilizing the growth rate and cell number. The chemostat is very similar to the industrial fermenters used to produce vitamins and antibiotics (see chapter 25). It has the advantage of maintaining the culture in a biochemically active state and preventing it from entering the death phase.

Other Methods of Analyzing Population Growth

Microbiologists have developed several alternative ways of analyzing bacterial growth qualitatively and quantitatively. One of the simplest methods for estimating the size of a population is through turbidometry. This technique relies on the simple observation that a tube of clear nutrient solution becomes cloudy, or **turbid,** as microbes grow in it. In general, the greater the turbidity, the larger the population size, which can be measured by means of sensitive instruments **(figure 7.17).**

Figure 7.17 Turbidity measurements as indicators of growth. **(a)** Holding a broth to the light is one method of checking for gross differences in cloudiness (turbidity). The broth on the left is transparent, indicating little or no growth; the broth on the right is cloudy and opaque, indicating heavy growth. **(b)** The eye is not sensitive enough to pick up fine degrees in turbidity; more sensitive measurements can be made with a spectrophotometer. (1) A tube with no growth will allow light to easily pass. Therefore more light will reach the photodetector and give a higher transmittance value. (2) In a tube with growth, the cells scatter the light, resulting in less light reaching the photodetector, and, therefore, gives a lower transmittance value. Both a newer digital and an older analog spectrophotometer are pictured.

Enumeration of Bacteria

Turbidity readings are useful for evaluating relative amounts of growth, but if a more quantitative evaluation is required, the viable colony count described in Insight 7.4 or some other enumeration (counting) procedure is necessary. The **direct,** or **total, cell count** involves counting the number of cells in a sample microscopically **(figure 7.18).** This technique, very similar to that used in blood cell counts, employs a special microscope slide (cytometer) calibrated to accept a tiny sample that is spread over a premeasured grid. The cell count from a cytometer can be used to estimate the total number of cells in a larger sample (for instance, of milk or water). One inherent inaccuracy in this method as well as in spectrophotometry is that no distinction can be made between dead and live cells, both of which are included in the count.

Figure 7.18 Direct microscopic count of bacteria. A small sample is placed on the grid under a cover glass. Individual cells, both living and dead, are counted. This number can be used to calculate the total count of a sample.

Counting can be automated by sensitive devices such as the *Coulter counter,* which electronically scans a culture as it passes through a tiny pipette. As each cell flows by, it is detected and registered on an electronic sensor **(figure 7.19).** A *flow cytometer* works on a similar principle, but in addition to counting, it can measure cell size and even differentiate between live and dead cells. When used in conjunction with fluorescent dyes and antibodies to tag cells, it has been used to differentiate between gram-positive and gram-negative bacteria. It has been adapted for use as a rapid method to identify pathogens in patient specimens and to differentiate blood cells. More sophisticated forms of the flow cytometer can actually sort cells of different types into separate compartments of a collecting device.

Case File 7   *Wrap-Up*

Because it requires a minimum temperature of at least 16.5°C to grow, *V. parahaemolyticus* is considered a mesophile. Historically, Alaskan waters have been too cold for the bacterium to thrive, and people have routinely eaten raw oysters without concern for their safety. But due to the warming of the waters of Prince William Sound, *V. parahaemolyticus* spread from its usual habitat to an area more than 900 kilometers (600 miles) farther north, where it contaminated the oysters and caused illness. This incident led to the closure of seven oyster farms in Alaska pending further investigation. In addition, as a result of this case, testing for *V. parahaemolyticus* is now routine throughout Alaska, and many oyster farmers have developed a new practice: When sea temperatures approach 15°C, baskets of oysters are lowered to the colder waters 100 feet below the surface to rid them of bacteria.

This case is only one of a number involving illnesses apparently influenced by rising temperatures around the globe. In Sweden, the number of cases of tick-borne encephalitis has increased due to warmer temperatures that facilitated the northward movement of ticks. In other areas, mosquitoes that spread malaria are being found at higher and higher altitudes as warmer summers expand their range upward. The World Health Organization estimated that 154,000 deaths worldwide in the year 2000 could ultimately be attributed to climate change (although only a fraction of these were due to infectious diseases). Not all the news is grim, though: A British study reported a drop in respiratory infections attributable to respiratory syncytial virus, most likely due to warming temperatures.

See: October 26, 2004. State of Alaska Epidemiology Bulletin No. 24. 2005. *New Engl. J. Med.* 353:1463–70.

Automatic counter

Sample in liquid

Bacterial cell

Tube

Counting orifice

Electronic detector

Figure 7.19 Coulter counter. As cells pass through this device, they trigger an electronic sensor that tallies their numbers.

Although flow cytometry can be used to count bacteria in natural samples without the need for culturing them, it requires fluorescent labeling of the cells you are interested in detecting, which is not always possible.

A variation of the polymerase chain reaction (PCR) (see Insight 7.2), called real-time PCR, allows scientists to quantify bacteria and other microorganisms that are present in environmental or tissue samples without isolating them and without culturing them.

7.3 Learning Outcomes—Can You ...

13. ... describe the major way that bacteria divide? Name another way used by fewer bacteria?
14. ... define doubling time and how it relates to exponential growth?
15. ... compare and contrast the four phases of growth in a bacterial growth curve?
16. ... identify three methods besides a growth curve to count bacteria?

 ## Chapter Summary

7.1 Microbial Nutrition

- Nutrition is a process by which all living organisms obtain substances from their environment to convert to metabolic uses.
- Although the chemical form of nutrients varies widely, all organisms require six elements—carbon, hydrogen, oxygen, nitrogen, phosphorus, and sulfur—to survive, grow, and reproduce.
- Nutrients are categorized by the amount required (macronutrients or micronutrients), by chemical structure (organic or inorganic), and by their importance to the organism's survival (essential or nonessential).
- Microorganisms are classified both by the chemical form of their nutrients and the energy sources they utilize.
- Nutrients are transported into microorganisms by two kinds of processes: active transport that expends energy and passive transport that occurs independently of energy input.

7.2 Environmental Factors That Influence Microbes

- The environmental factors that control microbial growth are temperature, pH, moisture, radiation, gases, and other microorganisms.
- Environmental factors control microbial growth mainly by their influence on microbial enzymes.
- Three cardinal temperatures for a microorganism describe its temperature range and the temperature at which it grows best. These are the minimum temperature, the maximum temperature, and the optimum temperature.
- Microorganisms are classified by their temperature requirements as psychrophiles, mesophiles, or thermophiles.

- Most eukaryotic microorganisms are aerobic, while bacteria vary widely in their oxygen requirements from obligately aerobic to anaerobic.
- Microorganisms live in association with other species that range from mutually beneficial symbiosis to parasitism and antagonism.
- Biofilms are examples of complex synergistic communities of microbes that behave differently than planktonic microorganisms.

7.3 The Study of Microbial Growth

- The splitting of a parent bacterial cell to form a pair of similar-size daughter cells is known as binary, or transverse, fission.
- Microbial growth refers both to increase in cell size and increase in number of cells in a population.
- The generation time is a measure of the growth rate of a microbial population. It varies in length according to environmental conditions.
- Microbial cultures in a nutrient-limited batch environment exhibit four distinct stages of growth: the lag phase, the exponential growth (log) phase, the stationary phase, and the death phase.
- Microbial cell populations show distinct phases of growth in response to changing nutrient and waste conditions.
- Population growth can be quantified by measuring turbidity, colony counts, and direct cell counts. Other techniques can be used to count bacteria without growing them.

 ## Multiple-Choice and True-False Questions   Knowledge and Comprehension

Multiple-Choice Questions. Select the correct answer from the answers provided.

1. The source of the necessary elements of life is
   a. an inorganic environmental reservoir.
   b. the sun.
   c. rocks.
   d. the air.

2. An organism that can synthesize all its required organic components from CO_2 using energy from the sun is a
   a. photoautotroph.
   b. photoheterotroph.
   c. chemoautotroph.
   d. chemoheterotroph.

3. Chemoautotrophs can survive on _____ alone.
   a. minerals
   b. CO_2
   c. minerals and CO_2
   d. methane

4. Which of the following statements is true for *all* organisms?
   a. They require organic nutrients.
   b. They require inorganic nutrients.
   c. They require growth factors.
   d. They require oxygen gas.

5. A pathogen would most accurately be described as a
   a. parasite.
   b. commensal.
   c. saprobe.
   d. symbiont.

6. Which of the following is true of passive transport?
   a. It requires a gradient.
   b. It uses the cell wall.
   c. It includes endocytosis.
   d. It only moves water.

7. A cell exposed to a hypertonic environment will _____ by osmosis.
   a. gain water
   b. lose water
   c. neither gain nor lose water
   d. burst

8. Psychrophiles would be expected to grow
   a. in hot springs.
   b. on the human body.
   c. at refrigeration temperatures.
   d. at low pH.

9. Superoxide ion is toxic to strict anaerobes because they lack
   a. catalase.
   b. peroxidase.
   c. dismutase.
   d. oxidase.

10. In a viable plate count, each _____represents a _____ from the sample population.
    a. cell, colony
    b. colony, cell
    c. hour, generation
    d. cell, generation

True-False Questions. If the statement is true, leave as is. If it is false, correct it by rewriting the sentence.

11. Active transport of a substance across a membrane requires a concentration gradient.

12. An organic nutrient essential to an organism's metabolism that it cannot synthesize is called a growth factor.

13. Biofilms consist of multiple species of bacteria.

14. An obligate halophile is an organism that requires high osmotic pressure.

15. An anaerobe can grow with or without oxygen.

Critical Thinking Questions   Application and Analysis

These questions are suggested as a *writing-to-learn* experience. For each question, compose a one- or two-paragraph answer that includes the factual information needed to completely address the question.

1. Name some functions of metallic ions in cells.

2. a. Compare and contrast passive and active forms of transport, using examples of what is being transported and the requirements for each.
   b. How are phagocytosis and pinocytosis similar? How are they different?

3. Compare the effects of isotonic, hypotonic, and hypertonic solutions on an amoeba and on a bacterial cell. If a cell lives in a hypotonic environment, what will occur if it is placed in a hypertonic one? Answer for the opposite case as well.

4. a. Classify a human with respect to oxygen requirements.
   b. What might be the habitat of an aerotolerant anaerobe?
   c. Where in the body are anaerobic habitats apt to be found?

5. Why is growth called exponential? What is the size of a population in 20 generations? Explain what is happening to the population at points A, B, C, and D in the following diagram.

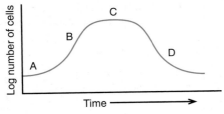

6. Is there a microbe that could grow on a medium that contains only the following compounds dissolved in water: $CaCO_3$, $MgNO_3$, $FeCl_2$, $ZnSO_4$, and glucose? Defend your answer.

7. How can you explain the observation that unopened milk will spoil even while refrigerated?

8. Patients with ketoacidosis associated with diabetes are especially susceptible to fungal infections. Can you explain why?

9. a. If an egg salad sandwich sitting in a warm car for 4 hours develops 40,960 bacterial cells, how many more cells would result with just one more hour of incubation? (Use the same criteria that were stated in the sample problem.)
   b. With 10 additional hours of incubation?
   c. What would the cell count be after 4 hours if the initial bacterial dose were 100?
   d. What do your answers tell you about using clean techniques in food preparation and storage (other than aesthetic considerations)?

10. Discuss the idea of biotechnology companies being allowed to isolate and own microorganisms taken from the earth's habitats and derive profits from them. Can you come up with a solution that encourages exploration yet also benefits the public?

Concept Mapping   Synthesis

Appendix D provides guidance for working with concept maps.

1. Supply your own lines (linkers) and linking words or phrases in this concept map, and provide the missing concepts in the empty box.

Visual Connections   Synthesis

These questions use visual images or previous content to make connections to this chapter's concepts.

1. **From chapter 6, figure 6.20a.** What type of symbiotic relationship is illustrated here?

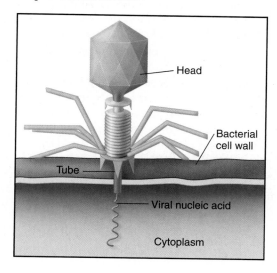

2. **Figure 7.8.** What effect will a patient's fever have on infection by a mesophile?

www.connect.microbiology.com

|MICROBIOLOGY

Enhance your study of this chapter with study tools and practice tests. Also ask your instructor about the resources available through ConnectPlus, including the media-rich eBook, interactive learning tools, and animations.

8

Microbial Metabolism
The Chemical Crossroads of Life

Case File 8

Two cases of laboratory-confirmed infection with *Salmonella enterica* serotype Typhimurium were reported to the Pennsylvania Department of Health (PDH) in February 2007. Both patients reported consuming unpasteurized, or raw, milk from the same dairy—Dairy A, located in York County, Pennsylvania. At the same time, the Pennsylvania Department of Agriculture (PDA) received several reports of diarrheal illness associated with consumption of raw milk from Dairy A. (In Pennsylvania, the PDA regulates raw-milk sales, issuing permits to dairies that adhere to milk sanitation regulations and displaying public notices explaining the potential hazards of consuming raw milk.)

On February 26, the PDH and the PDA initiated an investigation to identify the source of the salmonellosis outbreak and to determine how many cases could be traced to the initial source. Samples taken from the raw-milk bulk tank at Dairy A yielded *S. enterica* Typhimurium genetically identical to that seen in the patients. Stool samples of patients and family members were also tested for the presence of the pathogen, and food histories were obtained for each patient. By July 14, a total of 29 cases of diarrheal illness caused by *S. enterica* Typhimurium and associated with consumption of raw milk from Dairy A had been identified and grouped into three distinct time periods.

- How do you think milk can become contaminated by *Salmonella*, an organism that colonizes the digestive tract?
- How can milk be tested for contamination?

Continuing the Case appears on page 216.

Outline and Learning Outcomes

8.1 The Metabolism of Microbes
1. Describe the relationship among metabolism, catabolism, and anabolism.
2. Fully define the structure and function of enzymes.
3. Differentiate between an apoenzyme and a holoenzyme.

4. Differentiate between endoenzyme and exoenzyme, and between constitutive and regulated enzymes.
5. Diagram some different patterns of metabolism.
6. Describe how enzymes are controlled.

8.2 The Pursuit and Utilization of Energy

7. Name the chemical in which energy is stored in cells.
8. Create a general diagram of a redox reaction.
9. Identify electron carriers used by cells.

8.3 The Pathways

10. Name three basic catabolic pathways and give an estimate of how much ATP each of them yields.
11. Write a summary statement describing glycolysis.
12. Describe the Krebs cycle.
13. Discuss the significance of the electron transport system.
14. Point out how anaerobic respiration differs from aerobic respiration.
15. Provide a summary of fermentation.
16. Describe how noncarbohydrate compounds are catabolized.

8.4 Biosynthesis and the Crossing Pathways of Metabolism

17. Provide an overview of the anabolic stages of metabolism.
18. Define amphibolism.

8.5 It All Starts with Light

19. Summarize the process of photosynthesis in simple language.
20. Discuss the relationship between light-dependent and light-independent reactions.
21. Explain where the Calvin cycle fits into photosynthesis.
22. Speculate on the importance of the discovery of photosynthetic bacteria on the ocean floor.

8.1 The Metabolism of Microbes

Metabolism, from the Greek term *metaballein,* meaning change, pertains to all chemical reactions and physical workings of the cell. Although metabolism entails thousands of different reactions, most of them fall into one of two general categories. **Anabolism,** sometimes also called *biosynthesis,* is any process that results in synthesis of cell molecules and structures. It is a building and bond-making process that forms larger macromolecules from smaller ones, and it usually requires the input of energy. **Catabolism** is the opposite of anabolism. Catabolic reactions break the bonds of larger molecules into smaller molecules and often release energy. The linking of anabolism to catabolism ensures the efficient completion of many thousands of cellular processes.

In summary, metabolism performs these functions **(figure 8.1):**

1. assembles smaller molecules into larger macromolecules needed for the cell; in this process, ATP (energy) is utilized to form bonds (anabolism),
2. degrades macromolecules into smaller molecules, a process which yields energy (catabolism),
3. conserves energy in the form of ATP (adenosine triphosphate) or heat.

Metabolism has built-in controls for reducing or stopping a process that is not in demand and other controls for storing excess nutrients. The metabolic workings of the cell are indeed intricate and complex, but they are also elegant and efficient. It is this very organization that sustains life.

Enzymes: Catalyzing the Chemical Reactions of Life

A microbial cell could be viewed as a microscopic factory, complete with basic building materials, a source of energy, and a "blueprint" for running its extensive network of metabolic reactions. But the chemical reactions of life, even when highly organized and complex, cannot proceed without a special class of macromolecules called **enzymes.** Enzymes are a remarkable example of **catalysts,** chemicals that increase the rate of a chemical reaction without becoming part of the products or being consumed in the reaction. It is easy to think that an enzyme creates a reaction, but that is not true. Because of the great energy of some molecules, a reaction could occur spontaneously at some point even without an enzyme, but at a very slow rate. A study of the enzyme urease shows that it increases the rate of the breakdown of urea by a factor of 100 trillion as compared to an uncatalyzed reaction. Because most uncatalyzed metabolic reactions do not occur fast enough to sustain cell processes, enzymes, which speed up the rate of reactions, are indispensable to life. Other major characteristics of enzymes are summarized in **table 8.1.**

How Do Enzymes Work?

We have said that an enzyme speeds up the rate of a metabolic reaction, but just how does it do this? During a chemical reaction, reactants are converted to products by bond formation or breakage. A certain amount of energy is required to initiate every such reaction, which limits its rate. This resistance to a reaction, which must be overcome for a reaction to proceed, is measurable and is called the **energy of activation** or activation

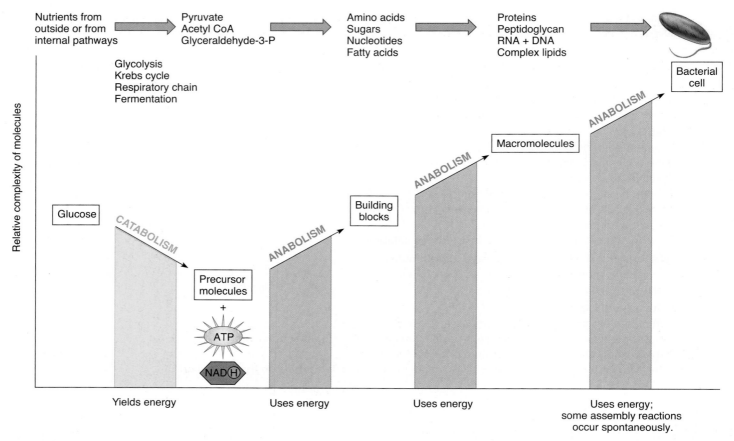

Figure 8.1 Simplified model of metabolism. Cellular reactions fall into two major categories. Catabolism involves the breakdown of complex organic molecules to extract energy and form simpler end products. Anabolism uses the energy to synthesize necessary macromolecules and cell structures from precursors.

energy. In the laboratory, overcoming this initial resistance can be achieved by:

1. increasing thermal energy (heating) to increase molecular velocity,

2. increasing the concentration of reactants to increase the rate of molecular collisions, or

3. adding a catalyst.

In most living systems, the first two alternatives are not feasible, because elevating the temperature is potentially harmful and higher concentrations of reactants are not practical. This leaves only the action of catalysts, and enzymes fill this need efficiently and potently **(Insight 8.1).**

At the molecular level, an enzyme promotes a reaction by serving as a physical site upon which the reactant molecules, called **substrates,** can be positioned for various interactions. The enzyme is much larger in size than its substrate, and it presents a unique active site that fits only that particular substrate. Although an enzyme binds to the substrate and participates directly in changes to the substrate, it does not become a part of the products, is not used up by the reaction, and can function over and over again. Enzyme speed, defined as the number of substrate molecules converted per enzyme per second, is well documented. Speeds range from several million for catalase to a thousand for lactate dehydrogenase. To further visualize the roles of enzymes in metabolism, we must next look at their structure.

Table 8.1 Checklist of Enzyme Characteristics

- Most composed of protein; may require cofactors
- Act as organic catalysts to speed up the rate of cellular reactions
- Lower the activation energy required for a chemical reaction to proceed (see Insight 8.1)
- Have unique characteristics such as shape, specificity, and function
- Enable metabolic reactions to proceed at a speed compatible with life
- Have an active site for target molecules called substrates
- Are much larger in size than their substrates
- Associate closely with substrates but do not become integrated into the reaction products
- Are not used up or permanently changed by the reaction
- Can be recycled, thus function in extremely low concentrations
- Are greatly affected by temperature and pH
- Can be regulated by feedback and genetic mechanisms

INSIGHT 8.1 Enzymes as Biochemical Levers

An analogy will allow us to envision the relationship of enzymes to the energy of activation. A large boulder sitting precariously on a cliff's edge contains a great deal of potential energy, but it will not fall to the ground and release this energy unless something disturbs it. It might eventually be disturbed spontaneously as the cliff erodes below it, but that could take a very long time. Moving it with a crowbar (to overcome the resistance of the boulder's weight) will cause it to tumble down freely by its own momentum. If we relate this analogy to chemicals, the reactants are the boulder on the cliff, the activation energy is the energy needed to move the boulder, the enzyme is the crowbar, and the product is the boulder at the bottom of the cliff. Like the crowbar, an enzyme permits a reaction to occur rapidly by getting over the energy "hump." Although this analogy concretely illustrates the concept of the energy of activation, it is imperfect in that the enzyme, unlike the person with the crowbar, does not actually add any energy to the system.

This phenomenon can be represented by plotting the energy of the reaction against the direction of the reaction. The curve of reaction is shown in the accompanying graph. Reactants must overcome the energy of activation (E_{act}) for the reaction to proceed. When a catalyst is present, it lowers the E_{act}. It does this by providing the reactants with an alternate pathway, requiring less energy, by which they can progress to the final state. Note that the products reach the same final energy state with or without an enzyme.

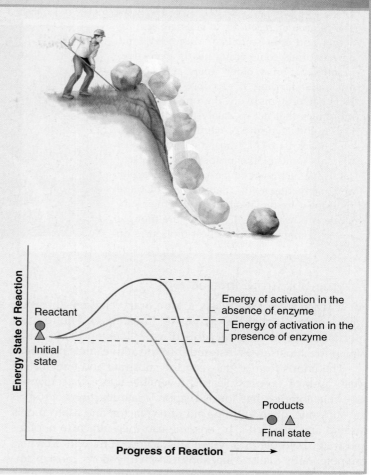

Enzyme Structure

The primary structure of most enzymes is protein—with some exceptions **(Insight 8.2)**, and they can be classified as simple or conjugated. Simple enzymes consist of protein alone, whereas conjugated enzymes **(figure 8.2)** contain protein and nonprotein molecules. A conjugated enzyme, sometimes referred to as a **holoenzyme,** is a combination of a protein, now called the **apoenzyme,** and one or more **cofactors.** Cofactors are either organic molecules, called **coenzymes,** or inorganic elements (metal ions). For example,

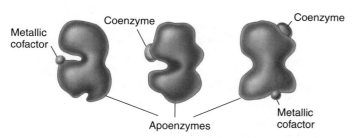

Figure 8.2 Conjugated enzyme structure. All have an apoenzyme (polypeptide or protein) component and one or more cofactors.

catalase, an enzyme that we learned in chapter 7 breaks down hydrogen peroxide, requires iron as a metallic cofactor.

Apoenzymes: Specificity and the Active Site

Apoenzymes range in size from small polypeptides with about 100 amino acids and a molecular weight of 12,000 to large polypeptide conglomerates with thousands of amino acids and a molecular weight of over 1 million. Like all proteins, an apoenzyme exhibits levels of molecular complexity called the primary, secondary, tertiary, and, in larger enzymes, quaternary organization **(figure 8.3).** As we saw in chapter 2, the first three levels of structure arise when a single polypeptide chain undergoes an automatic folding process and achieves stability by forming disulfide and other types of bonds. Folding causes the surface of the apoenzyme to acquire three-dimensional features that result in the enzyme's specificity for substrates. The actual site where the substrate binds is a crevice or groove called the **active site,** or **catalytic site,** and there can be from one to several such sites (see figure 8.3). Each type of enzyme has a different primary structure (type and sequence of amino acids), variations in folding, and unique active sites.

INSIGHT 8.2 Unconventional Enzymes

The molecular reactions of cells are still an active and rich source of discovery, and new findings come along nearly every few months that break older "rules" and change our understanding. It was once an accepted fact that proteins were the only biological molecules that act as catalysts, until biologists found a type of RNA termed **ribozymes,** which are parts of ribosomes. Ribozymes display some of the properties of protein catalysts, such as having a specific active site and interacting with a substrate. But these molecules are remarkable because their substrate is other RNA. Ribozymes are thought to be remnants of the earliest molecules on

earth that could have served as both catalysts and genetic material. In natural systems, ribozymes are involved in self-splicing or cutting of RNA molecules during final processing of the genetic code (see chapter 9). Further research has shown that ribozymes can be designed to handle other kinds of activities, such as inhibiting gene expression. Several companies have developed and are testing ribozyme-based therapies for treating cancer, certain types of infections, and AIDS.

A "hammerhead" ribozyme consisting of a single RNA strand curved around to form an active site (indentation between tetraloop and stem I).

Enzyme-Substrate Interactions

For a reaction to take place, a temporary enzyme-substrate union must occur at the active site **(figure 8.4)**. The fit is so specific that it is often described as a "lock-and-key" fit in which the substrate is inserted into the active site's pocket.

The bonds formed between the substrate and enzyme are weak and, of necessity, easily reversible. Once the enzyme-substrate complex has formed, appropriate reactions occur on the substrate, often with the aid of a cofactor, and a product is formed and released. The enzyme can then attach to another substrate molecule and repeat this action. Although enzymes can potentially catalyze reactions in both directions, most examples in this chapter depict them working in one direction only.

Cofactors: Supporting the Work of Enzymes

In chapter 7, you learned that microorganisms require specific metal ions called trace elements and certain organic growth factors. In many cases, the need for these substances arises from their roles as cofactors for enzymes. The metallic cofactors, including iron, copper, magnesium, manganese, zinc, cobalt, selenium, and many others, participate in precise functions between the enzyme and its substrate. In general, metals activate enzymes, help bring the active site and substrate close together, and participate directly in chemical reactions with the enzyme-substrate complex.

Coenzymes are a type of cofactor. They are organic compounds that work in conjunction with an apoenzyme to perform a necessary alteration of a substrate. The general function of a coenzyme is to remove a chemical group from one substrate molecule and add it to another substrate, thereby serving as a transient carrier of this group. The specific activities of coenzymes are many and varied. In a later section of this chapter, we shall see that coenzymes carry and transfer hydrogen atoms,

Figure 8.3 How the active site and specificity of the apoenzyme arise.

(a) As the polypeptide forms intrachain bonds and folds, it assumes a three-dimensional (tertiary) state with numerous surface features. Some enzymes have more than one active site.

(b) More complex enzymes have a quaternary structure consisting of several polypeptides bound by weak forces. Often the active site is formed by the junction of two polypeptides.

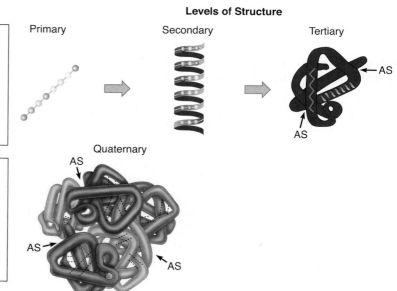

Levels of Structure

Primary Secondary Tertiary

AS

AS

Quaternary

AS

AS

AS

Figure 8.4 Enzyme-substrate reactions. **(a)** When the enzyme and substrate come together, the substrate (S) must show the correct fit and position with respect to the enzyme (E). **(b)** When the ES complex is formed, it enters a transition state. During this temporary but tight interlocking union, the enzyme participates directly in breaking or making bonds. **(c)** Once the reaction is complete, the enzyme releases the products.

electrons, carbon dioxide, and amino groups. One of the most important components of coenzymes is **vitamins,** which explains why vitamins are important to nutrition and may be required as growth factors for living things. Vitamin deficiencies prevent the complete holoenzyme from forming. Consequently, both the chemical reaction and the structure or function dependent upon that reaction are compromised.

Classification of Enzyme Functions

Enzymes are classified and named according to characteristics such as site of action, type of action, and substrate **(Insight 8.3).**

INSIGHT 8.3   The Enzyme Name Game

Most metabolic reactions require separate and unique enzymes. A standardized system of nomenclature and classification was developed to prevent discrepancies.

In general, an enzyme name is composed of two parts: a prefix or stem word derived from a certain characteristic—usually the substrate acted upon or the type of reaction catalyzed, or both—followed by the ending *-ase.*

The system classifies the enzyme in one of these six classes, on the basis of its general biochemical action:

1. *Oxidoreductases* transfer electrons from one substrate to another, and *dehydrogenases* transfer a hydrogen from one compound to another.
2. *Transferases* transfer functional groups from one substrate to another.
3. *Hydrolases* cleave bonds on molecules with the addition of water.
4. *Lyases* add groups to or remove groups from double-bonded substrates.

5. *Isomerases* change a substrate into its isomeric* form.
6. *Ligases* catalyze the formation of bonds with the input of ATP and the removal of water.

Each enzyme is also assigned a common name that indicates the specific reaction it catalyses. With this system, an enzyme that digests a carbohydrate substrate is a *carbohydrase;* a specific carbohydrase, *amylase,* acts on starch (amylose is a major component of starch). The enzyme *maltase* digests the sugar maltose. An enzyme that hydrolyzes peptide bonds of a protein is a *proteinase, protease,* or *peptidase,* depending on the size of the protein substrate. Some fats and other lipids are digested by *lipases.* DNA is hydrolyzed by *deoxyribonuclease,* generally shortened to *DNase.* A *synthetase* or *polymerase* bonds together many small molecules into large molecules. Other examples of enzymes are presented in **table 8.A.**

---
*An isomer is a compound that has the same molecular formula as another compound but differs in arrangement of the atoms.

Table 8.A A Sampling of Enzymes, Their Substrates, and Their Reactions

Common Name	Systematic Name	Enzyme Class	Substrates	Action
Lactase	β-D-galactosidase	Hydrolase	Lactose	Breaks lactose down into glucose and galactose
Penicillinase	Beta-lactamase	Hydrolase	Penicillin	Hydrolyzes beta-lactam ring
DNA polymerase	DNA nucleotidyl-transferase	Transferase	DNA nucleosides	Synthesizes a strand of DNA using the complementary strand as a model
Lactate dehydrogenase	Same as common name	Oxidoreductase	Pyruvic acid	Catalyzes the conversion of pyruvic acid to lactic acid
Oxidase	Cytochrome oxidase	Oxidoreductase	Molecular oxygen	Catalyzes the reduction of O_2 (addition of electrons and hydrogen)

Location and Regularity of Enzyme Action

Enzymes perform their tasks either inside or outside of the cell in which they were produced. After initial synthesis in the cell, **exoenzymes** are transported extracellularly, where they break down (hydrolyze) large food molecules or harmful chemicals. Examples of exoenzymes are cellulase, amylase, and penicillinase. By contrast, **endoenzymes** are retained intracellularly and function there. Most enzymes of the metabolic pathways are of this variety **(figure 8.5).**

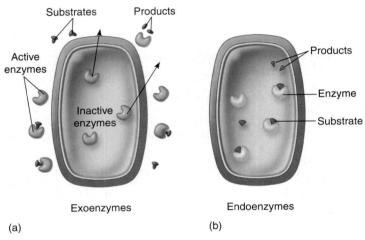

(a)

(b)

Figure 8.5 Types of enzymes, as described by their location of action. (a) Exoenzymes are released outside the cell to function. (b) Endoenzymes remain in the cell and function there.

In terms of their presence in the cell, enzymes are not all produced in equal amounts or at equal rates. Some, called **constitutive enzymes (figure 8.6a),** are always present and in relatively constant amounts, regardless of the amount of substrate. The enzymes involved in utilizing glucose, for example, are very important in metabolism and thus are constitutive. Other enzymes are **regulated enzymes (figure 8.6b),** the production of which is either turned on (induced) or turned off (repressed) in response to changes in concentration of the substrate. The level of inducible and repressible enzymes is controlled by the degree to which the genes for these proteins are transcribed into proteins, discussed in chapter 9.

Synthesis and Hydrolysis Reactions A growing cell is in a frenzy of activity, constantly synthesizing proteins, DNA, and RNA; forming storage polymers such as starch and glycogen; and assembling new cell parts. Such anabolic reactions require enzymes (ligases) to form covalent bonds between smaller substrate molecules. Also known as *dehydration reactions*, synthesis reactions typically require ATP and release one water molecule for each bond made **(figure 8.7a).** Catabolic reactions involving energy transactions, remodeling of cell structure, and digestion of macromolecules are also very active during cell growth. For example, digestion requires enzymes to break down substrates into smaller molecules so they can be used by the cell. Because the breaking of bonds requires the input of water, digestion is often termed a *hydrolysis* (hy-drol'-uh-sis) *reaction* **(figure 8.7b).**

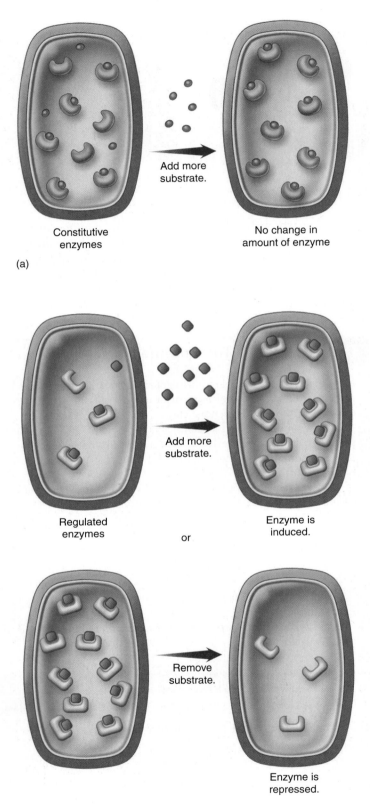

(a)

(b)

Figure 8.6 Constitutive and regulated enzymes.
(a) Constitutive enzymes are present in constant amounts in a cell. The addition of more substrate does not increase the numbers of these enzymes. (b) The concentration of regulated enzymes in a cell increases or decreases in response to substrate levels.

(a) **Dehydration Reaction.** Forming a glycosidic bond between two glucose molecules to generate maltose requires the removal of a water molecule and energy from ATP.

(b) **Hydrolysis Reaction.** Breaking a peptide bond between two amino acids requires a water molecule that adds an H and an OH to the amino acids.

Figure 8.7 **Examples of enzyme-catalyzed synthesis and hydrolysis reactions.**

Transfer Reactions by Enzymes   Other enzyme-driven processes that involve the simple addition or removal of a functional group are important to the overall economy of the cell. Oxidation-reduction and other transfer activities are examples of these types of reactions.

Some atoms and compounds readily give or receive electrons and participate in oxidation (the loss of electrons) or reduction (the gain of electrons). The compound that loses the electrons is **oxidized,** and the compound that receives the electrons is **reduced.** Such oxidation-reduction (redox) reactions are common in the cell and indispensable to the energy transformations discussed later in this chapter (see also Insight 2.2). Important components of cellular redox reactions are oxidoreductases, which remove electrons from one substrate and add them to another. Their coenzyme carriers are nicotinamide adenine dinucleotide (NAD) and flavin adenine dinucleotide (FAD). Oxidation and reduction are covered in more detail later in this chapter.

Other enzymes play a role in the molecular conversions necessary for the economical use of nutrients by directing the transfer of functional groups from one molecule to another. For example, *aminotransferases* convert one type of amino acid to another by transferring an amino group; *phosphotransferases* participate in the transfer of phosphate groups and are involved in energy transfer; *methyltransferases*

move a methyl (CH_3) group from substrate to substrate; and *decarboxylases* (also called carboxylases) catalyze the removal of carbon dioxide from organic acids in several metabolic pathways.

The Role of Microbial Enzymes in Disease   Many pathogens secrete unique exoenzymes that help them avoid host defenses or promote their multiplication in tissues. Because these enzymes contribute to pathogenicity, they are referred to as virulence factors, or toxins in some cases. *Streptococcus pyogenes* (a cause of throat and skin infections) produces a streptokinase that digests blood clots and apparently assists in invasion of wounds. Another exoenzyme from this bacterium is called streptolysin.[1] In mammalian hosts, streptolysin damages blood cells and tissues. It is also responsible for lysing red blood cells used in blood agar dishes, and this trait is used for identifying the bacteria growing in culture (see chapter 21). *Pseudomonas aeruginosa,* a respiratory and skin pathogen, produces elastase and collagenase, which digest elastin and collagen, two proteins found in connective tissue. These increase the severity of certain lung diseases and burn infections. *Clostridium perfringens,* an agent of gas gangrene, synthesizes lecithinase C, a lipase that profoundly damages

---

1. Even though most enzyme names end in *-ase* (see Insight 8.3), not all do.

cell membranes and accounts for the tissue death associated with this disease. Not all microbial enzymes digest tissues; some, such as penicillinase, inactivate penicillin and thereby protect a microbe from its effects.

The Sensitivity of Enzymes to Their Environment

The activity of an enzyme is highly influenced by the cell's environment. In general, enzymes operate only under the natural temperature, pH, and osmotic pressure of an organism's habitat. When enzymes are subjected to changes in these normal conditions, they tend to be chemically unstable, or **labile.** Low temperatures inhibit catalysis, and high temperatures denature the apoenzyme. **Denaturation** is a process by which the weak bonds that collectively maintain the native shape of the apoenzyme are broken. This disruption causes extreme distortion of the enzyme's shape and prevents the substrate from attaching to the active site. Such nonfunctional enzymes block metabolic reactions and thereby can lead to cell death. Low or high pH or certain chemicals (heavy metals, alcohol) are also denaturing agents.

Regulation of Enzymatic Activity and Metabolic Pathways

Metabolic reactions proceed in a systematic, highly regulated manner that maximizes the use of available nutrients and energy. The cell responds to environmental conditions by using those metabolic reactions that most favor growth and survival. Because enzymes are critical to these reactions, the regulation of metabolism is largely the regulation of enzymes by an elaborate system of checks and balances. Let us take a look at some general features of metabolic pathways.

Metabolic Pathways

Metabolic reactions rarely consist of a single action or step. More often, they occur in a multistep series or pathway, with each step catalyzed by an enzyme. An individual reaction is shown in various ways, depending on the purpose at hand **(figure 8.8).** The product of one reaction is often the reactant (substrate) for the next, forming a linear chain of reactions. Many pathways have branches that provide alternate methods for nutrient processing. Others take a cyclic form, in which the starting molecule is regenerated to initiate another turn of the cycle. On top of that, pathways generally do not stand alone; they are interconnected and merge at many sites.

Every pathway has one or more enzyme pacemakers (usually the first enzyme in the series) that set the rate of a pathway's progression. These enzymes respond to various control signals and, in so doing, determine whether a pathway proceeds. Regulation of pacemaker enzymes proceeds on two fundamental levels. Either the enzyme itself is directly inhibited or activated, or the amount of the enzyme in the system is altered (decreased or increased). Factors that affect the enzyme directly provide a means for the system to be quickly and finely controlled, whereas regulation at

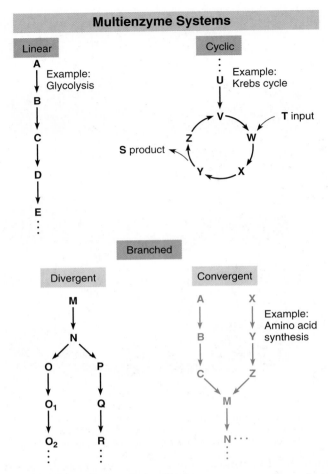

Figure 8.8 Patterns of metabolism. In general, metabolic pathways consist of a linked series of individual chemical reactions that produce intermediary metabolites and lead to a final product. These pathways occur in several patterns, including linear, cyclic, and branched. Anabolic pathways involved in biosynthesis result in a more complex molecule, each step adding on a functional group, whereas catabolic pathways involve the dismantling of molecules and can generate energy. Virtually every reaction in a series—represented by an arrow—involves a specific enzyme.

the genetic level (enzyme synthesis) provides a slower, less sensitive control.

Direct Controls on the Action of Enzymes

The bacterial cell has many ways of directly influencing the activity of its enzymes. It can inhibit enzyme activity by supplying a molecule that resembles the enzyme's normal substrate. The "mimic" can then occupy the enzyme's active site, preventing the actual substrate from binding there. Because the mimic cannot actually be acted on by the enzyme or function in the way the product would have, the enzyme is effectively shut down. This form of inhibition is called **competitive inhibition,** because the mimic is competing with the substrate for the binding site **(figure 8.9).** (In chapter 12, you will see that some antibiotics use the same

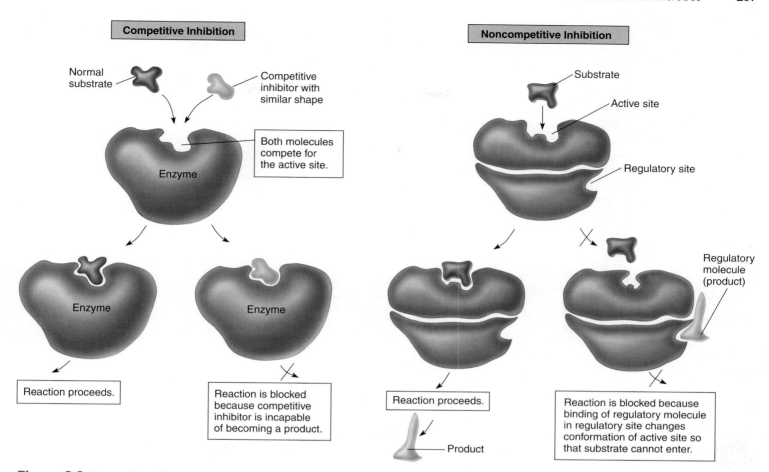

Figure 8.9 **Examples of two common control mechanisms for enzymes.**

strategy of competing with enzymatic active sites to shut down metabolic processes.)

Another form of inhibition can occur with special types of enzymes that have two binding sites—the active site and another area called the regulatory site (see figure 8.9). These enzymes are regulated by the binding of molecules other than the substrate in their regulatory sites. Often the regulatory molecule is the product of the enzymatic reaction itself. This provides a negative feedback mechanism that can slow down enzymatic activity once a certain concentration of product is produced. This is **noncompetitive inhibition,** because the regulator molecule does not bind in the same site as the substrate.

Controls on Enzyme Synthesis

Controlling enzymes by controlling their synthesis is another effective mechanism, because enzymes do not last indefinitely. Some wear out, some are deliberately degraded, and others are diluted with each cell division. For catalysis to continue, enzymes eventually must be replaced. This cycle works into the scheme of the cell, where replacement of enzymes can be regulated according to cell demand. The mechanisms of this system are genetic in nature; that is, they

require regulation of DNA and the protein synthesis machinery, topics we shall encounter once again in chapter 9.

Enzyme repression is a means to stop further synthesis of an enzyme somewhere along its pathway. As the level of the end product from a given enzymatic reaction has built to excess, the genetic apparatus responsible for replacing these enzymes is automatically suppressed **(figure 8.10).** The response time is longer than for feedback inhibition, but its effects are more enduring.

The inverse of enzyme repression is **enzyme induction.** In this process, enzymes appear (are induced) only when suitable substrates are present—that is, the synthesis of an enzyme is induced by its substrate. Both mechanisms are important genetic control systems in bacteria.

A classic model of enzyme induction occurs in the response of *Escherichia coli* to certain sugars. For example, if a particular strain of *E. coli* is inoculated into a medium whose principal carbon source is lactose, it will produce the enzyme lactase to hydrolyze it into glucose and galactose. If the bacterium is subsequently inoculated into a medium containing only sucrose as a carbon source, it will cease synthesizing lactase and begin synthesizing sucrase. This response enables the organism to adapt to a variety of nutrients, and it also

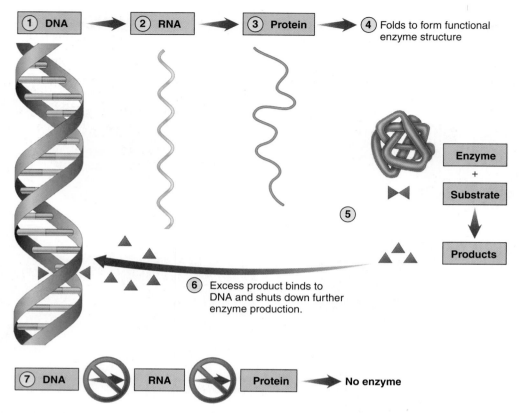

Figure 8.10 One type of genetic control of enzyme synthesis: enzyme repression. (1), (2), (3), (4), (5), The enzyme is synthesized continuously via uninhibited transcription and translation until enough product has been made. (6), (7), Excess product reacts with a site on DNA that regulates the enyzme's synthesis, thereby inhibiting further enzyme production.

prevents a microbe from wasting energy, making enzymes for which no substrates are present.

8.1 Learning Outcomes—Can You ...

1. ... describe the relationship among metabolism, catabolism, and anabolism?
2. ... fully define the structure and function of enzymes?
3. ... differentiate between an apoenzyme and a holoenzyme?
4. ... differentiate between endoenzyme and exoenzyme, and between constitutive and regulated enzymes?
5. ... diagram some different patterns of metabolism?
6. ... describe how enzymes are controlled?

8.2 The Pursuit and Utilization of Energy

In order to carry out the work of an array of metabolic processes, cells require constant input and expenditure of some form of usable energy. The energy comes directly from light or is contained in chemical bonds and released when substances are catabolized, or broken down. The energy is stored in ATP. For the most part, only chemical energy can routinely drive cell transactions, and chemical reactions are the universal basis of cellular energetics.

Energy in Cells

Cells manage energy in the form of chemical reactions that change molecules. This often involves activities such as the making or breaking of bonds and the transfer of electrons. Not all cellular reactions are equal with respect to energy. Some release energy, and others require it to proceed. For example, a reaction that proceeds as follows:

$$X + Y \xrightarrow{\text{Enzyme}} Z + \text{Energy}$$

releases energy as it goes forward. This type of reaction is termed **exergonic** (ex-er-gon'-ik). Energy of this type is considered free—it is available for doing cellular work. Energy transactions such as the following:

$$\text{Energy} + A + B \xrightarrow{\text{Enzyme}} C$$

are called **endergonic** (en-der-gon'-ik), because they are driven forward with the addition of energy. In cells, exergonic and endergonic reactions are often coupled, so that released energy is immediately put to use.

Summaries of metabolism might make it seem that cells "create" energy from nutrients, but they do not. What they actually do is extract chemical energy already present in nutrient fuels and apply that energy toward useful work in the cell, much like a gasoline engine releases energy as it

Figure 8.11 A simplified model of energy production.   The central events of cell energetics include the release of energy during the systematic dismantling of a fuel such as glucose. This is achieved by the shuttling of hydrogens and electrons to sites in the cell where their energy can be transferred to ATP. In aerobic metabolism, the final products are CO_2 and H_2O molecules.

burns fuel. The engine does not actually produce energy, but it converts some of the potential energy to do work.

At the simplest level, cells possess specialized enzyme systems that trap the energy present in the bonds of nutrients as they are progressively broken **(figure 8.11).** During exergonic reactions, energy released by bonds is stored in certain high-energy phosphate bonds such as in ATP. The ability of ATP to temporarily store and release the energy of chemical bonds fuels endergonic cell reactions. Before discussing ATP, we examine the process behind electron transfer: redox reactions.

A Closer Look at Biological Oxidation and Reduction

We stated earlier that biological systems often extract energy through **redox** reactions. Such reactions always occur in pairs, with an electron donor and an electron acceptor, which constitute a *redox pair.* The reaction can be represented as follows:

This process salvages electrons along with their inherent energy, and it changes the energy balance, leaving the previously reduced compound with less energy than the now oxidized one. The energy now present in the electron acceptor can be captured to **phosphorylate** (add an inorganic phosphate) to ADP or to some other compound. This process stores the energy in a high-energy molecule (ATP, for example). In many cases, the cell does not handle electrons as discrete entities but rather as parts of an atom such as hydrogen. For simplicity's sake, we will continue to use the term *electron transfer,* but keep in mind that hydrogens are often involved in the transfer process. The removal of hydrogens (a hydrogen atom consists of a single proton and a single electron) from a compound during a redox reaction is called dehydrogenation. The job of handling these protons and electrons falls to one or more carriers, which function as short-term repositories for the electrons until they can be transferred. As we shall see, dehydrogenations are an essential supplier of electrons for the respiratory electron transport system.

Electron Carriers: Molecular Shuttles

Electron carriers resemble shuttles that are alternately loaded and unloaded, repeatedly accepting and releasing electrons and hydrogens to facilitate the transfer of redox energy.

Reducing agent gives up electrons. Oxidizing agent accepts electrons. Oxidized cation Reduced anion

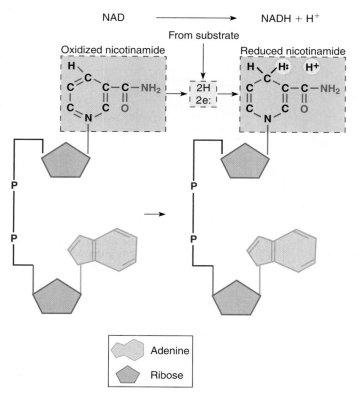

NAD ⟶ NADH + H⁺

From substrate

Oxidized nicotinamide   Reduced nicotinamide

Adenine

Ribose

Figure 8.12 Details of NAD reduction. The coenzyme NAD contains the vitamin nicotinamide (niacin) and the purine adenine attached to double ribose phosphate molecules (a dinucleotide). The principal site of action is on the nicotinamide (boxed areas). Hydrogens and electrons donated by a substrate interact with a carbon on the top of the ring. One hydrogen bonds there, carrying two electrons (H:), and the other hydrogen is carried in solution as H⁺ (a proton).

Most carriers are coenzymes that transfer both electrons and hydrogens, but some transfer electrons only. The most common carrier is NAD (nicotinamide adenine dinucleotide), which carries hydrogens (and a pair of electrons) from dehydrogenation reactions **(figure 8.12).** Reduced NAD can be represented in various ways. Because 2 hydrogens are removed, the actual carrier state is NADH + H⁺, but this is somewhat cumbersome, so we will represent it as "NADH." In catabolic pathways, electrons are extracted and carried through a series of redox reactions until the final electron acceptor at the end of a particular pathway is reached (see figure 8.11). In aerobic metabolism, this acceptor is molecular oxygen; in anaerobic metabolism, it is some other inorganic or organic compound. Other common redox carriers are FAD, NADP (NAD phosphate), and the compounds of the respiratory chain, which are fixed into membranes.

Adenosine Triphosphate: Metabolic Money

In what ways do cells extract chemical energy from electrons, store it, and then tap the storage sources? To answer these questions, we must look more closely at the powerhouse molecule, adenosine triphosphate. ATP has also been described

as metabolic money because it can be earned, banked, saved, spent, and exchanged. As a temporary energy repository, ATP provides a connection between energy-yielding catabolism and the other cellular activities that require energy. Some clues to its energy-storing properties lie in its unique molecular structure.

The Molecular Structure of ATP

ATP is a three-part molecule consisting of a nitrogen base (adenine) linked to a 5-carbon sugar (ribose), with a chain of three phosphate groups bonded to the ribose **(figure 8.13).** The type, arrangement, and especially the proximity of atoms in ATP combine to form a powerful high-energy molecule. The high energy of ATP originates in the orientation of the phosphate groups, which are relatively bulky and carry negative charges. The proximity of these repelling electrostatic charges imposes a strain that is most acute on the bonds between the last two phosphate groups. The strain on the phosphate bonds accounts for the energetic quality of ATP because removal of the terminal phosphates releases free energy.

Breaking the bonds between two successive phosphates of ATP yields adenosine diphosphate (ADP), which is then converted to adenosine monophosphate (AMP). AMP derivatives help form the backbone of RNA and are also a major component of certain coenzymes (NAD, FAD, and coenzyme A).

The Metabolic Role of ATP

ATP is the primary energy currency of the cell; and when it is used in a chemical reaction, it must then be replaced. Therefore, ATP utilization and replenishment is an ongoing cycle. In many instances, the energy released during ATP hydrolysis powers biosynthesis by activating individual subunits before they are enzymatically linked together. ATP is also used to

〜 Bond that releases energy when broken

Figure 8.13 The structure of adenosine triphosphate (ATP). Removing the left-most phosphate group yields ADP; removing the next one yields AMP.

Figure 8.14 ATP formation by substrate-level phosphorylation. The inorganic phosphate and the substrates form a bond with high potential energy. In a reaction catalyzed enzymatically, the phosphate is transferred to ADP, thereby producing ATP.

prepare molecules for catabolism such as when a 6-carbon sugar is phosphorylated during the early stages of glycolysis.

$$\text{Glucose} \xrightarrow[\quad\quad\quad\quad\quad]{\overset{\text{ATP}\quad\text{ADP}}{\curvearrowright}} \text{Glucose-6-phosphate}$$

When ATP is utilized, by the removal of the terminal phosphate to release energy plus ADP, ATP then needs to be re-created. The reversal of this process, that is, adding the terminal phosphate to ADP, will replenish ATP, but it requires an input of energy:

$$\text{ATP} \rightleftharpoons \text{ADP} + \text{P}_i + \text{Energy}$$

In heterotrophs, the energy infusion that regenerates a high-energy phosphate comes from certain steps of catabolic pathways, in which nutrients such as carbohydrates are degraded and yield energy. ATP is formed when substrates or electron carriers provide a high-energy phosphate that becomes bonded to ADP. Some ATP molecules are formed through *substrate-level phosphorylation.* In substrate-level phosphorylation, ATP is formed by transfer of a phosphate group from a phosphorylated compound (substrate) directly to ADP to yield ATP **(figure 8.14).**

Other ATPs are formed through *oxidative phosphorylation,* a series of redox reactions occurring during the final phase of the respiratory pathway. Phototrophic organisms have a system of *photophosphorylation,* in which the ATP is formed through a series of sunlight-driven reactions.

8.2 Learning Outcomes—Can You ...

7. ... name the chemical in which energy is stored in cells?
8. ... create a general diagram of a redox reaction?
9. ... identify electron carriers used by cells?

8.3 The Pathways

Now you have an understanding of all the tools a cell needs to *metabolize.* Metabolism uses *enzymes* to catalyze reactions that break down (*catabolize*) organic molecules to materials (*precursor molecules*) that cells can then use to build (*anabolize*) larger, more complex molecules that are particularly suited to them. This process is presented symbolically in figure 8.1, which is repeated as an icon in this section to guide the discussion. Another very important point about metabolism is that *reducing power* (the electrons available in NADH and FADH$_2$) and *energy* (stored in the bonds of ATP) are needed in large quantities for the anabolic parts of metabolism (the blue

bars in our figure). They are produced during the catabolic part of metabolism (the yellow bar below).

A series of biochemical reactions is called a pathway. The catabolic and anabolic pathways in a cell are interconnected and interdependent, though they do not simply work "backward and forward." It might seem more economical to use identical pathways, but having different enzymes and reactants allows anabolism and catabolism to proceed simultaneously without interference.

Metabolism starts with "nutrients" from the environment, usually discarded molecules from other organisms. Cells have to get the nutrients inside; to do this, they use the mechanisms discussed in chapter 7. Some of these require energy, which is available from catabolism already occurring in the cell. In the next step, intracellular nutrients have to be broken down to the appropriate precursor molecules. These catabolic pathways are discussed next.

Catabolism: Getting Materials and Energy

Nutrient processing is extremely varied, especially in bacteria, yet in most cases it is based on three basic catabolic pathways. Frequently, the nutrient is glucose. There are several pathways that can be used to break down glucose, but the most common one is **glycolysis** (gly-kol'-ih-sis). In previous discussions, microorganisms were categorized according to their requirement for oxygen gas, and this requirement is related directly to their mechanisms of energy release. **Figure 8.15** provides an overview of the three major pathways for producing the needed precursors and energy (i.e., catabolism).

As we shall see, **aerobic respiration** is a series of reactions (glycolysis, the Krebs[2] cycle, and the respiratory chain) that converts glucose to CO$_2$ and allows the cell to recover significant amounts of energy (review figure 8.11). Aerobic respiration relies on free oxygen as the final acceptor for electrons and hydrogens and produces a relatively large amount of ATP. Aerobic respiration is characteristic of many bacteria, fungi, protozoa, and animals, and it is the system we emphasize here. Facultative and aerotolerant anaerobes may use only the glycolysis scheme to incompletely oxidize (ferment) glucose. In this case, oxygen is not required, organic compounds are the final electron acceptors, and a relatively small amount of ATP is produced. While the growth of aerobic bacteria is usually limited by the availability of substrates, the growth of anaerobes is likely to be stopped when final electron acceptors run out. Some strictly anaerobic microorganisms metabolize by means of **anaerobic respiration.** This system involves the same three pathways as aerobic respiration, but it does not use molecular oxygen as the final electron acceptor; instead, NO$_3^-$, SO$_4^{2-}$, CO$_3^{3-}$, and other oxidized compounds are utilized. Aspects of fermentation and anaerobic respiration are covered in subsequent sections of this chapter.

---

2. Krebs is in honor of Sir Hans Krebs who, with F. A. Lipmann, delineated this pathway, an achievement for which they won the Nobel Prize in Physiology or Medicine in 1953.

Figure 8.15 Summary of the most common pathways of glucose metabolism. Glycolysis is the most common first step of metabolism. It yields two molecules of pyruvate as well as two ATPs and two NADHs. These products feed into either the Krebs cycle or fermentation. Note: Aerobic respiration may sometimes yield only 36 ATPs.

Aerobic Respiration

Aerobic respiration is a series of enzyme-catalyzed reactions in which electrons are transferred from fuel molecules such as glucose to oxygen as a final electron acceptor. This pathway is the principal energy-yielding scheme for aerobic heterotrophs, and it provides both ATP and metabolic intermediates for many other pathways in the cell, including those of protein, lipid, and carbohydrate synthesis.

Glucose: The Starting Compound

Carbohydrates such as glucose are good fuels because these compounds are readily oxidized; that is, they are superior hydrogen and electron donors. The enzymatic withdrawal of hydrogen from them also removes electrons that can be used in energy transfers. The end products of the conversion of these carbon compounds are energy-rich ATP and energy-poor carbon dioxide and water. Polysaccharides (starch, glycogen) and disaccharides (maltose, lactose) are stored

sources of glucose for the respiratory pathways. Although in our discussion we use glucose as the main starting compound, other hexoses (fructose, galactose) and fatty acid subunits can enter the pathways of aerobic respiration as well.

Glycolysis: The Starting Lineup

Glycolysis enzymatically converts glucose through several steps into pyruvic acid. Depending on the organism and the conditions, it may be only the first phase of aerobic respiration, or it may serve as the primary metabolic pathway (fermentation). Glycolysis provides a significant means to synthesize a small amount of ATP anaerobically and also to generate pyruvic acid, an essential intermediary metabolite.

Glycolysis proceeds along nine steps, starting with glucose and ending with pyruvic acid (pyruvate[3]). An overview of glycolysis will be presented here; **figure 8.16**

---

3. In biochemistry, the terms used for organic acids appear as either the acid form (pyruvic acid) or its salt (pyruvate).

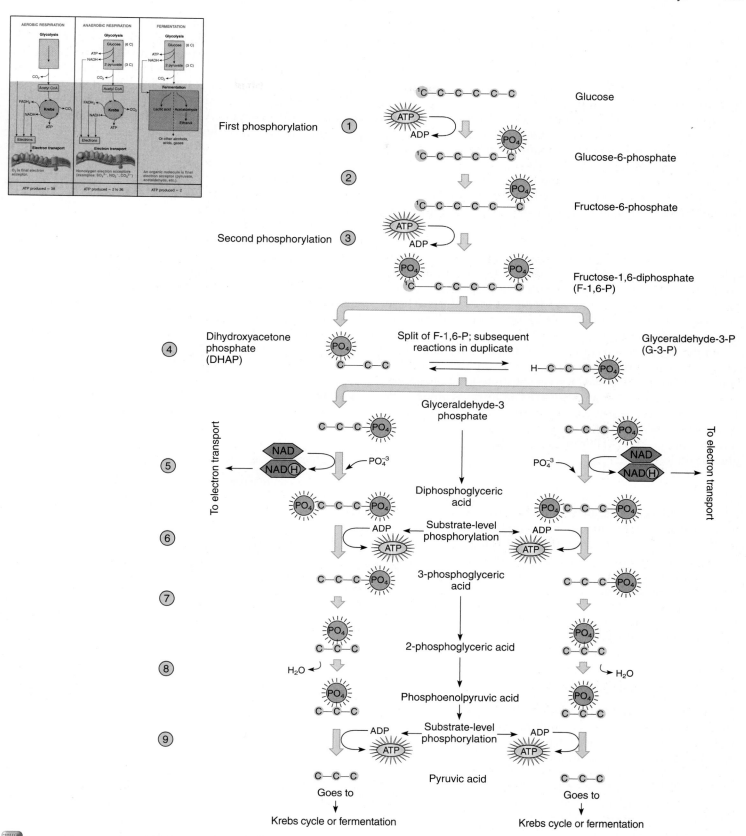

Process Figure 8.16 Summary of glycolysis.

contains the chemical structures and a visual representation of the reactions. Each of the nine reactions is catalyzed by a specific enzyme with a specific name, but we will not mention them here.

First, glucose is activated by adding a phosphate to it, resulting in glucose-6-phosphate. It is then converted (another reaction, another enzyme) to fructose-6-phosphate, and another phosphate is added. The resulting molecule—fructose diphosphate—is more symmetrical and can be split into two 3-carbon molecules **(figure 8.16, step 4)**. At this point, no oxidation-reduction has occurred and, in fact, 2 ATPs have been used. The two 3-carbon molecules are isomers of each other, and the next step involves converting the one (DHAP) to glyceraldehyde-3-P (G-3-P), resulting in two G-3-Ps.

From here to the end, everything that happens in glycolysis happens twice—once to each of the 3-C molecules. First, the G-3-Ps each receive another phosphate. At the same time, 2 NADs in the vicinity are reduced to NADHs. These NADHs will be used in the last step of catabolism (the electron transport system) to produce ATP.

In the last four steps of glycolysis **(figure 8.16, steps 6–9)**, the 3-carbon molecule is manipulated enzymatically to donate both of its phosphates to ADPs via substrate-level phosphorylation. This results in four new ATPs and two 3-carbon molecules with no phosphates, called pyruvic acid. But because 2 ATPs were expended in the early steps of glycolysis, the net yield of ATP from glycolysis of one glucose molecule is 2.

Pyruvic Acid—A Central Metabolite

Pyruvic acid occupies an important position in several pathways, and different organisms handle it in different ways **(figure 8.17)**. In strictly aerobic organisms and some anaerobes, pyruvic acid enters the Krebs cycle for further processing and energy release. Facultative anaerobes can adopt a fermentative metabolism, in which pyruvic acid is re-reduced into acids or other products.

The Krebs Cycle—A Carbon and Energy Wheel

As you have seen, the oxidation of glucose yields a comparatively small amount of energy and gives off pyruvic acid. Pyruvic acid is still energy-rich, containing a number of extractable hydrogens and electrons to power ATP synthesis, but this can be achieved only through the work of the second and third phases of respiration, in which pyruvic acid's hydrogens are transferred to oxygen, producing CO_2 and H_2O. In the following section, we examine the next phase of this process, which takes place in the cytoplasm of bacteria and in the mitochondrial matrix in eukaryotes.

To connect the glycolysis pathway to the Krebs cycle, for either aerobic or anaerobic respiration, the pyruvic acid is first converted to a starting compound for that cycle **(figure 8.18)**. This step involves the first oxidation-reduction reaction of this phase of respiration, and it also releases the first carbon dioxide molecule. It involves a cluster of enzymes and coenzyme A that participate in the dehydrogenation (oxidation) of pyruvic acid, the reduction of NAD to NADH, and the decarboxylation of pyruvic acid to a 2-carbon acetyl group. The acetyl group remains attached to coenzyme A, forming acetyl coenzyme A (acetyl CoA) that feeds into the Krebs cycle.

The NADH formed during this reaction will be shuttled into electron transport and used to generate ATP via oxidative phosphorylation. *Keep in mind that all reactions described actually happen twice for each glucose because of the two pyruvates that are released during glycolysis.*

The Krebs cycle as depicted in figure 8.18 always looks intimidating. Think of it as a series of eight reactions catalyzed by eight different enzymes.

Steps in the Krebs Cycle

As you learned earlier, a cyclic pathway is one in which the starting compound is regenerated at the end. The Krebs cycle has eight steps, beginning with citric acid formation and

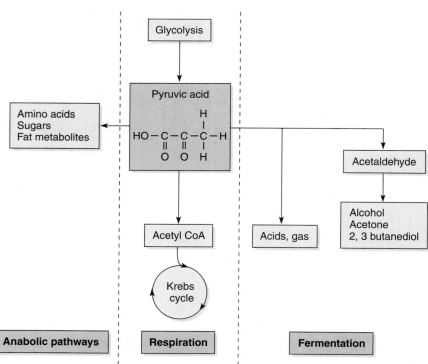

Figure 8.17 The fates of pyruvic acid (pyruvate). This metabolite is an important hub in the processing of nutrients by microbes. It may be fermented anaerobically to several end products or oxidized completely to CO_2 and H_2O through the Krebs cycle and the electron transport system. It can also serve as a source of raw material for synthesizing amino acids and carbohydrates.

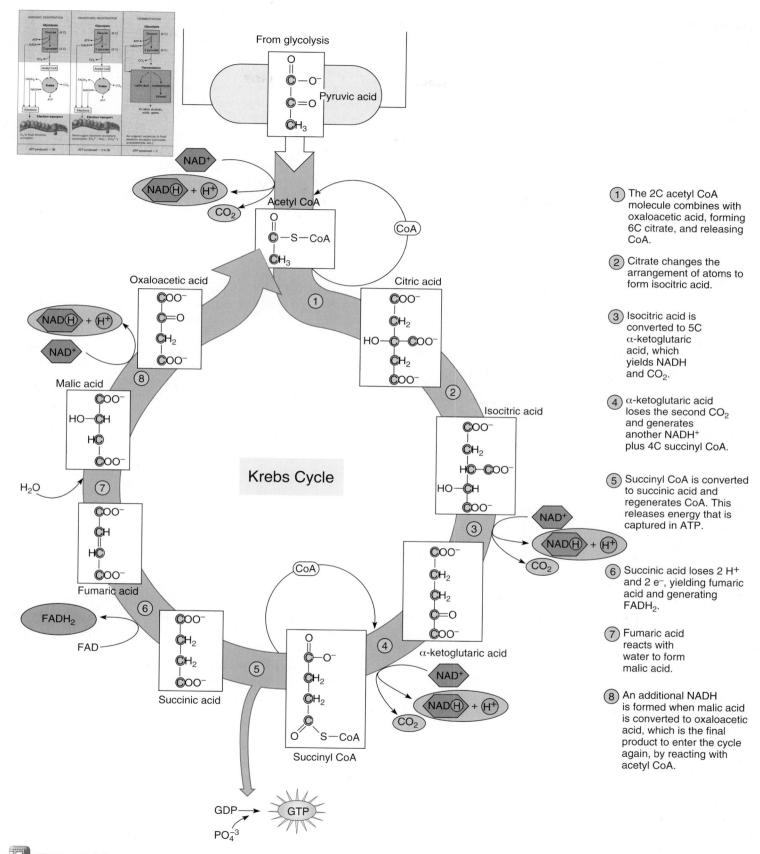

Figure 8.18 The reactions of a single turn of the Krebs cycle. Each glucose will produce two spins of this pathway. Note that this is an enlarged, more detailed view of the middle phase depicted in figure 8.15. It occurs in the cytoplasm of prokaryotes and the mitochondrial matrix of eukaryotes.

ending with oxaloacetic acid. As we take a single spin around the Krebs cycle, it will be helpful to keep track of

- the numbers of carbons (#C) of each substrate and product,
- reactions where CO_2 is generated,
- the involvement of the electron carriers NAD and FAD, and
- the site of ATP synthesis.

The reactions in the Krebs cycle follow:

1. Oxaloacetic acid (oxaloacetate; 4C) reacts with the acetyl group (2C) on acetyl CoA, thereby forming citric acid (citrate; 6C) and releasing coenzyme A so it can join with another acetyl group.
2. Citric acid is converted to its isomer, isocitric acid (isocitrate; 6C), to prepare this substrate for the decarboxylation and dehydrogenation of the next step.
3. Isocitric acid is acted upon by an enzyme complex including NAD or NADP (depending on the organism) in a reaction that generates NADH or NADPH, splits off a carbon dioxide, and leaves α-ketoglutaric acid (α-ketoglutarate; 5C).
4. Alpha-ketoglutaric acid serves as a substrate for the last decarboxylation reaction and yet another redox reaction involving coenzyme A and yielding NADH. The product is the high-energy compound succinyl CoA (4C).

At this point, the cycle has completed the formation of 3 CO_2 molecules that balance out the original 3-carbon pyruvic acid that began the Krebs. The remaining steps are needed not only to regenerate the oxaloacetic acid to start the cycle again but also to extract more energy from the intermediate compounds leading to oxaloacetic acid.

5. Succinyl CoA is the source of the one substrate-level phosphorylation in the Krebs cycle. In most microbes, it proceeds with the formation of ATP. The product of this reaction is succinic acid (succinate; 4C).
6. Succinic acid next becomes dehydrogenated, but in this case, the electron and H^+ acceptor is flavin adenine dinucleotide (FAD). The enzyme that catalyzes this reaction, succinyl dehydrogenase, is found in the bacterial cell membrane and mitochondrial cristae of eukaryotic cells. $FADH_2$ then directly enters the electron transport system. Fumaric acid (fumarate; 4C) is the product of this reaction.
7. The addition of water to fumaric acid (called hydration) results in malic acid (malate; 4C). This is one of the few reactions in respiration that directly incorporates water.
8. Malic acid is dehydrogenated (with formation of a final NADH), and oxaloacetic acid is formed. This step brings the cycle back to its original starting position, where oxaloacetic acid can react with acetyl coenzyme A.

The Krebs cycle serves to transfer the energy stored in acetyl CoA to NAD^+ and FAD by reducing them (transferring hydrogen ions to them). Thus, the main products of the

Case File 8 *Continuing the Case*

Around 1938, the United States adopted the widespread practice of *pasteurizing* milk, a process that uses heat to decrease the number of pathogenic organisms and is a reliable method of ensuring the safety of milk. Before that time, approximately 25% of food- and water-borne outbreaks of disease were attributable to milk; by 2001, less than 1% of outbreaks were associated with milk. Still, some people continue to consume unpasteurized milk, whether for convenience, taste preference, or supposed health benefits (although such benefits are not supported by scientific evidence). Therefore, at least 28 states allow some form of raw milk sales to the public.

Human pathogens are often shed in the feces of cows and can contaminate milk when they are present in or on the udders. Hygienic milking practices can reduce, but not eliminate, this risk. In states that regulate the sale of raw milk, the milk is tested on a regular basis for the presence of total bacteria as well as specific bacteria, especially *Salmonella*, *Campylobacter*, *E. coli* O157, and *Listeria monocytogenes*.

Among the many assays used to determine the safety of milk, one of the simplest to perform is the methylene blue reductase test, which indicates the number of microorganisms in a sample of milk. The test is based on the assumption that milk with a high bacterial load will have less free oxygen available due to its metabolism by the bacteria. When oxygen is present in the environment, methylene blue is oxidized and displays its familiar blue color; when no oxygen is present, methylene blue is colorless. The test is accomplished by adding 1 ml of a methylene blue solution to 10 ml of milk and sealing the tube to prevent any oxygen from entering. The milk is then incubated at 35°C to 37°C. As bacteria in the milk multiply, oxygen is consumed, and the methylene blue is reduced, turning it colorless and allowing the milk to appear white again. The time it takes for this to occur is known as the methylene blue reduction time (MBRT). The shorter the time, the greater the number of bacteria in the milk. High-quality milk has an MBRT of at least 6 hours, while an MBRT of 30 minutes indicates milk of very poor quality.

- Why do agencies perform the MBRT before moving on to more specific tests?
- What would be the result of a methylene blue reductase test if the milk were contaminated with a high number of obligate psychrophiles or thermophiles?

Krebs cycle are these reduced molecules (as well as 2 ATPs for each glucose molecule). The reduced coenzymes NADH and $FADH_2$ are vital to the energy production that will occur in electron transport. Along the way the 2-carbon acetyl CoA joins with a 4-carbon compound, oxaloacetic acid, and then participates in seven additional chemical transformations while "spinning off" the NADH and $FADH_2$. That's why we called the Krebs cycle the "carbon and energy wheel" in a preceding heading.

The Respiratory Chain: Electron Transport and Oxidative Phosphorylation

We now come to the energy chain, which is the final "processing mill" for electrons and hydrogen ions and the major generator of ATP. Overall, the electron transport system (ETS) consists of a chain of special redox carriers that receives electrons from reduced carriers (NADH, FADH₂) generated by glycolysis and the Krebs cycle and passes them in a sequential and orderly fashion from one redox molecule to the next (see figure 8.15). The flow of electrons down this chain is highly energetic and allows the active transport of hydrogen ions to the outside of the membrane where the respiratory chain is located. The step that finalizes the transport process is the acceptance of electrons and hydrogen by oxygen, producing water. Obviously, this process consumes oxygen (see Continuing the Case). Some variability exists from one organism to another, but the principal compounds that carry out these complex reactions are NADH dehydrogenase,

flavoproteins, coenzyme Q (ubiquinone), and **cytochromes** (sy'-toh-krohm). The cytochromes contain a tightly bound metal atom at their center that is actively involved in accepting electrons and donating them to the next carrier in the series. The highly compartmentalized structure of the respiratory chain is an important factor in its function. Note in **figure 8.19** that the electron transport carriers and enzymes are embedded in the cell membrane in prokaryotes. The equivalent structure for housing them in eukaryotes is the inner mitochondrial membranes pictured in **figure 8.20.** We will describe the electron transport system in both prokaryotes and eukaryotes.

Elements of Electron Transport: The Energy Cascade

The principal questions about the electron transport system are: How are the electrons passed from one carrier to another in the series? How is this progression coupled to ATP synthesis? and Where and how is oxygen utilized? Although the biochemical details of this process are rather complicated, the basic reactions consist of a number of redox reactions now familiar to us. In general, the carrier compounds and their enzymes are arranged in linear sequence and are reduced and oxidized in turn.

Figure 8.19 The electron transport system and oxidative phosphorylation in bacterial membranes. Starting at NADH dehydrogenase, electrons brought in from the Krebs cycle by NADH are passed along the chain of electron transport carriers. Each adjacent pair of transport molecules undergoes a redox reaction. Coupled to the transport of electrons is the simultaneous active transport of H⁺ into the periplasm by specific carriers. These processes set the scene for ATP synthesis and final H⁺ and e⁻ acceptance by oxygen.

Cell wall

Cytochromes

Cytoplasm

ATP synthase

ADP

ATP

Cell membrane with ETS

The sequence of electron carriers in the respiratory chain of most aerobic organisms is

1. NADH dehydrogenase, which is closely associated in a complex with the adjacent carrier, which is
2. flavin mononucleotide (FMN);
3. coenzyme Q;
4. cytochrome b;
5. cytochrome c_1;
6. cytochrome c; and
7. cytochromes a and a_3, which are complexed together.

Conveyance of the NADHs from glycolysis and the Krebs cycle to the first carrier sets in motion the remaining six steps. With each redox exchange, the energy level of the reactants is lessened. The released energy is captured and used by the **ATP synthase** complex, stationed along the membrane in close association with the ETS carriers. Each NADH that enters electron transport can give rise to 3 ATPs. This coupling of ATP synthesis to electron transport is termed **oxidative phosphorylation.** Because the electrons from $FADH_2$ from the Krebs cycle enter the cycle at a later point than the NAD and FMN complex reactions, there is less energy to release, and only 2 ATPs are the result.

The Formation of ATP and Chemiosmosis

What biochemical processes are involved in coupling electron transport to the production of ATP? We will first look at the system in prokaryotes, which have the components of electron transport embedded in a precise sequence on the cytoplasmic membrane. According to a widely accepted concept called **chemiosmosis,** as the electron transport carriers shuttle electrons, they actively pump hydrogen ions (protons) into the periplasmic space. This process sets up a concentration gradient of hydrogen ions called the *proton motive force (PMF).* The PMF consists of a difference in charge between the outside of the membrane (+) and the inside of the membrane (−) (see figure 8.19).

Separating the charge has the effect of a battery, which can temporarily store potential energy. This charge will be maintained by the impermeability of the membrane to H^+. The only site where H^+ can diffuse into the cytoplasm is at the ATP synthase complex, which sets the stage for the final processing of H^+ leading to ATP synthesis.

ATP synthase is a complex enzyme composed of two large units, F_0 and F_1 (see figures 8.19 and 8.20). It is embedded in the membrane, but part of it rotates like a motor and traps chemical energy. As the H^+ ions flow through the F_0

Figure 8.20 **The electron transport system and oxidative phosphorylation on the mitochondrial cristae.**

FMN
Coenzyme Q

(a) The electron transport system in eukaryotes is on the inner membrane of mitochondrial cristae.

+ Charged

− Charged

(b) As the carriers in the mitochondrial cristae transport electrons, they also actively pump H^+ ions (protons) to the intermembrane space, producing a chemical and charge gradient between the outer and inner mitochondrial compartments.

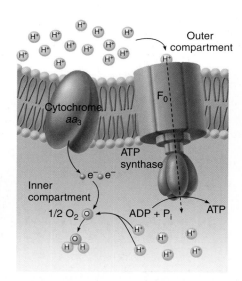

(c) The distribution of electric potential and the concentration gradient of protons across the membrane drive the synthesis of ATP by ATP synthase. The rotation of this enzyme couples diffusion of H^+ to the inner compartment with the bonding of ADP and P_i. The final event of electron transport is the reaction of the electrons with the H^+ and O_2 to form metabolic H_2O. This step is catalyzed by cytochrome oxidase (cytochrome aa_3).

center of the enzyme by diffusion, the F_1 compartments pull in ADP and P_i. Rotation causes a three-dimensional change in the enzyme that bonds these two molecules, thereby releasing ATP into the cytoplasm (see figure 8.19). The enzyme is then rotated back to the start position and will continue the process.

Eukaryotic ATP synthesis occurs by means of the same overall process. However, eukaryotes have the ETS stationed in mitochondrial membranes, between the inner mitochondrial matrix and the outer intermembrane space (see figure 8.20). This difference will affect the amount of ATP produced (discussed in the next section). In both cell types, the chemiosmotic theory has been supported by tests showing that oxidative phosphorylation is blocked if the mitochondrial or bacterial cell membranes are disrupted.

Potential Yield of ATPs from Oxidative Phosphorylation

The total of five NADHs (four from the Krebs cycle and one from glycolysis) can be used to synthesize:

15 ATPs for ETS (5 × 3 per electron pair)

and

15 × 2 = 30 ATPs per glucose

The single FADH produced during the Krebs cycle results in:

2 ATPs per electron pair

and

2 × 2 = 4 ATPs per glucose

Figure 8.21 summarizes the total of ATP and other products for the entire aerobic pathway. These totals are the potential yields possible but may not be fulfilled by many organisms.

Summary of Aerobic Respiration

Originally, we presented a summary equation for respiration. We are now in a position to tabulate the input and output of this equation at various points in the pathways and sum up the final ATP. Close examination of figure 8.21 will reveal several important facets of aerobic respiration:

1. The total possible yield of ATP is 40: 4 from glycolysis, 2 from the Krebs cycle, and 34 from electron transport. However, because 2 ATPs were expended in early glycolysis, this leaves a maximum of **38 ATPs.**

The actual totals may be lower in certain eukaryotic cells because energy is expended in transporting the NADH produced during glycolysis across the mitochondrial membrane. Certain aerobic bacteria come closest to achieving the full total of 38 because they lack mitochondria and thus do not have to use ATP in transport of NADH across the outer mitochondrial membrane.

2. Six carbon dioxide molecules are generated during the Krebs cycle.

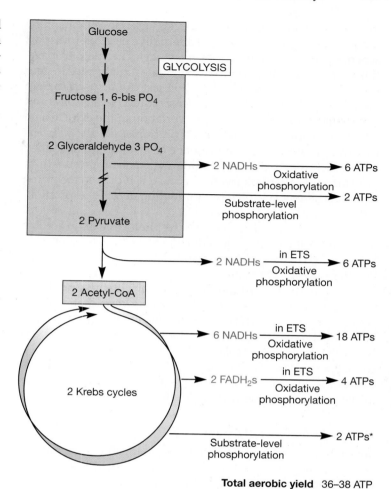

Figure 8.21 Theoretic ATP yield from aerobic respiration. To attain the theoretic maximum yield of ATP, one must assume a ratio of 3 for the oxidation of NADH and 2 for $FADH_2$. The actual yield is generally lower and varies between eukaryotes and prokaryotes and among prokaryotic species.

3. Six oxygen molecules are consumed during electron transport.

4. Six water molecules are produced in electron transport and 2 in glycolysis, but because 2 are used in the Krebs cycle, this leaves a net number of 6.

The Terminal Step

The terminal step, during which oxygen accepts the electrons, is catalyzed by cytochrome aa_3, also called cytochrome oxidase. This large enzyme complex is specifically adapted to receive electrons from cytochrome c, pick up hydrogens from the solution, and react with oxygen to form a molecule of water. This reaction, though in actuality more complex, is summarized as follows:

$$2H^+ + 2e^- + \tfrac{1}{2}O_2 \rightarrow H_2O$$

Most eukaryotic aerobes have a fully functioning cytochrome system, but bacteria exhibit wide-ranging variations in this part of the system. Some species lack one or more of the redox steps; others have several alternative electron transport schemes. Because many bacteria lack cytochrome *c* oxidase, this variation can be used to differentiate among certain genera of bacteria. An oxidase detection test can be used to help identify members of the genera *Neisseria* and *Pseudomonas* and some species of *Bacillus.* Another variation in the cytochrome system is evident in certain bacteria (*Klebsiella, Enterobacter*) that can grow even in the presence of cyanide because they lack cytochrome oxidase. Cyanide will cause rapid death in humans and other eukaryotes because it blocks cytochrome oxidase, thereby completely terminating aerobic respiration, but it is harmless to these bacteria.

A potential side reaction of the respiratory chain in aerobic organisms is the incomplete reduction of oxygen to superoxide ion (O_2^-) and hydrogen peroxide (H_2O_2). As mentioned in chapter 7, these toxic oxygen products can be very damaging to cells. Aerobes have neutralizing enzymes to deal with these products, including *superoxide dismutase* and *catalase.* One exception is the genus *Streptococcus*, which can grow well in oxygen yet lacks both cytochromes and catalase. The tolerance of these organisms to oxygen can be explained by the neutralizing effects of a special peroxidase. The lack of cytochromes, catalase, and peroxidases in anaerobes as a rule limits their ability to process free oxygen and contributes to its toxic effects on them.

Anaerobic Respiration

Some bacteria have evolved an anaerobic respiratory system that functions like the aerobic cytochrome system except that it utilizes oxygen-containing ions, rather than free oxygen, as the final electron acceptor in electron transport (see figure 8.15). Of these, the nitrate (NO_3^-) and nitrite (NO_2^-) reduction systems are best known. The reaction in species such as *Escherichia coli* is represented as:

$$\text{Nitrate reductase}$$
$$\downarrow$$
$$NO_3^- + NADH \rightarrow NO_2^- + H_2O + NAD^+$$
$$\text{nitrate} \qquad\qquad \text{nitrate}$$

The enzyme nitrate reductase catalyzes the removal of oxygen from nitrate, leaving nitrite and water as products. A test for this reaction is one of the physiological tests used in identifying bacteria.

Some species of *Pseudomonas* and *Bacillus* possess enzymes that can further reduce nitrite to nitric oxide (NO), nitrous oxide (N_2O), and even nitrogen gas (N_2). This process, called **denitrification,** is a very important step in recycling nitrogen in the biosphere. Other oxygen-containing nutrients reduced anaerobically by various bacteria are carbonates and sulfates. None of the anaerobic pathways produce as much ATP as aerobic respiration.

Fermentation

Of all the results of pyruvate metabolism, probably the most varied is fermentation. Technically speaking, **fermentation** is the incomplete oxidation of glucose or other carbohydrates in the absence of oxygen. This process uses organic compounds as the terminal electron acceptors and yields a small amount of ATP (see figure 8.15).

Over time, the term **fermentation** has acquired several looser connotations. Originally, Pasteur called the microbial action of yeast during wine production *ferments,* and to this day, biochemists use the term in reference to the production of ethyl alcohol by yeasts acting on glucose and other carbohydrates. Fermentation is also what bacteriologists call the formation of acid, gas, and other products by the action of various bacteria on pyruvic acid. The process is a common metabolic strategy among bacteria. Industrial processes that produce chemicals on a massive scale through the actions of microbes are also called fermentations (see chapter 25). Each of these usages is acceptable for one application or another.

It may seem that fermentation would yield only meager amounts of energy (2 ATPs maximum per glucose) and that would slow down growth. What actually happens, however, is that many bacteria can grow as fast as they would in the presence of oxygen. This rapid growth is made possible by an increase in the rate of glycolysis. From another standpoint, fermentation permits independence from molecular oxygen and allows colonization of anaerobic environments. It also enables microorganisms with a versatile metabolism to adapt to variations in the availability of oxygen. For them, fermentation provides a means to grow even when oxygen levels are too low for aerobic respiration.

Bacteria that digest cellulose in the rumens of cattle are largely fermentative. After initially hydrolyzing cellulose to glucose, they ferment the glucose to organic acids, which are then absorbed as the bovine's principal energy source. Even human muscle cells can undergo a form of fermentation that permits short periods of activity after the oxygen supply in the muscle has been exhausted. Muscle cells convert pyruvic acid into lactic acid, which allows anaerobic production of ATP to proceed for a time. But this cannot go on indefinitely, and after a few minutes, the accumulated lactic acid causes muscle fatigue.

Products of Fermentation in Microorganisms

Alcoholic beverages (wine, beer, whiskey) are perhaps the most prominent among fermentation products; others are solvents (acetone, butanol), organic acids (lactic, acetic), dairy products, and many other foods. Derivatives of proteins, nucleic acids, and other organic compounds are fermented to produce vitamins, antibiotics, and even hormones such as hydrocortisone.

Fermentation products can be grouped into two general categories: alcoholic fermentation products and acidic fermentation products **(figure 8.22). Alcoholic fermentation** occurs in yeast or bacterial species that have metabolic pathways for converting pyruvic acid to ethanol. This process involves a decarboxylation of pyruvic acid to acetaldehyde, followed by a reduction of the acetaldehyde to ethanol. In oxidizing the NADH formed during glycolysis, NAD is regener-

Figure 8.22 The chemistry of fermentation systems that produce acid and alcohol. In both cases, the final electron acceptor is an organic compound. In yeasts, pyruvic acid is decarboxylated to acetaldehyde, and the NADH given off in the glycolytic pathway reduces acetaldehyde to ethyl alcohol. In homolactic fermentative bacteria, pyruvic acid is reduced by NADH to lactic acid. Both systems regenerate NAD to feed back into glycolysis or other cycles.

ated, thereby allowing the glycolytic pathway to continue. These processes are crucial in the production of beer and wine, though the actual techniques for arriving at the desired amount of ethanol and the prevention of unwanted side reactions are important tricks of the brewer's trade **(Insight 8.4).** Note that the products of alcoholic fermentation are not only ethanol but also CO_2, a gas that accounts for the bubbles in champagne and beer (and the rising of bread dough).

The pathways of **acidic fermentation** are extremely varied. Lactic acid bacteria ferment pyruvate in the same way that humans do—by reducing it to lactic acid. If the product of this fermentation is mainly lactic acid, as in certain species of *Streptococcus* and *Lactobacillus*, it is termed *homolactic.* The souring of milk is due largely to the production of this acid by bacteria. When glucose is fermented to a mixture of lactic acid, acetic acid, and carbon dioxide, as is the case with *Leuconostoc* and other species of *Lactobacillus*, the process is termed *heterolactic fermentation.*

Many members of the family Enterobacteriaceae (*Escherichia, Shigella,* and *Salmonella*) possess enzyme systems for converting pyruvic acid to several acids simultaneously. **Mixed acid** fermentation produces a combination of acetic, lactic, succinic, and formic acids, and it lowers the pH of a medium to about 4.0. *Propionibacterium* produces primarily propionic acid, which gives the characteristic flavor to Swiss cheese while fermentation gas (CO_2) produces the holes. Some members also further decompose formic acid completely to carbon dioxide and hydrogen gases. Because enteric bacteria commonly occupy the intestine, this fermentative activity accounts for the accumulation of some types of gas—primarily CO_2 and H_2—in the intestine. Some bacteria reduce the organic acids and produce the neutral end product 2,3-butanediol.

We have provided only a brief survey of fermentation products, but it is worth noting that microbes can be harnessed to synthesize a variety of other substances by varying the raw materials provided them. In fact, so broad is the colloquial meaning of the word **fermentation** that the large-scale industrial syntheses by microorganisms often utilize entirely different mechanisms from those described here, and they even occur aerobically, particularly in antibiotic, hormone, vitamin, and amino acid production (see chapter 25).

INSIGHT 8.4   Pasteur and the Wine-to-Vinegar Connection

The microbiology of alcoholic fermentation was greatly clarified by Louis Pasteur after French winemakers hired him to uncover the causes of periodic spoilage in wines. Especially troublesome was the conversion of wine to vinegar and the resultant sour flavor. Up to that time, wine formation had been considered strictly a chemical process. After extensively studying beer making and wine grapes, Pasteur concluded that wine, both fine and not so fine, was the result of microbial action on the juices of the grape and that wine "disease" was caused by contaminating organisms that produced undesirable products such as acid. Although he did not know it at the time, the bacterial contaminants responsible for the acidity of the spoiled wines were likely to be *Acetobacter* or *Gluconobacter* introduced by the grapes, air, or wine-making apparatus. These common gram-negative genera further oxidized ethanol to acetic acid and are presently used in commercial vinegar production. The following formula shows how this is accomplished:

$$\underset{\text{Ethanol}}{\text{H}-\overset{\overset{\text{H}}{|}}{\underset{\underset{\text{H}}{|}}{\text{C}}}-\overset{\overset{\text{H}}{|}}{\underset{\underset{\text{H}}{|}}{\text{C}}}-\text{OH} \longrightarrow \underset{\text{Acetic acid}}{\text{H}-\overset{\overset{\text{H}}{|}}{\underset{\underset{\text{H}}{|}}{\text{C}}}-\overset{\text{O}}{\underset{\text{OH}}{\text{C}}} + 2\text{H}^+}$$

Pasteur's far-reaching solution to the problem is still with us today—mild heating, or **pasteurization,** of the grape juice to destroy the contaminants, followed by inoculation of the juice with a pure yeast culture. The topic of wine making is explored further in chapter 25.

Catabolism of Noncarbohydrate Compounds

We have given you one version of events for catabolism, using glucose, a carbohydrate, as our example. Other compounds serve as fuel, as well. The more complex polysaccharides are easily broken down into their component sugars, which can enter glycolysis at various points. Microbes also break down other molecules for their own use, of course. Two other major sources of energy and building blocks for microbes are lipids (fats) and proteins. Both of these must be broken down to their component parts to produce precursor metabolites and energy.

Recall from chapter 2 that fats are fatty acids joined to glycerol. Enzymes called **lipases** break these apart. The glycerol is then converted to dihydroxyacetone phosphate (DHAP), which can enter step 4 of glycolysis (see figure 8.16). The fatty acid component goes through a process called **beta oxidation.** Fatty acids have a variable number of carbons; in beta oxidation, 2-carbon units are successively transferred to coenzyme A, creating acetyl CoA, which enters the Krebs cycle. This process can yield a large amount of energy. Oxidation of a 6-carbon fatty acid yields 50 ATPs, compared with 38 for a 6-carbon sugar.

Proteins are chains of amino acids. Enzymes called **proteases** break proteins down to their amino acid components (see figure 8.7), after which the amino groups are removed by a reaction called **deamination (figure 8.23).** This

Figure 8.23 Deamination.   Removal of an amino group converts an amino acid to an intermediate of carbohydrate metabolism. Ammonium is a waste product.

leaves a carbon compound, which is easily converted to one of several Krebs cycle intermediates.

8.3 Learning Outcomes—Can You ...

10. ... name three basic catabolic pathways and give an estimate of how much ATP each of them yields?
11. ... write a summary statement describing glycolysis?
12. ... describe the Krebs cycle?
13. ... discuss the significance of the electron transport system?
14. ... point out how anaerobic respiration differs from aerobic respiration?
15. ... provide a summary of fermentation?
16. ... describe how noncarbohydrate compounds are catabolized?

8.4 Biosynthesis and the Crossing Pathways of Metabolism

Our discussion now turns from catabolism and energy extraction to anabolic functions and biosynthesis. In this section, we present aspects of intermediary metabolism, including amphibolic pathways, the synthesis of simple molecules, and the synthesis of macromolecules.

The Frugality of the Cell—Waste Not, Want Not

It must be obvious by now that cells have mechanisms for careful management of carbon compounds. Rather than being dead ends, most catabolic pathways contain strategic molecular intermediates (metabolites) that can be diverted into anabolic pathways. In this way, a given molecule can serve multiple purposes, and the maximum benefit can be derived from all nutrients and metabolites of the cell pool. The property of a system to integrate catabolic and anabolic pathways to improve cell efficiency is termed **amphibolism** (am-fee-bol′-izm).

At this point in the chapter, you can appreciate a more complex view of metabolism than that presented at the beginning, in figure 8.1. **Figure 8.24** demonstrates the amphibolic nature of intermediary metabolism. The pathways of glucose catabolism are an especially rich "metabolic marketplace." The principal sites of amphibolic interaction occur during glycolysis (glyceraldehyde-3-phosphate and pyruvic acid) and the Krebs cycle (acetyl coenzyme A and various organic acids).

Amphibolic Sources of Cellular Building Blocks

Glyceraldehyde-3-phosphate can be diverted away from glycolysis and converted into precursors for amino acid, carbohydrate, and triglyceride (fat) synthesis. (A precursor molecule is a compound that is the source of another compound.) Earlier we noted the numerous directions that pyruvic acid catabolism can take. In terms of synthesis, pyruvate also plays a pivotal role in providing intermediates for amino acids. In the event of an inadequate glucose supply, pyruvate serves as the starting point in glucose synthesis from various metabolic intermediates, a process called **gluconeogenesis** (gloo′-koh-nee′-oh-gen′-uh-sis).

The acetyl group that starts the Krebs cycle is another extremely versatile metabolite that can be fed into a number of synthetic pathways. This 2-carbon fragment can be converted as a single unit into one of several amino acids, or a number of these fragments can be condensed into hydrocarbon chains that are important building blocks for fatty acid and lipid synthesis. Note that the reverse is also true—fats can be degraded to acetyl through a process called

Figure 8.24 An amphibolic view of metabolism. Intermediate compounds such as pyruvic acid and acetyl coenzyme A serve an amphibolic function. With comparatively small modifications, these compounds can be converted into other compounds and enter a different pathway. Note that catabolism of glucose (center) furnishes numerous intermediates for anabolic pathways that synthesize amino acids, fats, nucleic acids, and carbohydrates. These building blocks can serve in further synthesis of larger molecules to construct various cell components.

beta oxidation, and thereby enter the Krebs cycle at acetyl coenzyme A.

Two metabolites of carbohydrate catabolism that the Krebs cycle produces, oxaloacetic acid and α-ketoglutaric acid, are essential intermediates in the synthesis of certain amino acids. This occurs through **amination,** the addition of an amino group to a carbon skeleton **(figure 8.25a).** A certain core group of amino acids can then be used to synthesize others. Amino acids and carbohydrates can be interchanged through **transamination (figure 8.25b).**

Pathways that synthesize the nitrogen bases (purines, pyrimidines), which are components of DNA and RNA, originate in amino acids and so can be dependent on intermediates from the Krebs cycle as well. Because the coenzymes NAD, NADP, FAD, and others contain purines and pyrimidines similar to the nucleic acids, their synthetic pathways are also dependent on amino acids. During times of carbohydrate deprivation, organisms can likewise convert amino acids to intermediates of the Krebs cycle by **deamination** and thereby derive energy from proteins (see figure 8.23).

Anabolism: Formation of Macromolecules

Monosaccharides, amino acids, fatty acids, nitrogen bases, and vitamins—the building blocks that make up the various macromolecules and organelles of the cell—come from two possible sources. They can enter the cell from the outside as nutrients, or they can be synthesized through various cellular pathways. The degree to which an organism can synthesize its own building blocks (simple molecules) is determined by its genetic makeup, a factor that varies tremendously from group to group. In chapter 7, you learned that autotrophs require only CO_2 as a carbon source, a few minerals to synthesize all cell substances, and no organic nutrients. Some heterotrophic organisms (*E. coli,* yeasts) are also very efficient in that they can synthesize all cellular substances from minerals and one organic carbon source such as glucose. Compare this with a strict parasite that has few synthetic abilities of its own and derives most precursor molecules from the host.

Whatever their source, once these building blocks are added to the metabolic pool, they are available for synthesis of polymers by the cell. The details of synthesis vary among the types of macromolecules, but all of them involve the formation of bonds by specialized enzymes and the expenditure of ATP.

Carbohydrate Biosynthesis

The role of glucose in bioenergetics is so crucial that its biosynthesis is ensured by several alternative pathways. Certain structures in the cell depend on an adequate supply of glucose as well. It is the major component of the cellulose cell walls of some eukaryotes and of certain storage granules (starch, glycogen). One of the intermediaries in glycolysis, glucose-6-P, is used to form glycogen. Monosaccharides other than glucose are important in the synthesis of bacterial cell walls. Peptidoglycan contains a linked polymer of muramic acid and glucosamine. Fructose-6-P from glycolysis is used to form these two sugars. Carbohydrates (deoxyribose, ribose) are also essential building blocks in nucleic acids. Polysaccharides are the predominant components of cell surface structures such as capsules and the glycocalyx, and they are commonly found in slime layers. Remember that most polymerization reactions occur via loss of a water molecule (see figure 2.15) and the input of energy (see figure 8.7).

Figure 8.25 Reactions that produce and convert amino acids. All of them require energy as ATP or NAD and specialized enzymes. **(a)** Through amination (the addition of an ammonium molecule [amino group]), a carbohydrate can be converted to an amino acid. **(b)** Through transamination (transfer of an amino group from an amino acid to a carbohydrate fragment), metabolic intermediates can be converted to amino acids that are in low supply. Contrast these to deamination in figure 8.23.

Amino Acids, Protein Synthesis, and Nucleic Acid Synthesis

Proteins account for a large proportion of a cell's constituents. They are essential components of enzymes, the cell membrane, the cell wall, and cell appendages. As a general rule, 20 amino acids are needed to make these proteins. Although some organisms (*E. coli,* for example) have pathways that will synthesize all 20 amino acids, others, especially animals, lack some or all of the pathways for amino acid synthesis and must acquire the essential ones from their diets. Protein synthesis itself is a complex process that requires a genetic blueprint and the operation of intricate cellular machinery, as you will see in chapter 9.

DNA and RNA are responsible for the hereditary continuity of cells and the overall direction of protein synthesis. Because nucleic acid synthesis is a major topic of genetics and is closely allied to protein synthesis, it will likewise be covered in chapter 9.

Assembly of the Cell

The component parts of a bacteria cell are being synthesized on a continuous basis, and catabolism is also taking place, as long as nutrients are present and the cell is in a nondormant state. When anabolism produces enough macromolecules to serve two cells, and when DNA replication produces duplicate copies of the cell's genetic material, the cell undergoes binary fission, which results in two cells from one parent cell. The two cells will need twice as many ribosomes, twice as many enzymes, and so on. The cell has created these during the initial anabolic phases we have described. Before cell division, the membrane(s) and the cell wall will have increased in size to create a cell that is almost twice as big as a "newborn" cell. Once synthesized, the phospholipid bilayer components of the membranes assemble themselves spontaneously with no energy input. But proteins and other components must be added to the membranes. Growth of the cell wall, accomplished by the addition and coupling of sugars and peptides, requires energy input. The catabolic processes provide all the energy for these complex building reactions.

8.4 Learning Outcomes—Can You ...

17. ... provide an overview of the anabolic stages of metabolism?
18. ... define amphibolism?

8.5 It All Starts with Light

As mentioned earlier, the ultimate source of most of the chemical energy in cells comes from the sun. Most organisms depend either directly or indirectly on the sunlight's energy,

which is converted into chemical energy through photosynthesis. (Some chemoautotrophs derive their energy and nutrients solely from inorganic substrates.) The other major products of photosynthesis are organic carbon compounds, which are produced from carbon dioxide through a process called carbon fixation.

Photosynthesis

With few exceptions, the energy that drives all life processes comes from the sun, but this source is directly available only to the cells of photosynthesizers. In the terrestrial biosphere, green plants are the primary photosynthesizers, and in aquatic ecosystems, where 80% to 90% of all photosynthesis occurs, algae, green and purple bacteria, and cyanobacteria fill this role. It was also recently discovered that bacteriophages that infect marine cyanobacteria actually carry out significant amounts of photosynthesis.

Photosynthetic organisms use light energy to produce high-energy glucose from low-energy CO_2 and water. They do this through a series of reactions involving light, pigment, CO_2, and water, which is used as a source for electrons.

Photosynthesis proceeds in two phases: the **light-dependent reactions,** which proceed only in the presence of sunlight, and the **light-independent reactions,** which proceed regardless of the lighting conditions (light or dark).

Solar energy is delivered in discrete energy packets called **photons** (also called quanta) that travel as waves. The wavelengths of light operating in photosynthesis occur in the visible spectrum between 400 (violet) and 700 nanometers (red). As this light strikes photosynthetic pigments, some wavelengths are absorbed, some pass through, and some are reflected. The activity that has greatest impact on photosynthesis is the absorbance of light by photosynthetic pigments. These include the **chlorophylls,** which are green; **carotenoids,** which are yellow, orange, or red; and **phycobilins,** which are red or blue-green.[4] By far the most important of these pigments are the bacterial chlorophylls, which contain a *photocenter* that consists of a magnesium atom held in the center of a complex ringed molecule called a *porphyrin.* As we will see, the chlorophyll molecule harvests the energy of photons and converts it to electron (chemical) energy. Accessory photosynthetic pigments such as carotenes trap light energy and shuttle it to chlorophyll, thereby functioning like antennae. These light-dependent reactions are catabolic (energy-producing) reactions, which pave the way for the next set of reactions, the light-independent reactions, which use the produced energy for synthesis (anabolism). During this phase, carbon atoms from CO_2 are fixed to the carbon backbones of organic molecules.

The detailed biochemistry of photosynthesis is beyond the scope of this text, but we will provide an overview of

4. The color of the pigment corresponds to the wavelength of light it reflects.

the general process as it occurs in green plants, algae, and cyanobacteria **(figure 8.26)**. Many of the basic activities (electron transport and phosphorylation) are biochemically similar to certain pathways of respiration.

Light-Dependent Reactions   The same systems that carry the photosynthetic pigments are also the sites for the light reactions. They occur in the **thylakoid** membranes of compartments called grana (singular: granum) in chloroplasts **(figure 8.27a)** and in specialized parts of the cell membranes in prokaryotes (see chapter 4). These systems exist as two separate complexes called *photosystem I* (P700) and *photosystem II* (P680)[5] **(figure 8.27c)**. Both systems contain chlorophyll and they are simultaneously activated by light, but the reactions in photosystem II help drive

---

5. The numbers refer to the wavelength of light to which each system is most sensitive.

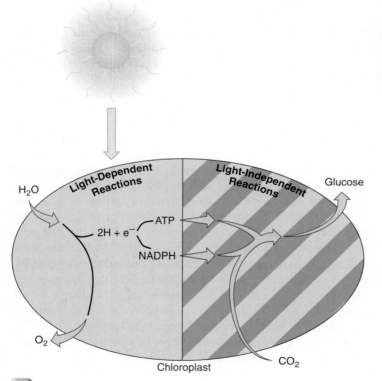

Figure 8.26 Overview of photosynthesis.   The general reactions of photosynthesis, divided into two phases called light-dependent reactions and light-independent reactions. The dependent reactions require light to activate chlorophyll pigment and use the energy given off during activation to split an H_2O molecule into oxygen and hydrogen, producing ATP and NADPH. The independent reactions, which occur either with or without light, utilize ATP and NADPH produced during the light reactions to fix CO_2 into organic compounds such as glucose.

Process Figure 8.27 The reactions of photosynthesis.

(a) **A cell of the motile alga *Chlamydomonas*, with a single large chloroplast (magnified cutaway view). The chloroplast contains membranous compartments called grana where chlorophyll molecules and the photosystems for the light reactions are located.**

(b) **A chlorophyll molecule, with a central magnesium atom held by a porphyrin ring.**

(c) **The main events of the light reaction shown as an exploded view in one granum.**

1. When light activates photosystem II, it sets up a chain reaction, in which electrons are released from chlorophyll.

2. These electrons are transported along a chain of carriers to photosystem I.

3. The empty position in photosystem II is replenished by photolysis of H_2O. Other products of photolysis are O_2 and H^+.

4. Pumping of H^+ into the interior of the granum produces conditions for ATP to be synthesized.

5. The final electron and H^+ acceptor is NADP, which receives these from photosystem I.

6. Both NADPH and ATP are fed into the stroma for the Calvin cycle.

photosystem I. Together the systems are activated by light, transport electrons, pump hydrogen ions, and form ATP and NADPH.

When photons enter the photocenter of the P680 system (PS II), the magnesium atom in chlorophyll becomes excited and releases 2 electrons. The loss of electrons from the photocenter has two major effects:

1. It creates a vacancy in the chlorophyll molecule forceful enough to split an H_2O molecule into hydrogen (H^+) (electrons and hydrogen ions) and oxygen (O_2). This splitting of water, termed **photolysis,** is the ultimate source of the O_2 gas that is an important product of photosynthesis. The electrons released from the lysed water regenerate photosystem II for its next reaction with light.

2. Electrons generated by the first photoevent are immediately boosted through a series of carriers (cytochromes) to the P700 system. At this same time, hydrogen ions accumulate in the internal space of the thylakoid complex, thereby producing an electrochemical gradient.

The P700 system (PS I) has been activated by light so that it is ready to accept electrons generated by the PS II. The electrons it receives are passed along a second transport chain to a complex that uses electrons and hydrogen ions to reduce NADP to NADPH. (Recall that reduction in this sense entails the addition of electrons and hydrogens to a substrate.)

A second energy reaction involves synthesis of ATP by a chemiosmotic mechanism similar to that shown in figures 8.19 and 8.20. Channels in the thylakoids of the granum actively pump H^+ into the inner chamber, producing a charge gradient. ATP synthase located in this same thylakoid uses the energy from H^+ transport to phosphorylate ADP to ATP. Because it occurs in light, this process is termed **photophosphorylation.** Both NADPH and ATP are released into the stroma of the chloroplast, where they drive the reactions of the **Calvin cycle.**

Light-Independent Reactions The subsequent photosynthetic reactions that do not require light occur in the chloroplast stroma or the cytoplasm of cyanobacteria. These reactions use energy produced by the light phase to synthesize glucose by means of the **Calvin cycle (figure 8.28).**

The cycle begins at the point where CO_2 is combined with a doubly phosphorylated 5-carbon acceptor molecule called ribulose-1,5-bisphosphate (RuBP). This process, called **carbon fixation,** generates a 6C intermediate compound that immediately splits into two 3-carbon molecules of 3-phosphoglyceric acid (PGA). The subsequent steps use the ATP and NADPH generated by the photosystems to form high-energy intermediates. First, ATP adds a second phosphate to 3-PGA and produces 1,3-bisphosphoglyceric acid (BPG). Then, during the same step, NADPH contributes its hydrogen to BPG, and one high-energy phosphate

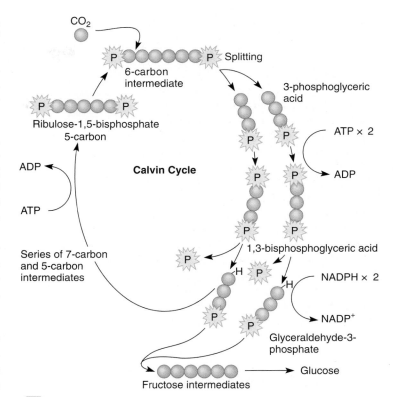

Figure 8.28 The Calvin cycle. The main events of the reactions in photosynthesis that do not require light. It is during this cycle that carbon is fixed into organic form using the energy (ATP and NADPH) released by the light reactions. The end product, glucose, can be stored as complex carbohydrates, or it can be used in various amphibolic pathways to produce other carbohydrate intermediates or amino acids.

is removed. These events give rise to glyceraldehyde-3-phosphate (PGAL). This molecule and its isomer dihydroxyacetone phosphate (DHAP) are key molecules in hexose synthesis leading to fructose and glucose. You may notice that this pathway is very similar to glycolysis, except that it runs in reverse (see figure 8.16). Bringing the cycle back to regenerate RuBP requires PGAL and several steps not depicted in **figure 8.28.**

Other Mechanisms of Photosynthesis The **oxygenic,** or oxygen-releasing, photosynthesis that occurs in plants, algae, and cyanobacteria is the dominant type on the earth. Other photosynthesizers such as green and purple bacteria possess bacteriochlorophyll, which is more versatile in capturing light. They have only a cyclic photosystem I, which routes the electrons from the photocenter to the electron carriers and back to the photosystem again. This pathway generates a relatively small amount of ATP, and it may not produce NADPH. As photolithotrophs, these bacteria use H_2, H_2S, or elemental sulfur rather than H_2O as a source of electrons and reducing power. As a consequence, they are **anoxygenic** (non-oxygen-producing), and many are strict anaerobes.

Case File 8   *Wrap-Up*

Of the 29 incidences of infection with *S. enterica* Typhimurium, the first cluster consisted of 15 cases with dates of onset between February 3 and March 5. Samples of raw milk collected from a bulk-milk tank at Dairy A (on February 20) and from the home of an ill person (on February 28) yielded the outbreak strain of *S. enterica* Typhimurium. On March 2, the PDH ordered the dairy to stop selling raw milk and advised the public not to consume raw milk or raw-milk products from the dairy. The dairy was allowed to resume sales after two consecutive samplings of raw milk from the milk tanks tested negative for the bacterium. A second outbreak occurred in late March and was linked to cheese made from raw milk purchased from Dairy A. The dairy was again ordered to cease raw-milk sales, and its state-issued permit to sell raw milk was suspended. The final cluster of 11 cases occurred during the summer of 2007, 10 of them among people living close to the dairy. Further investigation revealed that the dairy had, despite its suspended permit, been selling raw milk. Analysis of the milk from a bulk-milk tank and from the home of an ill person revealed the presence of the outbreak-related strain of *S. enterica* Typhimurium. The dairy was again ordered to halt distribution of raw milk, and its raw-milk permit was subsequently revoked.

Eight inspections of the dairy by the PDA during the first four months of 2007 revealed improper cleaning of milking equipment, insufficient supervision of workers, illnesses in lactating cows, and bird and rodent infestation, any of which could have contributed to the salmonellosis outbreak.

Agencies use "catch-all" kinds of tests like the MBRT as screening mechanisms. If bacteria are found, more specific tests can then be performed. Incubation temperatures of 35°C to 37°C are used, since most human pathogens multiply at that temperature. If for some reason the milk were contaminated with psychrophiles or thermophiles, they would likely go undetected because they would not grow to any significant extent over the time period of this test.

See: 2007. *MMWR*, 56: 1161–64.

While most of the mechanisms just described involve chlorophyll or bacteriochlorophyll as the light-absorbing pigment, archaea use a pigment called bacteriorhodopsin. You may recognize the root "rhodopsin," which is a pigment present in vertebrate eyes (in the rods and cones). This type of photosynthesis does not involve electron transport but instead uses a light-driven proton pump. Through chemiosmosis it generates ATP. Until recently it was thought that only archaea can photosynthesize in this manner, but in 2000 evidence became available that many "common" bacteria in the ocean—as many as 13% of surface marine bacteria—use a rhodopsin-like molecule, called proteorhodopsin, to photosynthesize.

In perhaps a more startling discovery, the first organisms to photosynthesize on light other than that from the sun were described in 2005. Green sulfur bacteria, common in the environment, are obligately anaerobic photoautotrophs, which you will recall means they derive their energy from light. Representatives of these bacteria were found at the bottom of the ocean, far from contact with any sunlight. They were found to perform photosynthesis using the very low levels of light given off by geothermal radiation coming from the undersea vents. This broadens our sense of the conditions under which organisms can live (an obligate photosynthesizer can live in the absence of the sun). Another dogma overturned!

8.5 Learning Outcomes—Can You ...

19. ... summarize the process of photosynthesis in simple language?
20. ... discuss the relationship between light-dependent and light-independent reactions?
21. ... explain where the Calvin cycle fits into photosynthesis?
22. ... speculate on the importance of the discovery of photosynthetic bacteria on the ocean floor?

Chapter Summary

8.1 The Metabolism of Microbes

- Metabolism is the sum of cellular chemical and physical activities. It consists of anabolism, synthetic reactions that convert small molecules into large molecules, and catabolism, in which large molecules are degraded and energy is produced.
- Metabolism is made possible by organic catalysts, or enzymes, that speed up reactions by lowering the energy of activation.

- Enzymes are not consumed and can be reused. Each enzyme acts specifically upon its matching molecule or substrate.
- Substrate attachment occurs in the special pocket called the active, or catalytic, site.
- Many pathogens secrete enzymes or toxins, which are referred to as virulence factors, that enable them to avoid host defenses.

- Enzymes are labile (unstable) and function only within narrow operating ranges of temperature, osmotic pressure, and pH, and they are especially vulnerable to denaturation.
- Enzymes are frequently the targets for physical and chemical agents used in control of microbes.
- Regulatory controls can act on enzymes directly or on the process that gives rise to the enzymes.

8.2 The Pursuit and Utilization of Energy

- Energy is the capacity of a system to perform work. It is consumed in endergonic reactions and is released in exergonic reactions.
- Extracting energy requires a series of electron carriers arrayed in a redox chain between electron donors and electron acceptors.

8.3 The Pathways

- Carbohydrates, such as glucose, are energy-rich because when catabolized they can yield a large number of electrons per molecule.
- Glycolysis is a pathway that degrades glucose to pyruvic acid without requiring oxygen.
- Pyruvic acid is processed in aerobic respiration via the Krebs cycle and its associated electron transport chain.
- Acetyl coenzyme A is the product of pyruvic acid processing that undergoes further oxidation and decarboxylation in the Krebs cycle, which generates ATP, CO_2, and H_2O.
- The respiratory chain completes energy extraction.
- The final electron acceptor in aerobic respiration is oxygen. In anaerobic respiration, compounds such as sulfate, nitrate, or nitrite serve this function.

- Bacteria serve as important agents in the nitrogen cycle (denitrification).
- Fermentation is anaerobic respiration in which both the electron donor and final electron acceptors are organic compounds.
- Production of alcohol, vinegar, and certain industrial solvents relies upon fermentation.
- Glycolysis and the Krebs cycle are central pathways that link catabolic and anabolic pathways, allowing cells to break down different classes of molecules in order to synthesize compounds required by the cell.
- Intermediates such as pyruvic acid are convertible into amino acids through amination.
- Amino acids can be deaminated and used as precursors to glucose and other carbohydrates (gluconeogenesis).
- Two-carbon acetyl molecules from pyruvate can be used in fatty acid synthesis.

8.4 Biosynthesis and the Crossing Pathways of Metabolism

- The ability of a cell or system to integrate catabolic and anabolic pathways to improve efficiency is called amphibolism.
- Macromolecules, such as proteins, carbohydrates, and nucleic acids, are made of building blocks from two possible sources: from outside the cell (preformed) or via synthesis in one of the anabolic pathways.

8.5 It All Starts with Light

- Photosynthesis converts the sun's energy into chemical energy and organic carbon compounds, which are produced from carbon dioxide.

Multiple-Choice and True-False Questions   Knowledge and Comprehension

Multiple-Choice Questions. Select the correct answer from the answers provided.

1. Catabolism is a form of metabolism in which ____ molecules are converted into ____ molecules.
   a. large, small
   b. small, large
   c. amino acid, protein
   d. food, storage

2. An enzyme
   a. becomes part of the final products.
   b. is nonspecific for substrate.
   c. is consumed by the reaction.
   d. is heat and pH labile.

3. An apoenzyme is where the ____ is located.
   a. cofactor
   b. coenzyme
   c. redox reaction
   d. active site

4. Many coenzymes are
   a. metals.
   b. vitamins.
   c. proteins.
   d. substrates.

5. To digest cellulose in its environment, a fungus produces a/an
   a. endoenzyme.
   b. exoenzyme.
   c. catalase.
   d. polymerase.

6. Energy is carried from catabolic to anabolic reactions in the form of
   a. ADP.
   b. high-energy ATP bonds.
   c. coenzymes.
   d. inorganic phosphate.

7. A product or products of glycolysis is/are
   a. ATP.
   b. H_2O.
   c. CO_2.
   d. both a and b

8. Fermentation of a glucose molecule has the potential to produce a net number of ____ ATPs.
   a. 4
   b. 2
   c. 40
   d. 0

9. Complete oxidation of glucose in aerobic respiration can yield a net output of ____ ATPs.
   a. 40
   b. 6
   c. 38
   d. 2

10. ATP synthase complexes can generate ____ ATPs for each NADH that enters electron transport.
    a. 1
    b. 2
    c. 3
    d. 4

True-False Questions. If the statement is true, leave as is. If it is false, correct it by rewriting the sentence.

11. All photosynthesis begins with light.

12. An enzyme lowers the activation energy required for a chemical reaction.

13. One cycle of fermentation yields more energy than one cycle of aerobic respiration.

14. Energy in biological systems is primarily chemical.

15. Exoenzymes are produced outside the cell.

Critical Thinking Questions   Application and Analysis

These questions are suggested as a *writing-to-learn* experience. For each question, compose a one- or two-paragraph answer that includes the factual information needed to completely address the question.

1. a. Describe the chemistry of enzymes and explain how the apoenzyme forms.
    b. Show diagrammatically the interaction of holoenzyme and its substrate and general products that can be formed from a reaction.

2. Explain how oxidation of a substrate proceeds without oxygen.

3. a. Describe the roles played by ATP and NAD in metabolism.
    b. What particular features of their structure lend them to these functions?

4. a. What is meant by the concept of the "final electron acceptor"?
    b. What are the final electron acceptors in aerobic, anaerobic, and fermentative metabolism?

5. Name the major ways that substrate-level phosphorylation is different from oxidative phosphorylation.

6. a. Outline the basic steps in glycolysis, indicating where ATP is used and given off.
    b. Where does NADH originate, and what is its fate in an aerobe?
    c. What is the fate of NADH in a fermentative organism?

7. Speculate on how organisms that live in permanently dark habitats, such as the human gut, benefit from photosynthesis.

8. Using the concept of fermentation, describe the microbial (biochemical) mechanisms that cause milk to sour.

9. Explain how it is possible for certain microbes to survive and grow in the presence of cyanide, which would kill many other organisms.

10. What adaptive advantages does a fermentative metabolism confer on a microbe?

Concept Mapping   Synthesis

Appendix D provides guidance for working with concept maps.

1. Supply your own linking words or phrases in this concept map, and provide the missing concepts in the empty box.

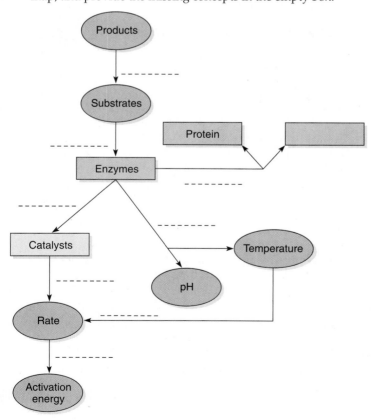

2. Construct your own concept map using the following words as the *concepts.* Supply the linking words between each pair of concepts.

    anabolism   nucleotides
    catabolism   DNA
    precursor molecules   ATP
    bacterial cell

Visual Connections   Synthesis

These questions use visual images or previous content to make connections to this chapter's concepts.

1. **From chapter 4, figure 4.12.** On the enlarged sections of both (a) and (b), draw protons in the proper compartment in such a way that creates a proton motive force.

(a)   (b)

www.connect.microbiology.com

Enhance your study of this chapter with study tools and practice tests. Also ask your instructor about the resources available through ConnectPlus, including the media-rich eBook, interactive learning tools, and animations.

Microbial Genetics

Case File 9

Acinetobacter baumannii is a gram-negative bacterium commonly found in soil and water. This bacterium is also frequently associated with nosocomial infections, diseases patients acquire while they are in a hospital. *A. baumannii* tends to thrive in hospital settings because the bacterium is resistant to environmental influences and can survive for months on such objects as faucets, toilets, bedclothes, doorknobs, sinks, and medical equipment. The spread of this bacterium is a concern for all medical facilities, but especially military ones, which have seen increasing numbers of bloodstream infections caused by *A. baumannii*, probably because combat conditions make controlling and treating them more difficult.

Additionally, *A. baumannii* infections have become problematic because increasing numbers of isolates show multiple drug resistance—that is, the bacteria are unfazed by the antibiotics commonly used to treat them. Many of the resistance genes found in *A. baumannii* are similar or identical to those seen in other genera of bacteria, such as *Pseudomonas*, *Salmonella*, and *Escherichia*, which also commonly occur in healthcare facilities.

- How might genes, such as those responsible for drug resistance, be transferred between bacterial species?
- Where could *A. baumannii* likely have acquired the genes for drug resistance?

Continuing the Case appears on page 263.

Outline and Learning Outcomes

9.1 Introduction to Genetics and Genes: Unlocking the Secrets of Heredity
1. Define the terms genome and gene.
2. Differentiate between genotype and phenotype.
3. Draw a picture of a length of DNA, including all important chemical groups.
4. Explain how DNA replication takes place.
5. Use Okazaki fragments to explain leading and lagging strands.

9.2   Applications of the DNA Code: Transcription and Translation
6. Relate the new and old versions of the "central dogma."
7. Identify important differences between RNA and DNA.
8. Draw a picture of the process of transcription.
9. List the three types of RNA directly involved in translation.
10. Define "codon" and "anticodon."
11. Identify on which molecules the promoter, the start codon, and the A and P sites appear.
12. Indicate how eukaryotic transcription and translation differ from these processes in prokaryotes.

9.3   Genetic Regulation of Protein Synthesis
13. List one or two important advantages to arranging genes in an operon.
14. Differentiate between repressible and inducible operons.
15. Name some antibiotic targets of the transcription and translation machinery.

9.4   Mutations: Changes in the Genetic Code
16. Define the term "mutation" and discuss its importance.
17. Differentiate among frameshift, nonsense, silent, and missense mutations.

9.5   DNA Recombination Events
18. Define recombinant.
19. Describe three forms of horizontal gene transfer used in bacteria.

9.1   Introduction to Genetics and Genes: Unlocking the Secrets of Heredity

Genetics is the study of the inheritance, or **heredity,** of living things. It is a wide-ranging science that explores

1. the transmission of biological properties (traits) from parent to offspring;
2. the expression and variation of those traits;
3. the structure and function of the genetic material; and
4. how this material changes.

This chapter will explore DNA, which is the genetic material, and the proteins and other products that it produces in a cell. Coming out of chapter 8, we should point out that the production of new DNA, RNA, and proteins is an example of an anabolic process.

The study of genetics takes place on several levels **(figure 9.1).** Organismal genetics observes the heredity of the whole organism or cell; chromosomal genetics examines the characteristics and actions of chromosomes; and molecular genetics deals with the biochemistry of the genes. All of these levels are useful areas of exploration, but in order to understand the expressions of microbial structure, physiology, mutations, and pathogenicity, we need to examine the operation of genes at the cellular and molecular levels. The study of microbial genetics provides a greater understanding of human genetics and an increased appreciation for the astounding advances in genetic engineering we are currently witnessing, which we will learn about in chapter 10.

Figure 9.1 Levels of genetic study.   The operations of genetics can be observed at the levels of organism, cell, chromosome, and DNA sequence (molecular level).

The Nature of the Genetic Material

For a species to survive, it must have the capacity of self-replication. In single-celled microorganisms, reproduction involves the division of the cell by means of binary fission or budding, but these forms of reproduction involve a more significant activity than just simple cleavage of the cell mass. Because the genetic material is responsible for inheritance, it must be accurately duplicated and separated into each daughter cell to ensure normal function. This genetic material itself is a long molecule of DNA that can be studied on several levels. Before we look at how DNA is copied, let us explore the organization of this genetic material, proceeding from the general to the specific.

The Levels of Structure and Function of the Genome

The **genome** is the sum total of genetic material of an organism. Although most of the genome exists in the form of chromosomes, genetic material can appear in nonchromosomal sites as well **(figure 9.2).** For example, bacteria and some fungi contain tiny extra pieces of DNA (plasmids), and certain organelles of eukaryotes (the mitochondria and chloroplasts) are equipped with their own DNA. Genomes of cells are composed exclusively of DNA, but viruses contain either DNA or RNA as the principal genetic material. Although the specific genome of an individual organism is unique, the general pattern of nucleic acid structure and function is similar among all organisms.

In general, a **chromosome** is a discrete cellular structure composed of a neatly packaged DNA molecule. The chromosomes of eukaryotes and bacterial cells differ in several respects. The structure of eukaryotic chromosomes consists of a DNA molecule tightly wound around histone proteins, whereas a bacterial chromosome is condensed and secured into a packet by means of histonelike proteins. Eukaryotic chromosomes are located in the nucleus; they vary in number from a few to hundreds; they can occur in pairs (diploid) or singles (haploid); and they have a linear appearance. In contrast, most bacteria have a single, circular (double-stranded) chromosome, although many bacteria have multiple circular chromosomes and some have linear chromosomes.

The chromosomes of all cells are subdivided into basic informational packets called genes. A **gene** can be defined from more than one perspective. In classical genetics, the term refers to the fundamental unit of heredity responsible for a given trait in an organism. In the molecular and biochemical sense, it is a site on the chromosome that provides information for a certain cell function. More specifically still, it has traditionally been characterized as a certain segment of DNA that contains the necessary code to make a **protein** or RNA molecule. With new findings in the area of gene expression, we now prefer to speak of a gene as a segment of DNA that contains code to make a group of related proteins or RNAs. More about this distinction later. Genes fall into three basic categories: **structural genes** that code for proteins, genes that code for the RNA machinery used in protein production,

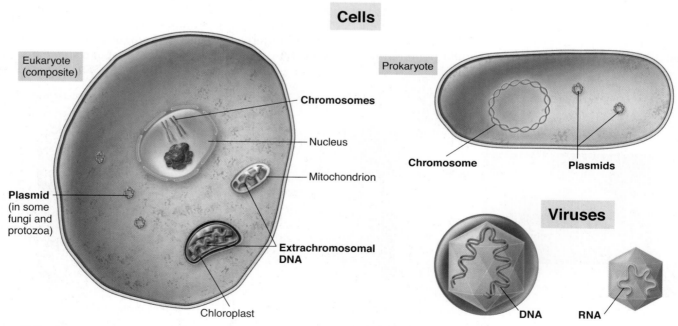

Figure 9.2 **The general location and forms of the genome in selected cell types and viruses (not to scale).**

and **regulatory genes** that control gene expression. The sum of all of these types of genes constitutes an organism's distinctive genetic makeup, or **genotype** (jee'-noh-tīp). The expression of the genotype creates traits (certain structures or functions) referred to as the **phenotype** (fee'-noh-tīp). Just as a person inherits a combination of genes (genotype) that gives a certain eye color or height (phenotype), a bacterium inherits genes that direct the formation of a flagellum, and a virus contains genes for its capsid structure. All organisms contain more genes in their genotypes than are manifested as a phenotype at any given time. In other words, the phenotype can change depending on which genes are "turned on" (expressed).

The Size and Packaging of Genomes

Genomes vary greatly in size. The smallest viruses have four or five genes; the bacterium *Escherichia coli* has a single chromosome containing 4,288 genes, and a human cell has about 20,000 to 25,000 genes on 46 chromosomes. The chromosome of *E. coli* would measure about 1 mm if unwound and stretched out linearly, and yet this fits within a cell that measures just over 1 micron across, making the stretched-out DNA 1,000 times longer than the cell **(figure 9.3)**. Still, the bacterial chromosome takes up only about one-third to one-half of the cell's volume. Likewise, if the sum of all DNA contained in the 46 human chromosomes were unraveled and laid end to end, it would measure about 6 feet. How can such elongated genomes fit into the minuscule volume of a cell, and in the case of eukaryotes, into an even smaller compartment, the nucleus? The answer lies in the intricate coiling of the DNA chain **(Insight 9.1).**

Figure 9.3 An *Escherichia coli* cell disrupted to release its DNA molecule. The cell has spewed out its single, uncoiled DNA strand into the surrounding medium.

The DNA Code: A Simple Yet Profound Message

Examining the function of DNA at the molecular level requires an even closer look at its structure. To do this we will imagine being able to magnify a small piece of a gene about 5 million times. What such fine scrutiny will disclose is one of the great marvels of biology. James Watson and Francis Crick put the pieces of the puzzle together in 1953 (see Insight 9.1) to discover that DNA is a gigantic molecule, a type of nucleic acid, with two strands combined into a double helix. The general structure of DNA is universal, except in some viruses that contain single-stranded DNA. The basic unit of DNA structure is a **nucleotide,** and a chromosome in a typical bacterium consists of several million nucleotides linked end to end. Each nucleotide is composed of **phosphate, deoxyribose** sugar, and a **nitrogenous base.** The nucleotides covalently bond to each other in a sugar-phosphate linkage that becomes the backbone of each strand. Each sugar attaches in a repetitive pattern to two phosphates. One of the bonds is to the number 5' (read "five prime") carbon on deoxyribose, and the other is to the 3' carbon, which confers a certain order and direction on each strand **(figure 9.4).**

The nitrogenous bases, **purines** and **pyrimidines,** attach by covalent bonds at the 1' position of the sugar **(figure 9.4a).** They span the center of the molecule and pair with appropriate complementary bases from the other strand. The paired bases are joined by hydrogen bonds. Such weak bonds are easily broken, allowing the molecule to be "unzipped" into its complementary strands. This feature is of great importance in gaining access to the information encoded in the nitrogenous base sequence. Pairing of purines and pyrimidines is not random; it is dictated by the formation of hydrogen bonds between certain bases. Thus, in DNA, the purine **adenine (A)** always pairs with the pyrimidine **thymine (T)**, and the purine **guanine (G)** always pairs with the pyrimidine **cytosine (C).** The bases are attracted to each other in this pattern because each has a complementary three-dimensional shape that matches its pair. Although the base-pairing partners generally do not vary, the sequence of base pairs along the DNA molecule can assume any order, resulting in an infinite number of possible nucleotide sequences.

Other important considerations of DNA structure concern the nature of the double helix itself. The halves are not oriented in the same direction. One side of the helix runs in the opposite direction of the other, in what is called an **antiparallel arrangement (figure 9.4b).** The order of the bond between the carbon on deoxyribose and the phosphates is used to keep track of the direction of the two sides of the helix. Thus, one helix runs from the 5' to 3' direction, and the other runs from the 3' to 5' direction. This characteristic is a significant factor in DNA synthesis and protein production.

INSIGHT 9.1   Deciphering the Structure of DNA

The search for the primary molecules of heredity was a serious focus throughout the first half of the 20th century. At first, many biologists thought that protein was the genetic material. An important milestone occurred in 1944 when Oswald Avery, Colin MacLeod, and Maclyn McCarty purified DNA and demonstrated at last that it was indeed the blueprint for life. This was followed by an avalanche of research, which continues today.

One area of extreme interest concerned the molecular structure of DNA. In 1951, American biologist James Watson and English physicist Francis Crick collaborated on solving the DNA puzzle. Although they did little of the original research, they were intrigued by several findings from other scientists. It had been determined by Erwin Chargaff that any model of DNA structure would have to contain deoxyribose, phosphate, purines, and pyrimidines arranged in a way that would provide variation and a simple way of copying itself. Watson and Crick spent long hours constructing models with cardboard cutouts and kept alert for any and every bit of information that might give them an edge.

Two English biophysicists, Maurice Wilkins and Rosalind Franklin, had been painstakingly collecting data on X-ray crystallographs of DNA for several years. With this technique, molecules of DNA bombarded by X rays produce a photographic image that can predict the three-dimensional structure of the molecule. After being shown some of this X-ray data, Watson and Crick noticed an unmistakable pattern: The molecule appeared to be a double helix. Gradually, the pieces of the puzzle fell into place, and a final model was assembled—a model that explained all of the qualities of DNA, including how it is copied. Although Watson and Crick were rightly hailed for the clarity of their solution, it must be emphasized that their success was due to the considerable efforts of a number of English and American scientists. This historic discovery showed that the tools of physics and chemistry have useful applications in biological systems, and it also spawned ingenious research in all areas of molecular genetics.

Since the discovery of the double helix in 1953, an extensive body of biochemical, microscopic, and crystallographic analysis has left little doubt that the model first proposed by Watson and Crick is correct. Newer techniques using scanning tunneling microscopy produce three-dimensional images of DNA magnified 2 million times. These images verify the helical shape and twists of DNA represented by models.

The men who cracked the code of life. Dr. James Watson (left) and Dr. Francis Crick (right) stand next to their model that finally explained the structure of DNA in 1953.

The first direct glimpse at DNA's structure. This false-color scanning tunneling micrograph of calf thymus gland DNA (2,000,000×) brings out the well-defined folds in the helix.

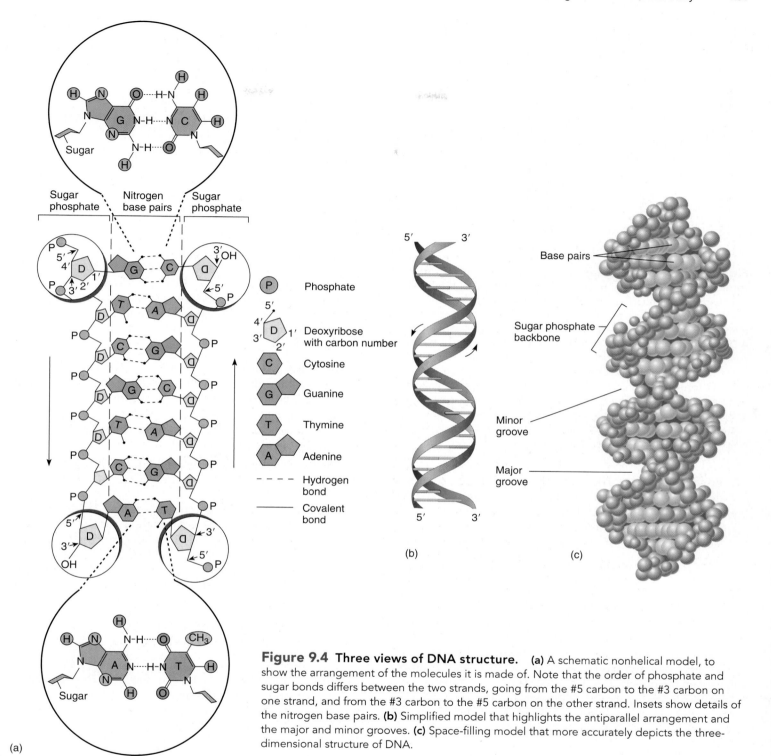

Figure 9.4 Three views of DNA structure. (a) A schematic nonhelical model, to show the arrangement of the molecules it is made of. Note that the order of phosphate and sugar bonds differs between the two strands, going from the #5 carbon to the #3 carbon on one strand, and from the #3 carbon to the #5 carbon on the other strand. Insets show details of the nitrogen base pairs. (b) Simplified model that highlights the antiparallel arrangement and the major and minor grooves. (c) Space-filling model that more accurately depicts the three-dimensional structure of DNA.

The Significance of DNA Structure

The arrangement of nitrogenous bases in DNA has two essential effects.

1. **Maintenance of the code during reproduction.** The constancy of base-pairing guarantees that the code will be retained during cell growth and division. When the two strands are separated, each one provides a template (pattern or model) for the replication (exact copying) of a new molecule **(figure 9.5).** Because the sequence of one strand automatically gives the sequence of its partner, the code can be duplicated with fidelity.

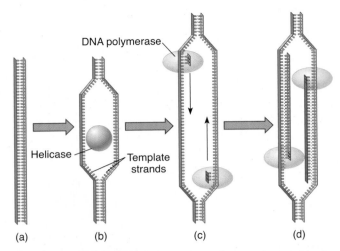

Figure 9.5 Simplified steps to show the semiconservative replication of DNA.   **(a, b)** The two strands of the double helix are unwound and separated by a helicase, which disrupts the hydrogen bonds and exposes the nitrogen base codes of DNA. Each single strand formed will serve as a template to synthesize a new strand of DNA. **(c)** A DNA polymerase proceeds along the DNA molecule, attaching the correct nucleotides according to the pattern of the template. An A on the template will pair with a T on the new molecule, and a C will pair with a G. **(d)** The resultant new DNA molecules contain one strand of the newly synthesized DNA and the original template strand. The integrity of the code is kept intact because the linear arrangement of the bases is maintained during this process. Note that the actual details of the process are presented in figure 9.6.

2. **Providing variety.** The order of bases along the length of the DNA strand constitutes the genetic program, or the language, of the DNA code. The message present in a gene is a precise sequence of these bases, and the genome is the collection of all DNA bases that, in an ordered combination, are responsible for the unique qualities of each organism.

It is tempting to ask how such a seemingly simple code can account for the extreme differences among forms as diverse as a virus, *E. coli,* and a human. The English language, based on 26 letters, can create an infinite variety of words, but how can an apparently complex genetic language such as DNA be based on just four nitrogen base "letters"? A mathematical example can explain the possibilities. For a segment of DNA that is 1,000 nucleotides long, there are $4^{1,000}$ different sequences possible. Carried out, this number would approximate 1.5×10^{602}, a number so huge that it provides nearly endless degrees of variation.

DNA Replication: Preserving the Code and Passing It On

The sequence of bases along the length of a gene constitutes the language of DNA. For this language to be preserved for hundreds of generations, it will be necessary for the genetic program to be duplicated and passed on to each offspring. This process of duplication is called DNA replication. In the following example, we will show replication in bacteria, but with some exceptions, it also applies to the process as it works

in eukaryotes and some viruses. Early in binary fission, the metabolic machinery of a bacterium initiates the duplication of the chromosome. This DNA replication must be completed during a single generation time (around 20 minutes in *E. coli*).

The Overall Replication Process

What features allow the DNA molecule to be exactly duplicated, and how is its integrity retained? DNA replication requires a careful orchestration of the actions of 30 different enzymes (partial list in **table 9.1**), which separate the strands of the existing DNA molecule, copy its template, and produce two complete daughter molecules. A simplified version of replication is shown in figure 9.5 and includes the following:

1. uncoiling the parent DNA molecule;
2. unzipping the hydrogen bonds between the base pairs, thus separating the two strands and exposing the nucleotide sequence of each strand (which is normally buried in the center of the helix) to serve as templates; and
3. synthesizing two new strands by attachment of the correct complementary nucleotides to each single-stranded template.

A critical feature of DNA replication is that each daughter molecule will be identical to the parent in composition, but neither one is completely new; the strand that serves as a template is an original parental DNA strand. The preservation of the parent molecule in this way, termed **semiconservative replication**—semi- meaning "half" as in "semicircle"— helps explain the reliability and fidelity of replication.

Refinements and Details of Replication

The process of synthesizing a new daughter strand of DNA using the parental strand as a template is carried out by the enzyme DNA polymerase III. The entire process of replication does, however, depend on several enzymes and can be most easily understood by keeping in mind a few points concerning both the structure of the DNA molecule and the limitations of DNA polymerase III:

1. The nucleotides that need to be read by DNA polymerase III are buried deep within the double helix. Accessing

Table 9.1   Some Enzymes Involved in DNA Replication and Their Functions

Enzyme	Function
Helicase	Unzipping the DNA helix
Primase	Synthesizing an RNA primer
DNA polymerase III	Adding bases to the new DNA chain; proofreading the chain for mistakes
DNA polymerase I	Removing primer, closing gaps, repairing mismatches
Ligase	Final binding of nicks in DNA during synthesis and repair
Topoisomerases I and II	Supercoiling and untangling

these nucleotides requires both that the DNA molecule be unwound and that the two strands of the helix be separated from one another.

2. DNA polymerase III is unable to *begin* synthesizing a chain of nucleotides but can only continue to add nucleotides to an already existing chain.

3. DNA polymerase III can only add nucleotides in one direction, so a new strand is always synthesized 5′ to 3′.

With these constraints in mind, the details of replication can be more easily understood.

The origin, or beginning point, of replication is a short sequence rich in adenine and thymine bases that, you will recall, are held together by only two hydrogen bonds rather than three. Because the origin of replication is AT-rich, less energy is required to separate the two strands than would be required if the origin were rich in guanine and cytosine. Prior to the start of replication, enzymes called **helicases** (unzipping enzymes) bind to the DNA at the origin. These enzymes untwist the helix and break the hydrogen bonds holding the two strands together, resulting in two separate strands, each of which will be used as a template for the synthesis of a new strand.

Replication begins when an RNA **primer** is synthesized and enters at the origin of replication **(figure 9.6, step 1)**. DNA polymerase III cannot begin synthesis unless it has

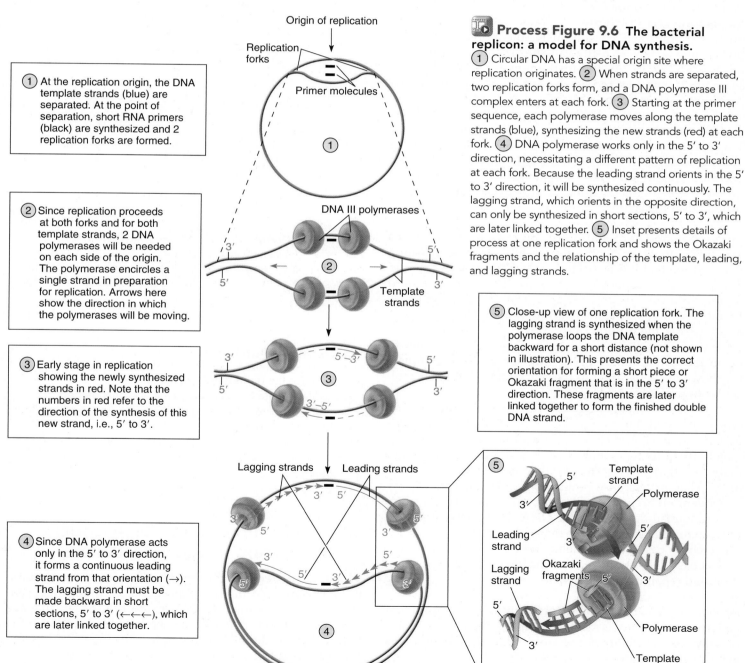

Process Figure 9.6 The bacterial replicon: a model for DNA synthesis.

(1) Circular DNA has a special origin site where replication originates. (2) When strands are separated, two replication forks form, and a DNA polymerase III complex enters at each fork. (3) Starting at the primer sequence, each polymerase moves along the template strands (blue), synthesizing the new strands (red) at each fork. (4) DNA polymerase works only in the 5′ to 3′ direction, necessitating a different pattern of replication at each fork. Because the leading strand orients in the 5′ to 3′ direction, it will be synthesized continuously. The lagging strand, which orients in the opposite direction, can only be synthesized in short sections, 5′ to 3′, which are later linked together. (5) Inset presents details of process at one replication fork and shows the Okazaki fragments and the relationship of the template, leading, and lagging strands.

(1) At the replication origin, the DNA template strands (blue) are separated. At the point of separation, short RNA primers (black) are synthesized and 2 replication forks are formed.

(2) Since replication proceeds at both forks and for both template strands, 2 DNA polymerases will be needed on each side of the origin. The polymerase encircles a single strand in preparation for replication. Arrows here show the direction in which the polymerases will be moving.

(3) Early stage in replication showing the newly synthesized strands in red. Note that the numbers in red refer to the direction of the synthesis of this new strand, i.e., 5′ to 3′.

(5) Close-up view of one replication fork. The lagging strand is synthesized when the polymerase loops the DNA template backward for a short distance (not shown in illustration). This presents the correct orientation for forming a short piece or Okazaki fragment that is in the 5′ to 3′ direction. These fragments are later linked together to form the finished double DNA strand.

(4) Since DNA polymerase acts only in the 5′ to 3′ direction, it forms a continuous leading strand from that orientation (→). The lagging strand must be made backward in short sections, 5′ to 3′ (←←←), which are later linked together.

this short strand of RNA to serve as a starting point for adding nucleotides. Because the bacterial DNA molecule is circular, opening of the circle forms two **replication forks,** each containing its own set of replication enzymes. The DNA polymerase III is a huge enzyme complex that encircles the replication fork and adds nucleotides in accordance with the template pattern. As synthesis proceeds, the forks continually open up to expose the template for replication **(figure 9.6, steps 2, 3).**

Because DNA polymerase is correctly oriented for synthesis *only* in the 5′ to 3′ direction of the new molecule (red) strand, only one strand, called the **leading strand,** can be synthesized as a continuous, complete strand. The strand with the opposite orientation (3′ to 5′) is termed the **lagging strand (figure 9.6, steps 4, 5).** Because it cannot be synthesized continuously, the polymerase adds nucleotides a few at a time in the direction away from the fork (5′ to 3′). As the fork opens up a bit, the next segment is synthesized backward to the point of the previous segment, a process repeated at both forks until synthesis is complete. In this way, the DNA polymerase is able to synthesize the two new strands simultaneously. This manner of synthesis produces one strand containing short fragments of DNA (100 to 1,000 bases long) called **Okazaki fragments.** These fragments are attached to the growing end of the lagging strand by another enzyme called DNA ligase.

Elongation and Termination of the Daughter Molecules

The addition of nucleotides proceeds at an astonishing pace, estimated in some bacteria to be 750 bases per second at each fork! As replication proceeds, the newly produced double strand loops down **(figure 9.7a).** DNA polymerase I removes the RNA primers used to initiate DNA synthesis and replaces them with DNA. When the forks come full circle and meet, ligases move along the lagging strand to begin the initial linking of the fragments and to complete synthesis and separation of the two circular daughter molecules **(figure 9.7b).**

Like any language, DNA is occasionally "misspelled" when an incorrect base is added to the growing chain. Studies have shown that such mistakes are made once in approximately 10^8 to 10^9 bases, but most of these are corrected. If not corrected, they are referred to as mutations (covered later in this chapter). Because continued cellular integrity is very dependent on accurate replication, cells have evolved their own proofreading function for DNA. DNA polymerase III, the enzyme that elongates the molecule, can detect incorrect, unmatching bases; excise them; and replace them with the correct base. DNA polymerase I can also proofread the molecule and repair damaged DNA.

Replication in Other Biological Systems
The replication pattern of eukaryotes is similar to that of prokaryotes. It also uses a variety of DNA polymerases, and replication proceeds in both directions from the point of origin.

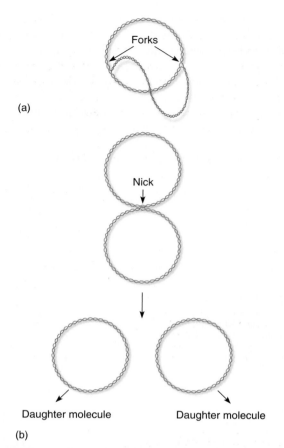

Figure 9.7 Completion of chromosome replication in bacteria. **(a)** As replication proceeds, one double strand loops down. **(b)** Final separation is achieved through repair and the release of two completed molecules. The daughter cells receive these during binary fission.

9.1 Learning Outcomes—Can You . . .

1. . . . define the terms genome and gene?
2. . . . differentiate between genotype and phenotype?
3. . . . draw a picture of a length of DNA, including all important chemical groups?
4. . . . explain how DNA replication takes place?
5. . . . use Okazaki fragments to explain leading and lagging strands?

9.2 Applications of the DNA Code: Transcription and Translation

We have explored how the genetic message in the DNA molecule is conserved through replication. Now we must consider the precise role of DNA in the cell. Given that the sequence of bases in DNA is a genetic code, just what is the nature of this code and how is it utilized by the cell? Although the genome is full of critical information, the molecule itself does not perform cell processes directly. Its stored information is conveyed to RNA molecules, which carry out instructions. The concept that genetic information flows from DNA to RNA to protein is a central theme of molecular biology **(figure 9.8a)**. More precisely, it states that the master code of DNA is first used to synthesize an RNA molecule via a process called **transcription,** and the information contained in the RNA is then used to produce proteins in a process known as **translation.** The principal exceptions to this pattern are found in RNA viruses, which convert RNA to other RNA, and in retroviruses, which convert RNA to DNA.

This "central dogma," which outlined the primary understanding of genetics during the first half century of the genetic revolution (since the 1950s), has very recently been shown to be incomplete. While it is true that proteins are made in accordance with this central dogma, there is more to the story **(figure 9.8b)**. In addition to the RNA that is used to produce proteins, a wide variety of RNAs are used to regulate gene function. Many of the genetic malfunctions that cause human disease are in fact found in these regulatory RNA segments—and not in genes for proteins as was once thought. The DNA that codes for these very crucial RNA molecules was called "junk" DNA until very recently. We say more about this in **Insight 9.2.**

The Gene-Protein Connection

The Triplet Code and the Relationship to Proteins

Several questions invariably arise concerning the relationship between genes and cell function. For instance, how does gene structure lead to the expression of traits in the individual, and what features of gene expression cause one organism to be so distinctly different from another? For answers, we must turn to the correlation between gene and protein structure. We know that each structural gene is a linear sequence of nucleotides that codes for a protein. Because each protein is different, each gene must also differ somehow in its composition. In fact, the language of DNA exists in the order of groups of three consecutive bases called triplets on one DNA strand **(figure 9.9)**. Thus, one gene differs from another in its composition of triplets. An equally important

(a)   (b)

Figure 9.8 Summary of the flow of genetic information in cells. DNA is the ultimate storehouse and distributor of genetic information. **(a)** DNA must be deciphered into a usable cell language. It does this by transcribing its code into RNA helper molecules that translate that code into protein. **(b)** Other sections of the DNA produce very important RNA molecules that regulate genes and their products.

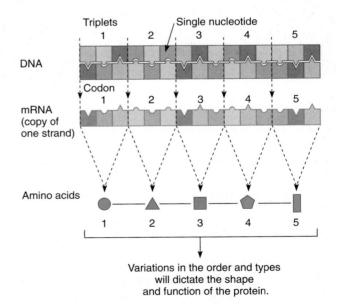

Figure 9.9 Simplified view of the DNA-protein relationship. The DNA molecule is a continuous chain of base pairs, but the sequence must be interpreted in groups of three base pairs (a triplet). Each triplet as copied into mRNA codons will translate into one amino acid; consequently, the ratio of base pairs to amino acids is 3:1.

INSIGHT 9.2 Small RNAs: An Old Dog Shows Off Some New(?) Tricks

Since the earliest days of molecular biology, RNA has been an overlooked worker of the cell, quietly ferrying the information in DNA to ribosomes to direct the formation of proteins. Current research, however, is showing a new, dynamic role for RNA in the cell that may forever change the reputation of this humble molecule.

Short lengths of RNA seem to have the ability to control the expression of certain genes. Some of these are called micro RNAs and some are called small interfering RNAs. They control gene expression by folding back on themselves after being transcribed, and by doing so they activate a system inside cells that degrades dsRNA. Cells do this in order to rid themselves of invading viruses (which are organisms that might have dsRNA). The micro RNAs also bind with mRNA of certain genes, thereby causing them to be degraded as well. The repressing nature of dsRNA was discovered quite accidentally when researchers were trying to induce expression of genes by providing them in dsRNA form; instead, genes matching those RNA sequences were shut down entirely through this clever regulatory system. In 2006, the Nobel Prize for Medicine or Physiology was awarded to the two American scientists, Andrew Fire and Craig Mello, who discovered this phenomenon.

A second type of regulation seems to occur when small RNAs alter the structure of chromosomes. As DNA and proteins coil together to form chromatin, small RNAs direct how tightly or loosely the chromatin is constructed. Just as a closed book cannot be read, DNA sequences contained within tightly coiled chromatin are generally inaccessible to the cell, silencing the expression of those genes. Antisense RNA is produced from the opposite strand of the DNA that produces mRNA. This antisense molecule has the ability to pair with the "sense," or messenger, RNA and thus keep it from being transcribed. Riboswitches, RNAs that attach to a chemical with one end and only then become available for translation on the other end, were isolated for the first time in 2002. One riboswitch has been found to regulate the expression of 26 important genes in the bacterium *Bacillus subtilis*. Riboswitches have probably been around since the early days of life on the planet. So, although they are new to us, they have been used to regulate gene expression for billions of years.

These newly discovered RNA molecules have answered some vexing questions that came out of the genome sequencing studies (led by the Human Genome Project). Most of the DNA in organisms was found *not* to code for functional proteins. In humans, the "junk" percentage was 98%! Yet, in bacteria as well as humans, the junk DNA was preserved in the same form for the last millions of years of evolution, suggesting it had a very important function. We now know that much of this "junk" DNA codes for these important RNA regulatory molecules.

Researchers have found that micro RNAs encoded by herpesviruses are probably responsible for shutting down viral replication during the latent (dormant) phase of the infection. In a practical application, measuring the amount and type of host micro RNAs—which are affected by viral infection—can help provide a more exact prognosis in patients with chronic infections such as those caused by cytomegalovirus. Importantly, molecules such as antisense RNA are being explored for their therapeutic uses. Researchers have transported siRNA into human T cells infected with HIV with some success. Also, small RNAs may have use in human genetic disorders in which defective human genes need to be shut down in order to restore a patient to health.

Our knowledge of the full role of small RNAs in the cell is just beginning. In the meantime, scientists will keep studying small RNAs while being mindful of the old adage, "Good things come in small packages."

---

part of this concept is that each triplet represents a code for a particular amino acid. When the triplet code is transcribed and translated, it dictates the type and order of amino acids in a polypeptide (protein) chain.

The final key points that connect DNA and an organism's traits are:

1. A protein's primary structure—the order and type of amino acids in the chain—determines its characteristic shape and function.
2. Proteins ultimately determine phenotype, the expression of all aspects of cell function and structure. Put more simply, living things are what their proteins make them. Regulatory RNAs help determine which proteins are made.
3. DNA is mainly a blueprint that tells the cell which kinds of proteins and RNAs to make and how to make them.

The Major Participants in Transcription and Translation

Transcription, the formation of RNA using DNA as a template, and translation, the synthesis of proteins using RNA as a template, are highly complex. A number of components participate: most prominently, messenger RNA, transfer RNA, regulatory RNAs, ribosomes, several types of enzymes, and a storehouse of raw materials. After first examining each of these components, we shall see how they come together in the assembly line of the cell.

RNAs: Tools in the Cell's Assembly Line

Ribonucleic acid is similar to DNA, but its general structure is different in several ways:

1. It is a single-stranded molecule that exists in helical form. This single strand can assume secondary and tertiary

Table 9.2 **Types of Ribonucleic Acid**

RNA Type	Contains Codes For	Function in Cell	Translated
Messenger (mRNA)	Sequence of amino acids in protein	Transports the DNA master code to the ribosome	Yes
Transfer (tRNA)	A cloverleaf tRNA to carry amino acids	Brings amino acids to ribosome during translation	No
Ribosomal (rRNA)	Several large structural rRNA molecules	Forms the major part of a ribosome and participates in protein synthesis	No
Micro (miRNA), antisense, riboswitch, and small interfering (siRNA)	Regulatory RNAs	Regulation of gene expression and coiling of chromatin	No
Primer	An RNA that can begin DNA replication	Primes DNA	No
Ribozymes	RNA enzymes, parts of splicer enzymes	Remove introns from other RNAs in eukaryotes	No

levels of complexity due to bonds within the molecule, leading to specialized forms of RNA (tRNA and rRNA—see figure 9.8*a*).

2. RNA contains **uracil (U),** instead of thymine, as the complementary base-pairing mate for adenine. This does not change the inherent DNA code in any way because the uracil still follows the pairing rules.

3. Although RNA, like DNA, contains a backbone that consists of alternating sugar and phosphate molecules, the sugar in RNA is **ribose** rather than deoxyribose.

The many functional types of RNA range from small regulatory pieces to large structural ones **(table 9.2** and Insight 9.2).

All types of RNA are formed through transcription of a DNA gene, but only mRNA is further translated into another type of molecule (protein).

Messenger RNA: Carrying DNA's Message

Messenger RNA (mRNA) is a transcript (copy) of a structural gene or genes in the DNA. It is synthesized by a process similar to synthesis of the leading strand during DNA replication, and the complementary base-pairing rules ensure that the code will be faithfully copied in the mRNA transcript. The message of this transcribed strand is later read as a series of triplets called **codons (figure 9.10),** and the length of the mRNA molecule

(a) Messenger RNA (mRNA)
A short piece of messenger RNA (mRNA) illustrates the general structure of RNA: single strandedness, repeating phosphate-ribose sugar backbone attached to single nitrogen bases; use of uracil instead of thymine.

Codon 1   Codon 2   Codon 3

ⓟ = Phosphate   Ⓡ = Ribose   U = Uracil

Figure 9.10 **Characteristics of transfer and messenger RNA.**

(b) Transfer RNA (tRNA)
Left: The tRNA strand loops back on itself to form intrachain hydrogen bonds. The result is a cloverleaf structure, shown here in simplified form. At its bottom is an anticodon that specifies the attachment of a particular amino acid at the 3′ end. Right: A three-dimensional view of tRNA structure.

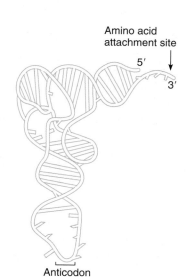

varies from about 100 nucleotides to several thousand. The details of transcription and the function of mRNA in translation will be covered shortly.

Transfer RNA: The Key to Translation

Transfer RNA (tRNA) is also a copy of a specific region of DNA; however, it differs from mRNA. It is uniform in length, being 75 to 95 nucleotides long, and it contains sequences of bases that form hydrogen bonds with complementary sections of the same tRNA strand. At these points, the molecule bends back upon itself into several **hairpin loops**, giving the molecule a secondary **cloverleaf** structure that folds even further into a complex, three-dimensional helix (see figure 9.10). This compact molecule is an adaptor that converts RNA language into protein language. The bottom loop of the cloverleaf exposes a triplet, the **anticodon**, that both designates the specificity of the tRNA and complements mRNA's codons. At the opposite end of the molecule is a binding site for the amino acid that is specific for that tRNA's anticodon. For each of the 20 amino acids, there is at least one specialized type of tRNA to carry it. Binding of an amino acid to its specific tRNA, a process known as "charging" the tRNA, takes place in two enzyme-driven steps: First an ATP activates the amino acid, and then this group binds to the acceptor end of the tRNA. Because tRNA is the molecule that will convert the master code on mRNA into a protein, the accuracy of this step is crucial.

The Ribosome: A Mobile Molecular Factory for Translation

The prokaryotic (70S) ribosome is a particle composed of tightly packaged **ribosomal RNA (rRNA)** and protein. The rRNA component of the ribosome is also a long polynucleotide molecule. It forms complex three-dimensional figures that contribute to the structure and function of ribosomes. The interactions of proteins and rRNA create the two subunits of the ribosome that engage in final translation of the genetic code (see figure 9.12). A metabolically active bacterial cell can contain up to 20,000 of these minuscule factories—all actively engaged in reading the genetic program, taking in raw materials, and producing proteins at an impressive rate. The 2009 Nobel Prize in Chemistry was awarded to three scientists who showed the chemical makeup of ribosomes, as well as the ways in which antibiotics bound to them.

Transcription: The First Stage of Gene Expression

During transcription, the DNA code is converted to RNA through several stages, directed by a huge and very complex enzyme system, **RNA polymerase (figure 9.11)**. Only one strand of the DNA—the **template strand**—contains meaningful instructions for synthesis of a functioning polypeptide. The strand of DNA that serves as a template varies from one gene to another.

Transcription is initiated when RNA polymerase recognizes a segment of the DNA called the **promoter region**. This region consists of two sequences of DNA just prior to the beginning of the gene to be transcribed. The first sequence, which occurs approximately 35 bases prior to the start of transcription, is tightly bound by RNA polymerase. Transcription is allowed to begin when the DNA helix begins to unwind at the second sequence, which is located about 10 bases prior to the start of transcription. As the DNA helix unwinds, the polymerase first pulls the early parts of the DNA into itself, a process called "DNA scrunching," and then, having acquired energy from the scrunching process, begins to advance down the DNA strand to continue synthesizing an RNA molecule complementary to the template strand of DNA. The nucleotide sequence of promoters differs only slightly from gene to gene, with all promoters being rich in adenine and thymine.

During elongation, which proceeds in the 5' to 3' direction (with regard to the growing RNA molecule), the mRNA is assembled by the addition of nucleotides that are complementary to the DNA template. Remember that uracil (U) is placed as adenine's complement. As elongation continues, the part of DNA already transcribed is rewound into its original helical form. At termination, the polymerases recognize another code that signals the separation and release of the mRNA strand, also called the **transcript.** How long is the mRNA? The smallest mRNA might consist of 100 bases; an average-size mRNA might consist of 1,200 bases; and a large one might consist of several thousand.

Translation: The Second Stage of Gene Expression

In translation, all of the elements needed to synthesize a protein, from the mRNA to the amino acids, are brought together on the ribosomes **(figure 9.12)**. The process occurs in five stages: initiation, elongation, termination, protein folding, and protein processing.

Initiation of Translation

The mRNA molecule leaves the DNA transcription site and is transported to ribosomes in the cytoplasm. Ribosomal subunits function by coming together and forming sites to hold the mRNA and tRNAs. The ribosomes of prokaryotes and eukaryotes are different sizes. Prokaryotic ribosomes, as well as the ribosomes in chloroplasts and mitochondria of eukaryotes, are of a 70S size, made up of a 50S (large) subunit and a 30S (small) subunit. The "S" is a measurement of sedimentation rates, which is how ribosomes are characterized. It is a nonlinear measure; therefore, 30S and 50S add up to 70S. Eukaryotic ribosomes are 80S (a large subunit of

1. Overall view of a gene. Each gene contains a specific promoter region and a leader sequence for guiding the beginning of transcription. This is followed by the region of the gene that codes for a polypeptide and ends with a series of terminal sequences that stop translation.

2. DNA is unwound at the promoter by RNA polymerase. Only one strand of DNA, called the template strand, is copied by the RNA polymerase. This strand runs in the 3' to 5' direction. Initially the enzyme pulls the DNA strand into itself.

3. The RNA polymerase begins to move along the strand. It adds complementary nucleotides as dictated by the DNA template, forming the single-stranded mRNA that reads in the 5' to 3' direction.

4. The polymerase continues transcribing until it reaches a termination site and the mRNA transcript is released for translation. Note that the section of the DNA that has been transcribed is rewound into its original configuration.

RNA polymerase binding site

Leader sequence | Initiation codon | Termination sequences

Promoter region

| T | A | C | G | A | C | T | G | A | T | G | C |
| A | T | G | C | T | G | A | C | T | A | C | G |

Intervening sequence of variable size

RNA polymerase

Template strand

3'   5'

5'   3'

Coding strand

Unwinding of DNA

Direction of transcription

3'

Nucleotide pool

5'

Early mRNA transcript

Termination sequence

Elongation

3'

5'

Late mRNA transcript

Process Figure 9.11 The major events in mRNA synthesis (transcription).

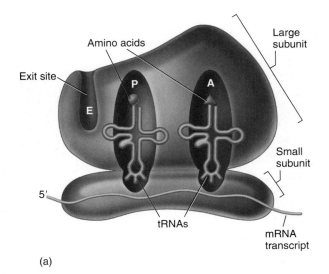

Amino acids

Exit site

Large subunit

P   A

E

Small subunit

5'

tRNAs

mRNA transcript

(a)

(b)

Figure 9.12 The "players" in translation.
(a) A ribosome serves as the stage for protein synthesis. Assembly of the small and large subunits results in specific sites for holding the mRNA and two tRNAs with their amino acids.
(b) Atomic-level view of an assembled ribosome. The ribosome is made of RNA (the double helix can be seen here in gray, for example) and of proteins (the purple parts).

60S and a 40S small subunit). The ribosome thus recognizes these molecules and stabilizes reactions between them. The small subunit binds to the 5′ end of the mRNA, and the large subunit supplies enzymes for making peptide bonds on the protein. The ribosome begins to scan the mRNA by moving in the 5′ to 3′ direction along the mRNA. The first codon it encounters is called the START codon, which is almost always AUG (and, rarely, GUG).

With the mRNA message in place on the assembled ribosome, the next step in translation involves entrance of tRNAs with their amino acids. The pool of cytoplasm contains a complete array of tRNAs, previously charged by having the correct amino acid attached. The step in which the complementary tRNA meets with the mRNA code is guided by the two sites on the large subunit of the ribosome called the P site (left) and the A site (right).[1] Think of these sites as shallow depressions in the larger subunit of the ribosome, each of which accommodates a tRNA. The ribosome also has an exit or E site where used tRNAs are released.

The Master Genetic Code: The Message in Messenger RNA

By convention, the master genetic code is represented by the mRNA codons and the amino acids they specify (**figure 9.13**). Except in a very few cases, this code is universal, whether for prokaryotes, eukaryotes, or viruses. It is worth noting that once the triplet code on mRNA is known, the original DNA sequence, the complementary tRNA code, and the types of amino acids in the protein are automatically known (**figure 9.14**). However, one cannot as easily predict (backward) from protein structure what the exact mRNA codons are because of a factor called **redundancy**,[2] meaning that a particular amino acid can be coded for by more than a single codon. Researchers can and do predict backward, however, a process assisted by their knowledge of the organism they are studying and which amino acid is likely to be represented by the codon.

In figure 9.13, the mRNA codons and their corresponding amino acid specificities are given. Because there are 64

---

1. P stands for peptide site; A stands for aminoacyl (amino acid) site; E stands for exit site.

2. This property is also called "degeneracy" by some books.

Second Base Position									
		U		**C**		**A**		**G**	
U	UUU	} Phenylalanine	UCU		UAU	} Tyrosine	UGU	} Cysteine	U
	UUC		UCC	Serine	UAC		UGC		C
	UUA	} Leucine	UCA		UAA	} STOP**	UGA	STOP**	A
	UUG		UCG		UAG		UGG	Tryptophan	G
C	CUU		CCU		CAU	} Histidine	CGU		U
	CUC	Leucine	CCC	Proline	CAC		CGC	Arginine	C
	CUA		CCA		CAA	} Glutamine	CGA		A
	CUG		CCG		CAG		CGG		G
A	AUU	Isoleucine	ACU		AAU	} Asparagine	AGU	} Serine	U
	AUC		ACC	Threonine	AAC		AGC		C
	AUA		ACA		AAA	} Lysine	AGA	} Arginine	A
	AUG	START ₍Methionine*	ACG		AAG		AGG		G
G	GUU		GCU		GAU	} Aspartic acid	GGU		U
	GUC	Valine	GCC	Alanine	GAC		GGC	Glycine	C
	GUA		GCA		GAA	} Glutamic acid	GGA		A
	GUG		GCG		GAG		GGG		G

First Base Position (left axis) · *Third Base Position* (right axis)

* This codon initiates translation.
**For these codons, which give the orders to stop translation, there are no corresponding tRNAs and no amino acids.

Figure 9.13　The genetic code: codons of mRNA that specify a given amino acid.　The master code for translation is found in the mRNA codons.

Figure 9.14 Interpreting the DNA code. If the DNA sequence is known, the mRNA codon can be surmised. If a codon is known, the anticodon and, finally, the amino acid sequence can be determined. The reverse is not as straightforward (determining the exact codon or anticodon from amino acid sequence) due to the redundancy of the code.

different triplet codes[3] and only 20 different amino acids, it is not surprising that some amino acids are represented by several codons. For example, leucine and serine can each be represented by any of six different triplets, and only tryptophan and methionine are represented by a single codon. In codons such as leucine, only the first two nucleotides are required to encode the correct amino acid, and the third nucleotide does not change its sense. This property, called **wobble,** is thought to permit some variation or mutation without altering the message.

The Beginning of Protein Synthesis

With mRNA serving as the guide, the stage is finally set for actual protein assembly. The correct tRNA (labeled 1 on **figure 9.15**) enters the P site and binds to the **start codon (AUG)** presented by the mRNA. Rules of pairing dictate that the anticodon of this tRNA must be complementary to the mRNA codon AUG; thus, the tRNA with anticodon UAC will first occupy site P. It happens that the amino acid carried by the initiator tRNA in bacteria is **formyl methionine** (fMet; see figure 9.13). Often fMet does not remain a permanent part of the finished protein but instead is cleaved from the finished peptide.

3. $64 = 4^3$ (the four different codons in all possible combinations of three).

Continuation and Completion of Protein Synthesis: Elongation and Termination

While reviewing the dynamic process of protein assembly, you will want to remain aware that the ribosome shifts its "reading frame" to the right along the mRNA from one codon to the next. This brings the next codon into place on the ribosome and makes a space for the next tRNA to enter the A position. A peptide bond is formed between the amino acids on the adjacent tRNAs, and the polypeptide grows in length.

Elongation begins with the filling of the A site by a second tRNA (**figure 9.15, step 2**). The identity of this tRNA and its amino acid is dictated by the second mRNA codon.

The entry of tRNA 2 into the A site brings the two adjacent tRNAs in favorable proximity for a peptide bond to form between the amino acids (aa) they carry. The fMet is transferred from the first tRNA to aa 2, resulting in two coupled amino acids called a dipeptide (**figure 9.15, step 2**).

For the next step to proceed, some room must be made on the ribosome, and the next codon in sequence must be brought into position for reading. This process is accomplished by **translocation,** the enzyme-directed shifting of the ribosome to the right along the mRNA strand, which causes the blank tRNA (1) to be discharged from the ribosome (**figure 9.15, step 3**) at the E site. This also shifts the tRNA holding the dipeptide into P position. Site A is temporarily left empty. The tRNA that has been released is now free to drift off into the cytoplasm and become recharged with an amino acid for later additions to this or another protein.

The stage is now set for the insertion of tRNA 3 at site A as directed by the third mRNA codon (**figure 9.15, step 4**). This insertion is followed once again by peptide bond formation between the dipeptide and aa 3 (making a tripeptide), splitting of the peptide from tRNA 2, and translocation. This releases tRNA 2, shifts mRNA to the next position, moves tRNA 3 to position P, and opens position A for the next tRNA (which will be called tRNA 4). From this point on, peptide elongation proceeds repetitively by this same series of actions out to the end of the mRNA.

The termination of protein synthesis is not simply a matter of reaching the last codon on mRNA. It is brought about by the presence of at least one special codon occurring just after the codon for the last amino acid. Termination codons—UAA, UAG, and UGA—are codons for which there is no corresponding tRNA. Although they are often called **nonsense codons,** they carry a necessary and useful message: *Stop here.* When this codon is reached, a special enzyme breaks the bond between the final tRNA and the finished polypeptide chain, releasing it from the ribosome.

Before newly made proteins can carry out their structural or enzymatic roles, they often require finishing touches. Even before the peptide chain is released from the ribosome, it begins folding upon itself to achieve its biologically active tertiary conformation. Other alterations,

① Entrance of tRNAs 1 and 2

② Formation of peptide bond

③ Discharge of tRNA 1 at E site

④ First translocation; tRNA 2 shifts into P site; enter tRNA 3 by ribosome

⑤ Formation of peptide bond

⑥ Discharge of tRNA 2; second translocation; enter tRNA 4

⑦ Formation of peptide bond

Process Figure 9.15 **The events in protein synthesis.**

called **posttranslational** modifications, may be necessary. Some proteins must have the starting amino acid (formyl methionine) clipped off; proteins destined to become complex enzymes have cofactors added; and some join with other completed proteins to form quaternary levels of structure.

The operation of transcription and translation is machine-like in its precision. Protein synthesis in bacteria is both efficient and rapid. At 37°C, 12 to 17 amino acids per second are added to a growing peptide chain. An average protein consisting of about 400 amino acids requires less than half a minute for complete synthesis. Further efficiency is gained when the translation of mRNA starts while transcription is still occurring **(figure 9.16)**. A single mRNA is long enough to be fed through more than one ribosome simultaneously. This permits the synthesis of hundreds of protein molecules from the same mRNA transcript arrayed along a chain of ribosomes. This **polyribosomal complex** is indeed an assembly line for mass production of proteins. It only occurs in prokaryotes, since there is no nucleus and transcription and translation both occur in the cytoplasm. (In eukaryotes transcription occurs in the nucleus.) Remember that all of the processes involved in gene expression are anabolic processes; protein synthesis consumes an enormous amount of energy. Nearly 1,200 ATPs are required just for synthesis of an average-size protein.

Eukaryotic Transcription and Translation: Similar Yet Different

Eukaryotes and prokaryotes share many similarities in protein synthesis. The start codon in eukaryotes is also AUG, but it codes for a different form of methionine. Another difference is that eukaryotic mRNAs code for just one protein, unlike bacterial mRNAs, which often contain information from several genes in series.

There are a few differences between prokaryotic and eukaryotic gene expression. As mentioned above, the presence of the DNA in a separate compartment (the nucleus) means that eukaryotic transcription and translation cannot be simultaneous. The mRNA transcript must pass through

Figure 9.16 Speeding up the protein assembly line in bacteria. **(a)** The mRNA transcript encounters ribosomal parts immediately as it leaves the DNA. **(b)** The ribosomal factories assemble along the mRNA in a chain, each ribosome reading the message and translating it into protein. Many products will thus be well along the synthetic pathway before transcription has even terminated. **(c)** Photomicrograph of a polyribosomal complex in action. Note that the protein "tails" vary in length depending on the stage of translation.

pores in the nuclear membrane and be carried to the ribosomes in the cytoplasm for translation.

We have given the simplified definition of a gene that works well for prokaryotes, but most eukaryotic genes (and, surprisingly, archaeal genes) do *not* exist as an uninterrupted series of triplets coding for a protein. A eukaryotic gene contains the code for a protein, but located along the gene are one to several intervening sequences of bases, called **introns,** that do not code for protein. Introns are interspersed between coding regions, called **exons,** that will be translated into protein **(figure 9.17).** We can use words as examples. A short section of colinear prokaryotic gene might read TOM SAW OUR DOG DIG OUT; a eukaryotic gene that codes for the same portion would read TOM SAW XZKP FPL OUR DOG QZWVP DIG OUT. The recognizable words are the exons, and the nonsense letters represent the introns.

This unusual genetic architecture, sometimes called a split gene, requires further processing before translation. Transcription of the entire gene with both exons and introns occurs first, producing a pre-mRNA. A series of adenosines is added to the mRNA molecule. This protects the molecule and eventually directs it out of the nucleus for translation. Next, a type of RNA and protein called a **spliceosome** recognizes the exon-intron junctions and enzymatically cuts through them. The action of this splicer enzyme loops the introns into lariat-shaped pieces, excises them, and joins the exons end to end. By this means, a strand of mRNA with no intron material is produced. This completed mRNA strand can then proceed to the cytoplasm to be translated.

Several different types of introns have been discovered, some of which do code for cell substances. As detailed in Insight 9.2, a great deal of non-protein-coding DNA is proving to be vital for cell function. In humans, this intron material represents 98% of the DNA and the discovery of its extreme importance has revolutionized the "genetic revolution." Another surprising finding from 2006 was the discovery of proteins that had sections that were in reverse order from the DNA sequence that encoded them. Previously it was considered a hard and fast rule that DNA sequence determined the mRNA and then the amino acid sequence once the introns were accounted for. This new data revealed that cellular machinery can flip stretches of amino acids around, essentially creating new proteins from the same gene. Many introns have been found to code for an enzyme called reverse transcriptase, which can convert RNA into DNA. Other introns are translated into endonucleases, enzymes that can snip DNA and allow insertions and deletions into the sequence.

Alternative Splicing and RNA Editing

A single primary transcript can be spliced into different mRNAs by the inclusion of different sets of exons, a process called alternative splicing. The generation of multiple transcripts from the same gene by alternative splicing allows for the production of more polypeptides than genes. This seems to occur only in higher eukaryotic organisms. Although many cases of alternative splicing have been documented, the recent completion of the sequence of the human genome now allows large-scale comparisons between sequences found in mRNAs and the genome. Initial assessments indicate that around 40% of human genes exhibit some form of alternative splicing. In some genes, alternative splicing allows for dozens or even hundreds of alternative mRNA transcripts from a single section of DNA. This greatly enhances the protein repertoire created from a single gene. This discovery led to the challenge of the one-gene one-product hypothesis. As stated at the beginning of this chapter, scientists now view that hypothesis more broadly, as one-gene one-family-of-related-products.

An even more dramatic posttranscriptional alteration of the message in eukaryotes

Figure 9.17 The split gene of eukaryotes.   Eukaryotic genes have an additional complicating factor in their translation. Their coding sequences, or exons (E), are interrupted at intervals by segments called introns (I) that are not part of that protein's code. Introns are transcribed but not translated, which necessitates their removal by RNA splicing enzymes before translation.

is the editing of mature transcripts to produce mRNA that is not truly encoded in the genome. First discovered as the insertion of uracil residues into some transcripts in protozoa, this was thought to be an anomaly. RNA editing has since been found in mammalian species, including humans. In this case, RNA editing involves the alteration of a sequence of nucleotides in the RNA after it has been transcribed from DNA but before it is translated into protein.

The Genetics of Animal Viruses

The genetic nature of viruses was described in chapter 6. Viruses essentially consist of one or more pieces of DNA or RNA enclosed in a protective coating. Above all, they are genetic parasites that require access to their host cell's genetic and metabolic machinery to be replicated, transcribed, and translated; and they also have the potential for genetically changing the cells. Because they contain only those genes needed for the production of new viruses, the genomes of viruses tend to be very compact and economical. In fact, this very simplicity makes them excellent subjects for the study of gene function.

The genetics of viruses is quite diverse. In many viruses, the nucleic acid is linear in form; in others, it is circular. The genome of most viruses exists in a single molecule, though in a few, it is segmented into several smaller molecules. Most viruses contain normal double-stranded (ds) DNA or single-stranded (ss) RNA, but other patterns exist. There are ssDNA viruses, dsRNA viruses, and retroviruses, which work backward by making dsDNA from ssRNA. In some instances, viral genes overlap one another, and in a few DNA viruses, both strands contain a translatable message.

A few generalities can be stated about viral genetics. In all cases, the viral nucleic acid penetrates the cell and is introduced into the host's gene-processing machinery at some point. In successful infection, an invading virus instructs the host's machinery to synthesize large numbers of new virus particles by a mechanism specific to a particular group. With few exceptions, replication of the DNA molecule of DNA animal viruses occurs in the nucleus, where the cell's DNA replication machinery lies and the genome of RNA viruses is replicated in the cytoplasm. In all viruses, viral mRNA is translated into viral proteins on host cell ribosomes using host tRNA.

9.2 Learning Outcomes—Can You . . .

6. . . . relate the new and old versions of the "central dogma"?
7. . . . identify important differences between RNA and DNA?
8. . . . draw a picture of the process of transcription?
9. . . . list the three types of RNA directly involved in translation?
10. . . . define "codon" and "anticodon"?
11. . . . identify on which molecules the promoter, the start codon, and the A and P sites appear?
12. . . . indicate how eukaryotic transcription and translation differ from these processes in prokaryotes?

9.3 Genetic Regulation of Protein Synthesis

In chapter 8, we surveyed the metabolic reactions in cells and the enzymes involved in those reactions. At that time, we mentioned that some enzymes are regulated and that one form of regulation occurs at the genetic level. Control mechanisms ensure that genes are active only when their products are required. One dramatic illustration of this is the expression of genes in outer space (Insight 9.3). In this way, enzymes will be produced as they are needed and prevent the waste of energy and materials in dead-end synthesis. Antisense RNAs, micro RNAs, and riboswitches (see Insight 9.2) provide regulation in both prokaryotes and eukaryotes. Prokaryotes have an additional strategy: They organize collections of genes into **operons.** Operons consist of a coordinated set of genes, all of which are regulated as a single unit. Operons are described as either inducible or repressible. The category each operon falls into is determined by how transcription is affected by the environment surrounding the cell. Many catabolic operons, or operons encoding enzymes that act in catabolism, are inducible, meaning that the operon is turned on (induced) by the substrate of the enzyme(s) for which the structural genes code. In this way, the enzymes needed to metabolize a nutrient (lactose, for example) are only produced when that nutrient is present in the environment. Repressible operons often contain genes coding for anabolic enzymes, such as those used to synthesize amino acids. In the case of these operons, several genes in series are turned off (repressed) by the product synthesized by the enzyme.

The Lactose Operon: A Model for Inducible Gene Regulation in Bacteria

The best understood cell system for explaining control through genetic induction is the **lactose (lac) operon.** This system, first described in 1961 by François Jacob and Jacques Monod, accounts for the regulation of lactose metabolism in *Escherichia coli.* Many other operons with similar modes of action have since been identified, and together they show us that the environment of a cell can have great impact on gene expression.

The lactose operon has three important features **(figure 9.18):**

1. the **regulator,** composed of the gene that codes for a protein capable of repressing the operon (a **repressor**);
2. the **control locus,** composed of two areas, the **promoter** (recognized by RNA polymerase) and the **operator,** a sequence that acts as an on/off switch for transcription; and
3. the **structural locus,** made up of three genes, each coding for a different enzyme needed to catabolize lactose.

One of the enzymes, β-galactosidase, hydrolyzes the lactose into its monosaccharides; another, permease, brings lactose across the cell membrane.

The operon provides an efficient strategy that permits genes for a particular metabolic pathway to be induced or repressed in unison by a single regulatory element. The promoter, operator, and structural components usually lie adjacent to one another, but the regulator can be at a distant site.

In inducible systems like the **lac** operon, the operon is normally in an *off mode* and does not initiate transcription when the appropriate substrate is absent **(figure 9.18a).** How is the operon maintained in this mode? The key is in the repressor protein that is coded by the regulatory gene. This relatively large molecule is **allosteric,** meaning it has two binding sites, one for the operator sequence on the DNA and another for lactose. In the absence of lactose, this repressor binds to the operator locus, thereby blocking the transcription of the structural genes lying downstream. Think of the repressor as a lock on the operator, and if the operator is locked, the structural genes cannot be transcribed. Importantly, the regulator gene lies upstream (to the left) of the

operator region and is transcribed constitutively because it is not controlled in tandem with the operon.

If lactose is added to the cell's environment, it triggers several events that turn the operon *on.* The binding of lactose to the repressor protein causes a conformational change in the repressor that dislodges it from the operator segment of the DNA **(figure 9.18b).** With the operator opened up, RNA polymerase can now bind to the promoter, and proceed. The structural genes are transcribed in a single unbroken transcript coding for all three enzymes. (During translation, however, each protein is synthesized separately.) Because lactose is ultimately responsible for stimulating protein synthesis, it is called the **inducer.**

As lactose is depleted, further enzyme synthesis is not necessary, so the order of events reverses. At this point, there is no longer sufficient lactose to inhibit the repressor;

(a) **Operon Off.** In the absence of lactose, a repressor protein (the product of a regulatory gene located elsewhere on the bacterial chromosome) attaches to the operator of the operon. This effectively locks the operator and prevents any transcription of structural genes downstream (to its right). Suppression of transcription (and consequently, of translation) prevents the unnecessary synthesis of enzymes for processing lactose.

(b) **Operon On.** Upon entering the cell, the substrate (lactose) becomes a genetic inducer by attaching to the repressor, which loses its grip and falls away. The RNA polymerase is now free to bind to the promoter and initiate transcription, and the enzymes produced by translation of the mRNA perform the necessary reactions on their lactose substrate.

Figure 9.18 **The lactose operon in bacteria: how inducible genes are controlled by substrate.**

hence, the repressor is again free to attach to the operator. The operator is locked, and transcription of the structural genes and enzyme synthesis related to lactose both stop.

A fine but important point about the **lac** operon is that it functions only in the absence of glucose or if the cell's energy needs are not being met by the available glucose. Glucose is the preferred carbon source because it can be used immediately in growth and does not require induction of an operon. When glucose is present, a second regulatory system ensures that the **lac** operon is inactive, regardless of lactose levels in the environment.

A Repressible Operon

Bacterial systems for synthesis of amino acids, purines and pyrimidines, and many other processes work on a slightly different principle—that of repression. Similar factors such as repressor proteins, operators, and a series of structural genes exist for this operon but with some important differences. Unlike the **lac** operon, this operon is normally in the *on* mode and will be turned *off* only when this nutrient is no longer required. The excess nutrient serves as a **corepressor** needed to block the action of the operon.

A growing cell that needs the amino acid arginine (arg) effectively illustrates the operation of a repressible operon. Under these conditions, the **arg** operon is set to *on* and arginine is being actively synthesized through the action of the operon's enzymatic products **(figure 9.19a).** In an active cell, the arginine will be used immediately, and the repressor will remain inactive (unable to bind the operator) because there is

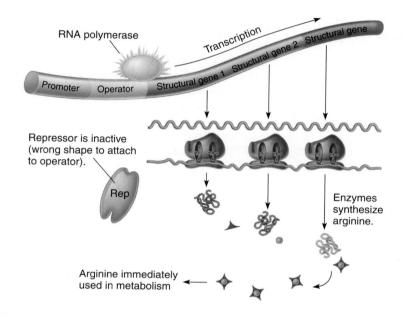

(a) **Operon On.** A repressible operon remains on when its nutrient products (here, arginine) are in great demand by the cell because the repressor is unable to bind to the operator at low nutrient levels.

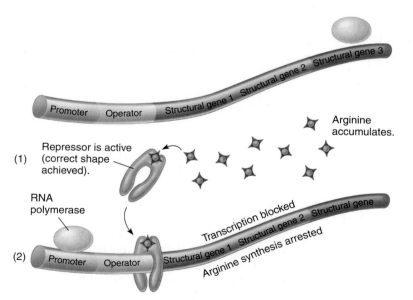

(b) **Operon Off.** The operon is repressed when (1) arginine builds up and, serving as a corepressor, activates the repressor. (2) The repressor complex affixes to the operator and blocks the RNA polymerase and further transcription of genes for arginine synthesis.

Figure 9.19 **Repressible operon: control of a gene through excess nutrient.**

INSIGHT 9.3   *Salmonella* in Space

In this chapter, you are learning the difference between phenotype and genotype, and that not all genes are expressed constitutively. Cheryl Nickerson and her team at Arizona State University found that for at least one bacterium, *Salmonella typhimurium,* outer space was a powerful force, making it much more virulent than it was in the lab on earth.

Nickerson and her team sent *Salmonella* into space aboard the shuttle *Atlantis* in 2006. When the shuttle returned after 12 days in space, the bacterium had altered the expression of 167 genes compared to strains that stayed behind on earth. When mice were infected with these bacteria, the space strains were almost three times as likely to kill them as the earth bacteria.

While this was widely reported at the time with such headlines as "Space Creates Mutant Superbugs," the bacteria did not mutate; in other words, their genotypes did not change significantly. But they regulated transcription in such a way that there was more or less expression from each of these 167 genes.

Later Nickerson's team conducted experiments that suggest that the direct cause of the regulatory changes was a lower amount of fluid shear experienced by the bacteria in space. They speculate that this can mimic conditions the bacteria experience as they dock in the brush border microvilli of the intestinal tract. Therefore, they believe they may have an insight into how to regulate the virulence of this pathogen even here on earth.

Others have speculated a bit more widely, suggesting that studies like these, including one in which human kidney cells were grown in orbit, raise larger questions about colonizing space. In these studies, the kidney cells changed the way they expressed more than 1,500 genes! So, many scientists wonder: How will cells, tissues, and bodies be different after long-term space stays? Indeed, what about organisms born in space, including, eventually, humans? How will their phenotypes be affected? Could we humans ourselves become alien, at least phenotypically?

---

too little free arginine to activate it. As the cell's metabolism begins to slow down, however, the synthesized arginine will no longer be used up and will accumulate. The free arginine is then available to act as a corepressor by attaching to the repressor. This reaction changes the shape of the repressor, making it capable of binding to the operator. Transcription stops; arginine is no longer synthesized **(figure 9.19b).**

In eukaryotic cells, gene function can be altered by intrinsic regulatory segments similar to operons. Some molecules, called transcription factors, insert on the grooves of the DNA molecule and enhance transcription of specific genes. Examples include zinc "fingers" and leucine "zippers." These transcription factors can regulate gene expression in response to environmental stimuli such as nutrients, toxin levels, or even temperature. Eukaryotic genes are also regulated during growth and development, leading to the hundreds of different tissue types found in higher multicellular organisms.

Phase Variation

When bacteria turn on or off a complement of genes that leads to obvious phenotypic changes, it is sometimes called **phase variation.** Phase variation is a type of phenotypic variation, but it has its own name because it has some special characteristics, the most important of which is that the phenotype is heritable, meaning it is passed down to subsequent generations, though during the subsequent generations it can change, again. But the process of turning on genes is often

mediated by regulatory proteins, as described with operons. The term phase variation is most often applied to traits affecting the bacterial cell surface and was originally coined to describe the ability of bacteria to change components of their surface that marked them for targeting by the host's immune system. Since these surface molecules also influenced the bacterium's ability to attach to surfaces, the ability to undergo phase variation allowed the microbes to adapt to—and stick in—different environments. Examples of phase variation include the ability of *Neisseria gonorrohoeae* strains to produce attachment fimbriae, and the ability of *Streptococcus pneumoniae* to produce a capsule.

Antibiotics That Affect Transcription and Translation

Naturally occurring cell nutrients are not the only agents capable of modifying gene expression. Some infection therapy is based on the concept that certain drugs react with DNA, RNA, or ribosomes and thereby alter genetic expression (see chapter 12). Treatment with such drugs is based on an important premise: that growth of the infectious agent will be inhibited by blocking its protein-synthesizing machinery selectively, without disrupting the cell synthesis of the patient receiving the therapy.

Drugs that inhibit protein synthesis exert their influence on transcription or translation. For example, the rifamycins used in therapy for tuberculosis bind to RNA polymerase, blocking the initiation step of transcription, and are selectively more active against bacterial RNA polymerase than the corresponding eukaryotic enzyme. Actinomycin D binds to bacterial DNA and halts mRNA chain elongation, but it also binds to human DNA. For this reason, it is very toxic and never used to treat bacterial infections, though it can be applied in tumor treatment.

The ribosome is a frequent target of antibiotics that inhibit ribosomal function and ultimately protein synthesis. The value and safety of these antibiotics again depend upon the differential susceptibility of prokaryotic and eukaryotic ribosomes. One problem with drugs that selectively disrupt prokaryotic ribosomes is that the mitochondria of humans contain a prokaryotic type of ribosome, and these drugs may inhibit the function of the host's mitochondria. One group of antibiotics (including erythromycin and spectinomycin) prevents translation by interfering with the attachment of mRNA to ribosomes. Chloramphenicol, lincomycin, and tetracycline bind to the ribosome in a way that blocks the elongation of the polypeptide, and aminoglycosides (such as streptomycin) inhibit peptide initiation and elongation. It is interesting to note that these drugs have served as important tools to explore genetic events because they can arrest specific stages in these processes.

9.3 Learning Outcomes—Can You ...

13. ... list one or two important advantages to arranging genes in an operon?
14. ... differentiate between repressible and inducible operons?
15. ... name some antibiotic targets of the transcription and translation machinery?

9.4 Mutations: Changes in the Genetic Code

As precise and predictable as the rules of genetic expression seem, permanent changes do occur in the genetic code. Indeed, genetic change is the driving force of evolution. In microorganisms, such changes may become evident in altered gene expression, such as the appearance or disappearance of anatomical or physiological traits. For example, a pigmented bacterium can lose its ability to form pigment, or a strain of the malarial parasite can develop resistance to a drug. Any change to the nucleotide sequence in the genome is called a mutation. Mutations are most noticeable when the genotypic change leads to a change in phenotype. Mutations can involve the loss of base pairs, the addition of base pairs, or a rearrangement in the order of base pairs. Do not confuse this with genetic recombination, in which microbes transfer whole segments of genetic information among themselves.

A microorganism that exhibits a natural, nonmutated characteristic is known as a **wild type,** or wild strain with respect to that trait. You might ask: "In a constantly changing population of microbes, what is the natural, nonmutated state?" For that reason most scientists prefer to define wild

type as the trait present in the highest numbers in a population. If a microorganism bears a mutation, it is called a **mutant strain.** Mutant strains can show variance in morphology, nutritional characteristics, genetic control mechanisms, resistance to chemicals, temperature preference, and nearly any type of enzymatic function. Mutant strains are very useful for tracking genetic events, unraveling genetic organization, and pinpointing genetic markers. A classic method of detecting mutant strains involves addition of various nutrients to a culture to screen for its use of that nutrient. For example, in a culture of a wild-type bacterium that is lactose-positive (meaning it has the necessary enzymes for fermenting this sugar), a small number of mutant cells have become lactose-negative, having lost the capacity to ferment this sugar. If the culture is plated on a medium containing indicators for fermentation, each colony can be observed for its fermentation reaction and the negative strain isolated. Another standard method of detecting and isolating microbial mutants is by replica plating **(figure 9.20).**

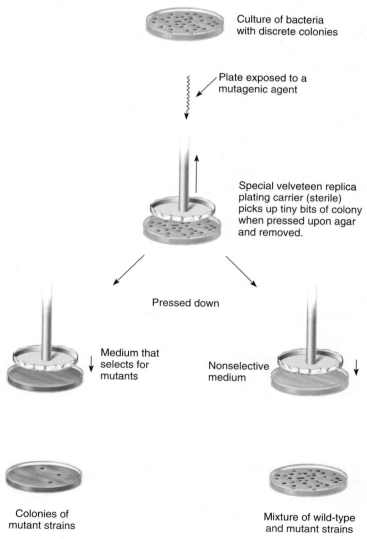

Figure 9.20 The general basis of replica plating. This method was developed by Joshua Lederberg for detecting and isolating mutant strains of microorganisms.

Causes of Mutations

Mutations can be spontaneous or induced, depending upon their origin. A **spontaneous mutation** is a random change in the DNA arising from errors in replication that occur randomly. The frequency of spontaneous mutations has been measured for a number of organisms. Mutation rates vary tremendously, from one mutation in 10^5 replications (a high rate) to one mutation in 10^{10} replications (a low rate). The rapid rate of bacterial reproduction allows these mutations to be observed more readily in bacteria than in most eukaryotes.

Induced mutations result from exposure to known **mutagens,** which are primarily physical or chemical agents that interact with DNA in a disruptive manner **(table 9.3).** The carefully controlled use of mutagens has proved a useful way to induce mutant strains of microorganisms for study.

Chemical mutagenic agents act in a variety of ways to change the DNA. Agents such as acridine dyes insert completely across the DNA helices between adjacent bases to produce mutations that distort the helix. Analogs[4] of the nitrogen bases (5-bromodeoxyuridine and 2-aminopurine, for example) are chemical mimics of natural bases that are incorporated into DNA during replication. Addition of these abnormal bases leads to mistakes in base-pairing. Many chemical mutagens also act as carcinogens, or cancer-causing agents, when vertebrates are exposed to them (see the discussion of the Ames test in a later section of this chapter).

Physical agents that alter DNA are primarily types of radiation. High-energy gamma rays and X rays introduce major physical changes into DNA, and it accumulates breaks that may not be repairable. Ultraviolet (UV) radiation induces abnormal bonds between adjacent pyrimidines that prevent normal replication. Exposure to large doses of radiation can be fatal, which is why radiation is so effective in microbial control; it can also be carcinogenic in animals. (The intentional use of UV to control microorganisms is described further in chapter 11.)

Categories of Mutations

Mutations range from large mutations, in which large genetic sequences are gained or lost, to small ones that affect only a single base on a gene. These latter mutations, which involve addition, deletion, or substitution of single bases, are called **point mutations.**

To understand how a change in DNA influences the cell, remember that the DNA code appears in a particular order of triplets (three bases) that is transcribed into mRNA codons, each of which specifies an amino acid. A permanent alteration in the DNA that is copied faithfully into mRNA and translated can change the structure of the protein. A change in a protein can likewise change the morphology and physiology of a cell. Some mutations have a harmful effect on the cell, leading to cell dysfunction or death; these are called lethal mutations. Neutral mutations produce neither adverse nor helpful changes. A small number of mutations are beneficial in that they provide the cell with a useful change in structure or physiology.

Any change in the code that leads to placement of a different amino acid is called a **missense mutation.** A missense mutation can do one of the following:

1. create a faulty, nonfunctional (or less functional) protein,
2. produce a protein that functions in a different manner, or
3. cause no significant alteration in protein function (see **table 9.4** to see how missense mutations look).

4. An analog is a chemical structured very similarly to another chemical except for minor differences in functional groups.

Table 9.3 Selected Mutagenic Agents and Their Effects

Agent	Effect
Chemical	
Nitrous acid, bisulfite	Removes an amino group from some bases
Ethidium bromide	Inserts between the paired bases
Acridine dyes	Cause frameshifts due to insertion between base pairs
Nitrogen base analogs	Compete with natural bases for sites on replicating DNA
Radiation	
Ionizing (gamma rays, X rays)	Form free radicals that cause single or double breaks in DNA
Ultraviolet	Causes cross-links between adjacent pyrimidines

Table 9.4 Categories of Point Mutations and Their Effects

(a)
							Normal gene
DNA	TAC	TGG	CTG	CTC	TAC	TTT...	
RNA	AUG	ACC	GAC	GAG	AUG	AAA...	
Protein	Met	Thr	Asp	Glu	Met	Lys...	

(b) Missense mutation: leading to amino acid switch (may or may not function well)
DNA	TAC	TGG	CTT	CTC	TAC	TTT...
RNA	AUG	ACC	GAA	GAG	AUG	AAA...
Protein	Met	Thr	Glu	Glu	Met	Lys...

(c) Base substitution: silent (no change in function)
DNA	TAC	TGG	CTA	CTC	TAC	TTT...
RNA	AUG	ACC	GAU	GAG	AUG	AAA...
Protein	Met	Thr	Asp	Glu	Met	Lys...

FRAMESHIFT MUTATION

(d) Frameshift and premature stop
DNA	TAC	TGC	TGC	TCT	ACT	TT
RNA	AUG	ACG	ACG	AGA	UGA	AA...
Protein	Met	Thr	Thr	Arg	STOP	

(e) Frameshift
DNA	TAC	TGG	GCT	GCT	CTA	CTT...
RNA	AUG	ACC	CGA	CGA	GAU	GAA...
Protein	Met	Thr	Arg	Arg	Asp	Glu...

Deletion mutation (d)
↓
Both lead to frameshifts and can lead to premature stop codons and/or poorly functioning protein
↑
Insertion mutation (e)

A **nonsense mutation,** on the other hand, changes a normal codon into a stop codon that does not code for an amino acid and stops the production of the protein wherever it occurs. A nonsense mutation almost always results in a nonfunctional protein. (**Table 9.4, row d,** shows a nonsense mutation resulting from a frameshift [described below].) A **silent mutation (table 9.4, row c)** alters a base but does not change the amino acid and thus has no effect. For example, because of the redundancy of the code, ACU, ACC, ACG, and ACA all code for threonine, so a mutation that changes only the last base will not alter the sense of the message in any way. A **back-mutation** occurs when a gene that has undergone mutation reverses (mutates back) to its original base composition.

Mutations also occur when one or more bases are inserted into or deleted from a newly synthesized DNA strand. This type of mutation, known as a **frameshift (table 9.4, rows d and e),** is so named because the reading frame of the mRNA has been changed. Frameshift mutations nearly always result in a nonfunctional protein because every amino acid after the mutation is different from what was coded for in the original DNA. Also note that insertion or deletion of bases in multiples of three (3, 6, 9, etc.) results in the addition or deletion of amino acids but does not disturb the reading frame. The effects of all of these types of mutations can be seen in table 9.4.

Repair of Mutations

Earlier we indicated that DNA has a proofreading mechanism to repair mistakes in replication that might otherwise become permanent (see page 240). Because mutations are potentially life-threatening, the cell has additional systems for finding and repairing DNA that has been damaged by various mutagenic agents and processes. Most ordinary DNA damage is resolved by enzymatic systems specialized for finding and fixing such defects.

DNA that has been damaged by ultraviolet radiation can be restored by photoactivation or light repair. This repair mechanism requires visible light and a light-sensitive enzyme, DNA photolyase, which can detect and attach to the damaged areas (sites of abnormal pyrimidine binding). Ultraviolet repair mechanisms are successful only for a relatively small number of UV mutations. Cells cannot repair severe, widespread damage and will die. In humans, the genetic disease *xeroderma pigmentosa* is due to nonfunctioning genes for enzymes responsible for excising pyrimidine dimers caused by UV light. Persons suffering from this rare disorder develop severe skin cancers; this relation provided early strong evidence for a link between cancer and mutations.

Mutations can be excised by a series of enzymes that remove the incorrect bases and add the correct ones. This process is known as **excision repair.** First, enzymes break the bonds between the bases and the sugar-phosphate strand at the site of the error. A different enzyme subsequently removes the defective bases one at a time, leaving a gap that will be filled in by DNA polymerase I and ligase **(figure 9.21).** A repair system can also locate mismatched bases that were missed during proof-

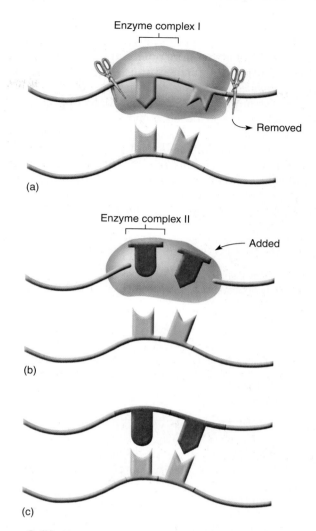

(a)

(b)

(c)

Figure 9.21 Excision repair of mutation by enzymes.
(a) The first enzyme complex recognizes one or several incorrect bases and removes them. **(b)** The second complex (DNA polymerase I and ligase) places correct bases and seals the gaps. **(c)** Repaired DNA.

reading: for example, C mistakenly paired with A, or G with T. The base must be replaced soon after the mismatch is made, or it will not be recognized by the repair enzymes.

The Ames Test

New agricultural, industrial, and medicinal chemicals are constantly being added to the environment, and exposure to them is widespread. The discovery that many such compounds are mutagenic and that many of these mutagens are linked to cancer is significant. Although animal testing has been a standard method of detecting chemicals with carcinogenic potential, a more rapid screening system called the **Ames test**[5] is also commonly used. In this ingenious test, the experimental subjects are bacteria whose gene expression and mutation rate can be readily observed and monitored.

5. Named for its creator, Bruce Ames.

The premise is that any chemical capable of mutating bacterial DNA could similarly mutate mammalian (and thus human) DNA and is therefore potentially hazardous.

One indicator organism in the Ames test is a mutant strain of *Salmonella typhimurium*[6] that has lost the ability to synthesize the amino acid histidine, a defect highly susceptible to back-mutation because the strain also lacks DNA repair mechanisms. Mutations that cause reversion to the wild strain, which is capable of synthesizing histidine, occur spontaneously at a very low rate. A test agent is considered a mutagen if it enhances the rate of back-mutation beyond levels that would occur spontaneously. One version of this testing procedure is outlined in **figure 9.22**. The Ames test

6. *S. typhimurium* inhabits the intestine of poultry and causes food poisoning in humans. It is used extensively in genetic studies of bacteria.

Culture of *Salmonella* bacteria, histidine (⁻)

In the control setup, bacteria are plated on a histidine-free medium containing liver enzymes but lacking the test agent.

The experimental plate is prepared the same way except that it contains the test agent.

(a) **Control Plate**
Minimal medium lacking histidine and test chemical

(b) **Test Plate**
Minimal medium with test chemical and no histidine

Incubation (12 h)
Any colonies that form have back-mutated to his(⁺)

his(⁺) colonies arising from spontaneous back-mutation

his(⁺) colonies in presence of the chemical

(c) The degree of mutagenicity of the chemical agent can be calculated by comparing the number of colonies growing on the control plate with the number on the test plate. Chemicals that induce an increased incidence of back-mutation (right side) are considered carcinogens.

Figure 9.22 The Ames test. This test is based on a strain of *Salmonella typhimurium* that cannot synthesize histidine [his(−)]. It lacks the enzymes to repair DNA so that mutations show up readily, and it has leaky cell walls that permit the ready entrance of chemicals. Many potential carcinogens (benzanthracene and aflatoxin, for example) are mutagenic agents only after being acted on by mammalian liver enzymes, so an extract of these enzymes is added to the test medium.

has proved invaluable for screening an assortment of environmental and dietary chemicals for mutagenicity and carcinogenicity without resorting to animal studies.

Positive and Negative Effects of Mutations

Many mutations are not repaired. How the cell copes with them depends on the nature of the mutation and the strategies available to that organism. Mutations are permanent and heritable and will be passed on to the offspring of organisms and new viruses and become a long-term part of the gene pool. Most mutations are harmful to organisms; others provide adaptive advantages.

If a mutation leading to a nonfunctional protein occurs in a gene for which there is only a single copy, as in haploid or simple organisms, the cell will probably die. This happens when certain mutant strains of *E. coli* acquire mutations in the genes needed to repair damage by UV radiation. Mutations of the human genome affecting the action of a single protein (mostly enzymes) are responsible for more than 3,500 diseases.

Although most spontaneous mutations are not beneficial, a small number contribute to the success of the individual and the population by creating variant strains with alternate ways of expressing a trait. Microbes are not "aware" of this advantage and do not direct these changes; they simply respond to the environment they encounter. Those organisms with beneficial mutations can more readily adapt, survive, and reproduce. In the long-range view, mutations and the variations they produce are the raw materials for change in the population and, thus, for evolution.

Mutations that create variants occur frequently enough that any population contains mutant strains for a number of characteristics, but as long as the environment is stable, these mutants will never comprise more than a tiny percentage of the population. When the environment changes, however, it can become hostile for the survival of certain individuals, and only those microbes bearing protective mutations will be equipped to survive in the new environment. In this way, the environment naturally selects certain mutant strains that will reproduce, give rise to subsequent generations, and in time, be the dominant strain in the population. Through these means, any change that confers an advantage during selection pressure will be retained by the population. One of the clearest models for this sort of selection and adaptation is acquired drug resistance in bacteria (see chapter 12). Bacteria have also developed a mechanism for increasing their adaptive capacity through genetic exchange, called genetic recombination, discussed in the next section.

9.4 Learning Outcomes—Can You . . .

16. . . . define the term "mutation" and discuss its importance?

17. . . . differentiate among frameshift, nonsense, silent, and missense mutations?

9.5 DNA Recombination Events

Genetic recombination through sexual reproduction is an important means of genetic variation in eukaryotes. Although bacteria have no exact equivalent to sexual reproduction, they exhibit a primitive means for sharing or recombining parts of their genome. An event in which one bacterium donates DNA to another bacterium is a type of genetic transfer termed **recombination,** the end result of which is a new strain different from both the donor and the original recipient strain. Recombination in bacteria depends in part on the fact that bacteria contain extrachromosomal DNA—that is, plasmids—and are adept at interchanging genes. Genetic exchanges have tremendous effects on the genetic diversity of bacteria. They provide additional genes for resistance to drugs and metabolic poisons, new nutritional and metabolic capabilities, and increased virulence and adaptation to the environment.

In general, any organism that contains (and expresses) genes that originated in another organism is called a **recombinant.**

Horizontal Gene Transfer in Bacteria

Any transfer of DNA that results in organisms acquiring new genes that did not come directly from parent organisms is called **horizontal gene transfer.** (Acquiring genes from parent organisms during reproduction is called vertical gene transfer.) Bacteria have been known to engage in horizontal gene transfer for decades. It is now becoming clear that eukaryotic organisms—including humans—also engage in horizontal gene transfer, often aided and abetted by microbes such as viruses. This revelation has upended traditional views about taxonomy and even "human-ness." Remember in chapter 1 the assertion that 40% to 50% of DNA in humans comes from nonhuman species, transferred to us via viruses? Here we will study the mechanisms used by bacteria to acquire genes horizontally.

DNA transfer between bacterial cells typically involves small pieces of DNA in the form of plasmids or chromosomal fragments. Plasmids are small, circular pieces of DNA that contain their own origin of replication and therefore can replicate independently of the bacterial chromosome. Plasmids are found in many bacteria (as well as some fungi) and typically contain, at most, only a few dozen genes. Although plasmids are not necessary for bacterial survival, they often carry useful traits, such as antibiotic resistance. Chromosomal fragments that have escaped from a lysed bacterial cell are also commonly involved in the transfer of genetic information between cells. An important difference between plasmids and fragments is that while a plasmid has its own origin of replication and is stably replicated and inherited, chromosomal fragments must integrate themselves into the bacterial chromosome in order to be replicated and eventually passed to progeny cells. While the process of genetic recombination is relatively rare in nature, its frequency can be increased in the laboratory, where the ability to shuffle genes between organisms is highly prized.

Depending on the mode of transmission, the means of genetic recombination in bacteria is called conjugation, transformation, or transduction. **Conjugation** requires the attachment of two related species and the formation of a bridge that can transport DNA. **Transformation** entails the transfer of naked DNA and requires no special vehicle. **Transduction** is DNA transfer mediated through the action of a bacterial virus **(table 9.5).**

Conjugation: Bacterial "Sex"

Conjugation is a mode of genetic exchange in which a plasmid or other genetic material is transferred by a donor to a recipient cell via a direct connection **(figure 9.23).** Both gram-negative and gram-positive cells can conjugate. In gram-negative cells, the donor has a plasmid **(fertility,** or **F′ factor)** that allows the synthesis of a conjugative **pilus.** The recipient cell has a recognition site on its surface. A cell's role in conjugation is denoted by F$^+$ for the cell that has the F plasmid and by F$^-$ for the cell that lacks it. Contact is made when a pilus grows out from the F$^+$ cell, attaches to the surface of the F$^-$ cell, contracts, and draws the two cells together

Table 9.5 Types of Horizontal Gene Transfer in Bacteria

Examples of Mode	Factors Involved	Direct or Indirect*	Genes Transferred
Conjugation	Donor cell with pilus Fertility plasmid in donor Both donor and recipient alive Bridge forms between cells to transfer DNA.	Direct	Drug resistance; resistance to metals; toxin production; enzymes; adherence molecules; degradation of toxic substances; uptake of iron
Transformation	Free donor DNA (fragment) Live, competent recipient cell	Indirect	Polysaccharide capsule; unlimited with cloning techniques
Transduction	Donor is lysed bacterial cell. Defective bacteriophage is carrier of donor DNA. Live recipient cell of same species as donor	Indirect	Toxins; enzymes for sugar fermentation; drug resistance

*Direct means the donor and recipient are in contact during exchange; indirect means they are not.

Figure 9.23 Conjugation: genetic transmission through direct contact between two cells.

Within the figure, the following labels appear:

Physical Conjugation

- F factor
- Bacterial chromosome
- F⁺
- Sex pilus makes contact with F⁻ recipient cell.
- F⁻
- Sex pilus contracts, bringing cells together.
- F⁺
- F⁻
- (1) The pilus of donor cell (top) attaches to receptor on recipient cell and retracts to draw the two cells together. This is the mechanism for gram-negative bacteria.

F Factor Transfer

- Bridge made with pilus
- Donor   Recipient
- F⁺   F⁻
- F factor (plasmid)
- Chromosome
- F⁺   F⁻
- F factor being copied
- F⁺   F⁺
- F factor
- (2) Transfer of the F factor, or conjugative plasmid

Hfr Transfer

- Donor   Recipient
- F factor
- Integration of F factor into chromosome
- Hfr cell
- Pilus
- Chromosome
- Partial copy of donor chromosome
- Bridge broken   Donated genes
- (3) High-frequency (Hfr) transfer involves transmission of chromosomal genes from a donor cell to a recipient cell. The donor chromosome is duplicated and transmitted in part to a recipient cell, where it is integrated into the chromosome.

(**figure 9.23;** see also figure 4.8). In both gram-positive and gram-negative cells, an opening is created between the connected cells, and the replicated DNA passes across from one cell to the other. Conjugation is a conservative process, in that the donor bacterium generally retains ("conserves") a copy of the genetic material being transferred.

There are hundreds of conjugative plasmids with some variations in their properties. One of the best understood plasmids is the F factor in *E. coli*, which exhibits these patterns of transfer:

1. The donor (F⁺) cell makes a copy of its F factor and transmits this to a recipient (F⁻) cell. The F⁻ cell is thereby changed into an F⁺ cell capable of producing a pilus and conjugating with other cells. No additional donor genes are transferred at this time.
2. In high-frequency recombination (Hfr) donors, the plasmid becomes integrated into the F⁺ donor chromosome.

The term **high-frequency recombination** was adopted to denote a cell with an integrated F factor that transmits its chromosomal genes. These genes become integrated into recipient chromosomes at a very high frequency.

The F factor can direct a more comprehensive transfer of part of the donor chromosome to a recipient cell. This transfer occurs through duplication of the DNA, after which one strand of DNA is retained by the donor, and the other strand is transported across to the recipient cell. The F factor may not be transferred during this process. The transfer of an entire chromosome takes about 100 minutes, but the pilus bridge between cells is ordinarily broken before this time, and rarely is the entire genome of the donor cell transferred.

Conjugation has great biomedical importance. Special **resistance (R) plasmids,** or **factors,** that bear genes for resisting antibiotics and other drugs are commonly shared among bacteria through conjugation. Transfer of R factors can confer multiple resistance to antibiotics such as tetracycline, chloramphenicol, streptomycin, sulfonamides, and penicillin. This phenomenon is discussed further in chapter 12. Other types of R factors carry genetic codes for resistance to heavy metals (nickel and mercury) or for synthesizing virulence factors (toxins, enzymes, and adhesion molecules) that increase the pathogenicity of the bacterial strain. Conjugation studies have also provided an excellent way to map the bacterial chromosome.

Transformation: Capturing DNA from Solution

One of the cornerstone discoveries in microbial genetics was made in the late 1920s by the English biochemist Frederick Griffith working with *Streptococcus pneumoniae* and laboratory mice. The pneumococcus exists in two major strains based on the presence of the capsule—the presence or absence of which affects colonial morphology and pathogenicity. Encapsulated strains have a smooth (S) colonial appearance and are virulent; strains lacking a capsule have a rough (R) appearance and are nonvirulent. (Recall from chapter 4 that the capsule protects a bacterium from the phagocytic host defenses.) To set the groundwork, Griffith showed that when mice were injected with a live, virulent

(S) strain, they soon died **(figure 9.24a)**. Mice injected with a live, nonvirulent (R) strain remained alive and healthy **(figure 9.24b)**. Next he tried a variation on this theme. First, he heat-killed an S strain and injected it into mice, which remained healthy **(figure 9.24c)**. Then came the ultimate test: Griffith injected both dead S cells and live R cells into mice, with the result that the mice died from pneumococcal blood infection **(figure 9.24d)**. If killed bacterial cells do not come back to life and the nonvirulent live strain was harmless, why did the mice die? Although he did not know it at the time, Griffith had demonstrated that dead S cells, while passing through the body of the mouse, broke open and released some of their DNA (by chance, that part containing the genes for making a capsule). A few of the live R cells subsequently picked up this loose DNA and were transformed by it into virulent, capsule-forming strains.

Later studies supported the concept that a chromosome released by a lysed cell breaks into fragments small enough to be accepted by a recipient cell and that DNA, even from a dead cell, retains its genetic code. This nonspecific acceptance by a bacterial cell of small fragments of soluble DNA from the surrounding environment is termed **transformation**.

Figure 9.24 Griffith's classic experiment in transformation. In essence, this experiment proved that DNA released from a killed cell can be acquired by a live cell. The cell receiving this new DNA is genetically transformed—in this case, from a nonvirulent strain to a virulent one.

Transformation is apparently facilitated by special DNA-binding proteins on the cell wall that capture DNA from the surrounding medium. Cells that are capable of accepting genetic material through this means are termed **competent.** The new DNA is processed by the cell membrane and transported into the cytoplasm, where some of it is inserted into the bacterial chromosome. Transformation is a natural event found in several groups of gram-positive and gram-negative bacterial species. Because transformation requires no special appendages and the donor and recipient cells do not have to be in direct contact, the process is useful for certain types of recombinant DNA technology. With this technique, foreign genes from a completely unrelated organism are inserted into a plasmid, which is then introduced into a competent bacterial cell through transformation. These recombinations can be carried out in a test tube, and human genes can be experimented upon and even expressed outside the human body by placing them in a microbial cell. This same phenomenon in eukaryotic cells, termed **transfection,** is an essential aspect of genetically engineered yeasts, plants, and mice, and it has been proposed as a future technique for curing genetic diseases in humans. These topics are covered in more detail in chapter 10.

A Note About the Term "Transformation"

Even in biology, the term "transformation" has more than one meaning, determined by the context of its use. Here we learn about transformation as a mechanism of horizontal gene transfer in bacteria. In the context of cancer and malignancy, a cell that is no longer normal but has lost its growth control mechanisms and becomes malignant is said to be "transformed." When this happens, a more complete description is that the cell has become malignantly transformed, but it is often just shortened to "transformed."

Transduction: The Case of the Piggyback DNA

Bacteriophages (bacterial viruses) have been previously described as destructive bacterial parasites. Viruses can in fact serve as genetic vectors (an entity that can bring foreign DNA into a cell). The process by which a bacteriophage serves as the carrier of DNA from a donor cell to a recipient cell is transduction. Although it occurs naturally in a broad spectrum of bacteria, the participating bacteria in a single transduction event must be the same species because of the specificity of viruses for host cells.

There are two versions of transduction. In **generalized transduction (figure 9.25),** random fragments of disintegrating host DNA are taken up by the phage during assembly. Virtually any gene from the bacterium can be transmitted through this means. In **specialized transduction (figure 9.26),** a highly specific part of the host genome is regularly incorporated into the virus. This specificity is explained by the prior existence of a temperate prophage inserted in a fixed site on the bacterial chromosome. When activated, the prophage DNA separates from the bacterial chromosome,

Process Figure 9.25 Generalized transduction: genetic transfer by means of a virus carrier. (1) A phage infects cell A (the donor cell) by normal means. (2) During replication and assembly, a phage particle incorporates a segment of bacterial DNA by mistake. (3) Cell A then lyses and releases the mature phages, including the genetically altered one. (4) The altered phage adsorbs to and penetrates another host cell (cell B), injecting the DNA from cell A rather than viral nucleic acid. (5) Cell B receives this donated DNA, which recombines with its own DNA. Because the virus is defective (biologically inactive as a virus), it is unable to complete a lytic cycle. The transduced cell survives and can use this new genetic material.

carrying a small segment of host genes with it. During a lytic cycle, these specific viral-host gene combinations are incorporated into the viral particles and carried to another bacterial cell.

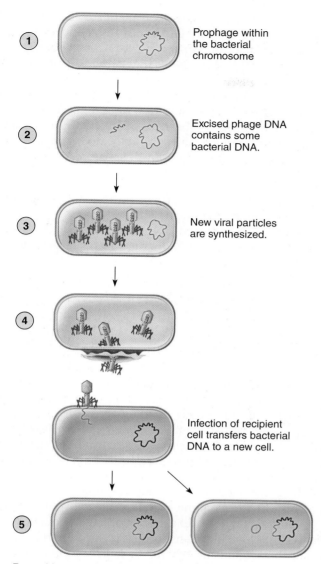

Process Figure 9.26 | Prophage within the bacterial chromosome

② Excised phage DNA contains some bacterial DNA.

③ New viral particles are synthesized.

④

Infection of recipient cell transfers bacterial DNA to a new cell.

⑤

Recombination results in two possible outcomes.

Process Figure 9.26 Specialized transduction: transfer of specific genetic material by means of a virus carrier.
① Specialized transduction begins with a cell that contains a prophage (a viral genome integrated into the host cell chromosome). ② Rarely, the virus enters a lytic cycle and, as it excises itself from its host cell, inadvertently includes some bacterial DNA. ③ Replication and assembly result in production of a chimeric virus, containing some bacterial DNA. ④ Release of the recombinant virus and subsequent infection of a new host result in transfer of bacterial DNA between cells. ⑤ Recombination can occur between the bacterial chromosome and the virus DNA, resulting in either bacterial DNA or a combination of viral and bacterial DNA being incorporated into the bacterial chromosome.

Several cases of specialized transduction have biomedical importance. The virulent strains of bacteria such as *Corynebacterium diphtheriae*, *Clostridium* spp., and *Streptococcus pyogenes* all produce toxins with profound physiological effects, whereas nonvirulent strains do not produce toxins. It turns out that toxicity arises from the expression of bacteriophage

Genes may be transferred between bacterial cells in three different ways: by conjugation, in which DNA is transferred between cells along a pilus; by transformation, the transfer of naked DNA; and by transduction, DNA transfer mediated through the action of a bacterial virus. All three modes of genetic transfer occur in *Acinetobacter*.

Had the resistance genes found in *A. baumannii* been unique (i.e., significantly different from resistance genes seen in other species), this would have suggested that they had first arisen within *A. baumannii*, with no genetic material contributed by other sources. Instead, the fact that many of the resistance genes were previously known to exist in other bacterial species indicated that they had probably been transferred to *A. baumannii* from one of these species. Since these other species are commonly found in healthcare facilities, the facilities themselves are the most likely setting for the transfer of genetic material between other bacterial species and *A. baumannii*.

genes that have been introduced by transduction. Only those bacteria infected with a temperate phage are toxin formers. (Details of toxin action are discussed in the organ-system-specific disease chapters.) Another instance of transduction is seen in staphylococcal transfer of drug resistance.

Transposons: "This Gene Is Jumpin'" One type of genetic transferral of great interest involves transposable elements, or **transposons.** Transposons have the distinction of shifting from one part of the genome to another and so are termed "jumping genes." When the idea of their existence in corn plants was first postulated by geneticist Barbara McClintock in 1951, it was greeted with nearly universal skepticism because it had long been believed that the location of a given gene was set and that genes did not or could not move around. Now it is evident that jumping genes are widespread among prokaryotic and eukaryotic cells and viruses.

All transposons share the general characteristic of traveling from one location to another on the genome—from one chromosomal site to another, from a chromosome to a plasmid, or from a plasmid to a chromosome **(figure 9.27).** Because transposons can occur in plasmids, they can also be transmitted from one cell to another in bacteria and a few eukaryotes. Some transposons replicate themselves before jumping to the next location, and others simply move without replicating first.

Transposons contain DNA that codes for the enzymes needed to remove and reintegrate the transposon at another site in the genome. Flanking the coding region of the DNA are sequences called tandem repeats, which mark the point at which the transposon is removed or reinserted into the genome. The smallest transposons consist of only these two genetic sequences and are often referred to as

Figure 9.27 Transposons: shifting segments of the genome. (1) A transposon exists as a small piece of DNA integrated into the host cell chromosome. (2) The transposon may excise itself and move from one location to another in the genome, maintaining itself at a single copy per cell. (3) It may also replicate prior to moving, leading to an increase in the copy number and a greater effect on the genome of the host. (4) Finally, the transposon may jump to a plasmid, which can then be transferred to another bacterial cell.

Case File 9   *Wrap-Up*

The multidrug resistance of *A. baumannii* is a serious concern in both military and civilian medical facilities and has led to several changes in their practices. Laboratory characterization of patient and environmental samples is in progress to determine the prominence of *A. baumannii* in soil samples and in medical facilities. Care facilities have increased surveillance for patients colonized with *A. baumannii*. Clinicians have had to treat infections most carefully and to consider new combinations of antimicrobials. Infection control measures have been introduced or revised, and use of alcohol-based hand sanitizers has been implemented. Finally, researchers and the pharmaceutical industry are continuing to search for new and innovative ways to treat all infectious diseases.

See: 2004. *MMWR* 53:1063–66.

insertion elements. A type of transposon called **retrotransposon** can transcribe DNA into RNA and then back into DNA for insertion in a new location. Other transposons contain additional genes that provide traits such as antibiotic resistance or toxin production.

The overall effect of transposons—to scramble the genetic language—can be beneficial or adverse, depending upon such variables as where insertion occurs in a chromosome, what kinds of genes are relocated, and the type of cell involved. In bacteria, transposons are known to be involved in

1. changes in traits such as colony morphology, pigmentation, and antigenic characteristics;
2. replacement of damaged DNA; and
3. the intermicrobial transfer of drug resistance (in bacteria).

Pathogenicity Islands: Special "Gifts" of Horizontal Gene Transfer?

Some of the horizontally transferred genes in bacteria have the ability to make their new hosts pathogenic, or able to cause disease. These are termed **pathogenicity islands.** These islands contain multiple genes that are coordinated to create a new trait on the bacterium, such as the ability to scavenge iron (important for the bacterium causing the plague, *Yersinia pestis*) or the ability to produce exotoxins (seen in *Staphylococcus aureus*). These islands of genes are thought to be transferred from other species because the G + C versus the A + T ratio of the DNA differs from that of the rest of the host bacterium's genome, a sure sign that it is "foreign" DNA. In addition, the islands are usually surrounded by sequences that look like bacteriophage sequences, or sequences that look like transposon enzymes. It is becoming apparent that organisms "share" their genes, sometimes in great chunks, with one another, essentially leap-frogging the evolution process by shuffling genes in this manner.

9.5 Learning Outcomes—Can You . . .

18. . . . define recombinant?
19. . . . describe three forms of horizontal gene transfer used in bacteria?

Chapter Summary

9.1 Introduction to Genetics and Genes: Unlocking the Secrets of Heredity

- Nucleic acids are molecules that contain the blueprints of life in the form of genes. DNA is the blueprint molecule for all cellular organisms. The blueprints of viruses, however, can be either DNA or RNA.
- The total amount of DNA in an organism is termed its genome (also genotype). Not all genes are expressed all the time; the ones that are expressed result in an organism's phenotype.
- The genome of prokaryotes is quite small compared with the genome of eukaryotes. Bacterial DNA consists of a few thousand genes in one circular chromosome. Eukaryotic genomes range from *thousands to tens of thousands* of genes.
- DNA copies itself just before cellular division by the process of semiconservative replication. Semiconservative replication means that each "old" DNA strand is the template upon which each "new" strand is synthesized.
- The circular bacterial chromosome is replicated at two forks as directed by DNA polymerase III. At each fork, two new strands are synthesized—one continuously and one in short fragments—and mistakes are proofread and removed.

9.2 Applications of the DNA Code: Transcription and Translation

- Information in DNA is converted to proteins by the process of transcription and translation. These proteins may be structural or functional in nature.
- The DNA code occurs in groups of three bases; this code is copied onto RNA as codons; the message determines the types of amino acids in a protein. This code is universal in all cells and viruses.
- DNA also contains a great number of non-protein-coding sequences. These sequences are often transcribed into RNA that serves to regulate cell function.
- Eukaryotes transcribe DNA in the nucleus, remove its introns, and translate it in the cytoplasm. Bacteria transcribe and translate simultaneously because the DNA is not sequestered in a nucleus and the bacterial DNA is free of introns.
- Eukaryotic cells can use alternative splicing mechanisms and RNA editing to create diverse products from a single gene sequence.

9.3 Genetic Regulation of Protein Synthesis

- Genes can be turned "on" and "off" by specific molecules, which expose or hide their nucleotide codes for transcribing proteins.
- Operons are collections of genes in bacteria that code for products with a coordinated function.
- Nutrients can combine with regulator gene products to turn a set of structural genes on (inducible genes) or off (repressible genes). The *lac* (lactose) operon is an example of an inducible operon. The *arg* (arginine) operon is an example of a repressible operon.
- The rifamycins, tetracyclines, and aminoglycosides are classes of antibiotics that interfere with transcription and translation processes in microorganisms.

9.4 Mutations: Changes in the Genetic Code

- Changes in the genetic code can occur by two means: mutation and recombination. Mutation means a change in the nucleotide sequence of the organism's genome.
- Recombination means the addition of genes from an outside source, such as a virus or another cell.
- Mutations can be either spontaneous or induced by exposure to some external mutagenic agent.
- All cells have enzymes that repair damaged DNA. When the degree of damage exceeds the ability of the enzymes to make repairs, mutations occur.
- Mutation-induced changes in DNA nucleotide sequences range from a single nucleotide to addition or deletion of large sections of genetic material.

9.5 DNA Recombination Events

- Genetic recombination occurs in eukaryotes through sexual reproduction and through horizontal gene transfer.
- In bacteria, recombination occurs only through horizontal gene transfer.
- The three main types of horizontal gene transfer in bacteria are transformation, conjugation, and transduction.
- Transposons are genes that can relocate from one part of the genome to another, causing rearrangement of genetic material.
- Some of the horizontally transferred genes in bacteria are pathogenicity islands, which confer the ability to cause disease on their hosts.

Multiple-Choice and True-False Questions Knowledge and Comprehension

Multiple-Choice Questions. Select the correct answer from the answers provided.

1. What is the smallest unit of heredity?
   - a. chromosome
   - b. gene
   - c. codon
   - d. nucleotide

2. The nitrogen bases in DNA are bonded to the
   - a. phosphate.
   - b. deoxyribose.
   - c. ribose.
   - d. hydrogen.

3. DNA replication is semiconservative because the _____ strand will become half of the _____ molecule.
   a. RNA, DNA
   b. template, finished
   c. sense, mRNA
   d. codon, anticodon

4. In DNA, adenine is the complementary base for _____, and cytosine is the complement for _____.
   a. guanine, thymine
   b. uracil, guanine
   c. thymine, guanine
   d. thymine, uracil

5. Transfer RNA is the molecule that
   a. contributes to the structure of ribosomes.
   b. adapts the genetic code to protein structure.
   c. transfers the DNA code to mRNA.
   d. provides the master code for amino acids.

6. As a general rule, the template strand on DNA will always begin with
   a. TAC.
   b. AUG.
   c. ATG.
   d. UAC.

7. The *lac* operon is usually in the _____ position and is activated by a/an _____ molecule.
   a. on, repressor
   b. off, inducer
   c. on, inducer
   d. off, repressor

8. Which genes can be transferred by all three methods of horizontal gene transfer?
   a. capsule production
   b. toxin production
   c. F factor
   d. drug resistance

9. Which of the following would occur through specialized transduction?
   a. acquisition of Hfr plasmid
   b. transfer of genes for toxin production
   c. transfer of genes for capsule formation
   d. transfer of a plasmid with genes for degrading pesticides

10. When genes are turned on differently under different environmental conditions, this represents a change in
    a. species.
    b. genotype.
    c. phenotype.
    d. growth rate.

True-False Questions: If the statement is true, leave as is. If it is false, correct it by rewriting the sentence.

11. The DNA pairs are held together primarily by covalent bonds.

12. Mutation usually has a negative outcome.

13. The lagging strand of DNA is replicated in short pieces because DNA polymerase can synthesize in only one direction.

14. Messenger RNA is formed by translation of a gene on the DNA template strand.

15. A nucleotide is composed of a 5-carbon sugar, a phosphate group, and a nitrogenous base.

Critical Thinking Questions   Application and Analysis

These questions are suggested as a *writing-to-learn* experience. For each question, compose a one- or two-paragraph answer that includes the factual information needed to completely address the question.

1. Describe what is meant by the antiparallel arrangement of DNA.

2. On paper, replicate the following segment of DNA:
   5' A T C G G C T A C G T T C A C 3'
   3' T A G C C G A T G C A A G T G 5'
   a. Show the direction of replication of the new strands and explain what the lagging and leading strands are.
   b. Explain how this is semiconservative replication. Are the new strands identical to the original segment of DNA?

3. Name several characteristics of DNA structure that enable it to be replicated with such great fidelity generation after generation.

4. Explain the following relationship: DNA formats RNA, which makes protein. Now talk about what happens when RNA is the desired end product instead of protein.

5. Compare the structure and functions of DNA and RNA.

6. The following sequence represents triplets on DNA:
   TAC CAG ATA CAC TCC CCT GCG ACT
   a. Give the mRNA codons and tRNA anticodons that correspond with this sequence, and then give the sequence of amino acids in the polypeptide.

   b. Provide another mRNA strand that can be used to synthesize this same protein.
   c. Looking at figure 9.13, give the type and order of the amino acids in the peptide.

7. Using the piece of DNA in question 6, show a deletion, an insertion, a substitution, and nonsense mutations. Which ones are frameshift mutations? Are any of your mutations nonsense? Missense? (Use the universal code to determine this.)

8. a. Summarize how bacterial and eukaryotic cells differ in gene structure, transcription, and translation.
   b. Discuss the roles of exons and introns.

9. Knowing that retroviruses operate on the principle of reversing the direction of transcription from RNA to DNA, propose a drug that might possibly interfere with their replication.

10. The enzymes required to carry out transcription and translation are themselves produced through these same processes. Speculate which may have come first in evolution—proteins or nucleic acids—and explain your choice.

Concept Mapping   Synthesis

Appendix D provides guidance for working with concept maps.

1. Supply your own linking words or phrases in this concept map, and provide the missing concepts in the empty boxes.

2. Construct your own concept map using the following words as the *concepts*. Supply the linking words between each pair of concepts.

ribozyme	rRNA
primer	transcription
riboswitch	translation
mRNA	DNA
tRNA	

Visual Connections   Synthesis

These questions use visual images or previous content to make connections to this chapter's concepts.

1. **Figure 9.15, step 1.** Label each of the parts of the illustration.

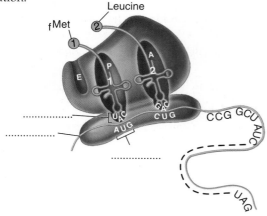

2. **From chapter 4, figure 4.7a.** Speculate on why these cells contain two chromosomes (shown in blue).

www.connect.microbiology.com

Enhance your study of this chapter with study tools and practice tests. Also ask your instructor about the resources available through ConnectPlus, including the media-rich eBook, interactive learning tools, and animations.

10

Genetic Engineering and Recombinant DNA

Case File 10

When the twin towers of the World Trade Center fell on the morning of September 11, 2001, every family affected by the attack asked the same question: "Did my loved one survive?" Weeks later, when the relative had not returned home, the answer should have been obvious. But it was only natural to hope that he or she might still walk in the door, especially since the devastation had left little concrete evidence. Starting in 2002, the New York City medical examiner's office began attempting to identify the human remains using tried-and-true methods of genetic analysis. However, these methods depend on relatively long pieces of undamaged human DNA, and little DNA of that description survived the catastrophic collapse and burn of the Trade Center. Frustrated with the slow pace of identification, officials decided to try two promising, but relatively unproven, experimental techniques.

- What methods of genetic analysis require only very small pieces of DNA rather than the longer pieces traditionally used?

- Where could investigators obtain—for purposes of comparison—DNA known to belong to a suspected victim of the World Trade Center disaster?

Continuing the Case appears on page 291.

Outline and Learning Outcomes

10.1 Basic Elements and Applications of Genetic Engineering
1. Provide examples of practical applications of genetic manipulation.

10.2 Tools and Techniques of Genetic Engineering
2. Explain the importance of restriction endonucleases to genetic engineering.
3. Describe how gel electrophoresis helps in the analysis of DNA.
4. Discuss Southern blots and how gene probes figure in them.
5. Outline the process of DNA sequencing.
6. List the steps in the polymerase chain reaction.

10.1 Basic Elements and Applications of Genetic Engineering

In chapter 9, we looked at the ways in which microorganisms duplicate, exchange, and use their genetic information. In scientific parlance, this is called **basic science** because no product or application is directly derived from it. Human beings being who they are, however, it is never long before basic knowledge is used to derive **applied science** or useful products and applications that owe their invention to the basic research that preceded them. As an example, basic science regarding the workings of the electron has led to the development of television, computers, and cell phones. None of these staples of modern life were envisioned when early physicists were deciphering the nature of subatomic particles, but without the knowledge of how electrons worked, our ability to harness them for our own uses never would have materialized.

The same scenario has played out with regard to genetics. The knowledge of how DNA was manipulated within the cell to carry out the goals of a microbe allowed scientists to utilize these processes to accomplish goals more to the liking of human beings. Contrary to being new ideas, the methods of genetic manipulation we will review are simply more efficient ways of accomplishing goals that humans have had for thousands of years.

Examples of human goals that have been more efficiently attained through the use of modern and not-so-modern genetic technologies can be seen in each of these scenarios:

1. A farmer mates his two largest pigs in the hopes of producing larger offspring. Unfortunately, he quite often ends up with small or unhealthy animals due to other genes that are transferred during mating. Genetic manipulation allows for the transfer of specific genes so that only advantageous traits are selected.

2. Courts have, for thousands of years, relied on a description of a person's phenotype (eye color, hair color, etc.) as a means of identification. By remembering that a phenotype is the product of a particular sequence of DNA, you can quickly see how looking at someone's DNA (perhaps from a drop of blood) gives a better clue as to his or her identification.

3. We have understood for a long time that many diseases are the result of a missing or dysfunctional protein, and we have generally treated the diseases by replacing the protein as best we can, usually resulting in only temporary relief and limited success. Examples include insulin-dependent diabetes, adenosine deaminase deficiency, and blood-clotting disorders. Genetic engineering offers the promise that fixing the underlying mutation responsible for the lack of a particular protein can treat these diseases far more successfully than we've been able to do in the past.

4. New results from whole-organism sequencing show us that RNA regulatory molecules might be even more useful in permanently "fixing" many diseases.

Information on genetic engineering and its biotechnological applications is growing at such an expanding rate that some new discovery or product is disclosed almost on a daily basis. To keep this subject somewhat manageable, we present essential concepts and applications, organized under the following six topics:

- Tools and Techniques of Genetic Engineering
- Methods in Recombinant DNA Technology
- Biochemical Products of Recombinant DNA Technology
- Genetically Modified Organisms
- Genetic Treatments
- Genome Analysis

10.1 Learning Outcomes—Can You ...

1. ... provide examples of practical applications of genetic manipulation?

10.2 Tools and Techniques of Genetic Engineering

DNA: The Raw Material

All of the intrinsic properties of DNA hold true whether the DNA is in a bacterium or a test tube. For example, the enzyme helicase is able to unwind the two strands of the double helix just as easily in the lab as it does in a bacterial cell. But in the laboratory we can take advantage of our knowledge of DNA chemistry to make helicase unnecessary. It turns out that when DNA is heated to just below boiling (90°C to 95°C), the two strands separate, revealing the information contained in their bases. With the nucleotides exposed, DNA can be more easily identified, replicated, or transcribed. If heat-denatured DNA is then slowly cooled, complementary nucleotides will hydrogen bond with one another and the strands will renature, or regain their familiar double-stranded form **(figure 10.1a)**. As we shall see, this process is a necessary feature of the polymerase chain reaction and in the application of nucleic acid probes described later.

Enzymes for Dicing, Splicing, and Reversing Nucleic Acids

The polynucleotide strands of DNA can also be clipped crosswise at selected positions by means of enzymes called **restriction endonucleases.**[1] These enzymes come from bacterial cells. They recognize foreign DNA and are capable of breaking the phosphodiester bonds between adjacent nucleotides on both strands of DNA, leading to a break in the DNA strand. In the bacterial cell, this ability protects against the incompatible DNA of bacteriophages or plasmids. In the biotechnologist's lab, the enzymes can be used to cleave DNA at desired sites and are necessary for the techniques of recombinant DNA technology.

So far, hundreds of restriction endonucleases have been discovered in bacteria. Each type has a known sequence of 4 to 10 base pairs as its target, so sites of cutting can be finely controlled. These enzymes have the unique property of rec-

---

1. The meaning of restriction is that the enzymes do not act upon the bacterium's own DNA; an *endo*nuclease nicks DNA internally, not at the ends.

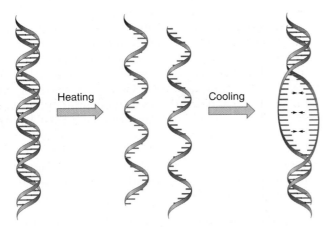

(a) DNA heating and cooling. DNA responds to heat by denaturing—losing its hydrogen bonding and thereby separating into its two strands. When cooled, the two strands rejoin at complementary regions. The two strands need not be from the same organism as long as they have matching sites.

Endonuclease	*Eco*RI	*Hind*III	*Hae*III
Cutting pattern	G A A T T C C T T A A G	A A G C T T T T C G A A	G G C C C C G G

(b) Examples of palindromes and cutting patterns.

(c) Action of restriction endonucleases. (1) A restriction endonuclease recognizes and cleaves DNA at the site of a specific palindromic sequence. Cleavage can produce staggered tails called sticky ends that accept complementary tails for gene splicing. (2) The sticky ends can be used to join DNA from different organisms by cutting it with the same restriction enzyme, ensuring that all fragments have complementary ends.

Figure 10.1 Some useful properties of DNA.

ognizing and clipping at base sequences called **palindromes (figure 10.1b).** Palindromes are sequences of DNA that are identical when read from the 5′ to 3′ direction on one strand and the 5′ to 3′ direction on the other strand.

Endonucleases are usually named by combining the first letter of the bacterial genus, the first two letters of the species, and the endonuclease number. Thus, *Eco*RI is the first endonuclease found in *Escherichia coli* (in the R strain), and *Hind*III is the third endonuclease discovered in *Haemophilus influenzae* Type d (see figure 10.1b).

Endonucleases are used in the laboratory to cut DNA into smaller pieces for further study as well as to remove and insert sequences during recombinant DNA techniques, described in a subsequent section. Endonucleases such as *Hae*III make straight, blunt cuts on DNA. But more often, the enzymes make staggered symmetrical cuts that leave short tails called "sticky ends." The enzymes cut four to five bases on the 3′ strand, and four to five bases on the 5′ strand, leaving overhangs on each end. Such adhesive tails will base-pair with complementary tails on other DNA fragments or plasmids **(figure 10.1c).** This effect makes it possible to splice genes into specific sites.

The pieces of DNA produced by restriction endonucleases are termed **restriction fragments.** Because DNA sequences vary, even among members of the same species, differences in the cutting pattern of specific restriction endonucleases give rise to restriction fragments of differing lengths, known as **restriction fragment length polymorphisms (RFLPs).** RFLPs allow the direct comparison of the DNA of two different organisms at a specific site, which, as we will see, has many uses.

Another enzyme, called a **ligase,** is necessary to seal the sticky ends together by rejoining the phosphate-sugar bonds cut by endonucleases. Its main application is in final splicing of genes into plasmids and chromosomes.

An enzyme called **reverse transcriptase** is best known for its role in the replication of the AIDS virus and other retroviruses. It also provides geneticists with a valuable tool for converting RNA into DNA. Copies called **complementary DNA,** or **cDNA,** can be made from messenger, transfer, ribosomal, and other forms of RNA. The technique provides a valuable means of synthesizing eukaryotic genes from mRNA transcripts **(figure 10.2).** The advantage is that the synthesized gene will be free of the intervening sequences (introns) that can complicate the management of eukaryotic and archaeal genes in genetic engineering.

Analysis of DNA

One way to produce a readable pattern of DNA fragments is through **gel electrophoresis.** In this technique, samples are placed in compartments (wells) in a soft agar gel and subjected to an electrical current. The phosphate groups in DNA give the entire molecule an overall negative charge, which causes the DNA to move toward the positive pole in

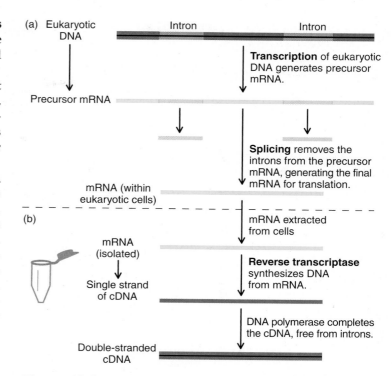

Figure 10.2 Making cDNA from eukaryotic mRNA.
In order for eukaryotic genes to be expressed by a prokaryotic cell, a copy of DNA without introns must be cloned. The cDNA encodes the same protein as the original DNA but lacks introns.

the gel. The rate of movement is based primarily on the size of the fragments. The larger fragments move more slowly and remain nearer the top of the gel, whereas the smaller fragments migrate faster and are positioned farther from the wells. The positions of DNA fragments are determined by staining the DNA fragments in the gel **(figure 10.3).** Electrophoresis patterns can be quite distinctive and are very useful in characterizing DNA fragments and comparing the degree of genetic similarities among samples as in a genetic fingerprint (discussed later).

Nucleic Acid Hybridization and Probes

Two different nucleic acids can **hybridize** by uniting at their complementary regions. All different combinations are possible: Single-stranded DNA can unite with other single-stranded DNA or RNA, and RNA can hybridize with other RNA. This property has allowed for the development of specially formulated tracers called **gene probes.** These probes consist of a short stretch of DNA of a known sequence that will base-pair with a stretch of DNA with a complementary sequence, if one exists in the test sample. Hybridization probes have practical value because they can detect specific nucleotide sequences in unknown samples. So that areas of hybridization can be visualized, the probes carry reporter

Figure 10.3 Revealing the patterns of DNA with electrophoresis. (a) After cleavage into fragments, DNA is loaded into wells on one end of an agarose gel. When an electrical current is passed through the gel (from the negative pole to the positive pole), the DNA, being negatively charged, migrates toward the positive pole. The larger fragments, measured in numbers of base pairs, migrate more slowly and remain nearer the wells than the smaller (shorter) fragments. (b) An actual stained gel reveals a separation pattern of the fragments of DNA. The size of a given DNA band can be determined by comparing the distance it traveled to the distance traveled by a set of DNA fragments of known size (lane 5).

molecules such as radioactive labels, which are isotopes that emit radiation, or luminescent labels, which give off visible light. Reactions can be revealed by placing photographic film in contact with the test reaction. Fluorescent probes contain dyes that can be visualized with ultraviolet radiation, and enzyme-linked probes react with substrate to release colored dyes.

When probes hybridize with an unknown sample of DNA or RNA, they tag the precise area and degree of hybridization and help determine the nature of nucleic acid present in a sample. In a method called the **Southern blot,**[2] DNA fragments are first separated by electrophoresis and then denatured and transferred to a special filter. A DNA probe is then incubated with the sample, and wherever this probe encounters the segment for which it is complementary, it will attach and form a hybrid. Development of the hybridization pattern will show up as one or more bands **(figure 10.4).** This method is a sensitive and specific way to isolate fragments from a complex mixture and to find specific gene sequences on DNA. The Southern

blot is also one of the important first steps for preparing isolated genes.

Probes are commonly used for diagnosing the cause of an infection from a patient's specimen and identifying a culture of an unknown bacterium or virus. A simple and rapid method called a hybridization test does not require electrophoresis. DNA from a test sample is isolated, denatured, placed on an absorbent filter, and combined with a microbe-specific probe **(figure 10.5).** The blot is then developed and observed for areas of hybridization. Commercially available diagnostic kits are now on the market for identifying intestinal pathogens such as *Salmonella, Campylobacter, Shigella, Clostridium difficile,* rotaviruses, and adenoviruses. Other bacterial probes exist for *Mycobacterium, Legionella, Mycoplasma,* and *Chlamydia;* viral probes are available for herpes simplex and zoster, papilloma (genital warts), hepatitis A and B, and AIDS. DNA probes have also been developed for human genetic markers and some types of cancer.

With another method, called **fluorescent *in situ* hybridization (FISH),** probes are applied to intact cells and observed microscopically for the presence and location of specific genetic marker sequences on genes. It is a very effective way to locate genes on chromosomes. *In situ* techniques can also

2. Named for its developer, E. M. Southern. The "northern" blot is a similar method used to analyze RNA, while the Western blot detects proteins.

① DNA samples are cut with restriction enzymes and loaded on agarose gel for electrophoresis.

Lane 1: Labeled size markers
Lane 2: DNA cut with restriction enzyme A
Lane 3: DNA with restriction enzyme B

Gel electrophoresis

DNA is denatured; gel is placed on sponge wick.

② DNA is separated by electrophoresis and visualized by staining and photography in UV light. (When large amounts of DNA are added to a well, it can only be seen as a smear rather than distinct bands.)

Weight
Paper towels
DNA-binding filter
Gel
Wick (sponge)
Buffer

③ DNA-binding filter, paper towels, and weight are placed on gel. Buffer passes upward by capillary action transferring DNA fragments to filter.

④ Filter is placed in heat-sealed food bag with solution containing radioactive probe.

Overlay filter with X-ray film

1 2 3
Developed X-ray film with DNA bands

⑤ Filter is washed to remove excess probe, then dried. Film is then exposed to produce photographic image of DNA bands.

Process Figure 10.4 Conducting a Southern blot hybridization test. The five-step process reveals the hybridized fragments on the X-ray film.

Master plate with colonies of bacteria containing cloned segments of foreign genes

Filter membrane

① Make replica of master plate on nitrocellulose filter.

② Treat filter with detergent to lyse bacteria.

Strands of bacterial DNA

③ Treat filter with sodium hydroxide (NaOH) to separate DNA into single strands.

Probes labeled with luminescence

④ Add probes labeled with luminescence.

Bound DNA probe — Gene of interest
Single-stranded DNA

⑤ Probe will hybridize with desired gene from bacterial cells.

Developed film

⑥ Wash filter to remove unbound probe and expose filter to X-ray film.

Colonies containing genes of interest

⑦ Developed film is compared with replica of master plate to identify colonies containing gene of interest.

Replica plate

Process Figure 10.5 A hybridization test relies on the action of microbe-specific probes to identify an unknown bacterium or virus.

INSIGHT 10.1   OK, the Genome's Sequenced—What's Next?

In early 2001, a press conference was held to announce that the human genome had been sequenced. The 3.1 billion base pairs that make up the DNA found in (nearly) every human cell had been identified and put in the proper order. Champagne corks popped, balloons fell, bands played, reporters reported on the significance of the occasion. Here for your perusal are a few FAQs.

Q: Who sequenced the genome?

A: Francis Collins was the head of the publicly funded Human Genome Project (HGP), while Craig Venter was the head of Celera Genomics, a private company that developed a new, more powerful method of DNA sequencing and competed with the HGP. A compromise was finally reached whereby both groups took credit for sequencing the genome.

Q: How big was this project?

A: The Human Genome Project was first discussed in the mid-1980s and got under way in 1990. Although the project was to have taken at least 15 years, advances in technology led to its being completed in just over 10. The 3.1 billion base pairs of DNA code for only about 20,000 to 25,000 genes, not the 100,000 or so that the genome was thought to contain only a few years ago.

Q: Will I ever see any benefits from this project?

A: Absolutely. Sequencing the genome was only the first step. Knowing what proteins are produced in the body, what they do, and how they interact with one another are essential to understanding the workings of the human body, in both health and disease. By knowing the genetic signatures of different diseases, we will be able to design extraordinarily sensitive diagnostic tests that detect not only a disease but particular subtypes of each malady. With a precise genetic identification of, for example, a tumor, treatment can be tailored to be as effective as possible, while dramatically reducing side effects.

Q: What's next?

A: The regulatory regions are the current area of excitement. The thinking is that areas within genes that are similar in mice and humans (known as regions of homology) are most important for the function of the gene and are the most likely targets for potential drugs or genetic treatments.

Q: Were there any surprises?

A: After the human genome was sequenced, a variety of other genomes were also sequenced. The information from all of these organisms revealed that the most important sequences may well be the ones in between the protein-coding genes. These regions regulate the genes.

Q: Where could I go to check out a really cool website on the human genome?

A: www.ornl.gov/hgmis/

Craig Venter, left, and Francis Collins celebrate mapping of the human genome.

be used to identify unknown bacteria living in natural habitats without having to culture them, and they can be used to detect RNA in cells and tissues.

Methods Used to Size, Synthesize, and Sequence DNA

The relative sizes of nucleic acids are usually denoted by the number of base pairs (bp) or nucleotides they contain. For example, the palindromic sequences recognized by endonucleases are usually 4 to 10 bp in length; an average gene in *E. coli* is approximately 1,300 bp, or 1.3 kilobases (kb); and its entire genome is approximately 4,700,000 bp, or 4,700 kb, or 4.7 megabases (Mb). The DNA of the human mitochondrion contains 16 kb, and the Epstein-Barr virus (a cause of infectious mononucleosis)

has 172 kb. Humans have approximately 3.1 billion base pairs arrayed along 46 chromosomes. The Human Genome Project had as its goal the description of the entire human genome **(Insight 10.1).**

DNA Sequencing: Determining the Exact Genetic Code Analysis of DNA by its size, restriction patterns, and hybridization characteristics is instructive, but the most detailed information comes from determining the actual order and types of bases in DNA. This process, called **DNA sequencing,** provides the identity and order of nucleotides for all types of DNA, including genomic, cDNA, artificial chromosomes, plasmids, and cloned genes. The most common sequencing technique was developed by Frederick Sanger and is based on the synthesis and analysis of a complementary strand of DNA in a test tube **(figure 10.6).**

① Isolated unknown DNA fragment

Original DNA to be sequenced

② DNA is denatured to produce single template strand.

③ Strand is labeled with specific primer molecule.

④ DNA polymerase and regular nucleotide mixture (ATP, CTP, GTP, and TTP) are added; ddG, ddA, ddC, and ddT are placed in separate reaction tubes with the regular nucleotides.

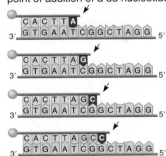

⑤ Newly replicated strands are terminated at the point of addition of a dd nucleotide.

⑥ A schematic view of how all possible positions on the fragment are occupied by a labeled nucleotide.

⑦ Running the reaction tubes in four separate gel lanes separates them by size and nucleotide type. They are visible because some sort of tracer was added during step 4. Reading from bottom to top, one base at a time, provides the correct DNA sequence.

(a)

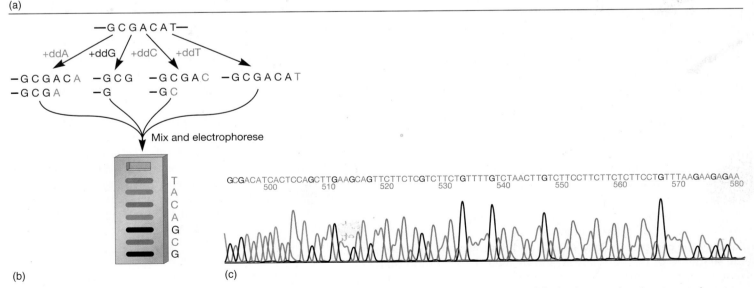

(b)

(c)

Process Figure 10.6 Steps in a Sanger DNA sequence technique. (a) Steps 1–6 are used for both manual and automated sequencing. Step 7 shows preparation of a gel for manual sequencing in which radiolabeled ddNTPs are used. (b) Part of an automated DNA sequencing run. Here the ddNTPs are labeled with fluorescent dyes. (c) Data generated during an automated DNA sequencing run.

The Sanger method has been modified to adapt to high-speed automated techniques, but we will describe the original method first since it makes it easier to visualize the outcomes of all sequencing methods.

The Sanger Method Because most DNA being sequenced is very long, it is made more manageable by cutting it into a large number of shorter fragments and separating them. The test strands, typically several hundred nucleotides long, are then denatured to expose single strands that will serve as templates to synthesize complementary strands. The fragments are divided into four separate tubes that contain primers to set the start point for the synthesis to begin on one of the strands. Primers are short strings of nulceotides, up to 20 bases long, that hybridize with the separated strand of DNA and allow DNA polymerase to start adding new bases. These take the place of RNA primers that would normally be synthesized by primase (in the cell). The primer is labeled with a fluorescent or radioactive tag, which allows it to be detected. The nucleotides will attach at the 3′ end of the primer, using the template strands as a guide, essentially the same way that DNA synthesis occurs in a cell.

The tubes are incubated with the necessary DNA polymerase and all four of the regular nucleotides needed to carry out the process of elongating the complementary strand. Each tube also contains a single type (A, T, G, or C) of dideoxynucleotide (dd), which is critical to the sequencing process. Dideoxynucleotides have no oxygen bound to the 3′ carbon of deoxyribose. This oxygen atom is needed for the chemical attachment of the next nucleotide in the growing DNA strand. As the reaction proceeds, strands elongate by adding normal nucleotides, but a small percentage of fragments will randomly incorporate the complementary dideoxynucleotide and be terminated. Eventually, all possible positions in the sequence will incorporate a terminal dideoxynucleotide, thus producing a series of strands that reflect the correct sequence.

The reaction products are placed into four wells (G, C, A, T) of a polyacrylamide gel **(figure 10.6a)**, which is sensitive enough to separate strands that differ by only a single nucleotide in length. Electrophoresis separates the fragments in order according to both size and lane, and only the fragments carrying the labeled nucleotides will be readable on the gel. The gel indicates the comparative orientation of the bases, which graduate in size from the smallest fragments that terminate early and migrate farthest (bottom of gel) to successively longer fragments (moving stepwise to the top). Reading the order of first appearance of a given gel fragment in the G, C, A, or T lanes provides the correct sequence of bases of the complementary strand, and it allows one to infer the sequence of the template strand as well. This method of sequencing is remarkably accurate, with only about one mistake in every 1,000 bases.

This process has been modified so that it can be automated, which makes it much faster and much cheaper.

When you can use an automated sequencer you can put all of the chain-terminating ddNTPs in a single reaction mixture, and just label them with different fluorescent colors. The resultant strands are run on a single gel and the computer reads the gel and provides a graph that gives the sequence of bases **(figure 10.6b)**. Automation of this process was absolutely necessary for sequencing the entire genomes of humans, mice, and other organisms (see Insight 10.1).

Polymerase Chain Reaction: A Molecular Xerox Machine for DNA

Some of the techniques used to analyze DNA and RNA are limited by the small amounts of test nucleic acid available. This problem was largely solved by the invention of a simple, versatile way to amplify DNA called the **polymerase chain reaction (PCR).** This technique rapidly increases the amount of DNA in a sample without the need for making cultures or carrying out complex purification techniques. It is so sensitive that it holds the potential to detect cancer from a single cell or to diagnose an infection from a single gene copy. It is comparable to being able to pluck a single DNA "needle" out of a "haystack" of other molecules and make unlimited copies of the DNA. The rapid rate of PCR makes it possible to replicate a target DNA from a few copies to billions of copies in a few hours.

To understand the idea behind PCR, it will be instructive to review figure 9.6, which describes synthesis of DNA as it occurs naturally in cells. The PCR method uses essentially the same events, with the opening up of the double strand, using the exposed strands as templates, the addition of primers, and the action of a DNA polymerase.

Initiating the reaction requires a few specialized ingredients **(figure 10.7)**. As we saw earlier, the primers are synthetic oligonucleotides (short DNA strands) of a known sequence of 15 to 30 bases that serve as landmarks to indicate where DNA amplification will begin. To keep the DNA strands separated, processing must be carried out at a relatively high temperature. This necessitates the use of special **DNA polymerases** isolated from thermophilic bacteria. Examples of these unique enzymes are Taq polymerase obtained from *Thermus aquaticus* (see Insight 7.2) and Vent polymerase from *Thermococcus litoralis.* Enzymes isolated from these thermophilic organisms remain active at the elevated temperatures used in PCR. Another useful component of PCR is a machine called a thermal cycler that automatically performs the cyclic temperature changes.

The PCR technique operates by repetitive cycling of three basic steps: denaturation, priming, and extension.

1. **Denaturation.** The first step involves heating target DNA to 94°C to separate it into two strands. Next, the

(a) In cycle 1, the DNA to be amplified is denatured, primed, and replicated by a polymerase that can function at high temperature. The two resulting strands then serve as templates for a second cycle of denaturation, priming, and synthesis.*

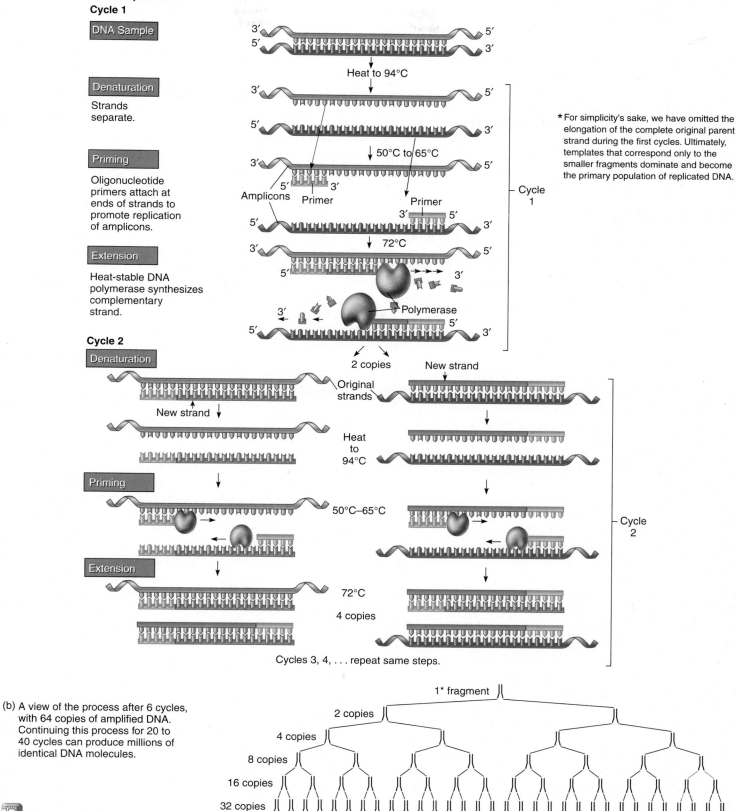

Cycle 1

DNA Sample

Heat to 94°C

Denaturation

Strands separate.

*For simplicity's sake, we have omitted the elongation of the complete original parent strand during the first cycles. Ultimately, templates that correspond only to the smaller fragments dominate and become the primary population of replicated DNA.

Priming

Oligonucleotide primers attach at ends of strands to promote replication of amplicons.

Amplicons   Primer   Primer

Extension

Heat-stable DNA polymerase synthesizes complementary strand.

Polymerase

Cycle 2

Denaturation

2 copies   New strand

Original strands

New strand

Heat to 94°C

Priming

50°C–65°C

Extension

72°C

4 copies

Cycles 3, 4, . . . repeat same steps.

(b) A view of the process after 6 cycles, with 64 copies of amplified DNA. Continuing this process for 20 to 40 cycles can produce millions of identical DNA molecules.

1* fragment

2 copies

4 copies

8 copies

16 copies

32 copies

64 copies

Figure 10.7 The polymerase chain reaction.

system is cooled to between 50°C and 65°C, depending on the exact nucleotide sequence of the primer.

2. **Priming.** Primers are added in a concentration that favors binding to the complementary strand of test DNA. This reaction prepares the two DNA strands, now called **amplicons,** for synthesis.

3. **Extension.** In the third phase, which proceeds at 72°C, DNA polymerase and raw materials in the form of nucleotides are added. Beginning at the free end of the primers on both strands, the polymerases extend the molecule by adding appropriate nucleotides and produce two complete strands of DNA.

It is through cyclic repetition of these steps that DNA becomes amplified. When the DNAs formed in the first cycle are denatured, they become amplicons to be primed and extended in the second cycle. Each subsequent cycle converts the new DNAs to amplicons and doubles the number of copies. The number of cycles required to produce a million molecules is 20, but the process is usually carried out to 30 or 40 cycles. One significant advantage of this technique has been its natural adaptability to automation. A PCR machine can perform 20 cycles on nearly 100 samples in 2 or 3 hours.

Once the PCR is complete, the amplified DNA can be analyzed by any of the techniques discussed earlier. A newer technique, called real-time PCR, can detect products during the reaction instead of at the end. PCR can be adapted to analyze RNA by initially converting an RNA sample to DNA with reverse transcriptase. This cDNA can then be amplified by PCR in the usual manner. It is by such means that ribosomal RNA and messenger RNA are readied for sequencing. The polymerase chain reaction has found prominence as a powerful workhorse of molecular biology, medicine, and biotechnology. It often plays an essential role in gene mapping, the study of genetic defects and cancer, forensics, taxonomy, and evolutionary studies.

For all of its advantages, PCR has some problems. A serious concern is the introduction and amplification of nontarget DNA from the surrounding environment, such as a skin cell from the technician carrying out the PCR reaction rather than material from the sample DNA that was supposed to be amplified. Such contamination can be minimized by using equipment and rooms dedicated for DNA analysis and maintained with the utmost degree of cleanliness. Problems with contaminants can also be reduced by using gene-specific primers and newer techniques such as nested PCR, which employs two primers instead on one.

10.2 Learning Outcomes—Can You . . .

2. . . . explain the importance of restriction endonucleases to genetic engineering?

3. . . . describe how gel electrophoresis helps in the analysis of DNA?

4. . . . discuss Southern blots and how gene probes figure in them?

5. . . . outline the process of DNA sequencing?

6. . . . list the steps in the polymerase chain reaction?

10.3 Methods in Recombinant DNA Technology: How to Imitate Nature

The primary intent of **recombinant DNA technology** is to deliberately remove genetic material from one organism and combine it with that of a different organism. Its origins can be traced to 1970, when microbiologists first began to duplicate the clever tricks bacteria do naturally with bits of extra DNA such as plasmids, transposons, and proviruses. As mentioned earlier, humans have been trying to artificially influence genetic transmission of traits for centuries. The discovery that bacteria can readily accept, replicate, and express foreign DNA made them powerful agents for studying the genes of other organisms in isolation. The practical applications of this work were soon realized by biotechnologists. Bacteria could be genetically engineered to mass produce substances such as hormones, enzymes, and vaccines that were difficult to synthesize by the usual industrial methods.

Figure 10.8 provides an overview of the recombinant DNA procedure. An important objective of this technique is to form genetic **clones.** Cloning involves the removal of a selected gene from an animal, plant, or microorganism (the genetic donor) followed by its propagation in a different host organism. Cloning requires that the desired donor gene first be selected, excised by restriction endonucleases, and isolated. The gene is next inserted into a **vector** (usually a plasmid or a virus) that will insert the DNA into a **cloning host.** The cloning host is usually a bacterium or a yeast that can replicate the gene and translate it into the protein product for which it codes. In the next section, we examine the elements of gene isolation, vectors, and cloning hosts and show how they participate in a complete recombinant DNA procedure.

Technical Aspects of Recombinant DNA and Gene Cloning

The first hurdles in cloning a target gene are to locate its exact site on the genetic donor's chromosome and to isolate it. Among the most common strategies for obtaining genes in an isolated state are:

1. The DNA is removed from cells and separated into fragments by endonucleases. Each fragment is then inserted into a vector and cloned. The cloned fragments undergo

Nucleus

Human, other mammal, microorganism, or plant cell identified.

DNA of interest is isolated.

DNA of interest is inserted into a cloning vector.

Cloning host receives vector, becomes a recombinant (may be a microbe used as a factory for the DNA or its expressed protein or an organism meant to be genetically altered, such as a plant).

Multiplication of cloning host is reproduced to amplify gene.

Cloning host translates foreign DNA into protein.

Cloning host provides abundant DNA for easy study.

Protein production
Pharmaceutical proteins
• insulin
• human growth hormone
Vaccines
• hepatitis B

Altered organisms with economically useful traits
Transgenic plants
• pest resistance
• herbicide resistance
• improved nutritional value

A source of DNA for study
Gene regulation
Gene function
Nucleotide sequencing

Figure 10.8 Methods and applications of genetic technology.   Practical applications of genetic engineering include the development of pharmaceuticals, genetically modified organisms, and forensic techniques.

A Note About Clones

Like so many words in biology, the word "clone" has two different, although related, meanings. In this chapter we will discuss genetic clones created within microorganisms. What we are cloning is *genes*. We use microorganisms to allow us to manipulate and replicate genes outside of the original host of that gene. You are much more likely to be familiar with the other type of cloning—which we will call whole-organism cloning. It is also known as reproductive cloning. This is the process of creating an identical organism using the DNA from an original. Dolly the sheep was the first cloned whole organism, and many others followed in her wake. These processes are beyond the scope of this book.

Southern blotting and are probed to identify desired sequences. This is a long and tedious process, because each fragment of DNA must be examined for the cloned gene.

2. A gene can be synthesized from isolated mRNA transcripts using reverse transcriptase (cDNA).

3. A gene can be amplified using PCR in many cases.

Although gene cloning and isolation can be very laborious, a fortunate outcome is that, once isolated, genes can be maintained in a cloning host and vector just like a microbial pure culture. **Genomic libraries** are collections of DNA clones that represent the entire genome of numerous organisms.

Cloning Vectors

Genes in isolation are not easily manipulated in the lab. They are typically spliced into a cloning vector, using restriction enzymes. Plasmids are excellent vectors because they are small, well characterized, easy to manipulate, and can be transferred into appropriate host cells through transformation. Bacteriophages also serve well because they have the natural ability to inject DNA into bacterial hosts through transduction. A common vector in early work was an *E. coli* plasmid that carries genetic markers for resistance to antibiotics, although it is restricted by the relatively small amount of foreign DNA it can accept. A modified phage vector, the *Charon*[3] phage, is missing large sections of its genome, so it can carry a fairly large segment of foreign DNA. The simple plasmids and bacteriophages that were a staple of early recombinant DNA methodologies evolved into newer, more advanced vectors. Today, thousands of unique cloning vectors are available commercially. Although every vector has characteristics that make it ideal for a specific project, all

---

3. Named for the mythical boatman in Hades who carried souls across the River Styx.

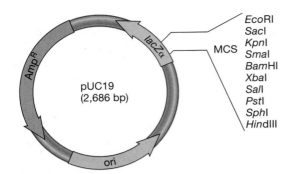

Figure 10.9 The cloning vector pUC19. The origin or replication is in yellow and the ampicillin-resistance gene is in tan.

vectors can be thought of as having three important attributes to consider **(figure 10.9):**

1. An origin of replication (ORI) is needed somewhere on the vector so that it will be replicated by the DNA polymerase of the cloning host.
2. The vector must accept DNA of the desired size. Early plasmids were limited to an insert size of less than 10 kb of DNA, far too small for most eukaryotic genes, with their sizable introns. Vectors called cosmids can hold 45 kb while complex **bacterial artificial chromosomes (BACs)** and **yeast artificial chromosomes (YACs)** can hold as much as 300 kb and 1,000 kb, respectively.
3. Vectors typically contain a gene that confers drug resistance to their cloning host. In this way, cells can be grown on drug-containing media, and only those cells that harbor a plasmid will be selected for growth.

Many vectors also have a site called a multicloning site (MCS), a region of DNA that is recognized by a wide variety of restriction enzymes.

Cloning Hosts

The best cloning hosts possess several key characteristics **(table 10.1).** The traditional cloning host is *Escherichia coli.*

Table 10.1	Desirable Features in a Microbial Cloning Host
Rapid turnover, fast growth rate	
Can be grown in large quantities using ordinary culture methods	
Nonpathogenic	
Genome that is well delineated (mapped)	
Capable of accepting plasmid or bacteriophage vectors	
Maintains foreign genes through multiple generations	
Will secrete a high yield of proteins from expressed foreign genes	

Because this bacterium was the original recombinant host, the protocols using it are well established, relatively easy, and reliable. Hundreds of specialized cloning vectors have been developed for it. The main disadvantage with this species is that the splicing of mRNA as well as the modification of proteins that would normally occur in the eukaryotic endoplasmic reticulum and Golgi apparatus are unavailable in this prokaryotic cloning host. One alternative host for certain industrial processes and research is the yeast *Saccharomyces cerevisiae,* which, being eukaryotic, already possesses mechanisms for processing and modifying eukaryotic gene products. Certain techniques may also employ different bacteria (*Bacillus subtilis*), animal cell cultures, and even live animals and plants to serve as cloning hosts. In our coverage, we present the recombinant process as it is performed in bacteria and yeasts.

Construction of a Recombinant, Insertion into a Cloning Host, and Genetic Expression

This section illustrates one example of recombinant DNA technology, in this case, to produce a drug called alpha-2a interferon (Roferon-A). This form of interferon is used to treat chronic hepatitis C (described in chapter 22) and cancers such as hairy-cell leukemia and Kaposi's sarcoma in AIDS patients (described in chapter 20). The human alpha interferon gene is a DNA molecule of approximately 500 bp that codes for a polypeptide of 166 amino acids. It was originally isolated and identified from human blood cells and prepared from processed mRNA transcripts that are free of introns. This step is necessary because the bacterial cloning host has none of the machinery needed to excise this nontranslated part of a gene.

The first step in cloning is to prepare the isolated interferon gene for splicing into an *E. coli* plasmid **(figure 10.10).** One way this is accomplished is to digest both the gene and the plasmid with the same restriction enzyme, resulting in complementary sticky ends on both the vector and the inserted DNA. In the presence of the endonuclease, the plasmid's circular molecule is nicked open and its sticky ends are exposed. When the gene and plasmid are placed together, their free ends base-pair, and a ligase makes the final covalent bonds. The resultant gene and plasmid combination is called a **recombinant.**

Following this procedure, the recombinant is introduced by transformation into the cloning host, a special laboratory strain of *E. coli* that lacks any extra plasmids that could complicate the expression of the gene. Because the recombinant plasmid enters only some of the cloning host cells, it is necessary to locate these recombinant clones. Cultures are plated out on medium containing ampicillin, and only those clones that carry the plasmid

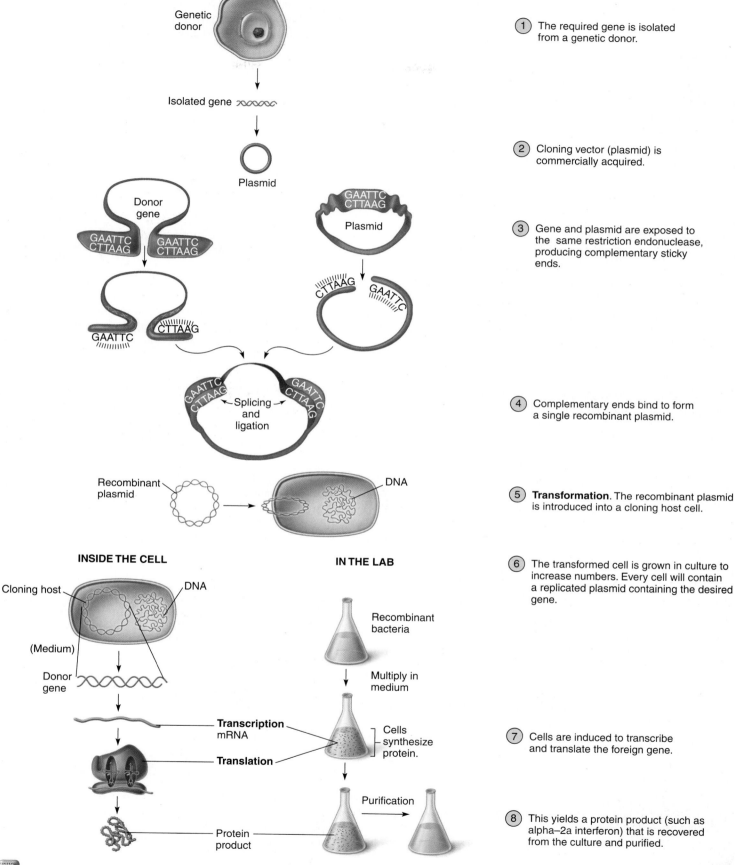

Process Figure 10.10 Using recombinant DNA for gene cloning.

with ampicillin resistance can form colonies **(figure 10.11)**. These recombinant colonies are selected from the plates and cultured. As the cells multiply, the plasmid is replicated along with the cell's chromosome. In a few hours of growth, there can be billions of cells, each containing the interferon gene. Once the gene has been successfully cloned and tested, this step does not have to be repeated—the recombinant strain can be maintained in culture for production purposes.

The bacteria's ability to express the eukaryotic gene is ensured, because the plasmid has been modified with the necessary transcription and translation recognition sequences. As the *E. coli* culture grows, it transcribes and translates the interferon gene, synthesizes the peptide, and secretes it into the growth medium. At the end of the process, the cloning cells and other chemical and microbial impurities are removed from the medium. Final processing to excise a terminal amino acid from the peptide yields the interferon product in a relatively pure form (see figure 10.10). The scale of this procedure can range from test tube size to gigantic industrial vats that can manufacture thousands of gallons of product (see chapter 25).

Although the process we have presented here produces interferon, some variation of it can be used to mass produce a variety of hormones, enzymes, and agricultural products such as pesticides. Recent advances even allow scientists to produce functions that weren't originally present in the bio-logical world. For instance, scientists are attempting to create microbes that produce hydrogen as fuel. Engineering new genetic capabilities is called **synthetic biology.**

10.3 Learning Outcomes—Can You ...

7. ... describe how you can clone a gene into a bacterium?
8. ... define recombinant in the context of this chapter?

10.4 Biochemical Products of Recombinant DNA Technology

Recombinant DNA technology is used by pharmaceutical companies to manufacture medications that cannot be manufactured by any other means. Diseases such as diabetes and dwarfism, caused by the lack of an essential hormone, are treated by replacing the missing hormone. Insulin of animal origin was once the only form available to treat diabetes, even though such animal products can cause allergic reactions in sensitive individuals. In contrast, dwarfism cannot be treated with animal growth hormones, so originally the only source of human growth hormone (HGH) was the pituitaries of cadavers. At one time, not enough HGH was available to treat the thousands of children in need. Another serious problem with using natural human products is the potential

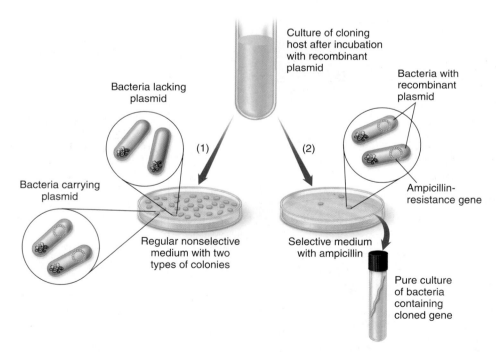

Figure 10.11 One method for screening clones of bacteria that have been transformed with the donor gene. (1) Plating the culture on nonselective medium will not separate the transformed cells from normal cells, which lack the plasmid. (2) Plating on selective medium containing ampicillin will permit only cells containing the plasmid to multiply. Colonies growing on this medium that carry the cloned gene can be used to make a culture for gene libraries, industrial production, and other processes. (Plasmids are shown disproportionate to size of cell.)

for infection. For example, infectious agents such as the prion responsible for Creutzfeldt-Jakob disease, described in chapter 19, can be transmitted in this manner. Similarly, clotting factor VIII, a protein needed for blood to clot properly, is missing in persons suffering from hemophilia A. Persons lacking factor VIII have received periodic injections of the missing protein, which historically had been collected from blood plasma. While the donated protein alleviated the symptoms of factor VIII deficiency, a tragic side effect was seen in the early 1980s, when a large percentage of the patients receiving plasma-derived factor VIII contracted HIV infections as a result of being exposed to the virus through the donated plasma.

Recombinant DNA technology changed the outcome of these and many other conditions by enabling large-scale manufacture of lifesaving hormones and enzymes of human origin. Recombinant human insulin can now be prescribed for diabetics, and recombinant HGH can now be administered to children with dwarfism and other conditions. HGH is also used to prevent the wasting syndrome that occurs in AIDS and cancer patients. In all of these applications, recombinant DNA technology has led to both a safer product and one that can be manufactured in quantities previously unfathomable. Other protein-based hormones, enzymes, and vaccines produced through recombinant DNA technology are summarized in **table 10.2**.

Nucleic acid products also have a number of medical applications. A new development in vaccine formulation involves using microbial DNA as a stimulus for the immune system. So far, animal tests using DNA vaccines for AIDS and influenza indicate that this may be a breakthrough in vaccine design. Recombinant DNA could also be used to produce DNA-based drugs for the types of gene and antisense therapy discussed in the genetic treatments section.

10.4 Learning Outcomes—Can You ...

9. ... provide several examples of recombinant products that have contributed to human health?

10.5 Genetically Modified Organisms

Recombinant organisms produced through the introduction of foreign genes are called **transgenic** or genetically modified organisms (GMOs). Foreign genes have been inserted into a variety of microbes, plants, and animals through recombinant DNA techniques developed especially for them. Transgenic "designer" organisms are available for a variety of biotechnological applications.

Table 10.2 Examples of Current Protein Products from Recombinant DNA Technology

Immune Treatments

Interferons—peptides used to treat some types of cancer, multiple sclerosis, and viral infections such as hepatitis and genital warts
Interleukins—types of cytokines that regulate the immune function of white blood cells; used in cancer treatment
Granulocyte-macrophage-colony-stimulating factor (GM-CSF)—used to stimulate bone marrow activity after bone marrow grafts
Tumor necrosis factor (TNF)—used to treat cancer
Granulocyte-colony-stimulating factor (Neupogen)—developed for treating cancer patients suffering from low neutrophil counts

Hormones

Erythropoietin (EPO)—a peptide that stimulates bone marrow used to treat some forms of anemia
Relaxin—an aid to childbirth
Human growth hormone (HGH)—stimulates growth in children with dwarfism; prevents wasting syndrome

Enzymes

rHDNase (Pulmozyme)—a treatment that can break down the thick lung secretions of cystic fibrosis
Tissue plasminogen activating factor (tPA)—can dissolve potentially dangerous blood clots
Antitrypsin—replacement therapy to benefit emphysema patients
PEG-SOD—a form of superoxide dismutase that minimizes damage to brain and other tissues after surgery or severe trauma

Vaccines

Vaccines for hepatitis B, human papillomavirus, and *Haemophilus influenzae* type b meningitis
Experimental malaria, AIDS, and other vaccines based on recombinant surface antigens

Miscellaneous

Factor VIII—needed as replacement blood-clotting factor in type A hemophilia
Bovine growth hormone or bovine somatotropin (BST)—given to cows to increase milk production
Apolipoprotein—to deter the development of fatty deposits in the arteries and to prevent strokes and heart attacks

INSIGHT 10.2   A Moment to Think

We are embarking on a very potentially troublesome journey, where we begin to reduce all other animals on this planet to genetically engineered products. . . . We will increasingly think of ourselves as just gene codes and blueprints and programs that can be tinkered with.

> Jeremy Rifkin, Foundation on Economic Trends

Never postpone experiments that have clearly defined future benefits for fear of dangers that can't be quantified [because] we can react rationally only to real (as opposed to hypothetical) risks.

> James Watson, Nobel Laureate and first head of the Human Genome Project

I've never been less well equipped intellectually to vote on an issue than I am on this.

> Unnamed U.S. Senator, prior to a vote on stem cell research and human cloning

Of these three statements, the third is without a doubt the most frightening. There are always several sides to every issue and the best we can hope for is that the people regulating genetic technology are as well informed as possible. Those who will determine the limits of genetic technology include not only scientists and politicians but voters and consumers as well. History is rife with both knee-jerk rejections to new technologies that have later proven to be invaluable (vaccinations) and complacency while dangerous products were made available to an ignorant and unsuspecting public (Fen-Phen, thalidomide). Ethical choices can be properly made only from a standpoint of intellectual awareness, and in this era of advertising, polling, and focus groups, people with a stake in genetic technology know that the most effective way to drum up support (both for or against) is not by carefully educating the public as to the uses and limits of our newfound powers but rather by publicizing exaggerated claims of frightening scenarios. Enlightenment is often a casualty of these advertising campaigns, and you as a student, voter, and potential consumer of bioengineered products need to realize that the truth lies somewhere between the photograph seen here and the blissful utopia often portrayed by some proponents of biotechnology.

Some of the issues that are hotly debated by the public are:

1. *The cultivation of recombinant plants.* Some are concerned that the engineered genes can jump species and have unintended consequences as they spread far afield from the original engineered crop. This argument extends to food crops; many consumers prefer not to buy foods that have been genetically engineered.
2. *Gene therapy.* Critics of somatic gene therapy point to past failures in treatment that resulted in patient deaths and suggest we should stop. Even more controversial is germline gene

Recombinant Microbes: Modified Bacteria and Viruses

One of the first practical applications of recombinant DNA in agriculture was to create a genetically altered strain of the bacterium *Pseudomonas syringae.* The wild strain ordinarily contains a gene that promotes ice or frost formation on moist plant surfaces. Genetic alteration of the frost gene using recombinant plasmids created a different strain that could prevent ice crystals from forming. A commercial product called Frostban has been successfully applied to stop frost damage in strawberry and potato crops. A strain of *Pseudomonas fluorescens* has been engineered with the gene from a bacterium (*Bacillus thuringiensis*) that codes for an insecticide. These recombinant bacteria are released to colonize plant roots and help destroy invading insects. All releases of recombinant microbes must be approved by the Environmental Protection Agency (EPA) and are closely monitored.

Although a number of recombinant proteins are produced by transformed bacterial hosts, many of the enzymes, hormones, and antibodies being used in drug therapy are currently being manufactured using mammalian cell cultures as the cloning and expression hosts. One of the primary advantages to this alternative procedure is that these cell cultures can modify the proteins (adding carbohydrates, for example) so that they are biologically more active. Some forms of reproductive hormones, human growth hormone, and interferon are products of cell culture.

Another significant bioengineering interest has been to create microbes to bioremediate disturbed environments. Biotechnologists have already developed and tested several types of bacteria that clean up oil spills and degrade pesticides and toxic substances (see chapter 25). The growing power of biotechnology has also caused some to wonder about possible sinister uses of this new ability **(Insights 10.2 and 10.3).**

Transgenic Plants: Improving Crops and Foods

Two unusual species of bacteria in the genus *Agrobacterium* are the original genetic engineers of the plant world. These pathogens live in soil and can invade injured plant tissues. Inside the wounded tissue, the bacteria transfer a discrete DNA fragment called T-DNA into the host cell. The DNA is integrated into the plant cell's chromosome, where it directs the synthesis of nutrients to feed the bacteria and hormones to stimulate plant growth. In the case of *Agrobacterium tumefaciens,* increased growth causes development of a tumor called **crown gall disease,** a mass of undifferentiated tissue on the stem. The other species, *Agrobacterium rhizogenes,* attacks the roots and transforms them into abnormally overgrown "hairy roots."

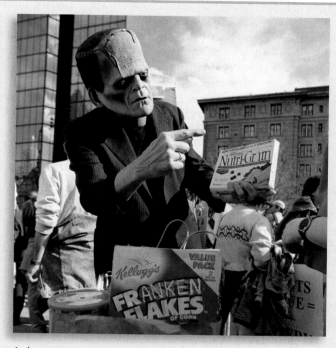

A demonstrator at a biotechnology conference protests the development and sale of genetically modified foods.

therapy, in which the genetic change is passed on to off-spring of the patient. This technique essentially creates new variations of "humanness," and so far is not being done.

3. *Genetic testing of individuals.* There are fears about who will own or use the information obtained by genome sequencing or other genetic examination techniques. Will insurance companies use the information about potential susceptibilities to disease to deny coverage? Will there be discrimination in hiring? What about genetic testing of fetuses? Will elective abortions become more common? On a more practical level, should we even know about all the potential diseases lurking in our genome, when we don't know whether they will actually manifest in disease. Will we cause needless anxiety and unnecessary testing and treatments?

4. *Synthetic biology.* Should we be creating our own versions of "life"? Some view these techniques as just the next logical step in engineering organisms that are more useful; others view it as a major philosophical and ethical issue.

We raise the questions without providing the answers here. The point is that we can choose to engage in calm and informed discussion of these issues, relying on evidence and reason, or we can choose to rely on emotion and misinformation that is disseminated by groups that have particular interests in particular outcomes. The more you know about biology the better you are able to draw your own reasoned conclusions.

INSIGHT 10.3 | DIYBio: Citizen Scientists

Meredith Patterson is a software engineer in San Francisco who saw a problem and wanted to solve it using genetic engineering. She is not a biologist and she has no lab. But she has a dining room—and she turned it into a home lab. She wants to create recombinant bacteria that contain a gene that fluoresces in the presence of melamine, the toxic chemical that turned up in infant formula in China in 2008, and in pet foods in the United States in 2007. Her idea is to make yogurt containing these bacteria so that melamine can be detected when the yogurt glows. She has none of the fancy equipment most genetics labs have: centrifuges, electrophoresis machines, etc. She gets the foreign DNA into her bacteria by zapping them with a $40 ultrasonic jewelry cleaner

instead of a fancy electroporator. Her centrifuge is a plastic salad spinner.

Meredith is part of a growing movement of do-it-yourself genetic engineers, sometimes called "biohackers." These self-styled geneticists are sometimes trained in biology but often are amateurs with a great interest in the subject. They are reminiscent of computer "geeks" in the 1970s who tinkered with computers in their garages and came up with technology that led to the personal computer industry. DIYers sometimes are passionately committed to innovation, reasoning that discoveries should not be limited to credentialed scientists working in universities or industry. So far, "garage" geneticists are building better rice plants, and even creating bacteria capable of performing simple logic operations, the kind of successes that are usually accomplished by large teams of well-funded scientists and engineers.

Companies and clubs have sprung up to support these amateur scientists. Microbes and genes are available for sale over the Internet. And eBay is selling an increasing array of used laboratory equipment. (Meredith Patterson finally gave up on her ultrasonic cleaner and bought an electroporator on eBay.) Competitions have sprung up that offer prizes to the best home-grown genetics breakthroughs.

While it is exhilarating to see this grassroots movement and the democratization of science, many have concerns that unexpected traits can be bred into organisms, or worse, that hackers with bad intentions will deliberately engineer dangerous organisms. What do you think?

The capacity of these bacteria, especially *A. tumefaciens,* to transfect host cells can be attributed to a large plasmid termed **Ti** (tumor-inducing). This plasmid inserts into the genomes of the infected plant cells and transforms them. Even after the bacteria in a tumor are dead, the plasmid genes remain in the cell nucleus and the tumor continues to grow. This plasmid is a perfect vector for inserting foreign genes into plant genomes. The procedure involves removing the Ti plasmid, inserting a previously isolated gene into it, and returning it to *Agrobacterium* **(figure 10.12).** Infection of the plant by the recombinant bacteria automatically transfers the plasmid with the foreign gene into the plant cells.

The movement toward release of engineered plants into the environment has led to some controversy. Many plant geneticists and ecologists are seriously concerned that transgenic plants will share their genes for herbicide, pesticide, and virus resistance with natural plants, leading to "superweeds" that could flourish and become indestructible. There is promising news, however. In 2008 a study found that rice that was bred through conventional methods had more unintentional genetic changes than did crops manipulated through genetic engineering. The United States Department of Agriculture is carefully regulating all releases of transgenic plants. See **table 10.3** for examples of plants that have been engineered.

Transgenic Animals: Engineering Embryos

Animals, too, can be genetically engineered. In fact, animals are so amenable to gene transfer that several hundred strains of transgenic animals have been introduced by research and industry. One reason for this movement toward animals is that, unlike bacteria and yeasts, they can express human genes in organs and organ systems that are very similar to those of humans. This advantage has led to the design of animal models to study human genetic diseases and then to use these natural systems to test new genetic therapies before they are used in humans. Animals such as sheep or goats can also be engineered to become "factories" capable of manufacturing proteins useful to humans and excreting them in their milk or semen, a process often referred to (when done to produce medically useful proteins) as "pharming."

Synthetic Biology

In recent years researchers have staked out entirely new territory in genetic manipulation: They are trying to create new organisms from scratch. This field is called synthetic biology. In Insight 6.2 you read about the creation of an "artificial" poliovirus and influenza virus. Viruses are simpler than cells, as you know, and now researchers are trying to create cells. One pioneer in the field is one of the same men who sequenced the human genome, Craig Venter. In 2010 he successfully created a self-replicating bacterial cell from four bottles of chemicals: the four nucleotides of DNA. This was a breakthrough of major proportions as it was the first time a living, replicating cell had been synthesized from chemicals. In an interesting side note, the researchers added some "letters" to the DNA code in the bacterium that spelled out their names, the name of the laboratory, and an e-mail address that you could write to if you managed to decode the genome. They also added some relevant quotations in the DNA, such as one from the Irish writer James Joyce: "To live, to err, to fall, to triumph, to recreate life out of life."

This kind of research activity raises some obvious ethical questions. For many it raises fears that whatever we create can get away from our control and have unintended consequences, as with Frankenstein in the famous Mary Shelley novel. Others argue that the potential benefits of being able

Genetically engineered *Agrobacterium* infects a target plant cell. Fusion of the bacterium with the plant cell wall permits entrance of the Ti plasmid and incorporation of the herbicide gene into a plant chromosome.

Growth and maturation of plant from transfected cells creates an herbicide-resistant form.

Figure 10.12 Bioengineering of plants.   Many techniques employ a natural tumor-producing bacterium called *Agrobacterium tumefaciens.*

Table 10.3 Examples of Engineered (Transgenic) Plants

Plant	Trait	Results	
Nicotiana tabacum (tobacco)	Herbicide resistance		Tobacco plants in the upper row have been transformed with a gene that provides protection against Buctril, a systemic herbicide. Plants in the lower row are normal and not transformed. Both groups were sprayed with Buctril and allowed to sit for 6 days. (The control plants at the beginning of each row were sprayed with a control mixture lacking Buctril.)
Pisum sativum (garden pea)	Pest protection		Pea plants were engineered with a gene that prevents digestion of the seed starch (see seeds on the left in the photo). This gene keeps tiny insects called weevils from feeding on the seeds. Seeds on the right are from plants that were not engineered and are suffering from weevil damage (note holes).
Oryza sativa (rice)	Added nutritional value		The golden rice grains seen in the photo have been genetically engineered to produce beta-carotene, a precursor to vitamin A. Lack of vitamin A leads to over 1 million deaths and 300,000 cases of blindness a year.

to design cells that create biofuels or medical or agricultural products outweigh such "theoretical" concerns. We talked more about this in Insight 10.2.

10.5 Learning Outcomes—Can You . . .

10. . . . compare and contrast recombinant bacteria, plants, and animals?

10.6 Genetic Treatments: Introducing DNA into the Body

Gene Therapy

We have known for decades that for certain diseases, the disease phenotype is due to the lack of a single specific protein. For example, type I diabetes is caused by a lack of insulin, leaving those with the disease unable to properly regulate their blood sugar. The initial treatment for this disease was simple: provide diabetics with insulin isolated from a different source, in most cases the pancreas of pigs or cows. While this treatment was adequate for most diabetics (especially in the short term), our increasingly sophisticated genetic engineering abilities made loitering around the slaughterhouse seem a decidedly low-tech solution to a high-tech problem. We've already discussed the first way in which genetic engineering has been used in

the treatment of disease, namely producing recombinant proteins in bacteria or yeast rather than isolating the protein from animals or humans. In fact, recombinant human insulin was the first genetically engineered drug to be approved for use in humans. The next logical step is to see if we can correct or repair a faulty gene in humans suffering from a fatal or debilitating disease, a process known as **gene therapy.**

The inherent benefit of this therapy is to permanently cure the physiological dysfunction by repairing the genetic defect. There are two strategies for this therapy. In *ex vivo* therapy, the normal gene is cloned in vectors such as retroviruses (mouse leukemia virus) or adenoviruses that are infectious but relatively harmless. Tissues removed from the patient are incubated with these genetically modified viruses to transfect them with the normal gene. The transfected cells are then reintroduced into the patient's body by transfusion **(figure 10.13).** In contrast, the *in vivo* type of therapy skips the intermediate step of incubating excised patient tissue. Instead, the naked DNA or a virus vector is directly introduced into the patient's tissues.

Experimentation with various types of gene therapy, or clinical testing, is performed on human volunteers with the particular genetic condition. Over 1,000 of these trials have been or are being carried out in the United States and other countries. Most trials target cancer, single-gene defects, and infections, and most gene deliveries are carried out by virus

1. Normal gene is isolated from healthy subject.

2. Gene is cloned.

3. Gene is inserted into retrovirus vector.

4. Bone marrow sample is taken from patient with genetic defect.

5. Marrow cells are infected with retrovirus.

6. Transfected cells are reinfused into patient.

7. Patient is observed for expression of normal gene.

Marrow cell

Process Figure 10.13 Protocol for the *ex vivo* type of gene therapy in humans.

vectors. So far, the therapeutic trials have been hampered by several difficulties relating to effectiveness and safety. Some of the safety issues have been related to the use of (seemingly safe) viruses as delivery vehicles. Newer studies are using polymer "capsules" that deliver genes without some of the safety issues.

The first gene therapy experiment in humans was initiated in 1990 by researchers at the National Institutes of Health. The subject was a 4-year-old girl suffering from a severe immunodeficiency disease caused by the lack of the enzyme adenosine deaminase (ADA). She was transfused with her own blood cells that had been engineered to contain a functional ADA gene. Later, other children were given the same type of therapy. So far, the children have shown remarkable improvement and continue to be healthy.

Several patients have been treated successfully for another type of severe combined immunodeficiency syndrome called X-1-linked SCID that is due to a missing enzyme required for mature immune cells. Full function has been restored to several hemophilic children, using a similar technique. In 2009, scientists successfully treated humans with a particular hereditary eye disease using genes surgically delivered to the eye using a virus vector. They later confirmed that the virus did not leave the eye and therefore concluded that viral vectors may indeed sometimes be appropriate. The ultimate sort of gene therapy is germline therapy, in which genes are inserted into an egg, sperm, or early embryo. In this type of therapy, the new gene will be present in all cells of the individual. The therapeutic gene is also heritable (that is, can be passed on to subsequent generations). Because of this last fact, germline gene therapy is still considered too controversial to use in humans.

DNA Technology as Genetic Medicine

Up to now, we have considered the use of genetic technology to replace a missing or faulty protein that is needed for normal cell function. A different problem arises when a disease results from the inappropriate expression of a protein. For example, Alzheimer's disease, most viral diseases, and many cancers occur when an unwanted gene is expressed rather than when a desirable gene is missing. The solution in cases such as this is to prevent transcription or translation of a gene, and scientists, as they often do, look for clues in bacteria. Bacteria have sophisticated ways of silencing genes.

Gene Silencing Strategies

Some genes in bacteria are repressed naturally when an antisense RNA binds to them, preventing translation at the ribosome. This **antisense RNA** has bases that are complementary to the sense strand of mRNA in the area surrounding the initiation site. When the antisense RNA binds to its particular mRNA, the now double-stranded RNA is inaccessible to the ribosome, resulting in a loss of translation of that mRNA.

Note that the term antisense as used in molecular genetics does *not* mean "no sense." It is used to describe any nucleic acid strand with a base sequence that is complementary to the "sense" or translatable strand. For example, DNA contains a template strand that is transcribed and a matching strand that is not usually transcribed. We can also apply this terminology to RNA. Messenger RNA is considered the translatable strand, and a strand with its complementary sequence of nucleotides would be the antisense strand. To illustrate: If an mRNA sequence read AUGCGAGAC, then an antisense RNA strand for it would read UACGCUCUG. In recent years, many studies have examined the use of antisense RNA to shut down faulty genes in humans, or to shut down virulence genes in the microbes infecting them. The first antisense treatment approved for use in humans is Vitravene, used to treat cytomegalovirus retinitis, blindness brought on by infection with cytomegalovirus in immunocompromised persons.

In chapter 9, you read about other clever strategies bacteria (as well as some eukaryotes) can use to regulate their own genes. Small interfering RNAs silence gene expression by folding back on themselves after being transcribed, which activates a system inside cells that degrades dsRNA **(figure 10.14).** The dsRNAs inside cells form a complex with an enzyme to form an "RNA-induced silencing complex," or RISC. The RNA unwinds and one strand is left in the complex, which then migrates to single-stranded RNA that is complementary to the RNA in the complex. The complex, since it contains an RNA-cutting enzyme, then cuts the target mRNA. Essentially, the RNA in the complex serves as a homing device to take the enzyme to the correct sequences. Ordinarily, cells do this in order to rid themselves of invading viruses (which are organisms that might have dsRNA). These interfering RNAs are currently being studied for their ability to treat serious microbial diseases such as HIV and hepatitis. There are also hopeful results in trials designed to shut down defective human genes that result in other serious diseases, such as Alzheimer's and cancer. The first successful human application of interfering RNAs was conducted at the University of Tennessee in 2010. There healthy human volunteers were given a nasal spray containing siRNA designed to silence a gene from respiratory syncytial virus (RSV). They used the spray for five days and then were infected with live RSV. Only 44% of those who had received the interfering RNA became infected, compared with 71% of control subjects.

10.6 Learning Outcomes—Can You ...

11. ... differentiate between somatic and germline gene therapy?
12. ... describe at least two gene silencing strategies?

10.7 Genome Analysis: Maps and Profiles

As was mentioned earlier, DNA technology has allowed us to accomplish many age-old goals by new and improved means. By remembering that phenotypes, whether human, bacterial, or even viral, are the result of specific sequences of DNA, we can easily see how DNA can be used to differentiate among organisms in the same way that observing any of these phenotypes can. Additionally, DNA can be used to "see" the phenotype of an organism no longer present, as when a criminal is identified by DNA extracted from a strand of hair left behind at a crime scene. Finally, possession of a particular sequence of DNA may indicate an increased risk of a genetic disease. Detection of this piece of DNA (known as a marker) can identify a person as being at increased risk for cancer or Alzheimer's disease long before symptoms arise. The ability to detect diseases before symptoms arise is especially important for diseases such as cancer, for which early treatment is sometimes the difference between life and death. With examples like this in mind, let's look at several ways in which new DNA technology is allowing us to accomplish goals in ways that were only dreamed of a few years ago.

Genome Mapping and Screening: An Atlas of the Genome

We have seen a variety of methods for accessing the genomes of organisms, but the most useful information comes from knowing the sequential makeup of the genetic material. Genetic engineers find it very informative to know the **locus,** or exact position, of a particular gene on a chromosome. They also seek information on the types and numbers of **alleles,** which are sites that vary from one individual to another. The process of determining location of loci and other qualities of genomic DNA is called **mapping.** Maps vary in resolution and

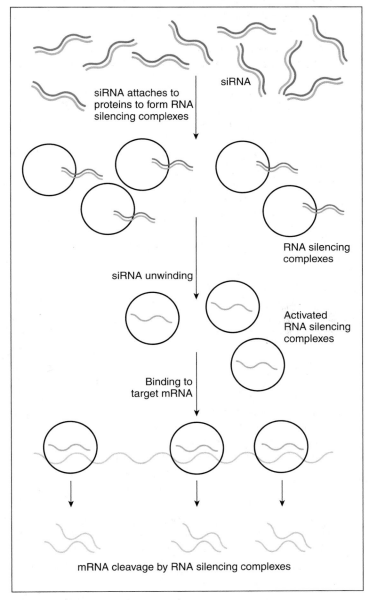

siRNA attaches to proteins to form RNA silencing complexes

siRNA

RNA silencing complexes

siRNA unwinding

Activated RNA silencing complexes

Binding to target mRNA

mRNA cleavage by RNA silencing complexes

Figure 10.14 RNA interference.   Double-stranded RNAs "interfere with" or silence genes when introduced to cells. After entering, the dsRNAs form complexes with endoribonucleases called RNA-induced silencing complexes, or RISCs in the diagram. The double strands unwind while associated with the RISCs and gravitate toward complementary RNA sequences. When they bind to the target sequences they are cleaved by the endonuclease portion of the RISC.

applications. **Linkage maps** show the relative proximity and order of genes on a chromosome and are relatively low resolution because only a few exact locations are mapped. **Physical maps** are more detailed arrays that not only depict the relative positions of distinct sections of DNA but also give the numerical size in base pairs. This technology uses restriction fragments and fluorescent hybridization probes to visualize the position of a particular selected site along a segment of DNA.

By far the most detailed maps are **sequence maps,** which are produced by the sequencers we discussed earlier. They give an exact order of bases in a plasmid, chromosome, or entire genome. Genome sequencing projects have been highly successful. As of 2010, the genome sequences of more than 2,000 viruses, close to 1,000 prokaryotes, and about a hundred eukaryotes had been published. The eukaryotic genomes include human, mouse, *Caenorhabditis elegans* (a nematode worm), yeast, fruit fly, *Arabidopsis* (a small flowering plant), and rice. One of the remarkable discoveries in this huge enterprise has been how similar the genomes of relatively unrelated organisms are. Humans share around 80% of their DNA codes with mice, about 60% with rice, and even 30% with the worm *C. elegans.*

The ease with which researchers can now sequence genomes was illustrated in the spring of 2003, when a previously unknown virus began causing severe acute respiratory syndrome (SARS) in Southeast Asia. Just 2 weeks after the first virus was isolated from patients, the genome was sequenced and made available to scientists rushing to create a diagnostic test, understand its virulence, and design a vaccine.

Although sequencing provides the ultimate genetic map, it does not automatically identify the exact genes and alleles. Analyzing and storing this massive amount of new data require specialized computers. Because the data consist of information of both biological and mathematical content, two whole new disciplines have grown up around managing these data: **genomics** (see Note) and **bioinformatics.** The job of genomics and bioinformatics is to analyze and classify genes, determine protein sequences, and ultimately determine the function of the genes. Determining this functional information is often called **annotating** the genome. In time, well-annotated genomes will provide a complete understanding of such phenomena as normal cell function, disease, development, aging, and many other issues. In addition, they will allow us to characterize the exact genetic mechanisms behind pathogens and allow new treatments to be developed against them.

DNA Profiles: A Unique Picture of a Genome

Although DNA is based on a structure of nucleotides, the exact way these nucleotides are combined is unique for each organism. It is now possible to apply DNA technology in a manner that emphasizes these differences and arrays the entire genome in a pattern for comparison. **DNA profiling** (also called DNA typing or fingerprinting) is best known as a tool of forensic science first devised in the mid-1980s by Alex Jeffreys of Great Britain **(figure 10.15).**

Several of the methods discussed previously in this chapter are involved in the creation of a DNA profile. Techniques such as the use of restriction endonucleases for cutting DNA precisely, PCR amplification for increasing the number of copies of a certain genome, electrophoresis to separate fragments, hybridization probes to locate specific loci and alleles, and the Southern blot technique for producing a visible record are all employed. Several different methods of DNA profiling are available, but all depend on distinguishing one sequence of DNA from another by comparing the sequence of the strands at specific loci.

One type of analysis depends on the ability of a restriction enzyme to cut DNA at a specific recognition site. If a given strand of DNA possesses the recognition site for a particular restriction enzyme, the DNA strand is cut, resulting in two smaller pieces of DNA. If the same strand from a different person does not contain the recognition site (perhaps due to a mutation many generations ago), it is not cut by the restriction enzyme and remains as a single large piece of DNA. When each of these DNA samples is digested with restriction enzymes and separated on an electrophoretic gel, the first displays two small bands while the second displays one larger band. This is an example of a restriction fragment length polymorphism, which was discussed earlier. All methods of DNA fingerprinting depend on some variation of this strategy to ferret out differences in DNA sequence at the same location in the genome. The type of polymorphism is also sometimes referred to as **single nucleotide polymorphism (SNP)** because only a single nucleotide is altered.

A Note About the New "-omics"

The ability to obtain the entire sequences of organisms has spawned new vocabulary that refers to the "total picture" of some aspect of a cell or organism.

genomics   The systematic study of an organism's genes and their functions.

proteomics   The study of an organism's complement of proteins (its "proteome") and functions mediated by the proteins.

metagenomics (also called "community genomics") The study of all the genomes in a particular ecological niche, as opposed to individual genomes from single species.

metabolomics   The study of the complete complement of small chemicals present in a cell at any given time. Provides a snapshot of the physiological state of the cell and the end products of its metabolism.

(a) Cells from different samples are processed to isolate their DNA. The DNA samples are exposed to endonucleases, which snip them at specific sites into a series of different fragments.

(b) Electrophoresis of DNA fragments separates them by size, with larger fragments nearer the wells. Although invisible to the unaided eye at this point, each well contains thousands of individual bands. After transferring the DNA fragments to a nylon membrane, specific DNA sequences are identified by hybridization of a fluorescently labeled nucleic acid probe.

(c) An actual DNA profile used in a rape trial. Control lanes with known markers are in lanes 1, 5, 8, and 9. The second lane contains a sample of DNA from the victim's blood. Evidence samples 1 and 2 (lanes 3 and 4) contain semen samples taken from the victim. Suspects 1 and 2 (lanes 6 and 7) were tested. Can you tell by comparing evidence and suspect lanes which individual committed the rape?

Figure 10.15 DNA profiles: the bar codes of life.

Case File 10   *Continuing the Case*

Faced with a dozen refrigerated semitrailers filled with human remains and at least 1,700 families hoping for closure, the medical examiner suggested two methods that rely on very small pieces of DNA: mini short tandem (DNA) repeats (mini-STR) and single nucleotide polymorphism (SNP). Although the New York State Health Department refused to certify these experimental methods, fearing incorrect identification, the city medical examiner's office pushed ahead.

Both methods involve genetically testing a portion of human remains and then comparing the results with DNA taken from tissue samples, such as hair and skin known to belong to the victim. As part of the investigation, family members pro-

vided toothbrushes, combs, razors, or other personal effects that contained the DNA of a person thought to have perished in the World Trade Center. SNP analysis is based on the fact that every person has between 3 million and 10 million variants in his or her 3 billion bases of DNA. Therefore, the chances of finding a variation in a small piece of DNA are relatively good. Mini-STR relies on a much smaller number of specific chromosomal regions—commonly 13—that typically show variability from person to person; in most cases, this is enough to conclusively identify human remains.

Tens of thousands of these differences at a single locus are known to exist throughout the genome. The human genome contains 10 million SNPs. These variations are currently a hot area of research and also commerce. Scientists are mapping SNPs and determining which ones put humans at greater risk of cancers and other diseases. Many companies have sprung up that will map SNPs and give you an estimated risk for a variety of diseases. An example of an SNP map is shown in **figure 10.16.**

Infectious disease laboratories are developing numerous test procedures to profile bacteria and viruses. Profiling is used to identify *Neisseria gonorrhoeae, Chlamydia,* the syphilis spirochete, and *Mycobacterium tuberculosis.* It was instrumental in identifying the anthrax strain used in the mail attacks of 2001. It is also an essential tool for determining genetic relationships between microbes, such as those involved in food-borne disease outbreaks (see Insight 22.3).

Knowing the complete nucleotide sequence of the human genome is really only half the battle. With few exceptions, all cells in an organism contain the same DNA, so knowing the sequence of that DNA, while certainly helpful, is of very little use when comparing two cells or tissues from the same organism. Recall that genes are expressed in response to both internal needs and external stimuli, and while the DNA content of a cell is static, the mRNA (and hence protein) content at any given time provides scientists with a profile of genes currently being expressed in the cell. What truly distinguishes a liver cell from a kidney cell or a healthy cell from a diseased cell are the genes expressed in each.

Twin advances in biology and electronics have allowed biologists to view the expression of genes in any given cell using a technique called DNA **microarray analysis.** Prior to the advent of this technology, scientists were able to track the expression of, at most, a few genes at a time. Microarrays are able to track the expression of thousands of genes at once and are able to do so in a single efficient experiment. Microarrays consist of a "chip"[4] made of glass, silicon, or nylon, onto which have been bound sequences from tens of thousands of different genes. A solution containing fluorescently labeled cDNA, representing all of the mRNA molecules in a cell at a given time, is added to the chip. The labeled cDNA is allowed to bind to any complementary DNA bound to the chip. Bound cDNA is then detected by exciting the fluorescent tag on the cDNA with a laser and recording the fluorescence with a detector linked to a computer. The computer can then interpret this data to determine what mRNAs are present in the cell under a variety of conditions **(figure 10.17).** In the example in this figure you see green, red, and yellow reactions. The green fluorescent tag was added to a control population of cells, let's say a bacterium growing in fluid culture. The red fluorescent tag was added to bacteria growing in a biofilm. The reactions appearing green are genes expressed only in fluid culture, the red reactions are genes expressed only in biofilms, and the yellow reactions were dual-labeled, meaning those genes are expressed under both conditions.

Possible uses of microarrays include developing extraordinarily sensitive diagnostic tests that search for a specific pattern of gene expression. As an example, being able to identify a patient's cancer as one of many subtypes (rather than just, for instance, breast cancer) will allow pharmacologists and doctors to treat each cancer with the drug that will be most effective. Again, we see that genetic technology can be a very effective way to reach long-held goals.

10.7 Learning Outcomes—Can You ...

13. ... outline the general steps in DNA profiling?
14. ... discuss the significance of single nucleotide polymorphisms (SNPs)?
15. ... describe the utility of DNA microarray analysis?

---

4. It's usually just a glass slide, but all microarray setups have come to be called chips.

Figure 10.16. The location of one pertinent set of SNPs on human chromosomes.   Genetic variations at the sites indicated can be used to estimate the risk of type 2 diabetes.

Chromosomes: 1 2 3 4 5 6 7 8 9 10 11 12 13 14 15 16 17 18 19 20 21 22 X Y

Case File 10   *Wrap-Up*

As investigators at the World Trade Center spent 2 years and millions of dollars working with the new genetic analysis techniques, they encountered many cases suggestive of a DNA match, but in the end they were able to make only a few unequivocal identifications. As of 2008, fewer than half of the 2,749 victims of the World Trade Center had been positively identified. As the researchers said, "We hit the limits of science." For now, they have cataloged their data and preserved the tissue samples, and are waiting until technology improves enough to identify the rest of the victims. Once that happens, acquiring the needed tissue samples from family members and creating a master database for potentially millions of individual fragments from thousands of victims will be a massive project.

See: 2005. *The New York Times.* April 3, p. 34.

Figure 10.17 Gene expression analysis using microarrays. Cloned genes from an organism are amplified by PCR, and after purification, samples are applied to a chip to generate a spotted microarray. mRNA from test and reference cultures are converted to cDNA by reverse transcriptase and labeled with two different fluorescent dyes. The labeled mixture is hybridized to the microarray and scanned.

 ## Chapter Summary

10.1 Basic Elements and Applications of Genetic Engineering
- The genetic revolution has produced a wide variety of technologies that allow humans to radically alter the blueprints of life.

10.2 Tools and Techniques of Genetic Engineering
- Genetic engineering utilizes a wide range of methods that physically manipulate DNA for purposes of visualization, sequencing, hybridizing, and identifying specific sequences.
- The tools of genetic engineering include restriction endonucleases, gel electrophoresis, DNA sequencing machines, and gene probes.
- The polymerase chain reaction (PCR) technique amplifies small amounts of DNA into much larger quantities for further analysis.

10.3 Methods in Recombinant DNA Technology: How to Imitate Nature
- Recombinant DNA techniques combine DNA from different sources to produce microorganism "factories" that produce hormones, enzymes, and vaccines on an industrial scale.

- Cloning is the process by which genes are removed from the original host and duplicated for transfer into a cloning host by means of cloning vectors.
- Plasmids, bacteriophages, and cosmids are types of cloning vectors used to transfer recombinant DNA into a cloning host.

10.4 Biochemical Products of Recombinant DNA Technology
- Bioengineered hormones, enzymes, and vaccines are safer and more effective than similar substances isolated directly from animals.

10.5 Genetically Modified Organisms
- Transgenic microorganisms are genetically designed for medical treatments and immunizations, crop improvement, pest reduction, and bioremediation.

10.6 Genetic Treatments: Introducing DNA into the Body
- Gene therapy is the replacement of faulty host genes with functional genes using delivery vehicles such as viruses or polymers. This treatment can be used to correct genetic disorders and acquired disease.

- Antisense DNA and interfering RNAs are used to block expression of undesirable host genes in plants and animals as well as those of intracellular parasites.
- DNA technology has advanced understanding of basic genetic principles that have significant applications in a wide range of disciplines, particularly medicine, evolution, forensics, and anthropology.

10.7 Genome Analysis: Maps and Profiles

- The Human Genome Project and other genome sequencing projects have revolutionized our understanding of organisms and led to two new biological disciplines, genomics and bioinformatics.
- DNA profiling is a technique by which organisms are identified for purposes of medical diagnosis, genetic ancestry, and forensics.
- Microarray analysis can determine what genes are transcribed in a given tissue. It is used to identify and devise treatments for diseases based on the phenotypic profile of the disease.

Multiple-Choice and True-False Questions Knowledge and Comprehension

Multiple-Choice Questions. Select the correct answer from the answers provided.

1. Which of the following is *not* essential to carry out the polymerase chain reaction?
   a. primers
   b. DNA polymerase
   c. gel electrophoresis
   d. high temperature

2. Which of the following is *not* a part of the Sanger method to sequence DNA?
   a. dideoxynucleotides
   b. DNA polymerase
   c. electrophoresis
   d. reverse transcriptase

3. The function of ligase is to
   a. rejoin segments of DNA.
   b. make longitudinal cuts in DNA.
   c. synthesize cDNA.
   d. break down ligaments.

4. The pathogen of plant roots that is used as a cloning host is
   a. *Pseudomonas.*
   b. *Agrobacterium.*
   c. *Escherichia coli.*
   d. *Saccharomyces cerevisiae.*

5. Which of the following sequences, when combined with its complement, could be clipped by an endonuclease?
   a. ATCGATCGTAGCTAGC
   b. AAGCTTTTCGAA
   c. GAATTC
   d. ACCATTGGTA

6. A region of DNA in a plasmid that is recognized by a wide variety of restriction enzymes is called the
   a. origin.
   b. regulator.
   c. multicloning site.
   d. vector.

7. The antisense DNA strand that complements mRNA AUGCGCGAC is
   a. UACGCUCUG.
   b. GTCTCGCAT.
   c. TACGCGCTG.
   d. DNA cannot complement mRNA.

8. Which of the following is a primary participant in cloning an isolated gene?
   a. restriction endonuclease
   b. vector
   c. host organism
   d. all of these

9. Single nucleotide polymorphisms are found in
   a. DNA.
   b. RNA.
   c. plasmids.
   d. siRNA.

10. Microarrays are used to monitor
    a. the rate of DNA replication.
    b. the presence of particular genes in DNA.
    c. antisense DNA.
    d. which genes are being expressed.

True-False Questions. If the statement is true, leave as is. If it is false, correct it by rewriting the sentence.

11. The synthetic unit of the polymerase chain reaction is the replica.

12. A nucleic acid probe can be used to identify unknown bacteria or viruses in clinical samples.

13. A DNA fragment with 450 bp will be closer to the top (negative pole) of an electrophoresis gel than one with 2,500 bp.

14. In order to detect recombinant cells, plasmids contain antibiotic resistance genes.

15. Plasmids are the only vector currently available for use in recombinant procedures.

Critical Thinking Questions   Application and Analysis

These questions are suggested as a *writing-to-learn* experience. For each question, compose a one- or two-paragraph answer that includes the factual information needed to completely address the question.

1. a. How would you make a copy of DNA from an mRNA transcript?
   b. Show how this process would look, using base notation.
   c. Why would it be an advantage to synthesize eukaryotic genes this way?

2. Outline the main steps in cloning a gene.

3. What is one way to determine whether a bacterial culture has received a recombinant plasmid?

4. Describe what a DNA profile is and why and how restriction fragments can be used to form a unique DNA pattern.

5. Discuss the most important difference between somatic cell gene therapy and germline gene therapy.

6. Give an example of a benefit of genetic engineering to society and a possible adverse outcome. Discuss.

7. Most of us would agree to growth hormone therapy for a child with dwarfism, but how do we deal with parents who want to give growth hormones to their 8-year-old son so that he will be "better at sports"?

8. a. If gene probes, profiling, and mapping could make it possible for you to know of future genetic diseases in you or one of your children, would you wish to use this technology to find out?
   b. What if it were used as a screen for employment or insurance?

9. The way that PCR amplifies DNA is similar to the doubling in a population of growing bacteria; a single DNA strand is used to synthesize 2 DNA strands, which become 4, then 8, then 16, and so on. If a complete cycle takes 3 minutes,
   a. how many strands of DNA would theoretically be present after 10 minutes?
   b. after 30 minutes?
   c. after 1 hour?

10. Describe any moral, ethical, or biological problems associated with eating tomatoes from an engineered plant or pork from a transgenic pig.

Concept Mapping   Synthesis

Appendix D provides guidance for working with concept maps.

1. Construct your own concept map using the following words as the *concepts*. Supply the linking words between each pair of concepts.

DNA	plasmid
restriction endonuclease	vector
palindrome	origin of replication
ligase	recombinant

Visual Connections   Synthesis

These questions use visual images or previous content to make connections to this chapter's concepts.

1. **From chapter 6, figure 6.22.** What has happened to the bacterial DNA in this illustration? What effect can this have on a bacterium? Is this temporary or permanent?

2. **From chapter 9, figure 9.25.** Study the series of events in this illustration. What do cell A (step 1) and cell B (step 5) now have in common?

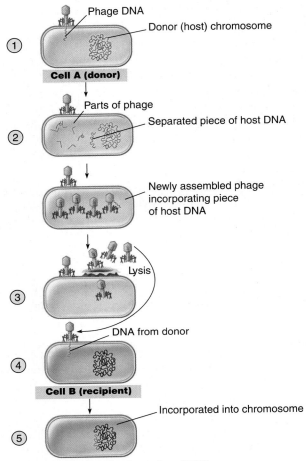

Cell survives and utilizes transduced DNA.

www.connect.microbiology.com

Enhance your study of this chapter with study tools and practice tests. Also ask your instructor about the resources available through ConnectPlus, including the media-rich eBook, interactive learning tools, and animations.

Physical and Chemical Control of Microbes

Case File 11

The popular interactive water fountain, or "sprayground," at Seneca Lake State Park closed for the remainder of the summer on August 17, 2005, after the New York State Health Commissioner announced that an outbreak of cryptosporidiosis had been traced to the park. Cryptosporidiosis results from ingesting water contaminated with the protozoan *Cryptosporidium parvum*. Symptoms include diarrhea, vomiting, fever, and abdominal cramps.

The sprayground itself is an 11,000-square-foot deck with hundreds of individual water jets, spouts, and hoses. After being sprayed into the air, water flows back into a holding tank below the play area before being recycled through the jets once again. This type of water playground has become immensely popular because even small children can play there, without the risk of drowning commonly associated with swimming pools.

■ Would *Cryptosporidium* be more or less resistant to physical and chemical methods of control than most other microbes?

■ What level of microbial control would be most appropriate in this case: disinfection, sterilization, antisepsis, or decontamination?

Continuing the Case appears on page 316.

Outline and Learning Outcomes

11.1 Controlling Microorganisms
1. Distinguish among the terms sterilization, disinfection, antisepsis, and decontamination.
2. Identify the microorganisms that are most resistant and least resistant to control measures.
3. Define "-static" and "-cidal."
4. Name four categories of cellular targets for physical and chemical agents.

11.2 Methods of Physical Control
5. Name six methods of physical control of microorganisms.
6. Discuss both moist and dry heat methods and identify multiple examples of both.
7. Define thermal death time and thermal death point.

8. Explain four different methods of moist heat control.
9. Explain two methods of dry heat control.
10. Identify advantages and disadvantages of cold and dessication.
11. Differentiate between the two types of radiation control methods.
12. Explain how filtration functions as a control method.
13. Identify some common uses of osmotic pressure as a control method.

11.3 Chemical Agents in Microbial Control

14. Name the desirable characteristics of chemical control agents.
15. Discuss several different halogen agents and their uses.
16. List advantages and disadvantages to phenolic compounds.
17. Explain the mode of action of alcohols.
18. Pinpoint the most appropriate applications of hydrogen peroxide agents.
19. Define surfactant and explain its mode of action.
20. Identify some heavy metal control agents and their most common applications.
21. Discuss the advantages and disadvantages of aldehyde agents.
22. Identify applications for ethylene oxide sterilization.

11.1 Controlling Microorganisms

Much of the time in our daily existence, we take for granted tap water that is drinkable, food that is not spoiled, shelves full of products to eradicate "germs," and drugs to treat infections. Controlling our degree of exposure to potentially harmful microbes is a monumental concern in our lives, and it has a long and eventful history **(Insight 11.1)**.

General Considerations in Microbial Control

The methods of microbial control used outside of the body are designed to result in four possible outcomes: steriliza-

tion, disinfection, antisepsis, or decontamination. **Sterilization** is the destruction of all microbial life. **Disinfection** destroys most microbial life, reducing contamination on inanimate surfaces. **Antisepsis** is the same as disinfection except a living surface is involved. **Decontamination** is the mechanical removal of most microbes from an animate or inanimate surface. A flowchart **(figure 11.1)** summarizes the major applications and aims in microbial control.

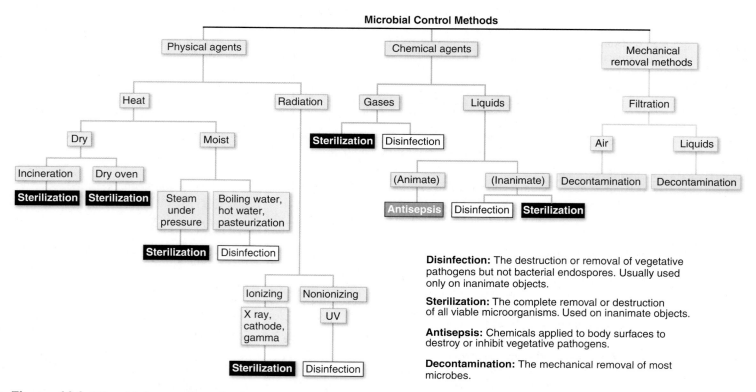

Disinfection: The destruction or removal of vegetative pathogens but not bacterial endospores. Usually used only on inanimate objects.

Sterilization: The complete removal or destruction of all viable microorganisms. Used on inanimate objects.

Antisepsis: Chemicals applied to body surfaces to destroy or inhibit vegetative pathogens.

Decontamination: The mechanical removal of most microbes.

Figure 11.1 Microbial control methods.

INSIGHT 11.1 Microbial Control in Ancient Times

No one knows for sure when humans first applied methods that could control microorganisms, but perhaps the starting point was the discovery and use of fire in prehistoric times. We do know that records describing simple measures to control decay and disease appear from civilizations that existed several thousand years ago. We know, too, that these ancient people had no concept that germs caused disease, but they did have a mixture of religious beliefs, skills in observing natural phenomena, and possibly, a bit of luck. This combination led them to carry out simple and sometimes rather hazardous measures that contributed to the control of microorganisms.

Salting, smoking, pickling, and drying foods and exposing food, clothing, and bedding to sunlight were prevalent practices among early civilizations. The Egyptians showed surprising sophistication and understanding of decomposition by embalming the bodies of their dead with strong salts and pungent oils. They introduced filtration of wine and water as well. The Greeks and Romans burned clothing and corpses during epi-

Illustration of protective clothing used by doctors in the 1700s to avoid exposure to plague victims. The beaklike portion of the hood contained volatile perfumes to protect against foul odors and possibly inhaling "bad air."

demics, and they stored water in copper and silver containers. The armies of Alexander the Great reportedly boiled their drinking water and buried their wastes. Burning sulfur to fumigate houses and applying sulfur as a skin ointment also date approximately from this era.

During the great plague pandemic of the Middle Ages, it was commonplace to bury corpses in mass graves, burn the clothing of plague victims, and ignite aromatic woods in the houses of the sick in the belief that fumes would combat the disease. In a desperate search for some sort of protection, those tending the sick wore peculiar garments and survivors anointed their bodies with herbs, strong perfume, and vinegar. These attempts may sound foolish and antiquated, but it now appears that they may have had some benefits. Burning wood releases formaldehyde, which could have acted as a disinfectant; herbs, perfume, and vinegar contain mild antimicrobial substances. Each of these early methods, although somewhat crude, laid the foundations for microbial control methods that are still in use today.

Relative Resistance of Microbial Forms

The primary targets of microbial control are microorganisms capable of causing infection or spoilage that are constantly present in the external environment and on the human body. This targeted population is rarely simple or uniform; in fact, it often contains mixtures of microbes with extreme differences in resistance and harmfulness. Contaminants that can have far-reaching effects if not adequately controlled include bacterial vegetative cells and endospores, fungal hyphae and spores, yeasts, protozoan trophozoites and cysts, worms, viruses, and prions. This schema compares the general resistance these forms have to physical and chemical methods of control:

Highest resistance
Prions; bacterial endospores
Moderate resistance
Protozoan cysts; some fungal sexual spores (zygospores); some viruses. In general, naked viruses are more resistant than enveloped forms. Among the most resistant viruses are the hepatitis B virus and the poliovirus. Bacteria with more resistant vegetative cells are *Mycobacterium tuberculosis*, *Staphylococcus aureus*, and *Pseudomonas* species.
Least resistance
Most bacterial vegetative cells; fungal spores (other than zygospores) and hyphae; enveloped viruses; yeasts; and protozoan trophozoites

Actual comparative figures on the requirements for destroying various groups of microorganisms are shown in **table 11.1.** Bacterial endospores have traditionally been considered the most resistant microbial entities, being as much as 18 times harder to destroy than their counterpart vegetative cells. Because of their resistance to microbial

Table 11.1 Comparative Resistance of Bacterial Endospores and Vegetative Cells to Control Agents

Method	Endospores*	Vegetative Forms*	Endospores Are ___ More Resistant**
Heat (moist)	120°C	80°C	1.5×
Radiation (X-ray) dosage	4,000 Grays	1,000 Grays	4×
Sterilizing gas (ethylene oxide)	1,200 mg/L	700 mg/L	1.7×
Sporicidal liquid (2% glutaraldehyde)	3 h	10 min	18×

*Values are based on methods (concentration, exposure time, intensity) that are required to destroy the most resistant pathogens in each group.

**The greater resistance of spores versus vegetative cells given as an average figure.

control, their destruction is the goal of *sterilization* because any process that kills endospores will invariably kill all less resistant microbial forms. Other methods of control (disinfection, antisepsis) act primarily upon microbes that are less hardy than endospores.

A Note About Prions

Prions are in a class of their own when it comes to "sterilization" procedures. This chapter defines "sterile" as the absence of all viable microbial life—but none of the procedures described in this chapter are necessarily sufficient to destroy prions. Prions are extraordinarily resistant to heat and chemicals. If instruments or other objects become contaminated with these unique agents, they must either be discarded as biohazards or, if this is not possible, a combination of chemicals and heat must be applied in accordance with CDC guidelines. The guidelines themselves are constantly evolving as new information becomes available. In the meantime, this chapter discusses sterilization using bacterial endospores as the toughest form of microbial life. When tissues, fluids, or instruments are suspected of containing prions, consultation with infection control experts and/or the CDC is recommended when determining effective sterilization conditions. Chapter 19 describes prions in detail.

Terminology and Methods of Microbial Control

Through the years, a growing terminology has emerged for describing and defining measures that control microbes. To complicate matters, the everyday use of some of these terms can at times be vague and inexact. For example, occasionally one may be directed to "sterilize" or "disinfect" a patient's skin, even though this usage does not fit the technical definition of either term. To lay the groundwork for the concepts in microbial control to follow, we present here a series of concepts, definitions, and usages in antimicrobial control.

Sterilization

Sterilization is a process that destroys or removes all viable microorganisms, including viruses. Any material that has been subjected to this process is said to be **sterile.** These terms should be used only in the strictest sense for methods that have been proved to sterilize. An object cannot be slightly sterile or almost sterile—it is either sterile or not sterile. Control methods that sterilize are generally reserved for inanimate objects, because sterilizing parts of the human body would call for such harsh treatment that it would be highly dangerous and impractical.

Sterilized products—surgical instruments, syringes, and commercially packaged foods, just to name a few—are

essential to human well-being. Although most sterilization is performed with a physical agent such as heat, a few chemicals called *sterilants* can be classified as sterilizing agents because of their ability to destroy spores.

In many situations, sterilization is neither practical nor necessary, and only certain groups of microbes need to be controlled. Some antimicrobial agents eliminate only the susceptible vegetative states of microorganisms but do not destroy the more resistant endospore and cyst stages. Keep in mind that the destruction of spores is not always a necessity, because most of the infectious diseases of humans and animals are caused by non-spore-forming microbes.

Disinfection refers to the use of a physical process or a chemical agent (a disinfectant) to destroy vegetative pathogens but not bacterial endospores. It is important to note that disinfectants are normally used only on inanimate objects because, in the concentrations required to be effective, they can be toxic to human and other animal tissue. Disinfection processes also remove the harmful products of microorganisms (toxins) from materials. Examples of disinfection include applying a solution of 5% bleach to an examining table, boiling food utensils used by a sick person, and immersing thermometers in an iodine solution between uses.

In modern usage, **sepsis** is defined as the growth of microorganisms in the blood and other tissues. The term **asepsis** refers to any practice that prevents the entry of infectious agents into sterile tissues and thus prevents infection. Aseptic techniques commonly practiced in health care range from sterile methods that exclude all microbes to *antisepsis*. In antisepsis, chemical agents called **antiseptics** are applied directly to exposed body surfaces (skin and mucous membranes), wounds, and surgical incisions to destroy or inhibit vegetative pathogens. Examples of antisepsis include preparing the skin before surgical incisions with iodine compounds, swabbing an open root canal with hydrogen peroxide, and ordinary hand washing with a germicidal soap.

The Agents Versus the Processes

The terms *sterilization, disinfection,* and so on refer to processes. You will encounter other terms that describe the agents used in the process. Two examples of these are the terms *bactericidal* and *bacteristatic.* The root *-cide,* meaning to kill, can be combined with other terms to define an antimicrobial agent aimed at destroying a certain group of microorganisms. For example, a **bactericide** is a chemical that destroys bacteria except for those in the endospore stage. It may or may not be effective on other microbial groups. A *fungicide* is a chemical that can kill fungal spores, hyphae, and yeasts. A *virucide* is any chemical known to inactivate viruses, especially on living tissue. A *sporicide* is an agent capable of destroying bacterial endospores. A sporicidal agent can also be a sterilant because it can destroy the most resistant of all microbes. **Germicide** and **microbicide** are additional terms for chemical agents that kill microorganisms.

The Greek words *stasis* and *static* mean to stand still. They can be used in combination with various prefixes to denote a condition in which microbes are temporarily prevented from multiplying but are not killed outright. Although killing or permanently inactivating microorganisms is the usual goal of microbial control, microbistasis does have meaningful applications. **Bacteristatic** agents prevent the growth of bacteria on tissues or on objects in the environment, and *fungistatic* chemicals inhibit fungal growth. Materials used to control microorganisms in the body (antiseptics and drugs) often have **microbistatic** effects because many microbicidal compounds can be highly toxic to human cells. Note that a *-cidal* agent doesn't necessarily result in sterilization.

Decontamination

Several applications in commerce and medicine do not require actual sterilization, disinfection, or antisepsis but are based on reducing the levels of microorganisms (the microbial load) so that the possibility of infection or spoilage is greatly decreased. Restaurants, dairies, breweries, and other food industries consistently handle large numbers of soiled utensils that could readily become sources of infection and spoilage. These industries must keep microbial levels to a minimum during preparation and processing. **Sanitization** is any cleansing technique that mechanically removes microorganisms as well as other debris to reduce contamination to safe levels. A sanitizer is a compound such as soap or detergent used to perform this task.

Cooking utensils, dishes, bottles, cans, and clothing that have been washed and dried may not be completely free of microbes, but they are considered safe for normal use (sanitary). Air sanitization with ultraviolet lamps reduces airborne microbes in hospital rooms, veterinary clinics, and laboratory installations. Note that some sanitizing processes (such as dishwashing machines) may be rigorous enough to sterilize objects, but this is not true of all sanitization methods. Also note that sanitization is often preferable to sterilization. In a restaurant, for example, you could be given a sterile fork with someone else's old food on it and a sterile glass with lipstick on the rim. On top of this, realize that the costs associated with sterilization would lead to the advent of the $50 fast-food meal. In a situation such as this, the advantage of being sanitary as opposed to sterile can be clearly seen.

It is often necessary to reduce the numbers of microbes on the human skin through **degermation.** This process usually involves scrubbing the skin or immersing it in chemicals, or both. It also emulsifies oils that lie on the outer cutaneous layer and mechanically removes potential pathogens on the outer layers of the skin. Examples of degerming procedures are the surgical handscrub, the application of alcohol wipes to the skin, and the cleansing of a wound with germicidal soap and water. The concepts of antisepsis and degermation clearly overlap, because a degerming procedure can simultaneously be antiseptic and vice versa.

Practical Concerns in Microbial Control

Numerous considerations govern the selection of a workable method of microbial control. These are among the most pressing concerns:

1. Does the application require sterilization, or is disinfection adequate? In other words, must spores be destroyed or is it necessary to destroy only vegetative pathogens?
2. Is the item to be reused or permanently discarded? If it will be discarded, then the quickest and least expensive method should be chosen.
3. If it will be reused, can the item withstand heat, pressure, radiation, or chemicals?
4. Is the control method suitable for a given application? (For example, ultraviolet radiation is a good sporicidal agent, but it will not penetrate solid materials.) Or, in the case of a chemical, will it leave an undesirable residue?
5. Will the agent penetrate to the necessary extent?
6. Is the method cost- and labor-efficient, and is it safe?

A remarkable variety of substances can require sterilization. They range from durable solids such as rubber to sensitive liquids such as serum, and even to entire office buildings, as seen in 2001 when the Hart Senate Office Building was contaminated with *Bacillus anthracis* endospores **(Insight 11.2).** Hundreds of situations requiring sterilization confront the network of persons involved in health care, whether technician, nurse, doctor, or manufacturer, and no universal method works well in every case.

Considerations such as cost, effectiveness, and method of disposal are all important. For example, disposable plastic items such as catheters and syringes that are used in invasive medical procedures have the potential for infecting the tissues. These must be sterilized during manufacture by a nonheating method (gas or radiation), because heat can damage plastics. After these items have been used, it is often necessary to destroy or decontaminate them before they are discarded because of the potential risk to the handler (from needlesticks). Steam sterilization, which is quick and sure, is a sensible choice at this point, because it does not matter if the plastic is destroyed.

What Is Microbial Death?

Death is a phenomenon that involves the permanent termination of an organism's vital processes. Signs of life in complex organisms such as animals are self-evident, and death is made clear by loss of nervous function, respiration, or heartbeat. In contrast, death in microscopic organisms that are composed of just one or a few cells is often hard to detect, because they reveal no conspicuous vital signs to begin with. Lethal agents (such as radiation and chemicals) do not necessarily alter the overt appearance of microbial cells. Even the loss of movement in a motile microbe cannot be used to indicate death. This fact has made it necessary to develop special qualifications that define and delineate microbial death.

INSIGHT 11.2   Decontaminating Congress

Choosing a microbial control technique is usually a straightforward process: Cultures are autoclaved, milk is pasteurized, and medical supplies may be irradiated. When letters containing spores of *Bacillus anthracis* were opened in the Hart Office Building of the U.S. Senate in 2001, the process got just a bit trickier. Among the many concerns of the Environmental Protection Agency, which was charged with the building's remediation, were these:

- Anthrax is a lethal disease.
- *Bacillus anthracis* is a spore-forming bacterium, making eradication difficult.
- The Hart Office Building is populated by thousands of people, who could quickly and easily spread endospores from office to office.
- The area to be decontaminated included heating and air-conditioning vents, carpeting, furniture, office equipment, sensitive papers, artwork, and the various belongings of quickly evacuated workers.

The goal of the project could be simply stated: Detect and remove all traces of a lethal, highly infectious, spore-forming bacterium from an enormous space filled with all manner of easily damaged material. Easier said than done.

With this goal in mind, the EPA first set to work to determine the extent of contamination. Samples were taken from 25 buildings on Capitol Hill. Nonporous surfaces were swabbed; furniture and carpets were vacuumed using a HEPA filter; air was pumped through a filter to remove any airborne spores. Samples were placed in sterile vials and double bagged before being transferred to the laboratory. Analysis of the samples revealed the presence of spores in many areas of the Hart Office

Workers in protective garments prepare the Hart Office Building for decontamination.

Building, including the mail-processing areas of 11 senators. Because spores were not found in the entrances to these offices, it was theorized that the spores spread primarily through the mail. The heaviest contamination was found in the office of Senator Tom Daschle, to whom the original anthrax-containing letter was addressed. Additional contamination was found in a conference room, stairwell, elevator, and restroom.

With the scope of the problem identified, the EPA set out to devise a strategy for remediation, keeping in mind the difficulty of killing spore-forming organisms and the myriad contents of the building, much of it delicate, expensive, and in many cases irreplaceable. It was decided that most areas would be cleaned by a combination of HEPA vacuuming followed by either treatment with liquid chlorine dioxide or Sandia decontamination foam, an antibacterial foam that combines surfactants with oxidizing agents. For the most heavily contaminated areas (Senator Daschle's office and parts of the heating and air-conditioning system), gaseous chlorine dioxide would be used. Chlorine dioxide has been accepted as a sterilant since 1988 and is used for, among other things, treatment of medical waste. Its use in this project was based primarily on the facts that it would (a) work and (b) be unlikely to harm the contents of the building. (It was even tested to ensure that it would not damage the ink making up the signature on a document.)

Before fumigation could begin, however, a method of evaluating the success of the remediation effort needed to be devised. Borrowing from a common laboratory technique, 3,000 small slips of paper covered with spores from the organism *Bacillus stearothermophilus* (which is generally considered harder to kill than *B. anthracis*) were dispersed throughout the building. If after the treatment was complete these spores were unable to germinate, then the fumigation could be considered a success.

On December 1, 2001, technicians prepared the 3,000-square-foot office for fumigation. This included constructing barriers to seal off the portion of building being fumigated and raising the humidity in the offices to approximately 75% to enable the gas to adhere to any lingering spores. Office machines (computers, copiers, for example) were turned on so that the fans inside the equipment would aid in spreading the gas. Finally, at 3:15 a.m., fumigation began. It ended 20 hours later; and, after the gas was neutralized and ventilated from the building, technicians entered to collect the test strips. Analyzing the results, it was clear that trace amounts of spores were still present but only in those areas that originally had the worst contamination (these areas were again cleaned with liquid chlorine dioxide). Senator Daschle's office got a makeover with new carpeting, paint, and furniture, and shortly thereafter the building was reoccupied. The senator also had his office equipment replaced as it was deemed too contaminated to be used.

The destructive effects of chemical or physical agents occur at the level of a single cell. As the cell is continuously exposed to an agent such as intense heat or toxic chemicals, various cell structures become dysfunctional, and the entire cell can sustain irreversible damage. At present, the most practical way to detect this damage is to determine if a microbial cell can still reproduce when exposed to a suitable environment. If the microbe has sustained metabolic or structural damage to such an extent that it can no longer reproduce, even under ideal environmental conditions, then it is no longer viable. The permanent loss of reproductive capability, even under optimum growth conditions, has become the accepted microbiological definition of death.

Factors That Affect Death Rate

The cells of a culture show marked variation in susceptibility to a given microbicidal agent. Death of the whole population is not instantaneous but begins when a certain threshold of microbicidal agent (some combination of time and concentration) is met. Death continues in a logarithmic manner as the time or concentration of the agent is increased (**figure 11.2a**). Because many microbicidal agents target the cell's metabolic processes, active cells (younger, rapidly dividing) tend to die more quickly than those that are less metabolically active (older, inactive). Eventually, a point is reached at which survival of any cells is highly unlikely; this point is equivalent to sterilization.

The effectiveness of a particular agent is governed by several factors besides time. These additional factors influence the action of antimicrobial agents:

1. The number of microorganisms (**figure 11.2b**). A higher load of contaminants requires more time to destroy.
2. The nature of the microorganisms in the population (**figure 11.2c**). In most actual circumstances of disinfection and sterilization, the target population is not a single species of microbe but a mixture of bacteria, fungi, spores, and viruses, presenting a broad spectrum of microbial resistance.
3. The temperature and pH of the environment.
4. The concentration (dosage, intensity) of the agent. For example, UV radiation is most effective at 260 nm, and most disinfectants are more active at higher concentrations.
5. The mode of action of the agent (**figure 11.2d**). How does it kill or inhibit the microorganism?
6. The presence of solvents, interfering organic matter, and inhibitors. Saliva, blood, and feces can inhibit the actions of disinfectants and even of heat.

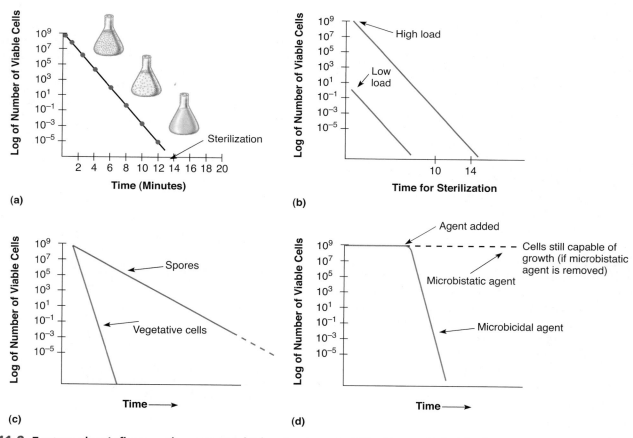

Figure 11.2 Factors that influence the rate at which microbes are killed by antimicrobial agents.   (a) Length of exposure to the agent. During exposure to a chemical or physical agent, all cells of a microbial population, even a pure culture, do not die simultaneously. Over time, the number of viable organisms remaining in the population decreases logarithmically, giving a straight-line relationship on a graph. The point at which the number of survivors is infinitesimally small is considered sterilization. **(b)** Effect of the microbial load. **(c)** Relative resistance of spores versus vegetative forms. **(d)** Action of the agent, whether microbicidal or microbistatic.

The influence of these factors is discussed in greater detail in subsequent sections.

How Antimicrobial Agents Work: Their Modes of Action

An antimicrobial agent's adverse effect on cells is known as its *mode* (or *mechanism*) *of action.* Agents affect one or more cellular targets, inflicting damage progressively until the cell is no longer able to survive. Antimicrobials have a range of cellular targets, with the agents that are least selective in their targeting tending to be effective against the widest range of microbes (examples include heat and radiation). More selective agents (drugs, for example) tend to target only a single cellular component and are much more restricted as to the microbes they are effective against.

The cellular targets of physical and chemical agents fall into four general categories:

1. the cell wall,
2. the cell membrane,
3. cellular synthetic processes (DNA, RNA), and
4. proteins.

The Effects of Agents on the Cell Wall

The cell wall maintains the structural integrity of bacterial and fungal cells. Several types of chemical agents damage the cell wall by blocking its synthesis, digesting it, or breaking down its surface. A cell deprived of a functioning cell wall becomes fragile and is lysed very easily. Detergents and alcohol can also disrupt cell walls, especially in gram-negative bacteria.

How Agents Affect the Cell Membrane

All microorganisms have a cell membrane composed of lipids and proteins, and many viruses have an outer membranous envelope. As we learned in previous chapters, a cell's membrane provides a two-way system of transport. If this membrane is disrupted, a cell loses its selective permeability and can neither prevent the loss of vital molecules nor bar the entry of damaging chemicals. Loss of those abilities leads to cell death. Detergents called **surfactants** (sir-fak'-tunt) work as microbicidal agents. Surfactants are polar molecules with hydrophilic and hydrophobic regions that can physically bind to the lipid layer and penetrate the internal hydrophobic region of membranes. In effect, this process "opens up" the once tight interface, leaving leaky spots that allow injurious chemicals to seep into the cell and important ions to seep out (**figure 11.3**).

Agents That Affect Protein and Nucleic Acid Synthesis

Microbial life depends upon an orderly and continuous supply of proteins to function as enzymes and structural molecules. As we saw in chapter 9, these proteins are synthesized via the ribosomes through a complex process called translation. For example, the antibiotic chloramphenicol binds to the ribosomes of bacteria in a way that stops peptide bonds from forming. In its presence, many bacterial cells are inhibited from forming proteins required in growth and metabolism and are thus inhibited from multiplying.

The nucleic acids are likewise necessary for the continued functioning of microbes. DNA must be regularly replicated and transcribed in growing cells, and any agent that either impedes these processes or changes the genetic code is potentially antimicrobial. Some agents bind irreversibly to DNA, preventing both transcription and translation; others are mutagenic agents. Gamma, ultraviolet, or X radiation causes mutations that result in permanent inactivation of DNA. Chemicals such as formaldehyde and ethylene oxide also interfere with DNA and RNA function.

Agents That Alter Protein Function

A microbial cell contains large quantities of proteins that function properly only if they remain in a normal three-dimensional configuration called the *native state.* The antimicrobial properties of some agents arise from their capacity to disrupt, or **denature,** proteins. In general, denaturation occurs when the bonds that maintain the secondary and tertiary structure of the protein are broken. Breaking these bonds will cause the protein to unfold or create random, irregular loops and coils (**figure 11.4**). One way that proteins can be denatured is through coagulation by moist heat (the same reaction seen in the irreversible solidification of the white of an egg when boiled). Chemicals such as strong organic solvents (alcohols, acids) and phenolics also coagulate proteins. Other antimicrobial agents, such as metallic ions, attach to

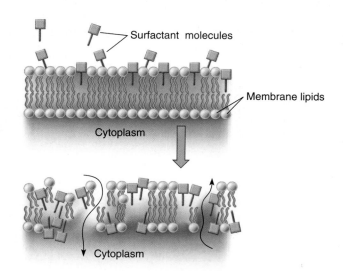

Figure 11.3 Mode of action of surfactants on the cell membrane.   Surfactants inserting in the lipid bilayer disrupt it and create abnormal channels that alter permeability and cause leakage both into and out of the cell.

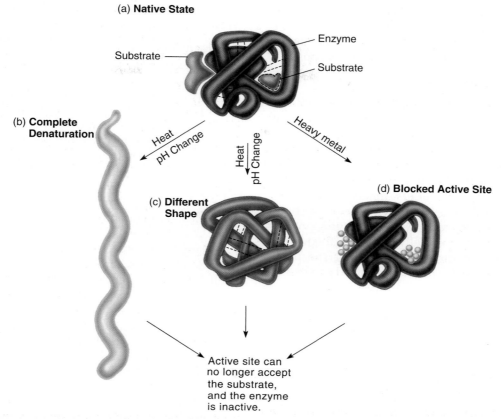

(a) Native State

Substrate

Enzyme

Substrate

(b) Complete Denaturation

Heat
pH Change

Heat
pH Change

Heavy metal

(d) Blocked Active Site

(c) Different Shape

Active site can no longer accept the substrate, and the enzyme is inactive.

Figure 11.4 Modes of action affecting protein function. **(a)** The native (functional) state is maintained by bonds that create active sites to fit the substrate. Some agents denature the protein by breaking all or some secondary and tertiary bonds. Results are **(b)** complete unfolding or **(c)** random bonding and incorrect folding. **(d)** Some agents react with functional groups on the active site and interfere with bonding.

the active site of the protein and prevent it from interacting with its correct substrate. Regardless of the exact mechanism, such losses in normal protein function can promptly arrest metabolism. Most antimicrobials of this type are nonselective as to the microbes they affect.

11.1 Learning Outcomes—Can You ...

1. ... distinguish among the terms sterilization, disinfection, antisepsis, and decontamination?
2. ... identify the microorganisms that are most resistant and least resistant to control measures?
3. ... define "-static" and "-cidal"?
4. ... name four categories of cellular targets for physical and chemical agents?

11.2 Methods of Physical Control

We can divide our methods of controlling microorganisms into two broad categories: physical and chemical. We'll start with physical methods. Microorganisms have adapted to the tremendous diversity of habitats the earth provides, even severe conditions of temperature, moisture, pressure, and light. For

microbes that normally withstand such extreme physical conditions, our attempts at control would probably have little effect. Fortunately for us, we are most interested in controlling microbes that flourish in the same environment in which humans live. The vast majority of these microbes are readily controlled by abrupt changes in their environment. Most prominent among antimicrobial physical agents is heat. Other less widely used agents include radiation, filtration, ultrasonic waves, and even cold. The following sections examine some of these methods and explore their practical applications in medicine, commerce, and the home.

Heat as an Agent of Microbial Control

A sudden departure from a microbe's temperature of adaptation is likely to have a detrimental effect on it. As a rule, elevated temperatures (exceeding the maximum growth temperature) are microbicidal, whereas lower temperatures (below the minimum growth temperature) are microbistatic. Heat can be applied in either moist or dry forms. *Moist heat* occurs in the form of hot water, boiling water, or steam (vaporized water). In practice, the temperature of moist heat usually ranges from 60°C to 135°C. As we shall see, the temperature of steam can be regulated by adjusting its pressure in a closed container. The expression *dry heat* denotes air with a low moisture content that has been heated by a flame or electric heating coil. In practice, the temperature of dry heat ranges from 160°C to several thousand degrees Celsius.

Mode of Action and Relative Effectiveness of Heat

Moist heat and dry heat differ in their modes of action as well as in their efficiency. Moist heat operates at lower temperatures and shorter exposure times to achieve the same effectiveness as dry heat **(table 11.2)**. Although many cellular structures are damaged by moist heat, its most microbicidal effect is the coagulation and denaturation of proteins, which quickly and permanently halts cellular metabolism.

Dry heat dehydrates the cell, removing the water necessary for metabolic reactions, and it also denatures proteins. However, the lack of water actually increases the stability of some protein conformations, necessitating the use of higher temperatures when dry heat is employed as a method of microbial control. At very high temperatures, dry heat oxidizes cells, burning them to ashes. This method is the one used in the laboratory when a loop is flamed or in industry when medical waste is incinerated.

Heat Resistance and Thermal Death of Spores and Vegetative Cells

Bacterial endospores exhibit the greatest resistance, and vegetative states of bacteria and fungi are the least resistant to both moist and dry heat. Destruction of spores usually requires temperatures above boiling, although resistance varies widely.

Vegetative cells also vary in their sensitivity to heat. Among bacteria, the death times with moist heat range from 50°C for 3 minutes (*Neisseria gonorrhoeae*) to 60°C for 60 minutes (*Staphylococcus aureus*). It is worth noting that vegetative cells of sporeformers are just as susceptible as vegetative cells of non-sporeformers and that pathogens are neither more nor less susceptible than nonpathogens. Other microbes, including fungi, protozoa, and worms, are rather similar in their sensitivity to heat. Viruses are surprisingly resistant to heat, with a tolerance range extending from 55°C for 2 to 5 minutes (adenoviruses) to 60°C for 600 minutes (hepatitis A virus). For practical purposes, all non-heat-resistant forms of bacteria, yeasts, molds, protozoa, worms, and viruses are destroyed by exposure to 80°C for 20 minutes.

Table 11.2	Comparison of Times and Temperatures to Achieve Sterilization with Moist and Dry Heat	
	Temperature (°C)	Time to Sterilize (Min)
Moist heat	121	15
	125	10
	134	3
Dry heat	121	600
	140	180
	160	120
	170	60

Practical Concerns in the Use of Heat: Thermal Death Measurements

Adequate sterilization requires that both temperature and length of exposure be considered. As we have seen, higher temperatures allow shorter exposure times, and lower temperatures require longer exposure times. A combination of these two variables constitutes the **thermal death time,** or TDT, defined as the shortest length of time required to kill all test microbes at a specified temperature. The TDT has been experimentally determined for the microbial species that are common or important contaminants in various heat-treated materials. Another way to compare the susceptibility of microbes to heat is the **thermal death point** (TDP), defined as the lowest temperature required to kill all microbes in a sample in 10 minutes.

Many perishable substances are processed with moist heat. Some of these products are intended to remain on the shelf at room temperature for several months or even years. The chosen heat treatment must render the product free of agents of spoilage or disease. At the same time, the quality of the product and the speed and cost of processing must be considered. For example, in the commercial preparation of canned green beans, one of the cannery's greatest concerns is to prevent growth of the agent of botulism. From several possible TDTs (that is, combinations of time and temperature) for *Clostridium botulinum* spores, the cannery must choose one that kills all spores but does not turn the beans to mush. Out of these many considerations emerges an optimal TDT for a given processing method. Commercial canneries heat low-acid foods at 121°C for 30 minutes, a treatment that sterilizes these foods. Because of such strict controls in canneries, cases of botulism due to commercially canned foods are rare.

Common Methods of Moist Heat Control

The four ways that moist heat is employed to control microbes are

1. steam under pressure,
2. nonpressurized steam,
3. pasteurization, and
4. boiling water.

Steam Under Pressure　At sea level, normal atmospheric pressure is 15 pounds per square inch (psi), or 1 atmosphere. At this pressure, water will boil (change from a liquid to a gas) at 100°C, and the resultant steam will remain at exactly that temperature, which is unfortunately too low to reliably kill all microbes. In order to raise the temperature of steam, the pressure at which it is generated must be increased. As the pressure is increased, the temperature at which water boils and the temperature of the steam produced both rise. For example, at a pressure of 20 psi (5 psi above normal), the temperature of steam is 109°C. As the pressure is increased to 10 psi above normal, the steam's temperature rises to 115°C, and at 15 psi above normal (a total of 2 atmospheres), it will be 121°C. It is not the pressure by itself that is killing microbes but the increased temperature it produces.

Such pressure-temperature combinations can be achieved only with a special device that can subject pure steam to pressures greater than 1 atmosphere. Health and commercial industries use an **autoclave** for this purpose, and a comparable home appliance is the pressure cooker. All autoclaves have a fundamentally similar design: a cylindrical metal chamber with an airtight door on one end and racks to hold materials **(figure 11.5)**. Its construction includes a complex network of valves, pressure and temperature gauges, and ducts for regulating and measuring pressure and conducting the steam into the chamber. Sterilization is achieved when the steam condenses against the objects in the chamber and gradually raises their temperature.

Experience has shown that the most efficient pressure-temperature combination for achieving sterilization is 15 psi, which yields 121°C. It is possible to use higher pressure to reach higher temperatures (for instance, increasing the pressure to 30 psi raises the temperature to 132°C), but doing so will not significantly reduce the exposure time and can harm the items being sterilized. It is important to avoid overpacking or haphazardly loading the chamber, which prevents steam from circulating freely around the contents and impedes the full contact that is necessary. The duration of the process is adjusted according to the bulkiness of the items in the load (thick bundles of material or large flasks of liquid) and how full the chamber is. The range of holding times varies from 10 minutes for light loads to 40 minutes for heavy or bulky ones; the average time is 20 minutes.

The autoclave is a superior choice to sterilize heat-resistant materials such as glassware, cloth (surgical dressings), rubber (gloves), metallic instruments, liquids, paper, some media, and some heat-resistant plastics. If the items are heat-sensitive (plastic Petri dishes) but will be discarded, the autoclave is still a good choice. However, the autoclave is ineffective for sterilizing substances that repel moisture (oils, waxes), or for those that are harmed by it (powders).

Nonpressurized Steam   Selected substances that cannot withstand the high temperature of the autoclave can be subjected to *intermittent sterilization*, also called **tyndallization.**[1] This technique requires a chamber to hold the materials and a reservoir for boiling water. Items in the chamber are exposed to free-flowing steam for 30 to 60 minutes. This temperature is not sufficient to reliably kill spores, so a single exposure will not suffice. On the assumption that surviving spores will germinate into less resistant vegetative cells, the

1. Named for the British physicist John Tyndall, who did early experiments with sterilizing procedures.

Figure 11.5   Steam sterilization with the autoclave.   **(a)** A tabletop autoclave. **(b)** Cutaway section, showing autoclave components.
Source: (b) From John J. Perkins, *Principles and Methods of Sterilization in Health Science*, 2nd ed., 1969. Courtesy of Charles C Thomas, Publisher, Springfield, Illinois.

items are incubated at appropriate temperatures for 23 to 24 hours, and then again subjected to steam treatment. This cycle is repeated for 3 days in a row. Because the temperature never gets above 100°C, highly resistant spores that do not germinate may survive even after 3 days of this treatment.

Intermittent sterilization is used most often to process heat-sensitive culture media, such as those containing sera, egg, or carbohydrates (which can break down at higher temperatures) and some canned foods. It is probably not effective in sterilizing items such as instruments and dressings that provide no environment for spore germination, but it certainly can disinfect them.

Pasteurization: Disinfection of Beverages Fresh beverages such as milk, fruit juices, beer, and wine are easily contaminated during collection and processing. Because microbes have the potential for spoiling these foods or causing illness, heat is frequently used to reduce the microbial load and destroy pathogens. **Pasteurization** is a technique in which heat is applied to liquids to kill potential agents of infection and spoilage, while at the same time retaining the liquid's flavor and food value.

Ordinary pasteurization techniques require special heat exchangers that expose the liquid to 71.6°C for 15 seconds (flash method) or to 63°C to 66°C for 30 minutes (batch method). The first method is preferable because it is less likely to change flavor and nutrient content, and it is more effective against certain resistant pathogens such as *Coxiella* and *Mycobacterium*. Although these treatments inactivate most viruses and destroy the vegetative stages of 97% to 99% of bacteria and fungi, they do not kill endospores or particularly heat-resistant microbes (mostly nonpathogenic lactobacilli, micrococci, and yeasts). Milk is not sterile after regular pasteurization. In fact, it can contain 20,000 microbes per milliliter or more, which explains why even an unopened carton of milk will eventually spoil. Newer techniques can also produce *sterile milk* that has a storage life of 3 months. This milk is processed with ultrahigh temperature (UHT)—134°C—for 1 to 2 seconds.

One important aim in pasteurization is to prevent the transmission of milk-borne diseases from infected cows or milk handlers. The primary targets of pasteurization are non-spore-forming pathogens: *Salmonella* species (a common cause of food infection), *Campylobacter jejuni* (acute intestinal infection), *Listeria monocytogenes* (listeriosis), *Brucella* species (undulant fever), *Coxiella burnetii* (Q fever), *Mycobacterium bovis*, *M. tuberculosis*, and several enteric viruses.

Pasteurization also has the advantage of extending milk storage time, and it can also be used by wineries and breweries to stop fermentation and destroy contaminants.

Boiling Water: Disinfection A simple boiling water bath or chamber can quickly decontaminate items in the clinic and home. Because a single processing at 100°C will not kill all resistant cells, this method can be relied on only for disinfection and not for sterilization. Exposing materials to boiling water for 30 minutes will kill most non-spore-forming pathogens, including resistant species such as the tubercle bacillus and staphylococci. Probably the greatest disadvantage with this method is that the items can be easily recontaminated when removed from the water. Boiling is also a recom-

mended method of disinfecting unsafe drinking water. In the home, boiling water is a fairly reliable way to sanitize and disinfect materials for babies, food preparation, and utensils, bedding, and clothing from the sickroom.

Dry Heat: Hot Air and Incineration

Dry heat is not as versatile or as widely used as moist heat, but it has several important sterilization applications. The temperatures and times employed in dry heat vary according to the particular method, but in general, they are greater than with moist heat. **Incineration** in a flame or electric heating coil is perhaps the most rigorous of all heat treatments. The flame of a Bunsen burner reaches 1,870°C at its hottest point, and furnaces/incinerators operate at temperatures of 800°C to 6,500°C. Direct exposure to such intense heat ignites and reduces microbes and other substances to ashes and gas.

Incineration of microbial samples on inoculating loops and needles using a Bunsen burner is a very common practice in the microbiology laboratory. This method is fast and effective, but it is also limited to metals and heat-resistant glass materials. This method also presents hazards to the operator (an open flame) and to the environment (contaminants on needle or loop often spatter when placed in flame). Tabletop infrared incinerators **(figure 11.6)** have replaced Bunsen burners in many labs for these reasons. Large incinerators are regularly employed in hospitals and research labs for complete destruction and disposal of infectious materials such as syringes, needles, cultural materials, dressings, bandages, bedding, animal carcasses, and pathology samples.

The hot-air oven provides another means of dry-heat sterilization. The so-called *dry oven* is usually electric (occasionally gas) and has coils that radiate heat within an enclosed compartment. Heated, circulated air transfers its heat to the materials in the oven. Sterilization requires exposure to 150°C to 180°C for 2 to 4 hours, which ensures thorough heating of the objects and destruction of spores.

Figure 11.6 Dry heat incineration. Infrared incinerator with shield to prevent spattering of microbial samples during flaming.

The dry oven is used in laboratories and clinics for heat-resistant items that do not sterilize well with moist heat. Substances appropriate for dry ovens are glassware, metallic instruments, powders, and oils that steam does not penetrate well. This method is not suitable for plastics, cotton, and paper, which may burn at the high temperatures, or for liquids, which will evaporate. Another limitation is the time required for it to work.

The Effects of Cold and Desiccation

The principal benefit of cold treatment is to slow growth of cultures and microbes in food during processing and storage. *It must be emphasized that cold merely retards the activities of most microbes.* Although it is true that some microbes are killed by cold temperatures, most are not adversely affected by gradual cooling, long-term refrigeration, or deep-freezing. In fact, freezing temperatures, ranging from −70°C to −135°C, provide an environment that can preserve cultures of bacteria, viruses, and fungi for long periods. Some psychrophiles grow very slowly even at freezing temperatures and can continue to secrete toxic products. Ignorance of these facts is probably responsible for numerous cases of food poisoning from frozen foods that have been defrosted at room temperature and then inadequately cooked. Pathogens able to survive several months in the refrigerator are *Staphylococcus aureus*, *Clostridium* species (sporeformers), *Streptococcus* species, and several types of yeasts, molds, and viruses. Outbreaks of *Salmonella* food infection traced backed to refrigerated foods such as ice cream, eggs, and tiramisu are testimony to the inability of freezing temperatures to reliably kill pathogens.

Vegetative cells directly exposed to normal room air gradually become dehydrated, or **desiccated.** Delicate pathogens such as *Streptococcus pneumoniae*, the spirochete of syphilis, and *Neisseria gonorrhoeae* can die after a few hours of air drying, but many others are not killed and some are even preserved. Endospores of *Bacillus* and *Clostridium* are viable for millions of years under extremely arid conditions. Staphylococci and streptococci in dried secretions and the tubercle bacillus surrounded by sputum can remain viable in air and dust for lengthy periods. Many viruses (especially nonenveloped) and fungal spores can also withstand long periods of desiccation. Desiccation can be a valuable way to preserve foods because it greatly reduces the amount of water available to support microbial growth.

It is interesting to note that a combination of freezing and drying—**lyophilization** (ly-off″-il-ih-za′-shun)—is a common method of preserving microorganisms and other cells in a viable state for many years. Pure cultures are frozen instantaneously and exposed to a vacuum that rapidly removes the water (it goes right from the frozen state into the vapor state). This method avoids the formation of ice crystals that would damage the cells. Although not all cells survive this process, enough of them do to permit future reconstitution of that culture.

As a general rule, chilling, freezing, and desiccation should not be construed as methods of disinfection or sterilization because their antimicrobial effects are erratic and uncertain, and one cannot be sure that pathogens subjected to them have been killed.

Radiation as a Microbial Control Agent

Another way in which energy can serve as an antimicrobial agent is through the use of radiation. **Radiation** is defined as energy emitted from atomic activities and dispersed at high velocity through matter or space. Although radiation exists in many states and can be described and characterized in various ways, we consider only those types suitable for microbial control: gamma rays, X rays, and ultraviolet radiation.

Modes of Action of Ionizing Versus Nonionizing Radiation

The actual physical effects of radiation on microbes can be understood by visualizing the process of **irradiation,** or bombardment with radiation, at the cellular level **(figure 11.7).**

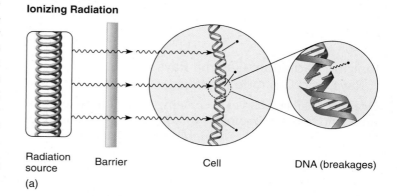

Ionizing Radiation

Radiation source   Barrier   Cell   DNA (breakages)
(a)

Nonionizing Radiation

(b)   DNA (abnormal bonds)

Radiation source   Barrier

UV does not penetrate. No effect on cell

(c)

Figure 11.7 Cellular effects of irradiation.   **(a)** Ionizing radiation can penetrate a solid barrier, bombard a cell, enter it, and dislodge electrons from molecules. Breakage of DNA creates massive mutations and damage to proteins prevents them from repairing it. **(b)** Nonionizing radiation enters a cell, strikes molecules, and excites them. The effect on DNA is mutation by formation of abnormal bonds. **(c)** A solid barrier cannot be penetrated by nonionizing radiation.

When a cell is bombarded by certain waves or particles, its molecules absorb some of the available energy, leading to one of two consequences: (1) If the radiation ejects orbital electrons from an atom, it causes ions to form; this type of radiation is termed **ionizing radiation.** It was previously believed that the most sensitive target for ionizing radiation is DNA, which undergoes mutations on a broad scale, but studies conducted in 2007 suggest that protein damage is the culprit. If proteins are not destroyed, apparently they can almost always repair the DNA. Secondary lethal effects appear to be chemical changes in organelles and the production of toxic substances. Gamma rays, X rays, and high-speed electrons are all ionizing in their effects. (2) **Nonionizing radiation,** best exemplified by ultraviolet (UV), excites atoms by raising them to a higher energy state, but it does not ionize them. This atomic excitation, in turn, leads to the formation of abnormal bonds within molecules such as DNA and is thus a source of mutations.

Figure 11.8 Foods commonly irradiated.   Regulations dictate that the universal symbol for irradiation must be affixed to all irradiated materials.

Ionizing Radiation: Gamma Rays, X Rays, and Cathode Rays

Over the past several years, ionizing radiation has become safer and more economical to use, and its applications have mushroomed. It is a highly effective alternative for sterilizing materials that are sensitive to heat or chemicals. Because it sterilizes in the absence of heat, irradiation is a type of **cold** (or low-temperature) **sterilization.**[2] Devices that emit ionizing rays include gamma-ray machines containing radioactive cobalt, X-ray machines similar to those used in medical diagnosis, and cathode-ray machines. Items are placed in these machines and irradiated for a short time with a carefully chosen dosage. The dosage of radiation is measured in *Grays* (which has replaced the older term, *rads*). Depending on the application, exposure ranges from 5 to 50 kiloGrays (kGray; a kiloGray is equal to 1,000 Grays). Although all ionizing radiation can penetrate liquids and most solid materials, gamma rays are most penetrating, X rays are intermediate, and cathode rays are least penetrating.

Applications of Ionizing Radiation

Foods have been subject to irradiation in limited circumstances for more than 50 years. From flour to pork and ground beef, to fruits and vegetables, radiation is used to kill not only bacterial pathogens but also insects and worms and even to inhibit the sprouting of white potatoes **(figure 11.8).** As soon as radiation is mentioned, however, consumer concern arises that food may be made less nutritious, unpalatable, or even unsafe by its having been subjected to ionizing

radiation. But irradiated food has been extensively studied, and each of these concerns has been addressed.

Irradiation may lead to a small decrease in the amount of thiamine (vitamin B1) in food, but this change is small enough to be inconsequential. The irradiation process does produce short-lived free radical oxidants, which disappear almost immediately (this same type of chemical intermediate is produced through cooking as well). Certain foods do not irradiate well and are not good candidates for this type of antimicrobial control. The white of eggs becomes milky and liquid, grapefruit gets mushy, and alfalfa seeds do not germinate properly. Lastly, it is important to remember that food is not made radioactive by the irradiation process, and many studies, in both animals and humans, have concluded that there are no ill effects from eating irradiated food. In fact, NASA relies on irradiated meat for its astronauts.

Sterilizing medical products with ionizing radiation is a rapidly expanding field. Drugs, vaccines, medical instruments (especially plastics), syringes, surgical gloves, tissues such as bone and skin, and heart valves for grafting all lend themselves to this mode of sterilization. After the anthrax attacks of 2001, mail delivered to certain Washington, D.C., ZIP Codes was irradiated with ionizing radiation. Its main advantages include speed, high penetrating power (it can sterilize materials through outer packages and wrappings), and the absence of heat. Its main disadvantages are potential dangers to radiation machine operators from exposure to radiation and possible damage to some materials.

Nonionizing Radiation: Ultraviolet Rays

Ultraviolet (UV) radiation ranges in wavelength from approximately 100 nm to 400 nm. It is most lethal from 240 nm to 280 nm (with a peak at 260 nm). In everyday

---

2. This is a possibly confusing use of the word "cold." In this context, it only means the absence of heat. Beer manufacturers have sometimes used this terminology as well. When they say that their product is "cold-filtered," they usually mean that it has been freed of contaminants via filtration, that is, in the absence of heat.

practice, the source of UV radiation is the germicidal lamp, which generates radiation at 254 nm. Owing to its lower energy state, UV radiation is not as penetrating as ionizing radiation. Because UV radiation passes readily through air, slightly through liquids, and only poorly through solids, the object to be disinfected must be directly exposed to it for full effect.

As UV radiation passes through a cell, it is initially absorbed by DNA. Specific molecular damage occurs on the pyrimidine bases (thymine and cytosine), which form abnormal linkages with each other called **pyrimidine dimers (figure 11.9).** These bonds occur between adjacent bases on the same DNA strand and interfere with normal DNA replication and transcription. The results are inhibition of growth and cellular death. In addition to altering DNA directly, UV radiation also disrupts cells by generating toxic photochemical products called free radicals. These highly reactive molecules interfere with essential cell processes by binding to DNA, RNA, and proteins.

Ultraviolet rays are a powerful tool for destroying fungal cells and spores, bacterial vegetative cells, protozoa, and viruses. Bacterial spores are about 10 times more resistant to radiation than are vegetative cells, but they can be killed by increasing the time of exposure.

Applications of Ultraviolet Radiation Ultraviolet radiation is usually directed at disinfection rather than sterilization. Germicidal lamps can cut down on the concentration of airborne microbes as much as 99%. They are used in hospital rooms, operating rooms, schools, food preparation areas, and dental offices. Ultraviolet disinfection of air has proved effective in reducing postoperative infections, preventing the transmission of infections by respiratory droplets, and curtailing the growth of microbes in food-processing plants and slaughterhouses.

Ultraviolet irradiation of liquids requires special equipment to spread the liquid into a thin, flowing film that is exposed directly to a lamp. This method can be used to treat drinking water **(figure 11.10)** and to purify other liquids (milk and fruit juices) as an alternative to heat. Ultraviolet treatment has proved effective in freeing vaccines and plasma from contaminants. The surfaces of solid, nonporous materials such as walls and floors, as well as meat, nuts, tissues for grafting, and drugs, have been successfully disinfected with UV.

One major disadvantage of UV is its poor powers of penetration through solid materials such as glass, metal, cloth, plastic, and even paper. Another drawback to UV is the damaging effect of overexposure on human tissues, including sunburn, retinal damage, cancer, and skin wrinkling.

Figure 11.9 Formation of pyrimidine dimers by the action of ultraviolet (UV) radiation. This shows what occurs when two adjacent thymine bases on one strand of DNA are induced by UV rays to bond laterally with each other. The result is a thymine dimer (shown in greater detail). Dimers can also occur between adjacent cytosines and thymine and cytosine bases. If they are not repaired, dimers can prevent that segment of DNA from being correctly replicated or transcribed. Massive dimerization is lethal to cells.

Figure 11.10 An ultraviolet (UV) treatment system for disinfection of water. Water flows through tunnels at a water treatment plant, past racks of UV lamps. This system has a capacity of several million gallons per day and can be used as an alternative to chlorination. Home systems that fit under the sink are also available.

Decontamination by Filtration: Techniques for Removing Microbes

Filtration is an effective method to remove microbes from air and liquids. In practice, a fluid is strained through a filter with openings large enough for the fluid to pass through but too small for microorganisms to pass through (**figure 11.11a**).

Most modern microbiological filters are thin membranes of cellulose acetate, polycarbonate, and a variety of plastic materials (Teflon, nylon) whose pore size can be carefully controlled and standardized. Ordinary substances such as charcoal, diatomaceous earth, or unglazed porcelain are also used in some applications. Viewed microscopically, most filters are perforated by very precise, uniform pores (**figure 11.11b**). The pore diameters vary from coarse (8 microns) to ultrafine (0.02 micron), permitting selection of the minimum particle size to be trapped. Those with even smaller pore diameters permit true sterilization by removing viruses, and some will even remove large proteins. A sterile liquid filtrate is typically produced by suctioning the liquid through a sterile filter into a presterilized container. These filters are also used to separate mixtures of microorganisms and to enumerate bacteria in water analysis (see chapter 25).

Applications of Filtration

Filtration is used to prepare liquids that cannot withstand heat, including serum and other blood products, vaccines, drugs, IV fluids, enzymes, and media. Filtration has been employed as an alternative method for decontaminating milk and beer without altering their flavor. It is also an important step in water purification. Its use extends to filtering out particulate impurities (crystals, fibers, and so on) that can cause severe reactions in the body. It has the disadvantage of not removing soluble molecules (toxins) that can cause disease.

Filtration is also an efficient means of removing airborne contaminants that are a common source of infection and spoilage. High-efficiency particulate air (HEPA) filters are widely used to provide a flow of decontaminated air to hospital rooms and sterile rooms. A vacuum with a HEPA filter was even used to remove anthrax spores from the Senate offices most heavily contaminated after the terrorist attack in late 2001 (see Insight 11.2).

Osmotic Pressure

In chapter 7 you learned about the effects of osmotic pressure on cells (see figure 7.5). This fact has long been exploited as a means of preserving food. Adding large amounts of salt or sugar to foods creates a hypertonic environment for bacteria in the foods, causing plasmolysis and making it impossible for the bacteria to multiply. People knew that these techniques worked long before the discovery of bacteria. This is why meats are "cured," or treated with high salt concentrations so they can be kept for long periods without refrigeration. High sugar concentrations in foods like jellies have the same effect.

(a)

(b)

Figure 11.11 Membrane filtration.   (a) Vacuum assembly for achieving filtration of liquids through suction. Inset shows filter as seen in cross section, with tiny passageways (pores) too small for the microbial cells to enter but large enough for liquid to pass through. **(b)** Scanning electron micrograph of filter, showing relative size of pores and bacteria trapped on its surface (5,900×).

11.2 Learning Outcomes—Can You ...

5. ... name six methods of physical control of microorganisms?

6. ... discuss both moist and dry heat methods and identify multiple examples of both?

7. ... define thermal death time and thermal death point?

8. ... explain four different methods of moist heat control?

9. ... explain two methods of dry heat control?

10. ... identify advantages and disadvantages of cold and dessication?

11. ... differentiate between the two types of radiation control methods?

12. ... explain how filtration functions as a control method?

13. ... identify some common uses of osmotic pressure as a control method?

11.3 Chemical Agents in Microbial Control

Chemical control of microbes probably emerged as a serious science in the 1800s, when physicians used chloride of lime and iodine solutions to treat wounds and to wash their hands before surgery. At the present time, more than 10,000 different antimicrobial chemical agents are manufactured; probably 1,000 of them are used routinely in the health care arena and the home. A genuine need exists to avoid infection and spoilage, but the abundance of products available to "kill germs," "disinfect," "antisepticize," "clean and sanitize," "deodorize," "fight plaque," and "purify the air" indicates a preoccupation with eliminating microbes from the environment that, at times, seems excessive **(Insight 11.3).**

INSIGHT 11.3   Pathogen Paranoia: "The Only Good Microbe Is a Dead Microbe"

The sensational publicity over outbreaks of infections such as H1N1 influenza, anthrax, and microbial food poisoning has monumentally influenced the public view of microorganisms. And, certainly, such knowledge can be seen as beneficial when it leads to well-reasoned and sensible choices, such as using greater care in hand washing, food handling, and personal hygiene. But sometimes a little knowledge can be dangerous. The trend also seems to have escalated into an obsessive fear of "germs" lurking around every corner and a fixation on eliminating microbes from the environment and the human body.

As might be expected, commercial industries have found a way to capitalize on those fears. Every year, the number of products that incorporate antibacterial or germicidal "protection" increases dramatically. A widespread array of cleansers and commonplace materials have already had antimicrobial chemicals added. First it was hand soaps and dishwashing detergents, and eventually the list grew to include shampoos, laundry aids, hand lotions, foot pads for shoes, deodorants, sponges and scrub pads, kitty litter, cutting boards, garbage bags, toys, toothpaste, water bottles, and ink pens.

One chemical agent routinely added to these products is a phenolic called *triclosan* (Irgasan). This substance is fairly mild and nontoxic and does indeed kill most pathogenic bacteria. However, it does not reliably destroy viruses or fungi and has been linked to cases of skin rashes due to hypersensitivity.

Medical experts are concerned that the widespread overuse of these antibacterial chemicals could favor the survival and growth of resistant strains of bacteria. We know that many pathogens such as *Mycobacterium tuberculosis* and *Pseudomonas* are naturally resistant to triclosan and that *E. coli* and *Staphylococcus aureus* have already demonstrated decreased sensitivity to it. The widespread use of this chemical may actually select for "super microbes" that survive ordinary disinfection. Another outcome of overuse of environmental germicides is to reduce the natural contact with microbes that is required to maintain the normal resident biota and stimulate immunities. Constant use of these agents could shift the balance in the normal biota of the body by killing off harmless or beneficial microbes. And there's one more thing. More and more

studies are showing that when some bacteria become resistant to antibacterial agents, including triclosan, they simultaneously become resistant to antibiotics such as tetracycline and erythromycin. In 2010 the FDA initiated a review of triclosan's safety.

Infectious disease specialists urge a happy medium approach. Instead of filling the home with questionable germicidal products, they encourage cleaning with traditional soaps and detergents, reserving more potent products to reduce the spread of infection among household members.

Ironically, at the same time that consumers are snapping up products of every kind that contain antimicrobials, they seem to be lax about the most effective antimicrobial technique: hand washing. The American Society for Microbiology and the Soap and Detergent Association have been studying handwashing behavior in public restrooms in Atlanta (Turner Field), Chicago (the Museum of Science and Industry), New York (Grand Central Station), and other places around the country. They found that although 92% of adults say they always wash their hands when using a public restroom, the actual percentage is more like 77%. (The study employed undercover observers who actually watched people in the restrooms.) Interestingly, women are more fastidious than men: 88% of women washed their hands after using the restroom compared with only 66% of men.

Antimicrobial chemicals occur in the liquid, gaseous, or even solid state, and they range from disinfectants and antiseptics to sterilants and preservatives (chemicals that inhibit the deterioration of substances). For the sake of convenience (and sometimes safety), many solid or gaseous antimicrobial chemicals are dissolved in water, alcohol, or a mixture of the two to produce a liquid solution. Solutions containing pure water as the solvent are termed **aqueous,** whereas those dissolved in pure alcohol or water-alcohol mixtures are termed **tinctures.**

Table 11.3 provides an overview of chemicals that are routinely used in health care.

Choosing a Microbicidal Chemical

The choice and appropriate use of antimicrobial chemical agents are of constant concern in medicine and dentistry. Although actual clinical practices of chemical decontamination vary widely, some desirable qualities in a germicide have been identified, including:

1. rapid action even in low concentrations,
2. solubility in water or alcohol and long-term stability,
3. broad-spectrum microbicidal action without being toxic to human and animal tissues,
4. penetration of inanimate surfaces to sustain a cumulative or persistent action,
5. resistance to becoming inactivated by organic matter,
6. noncorrosive or nonstaining properties,
7. sanitizing and deodorizing properties, and
8. affordability and ready availability.

As yet, no chemical can completely fulfill all of those requirements, but glutaraldehyde and hydrogen peroxide approach this ideal. At the same time, we should question the rather overinflated claims made about certain commercial agents such as mouthwashes and disinfectant air sprays.

Germicides are evaluated in terms of their effectiveness in destroying microbes in medical and dental settings. The three levels of chemical decontamination procedures are *high, intermediate,* and *low.* High-level germicides kill endospores and, if properly used, are sterilants. Materials that necessitate high-level control are medical devices—for example, catheters, heart-lung equipment, and implants—that are not

Table 11.3 Qualities of Chemical Agents Used in Health Care

Agent	Target Microbes	Level of Activity	Toxicity	Comments
Chlorine	Sporicidal (slowly)	Intermediate	Gas is highly toxic; solution irritates skin	Inactivated by organics; unstable in sunlight
Iodine	Sporicidal (slowly)	Intermediate	Can irritate tissue; toxic if ingested	Iodophors are milder forms
Phenolics	Some bacteria, viruses, fungi	Low to intermediate	Can be absorbed by skin; can cause CNS damage	Poor solubility; expensive
Chlorhexidine*	Most bacteria, some viruses, fungi	Low to intermediate	Low toxicity	Fast-acting, mild, has residual effects
Alcohols	Most bacteria, viruses, fungi	Intermediate	Toxic if ingested; a mild irritant; dries skin	Flammable, fast-acting
Hydrogen peroxide,* stabilized	Sporicidal	High	Toxic to eyes; toxic if ingested	Improved stability; works well in organic matter
Quaternary ammonium compounds	Some bactericidal, virucidal, fungicidal activity	Low	Irritating to mucous membranes; poisonous if taken internally	Weak solutions can support microbial growth; easily inactivated
Soaps	Certain very sensitive species	Very low	Nontoxic; few if any toxic effects	Used for removing soil, oils, debris
Mercurials	Weakly microbistatic	Low	Highly toxic if ingested, inhaled, absorbed	Easily inactivated
Silver nitrate	Bactericidal	Low	Toxic, irritating	Discolors skin
Glutaraldehyde*	Sporicidal	High	Can irritate skin; toxic if absorbed	Not inactivated by organic matter; unstable
Formaldehyde	Sporicidal	Intermediate to high	Very irritating; fumes damaging, carcinogenic	Slow rate of action; limited applications
Ethylene oxide gas*	Sporicidal	High	Very dangerous to eyes, lungs; carcinogenic	Explosive in pure state; good penetration; materials must be aerated
Dyes	Weakly bactericidal, fungicidal	Low	Low toxicity	Stains materials, skin

*These chemicals approach the ideal by having many of the following characteristics: broad spectrum, low toxicity, fast action, penetrating abilities, residual effects, stability, potency in organic matter, and solubility.

heat-sterilizable and are intended to enter body tissues during medical procedures. Intermediate-level germicides kill fungal (but not bacterial) spores, resistant pathogens such as the tubercle bacillus, and viruses. They are used to disinfect items (respiratory equipment, thermometers) that come into intimate contact with the mucous membranes but are noninvasive. Low levels of disinfection eliminate only vegetative bacteria, vegetative fungal cells, and some viruses. They are used to clean materials such as electrodes, straps, and pieces of furniture that touch the skin surfaces but not the mucous membranes.

Factors That Affect the Germicidal Activity of Chemicals

Factors that control the effect of a germicide include the nature of the microorganisms being treated, the nature of the material being treated, the degree of contamination, the time of exposure, and the strength and chemical action of the germicide (table 11.4). The modes of action of most germicides are to attack the cellular targets discussed earlier: proteins, nucleic acids, the cell wall, and the cell membrane.

A chemical's strength or concentration is expressed in various ways, depending on convention and the method of preparation. The content of many chemical agents can be expressed by more than one notation. In dilutions, a small volume of the liquid chemical (solute) is diluted in a larger volume of solvent to achieve a certain ratio. For example, a common laboratory phenolic disinfectant such as Lysol is usually diluted 1:200; that is, one part of chemical has been added to 200 parts of water by volume. Solutions such as chlorine that are effective

in very diluted concentrations are expressed in parts per million (ppm). In percentage solutions, the solute is added to water by weight or volume to achieve a certain percentage in the solution. Alcohol, for instance, is used in percentages ranging from 50% to 95%. In general, solutions of low dilution or high percentage have more of the active chemical (are more concentrated) and tend to be more germicidal, but expense and potential toxicity can necessitate using the minimum strength that is effective.

Another factor that contributes to germicidal effectiveness is the length of exposure. Most compounds require adequate contact time to allow the chemical to penetrate and to act on the microbes present. The composition of the material being treated must also be considered. Smooth, solid objects are more reliably disinfected than are those with pores or pockets that can trap soil. An item contaminated with common biological matter such as serum, blood, saliva, pus, fecal material, or urine presents a problem in disinfection. Large amounts of organic material can hinder the penetration of a disinfectant and, in some cases, can form bonds that reduce its activity. Adequate cleaning of instruments and other reusable materials ensures that the germicide or sterilant will better accomplish the job for which it was chosen.

Germicidal Categories According to Chemical Group

Several general groups of chemical compounds are widely used for antimicrobial purposes in medicine and commerce. Prominent agents include halogens, heavy metals, alcohols, phenolic compounds, oxidizers, aldehydes, detergents, and gases. These groups are surveyed in the following section from the standpoint of each agent's specific forms, modes of action, indications for use, and limitations.

The Halogen Antimicrobial Chemicals

The halogens are fluorine, bromine, chlorine, and iodine, a group of nonmetallic elements, all of which are found in group VII of the periodic table. These elements are highly effective components of disinfectants and antiseptics because they are microbicidal and not just microbistatic, and they are sporicidal with longer exposure. For these reasons, halogens are the active ingredients in nearly one-third of all antimicrobial chemicals currently marketed.

Chlorine and Its Compounds
Chlorine has been used for disinfection and antisepsis for approximately 200 years. The major forms used in microbial control are liquid and gaseous chlorine (Cl_2), hypochlorites (OCl), and chloramines (NH_2Cl). In solution, these compounds combine with water and release hypochlorous acid (HOCl), which oxidizes the sulfhydryl (S—H) group on the amino acid cysteine and interferes with disulfide (S—S) bridges on numerous enzymes. The resulting denaturation of the enzymes is permanent and suspends metabolic reactions. Chlorine kills not only bacteria and endospores but also fungi and viruses. Chlorine compounds are less effective if exposed to light, alkaline pH, and excess organic matter.

Table 11.4	Required Concentrations and Times for Chemical Destruction of Selected Microbes	
Organism	**Concentration**	**Time**
Agent: Chlorine		
Mycobacterium tuberculosis	50 ppm	50 sec
Entamoeba cysts (protozoa)	0.1 ppm	150 min
Hepatitis A virus	3 ppm	30 min
Agent: Ethyl Alcohol		
Staphylococcus aureus	70%	10 min
Escherichia coli	70%	2 min
Poliovirus	70%	10 min
Agent: Hydrogen Peroxide		
Staphylococcus aureus	3%	12.5 sec
Neisseria gonorrhoeae	3%	0.3 sec
Herpes simplex virus	3%	12.8 sec
Agent: Quaternary Ammonium Compound		
Staphylococcus aureus	450 ppm	10 min
Salmonella typhi	300 ppm	10 min
Agent: Ethylene Oxide Gas		
Streptococcus faecalis	500 mg/L	2–4 min
Influenza virus	10,000 mg/L	25 h

Chlorine Compounds in Disinfection and Antisepsis

Gaseous and liquid chlorine are used almost exclusively for large-scale disinfection of drinking water, sewage, and wastewater from such sources as agriculture and industry. Chlorination to a concentration of 0.6 to 1.0 parts of chlorine per million parts of water will usually ensure that water is safe to drink. This treatment rids the water of most pathogenic vegetative microorganisms without unduly affecting its taste (some people may debate this). In chapter 22, however, you will learn about pathogenic organisms that can survive water chlorination.

Hypochlorites are perhaps the most extensively used of all chlorine compounds. The scope of applications is broad, including sanitization and disinfection of food equipment in dairies, restaurants, and canneries and treatment of swimming pools, spas, drinking water, and even fresh foods. Hypochlorites are used in the allied health areas to treat wounds and to disinfect equipment, bedding, and instruments. Common household bleach is a weak solution (5%) of sodium hypochlorite that serves as an all-around disinfectant, deodorizer, and stain remover.

Chloramines (dichloramine, halazone) are being employed more frequently as an alternative to pure chlorine in treating water supplies. Because standard chlorination of water is now believed to produce unsafe levels of cancer-causing substances such as trihalomethanes, some water districts have been directed by federal agencies to adopt chloramine treatment of water supplies. Chloramines also serve as sanitizers and disinfectants, and for treating wounds and skin surfaces.

Iodine and Its Compounds

Iodine is a pungent chemical that forms brown-colored solutions when dissolved in water or alcohol. The two primary iodine preparations are *free iodine* in solution (I_2) and *iodophors*. Iodine rapidly penetrates the cells of microorganisms, where it apparently disturbs a variety of metabolic functions by interfering with the hydrogen and disulfide bonding of proteins (a mode of action similar to chlorine). All classes of microorganisms are killed by iodine if proper concentrations and exposure times are used. Iodine activity is not as adversely affected by organic matter and pH as chlorine is.

Applications of Iodine Solutions

Aqueous iodine contains 2% iodine and 2.4% sodium iodide; it is used as a topical antiseptic before surgery and occasionally as a treatment for burned and infected skin. A stronger iodine solution (5% iodine and 10% potassium iodide) is used primarily as a disinfectant for plastic items, rubber instruments, cutting blades, thermometers, and other inanimate items. Iodine tincture is a 2% solution of iodine and sodium iodide in 70% alcohol that can be used in skin antisepsis. Because iodine can be extremely irritating to the skin and toxic when absorbed, strong aqueous solutions and tinctures (5% to 7%) are no longer considered safe for routine antisepsis. Iodine tablets are available for disinfecting water during emergencies or destroying pathogens in impure water supplies.

Iodophors are complexes of iodine and alcohol. This formulation allows the slow release of free iodine and increases its degree of penetration. These compounds have largely replaced free iodine solutions in medical antisepsis because they are less prone to staining or irritating tissues. Common iodophor products marketed as Betadine, Povidone (PVP), and Isodine contain 2% to 10% of available iodine. They are used to prepare skin and mucous membranes for surgery and injections, in surgical handscrubs, to treat burns, and to disinfect equipment and surfaces. Although pure iodine is toxic to the eye, studies show that Betadine solution is an effective means of preventing eye infections in newborn infants, and it may replace antibiotics and silver nitrate as the method of choice.

Phenol and Its Derivatives

Phenol (carbolic acid) is an acrid, poisonous compound derived from the distillation of coal tar. First adopted by Joseph Lister in 1867 as a surgical germicide, phenol was the major antimicrobial chemical until other phenolics with fewer toxic and irritating effects were developed. Solutions of phenol are now used only in certain limited cases, but phenol remains one standard against which other phenolic disinfectants are rated. The *phenol coefficient* quantitatively compares a chemical's antimicrobic properties to those of phenol. Substances chemically related to phenol are often referred to as phenolics. Hundreds of these chemicals are now available.

Phenolics consist of one or more aromatic carbon rings with added functional groups **(figure 11.12).** Among the most important are alkylated phenols (cresols), chlorinated phenols, and bisphenols. In high concentrations, they are cellular poisons, rapidly disrupting cell walls and membranes and precipitating proteins; in lower concentrations, they inactivate certain critical enzyme systems. The phenolics are strongly microbicidal and will destroy vegetative bacteria (including the tuberculosis bacterium), fungi, and most viruses (not hepatitis B), but they are not reliably sporicidal. Their ability to act in the presence of organic matter and their detergent actions contribute to their usefulness. Unfortunately, the toxicity of many of the phenolics makes them too dangerous to use as antiseptics.

Applications of Phenolics

Phenol itself is still used for general disinfection of drains, cesspools, and animal quarters, but it is seldom applied as a

---

Case File 11   *Continuing the Case*

Unfortunately, the design of the Seneca Lake water playground allowed contaminants (e.g., vomit, feces, and dirt) to wash into the water-holding tanks supplying it. Testing revealed the presence of *Cryptosporidium* in those water tanks. Even though the water in the tanks was filtered and chlorinated, *Cryptosporidium* is small enough to pass through a filter and is also resistant to chlorine.

■ Besides using filters or chlorine, what other methods are available to disinfect water?

Figure 11.12 Some phenolics. All contain a basic aromatic ring, but they differ in the types of additional compounds such as Cl and CH₃.

medical germicide. The cresols are simple phenolic derivatives that are combined with soap for intermediate or low levels of disinfection in the hospital. Lysol and creolin, in a 1% to 3% emulsion, are common household versions of this type.

The bisphenols are also widely employed in commerce, clinics, and the home. One type, orthophenyl phenol, is the major ingredient in disinfectant aerosol sprays. This same phenolic is also found in some proprietary compounds (Lysol) often used in hospital and laboratory disinfection. One particular bisphenol, hexachlorophene, was once a common additive of cleansing soaps (pHisoHex) used in the hospital and home. When hexachlorophene was found to be absorbed through the skin and a cause of neurological damage, it was no longer available without a prescription. It is occasionally used to control outbreaks of skin infections.

Perhaps the most widely used phenolic is *triclosan,* chemically known as dichlorophenoxyphenol (see Insight 11.3). It is the antibacterial compound added to dozens of products, from soaps to kitty litter. It acts as both disinfectant and antiseptic and is broad-spectrum in its effects.

Chlorhexidine

The compound chlorhexidine (Hibiclens, Hibitane, Peridex) is a complex organic base containing chlorine and two phenolic rings. Its mode of action targets both cell membranes (lowering surface tension until selective permeability is lost) and protein structure (causing denaturation). At moderate to high concentrations, it is bactericidal for both gram-positive and gram-negative bacteria but inactive against spores. Its effects on viruses and fungi vary. It possesses distinct advantages over many other antiseptics because of its mildness, low toxicity, and rapid action, and it is not absorbed into deeper tissues to any extent. Alcoholic or aqueous solutions of chlorhexidine are now commonly used for hand scrubbing, preparing skin

sites for surgical incisions and injections, and whole-body washing. Chlorhexidine solution also serves as an obstetric antiseptic, a neonatal wash, a wound degermer, a mucous membrane irrigant, and a preservative for eye solutions. It is sold in many over-the-counter mouthwashes as well.

Alcohols as Antimicrobial Agents

Alcohols are colorless hydrocarbons with one or more —OH functional groups. Of several alcohols available, only ethyl and isopropyl are suitable for microbial control. Methyl alcohol is not particularly microbicidal, and more complex alcohols are either poorly soluble in water or too expensive for routine use. Alcohols are employed alone in aqueous solutions or as solvents for tinctures (iodine, for example).

Alcohol's mechanism of action depends in part upon its concentration. Concentrations of 50% and higher dissolve membrane lipids, disrupt cell surface tension, and compromise membrane integrity. Alcohol that has entered the cytoplasm denatures proteins through coagulation but only in alcohol-water solutions of 50% to 95%. Alcohol is the exception to the rule that higher concentrations of an antimicrobial chemical have greater microbicidal activity. Because water is needed for proteins to coagulate, alcohol shows a greater microbicidal activity at 70% concentration (that is, 30% water) than at 100% (0% water). Absolute alcohol (100%) dehydrates cells and inhibits their growth but is generally not a protein coagulant.

Although useful in intermediate- to low-level germicidal applications, alcohol does not destroy bacterial spores at room temperature. Alcohol can, however, destroy resistant vegetative forms, including tuberculosis bacteria and fungal spores, provided the time of exposure is adequate. Alcohol is generally more effective in inactivating enveloped viruses than nonenveloped viruses such as poliovirus and hepatitis A virus.

Applications of Alcohols Ethyl alcohol, also called ethanol or grain alcohol, is known for being germicidal, nonirritating, and inexpensive. Solutions of 70% to 95% are routinely used as skin degerming agents because the surfactant action removes skin oil, soil, and some microbes sheltered in deeper skin layers. One limitation to its effectiveness is the rate at which it evaporates. Ethyl alcohol is occasionally used to disinfect electrodes, face masks, and thermometers, which are first cleaned and then soaked in alcohol for 15 to 20 minutes. Isopropyl alcohol, sold as rubbing alcohol, is even more microbicidal and less expensive than ethanol, but these benefits must be weighed against its toxicity. It must be used with caution in disinfection or skin cleansing, because inhalation of its vapors can adversely affect the nervous system.

Hydrogen Peroxide and Related Germicides

Hydrogen peroxide (H_2O_2) is a colorless, caustic liquid that decomposes in the presence of light, metals, or catalase into water and oxygen gas. The germicidal effects of hydrogen peroxide are due to the direct and indirect actions of oxygen. Oxygen forms hydroxyl free radicals (—OH), which, like the superoxide radical (see chapter 7), are highly toxic and reactive to cells. Although most microbial cells produce catalase to inactivate the metabolic hydrogen peroxide, it cannot neutralize the amount of hydrogen peroxide entering the cell during disinfection and antisepsis. Hydrogen peroxide is bactericidal, virucidal, fungicidal, and, in higher concentrations, sporicidal.

Applications of Hydrogen Peroxide   As an antiseptic, 3% hydrogen peroxide serves a variety of needs, including skin and wound cleansing, bedsore care, and mouthwashing. It is especially useful in treating infections by anaerobic bacteria because of the lethal effects of oxygen on these forms. Hydrogen peroxide is also a versatile disinfectant for soft contact lenses, surgical implants, plastic equipment, utensils, bedding, and room interiors.

A number of clinical procedures involve delicate reusable instruments such as endoscopes and dental handpieces. Because these devices can become heavily contaminated by tissues and fluids, they need to undergo sterilization, not just disinfection, between patients to prevent transmission of infections such as hepatitis, tuberculosis, and genital warts. These very effective and costly diagnostic tools (a colonoscope may cost up to $30,000) have created another dilemma. They may trap infectious agents where they cannot be easily removed, and they are delicate, complex, and difficult to clean. Traditional methods are either too harsh (heat) to protect the instruments from damage or too slow (ethylene oxide) to sterilize them in a timely fashion between patients. The need for effective rapid sterilization has led to the development of low-temperature sterilizing cabinets that contain liquid chemical sterilants **(figure 11.13).** The major types of chemical sterilants used in these machines are powerful oxidizing agents such as hydrogen peroxide (35%) and peracetic acid (35%) that penetrate into delicate machinery, kill the most resistant microbes, and do not corrode or damage the working parts.

Vaporized hydrogen peroxide can also be used as a sterilant in enclosed areas. Hydrogen peroxide plasma sterilizers exist for those applications involving small industrial or medical items. For larger enclosed spaces, such as isolators and passthrough rooms, peroxide generators can be used to fill a room with hydrogen peroxide vapors at concentrations high enough to be sporicidal.

A cabinet for rapid (within 30 minutes) sterile processing of endoscopes and other microsurgical instruments

Figure 11.13 Sterile processing of invasive equipment protects patients.

(a)

Benzalkonium chloride

(b)

Figure 11.14 The structure of detergents.   **(a)** In general, detergents are polar molecules with a positively charged head and at least one long, uncharged hydrocarbon chain. The head contains a central nitrogen nucleus with various alkyl (R) groups attached. **(b)** A common quaternary ammonium detergent, benzalkonium chloride.

Another compound with effects similar to those of hydrogen peroxide is ozone (O_3), used to disinfect air, water, and industrial air conditioners and cooling towers.

Chemicals with Surface Action: Detergents

Detergents are polar molecules that act as **surfactants.** Most anionic detergents have limited microbicidal power. This includes most soaps. Much more effective are positively charged (cationic) detergents, particularly the quaternary ammonium compounds (usually shortened to *quats*).

The activity of cationic detergents arises from the amphipathic (two-headed) nature of the molecule. The positively charged end binds well with the predominantly negatively charged bacterial surface proteins while the long, uncharged hydrocarbon chain allows the detergent to disrupt the cell membrane **(figure 11.14).** Eventually the cell membrane loses selective permeability, leading to the death of the cell. Several other effects are seen but the loss of integrity of the cell membrane is most important.

The effects of detergents are varied. When used at high enough concentrations, quaternary ammonium compounds are effective against some gram-positive bacteria, viruses, fungi, and algae. In low concentrations, they exhibit only microbistatic effects. Drawbacks to the quats include their ineffectiveness against the tuberculosis bacterium, hepatitis virus, *Pseudomonas*, and spores at any concentration. Furthermore, their activity is greatly reduced in the presence of organic matter and they function best in alkaline solutions. As a result of these limitations, quats are rated only for low-level disinfection in the clinical setting.

Applications of Detergents and Soaps   Quaternary ammonium compounds **(quats)** include benzalkonium chloride, Zephiran, and cetylpyridinium chloride (Ceepryn). In dilutions ranging from 1:100 to 1:1,000, quats are mixed with cleaning agents to simultaneously disinfect and sanitize floors, furniture, equipment surfaces, and restrooms. They are used to clean restaurant eating utensils, food-processing equipment, dairy equipment, and clothing. They are common preservatives for ophthalmic solutions and cosmetics. Their level of disinfection is far too low for disinfecting medical instruments.

Soaps are alkaline compounds made by combining the fatty acids in oils with sodium or potassium salts. In usual practice, soaps are only weak microbicides, and they destroy only highly sensitive forms such as the agents of gonorrhea, meningitis, and syphilis. The common hospital pathogen *Pseudomonas* is so resistant to soap that various species grow abundantly in soap dishes.

Soaps function primarily as cleansing agents and sanitizers in industry and the home. The superior sudsing and wetting properties of soaps help to mechanically remove large amounts of surface soil, greases, and other debris that contains microorganisms. Soaps gain greater germicidal value when mixed with agents such as chlorhexidine or iodine. They can be used for cleaning instruments before heat sterilization, degerming patients' skin, routine hand washing by medical and dental personnel, and preoperative hand scrubbing. Vigorously brushing the hands with germicidal soap over a 15-second period is an effective way to remove dirt, oil, and surface contaminants as well as some resident microbes, but it will never sterilize the skin (**Insight 11.4** and **figure 11.15**).

INSIGHT 11.4   The Quest for Sterile Skin

More than a hundred years ago, before sterile gloves were a routine part of medical procedures, the hands remained bare during surgery. Realizing the danger from microbes, medical practitioners attempted to sterilize the hands of surgeons and their assistants to prevent surgical infections. Several stringent (and probably very painful) techniques involving strong chemical germicides and vigorous scrubbing were practiced. Here are a few examples.

In "Schatz's method," the hands and forearms were first cleansed by brisk scrubbing with liquid soap for 3 to 5 minutes, then soaked in a saturated solution of permanganate at a temperature of 110°F until they turned a deep mahogany brown. Next, the limbs were immersed in saturated oxalic acid until the skin became decolorized. Then, as if this were not enough, the hands and arms were rinsed with sterile limewater and washed in warm bichloride of mercury for 1 minute.

Or, there was "Park's method" (more like a torture). First, the surfaces of the hands and arms were rubbed completely with a mixture of cornmeal and green soap to remove loose dirt and superficial skin. Next, a paste of water and mustard flour was applied to the skin until it began to sting. This potion was rinsed off in sterile water, and the hands and arms were then soaked in

hot bichloride of mercury for a few minutes, during which the solution was rubbed into the skin.

Another method once earnestly suggested for getting rid of microorganisms was to expose the hands to a hot-air cabinet to "sweat the germs" out of skin glands. Pasteur himself advocated a quick flaming of the hands to maintain asepsis.

The old dream of sterilizing the skin was finally reduced to some basic realities: The microbes entrenched in the epidermis and skin glands cannot be completely eradicated even with the most intense efforts, and the skin cannot be sterilized without also seriously damaging it. Because this is true for both medical personnel and their patients, the chance always exists that infectious agents can be introduced during invasive medical procedures. Safe surgery had to wait until 1890, when rubber gloves were first made available for placing a sterile barrier around the hands. Of course, this did not mean that skin cleansing and antiseptic procedures were abandoned or downplayed. A thorough scrubbing of the skin, followed by application of an antiseptic, is still needed to remove the most dangerous source of infections—the superficial contaminants constantly picked up from whatever we touch.

(a)

(b)

Microbes on normal unwashed hands. **(a)** A scanning electron micrograph of a piece of skin from a fingertip shows clusters of bacteria perched atop a fingerprint ridge (47,000×). **(b)** Heavy growth of microbial colonies on a plate of blood agar. This culture was prepared by passing an open sterile plate around a classroom of 30 students and having each one touch its surface. After incubation, a mixed population of bacteria and fungi appeared.

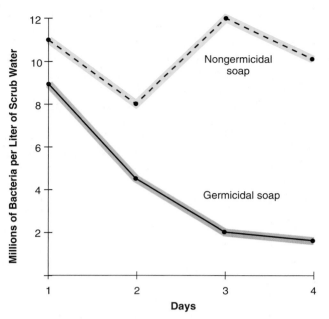

Figure 11.15 Graph showing effects of hand scrubbing.   Comparison of scrubbing over several days with a nongermicidal soap versus a germicidal soap. Germicidal soap has persistent effects on skin over time, keeping the microbial count low. Without germicide, soap does not show this sustained effect.

Heavy Metal Compounds

Various forms of the metallic elements mercury, silver, gold, copper, arsenic, and zinc have been applied in microbial control over several centuries. These are often referred to as heavy metals because of their relatively high atomic weight. However, from this list, only preparations containing mercury and silver still have any significance as germicides. Although some metals (zinc, iron) are actually needed in small concentrations as cofactors on enzymes, the higher molecular weight metals (mercury, silver, gold) can be very toxic, even in minute quantities (parts per million). This property of having antimicrobial effects in exceedingly small amounts is called an **oligodynamic** (ol'-ih-goh-dy-nam'-ik) **action (figure 11.16).** Heavy metal germicides contain either an inorganic or an organic metallic salt, and they come in the form of aqueous solutions, tinctures, ointments, or soaps.

Mercury, silver, and most other metals exert microbicidal effects by binding onto functional groups of proteins and inactivating them, rapidly bringing metabolism to a standstill (see figure 11.4c). This mode of action can destroy many types of microbes, including vegetative bacteria, fungal cells and spores, algae, protozoa, and viruses (but not endospores).

Unfortunately, there are several drawbacks to using metals in microbial control:

1. metals can be very toxic to humans if ingested, inhaled, or absorbed through the skin, even in small quantities, for the same reasons that they are toxic to microbial cells;

2. they often cause allergic reactions;
3. large quantities of biological fluids and wastes neutralize their actions; and
4. microbes can develop resistance to metals.

Health and environmental considerations have dramatically reduced the use of metallic antimicrobial compounds in medicine, dentistry, commerce, and agriculture.

Applications of Heavy Metals   Weak (0.001% to 0.2%) organic mercury tinctures such as thimerosal (Merthiolate) and nitro-mersol (Metaphen) are fairly effective antiseptics and infection preventives, but they should never be used on broken skin because they are harmful and can delay healing. The organic mercurials also serve as preservatives in cosmetics and ophthalmic solutions. Mercurochrome, that old staple of the medicine cabinet, is now considered among the poorest of antiseptics.

A silver compound with several applications is silver nitrate ($AgNO_3$) solution. German professor of obstetrics Carl Siegmund Franz Credé introduced it in the late 19th century for preventing gonococcal infections in the eyes of newborn infants who had been exposed to an infected birth canal (described in chapter 23). This preparation is not used as often now because many pathogens are resistant to it. It has been replaced by antibiotics in most instances. Solutions of silver nitrate (1% to 2%) can also be used as topical germicides on mouth ulcers and occasionally root canals. Silver sulfadiazine ointment, when added to dressings,

Silver amalgam   Gold foil

Figure 11.16 Demonstration of the oligodynamic action of heavy metals.   A pour plate inoculated with saliva has small fragments of heavy metals pressed lightly into it. During incubation, clear zones indicating growth inhibition developed around both fragments. The slightly larger zone surrounding the amalgam (used in tooth fillings) probably reflects the synergistic effect of the silver and mercury it contains.

effectively prevents infection in second- and third-degree burn patients, and pure silver is now incorporated into catheters to prevent urinary tract infections in the hospital. Colloidal silver preparations are mild germicidal ointments or rinses for the mouth, nose, eyes, and vagina. Silver ions are increasingly incorporated into many hard surfaces, such as plastics and steel, as a way to control microbial growth on items such as toilet seats, stethoscopes, and even refrigerator doors.

Aldehydes as Germicides

Organic substances bearing a —CHO functional group (a strong reducing group) on the terminal carbon are called aldehydes. Several common substances such as sugars and some fats are technically aldehydes. The two aldehydes used most often in microbial control are *glutaraldehyde* and *formaldehyde.*

Glutaraldehyde is a yellow liquid with a mild odor. The mechanism of activity involves cross-linking protein molecules on the cell surface. In this process, amino acids are alkylated, meaning that a hydrogen atom on an amino acid is replaced by the glutaraldehyde molecule itself **(figure 11.17).** It can also irreversibly disrupt the activity of enzymes within the cell. Glutaraldehyde is rapid and broad-spectrum and is one of the few chemicals officially accepted as a sterilant and high-level disinfectant. It kills spores in 3 hours and fungi and vegetative bacteria (even *Mycobacterium* and *Pseudomonas*) in a few minutes. Viruses, including the most resistant forms, appear to be inactivated after relatively short exposure times. Glutaraldehyde retains its potency even in the presence of organic matter, is noncorrosive, does not damage plastics, and is less toxic or irritating than formaldehyde. Its principal disadvantage is that it is somewhat unstable, especially with increased pH and temperature.

Formaldehyde is a sharp, irritating gas that readily dissolves in water to form an aqueous solution called **formalin.** Pure formalin is a 37% solution of formaldehyde gas dissolved in water. The chemical is microbicidal through its attachment to nucleic acids and functional groups of amino acids. Formalin is an intermediate- to high-level disinfectant, although it acts more slowly than glutaraldehyde. Formaldehyde's extreme toxicity (it is classified as a carcinogen) and irritating effects on the skin and mucous membranes greatly limit its clinical usefulness.

A third aldehyde, ortho-phthalaldehyde (OPA), is another high-level disinfectant. OPA is a pale blue liquid with a barely detectable odor and can be most directly compared to glutaraldehyde. It has a mechanism of action similar to glutaraldehyde, is stable, is nonirritating to the eyes and nasal passages, and, for most uses, is much faster acting than glutaraldehyde. It is effective against vegetative bacteria, including *Mycobacterium* and *Pseudomonas*, fungi, and viruses. Chief among its disadvantages are an inability to reliably destroy spores and, on a more practical note, its tendency to stain proteins, including those in human skin.

Applications of the Aldehydes
Glutaraldehyde is a milder chemical for sterilizing materials that are damaged by heat. Commercial products (Cidex, Sporicidin) diluted to 2% are used to sterilize respiratory therapy equipment, hemostats, fiberoptic endoscopes (laparoscopes, arthroscopes), and kidney dialysis equipment. Glutaraldehyde is employed on dental instruments (usually in combination with autoclaving) to inactivate hepatitis B and other blood-borne viruses. It also serves to preserve vaccines, sanitize poultry carcasses, and degerm cows' teats.

Formalin tincture (8%) has limited use as a disinfectant for surgical instruments, and formalin solutions have applications in aquaculture to kill fish parasites and control growth of algae and fungi. Any object that is intended to come into intimate contact with the body must be thoroughly rinsed to neutralize the formalin residue. It is, after all, one of the active ingredients in embalming fluid.

Gaseous Sterilants and Disinfectants

Processing inanimate substances with chemical vapors, gases, and aerosols provides a versatile alternative to heat or liquid chemicals. Currently, those vapors and aerosols having the broadest applications are ethylene oxide (ETO), propylene oxide, and chlorine dioxide.

Ethylene oxide is a colorless substance that exists as a gas at room temperature. It is very explosive in air, a feature that can be eliminated by combining it with a high percentage of carbon dioxide or fluorocarbon. Like the aldehydes, ETO is a very strong alkylating agent, and it reacts

Figure 11.17 Actions of glutaraldehyde. The molecule polymerizes easily. When these alkylating polymers react with amino acids, they cross-link and inactivate proteins.

Glutaraldehyde

Polymerization

Polyglutaraldehyde

Cross-linking with microbial protein

G−   G+

Amino groups in peptidoglycan

vigorously with functional groups of DNA and proteins. Through these actions, it blocks both DNA replication and enzymatic actions. Ethylene oxide is one of a very few gases generally accepted for chemical sterilization because, when employed according to strict procedures, it is a sporicide. A specially designed ETO sterilizer called a *chemiclave,* a variation on the autoclave, is equipped with a chamber, gas ports, and temperature, pressure, and humidity controls. Ethylene oxide is rather penetrating but relatively slow-acting, requiring from 90 minutes to 3 hours. Some items absorb ETO residues and must be aerated with sterile air for several hours after exposure to ensure dissipation of as much residual gas as possible. For all of its effectiveness, ETO has some unfortunate features. Its explosiveness makes it dangerous to handle; it can damage the lungs, eyes, and mucous membranes if contacted directly; and it is rated as a carcinogen by the government.

Chlorine dioxide is another gas that has of late been used as a sterilant. Despite the name, chlorine dioxide works in a completely different way from the chlorine compounds discussed earlier in the chapter. It is a strong alkylating agent, which disrupts proteins and is effective against vegetative bacteria, fungi, viruses, and endospores. Although chlorine dioxide is used for the treatment of drinking water, wastewater, food processing equipment, and medical waste, its most well-known use was in the decontamination of the Senate offices after the anthrax attack of 2001 (see Insight 11.2).

Applications of Gases and Aerosols Ethylene oxide (carboxide, cryoxide) is an effective way to sterilize and disinfect plastic materials and delicate instruments in hospitals and industries. It can sterilize prepackaged medical devices, surgical supplies, syringes, and disposable Petri dishes. Ethylene oxide has been used extensively to disinfect sugar, spices, dried foods, and drugs.

Propylene oxide is a close relative of ETO, with similar physical properties and mode of action, although it is less toxic. Because it breaks down into a relatively harmless substance, it is safer than ETO for sterilization of foods (nuts, powders, starches, spices).

Dyes as Antimicrobial Agents

Dyes are important in staining techniques and as selective and differential agents in media; they are also a primary source of certain drugs used in chemotherapy. Because aniline dyes such as crystal violet and malachite green are very active against gram-positive species of bacteria and various fungi, they are incorporated into solutions and ointments to treat skin infections (ringworm, for example). The yellow acridine dyes, acriflavine and proflavine, are sometimes utilized for antisepsis and wound treatment in medical and veterinary clinics. For the most part, dyes will continue to have limited applications because they stain and have a narrow spectrum of activity.

Acids and Alkalis

Conditions of very low or high pH can destroy or inhibit microbial cells; but they are limited in applications due to their corrosive, caustic, and hazardous nature. Aqueous solutions of ammonium hydroxide remain a common component of detergents, cleansers, and deodorizers. Organic acids are widely used in food preservation because they prevent spore germination and bacterial and fungal growth and because they are generally regarded as safe to eat. Acetic acid (in the form of vinegar) is a pickling agent that inhibits bacterial growth; propionic acid is commonly incorporated into breads and cakes to retard molds; lactic acid is added to sauerkraut and olives to prevent growth of anaerobic bacteria (especially the clostridia); and benzoic and sorbic acids are added to beverages, syrups, and margarine to inhibit yeasts.

For a look at the antimicrobial chemicals found in some common household products, see **table 11.5.**

11.3 Learning Outcomes—Can You . . .

14. . . . name the desirable characteristics of chemical control agents?
15. . . . discuss several different halogen agents and their uses?
16. . . . list advantages and disadvantages to phenolic compounds?
17. . . . explain the mode of action of alcohols?
18. . . . pinpoint the most appropriate applications of hydrogen peroxide agents?
19. . . . define surfactant and explain its mode of action?
20. . . . identify some heavy metal control agents and their most common applications?
21. . . . discuss the advantages and disadvantages of aldehyde agents?
22. . . . identify applications for ethylene oxide sterilization?

Case File 11 *Wrap-Up*

Estimates of the number of cases of cryptosporidiosis traceable to the Seneca Lake sprayground ranged as high as 3,800 people spread across 37 counties; fortunately, no fatalities were recorded. The total could have been even higher had the park not been shut down in mid-August.

Although *Cryptosporidium* is resistant to chlorine, it is susceptible to ultraviolet (UV) light. Therefore, to prevent a recurrence of cryptosporidiosis, the New York State Department of Health required that recirculated water in interactive fountains be disinfected using UV light. Installation of a donated $65,000 UV system allowed the park to reopen the following summer. Ultraviolet disinfection of water has long been used in Europe, but New York's 2006 ultraviolet disinfection requirements were the first in the United States.

See: 2006. *Ithaca J.,* vol. 192, p. 1B.

Table 11.5 Active Ingredients of Various Commercial Antimicrobial Products

Product	Specific Chemical Agent	Antimicrobial Category
Lysol Sanitizing Wipes	Dimethyl benzyl ammonium chloride	Detergent (quat)
Clorox Disinfecting Wipes	Dimethyl benzyl ammonium chloride	Detergent (quat)
Tilex Mildew Remover	Sodium hypochlorites	Halogen
Lysol Mildew Remover	Sodium hypochlorites	Halogen
Ajax Antibacterial Hand Soap	Triclosan	Phenolic
Dawn Antibacterial Hand Soap	Triclosan	Phenolic
Dial Antibacterial Hand Soap	Triclosan	Phenolic
Lysol Disinfecting Spray	Alkyl dimethyl benzyl ammonium saccharinate/ethanol	Detergent (quats)/alcohol
ReNu Contact Lens Solution	Polyaminopropyl biguanide	Chlorhexidine
Wet Ones Antibacterial Moist Towelettes	Benzethonium chloride	Detergents (quat)
Noxzema Triple Clean	Triclosan	Phenolic
Scope Mouthwash	Ethanol	Alcohol
Purell Instant Hand Sanitizer	Ethanol	Alcohol
Pine-Sol	Phenolics and surfactant	Mixed
Allergan Eye Drops	Sodium chlorite	Halogen

Chapter Summary

11.1 Controlling Microorganisms

- Microbial control methods involve the use of physical and chemical agents to eliminate or reduce the numbers of microorganisms from a specific environment to prevent the spread of infectious agents, retard spoilage, and keep commercial products safe.
- The population of microbes that cause spoilage or infection varies widely, so microbial control methods must be adjusted to fit individual situations.
- The type of microbial control is indicated by the terminology used. Sterilization agents destroy all viable organisms, including viruses. Antisepsis, disinfection, and decontamination reduce the numbers of viable microbes to a specified level.
- Antimicrobial agents are described according to their ability to destroy or inhibit microbial growth. Microbicidal agents cause microbial death. They are described by what they are -cidal for: sporocides, bactericides, fungicides, viricides.
- An antiseptic agent is applied to living tissue to destroy or inhibit microbial growth.
- A disinfectant agent is used on inanimate objects to destroy vegetative pathogens but not bacterial endospores.
- Sanitization reduces microbial numbers on inanimate objects to safe levels by physical or chemical means.
- Degermation refers to the process of mechanically removing microbes from the skin.

- Microbial death is defined as the permanent loss of reproductive capability in microorganisms.
- Antimicrobial agents attack specific cell sites to cause microbial death or damage. The four major cell targets are the cell wall, the cell membrane, biosynthesis pathways for DNA or RNA, or protein (enzyme) function.

11.2 Methods of Physical Control

- Physical methods of microbial control include heat, cold, radiation, drying, filtration, and osmotic pressure.
- Heat is the most widely used method of microbial control. It is used in combination with water (moist heat) or as dry heat (oven, flames).
- The thermal death time (TDT) is the shortest length of time required to kill all microbes at a specific temperature.
- The thermal death point (TDP) is the lowest temperature at which all microbes are killed in a specified length of time (10 minutes).
- Autoclaving, or steam sterilization, is the process by which steam is heated under pressure to sterilize a wide range of materials in a comparatively short time (minutes to hours).
- Boiling water and pasteurization of beverages disinfect but do not sterilize materials.
- Dry heat is microbicidal under specified times and temperatures. Flame heat, or incineration, is microbicidal.

- Chilling, freezing, and desiccation are microbistatic but not microbicidal. They are not considered true methods of disinfection because they are not consistent in their effectiveness.
- Ionizing radiation (cold sterilization) by gamma rays and X rays is used to sterilize medical products, meats, and spices. It damages DNA and cell organelles by producing disruptive ions.
- Ultraviolet light, or nonionizing radiation, has limited penetrating ability. It is therefore restricted to disinfecting air and certain liquids.
- Decontamination by filtration removes microbes from heat-sensitive liquids and circulating air. The pore size of the filter determines what kinds of microbes are removed.
- The addition of high amounts of salt or sugar to food results in preservation through osmotic pressure.

11.3 Chemical Agents in Microbial Control

- Chemical agents of microbial control are classified by their physical state and chemical nature.
- Chemical agents can be either microbicidal or microbistatic. They are also classified as high-, medium-, or low-level germicides.
- Factors that determine the effectiveness of a chemical agent include the type and numbers of microbes involved, the material involved, the strength of the agent, and the exposure time.
- Halogens are effective chemical agents at both microbicidal and microbistatic levels. Chlorine, iodine, and iodophors are examples.
- Phenols are strong microbicidal agents used in general disinfection. Milder phenol compounds, the bisphenols, are also used as antiseptics.
- Alcohols dissolve membrane lipids and destroy cell proteins. Their action depends upon their concentration, but they are generally only microbistatic.
- Hydrogen peroxide is a versatile microbicide that can be used as an antiseptic for wounds and a disinfectant for utensils. A high concentration is an effective sporicide.
- Surfactants are of two types: detergents and soaps. They reduce cell membrane surface tension, causing membrane rupture. Cationic detergents, or quats, are low-level germicides limited by the amount of organic matter present and the microbial load.
- Aldehydes are potent sterilizing agents and high-level disinfectants that irreversibly disrupt microbial enzymes.
- Ethylene oxide and chlorine dioxide are gaseous sterilants that work by alkylating protein and DNA.

Multiple-Choice and True-False Questions   Knowledge and Comprehension

Multiple-Choice Questions. Select the correct answer from the answers provided.

1. Microbial control methods that kill _____ are able to sterilize.
   a. viruses
   b. the tubercle bacillus
   c. endospores
   d. cysts

2. Sanitization is a process by which
   a. the microbial load on objects is reduced.
   b. objects are made sterile with chemicals.
   c. utensils are scrubbed.
   d. skin is debrided.

3. An example of an agent that lowers the surface tension of cells is
   a. phenol.
   b. chlorine.
   c. alcohol.
   d. formalin.

4. High temperatures _____ and low temperatures _____.
   a. sterilize, disinfect
   b. kill cells, inhibit cell growth
   c. denature proteins, burst cells
   d. speed up metabolism, slow down metabolism

5. Microbe(s) that is/are the target(s) of pasteurization include
   a. *Clostridium botulinum.*
   b. *Mycobacterium* species.
   c. *Salmonella* species.
   d. both b and c.

6. The primary mode of action of nonionizing radiation is to
   a. produce superoxide ions.
   b. make pyrimidine dimers.
   c. denature proteins.
   d. break disulfide bonds.

7. The most versatile method of sterilizing heat-sensitive liquids is
   a. UV radiation.
   b. exposure to ozone.
   c. beta propiolactone.
   d. filtration.

8. A chemical with sporicidal properties is
   a. phenol.
   b. alcohol.
   c. quaternary ammonium compound.
   d. glutaraldehyde.

9. Silver nitrate is used
   a. in antisepsis of burns.
   b. as a mouthwash.
   c. to treat genital gonorrhea.
   d. to disinfect water.

10. Detergents are
    a. high-level germicides.
    b. low-level germicides.
    c. excellent antiseptics.
    d. used in disinfecting surgical instruments.

True-False Questions. If the statement is true, leave as is. If it is false, correct it by rewriting the sentence.

11. The process of destroying non-spore-forming organisms on inanimate objects fits within the definition of disinfection.

12. The acceptable temperature-pressure combination for an autoclave is 131°C and 9 psi.

13. Ionizing radiation dislodges protons from atoms.

14. A microbicide is an agent that destroys microorganisms.

15. Prions are easily denatured by heat.

 ## Critical Thinking Questions Application and Analysis

These questions are suggested as a *writing-to-learn* experience. For each question, compose a one- or two-paragraph answer that includes the factual information needed to completely address the question.

1. Briefly explain how the type of microorganisms present will influence the effectiveness of exposure to antimicrobial agents.

2. a. Precisely what is microbial death?
   b. Why does a population of microbes not die instantaneously when exposed to an antimicrobial agent?

3. Describe four modes of action of antimicrobial agents, and give a specific example of how each works.

4. Explain the concepts of TDT and TDP, using examples. What are the minimum TDTs for vegetative cells and endospores?

5. Explain why desiccation and cold are not reliable methods of disinfection.

6. What is wrong with this statement: "Prior to vaccination, the patient's skin was sterilized with alcohol"? What would be the more correct wording?

7. For each item on the following list, give a reasonable method of sterilization. You cannot use the same method more than three times; the method must sterilize, not just disinfect; and the method must not destroy the item or render it useless unless there is no other choice. After considering a workable method, think of a method that would not work. Note: Where an object containing something is given, you must sterilize everything (for example, both the jar and the Vaseline in it). Some examples of methods are autoclave, ethylene oxide gas, dry oven, and ionizing radiation.

room air	fruit in plastic bags
serum	human hair (for wigs)
a pot of soil	a flask of nutrient agar
plastic Petri dishes	an entire room (walls, floor, etc.)
cloth dressings	rubber gloves
a cheese sandwich	disposable syringes
carcasses of cows with "mad cow" disease	metal instruments
inside of a refrigerator	mail contaminated with anthrax spores
wine	
a jar of Vaseline	

8. Can you think of situations in which the same microbe would be considered a serious contaminant in one case and completely harmless in another?

9. Devise an experiment that will differentiate between bactericidal and bacteristatic effects.

10. At the end of Section 11.1, in the discussion about agents that arrest protein function, it is stated that "Most antimicrobials of this type are nonselective as to the microbes they affect." Why would this be? What would the effect of these agents be on human skin or tissue, if applied there?

 ## Concept Mapping Synthesis

Appendix D provides guidance for working with concept maps.

1. Construct your own concept map using the following words as the *concepts*. Supply the linking words between each pair of concepts.

halogens	sporicidal
oligodynamic	chemical
surfactants	physical
alcohol	silver
phenolics	

Visual Connections   Synthesis

These questions use visual images or previous content to make connections to this chapter's concepts.

1. **From chapter 2, figure 2.20.** Study this illustration of a cell membrane. In what ways could alcohol (Hint: a solvent) damage this membrane? How would that harm the cell?

Glycolipid

Cell membrane

Globular protein   Protein

Cholesterol

Phospholipids

2. **From chapter 4, figure 4.21.** Why would many chemical control agents be ineffective in controlling this organism?

www.connect.microbiology.com

Enhance your study of this chapter with study tools and practice tests. Also ask your instructor about the resources available through ConnectPlus, including the media-rich eBook, interactive learning tools, and animations.

12

Drugs, Microbes, Host— The Elements of Chemotherapy

Case File 12

Nearly all the antibiotics used to stop bacterial infections are natural compounds that come from microbes themselves. For example, penicillin is derived from a fungus, while vancomycin, the antibiotic used when bacteria are resistant to many other drugs, comes from a bacterium. Furthermore, although many antibiotics are chemically synthesized to resemble natural antibiotics, the "models" for them are natural products of microbes themselves.

As more bacteria become resistant to traditional antibiotics, alternative drugs must be found. Recently, scientists discovered a completely new type of antibiotic that comes from *Hydra*, pictured above, a small freshwater creature famous for regenerating itself when its tissues are severed. While investigating defensive mechanisms on the skin of hydras in 2008, scientists at the University of Keil in Germany came across a protein that is active against both gram-negative and gram-positive bacteria. Most importantly, it works against some drug-resistant strains of bacteria. They named this protein hydramacin.

- Can you imagine why microbes produce chemicals that are inhibitory to other microbes?
- What enables a new drug to be effective against bacteria that are able to resist old drugs?
- How do you suppose the scientists figured out that the compound in *Hydra* acts against both gram-negative and gram-positive bacteria?

Continuing the Case appears on page 330.

Outline and Learning Outcomes

12.1 Principles of Antimicrobial Therapy
1. State the main goal of antimicrobial treatment.
2. Identify the sources for most currently used antimicrobials.

12.2 Interactions Between Drug and Microbe
3. Explain the concept of selective toxicity.
4. List the five major targets of antimicrobial agents.

   5. Identify which categories of drugs are most selectively toxic and why.
   6. Explain how drugs that inhibit protein synthesis can be selective.
   7. Define metabolic analog and discuss its relevance to antimicrobial action.

12.3 Survey of Major Antimicrobial Drug Groups
   8. Distinguish between broad-spectrum and narrow-spectrum antimicrobials and explain the significance of the distinction.
   9. Trace the evolution of penicillin antimicrobials, and identify which microbes they are effective against.
   10. Explain the significance of beta-lactamases, and where they are found.
   11. List other beta-lactam classes of antibiotics and give two examples.
   12. List some cell wall antibiotics that are not in the beta-lactam category.
   13. Identify two older and two newer antimicrobials that act by inhibiting protein synthesis.
   14. Explain how drugs targeting folic acid synthesis work.
   15. Identify the cellular target of quinolones and name two examples.
   16. Name two drugs that target the cellular membrane.
   17. Discuss how treatment of biofilm infections differs from that of nonbiofilm infections.
   18. Name the four main categories of antifungal agents and provide one example of each.
   19. Name four antiprotozoal drugs and three antihelminthic drugs.
   20. List the two major modes of actions of antiviral drugs.
   21. Discuss two possible ways that microbes acquire antimicrobial resistance.
   22. List five cellular or structural mechanisms that microbes use to resist antimicrobials.
   23. Discuss at least four novel antimicrobial strategies that are under investigation.

12.4 Interactions Between Drug and Host
   24. Distinguish between drug toxicity and allergic reactions to drugs.
   25. Explain what a superinfection is and how it occurs.

12.5 Considerations in Selecting an Antimicrobial Drug
   26. Describe two methods for testing antimicrobial susceptibility.
   27. Define therapeutic index and identify whether a high or a low index is preferable.

12.1 Principles of Antimicrobial Therapy

A hundred years ago in the United States, one out of three children was expected to die of an infectious disease before the age of 5. Early death or severe lifelong debilitation from scarlet fever, diphtheria, tuberculosis, meningitis, and many other bacterial diseases was a fearsome yet undeniable fact of life to most of the world's population. The introduction of modern drugs to control infections in the 1930s was a medical revolution that has added significantly to the life span and health of humans. It is no wonder that for many years, antibiotics in particular were regarded as miracle drugs. Although antimicrobial drugs have greatly reduced the incidence of certain infections, they have definitely not eradicated infectious disease and probably never will. In fact, many doctors are now warning that we are dangerously close to a post-antibiotic era, where the drugs we have are no longer effective. Part of the history of humans' struggle to chemically control disease is outlined in **Insight 12.1.**

   The goal of antimicrobial chemotherapy is deceptively simple: Administer a drug to an infected person, which destroys the infective agent without harming the host's cells. In actuality, this goal is rather difficult to achieve, because many (often contradictory) factors must be taken into account. The ideal drug should be easy to administer yet be able to reach the infectious agent anywhere in the body, be absolutely toxic to the infectious agent while simultaneously being nontoxic to the host, and remain active in the body as long as needed yet be safely and easily broken down and excreted. Additionally, microbes in biofilms often require different drugs than when they are not in biofilms. In short, the perfect drug does not exist; but by balancing drug characteristics against one another, a satisfactory compromise can be achieved **(table 12.1).**

Table 12.1   Characteristics of the Ideal Antimicrobial Drug
• Selectively toxic to the microbe but nontoxic to host cells
• Microbicidal rather than microbistatic
• Relatively soluble; functions even when highly diluted in body fluids
• Remains potent long enough to act and is not broken down or excreted prematurely
• Doesn't lead to the development of antimicrobial resistance
• Complements or assists the activities of the host's defenses
• Remains active in tissues and body fluids
• Readily delivered to the site of infection
• Reasonably priced
• Does not disrupt the host's health by causing allergies or predisposing the host to other infections

INSIGHT 12.1 From Witchcraft to Wonder Drugs

Early human cultures relied on various types of primitive medications such as potions, poultices, and mudplasters. Many were concocted from plant, animal, and mineral products that had been found—usually through trial and error or accident—to have some curative effect upon ailments and complaints. In one ancient Chinese folk remedy, a fermented soybean curd was applied to skin infections. The Greeks used wine and plant resins (myrrh and frankincense), rotting wood, and various mineral salts to treat diseases. Many folk medicines were effective, but some of them either had no effect or were even harmful. It is interesting that the Greek word *pharmakeutikos* originally meant the practice of witchcraft. These ancient remedies were handed down from generation to generation, but it was not until the Middle Ages that a specific disease was first treated with a specific chemical. Syphilitic patients were dosed with toxic arsenic and mercury compounds, a practice that continued into the 20th century and may have proved the ancient axiom: *Graviora quaedum sunt remedia periculus* ("Some remedies are worse than the disease").

An enormous breakthrough in the science of drug therapy came with the germ theory of infection by Robert Koch (see chapter 1). This allowed disease treatment to focus on a particular microbe, which in turn opened the way for Paul Ehrlich to formulate the first theoretical concepts in chemotherapy in the late 1800s. Ehrlich had observed that certain dyes affixed themselves to specific microorganisms and not to animal tissues. This observation led to the profound idea that if a drug was properly selective in its actions, it would zero in on and destroy a microbial target and leave human cells unaffected. His first discovery was an arsenic-based drug that was very toxic to the spirochete of syphilis but, unfortunately, to humans as well. Ehrlich systematically altered this parent molecule, creating numerous derivatives. Finally, on the 606th try, he arrived at a compound he called *salvarsan*. This drug had some therapeutic merit and was used for a few years, but it eventually had to be discontinued because it was still not selective enough in its toxicity.

Another pathfinder in early drug research was Gerhard Domagk, whose discoveries in the 1930s launched a breakthrough in therapy that marked the true beginning of broad-scale usage of antimicrobial drugs. Domagk showed that the red dye prontosil was chemically changed by the body into a compound with specific activity against bacteria. This substance was sulfonamide—the first *sulfa* drug. In a short time, the structure of this drug was determined and it became possible to synthesize it on a wide scale and to develop scores of other sulfonamide drugs. Although these drugs had immediate applications in therapy (and still do), still another fortunate discovery was needed before the golden age of antibiotics could really blossom.

The discovery of antibiotics dramatically demonstrates how developments in science and medicine often occur through a combination of accident, persistence, collaboration, and vision.

In 1928 in the London laboratory of Sir Alexander Fleming, a plate of *Staphylococcus aureus* became contaminated with the mold *Penicillium notatum*. Observing these plates, Fleming noted that the colonies of *Staphylococcus* were evidently being destroyed by some activity of the nearby mold colonies. Struck by this curious phenomenon, he extracted from the fungus a compound he called penicillin and showed that it was responsible for the inhibitory effects.

Although Fleming understood the potential for penicillin, he was unable to develop it. A decade after his discovery, English chemists Howard Florey and Ernst Chain worked out methods for industrial production of penicillin to help in the war effort. Clinical trials conducted in 1941 ultimately proved its effectiveness, and cultures of the mold were brought to the United States for an even larger-scale effort. When penicillin was made available to the world's population, it was a godsend. By the 1950s, the pharmaceutical industry had entered an era of drug research and development that soon made penicillin only one of a large assortment of antimicrobial drugs. But in time, because of extreme overuse and misunderstanding of its capabilities, it also became the model for one of the most serious drug problems—namely, drug resistance.

The father of modern antibiotics. A Scottish physician, Sir Alexander Fleming, accidently discovered penicillin when his keen eye noticed that colonies of bacteria were being lysed by a fungal contaminant. He studied the active ingredient and set the scene for the development of the drug 10 years later.

Chemotherapeutic agents are described with regard to their origin, range of effectiveness, and whether they are naturally produced or chemically synthesized. A few of the more important terms you will encounter are found in **table 12.2.**

In this chapter, we describe different types of antibiotic drugs, their mechanism of action, and the types of microbes on which they are effective. The organ system chapters 18 through 23 list specific disease agents and the drugs used to treat them.

The Origins of Antimicrobial Drugs

Nature is a prolific producer of antimicrobial drugs. Antibiotics, after all, are common metabolic products of aerobic bacteria and fungi. By inhibiting the growth of other microorganisms in the same habitat (antagonism), antibiotic producers presumably enjoy less competition for nutrients and space. The greatest numbers of current antibiotics are derived from bacteria in the genera *Streptomyces* and *Bacillus* and from molds in the genera *Penicillium* and *Cephalosporium.* Not only have chemists created new drugs by altering the structure of naturally occurring antibiotics, they are actively

Case File 12 *Continuing the Case*

Most currently used antibiotics are small molecules containing ring structures. But hydramacin is a protein consisting of 60 amino acids, and its structure is unlike that of any known antibiotic, although very similar to the proteins found in scorpion venom.

- Knowing that hydramacin's structure is similar to that of scorpion venom, what aspect of the compound should scientists thoroughly investigate before using it in humans?

searching for metabolic compounds with antimicrobial effects in species other than bacteria and fungi (discussed later).

12.1 Learning Outcomes—Can You ...

1. ... state the main goal of antimicrobial treatment?
2. ... identify the sources for most currently used antimicrobials?

Table 12.2 Terminology of Chemotherapy

Chemotherapeutic Drug	Any chemical used in the treatment, relief, or prophylaxis of a disease
Prophylaxis	Use of a drug to prevent imminent infection of a person at risk
Antimicrobial Chemotherapy	The use of chemotherapeutic drugs to control infection
Antimicrobials	All-inclusive term for any antimicrobial drug, regardless of its origin
Antibiotics	Substances produced by the natural metabolic processes of some microorganisms that can inhibit or destroy other microorganisms
Semisynthetic Drugs	Drugs that are chemically modified in the laboratory after being isolated from natural sources
Synthetic Drugs	Drugs produced entirely by chemical reactions
Narrow Spectrum (Limited Spectrum)	Antimicrobials effective against a limited array of microbial types—for example, a drug effective mainly on gram-positive bacteria
Broad Spectrum (Extended Spectrum)	Antimicrobials effective against a wide variety of microbial types—for example, a drug effective against both gram-positive and gram-negative bacteria

12.2 Interactions Between Drug and Microbe

The goal of antimicrobial drugs is either to disrupt the cell processes or structures of bacteria, fungi, and protozoa or to inhibit virus replication. Most of the drugs used in chemotherapy interfere with the function of enzymes required to synthesize or assemble macromolecules, or they destroy structures already formed in the cell. Above all, drugs should be **selectively toxic,** which means they should kill or inhibit microbial cells without simultaneously damaging host tissues. This concept of selective toxicity is central to antibiotic treatment, and the best drugs are those that block the actions or synthesis of molecules in microorganisms but not in vertebrate cells. Examples of drugs with excellent selective toxicity are those that block the synthesis of the cell wall in bacteria (penicillins). They have low toxicity and few direct effects on human cells because human cells lack the chemical peptidoglycan and are thus unaffected by this action of the antibiotic. Among the most toxic to human cells are drugs that act upon a structure common to both the infective agent and the host cell, such as the cell membrane (for example, amphotericin B, used to treat fungal infections). As the characteristics of the infectious agent become more and more similar to those of the host cell, selective toxicity becomes more difficult to achieve, and undesirable side effects are more likely to occur. The previous example briefly illustrates this concept. We examine the subject in more detail in a later section.

A Note About Chemotherapy

The word "chemotherapy" is commonly associated with the treatment of cancer. As you see in table 12.2, its official meaning is broader than that and can also be applied to antimicrobial treatment.

Mechanisms of Drug Action

If the goal of chemotherapy is to disrupt the structure or function of an organism to the point where it can no longer survive, then the first step toward this goal is to identify the structural and metabolic needs of a living cell. Once the requirements of a living cell have been determined, methods of removing, disrupting, or interfering with these requirements can be employed as potential chemotherapeutic strategies. The metabolism of an actively dividing cell is marked by the production of new cell wall components (in most cells), DNA, RNA, proteins, and cell membrane. Consequently, antimicrobial drugs are divided into categories based on which of these metabolic targets they affect. These categories are outlined in **figure 12.1** and include:

1. inhibition of cell wall synthesis,
2. inhibition of nucleic acid (RNA and DNA) structure and function,
3. inhibition of protein synthesis,
4. interference with cell membrane structure or function, and
5. inhibition of folic acid synthesis.

As you will see, these categories are not completely discrete, and some effects can overlap.

Antimicrobial Drugs That Affect the Bacterial Cell Wall

The cell walls of most bacteria contain a rigid girdle of peptidoglycan, which protects the cell against rupture from hypotonic environments. Active cells must constantly synthesize new peptidoglycan and transport it to its proper place in the cell envelope. Drugs such as penicillins and cephalosporins react with one or more of the enzymes required to complete this process, causing the cell to develop weak points at growth sites and to become osmotically

Figure 12.1 Primary sites of action of antimicrobial drugs on bacterial cells.

fragile **(figure 12.2)**. Antibiotics that produce this effect are considered bactericidal, because the weakened cell is subject to lysis. It is essential to note that many of these antibiotics are active only in young, growing cells, because old, inactive, or dormant cells do not synthesize peptidoglycan. (One exception is a class of antibiotics called the "-penems.")

Cycloserine inhibits the formation of the basic peptidoglycan subunits, and vancomycin hinders the elongation of the peptidoglycan. Penicillins and cephalosporins bind and block peptidases that cross-link the glycan molecules, thereby interrupting the completion of the cell wall **(figure 12.3)**. Penicillins that do not penetrate the outer membrane are less effective against gram-negative bacteria, but broad-spectrum penicillins and cephalosporins, such as carbenicillin or ceftriaxone, can access the cell walls of gram-negative species.

Antimicrobial Drugs That Affect Nucleic Acid Synthesis

As you learned in chapter 9, the metabolic pathway that generates DNA and RNA is a long, enzyme-catalyzed series of reactions. Like any complicated process, it is subject to breakdown at many different points along the way, and inhibition at any point in the sequence can block subsequent events. Antimicrobial drugs interfere with nucleic acid synthesis by blocking synthesis of nucleotides, inhibiting replication, or stopping transcription. Because functioning DNA and RNA are required for proper translation as well, the effects on protein metabolism can be far-reaching.

Other antimicrobials inhibit DNA synthesis. Chloroquine (an antimalarial drug) binds and cross-links the double helix. The newer broad-spectrum quinolones inhibit DNA unwinding enzymes or helicases, thereby stopping DNA transcription. Antiviral drugs that are analogs of purines and pyrimidines, including azidothymidine (AZT) and acyclovir, insert in the viral nucleic acid and block further replication.

Antimicrobial Drugs That Block Protein Synthesis

Most inhibitors of translation, or protein synthesis, react with the ribosome-mRNA complex. Although human cells also have ribosomes, the ribosomes of eukaryotes are different in size and structure from those of prokaryotes, so these antimicrobials usually have a selective action against bacteria. One potential therapeutic consequence of drugs that bind to the prokaryotic ribosome is the damage they can do to eukaryotic mitochondria, which contain a prokaryotic type of ribosome. Two possible targets of ribosomal inhibition are the 30S subunit and the 50S subunit **(figure 12.4)**. Aminoglycosides (streptomycin, gentamicin, for example) insert on sites on the 30S subunit and cause the misreading of the mRNA, leading to abnormal proteins. Tetracyclines block the attachment of tRNA on the A acceptor site and effectively stop further protein synthesis. Other antibiotics attach to sites on the 50S subunit in a way that prevents the formation of peptide bonds (chloramphenicol) or inhibits translocation of the subunit during translation (erythromycin).

Antimicrobial Drugs That Disrupt Cell Membrane Function

A cell with a damaged membrane invariably dies from disruption in metabolism or lysis and does not even have to be actively dividing to be destroyed. The antibiotic classes that damage cell membranes have specificity for particular microbial groups, based on differences in the types of lipids in their cell membranes.

Polymyxins interact with membrane phospholipids, distort the cell surface, and cause leakage of proteins and nitrogen bases, particularly in gram-negative bacteria. The polyene antifungal antibiotics (amphotericin B and nystatin) form

Peptidoglycan (cell wall)

Exposure to cephalosporin or penicillin

(a) Normal untreated cells.

10,000×

Weak points lacking peptidoglycan

Membrane bulges out as water diffuses into cell.

Membrane breaks.

Cell lyses.

10,000×

(b) Effects of treatment with penicillin. Left side depicts the stages in the breakdown of a *Staphylococcus* cell exposed to penicillin. Right view shows actual cells undergoing lysis and cell death.

Figure 12.2 Effects of antibiotics on bacterial cell walls.

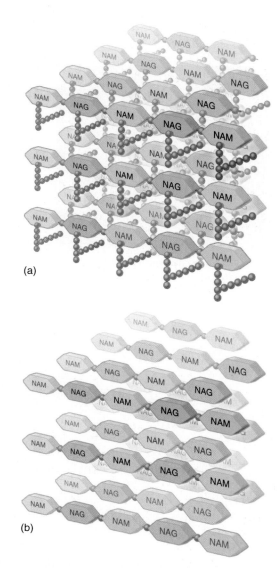

(a)

(b)

Figure 12.3 The mode of action of penicillins and cephalosporins on the bacterial cell wall. **(a)** Intact peptidoglycan has chains of NAM (*N*-acetyl muramic acid) and NAG (*N*-acetyl glucosamine) glycans cross-linked by peptide bridges. **(b)** These two drugs block the peptidases that link the cross-bridges between NAMs, thereby greatly weakening the cell wall meshwork.

complexes with the sterols on fungal membranes; these complexes cause abnormal openings and seepage of small ions. Unfortunately, this selectivity is not exact, and the universal presence of membranes in microbial and animal cells alike means that most of these antibiotics can be quite toxic to humans. Some newer drugs target both the cell membrane and the cell wall and are thus more selective.

Antimicrobial Drugs That Inhibit Folic Acid Synthesis

Sulfonamides and trimethoprim are drugs that act by mimicking the normal substrate of an enzyme in a process called

Figure 12.4 Sites of inhibition on the prokaryotic ribosome and major antibiotics that act on these sites. All have the general effect of blocking protein synthesis. Blockage actions are indicated by ✕.

competitive inhibition. They are supplied to the cell in high concentrations to ensure that a needed enzyme is constantly occupied with the **metabolic analog** rather than the true substrate of the enzyme. As the enzyme is no longer able to produce a needed product, cellular metabolism

INSIGHT 12.2 A Quest for Designer Drugs

Once the first significant drug was developed, the world immediately witnessed a scientific scramble to find more antibiotics. This search was advanced on several fronts. Hundreds of investigators began the laborious task of screening samples from soil, dust, muddy lake sediments, rivers, estuaries, oceans, plant surfaces, compost heaps, sewage, skin, and even the hair and skin of animals for antibiotic-producing bacteria and fungi. This intense effort has paid off over the past 50 years, because more than 10,000 antibiotics have been discovered (although surprisingly, only a relatively small number have actually been used clinically). Finding a new antimicrobial substance is only a first step. The complete pathway of drug development from discovery to therapy takes between 10 and 25 years at a cost of billions of dollars.

Antibiotics are products of fermentation pathways that occur in many bacteria and fungi. The role of antibiotics in the lives of these microbes must be important because the genes for antibiotic production are preserved in evolution. Some experts theorize that antibiotic-releasing microorganisms can inhibit or destroy nearby competitors or predators; others propose that antibiotics play a part in spore formation. Whatever benefit the microbes derive, these compounds have been extremely profitable for humans. Every year, the pharmaceutical industry farms vast quantities of microorganisms and harvests their products to treat diseases caused by other microorganisms. Researchers have facilitated the work of nature by selecting mutant species that yield more abundant or useful products, by varying the growth medium, or by altering the procedures for large-scale industrial production (see chapter 25).

Another approach in the drug quest is to chemically manipulate molecules by adding or removing functional groups. Drugs produced in this way are designed to have advantages over other, related drugs. Using this **semisynthetic** method, a natural product of the microorganism is joined with various preselected functional groups. The antibiotic is reduced to its basic molecular framework (called the nucleus), and to this nucleus specially selected side chains (R groups) are added. A case in point is the metamorphosis of the semisynthetic penicillins. The nucleus is an inactive penicillin derivative called aminopenicillanic acid, which has an opening on the number 6 carbon for addition of R groups. A particular carboxylic acid (R group) added to this nucleus can "fine-tune" the penicillin, giving it special characteristics. For instance, some R groups will make the product resistant to penicillinase (methicillin), some confer a broader activity spectrum (ampicillin), and others make the product acid-resistant (penicillin V). Cephalosporins and tetracyclines also exist in several semisynthetic versions. The potential for using bioengineering techniques to design drugs seems almost limitless, and, indeed, several drugs are produced by manipulating the genes of antibiotic producers.

A plate with several discrete colonies of soil bacteria was sprayed with a culture of *Escherichia coli* and incubated. Zones of inhibition (clear areas with no growth) surrounding several colonies indicate species that produce antibiotics.

Synthesizing penicillins. **(a)** The original penicillin G molecule is a fermentation product of *Penicillium chrysogenum* that appears somewhat like a house with a removable patio on the left. This house without the patio is the basic nucleus called aminopenicillanic acid. **(b)–(d)** Various new fixtures (R groups) can be added to change the properties of the drug. These R groups will produce different penicillins: **(b)** methicillin, **(c)** ampicillin, and **(d)** penicillin V.

Figure 12.5 The action of sulfa drugs. The metabolic pathway needed to synthesize tetrahydrofolic acid (THFA) contains two enzymes that are chemotherapeutic targets.

slows or stops. Sulfonamides and trimethoprim interfere with folate metabolism by blocking enzymes required for the synthesis of tetrahydrofolate, which is needed by bacterial cells for the synthesis of folic acid and the eventual production of DNA and RNA and amino acids. **Figure 12.5** illustrates sulfonamides' competition with PABA for the active site of the enzyme pteridine synthetase. Trimethoprim and sulfonamides are often given simultaneously to achieve a *synergistic effect*, which, in pharmacological terms, refers to an effect that is more than additive achieved by multiple drugs working together, thus requiring a lower dose of each.

The selective toxicity of these compounds is explained by the fact that mammals derive folic acid from their diet and so do not possess this enzyme system. Therefore, it is relatively easy to inhibit bacterial and protozoan parasites, which must synthesize folic acid, while leaving the human host unaffected.

12.2 Learning Outcomes—Can You ...

3. ... explain the concept of selective toxicity?
4. ... list the five major targets of antimicrobial agents?
5. ... identify which categories of drugs are most selectively toxic and why?
6. ... explain how drugs that inhibit protein synthesis can be selective?
7. ... define metabolic analog and discuss its relevance to antimicrobial action?

12.3 Survey of Major Antimicrobial Drug Groups

Scores of antimicrobial drugs are marketed in the United States. Although the medical and pharmaceutical literature contains a wide array of names for antimicrobials, most of them are variants of a small number of drug families. One of the most useful ways of categorizing antimicrobials, which you have already encountered in the previous section, is to designate them as either **broad-spectrum** or **narrow-spectrum.** Broad-spectrum drugs are effective against more than one group of bacteria, while narrow-spectrum drugs generally target a specific group. **Table 12.3** demonstrates that tetracyclines are broad-spectrum, while polymyxin and even penicillins are narrow-spectrum agents.

The rest of this section provides details about drugs based on which of the the five major mechanisms they target. There will also be a discussion of the special, and important, case of treating biofilms with antibiotics.

Antibacterial Drugs Targeting the Cell Wall

Penicillin and Its Relatives

The **penicillin** group of antibiotics, named for the parent compound, is a large, diverse group of compounds, most of which end in the suffix -*cillin*. Penicillins can either be completely synthesized in the laboratory from simple raw materials, or obtained naturally through microbial fermentation. The natural product can then be used either in unmodified form or to make semisynthetic derivatives. *Penicillium chrysogenum* is the major source of the drug. All penicillins consist of three parts: a thiazolidine ring, a *beta-lactam* (bey'-tuh-lak'-tam) ring, and a variable side chain that dictates its microbicidal activity **(figure 12.6).**

Subgroups and Uses of Penicillins The characteristics of certain penicillin drugs are shown in **table 12.4.** Penicillins G and V are the most important natural forms. Penicillin is considered the drug of choice for infections by known sensitive, gram-positive cocci (most streptococci) and some gram-negative bacteria (meningococci and the syphilis spirochete).

Certain semisynthetic penicillins such as ampicillin, carbenicillin, and amoxicillin have broader spectra and thus can be used to treat infections by gram-negative enteric rods. Many bacteria produce enzymes that are capable of destroying the beta-lactam ring of penicillin. The enzymes are referred to as **penicillinases** or *beta-lactamases*, and they make the bacteria that possess them

---

Table 12.3 Spectrum of Activity for Antibiotics

Bacteria	Mycobacteria	Gram-negative Bacteria	Gram-positive Bacteria	Chlamydias	Rickettsias
Examples of diseases	Tuberculosis	Salmonellosis, plague, gonorrhea	Strep throat, staph infections*	Chlamydia, trachoma	Rocky Mountain spotted fever
Spectrum of activity of various antibiotics	Isoniazid Streptomycin Tobramycin Polymyxin Carbapenems Tetracyclines Sulfonamides Cephalosporins Penicillins				
Are there normal biota in this group?	Yes	Yes	Yes	Probably	None known

*Note that some members of a bacterial group may not be affected by the antibiotics indicated, due to acquired or natural resistance. In other words, exceptions do exist.

Figure 12.6 Chemical structure of penicillins. All penicillins contain a thiazolidine ring (yellow) and a beta-lactam ring (red), but each differs in the nature of the side chain (R group), which is also responsible for differences in biological activity.

resistant to many penicillins. Researchers in 2008 counted 532 different beta-lactamases in bacteria. This points to how versatile bacteria can be in resisting our attacks on them. In response, scientists have created penicillinase-resistant penicillins such as methicillin, nafcillin, and cloxacillin, which are useful in treating infections caused by some penicillinase-producing bacteria. Mezlocillin and azlocillin have such an extended spectrum that they can be substituted for combinations of antibiotics. All of the "-cillin" drugs are relatively mild and well tolerated because of their specific mode of action on cell walls (which humans lack). The primary problems in therapy include allergy, which is altogether different from toxicity, and resistant strains of pathogens. Clavulanic acid is a chemical that inhibits beta-lactamase enzymes, thereby increasing the effectiveness of beta-lactam antibiotics in the presence of penicillinase-producing bacteria. For this reason, clavulanic acid is often added to semisynthetic penicillins to augment their effectiveness. For example, Clavamox is a combination of amoxicillin and clavulanate and is also marketed under the trade name Augmentin. Zosyn is a similar combination of tazobactam, a beta-lactamase inhibitor, and piperacillin that is used for a wide variety of systemic infections.

The Cephalosporin Group of Drugs

The **cephalosporins** are a group of antibiotics that were originally isolated in the late 1940s from the mold *Cephalosporium acremonium*. Cephalosporins are similar to penicillins; they have a beta-lactam structure that can be synthetically altered

Table 12.4 Characteristics of Selected Penicillin Drugs

Name	Spectrum of Action	Uses, Advantages	Disadvantages
Penicillin G	Narrow	Best drug of choice when bacteria are sensitive; low cost; low toxicity	Can be hydrolyzed by penicillinase; allergies occur; requires injection
Penicillin V	Narrow	Good absorption from intestine; otherwise, similar to penicillin G	Hydrolysis by penicillinase; allergies
Oxacillin, dicloxacillin	Narrow	Not susceptible to penicillinase; good absorption	Allergies; expensive
Methicillin, nafcillin	Narrow	Not usually susceptible to penicillinase	Poor absorption; allergies; growing resistance
Ampicillin	Broad	Works on gram-negative bacilli	Can be hydrolyzed by penicillinase; allergies; only fair absorption
Amoxicillin	Broad	Gram-negative infections; good absorption	Hydrolysis by penicillinase; allergies
Carbenicillin	Broad	Same as ampicillin	Poor absorption; used only parenterally
Azlocillin, mezlocillin, ticarcillin	Very broad	Effective against *Pseudomonas* species; low toxicity compared with aminoglycosides	Allergies, susceptible to many beta-lactamases

(figure 12.7) and have a similar mode of action. The generic names of these compounds are often recognized by the presence of the root *cef, ceph,* or *kef* in their names.

Subgroups and Uses of Cephalosporins

The cephalosporins are versatile. They are relatively broad-spectrum, resistant to most penicillinases, and cause fewer allergic reactions than penicillins. Although some cephalosporins are given orally, many are poorly absorbed from the intestine and must be administered **parenterally** (par-ehn′-tur-ah-lee), by injection into a muscle or a vein.

Five generations of cephalosporins exist, based upon their antibacterial activity. First-generation cephalosporins such as cephalothin and cefazolin are most effective against gram-positive cocci and a few gram-negative bacteria. Second-generation forms include cefaclor and cefonicid, which are more effective than the first-generation forms in treating infections by gram-negative bacteria such as *Enterobacter, Proteus,* and *Haemophilus.* Third-generation cephalosporins, such as cephalexin (Keflex) and cefotaxime, are broad-spectrum with especially well-developed activity against enteric bacteria that produce beta-lactamases. Ceftriaxone (Rocephin) is a semisynthetic broad-spectrum drug for treating a wide variety of respiratory, skin, urinary, and nervous system infections. The fourth-generation cephalosporins include cefpirome and cefepime. The fifth-generation drug ceftobiprole exhibits activity against methicillin-resistant *Staphylococcus aureus* and also against penicillin-resistant gram-positive and gram-negative bacteria.

*New improved versions of drugs are referred to as new "generations."

Figure 12.7 The structure of cephalosporins. Like penicillin, they have a beta-lactam ring (red), but they have a different main ring (yellow). However, unlike penicillins, they have two sites for placement of R groups (at positions 3 and 7). This makes possible several generations of molecules with greater versatility in function and complexity in structure.

Other Beta-Lactam Antibiotics

Newer antibiotics such as doripenem and imipenem belong to a new class of cell wall antibiotics called carbapenems. They are powerful but potentially dangerous, and reserved for use in hospitals when other drugs aren't working. Aztreonam, isolated from the bacterium *Chromobacterium violaceum,* is a narrow-spectrum drug for treating pneumonia, septicemia, and urinary tract infections by gram-negative aerobic bacilli. Aztreonam is especially useful when treating persons who are allergic to penicillin. Because of similarities in their chemical structure, allergies to penicillin often are accompanied by allergies to cephalosporins and carbapenems. The structure of aztreonam is chemically distinct so that persons with allergies to penicillin are not usually adversely affected by treatment with aztreonam.

Recently, the appearance of a gene called NDM-1 in gram-negatives has caused great concern since it confers resistance to carbapenems and is highly transmissible from bacterium to bacterium. This development has caused some scientists to declare that the end of the antibiotic era is upon us.

Other Drugs Targeting the Cell Wall

Bacitracin is a narrow-spectrum antibiotic produced by a strain of the bacterium *Bacillus subtilis.* Since it was first isolated, its greatest claim to fame has been as a major ingredient in a common drugstore antibiotic ointment (Neosporin) for combating superficial skin infections by streptococci and staphylococci. For this purpose, it is usually combined with neomycin (an aminoglycoside) and polymyxin.

Isoniazid (INH) is bactericidal to *Mycobacterium tuberculosis* but only against growing cells. It is generally used in combination with two or three additional drugs in active tuberculosis cases. **Vancomycin** is a narrow-spectrum antibiotic most effective in treating staphylococcal infections in cases of penicillin and methicillin resistance or in patients with an allergy to penicillins. Vancomycin belongs to the first generation of glycopeptide antibiotics, initially used in the 1960s but lately used more widely as gram-positive bacteria has become resistant to methicillin and consequently plaguing hospitals, and the community at large. Second-generation glycopeptides include telavancin (Vibativ) and oritavancin. **Fosfomycin tromethamine** is a phosphoric acid agent effective as alternate treatment for urinary tract infections caused by enteric bacteria. It works by inhibiting an enzyme necessary for cell wall synthesis.

Antibacterial Drugs Targeting Protein Synthesis

The Aminoglycoside Drugs

Antibiotics composed of one or more amino sugars and an aminocyclitol (6-carbon) ring are referred to as **aminoglycosides (figure 12.8)**. These complex compounds are exclusively the products of various species of soil **actinomycetes** in the genera *Streptomyces* **(figure 12.9)** and *Micromonospora.*

Subgroups and Uses of Aminoglycosides The aminoglycosides have a relatively broad antimicrobial spectrum because they inhibit protein synthesis. They are especially useful in treating infections caused by aerobic gram-negative rods and certain gram-positive bacteria. Streptomycin is among the oldest of the drugs and has gradually been replaced by newer forms with less mammalian toxicity. It is still the antibiotic of choice for treating bubonic plague and tularemia and is considered a good

Figure 12.8 The structure of streptomycin. Colored portions of the molecule show the general arrangement of an aminoglycoside.

Figure 12.9 A colony of *Streptomyces*, one of nature's most prolific antibiotic producers.

antituberculosis agent, especially in populations where newer drugs are not available. You will notice that many aminoglycoside drugs end with the suffix -*mycin*, but this suffix is used for drugs from other families as well (for example, vancomycin), so is not a useful way of remembering which category a drug fits into.

Tetracycline Antibiotics

In 1948, a colony of *Streptomyces* isolated from a soil sample was discovered to be giving off a substance, aureomycin, with strong antimicrobial properties. This antibiotic was used to synthesize its relatives terramycin and tetracycline. These natural parent compounds and semisynthetic derivatives are known as the **tetracyclines (figure 12.10a).** Their action of binding to ribosomes and blocking protein synthesis accounts for the broad-spectrum effects in the group.

Subgroups and Uses of Tetracyclines The scope of microorganisms inhibited by tetracyclines includes gram-positive and gram-negative rods and cocci, aerobic and anaerobic bacteria, mycoplasmas, rickettsias, and spirochetes. Although generic tetracycline is low in cost and easy to administer, its side effects—namely, gastrointestinal disruption due to changes in the normal biota of the gastrointestinal tract and deposition in hard tissues—can limit its use (see table 12.6).

(a) **Tetracyclines**

(b) **Erythromycin**

Figure 12.10 **Structures of two broad-spectrum antibiotics.** **(a)** Tetracyclines. These are named for their regular group of four rings. The several types vary in structure and activity by substitution at the four R groups. **(b)** Erythromycin, an example of a macrolide drug. Its central feature is a large lactone ring to which two hexose sugars are attached.

Glycylcyclines

Glycylcyclines are newer derivatives of tetracyclines. Their mode of action, like that of tetracyclines, is to bind to the 30S ribosomal subunit and block the entry of the tRNA bearing an amino acid into the A site of the ribosome. However, differences in the structure of the drug make it effective against bacteria that have become resistant to the tetracyclines. The first antibiotic licensed in this group is tigecycline, marketed as Tygacil.

Erythromycin, Clindamycin, and Telithromycin

Erythromycin is a macrolide[1] antibiotic first isolated in 1952 from a strain of *Streptomyces*. Its structure consists of a large lactone ring with sugars attached **(figure 12.10b).** This drug is relatively broad-spectrum and of fairly low toxicity. Its mode of action is to block protein synthesis by attaching to the ribosome. Newer semisynthetic macrolides include *clarithromycin* and *azithromycin*. Both drugs are useful for middle ear, respiratory, and skin infections and have also been approved for *Mycobacterium* (MAC) infections in AIDS patients. Clarithromycin has additional applications in controlling infectious stomach ulcers (see chapter 22).

Clindamycin is a broad-spectrum antibiotic derived from the less effective lincomycin. The tendency of clindamycin to cause adverse reactions in the gastrointestinal tract limits its applications to

1. serious infections in the large intestine and abdomen due to anaerobic bacteria (*Bacteroides* and *Clostridium*) that are unresponsive to other antibiotics,
2. infections with penicillin-resistant staphylococci, and
3. acne medications applied to the skin.

In 2004, the FDA approved the first representative of a new class of drugs called ketolides, which are similar to macrolides like erythromycin but have a different ring structure. The new drug, called telithromycin (trade name Ketek), was used for respiratory tract infections that are suspected to be caused by antibiotic-resistant bacteria such as *Streptococcus pneumoniae*. However, its usefulness has been limited as it was found to cause serious liver damage in some patients.

Synercid and Oxazolidinones

Synercid is a combined antibiotic from the streptogramin group of drugs. It is effective against *Staphylococcus* and *Enterococcus* species that cause endocarditis and surgical infections, including resistant strains. It is one of the main choices when other drugs are ineffective due to resistance. Synercid works by binding to sites on the 50S ribosome, inhibiting translation.

Another class of synthetic antibacterial drugs, oxazolidinones, was developed in 2000, and the first member of that class

---

1. Macrolide antibiotics get their name from the type of chemical ring structure (macrolide ring) they all possess.

was linezolid. These drugs work by a completely novel mechanism, inhibiting the initiation of protein synthesis. Because this class of drug is not found in nature, it is hoped that resistance among bacteria will be slow to develop. Linezolid (under the name Zyvox) is used to treat infections caused by two of the most difficult clinical pathogens, methicillin-resistant *Staphylococcus aureus* (MRSA) and vancomycin-resistant *Enterococcus* (VRE).

A class of drugs that was previously only used in veterinary medicine has now made the leap to human medicine, albeit in a fairly limited way. Drugs called pleuromutilins bind to the 50S subunit of bacterial ribosomes. The first representative of the pleuromutilins is retapamulin (Altabax) and is approved only for external application for the skin infection impetigo (see chapter 18).

Antibacterial Drugs Targeting Folic Acid Synthesis

The Sulfonamides, Trimethoprim, and Sulfones

The very first modern antimicrobial drugs were the **sulfonamides,** or sulfa drugs, named for sulfanilamide, an early form of the drug **(figure 12.11).** They are synthetic and do not originate from bacteria or fungi. Although thousands of sulfonamides have been formulated, only a few have gained any importance in chemotherapy. Because of its solubility, sulfisoxazole is the best agent for treating shigellosis, acute urinary tract infections, and certain protozoan infections. Silver sulfadiazine ointment and solution are prescribed for treatment of burns and eye infections. Another drug, trimethoprim (Septra, Bactrim), inhibits the enzymatic step immediately following the step inhibited by sulfonamides in the synthesis of folic acid. Because of this, trimethoprim is often given in combination with sulfamethoxazole to take advantage of the synergistic effect of the two drugs. This combination is one of the primary

treatments for *Pneumocystis (carinii) jiroveci* pneumonia (PCP) in AIDS patients.

Antibacterial Drugs Targeting DNA or RNA

Even though nucleic acids in prokaryotes and humans are chemically similar, DNA and RNA have proved to be useful targets for antimicrobials. Much excitement was generated by a new class of synthetic drugs chemically related to quinine called **fluoroquinolones.** These drugs exhibit several ideal traits, including high potency and broad spectrum. Even in minimal concentrations, quinolones inhibit a wide variety of gram-positive and gram-negative bacterial species. In addition, they are readily absorbed from the intestine. Just as with other drug families, there are multiple "generations" of quinolones. The first generation was typified by nalidixic acid, which is rarely used now. Second-generation quinolones include ciprofloxacin and ofloxacin. Ciprofloxacin received a great deal of publicity as the drug of choice for treating anthrax. Shortly after the first attacks in 2001, however, the Centers for Disease Control and Prevention changed their recommendation from ciprofloxacin to doxycycline (a protein synthesis inhibitor). The change in preferred drug was made not because ciprofloxacin was ineffective but rather to prevent the emergence of ciprofloxacin-resistant bacteria. Third-generation quinolones exhibited expanded activity against gram-positive organisms, including some that are resistant to other drugs. The most well-known example is levofloxacin. Fourth-generation quinolones are effective against anaerobic organisms; an example is trovafloxacin. Side effects that limit the use of quinolones can include seizures and other brain disturbances.

Another product of the genus *Streptomyces* is rifamycin, which is altered chemically into rifampin. It is somewhat limited in spectrum because the molecule cannot pass through the cell envelope of many gram-negative bacilli. It is mainly used to treat infections by several gram-positive rods and cocci and a few gram-negative bacteria. Rifampin figures most prominently in treating mycobacterial infections, especially tuberculosis and leprosy, but it is usually given in combination with other drugs to prevent development of resistance. A newer derivative of rifampin called Xifaxan was approved in 2004 for a very specific use: the treatment of traveler's diarrhea.

Antibacterial Drugs Targeting Cell Membranes

Every cell has a membrane. Some drugs target membranes, but they are not usually first-choice antimicrobials except in a few circumstances. *Bacillus polymyxa* is the source of the **polymyxins,** narrow-spectrum peptide antibiotics with a unique fatty acid component that contributes to their detergent activity. Only two polymyxins—B and E (also known as colistin)—have any routine applications, and even these are limited by their toxicity to the kidney. Either drug can

Figure 12.11 The structures of some sulfonamides.

be indicated to treat drug-resistant *Pseudomonas aeruginosa* and severe urinary tract infections caused by other gram-negative rods.

Daptomycin is a lipopeptide made by *Streptomyces*. It is most active against gram-positive bacteria, acting to disrupt multiple aspects of membrane function. Many experts are urging physicians to use these medications only when no other drugs are available to slow the development of drug resistance.

Antibiotics and Biofilms

As you read in chapter 7, biofilm inhabitants behave differently than their free-living counterparts. One of the major ways they differ—at least from a medical perspective—is that they are often unaffected by the same antimicrobials that work against them when they are free-living. When this was first recognized, it was assumed that it was a problem of penetration, that the (often charged) antimicrobial drugs could not penetrate the sticky extracellular material surrounding biofilm organisms. While that is a factor, there is something more important contributing to biofilm resistance: the different phenotype expressed by biofilm bacteria. Secured to surfaces they express different genes and therefore have different antibiotic susceptibility profiles.

Years of research have so far not yielded an obvious solution to this problem, though there are several partially successful strategies. One of these involves interrupting the quorum sensing pathways that mediate communication between cells and may change phenotypic expression. Daptomycin, a lipopeptide that is effective in deep tissue infections with resistant bacteria, has also shown some success in biofilm infection treatment. Also, some researchers have found that adding DNase to their antibiotics can help with penetration of the antibiotic through the extracellular debris—apparently some of which is DNA from lysed cells.

Many biofilm infections can be found on biomaterials inserted in the body, such as cardiac or urinary catheters. These can be impregnated with antibiotics prior to insertion to prevent colonization. This, of course, cannot be done with biofilm infections of natural tissues, such as the prostate or middle ear.

Interestingly, it appears that chemotherapy with some antibiotics—notably aminoglycosides—can cause bacteria to form biofilms at a higher rate than they otherwise would. Obviously there is much more to come in understanding biofilms and their control.

Agents to Treat Fungal Infections

Because the cells of fungi are eukaryotic, they present special problems in chemotherapy. For one, the great majority of chemotherapeutic drugs are designed to act on bacteria and are generally ineffective in combating fungal infections. For another, the similarities between fungal and human cells

often mean that drugs toxic to fungal cells are also capable of harming human tissues. A few agents with special antifungal properties have been developed for treating systemic and superficial fungal infections. Four main drug groups currently in use are the macrolide polyene antibiotics, the azoles, the echinocandins, and flucytosine (**figure 12.12**).

Polyenes bind to fungal membranes and cause loss of selective permeability. They are specific for fungal membranes because fungal membranes contain a particular sterol component called ergosterol, while human membranes do not. The toxicity of polyenes is not completely selective, however, because mammalian cell membranes contain compounds similar to ergosterol that bind polyenes to a small extent.

Macrolide polyenes, represented by amphotericin B (named for its acidic and basic—amphoteric—properties), have a structure that mimics the lipids in some cell membranes. Amphotericin B is an extremely versatile and effective antifungal. Not only does it work on most fungal infections, including skin and mucous membrane lesions caused by *Candida albicans*, but it is one of the few drugs that can be injected to treat systemic fungal infections such as histoplasmosis and cryptococcus meningitis. The **azoles** are broad-spectrum antifungal agents with a complex ringed structure. They interfere with sterol synthesis in fungi. The most effective drugs are ketoconazole, fluconazole, clotrimazole, and miconazole. Ketoconazole is used orally and topically for cutaneous mycoses, vaginal and oral candidiasis, and some systemic mycoses.

(a)

(b)   (c)

Figure 12.12 Some antifungal drug structures. **(a)** Polyenes. The example shown is amphotericin B, a complex steroidal antibiotic that inserts into fungal cell membranes. **(b)** Clotrimazole, one of the azoles. **(c)** Flucytosine, a structural analog of cytosine that contains fluoride.

Fluconazole can be used in selected patients for AIDS-related mycoses such as aspergillosis and cryptococcus meningitis. Clotrimazole and miconazole are used mainly as topical ointments for infections in the skin, mouth, and vagina.

The **echinocandins** are a class of antifungal that act by inhibiting fungal cell wall synthesis. They are most often used against *Candida* strains and *Aspergillus*. Two examples are caspofungin and micafungin.

Flucytosine is an analog of the nucleotide cytosine that has antifungal properties. It is rapidly absorbed after oral therapy, and it is readily dissolved in the blood and cerebrospinal fluid. Alone, it can be used to treat certain cutaneous mycoses. Many fungi are resistant to flucytosine, so it is usually combined with amphotericin B to effectively treat systemic mycoses.

There is one further class of antifungal drugs, which is only used topically. Griseofulvin is an antifungal product especially active in certain dermatophyte infections such as athlete's foot. The drug is deposited in the epidermis, nails, and hair, where it inhibits fungal growth by binding to microtubules. Because complete eradication requires several months and griseofulvin is relatively nephrotoxic, this therapy is given only for the most stubborn cases.

Antiparasitic Chemotherapy

The enormous diversity among protozoan and helminth parasites and their corresponding therapies reach far beyond the scope of this textbook; however, a few of the more common drugs are surveyed here and described again for particular diseases in the organ systems chapters.

Antimalarial Drugs: Quinine and Its Relatives

Quinine, extracted from the bark of the cinchona tree, was the principal treatment for malaria for hundreds of years, but it has been replaced by the synthesized quinolones, mainly chloroquine and primaquine, which have less toxicity to humans. Because there are several species of *Plasmodium* (the malaria parasite) and many stages in its life cycle, no single drug is universally effective for every species and stage, and each drug is restricted in application. For instance, primaquine eliminates the liver phase of infection, and chloroquine suppresses acute attacks associated with infection of red blood cells. Chloroquine is taken alone for prophylaxis and in combination with doxycycline or other antibiotics for the suppression of acute forms of malaria. Primaquine is administered to patients with relapsing cases of malaria.

Chemotherapy for Other Protozoan Infections

A widely used amoebicide, metronidazole (Flagyl), is effective in treating mild and severe intestinal infections and hepatic disease caused by *Entamoeba histolytica*. Given orally, it also has applications for infections by *Giardia lamblia* and *Trichomonas vaginalis* (described in chapters 22 and 23,

respectively). Other drugs with antiprotozoan activities are quinacrine (a quinine-based drug), sulfonamides, and tetracyclines.

Antihelminthic Drug Therapy

Treating helminthic infections has been one of the most difficult and challenging of all chemotherapeutic tasks. Flukes, tapeworms, and roundworms are much larger parasites than other microorganisms and, being animals, have greater similarities to human physiology. Also, the usual strategy of using drugs to block their reproduction is usually not successful in eradicating the adult worms. The most effective drugs immobilize, disintegrate, or inhibit the metabolism of all stages of the life cycle.

Mebendazole and albendazole are broad-spectrum antiparasitic drugs used in several roundworm intestinal infestations. These drugs work locally in the intestine to inhibit the function of the microtubules of worms, eggs, and larvae. This means the parasites can no longer utilize glucose, which leads to their demise. The compound pyrantel paralyzes the muscles of intestinal roundworms. Consequently, the worms are unable to maintain their grip on the intestinal wall and are expelled along with the feces by the normal peristaltic action of the bowel. Two newer antihelminthic drugs are praziquantel, a treatment for various tapeworm and fluke infections, and ivermectin, a veterinary drug now used for strongyloidiasis and oncocercosis in humans. Helminthic diseases are described in chapter 22 because these organisms spend at least some part of their life cycles in the digestive tract.

Antiviral Chemotherapeutic Agents

The chemotherapeutic treatment of viral infections presents unique problems. With viruses, we are dealing with an infectious agent that relies upon the host cell for the vast majority of its metabolic functions. Disrupting viral metabolism requires that we disrupt the metabolism of the host cell to a much greater extent than is desirable. Put another way, selective toxicity with regard to viral infection is difficult to achieve because a single metabolic system is responsible for the well-being of both virus and host. Although viral diseases such as measles, mumps, and hepatitis are routinely prevented by the use of effective vaccinations, epidemics of AIDS, influenza, and even the common cold attest to the need for more effective medications for the treatment of viral pathogens.

The first successful antiviral drugs were developed to target specific points in the infectious cycle of viruses. Three major modes of action are

1. barring penetration of the virus into the host cell,
2. blocking the transcription and translation of viral molecules, and
3. preventing the maturation of viral particles.

Table 12.5 presents a comprehensive overview of the most widely used antiviral drugs. Hundreds of new drugs are in development. The following paragraphs provide some additional detail about the principles in table 12.5. Although antiviral drugs protect uninfected cells by keeping viruses from being synthesized and released, most are unable to destroy extracellular viruses or those in a latent state.

Fuzeon (generic name enfuvirtide), an anti-HIV drug approved in 2003, keeps the virus from attaching to its cellular receptor and thereby prevents the initial fusion of HIV to the host cell. Relenza and Tamiflu medications can be effective treatments for influenza A and B and useful prophylactics as well. Because one action of these drugs is to inhibit the fusion and uncoating of the virus, they must be given rather early in an infection. Also, viruses can quickly become resistant to antivirals. The dominant flu virus circulating in 2009–2010 was mostly resistant to Tamiflu, for example.

Several antiviral agents mimic the structure of nucleotides and compete for sites on replicating DNA. The incorporation of these synthetic nucleotides inhibits further DNA synthesis. **Acyclovir** (Zovirax) and its relatives are synthetic purine compounds that block DNA synthesis in a small group of viruses, particularly the herpesviruses (see chapters 18 and 23). In the topical form, they are most effective in controlling the primary attack of facial or genital herpes. Intravenous or oral acyclovir therapy can reduce the severity of primary and recurrent genital herpes episodes. Some newer relatives (valacyclovir) are more effective and require fewer doses. Famciclovir is used to treat shingles and chickenpox caused by the herpes zoster virus, and ganciclovir is approved to treat cytomegalovirus infections of the eye. An interesting aspect of some of these antiviral agents (specifically valacyclovir and famciclovir) is that they are activated by an enzyme encoded by the virus itself, activating the drug only in virally infected cells. The enzyme thymidine kinase is used by the virus to process nucleosides before incorporating them into viral RNA or DNA. When the inactive drug enters a virally infected cell, it is activated by the virus' thymidine kinase to produce a working antiviral agent. In cells without viruses, the drug is never activated and DNA replication is allowed to continue unabated.

HIV is classified as a retrovirus, meaning it carries its genetic information in the form of RNA rather than DNA (HIV and AIDS are discussed in chapter 20). Upon infection, the RNA genome is used as a template by the enzyme **reverse transcriptase** to produce a DNA copy of the virus' genetic information. Because this particular reaction is not seen outside of the retroviruses, it offers two ideal targets for chemotherapy. The first is interfering with the synthesis of the new DNA strand, which is accomplished using *nucleoside reverse transcriptase inhibitors* (nucleotide analogs), while the second involves interfering with the action of the enzyme responsible for the synthesis, which is accomplished using *nonnucleoside reverse transcriptase inhibitors*.

Azidothymidine (AZT or zidovudine) is a thymine analog that exerts its effect by incorporating itself into the growing DNA chain of HIV and terminating synthesis, in a manner analogous to that seen with acyclovir. AZT is used at all stages of HIV infection, including prophylactically with people accidentally exposed to blood or other body fluids.

Nonnucleoside reverse transcriptase inhibitors (such as nevirapine) accomplish the same goal (preventing reverse transcription of the HIV genome) by binding to the reverse transcriptase enzyme itself, inhibiting its ability to synthesize DNA.

Assembly and release of mature viral particles are also targeted in HIV through the use of protease inhibitors. These drugs (indinavir, saquinavir), usually used in combination with nucleotide analogs and reverse transcriptase inhibitors, have been shown to reduce the HIV load to undetectable levels by preventing the maturation of virus particles in the cell. Refer to table 12.5 for a summary of HIV drug mechanisms and see chapter 20 for further coverage of this topic.

A sensible alternative to artificial drugs has been a human-based substance, **interferon (IFN)**. Interferon is a glycoprotein produced primarily by fibroblasts and leukocytes in response to various immune stimuli. It has numerous biological activities, including antiviral and anticancer properties. Studies have shown that it is a versatile part of animal host defenses, having a major role in natural immunities. (Its mechanism is discussed in chapter 14.)

Several types of interferon are currently produced by the recombinant DNA technology techniques outlined in chapter 10. Extensive clinical trials have tested its effectiveness in viral infections and cancer. It is currently most widely used in treatment of chronic hepatitis C infection and in the treatment of several cancers. Unfortunately, interferon treatment often results in serious side effects, including personality changes and dysfunction of the immune system.

Interactions Between Microbes and Drugs: The Acquisition of Drug Resistance

One unfortunate outcome of the use of antimicrobials is the development of microbial **drug resistance,** an adaptive response in which microorganisms begin to tolerate an amount of drug that would ordinarily be inhibitory. The ability to circumvent or inactivate antimicrobial drugs is due largely to the genetic versatility and adaptability of microbial populations. The property of drug resistance can be intrinsic as well as acquired. Intrinsic drug resistance can best be exemplified by the fact that bacteria must, of course, be resistant to any antibiotic that they themselves

Table 12.5 Actions of Antiviral Drugs

Mode of Action	Examples	Effects of Drug	
Inhibition of Virus Entry: Receptor/Fusion/Uncoating Inhibitors	Enfuvirtide (Fuzeon)	Blocks **HIV** infection by preventing the binding of viral GP-41 receptors to cell receptor ①, thereby preventing fusion of virus with cell	
	Amantadine and its relatives, zanamivir (Relenza), oseltamivir (Tamiflu)	Block entry of **influenza virus** by interfering with fusion of virus with cell membrane (also release); stop the action of influenza neuraminidase, required for entry of virus into cell (also assembly) ② ③	
Inhibition of Nucleic Acid Synthesis	Acyclovir (Zovirax), other "cyclovirs," vidarabine	Purine analogs that terminate DNA replication in **herpesviruses** ④	
	Ribavirin	Purine analog, used for **respiratory syncytial virus (RSV)** and some **hemorrhagic fever viruses**	
	Zidovudine (AZT), lamivudine (3T3), didanosine (ddI), zalcitabine (ddC), and stavudine (d4T)	Nucleotide analog reverse transcriptase (RT) inhibitors; stop the action of RT in **HIV**, blocking viral DNA production ⑤	
	Nevirapine, efavirenz, delavirdine	Nonnucleotide analog reverse transcriptase inhibitors; attach to **HIV** RT binding site, stopping its action ⑥	
Inhibition of Viral Assembly/Release	Indinavir, saquinavir	Protease inhibitors; insert into **HIV** protease, stopping its action and resulting in inactive noninfectious viruses ⑦	

produce. Of much greater importance is the acquisition of resistance to a drug by a microbe that was previously sensitive to the drug. In our context, the term *drug resistance* will refer to this last type of acquired resistance.

How Does Drug Resistance Develop?

Contrary to popular belief, antibiotic resistance is not a recent phenomenon. Resistance to penicillin developed in some bacteria as early as 1940, three years before the drug was even approved for public use. The scope of the problem became apparent in the 1980s and 1990s, when scientists and physicians observed treatment failures on a large scale.

Microbes become newly resistant to a drug after one of the following two events occurs: (1) spontaneous mutations in critical chromosomal genes, or (2) acquisition of entire new genes or sets of genes via horizontal transfer from another species. Chromosomal drug resistance usually results from spontaneous random mutations in bacterial populations. The chance that such a mutation will be advantageous is minimal, and the chance that it will confer resistance to a specific drug is lower still. Nevertheless, given the huge numbers of microorganisms in any population and the constant rate of mutation, such mutations do occur. The end result varies from slight changes in microbial sensitivity, which can be overcome by larger doses of the drug, to complete loss of sensitivity. There may be a third mechanism of acquiring resistance to a drug, which is a phenotypic, not a genotypic, adaptation. Recent studies suggest that bacteria can "go to sleep" when exposed to antibiotics, meaning they will slow or stop their metabolism so that they cannot be harmed by the antibiotic. They can then rev back up after the antibiotic concentration decreases. In the next sections we will focus on the two genetic changes that can result in acquired resistance.

Resistance occurring through horizontal transfer originates from plasmids called **resistance (R) factors** that are transferred through conjugation, transformation, or transduction. Studies have shown that plasmids encoded with drug resistance are naturally present in microorganisms before they have been exposed to the drug. Such traits are "lying in wait" for an opportunity to be expressed and to confer adaptability on the species. Many bacteria also maintain transposable drug resistance sequences (transposons) that are duplicated and inserted from one plasmid to another or from a plasmid to the chromosome. Chromosomal genes and plasmids containing codes for drug resistance are faithfully replicated and inherited by all subsequent progeny. This sharing of resistance genes accounts for the rapid proliferation of drug-resistant species. As you have read in earlier chapters, gene transfers are extremely frequent in nature, with genes coming from totally unrelated bacteria, viruses, and other organisms living in the body's normal biota and the environment.

We also have a new appreciation for where the reservoirs of antibiotic-resistance genes might be. Recently it was discovered that a wide variety of soil bacteria can not only survive in the presence of many antibiotics, but use the antibiotics as fuel. This indicates that there is a large population of natural environmental bacteria with capabilities that might be transferred to disease-causing bacteria. It is also clear that non-disease-causing inhabitants of our bodies and the bodies of our pets harbor many antibiotic-resistance genes that can and do easily jump to pathogenic bacteria with which they share space.

Specific Mechanisms of Drug Resistance

The two events that precipitate microbes becoming resistant to a drug (described earlier) have as their net effect one of the following actions, which actually cause the bacterium to be resistant (illustrated in **figure 12.13**):

1. New enzymes are synthesized; these inactivate the drug (only occurs when new genes are acquired).
2. Permeability or uptake of drug into bacterium is decreased (usually occurs via mutation).
3. Drug is immediately eliminated (usually occurs via acquisition of new genes).
4. Binding sites for drug are decreased in number or affinity (can occur via mutation or acquisition of new genes).
5. An affected metabolic pathway is shut down or an alternate pathway is used (occurs due to mutation of original enzyme(s)).

Some bacteria can become resistant indirectly by lapsing into dormancy or, in the case of penicillin, by converting to a cell wall-deficient form (L form) that penicillin cannot affect.

Drug Inactivation Mechanisms   Microbes inactivate drugs by producing enzymes that permanently alter drug structure. One example, bacterial exoenzymes called **beta-lactamases,** hydrolyze the beta-lactam ring structure of some penicillins and cephalosporins rendering the drugs inactive. Two beta-lactamases—penicillinase and cephalosporinase—disrupt the structure of certain penicillin or cephalosporin molecules so their activity is lost. So many strains of *Staphylococcus aureus* produce penicillinase that regular penicillin is rarely a possible therapeutic choice.

Decreased Drug Permeability or Increased Drug Elimination   The resistance of some bacteria can be due to a mechanism that prevents the drug from entering the cell and acting on its target. For example, the outer membrane of the cell wall of certain gram-negative bacteria is a natural blockade for some of the penicillin drugs. Resistance to the tetracyclines can arise from plasmid-encoded proteins that pump the drug out of the cell. Aminoglycoside resistance can arise in multiple ways; one of these is change in drug permeability caused by point mutations in the transport system or LPS machinery.

Figure 12.13 Examples of mechanisms of acquired drug resistance.

Many bacteria possess multidrug-resistant (MDR) pumps that actively transport drugs and other chemicals out of cells. These pumps are proteins encoded by plasmids or chromosomes. They are stationed in the cell membrane and expel molecules by a proton-motive force similar to ATP synthesis (see figure 12.13). They confer drug resistance on many gram-positive pathogens (*Staphylococcus, Streptococcus*) and gram-negative pathogens (*Pseudomonas, E. coli*). Because they lack selectivity, one type of pump can expel a broad array of antimicrobial drugs, detergents, and other toxic substances.

Change of Drug Receptors Because most drugs act on a specific target such as protein, RNA, DNA, or membrane structure, microbes can circumvent drugs by altering the nature of this target. Bacteria can become

INSIGHT 12.3   The Rise of Drug Resistance

Many people unrealistically assume that science will come to the rescue and solve the problem of drug resistance. If drug companies just keep making more and better antimicrobials, soon infectious diseases will be vanquished. This unfortunate attitude has vastly underestimated the extreme versatility and adaptability of microorganisms and the complexity of the task. It is a fact of nature that if a large number of microbes are exposed to a variety of drugs, there will always be some genetically favored individuals that survive and thrive. The AIDS virus (HIV) is so prone to drug resistance that it can become resistant during the first few weeks of therapy in a single individual. Ironically, thousands of patients die every year in the United States from infections that

lack effective drugs, and 60% of hospital infections are caused by drug-resistant microbes. For many years, concerned observers reported the gradual development of drug resistance in staphylococci, *Salmonella*, and gonococci. In 2007, the first case of completely drug-resistant tuberculosis occurred in Italy.

MRSA, VISA, VRSA

If you have had any experience in health care, you are familiar with MRSA, methicillin-resistant *Staphylococcus aureus*. For that matter, you will be familiar with it if you read newspapers or have children in school or, possibly, you may have had this dangerous infection. It usually manifests as a skin or tissue infection. These can also spread to the bloodstream. The significance of the bacterium being methicillin-resistant is that other drugs must be found to treat it. Vancomycin quickly became the last-ditch drug for MRSA. Predictably, in 1996, the first case of VISA—vancomycin intermediate *Staphylococcus aureus*—was reported in Japan. This designation means that the bacterium has a reduced sensitivity to vancomycin. In 2002, we saw the arrival of VRSA strains—vancomycin-resistant *S. aureus*—which are resistant to high concentrations of vancomycin. So far, both VISA and VRSA infections can be treated with combinations of other antibiotics.

The Hospital Factor

The clinical setting is a prolific source of drug-resistant strains of bacteria. This environment continually exposes pathogens to a variety of drugs. The hospital also maintains patients with weakened defenses, making them highly susceptible to pathogens. A classic example occurred with *Staphylococcus aureus* and penicillin. In the 1950s, hospital strains began to show resistance to this drug, and because of indiscriminate use, these strains became nearly 100% resistant in 30 years.

Drugs in Animal Feeds

Another practice that has contributed significantly to growing drug resistance is the addition of antimicrobials to livestock feed, with the idea of decreasing infections and thereby improving animal health and size. This practice has had serious impact in both the United States and Europe. Enteric bacteria such as *Salmonella*, *Escherichia coli*, and enterococci that live as normal intestinal biota of these animals readily share resistance plasmids and are constantly selected and amplified by exposure to drugs.

resistant to aminoglycosides when point mutations in ribosomal proteins arise (see figure 12.13). Erythromycin and clindamycin resistance is associated with an alteration on the 50S ribosomal binding site. Penicillin resistance in *Streptococcus pneumoniae* and methicillin resistance in *Staphylococcus aureus* are related to an

alteration in the binding proteins in the cell wall. Enterococci have acquired resistance to vancomycin through a similar alteration of cell wall proteins **(Insight 12.3).** Fungi can become resistant by decreasing their synthesis of ergosterol, the principal receptor for certain antifungal drugs.

These pathogens subsequently "jump" to humans and cause drug-resistant infections, oftentimes at epidemic proportions. A bill in Congress called the Preservation of Antibiotics for Medical Treatment Act was introduced in 2009, and as of the printing of this textbook, was still in committee.

Worldwide Drug Resistance

The drug dilemma has become a widespread problem, affecting all countries and socioeconomic groups. In general, the majority of infectious diseases, whether bacterial, fungal, protozoan, or viral, are showing increases in drug resistance. In parts of India, the main drugs used to treat cholera (furazolidone, ampicillin) went from being highly effective to essentially useless in 10 years. In Southeast Asia, 98% of gonococcus infections are multidrug resistant. Malaria, tuberculosis, and typhoid fever pathogens are gaining in resistance, with few alternative drugs to control them. To add to the problem, global travel and globalization of food products mean that drug resistance can be rapidly exported.

In countries with adequate money to pay for antimicrobials, most infections will be treated but at some expense. In the United States alone, the extra cost for treating the drug-resistant variety is around $10 billion per year. In many developing countries, drugs are mishandled by overuse and underuse, either of which can contribute to drug resistance. Many countries that do not regulate the sale of prescription drugs make them readily available to purchase over the counter. For example, the antituberculosis drug INH (isoniazid) is sometimes used as a "lung vitamin" to improve health, and antibiotics are taken in the wrong dose and at the wrong time for undiagnosed conditions. These countries serve as breeding grounds for drug resistance that can eventually be carried to other countries. This seems to have occurred with carbapenem resistance, which arose in India and now has spread to the West, causing physicians to fear there will soon be no treatments for some gram-negative infections.

It is clear that we are in a race with microbes and we are falling behind. If the trend is not contained, the world may return to a time when there are few effective drugs left. We simply cannot develop them as rapidly as microbes can develop resistance. In this light, it is essential to fight the battle on more than one front. **Table 12.A** summarizes the several critical strategies to give us an edge in controlling drug resistance.

Table 12.A Strategies to Limit Drug Resistance by Microorganisms

Drug Usage

- Physicians have the responsibility for making an accurate diagnosis and prescribing the correct drug therapy.
- Patients must comply with and carefully follow the physician's guidelines. It is important for the patient to take the correct dosage, by the best route, for the appropriate period. This diminishes the selection for mutants that can resist low drug levels and ensures elimination of the pathogen.
- For some combinations of drugs, administration of two or more drugs together increases the chances that at least one of them will be effective and that a resistant strain of either drug will not be able to persist. The basis for this combined therapy method lies in the unlikelihood of simultaneous resistance to several drugs.

Drug Research

- Research focuses on developing shorter-term, higher-dose antimicrobials that are more effective, less expensive, and have fewer side effects.
- Pharmaceutical companies continue to seek new antimicrobial drugs with structures that are not readily inactivated by microbial enzymes or drugs with modes of action that are not readily circumvented.

Long-Term Strategies

- Proposals to reduce the abuse of antibiotics range from educational programs for health workers to requiring written justification from the physician on all antibiotics prescribed.
- Especially valuable antimicrobials may be restricted in their use to only one or two types of infections.
- The addition of antimicrobials to animal feeds must be curtailed worldwide.
- Government programs that make effective therapy available to low-income populations should be increased.
- Vaccines should be used whenever possible to provide alternative protection.

Changes in Metabolic Patterns The action of antimetabolites can be circumvented if a microbe develops an alternative metabolic pathway or enzyme. Sulfonamide and trimethoprim resistance develop when microbes deviate from the usual patterns of folic acid synthesis. Fungi can acquire resistance to flucytosine by completely shutting off certain metabolic activities.

Natural Selection and Drug Resistance

So far, we have been considering drug resistance at the cellular and molecular levels, but its full impact is felt only if this resistance occurs throughout the cell population. Let us examine how this might happen and its long-term therapeutic consequences.

Any large population of microbes is likely to contain a few individual cells that are already drug resistant because of prior mutations or transfer of plasmids (**figure 12.14a**). As long as the drug is not present in the habitat, the numbers of these resistant forms will remain low because they have no particular growth advantage (and often are disadvantaged relative to their nonmutated counterparts). But if the population is subsequently exposed to this drug (**figure 12.14b**), sensitive individuals are inhibited or destroyed, and resistant forms survive and proliferate. During subsequent population growth, offspring of these resistant microbes will inherit this drug resistance. In time, the replacement population will have a preponderance of the drug-resistant forms and can eventually become completely resistant (**figure 12.14c**). In ecological terms, the environmental factor (in this case, the drug) has put selection pressure on the population, allowing the more "fit" microbe (the drug-resistant one) to survive, and the population has evolved to a condition of drug resistance.

New Approaches to Antimicrobial Therapy

Often, the quest for new antimicrobial strategies focuses on finding new targets in the bacterial cell and custom-designing drugs that aim for them. There are many interesting new strategies that have not yet resulted in a marketable drug—for example, (1) targeting iron-scavenging capabilities of bacteria, (2) using RNA interference strategies, (3) mimicking molecules called defense peptides, and (4) exploiting an old technology, using bacteriophages, the natural enemies of bacteria, to do the killing for us. The best example of a strategy aimed at iron-scavenging capabilities is recent work with *Staphylococcus aureus*. Scientists have found that this bacterium has a special pathway involving several proteins that punch holes in red blood cells and then "reach in" to bind the heme,

strip it of its iron, and use it for their own purposes. Researchers are currently investigating inhibitory substances that block the iron-collecting pathway, which would result in inevitable bacterial death. This approach may prove effective in wiping out antibiotic-resistant strains of *S. aureus*.

RNA interference, you recall from chapter 10, refers to small pieces of RNA that regulate the expression of genes. This is being exploited in attempts to shut down the metabolism of pathogenic microbes. There have been several human trials of RNA interference, including trials to evaluate the effectiveness of synthetic RNAs in treating hepatitis C and respiratory syncytial virus.

Many researchers are looking into proteins called host or bacterial defense peptides. Host defense peptides are peptides of 20–50 amino acids that are secreted as part of the mammalian innate immune system. They have names such as defensin, magainins, and protegrins. Some bacteria produce similar peptides. These are called bacteriocins and lantibiotics. Both host and bacterial defense peptides have multiple activities against bacteria—inserting in their membranes and also targeting other structures in the cells. For this reason researchers believe they may be more effective than narrowly targeted drugs in current use, and will be much less likely to foster resistance.

Sometimes the low-tech solution can be the best one. Eastern European countries have gained a reputation for using mixtures of bacteriophages as medicines for bacterial infections. There is little argument about the effectiveness of these treatments, though they have never been approved for use in the West. One recent human trial used a mixture of bacteriophages specific for *Pseudomonas aeruginosa* to treat ear infections caused by the bacterium. These infections are found in the form of biofilms and have been extremely difficult to treat. The phage preparation called Biophage-PA successfully treated patients who had experienced long-term antibiotic-resistant infections. Other researchers are incorpo-

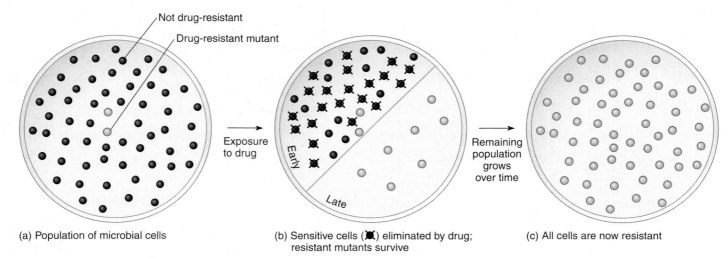

(a) Population of microbial cells

(b) Sensitive cells (✖) eliminated by drug; resistant mutants survive

(c) All cells are now resistant

Figure 12.14 The events in natural selection for drug resistance. **(a)** Populations of microbes can harbor some members with a prior mutation that confers drug resistance. **(b)** Environmental pressure (here, the presence of the drug) selects for survival of these mutants. **(c)** They eventually become the dominant members of the population.

rating phages into wound dressings. One clear advantage to bacteriophage treatments is the extreme specificity of the phages— only one species of bacterium is affected, leaving the normal inhabitants of the body alone.

There are new approaches being considered for antiviral treatment as well. In 2010, an siRNA treatment was successfully used to treat rhesus monkeys that had been infected with Ebola virus. This treatment, which blocked three vital genes of the virus, was the first ever successful strategy against Ebola.

Viruses mutate to become resistant to the drugs used to treat them even more quickly than do bacteria. As we learned earlier, current antivirals target parts of the virus that make it able to attach, multiply, or package itself. They are usually specific for one type of molecule, such as an enzyme. This makes it extremely likely that the molecule will incorporate a mutation quickly and then become resistant to the drug. The new investigative strategy is to exploit the one thing all viruses have in common: their complete dependence on the host cell. What if a drug targets a host protein, which would mutate much, much more slowly? For this strategy to work, a protein that was essential for viral reproduction but not necessary to the host cell function must be found. It turns out there are a lot of these. One promising host cell target is a protein called TSG101. It is a protein that the cell uses to transport materials internally, and that is hijacked by viruses to help them exit the cell. Crippling this protein has little effect on the human cell, and is devastating to the virus. The startling fact about this line of research is that it could yield a class of drugs that are active against viruses that have not even been discovered yet—as it is not dependent on particular attributes of a particular virus.

Helping Nature Along

Other novel approaches to controlling infections include the use of **probiotics** and **prebiotics.** Probiotics are preparations of live microorganisms that are fed to animals and humans to improve the intestinal biota. This can serve to replace microbes lost during antimicrobial therapy or simply to augment the biota that is already there. This is a slightly more sophisticated application of methods that have long been used in an empiric fashion, for instance, by people who consume yogurt because of the beneficial microbes it contains. Recent years have seen a huge increase in the numbers of probiotic products sold in ordinary grocery stores **(figure 12.15).** Experts generally find these products safe, and in some cases they can be effective. Probiotics are thought to be useful for the management of food allergies; their role in the stimulation of mucosal immunity is also being investigated.

Prebiotics are nutrients that encourage the growth of beneficial microbes in the intestine. For instance, certain sugars such as fructans are thought to encourage the growth of *Bifidobacterium* in the large intestine and to discourage the growth of potential pathogens. You can be

Figure 12.15 Examples of probiotic grocery items.

sure that you will hear more about prebiotics and probiotics as the concepts become increasingly well studied by scientists. Clearly, the use of these agents is a different type of antimicrobial strategy than we are used to, but it may have its place in a future in which traditional antibiotics are more problematic.

12.3 Learning Outcomes—Can You ...

8. ... distinguish between broad-spectrum and narrow-spectrum antimicrobials and explain the significance of the distinction?
9. ... trace the evolution of penicillin antimicrobials, and identify which microbes they are effective against?
10. ... explain the significance of beta-lactamases, and where they are found?
11. ... list other beta-lactam classes of antibiotics and give two examples.
12. ... list some cell wall antibiotics that are not in the beta-lactam category?
13. ... identify two older and two newer antimicrobials that act by ... inhibiting protein synthesis?
14. ... explain how drugs targeting folic acid synthesis work?
15. ... identify the cellular target of quinolones and name two examples?
16. ... name two drugs that target the cellular membrane?
17. ... discuss how treatment of biofilm infections differs from that of nonbiofilm infections?
18. ... name the four main categories of antifungal agents and provide one example of each?
19. ... name four antiprotozoal drugs and three antihelminthic drugs?
20. ... list the two major modes of actions of antiviral drugs?
21. ... discuss two possible ways that microbes acquire antimicrobial resistance?
22. ... list five cellular or structural mechanisms that microbes use to resist antimicrobials?
23. ... discuss at least four novel antimicrobial strategies that are under investigation?

12.4 Interaction Between Drug and Host

Until now, this chapter has focused on the interaction between antimicrobials and the microorganisms they target. During an infection, the microbe is living in or on a host; therefore, the drug is administered to the host though its target is the microbe. Therefore, the effect of the drug on the host must always be considered.

Although selective antimicrobial toxicity is the ideal constantly being sought, chemotherapy by its very nature involves contact with foreign chemicals that can harm human tissues. In fact, estimates indicate that at least 5% of all persons taking an antimicrobial drug experience some type of serious adverse reaction to it. The major side effects of drugs fall into one of three categories: direct damage to tissues through toxicity, allergic reactions, and disruption in the balance of normal microbial biota. The damage incurred by antimicrobial drugs can be short term and reversible or permanent, and it ranges in severity from cosmetic to lethal. **Table 12.6** summarizes drug groups and their major side effects.

Toxicity to Organs

Drugs can adversely affect the following organs: the liver (hepatotoxic), kidneys (nephrotoxic), gastrointestinal tract, cardiovascular system and blood-forming tissue (hemotoxic), nervous system (neurotoxic), respiratory tract, skin, bones, and teeth.

Because the liver is responsible for metabolizing and detoxifying foreign chemicals in the blood, it can be damaged by a drug or its metabolic products. Injury to liver cells can result in enzymatic abnormalities, fatty liver deposits, hepatitis, and liver failure. The kidney is involved in excreting drugs and their metabolites. Some drugs irritate the nephron tubules, creating changes that interfere with their filtration abilities. Drugs such as sulfonamides can crystallize in the kidney and form stones that can obstruct the flow of urine.

The most common complaint associated with oral antimicrobial therapy is diarrhea, which can progress to severe intestinal irritation or colitis. Although some drugs directly irritate the intestinal lining, the usual gastrointestinal complaints are caused by disruption of the intestinal microbiota (discussed in a subsequent section).

Many drugs given for parasitic infections are toxic to the heart, causing irregular heartbeats and even cardiac arrest in extreme cases. Some drugs hemolyze the red blood cells, others reduce white blood cell counts, and still others damage platelets or interfere with their formation, thereby inhibiting blood clotting.

Certain antimicrobials act directly on the brain and can cause seizures. Others, such as aminoglycosides, damage nerves (very commonly, the eighth cranial nerve), leading to dizziness, deafness, or motor and sensory disturbances. When drugs block the transmission of impulses to the diaphragm, respiratory failure can result.

The skin is a frequent target of drug-induced side effects. The skin response can be a symptom of drug allergy or a direct toxic effect. Some drugs interact with sunlight to cause

Table 12.6 Major Adverse Toxic Reactions to Common Drug Groups

Antimicrobial Drug	Primary Damage or Abnormality Produced
Antibacterials	
Penicillin G	Skin
Carbenicillin	Abnormal bleeding
Ampicillin	Diarrhea and enterocolitis
Cephalosporins	Inhibition of platelet function Decreased circulation of white blood cells Nephritis
Tetracyclines	Diarrhea and enterocolitis Discoloration of tooth enamel Reactions to sunlight (photosensitization)
Chloramphenicol	Injury to red and white blood cell precursors
Aminoglycosides (streptomycin, gentamicin, amikacin)	Diarrhea and enterocolitis Malabsorption Loss of hearing, dizziness, kidney damage
Isoniazid	Hepatitis Seizures Dermatitis
Sulfonamides	Formation of crystals in kidney; blockage of urine flow Hemolysis Reduction in number of red blood cells
Polymyxin	Kidney damage Weakened muscular responses
Quinolones (ciprofloxacin, norfloxacin)	Headache, dizziness, tremors, GI distress
Rifampin	Damage to hepatic cells Dermatitis
Antifungals	
Amphotericin B	Disruption of kidney function
Flucytosine	Decreased number of white blood cells
Antiprotozoan Drugs	
Metronidazole	Nausea, vomiting
Chloroquine	Vomiting Headache Itching
Antihelminthics	
Niclosamide	Nausea, abdominal pain
Pyrantel	Irritation Headache, dizziness
Antivirals	
Acyclovir	Seizures, confusion Rash
Amantadine	Nervousness, light-headedness Nausea
AZT	Immunosuppression, anemia

photodermatitis, a skin inflammation. Tetracyclines are con-traindicated (not advisable) for children from birth to 8 years of age because they bind to the enamel of the teeth, creating a permanent gray to brown discoloration **(figure 12.16).** Pregnant women should avoid tetracyclines because they can cause liver damage. They also cross the placenta and can be deposited in the developing fetal bones and teeth.

Allergic Responses to Drugs

One of the most frequent drug reactions is heightened sensitivity, or **allergy.** This reaction occurs because the drug acts as an antigen (a foreign material capable of stimulating the immune system) and stimulates an allergic response. This response can be provoked by the intact drug molecule or by substances that develop from the body's metabolic alteration of the drug. In the case of penicillin, for instance, it is not the penicillin molecule itself that causes the allergic response but a product, *benzylpenicilloyl.* Allergic reactions have been reported for every major type of antimicrobial drug, but the penicillins account for the greatest number of antimicrobial allergies, followed by the sulfonamides.

People who are allergic to a drug become sensitized to it during the first contact, usually without symptoms. Once the immune system is sensitized, a second exposure to the drug can lead to a reaction such as a skin rash (hives), respiratory inflammation, and, rarely, anaphylaxis, an acute, overwhelming allergic response that develops rapidly and can be fatal. (This topic is discussed in greater detail in chapter 16.)

Suppression and Alteration of the Microbiota by Antimicrobials

Most normal, healthy body surfaces, such as the skin, large intestine, outer openings of the urogenital tract, and oral cavity, provide numerous habitats for a virtual "garden" of microorganisms. These normal colonists or residents, called the **biota** or microbiota, consist mostly of harmless or beneficial bacteria, but a small number can potentially be

pathogens. Although we defer a more detailed discussion of this topic to chapter 13 and later chapters, here we focus on the general effects of drugs on this population.

If a broad-spectrum antimicrobial is introduced into a host to treat infection, it will destroy microbes regardless of their roles as normal biota, affecting not only the targeted infectious agent but also many others in sites far removed from the original infection **(figure 12.17).** When this therapy destroys beneficial resident species, other microbes that were once in small numbers begin to overgrow and cause disease. This complication is called a **superinfection.**

Some common examples demonstrate how a disturbance in microbial biota leads to replacement biota and superinfection. A broad-spectrum cephalosporin used to treat a urinary tract infection by *Escherichia coli* will cure the infection, but it will also destroy the lactobacilli in the vagina that normally maintain a protective acidic environment there. The drug has no effect, however, on *Candida albicans,* a yeast that also resides in normal vaginas. Released from the inhibitory environment provided by lactobacilli, the yeasts proliferate and cause symptoms. *Candida* can cause similar superinfections of the oropharynx (thrush) and the large intestine.

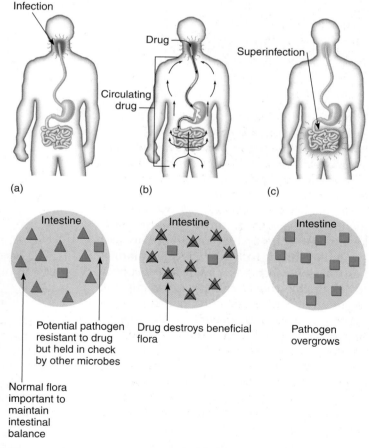

Figure 12.17 The role of antimicrobials in disrupting microbial biota and causing superinfections. **(a)** A primary infection in the throat is treated with an oral antibiotic. **(b)** The drug is carried to the intestine and is absorbed into the circulation. **(c)** The primary infection is cured, but drug-resistant pathogens have survived and create an intestinal superinfection.

Figure 12.16 Drug-induced side effect. An adverse effect of tetracycline given to young children is the permanent discoloration of tooth enamel.

Oral therapy with tetracyclines, clindamycin, and broad-spectrum penicillins and cephalosporins is associated with a serious and potentially fatal condition known as *antibiotic-associated colitis* (pseudomembranous colitis). This condition is due to the overgrowth in the bowel of *Clostridium difficile,* an endospore-forming bacterium that is resistant to the antibiotic. It invades the intestinal lining and releases toxins that induce diarrhea, fever, and abdominal pain. (You'll learn more about infectious diseases of the gastrointestinal tract, including *C. difficile,* in chapter 22.)

12.4 Learning Outcomes—Can You ...

24. ... distinguish between drug toxicity and allergic reactions to drugs?
25. ... explain what a superinfection is and how it occurs?

12.5 Considerations in Selecting an Antimicrobial Drug

Before actual antimicrobial therapy can begin, it is important that at least three factors be known:

1. the nature of the microorganism causing the infection,
2. the degree of the microorganism's susceptibility (also called sensitivity) to various drugs, and
3. the overall medical condition of the patient.

Identifying the Agent

Identification of infectious agents from body specimens should be attempted as soon as possible. It is especially important that such specimens be taken before any antimicrobial drug is given, just in case the drug eliminates the infectious agent. Direct examination of body fluids, sputum, or stool is a rapid initial method for detecting and perhaps even identifying bacteria or fungi. A doctor often begins the therapy on the basis of such immediate findings, or even on the basis of an informed best guess. For instance, if a sore throat appears to be caused by *Streptococcus pyogenes,* the physician might prescribe penicillin, because this species seems to be almost universally sensitive to it so far. If the infectious agent is not or cannot be isolated, epidemiologic statistics may be required to predict the most likely agent in a given infection. For example, *Streptococcus pneumoniae* accounts for the majority of cases of meningitis in children, followed by *Neisseria meningitidis* (discussed in detail in chapter 19).

Testing for the Drug Susceptibility of Microorganisms

Testing is essential in those groups of bacteria commonly showing resistance, such as *Staphylococcus* species, *Neisseria gonorrhoeae,*

Streptococcus pneumoniae, Enterococcus faecalis, and the aerobic gram-negative enteric bacilli. However, not all infectious agents require antimicrobial sensitivity testing. Drug testing in fungal or protozoan infections is difficult and is often unnecessary. When certain groups, such as group A streptococci and all anaerobes (except *Bacteroides*), are known to be uniformly susceptible to penicillin G, testing may not be necessary unless the patient is allergic to penicillin.

Selection of a proper antimicrobial agent begins by demonstrating the *in vitro* activity of several drugs against the infectious agent by means of standardized methods. In general, these tests involve exposing a pure culture of the bacterium to several different drugs and observing the effects of the drugs on growth.

The *Kirby-Bauer* technique is an agar diffusion test that provides useful data on antimicrobial susceptibility. In this test, the surface of a plate of special medium is spread with the test bacterium, and small discs containing a premeasured amount of antimicrobial are dispensed onto the bacterial lawn. After incubation, the zone of inhibition surrounding the discs is measured and compared with a standard for each drug (**table 12.7** and **figure 12.18**). The profile of antimicrobial sensitivity, or *antibiogram,* provides data for drug selection. The Kirby-Bauer procedure is less effective for bacteria that are anaerobic, highly fastidious, or slow-growing (*Mycobacterium*). An alternative diffusion system that provides additional information on drug effectiveness is the E-test (**figure 12.19**).

More sensitive and quantitative results can be obtained with tube dilution tests. First the antimicrobial is diluted serially in tubes of broth, and then each tube is inoculated with a small uniform sample of pure culture, incubated, and

Table 12.7   Results of a Sample Kirby-Bauer Test

Drug	Zone Sizes (mm) Required for: Susceptibility (S)	Zone Sizes (mm) Required for: Resistance (R)	Example Results (mm) for *Staphylococcus aureus*	Evaluation
Bacitracin	>13	<8	15	S
Chloramphenicol	>18	<12	20	S
Erythromycin	>18	<13	15	I
Gentamicin	>13	<12	16	S
Kanamycin	>18	<13	20	S
Neomycin	>17	<12	12	R
Penicillin G	>29	<20	10	R
Polymyxin B	>12	<8	10	R
Streptomycin	>15	<11	11	R
Vancomycin	>12	<9	15	S
Tetracycline	>19	<14	25	S

R = resistant, I = intermediate, S = sensitive

Kirby-Bauer Disc Diffusion Test*

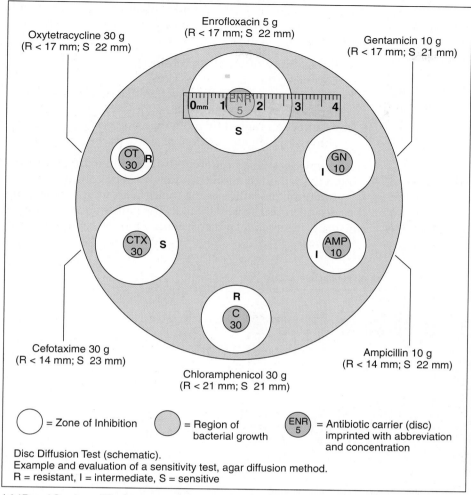

Enrofloxacin 5 g
(R < 17 mm; S 22 mm)

Oxytetracycline 30 g
(R < 17 mm; S 22 mm)

Gentamicin 10 g
(R < 17 mm; S 21 mm)

Cefotaxime 30 g
(R < 14 mm; S 23 mm)

Ampicillin 10 g
(R < 14 mm; S 22 mm)

Chloramphenicol 30 g
(R < 21 mm; S 21 mm)

◯ = Zone of Inhibition   ⬤ = Region of bacterial growth   (ENR 5) = Antibiotic carrier (disc) imprinted with abbreviation and concentration

Disc Diffusion Test (schematic).
Example and evaluation of a sensitivity test, agar diffusion method.
R = resistant, I = intermediate, S = sensitive

(a) *R and S values differ from table 12.7 due to differing concentrations of the antimicrobials.

(b)

Figure 12.18 Technique for preparation and interpretation of disc diffusion tests. **(a)** Standardized methods are used to seed a lawn of bacteria over the medium. A dispenser delivers several drugs onto a plate, followed by incubation. Interpretation of results: During incubation, antimicrobials become increasingly diluted as they diffuse out of the disc into the medium. If the test bacterium is sensitive to a drug, a zone of inhibition develops around its disc. Roughly speaking, the larger the size of this zone, the greater is the bacterium's sensitivity to the drug. The diameter of each zone is measured in millimeters and evaluated for susceptibility or resistance by means of a comparative standard (see table 12.7). **(b)** Results of test with *Escherichia hermannii* indicate a synergistic effect between ticarcillin (TIC) and AMC (note the expanded zone between these two drugs).

Figure 12.19 Alternative to the Kirby-Bauer procedure. Another diffusion test is the E-test, which uses a strip to produce the zone of inhibition. The advantage of the E-test is that the strip contains a gradient of drug calibrated in micrograms. This way, the MIC can be measured by observing the mark on the strip that corresponds to the edge of the zone of inhibition. (IP = imipenem and TZ = tazobactam)

examined for growth (turbidity). The smallest concentration (highest dilution) of drug that visibly inhibits growth is called the **minimum inhibitory concentration,** or **MIC.** The MIC is useful in determining the smallest effective dosage of a drug and in providing a comparative index against other antimicrobials **(figure 12.20).** In many clinical laboratories, these antimicrobial testing procedures are performed in automated machines that can test dozens of drugs simultaneously.

The MIC and Therapeutic Index

The results of antimicrobial sensitivity tests guide the physician's choice of a suitable drug. If therapy has already commenced, it is imperative to determine if the tests bear out the use of that particular drug. Once therapy has begun, it is important to observe the patient's clinical response, because the *in vitro* activity of the drug is not always correlated with its *in vivo* effect. When antimicrobial treatment fails, the failure is due to

1. the inability of the drug to diffuse into that body compartment (the brain, joints, skin),
2. resistant microbes in the infection that didn't make it into the sample collected for testing, or
3. an infection caused by more than one pathogen (mixed), some of which are resistant to the drug.

If therapy does fail, a different drug, combined therapy, or a different method of administration must be considered.

Many factors influence the choice of an antimicrobial drug besides microbial sensitivity to it. The nature and spectrum of the drug, its potential adverse effects, and the condition of the

Figure 12.20 Tube dilution test for determining the minimum inhibitory concentration (MIC).   (a) The antibiotic is diluted serially through tubes of liquid nutrient from right to left. All tubes are inoculated with an identical amount of a test bacterium and then incubated. The first tube on the left is a control that lacks the drug and shows maximum growth. The dilution of the first tube in the series that shows no growth (no turbidity) is the MIC. **(b)** Microbroth dilution in a multiwell plate adapted for eukaryotic pathogens. Here, amphotericin B, flucytosine, and several azole drugs are tested on a pathogenic yeast. Pink indicates growth and blue, no growth. Numbers indicate the dilution of the MIC, and Xs show the first well without growth.

patient can be critically important. When several antimicrobial drugs are available for treating an infection, final drug selection advances to a new series of considerations. In general, it is better to choose the narrowest-spectrum drug of those that are effective if the causative agent is known. This decreases the potential for superinfections and other adverse reactions.

Because drug toxicity is of concern, it is best to choose the one with high selective toxicity for the infectious agent and low human toxicity. The **therapeutic index (TI)** is defined as the ratio of the dose of the drug that is toxic to humans as compared to its minimum effective (therapeutic) dose. The closer these two figures are (the smaller the ratio), the greater is the potential for toxic drug reactions. For example, a drug that has a therapeutic index of:

$$\frac{10 \ \mu g/ml: \text{toxic dose}}{9 \ \mu g/\mu l \ (\text{MIC})} \quad \boxed{\text{TI} = 1.1}$$

is a riskier choice than one with a therapeutic index of:

$$\frac{10 \ \mu g/ml}{9 \ \mu g/ml} \quad \boxed{\text{TI} = 10}$$

When a series of drugs being considered for therapy have similar MICs, the drug with the highest therapeutic index usually has the widest margin of safety.

The physician must also take a careful history of the patient to discover any preexisting medical conditions that will influence the activity of the drug or the response of the patient. A history of allergy to a certain class of drugs precludes the use of that drug and any drugs related to it. Underlying liver or kidney disease will ordinarily necessitate the modification of drug therapy, because these organs play such an important part in metabolizing or excreting the drug. Infants, the elderly, and pregnant women require special precautions. For example, age can diminish gastrointestinal absorption and organ function, and most antimicrobial drugs cross the placenta and could affect fetal development.

The intake of other drugs must be carefully scrutinized, because incompatibilities can result in increased toxicity or failure of one or more of the drugs. For example, the combination of aminoglycosides and cephalosporins increases nephrotoxic effects; antacids reduce the absorption of isoniazid; and the interaction of tetracycline or rifampin with oral contraceptives can abolish the contraceptive's effect. Some drugs (penicillin with certain aminoglycosides, or amphotericin B with flucytosine) act synergistically, so that reduced doses of each can be used in combined therapy. Other concerns in choosing drugs include any genetic or metabolic abnormalities in the patient, the site of infection, the route of administration, and the cost of the drug.

The Art and Science of Choosing an Antimicrobial Drug

Even when all the information is in, the final choice of a drug is not always easy or straightforward. Consider the hypothetical case of an elderly alcoholic patient with pneu-monia caused by *Klebsiella* and complicated by diminished liver and kidney function. All drugs must be given parenterally because of prior damage to the gastrointestinal lining and poor absorption. Drug tests show that the infectious agent is sensitive to third-generation cephalosporins, gentamicin, imipenem, and azlocillin. The patient's history shows previous allergy to the penicillins, so these would be ruled out. Drug interactions occur between alcohol and the cephalosporins, which are also associated with serious bleeding in elderly patients, so this may not be a good choice. Aminoglycosides such as gentamicin are nephrotoxic and poorly cleared by damaged kidneys. Imipenem causes intestinal discomfort, but it has less toxicity and would be a viable choice.

In the case of a cancer patient with severe systemic *Candida* infection, there will be fewer criteria to weigh. Intravenous amphotericin B or fluconazole are the only possible choices, despite drug toxicity and other possible adverse side effects. In a life-threatening situation in which a dangerous chemotherapy is perhaps the only chance for survival, the choices are reduced and the priorities are different.

An Antimicrobial Drug Dilemma

We began this chapter with a view of the exciting strides made in chemotherapy during the past few years, but we must end it on a note of qualification and caution. There is now a worldwide problem in the management of antimicrobial drugs. The remarkable progress in treating many infectious diseases has spawned a view of antimicrobials as a "cure-all" for infections as diverse as the common cold and acne. And, although it is true that nothing is as dramatic as curing an infectious disease with the correct antimicrobial drug, in many instances, drugs have no effect or can be harmful. For example, roughly 200 million prescriptions for antimicrobials are written in the United States every year. A recent study disclosed that 75% of antimicrobial prescriptions are for pharyngeal, sinus, lung, and upper respiratory infections. A fairly high percentage of these are viral in origin and will have little or no benefit from antibacterial drugs.

In the past, many physicians tended to use a "shotgun" antimicrobial therapy for minor infections, which involves administering a broad-spectrum drug instead of a more specific narrow-spectrum one. This practice led to superinfections and other adverse reactions. Importantly, it also caused the development of resistance in "bystander" microbes (normal biota) that were exposed to the drug as well. This helped to spread antibiotic resistance to pathogens. With growing awareness of the problems of antibiotic resistance, this practice is much less frequent.

Tons of excess antimicrobial drugs produced in this country are exported to other countries, where controls are not as strict. Nearly 200 different antibiotics are sold over the counter in Latin America and Asian countries. It is common for people in these countries to self-medicate without understanding the correct medical indication. Drugs used in this way are largely ineffectual but, worse yet, they are known to be responsible for emergence of drug-resistant bacteria that subsequently cause epidemics.

In the final analysis, every allied health professional should be critically aware not only of the admirable and utilitarian nature of antimicrobials but also of their limitations.

12.5 Learning Outcomes—Can You. . .

26. . . . describe two methods for testing antimicrobial susceptibility?

27. . . . define therapeutic index and identify whether a high or a low index is preferable?

Case File 12   *Wrap-Up*

Short protein molecules have been isolated from various animal sources. Hydramacin is a particularly promising one. Of course, there is a long path between the laboratory discovery of a compound that inhibits bacteria and the production of a safe drug derived from that compound. One important phase of testing is to determine a compound's toxic effects on the patient. You learned in this chapter that the best antimicrobials are selectively toxic. Whether hydramacin, so closely related to scorpion venom, passes this test remains to be seen.

See: 2009. *J. Biol. Chem.* 284:3, 1896–1905.

Chapter Summary

12.1 Principles of Antimicrobial Therapy

- Antimicrobial chemotherapy involves the use of drugs to control infection on or in the body.
- Antimicrobial drugs are produced either synthetically or from natural sources. They inhibit or destroy microbial growth in the infected host. Antibiotics are the subset of antimicrobials produced by the natural metabolic processes of microorganisms.
- Antimicrobial drugs are classified by their range of effectiveness. Broad-spectrum antimicrobials are effective against many types of microbes. Narrow-spectrum antimicrobials are effective against a limited group of microbes.
- Bacteria and fungi are the primary sources of most currently used antibiotics. The molecular structures of these compounds can be chemically altered or mimicked in the laboratory.

12.2 Interactions Between Drug and Microbe

- Antimicrobials are classified into +/−20 major drug families, based on chemical composition, source or origin, and their site of action.
- The majority of antimicrobials are effective against bacteria, but a limited number are effective against protozoa, helminths, fungi, and viruses.
- There are five main cellular targets for antibiotics in microbes: cell wall synthesis, nucleic acid structure and function, protein synthesis, cell membranes, and folic acid synthesis.

12.3 Survey of Major Antimicrobial Drug Groups

- Penicillins, cephalosporins, carbapenems, and vancomycin block cell wall synthesis.
- Aminoglycosides, tetracyclines, erythromycin, and ketolides block protein synthesis in prokaryotes.
- Sulfonamides, trimethoprim, and the fluoroquinolones are synthetic antimicrobials effective against a broad range of microorganisms. They block steps in the synthesis of nucleic acids.
- Polymyxins and daptomycin are the major drugs that disrupt cell membranes.

- Bacteria in biofilms respond differently to antibiotics than when they are free-floating. It is therefore difficult to eradicate biofilms in the human body.
- Fungal antimicrobials, such as macrolide polyenes, azoles, echinocandins, and flucytosine, must be monitored carefully because of the potential toxicity to the infected host.
- There are fewer antiparasitic drugs than antibacterial drugs because parasites are eukaryotes like their human hosts and they have several life stages, some of which can be resistant to the drug.
- Antihelminthic drugs immobilize or disintegrate infesting helminths or inhibit their metabolism in some manner.
- Antiviral drugs interfere with viral replication by blocking viral entry into cells, blocking the replication process, or preventing the assembly of viral subunits into complete virions.
- Many antiviral agents are analogs of nucleotides. They inactivate the replication process when incorporated into viral nucleic acids. HIV antivirals interfere with reverse transcriptase or proteases to prevent the maturation of viral particles.
- Commercial interferon has some use against viral infections and cancer.
- Microorganisms are termed drug resistant when they are no longer inhibited by an antimicrobial to which they were previously sensitive.
- Most drug resistance is genetic; microbes acquire genes that code for methods of inactivating or escaping the antimicrobial, or acquire mutations that affect the drug's impact.
- Varieties of microbial drug resistance include drug inactivation, decreased drug uptake, decreased drug receptor sites, and modification of metabolic pathways formerly attacked by the drug.
- Widespread indiscriminate use of antimicrobials has resulted in an explosion of microorganisms resistant to all common drugs.

- Research strategies for new types of antibiotics include targeting iron-scavenging pathways of microbes, the use of RNA interference, mimicking natural defense peptides, and the use of bacteriophages.
- New targets for antiviral therapy may focus on host factors that the virus needs for its reproduction.
- Pro- and prebiotics are methods of crowding out pathogenic bacteria and providing a favorable environment for the growth of beneficial bacteria.

12.4 Interactions Between Drug and Host

- The three major side effects of antimicrobials are toxicity to organs, allergic reactions, and problems resulting from alteration of normal biota.
- Antimicrobials that destroy most but not all normal biota can allow the unaffected normal biota to overgrow, causing a superinfection.

12.5 Considerations in Selecting an Antimicrobial Drug

- The three major considerations necessary to choose an effective antimicrobial are the nature of the infecting microbe, the microbe's sensitivity to available drugs, and the overall medical status of the infected host.
- The Kirby-Bauer test identifies antimicrobials that are effective against a specific infectious bacterial isolate.
- The MIC (minimum inhibitory concentration) identifies the smallest effective dose of an antimicrobial toxic to the infecting microbe.
- The therapeutic index is a ratio of the amount of drug toxic to the infected host and the MIC. The smaller the ratio, the greater the potential for toxic host-drug reactions.
- The effectiveness of antimicrobial drugs has been compromised by several practices including inappropriate prescription, use of broad-spectrum instead of narrow-spectrum drugs, and sale of over-the-counter antimicrobials in other countries.

Multiple-Choice and True-False Questions   Knowledge and Comprehension

Multiple-Choice Questions. Select the correct answer from the answers provided.

1. A compound synthesized by bacteria or fungi that destroys or inhibits the growth of other microbes is a/an
   a. synthetic drug.
   b. antibiotic.
   c. antimicrobial drug.
   d. competitive inhibitor.

2. Which statement is *not* an aim in the use of drugs in antimicrobial chemotherapy? The drug should
   a. have selective toxicity.
   b. be active even in high dilutions.
   c. be broken down and excreted rapidly.
   d. be microbicidal.

3. Drugs that prevent the formation of the bacterial cell wall are
   a. quinolones.
   b. beta-lactams.
   c. tetracyclines.
   d. aminoglycosides.

4. Microbial resistance to drugs is acquired through
   a. conjugation.
   b. transformation.
   c. transduction.
   d. all of these.

5. R factors are _____ that contain a code for _____.
   a. genes, replication
   b. plasmids, drug resistance
   c. transposons, interferon
   d. plasmids, conjugation

6. Phage therapy is a technique that uses
   a. chemicals to destroy phages infecting human cells.
   b. chemicals to foster the growth of beneficial phages in the body.
   c. phages to foster the growth of normal biota.
   d. phages to target pathogenic bacteria in the body.

7. Most antihelminthic drugs function by
   a. weakening the worms so they can be flushed out by the intestine.
   b. inhibiting worm metabolism.
   c. blocking the absorption of nutrients.
   d. inhibiting egg production.

8. Which of the following modes of action would be most selectively toxic?
   a. interrupting ribosomal function
   b. dissolving the cell membrane
   c. preventing cell wall synthesis
   d. inhibiting DNA replication

9. The MIC is the _____ of a drug that is required to inhibit growth of a microbe.
   a. largest concentration
   b. standard dose
   c. smallest concentration
   d. lowest dilution

10. An antimicrobial drug with a ____ therapeutic index is a better choice than one with a _____ therapeutic index.
   a. low, high
   b. high, low

True-False Questions. If the statement is true, leave as is. If it is false, correct it by rewriting the sentence.

11. Most antiviral agents work by destroying active viruses.

12. Sulfonamide drugs work by disrupting protein synthesis.

13. Biofilms are difficult to treat and don't always respond to antibiotics.

14. An antibiotic that disrupts the host's normal biota can cause superinfection.

15. Drug resistance can occur when a patient's immune system becomes reactive to a drug.

Critical Thinking Questions   Application and Analysis

These questions are suggested as a *writing-to-learn* experience. For each question, compose a one- or two-paragraph answer that includes the factual information needed to completely address the question.

1. a. Using the diagram below as a guide, briefly explain how the three factors in drug therapy interact.
   b. What drug characteristics will make treatment most effective?
   c. Why is it better for a drug to be microbicidal than microbistatic?

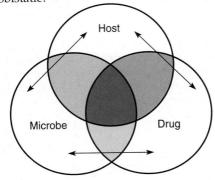

2. Why does the penicillin group of drugs have milder toxicity than other antibiotics?

3. Explain why there are fewer antifungal, antiparasitic, and antiviral drugs than antibacterial drugs.

4. Explain the phenomenon of drug resistance from the standpoint of microbial genetics (include a description of R factors).

5. Occasionally, one will hear the expression that a microbe has become "immune" to a drug.
   a. What is a better way to explain what is happening?
   b. Explain a simple test one could do to determine if drug resistance was developing in a culture.

6. Drugs are often given to dental patients with heart disease, or to healthy family members exposed to contagious infections.
   a. What word would you use to describe this use of drugs?
   b. What is the purpose of this form of treatment?
   c. Explain some potential undesired effects of this form of therapy.

7. A woman has been prescribed a broad-spectrum oral cephalosporin for a strep throat. What are some possible consequences in addition to cure of the infected throat?

8. You have been directed to take a sample from a growth-free portion of the zone of inhibition in the Kirby-Bauer test and inoculate it onto a plate of nonselective medium.
   a. What does it mean if growth occurs on the new plate?
   b. What if there is no growth?

9. a. Refer to figure 12.18*a* and interpret the results.
   b. Give the MICs for the tests in figure 12.20*a*.

10. a. Explain the basis for combined therapy.
    b. Give reasons why it could be helpful to use combined therapy in treating HIV infection.

Concept Mapping   Synthesis

Appendix D provides guidance for working with concept maps.

1. Supply your own linking lines *and* phrases in this concept map.

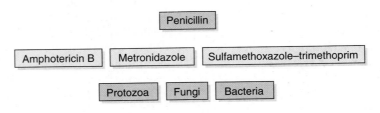

2. Use 6 to 10 words of your choice from the Chapter Summary to create a concept map. Finish it by providing linking words.

Visual Connections   Synthesis

These questions use visual images or previous content to make connections to this chapter's concepts.

1. **Figure 12.6.** Where could penicillinase affect each of these antibiotics?

2. **From chapter 6, figure 6.13.** How could an antiviral drug interfere with the activity illustrated in the figure? How is that effective in controlling the viral cycle?

Multiplication of double-stranded NA viruses.
The virus penetrates the host cell and releases DNA, which

1. enters the nucleus and
2. is transcribed in two phases. In the early phase viral DNA that codes for enzymes needed to replicate DNA is transcribed. In the late phase viral DNA that codes for structural proteins is transcribed.
3. The RNA transcripts move to the cytoplasm.
4. Viral mRNA is translated into structural proteins; proteins enter the nucleus.
5. Viral DNA is replicated repeatedly in the nucleus.
6. Viral DNA and proteins are assembled into a mature virus in the nucleus.
7. Because it is double-stranded, the viral DNA can insert itself into host DNA (latency).

www.connect.microbiology.com

Enhance your study of this chapter with study tools and practice tests. Also ask your instructor about the resources available through ConnectPlus, including the media-rich eBook, interactive learning tools, and animations.

13

Microbe-Human Interactions
Infection and Disease

Case File 13

Internet users have grown accustomed to using Google to search for all kinds of information: the definition of a word, the latest news about a celebrity, or the possible cause of an ache or pain. Now it turns out that Google may be one of the more powerful tools for predicting disease outbreaks—some say even more powerful than the best tools of the Centers for Disease Control and Prevention (CDC).

In 2008 Google launched Google Flu Trends, an application that compiles aggregated data from key word searches for clinical terms, such as *thermometer, chest congestion, muscle aches,* or *flu symptoms.* Google reports the data on a website, which then provides an early warning system for the locations of new flu outbreaks. Because the data are collected from searches performed each day, trends in flu symptoms become apparent much more quickly than when they are based on data reported during office visits or in lab reports from physicians around the country. When the CDC compared actual cases over the course of a year with Google's findings, the data from the two sources matched.

- Is there any possible downside to this approach to data collection?
- How might data collected in this way *not* be representative of a particular population?

Continuing the Case appears on page 388.

Outline and Learning Outcomes

13.1 The Human Host

1. Differentiate between colonization, infection, and disease.
2. Enumerate the sites where normal biota is found in humans.
3. Discuss how the Human Microbiome Project will change our understanding of normal biota.
4. Point out how microbial antagonism can be helpful to the human host.

13.2 The Progress of an Infection

5. Differentiate between pathogenicity and virulence.
6. Define opportunism.
7. List the steps a microbe has to take to get to the point where it can cause disease.

8. List several portals of entry.
9. Define infectious dose.
10. Describe three ways microbes cause tissue damage.
11. Differentiate between endotoxins and exotoxins.
12. Provide a definition of virulence factors.
13. Draw and label a curve representing the course of clinical infection.
14. Discuss the topic of reservoirs thoroughly.
15. List seven different modes of transmission of infectious agents.
16. Define nosocomial infection and list the three most common types.
17. List Koch's postulates, and when they might not be appropriate in establishing causation.

13.3 Epidemiology: The Study of Disease in Populations
18. Differentiate the science of epidemiology from traditional medical practice.
19. Identify the need for some diseases being denoted "notifiable."
20. Define incidence and prevalence.
21. Discuss point-source, common-source, and propagated epidemics and predict the shape of the epidemic curves associated with each.

13.1 The Human Host

The human body exists in a state of dynamic equilibrium with microorganisms. In the healthy individual, this balance is maintained as a peaceful coexistence and lack of disease. But on occasion, the balance tips in favor of the microorganism, and an infection or disease results. In this chapter, we explore each component of the host-parasite relationship, beginning with the nature and function of normal biota, moving to the stages of infection and disease, and closing with a study of epidemiology and the patterns of disease in populations. These topics will set the scene for chapters 14 and 15, which deal with the ways the host defends itself against assault by microorganisms, and also for chapters 18 through 23, which examine diseases affecting different organ systems.

Contact, Infection, Disease—A Continuum

The body surfaces are constantly exposed to microbes. Some microbes become implanted there as colonists (normal biota), some are rapidly lost (transients), and others invade the tissues. Such intimate contact with microbes inevitably leads to **infection,** a condition in which pathogenic microorganisms penetrate the host defenses, enter the tissues, and multiply. When the cumulative effects of the infection damage or disrupt tissues and organs, the **pathologic** state that results is known as a disease. A disease is defined as any deviation from health. There are hundreds of different diseases caused by such factors as infections, diet, genetics, and aging. In this chapter, however, we discuss only **infectious disease**—the disruption of a tissue or organ caused by microbes or their products.

The pattern of the host-parasite relationship can be viewed as a series of stages that begins with contact, progresses to infection, and ends in disease. Because of numerous factors relating to host resistance and degree of pathogenicity, not all contacts lead to colonization, not all colonizations lead to infection, and not all infections lead to disease. In fact, contamination without colonization and colonization without disease are the rule.

Resident Biota: The Human as a Habitat

With its constant source of nourishment and moisture, relatively stable pH and temperature, and extensive surfaces upon which to settle, the human body provides a favorable habitat for an abundance of microorganisms. In fact, it is so favorable that, cell for cell, microbes on the human body outnumber human cells at least ten to one! The large and mixed collection of microbes adapted to the body has been variously called the **normal (resident) biota,** or indigenous biota, though some microbiologists prefer to use the term *normal flora*. The normal residents include an array of bacteria, fungi, protozoa, and, to a certain extent, viruses and arthropods. These organisms have a profound effect on human biology.

Since it has become known that there are more unknown than known species that populate the human body, an effort is now underway to utilize **metagenomics** to identify the microbial profile inside and on humans. The **Human Microbiome Project** began in 2007 and is funded by the National Institutes of Health and is being conducted at laboratories all over the country. The aim is to collect genetic sequences in the gut, respiratory tract, skin, etc. to determine which microbes are there, even when they can't be grown in the laboratory. A secondary aim is to determine what role these normal biota play in health and disease. When the project is completed, in several years, this chapter will look completely different. Keep in mind that the microbes we discuss here are only those we can cultivate in the laboratory, although we know that many of them are indeed important. In fact, the science of "normal biota" is in its infancy.

Acquiring Resident Biota

The human body offers a seemingly endless variety of environmental niches, with wide variations in temperature, pH, nutrients, and oxygen tension occurring from one area to another. Because the body provides such a range of habitats, it should not be surprising that the body supports a wide range of microbes. As shown in **tables 13.1** and **13.2,** most areas of the body in contact with the outside environment harbor resident

Table 13.1 Sites That Harbor a Known Normal Biota

- Skin and its adjacent mucous membranes
- Respiratory tract
- Gastrointestinal tract (various parts)
- Outer opening of urethra
- External genitalia
- Vagina
- External ear canal
- External eye (lids, conjunctiva)

Table 13.2 Anatomical Sites and Fluids Thought to Be Sterile

All internal tissues and organs

Heart and circulatory system (?)
Liver
Kidneys and bladder
Brain and spinal cord
Muscles
Bones
Ovaries/testes
Glands (pancreas, salivary, thyroid)
Sinuses
Middle and inner ear
Internal eye

Fluids within an organ or tissue

Blood
Urine in kidneys, ureters, bladder
Cerebrospinal fluid
Saliva prior to entering the oral cavity
Semen prior to entering the urethra
Amniotic fluid surrounding the embryo and fetus

long before they are able to colonize a particular area. Of those microbes able to establish an ongoing presence, an even smaller number are able to remain without attracting the unwanted attention of the body's defenses. This last group of organisms has evolved, along with its human hosts, to produce a complex relationship in which the effects of normal biota are generally not deleterious to the host. Recall from chapter 7 that microbes exist in different kinds of relationships with their hosts. Normal biota are generally either in a commensal or a mutualistic association with their hosts. Although generally stable, the biota can fluctuate to a limited extent with general health, age, variations in diet, hygiene, hormones, and drug therapy. In fact, research in 2007 suggests that maintaining a healthy "crop" of normal biota is, in fact, the job of the appendix. Researchers speculate that when entire populations lost their gut flora, for example, when a cholera epidemic swept through an area, that the appendix contained a rich mix of gut bacteria that could repopulate the intestines. This was particularly important before humans lived in dense populations, when it could be difficult to come in contact with enough people to acquire a diverse normal biota.

We now know that bacterial biota benefits the human host in many ways. The very development of our organs is influenced by the presence of resident biota. They also prevent the overgrowth of harmful microorganisms. A common example

microorganisms, while internal organs and tissue, along with the fluids they contain, are generally microbe-free.

Table 13.3 provides a view of normal biota as of late 2010. The microbes listed were mostly identified by culturing them, a technique that we now know misses many, if not most, microbes in a habitat.

Second, it should be mentioned that scientists have recently reported detecting bacteria in blood from healthy humans and animals. Others have identified hundreds of species of bacteria in the lungs, also previously believed to be sterile. They are bacteria that cannot be cultivated on laboratory media and were only detected using microscopy and molecular identification techniques. For the purposes of this book, we consider the blood and other sites listed in table 13.2 to be sterile. Discoveries such as these remind us that science is a continuously changing body of knowledge, and no scientific truth is ever "final."

The vast majority of microbes that come in contact with the body are removed or destroyed by the host's defenses

A Note About Viruses as Normal Biota

Microbiologists have never known how to characterize the non-disease-causing viruses and viral sequences we know are present in mammalian organisms. As you read in previous chapters, DNA sequences that we know come from viruses account for anywhere from 8% to 90% of human DNA. Some of those are just genes left behind by viruses, of course, but some of those are also entire viruses. In 2006, researchers at Texas A & M showed that viruses called endogenous retroviruses (ERVs) are present in all mammals and are vital to healthy development of placentas in the sheep they studied.

They seem to have originated from infections of mammals from thousands of years ago and have remained in mammals because the proteins they produce provide some real benefit to their hosts. In this case, the ERVs studied in sheep seem to be vital to healthy development of placentas and embryos. When researchers blocked the action of the ERVs, sheep miscarried at a high rate. Apparently, over time, the sheep and the viruses have coevolved to their mutual benefit.

In 2008, researchers in Japan found that populations with high rates of infection with the human T-lymphotrophic virus (HTLV-1) had unusually low rates of stomach cancer, suggesting a mutualistic and protective role for the virus.

The role of "normal biota"—or coevolved—viruses in mammalian health will be an exciting area of research in coming years. Of course, viral sequences will be detected in the metagenomic search being conducted as part of the Human Microbiome Project.

Table 13.3 Life on Humans: Sites Containing Well-Established Biota and Representative Examples*

Anatomic Sites	Common Genera	Remarks
Skin	**Bacteria:** *Pseudomonas, Janthinobacterium,* other gram-negatives, very few gram-positives **Fungi:** *Candida, Pityrosporum* **Arthropods:** *Demodex* mite	Microbes live mainly in upper dead layers of epidermis, glands, and follicles Dependent on skin lipids for growth Present in sebaceous glands and hair follicles
Gastrointestinal Tract		
Oral cavity	**Bacteria:** *Streptococcus, Neisseria, Veillonella, Fusobacterium, Lactobacillus, Bacteroides, Actinomyces, Eikenella, Treponema, Haemophilus* **Fungi:** *Candida* species **Protozoa:** *Entamoeba gingivalis*	Colonize the epidermal layer of cheeks, gingiva, pharynx; surface of teeth; found in saliva in huge numbers Can cause thrush Inhabit the gingiva of persons with poor oral hygiene
Large intestine and rectum	**Bacteria:** *Bacteroides, Fusobacterium,* streptococci, *Lactobacillus,* coliforms (*Escherichia, Enterobacter*) **Fungi:** *Candida* **Protozoa:** *Entamoeba coli, Trichomonas hominis*	*Bifidobacterium, Clostridium,* fecal biota consists predominantly of anaerobes; other microbes are aerotolerant or facultative. Intestinal thrush Feed on waste materials in the large intestine
Upper Respiratory Tract	Biota resembles that of oral cavity	Nasal passages, throat, and pharynx
Lower Respiratory Tract	**Bacteria:** *Prevotella* spp.	Previously thought to be sterile; asthmatic lungs colonized by different species than healthy
Genital Tract	**Bacteria:** *Lactobacillus, Streptococcus, Corynebacterium, Escherichia* **Fungi:** *Candida*	In females, biota occupies the external genitalia and vaginal and cervical surfaces; internal reproductive structures thought to be sterile. Biota responds to hormonal changes during life. Cause of yeast infections
Urinary Tract	**Bacteria:** *Staphylococcus, Streptococcus, Corynebacterium, Lactobacillus*	In females, biota exists only in the first portion of the urethral mucosa; the remainder of the tract is sterile. In males, the entire reproductive and urinary tract is thought to be sterile except for a short portion of the anterior urethra.

*Information in this table subject to significant change as results of Human Microbiome Project become available.

is the fermentation of glycogen by lactobacilli, which keep the pH in the vagina quite acidic and prevent the overgrowth of the yeast *Candida albicans.*

The generally antagonistic effect "good" microbes have against intruder microorganisms is called **microbial antagonism.** Normal biota exist in a steady established relationship with the host and are unlikely to be displaced by incoming microbes. This antagonistic protection may simply be a result of a limited number of attachment sites in the host site, all of which are stably occupied by normal biota. Antagonism may also result from the chemical or physiological environment created by the resident biota, which is hostile to other microbes.

An increasing body of evidence suggests that the make-up of your intestinal biota can influence your tendency to be overweight. For example, scientists have found that obese humans have more bacteria in the group Firmicutes (see chapter 1) and fewer in the group Bacteroidetes. The ratios are reversed in people of normal weight. There is evidence that people harboring higher levels of Firmicutes in their intestines get more calories from their food than the other group. This area of investigation will certainly continue.

Characterizing the normal biota as beneficial or, at worst, commensal to the host presupposes that the host is in good health, with a fully functioning immune system, and that the biota is present only in its natural microhabitat within the body. Hosts with compromised immune systems could very easily experience disease caused by their (previously normal) biota **(table 13.4).** This outcome is seen when AIDS patients become sick with pneumococcal pneumonia, the causative agent of which (*Streptococcus pneumoniae*) is often carried as normal biota in the nasopharynx. **Endogenous** infections (those caused by biota that are already present in the body) can also occur when normal biota is introduced to a site that was previously sterile, as when *Escherichia coli* enters the bladder, resulting in a urinary tract infection.

Initial Colonization of the Newborn

The uterus and its contents are normally sterile during embryonic and fetal development and remain essentially germ-free until just before birth. The event that first exposes the infant to microbes is the breaking of the fetal membranes, at which time microbes from the mother's vagina can enter the womb. Comprehensive exposure occurs during the birth process itself, when the baby becomes colonized with the mother's vaginal biota **(figure 13.1).** (Babies born by cesarean section typically are colonized by adult skin biota.) Within 8 to 12 hours after delivery, the vaginally-delivered newborn typically has been colonized by bacteria such as streptococci, staphylococci, and lactobacilli, acquired primarily from its mother. The nature of the biota initially colonizing the baby's large intestine depends on whether the baby is bottle- or breast-fed. Bottle-fed infants (receiving milk or a milk-based formula) tend to acquire a mixed population of coliforms, lactobacilli, enteric streptococci, and staphylococci. In contrast, the intestinal biota of breast-fed infants consists primarily of *Bifidobacterium* species whose growth is favored by a growth factor from the milk. This bacterium metabolizes sugars into acids that protect the infant from infection by certain intestinal pathogens. The skin, gastrointestinal tract, and portions of the respiratory and genitourinary tracts all continue to be colonized as contact continues with family members, health care personnel, the environment, and food.

Figure 13.1 The origins of microbiota in newborns.
A vaginal birth exposes babies to the biota of the mother's reproductive tract. From the moment of birth, the infant will begin to acquire microbes from its environment.

Indigenous Biota of Specific Regions

Although we tend to speak of the biota as a single unit, it is a complex mixture of hundreds of species, differing somewhat in quality and quantity from one individual to another. Studies of the biota have shown that most people harbor certain specially adapted bacteria, fungi, and protozoa. The normal, indigenous biota present in specific body sites is presented in detail in chapters 18 through 23. Table 13.3 provides an overview.

For a look into the laboratory study of resident biota, see **Insight 13.1.**

13.1 Learning Outcomes—Can You ...

1. ... differentiate between colonization, infection, and disease?
2. ... enumerate the sites where normal biota is found in humans?
3. ... discuss how the Human Microbiome Project will change our understanding of normal biota?
4. ... point out how microbial antagonism can be helpful to the human host?

13.2 The Progress of an Infection

A microbe whose relationship with its host is parasitic and results in infection and disease is termed a **pathogen.** The type and severity of infection depend both on the pathogenicity of the organism and the condition of the host **(figure 13.2).** **Pathogenicity,** you will recall, is a broad concept that describes an organism's potential to cause infection or disease, and is used to divide pathogenic microbes into one of two groups. **True pathogens** (primary pathogens) are capable of causing disease in healthy persons with normal immune defenses. They are generally associated with a specific, recognizable disease, which may vary in severity from mild (colds) to severe (malarial) to fatal (rabies). Examples of true pathogens include the influenza virus, plague bacillus, and malarial protozoan.

A Note About Pathogens

Science has documented a total of 1,407 microbes that cause disease in humans. Of these, 538 are bacteria, 317 are fungi, 287 are helminths, 208 are viruses, and 57 are protozoa. Of course, we don't know how many pathogens we *don't* know about. And there are plenty of conditions and diseases that have no known cause as of yet.

Opportunistic pathogens cause disease when the host's defenses are compromised[1] or when they become established in a part of the body that is not natural to them. Opportunists are not considered pathogenic to a normal healthy person and, unlike primary pathogens, do not generally possess well-

---

1. People with weakened immunity are often termed *immunocompromised*.

Figure 13.2 Will disease result from an encounter between a (human) host and a microorganism? In most cases, all of the slider bars must be in the correct ranges and the microbe's toggle switch must be in the "yes" position while the host's toggle switch must be in the "no" position in order for disease to occur.

developed virulence properties. Examples of opportunistic pathogens include *Pseudomonas* species and *Candida albicans*. Factors that greatly predispose a person to infections, both primary and opportunistic, are shown in table 13.4.

The relative severity of the disease caused by a particular microorganism depends on the **virulence** of the microbe. Although the terms *pathogenicity* and *virulence* are often used interchangeably, virulence is the accurate term for describing the degree of pathogenicity. The virulence of a microbe is determined by its ability to

1. establish itself in the host, and
2. cause damage.

There is much involved in both of these steps. To establish themselves in a host, microbes must enter the host, attach firmly to host tissues, and survive the host defenses. To cause damage, microbes produce toxins or induce a host response that is actually injurious to the host. Any characteristic or structure of the microbe that contributes to the preceding activities is called a **virulence factor.** Virulence can be due to single or multiple factors. In some microbes, the causes of virulence are clearly established, but in others they are not. In the following section, we examine the effects of virulence fac-

tors while simultaneously outlining the stages in the progress of an infection.

Note that different healthy individuals have widely varying responses to the same microorganism. This is determined in part by genetic variation in the specific components of their defense systems. That is why the same infectious agent can cause severe disease in one individual and mild or no disease in another.

Table 13.4 Factors That Weaken Host Defenses and Increase Susceptibility to Infection*

- Old age and extreme youth (infancy, prematurity)
- Genetic defects in immunity, and acquired defects in immunity (AIDS)
- Surgery and organ transplants
- Underlying disease: cancer, liver malfunction, diabetes
- Chemotherapy/immunosuppressive drugs
- Physical and mental stress
- Other infections

*These conditions compromise defense barriers or immune responses.

INSIGHT 13.1   Life Without Microbiota

For years, questions lingered about how essential the microbiota is to normal life and what functions various members of the biota might serve. The need for animal models to further investigate these questions led eventually to development of laboratory strains of *germ-free*, or **axenic**, mammals and birds. The techniques and facilities required for producing and maintaining a germ-free colony are exceptionally rigorous. After the young mammals are taken from the mother aseptically by cesarean section, they are immediately transferred to a sterile isolator or incubator. The newborns must be fed by hand through gloved ports in the isolator until they can eat on their own, and all materials entering their chamber must be sterile. Rats, mice, rabbits, guinea pigs, monkeys, dogs, hamsters, and cats are some of the mammals raised in the germ-free state.

A dramatic characteristic of germ-free animals is that they live longer and have fewer diseases than normal controls, as long as they remain in a sterile environment. From this standpoint, it is clear that the biota is not needed for survival in this rarefied environment. At the same time, it is also clear that axenic life is highly impractical. Studies have revealed important facts about the effect of the biota on various organs and systems. For example, the biota contributes significantly to the development of the immune system. When germ-free animals are placed in contact with normal control animals, they gradually develop a biota similar to that of the controls. However, germ-free subjects are less tolerant of microorganisms and can die from infections

Table 13.A Effects of the Germ-Free State

Germ-Free Animals Display	Suggesting That:
Enlargement of the cecum; other degenerative diseases of the intestinal tract of rats, rabbits, chickens	Microbes are needed for normal intestinal development.
Vitamin deficiency in rats	Microbes are a significant nutritional source of vitamins.
Underdevelopment of immune system in most animals	Microbes are needed to stimulate development of certain host defenses.
Higher rates of autoimmune disease	Microbes are needed to "occupy" the immune system.

by relatively harmless species. This susceptibility is due to the immature character of the immune system of germ-free animals. Germ-free animals also have stunted intestinal tracts. **Table 13.A** summarizes some major conclusions arising from studies with germ-free animals.

In 2008 researchers found that *Bacteroides fragilis* in the gut produce a molecule that fends off colonization by *Helicobacter pylori*. When scientists isolated this molecule and fed it to mice, it protected them from colitis. And normal biota in the mouth apparently are important contributors to taste, according to a recent study. It seems that the thiols released from fruits and vegetables (and wines!), which give them their flavor, are released due to the action of oral bacteria. Germ-free experiments have clarified the dynamics of several infectious diseases. Perhaps the most striking discoveries were made in the case of oral diseases. For years, the precise involvement of microbes in dental caries had been ambiguous. Studies with germ-free rats, hamsters, and beagles confirmed that caries development is influenced by heredity, a diet high in sugars, and poor oral hygiene. Even when all these predisposing factors are present, however, germ-free animals still remain free of caries unless they have been inoculated with specific bacteria. Further discussion on dental diseases is found in chapter 22.

Sterile enclosure for rearing and handling germ-free laboratory animals.

Why is there variation? In chapter 7, we described coevolution as changes in genetic composition by one species in response to changes in another. Infectious agents evolve in response to their interaction with a host (as in the case of antibiotic resistance). Hosts evolve, too. And although their pace of change is much slower than that of a microbe, eventually changes show up in human populations due to their past experiences with pathogens. One striking example is sickle cell disease. Persons who are carriers of a mutation

in their hemoglobin gene (i.e., who inherited one mutated hemoglobin gene and one normal) have few or no sickle cell disease symptoms but are more resistant to malaria than people who have no mutations in their hemoglobin genes. When a person inherits two alleles for the mutation (from both parents), that person enjoys some protection from malaria but will suffer from sickle cell disease.

People of West African descent are much more likely to have one or two sickle cell alleles. Malaria is endemic in West

Africa. It seems the hemoglobin mutation is an adaptation of the human host to its long-standing relationship with the malaria protozoan.

In another example, AIDS researchers have found that people with a particular gene are less likely to be infected by HIV, and are slower to develop symptoms from it. Conversely, possessing a different gene gives you weaker cell-mediated immunity and that predisposes you to infections that others might not experience. These are examples of the variability represented by the slider bar in the lower left-hand corner of figure 13.2. Scientists have also found that bacteria in the human body respond to human stress hormones, such as norepinephrine. For example, when nerve cells in the gut produce this hormone, *E. coli* were found to increase their numbers up to ten-thousandfold. Other studies have found that some stress hormones can induce bacteria to adhere to hard surfaces, raising the possibility of biofilm formation, and that bacteria increase the expression of pathogenic genes in these hormones. These phenomena (depicted with the lower right slider bar in figure 13.2), suggest an intriguing new area of research into the prevention of microbial disease. Even though human factors are important, the Centers for Disease Control and Prevention has adopted a system of biosafety categories for pathogens based on their general degree of pathogenicity and the relative danger in handling them. This system is explained in more detail in **Insight 13.2.**

Becoming Established: Step One—Portals of Entry

To initiate an infection, a microbe enters the tissues of the body by a characteristic route, the **portal of entry,** usually a cutaneous or membranous boundary. The source of the infectious agent can be **exogenous,** originating from a source outside the body (the environment or another person or animal), or endogenous, already existing on or in the body (normal biota or a previously silent infection).

For the most part, the portals of entry are the same anatomical regions that also support normal biota: the skin, gastrointestinal tract, respiratory tract, and urogenital tract. The majority of pathogens have adapted to a specific portal of entry, one that provides a habitat for further growth and spread. This adaptation can be so restrictive that if certain pathogens enter the "wrong" portal, they will not be infectious. For instance, inoculation of the nasal mucosa with the influenza virus invariably gives rise to the flu, but if this virus contacts only the skin, no infection will result. Likewise, contact with athlete's foot fungi in small cracks in the toe webs can induce an infection, but inhaling the fungus spores will not infect a healthy individual. Occasionally, an infective agent can enter by more than one portal. For instance, *Mycobacterium tuberculosis* enters through both the respiratory and gastrointestinal tracts, and pathogens in the genera *Streptococcus* and *Staphylococcus* have adapted to invasion through several portals of entry such as the skin, urogenital tract, and respiratory tract.

Infectious Agents That Enter the Skin

The skin is a very common portal of entry. The actual sites of entry are usually nicks, abrasions, and punctures (many of which are tiny and inapparent) rather than unbroken skin. Intact skin is a very tough barrier that few microbes can penetrate. *Staphylococcus aureus* (the cause of boils), *Streptococcus pyogenes* (an agent of impetigo), the fungal dermatophytes, and agents of gangrene and tetanus gain access through damaged skin. The viral agent of cold sores (herpes simplex, type 1) enters through the mucous membranes near the lips.

Some infectious agents create their own passageways into the skin using digestive enzymes. For example, certain helminth worms burrow through the skin directly to gain access to the tissues. Other infectious agents enter through bites. The bites of insects, ticks, and other animals offer an avenue to a variety of viruses, rickettsias, and protozoa. An artificial means for breaching the skin barrier is contaminated hypodermic needles by intravenous drug abusers. Users who inject drugs are predisposed to a disturbing list of well-known diseases: hepatitis, AIDS, tetanus, tuberculosis, osteomyelitis, and malaria. Contaminated needles often contain bacteria from the skin or environment that induce heart disease (endocarditis), lung abscesses, and chronic infections at the injection site.

Although the conjunctiva, the outer protective covering of the eye, is ordinarily a relatively good barrier to infection, bacteria such as *Haemophilus aegyptius* (pinkeye), *Chlamydia trachomatis* (trachoma), and *Neisseria gonorrhoeae* have a special affinity for this membrane.

The Gastrointestinal Tract as Portal

The gastrointestinal tract is the portal of entry for pathogens contained in food, drink, and other ingested substances. They are adapted to survive digestive enzymes and abrupt pH changes. The best-known enteric agents of disease are gram-negative rods in the genera *Salmonella, Shigella, Vibrio,* and certain strains of *Escherichia coli.* Viruses that enter through the gut are poliovirus, hepatitis A virus, echovirus, and rotavirus. Important enteric protozoans are *Entamoeba histolytica* (amoebiasis) and *Giardia lamblia* (giardiasis). Recent research has also shown that the intestines contain a wide variety of plant bacteria (which enter on food). It is not known whether these organisms cause disease, but scientists speculate they may be responsible for complaints that doctors can't diagnose. The anus is a portal of entry in people who practice anal sex. See chapter 22 for details of these diseases.

The Respiratory Portal of Entry

The oral and nasal cavities are also the gateways to the respiratory tract, the portal of entry for the greatest number of pathogens. Because there is a continuous mucous membrane surface covering the upper respiratory tract, the sinuses, and the auditory tubes, microbes are often transferred from one site to another. The extent to which an agent is carried into the respiratory tree is based primarily

INSIGHT 13.2   Laboratory Biosafety Levels and Classes of Pathogens

Personnel handling infectious agents in the laboratory must be protected from possible infection through special risk management or containment procedures. These involve:

1. carefully observing standard laboratory aseptic and sterile procedures while handling cultures and infectious samples;
2. using large-scale sterilization and disinfection procedures;
3. refraining from eating, drinking, and smoking; and
4. wearing personal protective items such as gloves, masks, safety glasses, laboratory coats, boots, and headgear.

Some circumstances also require additional protective equipment such as biological safety cabinets for inoculations and specially engineered facilities to control materials entering and leaving the laboratory in the air and on personnel. **Table 13.B** summarizes the primary biosafety levels and agents of disease as characterized by the Centers for Disease Control and Prevention.

TABLE 13.B Primary Biosafety Levels and Agents of Disease

Biosafety Level	Facilities and Practices	Risk of Infection and Class of Pathogens
1	Standard, open bench, no special facilities needed; typical of most microbiology teaching labs; access may be restricted.	Low infection hazard; microbes not generally considered pathogens and will not colonize the bodies of healthy persons; *Micrococcus luteus, Bacillus megaterium, Lactobacillus, Saccharomyces.*
2	At least level 1 facilities and practices; plus personnel must be trained in handling pathogens; lab coats and gloves required; safety cabinets may be needed; biohazard signs posted; access restricted.	Agents with moderate potential to infect; class 2 pathogens can cause disease in healthy people but can be contained with proper facilities; most pathogens belong to class 2; includes *Staphylococcus aureus, Escherichia coli, Salmonella* spp., *Corynebacterium diphtheriae;* pathogenic helminths; hepatitis A, B, and rabies viruses; *Cryptococcus* and *Blastomyces.*
3	Minimum of level 2 facilities and practices; plus all manipulation performed in safety cabinets; lab designed with special containment features; only personnel with special clothing can enter; no unsterilized materials can leave the lab; personnel warned, monitored, and vaccinated against infection dangers.	Agents can cause severe or lethal disease especially when inhaled; class 3 microbes include *Mycobacterium tuberculosis, Francisella tularensis, Yersinia pestis, Brucella* spp., *Coxiella burnetii, Coccidioides immitis,* and yellow fever, WEE, and HIV.
4	Minimum of level 3 facilities and practices; plus facilities must be isolated with very controlled access; clothing changes and showers required for all people entering and leaving; materials must be autoclaved or fumigated prior to entering and leaving lab.	Agents are highly virulent microbes that pose extreme risk for morbidity and mortality when inhaled in droplet or aerosol form; most are exotic flaviviruses; arenaviruses, including Lassa fever virus; or filoviruses, including Ebola and Marburg viruses.

on its size. In general, small cells and particles are inhaled more deeply than larger ones. Infectious agents with this portal of entry include the bacteria of streptococcal sore throat, meningitis, diphtheria, and whooping cough and the viruses of influenza, measles, mumps, rubella, chickenpox, and the common cold. Pathogens that are inhaled into the lower regions of the respiratory tract (bronchioles and lungs) can cause **pneumonia,** an inflammatory condition of the lung. Bacteria (*Streptococcus pneumoniae, Klebsiella, Mycoplasma*) and fungi (*Cryptococcus* and *Pneumocystis*) are a few of the agents involved in pneumonias. Other agents causing unique recognizable lung diseases are

Mycobacterium tuberculosis and fungal pathogens such as *Histoplasma.* Chapter 21 describes infections of the respiratory system.

Urogenital Portals of Entry

The urogenital tract is the portal of entry for many pathogens that are contracted by sexual means (intercourse or intimate direct contact). **Sexually transmitted diseases (STDs)** account for an estimated 4% of infections worldwide, with approximately 13 million new cases occurring in the United States each year. The most recent available statistics for the estimated incidence of common STDs are provided in **table 13.5.**

The microbes of STDs enter the skin or mucosa of the penis, external genitalia, vagina, cervix, and urethra. Some can penetrate an unbroken surface; others require a cut or abrasion. The once predominant sexual diseases syphilis

and gonorrhea have been supplanted by a large and growing list of STDs led by genital warts, chlamydia, and herpes. Evolving sexual practices have increased the incidence of STDs that were once uncommon, and diseases that were not originally considered STDs are now so classified.[2] Other common sexually transmitted agents are HIV (AIDS virus), *Trichomonas* (a protozoan), *Candida albicans* (a yeast), and hepatitis B virus. STDs are described in detail in chapter 23, with the exception of HIV (see chapter 20) and hepatitis B (see chapter 22).

Not all urogenital infections are STDs. Some of these infections are caused by displaced organisms (as when normal biota from the gastrointestinal tract cause urinary tract infections) or by opportunistic overgrowth of normal biota ("yeast infections").

Pathogens That Infect During Pregnancy and Birth

The placenta is an exchange organ—formed by maternal and fetal tissues—that separates the blood of the developing fetus from that of the mother yet permits diffusion of dissolved nutrients and gases to the fetus. The placenta is ordinarily an effective barrier against microorganisms in the maternal circulation. However, a few microbes such as the syphilis spirochete can cross the placenta, enter the umbilical vein, and spread by the fetal circulation into the fetal tissues **(figure 13.3).**

Other infections, such as herpes simplex, can occur perinatally when the child is contaminated by the birth canal.

Table 13.5 Incidence of Common Sexually Transmitted Diseases	
STD	**Estimated Number of New Cases per Year in United States**
Human papillomavirus	6,000,000
Trichomoniasis	5,000,000
Chlamydiosis	3,000,000
Herpes simplex	1,600,000
Gonorrhea	356,000
Hepatitis B	77,000
AIDS	41,000
Syphilis	41,000

2. Amoebic dysentery, scabies, salmonellosis, and *Strongyloides* worms are examples.

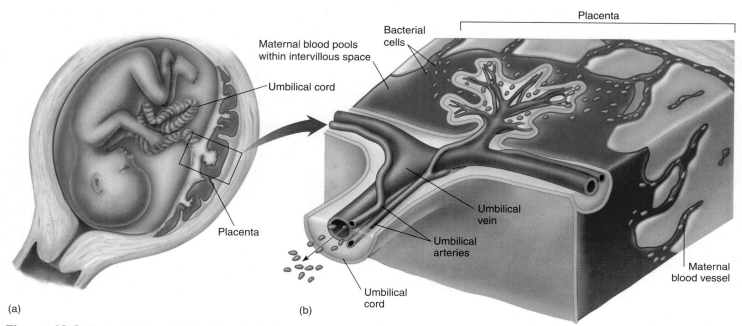

Figure 13.3 Transplacental infection of the fetus. **(a)** Fetus in the womb. **(b)** In a closer view, microbes are shown penetrating the maternal blood vessels and entering the blood pool of the placenta. They then invade the fetal circulation by way of the umbilical vein.

The common infections of fetus and neonate are grouped together in a unified cluster, known by the acronym TORCH, that medical personnel must monitor. TORCH stands for **t**oxoplasmosis, **o**ther diseases (hepatitis B, AIDS, and chlamydia), **r**ubella, **c**ytomegalovirus, and **h**erpes simplex virus. The most serious complications of TORCH infections are spontaneous abortion, congenital abnormalities, brain damage, prematurity, and stillbirths.

The Size of the Inoculum

Another factor crucial to the course of an infection is the quantity of microbes in the inoculating dose. For most agents, infection will proceed only if a minimum number, called the *infectious dose* (ID), is present. This number has been determined experimentally for many microbes. In general, microorganisms with smaller infectious doses have greater virulence. On the low end of the scale, the ID for rickettsia, the causative agent of Q fever, is only a single cell, and it is only about 10 infectious cells in tuberculosis, giardiasis, and coccidioidomycosis. The ID is 1,000 bacteria for gonorrhea and 10,000 bacteria for typhoid fever, in contrast to 1,000,000,000 bacteria in cholera. Numbers below an infec-tious dose will generally not result in an infection. But if the quantity is far in excess of the ID, the onset of disease can be extremely rapid.

Becoming Established: Step Two—Attaching to the Host

How Pathogens Attach

Adhesion is a process by which microbes gain a more stable foothold on host tissues. Because adhesion is dependent on binding between specific molecules on both the host and pathogen, a particular pathogen is limited to only those cells (and organisms) to which it can bind. Once attached, the pathogen is poised advantageously to invade the body compartments. Bacterial, fungal, and protozoal pathogens attach most often by mechanisms such as fimbriae (pili), surface proteins, and adhesive slimes or capsules; viruses attach by means of specialized receptors **(figure 13.4)**. In addition, parasitic worms are mechanically fastened to the portal of entry by suckers, hooks, and barbs. Adhesion methods of various microbes and the diseases they lead to are shown in **table 13.6**. Firm attachment to host tissues is

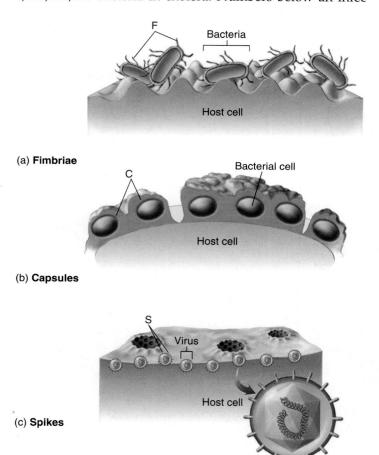

Figure 13.4 Mechanisms of adhesion by pathogens.
(a) Fimbriae (F), minute bristlelike appendages. **(b)** Adherent extracellular capsules (C) made of slime or other sticky substances. **(c)** Viral envelope spikes (S). See table 13.6 for specific examples.

Table 13.6 Adhesive Properties of Microbes

Microbe	Disease	Adhesion Mechanism
Neisseria gonorrhoeae	Gonorrhea	Fimbriae attach to genital epithelium.
Escherichia coli	Diarrhea	Fimbrial adhesin
Shigella	Dysentery	Fimbriae attach to intestinal epithelium.
Mycoplasma	Pneumonia	Specialized tip at ends of bacteria fuse tightly to lung epithelium.
Pseudomonas aeruginosa	Burn, lung infections	Fimbriae and slime layer
Streptococcus pyogenes	Pharyngitis, impetigo	Lipoteichoic acid and capsule anchor cocci to epithelium.
Streptococcus mutans, S. sobrinus	Dental caries	Dextran slime layer glues cocci to tooth surface after initial attachment.
Influenza virus	Influenza	Viral spikes attach to receptor on cell surface.
Poliovirus	Polio	Capsid proteins attach to receptors on susceptible cells.
HIV	AIDS	Viral spikes adhere to white blood cell receptors.
Giardia lamblia (protozoan)	Giardiasis	Small suction disc on underside attaches to intestinal surface.

almost always a prerequisite for causing disease since the body has so many mechanisms for flushing microbes and foreign materials from its tissues.

Becoming Established: Step Three—Surviving Host Defenses

Microbes that are not established in a normal biota relationship in a particular body site in a host are likely to encounter resistance from host defenses when first entering, especially from certain white blood cells called **phagocytes.** These cells ordinarily engulf and destroy pathogens by means of enzymes and antimicrobial chemicals (see chapter 14).

Antiphagocytic factors are a type of virulence factor used by some pathogens to avoid phagocytes. The antiphagocytic factors of resistant microorganisms help them to circumvent some part of the phagocytic process (see figure 13.5c). The most aggressive strategy involves bacteria that kill phagocytes outright. Species of both *Streptococcus* and *Staphylococcus* produce **leukocidins,** substances that are toxic to white blood cells. Some microorganisms secrete an extracellular surface layer (slime or capsule) that makes it physically difficult for the phagocyte to engulf them. *Streptococcus pneumoniae, Salmonella typhi, Neisseria meningitidis,* and *Cryptococcus neoformans* are notable examples. Some bacteria are well adapted to survival inside phagocytes after ingestion. For instance, pathogenic species of *Legionella, Mycobacterium,* and many rickettsias are readily engulfed but are capable of avoiding further destruction. The ability to survive intracellularly in phagocytes has special significance because it provides a place for the microbes to hide, grow, and be spread throughout the body.

Causing Disease

How Virulence Factors Contribute to Tissue Damage

Virulence factors from a microbe's perspective are simply adaptations it uses to invade and establish itself in the host. (You will remember from chapter 9 that many virulence factors can be found on pathogenicity islands, genetic regions that have been passed horizontally from other microbes.) These same factors determine the degree of tissue damage that occurs. The effects of a pathogen's virulence factors on tissues vary greatly. Cold viruses, for example, invade and multiply but cause relatively little damage to their host. At the other end of the spectrum, pathogens such as *Clostridium tetani* or HIV severely damage or kill their host. Microorganisms either inflict direct damage on hosts through the use of exoenzymes or toxins **(figure 13.5a,b),** or they cause damage indirectly when their presence causes an excessive or inappropriate host response **(figure 13.5c).** For convenience, we divide the "directly damaging" virulence factors into exoenzymes and toxins. Although this distinction is useful, there is often a very fine line between enzymes and toxins because many substances called toxins actually function as enzymes.

Microbial virulence factors are often responsible for inducing the host to cause damage, as well. The capsule

(a) **Exoenzymes**

(b) **Toxins**

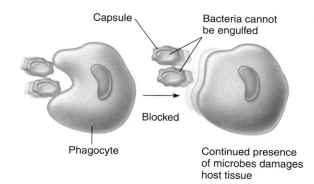

(c) **Blocked phagocytic response**

Figure 13.5 Three ways microbes damage the host.
(a) Exoenzymes. Bacteria produce extracellular enzymes that dissolve intracellular connections and penetrate through or between cells to underlying tissues. **(b)** Toxins (primarily exotoxins) secreted by bacteria diffuse to target cells, which are poisoned and disrupted. **(c)** Bacterium has a property that enables it to escape phagocytosis and remain as an "irritant" to host defenses, which are deployed excessively.

of *Streptococcus pneumoniae* is a good example. Its presence prevents the bacterium from being cleared from the lungs by phagocytic cells, leading to a continuous influx of fluids into the lung spaces, and the condition we know as pneumonia.

Extracellular Enzymes Many pathogenic bacteria, fungi, protozoa, and worms secrete **exoenzymes** that break down and inflict damage on tissues. Other enzymes dissolve the host's defense barriers and promote the spread of microbes to deeper tissues.

Examples of enzymes are:

1. mucinase, which digests the protective coating on mucous membranes and is a factor in amoebic dysentery;

2. keratinase, which digests the principal component of skin and hair, and is secreted by fungi that cause ringworm;

3. collagenase, which digests the principal fiber of connective tissue and is an invasive factor of *Clostridium* species and certain worms; and

4. hyaluronidase, which digests hyaluronic acid, the ground substance that cements animal cells together. This enzyme is an important virulence factor in staphylococci, clostridia, streptococci, and pneumococci.

Some enzymes react with components of the blood. Coagulase, an enzyme produced by pathogenic staphylococci, causes clotting of blood or plasma. By contrast, the bacterial kinases (streptokinase, staphylokinase) do just the opposite, dissolving fibrin clots and expediting the invasion of damaged tissues. In fact, one form of streptokinase (Streptase) is marketed as a therapy to dissolve blood clots in patients with problems with thrombi and emboli.[3]

Bacterial Toxins: A Potent Source of Cellular Damage

A **toxin** is a specific chemical product of microbes, plants, and some animals that is poisonous to other organisms. **Toxigenicity,** the power to produce toxins, is a genetically controlled characteristic of many species and is responsible for the adverse effects of a variety of diseases generally called **toxinoses.** Toxinoses in which the toxin is spread by the blood from the site of infection are called **toxemias** (teta-

nus and diphtheria, for example), whereas those caused by ingestion of toxins are **intoxications** (botulism). A toxin is named according to its specific target of action: Neurotoxins act on the nervous system; enterotoxins act on the intestine; hemotoxins lyse red blood cells; and nephrotoxins damage the kidneys.

Another useful scheme classifies toxins according to their origins **(figure 13.6).** A toxin molecule secreted by a living bacterial cell into the infected tissues is an **exotoxin.** A toxin that is not actively secreted but is shed from the outer membrane is an **endotoxin.** Other important differences between the two groups are summarized in **table 13.7.**

Exotoxins are proteins with a strong specificity for a target cell and extremely powerful, sometimes deadly, effects. They generally affect cells by damaging the cell membrane and initiating lysis or by disrupting intracellular function. **Hemolysins** (hee-mahl'-uh-sinz) are a class of bacterial exotoxin that disrupts the cell membrane of red blood cells (and some other cells, too). This damage causes the red blood cells to **hemolyze**—to burst and release hemoglobin pigment. Hemolysins that increase pathogenicity include the streptolysins of *Streptococcus pyogenes* and the alpha (α) and beta (β) toxins of *Staphylococcus aureus.* When colonies of bacteria growing on blood agar produce hemolysin, distinct zones appear around the colony. The pattern of hemolysis is often used to identify bacteria and determine their degree of pathogenicity.

The exotoxins of diphtheria, tetanus, and botulism, among others, attach to a particular target cell, become internalized, and interrupt an essential cell pathway. The consequences of

---

3. These conditions are intravascular blood clots that can cause circulatory obstructions.

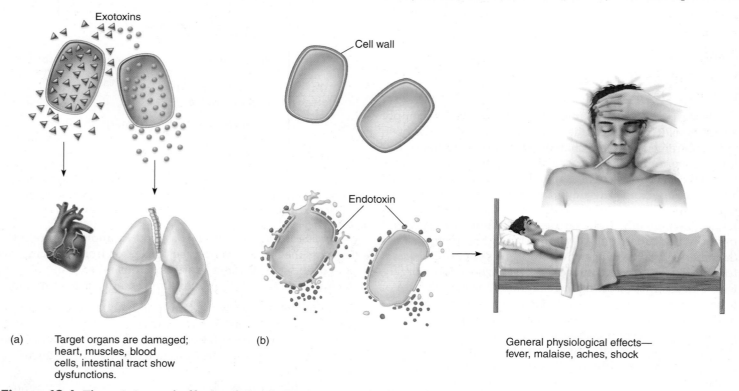

(a)   Target organs are damaged; heart, muscles, blood cells, intestinal tract show dysfunctions.

(b)

General physiological effects— fever, malaise, aches, shock

Figure 13.6 The origins and effects of circulating exotoxins and endotoxin.   (a) Exotoxins, given off by live cells, have highly specific targets and physiological effects. (b) Endotoxin, given off when the cell wall of gram-negative bacteria disintegrates, has more generalized physiological effects.

Table 13.7 Differential Characteristics of Bacterial Exotoxins and Endotoxin

Characteristic	Exotoxins	Endotoxin
Toxicity	Toxic in minute amounts	Toxic in high doses
Effects on the body	Specific to a cell type (blood, liver, nerve)	Systemic: fever, inflammation
Chemical composition	Small proteins	Lipopolysaccharide of cell wall
Heat denaturation at 60°C	Unstable	Stable
Toxoid formation	Can be converted to toxoid*	Cannot be converted to toxoid
Immune response	Stimulate antitoxins**	Does not stimulate antitoxins
Fever stimulation	Usually not	Yes
Manner of release	Secreted from live cell	Released by cell via shedding or during lysis
Typical sources	A few gram-positive and gram-negative	All gram-negative bacteria

*A toxoid is an inactivated toxin used in vaccines.

**An antitoxin is an antibody that reacts specifically with a toxin.

cell disruption depend upon the target. One toxin of *Clostridium tetani* blocks the action of certain spinal neurons; the toxin of *Clostridium botulinum* prevents the transmission of nerve-muscle stimuli; pertussis toxin inactivates the respiratory cilia; and cholera toxin provokes profuse salt and water loss from intestinal cells. More details of the pathology of exotoxins are found in later chapters on specific diseases.

In contrast to the category *exotoxin,* which contains many specific examples, the word *endotoxin* refers to a single substance. Endotoxin is actually a chemical called lipopolysaccharide (LPS), which is part of the outer membrane of gram-negative cell walls. Gram-negative bacteria shed these LPS molecules into tissues or into the circulation. Endotoxin differs from exotoxins in having a variety of systemic effects on tissues and organs. Depending upon the amounts present, endotoxin can cause fever, inflammation, hemorrhage, and diarrhea. Blood infection by gram-negative bacteria such as *Salmonella, Shigella, Neisseria meningitidis,* and *Escherichia coli* are particularly dangerous, in that it can lead to fatal endotoxic shock.

Inducing an Injurious Host Response   Despite the extensive discussion on direct virulence factors, such as enzymes and toxins, it is probably the case that more microbial diseases are the result of indirect damage, or the host's excessive or inappropriate response to a microorganism. This is an extremely important point because it means that pathogenicity is not a trait inherent in microorganisms, but is really a consequence of the interplay between microbe and host.

Of course, it is easier to study and characterize the microbes that cause direct damage through toxins or enzymes. For this reason, these true pathogens were the first to be fully understood as the science of microbiology progressed. But in the last 15 to 20 years, microbiologists have come to appreciate exactly how important the relationship between microbe and host is, and this has greatly expanded our understanding of infectious diseases.

The Process of Infection and Disease

Establishment, Spread, and Pathologic Effects

Aided by virulence factors, microbes eventually settle in a particular target organ and cause damage at the site. The type

---

A Note About Terminology

Words in medicine have great power and economy. A single technical term can often replace a whole phrase or sentence, thereby saving time and space in patient charting. The beginning student may feel overwhelmed by what seems like a mountain of new words. However, having a grasp of a few root words and a fair amount of anatomy can help you learn many of these words and even deduce the meaning of unfamiliar ones. Some examples of medical shorthand follow.

- The suffix *-itis* means an inflammation and, when affixed to the end of an anatomical term, indicates an inflammatory condition in that location. Thus, meningitis is an inflammation of the meninges surrounding the brain; encephalitis is an inflammation of the brain itself; hepatitis involves the liver; vaginitis, the vagina; gastroenteritis, the intestine; and otitis media, the middle ear. Although not all inflammatory conditions are caused by infections, many infectious diseases inflame their target organs.
- The suffix *-emia* is derived from the Greek word *haeima,* meaning blood. When added to a word, it means "associated with the blood." Thus, septicemia means sepsis (infection) of the blood; bacteremia, bacteria in the blood; viremia, viruses in the blood; and fungemia, fungi in the blood. It is also applicable to specific conditions such as toxemia, gonococcemia, and spirochetemia.
- The suffix *-osis* means "a disease or morbid process." It is frequently added to the names of pathogens to indicate the disease they cause: for example, listeriosis, histoplasmosis, toxoplasmosis, shigellosis, salmonellosis, and borreliosis. A variation of this suffix is *-iasis,* as in trichomoniasis and candidiasis.
- The suffix *-oma* comes from the Greek word *onkomas* (swelling) and means tumor. Although it is often used to describe cancers (sarcoma, melanoma), it is also applied in some infectious diseases that cause masses or swellings (tuberculoma, leproma).

INSIGHT 13.3 The Classic Stages of Clinical Infections

There are four distinct phases of infection and disease: the incubation period, the prodrome, the period of invasion, and the convalescent period.

The **incubation period** is the time from initial contact with the infectious agent (at the portal of entry) to the appearance of the first symptoms. During the incubation period, the agent is multiplying at the portal of entry but has not yet caused enough damage to elicit symptoms. Although this period is relatively well defined and predictable for each microorganism, it does vary according to host resistance, degree of virulence, and distance between the target organ and the portal of entry (the farther apart, the longer the incubation period). Overall, an incubation period can range from several hours in pneumonic plague to several years in leprosy. The majority of infections, however, have incubation periods ranging between 2 and 30 days.

The earliest notable symptoms of infection appear as a vague feeling of discomfort, such as head and muscle aches, fatigue, upset stomach, and general malaise. This short period (1–2 days) is known as the **prodromal stage.** The infectious agent next enters a **period of invasion,** during which it multiplies at high levels, exhibits its greatest toxicity, and becomes well established in its target tissue. This period is often marked by fever and other prominent and more specific signs and symptoms, which can include cough, rashes, diarrhea, loss of muscle control, swelling, jaundice, discharge of exudates, or severe pain, depending on the particular infection. The length of this period is extremely variable.

As the patient begins to respond to the infection, the symptoms decline—sometimes dramatically, other times slowly. During the recovery that follows, called the **convalescent period,** the patient's strength and health gradually return owing to the

healing nature of the immune response. During this period many patients stop taking their antibiotics, even though there are still pathogens in their system. And think about it—the ones still alive at this stage of treatment are the ones in the population with the most resistance to the antibiotic. In most cases, continuing the antibiotic dosing will take care of them. But stop taking the drug now and the bugs that are left to repopulate are the ones with the higher resistance.

The transmissibility of the microbe during these four stages must be considered on an individual basis. A few agents are released mostly during incubation (measles, for example); many are released during the invasive period (*Shigella*); and others can be transmitted during all of these periods (hepatitis B).

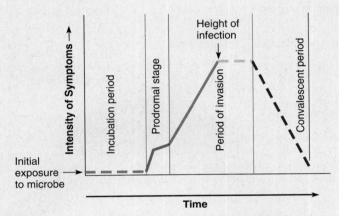

Stages in the course of infection and disease. Dashed lines represent periods with a variable length.

and scope of injuries inflicted during this process account for the typical stages of an infection **(Insight 13.3)**, the patterns of the infectious disease, and its manifestations in the body.

In addition to the adverse effects of enzymes, toxins, and other factors, multiplication by a pathogen frequently weakens host tissues. Pathogens can obstruct tubular structures such as blood vessels, lymphatic channels, fallopian tubes, and bile ducts. Accumulated damage can lead to cell and tissue death, a condition called **necrosis.** Although viruses do not produce toxins or destructive enzymes, they destroy cells by multiplying in and lysing them. Many of the cytopathic effects of viral infection arise from the impaired metabolism and death of cells (see chapter 6).

Patterns of Infection Patterns of infection are many and varied. In the simplest situation, a **localized infection,** the microbe enters the body and remains confined to a specific tissue **(figure 13.7a)**. Examples of localized infections are boils, fungal skin infections, and warts.

Many infectious agents do not remain localized but spread from the initial site of entry to other tissues. In fact, spreading is necessary for pathogens such as rabies and

hepatitis A virus, whose target tissue is some distance from the site of entry. The rabies virus travels from a bite wound along nerve tracts to its target in the brain, and the hepatitis A virus moves from the intestine to the liver via the circulatory system. When an infection spreads to several sites and tissue fluids, usually in the bloodstream, it is called a **systemic infection (figure 13.7b).** Examples of systemic infections are viral diseases (measles, rubella, chickenpox, and AIDS); bacterial diseases (brucellosis, anthrax, typhoid fever, and syphilis); and fungal diseases (histoplasmosis and cryptococcosis). Infectious agents can also travel to their targets by means of nerves (as in rabies) or cerebrospinal fluid (as in meningitis).

A **focal infection** is said to exist when the infectious agent breaks loose from a local infection and is carried into other tissues **(figure 13.7c)**. This pattern is exhibited by tuberculosis or by streptococcal pharyngitis, which gives rise to scarlet fever. In the condition called toxemia,[4] the infection itself remains localized at the portal of entry, but the toxins produced by the pathogens are carried by the blood to the actual target tissue.

4. Not to be confused with toxemia of pregnancy, which is a metabolic disturbance and not an infection.

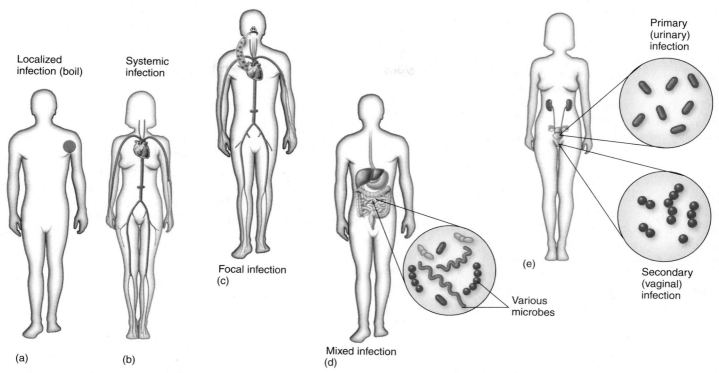

Figure 13.7 The occurrence of infections with regard to location, type of microbe, and order of infection. **(a)** A localized infection, in which the pathogen is restricted to one specific site. **(b)** Systemic infection, in which the pathogen spreads through circulation to many sites. **(c)** A focal infection occurs initially as a local infection, but circumstances cause the microbe to be carried to other sites systemically. **(d)** A mixed infection, in which the same site is infected with several microbes at the same time. **(e)** In a primary-secondary infection, an initial infection is complicated by a second one in the same or a different location and caused by a different microbe.

In this way, the target of the bacterial cells can be different from the target of their toxin.

An infection is not always caused by a single microbe. In a **mixed infection,** several agents establish themselves simultaneously at the infection site **(figure 13.7d).** In some mixed or synergistic infections, the microbes cooperate in breaking down a tissue. In other mixed infections, one microbe creates an environment that enables another microbe to invade. Gas gangrene, wound infections, dental caries, and human bite infections tend to be mixed. These are sometimes called **polymicrobial** diseases.

Some diseases are described according to a sequence of infection. When an initial, or **primary, infection** is complicated by another infection caused by a different microbe, the second infection is termed a **secondary infection (figure 13.7e).** This pattern often occurs in a child with chickenpox (primary infection) who may scratch his pox and infect them with *Staphylococcus aureus* (secondary infection). The secondary infection need not be in the same site as the primary infection, and it usually indicates altered host defenses.

Infections that come on rapidly, with severe but short-lived effects, are called **acute infections.** Infections that progress and persist over a long period of time are **chronic infections.**

Figure 13.8 is a summary of the pathway a microbe follows when it causes disease.

Figure 13.8 The steps involved when a microbe causes disease in a host.

Signs and Symptoms: Warning Signals of Disease

When an infection causes pathologic changes leading to disease, it is often accompanied by a variety of signs and symptoms. A **sign** is any objective evidence of disease as noted by an observer; a **symptom** is the subjective evidence of disease as sensed by the patient. In general, signs are more precise than symptoms, though both can have the same underlying cause. For example, an infection of the brain might present with the sign of bacteria in the spinal fluid and symptom of headache. Or a streptococcal infection might produce a sore throat (symptom) and inflamed pharynx (sign). Disease indicators that can be sensed and observed can qualify as either a sign or a symptom. When a disease can be identified or defined by a certain complex of signs and symptoms, it is termed a **syndrome.** Signs and symptoms with considerable importance in diagnosing infectious diseases are shown in **table 13.8.** Specific signs and symptoms for particular infectious diseases are covered in chapters 18 through 23.

Signs and Symptoms of Inflammation

The earliest symptoms of disease result from the activation of the body defense process called **inflammation.** The inflammatory response includes cells and chemicals that respond nonspecifically to disruptions in the tissue. This subject is discussed in greater detail in chapter 14, but as noted earlier, many signs and symptoms of infection are caused by the mobilization of this system. Some common symptoms of inflammation include fever, pain, soreness, and swelling. Signs of inflammation include **edema,** the accumulation of fluid in an afflicted tissue; **granulomas** and **abscesses,** walled-off collections of inflammatory cells and microbes in the tissues; and **lymphadenitis,** swollen lymph nodes.

Rashes and other skin eruptions are common symptoms and signs in many diseases, and because they tend to mimic each other, it can be difficult to differentiate among diseases on this basis alone. The general term for the site of infection or disease is **lesion.** Skin lesions can be restricted to the epidermis and its glands and follicles, or they can extend into the dermis and subcutaneous regions. The lesions of some infections undergo characteristic changes in appearance during the course of disease and thus fit more than one category (see Insight 18.3).

Signs of Infection in the Blood

Changes in the number of circulating white blood cells, as determined by special counts, are considered to be signs of possible infection. **Leukocytosis** (loo″-koh′-sy-toh′-sis) is an increase in the level of white blood cells, whereas **leukopenia** (loo″-koh-pee′-nee-uh) is a decrease. Other signs of infection revolve around the occurrence of a microbe or its products in the blood. The clinical term for blood infection, **septicemia,** refers to a general state in which microorganisms are multiplying in the blood and are present in large numbers. When small numbers of bacteria or viruses are found in the blood, the correct terminology is **bacteremia** or **viremia,** which means that these microbes are present in the blood but are not necessarily multiplying.

During infection, a normal host will invariably show signs of an immune response in the form of antibodies in the serum or some type of sensitivity to the microbe. This fact is the basis for several serological tests used in diagnosing infectious diseases such as AIDS or syphilis. Such specific immune reactions indicate the body's attempt to develop specific immunities against pathogens. We concentrate on this role of the host defenses in chapters 14 and 15.

Infections That Go Unnoticed

It is rather common for an infection to produce no noticeable symptoms, even though the microbe is active in the host tissue. In other words, although infected, the host does not manifest the disease. Infections of this nature are known as **asymptomatic, subclinical,** or *inapparent* because the patient experiences no symptoms or disease and does not seek medical attention. However, it is important to note that most infections are attended by some sort of sign. In the section on epidemiology, we further address the significance of subclinical infections in the transmission of infectious agents.

The Portal of Exit: Vacating the Host

Earlier, we introduced the idea that a parasite is considered *unsuccessful* if it does not have a provision for leaving its host and moving to other susceptible hosts. With few exceptions, pathogens depart by a specific avenue called the **portal of exit** (figure 13.8 and **figure 13.9).** In most cases, the pathogen is shed or released from the body through secretion, excretion, discharge, or sloughed tissue. The usually very high number of infectious agents in these materials increases the likelihood that the pathogen will reach other hosts. In many cases, the portal of exit is the same as the portal of entry, but some pathogens use a different route. As we see in the next section, the portal of exit concerns epidemiologists because it greatly influences the dissemination of infection in a population.

Table 13.8 Common Signs and Symptoms of Infectious Diseases	
Signs	**Symptoms**
Fever	Chills
Septicemia	Pain, ache, soreness, irritation
Microbes in tissue fluids	Malaise
Chest sounds	Fatigue
Skin eruptions	Chest tightness
Leukocytosis	Itching
Leukopenia	Headache
Swollen lymph nodes	Nausea
Abscesses	Abdominal cramps
Tachycardia (increased heart rate)	Anorexia (lack of appetite)
Antibodies in serum	Sore throat

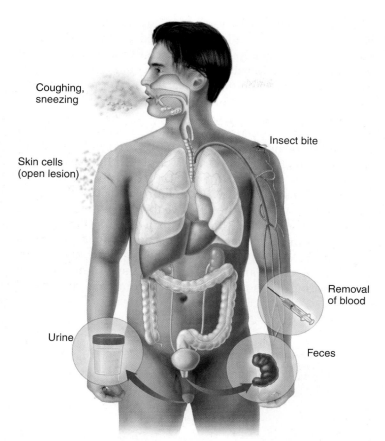

Coughing, sneezing

Skin cells (open lesion)

Insect bite

Removal of blood

Urine

Feces

Figure 13.9 Major portals of exit of infectious diseases.

Respiratory and Salivary Portals

Mucus, sputum, nasal drainage, and other moist secretions are the media of escape for the pathogens that infect the lower or upper respiratory tract. The most effective means of releasing these secretions are coughing and sneezing (see figure 13.13), although they can also be released during talking and laughing. Tiny particles of liquid released into the air form aerosols or droplets that can spread the infectious agent to other people. The agents of tuberculosis, influenza, measles, and chickenpox most often leave the host through airborne droplets. Droplets of saliva are the exit route for several viruses, including those of mumps, rabies, and infectious mononucleosis.

Skin Scales

The outer layer of the skin and scalp is constantly being shed into the environment. A large proportion of household dust is actually composed of skin cells. A single person can shed several billion skin cells a day. Skin lesions and their exudates can serve as portals of exit in warts, fungal infections, boils, herpes simplex, smallpox, and syphilis.

Fecal Exit

Feces are a very common portal of exit. Some intestinal pathogens grow in the intestinal mucosa and create an inflammation that increases the motility of the bowel. This increased

motility speeds up peristalsis, resulting in diarrhea, and the more fluid stool provides a rapid exit for the pathogen. A number of helminth worms release cysts and eggs through the feces (see chapter 22). Feces containing pathogens are a public health problem when allowed to contaminate drinking water or when used to fertilize crops.

Urogenital Tract

A number of agents involved in sexually transmitted infections leave the host in vaginal discharge or semen. This is also the source of neonatal infections such as herpes simplex, *Chlamydia,* and *Candida albicans,* which infect the infant as it passes through the birth canal. Less commonly, certain pathogens that infect the kidney are discharged in the urine: for instance, the agents of leptospirosis, typhoid fever, tuberculosis, and schistosomiasis.

Removal of Blood or Bleeding

Although the blood does not have a direct route to the outside, it can serve as a portal of exit when it is removed or released through a vascular puncture made by natural or artificial means. Blood-feeding animals such as ticks and fleas are common transmitters of pathogens (see Insight 20.2). The AIDS and hepatitis viruses are transmitted by shared needles or through small gashes in a mucous membrane caused by sexual intercourse. Blood donation is also a means for certain microbes to leave the host, though this means of exit is now unusual because of close monitoring of the donor population and blood used for transfusions.

The Persistence of Microbes and Pathologic Conditions

The apparent recovery of the host does not always mean that the microbe has been completely removed or destroyed by the host defenses. After the initial symptoms in certain chronic infectious diseases, the infectious agent retreats into a dormant state called **latency.** Throughout this latent state, the microbe can periodically become active and produce a recurrent disease. The viral agents of herpes simplex, herpes zoster, hepatitis B, AIDS, and Epstein-Barr can persist in the host for long periods. The agents of syphilis, typhoid fever, tuberculosis, and malaria also enter into latent stages. The person harboring a persistent infectious agent may or may not shed it during the latent stage. If it is shed, such persons are chronic carriers who serve as sources of infection for the rest of the population.

Some diseases leave **sequelae** in the form of long-term or permanent damage to tissues or organs. For example, meningitis can result in deafness, strep throat can lead to rheumatic heart disease, Lyme disease can cause arthritis, and polio can produce paralysis.

Reservoirs: Where Pathogens Persist

In order for an infectious agent to continue to exist and be spread, it must have a permanent place to reside. The

reservoir is the primary habitat in the natural world from which a pathogen originates. Often it is a human or animal carrier, although soil, water, and plants are also reservoirs. The reservoir can be distinguished from the infection **source,** which is the individual or object from which an infection is actually acquired. In diseases such as syphilis, the reservoir and the source are the same (the human body). In the case of hepatitis A, the reservoir (a human carrier) is usually different from the source of infection (contaminated food).

Living Reservoirs

Persons or animals with frank symptomatic infection are obvious sources of infection, but a **carrier** is, by definition, an individual who *inconspicuously* shelters a pathogen and spreads it to others without any notice. Although human carriers are occasionally detected through routine screening (blood tests, cultures) and other epidemiological devices, they are unfortunately very difficult to discover and control.

As long as a pathogenic reservoir is maintained by the carrier state, the disease will continue to exist in that population, and the potential for epidemics will be a constant threat. The duration of the carrier state can be short or long term, and it is important to remember that the carrier may or may not have experienced disease due to the microbe.

Several situations can produce the carrier state. **Asymptomatic** (apparently healthy) **carriers** are infected but they show no symptoms **(figure 13.10a).** A few asymptomatic infections (gonorrhea and genital warts, for instance) can carry out their entire course without overt manifestations. **Figure 13.10b** demonstrates three types of carriers who have had or will have the disease but do not at the time they transmit the organism. **Incubating carriers** spread the infectious agent during the incubation period. For example, AIDS patients can harbor and spread the virus for months and years before their first symptoms appear. Recuperating patients without symptoms are considered

Figure 13.10   **(a)** An asymptomatic carrier is infected without symptoms. **(b)** Incubation, convalescent, and chronic carriers can transmit the infection either before or after the period of symptoms. **(c)** A passive carrier is contaminated but not infected.

convalescent carriers when they continue to shed viable microbes and convey the infection to others. Diphtheria patients, for example, spread the microbe for up to 30 days after the disease has subsided.

An individual who shelters the infectious agent for a long period after recovery because of the latency of the infectious agent is a **chronic carrier.** Patients who have recovered from tuberculosis or hepatitis infections frequently carry the agent chronically. About one in 20 victims of typhoid fever continues to harbor *Salmonella typhi* in the gallbladder for several years, and sometimes for life. The most infamous of these was "Typhoid Mary," a cook who spread the infection to hundreds of victims in the early 1900s. (*Salmonella* infection is described in chapter 22.)

The **passive carrier** state is of great concern during patient care (see a later section on nosocomial infections). Medical and dental personnel who must constantly handle materials that are heavily contaminated with patient secretions and blood risk picking up pathogens mechanically and accidently transferring them to other patients **(figure 13.10c).** Proper handwashing, handling of contaminated materials, and aseptic techniques greatly reduce this likelihood.

Animals as Reservoirs and Sources   Up to now, we have lumped animals with humans in discussing living reservoirs or carriers, but animals deserve special consideration as vectors of infections. The word **vector** is used by epidemiologists to indicate a live animal that transmits an infectious agent from one host to another. (The term is sometimes misused to include any object that spreads disease.) The majority of vectors are arthropods such as fleas, mosquitoes, flies, and ticks, although larger animals can also spread infection—for example, mammals (rabies), birds (psittacosis), or lizards (salmonellosis).

By tradition, vectors are placed into one of two categories, depending on the animal's relationship with the microbe **(figure 13.11).** A **biological vector** actively participates in a pathogen's life cycle, serving as a site in which it can multiply or complete its life cycle. A biological vector communicates the infectious agent to the human host by biting, aerosol formation, or touch. In the case of biting vectors, the animal can

1. inject infected saliva into the blood (the mosquito) **(figure 13.11a),**
2. defecate around the bite wound (the flea), or
3. regurgitate blood into the wound (the tsetse fly).

A detailed discussion of arthropod vectors is found in Insight 20.2.

Mechanical vectors are not necessary to the life cycle of an infectious agent and merely transport it without being infected. The external body parts of these animals become contaminated when they come into physical contact with a source of pathogens. The agent is subsequently transferred to humans indirectly by an intermediate such as food or, occasionally, by direct contact (as in certain eye infections). Houseflies **(figure 13.11b)** are noxious mechanical vectors. They feed on decaying garbage and feces, and while they are feeding, their feet and mouthparts easily become contaminated. They also regurgitate juices onto food to soften and digest it. Flies spread more than 20 bacterial, viral, protozoan, and worm infections. Various flies transmit tropical ulcers, yaws, and trachoma. Cockroaches, which have similar unsavory habits, play a role in the mechanical transmission of fecal pathogens as well as contributing to allergy attacks in asthmatic children.

Many vectors and animal reservoirs spread their own infections to humans. An infection indigenous to animals but naturally transmissible to humans is a **zoonosis** (zoh"-uh-noh'-sis). In these types of infections, the human is essentially a dead-end host and does not contribute to the natural persistence of the microbe. Some zoonotic infections (rabies, for instance) can have multihost involvement, and others can have very complex cycles in the wild (see plague in chapter 20). Zoonotic spread of disease is promoted by close associations of humans with animals, and people in animal-oriented or outdoor professions are at greatest risk. At least 150 zoonoses exist worldwide; the most common ones are

(a) Biological vectors are infected. Example: The *Anopheles* mosquito carries the malaria protozoan in its gut and salivary glands and transmits it to humans when it bites.

(b) Mechanical vectors are not infected. Example: Flies can transmit cholera by landing on feces then landing on food or a drinking glass.

Figure 13.11 Two types of vectors.   **(a)** Biological vectors serve as hosts during pathogen development. One example is the mosquito, a carrier of malaria. **(b)** Mechanical vectors such as the housefly transport pathogens on their feet and mouthparts.

listed in **table 13.9.** Zoonoses make up a full 70% of all new emerging diseases worldwide. It is worth noting that zoonotic infections are impossible to completely eradicate without also eradicating the animal reservoirs. Attempts have been made to eradicate mosquitoes and certain rodents, and in 2004 China slaughtered tens of thousands of civet cats who were thought to be a source of the respiratory disease SARS.

A 2005 United Nations study warned that one of the most troublesome trends is the increase in infectious diseases due to environmental destruction. Deforestation and urban sprawl cause animals to find new habitats, often leading to new patterns of disease transmission. For example, the fatal Nipahvirus seems to have begun to infect humans although it previously only infected Asian fruit bats. The bats were pushed out of their forest habitats by the creation of palm plantations. They encountered domesticated pigs, passing the virus to them, and the pigs in turn transmitted it to their human handlers.

Nonliving Reservoirs

Clearly, microorganisms have adapted to nearly every habitat in the biosphere. They thrive in soil and water and often find their way into the air. Although most of these microbes are saprobic and cause little harm and considerable benefit to humans, some are opportunists and a few are regular pathogens. Because human hosts are in regular contact with these environmental sources, acquisition of pathogens from natural habitats is of diagnostic and epidemiological importance.

Table 13.9 Common Zoonotic Infections

Disease	Primary Animal Reservoirs
Viruses	
Rabies	All mammals
Yellow fever	Wild birds, mammals, mosquitoes
Viral fevers	Wild mammals
Hantavirus	Rodents
Influenza	Chickens, birds, swine
West Nile virus	Wild birds, mosquitoes
Bacteria	
Rocky Mountain spotted fever	Dogs, ticks
Psittacosis	Birds
Leptospirosis	Domestic animals
Anthrax	Domestic animals
Brucellosis	Cattle, sheep, pigs
Plague	Rodents, fleas
Salmonellosis	Variety of mammals, birds, and rodents
Tularemia	Rodents, birds, arthropods
Miscellaneous	
Ringworm	Domestic mammals
Toxoplasmosis	Cats, rodents, birds
Trypanosomiasis	Domestic and wild mammals
Trichinosis	Swine, bears
Tapeworm	Cattle, swine, fish

Soil harbors the vegetative forms of bacteria, protozoa, helminths, and fungi, as well as their resistant or developmental stages such as spores, cysts, ova, and larvae. Bacterial pathogens include the anthrax bacillus and species of *Clostridium* that are responsible for gas gangrene, botulism, and tetanus. Pathogenic fungi in the genera *Coccidioides* and *Blastomyces* are spread by spores in the soil and dust. The invasive stages of the hookworm *Necator* occur in the soil. Natural bodies of water carry fewer nutrients than soil does but still support pathogenic species such as *Legionella, Cryptosporidium,* and *Giardia.*

The Acquisition and Transmission of Infectious Agents

Infectious diseases can be categorized on the basis of how they are acquired. A disease is **communicable** when an infected host can transmit the infectious agent to another host and establish infection in that host. (Although this terminology is standard, one must realize that it is not the disease that is communicated but the microbe. Also be aware that the word *infectious* is sometimes used interchangeably with the word *communicable*, but this is not precise usage.) The transmission of the agent can be direct or indirect, and the ease with which the disease is transmitted varies considerably from one agent to another. If the agent is highly communicable, especially through direct contact, the disease is **contagious.** Influenza and measles move readily from host to host and thus are contagious, whereas Hansen's disease (leprosy) is only weakly communicable. Because they can be spread through the population, communicable diseases are our main focus in the following sections.

In contrast, a **noncommunicable** infectious disease does *not* arise through transmission of the infectious agent from host to host. The infection and disease are acquired through some other special circumstance. Noncommunicable infections occur primarily when a compromised person is invaded by his or her own microbiota (as with certain pneumonias, for example) or when an individual has accidental contact with a microbe that exists in a nonliving reservoir such as soil. Some examples are certain mycoses, acquired through inhalation of fungal spores, and tetanus, in which *Clostridium tetani* spores from a soiled object enter a cut or wound. Persons thus infected do not become a source of disease to others.

Patterns of Transmission in Communicable Diseases

The routes or patterns of disease transmission are many and varied. The spread of diseases is by direct or indirect contact with animate or inanimate objects and can be horizontal or vertical. The term *horizontal* means the disease is spread through a population from one infected individual to another; *vertical* signifies transmission from parent to offspring via the ovum, sperm, placenta, or milk. The extreme complexity of transmission patterns among microorganisms makes it very difficult to generalize. However, for easier organization, we will divide microorganisms into two major groups, as shown in **figure 13.12**: transmission by some form of direct contact or transmission by indirect routes, in which some vehicle is involved.

Modes of Contact Transmission

In order for microbes to be directly transferred, some type of contact must occur between the skin or mucous membranes of the infected person and that of the new infectee. It may help to think of this route as the portal of exit meeting the portal of entry without the involvement of an intermediate object, substance, or space. Most sexually transmitted diseases are spread directly. In addition, infections that result from kissing or bites by biological vectors are direct. Most obligate parasites are far too sensitive to survive for long outside the host and can be transmitted only through direct contact. Diseases transmitted vertically from mother to baby fit in this contact category also. The trickiest type of "contact" transmission is droplet contact, in which fine droplets are sprayed directly upon a person during sneezing or coughing (as distinguished from droplet nuclei that are transmitted some distance by air). While there is some space between the infecter and the infectee, it is still considered a form of contact because the two people have to be in each other's presence, as opposed to indirect forms of contact.

Routes of Indirect Transmission

For microbes to be indirectly transmitted, the infectious agent must pass from an infected host to an intermediate conveyor and from there to another host. This form of communication is especially pronounced when the infected individuals contaminate inanimate objects, food, or air through their activities. The transmitter of the infectious agent can be either openly infected or a carrier.

Indirect Spread by Vehicles: Contaminated Materials

The term **vehicle** specifies any inanimate material commonly used by humans that can transmit infectious agents. A *common vehicle* is a single material that serves as the source of infection for many individuals. Some specific types of vehicles are food, water, various biological products (such as blood, serum, and tissue), and fomites. A **fomite** is an inanimate object that harbors and transmits pathogens. The list of possible fomites is as long as your imagination allows.

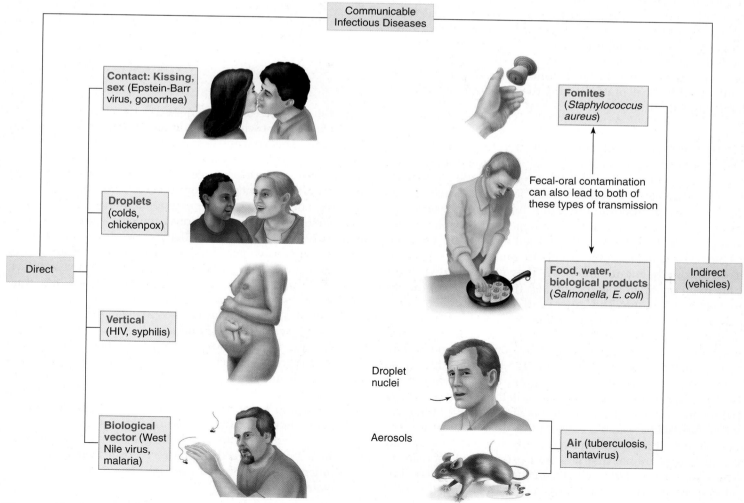

Figure 13.12 Summary of how communicable infectious diseases are transmitted.

Probably highest on the list would be objects commonly in contact with the public such as doorknobs, telephones, handheld remote controls, and faucet handles that are readily contaminated by touching. Shared bed linens, handkerchiefs, toilet seats, toys, eating utensils, clothing, personal articles, and syringes are other examples. Although paper money is impregnated with a disinfectant to inhibit microbes, pathogens are still isolated from bills as well as coins.

Outbreaks of food poisoning often result from the role of food as a common vehicle. The source of the agent can be soil, the handler, or a mechanical vector. Because milk provides a rich growth medium for microbes, it is a significant means of transmitting pathogens from diseased animals, infected milk handlers, and environmental sources of contamination. The agents of brucellosis, tuberculosis, Q fever, salmonellosis, and listeriosis are transmitted by contaminated milk. Water that has been contaminated by feces or urine can carry *Salmonella, Vibrio* (cholera) viruses (hepatitis A, polio), and pathogenic protozoans (*Giardia, Cryptosporidium*).

In the type of transmission termed the *oral-fecal route,* a fecal carrier with inadequate personal hygiene contaminates food during handling, and an unsuspecting person ingests it. Hepatitis A, amoebic dysentery, shigellosis, and typhoid fever are often transmitted this way. Oral-fecal transmission can also involve contaminated materials such as toys and diapers. It is really a special category of indirect transmission, which specifies that the way in which the vehicle became contaminated was through contact with fecal material and that it found its way to someone's mouth.

Indirect Spread by Vehicles: Air as a Vehicle Unlike soil and water, outdoor air cannot provide nutritional support for microbial growth and seldom transmits airborne pathogens. On the other hand, indoor air (especially in a closed space) can serve as an important medium for the suspension and dispersal of certain respiratory pathogens via droplet nuclei and aerosols. **Droplet nuclei** are dried microscopic residues created when microscopic pellets of mucus and saliva are ejected from the mouth and nose. They are generated forcefully in an unstifled sneeze or cough **(figure 13.13)** or mildly during vocalizations. The larger beads of moisture settle rapidly. If these settle in or on another person, it is considered droplet contact, as described earlier; but the smaller particles evaporate and remain suspended for longer periods. They can be encountered by a new host who is geographically or chronologically distant; thus, they are considered indirect contact. Droplet nuclei are implicated in the spread of hardier pathogens such as the tubercle bacillus and the influenza virus. **Aerosols** are suspensions of fine dust or moisture particles in the air that contain live pathogens. Q fever is spread by dust from animal quarters, and psittacosis is spread by aerosols from infected birds. An unusual outbreak of coccidioidomycosis (a lung infection) occurred during the 1994

Figure 13.13 The explosiveness of a sneeze. Special photography dramatically captures droplet formation in an unstifled sneeze. When such droplets dry and remain suspended in air, they are droplet nuclei.

Southern California earthquake. Epidemiologists speculate that disturbed hillsides and soil gave off clouds of dust containing the spores of *Coccidioides.*

In the disease chapters of this book (see chapters 18–23), the modes of transmission appearing in the pink boxes in figure 13.12 will be used to describe the diseases.

Nosocomial Infections: The Hospital as a Source of Disease

Infectious diseases that are acquired or develop during a hospital stay are known as **nosocomial** (nohz"-oh-koh'-mee-al) **infections.** This concept seems incongruous at first thought, because a hospital is regarded as a place to get treatment for a disease, not a place to acquire a disease. Yet it is not uncommon for a surgical patient's incision to become infected or a burn patient to develop a case of pneumonia in the clinical setting. The rate of nosocomial infections can be as low as 0.1% or as high as 20% of all admitted patients depending on the clinical setting, with an average of about 5%. In light of the number of admissions, this adds up to 2 to 4 million cases a year, which result in nearly 90,000 deaths. Nosocomial infections cost time and money as well as suffering. By one estimate, they amount to 8 million additional days of hospitalization a year and an increased cost of $5 to $10 billion.

So many factors unique to the hospital environment are tied to nosocomial infections that a certain number of infections are virtually unavoidable. After all, the hospital both attracts and creates compromised patients, and it serves as a collection point for pathogens. Some patients become infected when surgical procedures or lowered defenses permit resident biota to invade their bodies. Other patients acquire infections directly or indirectly from fomites, medical equipment, other patients, medical personnel, visitors, air, and water.

The health care process itself increases the likelihood that infectious agents will be transferred from one patient to another. Treatments using reusable instruments such as respirators and thermometers constitute a possible source of infectious agents. Indwelling devices such as catheters, prosthetic heart valves, grafts, drainage tubes, and tracheostomy tubes form ready portals of entry and habitats for infectious agents. Because such a high proportion of the hospital population receives antimicrobial drugs during their stay, drug-resistant microbes are selected for at a much greater rate than is the case outside the hospital.

The most common nosocomial infections involve the urinary tract, the respiratory tract, and surgical incisions (**figure 13.14**). Gram-negative intestinal biota (*Escherichia coli, Klebsiella, Pseudomonas*) are cultured in more than half of patients with nosocomial infections. Gram-positive bacteria (staphylococci and streptococci) and yeasts make up most of the remainder. True pathogens such as *Mycobacterium tuberculosis, Salmonella,* hepatitis B, and influenza virus can be transmitted in the clinical setting as well.

The federal government has taken steps to incentivize hospitals to control nosocomial transmission. In the fall of 2008 the Medicare and Medicaid programs announced they would not reimburse hospitals for nosocomial catheter-associated urinary tract infections, vascular catheter-associated bloodstream infections, and surgical site infections. It will be interesting to see whether this regulation has any effect on the rate of nosocomial infections.

Medical asepsis includes practices that lower the microbial load in patients, caregivers, and the hospital environment.

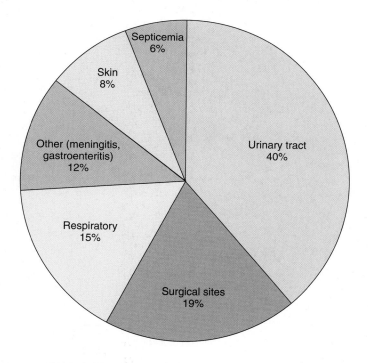

Figure 13.14 Most common nosocomial infections.
Relative frequency by target area.

These practices include proper hand washing, disinfection, and sanitization, as well as patient isolation. The goal of these procedures is to limit the spread of infectious agents from person to person. An even higher level of stringency is seen with *surgical asepsis,* which involves all of the strategies listed previously plus ensuring that all surgical procedures are conducted under sterile conditions. This includes sterilization of surgical instruments, dressings, sponges, and the like, as well as clothing personnel in sterile garments and scrupulously disinfecting the room surfaces and air.

Hospitals generally employ an *infection control officer* who not only implements proper practices and procedures throughout the hospital but is also charged with tracking potential outbreaks, identifying breaches in asepsis, and training other health care workers in aseptic technique. Among those most in need of this training are nurses and other caregivers whose work, by its very nature, exposes them to needlesticks, infectious secretions, blood, and physical contact with the patient. The same practices that interrupt the routes of infection in the patient can also protect the health care worker. It is for this reason that most hospitals have adopted universal precautions that recognize that all secretions from all persons in the clinical setting are potentially infectious and that transmission can occur in either direction.

Universal Blood and Body Fluid Precautions

Medical and dental settings require stringent measures to prevent the spread of nosocomial infections from patient to patient, from patient to worker, and from worker to patient. But even with precautions, the rate of such infections is rather high. Recent evidence indicates that more than one-third of nosocomial infections could be prevented by consistent and rigorous infection control methods.

Previously, control guidelines were disease-specific, and clearly identified infections were managed with particular restrictions and techniques. With this arrangement, personnel tended to handle materials labeled *infectious* with much greater care than those that were not so labeled. The AIDS epidemic spurred a reexamination of that policy. Because of the potential for increased numbers of undiagnosed HIV-infected patients, the Centers for Disease Control and Prevention laid down more stringent guidelines for handling patients and body substances. These guidelines have been termed **universal precautions (UPs),** because they are based on the assumption that all patient specimens could harbor infectious agents and so must be treated with the same degree of care. They also include body substance isolation (BSI) techniques to be used in known cases of infection.

It is worth mentioning that these precautions are designed to protect all individuals in the clinical setting—patients, workers, and the public alike. In general, they include techniques designed to prevent contact with pathogens and contamination and, if prevention is not possible, to take purposeful measures to decontaminate potentially infectious materials.

The universal precautions recommended for all health care settings are:

1. Barrier precautions, including masks and gloves, should be taken to prevent contact of skin and mucous membranes with patients' blood or other body fluids. Because gloves can develop small invisible tears, double gloving decreases the risk further. For protection during surgery, venipuncture, or emergency procedures, gowns, aprons, and other body coverings should be worn. Dental workers should wear eyewear and face shields to protect against splattered blood and saliva.

2. More than 10% of health care personnel are pierced each year by sharp (and usually contaminated) instruments. These accidents carry risks not only for AIDS but also for hepatitis B, hepatitis C, and other diseases. Preventing inoculation infection requires vigilant observance of proper techniques. All disposable needles, scalpels, or sharp devices from invasive procedures must immediately be placed in puncture-proof containers for sterilization and final discard. Under no circumstances should a worker attempt to recap a syringe, remove a needle from a syringe, or leave unprotected used syringes where they pose a risk to others. Reusable needles or other sharp devices must be heat-sterilized in a puncture-proof holder before they are handled. If a needlestick or other injury occurs, immediate attention to the wound, such as thorough degermation and application of strong antiseptics, can prevent infection.

3. Dental handpieces should be sterilized between patients, but if this is not possible, they should be thoroughly disinfected with a high-level disinfectant (peroxide, hypochlorite). Blood and saliva should be removed completely from all contaminated dental instruments and intraoral devices prior to sterilization.

4. Hands and other skin surfaces that have been accidently contaminated with blood or other fluids should be scrubbed immediately with a germicidal soap. Hands should likewise be washed after removing rubber gloves, masks, or other barrier devices.

5. Because saliva can be a source of some types of infections, barriers should be used in all mouth-to-mouth resuscitations.

6. Health care workers with active, draining skin or mucous membrane lesions must refrain from handling patients or equipment that will come into contact with other patients. Pregnant health care workers risk infecting their fetuses and must pay special attention to these guidelines. Personnel should be protected by vaccination whenever possible.

Isolation procedures for known or suspected infections should still be instituted on a case-by-case basis.

Which Agent Is the Cause? Using Koch's Postulates to Determine Etiology

An essential aim in the study of infection and disease is determining the precise **etiologic,** or causative, **agent.** In our modern technological age, we take for granted that a certain

infection is caused by a certain microbe, but such has not always been the case. More than a century ago, Robert Koch realized that in order to prove the germ theory of disease he would have to develop a standard for determining causation that would stand the test of scientific scrutiny. Out of his

① Specimen from patient ill with infection of unknown etiology is carried through an isolation procedure.

② A pure culture of the suspected agent is made.

Full microscopic and biological characterization

Inoculation of test subject

③

Observe animal for disease characteristics

Specimen taken

④

Pure culture and identification procedures

Process Figure 13.15 Koch's postulates: Is this the etiologic agent?   The microbe in the initial and second isolations and the disease in the patient and experimental animal must be identical for the postulates to be satisfied.

experimental observations on the transmission of anthrax in cows came a series of proofs, called **Koch's postulates,** that established the principal criteria for etiologic studies **(figure 13.15).** These postulates direct an investigator to

1. find evidence of a particular microbe in every case of a disease,
2. isolate that microbe from an infected subject and cultivate it in pure culture in the laboratory,
3. inoculate a susceptible healthy subject with the laboratory isolate and observe the same resultant disease, and
4. reisolate the agent from this subject.

Valid application of Koch's postulates requires attention to several critical details. Each isolated culture must be pure, observed microscopically, and identified by means of characteristic tests; the first and second isolates must be identical; and the pathologic effects, signs, and symptoms of the disease in the first and second subjects must be the same. Once established, these postulates were rapidly put to the test, and within a short time, they had helped determine the causative agents of tuberculosis, diphtheria, and plague. Today, most known infectious diseases have been directly linked to a known infectious agent.

Koch's postulates continue to play an essential role in modern epidemiology. Every decade, new diseases challenge the scientific community and require application of the postulates.

Koch's postulates are reliable for many infectious diseases, but they cannot be completely fulfilled in certain situations. For example, some infectious agents are not readily isolated or grown in the laboratory. If one cannot elicit a similar infection by inoculating it into an animal, it is very difficult to prove the etiology. It is difficult to satisfy Koch's postulates for viral diseases because viruses usually have a very narrow host range. Human viruses may only cause disease in humans, or perhaps in primates, though the disease symptoms in apes will often be different. To address this, T. M. Rivers proposed modified postulates for viral infections. These were used in 2003 to definitively determine the coronavirus cause of SARS **(Insight 13.4).**

It is also usually not possible to use Koch's postulates to determine causation in polymicrobial diseases. Diseases such as periodontitis and soft tissue abscesses are caused by complex mixtures of microbes. While it is theoretically possible to isolate each member and to re-create the exact proportions of individual cultures for step 3, it is not attempted in practice.

13.2 Learning Outcomes—Can You . . .

5. . . . differentiate between pathogenicity and virulence?
6. . . . define opportunism?
7. . . . list the steps a microbe has to take to get to the point where it can cause disease?
8. . . . list several portals of entry?
9. . . . define infectious dose?
10. . . . describe three ways microbes cause tissue damage?
11. . . . differentiate between endotoxins and exotoxins?
12. . . . provide a definition of virulence factors?

| INSIGHT 13.4 | Koch's Postulates Still Critical |

SARS (severe acute respiratory syndrome) hit the news in the winter of 2002, and though it was deadly, ultimately killing hundreds of people of the 8,000 or so it infected, it was contained in a period of 7 months, even though it was new to the medical community. The epidemic was brought to a halt quickly because the response by the scientific and medical personnel was lightning fast. By April of 2003, scientists had sequenced the entire genome of the suspected agent, a coronavirus. In May of 2003, Dutch scientists published a paper in the journal *Nature* with the title "Aetiology: Koch's Postulates Fulfilled for SARS Virus."

The set of Koch's postulates used in this study was that modified by Rivers in 1937 for viral diseases. There are six postulates in the modified version, not four as in the original Koch's postulates. In their SARS paper, the scientists noted that the first three postulates had been met by other researchers. The final three were examined in the work described in the article. The scientists inoculated two macaque monkeys with the SARS virus that had been isolated from a fatal human case and cultivated in cell culture. The two macaques became lethargic. One of them suffered respiratory distress, and both of them excreted virus from their noses and throats. At autopsy, the macaques were found to have histological signs of pneumonia that were indistinguishable from human cases (postulate 4). The virus that was recovered from the monkeys was shown by PCR and electron microscopy to be identical to the one used for inoculation (postulate 5). Finally, 2 weeks after infection, the macaques' blood tested positive for antibody to the SARS virus. This fulfilled the last postulate and gave scientists the proof they needed to rapidly design interventions targeted at this particular coronavirus.

Koch's Postulates as Modified by Rivers

1. Virus must be isolated from each diseased host.
2. Virus must be cultivated in cell culture.
3. Virus must be filterable, that is, must pass through pores small enough to impede bacteria and other microorganisms.
4. Virus must produce comparable disease when inoculated into the original host species or a related one.
5. The same virus must be reisolated from the new host.
6. There must be a specific immune response to the original virus in the new host.

---

13. . . . draw and label a curve representing the course of clinical infection?
14. . . . discuss the topic of reservoirs thoroughly?
15. . . . list seven different modes of transmission of infectious agents?
16. . . . define nosocomial infection and list the three most common types?
17. . . . list Koch's postulates, and when they might not be appropriate in establishing causation?

13.3 Epidemiology: The Study of Disease in Populations

So far, our discussion has revolved primarily around the impact of an infectious disease in a single individual. Let us now turn our attention to the effects of diseases on the community—the realm of **epidemiology.** By definition, this term involves the study of the frequency and distribution of disease and other health-related factors in defined populations. It involves many disciplines—not only microbiology but also anatomy, physiology, immunology, medicine, psychology, sociology, ecology, and statistics—and it considers all forms of disease, including heart disease, cancer, drug addiction, and mental illness.

A groundbreaking British nurse named Florence Nightingale helped to lay the foundations of modern epidemiology. She arrived in the Crimean war zone in Turkey in the mid-1850s, where the British were fighting and dying at an astonishing rate. Estimates suggest that 20% of the soldiers there died (by contrast, 2.6% of U.S. soldiers in the Vietnam war died). Even though this was some years before the discovery of the germ theory, Nightingale understood that filth contributed to disease and instituted methods that had never been seen in military field hospitals. She insisted that separate linens and towels be used for each patient, and that the floors be cleaned and the pipes of sewage unclogged. She kept meticulous notes of what was killing the patients and was able to demonstrate that many more men died of disease than of their traumatic injuries. This was indeed one of the earliest forays into epidemiology—trying to understand how diseases were being transmitted and using statistics to do so.

The techniques of epidemiology are also used to track behaviors, such as exercise or smoking. The epidemiologist is a medical sleuth who collects clues on the causative agent, pathology, sources, and modes of transmission and tracks the numbers and distribution of cases of disease in the community. In fulfilling these demands, the epidemiologist asks who, when, where, how, why, and what about diseases. The outcome of these studies helps public health departments develop prevention and treatment programs and establish a basis for predictions.

Who, When, and Where? Tracking Disease in the Population

Epidemiologists are concerned with all of the factors covered earlier in this chapter: virulence, portals of entry and exit, and the course of disease. But they are also interested in surveillance—that is, collecting, analyzing, and reporting data on the rates of occurrence, mortality, morbidity, and transmission of infections. Surveillance involves keeping data for a large number of diseases seen by the medical community and reported to public health authorities. By law, certain **reportable,** or notifiable, **diseases** must be reported to authorities; others are reported on a voluntary basis.

A well-developed network of individuals and agencies at the local, district, state, national, and international levels

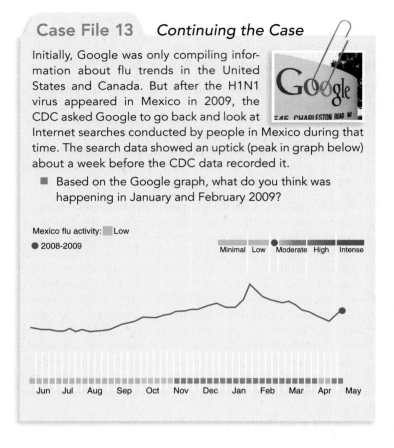

Case File 13   *Continuing the Case*

Initially, Google was only compiling information about flu trends in the United States and Canada. But after the H1N1 virus appeared in Mexico in 2009, the CDC asked Google to go back and look at Internet searches conducted by people in Mexico during that time. The search data showed an uptick (peak in graph below) about a week before the CDC data recorded it.

■ Based on the Google graph, what do you think was happening in January and February 2009?

keeps track of infectious diseases. Physicians and hospitals report all notifiable diseases that are brought to their attention. These reports are either made about individuals or in the aggregate, depending on the disease.

Traditionally, local public health agencies first receive the case data and determine how they will be handled. In most cases, health officers investigate the history and movements of patients to trace their prior contacts and to control the further spread of the infection as soon as possible through drug therapy, immunization, and education. In notifiable sexually transmitted diseases, patients are asked to name their partners so that these persons can be notified, examined, and treated. It is very important to maintain the confidentiality of the persons in these reports. The principal government agency responsible for keeping track of infectious diseases nationwide is the Centers for Disease Control and Prevention (CDC) in Atlanta, Georgia; the CDC is a part of the U.S. Public Health Service. The CDC publishes a weekly notice of diseases (the *Morbidity and Mortality Report*) that provides weekly and cumulative summaries of the case rates and deaths for about 50 notifiable diseases, highlights important and unusual diseases, and presents data concerning disease occurrence in the major regions of the United States. It is available to anyone at http://www.cdc.gov/mmwr/. Ultimately, the CDC shares its statistics on disease with the World Health Organization (WHO) for worldwide tabulation and control.

Epidemiological Statistics: Frequency of Cases

The **prevalence** of a disease is the total number of existing cases with respect to the entire population. It is often thought of as a snapshot and is usually reported as the percentage of the population having a particular disease at any given time. Disease **incidence** measures the number of new cases over a certain time period. This statistic, also called the case, or morbidity, rate, indicates both the rate and the risk of infection. The equations used to figure these rates are:

$$\text{Prevalence} = \frac{\text{Total number of cases in population}}{\text{Total number of persons in population}} \times 100 = \%$$

$$\text{Incidence} = \frac{\text{Number of new cases}}{\text{Total number of susceptible persons}} \text{ (Usually reported per 100,000 persons)}$$

The changes in incidence and prevalence are usually followed over a seasonal, yearly, and long-term basis and are helpful in predicting trends **(figure 13.16).** Statistics of concern to the epidemiologist are the rates of disease with regard to sex, race, or geographic region. Also of importance is the **mortality rate,** which measures the total number of deaths in a population due to a certain disease. Over the past century, the overall death rate from infectious

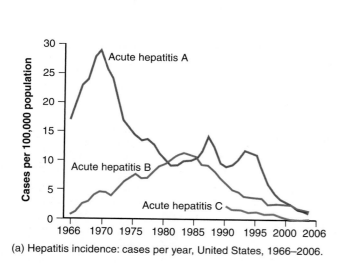

(a) Hepatitis incidence: cases per year, United States, 1966–2006.

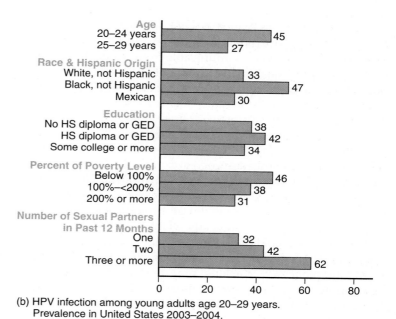

(b) HPV infection among young adults age 20–29 years. Prevalence in United States 2003–2004.

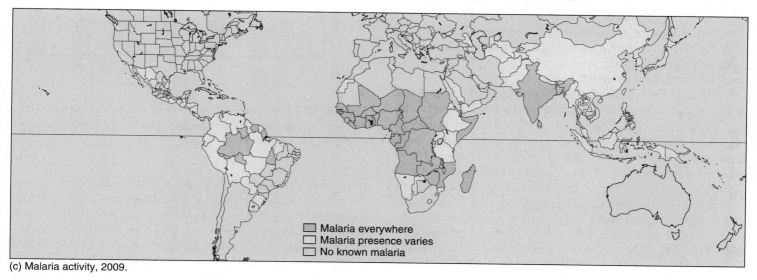

(c) Malaria activity, 2009.

Figure 13.16 Graphical representation of epidemiological data. The Centers for Disease Control and Prevention collects epidemiological data that are analyzed with regard to **(a)** time frame, **(b)** age and other characteristics, and **(c)** geographic region.

diseases in the developed world has dropped, although the number of persons afflicted with infectious diseases (the **morbidity rate**) has remained relatively high.

When there is an increase in disease in a particular geographical area, it can be helpful to examine the epidemic curve (incidence over time) to determine if the infection is a **point-source, common-source,** or **propagated epidemic**. A point-source epidemic, illustrated in **figure 13.17a,** is one in which the infectious agent came from a single source, and all of its "victims" were exposed to it from that source. The classic example of this is food illnesses brought on by exposure to a contaminated food item at a potluck dinner or restaurant. Common-source epidemics or outbreaks result from common exposure to a single source of infection that can occur over a period of time **(figure 13.17b)**. Think of a contaminated water plant that infects multiple people over the course of a week, or even of a single restaurant worker who is a carrier of hepatitis A and does not practice good hygiene. Lastly, a propagated epidemic **(figure 13.17c)** results from an infectious agent that is communicable from person to person and therefore is sustained—propagated—over time in a population. Influenza is the classic example of this. The point is that each of these types of spread become apparent from the shape of the outbreak or epidemic curves.

An additional term, the **index case,** refers to the first patient found in an epidemiological investigation. How the cases unfurl from this case helps explain the type of epidemic it is. The index case may not turn out to be the first case—as the investigation continues earlier cases may be found—but the index case is the case that brought the epidemic to the attention of officials. Monitoring statistics also makes it possible to define the frequency of a disease in the population. An infectious disease that exhibits a relatively steady frequency over a long time period in a particular geographic locale is **endemic (figure 13.18a)**. For example, Lyme disease is endemic to certain areas of the United States where the tick vector is found. A certain number of new cases are expected in these areas every year. When a disease is **sporadic,** occasional cases are reported at irregular intervals in random locales **(figure 13.18b)**. Tetanus and diphtheria are reported sporadically in the United States (fewer than 50 cases a year).

When statistics indicate that the prevalence of an endemic or sporadic disease is increasing beyond what is expected for that population, the pattern is described as an **epidemic (figure 13.18c)**. The time period is not defined—it can range from hours in food poisoning to years in syphilis—nor is an exact percentage of increase needed before an outbreak can qualify as an epidemic. Several epidemics occur every year in the United States, most recently among STDs such as chlamydia and gonorrhea. The spread of an epidemic across continents is a **pandemic,** as exemplified by AIDS and influenza **(figure 13.18d)**.

One important epidemiological truism might be called the "iceberg effect," which refers to the fact that only a small

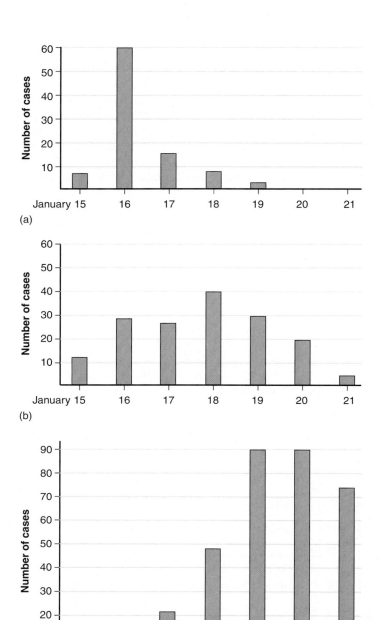

Figure 13.17 Different outbreak or epidemic curves with different shapes. (a) Point-source epidemic, (b) common-source epidemic, (c) propagated epidemic.

portion of an iceberg is visible above the surface of the ocean, with a much more massive part lingering unseen below the surface. Regardless of case reporting and public health screening, a large number of cases of infection in the community go undiagnosed and unreported. (For a list of reportable diseases in the United States, see **table 13.10.**) In the instance of salmonellosis, approximately 40,000 cases are reported

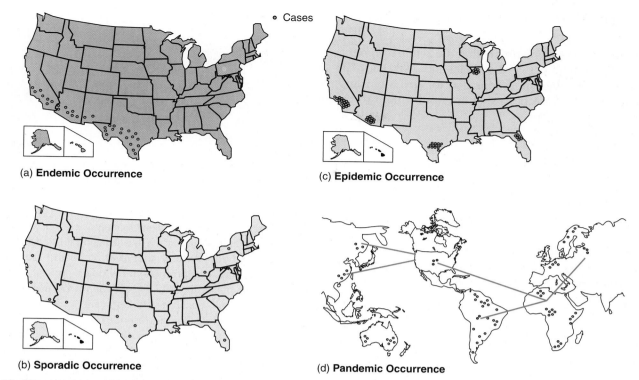

• Cases

(a) **Endemic Occurrence**

(c) **Epidemic Occurrence**

(b) **Sporadic Occurrence**

(d) **Pandemic Occurrence**

Figure 13.18 Patterns of infectious disease occurrence. **(a)** In endemic occurrence, cases are concentrated in one area at a relatively stable rate. **(b)** In sporadic occurrence, a few cases occur randomly over a wide area. **(c)** An epidemic is an increased number of cases that often appear in geographic clusters. The clusters may be local, as in the case of a restaurant-related food-borne epidemic, or nationwide, as is the case with *Chlamydia*. **(d)** Pandemic occurrence means that an epidemic ranges over more than one continent.

Table 13.10 Reportable Diseases in the United States*

- Anthrax
- Botulism
- Brucellosis
- Chancroid
- *Chlamydia trachomatis* genital infections
- Cholera
- Cryptosporidiosis
- Cyclosporiasis
- Dengue fever
- Diphtheria
- Ehrlichiosis
- Encephalitis/meningitis, arboviral
  - Encephalitis/meningitis, California serogroup viral
  - Encephalitis/meningitis, eastern equine
  - Encephalitis/meningitis, Powassan
  - Encephalitis/meningitis, St. Louis
  - Encephalitis/meningitis, western equine
  - Encephalitis/meningitis, West Nile

- Giardiasis
- Gonorrhea
- *Haemophilus influenzae* invasive disease
- Hansen's disease (leprosy)
- Hantavirus pulmonary syndrome
- Hemolytic uremic syndrome
- Hepatitis, viral, acute
  - Hepatitis A, acute
  - Hepatitis B, acute
  - Hepatitis B virus, perinatal infection
  - Hepatitis C, acute
- Hepatitis, viral, chronic
  - Chronic hepatitis B
  - Hepatitis C virus infection (past or present)
- HIV infection
- Influenza-associated pediatric mortality
- Legionellosis
- Listeriosis
- Lyme disease
- Malaria
- Measles

- Meningococcal disease
- Mumps
- Novel influenza A infections
- Pertussis
- Plague
- Poliomyelitis, paralytic
- Poliovirus infection
- Psittacosis
- Q fever
- Rabies
  - Rabies, animal
  - Rabies, human
- Rubella
- Rubella, congenital syndrome
- Salmonellosis
- Severe acute respiratory syndrome–associated coronavirus (SARS-CoV) disease
- Shiga toxin–producing *Escherichia coli* (STEC)
- Shigellosis
- Smallpox
- Spotted fever rickettsiosis
- Streptococcal disease, invasive, group A

- Streptococcal toxic shock syndrome
- *Streptococcus pneumoniae*, invasive disease
- Syphilis
- Syphilis, congenital
- Tetanus
- Toxic shock syndrome
- Trichinellosis
- Tuberculosis
- Tularemia
- Typhoid fever
- Vancomycin-intermediate *Staphylococcus aureus* (VISA)
- Vancomycin-resistant *Staphylococcus aureus* (VRSA)
- Varicella
- Vibriosis
- Viral hemorrhagic fevers
  - Arenavirus
  - Crimean-Congo hemorrhagic fever virus
  - Ebola virus
  - Lassa virus
  - Marburg virus
- Yellow fever

*Reportable to the CDC; other diseases may be reportable to state departments of health.
Source: Centers for Disease Control and Prevention, 2010.

each year. Epidemiologists estimate that the actual number is more likely somewhere between 400,000 and 4,000,000. The iceberg effect can be even more lopsided for sexually transmitted diseases or for infections that are not brought to the attention of reporting agencies.

13.3 Learning Outcomes—Can You ...

18. ... differentiate the science of epidemiology from traditional medical practice?

19. ... identify the need for some diseases being denoted "notifiable."

20. ... define incidence and prevalence?

21. ... discuss point-source, common-source, and propagated epidemics and predict the shape of the epidemic curves associated with each?

Case File 13 *Wrap-Up*

Epidemic tracking based on Internet searches reflects what is called "collective intelligence." It works because individuals using their personal computers tend to search for terms related to their immediate needs and intentions, and they generally do this before presenting in a doctor's office or emergency room. The methodology of Google search was published in the prestigious science journal *Nature*, and another independent study has been published about a similar search analysis conducted by Yahoo, showing that it was effective in predicting flu trends.

Some people worry that data collected from Internet searches may compromise individuals' privacy. However, Google maintains that Flu Trends cannot be used to identify individual users because the data are anonymous and are aggregated before being presented. Another potential drawback is that this data collection method is less likely to be useful for tracking epidemics in societies having a low percentage of computer ownership—namely, developing countries. However, considering the high stakes involved in identifying an epidemic quickly, Internet search term analysis holds great promise for public health. And, unlike most health innovations, it's free!

See: 2009. *Nature* 457:1012–14.

Chapter Summary

13.1 The Human Host

- Humans coexist with microorganisms from the moment of birth onward.
- Normal biota reside on the skin and in the respiratory tract, the gastrointestinal tract, the outer parts of the urethra, the vagina, the eye, and the external ear canal.
- The Human Microbiome Project is finding a much wider array of normal biota in more anatomical places than known previously

13.2 The Progress of an Infection

- The pathogenicity of a microbe refers to its ability to cause disease. Its virulence is the degree of damage it can inflict.
- True pathogens cause infectious disease in healthy hosts; opportunistic pathogens cause damage only when the host immune system is compromised in some way.
- The site at which a microorganism first contacts host tissue is called the portal of entry. Most pathogens have one preferred portal of entry, although some have more than one.
- The respiratory system is the portal of entry for the greatest number of pathogens.
- The infectious dose, or ID, refers to the minimum number of microbial cells required to initiate infection in the

host. Fimbriae and adhesive capsules allow pathogens to physically attach to host tissues.

- Antiphagocytic factors produced by microorganisms include leukocidins, capsules, and factors that resist digestion by white blood cells.
- Exoenzymes, toxins, and the ability to induce injurious host responses are the three main types of virulence factors pathogens utilize to combat host defenses and damage host tissue.
- Exotoxins and endotoxins differ in their chemical composition and tissue specificity.
- Inappropriate or extreme host responses are a major factor in most infectious diseases.
- Patterns of infection vary with the pathogen or pathogens involved. Examples are local, focal, and systemic.
- Mixed infections are more common than previously appreciated.
- Infections can be characterized by their sequence as primary or secondary and by their duration as either acute or chronic.
- The portal of exit by which a pathogen leaves its host is often but not always the same as the portal of entry.
- The portals of exit and entry determine how pathogens spread in a population.
- Some pathogens persist in the body in a latent state.

- The primary habitat of a pathogen is called its reservoir. A human reservoir is also called a carrier.
- Animals can be either reservoirs or vectors of pathogens. An infected animal is a biological vector. Uninfected animals, especially insects, that transmit pathogens mechanically are called mechanical vectors.
- Soil and water are nonliving reservoirs for pathogenic bacteria, protozoa, fungi, and worms.
- A communicable disease can be transmitted from an infected host to others, but not all infectious diseases are communicable.
- The spread of infectious disease from person to person is called horizontal transmission. The spread from parent to offspring is called vertical transmission.
- Infectious diseases are spread by either contact or indirect routes of transmission. Vehicles of indirect transmission include soil, water, food, air, and fomites (inanimate objects).
- Nosocomial infections are acquired in a hospital from surgical procedures, equipment, personnel, and exposure to drug-resistant microorganisms.

- Causative agents of infectious disease may be identified according to Koch's postulates.

13.3 Epidemiology: The Study of Disease in Populations

- Epidemiology is the study of the determinants and distribution of infectious and noninfectious diseases in populations.
- Data on specific, reportable diseases is collected by local, national, and worldwide agencies.
- The prevalence of a disease is the percentage of existing cases in a given population. The disease incidence, or morbidity rate, is the number of newly infected members in a population during a specified time period.
- Outbreaks and epidemics are described as point-source, common-source, or propagated based on the source of the pathogen.
- Disease frequency is described as sporadic, epidemic, pandemic, or endemic.

Multiple-Choice and True-False Questions   Knowledge and Comprehension

Multiple-Choice Questions. Select the correct answer from the answers provided.

1. The best descriptive term for the resident biota is
   a. commensals.   c. pathogens.
   b. parasites.   d. mutualists.

2. Resident biota is absent from the
   a. pharynx.   c. intestine.
   b. heart.   d. hair follicles.

3. Virulence factors include
   a. toxins.
   b. enzymes.
   c. capsules.
   d. all of these.

4. The specific action of hemolysins is to
   a. damage white blood cells.
   b. cause fever.
   c. damage red blood cells.
   d. cause leukocytosis.

5. The ____ is the time that lapses between encounter with a pathogen and the first symptoms.
   a. prodrome
   b. period of invasion
   c. period of convalescence
   d. period of incubation

6. A short period early in a disease that may manifest with general malaise and achiness is the
   a. period of incubation.
   b. prodrome.
   c. sequela.
   d. period of invasion.

7. A/an ____ is a passive animal transporter of pathogens.
   a. zoonosis   c. mechanical vector
   b. biological vector   d. asymptomatic carrier

8. An example of a noncommunicable infection is
   a. measles.
   b. leprosy.
   c. tuberculosis.
   d. tetanus.

9. A positive antibody test for HIV would be a ____ of infection.
   a. sign
   b. symptom
   c. syndrome
   d. sequela

10. An outbreak caused by a batch of bad potato salad at a picnic is a _____ outbreak.
    a. point-source
    b. common-source
    c. propagated
    d. all of the above

True-False Questions. If the statement is true, leave as is. If it is false, correct it by rewriting the sentence.

11. The presence of a few bacteria in the blood is called septicemia.

12. Resident microbiota is commonly found in the urethra.

13. A subclinical infection is one that is acquired in a hospital or medical facility.

14. The general term that describes an increase in the number of white blood cells is leukopenia.

15. The index case is the first case found in an epidemiological investigation.

Critical Thinking Questions   Application and Analysis

These questions are suggested as a *writing-to-learn* experience. For each question (except #7), compose a one- or two-paragraph answer that includes the factual information needed to completely address the question.

1. Differentiate between contamination, infection, and disease. What are the possible outcomes in each?

2. How are infectious diseases different from other diseases?

3. Explain several ways that true pathogens differ from opportunistic pathogens.

4. Describe the course of infection from contact with the pathogen to its exit from the host.

5. Compare and contrast: systemic versus local infections; primary versus secondary infections; infection versus intoxication.

6. a. List the main features of Koch's postulates.
   b. Why is it so difficult to prove them for some diseases?

7. Describe each of the following infections using correct technical terminology. (Descriptions may fit more than one category.) Use terms such as *primary, secondary, nosocomial, STD, mixed, latent, toxemia, chronic, zoonotic, asymptomatic, local, systemic, -itis, -emia.*

   Caused by needlestick in dental office

   Pneumocystis pneumonia in AIDS patient

   Bubonic plague from rat flea bite

   Diphtheria

   Undiagnosed chlamydiosis

   Acute necrotizing gingivitis

   Syphilis of long duration

   Large numbers of gram-negative rods in the blood

   A boil on the back of the neck

   An inflammation of the meninges

   Scarlet fever

8. Name 10 fomites that you came into contact with today.

9. Suggest several reasons why urinary tract, respiratory tract, and surgical infections are the most common nosocomial infections.

10. Can you explain how improvements in treatment of a disease such as AIDS can increase its prevalence?

Concept Mapping   Synthesis

Appendix D provides guidance for working with concept maps.

1. Supply your own linking words or phrases in this concept map, and provide the missing concepts in the empty boxes.

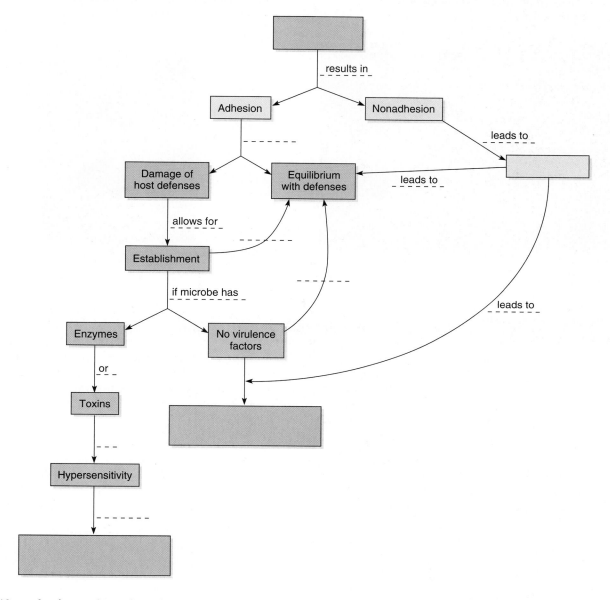

2. Use 6 to 10 words of your choice from the Chapter Summary to create a concept map. Finish it by providing linking words..

Visual Connections Synthesis

These questions use visual images or previous content to make connections to this chapter's concepts.

1. **From chapter 3, figure 3.7a.** What chemical is the organism in this illustration producing? How does this add to an organism's pathogenicity?

2. **From chapter 4, figure 4.11.** In what setting was this infection most likely acquired? What is this type of infection called? What could be the source of the microorganism?

Glycocalyx
slime

Catheter
surface

Cell
cluster

www.connect.microbiology.com

Enhance your study of this chapter with study tools and practice tests. Also ask your instructor about the resources available through ConnectPlus, including the media-rich eBook, interactive learning tools, and animations.

Host Defenses I
Overview and Nonspecific Defenses

Case File 14

War, famine, and political repression displace millions of people around the world. Some families are internally displaced, meaning that they must leave their homes but can still remain within their country; others become refugees, migrating to another country to find peace or safety. The United States receives a large share of these refugees. The largest numbers come from the Near East (especially Iraq and Iran) and southern Asia. Many also emigrate from eastern Asia, especially Burma, and from Africa, particularly Somalia and Sudan. In 2008, the United States received 60,191 refugees.

When refugees arrive in another country, they need housing, food, and medical attention. Since many refugees come from areas having high rates of diseases that are not common in the United States, health care workers follow a set of guidelines in order to provide the needed care. One of the first tests run is a CBC, or complete blood count, in which a quantity of blood is drawn and analyzed. One type of white blood cell, the eosinophil, is a particularly useful diagnostic tool for the refugee population. An elevated eosinophil count often means the patient has a worm or parasite infection.

- Why don't health care providers test refugees for very specific diseases rather than for increased eosinophils?
- Refugees arriving in the United States must also worry about encountering diseases they have not been exposed to before. What might some of these diseases be?

Continuing the Case appears on page 408.

Outline and Learning Outcomes

14.1 Defense Mechanisms of the Host in Perspective
1. Summarize what the three lines of defense are.
2. Identify three components of the first line of defense.

14.2 The Second and Third Lines of Defense: An Overview
3. Define marker, and discuss its importance in the second and third lines of defense.

14.3 Systems Involved in Immune Defenses

4. Name four body compartments that participate in immunity.
5. List the components of the reticuloendothelial system.
6. Fully describe the structure and function of the lymphatic system.
7. Differentiate between whole blood and plasma.
8. Name six kinds of blood cells that function in nonspecific immunity, and the most important function of each.
9. Name two kinds of lymphocytes involved in specific immunity.

14.4 The Second Line of Defense

10. List the four major categories of nonspecific immunity.
11. Outline the steps in inflammation.
12. Outline the steps in phagocytosis.
13. Discuss the mechanism of fever and what it accomplishes.
14. Name four types of antimicrobial proteins.
15. Compose one good overview sentence about the purpose and the mode of action of the complement system.

14.1 Defense Mechanisms of the Host in Perspective

The survival of the host depends upon an elaborate network of defenses that keep harmful microbes and other foreign materials from penetrating the body. Should they penetrate, additional host defenses are summoned to prevent them from becoming established in tissues. Defenses involve barriers, cells, and chemicals, and they range from nonspecific to specific and from inborn or innate to acquired. This chapter introduces the main lines of defense intrinsic to all humans. Topics included in this survey are the anatomical and physiological systems that detect, recognize, and destroy foreign substances and the general adaptive responses that account for an individual's long-term immunity or resistance to infection and disease.

In chapter 13, we explored the host-parasite relationship, with emphasis on the role of microorganisms in disease. In this chapter, we examine the other side of the relationship— that of the host defending itself against microorganisms. As previously stated, whether an encounter between a human and a microbe results in disease is dependent on many factors (see figure 13.2). The encounters occur constantly. In the battle against all sorts of invaders, microbial and otherwise, the body erects a series of barriers, sends in an army of cells, and emits a flood of chemicals to protect tissues from harm.

The host defenses are a multilevel network of innate, nonspecific protections and specific **immunities** referred to as the first, second, and third lines of defense **(figure 14.1).** The interaction and cooperation of these three levels of defense normally provide complete protection against infection. The **first line of defense** includes any barrier that blocks invasion at the portal of entry. This mostly nonspecific line of defense limits access to the internal tissues of the body. However, it is not considered a true immune response because it does not involve recognition of a specific foreign substance but is very general in action. The **second line of defense** is a more internalized system of protective cells and fluids that includes inflammation and phagocytosis. It acts rapidly at both the local and systemic levels once the first line of defense

has been circumvented. The highly specific **third line of defense** is acquired on an individual basis as each foreign substance is encountered by white blood cells called lymphocytes. The reaction with each different microbe produces unique protective substances and cells that can come into play if that microbe is encountered again. The third line of defense provides long-term immunity. It is discussed in detail in chapter 15. This chapter focuses on the first and second lines of defense.

The human systems are armed with various levels of defense that do not operate in a completely separate fashion; most defenses overlap and are even redundant in some of their effects. This literally bombards microbial invaders with an entire assault force, making their survival unlikely. Because of the interwoven nature of host defenses, we will introduce basic concepts of structure and function that will prepare you for later information on specific reactions of the immune system (see chapter 15).

Barriers: A First Line of Defense

A number of defenses are a normal part of the body's anatomy and physiology. These inborn, nonspecific defenses can be divided into physical, chemical, and genetic barriers that impede the entry of not only microbes but any foreign agent, whether living or not **(figure 14.2).**

Physical or Anatomical Barriers at the Body's Surface

The skin and mucous membranes of the respiratory and digestive tracts have several built-in defenses. The outermost layer (stratum corneum) of the skin is composed of epithelial cells that have become compacted, cemented together, and impregnated with an insoluble protein, keratin. The result is a thick, tough layer that is highly impervious and waterproof. Few pathogens can penetrate this unbroken barrier, especially in regions such as the soles of the feet or the palms of the hands, where the stratum corneum is much thicker than on other parts of the body. It is so obvious as to be overlooked: the

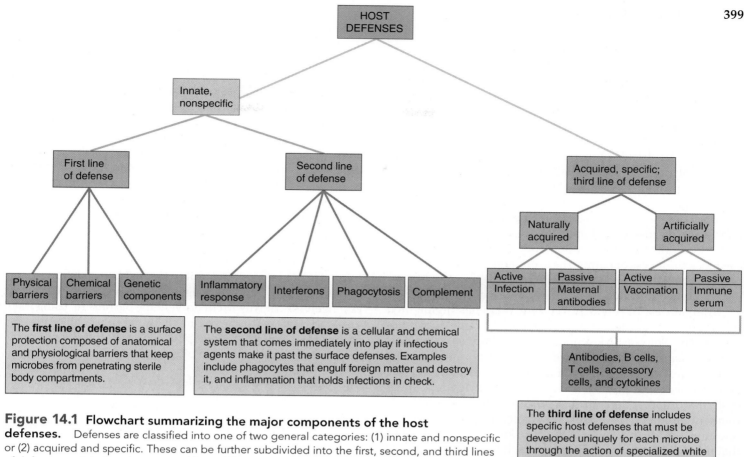

Figure 14.1 Flowchart summarizing the major components of the host defenses. Defenses are classified into one of two general categories: (1) innate and nonspecific or (2) acquired and specific. These can be further subdivided into the first, second, and third lines of defense, each being characterized by a different level and type of protection. The third line of defense is the most complex and is responsible for specific immunity.

skin separates our inner bodies from the microbial assaults of the environment. It is a surprisingly tough and sophisticated barrier. The top layer of cells is packed with keratin, a protective and waterproofing protein. In addition, outer layers of skin are constantly sloughing off, taking associated microbes with them. Other cutaneous barriers include hair follicles and skin glands. The hair shaft is periodically extruded, and the follicle cells are **desquamated** (des'-kwuh-mayt-ud). The flushing effect of sweat glands also helps remove microbes.

The mucous membranes of the digestive, urinary, and respiratory tracts and of the eye are moist and permeable. They do provide barrier protection but without a keratinized layer. The mucous coat on the free surface of some membranes impedes the entry and attachment of bacteria. Blinking and tear production (lacrimation) flush the eye's surface with tears and rid it of irritants. The constant flow of saliva helps carry microbes into the harsh conditions of the stomach. Vomiting and defecation also evacuate noxious substances or microorganisms from the body.

The respiratory tract is constantly guarded from infection by elaborate and highly effective adaptations. Nasal hair traps larger particles. The copious flow of mucus and fluids that occurs in allergy and colds exerts a flushing action. In the respiratory tree (primarily the trachea and bronchi), a ciliated epithelium (called the ciliary escalator) conveys

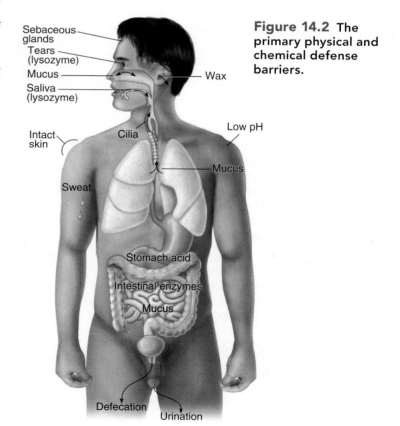

Figure 14.2 The primary physical and chemical defense barriers.

foreign particles entrapped in mucus toward the pharynx to be removed **(figure 14.3).** Irritation of the nasal passage reflexively initiates a sneeze, which expels a large volume of air at high velocity. Similarly, the acute sensitivity of the bronchi, trachea, and larynx to foreign matter triggers coughing, which ejects irritants.

The genitourinary tract derives partial protection via the continuous trickle of urine through the ureters and from periodic bladder emptying that flushes the urethra. Vaginal secretions provide cleansing of the lower reproductive tract in females.

The composition of resident microbiota and its protective effect were discussed in chapter 13. Even though the resident biota does not constitute an anatomical barrier, its presence can block the access of pathogens to epithelial surfaces and can create an unfavorable environment for pathogens by competing for limited nutrients or by altering the local pH.

A great deal of research in recent years has highlighted the importance of the gut microbiota on the development of nonspecific defenses (described in this chapter) as well as specific immunity. The presence of a robust commensal biota "trains" host defenses in such a way that commensals are kept in check and pathogens are eliminated. Evidence suggests that interruptions in this process, which may include frequent antibiotic treatments that affect the gut, can lead to immunologic disturbances in the gut. Some scientists believe that inflammatory bowel disease, which has been increasing in Western countries especially, may well be a result of our overzealous attempts to free our environment of microbes and to overtreat ourselves with antibiotics. The result, they say, is an "ill-trained" gut defense system that inappropriately responds to commensal biota.

Nonspecific Chemical Defenses

The skin and mucous membranes offer a variety of chemical defenses. Sebaceous secretions exert an antimicrobial effect, and specialized glands such as the meibomian glands of the eyelids lubricate the conjunctiva with an antimicrobial secretion. An additional defense in tears and saliva is **lysozyme,** an enzyme that hydrolyzes the peptidoglycan in the cell wall of bacteria. The high lactic acid and electrolyte concentrations of sweat and the skin's acidic pH and fatty acid content are also inhibitory to many microbes. Likewise, the hydrochloric acid in the stomach renders protection against many pathogens that are swallowed, and the intestine's digestive juices and bile are potentially destructive to microbes. Even semen contains an antimicrobial chemical that inhibits bacteria, and the vagina has a protective acidic pH maintained by normal biota.

Genetic Differences in Susceptibility

Some hosts are genetically immune to the diseases of other hosts. One explanation for this phenomenon is that some pathogens have such great specificity for one host species that they are incapable of infecting other species. For exam-

ple, humans can't acquire distemper from cats, and cats can't get mumps from humans. This specificity is particularly true of viruses, which can invade only by attaching to a specific host receptor. But it does not hold true for zoonotic infectious agents that attack a broad spectrum of animals. Genetic differences in susceptibility can also exist within members of one species, as described in chapter 13. Often these differences arise from mutations in the genes that code for components described in this chapter and the next, such as complement proteins, cytokines, and T-cell receptors.

The vital contribution of barriers is clearly demonstrated in people who have lost them or never had them. Patients with severe skin damage due to burns are extremely susceptible to infections; those with blockages in the salivary glands, tear ducts, intestine, and urinary tract are also at greater risk for infection. But as important as it is, the first line of defense alone is not sufficient to protect against infection. Because many pathogens find a way to circumvent the barriers by using their virulence factors (discussed in chapter 13), a whole new set of defenses—inflammation, phagocytosis, specific immune responses—are brought into play.

14.1 Learning Outcomes—Can You . . .

1. . . . summarize what the three lines of defense are?
2. . . . identify three components of the first line of defense?

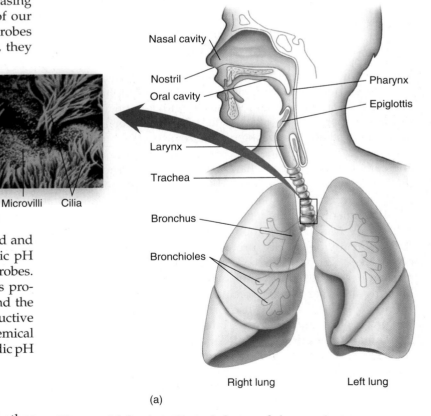

Figure 14.3 The ciliary defense of the respiratory tree. **(a)** The epithelial lining of the airways contains a brush border of cilia to entrap and propel particles upward toward the pharynx. **(b)** Tracheal mucosa (5,000×).

14.2 The Second and Third Lines of Defense: An Overview

Immunology encompasses the study of all features of the body's second and third lines of defense. Although this chapter is concerned, not surprisingly, with infectious microbial agents, be aware that immunology is central to the study of fields as diverse as cancer and allergy.

In the body, the mandate of the immune system can be easily stated. A healthy functioning immune system is responsible for

1. surveillance of the body,
2. recognition of foreign material, and
3. destruction of entities deemed to be foreign (**figure 14.4**).

Because infectious agents could potentially enter through any number of portals, the cells of the immune system constantly move about the body, searching for potential pathogens. This process is carried out primarily by white blood cells, which have been trained to recognize body cells (so-called **self**) and differentiate them from any foreign material in the body, such as an invading bacterial cell **(nonself)**. The ability to evaluate cells and macromolecules as either self or nonself is central to the functioning of the immune system.

While foreign substances must be recognized as a potential threat and dealt with appropriately, self cells and chemicals must not come under attack by the immune defenses.

The immune system evaluates cells by examining certain molecules on their surfaces called **markers**.[1] These markers, which generally consist of proteins and/or sugars, can be thought of as the cellular equivalent of facial characteristics in humans and allow the cells of the immune system to identify whether or not a newly discovered cell poses a threat. While cells deemed to be self are left alone, cells and other objects designated as foreign are marked for destruction by a number of methods, the most common of which is phagocytosis. There is a middle ground as well. Nonself proteins that are not harmful—such as those found in food we ingest and on commensal microorganisms—are generally recognized as such and the immune system is signalled not to react.

14.2 Learning Outcomes—Can You . . .

3. . . . define marker, and discuss its importance in the second and third lines of defense?

---

1. The term *marker* is also employed in genetics in a different sense—that is, to denote a detectable characteristic of a particular genetic mutant.

Contact with self cells

WBC — Normal self molecules

No reaction

Contact with a foreign cell

WBC — Pathogen recognition receptor (PRR) — PAMPs on microbe

Surveillance

Body compartments are screened by circulating WBCs.

Detection and recognition of foreign cell or virus

Destruction

Figure 14.4 Search, recognize, and destroy is the mandate of the immune system. White blood cells are equipped with a very sensitive sense of "touch." As they sort through the tissues, they feel surface markers that help them determine what is self and what is not. When self markers are recognized, no response occurs. However, when nonself is detected, a reaction to destroy it is mounted.

14.3 Systems Involved in Immune Defenses

Unlike many systems, the immune system does not exist in a single, well-defined site; rather, it encompasses a large, complex, and diffuse network of cells and fluids that permeate every organ and tissue. It is this very arrangement that promotes the surveillance and recognition processes that help screen the body for harmful substances.

The body is partitioned into several fluid-filled spaces called the intracellular, extracellular, lymphatic, cerebrospinal, and circulatory compartments. Although these compartments are physically separated, they have numerous connections. Their structure and position permit extensive interchange and communication. Among the body compartments that participate in immune function are

1. the **reticuloendothelial** (reh-tik″-yoo-loh-en″-doh-thee′-lee-al) **system (RES),**
2. the spaces surrounding tissue cells that contain **extracellular fluid (ECF),**
3. the **bloodstream,** and
4. the **lymphatic system.**

In the following section, we consider the anatomy of these main compartments and how they interact in the second and third lines of defense.

The Communicating Body Compartments

For effective immune responsiveness, the activities in one fluid compartment must be conveyed to other compartments. Let us see how this occurs by viewing tissue at the microscopic level **(figure 14.5).** At this level, clusters of tissue cells are in direct contact with the reticuloendothelial system (RES), which is described shortly, and the extracellular fluid (ECF). Other compartments (vessels) that penetrate at this level are blood and lymphatic capillaries. This close association allows cells and chemicals that originate in the RES and ECF to diffuse or migrate into the blood and lymphatics; any products of a lymphatic reaction can be transmitted directly into the blood through the connection between these two systems; and certain cells and chemicals originating in the blood can move through the vessel walls into the extracellular spaces and migrate into the lymphatic system.

The flow of events among these systems depends on where an infectious agent or foreign substance first intrudes. A typical progression might begin in the extracellular spaces and RES, move to the lymphatic circulation, and ultimately end up in the bloodstream. Regardless of which compartment is first exposed, an immune reaction in any one of them will eventually be communicated to the others at the microscopic level. An obvious benefit of such an integrated system is that no cell of the body is far removed from competent protection, no matter how isolated. Let us take a closer look at each of these compartments.

Immune Functions of the Reticuloendothelial System

The tissues of the body are permeated by a support network of connective tissue fibers, or a **reticulum,** that originates in the cellular basal lamina, interconnects nearby cells, and meshes with the massive connective tissue network surrounding all organs. This network, called the **reticuloendothelial system** (the **RES, figure 14.6**) is intrinsic to the immune function because it provides a passageway within and between tissues and organs. The RES consists of the thymus, where important white blood cells mature, and of the lymph nodes, tonsils, spleen, and lymphoid tissue in the mucosa of the gut and respiratory tract, where most of the RES "action" takes place. The lymphoid tissue in the gut is sometimes called GALT (gut-associated lymphoid tissue), and more generally lymphoid tissue associated with the mucosal surfaces anywhere is called MALT—mucosa-associated lymphoid tissue. The RES is heavily endowed with white blood cells called macrophages waiting to attack passing foreign intruders as they arrive in the skin, lungs, liver, lymph nodes, spleen, and bone marrow.

Dendritic cell
Lymphatic capillaries
Extracellular fluid
Tissue cell
Blood capillaries
Macrophage
Reticuloendothelium

Figure 14.5 Connections between the body compartments. The meeting of the major fluid compartments at the microscopic level.

Components and Functions of the Lymphatic System

The **lymphatic system** is a compartmentalized network of vessels, cells, and specialized accessory organs **(figure 14.7).** It begins in the farthest reaches of the tissues as

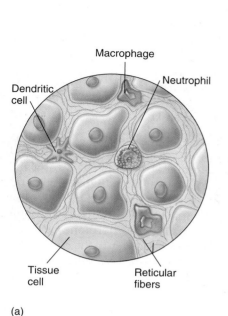

Macrophage

Dendritic cell

Neutrophil

Tissue cell

Reticular fibers

(a)

(b)

Figure 14.6 The reticuloendothelial system is a pervasive, continuous connective tissue framework throughout the body. **(a)** This system begins at the microscopic level with a fibrous support network (reticular fibers) enmeshing each cell. This web connects one cell to another within a tissue or organ and provides a niche for phagocytic white blood cells, which can crawl within and between tissues. **(b)** The degrees of shading in the body indicate variations in phagocyte concentration (darker = greater).

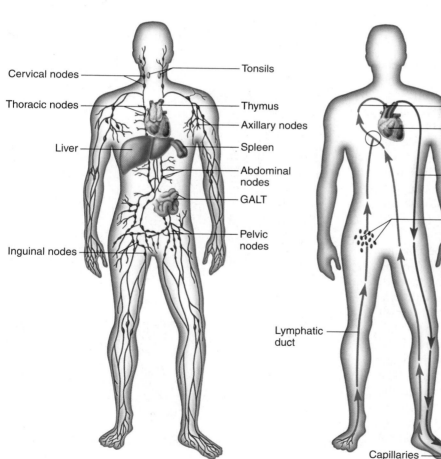

Cervical nodes

Thoracic nodes

Liver

Inguinal nodes

Tonsils

Thymus

Axillary nodes

Spleen

Abdominal nodes

GALT

Pelvic nodes

Vein

Heart

Artery

Lymph nodes

Lymphatic duct

Capillaries

Figure 14.7 General components of the lymphatic system.

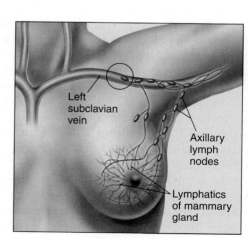

Left subclavian vein

Axillary lymph nodes

Lymphatics of mammary gland

(a) The lymphatic system consists of a branching network of vessels that extend into most body areas. Note the higher density of lymphatic vessels in the "dead-end" areas of the hands, feet, and breast, which are frequent contact points for infections. Other lymphatic organs include the lymph nodes, spleen, gut-associated lymphoid tissue (GALT), the thymus gland, and the tonsils.

(b) Comparison of the generalized circulation of the lymphatic system and the blood. Although the lymphatic vessels parallel the regular circulation, they transport in only one direction unlike the cyclic pattern of blood. Direct connection between the two circulations occurs at points near the heart where large lymph ducts empty their fluid into veins (circled area).

(c) Close-up to indicate a chain of lymph nodes near the axilla and breast and another point of contact between the two circulations (circled area).

tiny capillaries that transport a special fluid (lymph) through an increasingly larger tributary system of vessels and filters (lymph nodes), and it leads to major vessels that drain back into the regular circulatory system. Some major functions of the lymphatic system are

1. to provide an auxiliary route for the return of extracellular fluid to the circulatory system proper;
2. to act as a "drain-off" system for the inflammatory response; and
3. to render surveillance, recognition, and protection against foreign materials through a system of lymphocytes, phagocytes, and antibodies.

Lymphatic Fluid   Lymph is a plasmalike liquid carried by the lymphatic circulation. It is formed when certain blood components move out of the blood vessels into the extracellular spaces and diffuse or migrate into the lymphatic capillaries. Lymph is made up of water, dissolved salts, and 2% to 5% protein (especially antibodies and albumin). Like blood, it transports numerous white blood cells (especially lymphocytes) and miscellaneous materials such as fats, cellular debris, and infectious agents that have gained access to the tissue spaces.

Lymphatic Vessels   The system of vessels that transports lymph is constructed along the lines of blood vessels. As the lymph is never subjected to high pressure, the lymphatic vessels appear most similar to thin-walled veins rather than thicker-walled arteries. The tiniest vessels, lymphatic capillaries, accompany the blood capillaries and permeate all parts of the body except the central nervous system and certain organs such as bone, placenta, and thymus. Their thin walls are easily permeated by extracellular fluid that has escaped from the circulatory system. Lymphatic vessels are found in particularly high numbers in the hands, feet, and around the areola of the breast.

In the next section you will read about the bloodstream and blood vessels. Two overriding differences between the bloodstream and the lymphatic system should be mentioned. First, because one of the main functions of the lymphatic system is returning lymph to the circulation, the flow of lymph is in one direction only with lymph moving from the extremities toward the heart. Eventually, lymph will be returned to the bloodstream through the thoracic duct or the right lymphatic duct to the subclavian vein near the heart. The second difference concerns how lymph travels through the vessels of the lymphatic system. While blood is transported through the body by means of a dedicated pump (the heart), lymph is moved only through the contraction of the skeletal muscles through which the lymphatic ducts wend their way. This dependence on muscle movement helps to explain the swelling of the hands and feet that sometimes occurs during the night (when muscles are inactive) yet dissipates soon after waking.

Lymphoid Organs and Tissues   Other organs and tissues that perform lymphoid functions are the thymus, lymph nodes (glands), spleen, and clusters of tissues that appear in mucosal surfaces (MALT) A trait common to these organs is a loose connective tissue framework that houses aggregations of lymphocytes, the important class of white blood cells mentioned previously.

The Thymus: Site of T-Cell Maturation   The **thymus** originates in the embryo as two lobes in the pharyngeal region that fuse into a triangular structure. The size of the thymus is greatest proportionately at birth **(figure 14.8),** and it continues to exhibit high rates of activity and growth until puberty, after which it begins to shrink gradually through adulthood. Under the influence of thymic hormones, thymocytes develop specificity and are released into the circulation as mature T cells. The T cells subsequently migrate to and settle in other lymphoid organs (for example, the lymph nodes and spleen), where they occupy the specific sites described previously.

Children born without a thymus (DiGeorge syndrome, see chapter 16) or who have had their thymus surgically removed are severely immunodeficient and fail to thrive. Adults have developed enough mature T cells that removal

Thymus gland

Blood vessels

Cortex

Medulla

Figure 14.8 The thymus gland.   Immediately after birth, the thymus is a large organ that nearly fills the region over the midline of the upper thoracic region. In the adult, however, it is proportionately smaller (to compare, see figure 14.7a). Section shows the main anatomical regions of the thymus. Immature T cells enter through the cortex and migrate into the medulla as they mature.

of the thymus or reduction in its function has milder effects. Do not confuse the thymus with the thyroid gland, which is located nearby but has an entirely different function.

Lymph Nodes   Lymph nodes are small, encapsulated, bean-shaped organs stationed, usually in clusters, along lymphatic channels and large blood vessels of the thoracic and abdominal cavities (see figure 14.7). Major aggregations of nodes occur in the loose connective tissue of the armpit (axillary nodes), groin (inguinal nodes), and neck (cervical nodes). Both the location and architecture of these nodes clearly specialize them for filtering out materials that have entered the lymph and providing appropriate cells and niches for immune reactions.

Spleen   The spleen is a lymphoid organ in the upper left portion of the abdominal cavity. It is somewhat similar to a lymph node except that it serves as a filter for blood instead of lymph. While the spleen's primary function is to remove worn-out red blood cells from circulation, its most important immunologic function centers on the filtering of pathogens from the blood and their subsequent phagocytosis by resident macrophages. Although adults whose spleens have been surgically removed can live a relatively normal life, asplenic children are severely immunocompromised.

Miscellaneous Lymphoid Tissue   At many sites on or just beneath the mucosa of the gastrointestinal and respiratory tracts lie discrete bundles of lymphocytes. The positioning of this diffuse system provides an effective first-strike potential against the constant influx of microbes and other foreign materials in food and air. In the pharynx, a ring of tissues called the tonsils provides an active source of lymphocytes. The breasts of pregnant and lactating women also become temporary sites of antibody-producing lymphoid tissues. The intestinal tract houses the best-developed collection of lymphoid tissue, called **gut-associated lymphoid tissue,** or **GALT.** Examples of GALT include the appendix, the lacteals (special lymphatic vessels stationed in each intestinal villus), and **Peyer's patches,** compact aggregations of lymphocytes in the ileum of the small intestine. GALT provides immune functions against intestinal pathogens and is a significant source of some types of antibodies. Other, less well-organized collections of secondary lymphoid tissue include the mucosal-associated lymphoid tissue (MALT), skin-associated lymphoid tissue (SALT), and bronchial-associated lymphoid tissue (BALT).

Origin, Composition, and Functions of the Blood

The circulatory system consists of the circulatory system proper, which includes the heart, arteries, veins, and capillaries that circulate the blood, and the lymphatic system, which includes lymphatic vessels and lymphatic organs (lymph nodes) that circulate lymph. As you will see, these two circulations parallel, interconnect with, and complement one another.

The substance that courses through the arteries, veins, and capillaries is **whole blood,** a liquid consisting of **blood cells** (formed elements) suspended in **plasma.** One can visualize these two components with the naked eye when a tube of **unclotted** blood is allowed to sit or is spun in a centrifuge. The cells' density causes them to settle into an opaque layer at the bottom of the tube, leaving the plasma, a clear, yellowish fluid, on top **(figure 14.9).** In chapter 15, we introduce the concept of **serum.** This substance is essentially the same as plasma, except it is the clear fluid from clotted blood. Serum is often used in immune testing and therapy.

Fundamental Characteristics of Plasma   Plasma contains hundreds of different chemicals produced by the liver, white blood cells, endocrine glands, and nervous system and absorbed from the digestive tract. The main component of this fluid is water (92%), and the remainder consists of proteins such as albumin and globulins (including antibodies); other immunochemicals; fibrinogen and other clotting factors; hormones; nutrients (glucose, amino acids, fatty acids); ions (sodium, potassium, calcium, magnesium, chloride, phosphate, bicarbonate); dissolved gases (O_2 and CO_2); and waste products (urea). These substances support the normal physiological functions of nutrition, development, protection, homeostasis, and immunity. We return to the subject of plasma and its function in immune interactions later in this chapter and in chapter 15.

A Survey of Blood Cells   The production of blood cells, or **hematopoiesis** (hee"-mat-o-poy-ee'-sis), begins early in embryonic development in the yolk sac (an embryonic

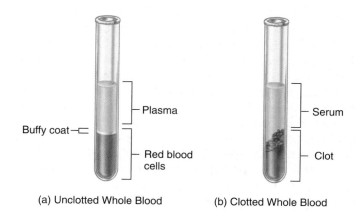

(a) Unclotted Whole Blood   (b) Clotted Whole Blood

Figure 14.9 The macroscopic composition of whole blood.   **(a)** When blood containing anticoagulants is allowed to sit for a period, it stratifies into a clear layer of plasma; a thin layer of off-white material called the buffy coat (which contains the white blood cells); and a layer of red blood cells in the bottom, thicker layer. **(b)** Serum is the clear fluid that separates from clotted blood.

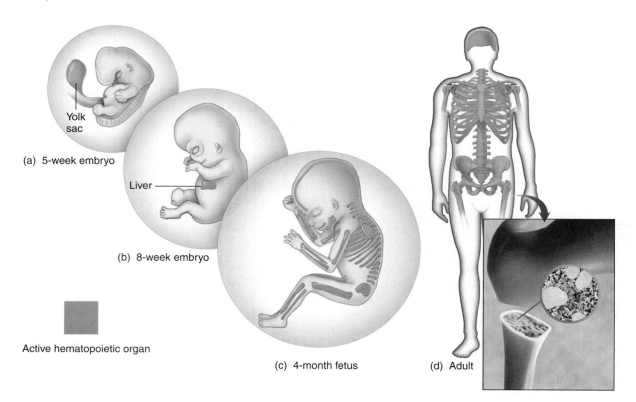

(a) 5-week embryo

Yolk sac

(b) 8-week embryo

Liver

Active hematopoietic organ

(c) 4-month fetus

(d) Adult

Figure 14.10 Stages in hematopoiesis. The sites of blood cell production change as development progresses from **(a, b)** yolk sac and liver in the embryo to **(c)** extensive bone marrow sites in the fetus and **(d)** selected bone marrow sites in the child and adult. **(Inset)** Red marrow occupies the spongy bone (circle) in these areas.

membrane). Later, it is taken over by the liver and lymphatic organs, and is finally assumed entirely and permanently by the red bone marrow **(figure 14.10).** Although much of a newborn's red marrow is devoted to hematopoietic function, the active marrow sites gradually recede, and by the age of 4 years, only the ribs, sternum, pelvic girdle, flat bones of the skull and spinal column, and proximal portions of the humerus and femur are devoted to blood cell production.

The relatively short life of blood cells demands a rapid turnover that is continuous throughout a human life span. The primary precursor of new blood cells is a pool of undifferentiated cells called pluripotential **stem cells**[2] maintained in the marrow. During development, these stem cells proliferate and **differentiate**—meaning that immature or unspecialized cells develop the specialized form and function of mature cells. The primary lines of cells that arise from this process produce red blood cells (RBCs, or erythrocytes), white blood cells (WBCs, or leukocytes), and platelets (thrombocytes). The white blood cell lines are programmed to develop into several secondary lines of cells during the final process of differentiation **(figure 14.11).** These committed lines of WBCs are largely responsible for immune function.

The **white blood cells,** or **leukocytes,** are traditionally evaluated by their reactions with hematologic stains that contain a mixture of dyes and can differentiate cells by color and morphology. When this stain used on blood smears is evaluated using the light microscope, the leukocytes appear either with or without noticeable colored granules in the cytoplasm and, on that basis, are divided into two groups: **granulocytes** and **agranulocytes.** Greater magnification reveals that even the agranulocytes have tiny granules in their cytoplasm, so some hematologists also use the appearance of the nucleus to distinguish them. Granulocytes have a lobed nucleus, and agranulocytes have an unlobed, rounded nucleus. Note both of these characteristics in circulating leukocytes shown in figure 14.11.

Granulocytes   The types of granular leukocytes present in the bloodstream are neutrophils, eosinophils, and basophils. All three are known for prominent cytoplasmic granules that stain with some combination of acidic dye (eosin) or basic dye (methylene blue). Although these granules are useful diagnostically, they also function in numerous physiological events. Refer to figure 14.11 to view the cell types described.

Neutrophils, also called polymorphonuclear neutrophils (PMNs), make up 55% to 90% of the circulating leukocytes—about 25 billion cells in the circulation at any given moment. The main work of the neutrophils is in production of toxic chemicals and in phagocytosis at the early stages of

---

2. Pluripotential stem cells can develop into several different types of blood cells; unipotential cells have already committed to a specific line of development.

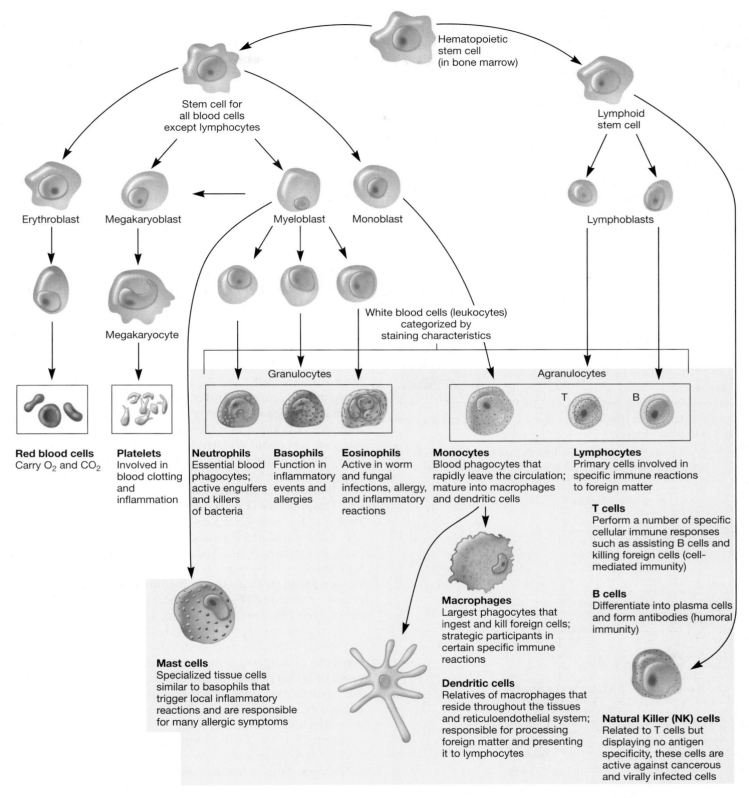

Figure 14.11 The development of blood cells and platelets. Undifferentiated stem cells in the red marrow differentiate to give rise to several different cell lines that become increasingly specialized until mature cells are released into circulation. Some cells migrate into the tissues to achieve fully functional status. The shaded areas indicate mature leukocytes (white blood cells).

a response. Their high numbers in both the blood and tissues suggest a constant challenge from resident microbiota and environmental sources. Most of the cytoplasmic granules carry digestive enzymes and other chemicals that degrade the phagocytosed materials (see the discussion of phagocytosis later in this chapter). The average neutrophil lives only about 8 days, spending much of this time in the tissues and only about 6 to 12 hours in circulation.

The role of the **eosinophil** (ee"-oh-sin'-oh-fil) in the immune system is complicated. Their granules contain peroxidase, lysozyme, and other digestive enzymes, as well as toxic proteins and inflammatory chemicals. The protective action of eosinophils is to attack and destroy large eukaryotic pathogens, but they are also involved in the formation of fetal tissue as well as in inflammation and allergic reactions. Among their most important targets are helminth worms and fungi. Eosinophils are among the earliest cells to accumulate

near sites of inflammation and allergic reactions, where they attract other leukocytes and release chemical mediators.

Basophils are the scarcest type of leukocyte, making up less than 0.5% of the total circulating WBCs in a normal individual. They share some morphological and functional similarities with widely distributed tissue cells called **mast cells.** Although these two cell types were once regarded as identical, mast cells are nonmotile elements bound to connective tissue around blood vessels, nerves, and epithelia, and basophils are motile elements derived from bone marrow.

Basophils parallel eosinophils in many of their actions, because they also contain granules with potent chemical mediators. Mast cells are first line defenders against the local invasion of pathogens, they recruit other inflammatory cells, and they are directly responsible for the release of histamine and other allergic stimulants during immediate allergies (see chapter 16).

Agranulocytes   Agranular leukocytes have globular, nonlobed nuclei and lack prominent cytoplasmic granules when viewed with the light microscope. The two general types are lymphocytes and monocytes.

Although lymphocytes are the cornerstone of the third line of defense, which is the subject of chapter 15, their origin and morphology are described here so their relationship to the other blood components is clear. **Lymphocytes** are the second most common WBC in the blood, comprising 20% to 35% of the total circulating leukocytes. The fact that their overall number throughout the body is among the highest of all cells indicates how important they are to immunity. One estimate suggests that about one-tenth of all adult body cells are lymphocytes, exceeded only by erythrocytes and fibroblasts. Lymphocytes exist as two functional types—the bursal-equivalent, or **B lymphocytes** (**B cells,** for short), and the thymus-derived, or **T lymphocytes** (**T cells,** for short). B cells were first demonstrated in and named for a special lymphatic gland of chickens called the **bursa of Fabricius,** the site for their maturation in birds. In humans, B cells mature in special bone marrow sites; humans do not have a bursa of Fabricius. T cells mature in the thymus gland in all birds and mammals. Both populations of cells are transported by the bloodstream and lymph and move about freely between lymphoid organs and connective tissue.

Lymphocytes are the key cells of the third line of defense—the specific immune response. When stimulated by foreign substances (antigens), lymphocytes are transformed into activated cells that neutralize and destroy that foreign substance. The contribution of B cells is mainly in **antibody-mediated immunity,** defined as protective molecules carried in the fluids of the body; for this reason, it used to be called "humoral immunity," as in "in the humors." When activated B cells divide, they form specialized **plasma cells,** which produce **antibodies,** large protein molecules that interlock with an antigen and participate in its destruction. Activated T cells engage in a spectrum of immune functions characterized as **cell-mediated immunity** in which T cells modulate immune functions and kill foreign cells. The action of both classes of lymphocytes accounts for the recognition and memory typical of immunity. Lymphocytes are so important to the defense of the body that most of chapter 15 is devoted to their reactions.

Case File 14   *Continuing the Case*

When screening refugees newly arrived in the United States, the Centers for Disease Control and Prevention recommends the use of the following flowchart. The first tests recommended are a CBC and an examination for ova and parasites (O & P) in the stool. Eosinophilia is defined as the presence of more than 400 eosinophils in 1 microliter of blood.

■ What does this chart advise health care providers to do once an eosinophilia-causing infection is treated?

*Eosinophilia—an absolute eosinophil count of >400 cells/pt
O & P—ova and parasite
CBC—complete blood count

Monocytes are generally the largest of all white blood cells and the third most common in the circulation (3% to 7%). Their cytoplasm holds many fine vacuoles containing digestive enzymes. Monocytes are discharged by the bone marrow into the bloodstream, where they live as phagocytes for a few days. Later they leave the circulation to undergo final differentiation into **macrophages (figure 14.12).** Unlike many other WBCs, the monocyte series is relatively long-lived and retains an ability to multiply. Macrophages are among the most versatile and important of cells. In general, they are responsible for

1. many types of specific and nonspecific phagocytic and killing functions (they assume the job of cellular house-keepers, "mopping up the messes" created by infection and inflammation);
2. processing foreign molecules and presenting them to lymphocytes; and
3. secreting biologically active compounds that assist, mediate, attract, and inhibit immune cells and reactions.

We touch upon these functions in several ensuing sections.

Another product of the monocyte cell line is **dendritic cells,** named for their long, thin cell processes. Immature dendritic cells move from the blood to the RES and lymphatic tissues, where they trap pathogens. Ingestion of bacteria and viruses stimulates dendritic cells to migrate to lymph nodes and the spleen. Here, they mature into highly effective processors and presenters of foreign proteins (see chapter 15).

Erythrocyte and Platelet Lines These elements stay in the circulatory system proper. Their development is also shown in figure 14.11.

Erythrocytes develop from stem cells in the bone marrow and lose their nucleus just prior to entering the circulation. The resultant red blood cells are simple, biconcave sacs of hemoglobin that transport oxygen and carbon dioxide to and from the tissues. These are the most numerous of circulating blood cells, appearing in stains as small pink circles. Red blood cells do not ordinarily have immune functions, though they can be the target of immune reactions (see chapter 16).

Platelets are formed elements in circulating blood that are *not* whole cells. In stains, platelets are blue-gray with fine red granules and are readily distinguished from cells by their small size. Platelets function primarily in hemostasis (plugging broken blood vessels to stop bleeding) and in releasing chemicals that act in blood clotting and inflammation.

14.3 Learning Outcomes—Can You ...

4. ... name four body compartments that participate in immunity?
5. ... list the components of the reticuloendothelial system?
6. ... fully describe the structure and function of the lymphatic system?
7. ... differentiate between whole blood and plasma?
8. ... name six kinds of blood cells that function in nonspecific immunity, and the most important function of each?
9. ... name two kinds of lymphocytes involved in specific immunity?

Alveolar macrophage   Lung alveolus cell

(a)

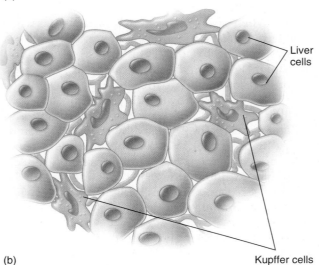
Liver cells

(b)   Kupffer cells

Langerhans dendritic cells

Epidermis

Dermis

(c)

Figure 14.12 Sites containing macrophages. **(a)** Scanning electron micrograph view of a lung with an alveolar macrophage. **(b)** Liver tissue with Kupffer cells. **(c)** Langerhans cells deep in the epidermis.

14.4 The Second Line of Defense

Now that we have introduced the principal anatomical and physiological framework of the immune system, we address some mechanisms that play important roles in host defenses: (1) inflammation, (2) phagocytosis, (3) fever, and (4) antimicrobial proteins. Because of the generalized nature of these defenses, they are primarily nonspecific in their effects, but they also support and interact with the specific immune responses described in chapter 15.

The Inflammatory Response: A Complex Concert of Reactions to Injury

At its most general level, the inflammatory response is a reaction to any traumatic event in the tissues. It is so commonplace that all of us manifest inflammation in some way every day. It appears in the nasty flare of a cat scratch, the blistering of a burn, the painful lesion of an infection, and the symptoms of allergy. When close to our external surfaces, it is readily identifiable by a classic series of signs and symptoms characterized succinctly by four Latin terms: **rubor, calor, tumor,** and **dolor.** Rubor (redness) is caused by increased circulation and vasodilation in the injured tissues; calor (warmth) is the heat given off by the increased flow of blood; tumor (swelling) is caused by increased fluid escaping into the tissues; and dolor (pain) is caused by the stimulation of nerve endings **(figure 14.13).** A fifth symptom, loss of function, has been added to give a complete picture of the effects of inflammation. Although these manifestations can be unpleasant, they serve an important warning that injury has taken place and set in motion responses that save the body from further injury.

It is becoming increasingly clear that some chronic diseases, such as cardiovascular disease, can be caused by chronic inflammation. While we speak of inflammation at a local site (such as a finger), inflammation can affect an entire system—such as blood vessels, lungs, skin, the joints, etc. Some researchers believe that the very act of aging is a consequence of increasing inflammation in multiple body systems.

Factors that can elicit inflammation include trauma from infection (the primary emphasis here), tissue injury or necrosis due to physical or chemical agents, and specific immune reactions. Although the details of inflammation are very complex, its chief functions can be summarized as follows:

1. to mobilize and attract immune components to the site of the injury,
2. to set in motion mechanisms to repair tissue damage and localize and clear away harmful substances, and
3. to destroy microbes and block their further invasion **(figure 14.14).**

The inflammatory response is a powerful defensive reaction, a means for the body to maintain stability and restore itself after an injury. But when it is chronic, it has the potential to actually *cause* tissue injury, destruction, and disease **(Insight 14.1).**

The Stages of Inflammation

The process leading to inflammation is a dynamic, predictable sequence of events that can be acute, lasting from a few minutes or hours, to chronic, lasting for days, weeks, or years. Once the initial injury has occurred, a chain reaction takes place at the site of damaged tissue, summoning beneficial cells and fluids into the injured area. As an example, we will look at an injury at the microscopic level and observe the flow of major events (see figure 14.14).

Vascular Changes: Early Inflammatory Events

Following an injury, some of the earliest changes occur in the vasculature (arterioles, capillaries, venules) in the vicinity of the damaged tissue. These changes are controlled by nervous stimulation, **chemical mediators,** and **cytokines** released by blood cells, tissue cells, and platelets in the injured area. Some mediators are **vasoactive**—that is, they affect the endothelial cells and smooth muscle cells of blood vessels, and others are **chemotactic factors,** also called **chemokines,** that affect white blood cells. Inflammatory mediators cause fever, stimulate lymphocytes, prevent virus spread, and cause allergic symptoms **(Insight 14.2).** Although the constriction of arterioles is stimulated first, it lasts for only a few seconds or minutes and is followed in quick succession by the opposite reaction, vasodilation. The overall effect of vasodilation is to increase the flow of blood into the area, which facilitates the influx of immune components and also causes redness and warmth.

Edema: Leakage of Vascular Fluid into Tissues

Some vasoactive substances cause the endothelial cells in the walls of postcapillary venules to contract and form gaps through which blood-borne components exude into the extracellular spaces. The fluid part that escapes is called the **exudate.** Accumulation of this fluid in the tissues gives rise to local swelling and hardness called **edema.** The edematous exudate contains varying amounts of plasma

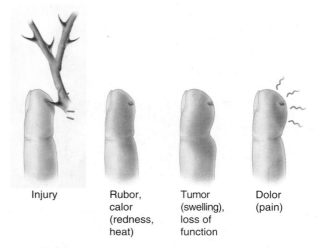

| Injury | Rubor, calor (redness, heat) | Tumor (swelling), loss of function | Dolor (pain) |

Figure 14.13 The response to injury. This classic checklist encapsulates the reactions of the tissues to an assault. Each of the events is an indicator of one of the mechanisms of inflammation described in this chapter.

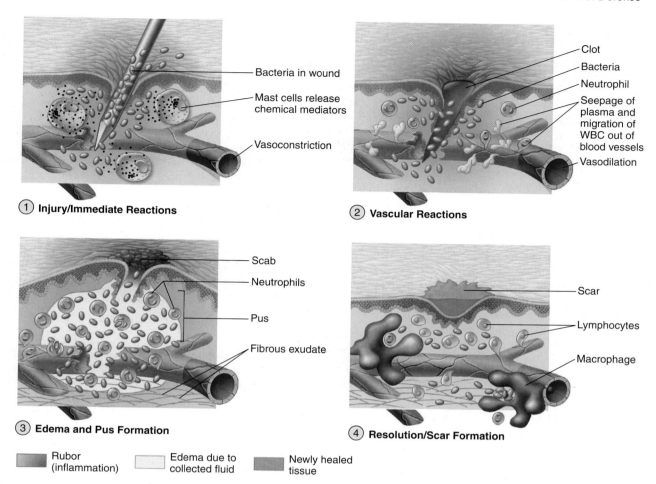

1 **Injury/Immediate Reactions**

- Bacteria in wound
- Mast cells release chemical mediators
- Vasoconstriction

2 **Vascular Reactions**

- Clot
- Bacteria
- Neutrophil
- Seepage of plasma and migration of WBC out of blood vessels
- Vasodilation

3 **Edema and Pus Formation**

- Scab
- Neutrophils
- Pus
- Fibrous exudate

4 **Resolution/Scar Formation**

- Scar
- Lymphocytes
- Macrophage

Rubor (inflammation) Edema due to collected fluid Newly healed tissue

Process Figure 14.14 The major events in inflammation. ① Injury → Reflex narrowing of the blood vessels (vasoconstriction) lasting for a short time → Release of chemical mediators into area. ② Increased diameter of blood vessels (vasodilation) → Increased blood flow → Increased vascular permeability → Leakage of fluid (plasma) from blood vessels into tissues (exudate formation). ③ Edema → Infiltration of site by neutrophils and accumulation of pus. ④ Macrophages and lymphocytes → Repair, either by complete resolution and return of tissue to normal state or by formation of scar tissue.

INSIGHT 14.1 When Inflammation Gets Out of Hand

Not every aspect of inflammation is protective or results in the proficient resolution of tissue damage. As one looks over a list of diseases, it is rather striking how many of them are due in part or even completely to an overreactive or dysfunctional inflammatory response.

Some -itis reactions mentioned in chapter 13 are a case in point. Inflammatory exudates that build up in the brain in African trypanosomiasis, cryptococcosis, and other brain infections can be so injurious to the nervous system that impairment is permanent. Frequently, an inflammatory reaction that walls off the pathogen leads to an abscess, a swollen mass of neutrophils and dead, liquefied tissue that can harbor live pathogens in the center. Abscesses are a prominent feature of staphylococcal, amoebic, and enteric infections.

Other pathologic manifestations of chronic diseases—for example, the tubercles of tuberculosis, the lesions of late syphilis, the disfiguring nodules of leprosy, and the cutaneous ulcers of leishmaniasis—are due to an aberrant tissue response called **granuloma formation.** Granulomas develop not only in response to microbes but also in response to inanimate foreign bodies (sutures and mineral grains that are difficult to break down). This condition is initiated when neutrophils ineffectively and incompletely phagocytose the pathogens or materials involved in an inflammatory reaction. The macrophages then enter to clean up and attempt to phagocytose the dead neutrophils and foreign substances, but they fail to completely manage them. They respond by storing these ingested materials in vacuoles and becoming inactive. Over a given time period, large numbers of adjacent macrophages fuse into giant, inactive multinucleate cells called foreign body giant cells. These sites are further infiltrated with lymphocytes. The resultant collections make the tissue appear granular—hence, the name. A granuloma can exist in the tissue for months, years, or even a lifetime.

Medical science is rapidly searching for new applications for the massive amount of new information on inflammatory mediators. One highly promising area appears to be the use of chemokine inhibitors that could reduce chemotaxis and the massive, destructive influx of leukocytes. Such therapy could ultimately be used for certain cancers, hardening of arteries, and Alzheimer's disease.

INSIGHT 14.2   The Dynamics of Inflammatory Mediators

Hundreds of small, active molecules are constantly being secreted to regulate, stimulate, suppress, and otherwise control the many aspects of cell development, inflammation, and immunity. These substances are the products of several types of cells, including monocytes, macrophages, lymphocytes, fibroblasts, mast cells, platelets, and endothelial cells of blood vessels. Their effects may be local or systemic, short term or long-lasting, nonspecific or specific, protective or pathologic.

In recent times, the field of cytokines has become so increasingly complex that we can include here only an overview of the major groups of important cytokines and other mediators. The major functional types can be categorized into

1. cytokines that mediate nonspecific immune reactions such as inflammation and phagocytosis,
2. cytokines that regulate the growth and activation of lymphocytes,
3. cytokines that activate immune reactions during inflammation,
4. hematopoiesis factors for white blood cells,
5. vasoactive mediators, and
6. miscellaneous inflammatory mediators.

Nonspecific Mediators of Inflammation and Immunity

- **Tumor necrosis factor (TNF),** a substance from macrophages, lymphocytes, and other cells that increases chemotaxis and phagocytosis and stimulates other cells to secrete inflammatory cytokines. It also serves as an endogenous pyrogen that induces fever, increases blood coagulation, suppresses bone marrow, and suppresses appetite.
- **Interferon (IFN),** produced by leukocytes, fibroblasts, and other cells, inhibits virus replication and cell division and increases the action of certain lymphocytes that kill other cells.
- **Interleukin* (IL) 1,** a product of macrophages and dendritic cells that has many of the same biological activities as TNF, such as inducing fever and activation of certain white blood cells.
- **Interleukin-6,** secreted by macrophages and T cells. Its primary effects are to stimulate the growth of B cells and to increase the synthesis of liver proteins.
- **Various chemokines.** By definition, chemokines are cytokines that stimulate the movement and migration of white blood cells (chemotactic factors).

Cytokines That Regulate Lymphocyte Growth and Activation

- **Interleukin-2,** the primary growth factor from T cells. Interestingly, it acts on the same cells that secrete it. It stimulates mitosis and secretion of other cytokines. In B cells, it is a growth factor and stimulus for antibody synthesis.
- **Interleukin-4,** a stimulus for the production of allergy antibodies; inhibits macrophage actions; favors development of T cells.
- **Granulocyte colony-stimulating factor (G-CSF),** produced by T cells, macrophages, and neutrophils. It stimulates the activation and differentiation of neutrophils.
- **Macrophage colony-stimulating factor (M-CSF),** produced by a variety of cells. M-CSF promotes the growth and development of macrophages from undifferentiated precursor cells.

Cytokines That Activate Specific Immune Reactions

- **Interferon gamma,** a T-cell-derived mediator whose primary function is to activate macrophages. It also promotes the differentiation of T and B cells, activates neutrophils, and stimulates diapedesis.
- **Interleukin-5** activates eosinophils and B cells; **interleukin-10** inhibits macrophages and stimulates B cells; and **interleukin-12** activates T cells and killer cells.

Vasoactive Mediators

- **Histamine,** a vasoactive mediator produced by mast cells and basophils that causes vasodilation, increased vascular permeability, and mucus production. It functions primarily in inflammation and allergy.
- **Serotonin,** a mediator produced by platelets and intestinal cells that causes smooth muscle contraction, inhibits gastric secretion, and acts as a neurotransmitter.
- **Bradykinin,** a vasoactive amine from the blood or tissues that stimulates smooth muscle contraction and increases vascular permeability, mucus production, and pain. It is particularly active in allergic reactions.

Miscellaneous Inflammatory Mediators

- **Prostaglandins,** produced by most body cells; complex chemical mediators that can have opposing effects (for example, dilation or constriction of blood vessels) and are powerful stimulants of inflammation and pain.
- **Leukotrienes** stimulate the contraction of smooth muscle and enhance vascular permeability. They are implicated in the more severe manifestations of immediate allergies (constriction of airways).
- **Platelet-activating factor,** a substance released from basophils, causes the aggregation of platelets and the release of other chemical mediators during immediate allergic reactions.

*_Interleukin_ is a term that refers to a group of small peptides originally isolated from leukocytes. There are currently more than 30 named interleukins. We now know that other cells besides leukocytes can synthesize them and that they have a variety of biological activities. Functions of some selected examples are presented in chapter 15.

proteins, such as globulins, albumin, the clotting protein fibrinogen, blood cells, and cellular debris. Depending on its content, the exudate may be clear (called **serous**), or it may contain red blood cells or pus. Pus is composed mainly of white blood cells and the debris generated by phagocytosis. In some types of edema, the fibrinogen is converted to fibrin threads that enmesh the injury site. Within an hour, multitudes of neutrophils responding chemotactically to special signaling molecules converge on the injured site (see figure 14.14, step 3).

Unique Dynamic Characteristics of White Blood Cells

In order for WBCs to leave the blood vessels and enter the tissues, they adhere to the inner walls of the smaller blood vessels. From this position, they are poised to migrate out of the blood into the tissue spaces by a process called **diapedesis** (dye"-ah-puh-dee'-sis).

Diapedesis, also known as transmigration, is aided by several related characteristics of WBCs. For example, they are actively motile and readily change shape. This phenomenon is also assisted by the nature of the endothelial cells lining the venules. They contain complex adhesive receptors that capture the WBCs and participate in their transport from the venules into the extracellular spaces (**figure 14.15**).

Another factor in the migratory habits of these WBCs is **chemotaxis**, defined as the tendency of cells to migrate in response to a specific chemical stimulus given off at a site of injury or infection (see inflammation and phagocytosis later in this chapter). Through this means, cells swarm from many compartments to the site of infection and remain there to perform general and specific immune functions. These basic properties are absolutely essential for the sort of intercommunication and deployment of cells required for most immune reactions (see figure 14.15).

The Benefits of Edema and Chemotaxis Both the formation of edematous exudate and the infiltration of neutrophils are physiologically beneficial activities. The influx of fluid dilutes toxic substances, and the fibrin clot can effectively trap microbes and prevent their further spread. The neutrophils that aggregate in the inflamed site are immediately involved in phagocytosing and destroying bacteria, dead tissues, and particulate matter (by mechanisms discussed in a later section on phagocytosis). In some types of inflammation, accumulated phagocytes contribute to **pus**, a whitish mass of cells, liquefied cellular debris, and bacteria. Certain bacteria (streptococci, staphylococci, gonococci, and meningococci) are especially powerful attractants for neutrophils and are thus termed **pyogenic**, or pus-forming, bacteria.

Late Reactions of Inflammation Sometimes a mild inflammation can be resolved by edema and phagocytosis. Inflammatory reactions that are more long-lived attract a collection of monocytes, lymphocytes, and macrophages to the reaction site. Clearance of pus, cellular debris, dead neutrophils, and damaged tissue is performed by macrophages, the only cells

(a)

(b)

Figure 14.15 Diapedesis and chemotaxis of leukocytes. **(a)** View of a venule depicts white blood cells squeezing themselves between spaces in the blood vessel wall via diapedesis. This process, shown in cross section, indicates how the pool of leukocytes adheres to the endothelial wall. From this site, they are poised to migrate out of the vessel into the tissue space. **(b)** This photograph captures neutrophils in the process of diapedesis.

that can engulf and dispose of such large masses. At the same time, B lymphocytes react with foreign molecules and cells by producing specific antimicrobial proteins (antibodies), and T lymphocytes kill intruders directly. Late in the process, the tissue is completely repaired, if possible, or replaced by connective tissue in the form of a scar (see figure 14.14, step 4). If the inflammation cannot be relieved or resolved in this way, it can become chronic and create a long-term pathologic condition.

Phagocytosis: Cornerstone of Inflammation and Specific Immunity

By any standard, a phagocyte represents an impressive piece of living machinery, meandering through the tissues to seek, capture, and destroy a target. The general activities of phagocytes are

1. to survey the tissue compartments and discover microbes, particulate matter (dust, carbon particles, antigen-antibody complexes), and injured or dead cells;
2. to ingest and eliminate these materials; and
3. to extract immunogenic information (antigens) from foreign matter.

It is generally accepted that all cells have some capacity to engulf materials, but **professional phagocytes** do it for a living. The three main types of phagocytes are neutrophils, monocytes, and macrophages.

Neutrophils and Eosinophils

As previously stated, neutrophils are general-purpose phagocytes that react early in the inflammatory response to bacteria and other foreign materials and to damaged tissue. A common sign of bacterial infection is a high neutrophil count in the blood (neutrophilia), and neutrophils are also a primary component of pus. Eosinophils are attracted to sites of parasitic infections and antigen-antibody reactions, though they play only a minor phagocytic role.

Monocytes and Macrophages: Kings of the Phagocytes

After emigrating out of the bloodstream into the tissues, monocytes are transformed by various inflammatory mediators into macrophages. This process is marked by an increase in size and by enhanced development of lysosomes and other organelles **(figure 14.16).** At one time, macrophages were classified as either fixed (adherent to tissue) or wandering, but this terminology can be misleading. All macrophages retain the capacity to move about. Whether they reside in a specific organ or wander depends upon their stage of development and the immune stimuli they receive. Specialized macrophages called **histiocytes** migrate to a certain tissue and remain there during their life span. Examples are alveolar (lung) macrophages; the Kupffer cells in the liver; dendritic cells in the skin (see figure 14.12); and

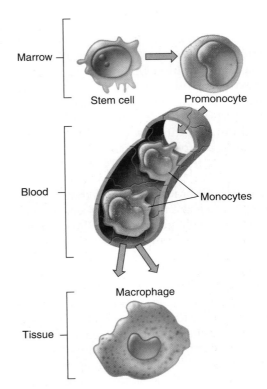

Figure 14.16 The developmental stages of monocytes and macrophages. The cells progress through maturational stages in the bone marrow and peripheral blood. Once in the tissues, a macrophage can remain nomadic or take up residence in a specific organ.

macrophages in the spleen, lymph nodes, bone marrow, kidney, bone, and brain. Other macrophages do not reside permanently in a particular tissue and drift nomadically throughout the RES. Not only are macrophages dynamic scavengers, but they also process foreign substances and prepare them for reactions with B and T lymphocytes (see chapter 15).

Mechanisms of Phagocytic Recognition, Engulfment, and Killing

The term **phagocyte** literally means "eating cell." But phagocytosis (the name for what a phagocytes do) is more than just the physical process of engulfment, because phagocytes also actively attack and dismantle foreign cells with a wide array of antimicrobial substances. Phagocytosis can occur as an isolated event performed by a lone phagocytic cell responding to a minor irritant in its area or as part of the orchestrated events of inflammation described in the previous section. The events in phagocytosis include chemotaxis, ingestion, phagolysosome formation, destruction, and excretion **(figure 14.17).**

Chemotaxis and Ingestion Phagocytes migrate into a region of inflammation with a deliberate sense of direction, attracted by a gradient of stimulant products from the parasite and host tissue at the site of injury. Phagocytes and

Process Figure 14.17 The phases of phagocytosis. ① Phagocyte is attracted to bacteria. ② Close-up view of process showing bacteria adhering to phagocyte PRRs by their PAMPs. ③ Vacuole is formed around bacteria during engulfment. ④ Phagosome digestive vacuole results. ⑤ Lysosomes fuse with phagosome, forming a phagolysosome. ⑥ Enzymes and toxic oxygen products kill and digest bacteria. ⑦ Undigested particles are released. Inset: Scanning electron micrograph of a macrophage actively engaged in devouring bacteria (10,000×).

other defensive cells are now known to be able to recognize some microorganisms as foreign because of signal molecules that the microbes have on their surfaces. These are called **pathogen-associated molecular patterns,** or **PAMPs.** They are molecules shared by many microorganisms, but not present in mammals, and therefore serve as "red flags" for phagocytes and other cells of innate immunity.

Bacterial PAMPs include peptidoglycan and lipopolysaccharide. Double-stranded RNA, which is found only in some viruses, is also a PAMP. On the host side, phagocytes, dendritic cells, endothelial cells, and even lymphocytes possess molecules on their surfaces, called **pattern recognition receptors (PRRs),** that recognize and bind PAMPs. The cells possess these PRRs all the time, whether or not they have encountered PAMPs before. This is different than the situation with specific immunity. One category of PRRs is the **toll-like receptors (figure 14.18)** (called "toll-like" because similar proteins called "toll" were originally discovered in fruit flies). The receptors not only recognize PAMPs, but upon binding, set in motion a cascade of events inside the host cell that amplifies and orchestrates the defensive response, including initiating the specific immune response. (There are a lot of acronyms in immunology and especially in this last paragraph. Don't let them get away from you; keep up with them. If you know what all the acronyms stand for and what they do, you are a good deal of the way there in understanding host defenses!)

On the scene of an inflammatory reaction, phagocytes often trap cells or debris against the fibrous network of connective tissue or the wall of blood and lymphatic vessels. Once the phagocyte has made contact with its prey, it extends pseudopods that enclose the cells or particles in a pocket and internalize them in a vacuole called a **phagosome.** It also secretes more cytokines to further amplify the innate response.

Phagolysosome Formation and Killing   In a short time, **lysosomes** migrate to the scene of the phagosome and fuse with it to form a **phagolysosome.** Other granules containing antimicrobial chemicals are released into the phagolysosome, forming a potent brew designed to poison and then dismantle the ingested material. The destructiveness of phagocytosis is evident by the death of bacteria within 30 minutes after contacting this battery of antimicrobial substances.

Destruction and Elimination Systems   Two separate systems of destructive chemicals await the microbes in the phagolysosome. The oxygen-dependent system (known

as the respiratory burst, or oxidative burst) involves several substances that were described in chapters 7 and 11. Myeloperoxidase, an enzyme found in granulocytes, forms halogen ions (OCl^-) that are strong oxidizing agents. Other products of oxygen metabolism such as hydrogen peroxide, the superoxide anion (O_2^-), activated or so-called singlet oxygen ($^{\bullet}O_2$), and the hydroxyl free radical ($OH^{\bullet}$) separately and together have formidable killing power. Other mechanisms that come into play are the liberation of lactic acid, lysozyme, and **nitric oxide** (NO), a powerful mediator that kills bacteria and inhibits viral replication. Cationic proteins that injure bacterial cell membranes and a number of proteolytic and other hydrolytic enzymes complete the job. The small bits of undigestible debris are released from the macrophage by exocytosis.

Fever: An Adjunct to Inflammation

An important systemic component of inflammation—and innate immunity in general—is fever, defined as an abnormally elevated body temperature. Although fever is a nearly universal symptom of infection, it is also associated with certain allergies, cancers, and other organic illnesses. Fevers whose causes are unknown are called fevers of unknown origin, or FUO.

The body temperature is normally maintained by a control center in the hypothalamus region of the brain. This thermostat regulates the body's heat production and heat loss and sets the core temperature at around 37°C (98.6°F) with slight fluctuations (1°F) during a daily cycle. Fever is initiated when circulating substances called pyrogens (py'-rohjenz) reset the hypothalamic thermostat to a higher setting. This change signals the musculature to increase heat production and peripheral arterioles to decrease heat loss through vasoconstriction **(Insight 14.3).** Fevers range in severity from low-grade (37.7°C to 38.3°C, or 100°F to 101°F) to moderate (38.8°C to 39.4°C, or 102°F to 103°F) to high (40.0°C to 41.1°C, or 104°F to 106°F). Pyrogens are described as **exogenous** (coming from outside the body) or **endogenous** (originating internally). Exogenous pyrogens are products of infectious agents such as viruses, bacteria, protozoans, and fungi. One well-characterized exogenous pyrogen is endotoxin, the lipopolysaccharide found in the cell walls of gram-negative bacteria. Blood, blood products, vaccines, or injectable solutions can also contain exogenous pyrogens. Endogenous pyrogens are liberated by monocytes, neutrophils, and macrophages during the process of phagocytosis and appear to be a natural part of the immune response. Two potent pyrogens released by macrophages are interleukin-1 (IL-1) and tumor necrosis factor (TNF).

Benefits of Fever   The association of fever with infection strongly suggests that it serves a beneficial role, a view still being debated but gaining acceptance. Aside from its practical and medical importance as a sign of a physiologi-

Figure 14.18 Phagocyte detection and signaling with pattern recognition receptors.   The example here shows the actions of a toll-like receptor that spans the membrane of many cells of the immune system. When a molecule specific to a particular class of pathogen is recognized by a receptor, the toll-like receptors merge and bind the foreign molecule. This induces production of chemicals that stimulate an immune response.

INSIGHT 14.3   Some Facts About Fever

Fever is such a prevalent reaction that it is a prominent symptom of hundreds of diseases. For thousands of years, people believed fever was part of an innate protective response. Hippocrates offered the idea that it was the body's attempt to burn off a noxious agent. Sir Thomas Sydenham wrote in the 17th century: "Why, fever itself is Nature's instrument!" So widely held was the view that fever could be therapeutic that pyretotherapy (treating disease by inducing an intermittent fever) was once used to treat syphilis, gonorrhea, leishmaniasis (a protozoan infection), and cancer. This attitude fell out of favor when drugs for relieving fever (aspirin) first came into use in the early 1900s, and an adverse view of fever began to dominate.

Changing Views of Fever

In recent times, the medical community has returned to the original concept of fever as more healthful than harmful. Experiments with vertebrates indicate that fever is a universal reaction, even in cold-blooded animals such as lizards and fish. A study with febrile (feverish) mice and frogs indicated that fever increases the rate of antibody synthesis. Work with tissue cultures showed that increased temperatures stimulate the activities of T cells and increase the effectiveness of interferon. Artificially infected rabbits and pigs allowed to remain febrile survive at a higher rate than those given suppressant drugs. Fever appears to enhance phagocytosis of staphylococci by neutrophils in guinea pigs and humans. In recent years, malaria-induced fevers have been experimentally studied as a way to treat HIV infection.

Hot and Cold: Why Do Chills Accompany Fever?

Fever almost never occurs as a single response; it is usually accompanied by chills. What causes this oddity—that a person flushed with fever periodically feels cold and trembles uncontrollably? The explanation lies in the natural physiological interaction between the thermostat in the hypothalamus and the temperature of the blood. For example, if the thermostat has been set (by pyrogen) at 102°F but the blood temperature is 99°F, the muscles are stimulated to contract involuntarily (shivering) as a means of producing heat. In addition, the vessels in the skin constrict, creating a sensation of cold, and the piloerector muscles in the skin cause "goose bumps" to form.

---

cal disruption, increased body temperature has additional benefits:

- Fever inhibits multiplication of temperature-sensitive microorganisms such as the poliovirus, cold viruses, herpes zoster virus, systemic and subcutaneous fungal pathogens, *Mycobacterium* species, and the syphilis spirochete.
- Fever impedes the nutrition of bacteria by reducing the availability of iron. It has been demonstrated that during fever, the macrophages stop releasing their iron stores, which could retard several enzymatic reactions needed for bacterial growth.
- Fever increases metabolism and stimulates immune reactions and naturally protective physiological processes. It speeds up hematopoiesis, phagocytosis, and specific immune reactions.

Treatment of Fever   With this revised perspective on fever, whether to suppress it or not can be a difficult decision. Some advocates feel that a slight to moderate fever in an otherwise healthy person should be allowed to run its course, in light of its potential benefits and minimal side effects. All medical experts do agree that high and prolonged fevers or fevers in patients with cardiovascular disease, seizures, or respiratory ailments are risky and must be treated immediately with fever-reducing drugs. The classic therapy for fever is an antipyretic drug such as aspirin or acetaminophen (Tylenol) that lowers the setting of the hypothalamic center and restores normal temperature. Any physical technique that increases heat loss (tepid baths, for example) can also help reduce the core temperature.

Antimicrobial Proteins: (1) Interferon

Interferon (IFN) was described in chapter 12 as a small protein produced naturally by certain white blood and tissue cells that is used in therapy against certain viral infections and cancer. Although the interferon system was originally thought to be directed exclusively against viruses, it is now known to be involved also in defenses against other microbes and in immune regulation and intercommunication. Three major types are **interferons alpha** and **beta,** products of many cells, including lymphocytes, fibroblasts, and macrophages; and **interferon gamma,** a product of T cells.

All three classes of interferon are produced in response to viruses, RNA, immune products, and various antigens. Their biological activities are extensive. In all cases, they bind to cell surfaces and induce changes in genetic expression, but the exact results vary. In addition to antiviral effects discussed in the next section, all three IFNs can inhibit the expression of cancer genes and have tumor suppressor effects. IFN alpha and beta stimulate phagocytes, and IFN gamma is an immune regulator of macrophages and T and B cells.

Characteristics of Antiviral Interferon

When a virus binds to the receptors on a host cell, a signal is sent to the nucleus that directs the cell to synthesize interferon. After transcribing and translating the interferon gene, newly synthesized interferon molecules are rapidly secreted by the cell into the extracellular space, where they bind to other host cells. The binding of interferon to a second cell induces the production of proteins in that cell that inhibit viral multiplication either by degrading the viral RNA or by preventing the translation of viral proteins **(figure 14.19).** Interferon is not virus-specific, so its synthesis in response to one type of virus will also protect against other types. Because this protein is an inhibitor of viruses, it has been a valuable treatment for a number of virus infections.

Other Roles of Interferon

Interferons are also important immune regulatory cytokines that activate or instruct the development of white blood cells. For example, interferon alpha produced by T lymphocytes activates a subset of cells called natural killer (NK) cells. In addition, one type of interferon beta plays a role in the maturation of B and T lymphocytes and in inflammation. Interferon gamma inhibits cancer cells, stimulates B lymphocytes, activates macrophages, and enhances the effectiveness of phagocytosis.

Antimicrobial Proteins: (2) Complement

Among its many overlapping functions, the immune system has another complex and multiple-duty system called **complement** that, like inflammation and phagocytosis, is brought into play at several levels. The complement system, named for its property of "complementing" immune reactions, consists of at least 26 blood proteins that work in concert to destroy bacteria and certain viruses. Some knowledge of this important system will help in your understanding of topics in chapter 15.

The concept of a cascade reaction is helpful in understanding how complement functions. A **cascade reaction** is a sequential physiological response like that of blood clotting, in which the first substance in a chemical series activates the next substance, which activates the next, and so on, until a desired end product is reached. There are three different complement pathways, distinguished by how they become activated. The final stages of the three pathways are the same and yield a similar end result. The **classical pathway** is activated mainly by the presence of antibody bound to microorganisms, although in some cases it can occur in the absence of antibody. The **lectin pathway** is activated when a host serum protein binds a sugar called mannan present in the walls of fungi and other microbes. (Proteins that bind carbohydrates are called lectins.) The **alternative pathway** begins when complement proteins bind to normal cell wall and surface components of microbes. For our discussion, we will focus on one pathway and point out how the others differ in **table 14.1.** Note that because the complement numbers (C1–C9) are based on the order of their discovery, factors C1–C4 do not appear in numerical order during activation (see table 14.1).

Overall Stages in the Complement Cascade

In general, the complement cascade includes the four stages of **initiation, amplification and cascade, polymerization,** and **membrane attack.** At the outset, an initiator (such as microbes, or antibodies, see table 14.1) reacts with the first complement chemical, which propels the reaction on its course. There is a recognition site on the surface of the target

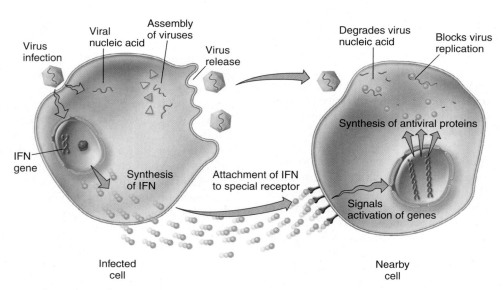

Figure 14.19 The antiviral activity of interferon.   When a cell is infected by a virus, its nucleus is triggered to transcribe and translate the interferon (IFN) gene. Interferon diffuses out of the cell and binds to IFN receptors on nearby uninfected cells, where it induces production of proteins that eliminate viral genes and block viral replication. Note that the original cell is not protected by IFN and that IFN does not prevent viruses from invading the protected cells.

Table 14.1 Complement Pathways

Pathway	Activators	Host Components That Initially Bind	Complement Proteins Involved
Classical (Rapid, efficient)	Complement-fixing antibodies (IgG, IgM) (sometimes microbe surface components)	C1 complex	C1 complex / C4 / C2 / C3
Lectin (Enters classical pathway)	Mannans	Mannose-binding lectin	C2 / C4
Alternative (Slower, less efficient)	Bacterial or fungal cell wall / Viruses / Parasite surfaces	C3	C3 / Factor B / Factor D / Properdin

C5 / C6 / C7 / C8 / C9 — Membrane attack complex

cell where the initial C components will bind. Through a stepwise series, each component reacts with another on or near the recognition site. In the C2–C5 series, enzymatic cleavage produces several inflammatory mediators. Other details of the pathways differ, but whether classical, lectin, or alternative, the functioning end product is a large ring-shaped protein termed the **membrane attack complex.** This complex can digest holes in the cell membranes of bacteria, cells, and enveloped viruses, thereby destroying them (**figure 14.20,** steps 4 and 5).

The **classical pathway** is a part of the specific immune response covered in chapter 15. It is initiated either by the foreign cell membrane of a parasite or a surface antibody. The first chemical, C1, is a large complex of three molecules, C1q, C1r, and C1s. When the C1q subunit has recognized and bound to surface receptors on the membrane, the C1r subunit cleaves the C1s proenzyme, and an activated enzyme emerges. During amplification, the C1s enzyme has as its primary targets proenzymes C4 and C2. Through the enzyme's action, C4 is converted into C4a and C4b, and C2 is converted into C2a and C2b. C4b and C2b fragments remain attached as an enzyme, C3 convertase, whose substrate is factor C3. The cleaving of C3 yields subunits C3a and C3b. C3b has the property of binding strongly with the cell membrane in close association with the component C5, and it also forms an enzyme complex with C4b–C2b that converts C5 into two fragments, C5a and C5b. C5b will form the nucleus for the membrane attack complex. This is the point at which the two pathways merge. From this point on, C5b reacts with C6 and C7 to form a stable complex inserted in the membrane. Addition of C8 to the complex causes the polymerization of several C9 molecules into a giant ring-shaped membrane attack complex that bores ring-shaped holes in the membrane. If the target is a cell, this reaction causes it to disintegrate (see figure 14.20, step 4). If the target is an enveloped virus, the

envelope is perforated and the virus inactivated. The end result of complement action is multifaceted. Gram-negative bacteria and infected host cells may be lysed. Phagocytes will be attracted to the site in greater numbers. Overall inflammation will be amplified by the action of complement. In recent years, the excessive actions of complement have been implicated as aggravators of several autoimmune diseases, such as lupus, rheumatoid arthritis, and myasthenia gravis.

Antimicrobial Proteins: (3) Iron-Binding Proteins and (4) Antimicrobial Peptides

Both humans and bacteria require iron for their enzymes, and therefore their metabolisms, to function properly. Because there is not an abundance of available iron in the human body, it becomes a rate-limiting factor in the growth of bacteria that have invaded a host. There is generally a great deal of iron in the body, but several host iron-binding proteins keep it bound tightly so that it is not available for microbial use. **Hemoglobin** is probably the most familiar iron-binding protein. It is located within red blood cells. **Transferrin,** found in blood and tissue fluids, and **lactoferrin,** found in milk and saliva, also bind iron. A fourth protein is ferritin, found in every cell type. These four proteins make sure that most of the iron in the body is bound tightly, sequestered for use in the body's physiological reactions.

Predictably, bacteria have evolved mechanisms for "grabbing away" some of this bound iron. Many possess proteins called **siderophores.** These proteins are capable of scavenging iron from the iron-binding proteins described above because they can bind the iron more tightly than the human proteins. As you see, it becomes a tug-of-war for iron between pathogens and body proteins. Recall from the section on fever that raised temperatures make iron even less available to pathogens in the body.

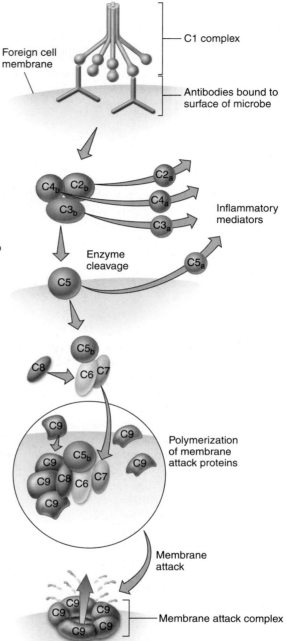

1. **Initiation.** The classical pathway begins when C1 components bind to antibodies bound to a foreign cell.

2. **Amplification and cascade.** The C1 complex is an enzyme that activates a second series of components, C4 and C2. When these have been enzymatically cleaved into separate molecules, they become a second enzyme complex that activates C3. At this same site, C3 binds to C5 and cleaves it to form a product that is tightly bound to the membrane.

3. **Polymerization.** $C5_b$ is a reactive site for the final assembly of an attack complex. In series, C6, C7, and C8 aggregate with C5 and become integrated into the membrane. They form a substrate upon which the final component, C9, can bind. Up to 15 of these C9 units ring the central core of the complex.

4. **Membrane attack.** The final product of these reactions is a large, donut-shaped enzyme that punctures small pores through the membrane, leading to cell lysis.

5. An electron micrograph (187,000×) of a cell reveals multiple puncture sites over its surface. The lighter, ringlike structures are the actual enzyme complex.

Process Figure 14.20 Steps in the classical complement pathway at a single site. All complement pathways function in a similar way, but the details differ. The classical pathway is illustrated here.

Case File 14   *Wrap-Up*

Very often, the first step in diagnosis is to detect the body's reaction to an infection. A signal that something is going on often points the physician in the right direction, saving the time, expense, discomfort, and inconvenience involved in undergoing multiple tests. Especially for refugees who are asymptomatic, multiple tests for every possible infection are not called for. Rather, the most common infections can be diagnosed based on a CBC, which will show the body's reaction to any infection, plus a stool test, which may yield the parasites or ova themselves.

Of course, a CBC can yield vital diagnostic information about any person. For example, eosinophilia often occurs in the United States in people who become infected with *Trichinella*. This infection, which was formerly associated with consuming undercooked pork, is now most often caused by eating bear meat.

See: http://www.cdc.gov/ncidod/dq/refugee/rh_guide/ip/domestic.htm

Antimicrobial peptides have only recently been appreciated. They are short proteins, of between 12 and 50 amino acids, which have the capability of inserting themselves into prokaryotic membranes. Through this mechanism and others, they kill the microbes. They have names like defensin, magainins, and protegrins. They are part of the innate immune system, and also have an effect on other actions of nonspecific and specific immunity. Many researchers are trying to turn these antimicrobial peptides into practical use as therapeutic drugs. Their ability to modulate immune responses would distinguish them from other antibiotics on the market.

14.4 Learning Outcomes—Can You ...

10. ... list the four major categories of nonspecific immunity?
11. ... outline the steps in inflammation?
12. ... outline the steps in phagocytosis?
13. ... discuss the mechanism of fever and what it accomplishes?
14. ... name four types of antimicrobial proteins?
15. ... compose one good overview sentence about the purpose and the mode of action of the complement system?

Chapter Summary

14.1 Defense Mechanisms of the Host in Perspective

- The interconnecting network of host protection against microbial invasion is organized into three lines of defense.
- The first line of defense consists of physical and chemical barricades associated with the skin and mucous membranes.
- The second line encompasses all the nonspecific cells and chemicals found in the tissues and blood.
- The third line, the specific immune response, is customized to react to specific antigens of a microbial invader.

14.2 The Second and Third Lines of Defense: An Overview

- The immune system operates as a surveillance system that discriminates between the host's self identity markers and the nonself identity markers of foreign cells.

14.3 Systems Involved in Immune Defenses

- The immune system is a complex collection of fluids and cells that penetrate every organ, tissue space, fluid compartment, and vascular network of the body. The four major subdivisions of this system are the RES, the ECF, the lymphatic system, and the blood vascular system.
- The RES, or reticuloendothelial system, is a network of connective tissue fibers inhabited by macrophages ready to attack and ingest microbes that have managed to bypass the first line of defense.
- The ECF, or extracellular fluid, compartment surrounds all tissue cells and is penetrated by both blood and lymph vessels, which bring all components of the second and third line of defense to attack infectious microbes.
- The lymphatic system has three functions: (1) it returns tissue fluid to general circulation; (2) it carries away excess fluid in inflamed tissues; (3) it concentrates and processes foreign invaders and initiates the specific immune response. Important sites of lymphoid tissues are lymph nodes, spleen, thymus, tonsils, and GALT.
- The blood contains both specific and nonspecific defenses. Nonspecific cellular defenses include the granulocytes, macrophages, and dendritic cells. The two major components of the specific immune response are the T lymphocytes, which provide specific cell-mediated immunity, and the B lymphocytes, which produce specific antibody-mediated immunity.

14.4 The Second Line of Defense

- Nonspecific immune reactions are generalized responses to invasion, regardless of the type. These include inflammation, phagocytosis, fever, and an array of antimicrobial proteins.
- The four symptoms of inflammation are rubor (redness), calor (heat), tumor (edema), and dolor (pain). Loss of function often accompanies these.
- Macrophages are activated monocytes. Along with neutrophils (PMNs), they are the key phagocytic agents of nonspecific response to disease.
- Fever is another component of nonspecific immunity. It is caused by both endogenous and exogenous pyrogens. Fever increases the rapidity of the host immune responses and reduces the viability of many microbial invaders.
- There are four main types of antimicrobial proteins: the complement system, interferons, iron-binding proteins, and antimicrobial peptides

Multiple-Choice and True-False Questions   Knowledge and Comprehension

Multiple-Choice Questions. Select the correct answer from the answers provided.

1. An example of a nonspecific chemical barrier to infection is
   a. unbroken skin.
   b. lysozyme in saliva.
   c. cilia in respiratory tract.
   d. all of these.

2. Which nonspecific host defense is associated with the trachea?
   a. lacrimation
   b. ciliary lining
   c. desquamation
   d. lactic acid

3. Which of the following blood cells function primarily as phagocytes?
   a. eosinophils
   b. basophils
   c. lymphocytes
   d. neutrophils

4. Which of the following is not a lymphoid tissue?
   a. spleen
   b. thyroid gland
   c. lymph nodes
   d. GALT

5. What is included in GALT?
   a. thymus
   b. Peyer's patches
   c. tonsils
   d. breast lymph nodes

6. Monocytes are _____ leukocytes that develop into _____.
   a. granular, phagocytes
   b. agranular, mast cells
   c. agranular, macrophages
   d. granular, T cells

7. An example of an exogenous pyrogen is
   a. interleukin-1.
   b. complement.
   c. interferon.
   d. endotoxin.

8. Which of the following is an antimicrobial protein that has a much greater role in the third line of defense than in the second line of defense?
   a. antibody
   b. complement
   c. protegrin
   d. interferon

9. Which of the following substances is *not* produced by phagocytes to destroy engulfed microorganisms?
   a. hydroxyl radicals
   b. superoxide anion
   c. hydrogen peroxide
   d. bradykinin

10. Which of the following is the end product of the complement system?
    a. properdin
    b. cascade reaction
    c. membrane attack complex
    d. complement factor C9

True-False Questions. If the statement is true, leave as is. If it is false, correct it by rewriting the sentence.

11. The liquid component of clotted blood is called plasma.

12. Pyogenic bacteria are commonly associated with fever.

13. Communication between cells of the immune system is accomplished using chemical signals.

14. Lysozyme is an enzyme found in tears and saliva that hydrolyzes peptidoglycan in bacterial cell walls.

15. The immune system uses DNA content to distinguish self from nonself.

Critical Thinking Questions   Application and Analysis

These questions are suggested as a *writing-to-learn* experience. For each question, compose a one- or two-paragraph answer that includes the factual information needed to completely address the question.

1. Suggest some reasons for so much redundancy of action and so many interacting aspects of immune responses.

2. a. Use the pointers in the figure to describe the major components of the first line of defense.
   b. What effects do these defenses have on microbes?

3. a. Describe the main elements of the process through which the immune system distinguishes self from nonself.
   b. How is surveillance of the tissues carried out?

   c. What is responsible for this surveillance?
   d. What does the term *foreign* mean in reference to the immune system?

4. a. Differentiate between granulocytes and agranulocytes.
   b. Describe the main cell types in each group, their functions, and their incidence in the circulation.

5. a. What is lymph, and how is it formed?
   b. Why are white cells but not red cells normally found in it?

6. In what ways is a phagocyte a tiny container of disinfectants?

7. Describe the mechanism by which interferon acts as an antiviral compound.

8. Patients with a history of tuberculosis often show scars in the lungs and experience recurrent infection. Account for these effects on the basis of the inflammatory response.

9. Macrophages perform the final job of removing tissue debris and other products of infection. Indicate some of the possible effects when these scavengers cannot successfully complete the work of phagocytosis.

10. List four common PAMPs, and discuss what trait most PAMPs have in common.

Concept Mapping   Synthesis

Appendix D provides guidance for working with concept maps.

1. Construct your own concept map using the following words as the *concepts*. Supply the linking words between each pair of concepts.

defenses	inflammation
leukocytes	antibodies
lymphocytes	neutrophils
monocytes	fever
macrophages	

Visual Connections   Synthesis

These questions use visual images or previous content to make connections to this chapter's concepts.

1. **From chapter 10, figure 10.8; and from chapter 14, figure 14.19.** Study the two illustrations. Is there any way you could apply the technique illustrated on the left to achieve the same outcome seen in figure 14.19 on the right? Explain your answer.

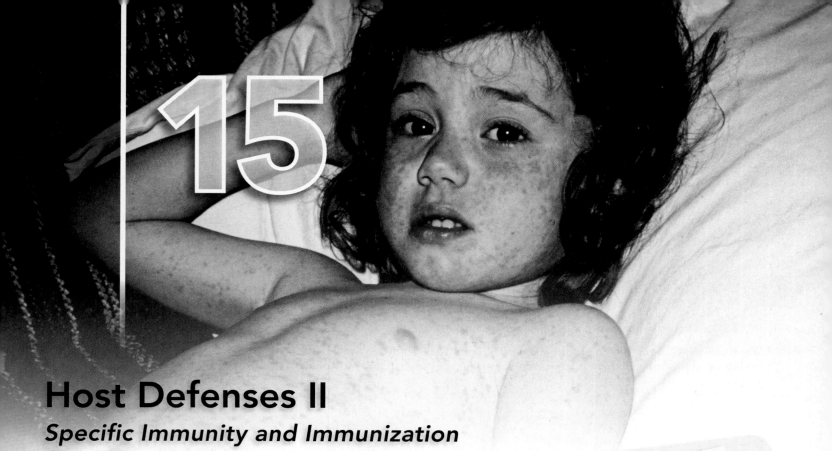

Host Defenses II
Specific Immunity and Immunization

Case File 15

The Ohio State Department of Health confirmed a diagnosis of measles in a 6-year-old girl who was hospitalized in Cincinnati while visiting relatives in May 2005. Because the patient was a resident of Indiana, the Indiana State Department of Health initiated an investigation that eventually identified a total of 34 cases of measles occurring between May 16 and June 24. Of the 34 infected persons, 33 had participated in a church gathering in northwestern Indiana on May 15—or were family members of a participant. The final case occurred in a phlebotomist who worked at a hospital where one of the measles patients had been admitted; childhood school records indicated that he had received only one of two recommended doses of measles vaccine.

Three of the 34 patients were hospitalized, two with dehydration and one with pneumonia requiring 6 days of mechanical respiratory support. Complications seen in the 31 nonhospitalized patients included 16 cases of diarrhea and 2 cases of otitis media (ear infection). State and local health departments in Ohio, Indiana, and Illinois (where one patient lived) immediately began tracing the contacts of all 34 patients to determine the outbreak's epidemiology.

- What type of infectious agent is responsible for measles? How is measles spread?
- Does this look like a point-source epidemic or a propagated epidemic? (See chapter 13 for a review of epidemiology.)

Continuing the Case appears on page 451.

Outline and Learning Outcomes

15.1 Specific Immunity: The Third and Final Line of Defense
    1. Describe how the third line of defense is different from the other two.
    2. List the four stages of a specific immune response.

15.2 Step I: Lymphocyte Development
    3. Discuss four major immune functions of cell markers.
    4. Describe the major histocompatibility complex in two sentences.

5. Contrast the way T cells recognize antigen with the way B cells do.
6. Summarize the maturation process of both B cells and T cells.
7. Explain how our bodies are equipped with lymphocytes capable of responding to nearly any antigen imaginable.
8. Outline the processes of clonal selection and expansion.
9. Describe the B-cell receptor and the T-cell receptor.

15.3 Step II: Presentation of Antigens
10. Compare the terms antigen, immunogen, and epitope.
11. List characteristics of antigens that optimize their immunogenicity.
12. List the types of cells that can act as antigen-presenting cells.

15.4 Steps III and IV: B-Cell Response
13. Diagram the steps in the B-cell response.
14. Make a detailed drawing of an antibody molecule.
15. Explain the various end results of antibody binding to an antigen.
16. List the five types of antibodies and important facts about each.
17. Describe the memory response.

15.5 Steps III and IV: T-Cell Response
18. List the three major types of cells T cells will differentiate into after stimulation.
19. Describe the main functions of these three types of T cells.
20. Explain how T_C cells kill other cells.

15.6 Specific Immunity and Vaccination
21. List and define the four different descriptors of specific immune states.
22. Discuss the qualities of an effective vaccine.
23. Name the two major categories of vaccines and then the subcategories under each.
24. Discuss the pros and cons of killed (or inactivated) versus attenuated vaccines.
25. Describe the principle behind DNA vaccines.
26. Explain the principle of herd immunity.

15.1 Specific Immunity: The Third and Final Line of Defense

In chapter 14, we described the capacity of the immune system to survey, recognize, and react to foreign cells and molecules and we overviewed the characteristics of nonspecific host defenses, blood cells, phagocytosis, inflammation, and complement. In addition, we introduced the concepts of acquired immunity and specificity. In this chapter, we take a closer look at those topics.

When host barriers and nonspecific defenses fail to control an infectious agent, a person with a normally functioning immune system has a mechanism to resist the pathogen—the third, specific line of immunity. Immunity is the resistance developed after contracting childhood ailments such as chickenpox or measles that provides long-term protection against future attacks. This sort of immunity is not innate but adaptive; it is acquired only after an immunizing event such as an infection. The absolute need for acquired or adaptive immunity is impressively documented in children who have genetic defects in this system or in AIDS patients who have lost it. Even with heroic measures to isolate the patient, combat infection, or restore lymphoid tissue, the victim is constantly vulnerable to life-threatening infections.

Acquired specific immunity is the product of a dual system that we have previously mentioned—the B and T lymphocytes. During development, these lymphocytes undergo a selective process that specializes them for reacting only to one specific antigen or immunogen. During this time, **immunocompetence,** the ability of the body to react with countless foreign substances, develops. An infant is born with the theoretical potential to react to millions of different substances.

Antigens or immunogens figure very prominently in specific immunity. They are defined as molecules that stimulate a response by T and B cells. They are usually protein or polysaccharide molecules on or inside all cells and viruses, including our own. (Environmental chemicals can also be antigens. These are covered in chapter 16.) In fact, any exposed or released protein or polysaccharide is potentially an antigen, even those on our own cells. For reasons we discuss later, our own antigens do not usually evoke a response from our own immune systems. So it is acceptable to think of antigens as *foreign* molecules that stimulate an immune response.

In chapter 14, we discussed pathogen-associated molecular patterns (PAMPs) that stimulate responses by phagocytic cells during an innate defense response. While PAMPs are molecules shared by many types of microbes that stimulate a nonspecific response, antigens are highly individual and stimulate specific immunity. The two types of molecules do share two characteristics: (1) they are "parts" of foreign cells (microbes or other foreign materials), and (2) they provoke a defensive reaction from the host.

Two features that most characterize this third line of defense are **specificity** and **memory.** Unlike mechanisms such as anatomical barriers or phagocytosis, acquired immunity is highly selective. For example, the antibodies produced during an infection against the chickenpox virus will function against that virus and not against the measles virus. The property of memory refers to the rapid mobilization of lymphocytes that have been programmed to "recall" their first engagement with the invader and rush to the attack once again.

The elegance and complexity of immune function are largely due to lymphocytes working closely together with macrophages. To simplify and clarify the network of immunologic development and interaction, we present it here as a series of stages, with each stage covered in a separate section (**figure 15.1**). The principal stages are:

   I. lymphocyte development and differentiation;
  II. the presentation of antigens;
 III. the challenge of B and T lymphocytes by antigens;
  IV. B-lymphocyte response: the production and activities of antibodies; and
  IV. T-lymphocyte response: cell-mediated immunity.

This sequence is illustrated below and in figure 15.1. We will give an overview here and spend the rest of the chapter filling in the details.

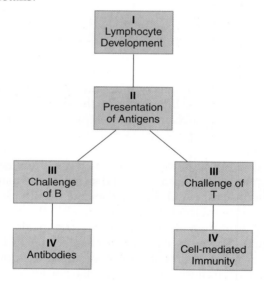

Development of the Dual Lymphocyte System

Lymphocytes are central to immune responsiveness. They undergo development that begins in the embryonic yolk sac and shifts to the liver and bone marrow. Although all lymphocytes arise from the same basic stem cell type, at some point in development they diverge into two distinct types. Final maturation of B cells occurs in specialized bone marrow sites, and that of T cells occurs in the thymus. Both cell types subsequently migrate to separate areas in the lymphoid organs (for instance, nodes and spleen). B and T cells constantly recirculate through the circulatory system and lymphatics, migrating into and out of the lymphoid organs.

Entrance and Presentation of Antigens and Clonal Selection

When foreign cells, such as pathogens (carrying antigens), cross the first line of defense and enter the tissue, resident phagocytes migrate to the site. Tissue macrophages ingest the pathogen and induce an inflammatory response in the tissue if appropriate. Tissue dendritic cells ingest the antigen and migrate to the nearest lymphoid organ (often the draining lymph nodes). Here they process and present antigen to T lymphocytes. Pieces of the pathogen also drain into these lymph nodes. Both macrophages and dendritic cells are thus **antigen-presenting cells.** The antigens activate B cells. In most cases, the response of B cells also requires the additional assistance of special classes of T cells called T helper cells.

Activation of Lymphocytes and Clonal Expansion

When challenged by immunogen, both B cells and T cells further proliferate and differentiate. The multiplication of a particular lymphocyte creates a clone, or group of genetically identical cells, some of which are memory cells that will ensure future reactiveness against that antigen. Because the B-cell and T-cell responses differ significantly from this point on in the sequence, they are summarized separately.

Products of B Lymphocytes: Antibody Structure and Functions

One B cell divides, giving rise to plasma cells, each with the same reactive profile. Plasma cells release antibodies into the tissue and blood. When these antibodies attach to the antigen for which they are specific, the antigen is marked for destruction or neutralization.

How T Cells Respond to Antigen: Cell-Mediated Immunity (CMI)

T-cell types and responses are extremely varied. When activated (sensitized) by antigen, a T cell gives rise to one of three different types of progeny, each involved in a cell-mediated immune function. The three main functional types of T cells are:

   1. helper T cells that activate macrophages, assist B-cell processes, and help activate cytotoxic T cells;
   2. regulatory T cells that control the T-cell response; and
   3. cytotoxic T cells that lead to the destruction of infected host cells and other "foreign" cells.

Although T cells secrete cytokines that help destroy pathogens and regulate immune responses, they do not produce antibodies.

15.1 Learning Outcomes—Can You . . .

   1. . . . describe how the third line of defense is different from the other two?
   2. . . . list the four stages of a specific immune response?

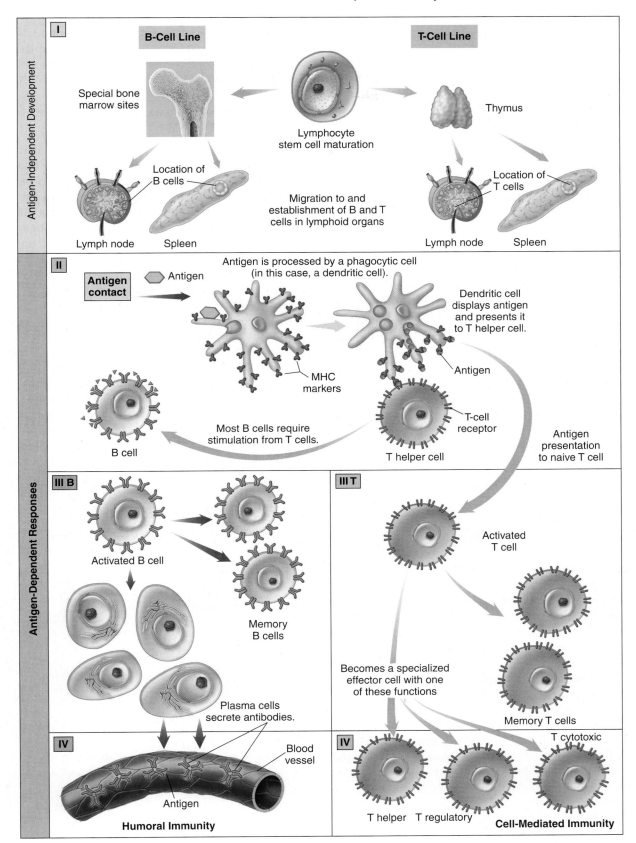

Figure 15.1 Overview of the stages of lymphocyte development and function.   **I.** Development of B- and T-lymphocyte specificity and migration to lymphoid organs. **II.** Antigen processing by dendritic cell and presentation to lymphocytes; assistance to B cells by T cells. **III.** Lymphocyte activation, clonal expansion, and formation of memory B and T cells. **IV.** End result of lymphocyte activation. Left-hand side: antibody release; right-hand side: cell-mediated immunity. Details of these processes are covered in each corresponding section heading.

15.2 Step I: Lymphocyte Development

Before we examine lymphocyte development and function in greater detail, we must initially review concepts such as the unique structure of molecules (especially proteins), the characteristics of cell surfaces (membranes and envelopes), the ways that genes are expressed, and immune recognition and identification of self and nonself. Ultimately, the shape and function of protein receptors and markers protruding from the surfaces of cells are the result of genetic expression, and these molecules are responsible for specific immune recognition and, thus, immune reactions.

Markers on Cell Surfaces Involved in Recognition of Self and Nonself

Chapter 14 touched on the fundamental idea that cell markers (sometimes called receptors) confer specificity and identity. A given cell can express several different markers, each type playing a distinct and significant role in detection, recognition, and cell communication. Major functions of immune system markers are:

1. attachment to nonself or foreign antigens;
2. binding to cell surface receptors that indicate self, such as MHC molecules (discussed in next paragraph);
3. receiving and transmitting chemical messages to coordinate the response; and
4. aiding in cellular development.

Because of their importance in the immune response, we concentrate here on the major markers of lymphocytes and macrophages.

Major Histocompatibility Complex

One set of genes that codes for human cell receptors is the **major histocompatibility complex (MHC).** This gene complex gives rise to a series of glycoproteins (called MHC molecules) found on all cells except red blood cells. The MHC is also known as the human leukocyte antigen (HLA) system. This marker complex plays a vital role in recognition of self by the immune system and in rejection of foreign tissue.

Three classes of MHC genes have been identified. Class I genes code for markers that appear on all nucleated cells. They display unique characteristics of self and allow for the recognition of self molecules and the regulation of immune reactions. The system is rather complicated in its details, but in general, each human being inherits a particular combination of class I MHC (HLA) genes in a relatively predictable fashion. Although millions of different combinations and variations of these genes are possible among humans, the closer the blood relationship, the greater the probability for similarity in MHC profile. Individual differences in the exact inheritance of MHC genes, however, make it fairly unlikely that even closely related persons will express an identical MHC profile. Class II MHC genes also code for immune regulatory markers. These markers are found on macrophages, dendritic cells, and B cells and are involved in presenting antigens to

T cells during cooperative immune reactions. Class III MHC genes encode proteins involved with the complement system among others. We'll focus on classes I and II in this chapter. See **figure 15.2** for depictions of the first two MHC classes.

Lymphocyte Receptors and Specificity to Antigen

The part lymphocytes play in immune surveillance and recognition emphasizes the essential role of their markers. These markers are even more frequently called receptors, a name that emphasizes that their major role is to "accept" or "grasp" antigens in some form. B cells have receptors that bind antigens, and T cells have receptors that bind antigens that have been processed and complexed with MHC molecules on the presenting cell surface. Antigen molecules exist in great diversity; there are potentially millions and even billions of unique types. The many sources of antigens include microorganisms as well as an endless array of chemical compounds in the environment. One of the most fascinating questions in immunology is: How can the lymphocyte receptors be varied to react with such a large number of different antigens? After all, it is generally accepted that there will have to be a different lymphocyte receptor for each unique antigen. Some questions that naturally follow are: How can a cell accommodate enough genetic information to respond to millions or even billions of antigens? When, where, and how does the capacity to distinguish self from foreign tissue arise? To answer these questions, we must first introduce a central theory of immunity.

The Development of Lymphocyte Diversity
Specific Events in B-Cell Maturation

The site of B-cell maturation was first discovered in birds, which have an organ in the intestine called the bursa. For

Class I MHC molecule
found on all nucleated
human cells

Class II MHC
found on some types
of white blood cells

Figure 15.2 Classes I and II of molecules of the human major histocompatibility complex.

Table 15.1 Contrasting Properties of B Cells and T Cells

	B Cells	T Cells
Site of Maturation	Bone marrow	Thymus
Specific Surface Markers	Immunoglobulin	T-cell receptor Several CD molecules
Circulation in Blood	Low numbers	High numbers
Receptors for Antigen	B-cell receptor (immunoglobulin)	T-cell receptor
Distribution in Lymphatic Organs	Cortex (in follicles)	Paracortical sites (interior to the follicles)
Require Antigen Presented with MHC	No	Yes
Product of Antigenic Stimulation	Plasma cells and memory cells	Several types of sensitized T cells and memory cells
General Functions	Production of antibodies to inactivate, neutralize, target antigens	Cells function in helping other immune cells, suppressing, killing abnormal cells; hypersensitivity; synthesize cytokines

some time, the human bursal equivalent was not established. Now it is known to be certain bone marrow sites that harbor *stromal cells*. These huge cells nurture the lymphocyte stem cells and provide chemical signals that initiate B-cell development. As a result of gene modification and selection, hundreds of millions of distinct B cells develop. These naive lymphocytes circulate through the blood, "homing" to specific sites in the lymph nodes, spleen, and gut-associated lymphoid tissue (GALT), where they adhere to specific binding molecules. Here they will come into contact with antigens throughout life. B cells have immunoglobulins as surface receptors **(table 15.1).**

Specific Events in T-Cell Maturation

The maturation of T cells and the development of their specific receptors are directed by the thymus gland and its hormones. In addition to the antigen-specific T-cell receptor, all mature T lymphocytes express coreceptors called CD3. CD3 molecules surround the T-cell receptor and assist in binding. T cells also express either a CD4 or a CD8 coreceptor. CD4 is an accessory receptor protein on T helper cells that binds to MHC class II molecules. CD8 is found on cytotoxic T cells, and it binds MHC class I molecules. Like B cells, T cells also constantly circulate between the lymphatic and general circulatory systems, migrating to specific T-cell areas of the lymph nodes and spleen. It has been estimated that more than 10^9 T cells pass between the lymphatic and general circulations per day.

The Origin of Immunological Diversity

Research findings have shown that lymphocytes use slightly more than 500 gene segments to produce the tremendous repertoire of specific receptors they must display for antigens. This is accomplished through extensive genetic rearrangement of receptor molecules. Early undifferentiated lymphocytes in the embryo, fetus, and adult bone marrow undergo a continuous series of divisions and genetic changes

that generate hundreds of millions of different types of B and T cells, each different because the variable regions of their receptors are carrying a particular receptor specificity **(figure 15.3).**

The mechanism, generally true for both B and T cells, can be summarized as follows: In the bone marrow, stem cells can become granulocytes, monocytes, or lymphocytes. The lymphocytes then become either T cells or B cells. Cells destined to become B cells stay in the bone marrow; T cells migrate to the thymus. Here they build their unique antigen receptor. Both B and T cells then migrate to secondary lymphoid tissues **(figure 15.4).** The secondary lymphoid tissues are resupplied with B and T cells because some self-destruct if they are not used and others become activated and leave.

By the time T and B cells reach the lymphoid tissues, each one is already equipped to respond to a single unique antigen. This amazing diversity is generated by extensive rearrangements of the gene segments that code for the antigen receptors on the T and B cells (see figure 15.3). In time, every possible recombination occurs, leading to a huge assortment of lymphocytes.[1] Each genetically unique line of lymphocytes arising from these recombinations is termed a **clone.** Keep in mind that the rearranged genetic code is expressed as a protein receptor of unique configuration on the surface of the lymphocyte, something like a "sign post" announcing its specificity and reactivity for an antigen. This *proliferative* stage of lymphocyte development does not require the actual presence of foreign antigens.

Clonal Selection

The second stage of development—**clonal selection** and expansion—does require stimulation by an antigen such as a microbe. When this antigen enters the immune surveillance system, it encounters specific lymphocytes ready to recognize it. Such contact stimulates that clone to undergo

---

1. Estimates of the theoretical number of possible variations that may be created vary from 10^{14} to 10^{18} different specificities.

(a)

Process Figure 15.3 Structure and genetics of immunoglobulins. **(a)** Simple model of an immunoglobulin molecule. The main components are four polypeptide chains—two identical light chains and two identical heavy chains bound by disulfide bonds as shown. Each chain consists of a variable region (V) and a constant region (C). The variable regions of light and heavy chains form a binding site for antigen. **(b)** The final gene that codes for a heavy or light chain is assembled by splicing blocks of genetic material from several regions ((1), (2), (3)). These genes are transcribed and translated into the polypeptides that join to form the final molecule ((4)).

1. The heavy-chain genes are composed of four separate segments (V, D, J, and C) that are (2) transcribed and translated to form the heavy polypeptide chains.

3. The light-chain genes are put together like heavy ones, except that the final gene is spliced from three gene groups (V, J, and C), making smaller polypeptides.

Precisely shaped binding sites

4. During final assembly, first the heavy and light chains are bound, and then the heavy-light combinations are connected to form the immunoglobulin molecule.

(b)

Figure 15.4 Major stages in the development of B and T cells.

mitotic divisions and expands it into a larger population of lymphocytes all bearing the same specificity **(figure 15.5).** This increases the capacity of the immune response to that antigen. Two important generalities one can derive from the phenomenon of clonal selection are (1) lymphocyte specificity is pre-programmed, existing in the genetic makeup before an antigen has ever entered the tissues, and (2) each genetically distinct lymphocyte expresses only a single specificity and can react to only one type of antigen. Other important features of the lymphocyte response system are expanded in later sections.

One potentially problematic outcome of random genetic assortment is the development of clones of lymphocytes able to react to *self.* This outcome could lead to severe damage when the immune system actually perceives self molecules as foreign and mounts a harmful response against the host's tissues. Any such clones are destroyed during development through clonal *deletion.* The removal of such potentially harmful clones is the basis of immune tolerance or tolerance to self. Since humans are exposed to many new antigenic substances during their lifetimes, T cells and B cells in the periphery of the body have mechanisms for *not* reacting to innocuous antigens. Some diseases (autoimmunity) are thought to be caused by the loss of immune tolerance through the survival of certain "forbidden clones" or failure of these other systems (see chapter 16).

The Specific B-Cell Receptor: An Immunoglobulin Molecule

In the case of B lymphocytes, the receptor genes that undergo the recombination described are those governing **immunoglobulin** (im"-yoo-noh-glahb'-yoo-lin) **(Ig)** synthesis. Immunoglobulins are large glycoprotein molecules that serve as the antigen receptors of B cells and, when secreted, as antibodies. The basic immunoglobulin molecule is a composite of four polypeptide chains: a pair of identical heavy (H) chains and a pair of identical light (L) chains (see figure 15.3). One light chain is bonded to one heavy chain, and the two heavy chains are bonded to one another with disulfide bonds, creating a symmetrical, Y-shaped arrangement.

The ends of the forks formed by the light and heavy chains contain pockets, called the **antigen binding sites.**

These sites can be highly variable in shape to fit a wide range of antigens. This extreme versatility is due to **variable regions (V)** in antigen binding sites, where amino acid composition is highly varied from one clone of B lymphocytes to another, a result of the genetic reassortment we discussed above. The remainder of the light chains and heavy chains consist of constant regions (C) whose amino acid content does not vary greatly from one antibody to another.

T-Cell Receptors

The T-cell receptor for antigen belongs to the same protein family as the B-cell receptor. It is similar to B cells in being formed by genetic modification, having variable and constant regions, being inserted into the membrane, and having an antigen binding site formed from two parallel polypeptide

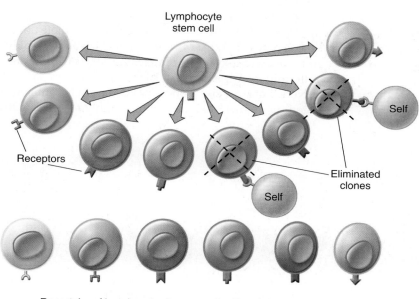

Repertoire of lymphocyte clones, each with unique receptor display

(a) Antigen-Independent Period

1. During development of early lymphocytes from stem cells, a given stem cell undergoes rapid cell division to form numerous progeny.

During this period of cell differentiation, random rearrangements of the genes that code for cell surface protein receptors occur. The result is a large array of genetically distinct cells, each bearing a different receptor that is specific to react with only a single type of foreign molecule or antigen.

2. At this same time, any lymphocytes that develop a specificity for self molecules and could be harmful are eliminated from the pool of diversity. This is called immune tolerance.

3. The specificity for a single antigen molecule is programmed into the lymphocyte and is set for the life of a given cell. The end result is an enormous pool of mature but naive lymphocytes that are ready to further differentiate under the influence of certain organs and immune stimuli.

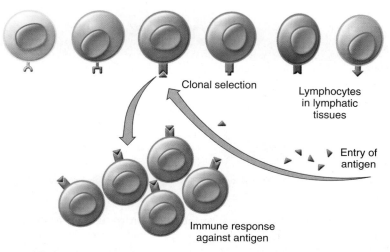

(b) Antigen-Dependent Period

4. Mature lymphocytes come to populate the lymphatic organs, where they will finally encounter antigens. These antigens will become the stimulus for the lymphocytes' final activation and immune function. Entry of a specific antigen selects only the lymphocyte that carries matching surface receptors. This will trigger proliferation, which results in large numbers of cells bearing identical antigen-specific receptors.

Figure 15.5 Overview of the clonal selection theory of lymphocyte development and diversity.

Figure 15.6 Proposed structure of the T-cell receptor and surrounding structures. The structure of this polypeptide is similar to that of an immunoglobulin. V stands for variable region and C for constant region. The four blue bars are CD3 molecules; the coreceptor CD4 is also shown.

chains **(figure 15.6).** Unlike the immunoglobulins, the T-cell receptor is relatively small and is never secreted. Various other receptors and markers that are not antigen-specific are described in a later section.

15.2 Learning Outcomes—Can You ...

3. ... discuss four major immune functions of cell markers?
4. ... describe the major histocompatibility complex in two sentences?
5. ... contrast the way T cells recognize antigen with the way B cells do?
6. ... summarize the maturation process of both B cells and T cells?
7. ... explain how our bodies are equipped with lymphocytes capable of responding to nearly any antigen imaginable?
8. ... outline the processes of clonal selection and expansion?
9. ... describe the B-cell receptor and the T-cell receptor?

15.3 Step II: Presentation of Antigens

Entrance and Processing of Antigens

Having reviewed the characteristics of lymphocytes, let us more deeply examine the properties of antigens, the substances that cause them to react. As discussed earlier, an **antigen (Ag)** is a substance that provokes an immune response in specific lymphocytes. The property of behaving as an antigen is called **antigenicity.** The term **immunogen** is another term of reference for a substance that can elicit an immune response. To be perceived as an antigen or immunogen, a substance must meet certain requirements in foreignness, shape, size, and accessibility.

Characteristics of Antigens

One important characteristic of an antigen is that it be perceived as foreign, meaning that it is not a normal constituent of the body. Whole microbes or their parts, cells, or sub-

stances that arise from other humans, animals, plants, and various molecules all possess this quality of foreignness and thus are potentially antigenic to the immune system of an individual **(figure 15.7).** Molecules of complex composition such as proteins and protein-containing compounds prove to be more immunogenic than repetitious polymers composed of a single type of unit. Most materials that serve as antigens fall into these chemical categories:

- Proteins and polypeptides (enzymes, cell surface structures, hormones, exotoxins)
- Lipoproteins (cell membranes)
- Glycoproteins (blood cell markers)
- Nucleoproteins (DNA complexed to proteins but not pure DNA)
- Polysaccharides (certain bacterial capsules) and lipopolysaccharides

Effects of Molecular Shape and Size To initiate an immune response, a substance must also be large enough to "catch the attention" of the surveillance cells. Molecules with a molecular weight (MW) of less than 1,000 are seldom complete antigens, and those between 1,000 MW and 10,000 MW are weakly so. Complex macromolecules approaching 100,000 MW are the most immunogenic, a category also dominated by large proteins. Note that large size alone is not sufficient for antigenicity; glycogen, a polymer of glucose with a highly repetitious struc-

(a)

Microbial cells, viruses

Foreign human or animal cells

Plant molecules

(b)

(1)

(2)

(3)

(c)

Figure 15.7 Characteristics of antigens. **(a)** Whole cells and viruses make good immunogens. **(b)** Complex molecules with several epitopes make good immunogens. **(c)** Poor immunogens include small molecules not attached to a carrier molecule (1), simple molecules (2), and large but repetitive molecules (3).

ture, has a molecular weight over 100,000 and is not normally antigenic, whereas insulin, a protein with a molecular weight of 6,000, can be antigenic.

A lymphocyte's capacity to discriminate differences in molecular shape is so fine that it recognizes and responds to only a portion of the antigen molecule. This molecular fragment, called the **epitope,** is the primary signal that the molecule is foreign **(figure 15.7b).**

A Note About Epitopes and Antigens

While up to now we have been calling the immunogenic substance "the antigen," it is more precisely termed the epitope. You could say, for instance, "the antigenic portion of the protein on a microbe is the epitope." You will also note that in practice, clinicians, and even other parts of this book, use the word "antigen" when the precise term is "epitope." You will know, however, that the part of the molecule that is actually recognized by the immune system is the epitope. This means, also, that every epitope can be recognized by B- and T-cell receptors that were formed during genetic reassortment. The particular tertiary structure and shape of this determinant must conform like a key to the receptor "lock" of the lymphocyte, which then responds to it. Certain amino acids accessible at the surface of proteins or protruding carbohydrate side chains are typical examples. Many foreign cells and molecules are very complex antigenically, with numerous component parts, each of which will elicit a separate and different lymphocyte response. Examples of these multiple, or *mosaic*, antigens include bacterial cells containing cell wall, membrane, flagellar, capsular, and toxin antigens, as well as viruses. T-cell antigen receptors recognize these small pieces of antigens—epitopes—in combination with MHC molecules.

Small foreign molecules that consist only of a determinant group and are too small by themselves to elicit an immune response are termed **haptens.** However, if such an incomplete antigen is linked to a larger carrier molecule, the combination develops immunogenicity **(figure 15.8).** The carrier group contributes to the size of the complex and enhances the proper spatial orientation of the determinative group, while the hapten serves as the epitope. Haptens include such molecules as

drugs, metals, and ordinarily innocuous household, industrial, and environmental chemicals. Many haptens develop antigenicity in the body by combining with large carrier molecules such as serum proteins (see allergy in chapter 16).

Because each human being is genetically and biochemically unique (except for identical twins), the proteins and other molecules of one person can be antigenic to another. **Alloantigens** are cell surface markers and molecules that occur in some members of the same species but not in others. Alloantigens are the basis for an individual's blood group and major histocompatibility profile, and they are responsible for incompatibilities that can occur in blood transfusion or organ grafting.

Some bacterial toxins, which belong to a group of immunogens called **superantigens,** are potent stimuli for T cells. Their presence in an infection activates T cells at a rate 100 times greater than ordinary antigens. The result can be an overwhelming release of cytokines and cell death. Such diseases as toxic shock syndrome and certain autoimmune diseases are associated with this class of antigens.

Antigens that evoke allergic reactions, called **allergens,** are characterized in detail in chapter 16.

Cooperation in Immune Reactions to Antigens

The basis for most immune responses is the encounter between antigens and white blood cells. Microbes and other foreign substances enter most often through the respiratory or gastrointestinal mucosa and less frequently through other mucous membranes, the skin, or across the placenta. Antigens introduced intravenously become localized in the liver, spleen, bone marrow, kidney, and lung. If introduced by some other route, antigens are carried in lymphatic fluid and concentrated by the lymph nodes. The lymph nodes and spleen are important in concentrating the antigens and circulating them thoroughly through all areas populated by lymphocytes so that they come into contact with the proper clone.

The Role of Antigen Processing and Presentation

In most immune reactions, the antigen must be further acted upon and formally presented to lymphocytes by cells called

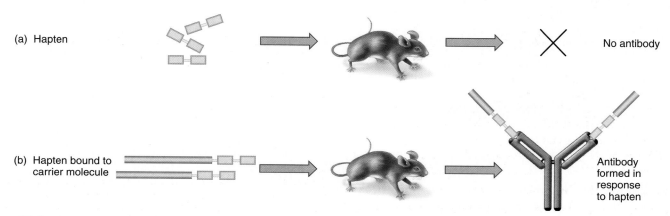

Figure 15.8   The hapten-carrier phenomenon.   **(a)** Haptens are too small to be discovered by an animal's immune system; no response. **(b)** A hapten bound to a large molecule will serve as an epitope and stimulate a response and an antibody that is specific for it.

antigen-presenting cells (APCs). Three different cells can serve as APCs: macrophages, B cells, and **dendritic** (den'-drih-tik) **cells.** Dendritic cells engulf the antigen and modify it so that it will be more immunogenic and recognizable to T lymphocytes. After processing is complete, the antigen is bound to the MHC receptor and moved to the surface of the APC so that it will be readily accessible to T lymphocytes during presentation **(figure 15.9).**

Presentation of Antigen to the Lymphocytes and Its Early Consequences

For lymphocytes to respond to the APC-bound antigen, certain conditions must be met. T-cell-dependent antigens, usually protein-based, require recognition steps between the APC, antigen, and lymphocytes. APCs (often dendritic cells that have engulfed antigen) activate CD4 T helper cells in the lymph nodes. This class of T cell bears an antigen-specific T-cell receptor that binds to a piece of the antigen (epitope) and the CD4 molecule, which binds to MHC class II (figure 15.9). Once identification has occurred, a molecule on the APC activates this T helper (T_H) cell. The T_H cell, in turn, produces a cytokine, **interleukin-2 (IL-2),** which is a growth factor for the T helper cells and cytotoxic T cells. These T helper cells can then help activate B cells. The manner in which B and T cells subsequently become activated by the APC–T helper cell complex and their individual responses to antigen are addressed in later sections.

A few antigens can trigger a response from B lymphocytes without the cooperation of APCs or T helper cells. These T-cell-independent antigens are usually simple molecules such as carbohydrates with many repeating and invariable determinant groups. Examples include lipopolysaccharide

Process Figure 15.9 Interactions between antigen-presenting cells (APCs) and T helper (CD4) cells required for T-cell activation. For T cells to recognize foreign antigens, they must have the antigen processed and presented by a professional APC such as a dendritic cell.

from the cell wall of *Escherichia coli,* polysaccharide from the capsule of *Streptococcus pneumoniae,* and molecules from rabies and Epstein-Barr virus. Because so few antigens are of this type, most B-cell reactions require T helper cells.

15.3 Learning Outcomes—Can You ...

10. ... compare the terms antigen, immunogen, and epitope?
11. ... list characteristics of antigens that optimize their immunogenicity?
12. ... list the types of cells that can act as antigen-presenting cells?

15.4 Steps III and IV: B-Cell Response

Activation of B Lymphocytes: Clonal Expansion and Antibody Production

The immunologic activation of most B cells requires a series of events (**figure 15.10**).

1. **Binding of epitope.** In this case, a precommitted B cell binds the only epitope its receptor fits.
2. **Antigen processing and presentation.** The antigen is endocytosed by the B cell and degraded into smaller

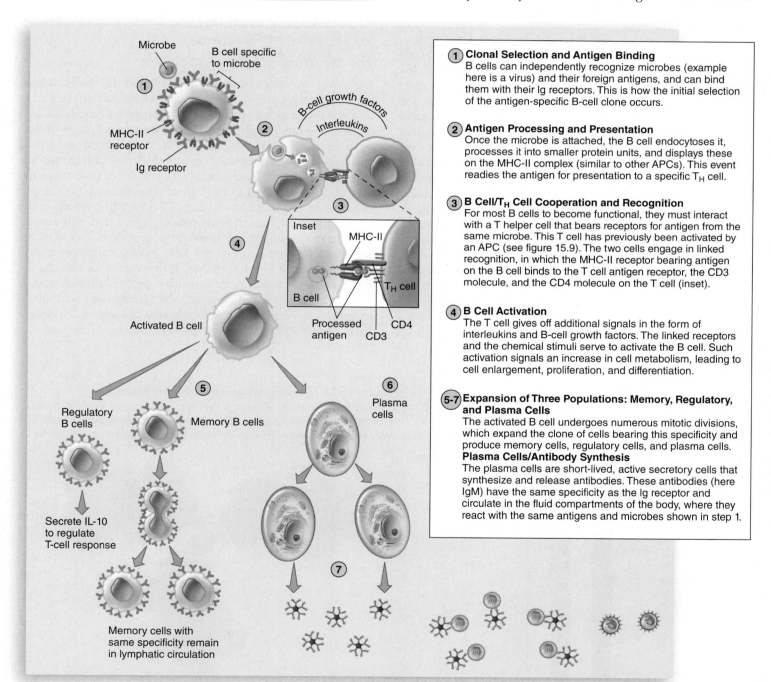

1 Clonal Selection and Antigen Binding
B cells can independently recognize microbes (example here is a virus) and their foreign antigens, and can bind them with their Ig receptors. This is how the initial selection of the antigen-specific B-cell clone occurs.

2 Antigen Processing and Presentation
Once the microbe is attached, the B cell endocytoses it, processes it into smaller protein units, and displays these on the MHC-II complex (similar to other APCs). This event readies the antigen for presentation to a specific T$_H$ cell.

3 B Cell/T$_H$ Cell Cooperation and Recognition
For most B cells to become functional, they must interact with a T helper cell that bears receptors for antigen from the same microbe. This T cell has previously been activated by an APC (see figure 15.9). The two cells engage in linked recognition, in which the MHC-II receptor bearing antigen on the B cell binds to the T cell antigen receptor, the CD3 molecule, and the CD4 molecule on the T cell (inset).

4 B Cell Activation
The T cell gives off additional signals in the form of interleukins and B-cell growth factors. The linked receptors and the chemical stimuli serve to activate the B cell. Such activation signals an increase in cell metabolism, leading to cell enlargement, proliferation, and differentiation.

5-7 Expansion of Three Populations: Memory, Regulatory, and Plasma Cells
The activated B cell undergoes numerous mitotic divisions, which expand the clone of cells bearing this specificity and produce memory cells, regulatory cells, and plasma cells.
Plasma Cells/Antibody Synthesis
The plasma cells are short-lived, active secretory cells that synthesize and release antibodies. These antibodies (here IgM) have the same specificity as the Ig receptor and circulate in the fluid compartments of the body, where they react with the same antigens and microbes shown in step 1.

Process Figure 15.10 Events in B-cell activation and antibody synthesis.

peptide determinants. The antigen is then bound to the MHC-II receptors on the surface of the B cell.

3. **B-cell/T-cell recognition and cooperation.** The MHC/Ag complex is recognized and bound by a T_H cell. The B cell receives chemical signals from macrophages and T cells (interleukins).

4. **B-cell activation.** The combination of these stimuli on the membrane receptors causes a signal to be transmitted internally to the B-cell nucleus. These events trigger B-cell activation. An activated B cell undergoes an increase in DNA synthesis, organelle bulk, and overall size in preparation for entering the cell cycle and dividing.

5–6. **Clonal expansion.** A stimulated B cell multiplies through successive mitotic divisions and produces a large population of genetically identical daughter cells. Some cells that stop short of becoming fully differentiated are **memory cells,** which remain for long periods to react with that same antigen at a later time. This reaction also expands the clone size, so that during subsequent exposure to that antigen there are more cells with that specificity. This expansion of the clone size accounts for the increased speed and intensity of the memory response. Secondly, a group of cells that is important in minimizing the immune response, regulatory B cells, is created. The third type of progeny are large, specialized, terminally differentiated B cells called **plasma cells.**

7. **Regulatory B-cell activity. Regulatory B cells** are thought to secrete interleukin-10, a cytokine which suppresses helper T cells. Often this serves to dampen autoimmune reactions of the T-cell system. When B_{reg} cells don't function properly, the immune system attacks self inappropriately. Conversely, B_{reg} cells may have a role in some cancers. In those cases they work too well

and dampen the immune response to cancerous cells. For these reasons, researchers are studying how to modulate B_{reg} cells to combat these two types of disease.

8. **Antibody production and secretion.** The primary action of plasma cells is to secrete into the surrounding tissues copious amounts of antibodies with the same specificity as the original receptor (figure 15.10). Although an individual plasma cell can produce around 2,000 antibodies per second, production does not continue indefinitely. The plasma cells do not survive for long and deteriorate after they have synthesized antibodies.

Products of B Lymphocytes: Antibody Structure and Functions

The Structure of Immunoglobulins

Earlier we saw that a basic immunoglobulin (Ig) molecule contains four polypeptide chains connected by disulfide bonds. Let us view this structure once again, using an IgG molecule as a model. Two functionally distinct segments called *fragments* can be differentiated. The two "arms" that bind antigen are termed antigen binding fragments (FAbs), and the rest of the molecule is the crystallizable fragment (Fc), so called because it was the first to be crystallized in pure form. The amino-terminal end of each FAb fragment (consisting of the variable regions of the heavy and light chains) folds into a groove that will accommodate one epitope. The presence of a special region at the site of attachment between the FAb and Fc fragments allows swiveling of the FAb fragments. In this way, they can change their angle to accommodate nearby antigen sites that vary slightly in distance and position. The Fc fragment is involved in binding to various cells and molecules of the immune system itself. **Figure 15.11** shows two views of antibody structure.

Figure 15.11 Working models of antibody structure.
(a) Diagrammatic view of IgG depicts the principal functional areas (FAbs and Fc) of the molecule. **(b)** Realistic model of immunoglobulin shows the tertiary and quaternary structure achieved by additional intrachain and interchain bonds.

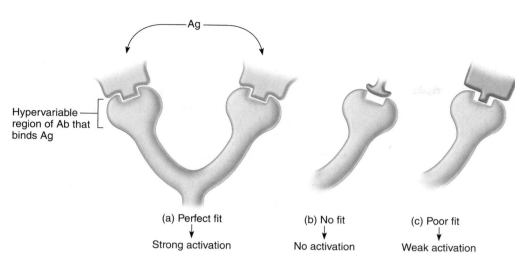

Hypervariable region of Ab that binds Ag

Ag

(a) Perfect fit
↓
Strong activation

(b) No fit
↓
No activation

(c) Poor fit
↓
Weak activation

Figure 15.12 Antigen-antibody binding. The union of antibody (Ab) and antigen (Ag) is characterized by a certain degree of fit and is supported by a multitude of weak linkages, especially hydrogen bonds and electrostatic attraction. The better the fit—that is, antigen in **(a)** versus antigen in **(c)**—the stronger the stimulation of the lymphocyte during the activation stage.

Antibody-Antigen Interactions and the Function of the FAb

The site on the antibody where the epitope binds is composed of a *hypervariable region* whose amino acid content can be extremely varied. Antibodies differ somewhat in the exactness of this groove for antigen, but a certain complementary fit is necessary for the antigen to be held effectively **(figure 15.12).** The specificity of antigen binding sites for antigens is very similar to enzymes and substrates (in fact, some antibodies are used as enzymes, as you learned in Insight 8.2). Because the specificity of the two FAb sites is identical, an Ig molecule can bind epitope on the same cell or on two separate cells and thereby link them.

The principal activity of an antibody is to unite with, immobilize, call attention to, or neutralize the antigen for which it was formed **(figure 15.13).** Antibodies called opsonins stimulate **opsonization** (ahp"-son-uh-zaz'-shun),

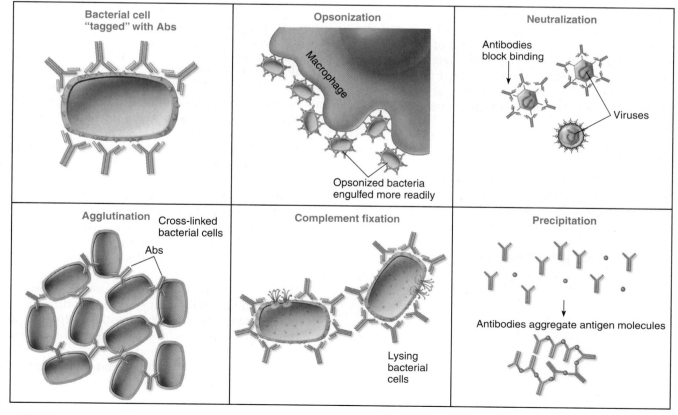

Figure 15.13 Summary of antibody functions. Complement fixation, agglutination, and precipitation are covered further in chapter 17.

a process in which microorganisms or other particles are coated with specific antibodies so that they will be more readily recognized by phagocytes, which dispose of them. Opsonization has been likened to putting handles on a slippery object to provide phagocytes a better grip. The capacity for antibodies to aggregate, or **agglutinate,** antigens is the consequence of their cross-linking cells or particles into large clumps. Agglutination renders microbes immobile and enhances their phagocytosis. This is a principle behind certain immune tests discussed in chapter 17. The interaction of an antibody with complement can result in the specific rupturing of cells and some viruses. In **neutralization** reactions, antibodies fill the surface receptors on a virus or the active site on a microbial enzyme to prevent it from attaching normally. An **antitoxin** is a special type of antibody that neutralizes bacterial exotoxins.[2] Note that not all antibodies are protective; some neither benefit nor harm, and a few actually cause diseases.

Functions of the Fc Fragment

Although the FAb fragments bind antigen, the Fc fragment has a different binding function. In most classes of immunoglobulin, the Fc end contains an effector portion that can bind to receptors on the membranes of cells, such as macrophages, neutrophils, eosinophils, mast cells, basophils, and lymphocytes. The effect of an antibody's Fc fragment binding to a cell depends upon that cell's role. In the case of opsonization, the attachment of antibody to foreign cells and viruses exposes the Fc fragments to phagocytes. Certain antibodies have regions on the Fc portion for fixing complement; and in some immune reactions, the binding of Fc causes the release of cytokines. For example, the Fc end of the antibody of allergy (IgE) binds to basophils and mast cells, which causes the release of allergic mediators such as histamine. The size and amino acid composition of Fc also determine an antibody's permeability, its distribution in the body, and its class.

Accessory Molecules on Immunoglobulins

All antibodies contain molecules in addition to the basic polypeptides. Varying amounts of carbohydrates are affixed to the constant regions in most instances **(table 15.2).** Two additional accessory molecules are the *J chain,* which joins the monomers[3] of IgA and IgM, and the *secretory component,* which helps move IgA across mucous membranes.

---

2. There are other uses for the term antitoxin, notably substances used to counteract snake bites, etc. But in immunology, an antitoxin is an antibody that binds to microbial toxins.

3. "Monomer" means "one unit" or "one part." Accordingly, "dimer" means "two units," pentamer means "five units," and polymer means "many units."

The Classes of Immunoglobulins

Immunoglobulins exist as structural and functional classes called *isotypes* (compared and contrasted in table 15.2). The differences in these classes are due primarily to variations in the Fc fragment. The classes are differentiated with shorthand names (Ig, followed by a letter: IgG, IgA, IgM, IgD, IgE).

The structure of IgG has already been presented. It is a monomer produced by plasma cells in a primary response and by memory cells responding the second time to a given antigenic stimulus. It is by far the most prevalent antibody circulating throughout the tissue fluids and blood. It has numerous functions: It neutralizes toxins, opsonizes, and fixes complement; and it is the only antibody capable of crossing the placenta.

The two forms of IgA are (1) a monomer that circulates in small amounts in the blood and (2) a dimer that is a significant component of the mucous and serous secretions of the salivary glands, intestine, nasal membrane, breast, lung, and genitourinary tract. The dimer, called secretory IgA, is formed by two monomers held together by a J chain. To facilitate the transport of IgA across membranes, a secretory piece is later added. IgA coats the surface of these membranes and appears free in saliva, tears, colostrum, and mucus. It provides the most important specific local immunity to enteric, respiratory, and genitourinary pathogens. During lactation the breast becomes a site for the proliferation of lymphocytes that produce IgA. The very earliest secretion of the breast, a thin, yellow milk called **colostrum,** is very high in IgA. These antibodies form a protective coating in the gastrointestinal tract of a nursing infant that guards against infection by a number of enteric pathogens (*Escherichia coli, Salmonella,* poliovirus, rotavirus). Protection at this level is especially critical because an infant's own IgA and natural intestinal barriers are not yet developed. As with immunity in utero, the necessary antibodies will be donated only if the mother herself has active immunity to the microbe through a prior infection or vaccination.

IgM is a huge molecule composed of five monomers (making it a pentamer) attached by the Fc portions to a central J chain. With its 10 binding sites, this molecule has tremendous capacity for binding antigen. IgM is the first class synthesized following the host's first encounter with antigen. Its complement-fixing qualities make it an important antibody in many immune reactions. It circulates mainly in the blood and does not cross the placental barrier.

IgD is a monomer found in minuscule amounts in the serum, and it does not fix complement, opsonize, or cross the placenta. Its main function is that it is the receptor for antigen on B cells, usually along with IgM. It seems to be the triggering molecule for B-cell activation.

IgE is also an uncommon blood component unless one is allergic or has a parasitic worm infection. Its Fc region inter-

Table 15.2 Characteristics of the Immunoglobulin (Ig) Classes

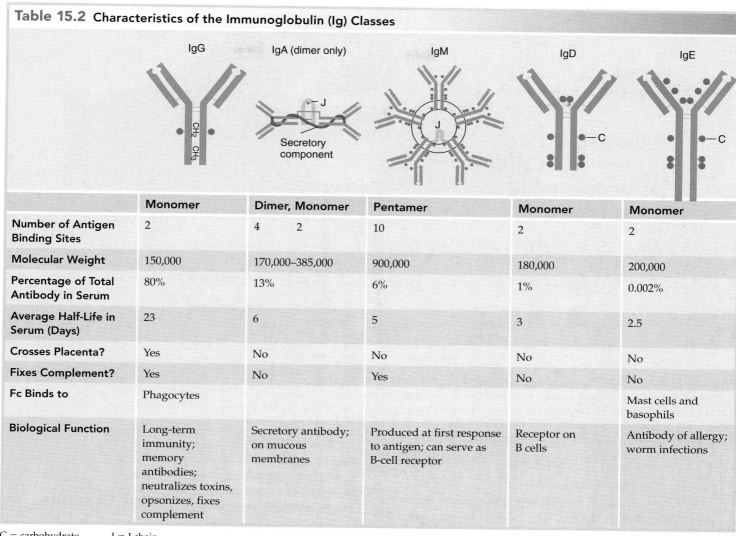

	Monomer	Dimer, Monomer		Pentamer	Monomer	Monomer
	IgG	IgA (dimer only)		IgM	IgD	IgE
Number of Antigen Binding Sites	2	4	2	10	2	2
Molecular Weight	150,000	170,000–385,000		900,000	180,000	200,000
Percentage of Total Antibody in Serum	80%	13%		6%	1%	0.002%
Average Half-Life in Serum (Days)	23	6		5	3	2.5
Crosses Placenta?	Yes	No		No	No	No
Fixes Complement?	Yes	No		Yes	No	No
Fc Binds to	Phagocytes					Mast cells and basophils
Biological Function	Long-term immunity; memory antibodies; neutralizes toxins, opsonizes, fixes complement	Secretory antibody; on mucous membranes		Produced at first response to antigen; can serve as B-cell receptor	Receptor on B cells	Antibody of allergy; worm infections

C = carbohydrate.   J = J chain.

acts with receptors on mast cells and basophils. Its biological role is to stimulate an inflammatory response through the release of potent physiological substances by the basophils and mast cells. Because inflammation enlists blood cells such as eosinophils and lymphocytes to the site of infection, it is an important defense against parasites. Unfortunately, IgE has another, more insidious effect—that of mediating anaphylaxis, asthma, and certain other allergies (explained in chapter 16).

Monitoring Antibody Production over Time: Primary and Secondary Responses to Antigens

We can learn a great deal about how the immune system reacts to an antigen by studying the levels of antibodies in serum over time **(figure 15.14)**. This level is expressed quantitatively as the **titer** (ty'-tur), or concentration of antibodies. Upon the first exposure to an antigen, the system undergoes a **primary response.** The earliest part of this response, the *latent period,* is marked by a lack of antibodies for that antigen, but much activity is occurring. During this time, the antigen is being concentrated in lymphoid tissue and is being processed by the correct clones of B lymphocytes. As plasma cells synthesize antibodies, the serum titer increases to a certain plateau and then tapers off to a low level over a few weeks or months. It turns out that, early in the primary response, most of the antibodies are the IgM type, which is the first class to be secreted by plasma cells. Later, the class of the antibodies (but not their specificity) is switched to IgG or some other class (IgA or IgE).

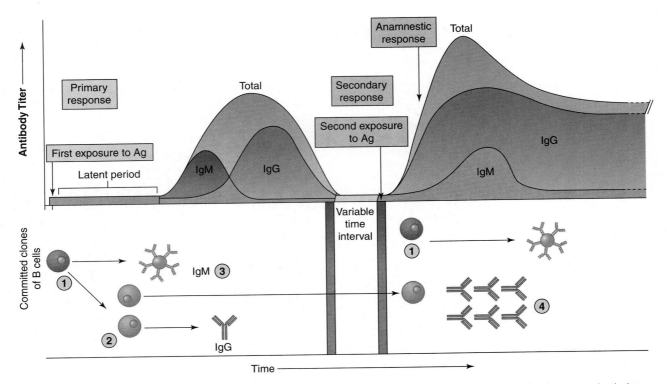

Process Figure 15.14 Primary and secondary responses to antigens. *(Top)* The pattern of antibody titer and subclasses as monitored during initial and subsequent exposure to the same antigen. *(Bottom)* A view of the B-cell responses that account for the pattern. Depicted are ① clonal selection, ② production of memory cells, and the predominant antibody class occurring at ③ first and ④ second contact with antigen. Note that residual memory cells remaining from the primary response are ready to act immediately, which produces the rapid rise of antibody levels early in the secondary period.

When the immune system is exposed again to the same immunogen within weeks, months, or even years, a **secondary response** occurs. The rate of antibody synthesis, the peak titer, and the length of antibody persistence are greatly increased over the primary response. The speed and intensity seen in this response are attributable to the memory B cells that were formed during the primary response. Because of its association with recall, the secondary response is also called the **anamnestic response.** The advantage of this response is evident: It provides a quick and potent strike against subsequent exposures to infectious agents. This memory effect is the fundamental basis for vaccination, which we discuss later.

15.4 Learning Outcomes—Can You. . .

13. . . . diagram the steps in the B-cell response?

14. . . . make a detailed drawing of an antibody molecule?

15. . . . explain the various end results of antibody binding to an antigen?

16. . . . list the five types of antibodies and important facts about each?

17. . . . describe the memory response?

15.5 Steps III and IV: T-Cell Response

Cell-Mediated Immunity (CMI)

During the time that B cells have been actively responding to antigens, the T-cell limb of the system has been similarly engaged. The responses of T cells, however, are **cell-mediated immunities,** which require the direct involvement of T lymphocytes throughout the course of the reaction. These reactions are among the most complex and diverse in the immune system and involve several subsets of T cells whose particular actions are dictated by the APCs that activate them. T cells are restricted; that is, they require some type of MHC (self) recognition before they can be activated, and all produce cytokines with a spectrum of biological effects.

Rather than making antibodies to control foreign antigens, T cells stimulate other T cells, B cells, and phagocytes.

The Activation of T Cells and Their Differentiation into Subsets

The mature T cells in lymphoid organs are primed to react with antigens that have been processed and presented to them by dendritic cells and macrophages. They recognize an antigen only when it is presented in association with an MHC carrier (see figure 15.9). T cells with CD4 receptors recognize endocytosed peptides presented on MHC-II, and T cells with CD8 receptors recognize peptides presented on MHC-I.

A T cell is initially sensitized when an antigen/MHC complex is bound to its receptors. As with B cells, activated T cells transform in preparation for mitotic divisions, and they differentiate into one of the subsets of effector cells and memory cells that can respond quickly to MHC plus antigen on APCs upon subsequent contact **(table 15.3).** Memory T cells are some of the longest-lived blood cells known (70 years in one well-documented case).

T Helper (T$_H$) Cells Helper cells play a central role in regulating immune reactions to antigens, including those of B cells and other T cells. They are also involved in activating macrophages. They do this directly by receptor contact and indirectly by releasing cytokines like interferon gamma (IFNγ). T helper cells secrete interleukin-2, which stimulates the primary growth and activation of many types of T cells, including cytotoxic T cells. Some T helper cells secrete interleukins-4, -5, and -6, which stimulate various activities of B cells. T helper cells are the most prevalent type of T cell in the blood and lymphoid organs, making up about 65% of this population. The severe depression of this class of T cells (with CD4 receptors) by HIV is what largely accounts for the immunopathology of AIDS.

When T helper (CD4) cells are stimulated by antigen/MHC complex, they differentiate into either T helper 1 (T$_H$1) cells, T helper 2 (T$_H$2) cells, or T helper 17 (T$_H$17) cells, probably depending on what type of cytokines the antigen-presenting cells secrete. A T$_H$1 cell will activate phagocytic cells to be better at inducing inflammation, resulting in a delayed hypersensitivity reaction. If the APC secretes another set of cytokines, the T cell will differentiate into a T$_H$2 cell. These cells have the functions of secreting substances that influence B-cell differentiation and enhancing the antibody response. One of their important roles is to respond to extracellular microbes, helminths, and allergens. T$_H$17 cells are so-named because they secrete interleukin-17, which leads to the production of other cytokines that promote inflammation. Inflammation is useful, of course, but when excessive or inappropriate may lead to inflammatory diseases such as Crohn's disease or psoriasis. T$_H$17 may be critical to these conditions.

Regulatory T (T$_R$) Cells: Cells That Maintain the Happy Medium T$_R$ cells are also broadly in the T$_H$ class, in that they also carry CD4 markers. But they are usually put in their own category. They act to control the inflammatory process, to prevent autoimmunity, and to make sure the immune response doesn't inappropriately target normal flora. Please remember that regulatory B cells also regulate the degree of response from T cells. So B cells are involved in two ways in the T-cell response: They can become activated to become plasma cells by cytokines from activated T cells, and already activated regulatory B cells can secrete their own cytokines to dampen the T-cell response.

Cytotoxic T (T$_C$) Cells: Cells That Kill Other Cells Cytotoxicity is the capacity of certain T cells to kill a specific target cell. It is a fascinating and powerful property that accounts for much of our immunity to foreign cells and cancer, and yet, under some circumstances, it can lead to disease. For a CD8 **killer T cell** to become activated, it must recognize a foreign peptide complexed with self MHC-I presented to it and mount a direct attack upon the target cell. After activation, the T$_C$ cell severely injures the target cell **(figure 15.15).** This process involves the secretion of **perforins**[4] and **granzymes.** Perforins are proteins that can punch holes in the membranes of target cells. Granzymes are enzymes that attack proteins of target cells. The action of the perforins causes ions to leak

---

4. **perforin** From the term *perforate* or to penetrate with holes.

Table 15.3 Characteristics of Subsets of T Cells

Types	Primary Receptors on T Cell	Functions/Important Features
T helper cell 1 (T$_H$1)	CD4	Activates the cell-mediated immunity pathway, secretes tumor necrosis factor and interferon gamma, also responsible for delayed hypersensitivity (allergy occurring several hours or days after contact)
T helper cell 2 (T$_H$2)	CD4	Drives B-cell proliferation, secretes IL-4, IL-5, IL-13
T helper cell 17 (T$_H$17)	CD4	Promotes inflammation, secretes IL-17
T regulatory cell (T$_R$)	CD4	Controls specific immune response, prevents autoimmunity
T cytotoxic cell (T$_C$)	CD8	Destroys a target foreign cell by lysis; important in destruction of complex microbes, cancer cells, virus-infected cells; graft rejection; requires MHC-I for function

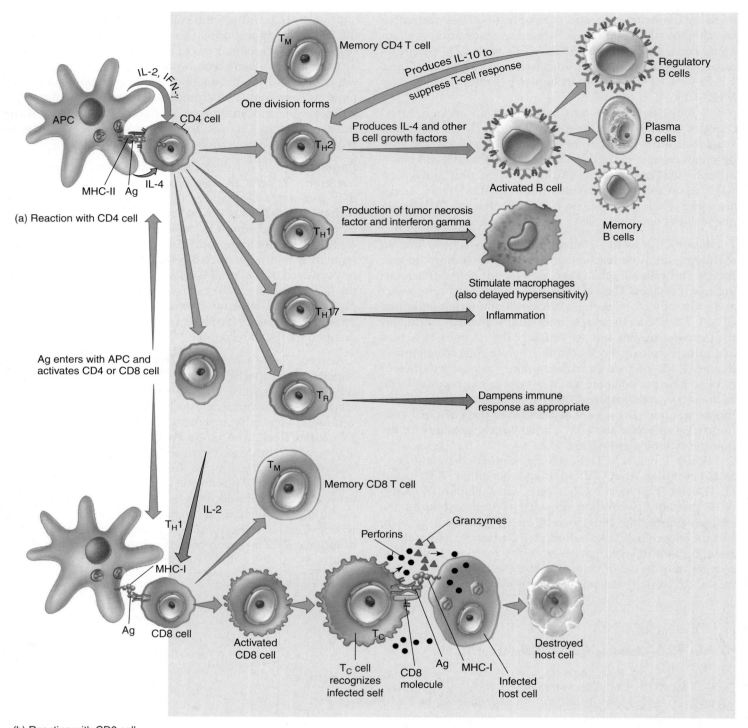

(a) Reaction with CD4 cell

(b) Reaction with CD8 cell

Figure 15.15 Overall scheme of T-cell activation and differentiation into different types of T cells. Antigen-presenting cells present antigenic peptides to T cells bearing either CD4 or CD8 markers. Upon binding antigen/MHC-I complex, CD8 cells lead to the apoptosis of those cells. CD4 cells bind antigen/MHC-II complexes on APCs and, depending on the type of cytokine released by the APC, become either memory cells, T_H1, T_H2, T_H17, or T_R cells. Regulatory B cells of the same specificity can dampen the activation of T cells.

out of target cells and creates a passageway for granzymes to enter. These events are usually followed by targeted cell death through a process called *apoptosis*.

Target cells that T_C cells can destroy include the following:

- Virally infected cells (figure 15.15). Cytotoxic cells recognize these because of telltale virus peptides expressed on their surface. Cytotoxic defenses are an essential protection against viruses.
- Cancer cells. T cells constantly survey the tissues and immediately attack any abnormal cells they encounter **(figure 15.16).** The importance of this function is clearly demonstrated in the susceptibility of T-cell-deficient people to cancer (chapter 16).
- Cells from other animals and humans. Cytotoxic CMI is the most important factor in graft rejection. In this instance, the T_C cells attack the foreign tissues that have been implanted into a recipient's body.

Additional Cells With Orders to Kill Natural killer (NK) cells are a type of lymphocyte related to T cells that lack specificity for antigens. They circulate through the spleen, blood, and lungs and are probably the first killer cells to attack cancer cells and virus-infected cells. They destroy such cells by similar mechanisms as T cells. They are not considered part of specific cell-mediated immunity although their activities are acutely sensitive to cytokines such as interleukin-12 and interferon. Finally, there is a hybrid kind of cell that is part killer cell and part T cell, with T-cell receptors for antigen and the ability to

Figure 15.16 A cytotoxic T cell (lower blue cell) has mounted a successful attack on a tumor cell (larger yellow cell). These small killer cells perforate their cellular targets with holes that lead to lysis and death.

release large amounts of cytokines very quickly, leading to cell death. These cells are called natural killer T cells, or NK cells. They have recently been implicated as a cause of asthma.

As you can see, the T-cell system is very complex. In summary, T cells differentiate into five different types of cells (and also memory cells), each of which contributes to the orchestrated immune response, under the influence of a multitude of cytokines. The T-cell system is summarized in figure 15.15. You can compare it with the B-cell system depicted in figure 15.10.

15.5 Learning Outcomes—Can You ...

18. ... list the three major types of cells T cells will differentiate into after stimulation?
19. ... describe the main functions of these three types of T cells?
20. ... explain how T_C cells kill other cells?

15.6 Specific Immunity and Vaccination

Specific immunity in humans and other mammals is categorized using two different sets of criteria which, when combined, result in four specific descriptors of the immune state. Immunity can either be active or passive. Also, it can be either natural or artificial.

Active immunity occurs when an individual receives an immune stimulus (antigen) that activates the B and T cells, causing the body to produce immune substances such as antibodies. Active immunity is marked by several characteristics: (1) it creates a memory that renders the person ready for quick action upon reexposure to that same antigen; (2) it requires several days to develop; and (3) it lasts for a relatively long time, sometimes for life. Active immunity can be stimulated by natural or artificial means.

Passive immunity occurs when an individual receives immune substances (antibodies) that were produced actively in the body of another human or animal donor. The recipient is protected for a short time even though he or she has not had prior exposure to the antigen. It is characterized by (1) lack of memory for the original antigen; (2) lack of production of new antibodies against that disease; (3) immediate onset of protection; and (4) short-term effectiveness, because antibodies have a limited period of function and, ultimately, the recipient's body disposes of them. Passive immunity can also be natural or artificial in origin.

Passive immunity can also come in the form of monoclonal antibodies **(Insight 15.1).**

Natural immunity encompasses any immunity that is acquired during the normal biological experiences of an individual rather than through medical intervention.

Artificial immunity is protection from infection obtained through medical procedures. This type of immunity is induced by immunization with vaccines and immune serum.

INSIGHT 15.1   Monoclonal Antibodies: Variety Without Limit

The value of antibodies as tools for locating or identifying antigens is well established. For many years, antiserum extracted from human or animal blood was the main source of antibodies for tests and therapy, but most antiserum has a basic problem. It contains **polyclonal antibodies,** meaning that it is a mixture of different antibodies because it reflects dozens of immune reactions from a wide variety of B-cell clones. This characteristic is to be expected, because several immune reactions may be occurring simultaneously, and even a single species of microbe (with its many epitopes) can stimulate several different types of antibodies. Certain applications in immunology require a pure preparation of **monoclonal antibodies (MAbs)** that originate from a single clone and have a single specificity for antigen.

Monoclonal antibodies are made possible by hybridizing cancer cells and activated B cells in the lab. This technique began with the discovery that tumors isolated from multiple myelomas in mice consist of identical plasma cells. These monoclonal plasma cells create a strikingly pure form of antibodies with a single specificity and continue to divide indefinitely. Immunologists recognized the potential in these plasma cells and devised a **hybridoma** approach to creating MAbs. The basic idea behind this approach is to hybridize or fuse a myeloma cell with a normal plasma cell from a mouse spleen to create an immortal cell that secretes a supply of functional antibodies with a single specificity.

Early monoclonal antibodies were useful for research but were not used in medical therapy because the antibodies were of mouse origin. The human immune system usually quickly cleared these foreign proteins. Advances allowed the MAbs to be "humanized," either through hybridizing the mouse Fab portion with a human Fc portion (creating half-mouse, half-human MAbs) or by producing fully human MAbs through the very newest molecular biology techniques.

Currently, MAbs are used therapeutically to treat certain cancers and autoimmune diseases such as rheumatoid arthritis. One MAb drug is used to prevent RSV disease (a viral respiratory infection) in high-risk children.

Summary of the technique for producing monoclonal antibodies by hybridizing myeloma tumor cells with normal plasma cells. **(a)** A normal mouse is inoculated with an antigen having the desired specificity, and activated cells are isolated from its spleen. A special strain of mouse provides the myeloma cells. **(b)** The two cell populations are mixed with polyethylene glycol, which causes some cells in the mixture to fuse and form hybridomas. **(c)** Surviving cells are cultured and separated into individual wells. **(d)** Tests are performed on each hybridoma to determine the specificity of the antibody (Ab) it secretes. **(e)** A hybridoma with the desired specificity is grown in tissue culture; antibody product is then isolated and purified.

Figure 15.17 illustrates the various possible combinations of acquired immunities.

Natural Active Immunity: Getting the Infection

After recovering from infectious disease, a person will generally be actively resistant to reinfection for a period that varies according to the disease. In the case of childhood viral infections such as measles, mumps, and rubella, this natural active stimulus provides nearly lifelong immunity. Other diseases result in a less extended immunity of a few months to years (such as pneumococcal pneumonia and shigellosis), and reinfection is possible. Even a subclinical infection can

Acquired Immunity

Natural Immunity
is acquired through the normal life experiences of
a human and is not induced through medical means.

Artificial Immunity
is that produced purposefully through
medical procedures (also called immunization).

Active Immunity
is the consequence of
a person developing his
own immune response
to a microbe.

Passive Immunity
is the consequence of
one person receiving
preformed immunity
made by another person.

Active Immunity
is the consequence of a
person developing his
own immune response
to a microbe.

Passive Immunity
is the consequence
of one person receiving
preformed immunity
made by another person.

Figure 15.17 Categories of acquired immunities. Natural immunities, which occur during the normal course of life, are either active (acquired from an infection and then recovering) or passive (antibodies donated by the mother to her child). Artificial immunities are acquired through medical practices and can be active (vaccinations with antigen to stimulate an immune response) or passive (immune therapy with a serum containing antibodies).

stimulate natural active immunity. This probably accounts for the fact that some people are immune to an infectious agent without ever having been noticeably infected with or vaccinated for it.

Natural Passive Immunity: Mother to Child

Natural, passively acquired immunity occurs only as a result of the prenatal and postnatal mother-child relationship. During fetal life, IgG antibodies circulating in the maternal bloodstream are small enough to pass or be actively transported across the placenta. Antibodies against tetanus, diphtheria, pertussis, and several viruses regularly cross the placenta. This natural mechanism provides an infant with a mixture of many maternal antibodies that can protect it for the first few critical months outside the womb, while its own immune system is gradually developing active immunity. Depending on the microbe, passive protection lasts anywhere from a few months to a year. But eventually, the infant's body clears the antibody. Most childhood vaccinations are timed so that there is no lapse in protection against common childhood infections.

Another source of natural passive immunity comes to the baby by way of mother's milk. Although the human infant acquires 99% of natural passive immunity in utero and only about 1% through nursing, the milk-borne antibodies provide a special type of intestinal protection that is not available from transplacental antibodies.

Artificial Active Immunization: Vaccination:

The term *vaccination* originated from the Latin word *vacca* (cow), because the cowpox virus was used in one of the first preparations for active immunization against smallpox **(Insight 15.2).** Vaccination exposes a person to a specially prepared microbial (antigenic) stimulus, which then triggers the immune system to produce antibodies and lymphocytes to protect the person upon future exposure to that microbe. As with natural active immunity, the degree and length of protection vary. Commercial vaccines are currently available for many diseases. Also, vaccines are being developed for cancer. Some of these vaccines are not targeted to microbes at all. Also, some are designed to be used as treatment rather than prevention.

Artificial Passive Immunization: Immunotherapy

In immunotherapy, a patient who is ill with a particular infection, or at risk for acquiring it, is administered a preparation that contains specific antibodies against that infectious agent. In the past, these therapeutic substances were obtained by vaccinating animals (horses, in particular), then taking blood and extracting the serum. However, horse serum is now used only in limited situations because of the potential for hypersensitivity to it. Pooled human serum from donor blood (gamma globulin) and immune serum globulins containing high quantities of antibodies are more frequently used.

INSIGHT 15.2   The Lively History of Active Immunization

The basic notion of immunization has existed for thousands of years. It probably stemmed from the observation that persons who had recovered from certain communicable diseases rarely if ever got a second case. Undoubtedly, the earliest crude attempts involved bringing a susceptible person into contact with a diseased person or animal. The first recorded attempt at immunization occurred in sixth-century China. It consisted of drying and grinding up smallpox scabs and blowing them with a straw into the nostrils of vulnerable family members. By the 10th century, this practice had changed to the deliberate inoculation of dried pus from the smallpox pustules of one patient into the arm of a healthy person, a technique later called **variolation** (variola is the smallpox virus). This method was used in parts of the Far East for centuries before Lady Mary Montagu brought it to England in 1721. Although the principles of the technique had some merit, unfortunately many recipients and their contacts died of smallpox. This outcome vividly demonstrates a cardinal rule for a workable vaccine: It must contain an antigen that will provide protection but not cause the disease. Variolation was so controversial that any English practitioner caught doing it was charged with a felony.

Eventually, this human experimentation paved the way for the first really effective vaccine, developed by the English physician Edward Jenner in 1796. Jenner conducted the

Detail from "The Cowpock," an 1808 etching that caricatured the worst fears of the English public concerning Edward Jenner's smallpox vaccine.

first scientifically controlled study, one that had a tremendous impact on the advance of medicine. His work gave rise to the words **vaccine** and *vaccination* (from L., *vacca*, cow), which now apply to any immunity obtained by inoculation with selected antigens. Jenner was inspired by the case of a dairymaid who had been infected by a pustular infection called cowpox. This related virus afflicts cattle but causes a milder condition in humans. She explained that she and other milkmaids had remained free of smallpox. Other residents of the region expressed a similar confidence in the cross-protection of cowpox. To test the effectiveness of this new vaccine, Jenner prepared material from human cowpox lesions and inoculated a young boy. When challenged 2 months later with an injection of crusts from a smallpox patient, the boy proved immune.

Jenner's discovery—that a less pathogenic agent could confer protection against a more pathogenic one—is especially remarkable in view of the fact that microscopy was still in its infancy and the nature of viruses was unknown. At first, the use of the vaccine was regarded with some fear and skepticism (see illustration). When Jenner's method proved successful and word of its significance spread, it was eventually adopted in many other countries. In 1973, the World Health Organization declared that smallpox had been eradicated. As a result, smallpox vaccination had been discontinued until recently, due to the threat of bioterrorism.

Immune serum globulins are used to protect people who have been exposed to hepatitis, measles, and rubella. More specific immune serum, obtained from patients recovering from a recent infection, is useful in preventing and treating hepatitis B, rabies, pertussis, and tetanus.

An outline summarizing the system of host defenses covered in chapters 14 and 15 was presented in figure 14.1. You may want to use this resource to review major aspects of immunity.

Immunization: Methods of Manipulating Immunity for Therapeutic Purposes

Methods that actively or passively immunize people are widely used in disease prevention and treatment. In the case of passive immunization, a patient is given preformed antibodies, which is actually a form of **immunotherapy.** In the case of active immunization, a patient is vaccinated with a microbe or its antigens, providing a form of advance protection.

Passive Immunization

As mentioned earlier, the first attempts at passive immunization involved the transfusion of horse serum containing antitoxins to prevent tetanus and to treat patients exposed to diphtheria. Since then, antisera from animals have been replaced with products of human origin that function with various degrees of specificity. Immune serum globulin (ISG), sometimes called *gamma globulin,* contains immunoglobulin extracted from the pooled blood of at least 1,000 human donors. The method of processing ISG concentrates the antibodies to increase potency and eliminates potential pathogens (such as the hepatitis B and HIV viruses). It is a treatment of choice in preventing measles and hepatitis A and in replacing antibodies in immunodeficient patients. Most forms of ISG are injected intramuscularly to minimize adverse reactions, and the protection it provides lasts 2 to 3 months.

A preparation called specific immune globulin (SIG) is derived from a more defined group of donors. Companies that prepare SIG obtain serum from patients who are convalescing and in a hyperimmune state after such infections as pertussis, tetanus, chickenpox, and hepatitis B. These globulins are preferable to ISG because they contain higher titers of specific antibodies obtained from a smaller pool of patients. Although useful for prophylaxis in persons who have been exposed or may be exposed to infectious agents, these sera are often limited in availability.

When a human immune globulin is not available, anti-sera and antitoxins of animal origin can be used. Sera produced in horses are available for diphtheria, botulism, and spider and snake bites. Unfortunately, the presence of horse antigens can stimulate allergies such as serum sickness or anaphylaxis (see chapter 16). Although donated immunities only last a relatively short time, they act immediately and can protect patients for whom no other useful medication or vaccine exists.

Artificial Active Immunity: Vaccination

Active immunity can be conferred artificially by **vaccination**—exposing a person to material that is antigenic but not pathogenic. The discovery of vaccination was one of the farthest reaching and most important developments in medical science (see Insight 15.2). The basic principle behind vaccination is to stimulate a primary and secondary anamnestic response that primes the immune system for future exposure to a virulent pathogen. If this pathogen enters the body, the immune response will be immediate, powerful, and sustained.

Vaccines have profoundly reduced the prevalence and impact of many infectious diseases that were once common and often deadly. In this section, we survey the principles of vaccine preparation and important considerations surrounding vaccine indication and safety. (Vaccines are also given specific consideration in later chapters on infectious diseases and organ systems.)

More recently, vaccines have been developed for threats to human health that do not involve microbes at all **(Insight 15.3).**

Principles of Vaccine Preparation A vaccine must be considered from the standpoints of antigen selection, effectiveness, ease in administration, safety, and cost. In natural immunity, an infectious agent stimulates a relatively long-term protective response. In artificial active immunity, the objective is to obtain this same response with a modified version of the microbe or its components. Qualities of an

---

INSIGHT 15.3   Manipulating the Immune System to Fight Lots of Things Besides Infections

Some new vaccines in development seem to violate two important principles of immunization: (1) They are not targeted at microbes at all, and (2) they are not designed to prevent a disease. The new "vaccines" are cancer vaccines. Note that two approved cancer vaccines do have the traits of traditional vaccines. In 2006, a vaccine for human papillomavirus (HPV) was approved. This vaccine can prevent cervical cancer, because most cervical cancers are caused by HPV. The vaccine against hepatitis B can also prevent liver cancer. In that sense, they bear the designation *cancer vaccines.* They prevent the cancer by preventing infection with cancer-causing viruses.

Other vaccines are in development that are aimed at cancers that are not associated with microbial infection. A vaccine called Provenge has been in the works for some years. This vaccine is therapeutic rather than preventive. It is intended for patients who already have prostate cancer. It stimulates the immune system to more effectively fight malignant cells. Studies found that it extended the lives of patients by several months.

One experimental approach to the treatment of cervical cancer exploits an unrelated microbe and its ability to infect—and deploy—antigen-presenting cells. A vaccine company engineered a strain of *Listeria monocytogenes* to carry an epitope found on the surface of cervical cancer cells. Women with the cancer were injected with the engineered bacterium, which homes into antigen-presenting cells, promptly causing the APCs to display the cervical cancer marker, initiating the cascade of a specific immune response against those cancer cells.

Regulatory T cells are at the heart of several anticancer strategies in development. It appears that cancer patients with higher supplies of regulatory T cells don't fare as well as patients with lower numbers, due to the immune-dampening effects of the T_R cells. Treating these patients with a drug that reduces the number of T_R cells has caused marked improvement in their cancers in

many cases. Likewise, increasing the number of T_R cells is being studied as a more fine-tuned method of dampening autoimmunity in diseases such as rheumatoid arthritis.

The vaccine approach is now being pioneered to treat cocaine addiction, cigarette smoking, high blood pressure, and even obesity. Scientists are fighting these diseases by getting the body to produce antibodies to either the addictive substances, or to hormones in the body that are going awry and causing disease. For example, researchers managed to get the body to produce antibodies to cocaine molecules, by conjugating the (too small) cocaine particles to a protein derived from a *Vibrio cholerae* bacterium. And another group is "inoculating" humans with the hormone angiotensin, which regulates the width of blood vessels. When antibodies are produced, the vessels relax and blood pressure is lowered.

It looks like we are on the verge of a revolution in how we think about vaccines, and how we treat cancers and even addictions as well.

Table 15.4 Checklist of Requirements for an Effective Vaccine

- It should have a low level of adverse side effects or toxicity and not cause serious harm.
- It should protect against exposure to natural, wild forms of pathogen.
- It should stimulate both antibody (B-cell) response and cell-mediated (T-cell) response.
- It should have long-term, lasting effects (produce memory).
- It should not require numerous doses or boosters.
- It should be inexpensive, have a relatively long shelf life, and be easy to administer.

effective vaccine are listed in **table 15.4.** Vaccine preparations can be broadly categorized as either whole organism or part-of-organism preparations. These categories also have subcategories:

1. whole cells or viruses
   a. live, attenuated cells or viruses
   b. killed cells or inactivated viruses
2. antigenic molecules derived from bacterial cells or viruses (subunits)
   a. subunits derived from cultures of cells or viruses
   b. subunits chemically synthesized to mimic natural molecules

c. subunits manufactured via genetic engineering
d. any of these subunits can be conjugated with proteins from other microbes to make them more immunogenic. These are called **conjugated vaccines.**

These categories are also shown in **figure 15.18.**

Note: As of 2008 there were no vaccines available in the United States that consisted of killed whole bacteria. The last two available were those for cholera and plague.

Whole cells or viruses are very effective immunogens, since they are so large and complex. Depending on the vaccine, these are either killed or attenuated. **Killed vaccines** (viruses are termed "inactivated" instead of "killed") are prepared by cultivating the desired strain or strains of a bacterium or virus and treating them with formalin, radiation, heat, or some other agent that does not destroy antigenicity. The hepatitis A vaccine and three forms of the influenza vaccine contain inactivated viruses. Because the microbe does not multiply, killed vaccines often require a larger dose and more boosters to be effective.

A number of vaccines are prepared from live, **attenuated** microbes. Attenuation is any process that substantially lessens or negates the virulence of viruses or bacteria. It is usually achieved by modifying the growth conditions or manipulating microbial genes in a way that eliminates virulence factors. Attenuation methods include long-term cultivation, selection of mutant strains that grow at colder temperatures (cold mutants), passage of the microbe through unnatural hosts or

Figure 15.18 Strategies in vaccine design. **(a)** Whole cells or viruses, killed or attenuated. **(b)** Acellular or subunit vaccines, which are made of various molecules or cell parts, are immunogenic.

(a) **Whole Cell Vaccines**

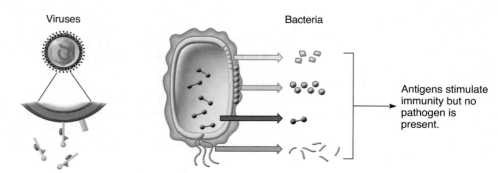

(b) **Subunit Vaccines**

tissue culture, and removal of virulence genes. The vaccine for tuberculosis (BCG) was obtained after 13 years of subculturing the agent of bovine tuberculosis. Vaccines for measles, mumps, polio (Sabin), and rubella contain live, nonvirulent viruses. The advantages of live preparations are:

1. Viable microorganisms can multiply and produce infection (but not disease) like the natural organism.
2. They confer long-lasting protection.
3. They usually require fewer doses and boosters than other types of vaccines.
4. They are particularly effective at inducing cell-mediated immunity.

Disadvantages of using live microbes in vaccines are that they require special storage facilities, can be transmitted to other people, and can conceivably mutate back to a virulent strain.

If the exact epitopes that stimulate immunity are known, it is possible to produce a vaccine based on a selected component of a microorganism. These vaccines for bacteria are called **subunit vaccines.** The antigen used in these vaccines may be taken from cultures of the microbes, produced by genetic engineering, or synthesized chemically.

Examples of component antigens currently in use are the capsules of the pneumococcus and meningococcus, the protein surface antigen of anthrax, and the surface proteins of hepatitis B virus. A special type of vaccine is the **toxoid,** which consists of a purified bacterial exotoxin that has been chemically denatured. By eliciting the production of antitoxins that can neutralize the natural toxin, toxoid vaccines provide protection against diseases such as diphtheria, tetanus, and pertussis. **Table 15.5** presents a list of the currently licensed vaccines in the United States that are used for single diseases.

Table 15.5 Single Disease Vaccines Available in United States

	Vaccines Available	Type
Subunit vaccines		
Anthrax	BioThrax	Subunit (recombinant)
Hepatitis B	Engerix-B	Subunit (recombinant)
	Recombivax HB	Subunit (recombinant)
Influenza	Fluvirin	Subunit
Meningococcal meningitis	Menomune	Subunit (polysaccharide)
Typhoid	Typhim Vi	Subunit (polysaccharide)
Human papillomavirus	Gardasil	Subunit (protein)
Pneumococcal pneumonia	Prevnar	Polysaccharide subunits of 7 strains
	Pneumovax 23	Polysaccharide subunits of 23 strains
Subunit conjugated vaccines		
Haemophilus influenzae b	ActHIB	Conjugate of tetanus protein and Hib polysaccharide
	HibTITER	Conjugate of diphtheria protein and Hib polysaccharide
	PedvaxHIB	Conjugate of *Neisseria* protein and Hib polysaccharide
Meningococcal meningitis	Menactra	Conjugate of diphtheria protein and *N. meningitidis* polysaccharide
Inactivated virus vaccines		
Hepatitis A	Havrix	Inactivated
	Vaqta	Inactivated
Influenza	Fluarix	Inactivated
	Fluzone	Inactivated
	FluLaval	Inactivated
Japanese encephalitis	JE-Vax	Inactivated
Polio	IPOL	Inactivated
Rabies	Imovax Rabies	Inactivated
	RabAvert	Inactivated
Attenuated virus vaccines		
Chickenpox	Varivax	Attenuated virus
Influenza	FluMist	Attenuated virus (nasal spray)
Measles	Attenuvax	Attenuated
Mumps	Mumpsvax	Attenuated
Rotavirus	RotaTeq	Attenuated
Rubella	Meruvax II	Attenuated
Shingles	Zostavax	Attenuated
Smallpox and monkeypox	Dryvax	Attenuated
Yellow fever	YF-Vax	Attenuated
Attenuated whole bacteria vaccines		
Tuberculosis	BCG	Attenuated
Typhoid	Vivotif Berna	Attenuated

As you may know, some childhood vaccines are given as complexes—such as the MMR vaccine, used for measles, mumps, and rubella. This trend has increased in recent years, and there are a wide variety of vaccine combinations available in a single administration. These are listed in **table 15.6.**

Development of New Vaccines

Despite considerable successes, dozens of bacterial, viral, protozoan, and fungal diseases still remain without a functional vaccine. At the present time, no reliable vaccines are available for malaria, HIV/AIDS, various diarrheal diseases, respiratory diseases, and worm infections that affect over 200 million people per year worldwide. Worse than that, even those vaccines that are available are out of reach for much of the world's population.

Infections that are difficult to design a vaccine for are the latent or persistent viral infections, such as some herpesviruses and cytomegaloviruses. In these cases, the host's natural immunity is not capable of clearing the infection, so artificial immunity must actually outperform the host's response to a natural infection. This has proved to be very difficult. Currently, much attention is being focused on newer strategies for vaccine preparation that employ antigen synthesis, recombinant DNA, and gene cloning technology.

Genetically Engineered Vaccines

Some of the genetic engineering concepts introduced in chapter 10 offer novel approaches to vaccine development. These methods are particularly effective in designing vaccines for obligate parasites that are difficult or expensive to culture, such as the syphilis spirochete or the malaria parasite. This technology provides a means of isolating the genes that encode various microbial antigens, inserting them into plasmid vectors, and cloning them in appropriate hosts. The outcome of recombination can be varied as desired. For instance, the cloning host can be stimulated to synthesize and

secrete a protein product (antigen), which is then harvested and purified. Certain vaccines for hepatitis are currently being prepared in this way.

Another ingenious technique using genetic recombination has been nicknamed the *Trojan horse* vaccine. The term derives from an ancient legend in which the Greeks sneaked soldiers into the fortress of their Trojan enemies by hiding them inside a large, mobile wooden horse. In the microbial equivalent, genetic material from a selected infectious agent is inserted into a live carrier microbe that is nonpathogenic. In theory, the recombinant microbe will multiply and express the foreign genes, and the vaccine recipient will be immunized against the microbial antigens. Vaccinia, the virus originally used to vaccinate for smallpox, and adenoviruses have proved practical agents for this technique. Vaccinia is used as the carrier in experimental vaccines for AIDS, herpes simplex 2, leprosy, and tuberculosis.

DNA vaccines are also a very promising new approach to immunization. The technique in these formulations is very similar to gene therapy as described in chapter 10, except in this case, microbial (not human) DNA is inserted into a plasmid vector and inoculated into a recipient **(figure 15.19).** The expectation is that the human cells will take up some of the plasmids and express the microbial DNA in the form of proteins. Because these proteins are foreign, they will be recognized during immune surveillance and cause B and T cells to be sensitized and form memory cells.

Experiments with animals have shown that these vaccines are very safe and that only a small amount of the foreign antigen need be expressed to produce effective immunity. Another advantage to this method is that any number of potential microbial proteins can be expressed, making the antigenic stimulus more complex and improving the likelihood that it will stimulate both antibody and cell-mediated immunity. At the present time, over 30 DNA-based vaccines are being tested in animals. Vaccines for HIV, Lyme disease, hepatitis C, herpes simplex, influenza, tuberculosis, papillomavirus, malaria, and SARS are undergoing clinical trials, most with encouraging results.

Route of Administration and Side Effects of Vaccines

Most vaccines are injected by subcutaneous, intramuscular, or intradermal routes. One form of the influenza vaccine comes in the form of a nasal spray. Oral (or nasal) vaccines are available for only a few diseases, but they have some distinct advantages. An oral or nasal dose of a vaccine can stimulate protection (IgA) on the mucous membrane of the portal of entry. Oral and nasal vaccines are also easier to give than are injections, are more readily accepted, and are well tolerated.

Some vaccines require the addition of a special binding substance, or **adjuvant** (ad'-joo-vunt). An adjuvant is any compound that enhances immunogenicity and prolongs antigen retention at the injection site. The adjuvant precipitates the antigen and holds it in the tissues so that it will be released gradually. Its gradual release presumably facilitates

Table 15.6 Multiple Disease Vaccines

Diseases	Vaccines
Diphtheria, tetanus	Decavac DT and TT (generics)
Diphtheria, pertussis, tetanus	DTaP (Daptacel, Infanrix, Tripedia) Tdap (Boostrix, Adacel)
Diphtheria, pertussis, tetanus, *Haemophilus influenzae* b	TriHIBit
Diphtheria, pertussis, tetanus, hepatitis B, polio	Pediarix
Hepatitis A, hepatitis B	Twinrix
Hepatitis B, *Haemophilus influenzae* b	Comvax
Measles, mumps, rubella	MMR II
Measles, mumps, rubella, chickenpox	ProQuad

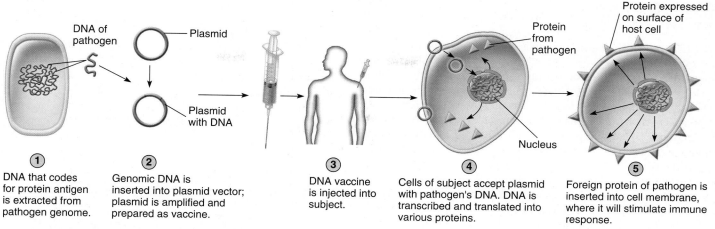

① DNA that codes for protein antigen is extracted from pathogen genome.

② Genomic DNA is inserted into plasmid vector; plasmid is amplified and prepared as vaccine.

③ DNA vaccine is injected into subject.

④ Cells of subject accept plasmid with pathogen's DNA. DNA is transcribed and translated into various proteins.

⑤ Foreign protein of pathogen is inserted into cell membrane, where it will stimulate immune response.

Process Figure 15.19 DNA vaccine preparation. DNA vaccines contain all or part of the pathogen's DNA, which is used to "infect" a recipient's cells. Processing of the DNA leads to production of an antigen protein that can stimulate a specific response against that pathogen.

contact with antigen-presenting cells and lymphocytes. Common adjuvants are alum (aluminum hydroxide salts), Freund's adjuvant (emulsion of mineral oil, water, and extracts of mycobacteria), and beeswax.

Vaccines must go through many years of trials in experimental animals and human volunteers before they are licensed for general use. Even after they have been approved, like all therapeutic products, they are not without complications. The most common of these are local reactions at the injection site, fever, allergies, and other adverse reactions. Relatively rare reactions (about 1 case out of 220,000 vaccinations) are panencephalitis (from measles vaccine), backmutation to a virulent strain (from polio vaccine), disease due to contamination with dangerous viruses or chemicals, and neurological effects of unknown cause (from pertussis and swine flu vaccines). Some patients experience allergic reactions to the medium (eggs or tissue culture) rather than to vaccine antigens. Some recent studies have attempted to link childhood vaccinations to later development of diabetes, asthma, and autism. After thorough examination of records, epidemiologists have found no convincing evidence for a vaccine connection to these diseases **(Insight 15.4).**

When known or suspected adverse effects have been detected, vaccines are altered or withdrawn. Recently, the whole-cell pertussis vaccine was replaced by the acellular capsule (aP) form when it was associated with adverse neurological effects. The first oral rotavirus vaccine had to be withdrawn when children experienced intestinal blockage. An improved version was licensed in 2006. Polio vaccine was switched from live oral to inactivated when occasional cases of paralytic disease occurred from back-mutated vaccine stocks. Vaccine companies have also phased out certain preservatives, such as thimerosal, that are thought to cause allergies and other potential side effects.

Professionals involved in giving vaccinations must understand their inherent risks but also realize that the risks from the infectious disease almost always outweigh the chance of an adverse vaccine reaction. The greatest caution must be exer-

cised in giving live vaccines to immunocompromised or pregnant patients, the latter because of possible risk to the fetus.

To Vaccinate: Why, Whom, and When?

Vaccination confers long-lasting, sometimes lifetime, protection in the individual, but an equally important effect is to protect the public health. Vaccination is an effective method of establishing **herd immunity** in the population. According to this concept, individuals immune to a communicable infectious disease will not harbor it, thus reducing the occurrence of that pathogen. With a larger number of immune individuals in a population (herd), it will be less likely that an unimmunized member of the population will encounter the agent. In effect, collective immunity through mass immunization confers indirect protection on the nonimmune members (such as children). Herd immunity maintained through immunization is an important force in preventing epidemics (see also **Insight 15.4**).

Case File 15   *Continuing the Case*

One of the people present at the church gathering on May 15 was a 17-year-old girl who had never been immunized for measles and who had worked from May 4 through 14 as a missionary in Bucharest, Romania, where a large measles outbreak was later reported. The day before the gathering, the girl had returned to the United States, traveling on both international and domestic commercial airliners. When she arrived, she was experiencing fever, cough, conjunctivitis, and coldlike symptoms; family members later recalled that she had exhibited a rash the next day.

■ What are some possible reasons for the girl never having been immunized for measles?

■ What is herd immunity? Why did herd immunity protect the girl from infection with measles in the United States but not in Romania?

INSIGHT 15.4   How Anti-Vaxxers Were Misled

In 1998, a British physician published a paper that seemed to establish a link between vaccination with the MMR vaccine and the occurrence of bowel disease associated with autism. The effect was immediate: MMR vaccination rates in the United Kingdom fell from 92% to 80%. Consequently, measles infections have increased. In 1998, there were 56 measles cases in the United Kingdom; in 2008 there were 1,348. And the antivaccination campaign spread quickly to the United States. Celebrities such as Jenny McCarthy launched public relations campaigns to warn the public about the risks of autism from vaccinations.

Let's examine the data: Wakefield's 1998 study followed just 12 children. In 2004, 10 of the coauthors on the paper asked that the paper be withdrawn, saying that the data were insufficient. And in 2009, two disturbing facts came to light. The *Times* of London found that the data in the paper had been altered to support Wakefield's hypothesis. In most of the cases, the problems Wakefield cited as a result of the vaccination were present before the vaccination. Hospital pathologists testified that the majority of the cases were normal, and that the data were altered for publication. Second, Wakefield was receiving money from lawyers who represent families suing vaccine manufacturers for alleged harm done them by the vaccines. The medical journal that published the original paper completely retracted the paper in February 2010. In May 2010, the General Medical Council of Britain found Wakefield guilty of serious ethical violations and removed his medical license.

Many subsequent well-controlled studies of the link between autism and the MMR vaccine, and/or of the thimerosal preservative used in it, have shown no association between the disease and the vaccination. In contrast, the price of not being vaccinated has become painfully clear. Outbreaks of measles, mumps, diphtheria, polio, typhoid fever, and whooping cough have popped up all over this country, in college dormitories, in antivaccination religious communities, and in jet airplanes.

These outbreaks are often attributed to a decrease in the level of herd immunity, a phenomenon in which a certain percentage of the population is vaccinated, which means that the microbe is unable to maintain its circulation through the population. Think about it—this means that getting vaccinated serves the common good as well as your individual good. At a time when most of the world's population is clamoring for vaccines, some in the developed world are refusing vaccination, essentially relying on others' willingness to be vaccinated to keep them and their children safe.

Some have speculated that vaccination has done too good of a job—at least in terms of being so effective for so long that

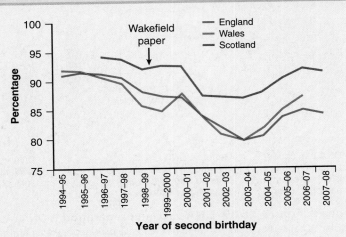

(a) Percent of two-year-olds receiving MMR vaccine—England, Wales, and Scotland, 1994–2008.

(b) Annual laboratory-confirmed measles cases, London and the rest of England and Wales, 1995–2008.

many young parents have no memory of the prevaccination era and don't appreciate the much greater risk of not vaccinating compared to vaccinating. In the decade before measles vaccination began, 3 to 4 million cases occurred each year in the United States. Typically 300 to 400 children died annually and 1,000 more were chronically disabled due to measles encephalitis. Put simply, childhood vaccines save the lives of 2.5 million children a year (worldwide), according to UNICEF. Combine that fact with the shaky nature of the original (Wakefield's) claims, and the stacks of studies that show no link between autism and vaccination, and the evidence is clear: Vaccinate.

Until recently, vaccination was recommended for all typical childhood diseases for which a vaccine is available and for adults only in certain special circumstances (health workers, travelers, military personnel). It has become apparent to public health officials that vaccination of adults is often needed in order to boost an older immunization, protect against "adult" infections (such as pneumonia in elderly people), or provide special protection in people with certain medical conditions.

In **table 15.7,** the current recommended schedule for childhood and adolescent immunizations is provided.

Table 15.7 Recommended Immunization Schedule United States 2010

Persons Aged 0–6 Years

Vaccine ▼ Age ▶	Birth	1 month	2 months	4 months	6 months	12 months	15 months	18 months	19–23 months	2–3 years	4–6 years
Hepatitis B	HepB	HepB			HepB						
Rotavirus			RV	RV	RV[2]						
Diphtheria, Tetanus, Pertussis			DTaP	DTaP	DTaP		DTaP				DTaP
Haemophilus influenzae type b			Hib	Hib	Hib[4]	Hib					
Pneumococcal			PCV	PCV	PCV	PCV				PPSV	
Inactivated Poliovirus			IPV	IPV		IPV					IPV
Influenza						Influenza (Yearly)					
Measles, Mumps, Rubella						MMR					MMR
Varicella						Varicella					Varicella
Hepatitis A						HepA (2 doses)				HepA Series	
Meningococcal										MCV	

Range of recommended ages for all children except certain high-risk groups

Range of recommended ages for certain high-risk groups

Persons Aged 7–18 Years

Vaccine ▼ Age ▶	7–10 years	11–12 years	13–18 years
Diphtheria, Tetanus, Pertussis		Tdap	Tdap
Human Papillomavirus		HPV (3 doses)	HPV Series
Meningococcal	MPSV4	MCV	MCV
Influenza	Influenza (Yearly)		
Pneumococcal	PPSV		
Hepatitis A	HepA Series		
Hepatitis B	Hep B Series		
Inactivated Poliovirus	IPV Series		
Measles, Mumps, Rubella	MMR Series		
Varicella	Varicella Series		

Range of recommended ages for all children except certain high-risk groups

Range of recommended ages for catch-up immunization

Range of recommended ages for certain high-risk groups

Table 15.8 Recommended Immunization Schedule United States 2010

Adults

Vaccine ▼ Age ▶	19–49 years	50–64 years	65 years
Diphtheria, Tetanus, Pertussis (Td/Tdap)	Substitute 1-time dose of Tdap for Td booster; then boost with Td every 10 yrs		Td booster every 10 yrs
Human Papillomavirus (HPV)	3 doses (females)		
Measles, Mumps, Rubella (MMR)	1 or 2 doses	1 dose	
Varicella	2 doses		
Influenza	1 dose annually	1 dose annually	
Pneumococcal (polysaccharide)	1–2 doses		1 dose
Hepatitis A	2 doses		
Hepatitis B	3 doses		
Meningococcal	1 or more doses		

Table 15.8 contains the recommended adult immunization schedule. As you have seen, some vaccines are mixtures of antigens from several pathogens, notably Pediarix (DTaP, IPV, and HB). It is also common for several vaccines to be given simultaneously, as occurs in military recruits who receive as many as 15 injections within a few minutes and children who receive boosters for DTaP and polio at the same time they receive the MMR vaccine.

15.6 Learning Outcomes—Can You . . .

21. . . . list and define the four different descriptors of specific immune states?
22. . . . discuss the qualities of an effective vaccine?
23. . . . name the two major categories of vaccines and then the subcategories under each?
24. . . . discuss the pros and cons of killed (or inactivated) versus attenuated vaccines?
25. . . . describe the principle behind DNA vaccines?
26. . . . explain the principle of herd immunity?

Case File 15   *Wrap-Up*

Measles is caused by a virus known simply as the measles virus, and is spread mainly through droplet contact. Although 30 to 40 million cases of measles occur annually worldwide, resulting in about 400,000 deaths per year, widespread vaccination has made measles in the United States nearly unheard of, with only a few cases reported per year. This propagated outbreak was the largest in the United States since 1996. Its severity was due almost entirely to the fact that only one of the 33 people infected had been adequately vaccinated against measles. State and local health departments in Indiana, Ohio, and Illinois worked to control the outbreak through multiple measures, including voluntary isolation of patients, administration of vaccine and immunoglobulin to susceptible contacts, voluntary home quarantine of susceptible individuals who refused vaccination, and alerting hospitals and the media to the measles outbreak.

In the United States, the Advisory Committee on Immunization Practices (ACIP), composed of a group of 15 experts, advises the U.S. Department of Health and Human Services and the CDC on the control of vaccine-preventable diseases. This committee has long advocated that (1) all persons who travel internationally be vaccinated against measles, (2) all school-aged children in the United States receive two doses of measles vaccine, and (3) all hospital workers be fully vaccinated against the disease. Indiana is one of a number of states that allow nonmedical exemption from vaccination for philosophical or religious reasons, although these persons are 22 times more likely to acquire measles than are those who are vaccinated. If the three recommendations of the ACIP had been followed, this outbreak would have been prevented.

Since this outbreak, others have occurred in the United States, including one in 2008 that affected more than 125 people. It seems that, in addition to people who have general philosophical or religious reasons for refusing vaccines, a growing number of individuals believe (incorrectly) that vaccinations are harmful or may cause autism, setting in place the circumstances for more frequent outbreaks. Americans generally enjoy some degree of herd immunity, the phenomenon that protects unvaccinated individuals because almost everyone they come in contact with has been immunized and therefore will not transmit the microbe, because of the high vaccination rate. This is not always the case in third-world countries. Fears about immunization in this country could jeopardize the vaccination coverage rate, and thus, herd immunity.

See: 2005. *MMWR* 54:1073–75.

Chapter Summary

15.1 Specific Immunity: The Third and Final Line of Defense

- Acquired specific immunity is an elegant but complex matrix of interrelationships between lymphocytes and antigen-presenting cells consisting of several stages.
- Stage I. Lymphocytes originate in hematopoietic tissue but go on to diverge into two distinct types: B cells, which produce antibody, and T cells, which destroy cells and produce cytokines that mediate and coordinate the entire immune response.
- Stage II. Antigen-presenting cells detect invading pathogens and present these antigens to lymphocytes, which recognize the antigen and initiate the specific immune response.
- Stage III. Lymphocytes proliferate, producing clones of progeny that include groups of responder cells, regulator cells, and memory cells.
- Stage IV. Activated B lymphocytes become plasma cells that produce and secrete large quantities of antibodies. Regulatory B cells are also produced. Activated T lymphocytes (one of three subtypes), regulate and participate directly in the specific immune responses.

15.2 Step I: Lymphocyte Development

- The surfaces of all cell membranes contain protein markers or receptors. These function in identification, communication, and cell development. Some are also self identity markers.
- Human identity markers are genetically determined by MHCs. MHC-I codes for identity markers on all nucle-ated host cells. MHC-II codes for identity receptors on dendritic cells, macrophages, and B cells.
- During development, both B and T cells develop millions of genetically different clones. Together these clones possess enough genetic variability to respond to many millions of different antigens. Each clone, however, can respond to only one specific antigen.
- Binding of antigen to a particular clone is called clonal selection. That clone is exclusively amplified in a process called clonal expansion, which leads to an army of cells with that individual specificity.

15.3 Step II: Presentation of Antigens

- Immature lymphocytes released from hematopoietic tissue migrate (home) to one of two sites for further development. B cells mature in the stromal cells of the bone marrow. T cells mature in the thymus.
- Antigens or immunogens are proteins or other complex molecules of high molecular weight that trigger the immune response in the host.
- Lymphocytes respond to a specific portion of an antigen called the epitope. A given microorganism has many such epitopes, all of which stimulate individual specific immune responses.
- Haptens are molecules that are too small to trigger an immune response alone but can be immunogenic when they attach to a larger substance, such as host serum protein.

- Antigen-presenting cells (APCs) such as dendritic cells and macrophages engulf and process foreign antigen and bind the epitope to MHC class II molecules on their cell surface for presentation to CD4 T lymphocytes. Physical contact between the APC, T cells, and B cells activates these lymphocytes to proceed with their respective immune responses.

15.4 Steps III and IV: B-Cell Response

- B cells produce five classes of antibody: IgM, IgG, IgA, IgD, and IgE. IgM and IgG predominate in plasma. IgA predominates in body secretions. IgD is expressed on B cells as an antigen receptor. IgE binds to mast cells and basophils in tissues, promoting inflammation.
- Antibodies bind physically to the specific antigen that stimulates their production, thereby immobilizing the antigen and enabling it to be destroyed by other components of the immune system.
- The memory response means that the second exposure to antigen calls forth a much faster and more vigorous response than the first.

15.5 Steps III and IV: T-Cell Response

- T cells do not produce antibodies. Instead, they produce different cytokines that play diverse roles in the immune response.
- The three main classes of T cells are T helper cells, T regulatory cells, and T cytotoxic cells. Each subset of T cell produces a distinct set of cytokines that stimulate lymphocytes or destroy foreign cells. T helper cells release cytokines that stimulate macrophages and B cells,

among other functions. T regulatory cells guard against excessive or inappropriate inflammation and immunity. Cytotoxic T cells can kill targeted cells directly.
- Natural killer (NK) cells are not themselves specific, but they participate in specific immune responses. NK cells recognize antigen and act as killer cells.

15.6 Specific Immunity and Vaccination

- Active immunity means that your body produces antibodies to a disease agent. If you contract the disease, you can develop natural active immunity. If you are vaccinated, your body will produce artificial active immunity.
- In passive immunity, you receive antibodies from another person. Natural passive immunity comes from the mother. Artificial passive immunity is administered medically.
- Knowledge of the specific immune response has a practical application: commercial production of antisera and vaccines.
- Artificial passive immunity usually involves administration of antiserum and, occasionally, B and T cells. Antibodies collected from donors (human or otherwise) are injected into people who need protection immediately.
- Artificial active agents are vaccines that provoke a protective immune response in the recipient but do not cause the actual disease. Vaccination is the process of challenging the immune system with a specially selected antigen. Vaccines currently in use consist either of whole cells or viruses, or of subunits from them that are immunogenic.
- Vaccination programs seek to protect the individual directly through raising the antibody titer and indirectly through the development of herd immunity.

Multiple-Choice and True-False Questions   Knowledge and Comprehension

Multiple-Choice Questions. Select the correct answer from the answers provided.

1. The primary B-cell receptor is
   a. IgD.
   b. IgA.
   c. IgE.
   d. IgG.

2. In humans, B cells mature in the _____ and T cells mature in the _____.
   a. GALT, liver
   b. bursa, thymus
   c. bone marrow, thymus
   d. lymph nodes, spleen

3. Small, simple molecules are _____ antigens.
   a. poor
   b. never
   c. good
   d. heterophilic

4. The cross-linkage of antigens by antibodies is known as
   a. opsonization.
   b. a cross-reaction.
   c. agglutination.
   d. complement fixation.

5. T_____ cells assist in the functions of certain B cells and other T cells.
   a. sensitized
   b. cytotoxic
   c. helper
   d. natural killer

6. T_C cells are important in controlling
   a. virus infections.
   b. allergy.
   c. autoimmunity.
   d. all of these.

7. Which of the following can serve as antigen-presenting cells (APCs)?
   a. T cells
   b. B cells
   c. macrophages
   d. dendritic cells
   e. b, c, and d

8. A vaccine that contains parts of viruses is called
   a. acellular.
   b. recombinant.
   c. subunit.
   d. attenuated.

9. Conjugated vaccines combine antigens and
   a. antibodies.
   b. adjuvants.
   c. epitopes.
   d. foreign proteins.

10. Widespread immunity that protects the population from the spread of disease is called
    a. seropositivity.
    b. cross-reactivity.
    c. epidemic prophylaxis.
    d. herd immunity.

True-False Questions. If the statement is true, leave as is. If it is false, correct it by rewriting the sentence.

11. Cell surface markers are also often called receptors.

12. Antibodies are secreted by monocytes.

13. Vaccination could be described as artificial passive immunity.

14. IgE antibodies are found in body secretions.

15. The process of reducing the virulence of microbes so that they can be used in vaccines is called denaturation.

Critical Thinking Questions   Application and Analysis

These questions are suggested as a *writing-to-learn* experience. For each question, compose a one- or two-paragraph answer that includes the factual information needed to completely address the question.

1. a. What function do B-cell and T-cell receptors play in specific immune responses?
   b. How can receptors be made to vary so widely?
2. Describe the major histocompatibility complex, and explain how it participates in immune reactions.
3. Explain the clonal selection theory of antibody specificity and diversity.
4. Describe three ways that B cells and T cells are similar and at least five major ways in which they are different.
5. Describe the actions of an antigen-presenting cell.
6. a. Describe the structure of immunoglobulin.
   b. What are the functions of the FAb and Fc portions?
   c. Describe four or five ways that antibodies function in immunity.
   d. Describe the attachment of Abs to Ags. (What eventually happens to the Ags?)

7. a. Contrast the primary and secondary response to Ag.
   b. Explain the type, order of appearance, and amount of immunoglobulin in each response and the reasons for them.
   c. What causes the latent period? The anamnestic response?
8. a. Describe the concept of herd immunity.
   b. How does vaccination contribute to its development in a community?
9. a. Give some possible explanations for the need to have immune tolerance.
   b. Why would it be necessary for the T cells to bind both antigen and self (MHC) receptors?
10. Explain why most immune reactions result in a polyclonal collection of antibodies.

Concept Mapping   Synthesis

Appendix D provides guidance for working with concept maps.

1. Supply your own linking lines, as well as the linking words or phrases, in this concept map, and provide the missing concepts in the empty boxes.

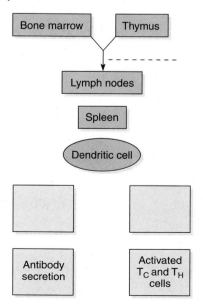

2. Construct your own concept map using the following words as the *concepts*. Supply the links and the linking words between each pair of concepts.

active immunity	vaccines
passive immunity	interferon
natural immunity	inflammation
artificial immunity	memory
innate immunity	

Visual Connections   Synthesis

These questions use visual images or previous content to make connections to this chapter's concepts.

1. **Figure 15.14.** In this figure describing primary and secondary responses to antigen, indicate where a vaccination might be most effective, and also indicate where natural infection would play a role.

www.connect.microbiology.com

Enhance your study of this chapter with study tools and practice tests. Also ask your instructor about the resources available through ConnectPlus, including the media-rich eBook, interactive learning tools, and animations.

Disorders in Immunity

Case File 16

Case File 16

A 67-year-old patient at a Florida hospital was given a blood transfusion as part of a minor surgical procedure. Shortly after receiving the donated blood, the patient experienced a hemolytic transfusion reaction and died that same day, December 29, 2007.

Hemolytic transfusion reactions are responsible for the majority of transfusion-related deaths. This type of reaction occurs when antibodies in the recipient's blood recognize red blood cells in the donated blood, eventually resulting in the destruction of the red blood cells. By comparison, if the donated blood is correctly matched to the blood type of the recipient, the donated blood is perceived as the patient's own, and no reaction occurs.

In the Florida case, the medical team had anticipated the potential need for blood during or after surgery, and the patient's blood had been typed 11 days earlier in his hospital room. Initial investigation into the case indicated that the donated blood matched the patient's blood type.

- What feature of the red blood cell is responsible for its blood type?
- Since the donor and the patient's blood types matched, how could a hemolytic transfusion reaction have occurred?

Continuing the Case appears on page 471.

Outline and Learning Outcomes

16.1 The Immune Response: A Two-Sided Coin
1. Name the two major categories of immune dysfunction.
2. Identify the four types of overreaction to antigens.

16.2 Type I Allergic Reactions: Atopy and Anaphylaxis
3. Define allergen and distinguish among inhalant, ingestant, and contactant types.
4. Describe the sequence of events after secondary exposures to allergens.
5. Explain why systemic anaphylaxis is so serious.

16.1 The Immune Response: A Two-Sided Coin

Humans possess a powerful and intricate system of defense, which by its very nature also carries the potential to cause injury and disease. In most instances, a defect in immune function is expressed in commonplace but miserable symptoms such as those of hay fever and dermatitis. But abnormal or undesirable immune functions are also actively involved in debilitating or life-threatening diseases such as asthma, anaphylaxis, diabetes, rheumatoid arthritis, and graft rejection.

With few exceptions, our previous discussions of the immune response have centered around its numerous beneficial effects. The precisely coordinated system that seeks out, recognizes, and destroys an unending array of foreign materials is clearly protective, but it also presents another side—a side that promotes rather than prevents disease. In this chapter, we survey **immunopathology**, the study of disease states associated with overreactivity or underreactivity of the immune response **(figure 16.1)**. Over-

Figure 16.1 Overview of disorders of the immune system.   Just as the system of T cells and B cells provides necessary protection against infection and disease, the same system can cause serious and debilitating conditions by overreacting or underreacting to immune stimuli.

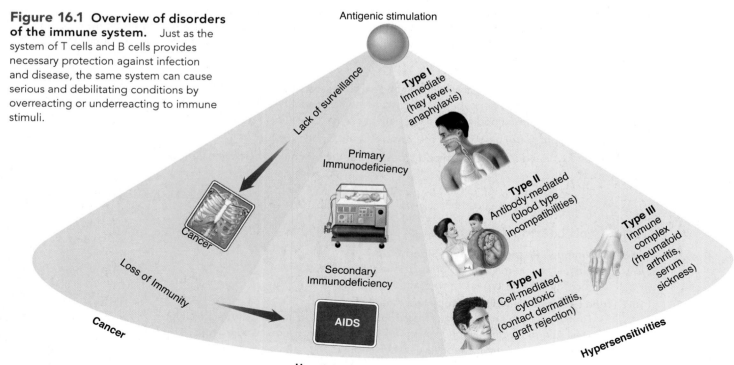

reactivity (look for pink background in figure 16.1) takes the forms of allergy, hypersensitivity and autoimmunity. In the cases of allergies and *autoimmunity*, the tissues are innocent bystanders attacked by immunologic functions that can't distinguish one's own tissues from those expressing foreign material. In **immuno-deficiency diseases** (the blue background in figure 16.1), immune function is incompletely developed, suppressed, or destroyed. Cancer falls into a special category (green background), because it is both a cause and an effect of immune dysfunction. As we shall see, one fascinating by-product of studies of immune disorders has been our increased understanding of the basic workings of the immune system.

Overreactions to Antigens: Four Types

The most widely accepted classification of the four types of allergy and hypersensitivity, first introduced by immunologists P. Gell and R. Coombs, includes four major categories: type I ("common" allergy and anaphylaxis), type II (IgG- and IgM-mediated cell damage), type III (immune complex), and type IV (delayed hypersensitivity) **(table 16.1)**. In general, types I, II, and III involve a B-cell–immunoglobulin response, and type IV involves a T-cell response (see figure 16.1). The antigens that elicit these reactions can be exogenous, originating from outside the body (microbes, pollen grains, and foreign cells and proteins), or endogenous, arising from self tissue (autoimmunities).

One of the reasons allergies are easily mistaken for infections is that both involve damage to the tissues and thus trigger the inflammatory response, as described in chapter 14. Many symptoms and signs of inflammation (redness, heat, skin eruptions, edema, and granuloma) are prominent features of allergies.

16.1 Learning Outcomes—Can You ...

1. ... name the two major categories of immune dysfunction?
2. ... identify the four types of overreaction to antigens?

16.2 Type I Allergic Reactions: Atopy and Anaphylaxis

Allergy/Hypersensitivity

The term **allergy** means a condition of altered reactivity or exaggerated immune response that is manifested by inflammation. Although it is sometimes used interchangeably with hypersensitivity, some experts refer to immediate reactions such as hay fever as allergies and to delayed reactions as hypersensitivities. Allergic individuals are acutely sensitive to repeated contact with antigens, called **allergens,** that do not noticeably affect nonallergic individuals. Although the general effects of hypersensitivity are detrimental, we must be aware that it involves the very same types of immune reactions as those at work in protective immunities. These include humoral and cell-mediated actions, the inflammatory response, phagocytosis, and complement. Such an association means that all humans have the potential to develop hypersensitivity under particular circumstances.

All type I allergies share a similar physiological mechanism, are immediate in onset, and are associated with exposure to specific antigens. However, it is convenient to recognize two levels of severity: **Atopy** is any chronic local allergy such as hay fever or asthma; **anaphylaxis** (an"-uh-fih-lax'-us) is a systemic, sometimes fatal reaction that involves airway obstruction and circulatory collapse. In the following sections, we consider the epidemiology of type I allergies, allergens and routes of inoculation, mechanisms of disease, and specific syndromes.

Epidemiology and Modes of Contact with Allergens

Allergies exert profound medical and economic impact. Allergists (physicians who specialize in treating allergies)

Table 16.1 Hypersensitivity States

Type		Systems and Mechanisms Involved	Examples
I	Immediate hypersensitivity	IgE-mediated; involves mast cells, basophils, and allergic mediators	Anaphylaxis, allergies such as hay fever, asthma
II	Antibody-mediated	IgG, IgM antibodies act upon cells with complement and cause cell lysis; includes some autoimmune diseases	Blood group incompatibility; pernicious anemia; myasthenia gravis
III	Immune complex–mediated	Antibody-mediated inflammation; circulating IgG complexes deposited in basement membranes of target organs; includes some autoimmune diseases	Systemic lupus erythematosus; rheumatoid arthritis; serum sickness; rheumatic fever
IV	T-cell-mediated	Delayed hypersensitivity and cytotoxic reactions in tissues; includes some autoimmune diseases	Infection reactions; contact dermatitis; graft rejection

estimate that about 10% to 30% of the population is prone to atopic allergy. It is generally acknowledged that self-treatment with over-the-counter medicines accounts for significant underreporting of cases. The 35 million people afflicted by hay fever (15% to 20% of the population) spend about half a billion dollars annually for medical treatment. The monetary loss due to employee debilitation and absenteeism is immeasurable. The majority of type I allergies are relatively mild, but certain forms such as asthma and anaphylaxis may require hospitalization and can cause death. Millions of people in the United States suffer from asthma.

The predisposition for type I allergies has a strong familial association. Be aware that what is hereditary is a generalized *susceptibility*, not the allergy to a specific substance. For example, a parent who is allergic to ragweed pollen can have a child who is allergic to cat hair. The prospect of a child's developing atopic allergy is at least 25% if one parent is atopic, increasing up to 50% if grandparents or siblings are also afflicted. The actual basis for atopy appears to be a genetic program that favors allergic antibody (IgE) production, increased reactivity of mast cells, and increased susceptibility of target tissue to allergic mediators. Allergic persons often exhibit a combination of syndromes, such as hay fever, eczema, and asthma.

The "hygiene hypothesis" provides one explanation for the occurrence of allergies. Researchers have found that the combination of being delivered by caesarean section *and* a maternal history of allergy elevates the risk that a child will be allergic to foods by a factor of eight. By themselves, neither factor leads to a significant increase in risk. Scientists suggest that the caesarean section has kept the baby from being exposed to vaginal and stool bacteria. Additional work shows that babies need to be exposed to commensal bacteria in order for the IgA system to develop normally. As one author notes: "We must keep in mind that the current epidemic of allergy in industrialized countries is a small price to pay for the remarkable reduction of infant mortality provided by the elimination of pathogens through improved hygiene. Having too few microbes in our immediate environment seems to be problematic, but having many pathogens is far, far worse."[1]

Also, newborn babies that are breastfed exclusively for the first four months of life have a lower risk of asthma and eczema, especially if they have a family history of allergy. This is thought to come from the presence of cytokines and growth factors in human milk that act on the baby's gut mucosa to induce tolerance, rather than reactivity, to allergens. In some persons, atopic allergies last for a lifetime; others "outgrow" them, and still others suddenly develop them later in life. Some features of allergy are not yet completely explained.

1. 2007. *American Scientist;* January–February. 28–35.

The Nature of Allergens and Their Portals of Entry

As with other antigens, allergens have certain immunogenic characteristics. Not unexpectedly, proteins are more allergenic than carbohydrates, fats, or nucleic acids. Some allergens are haptens, nonproteinaceous substances with a molecular weight of less than 1,000 that can form complexes with carrier molecules in the body (shown in figure 15.8). Organic and inorganic chemicals found in industrial and household products, cosmetics, food, and drugs are commonly of this type. **Table 16.2** lists a number of common allergenic substances.

Allergens typically enter through epithelial portals in the respiratory tract, gastrointestinal tract, and skin. The mucosal surfaces of the gut and respiratory system present a thin, moist surface that is normally quite penetrable. The dry, tough keratin coating of skin is less permeable, but access still occurs through tiny breaks, glands, and hair follicles. It is worth noting that the organ of allergic expression may or may not be the same as the portal of entry.

Airborne environmental allergens such as pollen, house dust, dander (shed skin scales), or fungal spores are termed *inhalants*. Each geographic region harbors a particular combination of airborne substances that varies with the season and humidity **(figure 16.2a)**. Pollen, the most common offender, is given off seasonally by the reproductive structures of pines and flowering plants (weeds, trees, and grasses). Unlike pollen, mold spores are released throughout the year and are especially profuse in moist areas of the home and garden. Airborne animal hair and dander (skin flakes), feathers, and the saliva of dogs and cats are common sources of allergens. The component of house dust that appears to account for most dust allergies is not soil or other debris but the decomposed bodies and feces of tiny mites that commonly live in this dust **(figure 16.2b)**. Some people are allergic to their work, in the sense that they are exposed to allergens on the

Table 16.2	Common Allergens, Classified by Portal of Entry		
Inhalants	**Ingestants**	**Injectants**	**Contactants**
Pollen	Food (milk,	Hymenopteran	Drugs
Dust	peanuts,	venom (bee,	Cosmetics
Mold spores	wheat,	wasp)	Heavy metals
Dander	shellfish,	Drugs	Detergents
Animal hair	soybeans,	Vaccines	Formalin
Insect parts	nuts, eggs,	Serum	Latex
Formalin	fruits)	Enzymes	Glue
Drugs	Food additives	Hormones	Solvents
	Drugs (aspirin,		Dyes
	penicillin)		

**National Allergy Bureau
Pollen and Mold Report**

Location: Sacramento, California   Date: June 04, 2003
Counting Station: Allergy Medical Group of the North Area

Trees	Moderate severity	Total count: 41 / m³
Weeds	High severity	Total count: 64 / m³
Grass	High severity	Total count: 60 / m³
Mold	Low severity	Total count: 4,219 / m³

(a)

(b)

(c)

Figure 16.2 Monitoring airborne allergens. **(a)** The air in heavily vegetated places with a mild climate is especially laden with allergens such as pollen and mold spores. These counts vary seasonally. **(b)** Because the dust mite *Dermatophagoides* feeds primarily on human skin cells in house dust, these mites are found in abundance in bedding and carpets. Airborne mite feces and particles from their bodies are an important source of allergies. **(c)** Scanning electron micrograph of a single pollen grain from a rose (6,000×). Millions of these are released from a single flower.

job. Examples include florists, woodworkers, farmers, drug processors, welders, and plastics manufacturers whose work can aggravate inhalant and contact allergies.

Allergens that enter by mouth, called *ingestants,* often cause food allergies. *Injectant* allergies are an important adverse side effect of drugs or other substances used in diagnosing, treating, or preventing disease. A natural source of injectants is venom from stings by hymenopterans, a family of insects that includes honeybees and wasps. *Contactants* are allergens that enter through the skin. Many contact allergies are of the type IV, delayed variety discussed later in this chapter. It is also possible to be exposed to certain allergens, penicillin among them, during sexual intercourse due to the presence of allergens in the semen.

Mechanisms of Type I Allergy: Sensitization and Provocation

What causes some people to sneeze and wheeze every time they step out into the spring air, while others suffer no ill effects? In order to answer this question, we must examine what occurs in the tissues of the allergic individual that does not occur in the normal person. In general, type I allergies develop in stages **(figure 16.3)**. The initial encounter with an allergen provides a **sensitizing dose** that primes the immune system for a subsequent encounter with that allergen but generally elicits no signs or symptoms. The memory cells and immunoglobulin are then ready to react with a subsequent provocative dose of the same allergen. It is this dose that precipitates the signs and symptoms of allergy. Despite numerous anecdotal reports of people showing an allergy upon first contact with an allergen, it is generally believed that these individuals unknowingly had contact at some previous time. Fetal exposure to allergens from the mother's bloodstream is one possibility, and foods can be a prime source of "hidden" allergens such as penicillin.

The Physiology of IgE-Mediated Allergies

During primary contact and sensitization, the allergen penetrates the portal of entry **(figure 16.3*a*)**. When large particles such as pollen grains, hair, and spores encounter a moist membrane, they release molecules of allergen that pass into the tissue fluids and lymphatics. The lymphatics then carry the allergen to the lymph nodes, where specific clones of B cells recognize it, are activated, and proliferate into plasma cells. These plasma cells produce immunoglobulin E (IgE), the antibody of allergy. IgE is different from other immunoglobulins in having an Fc region with great affinity for mast cells and basophils. The binding of IgE to these cells in the tissues sets the scene for the reactions that occur upon repeated exposure to the same allergen **(figure 16.3b)**.

The Role of Mast Cells and Basophils

The most important characteristics of mast cells and basophils relating to their roles in allergy are:

1. Their ubiquitous location in tissues. Mast cells are located in the connective tissue of virtually all organs, but particularly high concentrations exist in the lungs, skin, gastrointestinal tract, and genitourinary tract. Basophils circulate in the blood but migrate readily into tissues.

2. Their capacity to bind IgE during sensitization (see figure 16.3). Each cell carries 30,000 to 100,000 cell receptors that bind 10,000 to 40,000 IgE antibodies.

3. Their cytoplasmic granules (secretory vesicles), which contain physiologically active cytokines (histamine, serotonin—introduced in chapter 14).

4. Their tendency to **degranulate** (see figures 16.3b and 16.4), or release the contents of the granules into the tissues when triggered by a specific allergen through the IgE bound to them.

Let us now see what occurs when sensitized cells are challenged with allergen a second time.

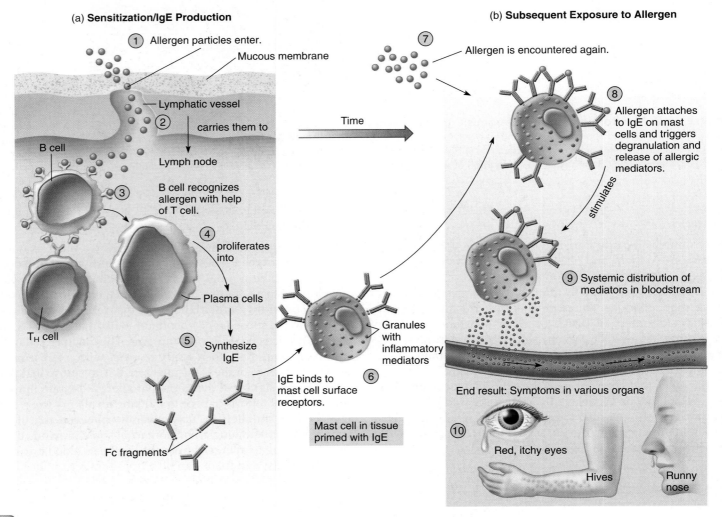

(a) Sensitization/IgE Production

1 Allergen particles enter.
Mucous membrane

Lymphatic vessel

2 carries them to

Lymph node

B cell

3 B cell recognizes allergen with help of T cell.

4 proliferates into

Plasma cells

T_H cell

5 Synthesize IgE

Fc fragments

IgE binds to mast cell surface receptors. 6

Granules with inflammatory mediators

Mast cell in tissue primed with IgE

Time

(b) Subsequent Exposure to Allergen

7 Allergen is encountered again.

8 Allergen attaches to IgE on mast cells and triggers degranulation and release of allergic mediators.

stimulates

9 Systemic distribution of mediators in bloodstream

End result: Symptoms in various organs

10 Red, itchy eyes

Hives

Runny nose

Process Figure 16.3 A schematic view of cellular reactions during the type I allergic response. **(a)** Sensitization (initial contact with sensitizing dose), 1–6. **(b)** Provocation (later contacts with provocative dose), 7–10.

The Second Contact with Allergen

After sensitization, the IgE-primed mast cells can remain in the tissues for years. Even after long periods without contact, a person can retain the capacity to react immediately upon reexposure. The next time allergen molecules contact these sensitized cells, they bind across adjacent receptors and stimulate degranulation. As chemical mediators are released, they diffuse into the tissues and bloodstream. Cytokines give rise to numerous local and systemic reactions, many of which appear quite rapidly (see figure 16.3*b*). The symptoms of allergy are not caused by the direct action of allergen on tissues but by the physiological effects of mast cell mediators on target organs.

Cytokines, Target Organs, and Allergic Symptoms

Numerous substances involved in mediating allergy (and inflammation) have been identified. The principal chemical mediators produced by mast cells and basophils are histamine, serotonin, leukotriene, platelet-activating factor, prostaglandins, and bradykinin **(figure 16.4).** These chemicals, acting alone or in combination, account for the tremendous scope of allergic symptoms. For some theories pertaining to this function of the allergic response, see **Insight 16.1.** Targets of these mediators include the skin, upper respiratory tract, gastrointestinal tract, and conjunctiva. The general responses of these organs include rashes, itching, redness, rhinitis,

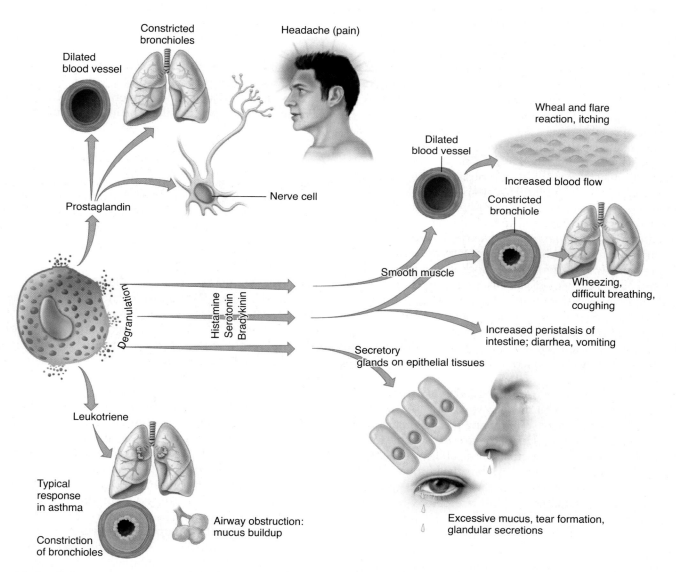

Figure 16.4 The spectrum of reactions to inflammatory cytokines released by mast cells and the common symptoms they elicit in target tissues and organs. Note the extensive overlapping effects.

INSIGHT 16.1   Of What Value Is Allergy?

Why would humans and other mammals evolve an allergic response that is capable of doing so much harm and even causing death? It is unlikely that this limb of immunity exists merely to make people miserable; it must have a role in protection and survival. What are the underlying biological functions of IgE, mast cells, and the array of potent cytokines? Analysis has revealed that, although allergic persons have high levels of IgE, trace quantities are present even in the sera of nonallergic individuals, just as mast cells and inflammatory chemicals are also part of normal human physiology. It is generally believed

that one important function of this system is to defend against helminth worms and other multicellular organisms that are ubiquitous human parasites. In chapter 14, you learned that inflammatory mediators serve valuable functions, such as increasing blood flow and vascular permeability to summon essential immune components to an injured site. They are also responsible for increased mucus secretion, gastric motility, sneezing, and coughing, which help expel noxious agents. The difference is that, in allergic persons, the quantity and quality of these reactions are excessive and uncontrolled.

sneezing, diarrhea, and shedding of tears. Systemic targets include smooth muscle, mucus glands, and nervous tissue. Because smooth muscle is responsible for regulating the size of blood vessels and respiratory passageways, changes in its activity can profoundly alter blood flow, blood pressure, and respiration. Pain, anxiety, agitation, and lethargy are also attributable to the effects of mediators on the nervous system.

Histamine is the most profuse and fastest-acting allergic mediator. It is a potent stimulator of smooth muscle, glands, and eosinophils. Histamine's actions on smooth muscle vary with location. It *constricts* the smooth muscle layers of the small bronchi and intestine, thereby causing labored breathing and increased intestinal motility. In contrast, histamine *relaxes* vascular smooth muscle and dilates arterioles and venules. It is responsible for the *wheal and flare* reaction in the skin (see figure 16.6), pruritus (itching), and headache. More severe reactions such as anaphylaxis can be accompanied by edema and vascular dilation, which lead to hypotension, tachycardia, circulatory failure, and, frequently, shock. Salivary, lacrimal, mucus, and gastric glands are also histamine targets.

Although the role of **serotonin** in human allergy is uncertain, its effects appear to complement those of histamine. In experimental animals, serotonin increases vascular permeability, capillary dilation, smooth muscle contraction, intestinal peristalsis, and respiratory rate, but it diminishes central nervous system activity.

Before the specific types were identified, **leukotriene** (loo"-koh-try'-een) was known as the "slow-reacting substance of anaphylaxis" for its property of inducing gradual contraction of smooth muscle. This type of leukotriene is responsible for the prolonged bronchospasm, vascular permeability, and mucus secretion of the asthmatic individual. Other leukotrienes stimulate the activities of polymorphonuclear leukocytes.

Platelet-activating factor is a lipid released by basophils, neutrophils, monocytes, and macrophages. The physiological response to stimulation by this factor is similar to that of histamine, including increased vascular permeability, pulmonary smooth muscle contraction, pulmonary edema, hypotension, and a wheal and flare response in the skin.

Prostaglandins are a group of powerful inflammatory agents. Normally, these substances regulate smooth muscle contraction (for example, they stimulate uterine contractions during

delivery). In allergic reactions, they are responsible for vasodilation, increased vascular permeability, increased sensitivity to pain, and bronchoconstriction. Certain anti-inflammatory drugs work by preventing the actions of prostaglandins.

Bradykinin is related to a group of plasma and tissue peptides known as kinins that participate in blood clotting and chemotaxis. In allergy, it causes prolonged smooth muscle contraction of the bronchioles, dilatation of peripheral arterioles, increased capillary permeability, and increased mucus secretion.

Specific Diseases Associated with IgE- and Mast-Cell-Mediated Allergy

The mechanisms just described are basic to hay fever, allergic asthma, food allergy, drug allergy, eczema, and anaphylaxis. In this section, we cover the main characteristics of these conditions, followed by methods of detection and treatment.

Atopic Diseases

Hay fever is a generic term for allergic rhinitis, a seasonal reaction to inhaled plant pollen or molds, or a chronic, year-round reaction to a wide spectrum of airborne allergens or inhalants (see table 16.2). The targets are typically respiratory membranes, and the symptoms include nasal congestion; sneezing; coughing; profuse mucus secretion; itchy, red, and teary eyes; and mild bronchoconstriction.

Asthma is a respiratory disease characterized by episodes of impaired breathing due to severe bronchoconstriction. The airways of asthmatic people are exquisitely responsive to minute amounts of inhalant allergens, food, or other stimuli, such as infectious agents. The symptoms of asthma range from occasional, annoying bouts of difficult breathing to fatal suffocation. Labored breathing, shortness of breath, wheezing, cough, and ventilatory **rales** are present to one degree or another. The respiratory tract of an asthmatic person is chronically inflamed and severely overreactive to allergy chemicals, especially leukotrienes and serotonin from pulmonary mast cells. Natural killer T (NKT) cells also seem to be important in asthma. One hypothesis is that once the allergen initiates the response, NKT cells are called in and add to the cytokine storm in the lungs. Other pathologic components are thick mucus plugs in the air sacs and lung damage that can result in long-term respiratory compromise. An imbalance in the nervous control of the respiratory smooth muscles is apparently involved in asthma, and the episodes are influenced by the psychological state of the person, which strongly supports a neurological connection.

The number of asthma sufferers in the United States is estimated at more than 10 million, with nearly one-third of them children. For reasons that are not completely understood, asthma is on the increase, and deaths from it have doubled since 1982, even though effective agents to control it are more available now than they have ever been before. It has been suggested that more highly insulated buildings, mandated by energy efficiency regulations, have created indoor air conditions that harbor higher concentrations of contaminants, including insect remains and ozone.

Atopic dermatitis is an intensely itchy inflammatory condition of the skin, sometimes also called **eczema.** Sensitization occurs through ingestion, inhalation, and, occasionally, skin contact with allergens. It usually begins in infancy with reddened, vesicular, weeping, encrusted skin lesions **(figure 16.5a).** It then progresses in childhood and adulthood to a dry, scaly, thickened skin condition. Lesions can occur on the face, scalp, neck, and inner surfaces of the limbs and trunk. The itchy, painful lesions cause considerable discomfort, and they are often predisposed to secondary bacterial infections. An anonymous writer once aptly described eczema as "the itch that rashes" or "one scratch is too many but one thousand is not enough."

Food Allergy

The ordinary diet contains a vast variety of compounds that are potentially allergenic. Although the mode of entry is intestinal, food allergies can also affect the skin and respiratory tract. Gastrointestinal symptoms include vomiting, diarrhea, and abdominal pain. In severe cases, nutrients are poorly absorbed, leading to growth retardation and failure to thrive in young children. Other manifestations of food allergies include eczema, hives **(figure 16.5b),** rhinitis, asthma, and occasionally, anaphylaxis. Classic food hypersensitivity involves IgE and degranulation of mast cells, but not all reactions involve this mechanism. The most common food allergens come from peanuts, fish, cow's milk, eggs, shellfish, and soybeans. (Do not confuse food allergy with food intolerance. Many people are lactose intolerant, for example, due to a deficiency in the enzyme that degrades the milk sugar.)

Drug Allergy

Modern chemotherapy has been responsible for many medical advances. Unfortunately, it has also been hampered by the fact that drugs are foreign compounds capable of stimulating allergic reactions. In fact, allergy to drugs is one of the most common side effects of treatment (present in 5% to 10% of hospitalized patients). Depending on the allergen, route of entry, and individual sensitivities, virtually any tissue of the body can be affected, and reactions range from mild atopy to fatal anaphylaxis. Compounds implicated most often are antibiotics (penicillin is number one in prevalence), synthetic antimicrobials (sulfa drugs), aspirin, opiates, and contrast dye used in X rays. The actual allergen is not the intact drug itself but a hapten given off when the liver processes the drug. Some forms of penicillin sensitivity are due to the presence of small amounts of the drug in meat, milk, and other foods and to exposure to *Penicillium* mold in the environment.

Figure 16.5 Skin manifestations in atopic allergies. **(a)** Atopic dermatitis, or eczema. Vesicular, encrusted lesions are typical in afflicted infants. This condition is prevalent enough to account for 1% of pediatric care. **(b)** Skin rash caused by an allergy to strawberries. The slightly raised red lesions, termed urticaria or hives, can sometimes merge to form a solid red rash.

(a)

(b)

Anaphylaxis: An Overpowering Systemic Reaction

The term **anaphylaxis,** or anaphylactic shock, was first used to denote a reaction of animals injected with a foreign protein. Although the animals showed no response during the first contact, upon reinoculation with the same protein at a later time, they exhibited acute symptoms—itching, sneezing, difficult breathing, prostration, and convulsions—and many died in a few minutes. Two clinical types of anaphylaxis are seen in humans. *Cutaneous anaphylaxis* is the wheal and flare inflammatory reaction to the local injection of allergen. *Systemic anaphylaxis,* on the other hand, is characterized by sudden respiratory and circulatory disruption that can be fatal in a few minutes. In humans, the allergen and route of entry are variable, though bee stings and injections of antibiotics or serum are implicated most often. Bee venom is a complex material containing several allergens and enzymes that can create a sensitivity that can last for decades after exposure.

The underlying physiological events in systemic anaphylaxis parallel those of atopy, but the concentration of chemical mediators and the strength of the response are greatly amplified. The immune system of a sensitized person exposed to a provocative dose of allergen responds with a sudden, massive release of chemicals into the tissues and blood, which act rapidly on the target organs. Anaphylactic persons have been known to die in 15 minutes from complete airway blockage.

Diagnosis of Allergy

Because allergy mimics infection and other conditions, it is important to determine if a person is actually allergic. If possible or necessary, it is also helpful to identify the specific allergen or allergens. Allergy diagnosis involves several levels of tests, including nonspecific, specific, *in vitro,* and *in vivo* methods.

A new test that can distinguish whether a patient has experienced an allergic attack measures elevated blood levels of tryptase, an enzyme released by mast cells that increases during an allergic response. Several types of specific *in vitro* tests can determine the allergic potential of a patient's blood sample. A differential blood cell count can indicate the levels of basophils and eosinophils—a higher level of these indicates allergy. The leukocyte histamine-release test measures the amount of histamine released from the patient's basophils when exposed to a specific allergen. The most widely used blood test is a radioallergosorbent (RAST) test, which measures levels of IgE to specific allergens. It can't be used for all allergens, but recently more tests have become available for food allergens.

Skin Testing

A tried and true *in vivo* method to detect precise atopic or anaphylactic sensitivities is skin testing. With this technique, a patient's skin is injected, scratched, or pricked with a small amount of a pure allergen extract. There are hundreds of these allergen extracts containing common airborne allergens (plant and mold pollen) and more unusual allergens (mule dander, theater dust, bird feathers). Unfortunately, skin tests for food allergies using food extracts are unreliable in most cases. In patients with numerous allergies, the allergist maps the skin on the inner aspect of the forearms or back and injects the allergens intradermally according to this predetermined pattern (**figure 16.6a**). Approximately 20 minutes after antigenic challenge, each site is appraised for a wheal response indicative of histamine release. The diameter of the wheal is measured and rated on a scale of 0 (no reaction) to 4+ (greater than 15 mm). **Figure 16.6b** shows skin test results for a person with extreme inhalant allergies.

(a)

Figure 16.6 A method for conducting an allergy skin test. The forearm (or back) is mapped and then injected with a selection of allergen extracts. The allergist must be very aware of potential anaphylaxis attacks triggered by these injections. **(a)** Close-up of skin wheals showing a number of positive reactions (dark lines are measurer's marks). **(b)** An actual skin test record for some common environmental allergens [not related to **(a)**].

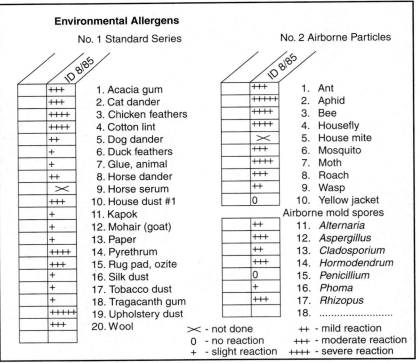

Environmental Allergens

No. 1 Standard Series

ID 8/85	
+++	1. Acacia gum
+++	2. Cat dander
++++	3. Chicken feathers
++++	4. Cotton lint
++	5. Dog dander
+	6. Duck feathers
+	7. Glue, animal
++	8. Horse dander
✕	9. Horse serum
+++	10. House dust #1
+	11. Kapok
+	12. Mohair (goat)
+	13. Paper
++++	14. Pyrethrum
+++	15. Rug pad, ozite
+	16. Silk dust
+	17. Tobacco dust
+	18. Tragacanth gum
+++++	19. Upholstery dust
+++	20. Wool

No. 2 Airborne Particles

ID 8/85	
+++	1. Ant
+++++	2. Aphid
++++	3. Bee
++++	4. Housefly
✕	5. House mite
+++	6. Mosquito
++++	7. Moth
+++	8. Roach
++	9. Wasp
0	10. Yellow jacket

Airborne mold spores

++	11. *Alternaria*
+++	12. *Aspergillus*
++	13. *Cladosporium*
+++	14. *Hormodendrum*
0	15. *Penicillium*
+	16. *Phoma*
+++	17. *Rhizopus*
	18. ....

✕ - not done   ++ - mild reaction
0 - no reaction   +++ - moderate reaction
+ - slight reaction   ++++ - severe reaction

(b)

Figure 16.7 **Strategies for circumventing allergy attacks.**

Treatment and Prevention of Allergy

In general, the methods of treating and preventing type I allergy involve:

1. avoiding the allergen, although this may be very difficult in many instances;
2. taking drugs that block the action of lymphocytes, mast cells, or chemical mediators; and
3. using "vaccine" to short-circuit the allergic reaction.

Taking Drugs to Block Allergy

The aim of antiallergy medication is to block the progress of the allergic response somewhere along the route between IgE production and the appearance of symptoms **(figure 16.7).** Oral anti-inflammatory drugs such as corticosteroids inhibit the activity of lymphocytes and thereby reduce the production of IgE, but they also have dangerous side effects and should not be taken for prolonged periods. Some drugs block the degranulation of mast cells and reduce the levels of inflammatory cytokines. The most effective of these are diethylcarbamazine and cromolyn. Asthma and rhinitis sufferers can find relief with a drug that blocks synthesis of leukotriene and a monoclonal antibody that inactivates IgE (Xolair).

Widely used medications for preventing symptoms of atopic allergy are **antihistamines,** the active ingredients in most over-the-counter allergy-control drugs. Antihistamines interfere with histamine activity by binding to histamine receptors on target organs. Most of them have major side effects, however, such as drowsiness. Newer antihistamines lack this side effect because they do not cross the blood-brain barrier. Other drugs that relieve inflammatory symptoms are aspirin and acetaminophen, which reduce pain by interfering with prostaglandin, and theophylline, a bronchodilator that reverses

spasms in the respiratory smooth muscles. Persons who suffer from anaphylactic attacks are urged to carry at all times injectable epinephrine (adrenaline) and an identification tag indicating their sensitivity. An aerosol inhaler containing epinephrine can also provide rapid relief. Epinephrine reverses constriction of the airways and slows the release of allergic mediators.

Allergy "Vaccines"

Approximately 70% of allergic patients benefit from controlled injections of specific allergens as determined by skin tests. This technique, called **desensitization** or **hyposensitization,** is a therapeutic way to prevent reactions between allergen, IgE, and mast cells. The allergen preparations contain pure, preserved suspensions of plant antigens, venoms, dust mites, dander, and molds (but so far, hyposensitization for foods has not proved very effective). The immunologic basis of this treatment is open to differences in interpretation. One theory suggests that injected allergens stimulate the formation of high levels of allergen-specific IgG **(figure 16.8)** instead of

Figure 16.8 The blocking antibody theory for allergic desensitization.
An injection of allergen causes IgG antibodies to be formed instead of IgE; these blocking antibodies cross-link and effectively remove the allergen before it can react with the IgE in the mast cell.

IgE. It has been proposed that these IgG **blocking antibodies** remove allergen from the system before it can bind to IgE, thus preventing the degranulation of mast cells. It is also possible that allergen delivered in this fashion combines with the IgE itself and takes it from circulation before it can react with the mast cells.

A newer experimental therapy is the first allergy shot to be developed that does not contain the allergen itself. This injection instead contains a "decoy," an innocuous molecule that merely resembles a bacterium. It engages the components of the immune system that are active in allergy, causing them to stop reacting inappropriately to specific allergens. It is thought that it will act against a variety of different allergies.

16.2 Learning Outcomes—Can You . . .

3. . . . define allergen and distinguish among inhalant, ingestant, and contactant types?
4. . . . describe the sequence of events after secondary exposures to allergens?
5. . . . explain why systemic anaphylaxis is so serious?
6. . . . briefly describe two methods for diagnosing allergies?
7. . . . discuss the mechanism of action of "allergy shots"?

16.3 Type II Hypersensitivities: Reactions That Lyse Foreign Cells

The diseases termed type II hypersensitivities are a complex group of syndromes that involve complement-assisted destruction (lysis) of cells by antibodies (IgG and IgM) directed against those cells' surface antigens. This category includes transfusion reactions and some types of autoimmunities (discussed in a later section). The cells targeted for destruction are often red blood cells, but other cells can be involved.

Chapters 14 and 15 described the functions of unique surface markers on cell membranes. Ordinarily, these molecules play essential roles in transport, recognition, and development, but they become medically important when the tissues of one person are placed into the body of another person. Blood transfusions and organ donations introduce alloantigens (molecules that differ in the same species) on donor cells that are recognized by the lymphocytes of the recipient. These reactions are not really immune dysfunctions as allergy and autoimmunity are. The immune system is in fact working normally, but it is not equipped to distinguish between the desirable foreign cells of a transplanted tissue and the undesirable ones of a microbe.

The Basis of Human ABO Antigens and Blood Types

The existence of human blood types was first demonstrated by an Austrian pathologist, Karl Landsteiner, in 1904. While studying incompatibilities in blood transfusions, he found that the serum of one person could clump the red blood cells of another. Landsteiner identified four distinct types, subsequently called the **ABO blood groups.**

Like the MHC antigens on white blood cells, the ABO antigen markers on red blood cells are genetically determined and composed of glycoproteins. These ABO antigens are inherited as two (one from each parent) of three alternative **alleles:** A, B, or O. A and B alleles are dominant over O and codominant with one another. As **table 16.3** indicates, this mode of inheritance gives rise to four blood types (phenotypes), depending on the particular combination of genes. Thus, a person with an *AA* or *AO* genotype has type A blood; genotype *BB* or *BO* gives type B; genotype *AB* produces type AB; and genotype *OO* produces type O. Some important points about the blood types are:

1. they are named for the dominant antigen(s),
2. the RBCs of type O persons have antigens but not A and B antigens, and
3. tissues other than RBCs carry A and B antigens.

A diagram of the AB antigens and blood types is shown in **figure 16.9.** The A and B genes each code for an enzyme

				Incidence of Type in United States		
Genotype	Blood Type	Antigen Present on Erythrocyte Membranes	Antibody in Plasma	Among Whites (%)	Among Asians (%)	Among Those of African and Caribbean Descent (%)
AA, AO	A	A	Anti-B	41	28	27
BB, BO	B	B	Anti-A	10	27	20
AB	AB	A and B	Neither anti-A nor anti-B	4	5	7
OO	O	Neither A nor B	Anti-A and anti-B	45	40	46

Table 16.3 Characteristics of ABO Blood Groups

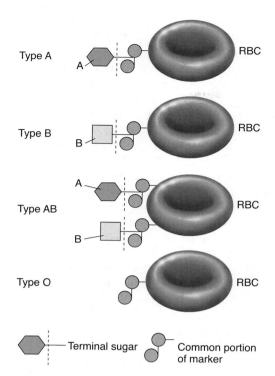

Figure 16.9 The genetic/molecular basis for the A and B antigens (receptors) on red blood cells. In general, persons with blood types A, B, and AB inherit a gene for the enzyme that adds a certain terminal sugar to the basic RBC receptor. Type O persons do not have such an enzyme and lack the terminal sugar.

that adds a terminal carbohydrate to RBC surface molecules during maturation. RBCs of type A contain an enzyme that adds *N*-acetylgalactosamine to the molecule; RBCs of type B have an enzyme that adds D-galactose; RBCs of type AB contain both enzymes that add both carbohydrates; and RBCs of type O lack the genes and enzymes to add a terminal molecule.

Antibodies Against A and B Antigens

Although an individual does not normally produce antibodies in response to his or her own RBC antigens, the serum can contain antibodies that react with blood of another antigenic type even though contact with this other blood type has *never* occurred. These preformed antibodies account for the immediate and intense quality of transfusion reactions. As a rule, type A blood contains antibodies (anti-B) that react against the B antigens on type B and AB red blood cells. Type B blood contains antibodies (anti-A) that react with A antigen on type A and AB red blood cells. Type O blood contains antibodies against both A and B antigens. Type AB blood does not contain antibodies

Case File 16 — *Continuing the Case*

When the body recognizes that transfused blood is of a different type, a transfusion reaction ensues, which may range from a low-grade fever to massive hemolysis and death. The risk of such a reaction requires that blood typing be done on every patient receiving blood to ensure that only the correct type is transfused.

As the investigation into the elderly Florida man's death continued, incorrect typing of the patient's blood was ruled out. Another possibility investigators considered was that other, rarer red blood cell antigens, such as MN or Kell, could have been incompatible between the donor and the recipient, leading to the fatal transfusion reaction. But this also turned out not to be the cause. Eventually, the investigation placed the blame on poor record keeping.

According to the hospital policy in place at the time, phlebotomists—healthcare workers trained to draw blood—were to use at least two separate patient identifiers, such as the patient's name and his or her medical records number, when drawing blood and when labeling the collection container. Furthermore, the phlebotomist was supposed to handwrite the medical records number from the patient's armband on the blood collection tube. In this case, the staff person who drew the blood did not transcribe the medical records number from the patient's armband to the blood tube label. Although the name on the tube was that of the patient, the blood within the tube was actually that of his hospital roommate. When the patient was transfused with blood that had been typed and cross-matched based on this mistaken identification, the transfusion reaction ensued.

against either A or B antigens[2] (see table 16.3). What is the source of these anti-A and anti-B antibodies? It appears that they develop in early infancy because of exposure to certain antigens that are widely distributed in nature. These antigens are surface molecules on bacteria and plant cells that mimic the structure of A and B antigens. Exposure to these sources stimulates the production of corresponding antibodies.

Clinical Concerns in Transfusions

The presence of ABO antigens and A, B antibodies underlie several clinical concerns in giving blood transfusions. First, the individual blood types of donor and recipient must be determined. By use of a standard technique, drops of blood are mixed with antisera that contain antibodies against the

---

2. Why would this be true? The answer lies in the first sentence of the paragraph.

A and B antigens and are then observed for the evidence of agglutination (**figure 16.10**).

Knowing the blood types involved makes it possible to determine which transfusions are safe to do. The general rule of compatibility is that the RBC antigens of the donor must not be agglutinated by antibodies in the recipient's blood (**figure 16.11**). The ideal practice is to transfuse blood that is a perfect match (A to A, B to B). But even in this event, blood samples must be cross-matched before the transfusion because other blood group incompatibilities can exist. This test involves mixing the blood of the donor with the serum of the recipient to check for agglutination.

Under certain circumstances (emergencies, the battlefield), the concept of universal transfusions can be used. To appreciate how this works, we must apply the rule stated in the previous paragraph. Type O blood lacks A and B antigens and will not be agglutinated by other blood types, so it could theoretically be used in any transfusion. Hence, a person with this blood type is called a **universal donor.** Because type AB blood lacks agglutinating antibodies, an individual with this blood could conceivably receive any type of blood. Type AB persons are consequently called *universal recipients.* Although both types of transfusions involve antigen-antibody incompatibilities, these are of less concern because of the dilution of the donor's blood in the body of the recipient. Additional RBC markers that can be significant in transfusions are the Rh, MN, and Kell antigens (see next sections).

Transfusion of the wrong blood type causes differing degrees of adverse reaction. The most severe reaction is massive hemolysis when the donated red blood cells react with recipient antibody and trigger the complement cascade (see figure 16.11). The resultant destruction of red cells leads to systemic shock and kidney failure brought on by the blockage of glomeruli (blood-filtering apparatus) by cell debris. Death is a common outcome. Other reactions caused by RBC destruction are fever, anemia, and jaundice. A transfusion reaction is managed by immediately halting the transfusion, administering drugs to remove hemoglobin from the blood,

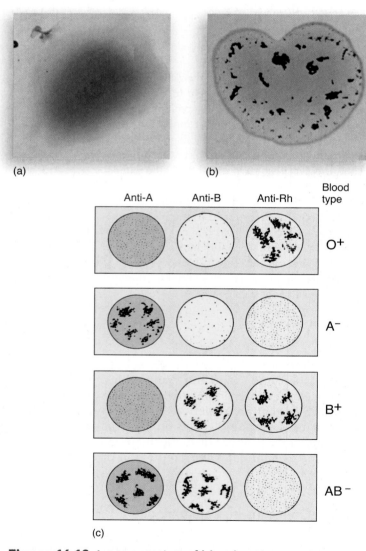

(a)

(b)

(c)

Figure 16.10 Interpretation of blood typing. In this test, a drop of blood is mixed with a specially prepared antiserum known to contain antibodies against the A, B, or Rh antigens. **(a)** If that particular antigen is not present, the red blood cells in that droplet do not agglutinate and form an even suspension. **(b)** If that antigen is present, agglutination occurs and the RBCs form visible clumps. **(c)** Several patterns and their interpretations. Anti-A, anti-B, and anti-Rh are shorthand for the antiserum applied to the drops. (In general, O⁺ is the most common blood type, and AB⁻ is the rarest.)

Figure 16.11 Microscopic view of a transfusion reaction. **(a)** Incompatible blood. The red blood cells of the type A donor contain antigen A, while the serum of the type B recipient contains anti-A antibodies that can agglutinate donor cells. **(b)** Agglutination complexes can block the circulation in vital organs. **(c)** Activation of the complement by antibody on the RBCs can cause hemolysis and anemia. This sort of incorrect transfusion is very rare because of the great care taken by blood banks to ensure a correct match.

and beginning another transfusion with red blood cells of the correct type.

The Rh Factor and Its Clinical Importance

Another RBC antigen of major clinical concern is the **Rh factor** (or D antigen). This factor was first discovered in experiments exploring the genetic relationships among animals. Rabbits inoculated with the RBCs of rhesus monkeys produced an antibody that also reacted with human RBCs. Further tests showed that this monkey antigen (termed Rh for rhesus) was present in about 85% of humans and absent in the other 15%. The details of Rh inheritance are more complicated than those of ABO, but in simplest terms, a person's Rh type results from a combination of two possible alleles—a dominant one that codes for the factor and a recessive one that does not. A person inheriting at least one Rh gene will be Rh$^+$; only those persons inheriting two recessive genes are Rh$^-$. The "+" or "−" appearing after a blood type refers to the Rh status of the person, as in O$^+$ or AB$^-$ (see figure 16.10c). However, unlike the ABO antigens, exposure to environmental antigens does not sensitize Rh$^-$ persons to the Rh factor. The only ways one can develop antibodies against this factor are through placental sensitization or transfusion.

Hemolytic Disease of the Newborn and Rh Incompatibility

The potential for placental sensitization occurs when a mother is Rh$^-$ and her unborn child is Rh$^+$. The obvious intimacy between mother and fetus makes it possible for fetal RBCs to leak into the mother's circulation during childbirth, when the detachment of the placenta creates avenues for fetal blood to enter the maternal circulation. The mother's immune system detects the foreign Rh factors on the fetal RBCs and is sensitized to them by producing antibodies and memory B cells. The first Rh$^+$ child is usually not affected because the process begins so late in pregnancy that the child is born before maternal sensitization is completed. However, the mother's immune system has been strongly primed for a second contact with this factor in a subsequent pregnancy **(figure 16.12a).**

In the next pregnancy with an Rh$^+$ fetus, fetal blood cells escape into the maternal circulation late in pregnancy and elicit a memory response. The fetus is at risk when the maternal anti-Rh antibodies cross the placenta into the fetal circulation, where they affix to fetal RBCs and cause complement-mediated lysis. The outcome is a potentially fatal **hemolytic disease of the newborn (HDN)** called *erythroblastosis fetalis* (eh-rith"-roh-blas-toh'-sis fee-tal'-is). This term is derived from the presence of immature nucleated RBCs called erythroblasts in the blood. They are released into the infant's circulation to compensate for the massive destruction of RBCs stimulated by maternal antibodies. Additional symptoms are severe anemia, jaundice, and enlarged spleen and liver.

Maternal-fetal incompatibilities are also possible in the ABO blood group, but adverse reactions occur less frequently than with Rh sensitization because the antibodies to these blood group antigens are IgM rather than IgG and are unable to cross the placenta in large numbers. In fact, the maternal-fetal relationship is a fascinating instance of foreign tissue not being rejected, despite the extensive potential for contact **(Insight 16.2).**

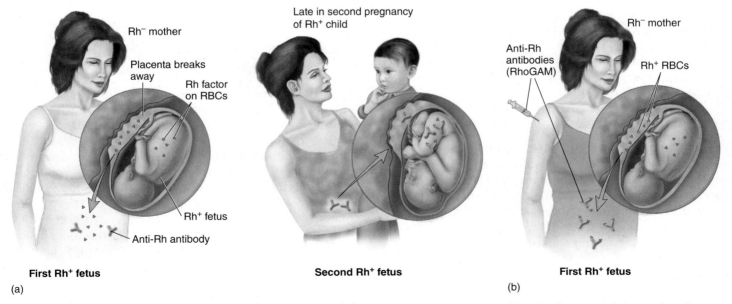

Figure 16.12 Development and control of Rh incompatibility. (a) A naturally occurring blood cell incompatibility results when an Rh$^+$ fetus develops within an Rh$^-$ mother. Initial sensitization of the maternal immune system occurs when fetal blood passes the placental barrier. In most cases, the fetus develops normally. However, a subsequent pregnancy with an Rh$^+$ fetus results in a severe fetal hemolysis. (b) Control of incompatibility: Anti-Rh antibody (RhoGAM) can be administered to Rh$^-$ mothers during pregnancy to help bind, inactivate, and remove any Rh factor that may be transferred from the fetus. In some cases, RhoGAM is administered before sensitization occurs.

INSIGHT 16.2 | **Why Doesn't a Mother Reject Her Fetus?**

Think of it: Even though mother and child are genetically related, the father's genetic contribution guarantees that the fetus will contain molecules that are antigenic to the mother. In fact, consider the practice of implanting one woman with the fertilized egg of another woman: The surrogate mother is carrying a fetus that has no genetic relationship to her. Yet, even with this essentially foreign body inside the mother, dangerous immunologic reactions such as Rh incompatibility are rather rare. In

what ways do fetuses avoid the surveillance of the mother's immune system? The answer appears to lie in the placenta and embryonic tissues. The fetal components that contribute to these tissues are not strongly antigenic, and they form a barrier that keeps the fetus isolated in its own antigen-free environment. The placenta is surrounded by a dense, many-layered envelope that prevents the passage of maternal cells, and it actively absorbs, removes, and inactivates circulating antigens.

Preventing Hemolytic Disease of the Newborn

Once sensitization of the mother to Rh factor has occurred, all other Rh^+ fetuses will be at risk for hemolytic disease of the newborn. Prevention requires a careful family history of an Rh^- pregnant woman. It can predict the likelihood that she is already sensitized or is carrying an Rh^+ fetus. It must take into account other children she has had, their Rh types, and the Rh status of the father. If the father is also Rh^- the child will be Rh^- and free of risk; but if the father is Rh^+, the probability that the child will be Rh^+ is 50% or 100%, depending on the exact genetic makeup of the father. If there is any possibility that the fetus is Rh^+, the mother must be passively immunized with antiserum containing antibodies against the Rh factor (Rh_0 [D] *immune globulin,* or RhoGAM).[3] This antiserum, injected at 28 to 32 weeks and again immediately after delivery, reacts with any fetal RBCs that have escaped into the maternal circulation, thereby preventing the sensitization of the mother's immune system to Rh factor **(figure 16.12b).** Anti-Rh antibody must be given with each pregnancy that involves an Rh^+ fetus. It is ineffective if the mother has already been sensitized by a prior Rh^+ fetus or an incorrect blood transfusion, which can be determined by a serological test.

As in ABO blood types, the Rh factor should be matched for a transfusion, although it is acceptable to transfuse Rh^- blood if the Rh type is not known.

Other RBC Antigens

Although the ABO and Rh systems are of greatest medical significance, about 20 other red blood cell antigen groups have been discovered. Examples are the *MN, Ss, Kell,* and *P* blood groups. Because of incompatibilities that these blood groups present, transfused blood is screened to prevent possible cross-reactions. The study of these blood antigens (as well as ABO and Rh) has given rise to other useful applications. For example, they can be useful in forensic medicine (crime detection), studying ethnic ancestry, and tracing prehistoric migrations in anthropology. Many blood cell antigens are remarkably hardy and can be detected in dried blood stains,

semen, and saliva. Even the 3,300-year-old mummy of King Tutankhamen has been typed A_2MN!

In section 16.6 you will read about special cases of type II hypersensitivity in which it is directed against self. Rheumatoid arthritis involves several types of hypersensitivity, including type II, and the symptoms of multiple sclerosis are caused by a combination of type II and type IV hypersensitivities.

16.3 Learning Outcomes—Can You . . .

8. . . . list the major immune system components involved in type II hypersensitivity?
9. . . . explain the basis for the ABO blood groups, and what type of antibody to the ABO antigens different individuals might have?
10. . . . identify which blood types are considered universal donors and universal recipients?
11. . . . explain under what circumstance the Rh factor can be problematic for newborn babies?

16.4 Type III Hypersensitivities: Immune Complex Reactions

Type III hypersensitivity involves the reaction of soluble antigen with antibody and the deposition of the resulting complexes in basement membranes of epithelial tissue. It is similar to type II, because it involves the production of IgG and IgM antibodies after repeated exposure to antigens and the activation of complement. Type III differs from type II because its antigens are not attached to the surface of a cell. The interaction of these antigens with antibodies produces free-floating complexes that can be deposited in the tissues, causing an **immune complex reaction** or disease. This category includes therapy-related disorders (serum sickness and the Arthus reaction) and a number of autoimmune diseases (such as glomerulonephritis and lupus erythematosus).

Mechanisms of Immune Complex Disease

After initial exposure to a profuse amount of antigen, the immune system produces large quantities of antibodies that

---

3. RhoGAM: Immunoglobulin fraction of human anti-Rh serum, prepared from pooled human sera.

circulate in the fluid compartments. When this antigen enters the system a second time, it reacts with the antibodies to form antigen-antibody complexes **(figure 16.13).** These complexes summon various inflammatory components such as complement and neutrophils, which would ordinarily eliminate Ag-Ab complexes as part of the normal immune response. In an immune complex disease, however, these complexes are so abundant that they deposit in the **basement membranes**[4] of epithelial tissues and become inaccessible. In response to these events, neutrophils release lysosomal granules that digest tissues and cause a destructive inflammatory condition. The symptoms of type III hypersensitivities are due in great measure to this pathologic state.

Types of Immune Complex Disease

During the early tests of immunotherapy using animals, hypersensitivity reactions to serum and vaccines were common. In addition to anaphylaxis, two syndromes, the **Arthus reaction**[5] and **serum sickness,** were identified. These syn-

4. Basement membranes are the bottom layers of epithelia that normally filter out circulating antigen-antibody complexes.

5. Named after Maurice Arthus, the physiologist who first identified this localized inflammatory response.

dromes are associated with certain types of passive immunization (especially with animal serum).

Serum sickness and the Arthus reaction are like anaphylaxis in that all of them require sensitization and preformed antibodies. Characteristics that set serum sickness and Arthus apart from anaphylaxis are:

1. they depend on IgG, IgM, or IgA (precipitating antibodies) rather than IgE;
2. they require large doses of antigen (not a minuscule dose as in anaphylaxis); and
3. their symptoms are delayed (a few hours to days).

The Arthus reaction and serum sickness differ from each other in some important ways. The Arthus reaction is a *localized* dermal injury due to inflamed blood vessels in the vicinity of any injected antigen. Serum sickness is a *systemic* injury initiated by antigen-antibody complexes that circulate in the blood and settle into membranes at various sites.

The Arthus Reaction

The Arthus reaction is usually an acute response to a second injection of vaccines (boosters) or drugs at the same site as the first injection. In a few hours, the area becomes red, hot

Immune complexes

Lodging of complexes in basement membrane

Neutrophils

Ag-Ab complexes

Basement membrane

Epithelial tissue

Blood vessels Heart/Lungs Joints Skin Kidney

Major organs that can be targets of immune complex deposition

Steps:

1. Antibody combines with excess soluble antigen, forming large quantities of Ag-Ab complexes.

2. Circulating immune complexes become lodged in the basement membrane of epithelia in sites such as kidney, lungs, joints, skin.

3. Fragments of complement cause release of histamine and other mediator substances.

4. Neutrophils migrate to the site of immune complex deposition and release enzymes that cause severe damage in the tissues and organs involved.

Process Figure 16.13 Pathogenesis of immune complex disease.

to the touch, swollen, and very painful. These symptoms are mainly due to the destruction of tissues in and around the blood vessels and the release of histamine from mast cells and basophils. Although the reaction is usually self-limiting and rapidly cleared, intravascular blood clotting can occasionally cause necrosis and loss of tissue.

Serum Sickness

Serum sickness was named for a condition that appeared in soldiers after repeated injections of horse serum to treat tetanus. It can also be caused by injections of animal hormones and drugs. The immune complexes enter the circulation; are carried throughout the body; and are eventually deposited in blood vessels of the kidney, heart, skin, and joints (see figure 16.13). The condition can become chronic, causing symptoms such as enlarged lymph nodes, rashes, painful joints, swelling, fever, and renal dysfunction.

Autoimmune diseases at least partially caused by type III hypersensitivities are systemic lupus erythematosus, rheumatoid arthritis, Graves' disease, and myasthenia gravis (see section 16.6 and table 16.4).

16.4 Learning Outcomes—Can You ...

12. ... specify how type III hypersensitivity is similar to, and also different from, type II hypersensitivity?

13. ... provide highlights about the Arthus reaction and serum sickness?

16.5 Type IV Hypersensitivities: Cell-Mediated (Delayed) Reactions

The adverse immune responses we have covered so far are explained primarily by B-cell involvement and antibodies. A notable difference exists in type IV hypersensitivity, which involves primarily the T-cell branch of the immune system. Type IV immune dysfunction has traditionally been known as delayed hypersensitivity because the symptoms arise one to several days following the second contact with an antigen. In general, type IV diseases result when T cells respond to antigens displayed on self tissues or transplanted foreign cells. Examples of type IV hypersensitivity include delayed allergic reactions to infectious agents, contact dermatitis, and graft rejection.

Delayed-Type Hypersensitivity

Infectious Allergy

A classic example of a delayed-type hypersensitivity occurs when a person sensitized by tuberculosis infection is injected with an extract (tuberculin) of the bacterium *Mycobacterium tuberculosis*. The so-called tuberculin reaction is an acute skin inflammation at the injection site appearing within 24 to 48 hours. So useful and diagnostic is this technique for detecting present or prior tuberculosis that it is the chosen screening

Figure 16.14 Positive tuberculin test. Intradermal injection of tuberculin extract in a person sensitized to tuberculosis yields a slightly raised red bump greater than 10 mm in diameter.

device (see chapter 21). Other infections that use similar skin testing are leprosy, syphilis, histoplasmosis, toxoplasmosis, and candidiasis. This form of hypersensitivity arises from time-consuming cellular events involving a specific class of T cells (T_H1) that receive the processed allergens from dendritic cells. Activated T_H cells release cytokines that recruit various inflammatory cells such as macrophages, neutrophils, and eosinophils. The buildup of fluid and cells at the site gives rise to a red papule (for example, see **figure 16.14**). In a chronic infection (tertiary syphilis, for example), extensive damage to organs can occur through granuloma formation.

Contact Dermatitis

The most common delayed allergic reaction, contact dermatitis, is caused by exposure to resins in poison ivy or poison oak **(Insight 16.3),** to simple haptens in household and personal articles (jewelry, cosmetics, elasticized undergarments), and to certain drugs. Like immediate atopic dermatitis, the reaction to these allergens requires a sensitizing and a provocative dose. The allergen first penetrates the outer skin layers, is processed by Langerhans cells (skin dendritic cells), and is presented to T cells. When subsequent exposures attract lymphocytes and macrophages to this area, these cells give off enzymes and inflammatory cytokines that severely damage the epidermis in the immediate vicinity **(figure 16.15a).** This response accounts for the intensely itchy papules and blisters that are the early symptoms **(figure 16.15b).** As healing progresses, the epidermis is replaced by a thick, keratinized layer. Depending on the dose and the sensitivity of the individual, the time from initial contact to healing can be a week to 10 days.

T Cells and Their Role in Organ Transplantation

Transplantation or grafting of organs and tissues is a common medical procedure. Although it is life-giving, this technique

1. Lipid-soluble chemicals are absorbed by the skin.

2. Dendritic cells close to the epithelium pick up the allergen and process it.

3. Previously sensitized T_H1 (CD4) cells recognize the presented allergen.

4. Sensitized T_H1 cells are activated to secrete cytokines (IFN, TNF) that

5. attract macrophages and cytotoxic T cells to the site.

6. Macrophage releases mediators that stimulate a strong, local inflammatory reaction. Cytotoxic T cells directly kill cells and damage the skin. Fluid-filled blisters result.

Process Figure 16.15 Contact dermatitis. **(a)** Genesis of contact dermatitis. **(b)** Contact dermatitis from poison oak, showing various stages of involvement: blister, scales, and thickened patches.

is plagued by the natural tendency of lymphocytes to seek out foreign antigens and mount a campaign to destroy them. The bulk of the damage that occurs in graft rejections can be attributed to expression of cytotoxic T cells and other killer cells. This section covers the mechanisms involved in graft rejection, tests for transplant compatibility, reactions against grafts, prevention of graft rejection, and types of grafts.

The Genetic and Biochemical Basis for Graft Rejection

In chapter 15, we discussed the role of major histocompatibility (MHC or HLA) genes and surface markers in immune function. In general, the genes and markers in MHC classes I and II are extremely important in recognizing self and in regulating the immune response. These molecules also set the events of graft rejection in motion. The MHC genes of humans are inherited from among a large pool of genes, so the cells of each person can exhibit variability in the pattern of cell surface molecules. The pattern is identical in different cells of the same person and can be similar in related siblings and parents, but the more distant the relationship, the less likely that the MHC genes and markers will be similar. When donor tissue (a graft) displays surface molecules of a different MHC class, the T cells of the recipient (called the host) will recognize its foreignness and react against it.

T-Cell-Mediated Recognition of Foreign MHC Receptors

Host Rejection of Graft When the cytotoxic T cells of a host recognize foreign class I MHC markers on the surface of grafted cells, they release interleukin-2 as part of a general immune mobilization. Receipt of this stimulus amplifies helper and cytotoxic T cells specific to the foreign antigens on the donated cells. The cytotoxic cells bind to the grafted

INSIGHT 16.3 Pretty, Pesky, Poisonous Plants

As a cause of allergic contact dermatitis (affecting about 10 million people a year), nothing can compare with a single family of plants belonging to the genus *Toxicodendron*. At least one of these plants—either poison ivy, poison oak, or poison sumac—flourishes in the forests, woodlands, or along the trails of most regions of America. The allergen in these plants, an oil called urushiol, has such extreme potency that a pinhead-size amount could spur symptoms in 500 people, and it is so long lasting that botanists must be careful when handling 100-year-old plant specimens. Although degrees of sensitivity vary among individuals, it is estimated that 85% of all Americans are potentially hypersensitive to this compound. Some people are so acutely sensitive that even the most minuscule contact, such as handling pets or clothes that have touched the plant or breathing vaporized urushiol, can trigger an attack.

Humans first become sensitized by contact during childhood. Individuals at great risk (firefighters, hikers) are advised to determine their degree of sensitivity using a skin test, so that they can be adequately cautious and prepared. Commercial products are available for blocking or washing away the urushiol. Allergy researchers have tested oral vaccines containing a form of urushiol, which seemed to desensitize experimental animals. An effective method using poison ivy desensitization injection is currently available to people with extreme sensitivity.

Poison oak

Poison sumac

Poison ivy

Learning to identify these common plants can prevent exposure and sensitivity. One old saying that might help warns, "Leaves of three, let it be; berries white, run with fright."

---

tissue and secrete lymphokines that begin the rejection process within 2 weeks of transplantation. Late in this process, antibodies formed against the graft tissue contribute to immune damage. A final blow is the destruction of the vascular supply, promoting death of the grafted tissue.

Graft Rejection of Host
In certain severe immunodeficiencies, the host cannot or does not reject a graft. But this failure may not protect the host from serious damage because graft incompatibility is a two-way phenomenon. Some grafted tissues (especially bone marrow) contain an indigenous population called passenger lymphocytes. This makes it quite possible for the graft to reject the host, causing **graft versus host disease (GVHD).** Because any host tissue bearing MHC markers foreign to the graft can be attacked, the effects of GVHD are widely systemic and toxic. A papular, peeling skin rash is the most common symptom. Other organs affected are the liver, intestine, muscles, and mucous membranes. Previously, GVHD occurred in approximately 30% of bone marrow transplants within 100 to 300 days of the graft. This percentage is declining as better screening and selection of tissues are developed.

Classes of Grafts
Grafts are generally classified according to the genetic relationship between the donor and the recipient. Tissue transplanted from one site on an individual's body to another site on his or her body is known as an **autograft.** Typical examples are skin replacement in burn repair and the use of a vein to fashion a coronary artery bypass. In an **isograft,** tissue from an identical twin is used. Because isografts do not contain foreign antigens, they are not rejected. **Allografts,** the most common type of grafts, are exchanges between genetically different individuals belonging to the same species (two humans). A close genetic correlation is sought for most allograft transplants (see next section). A **xenograft** is a tissue exchange between individuals of different species.

Types of Transplants

Today, transplantation is a recognized medical procedure whose benefit is reflected in the fact that at the end of 2007 approximately 180,000 people in the United States were living with a functional kidney, liver, heart, or lung transplant. The procedure has been performed on every major organ,

INSIGHT 16.4   The Mechanics of Bone Marrow Transplantation

In some ways, bone marrow is the most exceptional form of transplantation. It does not involve invasive surgery in either the donor or recipient, and it permits the removal of tissue from a living donor that is fully replaceable. While the donor is sedated, a bone marrow/blood sample is aspirated by inserting a special needle into an accessible marrow cavity. The most favorable sites are the crest and spine of the ilium (major bone of the pelvis). During this procedure, which lasts 1 to 2 hours, 3% to 5% of the donor's marrow is withdrawn in 20 to 30 separate extractions. Between 500 and 800 milliliters of marrow are removed. The donor may experience some pain and soreness, but there are rarely any serious complications. In a few weeks, the depleted marrow will naturally replace itself. Implanting the harvested bone marrow is rather convenient, because it is not necessary to place it directly into the marrow cavities of the recipient. Instead, it is dripped intravenously into the circulation, and the new marrow cells automatically settle in the appropriate bone marrow regions. The survival and permanent establishment of the marrow cells are increased by administering various growth factors and stem cell stimulants to the patient.

Removal of a bone marrow sample for transplantation. Samples are removed by inserting a needle into the spine or crest of the ilium. (The ilium is a prolific source of bone marrow.)

including parts of the brain. The most frequent transplant operations involve skin, liver, heart, kidney, coronary artery, cornea, and bone marrow. The sources of organs and tissues are live donors (kidney, skin, bone marrow, liver), cadavers (heart, kidney, cornea), and fetal tissues. In the past decade, we have witnessed some unusual types of grafts. For instance, the fetal pancreas has been implanted as a potential treatment for diabetes, and fetal brain tissues have been implanted for Parkinson disease. Part of a liver has been transplanted from a live parent to a child, and parents have donated a lobe from their lungs to help restore function in their children with severe cystic fibrosis.

Recent advances in stem cell technology have made it possible to isolate stem cells directly from the blood of donors without bone marrow sampling. Another potential source is the umbilical cord blood from a newborn infant. These have expanded the possibilities for treatment and survival.

Bone marrow transplantation is a rapidly growing medical procedure for patients with immune deficiencies, aplastic anemia, leukemia and other cancers, and radiation damage. Before bone marrow from a closely matched donor can be infused **(Insight 16.4)**, the patient is pretreated with chemotherapy and whole-body irradiation, a procedure designed to destroy the person's own blood stem cells and thus prevent rejection of the new marrow cells. Within 2 weeks to a month after infusion, the grafted cells are established in the host. Because donor lymphoid cells can still cause GVHD, antirejection drugs may be necessary. An amazing consequence of bone marrow transplantation is that a recipient's blood type may change to the blood type of the donor.

Autoimmune diseases in which type IV hypersensitivities play a role are rheumatoid arthritis, type 1 diabetes, and multiple sclerosis (see next section and table 16.4). As you read in chapter 15, certain B cells called regulatory B cells have a role in controlling the T-cell response. It is thought that when the B_{reg} cells malfunction, T cells are able to respond inappropriately as discussed in this section and the next.

16.5 Learning Outcomes—Can You ...

14. ... describe the pathogenesis of contact dermatitis?
15. ... provide the names for four different sources of graft material?

16.6 An Inappropriate Response Against Self: Autoimmunity

The immune diseases we have covered so far are all caused by foreign antigens. In the case of autoimmunity, an individual actually develops hypersensitivity to him- or herself. This pathologic process accounts for **autoimmune diseases,** in which **autoantibodies,** T cells, and, in some cases, both, mount an abnormal attack against self antigens. The scope of autoimmune diseases is extremely varied. In general, they are either *systemic,* involving several major organs, or *organ-specific,* involving only one organ or tissue. There are more than 80 recognized autoimmune diseases. Some major diseases, their targets, and basic pathology are presented in

Table 16.4 Selected Autoimmune Diseases

Disease	Target	Type of Hypersensitivity	Characteristics
Systemic lupus erythematosus (SLE)	Systemic	III	Inflammation of many organs; antibodies against red and white blood cells, platelets, clotting factors, nucleus DNA
Rheumatoid arthritis and ankylosing spondylitis	Systemic	II, III, and IV	Vasculitis; frequent target is joint lining; antibodies against other antibodies (rheumatoid factor), T-cell cytokine damage
Graves' disease	Thyroid	III	Antibodies against thyroid-stimulating hormone receptors
Myasthenia gravis	Muscle	III	Antibodies against the acetylcholine receptors on the nerve-muscle junction alter function.
Type 1 diabetes	Pancreas	IV	T cells attack insulin-producing cells.
Multiple sclerosis	Myelin	II and IV	T cells and antibodies sensitized to myelin sheath destroy neurons.

table 16.4. (For a reminder of hypersensitivity types, refer to table 16.1.)

Genetic and Gender Correlation in Autoimmune Disease

In most cases, the precipitating cause of autoimmune disease remains obscure, but we do know that susceptibility is determined by genetics and influenced by gender. Cases cluster in families, and even unaffected members tend to develop the autoantibodies for that disease. More direct evidence comes from studies of the major histocompatibility gene complex. Particular genes in the class I and II major histocompatibility complex coincide with certain autoimmune diseases. For example, autoimmune joint diseases such as rheumatoid arthritis and ankylosing spondylitis are more common in persons with the B-27 HLA type; systemic lupus erythematosus, Graves' disease, and myasthenia gravis are associated with the B-8 HLA antigen. Why autoimmune diseases (except ankylosing spondylitis) afflict more females than males also remains a mystery. Research has centered on the role that X-chromosome inactivation in females may play; serum from women with autoimmune diseases is often reactive with Barr bodies, a remnant of X-chromosome inactivation in nuclei.

The Origins of Autoimmune Disease

Because otherwise healthy individuals show (very low levels of) autoantibodies, it is suspected that there is a function for them. A moderate, regulated amount of autoimmunity is probably required to dispose of old cells and cellular debris. Disease apparently arises when this regulatory or recognition apparatus goes awry. Attempts to explain the origin of autoimmunity include the following theories.

The *sequestered antigen theory* explains that during embryonic growth, some tissues are immunologically privileged; that is, they are sequestered behind anatomical barriers and cannot be scanned by the immune system.

Examples of these sites are regions of the central nervous system, which are shielded by the meninges and blood-brain barrier; the lens of the eye, which is enclosed by a thick sheath; and antigens in the thyroid and testes, which are sequestered behind an epithelial barrier. Eventually the antigen becomes exposed by means of infection, trauma, or deterioration and is perceived by the immune system as a foreign substance.

According to the **clonal selection theory,** the immune system of a fetus develops tolerance by eradicating all self-reacting lymphocyte clones, called *forbidden clones,* while retaining only those clones that react to foreign antigens. Some of these forbidden clones may survive; and because they have not been subjected to this tolerance process, they can attack tissues with self antigens.

The *theory of immune deficiency* proposes that mutations in the receptor genes of some lymphocytes render them reactive to self or that a general breakdown in the normal suppression of the immune response sets the scene for inappropriate immune responses.

Inappropriate expression of MHC II markers on cells that don't normally express them has been found to cause abnormal immune reactions to self. In a related phenomenon, T-cell activation may incorrectly "turn on" B cells that can react with self antigens. This phenomenon is called the *bystander effect.*

Some autoimmune diseases appear to be caused by *molecular mimicry,* in which microbial antigens bear molecular determinants similar to normal human cells. An infection could cause formation of antibodies that can cross-react with tissues. This is one purported explanation for the pathology of rheumatic fever. Another probable example of mimicry leading to autoimmune disease is the skin condition psoriasis. Although the etiology of this condition is complex and involves the inheritance of certain types of MHC alleles, infection with group A streptococci also plays a role. Scientists report that T cells primed to react with streptococcal surface proteins also react with keratin cells in the skin, causing them to proliferate. For this reason, psoriasis patients often report flare-ups after a strep throat infection.

Autoimmune disorders such as type 1 diabetes and multiple sclerosis are possibly triggered by *viral infection*. Viruses can noticeably alter cell receptors, thereby causing immune cells to attack the tissues bearing viral receptors.

Another theory of autoimmunity involves a protein called the **autoimmune regulator,** known as AIRE. In healthy subjects, this protein directs the transcription of many self antigens in the thymus. Their expression there instructs the immune system not to respond to them. Many patients with autoimmune diseases display defects in this protein. In those cases, the immune response is not instructed to ignore those self antigens.

Examples of Autoimmune Disease

Systemic Autoimmunities

One of the most severe chronic autoimmune diseases is systemic lupus erythematosus (SLE, or lupus). This name originated from the characteristic butterfly-shaped rash that drapes across the nose and cheeks **(figure 16.16a).** Apparently, ancient physicians thought the rash resembled a wolf bite (*lupus* is Latin for wolf). Although the manifestations of the disease vary considerably, all patients produce autoantibodies against a great variety of organs and tissues. The organs most involved are the kidneys, bone marrow, skin, nervous system, joints, muscles, heart, and GI tract. Antibodies to intracellular materials such as the nucleoprotein of the nucleus and mitochondria are also common.

In SLE, autoantibody-autoantigen complexes appear to be deposited in the basement membranes of various organs. Kidney failure, blood abnormalities, lung inflammation, myocarditis, and skin lesions are the predominant symptoms. One form of chronic lupus (called discoid) is influenced by exposure to the sun and primarily afflicts the skin. The etiology of lupus is still a puzzle. It is not known how such a generalized loss of self-tolerance arises, though viral infection or loss of normal immune response suppression are suspected. The diagnosis of SLE can usually be made with blood tests. Antibodies against the nucleus and various tissues (detected by indirect fluorescent antibody or radioimmune assay techniques) are common, and a positive test for the lupus factor (an antinuclear factor) is also very indicative of the disease.

Rheumatoid arthritis, another systemic autoimmune disease, incurs progressive, debilitating damage to the joints. In some patients, the lung, eye, skin, and nervous system are also involved. In the joint form of the disease, autoantibodies form immune complexes that bind to the synovial membrane of the joints and activate phagocytes and stimulate release of cytokines. Chronic inflammation leads to scar tissue and joint destruction. The joints in the hands and feet are affected first, followed by the knee and hip joints **(figure 16.16b).** The precipitating cause in rheumatoid arthritis is not known, though infectious agents such as Epstein-Barr virus have been suspected. The most common feature of the disease is the presence of an IgM antibody, called rheumatoid factor (RF), directed against other antibodies. This does not cause

(a)

(b)

Figure 16.16 **Common autoimmune diseases.** **(a)** Systemic lupus erythematosus. One symptom is a prominent rash across the bridge of the nose and on the cheeks. These papules and blotches can also occur on the chest and limbs. **(b)** Rheumatoid arthritis commonly targets the synovial membrane of joints. Over time, chronic inflammation causes thickening of this membrane, erosion of the articular cartilage, and fusion of the joint. These effects severely limit motion and can eventually swell and distort the joints.

the disease but is used mainly in diagnosis. The symptoms are complicated by a type IV delayed hypersensitivity response. Cytokines, especially tumor necrosis factor (TNF), seem to cause a lot of the damage, and some of the newer drugs target TNF specifically.

Autoimmunities of the Endocrine Glands

On occasion, the thyroid gland is the target of autoimmunity. The underlying cause of **Graves' disease** is the attachment of autoantibodies to receptors on the follicle cells that secrete the hormone thyroxin. The abnormal stimulation of these cells causes the overproduction of this hormone and the symptoms of hyperthyroidism.

The pancreas and its hormone, insulin, are other autoimmune targets. Insulin, secreted by the beta cells in the pancreas, regulates and is essential to the utilization of glucose by cells. **Diabetes mellitus** is caused by a dysfunction in insulin production or utilization. Type 1 diabetes is associated with sensitized cytotoxic T cells that damage the beta cells. A complex inflammatory reaction leading to lysis of these cells greatly reduces the amount of insulin secreted.

A recent experimental study actually "cured" people of their type 1 diabetes by wiping out their immune systems with powerful drugs, after some of their bone marrow stem cells had been removed. When scientists then re-infused these patients with their own stem cells, a functional immune system was rebuilt that did not attack pancreatic cells. We can expect to see more examples of these types of treatments as our understanding of autoimmunity increases.

Neuromuscular Autoimmunities

Myasthenia gravis is named for the pronounced muscle weakness that is its principal symptom. Although the disease afflicts all skeletal muscle, the first effects are usually felt in the muscles of the eyes and throat. Eventually, it can progress to complete loss of muscle function and death. The classic syndrome is caused by autoantibodies binding to the receptors for acetylcholine, a chemical required to transmit a nerve impulse across the synaptic junction to a muscle **(figure 16.17)**. The immune attack so severely damages the muscle cell membrane that transmission is blocked and paralysis ensues. Current treatment usually includes immunosuppressive drugs and therapy to remove the autoantibodies from the circulation. Experimental therapy using immunotoxins to destroy lymphocytes that produce autoantibodies shows some promise.

Multiple sclerosis (MS) is a paralyzing neuromuscular disease associated with lesions in the insulating myelin sheath that surrounds neurons in the white matter of the central nervous system. The underlying pathology involves damage to the sheath by both T cells and autoantibodies that severely compromises the capacity of neurons to send impulses. The principal motor and sensory symptoms are muscular weakness and tremors, difficulties in speech and vision, and some degree of paralysis. Most MS patients first experience symptoms as young adults, and they tend to experience remissions (periods of relief) alternating with recurrences of disease throughout their lives. Convincing evidence from studies of the brain tissue of MS patients points to a strong connection between the disease and infection with human herpesvirus 6. The disease can be treated passively with monoclonal antibodies that target T cells, and a vaccine containing the myelin protein has shown beneficial effects. Immunosuppressants such as cortisone and interferon beta may also alleviate symptoms.

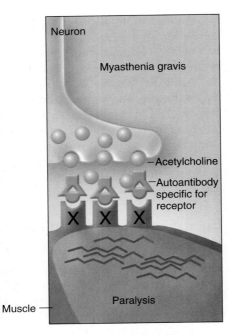

Figure 16.17 Mechanism for involvement of autoantibodies in myasthenia gravis. Antibodies developed against receptors on the postsynaptic membrane block them so that acetylcholine cannot bind and muscle contraction is inhibited.

16.6 Learning Outcomes—Can You ...

16. ... name and describe at least three different theories of autoimmunity?

17. ... describe the pathogenesis of at least three autoimmune diseases?

16.7 Immunodeficiency Diseases: Hyposensitivity of the Immune System

It is a marvel that development and function of the immune system proceed as normally as they do. On occasion, however, an error occurs and a person is born with or develops weakened immune responses. The predominant consequences of immunodeficiencies are recurrent, overwhelming infections, often with opportunistic microbes. Immunodeficiencies fall into two general categories: *primary diseases,* present at birth (congenital) and usually stemming from genetic errors, and *secondary diseases,* acquired after birth and caused by natural or artificial agents **(table 16.5)**.

Primary Immunodeficiency Diseases

Deficiencies affect both specific immunities such as antibody production and less-specific ones such as phagocytosis. Consult **figure 16.18** to survey the places in the normal sequential development of lymphocytes where defects can occur and the possible consequences. In many cases, the deficiency is due to an inherited abnormality, though the exact nature of the abnormality is not known for a number of diseases. Because the development of B cells and T cells diverges at some point, an individual can lack one or both cell lines. It must be emphasized, however, that some deficiencies affect other cell functions. For example, a T-cell deficiency can affect B-cell function because of the role of T helper cells. In some deficiencies, the lymphocyte in question is completely absent or is present at very low levels, whereas in others, lymphocytes are present but do not function normally.

Table 16.5 General Categories of Immunodeficiency Diseases with Selected Examples	
Primary Immune Deficiencies (Genetic)	**Secondary Immune Deficiencies (Acquired)**

B-cell defects (low levels of B cells and antibodies)
  Agammaglobulinemia (X-linked, non-sex-linked)
  Hypogammaglobulinemia
  Selective immunoglobulin deficiencies
T-cell defects (lack of all classes of T cells)
  Thymic aplasia (DiGeorge syndrome)
  Chronic mucocutaneous candidiasis
**Combined B-cell and T-cell defects (usually caused by lack
  or abnormality of lymphoid stem cell)**
  Severe combined immunodeficiency disease (SCID)
  X-SCIDI due to an interleukin defect
  Adenosine deaminase (ADA) deficiency
  Wiskott-Aldrich syndrome
  Ataxia-telangiectasia
Phagocyte defects
  Chédiak-Higashi syndrome
  Chronic granulomatous disease of children
  Lack of surface adhesion molecules
Complement defects
  Lacking one of C components
  Hereditary angioedema
  Associated with rheumatoid diseases
	From natural causes
	  Infections (AIDS) or cancers
	  Nutrition deficiencies
	  Stress
	  Pregnancy
	  Aging
	From immunosuppressive agents
	  Irradiation
	  Severe burns
	  Steroids (cortisones)
	  Drugs to treat graft rejection and cancer
	  Removal of spleen

Figure 16.18 The stages of development and the functions of B cells and T cells, whose failure causes immunodeficiencies.   Dotted lines represent the phases in development where breakdown can occur.

Clinical Deficiencies in B-Cell Development or Expression

Genetic deficiencies in B cells usually appear as an abnormality in immunoglobulin expression. In some instances, only certain immunoglobulin classes are absent; in others, the levels of all types of immunoglobulins (Ig) are reduced. A significant number of B-cell deficiencies are X-linked (also called sex-linked) recessive traits, meaning that the gene occurs on the X chromosome and the disease appears primarily in male children.

The term **agammaglobulinemia** literally means the absence of gamma globulin, the fraction of serum that contains immunoglobulins. Because it is very rare for Ig to be completely absent, some physicians prefer the term **hypogammaglobulinemia.** T-cell function in these patients is usually normal. The symptoms of recurrent, serious bacterial infections usually appear about 6 months after birth. The bacteria most often implicated are pyogenic cocci, *Pseudomonas,* and *Haemophilus influenzae;* and the most common infection sites are the lungs, sinuses, meninges, and blood. Many Ig-deficient patients can have recurrent infections with viruses and protozoa, as well. Patients often manifest a wasting syndrome and have a reduced life span, but modern therapy has improved their prognosis. The current treatment for this condition is passive immunotherapy with immune serum globulin and continuous antibiotic therapy.

The lack of a particular class of immunoglobulin is a relatively common condition. Although genetically controlled, its underlying mechanisms are not yet clear. IgA deficiency is the most prevalent, occurring in about one person in 600. Such persons have normal quantities of B cells and other immunoglobulins, but they are unable to synthesize IgA. Consequently, they lack protection against local microbial invasion of the mucous membranes and suffer recurrent respiratory and gastrointestinal infections. The usual treatment using Ig replacement does not work, because conventional preparations are high in IgG, not IgA.

Clinical Deficiencies in T-Cell Development or Expression

Due to their critical role in immune defenses, a genetic defect in T cells results in a broad spectrum of disease, including severe opportunistic infections, wasting, and cancer. In fact, a dysfunctional T-cell line is usually more devastating than a defective B-cell line because T helper cells are required to assist in most specific immune reactions. The deficiency can occur anywhere along the developmental spectrum, from thymus to mature, circulating T cells.

Abnormal Development of the Thymus   The most severe of the T-cell deficiencies involve the congenital absence or immaturity of the thymus gland. Thymic aplasia, or **DiGeorge syndrome,** results when the embryonic third and fourth pharyngeal pouches fail to develop. Some cases are associated with a deletion in chromosome 22. The accompanying lack of cell-mediated immunity makes children highly

susceptible to persistent infections by fungi, protozoa, and viruses. Common, usually benign childhood infections such as chickenpox, measles, or mumps can be overwhelming and fatal in these children. Vaccinations using attenuated microbes pose a danger. Other symptoms of thymic failure are reduced growth, wasting of the body, unusual facial characteristics **(figure 16.19),** and an increased incidence of lymphatic cancer. These children can have reduced antibody levels, and they are unable to reject transplants. The major therapy for them is a transplant of thymus tissue.

Severe Combined Immunodeficiencies: Dysfunction in B and T Cells

Severe combined immunodeficiencies (SCIDs) are the most dire and potentially lethal of the immunodeficiency diseases because they involve dysfunction in both lymphocyte systems. Some SCIDs are due to the complete absence of the lymphocyte stem cell in the marrow; others are attributable to the dysfunction of B cells and T cells later in development. Infants with SCID usually manifest the T-cell deficiencies within days after birth by developing candidiasis, sepsis, pneumonia, or systemic viral infections. This debilitating condition appears to have several forms. In the two most common forms, Swiss-type agammaglobulinemia and thymic alymphoplasia, the numbers of all types of lymphocytes are extremely low, the blood antibody content is greatly diminished, and the thymus and cell-mediated

Figure 16.19 Facial characteristics of a child with DiGeorge syndrome.   Typical defects include low-set, deformed earlobes; wide-set, slanted eyes; a small, bowlike mouth; and the absence of a philtrum (the vertical furrow between the nose and upper lip).

INSIGHT 16.5 An Answer to the Bubble Boy Mystery

David Vetter, the most famous SCID child, lived all but the last 2 weeks of his life in a sterile environment to isolate him from the microorganisms that could have quickly ended his life. When medical tests performed before birth had indicated that David might inherit this disease, he was delivered by cesarean section and immediately placed in a sterile isolette. From that time, he lived in various plastic chambers—ranging from room-size to a special suit that allowed him to walk outside. Remarkably, he developed into a well-adjusted child, even though his only physical contact with others was through special rubber gloves. When he was 12, his doctors decided to attempt a bone marrow transplant that might allow him to live free of his bubble prison. David was transplanted with his sister's bone marrow, but the marrow harbored a common herpesvirus called Epstein-Barr virus. Because he lacked any form of protective immunities against this oncogenic virus, a cancer spread rapidly through his body. Despite the finest medical care available, David died a short time later from the metastatic cancer.

After several years of study, researchers discovered the basis for David's immunodeficiency. He had inherited a form that arises from a defective genetic code in the receptors for interleukin-2, interleukin-4, and interleukin-7. The defect prevents the receptors on T cells and B cells from receiving the appropriate interleukin signals for growth, development, and reactivity. The end result is that both cytotoxic immunities and antibody-producing systems are shut down, leaving the body defenseless against infections and cancer.

David Vetter, the boy in the plastic bubble.

immunity are poorly developed. Both diseases are due to a genetic defect in the development of the lymphoid cell line.

A rarer form of SCID is **adenosine deaminase (ADA) deficiency,** which is caused by an autosomal recessive defect in the metabolism of adenosine. In this case, lymphocytes develop but a metabolic product builds up abnormally and selectively destroys them. Infants with ADA deficiency are subject to recurrent infections and severe wasting typical of severe deficiencies. A small number of SCID cases are due to a developmental defect in receptors for B and T cells. An X-linked deficiency in interleukin receptors was responsible for the disease of David, the child in the "plastic bubble" **(Insight 16.5).** Another condition, *bare lymphocyte syndrome,* is caused by the lack of genes that code for class II MHC receptors.

Because of their profound lack of specific adaptive immunities, SCID children require the most rigorous kinds of aseptic techniques to protect them from opportunistic infections. Aside from life in a sterile plastic bubble, the only serious option for their longtime survival is total replacement or correction of dysfunctional lymphoid cells. Some infants can benefit from fetal liver or stem cell grafts. Although transplanting compatible bone marrow has been about 50% successful in curing the disease, it is complicated by graft versus host disease. The condition of some ADA-deficient patients has been partly corrected by periodic transfusions of blood containing large amounts of the normal enzyme. A more lasting treatment for both X-linked and ADA types of SCID is gene therapy—insertion of normal genes to replace the defective genes (see chapter 10). Although there have been some problems with gene therapy trials, to date the most successful gene therapy treatments have been used for SCID.

Secondary Immunodeficiency Diseases

Secondary acquired deficiencies in B cells and T cells are caused by one of four general agents:

1. infection,
2. organic disease,
3. chemotherapy, or
4. radiation.

The most recognized infection-induced immunodeficiency is **AIDS.** This syndrome is caused when several types of immune cells, including T helper cells, monocytes, macrophages, and antigen-presenting cells, are infected by the human immunodeficiency virus (HIV). It is generally thought that the depletion of T helper cells and functional impairment of immune responses ultimately account for the cancers and opportunistic protozoan, fungal, and viral infections associated with this disease. See chapter 20 for an extensive discussion of AIDS. Other infections that can deplete immunities are measles, leprosy, and malaria.

Cancers that target the bone marrow or lymphoid organs can be responsible for extreme malfunction of both humoral and cellular immunity. In leukemia, the massive number of cancer cells compete for space and literally

Case File 16   *Wrap-Up*

In the United States, 54 people died from hemolytic transfusion reactions in 2008. Administrative or clerical mistakes are the most common cause of this type of reaction, but adherence to strict record-keeping procedures has helped decrease the incidence. Blood is now commonly labeled with a barcode that can be quickly and accurately scanned, reducing mistakes due to poor handwriting. In some hospitals, radio-frequency identification, or RFID, is used to manage the blood supply. RFID technology relies on small electronic chips to identify each bag of donated blood, while a similar chip, embedded in the patient's armband, broadcasts the patient's blood type. Medical personnel are alerted to a potential transfusion reaction by an audible alarm that sounds if the chips in the patient's armband and on the blood bag do not match.

See: Bert Fish Medical Center Clinical Laboratory. 2008. Statement of Deficiencies and Plan of Correction. Florida Agency for Health Care Administration, St. Petersburg, FL 33701.

displace the normal cells of the bone marrow and blood. Plasma cell tumors produce large amounts of nonfunctional antibodies, and thymus gland tumors cause severe T-cell deficiencies.

An ironic outcome of lifesaving medical procedures is the possible suppression of a patient's immune system. For instance, some immunosuppressive drugs that prevent graft rejection by T cells can likewise suppress beneficial immune responses. Although radiation and anticancer drugs are the first line of therapy for many types of cancer, both agents are extremely damaging to the bone marrow and other body cells.

16.7 Learning Outcomes—Can You . . .

18. . . . distinguish between primary and secondary immunodeficiencies?

19. . . . explain what severe combined immunodeficiency is and discuss currently available therapeutic approaches?

20. . . . name three conditions that can cause secondary immunodeficiencies?

Chapter Summary

16.1 The Immune Response: A Two-Sided Coin
- Immunopathology is the study of diseases associated with excesses and deficiencies of the immune response. Such diseases include allergies, autoimmunity, grafts, transfusions, immunodeficiency disease, and cancer.
- There are four categories of hypersensitivity reactions: type I (allergy and anaphylaxis), type II (IgG and IgM tissue destruction), type III (immune complex reactions), and type IV (delayed hypersensitivity reactions).

16.2 Type I Allergic Reactions: Atopy and Anaphylaxis
- An allergy or hypersensitivity is an exaggerated immune response that injures or inflames tissues.
- Antigens that trigger hypersensitivity reactions are allergens. They can be either exogenous (originate outside the host) or endogenous (involve the host's own tissue).
- Type I hypersensitivity reactions result from excessive IgE production in response to an exogenous antigen.
- The two kinds of type I hypersensitivities are atopy, a chronic, local allergy, and anaphylaxis, a systemic, potentially fatal allergic response.
- The predisposition to type I hypersensitivities is inherited, but age, geographic locale, and infection also influence allergic response.
- Type I allergens include inhalants, ingestants, injectants, and contactants.
- The portals of entry for type I antigens are the skin, respiratory tract, gastrointestinal tract, and genitourinary tract.

- Type I hypersensitivities are set up by a sensitizing dose of allergen and expressed when a second provocative dose triggers the allergic response. The time interval between the two can be many years.
- The primary participants in type I hypersensitivities are IgE, basophils, mast cells, and agents of the inflammatory response.
- Allergies are diagnosed by a variety of *in vitro* and *in vivo* tests that assay specific cells, IgE, and local reactions.
- Allergies are treated by medications that interrupt the allergic response at certain points. Allergic reactions can often be prevented by desensitization therapy.

16.3 Type II Hypersensitivities: Reactions That Lyse Foreign Cells
- Type II hypersensitivity reactions occur when preformed antibodies react with foreign cell-bound antigens. The most common type II reactions occur when transfused blood is mismatched to the recipient's ABO type. IgG or IgM antibodies attach to the foreign cells, resulting in complement fixation. The resultant formation of membrane attack complexes lyses the donor cells.
- Complement, IgG, and IgM antibodies are the primary mediators of type II hypersensitivities.
- The concepts of universal donor (type O) and universal recipient (type AB) apply only under emergency circumstances. Cross-matching donor and recipient blood is necessary to determine which transfusions are safe to perform.

- Type II hypersensitivities can also occur when Rh$^-$ mothers are sensitized to Rh$^+$ RBCs of their unborn babies and the mother's anti-Rh antibodies cross the placenta, causing hemolysis of the newborn's RBCs. This is called hemolytic disease of the newborn, or erythroblastosis fetalis.

16.4 Type III Hypersensitivities: Immune Complex Reactions

- Type III hypersensitivity reactions occur when large quantities of antigen react with host antibody to form small, soluble immune complexes that settle in tissue cell membranes, causing chronic destructive inflammation. The reactions appear hours or days after the antigen challenge.
- The mediators of type III hypersensitivity reactions include soluble IgA, IgG, or IgM, and agents of the inflammatory response.
- Two kinds of type III hypersensitivities are localized (Arthus) reactions and systemic (serum sickness).

16.5 Type IV Hypersensitivities: Cell-Mediated (Delayed) Reactions

- Type IV hypersensitivity reactions occur when cytotoxic T cells attack either self tissue or transplanted foreign cells. Type IV reactions are also termed delayed hypersensitivity reactions because they occur hours to days after the antigenic challenge.
- Type IV hypersensitivity reactions are mediated by T lymphocytes and are carried out against foreign cells that show both a foreign MHC and a nonself receptor site.
- Examples of type IV reactions include the tuberculin reaction, contact dermatitis, and mismatched organ transplants (host rejection and GVHD reactions).
- The four classes of transplants or grafts are determined by the degree of MHC similarity between graft and host.

From most to least similar, these are autografts, isografts, allografts, and xenografts.
- Graft rejection can be minimized by tissue matching procedures, immunosuppressive drugs, and use of tissues that do not provoke a type IV response.

16.6 An Inappropriate Response Against Self: Autoimmunity

- Autoimmune hypersensitivity reactions occur when autoantibodies or host T cells mount an abnormal attack against self antigens.
- Susceptibility to autoimmune disease appears to be influenced by gender and by genes in the MHC complex.
- Autoimmune disease may be an excessive response of a normal immune function, the appearance of sequestered antigens, "forbidden" clones of lymphocytes that react to self antigens, or the result of alterations in the immune response caused by infectious agents, particularly viruses.
- Examples of autoimmune diseases include systemic lupus erythematosus, rheumatoid arthritis, diabetes mellitus, myasthenia gravis, and multiple sclerosis.

16.7 Immunodeficiency Diseases: Hyposensitivity of the Immune System

- Immunodeficiency diseases occur when the immune response is reduced or absent.
- Primary immune diseases are genetically induced deficiencies of B cells, T cells, the thymus gland, or combinations of these.
- Secondary immune diseases are caused by infection, organic disease, chemotherapy, or radiation.
- The best-known infection-induced immunodeficiency is AIDS.

Multiple-Choice and True-False Questions   Knowledge and Comprehension

Multiple-Choice Questions. Select the correct answer from the answers provided.

1. Pollen is which type of allergen?
   a. contactant   c. injectant
   b. ingestant   d. inhalant

2. B cells are responsible for which allergies?
   a. asthma   c. tuberculin reactions
   b. anaphylaxis   d. both a and b

3. The contact with allergen that results in symptoms is called the
   a. sensitizing dose.   c. provocative dose.
   b. degranulation dose. d. desensitizing dose.

4. The direct, immediate cause of allergic symptoms is the action of
   a. the allergen directly on smooth muscle.
   b. the allergen on B lymphocytes.
   c. allergic mediators released from mast cells and basophils.
   d. IgE on smooth muscle.

5. Theoretically, type _____ blood can be donated to all persons because it lacks _____.
   a. AB, antibodies   c. AB, antigens
   b. O, antigens   d. O, antibodies

6. An example of a type III immune complex disease is
   a. serum sickness.   c. graft rejection.
   b. contact dermatitis. d. atopy.

7. Type II hypersensitivities are due to
   a. IgE reacting with mast cells.
   b. activation of cytotoxic T cells.
   c. IgG-allergen complexes that clog epithelial tissues.
   d. complement-induced lysis of cells in the presence of antibodies.

8. Production of autoantibodies may be due to
   a. emergence of forbidden clones of B cells.
   b. production of antibodies against sequestered tissues.
   c. infection-induced change in receptors.
   d. all of these are possible.

9. Rheumatoid arthritis is an _____ that affects the _____.
   a. immunodeficiency disease, muscles
   b. autoimmune disease, nerves
   c. allergy, cartilage
   d. autoimmune disease, joints

10. Which disease would be most similar to AIDS in its pathology?
    a. X-linked agammaglobulinemia
    b. SCID
    c. ADA deficiency
    d. DiGeorge syndrome

True-False Questions. If the statement is true, leave as is. If it is false, correct it by rewriting the sentence.

11. T cells are associated with type IV allergies.

12. A positive tuberculin skin test is an example of antibody-mediated inflammation.

13. Contact dermatitis can be caused by proteins found in foods.

14. Antibody-mediated degranulation of mast cells is involved in anaphylaxis.

15. Rejection of transplanted tissue is dependent on MHC/HLA markers.

Critical Thinking Questions   Application and Analysis

These questions are suggested as a *writing-to-learn* experience. For each question, compose a one- or two-paragraph answer that includes the factual information needed to completely address the question.

1. Describe several factors that influence types and severity of allergic responses.

2. a. How are atopic allergies similar to anaphylaxis?
   b. How are they different?

3. a. Trace the course of a pollen grain through sensitization and provocation in type I allergies.
   b. Include in the discussion the role of mast cells, basophils, IgE, and allergic mediators.
   c. Outline the target organs and symptoms of the principal atopic diseases and their diagnosis and treatment.

4. a. Describe the allergic response that leads to anaphylaxis. Include its usual causes, how it is diagnosed and treated, and two effective physiological targets for treatment.
   b. Explain how hyposensitization is achieved and suggest two mechanisms by which it might work.

5. Explain the rules of transfusion. Illustrate what will happen if type A blood is accidently transfused into a type B person.

6. a. Contrast type II and type III hypersensitivities with respect to type of antigen, antibody, and manifestations of disease.
   b. What is immune complex disease?

7. Why can T-cell deficiencies have greater impact than B-cell deficiencies?

8. A 3-week-old neonate develops severe eczema after being given penicillin therapy for the first time. Can you explain what has happened?

9. Why would it be advisable for an Rh⁻ woman who has had an abortion, miscarriage, or an ectopic pregnancy to be immunized against the Rh factor?

10. a. Explain why babies with agammaglobulinemia do not develop opportunistic infections until about 6 months after birth.
    b. Explain why people with B-cell deficiencies can benefit from artificial passive immunotherapy. Explain whether vaccination would work for them.

Concept Mapping   Synthesis

Appendix D provides guidance for working with concept maps.

1. Construct your own concept map using the following terms as the *concepts*. Supply the linking words between each pair of concepts.

lysed cells	allergens
degranulation release of mediators	cell-bound antibody
immune complexes	processed antigen
damage by T cells	soluble antigen

Visual Connections   Synthesis

These questions use visual images or previous content to make connections to this chapter's concepts.

1. **From chapter 15, figure 15.15.** How would a person's immunity be affected if he or she had a deficiency in CD8 cells? Would a deficiency in CD4 cells have a greater or lesser effect? Explain your answer.

2. **Figure 16.10c.** Draw the agglutination patterns for the other four common blood types.

Diagnosing Infections

Hepatitis C is a chronic liver infection that can be either silent (with no noticeable symptoms) or debilitating. Either way, 80% of infected persons experience continuing liver destruction. Chronic hepatitis C infection is the leading cause of liver transplants in the United States. The virus that causes it is blood-borne, and therefore patients who undergo frequent procedures involving transfer of blood are particularly susceptible to infection. Kidney dialysis patients belong to this group. In 2008, a for-profit hemodialysis facility in New York was shut down after nine of its patients were confirmed as having become infected with hepatitis C while undergoing hemodialysis treatments there between 2001 and 2008.

When the investigation was conducted in 2008, investigators found that 20 of the facility's 162 patients had been documented with hepatitis C infection at the time they began their association with the clinic. All the current patients were then offered hepatitis C testing, to determine how many had acquired hepatitis C during the time they were receiving treatment at the clinic. They were considered positive if enzyme-linked immunosorbent assay (ELISA) tests showed the presence of antibodies to the hepatitis C virus.

- Health officials did not test the workers at the hemodialysis facility for hepatitis C because they did not view them as likely sources of the nine new infections. Why not?
- Why do you think patients were tested for antibody to the virus instead of for the presence of the virus itself?

Continuing the Case appears on page 504.

Outline and Learning Outcomes

17.1 Preparation for the Survey of Microbial Diseases
1. Name the three major categories of microbe identification techniques.

17.2 On the Track of the Infectious Agent: Specimen Collection
2. Identify some important considerations about collecting samples from patients for microbial identification.
3. Explain the ideas behind presumptive versus confirmatory data.

17.1 Preparation for the Survey of Microbial Diseases

In chapters 18 through 23, the most clinically significant bacterial, fungal, parasitic, and viral diseases are covered. The chapters survey the most prevalent infectious conditions and the organisms that cause them. This chapter gets us started with an introduction to the how-to of diagnosing the infections.

For many students (and professionals), the most pressing topic in microbiology is *how to identify unknown bacteria* in patient specimens or in samples from nature. Methods microbiologists use to identify bacteria to the level of genus and species fall into three main categories: **phenotypic,** which includes a consideration of morphology (microscopic and macroscopic) as well as bacterial physiology or biochemistry; **immunologic,** which entails serological analysis; and **genotypic** (or genetic) techniques. Data from a cross section of such tests can produce a unique profile of each bacterium. Increasingly, genetic means of identification are being used as a sole resource for identifying bacteria. As universally used databases become more complete because of submissions from scientists and medical personnel worldwide, genetic analyses provide a more accurate and speedy way of identifying microbes than was possible even a decade ago. There are still many organisms, however, that must be identified in the "old-fashioned" way—via biochemical, serological, and morphological means. Serology is so reliable for some diseases that it may never be replaced. All of these methods—phenotypic, genotypic, and serological—are described in this chapter.

Phenotypic Methods

Microscopic Morphology

Traits that can be valuable aids to identification are combinations of cell shape and size; Gram stain reaction; acid-fast reaction; and special structures, including endospores, granules, and capsules. Electron microscope studies can pinpoint additional structural features (such as the cell wall, flagella, pili, and fimbriae).

Macroscopic Morpholog

Traits that can be assessed with the naked eye are also useful in diagnosis. These include the appearance of colonies, including texture, size, shape, pigment, speed of growth, and patterns of growth in broth and gelatin media.

Physiological/Biochemical Characteristics

These have been the traditional mainstay of bacterial identification. Enzymes and other biochemical properties of bacteria are fairly reliable and stable expressions of the chemical identity of each species. Dozens of diagnostic tests exist for determining the presence of specific enzymes and to assess nutritional and metabolic activities. Examples include tests for fermentation of sugars; capacity to digest or metabolize complex polymers such as proteins and polysaccharides; production of gas; presence of enzymes such as catalase, oxidase, and decarboxylases; and sensitivity to antimicrobic drugs. Special rapid identification test systems that record the major biochemical reactions of a culture have streamlined data collection.

Chemical Analysis

This involves analyzing the types of specific structural substances that the microorganism contains, such as the chemical composition of peptides in the cell wall and lipids in membranes.

Genotypic Methods

Examining the genetic material itself has revolutionized the identification and classification of bacteria. There are many advantages of genotypic methods over phenotypic methods, when they are available. The primary advantage is that actually culturing the microorganisms is not always necessary. In recent decades, scientists have come to realize that there are many more microorganisms that we can't grow in the lab compared with those that we can **(Insight 17.1).** Another advantage is that genotypic methods are increasingly automated, and results are obtained very quickly, often with more precision than with phenotypic methods.

Immunologic Methods

Bacteria and other microbes have surface and other molecules called antigens that are recognized by the immune system. One immune response to antigens is the production of molecules called antibodies that are designed to bind tightly to the antigens. The nature of the antibody response is also exploited

INSIGHT 17.1   The Uncultured

By the 1990s, it was clear to microbiologists that culture-based (phenotypic) methods for identifying bacteria were becoming inadequate. This was first confirmed by environmental researchers, who came to believe that at most 1% (and in some environments it was 0.001%) of microbes present in lakes, soil, and saltwater environments could be grown in laboratories and, therefore, were unknown and unstudied. These microbes are termed **viable noncultured,** or **VNC.**

Although it took microbiologists many years to come to this realization, once they did, it made sense. Scientists had spent several decades (since microbes could first routinely be grown) concocting recipes for media and having great success in growing all kinds of bacteria from all kinds of environments. They had plenty to do, just in identifying and studying those. By the 1990s, the advent of non-culture-dependent tools, such as gene probing and PCR, revealed vast numbers of species that had never before turned up on a culture dish. That this vast zoo of microbes was revealed in environmental samples was not surprising due to the huge array of microenvironments that would have had to have been reproduced in media for them to be grown in the lab.

But medical microbiologists felt fairly confident that they could culture microbes from a human, since the "environment" of human tissues is well understood. Although some human-inhabiting microbes cannot be grown in culture, we never suspected that we were missing a large proportion of them. In 1999, three Stanford University scientists applied PCR techniques to a collection of subgingival plaque harvested from one of their own mouths. They used a wide library of DNA fragments as probes, essentially "fishing" for new isolates. Oral biologists had previously recovered about 500 bacterial strains from this site; the Stanford scientists found 30 species that had never before been cultured or described. This discovery shook the medical world and led to increased investigation of "normal" human biota, using non-culture-based methods to find VNCs in the human body. Discoveries like these eventually led to **The Human Microbiome Project,** which began in 2007. This is a collective effort of scientists in laboratories all over the country. The aim is to collect genetic sequences in the gut, respiratory tract, skin, and the like, to determine which microbes are there, even when they can't be grown in the laboratory. A secondary aim is to determine what role these normal biota play in health and disease.

The new realization that our bodies are hosts to a wide variety of microbes about which we know nothing has several implications. As evolutionary microbiologist Paul Ewald has said, "What are all those microbes doing in there?" He points out that many oral microbes previously assumed to be innocuous are now associated with cancer and heart disease. Many of the diseases that we currently think of as noninfectious will likely be found to have an infectious cause once we learn to look for VNCs.

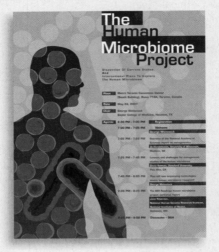

for diagnosis when a patient's blood (or other tissue) is tested for the presence of specific antibodies to a suspected pathogen. This is often easier than testing for the microbe itself, especially in the case of viral infections. Most HIV testing entails examination of a person's blood for presence of antibody to the virus. Laboratory kits based on this technique are available for immediate identification of a number of pathogens.

17.1 Learning Outcomes—Can You . . .

1. . . . name the three major categories of microbe identification techniques?

17.2 On the Track of the Infectious Agent: Specimen Collection

Regardless of the method of diagnosis, specimen collection is the common point that guides the health care decisions of every member of a clinical team. Indeed, the success of identification and treatment depends on how specimens are collected, handled, and stored. Specimens can be taken by a clinical laboratory scientist or medical technologist, nurse, physician, or even by the patient. However, it is imperative that general aseptic procedures be used, including sterile sample containers and other tools to prevent contamination from the environment or the patient. **Figure 17.1** delineates the most common sampling sites and procedures.

In sites that normally contain resident microbiota, care should be taken to sample only the infected site and not surrounding areas. For example, throat and nasopharyngeal swabs should not touch the tongue, cheeks, or saliva. Saliva is an especially undesirable contaminant because it contains millions of bacteria per milliliter, most of which are normal biota. Saliva samples are occasionally taken for dental diagnosis by having the patient expectorate into a container. Depending on the nature of a skin lesion, skin can be swabbed or scraped with a scalpel to expose deeper layers. The mucus lining of the vagina, cervix, or urethra can be sampled with a swab or applicator stick.

Urine is taken aseptically from the bladder with a thin tube called a catheter. Another method, called a "clean catch," is taken by washing the external urethra and collecting the urine midstream. The latter method inevitably incorporates a few normal biota into the sample, but these can usually be differentiated from pathogens in an actual infection. Sometimes diagnostic techniques require first-voided "dirty catch" urine. Sputum, the mucus secretion

(a)

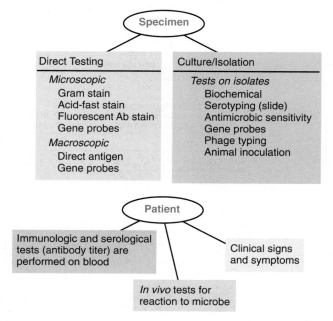

Figure 17.1 Sampling sites and methods of collection for clinical laboratories. **(a)** Sites for collection. **(b)** Sterile transport swab with carrier—sometimes called a Culturette.

that coats the lower respiratory surfaces, especially the lungs, is discharged by coughing or taken by catheterization to avoid contamination with saliva. Sterile materials such as blood, cerebrospinal fluid, and tissue fluids must be taken by sterile needle aspiration. Antisepsis of the puncture site is extremely important in these cases. Additional sources of specimens are the eye, ear canal, nasal cavity (all by swab), and diseased tissue that has been surgically removed (biopsied).

After proper collection, the specimen is promptly transported to a lab and stored appropriately (usually refrigerated) if it must be held for a time. Nonsterile samples in particular, such as urine, feces, and sputum, are especially prone to deterioration at room temperature. Special swab and transport systems are designed to collect the specimen and maintain it in stable condition for several hours. These devices contain nonnutritive maintenance media (so the microbes survive but do not grow), a buffering system, and an anaerobic environment to prevent possible destruction of oxygen-sensitive bacteria.

Overview of Laboratory Techniques

The routes taken in specimen analysis are the following: (1) direct tests using microscopic, immunologic, or genetic methods that provide immediate clues as to the identity of

the microbe or microbes in the sample; and (2) cultivation, isolation, and identification of pathogens using a wide variety of general and specific tests **(figure 17.2)**. Most test results

Figure 17.2 A scheme of specimen isolation and identification.

fall into two categories: presumptive data, which place the isolated microbe (isolate) in a preliminary category such as a genus, and more specific, confirmatory data, which provide more definitive evidence of a species. Some tests are more important for some groups of bacteria than for others. The total time required for analysis ranges from a few minutes in a streptococcal sore throat to several weeks in tuberculosis.

Results of specimen analysis are entered in a summary patient chart (**figure 17.3**) that can be used in assessment and treatment regimens. This looks like a boring form but take the time to read it! Understanding what the microbiology lab needs can help nurses and other caregivers understand what is needed and help accomplish it.

Some diseases are diagnosed without the need to identify microbes from specimens. Serological tests on a patient's serum can detect signs of an antibody response. One method that clarifies whether a positive test indicates current or prior infection is to take two samples several days apart to

MICROBIOLOGY UNIT

DATE, TIME & PERSON COLLECTING	SPECIMEN NUMBER	ANTIBIOTIC THERAPY	TENTATIVE DIAGNOSIS

SOURCE OF SPECIMEN

☐ THROAT
☐ SPUTUM
☐ STOOL
☐ CERVIX
☐ AEROSOL INDUCED SPUTUM
☐ WOUND - SPECIFY SITE _____
☐ OTHER - SPECIFY _____

☐ BLOOD
☐ URINE - CLEAN CATCH
☐ URINE - CATH
☐ BRONCHIAL WASHING

TEST REQUEST

☐ GRAM STAIN
☐ ROUTINE CULTURE
☐ SENSITIVITY
☐ MIC
☐ ANAEROBIC CULTURE
☐ R/O GROUP A STREP
☐ WRIGHT STAIN (WBC)

☐ ACID FAST SMEAR
☐ ACID FAST CULTURE
☐ FUNGUS WET MOUNT
☐ FUNGUS CULTURE
☐ PARASITE STUDIES
☐ OCCULT BLOOD
☐ PCR ANALYSIS

DO NOT WRITE BELOW THIS LINE -# FOR LAB USE ONLY

GRAM STAIN   (4+ NUMEROUS; 3+ MANY; 2+ MODERATE; 1+FEW; 0 NONE SEEN)

COCCI: GRAM POS._____ GRAM NEG._____ W B C_____
BACILLI: GRAM POS._____ GRAM NEG._____ EPITHELIAL CELLS_____
INTRACELLULAR & EXTRACELLULAR GRAM-NEGATIVE DIPLOCOCCI_____
YEAST_____   ☐ No organisms seen.

FUNGUS: WET MOUNT ☐ No mycotic elements or budding structures seen.
            ☐ _____
        CULTURE   ☐ _____

AFB: SMEAR   ☐ No acid fast bacilli seen.
            ☐ _____
        CULTURE ☐ _____

PARASITE   DIRECT:_____
STUDIES: CONCENTRATE:_____
            PERMANENT:_____

OCCULT BLOOD:
            APPEARANCE OF STOOL:_____
            OCCULT BLOOD:_____
COLONY COUNT: Urine organisms/ml.   ☐ _____ ☐ > 100,000
MISCELLANEOUS RESULTS:
☐ NO GROWTH IN: ☐ 2 DAYS ☐ 3 DAYS ☐ 5 DAYS ☐ 7 DAYS
☐ NORMAL FLORA ISOLATED
☐ NO ENTEROPATHOGENS ISOLATED
☐ SPUTUM UNACCEPTABLE FOR CULTURE — REPRESENTS SALIVA — NEW SPECIMEN REQUESTED
☐ URINE > 2 COLONY TYPES PRESENT REPRESENT CONTAMINATION — NEW SPECIMEN REQUESTED

CULTURE RESULTS

1+ FEW   3+ MANY
2+ MODERATE   4+ NUMEROUS

ANAEROBES	☐ BACTEROIDES
	☐ CLOSTRIDIUM
	☐ PEPTOSTREPTOCOCCUS
	☐
	☐

ENTERICS	☐ ESCHERICHIA COLI
	☐ ENTEROBACTER
	☐ KLEBSIELLA
	☐ PROTEUS
	☐

STAPH-YLOCOCCUS	☐ AUREUS
	☐ EPIDERMIDIS
	☐ SAPROPHYTICUS

STREP-TOCOCCUS	☐ GROUP A
	☐ GROUP B
	☐ GROUP D ENTEROCOCCI
	☐ GROUP D NON ENTEROCOCCI
	☐ PNEUMONIAE
	☐ VIRIDANS
	☐

| YEAST | ☐ CANDIDA |
| | ☐ |

OTHER ISOLATES	☐ PSEUDOMONAS
	☐ HAEMOPHILUS
	☐ GARDNERELLA VAGINALIS
	☐ NEISSERIA
	☐ CL. DIFFICILE
	☐

SENSITIVITY TESTS

NOTE: Bacteria with intermediate susceptibility may not respond satisfactorily to therapy.	AMIKACIN	AMPICILLIN	BETA LACTAMASE PRODUCTION	CARBENICILLIN	CEFAZOLIN	CEFOTAXIME	CEFOXITIN	CEFUROXIME	CHLORAMPHENICOL	CLINDAMYCIN	ERYTHROMYCIN	GENTAMICIN	METHICILLIN	METRONIDAZOLE	NITROFURANTOIN	PENICILLIN	IMMUNOLOGY	TETRACYCLINE	TOBRAMYCIN	TRIMETHO PRIM SULFAME THOXAZOLE	VANCOMYCIN	CIPROFLOX
A																						
B																						
C																						

☐ COMMENTS: _____

DATE _____ TECHNOLOGIST _____

706-30A

Figure 17.3 Example of a clinical form used to report data on a patient's specimens.

see if the antibody titer is rising. Skin testing can pinpoint a delayed allergic reaction to a microorganism. These tests are also important in screening the general population for exposure to an infectious agent such as rubella or tuberculosis.

Because diagnosis is both a science and an art, the ability of the practitioner to interpret signs and symptoms of disease can be very important. AIDS, for example, is usually diagnosed by serological tests and a complex of signs and symptoms without ever isolating the virus. Some diseases (athlete's foot, for example) are diagnosed purely by the typical presenting symptoms and may require no lab tests at all.

17.2 Learning Outcomes—Can You ...

2. ... identify some important considerations about collecting samples from patients for microbial identification?
3. ... explain the ideas behind presumptive versus confirmatory data?

17.3 Phenotypic Methods

Immediate Direct Examination of Specimen

Direct microscopic observation of a fresh or stained specimen is one of the most rapid methods of determining presumptive and sometimes confirmatory characteristics. Stains most often employed for bacteria are the Gram stain (see Insight 4.2) and the acid-fast stain (see figure 21.16). For many species these ordinary stains are useful, but they do not work with certain organisms. Direct fluorescence antibody (DFA) tests can highlight the presence of the microbe in patient specimens by means of labeled antibodies **(figure 17.4).** DFA tests are particularly useful for bacteria, such as the syphilis spirochete, that are not readily cultivated in the laboratory or if rapid diagnosis is essential for the survival of the patient.

Another way that specimens can be analyzed is through *direct antigen testing,* a technique similar to direct fluorescence in that known antibodies are used to identify antigens on the surface of bacterial isolates. But in direct antigen testing, the reactions can be seen with the naked eye. Quick test kits that greatly speed clinical diagnosis are available for *Staphylococcus aureus, Streptococcus pyogenes, Neisseria gonorrhoeae, Haemophilus influenzae,* and *Neisseria meningitidis.* However, when the microbe is very sparse in the specimen, direct testing is like looking for a needle in a haystack, and more sensitive methods are necessary.

Cultivation of Specimen

Isolation Media

Such a wide variety of media exist for microbial isolation that a certain amount of preselection must occur, based on the nature of the specimen. In cases in which the suspected pathogen is present in small numbers or is easily overgrown, the specimen can be initially enriched with specialized media. In specimens such as urine and feces that have high bacterial counts and a diversity of species, selective media are used.

Figure 17.4 Direct fluorescence antigen test. (a) Results for *Treponema pallidum,* the syphilis spirochete, and an unrelated spirochete. **(b)** Photomicrograph of this technique used on a blood sample from a syphilitic patient.

In most cases, specimens are also inoculated into differential media that define such characteristics as reactions in blood (blood agar) and fermentation patterns (mannitol salt and MacConkey agar). A patient's blood is usually cultured in a special bottle of broth that can be periodically sampled for growth. Numerous other examples of isolation, differential, and biochemical media were presented in chapter 3. So that subsequent steps in identification will be as accurate as possible, all work must be done from isolated colonies or pure cultures, because working with a mixed or contaminated culture gives misleading and inaccurate results. From such isolates, clinical microbiologists obtain information about a pathogen's microscopic morphology and staining reactions, cultural appearance, motility, oxygen requirements, and biochemical characteristics.

Biochemical Testing

The physiological reactions of bacteria to nutrients and other substrates provide excellent indirect evidence of the types of enzyme systems present in a particular species. Many of these tests are based on an enzymatic reaction (a step in the bacterium's metabolic pathway) that is visualized by a color change.

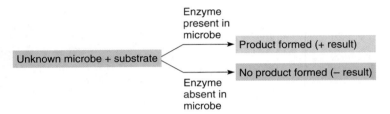

The microbe is cultured in a medium with a special substrate and then tested for a particular end product. The presence of the end product (made visible by a color dye) indicates that the enzyme is expressed in that species; its absence means it lacks the enzyme for utilizing the substrate in that particular way. These types of reactions are particularly meaningful in bacteria, which are haploid and generally express their genes for utilizing a given nutrient.

Among the prominent biochemical tests are carbohydrate fermentation (acid and/or gas); hydrolysis of gelatin, starch, and other polymers; enzyme actions such as catalase, oxidase, and coagulase; and various by-products of metabolism. Many are presently performed with rapid, miniaturized systems that can simultaneously determine up to 23 characteristics in small individual cups or spaces **(figure 17.5)**. An

Figure 17.5 Rapid tests. The API 20E manual biochemical system for microbial identification. Samples of a single bacterial culture are placed in the 20 different cups, which already contain chemicals designed to test for a particular enzyme. Different bacterial cultures were used in strip a and strip b. The culture in **(a)** was positive for every tested enzyme; the culture in **(b)** was negative for each one.

important plus, given the complexity of biochemical profiles, is that such systems are readily adapted to computerized analysis.

Common schemes exist for identifying bacteria. These are based on easily recognizable characteristics such as motility, oxygen requirements, Gram stain reactions, shape, spore formation, and various biochemical reactions. Schemes can be set up as flowcharts **(figure 17.6)** that trace a route of identification by offering pairs of opposing characteristics (positive versus negative, for example) from which to select. Flowcharts that offer two choices at each level are called **dichotomous keys.** Eventually, an endpoint is reached, and the name of a genus or species that fits that particular combination of characteristics appears. Diagnostic tables that provide more complete information are preferred by many laboratories because variations from the general characteristics used on the flowchart can be misleading.

Miscellaneous Tests

When morphological and biochemical tests are insufficient to complete identification, other tests come into play.

Bacteria host viruses called bacteriophages that are very species- and strain-specific. Such selection by a virus for its host is useful in typing some bacteria, primarily *Salmonella*. The technique of phage typing involves inoculating a lawn of cells onto a Petri dish, mapping it off into blocks, and applying a different phage to each block. Cleared areas corresponding to lysed cells indicate sensitivity to that phage. Phage typing is often used for tracing strains of bacteria in epidemics.

Animals must be inoculated to cultivate bacteria such as *Mycobacterium leprae* and significant quantities of *Treponema pallidum*, whereas avian embryos and cell cultures are used to grow rickettsias, chlamydias, and viruses. Animal inoculation is also occasionally used to test bacterial or fungal virulence.

Antimicrobial sensitivity tests are not only important in determining the drugs to be used in treatment (see figure 12.18), but the patterns of sensitivity can also be used in presumptive identification of some species of *Streptococcus*, *Pseudomonas*, and *Clostridium*. Antimicrobials are also used as selective agents in many media.

Determining Clinical Significance of Cultures

Questions that can be difficult but necessary to answer in this era of debilitated patients and opportunists are: Is an isolate clinically important? and How do you decide whether it is a contaminant or just part of the normal biota? The number of microbes in a sample is one useful criterion. For example, a few colonies of *Escherichia coli* in a urine sample can simply indicate normal biota, whereas several

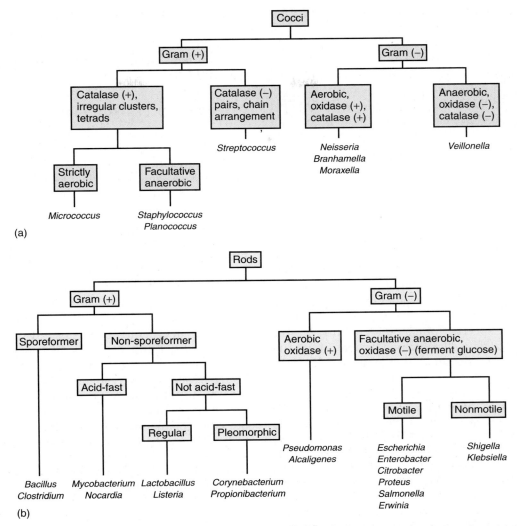

Figure 17.6 Flowchart to separate primary genera of gram-positive and gram-negative bacteria. (a) Cocci and (b) rods commonly involved in human diseases.

hundred can mean active infection. In contrast, the presence of a single colony of a true pathogen such as *Mycobacterium tuberculosis* in a sputum culture or an opportunist in sterile sites such as cerebrospinal fluid or blood is highly suggestive of its role in disease. Furthermore, the repeated isolation of a relatively pure culture of any microorganism can mean it is an agent of disease, though care must be taken in this diagnosis. Another problem facing clinical laboratory personnel is that of differentiating a pathogen from species in the normal biota that are similar in morphology to their more virulent relatives.

17.3 Learning Outcomes—Can You . . .

4. . . . list at least three different tests that fall in the direct identification category?

5. . . . explain the main principle behind biochemical tests?

17.4 Genotypic Methods

DNA Analysis Using Genetic Probes

The exact order and arrangement of the DNA code is unique to each organism. With a technique called *hybridization*, it is possible to identify a bacterial species by analyzing segments of its DNA. This requires small fragments of single-stranded DNA (or RNA) called **probes** that are known to be complementary to the specific sequences of DNA from a particular microbe. Several variations on the principle are used in infectious disease diagnosis. In the oldest method, unknown test DNA is extracted from cells in specimens or cultures and is bound to special blotter paper. After several different probes have been added to the blotter, it is observed for visible signs that the probes have become fixed (hybridized) to the test DNA. The identity of the source organism can be determined by the identity of the (known) probe used in the hybridization.

Hybridization techniques have been made easier by incorporating the probes on beads and looking for binding of test DNA (much like Ab-Ag agglutination) or by innovations that make it possible to "read" the results in liquid phase, in test tubes. These tests have become more convenient and portable, and they have become safer, too. Previously the only way to label a probe so that its binding would become visible was by binding a radioactive element to it. Now probes can be made fluorescent or labeled with chemically luminescent materials that can be measured by "light meters."

Nucleic Acid Sequencing and rRNA Analysis

You may remember from chapter 1 that one of the most viable indicators of evolutionary relatedness and affiliation is comparison of the sequence of nitrogen bases in 16s ribosomal RNA, a part of the small subunit of ribosomes. This is because parts of the 16s rRNA are highly conserved across species and across time. But because other parts of the rRNA are highly variable between species, it is also perfectly suited for differentiating one species from another, in other words, the diagnosis of infections. Cells obtained from a patient site can be lysed, their rRNA obtained and sequenced directly, but more often the correct rRNA is "fished out" using a particular PCR primer, and then sequenced (see below).

The property of dyes such as fluorescein and rhodamine to emit visible light in response to ultraviolet radiation was discussed in chapter 3. This property of fluorescence has found numerous applications in diagnostic testing. For instance, a technique called FISH (fluorescent *in situ* hybridization) has been developed to identify hybridization with

16s RNA without first culturing the organism. The turnaround time for identifying which organisms are present in blood cultures has been reduced from 24 h to 90 minutes, using a new technique called peptide nucleic acid FISH **(figure 17.7).**

Polymerase Chain Reaction

Many nucleic acid assays use the **polymerase chain reaction (PCR).** This method can amplify DNA present in samples even in tiny amounts, which greatly improves the sensitivity of the test (see figure 10.7). PCR tests are being used for a wide variety of bacteria, viruses, protozoa, and fungi. The sensitivity of PCR has been improved with various innovations in recent years. PCR diagnostic tests have been developed for important pathogens and situations for which waiting for culture or for offsite lab results would compromise care. Thus, clinics can choose to test high-risk clients for HIV using in-office PCR rather than the conventional ELISA followed by a Western blot (discussed later in this chapter). Likewise, hospitals can use PCR to diagnose methicillin-resistant *S. aureus* in patients in order to quickly institute isolation practices.

Since the terrorist attacks of September 11, 2001, very rapid identification of pathogens in the environment has been a research priority in the United States. This has led to a type of microbial identification system called a **biosensor.** These apparatuses often employ PCR techniques. Samples can either be manually loaded into a machine so that rapid PCR is conducted, or the machines can "sample" the environment by retrieving air or fluid samples on a regular basis and subjecting them to genomic techniques so personnel can continuously monitor the pathogen census in an environment.

Figure 17.7 PNA FISH testing for *S. aureus*.   These tests can identify bloodborne pathogens more quickly than other methods.

17.5 Immunologic Methods

The antibodies formed during an immune reaction are important in combating infection, but they hold additional practical value. Characteristics of antibodies (such as their quantity or specificity) can reveal the history of a patient's contact with microorganisms or other antigens. This is the underlying basis of serological testing. **Serology** is the branch of immunology that traditionally deals with *in vitro* diagnostic testing of serum. Serological testing is based on the familiar concept that antibodies have extreme specificity for antigens, so when a particular antigen is exposed to its specific antibody, it will fit like a hand in a glove. The ability to visualize this interaction by some means provides a powerful tool for detecting, identifying, and quantifying antibodies—or for that matter, antigens. The scheme works both ways, depending on the situation. One can detect or identify an unknown antibody using a known antigen, or one can use an antibody of known specificity to help detect or identify an unknown antigen **(figure 17.8).** Modern serological testing has grown into a field that tests more than just serum. Urine, cerebrospinal fluid, whole tissues, and saliva can also be used to determine the immunologic status of patients. These and other immune tests are helpful in confirming a suspected diagnosis or in screening a certain population for disease.

General Features of Immune Testing

The strategies of immunologic tests are diverse, and they underline some of the brilliant and imaginative ways that antibodies and antigens can be used as tools. We summarize them under the headings of agglutination, precipitation, complement fixation, fluorescent antibody tests, and immunoassay tests. First we provide an overview of the general characteristics of immune testing, and we then look at each type separately.

(a) In serological diagnosis of disease, a blood sample is scanned for the presence of antibody using an antigen of known specificity. A positive reaction is usually evident as some visible sign, such as color change or clumping, that indicates a specific interaction between antibody and antigen. (The reaction at the molecular level is rarely observed.)

(b) An unknown microbe is mixed with serum containing antibodies of known specificity, a procedure known as serotyping. Microscopically or macroscopically observable reactions indicate a correct match between antibody and antigen and permit identification of the microbe.

Figure 17.8 Basic principles of serological testing using antibodies and antigens.

The most effective serological tests have a high degree of specificity and sensitivity (**figure 17.9**). *Specificity* is the property of a test to focus on only a certain antibody or antigen and not to react with unrelated or distantly related ones. Better said, specificity is the degree to which a test does not (falsely) detect people who do not have a condition. *Sensitivity* means that the test can detect even very small amounts of antibodies or antigens that are the targets of the test. In other words, sensitivity is the degree to which a test will detect every positive person.

Visualizing Antigen-Antibody Interactions

The primary basis of most tests is the binding of an antibody (Ab) to a specific molecular site on an antigen (Ag). Because this reaction cannot be readily seen without an electron microscope, tests involve some type of endpoint reaction visible to the naked eye or with regular magnification that tells whether the result is positive or negative. In the case of large antigens such as cells, Ab binds to Ag and creates large clumps or aggregates that are visible macroscopically or microscopically (**figure 17.10a**). Smaller Ag-Ab complexes that do not result in readily observable changes will require special indicators in order to be visualized. Endpoints are often revealed by dyes or fluorescent reagents that can tag molecules of interest.

An antigen-antibody reaction can be used to read a **titer,** or the quantity of antibodies in the serum. Titer is determined by serially diluting a sample in tubes or in a multiple-welled microtiter plate and mixing it with antigen (**figure 17.10b**). It is expressed as the highest dilution of serum that produces a visible reaction with an antigen. The more a sample can be diluted and yet still react with antigen, the greater is the concentration of antibodies in that sample and the higher is its titer. Interpretation of testing results is discussed in **Insight 17.2.**

Agglutination and Precipitation Reactions

The essential differences between agglutination and precipitation are in size, solubility, and location of the antigen. In agglutination, the antigens are whole cells such as red blood cells or bacteria with determinant groups on the surface. In precipitation, the antigen is a soluble molecule. In both instances, when Ag and Ab are optimally combined so that neither is in excess, one antigen is interlinked by several antibodies to form an insoluble, three-dimensional aggregate so large that it cannot remain suspended and it settles out.

Agglutination Testing

Agglutination is discernible because the antibodies cross-link the antigens to form visible clumps. **Agglutination** tests are performed routinely by blood banks to determine ABO and Rh (Rhesus) blood types in preparation for transfusions. In this type of test, antisera containing antibodies against the blood group antigens on red blood cells are mixed with a small sample of blood and read for the presence or absence of clumping. Numerous variations of agglutination testing exist. The rapid plasma reagin (RPR) test is one of several tests commonly used to test for antibodies

---

INSIGHT 17.2   When Positive Is Negative: How to Interpret Serological Test Results

What if a patient's serum gives a positive reaction—is **seropositive**—in a serological test? In most situations, it means that antibodies specific for a particular microbe have been detected in the sample. But one must be cautious in proceeding to the next level of interpretation. The mere presence of antibodies does not necessarily indicate that the patient has a disease, but only that he or she has possibly had contact with a microbe or its antigens through infection or vaccination. In screening tests for determining a patient's history (rubella, for instance), knowing that a certain titer of antibodies is present can be significant because it shows that the person has some protection.

When the test is being used to diagnose current disease, however, a series of tests to show a rising titer of antibodies is necessary. The accompanying figure indicates how such a test can be used to diagnose patients who have nonspecific symptoms that could fit several diseases. Lyme disease, for instance, can be mistaken for arthritis or viral infections. In the first group, note that the antibody titer against *Borrelia burgdorferi,* the causative agent, increased steadily over a 6-week period. A control group that shared similar symptoms did not exhibit a rise in titer for antibodies to this microbe. Clinicians call samples collected early and late in an infection *acute* and *convalescent* sera.

Another important consideration in testing is the occasional appearance of biological false positives. These are results in which a patient's serum shows a positive reaction, even though, in reality, he or she is not or has not been infected by the microbe. False positives, such as those in syphilis and AIDS testing, arise when antibodies or other substances present in the serum cross-react with the test reagents, producing a positive result. Such false results may require retesting by a method that greatly minimizes cross-reactions.

Figure 17.9 Specificity and sensitivity in immune testing. **(a)** This test shows specificity in which an antibody (Ab) attaches with great exactness with only one type of antigen (Ag). **(b)** Sensitivity is demonstrated by the fact that Ab can pick up antigens even when the antigen is greatly diluted.

(a) Agglutination involves clumping of whole cells; precipitation is the formation of antigen-antibody complexes in cell-free solution. Both reactions can be observed by noticeable clumps or precipitates in test tubes (see (b) and figure 17.9a).

*Although IgG is shown as the Ab, IgM is also involved in these reactions.

(b) The tube agglutination test. A sample of patient's serum is serially diluted with saline. The dilution is made in a way that halves the number of antibodies in each subsequent tube. An equal amount of the antigen (here, blue bacterial cells) is added to each tube. The control tube has antigen, but no serum. After incubation and centrifugation, each tube is examined for agglutination clumps as compared with the control, which will be cloudy and clump-free. The titer is equivalent to the denominator of the dilution of the last tube in the series that shows agglutination.

Figure 17.10 Cellular/molecular view of agglutination and precipitation reactions that produce visible antigen-antibody complexes.

to syphilis. The *Weil-Felix reaction* is an agglutination test sometimes used in diagnosing rickettsial infections. In general, agglutination tests for identifying infections have been largely replaced in the developed world by fluorescent or genetic methods, but they are still widely used, and extremely useful, in the developing world where newer technologies are not available.

Precipitation Tests

In precipitation reactions, the soluble antigen is precipitated (made insoluble) by an antibody. This reaction is observable in a test tube in which antiserum has been carefully laid over an antigen solution. At the point of contact, a cloudy or opaque zone forms.

One example of this technique is the VDRL (Venereal Disease Research Laboratory) test that also detects antibodies to syphilis. Although it is a good screening test, it tests for reaction to a surrogate antigen (cardiolipin) that may give rise to false positive results. Although precipitation is a useful detection tool, the precipitates are so easily disrupted in liquid media that most precipitation reactions are now conducted with antigen or antibody that is anchored to a large insoluble particle so that the reactions are visible without magnification. Such is the case with the rapid plasma reagin test (RPR) for syphilis, which is basically the VDRL test made visible to the naked eye **(figure 17.11)**.

The Western Blot for Detecting Proteins

The **Western blot test** involves the electrophoretic separation of proteins, followed by an immunoassay to detect these proteins. This test is a counterpart of the Southern blot test for identifying DNA, described in chapter 10. It

is a highly specific and sensitive way to identify or verify a particular protein (antibody or antigen) in a sample **(figure 17.12)**. First, the test material is electrophoresed in a gel to separate out particular bands. The gel is then

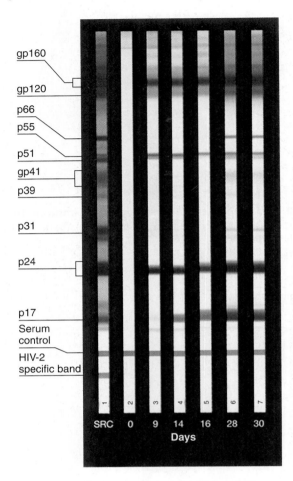

Successive tests on an HIV+ patient over 30 days reveal an increase in band intensity over time. This is due to continued formation of anti-HIV antibodies.

Figure 17.12 The Western blot procedure. Examples shown here test for antibodies to several HIV antigens. The test strips are prepared by electrophoresing the major HIV surface and core antigens and then blotting them onto special filters. The test strips are incubated with a serum sample and developed with a radioactive or colorimetric label. Sites where HIV antigens have bound antibodies show up as bands. A positive control strip (SRC) containing antibodies for all HIV antigens serves as a comparison.

Interpretation of bands to report a positive test
Labels correspond with glycoproteins (gp) or proteins (p) that are part of HIV-1 antigen structure.
- The test is considered positive if bands occur at two locations: gp160 or gp120 and p31 or p24.
- The test is considered negative if no bands are present for any HIV antigen.
- The test is considered indeterminate if bands are present but not at the primary locations. This result may require retesting at a later date.

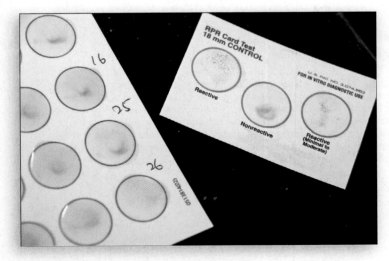

Figure 17.11 The Rapid plasma reagin test. The test uses an antigen complexed to microparticles so that blood from people who have syphilis will precipitate with the antigen-bound complexes.

transferred to a special blotter that binds the reactants in place. The blot is developed by incubating it with a solution of antigen or antibody that has been labeled with radioactive, fluorescent, or luminescent labels. Sites of specific binding will appear as a pattern of bands that can be compared with known positive and negative samples. This is currently the second (verification) test for people who are antibody-positive for HIV in the ELISA test (described in a later section), because it tests more types of antibodies and is less subject to misinterpretation than are other antibody tests. The technique has significant applications for detecting microbes and their antigens in specimens.

Complement Fixation

An antibody that requires complement to complete the lysis of its antigenic target cell is termed a **lysin** or cytolysin (see chapter 14 for a discussion of complement). When lysins act in conjunction with the intrinsic complement system on red blood cells, the cells hemolyze (lyse and release their hemoglobin). This lysin-mediated hemolysis is the basis of a group of tests called complement fixation, or CF **(figure 17.13).**

Complement fixation testing uses four components—antibody, antigen, complement, and sensitized sheep red blood cells—and it is conducted in two stages. In the first stage, the test antigen is allowed to react with the test antibody (at least one must be of known identity) in the absence of complement. If the Ab and Ag are specific for each other, they form complexes. To this mixture, purified complement proteins from guinea pig blood are added. If antibody and antigen have complexed during the previous step, they attach, or fix, the complement to them, thus preventing it from participating in further reactions. The extent of this complement fixation is determined in the second stage by means of sheep RBCs with surface lysin molecules. The sheep RBCs serve as an indicator complex that can also fix complement. Contents of the stage 1 tube are mixed with the stage 2 tube and observed for hemolysis, which can be observed with the naked eye as a clearing of the solution. If hemolysis *does not* occur, it means that the complement was used up by the first stage Ag-Ab complex and that the unknown antigen or antibody was indeed present. This result is considered positive. If hemolysis *does* occur, it means that unfixed complement from tube 1 reacted with the RBC complex instead,

Figure 17.13 Complement fixation test.   In this example, two serum samples are being tested for antibodies to a certain infectious agent. In reading this test, one observes the cloudiness of the tube. If it is cloudy, the RBCs are not hemolyzed and the test is positive. If it is clear and pink, the RBCs are hemolyzed and the test is negative.

thereby causing lysis of the sheep RBCs. This result is negative for the antigen or antibody that was the target of the test. Complement fixation tests are invaluable in diagnosing fungal diseases such as coccidioidomycosis, and histoplasmosis. It is also used to detect antibodies to *Coxiella burnetii*, the cause of Q fever.

The antistreptolysin O (ASO) titer test measures the levels of antibody against the streptolysin toxin, an important hemolysin of group A streptococci. It employs a technique related to complement fixation. A serum sample is exposed to known suspensions of streptolysin and then allowed to incubate with RBCs. Lack of hemolysis indicates antistreptolysin antibodies in the patient's serum that have neutralized the streptolysin and prevented hemolysis. This is an important verification procedure for scarlet fever, rheumatic fever, and other related streptococcal syndromes (see chapter 21).

Miscellaneous Serological Tests

In *toxin neutralization* tests, a test serum is incubated with the microbe that produces the toxin. If the serum inhibits the growth of the microbe, one can conclude that antitoxins are present. This test is mainly used to check the accuracy of other, more convenient, laboratory tests.

Serotyping is an antigen-antibody technique for identifying, classifying, and subgrouping certain bacteria into categories called serotypes, using antisera for cell antigens such as the capsule, flagellum, and cell wall. It is widely used in typing *Salmonella* species and strains and is the basis for identifying the numerous serotypes of streptococci. The Quellung test, which identifies serotypes of the pneumococcus, involves a precipitation reaction in which antibodies react with the capsular polysaccharide. Although the reaction makes the capsule seem to swell, it is actually creating a zone of Ag-Ab complex on the cell's surface.

Fluorescent Antibodies and Immunofluorescence Testing

The fundamental tool in immunofluorescence testing is a fluorescent antibody—a monoclonal antibody labeled by a fluorescent dye.

The two ways that fluorescent antibodies (FAbs) can be used for diagnosis are shown in **figure 17.14**. In *direct testing*, an unknown test specimen or antigen is fixed to a slide and exposed to a fluorescent antibody solution of known composition. If the antibodies are complementary to antigens in the material, they will bind to it. After the slide is rinsed to remove unattached antibodies, it is observed with the fluorescent microscope. Fluorescing cells or particles indicate the presence of Ab-Ag complexes and a positive result. These tests are valuable for identifying and locating antigens on the surfaces of cells or in tissues and in identifying the disease agents of syphilis, gonorrhea, chlamydiosis, whooping cough, Legionnaires' disease, plague, trichomoniasis, meningitis, and listeriosis.

In *indirect testing* methods, the fluorescent antibodies are antibodies made to react with the Fc region of another antibody (remember that antibodies can be antigenic). In this scheme, an antigen of known character (a bacterial cell, for example) is combined with a test serum of unknown antibody content. The fluorescent antibody solution that can react with the unknown antibody is applied and rinsed off to visualize whether the serum contains antibodies that have affixed to the antigen. A positive test shows fluorescing aggregates or cells, indicating that the fluorescent antibodies have combined with the unlabeled antibodies. In a negative test, no fluorescent complexes will appear. This technique is frequently used to diagnose syphilis (FTA-ABS) and various viral infections.

Immunoassays

The elegant tools of the microbiologist and immunologist are being used increasingly in athletics, criminology, government, and business to test for trace amounts of substances such as hormones, metabolites, and drugs. But traditional techniques

Visible fluorescence

Fluorescent microscopy

Unknown antigen (usually cell or tissue)

+

Antibody labeled with fluorescent dye

(a) Direct Testing

Ab2 fluorescently labeled; specific for Ab1

Ab1 in serum

Known Ag

No Ab in serum

Ab2 attaches to Ab1— visible fluorescence

Positive

Ab2 cannot attach— no fluorescence

(b) Indirect Testing

Negative

(c) Indirect Immunofluorescence Testing

Figure 17.14 Immunofluorescence testing. **(a)** Direct: Unidentified antigen (Ag) is directly tagged with fluorescent Ab. **(b)** Indirect: Ag of known identity is used to assay unknown Ab; a positive reaction occurs when the second Ab (with fluorescent dye) affixes to the first Ab. **(c)** An indirect immunofluorescent stain of cells infected with two different viruses. Cells fluorescing green contain cytomegalovirus; cells fluorescing yellow contain adenovirus.

in serology are not refined enough to detect a few molecules of these chemicals. Extremely sensitive alternative methods that permit rapid and accurate measurement of trace antigen or antibody are called **immunoassays.** Many of these tests are based on specifically formulated monoclonal antibodies.

Radioimmunoassay (RIA)

Antibodies or antigens labeled with a radioactive isotope can be used to pinpoint minute amounts of a corresponding antigen or antibody. Although very complex in practice, these assays compare the amount of label present in a sample before and after incubation with a known, labeled antigen or antibody. The labeled substance competes with its natural, nonlabeled partner for a reaction site. Large amounts of a bound labeled component indicate that the unknown test substance was not present. The amount of radioactivity is measured with an isotope counter or a photographic emulsion (autoradiograph). Radioimmunoassay has been employed to measure the levels of insulin and other hormones and to diagnose allergies, chiefly by the radioimmunosorbent test (RIST) for measurement of IgE in allergic patients and the radioallergosorbent test (RAST) to standardize allergenic extracts.

Enzyme-Linked Immunosorbent Assay (ELISA)

The **ELISA** test, also known as enzyme immunoassay (EIA), contains an enzyme-antibody complex that can be used as a color tracer for antigen-antibody reactions. The enzymes used most often are horseradish peroxidase and alkaline phosphatase, both of which release a dye (chromogen) when exposed to their substrate. This technique also relies on a solid support such as a plastic microtiter plate that can *adsorb* (attract on its surface) the reactants **(figure 17.15).**

The *indirect ELISA* test is used to detect antibodies in a serum sample. As with other indirect tests, the final positive reaction is achieved by means of an antibody-antibody reaction. The indicator antibody is complexed to an enzyme that produces a color change with positive serum samples **(figure 17.15a,b).** The starting reactant is a known antigen that is adsorbed to the surface of a well. To this, an unknown serum is added. After rinsing, an enzyme-Ab reagent that can react with the unknown test antibody is placed in the well. The substrate for the enzyme is then added, and the wells are

(a) **Indirect ELISA,** comparing a positive versus negative reaction. This is the basis for HIV screening tests.

(b) **Microtiter ELISA Plate with 96 Tests for HIV Antibodies.** Colored wells indicate a positive reaction.

(c) **Capture or Antibody Sandwich ELISA Method.** Note that an antigen is trapped between two antibodies. This test is used to detect hantavirus and measles virus.

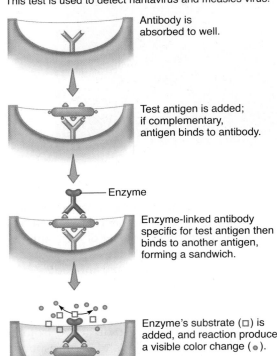

Antibody is absorbed to well.

Test antigen is added; if complementary, antigen binds to antibody.

Enzyme

Enzyme-linked antibody specific for test antigen then binds to another antigen, forming a sandwich.

Enzyme's substrate (□) is added, and reaction produces a visible color change (●).

Figure 17.15 Methods of ELISA testing.

scanned for color changes. Color development indicates that all the components reacted and that the antibody was present in the patient's serum. This is the common screening test for the antibodies to HIV, various rickettsial species, hepatitis A and C, the cholera vibrio, and *Helicobacter,* a cause of gastric ulcers. Because false positives can occur, a verification test may be necessary (such as Western blot for HIV).

In *direct ELISA* (or sandwich) tests, a known antibody is adsorbed to the bottom of a well and incubated with a solution containing unknown antigen **(figure 17.15c).** After excess unbound components have been rinsed off, an enzyme-antibody indicator that can react with the antigen is added. If antigen is present, it will attract the indicator-antibody and hold it in place. Next, the substrate for the enzyme is placed in the wells and incubated. Enzymes affixed to the antigen will hydrolyze the substrate and release a colored dye. Thus, any color developing in the wells is a positive result. Lack of color means that the antigen was not present and that the subsequent rinsing removed the enzyme-antibody complex. The direct technique is used to detect antibodies to hantavirus, rubella virus, and *Toxoplasma.*

A newer technology uses electronic monitors that directly read out antigen-antibody reactions. Without belaboring the technical aspects, these systems contain computer chips that sense the minute changes in electrical current given off when an antibody binds to antigen. The potential for sensitivity is extreme; it is thought that amounts as small as 12 molecules of a substance can be detected in a sample. In another procedure, antibody substrate molecules are incubated with sample and then exposed to the enzyme alkaline phosphatase. If the antibody is bound, the enzyme reacts with the substrate and causes visible light to be emitted. The light can be detected by machines or photographic films.

Some of the newer ELISA kits that use reporting mechanisms (i.e., labels) that don't come from enzymes but come from light-emitting substances should probably not be called "enzyme-linked" assays, but the name sticks since the principle is the same.

Case File 17   *Wrap-Up*

Eventually the hemodialysis facility in New York was shut down permanently. While not all of the new infections could be traced to poor infection control practices, some of them were. In addition to losing its certificate to operate, the facility paid a civil settlement to the state of New York.

Enveloped viruses, you will recall from chapter 11, are not usually very hardy in the environment, and are highly susceptible to disinfection procedures. Even though the viruses would have probably enjoyed some degree of protection from the organic medium (blood) they were in, they would not be expected to survive for long periods of time in the dialysis equipment or on other surfaces. This would be relevant as investigators compared the times and days of facility usage between patients who were the source of the infections and those who became infected later.

See: 2009. *MMWR* 58(08): 18994.

In Vivo Testing

Probably the first immunologic tests were performed not in a test tube but on the body itself. A classic example of one such technique is the **tuberculin test,** which uses a small amount of purified protein derivative (PPD) from *Mycobacterium tuberculosis* injected into the skin. The appearance of a red, raised, thickened lesion in 48 to 72 hours can indicate previous exposure to tuberculosis (shown in figure 16.14). In practice, *in vivo* tests employ principles similar to serological tests, except in this case an antigen or an antibody is introduced into a patient to elicit some sort of visible reaction. Like the tuberculin test, some of these diagnostic skin tests are useful for evaluating infections due to fungi (coccidioidin and histoplasmin tests, for example) or allergens. Allergic reactions and other immune system disorders are the topics of chapter 16.

A Note About Imaging in Diagnosis

Even though the three categories we highlighted here—phenotypic, genotypic, and immunologic—are far and away the most common means of diagnosing infectious diseases, special circumstances sometimes call for special techniques. Infections associated with hip implants, for example, may be difficult to access through blood samples. The bacteria may be growing in biofilms on the implanted materials, or they may be growing in an abscess deep in the hip joint. Magnetic resonance imaging, computerized tomography (CT scans), and positron emission tomography (PET scans) have been increasingly employed to find areas of localized infection in deep tissue, which can later be biopsied to aspirate samples for culture. In the event no infection is found on the image, the patient has been spared an invasive procedure. This seems very new and "high tech," but imaging in the form of X-rays has been used for centuries in the diagnosis of tuberculosis.

A Viral Example

All of the methods discussed so far—phenotypic, genotypic, and immunologic—are applicable to the different types of microorganisms. Viruses sometimes present special difficulties because they are not cells and they are more labor intensive to culture in the laboratory. **Figure 17.16** presents an overview of various techniques that might be used to diagnose viral infections. It provides one example of the variety of methods that can be employed for many infections regardless of their cause.

17.5 Learning Outcomes—Can You . . .

8. . . . give a thorough definition of the term serology?
9. . . . differentiate between sensitivity and specificity?
10. . . . discuss the concepts of agglutination and precipitation and when each is appropriate?
11. . . . list the steps of a Western blot?
12. . . . describe how complement fixation works?
13. . . . list the steps of an ELISA and explain the difference between a direct and an indirect test?

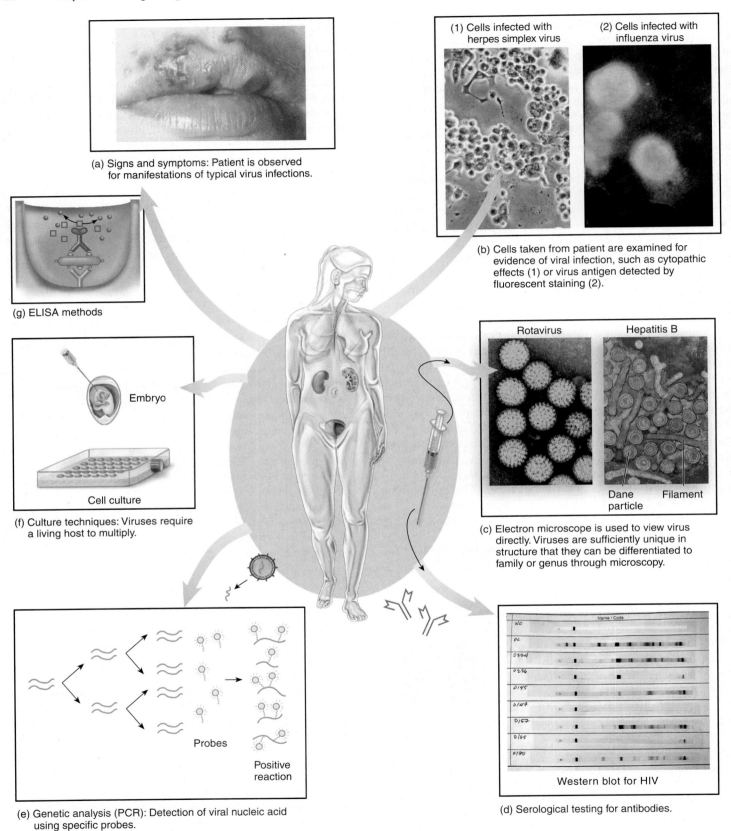

(a) Signs and symptoms: Patient is observed for manifestations of typical virus infections.

(1) Cells infected with herpes simplex virus   (2) Cells infected with influenza virus

(b) Cells taken from patient are examined for evidence of viral infection, such as cytopathic effects (1) or virus antigen detected by fluorescent staining (2).

(g) ELISA methods

Embryo

Cell culture

(f) Culture techniques: Viruses require a living host to multiply.

Rotavirus   Hepatitis B

Dane particle   Filament

(c) Electron microscope is used to view virus directly. Viruses are sufficiently unique in structure that they can be differentiated to family or genus through microscopy.

Probes

Positive reaction

(e) Genetic analysis (PCR): Detection of viral nucleic acid using specific probes.

Western blot for HIV

(d) Serological testing for antibodies.

Figure 17.16 Summary of methods used to diagnose viral infections.

Chapter Summary

17.1 Preparation for the Survey of Microbial Diseases

- Microbiologists use three categories of techniques to diagnose infections: *phenotypic, genotypic,* and *immunologic.*

17.2 On the Track of the Infectious Agent: Specimen Collection

- The first step in clinical diagnosis (after observing the patient) is obtaining a sample. If this step is not performed correctly, the test will not be accurate no matter how "sensitive."

17.3 Phenotypic Methods

- The main phenotypic methods include the direct examination of specimens, observing the growth of specimen cultures on special media, and biochemical testing of specimen cultures.

17.4 Genotypic Methods

- The use of genotypic methods has been increasing rapidly. These include genetic probing, nucleic acid sequencing, rRNA analysis, and PCR-based methods.

17.5 Immunologic Methods

- Serological tests can test for either antigens or antibodies. Most are *in vitro* assessments of antigen-antibody reactivity from a variety of body fluids. The basis of these tests is an antigen-antibody reaction made visible through the processes of agglutination, precipitation, complement fixation, fluorescent antibody, and immunoassay techniques.
- One measurement is the *titer,* described as the concentration of antibody in serum. It is the highest dilution of serum that gives a visible antigen-antibody reaction. The higher the titer, the greater the level of antibody present.
- In precipitation reactions, soluble antigen and antibody react to form insoluble, visible precipitates. Precipitation reactions can also be visualized by adding radioactive or enzyme markers to the antigen-antibody complex.

- Agglutination reactions occur between antibody and antigens bound to cells. This results in visible clumps caused by large antibody-antigen complexes. In viral hemagglutination testing, the antibody reacts with the antigen and inhibits it from agglutinating red blood cells.

- In immunoelectrophoresis techniques such as the Western blot, proteins that have been separated by electrical current are identified by labeled antibodies. HIV infections are verified with this method.

- Complement fixation involves a two-part procedure in which complement fixes to a specific antibody if present or to red blood cell antigens if antibody is absent. Lack of RBC hemolysis is indicative of a positive test.

- Serological tests can measure the degree to which host antibody binds directly to antigens, such as disease agents or toxins. This is the principle behind tests for syphilis and rheumatic fever.

- Direct fluorescence antibody tests indicate presence of an antigen and are useful in identifying infectious agents. Indirect fluorescence tests indicate the presence of a particular antibody and can diagnose infection.

- Immunoassays can detect very small quantities of antigen, antibody, or other substances.

- The ELISA test uses enzymes and dyes to detect antigen-antibody complexes. It is widely used to detect viruses, bacteria, and antibodies in HIV infection.

- *In vivo* serological testing, such as the tuberculin test, involves subcutaneous injection of antigen to elicit a visible immune response in the host.

Multiple-Choice and True-False Questions   Knowledge and Comprehension

Multiple-Choice Questions. Select the correct answer from the answers provided.

1. The most likely interpretation of the isolation of two colonies of *E. coli* on a plate streaked from a urine sample is
   a. probable infection.
   b. normal biota.
   c. contamination.

2. The most likely interpretation of the isolation of 50 colonies of *Streptococcus pneumoniae* is
   a. probable infection.
   b. normal biota.
   c. contamination.

3. The most likely interpretation of the isolation of 80 colonies of various streptococci on a culture from a throat swab is
   a. probable infection.
   b. normal biota.
   c. contamination.

4. The most likely interpretation of colonies of black bread mold on selective media used to isolate bacteria from stool is
   a. probable infection.
   b. normal biota.
   c. contamination.

5. Which of the following methods can identify different strains of a microbe?
   a. microscopic examination
   b. radioimmunoassay
   c. DNA typing
   d. agglutination test

6. In agglutination reactions, the antigen is a _____ ; in precipitation reactions, it is a _____ .
   a. soluble molecule, whole cell
   b. whole cell, soluble molecule
   c. bacterium, virus
   d. protein, carbohydrate

7. Which reaction requires complement?
   a. hemagglutination
   b. precipitation
   c. hemolysis
   d. toxin neutralization

8. A patient with a _____ titer of antibodies to an infectious agent generally has greater protection than a patient with a _____ titer.
   a. high, low
   b. low, high
   c. negative, positive
   d. old, new

9. Direct immunofluorescence tests use a labeled antibody to identify
   a. an unknown microbe.
   b. an unknown antibody.
   c. fixed complement.
   d. agglutinated antigens.

10. The Western blot test can be used to identify
    a. unknown antibodies.
    b. unknown antigens.
    c. specific DNA.
    d. both a and b.

True-False Questions. If the statement is true, leave as is. If it is false, correct it by rewriting the sentence.

11. Complement fixation is an example of an *in vivo* serological test.

12. A PNA FISH test utilizes both fluorescence and nucleic acids.

13. DNA probes are used to search for complementary segments of DNA.

14. Biochemical identification methods are based on a microbe's utilization of nutrients.

15. All microorganisms that grow from a clinical sample should be considered significant.

Critical Thinking Questions   Application and Analysis

These questions are suggested as a *writing-to-learn* experience. For each question, compose a one- or two-paragraph answer that includes the factual information needed to completely address the question.

1. Why do specimens need to be taken aseptically even when nonsterile sites are being sampled and selective media are to be used?

2. a. What is involved in direct specimen testing?
   b. In presumptive and confirmatory tests?
   c. In cultivating and isolating the pathogen?
   d. In biochemical testing?
   e. In gene probes?

3. Differentiate between the serological tests used to identify isolated cultures of pathogens and those used to diagnose disease from patients' serum.

4. Why is speed so important in the clinical laboratory?

5. Summarize the important points in determining if a clinical isolate is involved in infection.

6. a. What does seropositivity mean?
   b. Would a high rate of false-positives decrease the sensitivity or specificity of a test?

7. a. Explain the differences between direct and indirect procedures in serological or immunoassay tests.
   b. How is fluorescence detected?
   c. How is the reaction in a radioimmunoassay detected?
   d. How does a positive reaction in an ELISA test appear? How many wells are positive in figure 17.15*b*?

8. See Insight 17.1. How would you explain to a junior high biology class that in the next decade some diseases currently thought to be noninfectious will probably be found to be caused by microbes?

9. Why do some tests for antibody in serum (such as for HIV and syphilis) require backup verification with additional tests at a later date?

10. Why do we interpret positive hemolysis in the complement fixation test to mean negative for the test substance?

Concept Mapping Synthesis

Appendix D provides guidance for working with concept maps.

1. Supply your own linking words or phrases in this concept map, and provide the missing concepts in the empty boxes.

 Visual Connections Synthesis

These questions use visual images or previous content to make connections to this chapter's concepts.

1. **From chapter 3, figure 3.9b.** What biochemical characteristic does this figure illustrate? How could this characteristic be used to begin the identification of these two organisms? Explain your answer.

2. **From chapter 16, figure 16.15b.** Imagine that this patient is being seen by his or her physician for this unknown rash. What rapid phenotypic test could suggest that this condition is caused by a bacterium? Could a rapid immunoassay or fluorescent procedure be used to identify a specific viral cause? Explain your answer.

 www.connect.microbiology.com

Enhance your study of this chapter with study tools and practice tests. Also ask your instructor about the resources available through ConnectPlus, including the media-rich eBook, interactive learning tools, and animations.

18

Infectious Diseases Affecting the Skin and Eyes

Case File 18

Over the past several years, methicillin-resistant *Staphylococcus aureus* (MRSA) has become infamous as the cause of skin infections among football players, wrestlers, fencers, and other athletes who share equipment or engage in contact sports. MRSA strains are resistant to many drugs, including methicillin, a penicillin derivative commonly used to treat staphylococcal infections. Clinicians now distinguish between HA (hospital-acquired) MRSA and CA (community-acquired) MRSA. Spread of the bacterium from the initial infection site can lead to serious (often fatal) involvement of the heart, lungs, and bones.

Humans are not the only victims of MRSA. On January 29, 2008, the San Diego Zoo reported a MRSA outbreak involving a newborn African elephant and three of its human caretakers. The humans exhibited cutaneous pustules that were laboratory confirmed as MRSA infection. An investigation was initiated to determine the course and scope of the outbreak.

■ Was this an instance of HA-MRSA or CA-MRSA?

■ How is *S. aureus* commonly spread?

Continuing the Case appears on page 521.

Outline and Learning Outcomes

18.1 The Skin and Its Defenses
1. Describe the important anatomical features of the skin.
2. List the natural defenses present in the skin.

18.2 Normal Biota of the Skin
3. List the types of normal biota presently known to occupy the skin.

18.3 Skin Diseases Caused by Microorganisms
4. List the possible causative agents, modes of transmission, virulence factors, diagnostic techniques, and prevention/treatment for each of the diseases of the skin. These are: acne, impetigo, cellulitis, staphylococcal scalded skin syndrome, gas gangrene, vesicular/pustular rash diseases, maculopapular rash diseases, wartlike eruptions, large pustular skin lesions, and cutaneous mycoses.

18.1   The Skin and Its Defenses

The skin makes contact directly with the environment—not only with solid objects but also with water and other fluids, and with the atmosphere. What's more, many infectious diseases include skin eruptions or lesions as part of the course of illness and often as a major symptom, even if the infective agent does not enter via the skin. Prior to more sophisticated diagnostic methods, the appearance of a skin rash was often the best clue to the type of disease being experienced by a patient. This is still true in many instances.

The eye surface, like the skin, is also exposed constantly to the environment. For this reason, we include diseases of both organ systems in this chapter. The organs under consideration in this chapter form the boundary between the organism and the environment. The skin, together with the hair, nails, and sweat and oil glands, forms the **integument.** The skin has a total surface area of 1.5 to 2 square meters. Its thickness varies from 1.5 millimeters at places such as the eyelids to 4 millimeters on the soles of the feet. Several distinct layers can be found in this thickness, and we summarize them here. Follow **figure 18.1** as you read.

The outermost portion of the skin is the epidermis, which is further subdivided into four or five distinct layers. On top is a thick layer of epithelial cells called the stratum corneum, about 25 cells thick. The cells in this layer are dead and have migrated from the deeper layers during the normal course of cell division. They are packed with a protein called keratin, which the cells have been producing ever since they arose from the deepest level of the epidermis. Because this process is continuous, the

Figure 18.1   A cross section of skin.

entire epidermis is replaced every 25 to 45 days. Keratin gives the cells their ability to withstand damage, abrasion, and water penetration; the surface of the skin is termed **keratinized** for this reason. Below the stratum corneum are three or four more layers of epithelial cells. The lowest layer, the stratum basale, or basal layer, is attached to the underlying dermis and is the source for all of the cells that make up the epidermis.

The dermis, underneath the epidermis, is composed of connective tissue instead of epithelium. This means that it is a rich matrix of fibroblast cells and fibers such as collagen, and it contains macrophages and mast cells. The dermis also harbors a dense network of nerves, blood vessels, and lymphatic vessels. Damage to the epidermis generally does not result in bleeding, whereas damage deep enough to penetrate the dermis results in broken blood vessels. Blister formation, the result of friction trauma or burns, causes a separation between the dermis and epidermis.

The "roots" of hairs, called follicles, are in the dermis. **Sebaceous** (oil) **glands** and scent glands are associated with the hair follicle. Separate sweat glands are also found in this tissue. All of these glands have openings on the surface of the skin, so they pass through the epidermis as well.

It could be said that the skin is its own defense—in other words, the very nature of its keratinized surface prevents most microorganisms from penetrating into sensitive deeper tissues. Millions of cells from the stratum corneum slough off every day, and attached microorganisms slough off with them. The skin is also brimming with antimicrobial substances. Perhaps the most effective skin defense against infection is the one most recently discovered. In the past 20 years, small molecules called **antimicrobial peptides** have been identified in epithelial cells. These are positively charged chemicals that act by disrupting (negatively charged) membranes of bacteria. There are many different types of these peptides, and they seem to be chiefly responsible for keeping the microbial count on skin relatively low.

The sebaceous glands' secretion, called **sebum,** has a low pH, which makes the skin inhospitable to most microorganisms. Sebum is oily due to its high concentration of lipids. The lipids can serve as nutrients for normal microbiota, but breakdown of the fatty acids contained in lipids leads to toxic by-products that inhibit the growth of microorganisms not adapted to the skin environment. This mechanism helps control the growth of potentially pathogenic bacteria. Sweat is also inhibitory to microorganisms, because of both its low pH and its high salt concentration. **Lysozyme** is an enzyme found in sweat (and tears and saliva) that specifically breaks down peptidoglycan, which you learned in chapter 4 is a unique component of eubacterial cell walls.

18.1 Learning Outcomes—Can You ...

1. ... describe the important anatomical features of the skin?
2. ... list the natural defenses present in the skin?

18.2 Normal Biota of the Skin

Microbes that do live on the skin surface as normal biota must be capable of living in the dry, salty conditions they find there. Microbes are rather sparsely distributed over dry, flat areas of the body such as on the back, but they can grow into dense populations in moist areas and skin folds, such as the underarm and groin areas. The normal microbiota also live in the protected environment of the hair follicles and glandular ducts.

As discussed in chapter 13, we don't know how many species call the skin "home" because the majority of them are probably not cultivable. Early data have begun to emerge from the Human Microbiome Project (HMP). It came as a surprise that the two dominant genera on human skin are *Pseudomonas* and *Janthinobacterium,* both gram-negative rods. Neither was thought to be predominant on skin before the genomic methodology was applied. Fewer than 5% of the microbes on skin were found to be either *Staphylococcus epidermidis* or *Propionibacterium acnes,* the species long thought to be the most numerous normal biota on skin. **Figure 18.2** shows what types of bacteria were found by the HMP. It may be important that both *Pseudomonas* and *Janthinobacterium* are known to be adept at forming biofilms. Another important finding from the HMP is that there is a rich diversity of microbes—many of them well-known to be pathogenic—living under the skin. Their role in dermatologic diseases of all kinds is now being investigated. (Of course, we always knew microbes lived under the skin: Have you ever done a lab exercise in which you culture your hands before and after you wash them? Invariably more bacteria grow after the handwashing, indicating that removing the external layers exposes a richer diversity of microbial life.) In all, HMP researchers found 113 kinds of "normal biota" on human skin (sampled from various body sites. The forearm yielded the most diverse group of microbes (44 species) while

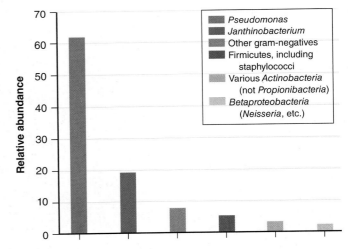

Figure 18.2 Relative abundance of different types of bacteria on the skin, as found by the Human Microbiome Project. Source: Data adapted from Grice et al., *Genome Research*, 2008, 18: 1043–1050.

the skin behind the ear hosted only 15. Scientists further found that swabbing the same people 10 months later yielded different microbes than in the original sample. The skin microbiota is more dynamic and more diverse than we ever imagined.

Defenses and Normal Biota of the Skin

	Defenses	Normal Biota
Skin	Keratinized surface, sloughing, low pH, high salt, lysozyme	*Pseudomonas, Janthinobacterium,* other gram-negatives, very few gram-positives

18.2 Learning Outcomes—Can You. . .

3. . . . list the types of normal biota presently known to occupy the skin?

18.3 Skin Diseases Caused by Microorganisms

Acne

The term *acne* encompasses all follicle-associated lesions, from the isolated pimple to severe widespread acne. Normally, the sebaceous glands associated with hair follicles (see figure 18.1) are a self-contained system for protecting, softening, and lubricating the skin. As hair and skin grow, dead epidermal cells and sebum work their way upward and are discharged from the pore to the skin surface.

Skin prone to pimples and acne has a structure that traps the mass of sebum and dead cells, clogging the pores. An exaggerated process of keratinization occurs in skin cells in and around the follicle, which also helps to block the pore. An added factor is overproduction of sebum when the sebaceous gland is stimulated by hormones (especially male). *Propionibacterium acnes* present in the follicle releases lipases to digest this surplus of oil. The combination of digestive products (fatty acids) and bacterial antigens stimulates an intense local inflammation that eventually can burst the follicle. In time, the lesion can erupt on the surface.

Different types of lesions are associated with this process. When the skin initially swells over the pore leading out of a hair follicle, it is called a **comedo**. If the pore is closed, this comedo is commonly called a whitehead. If the pore remains open to the surface but is blocked with a dark plug of sebum, it appears as a blackhead. When the lesion erupts on the surface, it is called a pustule or papule. At this point, the lesion contains sebum and pus, a collection of bacteria, dead skin cells, and white blood cells from the inflammatory reaction. Pustules that come to involve deeper layers of skin are called

A Note About the Chapter Organization

Beginning in this chapter, we discuss all the conditions caused by microbial infection. The chapter organization mirrors the clinical experience. Patients present themselves to health care practitioners with a set of symptoms, and the health care team makes an "anatomical" diagnosis—such as a *generalized vesicular rash*. The anatomical diagnosis allows practitioners to narrow down the list of possible causes to microorganisms that are known to be capable of creating such a condition. Then the proper tests can be performed to arrive at an etiologic diagnosis (that is, determining the exact microbial cause). So the order of events is (1) anatomical diagnosis based on signs and symptoms; (2) consideration of a number of agents that are known to cause disease in that anatomical location (often called the differential diagnosis); followed by (3) the etiologic diagnosis. In practice, this process may be shortened. For instance, if a patient has a disease such as mumps, the distinctive signs and symptoms of that disease may allow the practitioner to make the anatomical and the etiologic diagnosis at the same time, followed by confirmation of the etiology through laboratory methods, if necessary. In other cases, such as the common cold, the physician may consider only the anatomical diagnosis and never advance to the etiologic diagnosis because a cold is a mild self-limiting disease.

The chapters are organized by anatomical diagnosis (for example, Microbial Diseases of the Skin and Eyes). Specific diseases and the microorganisms that cause them are then detailed. Some diseases are the result of infection by a single type of microorganism. Hansen's disease is an example of this type of disease. In other cases, single diseases or conditions can be caused by many different microorganisms, including bacteria, viruses, and so on. The classic examples are pneumonia in the respiratory tract, meningitis in the central nervous system, and diarrhea in the gastrointestinal system. In this chapter, for instance, a maculopapular rash may be caused by the measles virus, the rubella virus, or a parvovirus. A Disease Table at the end of each disease/condition makes it clear whether a single microorganism or multiple agents are to be considered in the diagnosis.

cysts, and they can be quite painful. Widespread lesions of this type are called cystic acne.

▶ Causative Agent

Propionibacterium acnes is the bacterium associated with acne, but the "cause" of acne is multifactorial, requiring other conditions to be just right before the presence of this otherwise benign bacterium results in acne.

The bacterium is an anaerobic or aerotolerant gram-positive rod arranged in short chains or clumps. It releases a variety of enzymes that contribute to its virulence. The most important of these appears to be lipase, although it also releases proteases, neuraminidase, and a hyaluronidase. In addition, it secretes a low molecular weight protein that is a strong attractant for white blood cells (contributing to inflammation).

The complete genome sequence of the bacterium was published in 2004. This will allow researchers to identify additional virulence factors and to design more precise therapies for it.

▶ Transmission and Epidemiology

P. acnes is normal biota in small numbers on human skin, so it is not a transmissible infection. The epidemiology of a condition refers to its distribution in populations and usually takes into consideration the mode of transmission of the microorganism, the degree of susceptibility of different hosts, environmental parameters such as climate and geography, and even the behavior of current and potential hosts. When speaking of the epidemiology of acne we are really considering what groups have the combination of factors that can result in acne rather than the distribution of *P. acnes*. About 85% of adolescents and young adults experience acne of some degree at some time in their lives. More severe forms of adolescent acne are more common in males than females, probably because male hormones, or androgens, aggravate the condition. Females produce male hormones as well, but during adolescence males have a higher incidence of moderate to severe acne. Evidence exists that acne extending into adulthood, or beginning in adulthood, is more common in women.

▶ Prevention and Treatment

There is no effective prevention of acne; it is not the result of poor hygiene or even of eating the wrong foods. For many years, the only treatment options were (1) topical agents that enhanced the sloughing of skin cells, which could help to prevent comedo formation or to keep comedos from becoming pustules or papules; and (2) either topical or oral antibiotics, such as erythromycin or tetracycline. It has become apparent that such long-term use of antibiotics causes a high rate of antibiotic resistance in skin bacteria (in the case of topical application) or in whole-body normal biota. This result should have been predicted because oral antibiotics are typically given for long periods of time in low, sublethal doses—the perfect set of conditions for creating antibiotic resistance in bacteria. It has even been shown that live-in family members of people taking antibiotics for their acne also eventually harbor skin bacteria resistant to the same antibiotic the acne patient is taking. In this way, resistant bacteria can spread beyond the original host.

Females are often prescribed oral contraceptive pills (containing estrogen) to treat their acne. This treatment is somewhat controversial because of the dangers of estrogen use. For patients with severe acne and for whom other treatment options have failed, generic forms of Accutane (isotretinoin) may be prescribed. Accutane itself was recently removed from the market. These drugs can have severe side effects, the most severe of which impact fetuses. These are called **teratogenic** (ter-at'-oh-jen"-ik) effects. Because of this, women taking the drugs should also be using two different methods of birth control. Other side effects include psychological depression, and patients must be closely monitored.

Disease Table 18.1 Acne

Causative Organism(s)	*Propionibacterium acnes*
Most Common Mode(s) of Transmission	Endogenous
Virulence Factors	Lipase, inflammatory mediator, other enzymes
Culture/Diagnosis	Based on clinical picture
Prevention	None
Treatment	Antibiotics (topical or oral), isotretinoin, benzoyl peroxide

Impetigo

Impetigo is a superficial bacterial infection that causes the skin to flake or peel off (**figure 18.3;** see also **Insight 18.1**). It is not a serious disease but is highly contagious, and children are the primary victims. Impetigo can be caused by either *Staphylococcus aureus* or *Streptococcus pyogenes*, and some cases are probably caused by a mixture of the two. As you may know, these two bacteria cause a wide variety of skin conditions. We've summarized them in Insight 18.1. It has been suggested that *S. pyogenes* begins all cases of the disease, and in some cases *S. aureus* later takes over and becomes the predominant bacterium cultured from lesions. Because

Figure 18.3 Impetigo lesions on the face.

S. aureus produces a bacteriocin (toxin) that can destroy *S. pyogenes*, it is possible that *S. pyogenes* is often missed in culture-based diagnosis.

▶ Signs and Symptoms

The "lesion" of impetigo looks variously like peeling skin, crusty and flaky scabs, or honey-colored crusts. Lesions are most often found around the mouth, face, and extremities, though they can occur anywhere on the skin. It is very superficial and it itches. The symptomatology does not indicate whether the infection is caused by *Staphylococcus* or *Streptococcus*.

Impetigo Caused by *Staphylococcus aureus*

Staphylococcus aureus is one of the most exquisitely tuned microorganisms for causing disease in humans. It is responsible for a long list of different diseases in addition to the ones highlighted in this chapter. *S. aureus* can cause pneumonias, food poisoning, serious bloodstream infections, bone infections, toxic shock syndrome, and meningitis. It is a gram-positive coccus that grows in clusters, like a bunch of grapes (**figure 18.4a**). It is nonmotile. Much of its destructiveness is due to its array of **superantigens** (see Insight 18.1).

S. aureus in culture produces large, round, opaque colonies (**figure 18.4b**) at an optimum of 37°C, although it can grow at any temperature between 10°C and 46°C. The species is a facultative anaerobe whose growth is enhanced in the presence of O_2 and CO_2. Its nutrient requirements can be satisfied by routine laboratory media, and most strains are metabolically versatile—that is, they can digest proteins and lipids and ferment a variety of sugars. This species is considered the sturdiest of all non-spore-forming pathogens, with well-developed capacities to withstand high salt (7.5% to 10%), extremes in pH, and high temperatures (up to 60°C for 60 minutes). *S. aureus* also remains viable after months of air drying and resists the effect of many disinfectants and antibiotics. These properties contribute to the reputation of *S. aureus* as a troublesome hospital pathogen.

▶ Pathogenesis and Virulence Factors

The most important virulence factors relevant to *S. aureus* impetigo are exotoxins called exfoliative toxins A and B, which are coded for by a phage that infects some *S. aureus* strains. At least one of the toxins attacks a protein that is very important for epithelial cell-to-cell binding in the outermost layer of the skin. Breaking up this protein leads to the characteristic blistering seen in the condition. The breakdown of skin architecture also facilitates the spread of the bacterium. All pathogenic *S. aureus* strains typically produce **coagulase**, an enzyme that coagulates plasma and blood. It is thought that this enzyme causes fibrin to be deposited around the bacteria, concentrating the exotoxins in an area of local damage. Because 97% of all human isolates of *S. aureus* produce this enzyme, its presence is considered the most diagnostic species characteristic.

Other enzymes expressed by *S. aureus* include hyaluronidase, which digests the intercellular "glue" (hyaluronic acid) that binds connective tissue in host tissues; staphylokinase, which digests blood clots; a nuclease that digests DNA (DNase); and lipases that help the bacteria colonize oily skin surfaces.

▶ Culture and/or Diagnosis

Doctors usually diagnose impetigo by looking at it, and they treat it with antibiotics that target both probable causes of it. But when the etiologic agent requires identification (for instance, if initial treatment fails), well-established methods exist for looking for *S. aureus*. Primary isolation of *S. aureus* is achieved by inoculation on sheep or rabbit blood agar. For

(a)   (b)

Inner zone of hemolysis

Outer zone of hemolysis

Figure 18.4 *Staphylococcus aureus*. (a) Scanning electron micrograph of *S. aureus*. (b) Blood agar plate growing *S. aureus*. Some strains show two zones of hemolysis, caused by two different hemolysins. The inner zone is clear, whereas the outer zone is fuzzy and appears only if the plate has been refrigerated after growth.

INSIGHT 18.1   The Skin Predators: *Staphylococcus* and *Streptococcus* and Their Superantigens

The relatively hostile environment of the skin makes it difficult for many microorganisms to set up shop there. But two genera of gram-positive bacteria, *Staphylococcus* and *Streptococcus*, are uniquely suited to causing disease there. Many of these diseases are described in this chapter. Here we discuss some very common skin conditions caused by the two bacteria.

Staphylococcus aureus: Folliculitis, Furuncles, and Carbuncles

Currently, 33 species have been placed in the genus *Staphylococcus*. Of these, the most important human pathogen is probably *S. aureus*. Elsewhere in this chapter, we have discussed some of the other staphylococcal skin conditions (impetigo, cellulitis, and scalded skin syndrome), but other common skin diseases have *S. aureus* as a cause. **Folliculitis** is a mild, superficial inflammation of hair follicles or glands. Although these lesions are usually resolved with no complications, they can lead to infections of subcutaneous tissues. An *abscess* is a more serious localized staphylococcal skin infection, which appears as an inflamed, fibrous lesion enclosing a core of pus. There are two types: furuncles and carbuncles. A **furuncle** results when the inflammation of a single hair follicle or sebaceous gland progresses into a large, red, and extremely tender abscess or pustule. Furuncles often occur in clus-

ters on parts of the body such as the buttocks, axillae, and back of the neck, where skin rubs against other skin or clothing. They are also commonly called *boils*. A **carbuncle** is a larger and deeper lesion, sometimes as big as a baseball, created by aggregation and interconnection of a cluster of furuncles. It is usually found in areas of thick, tough skin such as on the back of the neck. Carbuncles are extremely painful and can even be fatal in elderly patients when they give rise to systemic disease.

Streptococcus pyogenes: Erysipelas

In addition to impetigo and cellulitis, at least two other important *S. pyogenes* diseases begin on the skin. One fairly invasive manifestation is **erysipelas.** The pathogen usually enters through a small wound or incision on the face or extremities and eventually

Furuncle

Carbuncle

Erysipelas

heavily contaminated specimens, selective media such as mannitol salt agar are used. In addition to culturing, the specimen can be Gram stained, and irregular clusters of gram-positive cocci can be observed. Because differentiating among gram-positive cocci, including *S. epidermidis*, is not possible using colonial and morphological characteristics alone, other tests are required. The production of catalase, an enzyme that breaks down hydrogen peroxide accumulated during oxidative metabolism, can be used to differentiate the staphylococci, which produce it, from the streptococci, which do not. The ability of *Staphylococcus* to grow anaerobically and to ferment sugars separates it from *Micrococcus*, a non-pathogenic genus that is a common specimen contaminant.

One key technique for separating *S. aureus* from other species of *Staphylococcus* is the coagulase test **(figure 18.5)**. By definition, any isolate that coagulates plasma is *S. aureus*; all others are coagulase negative. Rapid multitest systems are used routinely to collect other physiological information **(figure 18.6)**.

Plasma and Three Different Bacteria

Coagulase-negative

Coagulase-positive

Coagulase-positive

Figure 18.5 The coagulase test.
Staphylococcal coagulase is an enzyme that reacts with factors in plasma to initiate clot formation. In the coagulase test, a tube of plasma is inoculated with the bacterium. If it remains liquid, the test is negative. If the plasma develops a lump or becomes completely clotted, the test is positive.

spreads to the dermis and subcutaneous tissues. Early symptoms are edema and redness of the skin near the portal of entry, and fever and chills. The lesion begins to spread outward, producing a slightly elevated edge that is noticeably red and hot. Depending on the depth of the lesion and how the infection progresses, cutaneous lesions can remain superficial or can produce long-term systemic complications. Severe cases involving large areas of skin are occasionally fatal.

Both *Streptococcus pyogenes* and *Staphylococcus aureus:* Necrotizing Fasciitis

As you will read in this chapter, both *S. pyogenes* and *S. aureus* can lead to impetigo and cellulitis. Often, both of the pathogens are isolated from lesions. The same is true for a very invasive infection called necrotizing fasciitis. The disease has been known for hundreds of years, but in recent years small outbreaks of the disease have received heavy publicity as the "flesh-eating disease." Cases of this disease are rather rare, but its potential for harm is high. It can begin with an innocuous cut in the skin and spread rapidly into nearby tissue, causing severe disfigurement and even death.

There is really no mystery to the pathogenesis of necrotizing fasciitis. It begins very much like impetigo and other skin infections: Streptococci and/or staphylococci on the skin are readily introduced into small abrasions or cuts, where they begin to grow rapidly. The particular strains of bacteria that cause this condition have great toxigenicity and invasiveness because of special enzymes and toxins. The enzymes digest the connective tissue in skin, and the toxins poison the epidermal and dermal tissue. As the flesh is killed, it separates and sloughs off, forming a pathway for the bacteria to spread into deeper tissues such as muscle. More dangerous cases involve polymicrobial infections that can include anaerobic bacteria and the systemic spread of the toxin to other organs. Some patients have lost parts of their limbs and faces, and others have suffered amputation, but early diagnosis and treatment can prevent these complications.

Why are these two bacteria particularly nasty? Because they both possess an array of superantigens. Superantigens are antigens that are capable of stimulating a huge array of T cells, even those with the incorrect specificity. This results in a massive release of cytokines such as tumor necrosis factor and interleukins that lead to extensive damage and sometimes death. Several different bacteria and viruses carry antigens capable of this; these two bacteria are chock full of them.

Necrotizing fasciitis

All tests: positive

All tests: negative

Figure 18.6 Miniaturized test system used in further identification of *Staphylococcus* isolates.   A single isolate is used to inoculate all the cupules on a strip. The cupules contain substrates that detect phosphatase production (PHS), urea hydrolysis (URE), glucosidase production (GLS), mannose fermentation (MNE), mannitol fermentation (MAN), trehalose fermentation (TRE), salicin fermentation (SAL), glucuronidase production (GLC), arginine hydrolysis (ARG), and galactosidase production (NGP).

Impetigo Caused by *Streptococcus pyogenes*

Streptococcus pyogenes is thoroughly described in chapter 21. The important features are briefly summarized here and the features pertinent to impetigo are listed in **Disease Table 18.2.**

S. *pyogenes* is a gram-positive coccus in Lancefield group A and is beta-hemolytic on blood agar. In addition to impetigo, it causes streptococcal pharyngitis (strep throat), scarlet fever, pneumonia, puerperal fever, necrotizing fasciitis, serious bloodstream infections, and poststreptococcal conditions such as rheumatic fever.

If the precise etiologic agent must be identified, there are well-established methods for identifying group A streptococci. Refer to chapter 21.

▶ Pathogenesis and Virulence Factors

The symptoms of *S. pyogenes* impetigo are indistinguishable from those caused by *S. aureus*. Like *S. aureus*, this bacterium possesses a huge arsenal of enzymes and toxins. As mentioned earlier, it anchors itself to surfaces (including skin) using a variety of adhesive elements on its surface (LTA, M protein and other proteins, and a hyaluronic acid capsule). M protein also protects it from phagocytosis. Like *S. aureus*, it possesses hyaluronidase.

S. *pyogenes* has a clever system to exploit host factors to increase its ability to spread in tissues. The bacterium's M protein has a high-affinity binding site for plasminogen—a host plasma protein that, when activated (cleaved), becomes plasmin **(figure 18.7)**. Plasmin itself is a protein-splitting enzyme that digests fibrin and other tissue proteins. But *S. pyogenes* doesn't wait for the normal course of

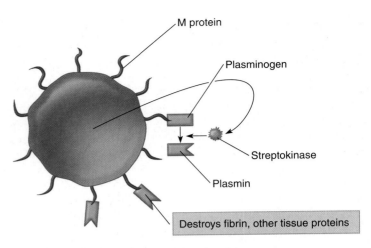

Figure 18.7 Plasmin activation by *S. pyogenes.*
The bacterium binds host plasminogen, then secretes an enzyme (streptokinase) that cleaves it, creating plasmin, which has tissue-degrading power. In the figure, bacterial components are red and host components are green.

events in which another host protein activates the plasminogen. Instead, it secretes an enzyme called streptokinase, which is a plasminogen activator. So the bacterium coats itself with host plasminogen, then uses its own enzyme (streptokinase) to activate it. It turns itself into a tissue degrader.

Rarely, impetigo caused by *S. pyogenes* can be followed by acute poststreptococcal glomerulonephritis (see chapter 21). The strains that cause impetigo never cause rheumatic fever, however.

Disease Table 18.2 Impetigo

Causative Organism(s)	*Staphylococcus aureus*	*Streptococcus pyogenes*
Most Common Modes of Transmission	Direct contact, indirect contact	Direct contact, indirect contact
Virulence Factors	Exfoliative toxin A, coagulase, other enzymes	Streptokinase, plasminogen-binding ability, hyaluronidase, M protein
Culture/Diagnosis	Routinely based on clinical signs, when necessary, culture and Gram stain, coagulase and catalase tests, multitest systems, PCR	Routinely based on clinical signs, when necessary, culture and Gram stain, coagulase and catalase tests, multitest systems, PCR
Prevention	Hygiene practices	Hygiene practices
Treatment	Topical mupirocin or pleuromutilin, oral cephalexin	Topical mupirocin or pleuromutilin, oral cephalexin
Distinguishing Features	Seen more often in older children, adults	Seen more often in newborns; may have some involvement in all impetigo (preceding *S. aureus* in staphylococcal impetigo)

▶ Transmission and Epidemiology of Impetigo

Impetigo, whether it is caused by *S. pyogenes, S. aureus,* or both, is highly contagious and transmitted through direct contact but also via fomites and mechanical vector transmission. It affects mostly preschool children, but all ages can acquire the disease. The peak incidence is in the summer and fall. *S. pyogenes* is more often the cause of impetigo in newborns, and *S. aureus* is more often the cause of impetigo in older children, but both can cause infection in either age group.

▶ Prevention

The only current prevention for impetigo is good hygiene. Vaccines are in development for both of the etiologic agents, but none are currently available.

▶ Treatment

Impetigo is usually treated with a drug that will kill either bacterium, *S. pyogenes* or *S. aureus,* eliminating the need to determine the exact etiologic agent. The drug of choice is topical mupirocin (brand name Bactroban), a protein synthesis inhibitor, or a newer topical drug called retapamulin (brand name Altabax), which is a pleuromutilin, and also a protein synthesis inhibitor. In cases of widespread skin involvement, oral antibiotics such as cephalexin may be used.

The treatment of nonimpetigo *S. pyogenes* infections is usually straightforward because this organism is sensitive to penicillin. *S. aureus* infections are another story. Although *S. aureus* impetigo is usually easily treated, other *S. aureus* diseases can be very difficult to treat effectively. We discuss these difficulties later in this chapter **(Disease Table 18.2)**.

Cellulitis

Cellulitis is a condition caused by a fast-spreading infection in the dermis and in the subcutaneous tissues below. It causes pain, tenderness, swelling, and warmth. Fever and swelling of the lymph nodes draining the area may also occur. Frequently, red lines leading away from the area are visible (a phenomenon called *lymphangitis*); this symptom is the result of microbes and inflammatory products being carried by the lymphatic system. Bacteremia could develop with this disease, but uncomplicated cellulitis has a good prognosis.

Cellulitis generally follows introduction of bacteria or fungi into the dermis, either through trauma or by subtle means (with no obvious break in the skin). Symptoms take several days to develop. The most common causes of the

---

A Note About MRSA

Everyone who has any recent work experience in health care knows the term *MRSA*, which stands for methicillin-resistant *Staphylococcus aureus*. MRSAs are *S. aureus* strains that are resistant to penicillin derivatives. (Methicillin is a penicillin derivative that is used only in the laboratory for testing purposes.) We first introduced MRSA in chapter 12, in Insight 12.3. Now it is very common for nosocomial infections to be caused by MRSA. These MRSA strains must be treated very aggressively with vancomycin or other new antibiotics (telavancin, tigecycline, or ceftobiprole) because they are resistant to multiple first-line and second-line antibiotics.

During the period between 2004 and 2006, a disturbing *S. aureus* trend that had been bubbling under the surface emerged into the public eye. While the health care establishment had grown accustomed to (though not complacent about) hospital-acquired MRSA (HA-MRSA), people who had no recent history in hospitals or health care facilities started turning up with MRSA infections. These infections are classified as *community-acquired* and given the acronym CA-MRSA. They turned up in tattoo parlors in Ohio and Kentucky, in the locker rooms of professional football teams, and in multiple schools and prisons. Currently more than 90,000 people per year in the United States get a MRSA infection. In 2007 the CDC predicted that soon, deaths from MRSA may exceed those from AIDS in this country, which currently number around 14,000/year.

The infection can begin as a boil or may invade a tiny cut. Many people report having had a "spider bite" because of the red swollen appearance of an early lesion. The good news is that CA-MRSA is susceptible to a wider array of antibiotics than the HA-MRSA. But how long will that last?

Case File 18   *Continuing the Case*

After the elephant calf was born at the zoo on November 28, 2007, its mother was unable to provide enough milk, so the calf was separated from her on December 24. A variety of zoo caretakers—nursery staff, elephant keepers, nutritionists, veterinarians, and veterinary technicians—bottle-fed the calf and played with it daily. These activities undoubtedly helped spread the bacterium, since *Staphylococcus aureus* is most commonly spread through contact with skin lesions. Some of the caretakers would also lie alongside the calf and blow into its trunk to encourage it to drink from a bottle. Because the calf was still not receiving sufficient nutrients through bottle feeding, surgeons inserted a central feeding line into a vein on the calf's neck. Three days later, cellulitis developed at the surgical site, and shortly thereafter pustules appeared on the calf's leg and elbow. Samples from all three locations were laboratory confirmed as MRSA on January 26. Treatment with topical, oral, and intravenous antibiotics successfully resolved the infection, but the calf failed to thrive and was euthanized on February 4.

Disease Table 18.3 Cellulitis

Causative Organism(s)	*Staphylococcus aureus*	*Streptococcus pyogenes*	Other bacteria or fungi
Most Common Modes of Transmission	Parenteral implantation	Parenteral implantation	Parenteral implantation
Virulence Factors	Exfoliative toxin A, coagulase, other enzymes	Streptokinase, plasminogen-binding ability, hyaluronidase, M protein	–
Culture/Diagnosis	Based on clinical signs	Based on clinical signs	Based on clinical signs
Prevention	–	–	–
Treatment	Oral or IV antibiotic (cephalexin); surgery sometimes necessary	Oral or IV antibiotic penicillin; surgery sometimes necessary	Aggressive treatment with oral or IV antibiotic (cephalexin or penicillin); surgery sometimes necessary
Distinguishing Features	–	–	More common in immunocompromised

condition in healthy people are *Staphylococcus aureus* and *Streptococcus pyogenes*, although almost any bacterium and some fungi can cause this condition in an immunocompromised patient. In infants, group B streptococci are a frequent cause (see chapter 23).

People who are immunocompromised or who have cardiac insufficiency are at higher risk for this condition than are healthy persons. They also risk complications, such as spread to the bloodstream, rapid spreading through adjacent tissues, and, especially in children, meningitis. Occasionally, cellulitis is a complication of varicella (chickenpox) infections.

Mild cellulitis responds well to oral antibiotics chosen to be effective against both *S. aureus* and *S. pyogenes.* More involved infections and infections in immunocompromised people require intravenous antibiotics. If there are extensive areas of tissue damage, surgical debridement (duh-breed'-munt) is warranted **(Disease Table 18.3).**

Staphylococcal Scalded Skin Syndrome (SSSS)

This syndrome is another **dermolytic** condition caused by *Staphylococcus aureus.* It affects mostly newborns and babies, although children and adults can experience the infection. Newborns are susceptible when sharing a nursery with another newborn who is colonized with *S. aureus.* Transmission may occur when caregivers carry the bacterium from one baby to another. Adults in the nursery can also directly transfer *S. aureus* because approximately 30% of adults are

asymptomatic carriers. Carriers can harbor the bacteria in the nasopharynx, axilla, perineum, and even the vagina. (Fortunately, only about 5% of *S. aureus* strains are lysogenized by the type of phage that codes for the toxins responsible for this disease.)

This condition can be thought of as a systemic form of impetigo. Like impetigo, it is an exotoxin-mediated disease. The phage-encoded exfoliative toxins A and B are responsible for the damage. Unlike impetigo, the toxins enter the bloodstream from some focus of infection (the throat, the eye, or sometimes an impetigo infection) and then travel to the skin throughout the body. These toxins cause **bullous lesions,** which often appear first around the umbilical cord (in neonates) or in the diaper or axilla area. The lesions begin as red areas, take on the appearance of wrinkled tissue paper, and then form very large blisters. Fever may precede the skin manifestations. Eventually, the top layers of epidermis peel off completely. The split occurs in the epidermal tissue layers just above the stratum basale (see figure 18.1). Widespread **desquamation** of the skin follows, leading to the burned appearance referred to in the name **(figure 18.8).**

At this point, the protective keratinized layer is gone, and the patient is vulnerable to secondary infections, cellulitis, and bacteremia. In the absence of these complications, young patients nearly always recover if treated promptly. Adult patients have a higher mortality rate—as high as 50%. Once a tentative diagnosis of SSSS is made, immediate antibiotic therapy should be instituted.

(a)

(b)

- Epidermis

- Space where separation has occurred

- Dermis

Figure 18.8 Staphylococcal scalded skin syndrome (SSSS) in a newborn child. **(a)** Exfoliative toxin produced in local infections causes blistering and peeling away of the outer layer of skin. **(b)** Photomicrograph of a segment of skin affected with SSSS. The point of epidermal shedding, or desquamation, is in the epidermis. The lesions will heal well because the level of separation is so superficial.

It is important, however, to differentiate this disease from a similar skin condition called *toxic epidermal necrolysis* (*TEN*), which is caused by a reaction to antibiotics, barbiturates, or other drugs. TEN has a significant mortality rate. The treatments for the two diseases are very different, so it is important to distinguish between them before instituting therapy. In TEN, the split in skin tissue occurs *between* the dermis and the epidermis, not within the epidermis as is the case with SSSS. Histological examination of tissue from a lesion is usually a better way to diagnose the disease than reliance on culture. Because SSSS is caused by the dissemination of exotoxin, *S. aureus* may not be found in lesions. Nevertheless, culture should be attempted so that antibiotic sensitivities can be established.

Disease Table 18.4 Scalded Skin Syndrome

Causative Organism(s)	*Staphylococcus aureus*
Most Common Modes of Transmission	Direct contact, droplet contact
Virulence Factors	Exfoliative toxins A and B
Culture/Diagnosis	Histological sections; culture performed but false negatives common because toxins alone are sufficient for disease
Prevention	Eliminate carriers in contact with neonates
Treatment	Immediate systemic antibiotics (cloxacillin or cephalexin)
Distinguishing Features	Split in skin occurs *within* epidermis

Gas Gangrene

Clostridium perfringens, a gram-positive endospore-forming bacterium, as well as some related species, causes a serious condition called **gas gangrene,** or clostridial **myonecrosis** (my″-oh-neh-kro′-sis). The spores of these species can be found in soil, on human skin, and in the human intestine and vagina. The bacteria are anaerobic, and they require anaerobic conditions to manufacture and release the exotoxins that mediate the damage in the disease.

▶ Signs and Symptoms

Two forms of gas gangrene have been identified. In anaerobic cellulitis, the bacteria spread within damaged necrotic muscle tissue, producing toxin and gas, but the infection remains localized and does not spread into healthy tissue. The pathology of true myonecrosis is more destructive. Toxins produced in large muscles, such as the thigh, shoulder, and buttocks, diffuse into nearby healthy tissue and cause local necrosis there. This damaged tissue then serves as a focus for continued clostridial growth, toxin formation, and gas production. The disease can quickly progress through an entire limb or body area, destroying tissues as it goes **(figure 18.9).** Initial symptoms of pain, edema, and a bloody exudate in the lesion are followed by fever, tachycardia, and blackened necrotic tissue filled with bubbles of gas. Gangrenous infections of the uterus, due to septic abortions, and clostridial septicemia are particularly serious complications. If treatment is not begun early, the disease is invariably fatal.

Figure 18.9 The clinical appearance of myonecrosis in a compound fracture of the leg.

Figure 18.10 Growth of *Clostridium perfringens* (plump rods), causing gas formation and separation of the fibers. A microscopic analysis of clostridial myonecrosis, showing a histological section of gangrenous skeletal muscle.

▶ Pathogenesis and Virulence Factors

Because clostridia are not highly invasive, infection requires damaged or dead tissue, which supplies growth factors, and an anaerobic environment. The low-oxygen environment results from an interrupted blood supply and the presence of aerobic bacteria, which deplete oxygen. Such conditions stimulate spore germination, rapid vegetative growth in the dead tissue, and release of exotoxins. *C. perfringens* produces several active exotoxins; the most potent one, *alpha toxin,* causes red blood cell rupture, edema, and tissue destruction **(figure 18.10).** Additional virulence factors that enhance tissue destruction are collagenase, hyaluronidase, and DNase. The gas formed in tissues, resulting from fermentation of muscle carbohydrates, can also destroy muscle structure.

▶ Transmission and Epidemiology

The conditions that may predispose a person to gangrene are surgical incisions, compound fractures, diabetic ulcers, septic abortions, puncture and gunshot wounds, and crushing injuries contaminated by spores from the body or the environment.

▶ Prevention and Treatment

One of the most effective ways to prevent clostridial wound infections is immediate and rigorous cleansing and surgical repair of deep wounds, decubitus ulcers (bedsores), compound fractures, and infected incisions. Debridement of diseased tissue eliminates the conditions that promote the spread of gangrenous infection. This procedure is most difficult in the intestine or body cavity, where only limited amounts of tissue can be removed. Surgery is supplemented by large doses of antibiotics to control infection. Hyperbaric oxygen therapy, in which the affected part is exposed to an increased oxygen mix in a pressurized chamber, can also

lessen the severity of infection. This works because under greater pressure your blood can carry more oxygen, thereby inhibiting the growth of anaerobic bacteria.

Extensive myonecrosis of a limb may call for amputation. Because there are so many different antigenic subtypes in this bacterial group, active immunization is not possible.

Disease Table 18.5 Gas Gangrene

Causative Organism(s)	*Clostridium perfringens,* other species
Most Common Modes of Transmission	Vehicle (soil), endogenous transfer from skin, GI tract, reproductive tract
Virulence Factors	Alpha toxin, other exotoxins, enzymes, gas formation
Culture/Diagnosis	Gram stain, CT scans (abdominal infections), X ray, clinical picture
Prevention	Clean wounds, debride dead tissue
Treatment	Penicillin and clindamycin, surgical removal, oxygen therapy

Vesicular or Pustular Rash Diseases

There are two diseases that present as generalized "rashes" over the body in which the individual lesions contain fluid. The lesions are often called *pox,* and the two diseases are chickenpox and smallpox. Chickenpox is very common and mostly benign, but even a single case of smallpox constitutes a public health emergency. Both are viral diseases.

Chickenpox

Most people think of chickenpox as a mild disease, and in most people it is. In immunocompromised people it can be life-threatening, however. Before the introduction of the vaccine in 1995, it was not unheard of for some families to hold "chickenpox parties." When one child in a group of acquaintances had chickenpox, other children would be brought together to play with them so that all the children could get chickenpox and be done with it. Parents wanted to ensure that their children got the disease while they were young because they knew that getting the disease at an older age could lead to more serious disease.

▶ Signs and Symptoms

After an incubation period of 10 to 20 days, the first symptoms to appear are fever and an abundant rash that begins on the scalp, face, and trunk and radiates in sparse crops to the extremities. Skin lesions progress quickly from macules and papules to itchy vesicles filled with a clear fluid. In several days, they encrust and drop off, usually healing completely but sometimes leaving a tiny pit or scar. Lesions number from a few to hundreds and are more abundant in adolescents and adults than in young children. **Figure 18.11a** contains images of the chickenpox lesions in a child and in an adult. The lesion distribution is *centripetal*, meaning that there are more in the center of the body and fewer on the extremities, in contrast to the distribution seen with smallpox. The illness usually lasts 4 to 7 days; new lesions stop appearing after about 5 days. Patients are considered contagious until all of the lesions have crusted over.

Most cases resolve without event within 2 to 3 weeks of onset. Some patients may experience secondary infections of the lesions with group A streptococci or staphylococci, and these require antibiotic therapy. Immunocompromised patients, as well as some adults and adolescents, may experience pneumonia as a result of chickenpox. The immunocompromised may also experience infection of the heart, liver, and kidney, resulting in a 20% mortality rate for this population.

Approximately 0.1% of chickenpox cases are followed by encephalopathy, or inflammation of the brain caused by the virus. It can be fatal, but in most cases recovery is complete.

Women who become infected with chickenpox during the early months of pregnancy are at risk for infecting the fetus. These babies may be born with serious birth defects

(a)   (b)

Figure 18.11 Images of chickenpox and smallpox. (a) Chickenpox. (b) Smallpox.

such as cataracts and missing limbs. Also, women who develop chickenpox just before or after giving birth may have passed the infection to the baby just before birth, resulting in serious infection in the newborn infant.

Shingles

After recuperation from chickenpox the virus enters into the sensory endings that innervate dermatomes, regions of the skin supplied by the cutaneous branches of nerves, especially the thoracic (**figure 18.12a**) and trigeminal nerves. From here it becomes latent in the ganglia and may reemerge as **shingles** (also known as **herpes zoster**) with its characteristic asymmetrical distribution on the skin of the trunk or head (**figure 18.12b**).

Shingles develops abruptly after reactivation by such stimuli as psychological stress, X-ray treatments, immunosuppressive and other drug therapy, surgery, or a developing malignancy. The virus is believed to migrate down the ganglion to the skin, where multiplication resumes and produces crops of tender, persistent vesicles. Inflammation of the ganglia and the pathways of nerves can cause pain and tenderness that can last for several months. Involvement of cranial nerves can lead to eye inflammation and ocular and facial paralysis.

▶ Causative Agent

Human herpesvirus 3 (HHV-3, also called **varicella** (var"-ih'sel'-ah) causes chickenpox, as well as the condition called herpes zoster or shingles. The virus is sometimes referred to as the varicella-zoster virus (VZV). Like other herpesviruses, it is an enveloped DNA virus.

▶ Pathogenesis and Virulence Factors

HHV-3 enters the respiratory tract, attaches to respiratory mucosa, and then invades and enters the bloodstream. The viremia disseminates the virus to the skin, where the virus causes adjacent cells to fuse and eventually lyse, resulting in the characteristic lesions. The virus enters the sensory nerves at this site, traveling to the ganglia.

The ability of HHV-3 to remain latent in ganglia is an important virulence factor, because resting in this site protects it from attack by the immune system and provides a reservoir of virus for the reactivation condition of shingles.

▶ Transmission and Epidemiology

Humans are the only natural hosts for HHV-3. The virus is harbored in the respiratory tract but is communicable from both respiratory droplets and the fluid of active skin lesions. People can acquire a chickenpox infection by being exposed to the fluid of shingles lesions. (It is not possible to "get" shingles from someone with shingles. If you are not immune to HHV-3, you can acquire HHV-3, which will manifest as chickenpox or, very occasionally, as an asymptomatic infection. Once you have the virus, whether you experience shingles or not is dependent on your own host factors.)

Infected persons are most infectious a day or two prior to the development of the rash. Only in rare instances will a person acquire chickenpox more than once. Chickenpox is so contagious that if you are exposed to it you almost certainly will get it. Some people have a subclinical case of it, meaning that their lesions never erupt. But they will have lifelong immunity (and will likely harbor the virus in their ganglia and be subject to shingles). When people think they have never had chickenpox, yet they don't seem to get it when exposed to infected persons, it is likely that they have had a subclinical case at some time in their lives.

Epidemics of the disease used to occur in winter and early spring. The introduction of the vaccine in 1995 reduced the occurrence of the disease, so it now occurs only sporadically.

▶ Prevention

Live attenuated vaccine was licensed in 1995. It consists of a weakened form of the Oka strain of the virus, which was

Figure 18.12 Varicella-zoster virus reemergence as shingles. **(a)** Dermatomes served by the thoracic nerves. **(b)** Clinical appearance of shingles lesions.

INSIGHT 18.2   Smallpox: An Ancient Scourge Becomes a Modern Threat

In earlier editions of this book, you could have read that smallpox had been eliminated from the earth and that this feat was one of the greatest triumphs of modern medicine. Today, soldiers, health care workers, and even former President George W. Bush have been vaccinated against this "vanquished" disease. What happened to cause this shift in thought, and how concerned should each of us be?

Historians note that smallpox epidemics have occurred for thousands of years. The 20th century saw one of humankind's greatest achievements when, through a massive worldwide health campaign that focused on immunization and isolation, the last case of smallpox was seen in Somalia in 1977. In 1980, with the war against smallpox "won," a committee of World Health Organization (WHO) experts recommended that laboratories worldwide destroy their stocks of variola virus or transfer them to one of two laboratories, the Institute of Virus Preparation in Moscow or the Centers for Disease Control and Prevention in the United States. At the time, all countries reported full compliance with the WHO request. Although the WHO committee recom-

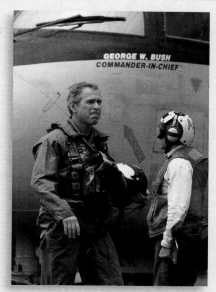

George W. Bush was the first president in many years to be vaccinated against smallpox.

mended that even the two remaining stockpiles of virus be destroyed in 1999, scientific and governmental organizations balked at destroying a potential useful research subject. Besides, many had reservations about carrying out the first *intentional* extinction of another species.

Concerns have since been expressed about the existence of smallpox stocks in other regions of the world. In fact, Iraqi prisoners captured in the 1991 Gulf War are reported to have had high levels of antibody to smallpox, which suggested they had been immunized, perhaps as protection against Iraqi biological weapons. And since the anthrax bioterror incident, which followed closely on the heels of the events of September 11, 2001, the U.S. government has taken the possibility of smallpox bioterrorism very seriously.

If smallpox is being contemplated as a weapon, it would not be the first time. During the French and Indian Wars (1754–1767), British soldiers were instructed to distribute blankets that had been used by smallpox patients to Native Americans in an attempt to infect them. Whether they actually did or not, bioterror and biowarfare are not new ideas, after all.

isolated from a Japanese boy named Oka. It is recommended as a single dose between the ages of 12 and 18 months.

In 2006, the FDA approved a unique vaccine called Zostavax®. It is intended for adults ages 60 and over and is for the prevention of shingles.

▶ Treatment

Uncomplicated varicella is self-limiting and requires no therapy aside from alleviation of discomfort. Secondary bacterial infection, as just noted, is treated with topical or systemic antibiotics. Oral acyclovir or related antivirals should be administered to people considered to be at risk for serious complications within 24 hours of onset of the rash. The acyclovir may diminish viral load and prevent complications.

Special Note About Reye's Syndrome

In the 1980s, researchers made a connection between aspirin and a serious condition that occurred in children, usually following a febrile (feb'-ruhl) viral infection, especially influenza or chickenpox. The condition is the result of an interaction of three factors: recent viral infection, age less than 15 years, and the use of salicylates (common aspirin).

The syndrome can be mild or severe. It usually begins with vomiting and nausea and is followed by a sudden change in mental status caused by encephalopathy. This condition results in a variety of central nervous system symptoms, also ranging from mild to severe, such as amnesia,

disorientation, seizures, coma, and respiratory arrest. The incidence has decreased dramatically since the public became aware that they should not administer salicylates to children with fever. Now there are at most 2 cases per year in the United States, evidence that public education *can* work.

Smallpox

Largely through the World Health Organization's comprehensive global efforts, naturally occurring smallpox is now a disease of the past. However, after the terrorist attacks on the United States on September 11, 2001, and the anthrax bioterrorism shortly thereafter, the U.S. government began taking the threat of smallpox bioterrorism very seriously. Vaccination, which had been discontinued, was once again offered to certain U.S. populations. After languishing in obscurity since its elimination from humans in the 1970s, smallpox was back in the news (**Insight 18.2**).

▶ Signs and Symptoms

Infection begins with fever and malaise, and later a rash begins in the pharynx, spreads to the face, and progresses to the extremities. Initially the rash is *macular,* evolving in turn to *papular, vesicular,* and *pustular* before eventually crusting over, leaving nonpigmented sites pitted with scar tissue (**Insight 18.3** for a description of these terms). There are two principal forms of smallpox, variola minor and variola major. Variola

INSIGHT 18.3   Naming Skin Lesions

There seems to be no end to the types of lesions or irregularities that can occur on the skin. Dermatology, the study of the skin, is a branch of medicine that relies heavily on visual characteristics for initial diagnoses. The many types of skin lesions or irregularities have been given specific descriptive names for this purpose. None of these names points to an exact etiologic cause, but because certain infectious agents generally cause distinctive types of lesions, the list of possible causes can be narrowed considerably once the "style" of irregularity is identified and named. **Table 18.A** contains a list of the more common descriptors of skin bumps, lesions, and irregularities.

Table 18.A   Skin Terms

Descriptive Name	Appearance	Examples
Macule	Flat, well-demarcated lesion characterized mainly by color change	Freckle, tinea versicolor (fungus infection)
Papule	Small elevated, solid bump	Warts, cutaneous leishmaniasis
Maculopapular Rash	Flat to slightly raised colored bump	Measles, rubella, fifth disease, roseola
Plaque	Elevated flat-topped lesion larger than 1 cm (i.e., a wider papule)	Psoriasis
Vesicle	Elevated lesion filled with clear fluid	Chickenpox
Bulla	Large (wide) vesicle	Blister, gas blisters in gangrene
Pustule	Small elevated lesion filled with purulent fluid (pus)	Acne, smallpox, mucocutaneous leishmaniasis, cutaneous anthrax
Cyst	Raised, encapsulated lesion, usually solid or semisolid when palpated	Severe acne
Purpura	Reddish-purple discoloration due to blood in small areas of tissue; does not blanch when pressed	Meningococcal bloodstream infection
Petechiae	Small purpura	Meningococcal bloodstream infection
Scale	Flaky portions of skin separated from deeper portions	Ringworm of body and scalp, athlete's foot

major is a highly virulent form that causes toxemia, shock, and intravascular coagulation. People who have survived any form of smallpox nearly always develop lifelong immunity.

It is vitally important for health care workers to be able to recognize the early signs of smallpox. The diagnosis of even a single suspected case must be treated as a health and law enforcement emergency. The symptoms of variola major progress as follows: After the prodrome period of high fever and malaise, a rash emerges, first in the mouth. Severe abdominal and back pain sometimes accompany this phase of the disease. As lesions develop, they break open and spread virus into the mouth and throat, making the patient highly contagious. A rash appears on the skin and spreads throughout the body within 24 hours. A distribution of the rash on the body is shown in figure 18.11*b*.

By the third or fourth day of the rash, the bumps become larger and fill with a thick opaque fluid. A major distinguishing feature of this disease is that the pustules are indented in the middle **(Disease Table 18.6)**. Also, patients report that the

lesions feel as if they contain a BB pellet. Within a few days, these pustules begin to scab over. After 2 weeks, most of the lesions will have crusted over; the patient remains contagious until the last scabs fall off because the crusts contain the virus. During the entire rash phase, the patient is very ill.

A patient with variola minor has a rash that is less dense and is generally less ill than someone with variola major.

▶ Causative Agent

The causative agent of smallpox, the variola virus, is an orthopoxvirus, an enveloped DNA virus. Variola is shaped like a brick and is 200 nanometers in diameter. Other members of this group are the monkeypox virus and the vaccinia virus from which smallpox vaccine is made. Variola is a hardy virus, surviving outside the host longer than most viruses.

▶ Pathogenesis and Virulence Factors

The infection begins by implantation of the virus in the nasopharynx. The virus invades the mucosa and multiplies in the regional lymph nodes, leading to viremia. Variola multiplies

Disease Table 18.6 Vesicular/Pustular Rash Diseases

Disease	Chickenpox	Smallpox
Causative Organism(s)	Human herpesvirus 3 (varicella-zoster virus)	Variola virus
Most Common Modes of Transmission	Droplet contact, inhalation of aerosolized lesion fluid	Droplet contact, indirect contact
Virulence Factors	Ability to fuse cells, ability to remain latent in ganglia	Ability to dampen, avoid immune response
Culture/Diagnosis	Based largely on clinical appearance	Based largely on clinical appearance
Prevention	Live attenuated vaccine; there is also vaccine to prevent reactivation of latent virus (shingles)	Live virus vaccine (vaccinia virus)
Treatment	None in uncomplicated cases; acyclovir for high risk	–
Distinguishing Features	No fever prodrome; lesions are superficial; in centripetal distribution (more in center of body)	Fever precedes rash, lesions are deep and in centrifugal distribution (more on extremities)
Appearance of Lesions		

within white blood cells and then travels to the small blood vessels in the dermis. The lesions occur at the dermal level, which is the reason that scars remain after the lesions are healed.

Much of the research on smallpox was suspended after its eradication from the human population. However, the virus genome has been sequenced, and scientists are once again studying how it causes damage to the host. It is turning out to be more difficult than expected to determine why it is so virulent. Scientists discovered the puzzling fact that the much tamer vaccinia virus has *more* genes that code for immune-evasion proteins than does the virulent variola virus.

▶ Transmission and Epidemiology

Before the eradication of smallpox, almost everyone contracted the disease over the course of their lifetime, either surviving with lifelong immunity or dying. It is spread primarily through droplets, although fomites such as contaminated bedding and clothing can also spread it. Traditionally the incidence of smallpox was highest in the winter and early spring.

In the early 1970s, smallpox was endemic in 31 countries. Every year, 10 to 15 million people contracted the disease, and approximately 2 million people died from it. By 1977,

after 11 years of intensive effort by the world health community, the last natural case occurred in Somalia.

▶ Prevention

In the 18th century, English physician Edward Jenner noticed that milkmaids who contracted a limited disease called cowpox, or vaccinia (from *vacca*, the Latin word for cow), seemed to be unaffected when smallpox swept through a locale. He no doubt also knew of the ages-old practice of *variolation*, the purposeful introduction of actual smallpox pus or scabs into healthy people, either through injection or inhalation, to protect them from natural infections. Variolation had been practiced for centuries in places such as Africa, India, Turkey, and China, because it was evident that those who recovered from the natural disease were protected from reinfection. This crude precursor of vaccination was dangerous, however; up to 10% of people who were variolated came down with severe smallpox, and some died from it. Still, with smallpox a constant threat, many people thought it worth the risk.

Jenner must have been aware of this practice; he combined his knowledge with his observation that the milkmaids' more limited lesions resembled those of smallpox and that these women then seemed to escape smallpox infection. He tested his theory by inoculating a young boy with material from cowpox lesions. That boy proved to be immune to both cowpox and smallpox—and the name *vaccination* was given to the practice of immunization.

To this day, the vaccination for smallpox is based on the vaccinia virus. Immunizations were stopped in the United States in 1972. Since the terrorist events of 2001 the United States has made sure to warehouse enough smallpox vaccine for every person in the country, and to prepare a rapid smallpox response plan. Most military branches are requiring that their personnel take the vaccination before deploying to certain parts of the world. In 2007 a new vaccine was approved by the Food and Drug Administration; it is called ACAM 2000.

Vaccination is also useful for postexposure prophylaxis, meaning that it can prevent or lessen the effects of the disease after you have already been infected with it.

Another chapter was added to the smallpox story in 2003, when dozens of people came down with a disease called monkeypox, caused by the monkey variant of the smallpox virus. They had apparently caught the disease from their pet prairie dogs, which had seemingly caught it from an exotic species of African rat. Both of these animals were imported to the United States as part of the exotic pet trade. The U.S. government recommended that people exposed to infected animals be vaccinated with the vaccinia vaccine.

▶ Treatment

There is no treatment for smallpox. Some advocate the use of cidofovir, which is labeled for use in cytomegalovirus infection. If lesions become infected secondarily with bacteria, antibiotics can be used for that complication **(Disease Table 18.6).**

Maculopapular Rash Diseases

Insight 18.3 contains a description of the different infectious conditions that can result in a rash of some sort on the skin. The infectious conditions described in this section are those with their major manifestations on the skin. (Meningococcal meningitis, for instance, can result in a diffuse rash on the skin, but its major manifestations are in the central nervous system, so it is discussed in chapter 19.) In this section, we examine measles, rubella, "fifth disease," and roseola. They all cause skin eruptions classified as maculopapular.

Measles

Most of us living in the United States don't think twice about measles. It is just another vaccination we get when we are children. But every year hundreds of thousands of children in the developing world die from this disease (at last count 540 a day), even though an extremely effective vaccine has been available since 1964. Health campaigns all over the world seek to make measles vaccine available to all, and have been very effective. Since 2002 worldwide deaths from measles have dropped 74%. It seems that more work and education needs to be done in developed countries now. Many parents are opting not to have their children vaccinated, due to unfounded fears about the link between the vaccine and autism (see Insight 15.4).

We would do well to remember that before the vaccine was introduced, measles killed 6 million people each year.

Measles is also known as **rubeola.** Be very careful not to confuse it with the next maculopapular rash disease, rubella.

▶ Signs and Symptoms

The initial symptoms of measles are sore throat, dry cough, headache, conjunctivitis, lymphadenitis, and fever. In a short time, unusual oral lesions called *Koplik's spots* appear as a prelude to the characteristic red maculopapular **exanthem** (eg-zan'-thum) that erupts on the head and then progresses to the trunk and extremities until most of the body is covered **(figure 18.13).** The rash gradually coalesces into red patches that fade to brown.

In a small number of cases, children develop laryngitis, bronchopneumonia, and bacterial secondary infections such as ear and sinus infections. Children afflicted with leukemia or thymic deficiency are especially predisposed to pneumonia because of their lack of a natural T-cell defense.

In a small percentage of cases, the virus can cause pneumonia. Affected patients are very ill and often have a characteristic dusky skin color from lack of oxygen. Occasionally (1 in 100 cases), measles progresses to encephalitis, resulting in various CNS changes ranging from disorientation to coma. Permanent brain damage or epilepsy can result.

A large number of measles patients experience secondary bacterial infections with *Haemophilus influenzae, Streptococcus pneumoniae,* or other streptococci or staphylococci. These can also lead to pneumonia or upper respiratory tract complications.

The most serious complication is **subacute sclerosing panencephalitis (SSPE),** a progressive neurological degeneration of the cerebral cortex, white matter, and brain stem. Its incidence is approximately one case in a million measles infections, and it afflicts primarily male children and adolescents. The pathogenesis of SSPE appears to involve a defective virus, one that has lost its ability to form a capsid and be released from an infected cell. Instead, it spreads unchecked through the brain by cell fusion, gradually destroying neurons and accessory cells and breaking down myelin. The disease is known for profound intellectual and neurological impairment. The course of the disease invariably leads to coma and death in a matter of months or years.

Measles during pregnancy has been associated with spontaneous miscarriage and low-birthweight babies, but severe birth defects have not been reported.

Figure 18.13 The rash of measles.

▶ Causative Agent

The measles virus is a member of the *Morbillivirus* genus. It is a single-stranded enveloped RNA virus in the Paramyxovirus family.

▶ Pathogenesis and Virulence Factors

The virus implants in the respiratory mucosa and infects the tracheal and bronchial cells. From there it travels to the lymphatic system, where it multiplies and then enters the bloodstream. Viremia carries the virus to the skin and to various organs.

The measles virus induces the cell membranes of adjacent host cells to fuse into large **syncytia** (sin-sish'-uh), giant cells with many nuclei. These cells no longer perform their proper function. The virus seems proficient at disabling many aspects of the host immune response, especially cell-mediated immunity and delayed-type hypersensitivity. The host may be left vulnerable for many weeks after infection; this immune response disruption is one of the reasons that secondary bacterial infections are so common.

▶ Transmission and Epidemiology

Measles is one of the most contagious infectious diseases, transmitted principally by respiratory droplets. Epidemic spread is favored by crowding, low levels of herd immunity, malnutrition, and inadequate medical care. There is no reservoir other than humans, and a person is infectious during the periods of incubation, prodrome phase, and the skin rash but usually not during convalescence. Only relatively large, dense populations of susceptible individuals can sustain the continuous chain necessary for transmission.

▶ Culture and Diagnosis

The disease can be diagnosed on clinical presentation alone; but if further identification is required, an ELISA test is available that tests for patient IgM to measles antigen, indicating a current infection. For best results, blood should be drawn on the third day of onset or later, because before that time titers of IgM may not be high enough to be detected by the test. Also, the method of comparing acute and convalescent sera may be used to confirm a measles infection after the fact. As you may recall from chapter 17, much higher IgG titers 14 days after onset when compared to titers at day 1 or 2 are a clear indication of current or recent infection. This knowledge allows health care providers to be on the lookout for complications and to be ahead of the game if a person who has had contact with the patient presents with similar symptoms.

▶ Prevention

The MMR vaccine (for measles, mumps, and rubella) contains live attenuated measles virus, which confers protection for about 20 years. Measles immunization is recommended for all healthy children at the age of 12 to 15 months, with a booster before the child enters school. Failing that, the preadolescent health check serves as a good time to get the second dose of measles vaccine.

▶ Treatment

Treatment relies on reducing fever, suppressing cough, and replacing lost fluid. Complications require additional remedies to relieve neurological and respiratory symptoms and to sustain nutrient, electrolyte, and fluid levels. Therapy includes antibiotics for bacterial complications and doses of immune globulin. Vitamin A supplements are recommended by some physicians; they have been found effective in reducing the symptoms and decreasing the rate of complications.

Rubella

This disease is also known as German measles. Rubella is derived from the Latin for "little red," and that's a good way to remember it because it causes a relatively minor rash disease with few complications. Sometimes it is called the 3-day measles. The only exception to this mild course of events is when a fetus is exposed to the virus while in its mother's womb (in utero). Serious damage can occur, and for that reason women of childbearing years must be sure to have been vaccinated well before they plan to conceive.

▶ Signs and Symptoms

The two clinical forms of rubella are referred to as postnatal infection, which develops in children or adults, and **congenital** (prenatal) infection of the fetus, expressed in the newborn as various types of birth defects.

Postnatal Rubella During an incubation period of 2 to 3 weeks, the rubella virus multiplies in the respiratory epithelium, infiltrates local lymphoid tissue, and enters the bloodstream. Early symptoms include malaise, mild fever, sore throat, and lymphadenopathy. The rash of pink macules and papules first appears on the face and progresses down the trunk and toward the extremities, advancing and resolving in about 3 days. The rash is milder looking than the measles rash (see Disease Table 18.7). Adult rubella is often accompanied by joint inflammation and pain rather than a rash. Very occasionally, complications such as arthralgia/arthritis, or even encephalitis, can occur but more often in adults than in children.

Congenital Rubella Rubella is a strongly **teratogenic** virus. Transmission of the rubella virus to a fetus in utero can result in a serious complication called **congenital rubella (figure 18.14)**. The mother is able to transmit the virus even if

Figure 18.14 An infant born with congenital rubella can manifest a papular pink or purple rash.

she is asymptomatic. Fetal injury varies according to the time of infection. Infection in the first trimester is most likely to induce miscarriage or multiple permanent defects in the newborn. The most common of these is deafness and may be the only defect seen in some babies. Other babies may experience cardiac abnormalities, ocular lesions, deafness and mental and physical retardation in varying combinations. Less drastic sequelae that usually resolve in time are anemia, hepatitis, pneumonia, carditis, and bone infection.

▶ Causative Agent

The rubella virus is a *Rubivirus,* in the family Togavirus. It is a nonsegmented single-stranded RNA virus with a loose lipid envelope. There is only one known serotype of the virus, and humans are the only natural host. Its envelope contains two different viral proteins.

▶ Pathogenesis and Virulence Factors

The course of disease in postnatal rubella is mostly unremarkable. But when exposed to a fetus, the virus creates havoc. It has the ability to stop mitosis, which is an important process in a rapidly developing embryo and fetus. It also induces apoptosis of normal tissue cells. This inappropriate cell death can do irreversible harm to organs it affects. And last, the virus damages vascular endothelium, leading to poor development of many organs.

▶ Transmission and Epidemiology

Rubella is an endemic disease with worldwide distribution. Infection is initiated through contact with respiratory secretions and occasionally urine. The virus is shed during the prodromal phase and up to a week after the rash appears. Congenitally infected infants are contagious for a much longer period of time. Because the virus is only moderately communicable, close living conditions are required for its spread. This disease is well-controlled in the United States, with fewer than 10 cases reported in each of the last several years. Most cases are reported among adolescents and young adults in military training camps, colleges, and summer camps. The greatest concern is that nonimmune women of childbearing age might be caught up in this cycle, raising the prospect of congenital rubella.

▶ Culture and Diagnosis

Diagnosing rubella relies on the same twin techniques discussed earlier for measles. Because it mimics other diseases, rubella should not be diagnosed on clinical grounds alone. IgM antibody to rubella virus can be detected early using an ELISA technique or a latex-agglutination card. Other conditions and infections can lead to false positives, however, and the IgM test should be augmented by an acute and convalescent measurement of IgG antibody. It is important to know whether the infection is indeed rubella, especially in women, because if so, they will be immune to reinfection.

▶ Prevention

The attenuated rubella virus vaccine is usually given to children in the combined form (MMR vaccination) at 12 to 15 months and a booster at 4 or 6 years of age. The vaccine for rubella can be administered on its own, without the measles and mumps components.

Many health care providers recommend screening adult women of childbearing age for antibodies to rubella, which would indicate either that they had had the infection or that they had been immunized. The current recommendation for nonpregnant, antibody-negative women is immediate immunization. Because the vaccine contains live virus, and because a teratogenic effect is theoretically possible, the vaccine is administered on the condition that the patient not become pregnant for 3 months afterward. The vaccine is not given to pregnant women.

▶ Treatment

Postnatal rubella is generally benign and requires only symptomatic treatment. No specific treatment is available for the congenital manifestations.

Fifth Disease

This disease, more precisely called *erythema infectiosum,* is so named because about 100 years ago it was the fifth of the diseases recognized by doctors to cause rashes in children. The first four were scarlet fever (see chapter 21), measles, rubella, and another rash that was thought to be distinct but was probably not. Fifth disease is a very mild disease that often results in a characteristic "slapped-cheek" appearance because of a confluent reddish rash that begins on the face. Within 2 days, the rash spreads on the body but is most prominent on the arms, legs, and trunk. The rash is maculopapular and the blotches tend to run together rather than to appear as distinct bumps. The illness is rather mild, featuring low-grade fever and malaise and lasting 5 to 10 days. The rash may persist for days to weeks, and it tends to recur under stress or with exposure to sunlight. As with almost any infectious agent, it can cause more serious disease in people with underlying immune disease.

The causative agent is parvovirus B19. You may have heard of "parvo" as a disease of dogs, but strains of this virus group infect humans as well. Fifth disease is usually diagnosed by the clinical presentation, but sometimes it is helpful to rule out rubella by testing for IgM against rubella. Specific serological tests for fifth disease are available if they are considered necessary.

This infection is very contagious. It is transmitted through respiratory droplets or even direct contact. It can be transmitted through the placenta, with a range of possible effects, from no symptoms to stillbirth. There is no vaccine and no treatment for this usually mild disease.

Roseola

This disease is common in young children and babies. It is sometimes known as "sixth disease." It can result in a maculopapular rash, but a high percentage (up to 70%) of cases proceed without the rash stage. Children sick with this disease exhibit a high fever (up to 41°C, or 105°F) that comes on quickly and lasts for up to 3 days. Seizures may occur during this period, but other than that patients remain alert and do not act terribly ill. On the fourth day, the fever disappears, and it is at this point that a rash can appear, first on the chest and trunk and less prominently on the face and limbs. By the time the rash appears, the disease is almost over.

Roseola is caused by a human herpesvirus called HHV-6, and sometimes by HHV-7. Like all herpesviruses, it can remain latent in its host indefinitely after the disease has cleared. Very occasionally, the virus reactivates in childhood or adulthood, leading to mononucleosis-like or hepatitis-like symptoms. Immunocompetent hosts generally do not experience reactivation. It is thought that 100% of the U.S. population is infected with this virus by adulthood. Some people experienced the disease roseola when they became infected, and some of them did not. The suggestion has been made that this virus causes other disease conditions later in life, such as multiple sclerosis. No vaccine and no treatment exist for roseola.

These two HHV viruses can cause severe disseminated disease in AIDS patients and other people with compromised immunity.

Scarlet Fever

To complete our survey of infections that can cause maculopapular rashes, we include a disease that has primary symptoms elsewhere but can produce a distinctive red rash on the skin as well. Scarlet fever is most often the result of a respiratory infection with *Streptococcus pyogenes* (most often, pharyngitis). Occasionally, scarlet fever will follow a streptococcal skin infection, such as impetigo or cellulitis. If the *S. pyogenes* strain contains a bacteriophage carrying a gene for an exotoxin called erythrogenic toxin, scarlet fever can result. More details on scarlet fever are given in chapter 21; it is included here mainly for purposes of differentiating the rash from the others in this group (**Disease Table 18.7**).

Disease Table 18.7 Maculopapular Rash Diseases

Disease	Measles (Rubeola)	Rubella	Fifth Disease	Roseola	Scarlet Fever
Causative Organism(s)	Measles virus	Rubella virus	Parvovirus B19	Human herpesvirus 6 or 7	*Streptococcus pyogenes* (lysogenized)
Most Common Modes of Transmission	Droplet contact	Droplet contact	Droplet contact, direct contact	?	Droplet or direct contact
Virulence Factors	Syncytium formation, ability to suppress CMI	In fetuses: inhibition of mitosis, induction of apoptosis, and damage to vascular endothelium	–	Ability to remain latent	Erythrogenic toxin
Culture/ Diagnosis	ELISA for IgM, acute/convalescent IgG	Acute IgM, acute/convalescent IgG	Usually diagnosed clinically	Usually diagnosed clinically	Examination of skin lesions, throat culture (beta-hemolytic on blood agar, sensitive to bacitracin, rapid antigen tests)
Prevention	Live attenuated vaccine (MMR)	Live attenuated vaccine (MMR)	–	–	Hygiene practices
Treatment	No antivirals; vitamin A, antibiotics for secondary bacterial infections	–	–	–	Penicillin, cephalexin in penicillin-allergic
Distinguishing Features of the Rashes	Starts on head, spreads to whole body, lasts over a week	Milder red rash, lasts approximately 3 days	"Slapped-face" rash first, spreads to limbs and trunk, tends to be confluent rather than distinct bumps	High fever precedes rash stage—rash not always present	Sandpaper feel to affected skin; severe sore throat
Appearance of Lesions					

Wartlike Eruptions

All types of warts are caused by viruses. Most common warts you have seen on yourself and others are probably caused by one of more than 100 human papillomaviruses, or HPVs. HPVs are also the cause of genital warts, described in chapter 23. Another virus in the poxvirus family causes a condition called **molluscum contagiosum,** which causes bumps that may look like warts.

Warts

Warts, also known as **papillomas,** afflict nearly everyone. Children seem to get them more frequently than adults, and there is speculation that people gradually build up immunity to the various HPVs that they encounter over time, as is the case with the viruses that cause the common cold.

The warts are benign, squamous epithelial growths. Some HPVs can infect mucous membranes; others invade skin. The appearance and seriousness of the infection vary somewhat from one anatomical region to another. Painless, elevated, rough growths on the fingers and occasionally on other body parts are called common, or seed, warts **(Disease Table 18.8).** These growths commonly occur in children and young adults. Just as certain types of HPVs are associated with particular outcomes in the genital area, common warts are most often caused by HPV-2, -4, -27, and -29. **Plantar warts** are often caused by HPV-1. They are deep, painful papillomas on the soles of the feet. Flat warts (HPV types 3, 10, 28, and 49) are smooth, skin-colored lesions that develop on the face, trunk, elbows, and knees.

The warts contain variable amounts of virus. Transmission occurs through direct contact, and often warts are transmitted from one part of the body to another by autoinoculation. Because the viruses are fairly stable in the environment, they can also be transmitted indirectly from towels or from a shower stall, where they persist inside the protective covering of sloughed-off keratinized skin cells. The incubation period can be from 1 to 8 months. Almost all nongenital warts are harmless, and they tend to resolve themselves over time. Rarely, a wart can become malignant when caused by a particular type of HPV.

The warts caused by papillomaviruses are usually distinctive enough to permit reliable clinical diagnosis without much difficulty. However, a biopsy and histological examination can help clarify ambiguous cases. Warts disappear on their own 60% to 70% of the time, usually over the course of 2 to 3 years. Physicians do approve of home remedies for resolving warts. These include nonprescription salicylic acid preparations, as well as the use of adhesive tape. Yes, you read that right: well-controlled medical studies have shown that adhesive tape (even duct tape!) can cause warts to disappear, presumably because the tape creates an airtight atmosphere that stops virus reproduction. But a psychological component, similar to a placebo effect, cannot be ruled out. (Neither of these treatments should be used for genital warts; see chapter 23.) Physicians have other techniques for removing warts, including a number of drugs and/or cryosurgery. No treatment guarantees that the viruses are eliminated; therefore, warts can always grow back.

Molluscum contagiosum

This disease is distributed throughout the world, with highest incidence occurring on certain Pacific islands, although its incidence in North America has been increasing since the 1980s. Skin lesions take the form of smooth, waxy nodules on the face, trunk, and limbs. The firm nodules may be indented in the middle (see Disease Table 18.8), and they contain a milky

Disease Table 18.8   Wart and Wartlike Eruptions

Causative Organism(s)	Human papillomaviruses	Molluscum contagiosum viruses
Most Common Modes of Transmission	Direct contact, autoinoculation, indirect contact	Direct contact, including sexual contact, autoinoculation
Virulence Factors	–	–
Culture/Diagnosis	Clinical diagnosis, also histology, microscopy, PCR	Clinical diagnosis, also histology, microscopy, PCR
Prevention	Avoid contact	Avoid contact
Treatment	Home treatments, cryosurgery (virus not eliminated)	Usually none, although mechanical removal can be performed (virus not eliminated)
Appearance of Lesions		

fluid containing epidermal cells filled with viruses in intracytoplasmic inclusion bodies. This condition is common in children, where it most often causes nodules on the face, arms, legs, and trunk. In adults, it appears mostly in the genital areas. In immunocompromised patients, the lesions can be more disfiguring and more widespread on the body. It is particularly common in AIDS patients and often presents as facial lesions.

The molluscum contagiosum virus is a poxvirus, containing double-stranded DNA and possessing an envelope. It is spread via direct contact and also through fomites. Adults who acquire this infection usually acquire it through sexual contact. Autoinoculation can spread the virus from existing lesions to new places on the body, resulting in new nodules.

The condition may be diagnosed on clinical appearance alone, or a skin biopsy may be performed and histological analysis undertaken. A clinician can perform a more simple "squash procedure," in which fluid from the lesion is extracted onto a microscope slide, squashed by another microscope slide, stained, and examined for the presence of the characteristic inclusion bodies in the epithelial cells. PCR can also be used to detect the virus in skin lesions. In most cases, no treatment is indicated, although a physician may remove the lesions or treat them with a topical chemical. Treatment of lesions does not ensure elimination of the virus **(Disease Table 18.8).**

Large Pustular Skin Lesions

Leishmaniasis

Two infections that result in large lesions (greater than a few millimeters across) deserve mention in this chapter on skin infections. The first is leishmaniasis, a zoonosis transmitted among various mammalian hosts by female sand flies. This infection can express itself in several different forms, depending on which species of the protozoan *Leishmania* is involved. Cutaneous leishmaniasis is a localized infection of the capillaries of the skin caused by *L. tropica,* found in Mediterranean, African, and Indian regions. A form of mucocutaneous leishmaniasis called espundia is caused by *L. brasiliensis,* endemic to parts of Central and South America. It affects both the skin and mucous membranes. Another form of this infection is systemic leishmaniasis.

Leishmania is transmitted to the mammalian host by the sand fly when it ingests the host's blood. The disease is endemic to equatorial regions that provide favorable conditions for the sand fly. Numerous wild and domesticated animals, especially dogs, serve as reservoirs for the protozoan. Although humans are usually accidental hosts, the flies freely feed on them. At particular risk are travelers or immigrants who have never had contact with the protozoan and lack specific immunity.

Leishmania infection begins when an infected fly injects the motile forms of the protozoan into the host while feeding. After being engulfed by macrophages, the parasite converts to a nonmotile reproductive form and multiplies in the macrophage. The manifestations of the disease vary with the fate of the macrophages. If they remain fixed, the infection stays localized in the skin or mucous membranes, but if the infected macrophages migrate, systemic disease occurs.

In cutaneous leishmaniasis, a small red papule occurs at the site of the bite and spreads laterally into a large ulcer **(Disease Table 18.9).** The edges of the ulcer are raised and the

Disease Table 18.9 Large Pustular Skin Lesions

Disease	Leishmaniasis	Cutaneous Anthrax
Causative Organism(s)	*Leishmania* spp.	*Bacillus anthracis*
Most Common Modes of Transmission	Biological vector	Direct contact with endospores
Virulence Factors	Multiplication within macrophages	Endospore formation; capsule, lethal factor, edema factor (see chapter 20)
Culture/Diagnosis	Culture of protozoa, microscopic visualization	Culture on blood agar; serology, PCR performed by CDC
Prevention	Avoiding sand fly	Avoid contact; vaccine available but not widely used
Treatment	Sodium stibogluconate	Ciprofloxacin, doxycycline, levofloxacin
Distinguishing Features	Mucocutaneous and systemic forms	Can be fatal
Appearance of Lesions		

base is moist. It can be filled with a serous/purulent exudate or covered with a crust. Satellite lesions may occur. Mucocutaneous leishmaniasis usually begins with a skin lesion on the head or face and then progresses to single or multiple lesions, usually in the mouth and nose. Lesions can be quite extensive, eventually involving and disfiguring the hard palate, the nasal septum, and the lips.

There is no vaccine; avoiding the sand fly is the only prevention. The disease can be treated with chemicals such as sodium stibogluconate. Other antimicrobials may be indicated for secondary infections of the lesions.

Cutaneous Anthrax

This form of anthrax is the most common and least dangerous version of infection with *Bacillus anthracis*. (The spectrum of anthrax disease is discussed fully in chapter 20.) It is caused by endospores entering the skin through small cuts or abrasions. Germination and growth of the pathogen in the skin are marked by the production of a papule that becomes increasingly necrotic and later ruptures to form a painless, black **eschar** (ess'-kar) (see Disease Table 18.9). In the fall of 2001, 11 cases of cutaneous anthrax occurred in the United States as a result of bioterrorism (along with 11 cases of inhalational anthrax). Mail workers and others contracted the infection when endospores were sent through the mail. The infection can be naturally transmitted by contact with hides of infected animals (especially goats).

Left untreated, even the cutaneous form of anthrax is fatal approximately 20% of the time. A vaccine exists but is recommended only for high-risk persons and the military. Upon suspicion of cutaneous anthrax, ciprofloxacin, levofloxacin and/or doxycycline should be used initially. If the isolate is found to be sensitive to penicillin, patients can be switched to that drug **(Disease Table 18.9)**.

Ringworm (Cutaneous Mycoses)

A group of fungi that is collectively termed **dermatophytes** causes a constellation of integument conditions. These mycoses are strictly confined to the nonliving epidermal tissues (stratum corneum) and their derivatives (hair and nails). All these conditions have different names that begin with the word **tinea** (tin'-ee-ah), which derives from the erroneous belief that they were caused by worms. That misconception is also the reason these diseases are often called *ringworm*—ringworm of the scalp (tinea capitis), beard (tinea barbae), body (tinea corporis), groin (tinea cruris), foot (tinea pedis), and hand (tinea manuum). (Don't confuse these "tinea" terms with genus and species names. It is simply an old practice for naming conditions.) Most of these conditions are caused by one of three different dermatophytes, which are discussed here.

One fungal infection is even more superficial than the others; it infects only the most superficial layers of the stratum corneum and causes a condition called **tinea versicolor.** It is not a ringworm but is nevertheless included at the end of this section.

▶ Signs and Symptoms of the Cutaneous Mycoses

Ringworm of the Scalp (Tinea Capitis)   This mycosis results from the fungal invasion of the scalp and the hair of the head, eyebrows, and eyelashes **(figure 18.15)**. Very common in children, tinea capitis is acquired from other children and adults or from domestic animals. Manifestations range from small scaly patches to a severe inflammatory reaction to destruction of the hair follicle and temporary or permanent hair loss.

Ringworm of the Beard (Tinea Barbae)   This tinea, also called *barber's itch*, affects the chin and beard of adult males. Although once a common aftereffect of unhygienic barbering, it is now contracted mainly from animals.

Ringworm of the Body (Tinea Corporis)   This extremely prevalent infection of humans can appear nearly anywhere on the body's glabrous (smooth and bare) skin. The principal sources are other humans, animals, and soil, and it is transmitted primarily by direct contact and fomites (clothing, bedding). The infection usually appears as one or more scaly reddish rings on the trunk, hip, arm, neck, or face **(figure 18.16)**. The ringed pattern is formed when the infection radiates from the original site of invasion into the surrounding skin. Depend-

Figure 18.15 Ringworm of the scalp.   Hair loss can accompany these lesions.

Figure 18.16 Ringworm of the body.

ing on the causal species and the health and hygiene of the patient, lesions vary from mild and diffuse to florid and pustular.

Ringworm of the Groin (Tinea Cruris) Sometimes known as *jock itch,* crural ringworm occurs mainly in males on the groin, perianal skin, scrotum, and, occasionally, the penis. The fungus thrives under conditions of moisture and humidity created by sweating. It is transmitted primarily from human to human and is pervasive among athletes and persons living in close quarters (ships, military installations).

Ringworm of the Foot (Tinea Pedis) Tinea pedis has more colorful names as well, including athlete's foot and jungle rot. The disease is clearly connected to wearing shoes because it is uncommon in cultures where people customarily go bare-

foot. Conditions that encase the feet in a closed, warm, moist environment increase the possibility of infection. Tinea pedis is a known hazard in shared facilities such as shower stalls, public floors, and locker rooms. Infections begin with blisters between the toes that burst, crust over, and can spread to the rest of the foot and nails **(figure 18.17a)**.

Ringworm of the Hand (Tinea Manuum) Infection of the hand by dermatophytes is often associated with concurrent infection of the foot. Lesions usually occur on the fingers and palms of one hand, and they vary from white and patchy to deep and fissured.

Ringworm of the Nail (Tinea Unguium) Fingernails and toenails, being masses of keratin, are often sites for persistent fungus colonization. The first symptoms are usually superficial white patches in the nail bed. A more invasive form causes thickening, distortion, and darkening of the nail **(figure 18.17b)**.

▶ Causative Agents

There are about 39 species in the genera *Trichophyton, Microsporum,* and *Epidermophyton* that can cause the preceding conditions. The causative agent of a given type of ringworm varies from one geographic location to another and is not restricted to a particular genus and species. These fungi are so closely related and morphologically similar that they can be difficult to differentiate. Various species exhibit unique macroconidia, microconidia, and unusual types of hyphae. In general, *Trichophyton* produces thin-walled, smooth macroconidia and numerous microconidia **(figure 18.18a);**

(a)

(b)

Figure 18.17 Ringworm of the extremities.
(a) *Trichophyton* infection spreading over the foot in a "moccasin" pattern. The chronicity of tinea pedis is attributed to the lack of fatty-acid-forming glands in the feet. **(b)** Ringworm of the nails. Invasion of the nail bed causes some degree of thickening, accumulation of debris, cracking, and discoloration; nails can be separated from underlying structures as shown here.

(a)

(b)

(c)

Figure 18.18 Examples of dermatophyte spores. **(a)** Regular, numerous microconidia of *Trichophyton*. **(b)** Macroconidia of *Microsporum canis*, a cause of ringworm in cats, dogs, and humans. **(c)** Smooth-surfaced macroconidia in clusters characteristic of *Epidermophyton*.

Microsporum produces thick-walled, rough macroconidia and sparser microconidia **(figure 18.18b)**; and *Epidermophyton* has ovoid, smooth, clustered macroconidia and no microconidia **(figure 18.18c).**

The presenting symptoms of a cutaneous mycosis occasionally are so dramatic and suggestive of these genera that no further testing is necessary. In most cases, however, direct microscopic examination and culturing are required. Diagnosis of tinea of the scalp caused by some species is aided by use of a long-wave ultraviolet lamp that causes infected hairs to fluoresce. Samples of hair, skin scrapings, and nail debris treated with heated potassium hydroxide (KOH) show a thin, branching fungal mycelium if infection is present.

▶ Pathogenesis and Virulence Factors

The dermatophytes have the ability to invade and digest keratin, which is naturally abundant in the cells of the stratum corneum. The fungi do not invade deeper epidermal layers. Important factors that promote infection are the hardiness of the dermatophyte spores (they can last for years on fomites); presence of abraded skin, and intimate contact. Most infections exhibit a long incubation period (months), followed by localized inflammation and allergic reactions to fungal proteins. As a general rule, infections acquired from animals and soil cause more severe reactions than do infections acquired from other humans, and infections eliciting stronger immune reactions are resolved faster.

▶ Transmission and Epidemiology

Transmission of the fungi that cause these diseases is direct and indirect contact with other humans or with infected animals. Some of these fungi can be acquired from the soil.

▶ Prevention and Treatment

The only way to prevent these infections is to avoid contact with the dermatophytes, which is impractical. Keeping susceptible skin areas dry is helpful. Treatment of ringworm is based on the knowledge that the dermatophyte is feeding on dead epidermal tissues. These regions undergo constant replacement from living cells deep in the epidermis, so if multiplication of the fungus can be blocked, the fungus will eventually be sloughed off along with the skin or nail. Unfortunately, this takes time. By far the most satisfactory choice for therapy is a topical antifungal agent. Ointments containing tolnaftate, miconazole, itraconazole, terbinafine, or thiabendazole are applied regularly for several weeks. Some drugs work by speeding up loss of the outer skin layer. Intractable infections can be treated with griseofulvin, but placing a patient on this drug, which is toxic to the liver and the kidneys, for the long periods needed is probably too risky in most cases. Gentle debridement of skin can have some benefit.

Superficial Mycoses

Agents of **superficial mycoses** involve the outer epidermal surface and are ordinarily innocuous infections with cosmetic rather than inflammatory effects. Tinea versicolor is caused by the yeast genus *Malassezia,* a genus that has at least 10 species living on human skin. The yeast feeds on the high oil content of the skin glands. Even though these yeasts are very common (carried by nearly 100% of humans tested), in some people its growth elicits mild, chronic scaling and interferes with production of pigment by melanocytes. The trunk, face, and limbs may take on a mottled appearance **(figure 18.19).** The disease is most pronounced in young people who are frequently exposed to the sun, because the area affected doesn't tan well. Other superficial skin conditions in which *Malassezia* is implicated are folliculitis, psoriasis, and seborrheic dermatitis (dandruff). It is also occasionally associated with systemic infections and catheter-associated sepsis in compromised patients **(Disease Table 18.10).**

18.3 Learning Outcomes—Can You ...

4. ... list the possible causative agents, modes of transmission, virulence factors, diagnostic techniques, and prevention/treatment for each of the diseases of the skin? These are: acne, impetigo, cellulitis, staphylococcal scalded skin syndrome, gas gangrene, vesicular/pustular rash diseases, maculopapular rash diseases, wartlike eruptions, large pustular skin lesions, and cutaneous mycoses.
5. ... discuss the spectrum of skin and tissue diseases caused by *Staphylococcus aureus* and *Streptococcus pyogenes*?
6. ... provide an update of the status of MRSA infections in the United States?
7. ... discuss the relative dangers of rubella and rubeola viruses in different populations?

Figure 18.19 Tinea versicolor.   Mottled, discolored skin pigmentation is characteristic of superficial skin infection by *Malassezia furfur.*

Disease Table 18.10 Cutaneous and Superficial Mycoses

Disease	Cutaneous Infections	Superficial Infections (Tinea Versicolor)
Causative Organism(s)	*Trichophyton, Microsporum, Epidermophyton*	*Malassezia* species
Most Common Modes of Transmission	Direct and indirect contact, vehicle (soil)	Endogenous "normal biota"
Virulence Factors	Ability to degrade keratin, invoke hypersensitivity	–
Culture/Diagnosis	Microscopic examination, KOH staining, culture	Usually clinical, KOH can be used
Prevention	Avoid contact	None
Treatment	Topical tolnaftate, itraconazole, terbinafine, miconazole, thiabendazole	Topical antifungals

18.4 The Surface of the Eye and Its Defenses

The eye is a complex organ with many different tissue types, but for the purposes of this chapter we consider only its exposed surfaces, the *conjunctiva* and the *cornea* **(figure 18.20).** The **conjunctiva** is a very thin membranelike tissue that covers the eye (except for the cornea) and lines the eyelids. It secretes an oil- and mucus-containing fluid that lubricates and protects the eye surface. The **cornea** is the dome-shaped central portion of the eye lying over the iris (the colored part of the eye). It has five to six layers of epithelial cells that can regenerate quickly if they are superficially damaged. It has been called "the windshield of the eye."

The eye's best defense is the film of tears, which consists of an aqueous fluid, oil, and mucus. The tears are formed in the lacrimal gland at the outer and upper corner of each eye **(figure 18.21),** and they drain into the lacrimal duct at the inner corner. The aqueous portion of tears contains sugars, lysozyme, and lactoferrin. These last two substances have antimicrobial properties. The mucus layer contains proteins and sugars and plays a protective role. And, of course, the flow of the tear film prevents the attachment of microorganisms to the eye surface.

Because the eye's primary function is vision, anything that hinders vision would be counterproductive. For that reason, inflammation does not occur in the eye as readily as it does elsewhere in the body. Flooding the eye with fluid containing

Figure 18.20 The anatomy of the eye.

Figure 18.21 The lacrimal apparatus of the eye.

a large number of light-diffracting objects such as lymphocytes and phagocytes in response to every irritant would mean almost constantly blurred vision. So even though the eyes are relatively vulnerable to infection (not being covered by keratinized epithelium), the evolution of the vertebrate eye has of necessity favored reduced innate immunity. This characteristic is sometimes known as **immune privilege**.

The specific immune response, involving B and T cells, is also somewhat restricted in the eye. The anterior chamber (see figure 18.20) is largely cut off from the blood supply. Lymphocytes that do gain access to this area are generally less active than lymphocytes elsewhere in the body.

18.4 Learning Outcomes—Can You ...

8. ... describe the important anatomical features of the eye?
9. ... list the natural defenses present in the eye?

18.5 Normal Biota of the Eye

The normal biota of the eye—so far as is currently known—is generally sparse. When people are tested, up to 20% have no recoverable (i.e., culturable) bacteria in their eyes. The few bacteria that are found resemble the normal biota of the skin—namely, diphtheroids, coagulase-negative staphylococci, *Micrococcus,* nonhemolytic streptococci, and some yeast. *Neisseria* species can also live on the surface of the eye.

	Defenses	Normal Biota
Defenses and Normal Biota of the Eyes		
Eyes	Mucus in conjunctiva and in tears, lysozyme and lactoferrin in tears	Sparsely populated with *Staphylococcus aureus*, *Staphylococcus epidermidis*, and *Corynebacterium* species.

18.5 Learning Outcomes—Can You ...

10. ... list the types of normal biota presently known to occupy the eye?

18.6 Eye Diseases Caused by Microorganisms

In this section, we cover the infectious agents that cause diseases of the surface structures of the eye—namely, the cornea and conjunctiva.

Conjunctivitis

Infection of the conjunctiva is relatively common. It can be caused by specific microorganisms that have a predilection for eye tissues, by contaminants that proliferate due to the presence of a contact lens or an eye injury, or by accidental inoculation of the eye by a traumatic event.

▶ Signs and Symptoms

Just as there are many different causes of conjunctivitis, there are many different clinical presentations. Inflammation of this tissue almost always causes a discharge of some sort. Most bacterial infections produce a milky discharge, whereas viral infections tend to produce a clear exudate. It is typical for a patient to wake up in the morning with an eye "glued" shut by secretions that have accumulated and solidified through the night. Some conjunctivitis cases are caused by an allergic response, and these often produce copious amounts of clear fluid as well. The pain generally is mild, although often patients report a gritty sensation in their eye(s). Redness and eyelid swelling are common, and in some cases patients report photophobia (sensitivity to light). The informal name for common conjunctivitis is pinkeye.

▶ Causative Agents and Their Transmission

Cases of neonatal eye infection with *Neisseria gonorrhoeae* or *Chlamydia trachomatis* are usually transmitted vertically from a genital tract infection in the mother (discussed in chapter 23). Either one of these eye infections can lead to serious eye damage if not treated promptly **(figure 18.22).** Note that herpes simplex can also cause neonatal conjunctivitis, but it is usually accompanied by generalized herpes infection (covered in chapter 23).

Bacterial conjunctivitis in other age groups is most commonly caused by *Staphylococcus epidermidis, Streptococcus pyogenes,* or *Streptococcus pneumoniae,* although *Haemophilus influenzae* and *Moraxella* species are also frequent causes. *N. gonorrhoeae* and *C. trachomatis* can also cause conjunctivitis in adults. These infections may result from autoinoculation from a genital infection or from sexual activity, although *N. gonorrhoeae* can be part of the normal biota in the respiratory tract. A wide variety of bacteria, fungi, and protozoa can contaminate contact lenses and lens cases and then be

Figure 18.22 Neonatal conjunctivitis.

transferred to the eye, resulting in disease that may be very serious. This means of infection is considered vehicle transmission, with the lens or the solution being the vehicle.

Viral conjunctivitis is commonly caused by adenoviruses, although other viruses may be responsible. (Herpesvirus infection of the eye is discussed later on.) Both bacterial and viral conjunctivitis are transmissible by direct and even indirect contact and are usually highly contagious.

A Note About *Sties*

A sty in the eye is the most common condition seen by eye doctors. What most people call a sty may be one of two different conditions. A *hordeolum* is an infection of an oil gland at the edge of the eyelid (much like a pimple). A *chalazion* is a noninfectious inflammation of an oil gland. Both of these conditions are distinct from conjunctivitis.

▶ Prevention and Treatment

Good hygiene is the only way to prevent conjunctivitis in adults and children other than neonates. Newborn children in the United States are administered antimicrobials in their eyes after delivery to prevent neonatal conjunctivitis from either *N. gonorrhoeae* or *C. trachomatis*. Treatment of those infections, if they are suspected, is started before lab results are available and usually is accomplished with erythromy-

cin, both topical and oral. If *N. gonorrhoeae* is confirmed, oral therapy is usually switched to ceftriaxone. If antibacterial therapy is prescribed for other conjunctivitis cases, it should cover all possible bacterial pathogens. Ciprofloxacin eyedrops are a common choice. Erythromycin or gentamicin are also often used. Because conjunctivitis is usually diagnosed based on clinical signs, a physician may prescribe prophylactic antibiotics even if a viral cause is suspected. If symptoms don't begin improving within 48 hours, more extensive diagnosis may be performed. **Disease Table 18.11** lists the most common causes of conjunctivitis; keep in mind that other microorganisms can also cause conjunctival infections.

Trachoma

Ocular trachoma is a chronic *Chlamydia trachomatis* infection of the epithelial cells of the eye. It is an ancient disease and a major cause of blindness in certain parts of the world. Although a few cases occur annually in the United States, several million cases occur endemically in parts of Africa and Asia. Transmission is favored by contaminated fingers, fomites, fleas, and a hot, dry climate. It is caused by a different *C. trachomatis* strain than the one that causes simple conjunctivitis. Ongoing infection or many recurrent infections with this strain eventually lead to chronic inflammatory damage and scarring.

The first signs of infection are a mild conjunctival discharge and slight inflammation of the conjunctiva. These symptoms are followed by marked infiltration of lymphocytes and macrophages into the infected area. As these cells build up, they impart a pebbled (rough) appearance to the inner aspect of the

Disease Table 18.11 Conjunctivitis

Disease	Neonatal Conjunctivitis	Bacterial Conjunctivitis	Viral Conjunctivitis
Causative Organism(s)	*Chlamydia trachomatis* or *Neisseria gonorrhoeae*	*Streptococcus pyogenes, Streptococcus pneumoniae, Staphylococcus aureus, Haemophilus influenzae, Moraxella,* and also *Neisseria gonorrhoeae, Chlamydia trachomatis*	Adenoviruses and others
Most Common Modes of Transmission	Vertical	Direct, indirect contact	Direct, indirect contact
Virulence Factors	–	–	–
Culture/Diagnosis	Gram stain and culture	Clinical diagnosis	Clinical diagnosis
Prevention	Screen mothers, apply antibiotic or silver nitrate to newborn eyes	Hygiene	Hygiene
Treatment	Topical and oral antibiotics	Broad-spectrum topical antibiotic, often ciprofloxacin	None, although antibiotics often given because type of infection not distinguished
Distinguishing Features	In babies <28 days old	Mucopurulent discharge	Serous (clear) discharge

Figure 18.23 Ocular trachoma caused by *C. trachomatis*.

Figure 18.24 *Acanthamoeba* infection of the eye.

upper eyelid **(figure 18.23).** In time, a vascular pseudomembrane of exudates and inflammatory leukocytes forms over the cornea, a condition called *pannus*, which lasts a few weeks. Chronic and secondary infections can lead to corneal damage and impaired vision. Early treatment of this disease with azithromycin is highly effective and prevents all of the complications. It is a tragedy that in this day of sophisticated preventive medicine, millions of children worldwide will develop blindness for lack of a few dollars' worth of antibiotics.

HSV-2 can also occur as a result of a sexual encounter with the virus or transfer of the virus from the genital to eye area or if an individual has a recurrent oral infection with HSV-2. Preliminary symptoms are a gritty feeling in the eye, conjunctivitis, sharp pain, and sensitivity to light. Some patients develop characteristic branched or opaque corneal lesions as well. In 25% to 50% of cases, this keratitis is recurrent and chronic and can interfere with vision. Blindness due to herpes is the leading infectious cause of blindness in the United States.

The viral condition is treated with trifluridine or acyclovir or both.

In the last few years, another form of keratitis has been increasing in incidence. An amoeba called *Acanthamoeba* has been causing serious keratitis cases, especially in people who wear contact lenses. This free-living amoeba is everywhere—it lives in tap water, freshwater lakes, and the like. The infections are usually associated with less-than-rigorous contact lens hygiene, or previous trauma to the eye **(figure 18.24).**

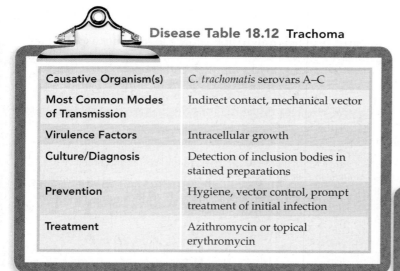

Disease Table 18.12 Trachoma

Causative Organism(s)	*C. trachomatis* serovars A–C
Most Common Modes of Transmission	Indirect contact, mechanical vector
Virulence Factors	Intracellular growth
Culture/Diagnosis	Detection of inclusion bodies in stained preparations
Prevention	Hygiene, vector control, prompt treatment of initial infection
Treatment	Azithromycin or topical erythromycin

Keratitis

Keratitis is a more serious eye infection than conjunctivitis. Invasion of deeper eye tissues occurs and can lead to complete corneal destruction. Any microorganism can cause this condition, especially after trauma to the eye, but this section focuses on one of the more common causes: herpes simplex virus. It can cause keratitis in the absence of predisposing trauma.

The usual cause of herpetic keratitis is a "misdirected" reactivation of (oral) herpes simplex virus type 1 (HSV-1). The virus, upon reactivation, travels into the ophthalmic rather than the mandibular branch of the trigeminal nerve. Infections with

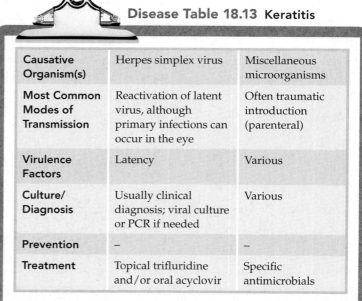

Disease Table 18.13 Keratitis

Causative Organism(s)	Herpes simplex virus	Miscellaneous microorganisms
Most Common Modes of Transmission	Reactivation of latent virus, although primary infections can occur in the eye	Often traumatic introduction (parenteral)
Virulence Factors	Latency	Various
Culture/Diagnosis	Usually clinical diagnosis; viral culture or PCR if needed	Various
Prevention	–	–
Treatment	Topical trifluridine and/or oral acyclovir	Specific antimicrobials

River Blindness

River blindness is a chronic parasitic (helminthic) infection. It is endemic in dozens of countries in Latin America, Africa, Asia, and the Middle East. At any given time, approximately 37 million people are infected with the worm called *Onchocerca volvulus* (ong"-koh'ser'-kah'volv'-yoo'lus). This organism is a filarial (threadlike) helminthic worm transmitted by small biting vectors called *black flies*. These voracious flies often attack in large numbers, and it is not uncommon in endemic areas to be bitten several hundred times a day. The disease gets its name from the habitat where these flies are most often found, rural settlements along rivers bordered with over-hanging vegetation.

The *Onchocerca* larvae are deposited into a bite wound and develop into adults in the immediate subcutaneous tissues, where disfiguring nodules form within 1 to 2 years after initial contact. Microfilariae given off by the adult female migrate via the bloodstream to many locations but especially to the eyes. While the worms are in the blood, they can be transmitted to other feeding black flies.

Some cases of onchocerciasis result in a severe itchy rash that can last for years. It was previously thought that the condition was caused by degeneration of the worms and the inflammation and granulomatous lesion formation that result from the release of their antigens. It is in fact the case that the worms eventually invade the entire eye, producing much inflammation and permanent damage to the retina and optic nerve. In 1999, researchers first discovered large colonies of bacteria called *Wolbachia* living *inside* the *Onchocerca* worms. There is convincing evidence that the damage caused to human tissues is induced by the bacteria rather than by the worms. Of course, the worms serve as the delivery system to the human as it does not appear that the bacteria can infect humans on their own. These bacteria enjoy a mutualistic relationship with their hosts; they are essential for normal *Onchocerca* development.

In regions of high prevalence, it is not unusual for an ophthalmologist to see microfilariae wiggling in the anterior chamber during a routine eye checkup. Microfilariae die in several months, but adults can exist for up to 15 years in skin nodules.

River blindness has been a serious problem in many areas of Africa. In some villages, nearly half of the residents are affected by the disease. A campaign to eradicate onchocerciasis is currently underway, supported by the Carter Center, an organization run by former U.S. President Jimmy Carter. The approach is to treat people with *ivermectin*, a potent antifilarial drug, and to use insecticides to control the black flies. Eliminating the protozoan will still eliminate the disease. The drug company that manufactures ivermectin has promised to provide the drug for free for as long as the need for it exists.

Case File 18   *Wrap-Up*

To determine the scope of this community-acquired MRSA outbreak, investigators obtained rectal and trunk cultures from the other 11 African elephants at the zoo and nasal cultures from 53 of 55 elephant caretakers. While no other elephants tested positive for MRSA, epidemiological investigation identified two caretakers as carriers and revealed a total of 20 suspected (based on signs and symptoms alone) or confirmed (through laboratory testing) MRSA infections among the caretakers. The strain was identified as MRSA USA 300, the most common strain implicated in CA-MRSA infection. This strain was identical to that isolated from the elephant calf and from the wounds on three of the caretakers.

Examination of work records showed that the calf had become infected with MRSA after being exposed to caretakers carrying the same strain. Investigators surmised that transmission then occurred from the calf to other human caretakers, since activities involving direct contact between the calf and a caretaker were those that most often resulted in infection. It was also noted that veterinary staff workers were more likely to wear personal protective equipment and were thus less likely to be infected than were the nursery staff or the elephant keepers.

See: CDC. 2009. *MMWR* 58:194–98.

Disease Table 18.14 River Blindness

Causative Organism(s)	*Wolbachia* plus *Onchocerca volvulus*
Most Common Modes of Transmission	Biological vector
Virulence Factors	Induction of inflammatory response
Culture/Diagnosis	"Skin snips": small piece of skin in NaCl solution examined under microscope and microfilariae counted
Prevention	Avoiding black fly
Treatment	Ivermectin
Distinguishing Features	Worms often visible in eye

18.6 Learning Outcomes—Can You ...

11. ... list the possible causative agents, modes of transmission, virulence factors, diagnostic techniques, and prevention/treatment for each of the diseases of the eye? These are: conjunctivitis, trachoma, keratitis, and river blindness.

► Summing Up

Taxonomic Organization Microorganisms Causing Diseases of the Skin and Eyes

Microorganism	Disease	Chapter Location
Gram-positive bacteria		
Propionibacterium acnes	Acne	Acne, p. 515
Staphylococcus aureus	Impetigo, cellulitis, scalded skin syndrome, folliculitis, abscesses (furuncles and carbuncles), necrotizing fasciitis	Impetigo, p. 516 Cellulitis, p. 521 Scalded skin syndrome, p. 522, Insight 18.1, p. 518, Note on p. 521
Streptococcus pyogenes	Impetigo, cellulitis, erysipelas, necrotizing fasciitis, scarlet fever	Impetigo, p. 520 Cellulitis, p. 521, Insight 18.1, p. 518
Clostridium perfringens	Gas gangrene	Gas gangrene, p. 523
Bacillus anthracis	Cutaneous anthrax	Large pustular skin lesions, p. 543
Gram-negative bacteria		
Neisseria gonorrhoeae	Neonatal conjunctivitis	Conjunctivitis, p. 540
Chlamydia trachomatis	Neonatal conjunctivitis, trachoma	Conjunctivitis, p. 540 Trachoma, p. 541
Wolbachia (in combination with *Onchocerca*)	River blindness	River blindness, p. 543
DNA viruses		
Human herpesvirus 3 (varicella) virus	Chickenpox	Vesicular or pustular rash diseases, p. 525
Variola virus	Smallpox	Vesicular or pustular rash diseases, p. 527
Parvovirus B19	Fifth disease	Maculopapular rash diseases, p. 532
Human herpesvirus 6 and 7	Roseola	Maculopapular rash diseases, p. 532
Human papillomavirus	Warts	Warts and wartlike eruptions, p. 534
Molluscum contagiosum virus	Molluscum contagiosum	Warts and wartlike eruptions, p. 534
Herpes simplex virus	Keratitis	Keratitis, p. 542
RNA viruses		
Measles virus	Measles	Maculopapular rash diseases, p. 530
Rubella virus	Rubella	Maculopapular rash diseases, p. 531
Fungi		
Trichophyton	Ringworm	Ringworm, p. 536
Microsporum	Ringworm	Ringworm, p. 536
Epidermophyton	Ringworm	Ringworm, p. 536
Malassezia species	Superficial mycoses	Superficial mycoses, p. 538
Protozoa		
Leishmania spp.	Leishmaniasis	Large pustular skin lesions, p. 535
Acanthamoeba		
Helminths		
Onchocerca volvulus (in combination with *Wolbachia*)	River blindness	River blindness, p. 543

INFECTIOUS DISEASES AFFECTING
The Skin and Eyes

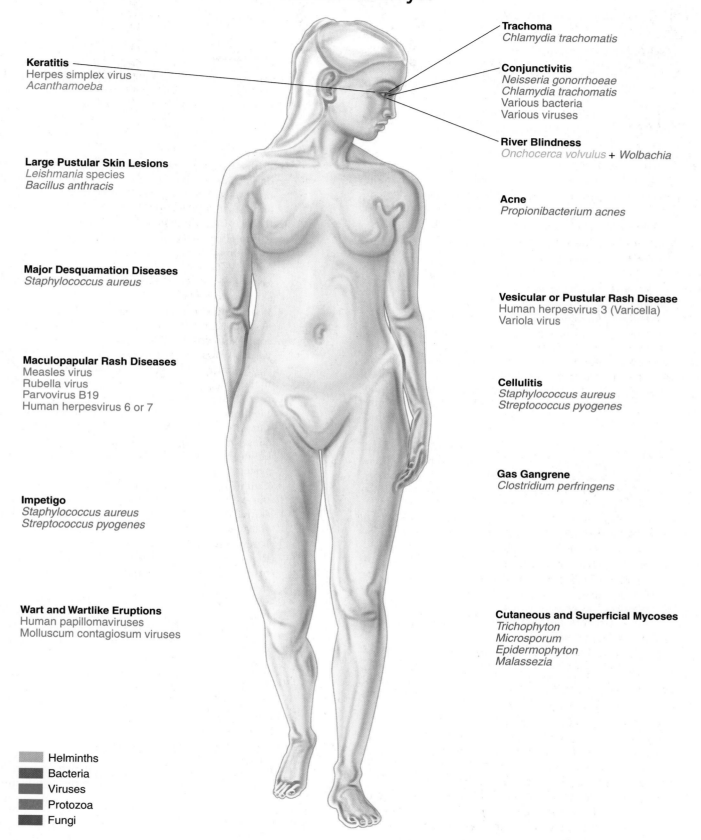

Keratitis
Herpes simplex virus
Acanthamoeba

Large Pustular Skin Lesions
Leishmania species
Bacillus anthracis

Major Desquamation Diseases
Staphylococcus aureus

Maculopapular Rash Diseases
Measles virus
Rubella virus
Parvovirus B19
Human herpesvirus 6 or 7

Impetigo
Staphylococcus aureus
Streptococcus pyogenes

Wart and Wartlike Eruptions
Human papillomaviruses
Molluscum contagiosum viruses

Trachoma
Chlamydia trachomatis

Conjunctivitis
Neisseria gonorrhoeae
Chlamydia trachomatis
Various bacteria
Various viruses

River Blindness
Onchocerca volvulus + *Wolbachia*

Acne
Propionibacterium acnes

Vesicular or Pustular Rash Disease
Human herpesvirus 3 (Varicella)
Variola virus

Cellulitis
Staphylococcus aureus
Streptococcus pyogenes

Gas Gangrene
Clostridium perfringens

Cutaneous and Superficial Mycoses
Trichophyton
Microsporum
Epidermophyton
Malassezia

Helminths
Bacteria
Viruses
Protozoa
Fungi

System Summary Figure 18.25

Chapter Summary

18.1 The Skin and Its Defenses

- The epidermal cells contain the protein keratin, which "waterproofs" the skin and protects it from microbial invasion.
- Other defenses include antimicrobial peptides, low pH sebum, high salt and lysozyme in sweat, and antimicrobial peptides.

18.2 Normal Biota of the Skin

- The skin has a diverse array of microbes as its normal biota, especially pseudomonads and *Janthinobacterium*. This is a major departure from the pre–Human Microbiome Project understanding of normal biota.

18.3 Skin Diseases Caused by Microorganisms

- **Acne:** A syndrome of follicle-associated lesions caused by microbial digestion of excess sebum trapped in pores of the skin. *Propionibacterium acnes* is the main causative agent.
- **Impetigo:** A highly contagious superficial bacterial infection that can cause skin to peel or flake off; transmitted by direct contact and via fomites and mechanical vectors. Causative organisms can be either *Staphylococcus aureus* or *Streptococcus pyogenes* or both.
- **Cellulitis:** Results from a fast-spreading infection of the dermis and subcutaneous tissue below. Most commonly caused by the introduction of *S. aureus* or *S. pyogenes* into dermis.
- **Staphylococcal Scalded Skin Syndrome (SSSS):** Caused by *S. aureus*. Affects mostly newborns and babies and is similar to a systemic form of impetigo. *Toxic epidermal necrolysis (TEN)* is a similar manifestation caused by a reaction to antibiotics, barbiturates, or other drugs.
- **Gas Gangrene:** Also called clostridial myonecrosis, can be manifested in two forms: anaerobic cellulitis or myonecrosis. The spore-forming anaerobe, *Clostridium perfringens,* is the most common causative organism.
- **Vesicular or Pustular Rash Diseases**
  - **Chickenpox:** Skin lesions progress quickly from macules and papules to itchy vesicles filled with clear fluid. Patients are considered contagious until all lesions have crusted over.
  - **Shingles:** Recuperation from chickenpox is associated with the virus becoming latent in the ganglia and may reemerge as shingles. Human herpesvirus 3, an enveloped DNA virus, causes chickenpox, as well as herpes zoster or shingles.
  - **Smallpox:** Naturally occurring smallpox has been eradicated from the world. The causative agent of smallpox, the variola virus, is an orthopoxvirus, an enveloped DNA virus.
- **Maculopapular Rash Diseases**
  - **Measles:** Measles or *rubeola* results in oral lesions called *Koplik's spots* and characteristic red maculopapular exanthem that erupts on the head and then progresses to the trunk and extremities until most of body is covered. The most serious complication is sub-

acute sclerosing panencephalitis (SSPE). The measles virus is a member of the *Morbillivirus* genus. The MMR vaccine (measles, mumps, and rubella) contains live attenuated measles virus.
  - **Rubella:** Also known as German measles, can appear in two forms: postnatal and congenital (prenatal) infection of the fetus. The MMR vaccination contains protection from rubella.
  - **Fifth Disease:** Also called *erythema infectiosum,* fifth disease is a very mild but highly contagious disease that often results in characteristic "slapped-cheek" appearance because of a confluent reddish rash that begins on the face. Causative agent is parvovirus B19.
  - **Roseola:** Can result in a maculopapular rash; is caused by a human herpesvirus called HHV-6 and sometimes by HHV-7.
  - **Scarlet Fever:** May accompany infection of throat or skin with *Streptococcus pyogenes.*
  - **Wartlike Eruptions:** Most common warts are caused by human papillomavirus or a poxvirus, molluscum contagiosum, which causes bumps that may look like warts. Warts, or papillomas, are benign, squamous epithelial growths. Rarely, a skin wart can become malignant when caused by a particular type of HPV.
- **Larger Pustular Skin Lesions**
  - **Leishmaniasis:** A zoonosis transmitted by the female sand fly when it ingests host's blood. A protozoan causes this equatorial disease, and the infection can be localized in the skin or mucous membranes, or be systemic.
  - **Cutaneous Anthrax:** Most common and least dangerous version of infection with *Bacillus anthracis.* The skin shows a papule that becomes necrotic and later ruptures to form a painless, black eschar.
  - **Ringworm (Cutaneous Mycoses):** A group of fungi that are collectively termed dermatophytes cause mycoses to the nonliving epidermal tissues, hair, and nails. Diseases are often called "ringworm"—ringworm of the scalp (tinea capitis), beard (tinea barbae), body (tinea corporis), groin (tinea cruris), foot (tinea pedis), and hand (tinea manuum). Species in the genera *Trichophyton, Microsporum,* and *Epidermophyton* cause the cutaneous mycoses.
  - **Superficial Mycosis:** Agents of superficial mycoses involve the outer epidermis. Tinea versicolor is caused by the yeast genus *Malassezia,* a normal inhabitant of human skin that feeds on the high oil content of the skin glands.

18.4 The Surface of the Eye and Its Defenses

- The flushing action of the tears, which contain lysozyme and lactoferrin, is the major protective feature of the eye.

18.5 Normal Biota of the Eye

- The eye has similar microbes as the skin but in lower numbers.

18.6 Eye Diseases Caused by Microorganisms

- **Conjunctivitis:** Infection of the conjunctiva (commonly called pinkeye) has many different clinical presentations. Neonatal eye infection is usually associated with *Neisseria gonorrhoeae* or *Chlamydia trachomatis;* they are transmitted vertically via a genital tract infection in the mother. Bacterial conjunctivitis in other age groups is most commonly caused by *Staphylococcus epidermidis* or by *Streptococcus pyogenes, Streptococcus pneumoniae, Haemophilus influenzae,* or *Moraxella* species. Viral conjunctivitis is commonly caused by adenoviruses. Both bacterial and viral conjunctivitis are highly contagious.

- **Trachoma:** Ocular trachoma is a chronic *Chlamydia trachomatis* infection of the epithelial cells of the eye and a major cause of blindness in certain parts of the world. Trachoma and simple conjunctivitis are caused by different strains of *C. trachomatis.*
- **Keratitis:** A more serious eye infection than conjunctivitis. Herpes simplex viruses (HSV-1 and HSV-2) and *Acanthamoeba* cause two different forms of the disease.
- **River Blindness:** A chronic parasitic helminth infection endemic in dozens of countries in Latin America, Africa, Asia, and the Middle East. The condition is caused by a symbiotic pair, the bacterium *Wolbachia* living inside the helminth *Onchocerca.* The worm is transmitted to humans by small biting black flies.

Multiple-Choice and True-False Questions   Knowledge and Comprehension

Multiple-Choice Questions. Select the correct answer from the answers provided.

1. An effective treatment for a cutaneous mycosis like tinea pedis would be
   a. penicillin.
   b. miconazole.
   c. griseofulvin.
   d. doxycycline.

2. What is the antimicrobial enzyme found in sweat, tears, and saliva that can specifically break down peptidoglycan?
   a. lysozyme
   b. beta-lactamase
   c. catalase
   d. coagulase

3. Which of the following is probably the most important defense factor for skin?
   a. phagocytes
   b. sebum
   c. dryness
   d. antimicrobial peptides

4. Name the organism(s) most commonly associated with cellulitis.
   a. *Staphylococcus aureus*   d. both a and b
   b. *Propionibacterium acnes*   e. both a and c
   c. *Streptococcus pyogenes*

5. Due to a highly successful vaccination program, the WHO has managed the worldwide eradication of the naturally occurring disease
   a. chickenpox.
   b. anthrax.
   c. smallpox.
   d. German measles.

6. Warts are caused by
   a. human herpesvirus 3.
   b. papillomavirus.
   c. herpes simplex virus.
   d. morbillivirus.

7. Herpesviruses can cause all of the following diseases, except
   a. chickenpox.
   b. shingles.
   c. keratitis.
   d. smallpox.
   e. roseola.

8. Which disease is incorrectly matched with the causative agent?
   a. viral conjunctivitis—adenovirus
   b. river blindness—*Onchocerca volvulus*
   c. smallpox—variola virus
   d. gas gangrene—*Staphylococcus aureus*

9. Dermatophytes are fungi that infect the epidermal tissue by invading and attacking
   a. collagen.
   b. keratin.
   c. fibroblasts.
   d. sebaceous glands.

10. Poor contact lens hygiene is likely to get you a case of
    a. herpetic keratitis.
    b. *Wolbachia* infection.
    c. *Acanthamoeba* keratitis.
    d. ophthalmic gonorrhea.

True-False Questions. If the statement is true, leave as is. If it is false, correct it by rewriting the sentence.

11. The enzyme catalase is associated with pathogenic strains of *Staphylococcus aureus.*

12. Fifth disease can be treated with acyclovir and prevented by immunization.

13. Measles can potentially be eradicated because humans are the only reservoir.

14. The blistering and peeling of the skin in scalded skin syndrome are due to the ability of *Staphylococcus aureus* to produce catalase.

15. Staphylocci and streptococci dominate the normal skin biota.

Critical Thinking Questions   Application and Analysis

These questions are suggested as a *writing-to-learn* experience. For each question, compose a one- or two-paragraph answer that includes the factual information needed to completely address the question.

1. Discuss the reasons the Human Microbiome Project is a step forward in characterizing normal and pathogenic biota in humans.

2. The cause of acne appears to be multifactorial. Describe the factors necessary that may result in an outbreak of acne.

3. a. What are some of the most common conditions that can lead to the onset of gas gangrene?
   b. Describe the key physiological characteristics of the causative organism that mediate the damage observed in this disease.
4. a. What is the causative agent of chickenpox?
   b. How is the occurrence of shingles related to chickenpox?
5. a. Name the three genera of fungi associated with tinea.
   b. Discuss the treatment options available for treating tinea.
6. Why would antibiotics in the penicillin family be ineffective in treating fungal infections?
7. a. How are warts contracted? List the different forms of transmission.
   b. Describe the causative agent(s).
   c. What are some of the methods used to treat warts?

8. a. Name the person credited with developing the first vaccine.
   b. What microorganism was used to create this vaccine?
   c. What was the disease that this vaccine was made against?
   d. What is "variolation"?
9. Smallpox has been widely reported as a possible bioterror weapon. Given what you know about the etiology of the disease and the current state of the world's immunity to smallpox, discuss how effective (or ineffective) a smallpox weapon might be. What kind of defense could be mounted against such an attack?
10. Despite the availability of the measles vaccine, outbreaks of measles still occur. Discuss some of the reasons for these occurrences.

Concept Mapping

Appendix D provides guidance for working with concept maps.

1. Supply your own linking words or phrases in this concept map, and provide the missing concepts in the empty boxes.
2. Use 6 to 10 words from the Chapter Summary to create a concept map. Finish it by providing linking words.

Visual Connections   Synthesis

These questions use visual images or previous content to make connections to this chapter's concepts.

1. **From chapter 13, figure 13.5a.** How does this figure help explain impetigo caused by *Staphylococcus aureus or Streptococcus pyogenes*?

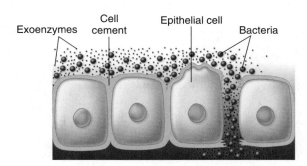

2. **From this chapter, figure 18.2.** Looking at this chart, and knowing the spectrum of activity for tetracycline, what do you think the long-term use of this antibiotic for acne would do to the normal biota on skin?

www.connect.microbiology.com

Enhance your study of this chapter with study tools and practice tests. Also ask your instructor about the resources available through ConnectPlus, including the media-rich eBook, interactive learning tools, and animations.

19

Infectious Diseases Affecting the Nervous System

Case File 19

An Indiana husband and wife, both feeling ill, went to separate hospitals to be examined, and several potential diagnoses were suggested. A few days later, on July 11, 2008, both patients were evaluated at the same hospital. There, physicians were able to make a preliminary diagnosis of botulism based on the couple's shared symptoms, which included cranial nerve palsy and descending flaccid paralysis. Both patients required mechanical ventilation. During a search of the couple's refrigerator, local health officials found an unlabeled bag of leftover chili sauce that, when analyzed, contained botulin, the bacterial toxin that causes botulism. Botulin is produced by *Clostridium botulinum,* an endospore-forming bacterium. Because botulism is a reportable disease, the facts of the case were forwarded to the Indiana State Department of Health and the Centers for Disease Control and Prevention (CDC).

Four days earlier, the CDC had received a similar report from Texas, where two siblings had been diagnosed with botulism, again only after being examined at the same hospital. Both children had eaten Castleberry's Hot Dog Chili Sauce for lunch on June 28. Although the can from this meal had been discarded, another can, bought at the same time, was found in the home.

Based on these two cases, the CDC suspected a common source epidemic.

■ What conditions encourage the germination of *Clostridium botulinum* endospores?

■ What is a common source epidemic?

Continuing the Case appears on page 576.

Outline and Learning Outcomes

19.1 The Nervous System and Its Defenses
1. Describe the important anatomical features of the nervous system.
2. List the natural defenses present in the nervous system.

19.2 Normal Biota of the Nervous System
3. Talk about the normal biota of the nervous system and the background behind it.

19.1 The Nervous System and Its Defenses

The nervous system can be thought of as having two component parts: the central nervous system (CNS), consisting of the brain and spinal cord, and the peripheral nervous system (PNS), which contains the nerves that emanate from the brain and spinal cord to sense organs and to the periphery of the body **(figure 19.1).** The nervous system performs three important functions—sensory, integrative, and motor. The sensory function is fulfilled by sensory receptors at the ends of peripheral nerves. They generate nerve impulses that are transmitted to the central nervous system. There, the impulses are translated, or integrated, into sensation or thought, which in turn drives the motor function. The motor function necessarily involves structures outside of the nervous system, such as muscles and glands.

The brain and the spinal cord are dense structures made up of cells called **neurons.** They are both surrounded by bone. The brain is situated inside the skull, and the spinal cord lies within the spinal column **(figure 19.2),** which is composed of a stack of interconnected bones called vertebrae. The soft tissue of the brain and spinal cord is encased within a tough casing of three membranes called the **meninges.** The layers of membranes, from outer to inner, are the dura mater, the arachnoid mater, and the pia mater. Between the arachnoid mater and pia mater is the subarachnoid space (that is, the space under the arachnoid mater). The subarachnoid space is filled with a clear serumlike fluid called cerebrospinal fluid (CSF). The CSF provides nutrition to the CNS, while

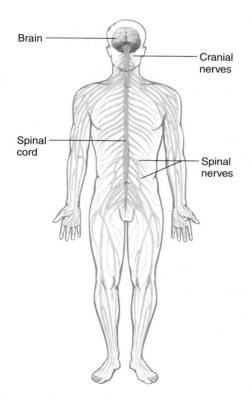

Figure 19.1 Nervous system.   The central nervous system and the peripheral nerves.

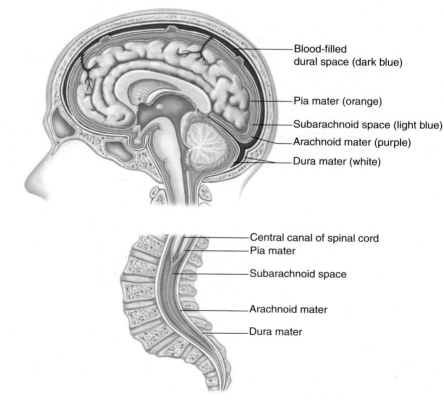

Figure 19.2 Detailed anatomy of the brain and spinal cord.

also providing a liquid cushion for the sensitive brain and spinal cord. The meninges are a common site of infection, and microorganisms can often be found in the CSF when meningeal infection (**meningitis**) occurs.

The PNS consists of cranial and spinal nerves (see figure 19.1). Nerves, or neurons, are bundles of cellular fibers in the form of axons and dendrites that receive and transmit nerve signals. The axons and dendrites of adjacent neurons communicate with each other over a very small space, called a synapse. Chemicals called neurotransmitters are released from one cell and act on the next cell in the synapse.

The defenses of the nervous system are mainly structural. The bony casings of the brain and spinal cord protect them from traumatic injury. The cushion of surrounding CSF also serves a protective function. The entire nervous system is served by the vascular system, but the interface between the blood vessels serving the brain and the brain itself is different from that of other areas of the body and provides a third structural protection. The cells that make up the walls of the blood vessels allow very few molecules to pass through. In other parts of the body, there is freer passage of ions, sugars, and other metabolites through the walls of blood vessels. The restricted permeability of blood vessels in the brain is called the **blood-brain barrier,** and it prohibits most microorganisms from passing into the central nervous system. The drawback of this phenomenon is that drugs and antibiotics are difficult to introduce into the CNS when needed.

The CNS is considered an "immunologically privileged" site. These sites are able to mount only a partial, or at least a different, immune response when exposed to immunologic challenge. The functions of the CNS are so vital for the life of an organism that even temporary damage that could potentially result from "normal" immune responses would be very detrimental. The uterus and parts of the eye are other immunologically privileged sites. Cells in the CNS express lower levels of MHC antigens. Complement proteins are also in much lower quantities in the CNS. Researchers now think that MHC markers and complement proteins play a role in the development, regulation and repair of neurons and nervous tissues, through their signaling mechanisms. They speculate that malfunctions with, or absence of these molecules in, the CNS may be responsible for a variety of conditions such as schizophrenia or autism. Other specialized cells in the central nervous system perform defensive functions. Microglia are a type of cell having phagocytic capabilities, and brain macrophages also exist in the CNS, although the activity of both of these types of cells is thought to be reduced when compared with phagocytic cells elsewhere in the body.

19.1 Learning Outcomes—Can You ...

1. ... describe the important anatomical features of the nervous system?
2. ... list the natural defenses present in the nervous system?

19.2 Normal Biota of the Nervous System

It is still believed that there is no normal biota in either the CNS or PNS, and that finding microorganisms of any type in these tissues represents a deviation from the healthy state. Viruses such as herpes simplex live in a dormant state in the nervous system between episodes of acute disease, but they are not considered normal biota. The Human Microbiome Project is not sampling this system.

19.2 Learning Outcomes—Can You ...

3. ... talk about the normal biota of the nervous system and the background behind it?

Nervous System Defenses and Normal Biota		
	Defenses	**Normal Biota**
Nervous System	Bony structures, blood-brain barrier, microglial cells, and macrophages	None

19.3 Nervous System Diseases Caused by Microorganisms

Meningitis

Meningitis, an inflammation of the meninges, is an excellent example of an anatomical syndrome. Many different microorganisms can cause an infection of the meninges, and they produce a similar constellation of symptoms. Noninfectious causes of meningitis exist as well, but they are much less common than the infections listed here.

The more serious forms of acute meningitis are caused by bacteria, but it is thought that their entrance to the CNS is often facilitated by coinfection or previous infection with respiratory viruses. Meningitis in neonates is most often caused by different microorganisms, and therefore it is described separately in the following section.

Whenever meningitis is suspected, lumbar puncture (spinal tap) is performed to obtain CSF, which is then examined by Gram stain and/or culture. Most physicians will begin treatment with a broad-spectrum antibiotic immediately and shift treatment if necessary after a diagnosis has been confirmed.

▶ Signs and Symptoms

No matter the cause, meningitis results in these typical symptoms: headache, painful or stiff neck, fever, and usually an increased number of white blood cells in the CSF. Specific microorganisms may cause additional, and sometimes characteristic, symptoms, which are described in the individual sections that follow.

Like many other infectious diseases, meningitis can manifest as acute or chronic disease. Some microorganisms are more likely to cause acute meningitis, and others are more likely to cause chronic disease.

In a normal healthy patient, it is very difficult for microorganisms to gain access to the nervous system. Those that are successful usually have specific virulence factors.

Neisseria meningitidis

Neisseria meningitidis appears as gram-negative diplococci lined up side by side **(figure 19.3)** and is commonly known as the meningococcus. It is often associated with epidemic forms of meningitis. This organism causes the most serious form of acute meningitis, and it is responsible for about 25% of all meningitis cases, most of them in children younger than age 2. Although 12 different strains of capsular antigens exist, serotypes A, B, and C are responsible for most cases of infection.

▶ Pathogenesis and Virulence Factors

Bacteria entering the blood vessels rapidly permeate the meninges and produce symptoms of meningitis. Meningitis is marked by fever, sore throat, headache, stiff neck, convulsions, and vomiting. The most serious complications of meningococcal infection are due to meningococcemia **(figure 19.4),** which can accompany meningitis but can also occur on its own. The pathogen releases endotoxin into the generalized circulation, which is a potent stimulus for certain white blood cells. Damage to the blood vessels caused by cytokines released by the white blood cells leads to vascular collapse, hemorrhage, and crops of lesions called **petechiae** (pee-tee'-kee-ay) on the trunk and appendages.

In a small number of cases, meningococcemia becomes a fulminant disease with a high mortality rate. Recent evidence suggests that persons who experience meningitis, rather than mild infection, have a genetic predisposition to it. These patients have changes in the genes that encode toll-like receptors (see chapter 14). The changes make it less likely that the host will initiate an early defensive response to the bacterium.

The disease has a sudden onset, marked by fever higher than 40°C, chills, delirium, severe widespread ecchymosis (ek"-ih'moh'seez) (areas of bleeding under the skin), shock, and coma. Generalized intravascular clotting, cardiac failure, damage to the adrenal glands, and death can occur within a few hours. The bacterium has an IgA protease and a capsule, both of which counter the body's defenses.

▶ Transmission and Epidemiology

Because meningococci do not survive long in the environment, these bacteria are usually acquired through close contact with secretions or droplets. Upon reaching their portal of entry in the nasopharynx, the meningococci attach there using pili. In many people, this can result in simple asymptomatic colonization. In the more vulnerable individual, however, the meningococci are engulfed by epithelial cells of the mucosa and penetrate into the nearby blood vessels, along the way damaging the epithelium and causing pharyngitis.

Meningococcal meningitis has a sporadic or epidemic incidence in late winter or early spring. The continuing reservoir of infection is humans who harbor the pathogen in the nasopharynx. The carriage state, which can last from a few days to several months, exists in 3% to 30% of the

Figure 19.4 Dissemination of the meningococcus from a nasopharyngeal infection. Bacteria spread to the roof of the nasal cavity, which borders a highly vascular area at the base of the brain. From this location, they can enter the blood and escape into the cerebrospinal fluid. Infection of the meninges leads to meningitis and an inflammatory purulent exudate over the brain surface.

Figure 19.3 Transmission electron micrograph of *Neisseria* (52,000×). This cross section makes the bacteria appear more spherical than usual.

adult population and can exceed 50% in institutional settings. The scene is set for transmission when carriers live in close quarters with nonimmune individuals, as might be expected in families, day care facilities, college dormitories, and military barracks. The highest risk groups are young children (6 to 36 months old) and older children and young adults (10 to 20 years old).

Every year, in what is called "the meningitis belt" in sub-Saharan Africa, a meningococcal epidemic sweeps through, coinciding with the dry season which runs from approximately December to May. In 2009, a particularly large outbreak killed more than 2,100 people in Niger and Nigeria and infected tens of thousands. Many more would have been affected except for a massive mobilization of vaccine. In the space of 4 months, 7.5 million people were vaccinated.

▶ Culture and Diagnosis

Suspicion of bacterial meningitis constitutes a medical emergency, and differential diagnosis must be done with great haste and accuracy. It is most important to confirm (or rule out) meningococcal meningitis, because it can be rapidly fatal. Treatment (described in the following section) is usually begun with this bacterium in mind until it can be ruled out. Cerebrospinal fluid, blood, or nasopharyngeal samples are stained and observed directly for the typical gram-negative diplococci. Cultivation may be necessary to differentiate the bacterium from other species. Specific rapid tests are also available for detecting the capsular polysaccharide or the cells directly from specimens without culturing.

It is usually necessary to differentiate this species from normal *Neisseria* that also live in the human body and can be present in infectious fluids. Immediately after collection, specimens are streaked on Modified Thayer-Martin medium (MTM) or chocolate agar and incubated in a high CO_2 atmosphere. Presumptive identification of the genus is obtained by a Gram stain and oxidase testing on isolated colonies **(figure 19.5)**. Further testing may be necessary to differentiate *N. meningitidis* and *N. gonorrhoeae* from one another, from other oxidase-positive species, and from normal biota of the oropharynx that can be confused with the pathogens. If no samples were obtained prior to antibiotic treatment, a PCR test is the best bet for identifying the pathogen.

▶ Prevention and Treatment

The infection rate in most populations is about 1%, so well-developed natural immunity to the meningococcus appears to be the rule. A sort of natural immunization occurs during the early years of life as one is exposed to the meningococcus and its close relatives. Resistance is due to opsonizing antibodies that develop against the capsular polysaccharides in groups A and C and against membrane antigens to group B. Because even treated meningococcemial disease has a mortality rate of up to 15%, it is vital that chemotherapy begin as soon as possible with one or more drugs. Penicillin G is the most potent of the drugs available for meningococcal infections; it

Figure 19.5 **The oxidase test.** A drop of oxidase reagent is placed on a suspected *Neisseria* or *Branhamella* colony. If the colony reacts with the chemical to produce a purple to black color, it is oxidase-positive; those that remain white to tan are oxidase-negative. Because several species of gram-negative rods are also oxidase-positive, this test is presumptive for these two genera only if a Gram stain has verified the presence of gram-negative cocci.

is generally given in high doses intravenously. Patients may also require treatment for shock and intravascular clotting.

When family members, medical personnel, or children in day care or school have come in close contact with infected people, preventive therapy with rifampin or tetracycline may be warranted. A new vaccine was licensed in 2005 and is recommended for children at elevated risk during their preadolescent visit. The vaccine is effective against groups A, C, Y, and W-135 and is conjugated to diphtheria toxoid as an adjuvant. It is thought to provide protection for 10 years. In European countries, serogroup B is more common than A, C, Y, and W-135. There is no vaccine for this serogroup.

Streptococcus pneumoniae

You will see in chapter 21 that *Streptococcus pneumoniae* causes the majority of bacterial pneumonias. (It is also referred to as the **pneumococcus.**) Pneumococcal meningitis is also caused by this bacterium; indeed, it is the most frequent cause of community-acquired meningitis and is also very severe. It does not cause the petechiae associated with meningococcal meningitis, and that difference is useful diagnostically. As many as 25% of pneumococcal meningitis patients will also have pneumococcal pneumonia. Pneumococcal meningitis is most likely to occur in patients with underlying susceptibility, such as alcoholic patients and patients with sickle-cell disease or those with absent or defective spleen function.

This bacterium is covered thoroughly in chapter 21, because it is a common cause of ear infections and pneumonia. It obviously has the potential to be highly pathogenic, while at the same time appearing as normal biota in many people. It can penetrate the respiratory mucosa; gain access to the bloodstream; and then, under certain conditions, enter the meninges.

Like the meningococcus, this bacterium has a polysaccharide capsule that protects it against phagocytosis. It also produces an alpha-hemolysin and hydrogen peroxide, both of which have been shown to induce damage in the CNS. It also appears capable of inducing brain cell apoptosis.

The bacterium is a small gram-positive flattened coccus that appears in end-to-end pairs. It has a distinctive appearance in a Gram stain of cerebrospinal fluid. Staining or culturing the nasopharynx is not useful because it is often normal biota there. It is also alpha-hemolytic on blood agar. Treatment requires a drug to which the bacterium is not resistant; penicillin is therefore not a good choice. Cefotaxime is often used, but drug susceptibilities must always be tested. It is recommended that a steroid be administered 20 minutes prior to antibiotic administration. This will dampen the inflammatory response to cell wall components that are released by antibiotic treatment of the gram-positive bacterium.

As mentioned in chapter 21, two vaccines are available for *S. pneumoniae*: a seven-valent conjugated vaccine (Prevnar), which is now recommended as part of the childhood immunization schedule, and a 23-valent polysaccharide vaccine (Pneumovax), which is available for adults.

Haemophilus influenzae

Haemophilus influenzae was originally named when it was isolated from patients with "flu" about 100 years ago. For over 40 years, it was erroneously proclaimed the causative agent until the real agent, the influenza virus, was discovered. This species eventually was shown to be an agent of acute bacterial meningitis in humans. The meningitis caused by this bacterium is severe. Before the vaccine was introduced in 1988, it was a very common cause of severe meningitis and death. In the course of the last 13 years, meningitis caused by this bacterium is virtually unknown in the United States, a situation that can always change if vaccine coverage falls. The disease is often called Hib because it is caused primarily by the B serotype. Routine vaccination with a subunit vaccine (Hib containing capsular polysaccharide conjugated to a protein) is recommended for all children, beginning at age 2 months, with three follow-up boosters.

Listeria monocytogenes

Listeria monocytogenes is a gram-positive bacterium that ranges in morphology from coccobacilli to long filaments in palisades formation **(figure 19.6)**. Cells do not produce capsules or spores and have from one to four flagella. *Listeria* is not fastidious and is resistant to cold, heat, salt, pH extremes, and bile. It grows inside host cells and can move directly from an infected host cell to an adjacent healthy cell.

Listeriosis in healthy adults is often a mild or subclinical infection with nonspecific symptoms of fever, diarrhea, and sore throat. However, listeriosis in elderly or immunocompromised patients, fetuses, and neonates (described later) usually affects the brain and meninges and results in

Figure 19.6 *Listeria monocytogenes.* The bacterium is generally rod shaped. In Gram stains, individual cells tend to stack up in structures called palisades.

septicemia. The death rate is around 20%. Pregnant women are especially susceptible to infection, which can be transmitted to the infant prenatally when the microbe crosses the placenta or postnatally through the birth canal. Intrauterine infections are widely systemic and usually result in premature abortion and fetal death.

The distribution of *L. monocytogenes* is so broad that its reservoir has been difficult to determine. It has been isolated all over the world from water, soil, plant materials, and the intestines of healthy mammals (including humans), birds, fish, and invertebrates. Apparently, the primary reservoir is soil and water, and animals, plants, and food are secondary sources of infection. Most cases of listeriosis are associated with ingesting contaminated dairy products, poultry, and meat. Recent epidemics have spurred an in-depth investigation into the prevalence of *L. monocytogenes* in these sources. A 2003 U.S. government report concluded that consumers are exposed to low to moderate levels of *L. monocytogenes* on a regular basis. The pathogen has been isolated in 10% to 15% of ground beef and in 25% to 30% of chicken and turkey carcasses and is also present in 5% to 10% of luncheon meats, hot dogs, and cheeses.

In late 2002, *Listeria* contamination of a poultry processing plant in Pennsylvania led to the recall of 27.4 million pounds of processed chicken and turkey, the largest meat recall in U.S. history. In 2008, Canada experienced a massive listeriosis outbreak that was traced to a meat processing plant in Toronto; 22 deaths resulted from this contamination of luncheon meats.

Diagnosing listeriosis is hampered by the difficulty in isolating it. The chances of isolation, however, can be improved by using a procedure called *cold enrichment,* in which the specimen is held at 4°C and periodically plated onto media, but this procedure can take 4 weeks. Rapid diagnostic kits using ELISA, immunofluorescence, and gene probe technology are now available for direct testing of dairy products and cultures. Antibiotic therapy should be started as soon as listeriosis is suspected. Ampicillin and trimethoprim-sulfamethoxazole are the first choices, followed by erythromycin. Prevention can be improved by adequate pasteurization temperatures and by proper washing, refrigeration, and cooking of foods that are suspected of being contaminated with animal manure or sewage. Pregnant women are cautioned by the U.S. Food and Drug Administration not to eat soft, unpasteurized cheeses.

Cryptococcus neoformans

The fungus *Cryptococcus neoformans* causes a more chronic form of meningitis with a more gradual onset of symptoms, although in AIDS patients the onset may be fast and the course of the disease more acute. It is sometimes classified as a meningoencephalitis. Headache is the most common symptom, but nausea and neck stiffness are very common. This fungus is a widespread resident of human habitats. It has a spherical to ovoid shape, with small, constricted buds and a large capsule that is important in its pathogenesis **(figure 19.7).**

▶ Transmission and Epidemiology

The primary ecological niche of *C. neoformans* is the bird population. It is prevalent in urban areas where pigeons congregate, and it proliferates in the high-nitrogen environment of droppings that accumulate on pigeon roosts. Masses of dried yeast cells are readily scattered into the air and dust. Its role as an opportunist is supported by evidence that healthy humans have strong resistance to it and that frank infection occurs primarily in debilitated patients. Most cryptococcal infections cause symptoms in the respiratory and central nervous systems.

By far the highest rates of cryptococcal meningitis occur among patients with AIDS. This meningitis is frequently fatal. Other conditions that predispose individuals to infection are steroid treatment, diabetes, and cancer. It is not considered communicable among humans.

The primary portal of entry for *C. neoformans* is the respiratory tract, but most lung infections are subclinical and rapidly resolved.

▶ Pathogenesis and Virulence Factors

The escape of the yeasts into the blood is intensified by weakened host defenses and results in severe complication. *Cryptococcus* shows an extreme affinity for the meninges and brain. The tumorlike masses formed in these locations can cause headache, mental changes, coma, paralysis, eye disturbances, and seizures. In some cases, the infection disseminates into the skin, bones, and viscera **(figure 19.8).**

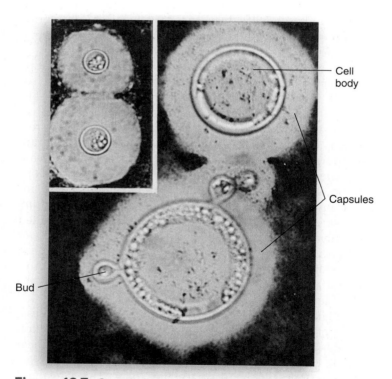

Figure 19.7 *Cryptococcus neoformans* **from infected spinal fluid stained negatively with India ink.**   Halos around the large spherical yeast cells are thick capsules. Also note the buds forming on one cell. Encapsulation is a useful diagnostic sign for cryptococcosis, although the capsule is fragile and may not show up in some preparations (150×).

Figure 19.8 **Cryptococcosis.**   A late disseminated case of cutaneous cryptococcosis in which fungal growth produces a gelatinous exudate. The texture is due to the capsules surrounding the yeast cells.

▶ Culture and/or Diagnosis

The first step in diagnosis of cryptococcosis is negative staining of specimens to detect encapsulated budding yeast cells that do not occur as pseudohyphae. Isolated colonies can be used to perform screening tests that presumptively differentiate *C. neoformans* from other cryptococcal species. Confirmatory results include a negative nitrate assimilation, pigmentation on birdseed agar, and fluorescent antibody tests. Cryptococcal antigen can be detected in a specimen by means of serological tests, and DNA probes can make a positive genetic identification.

▶ Prevention and Treatment

Systemic cryptococcosis requires immediate treatment with amphotericin B and fluconazole over a period of weeks or months. There is no prevention.

Coccidioides immitis

The morphology of *Coccidioides immitis* is very distinctive. At 25°C, it forms a moist white to brown colony with abundant, branching, septate hyphae. These hyphae fragment into thick-walled, blocklike **arthroconidia** (arthrospores) at maturity **(figure 19.9a).** On special media incubated at 37°C to 40°C, an arthrospore germinates into the parasitic phase, a small, spherical cell called a spherule **(figure 19.9b)** that can be found in infected tissues as well. This structure swells into a giant sporangium that cleaves internally to form numerous endospores that look like bacterial endospores but lack their resistance traits.

▶ Pathogenesis and Virulence Factors

This is a true systemic fungal infection of high virulence, as opposed to an opportunistic infection. It usually begins with pulmonary infection but can disseminate quickly throughout the body. Coccidioidomycosis of the meninges is the most serious manifestation. All persons inhaling the arthrospores probably develop some degree of infection, but certain groups have a genetic susceptibility that gives rise to more serious disease. After the arthrospores are inhaled, they develop into spherules in the lungs. These spherules release scores of endospores into the lungs. At this point the patient either experiences mild respiratory symptoms, which resolve themselves, or the endospores cause disseminated disease. Disseminated disease can include meningitis, osteomyelitis, and skin granulomas.

▶ Transmission and Epidemiology

C. immitis occurs endemically in various natural reservoirs and casually in areas where it has been carried by wind and animals. Conditions favoring its settlement include high carbon and salt content and a semiarid, relatively hot climate. The fungus has been isolated from soils, plants, and a large number of vertebrates. The natural history of *C. immitis* follows a cyclic pattern—a period of dormancy in winter and spring, followed by growth in summer and fall. Growth and spread are greatly increased by cycles of drought and heavy rains.

Skin testing has disclosed that the highest incidence of coccidioidomycosis, estimated at 100,000 cases per year,

(a) Arthrospores

(b) Spherules containing endospores

Figure 19.9 Two phases of *Coccidioides* infection.   **(a)** Arthrospores are present in the environment and are inhaled. **(b)** In the lungs, the brain, or other tissues, arthrospores develop into spherules that are filled with endospores. Endospores are released and induce damage.

occurs in the southwestern United States (figure 19.10), although it also occurs in Mexico and parts of Central and South America. Especially concentrated reservoirs exist in the San Joaquin Valley of California and in southern Arizona. Outbreaks are usually associated with farming activity, archeological digs, construction, and mining. A highly unusual outbreak of coccidioidomycosis was traced to the Northridge, California, earthquake in 1994. Clouds of dust bearing loosened spores were given off by landslides, and local winds then carried the dust into the outlying residential areas.

▶ Culture and Diagnosis

Diagnosis of coccidioidomycosis is straightforward when the highly distinctive spherules are found in sputum, spinal fluid, and biopsies. This finding is further supported by isolation of typical mycelia and arthrospores on Sabouraud's agar. Newer specific antigen tests have been effective tools to identify and differentiate *Coccidioides* from other fungi. All cultures must be grown in closed tubes or bottles and opened in a biological containment hood to prevent laboratory infections.

▶ Prevention and Treatment

The majority of patients do not require treatment. In people with disseminated disease, however, amphotericin B is administered intravenously; alternatively, oral or IV itraconazole is used. Minimizing contact with the fungus in its natural habitat has been of some value. For example, oiling dirt roads and planting vegetation help reduce spore aerosols, and using dust masks while excavating soil prevents workers from inhaling spores.

Viruses

A wide variety of viruses can cause meningitis. Because no bacteria or fungi are found in the CSF in viral meningitis, the condition is often called *aseptic meningitis.* Aseptic meningitis may also have noninfectious causes.

By far the majority of cases of viral meningitis occur in children, and 90% are caused by enteroviruses. But many other viruses also gain access to the central nervous system on occasion. An initial infection with herpes simplex type 2 is sometimes known to cause meningitis. Also, other herpesviruses such as HHV-6 and HHV-7 and also HHV-3 (the chickenpox virus) and cytomegalovirus (CMV) can infect the meninges, resulting in symptoms. Arboviruses, arenaviruses, and adenoviruses have also been found in meningitis cases. Finally, HIV infection may manifest as meningitis.

Viral meningitis is generally milder than bacterial or fungal meningitis, and it is usually resolved within 2 weeks. The mortality rate is less than 1%. Diagnosis begins with the failure to find bacteria, fungi, or protozoa in CSF and can be confirmed, depending on the virus, by viral culture or specific antigen tests. In most cases, no treatment is indicated. Acyclovir can be used when the causative agent is a herpesvirus; and, of course, if HIV is the cause the entire HIV antiviral regimen is called for (HIV is discussed in chapter 20). **Disease Table 19.1** summarizes the agents causing meningitis.

Neonatal Meningitis

Meningitis in newborns is almost always a result of infection transmitted by the mother, either in utero or (more fre-

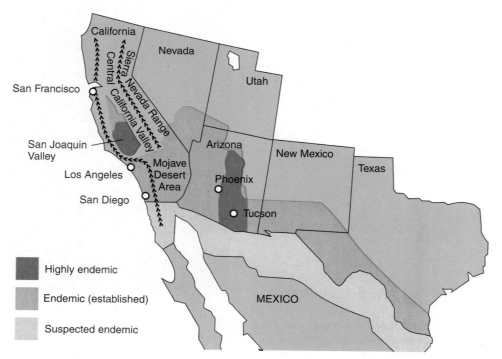

Figure 19.10 **Areas in the United States endemic for *Coccidioides immitis.***

Disease Table 19.1 Meningitis

Causative Organism(s)	*Neisseria meningitidis*	*Streptococcus pneumoniae*	*Haemophilus influenzae*	*Listeria monocytogenes*	*Cryptococcus neoformans*	*Coccidioides immitis*	Viruses
Most Common Modes of Transmission	Droplet contact	Droplet contact	Droplet contact	Vehicle (food)	Vehicle (air, dust)	Vehicle (air, dust, soil)	Droplet contact
Virulence Factors	Capsule, endotoxin, IgA protease	Capsule, induction of apoptosis, hemolysin and hydrogen peroxide production	Capsule	Intracellular growth	Capsule, melanin production	Granuloma (spherule) formation	Lytic infection of host cells
Culture/ Diagnosis	Gram stain/ culture of CSF, blood, rapid antigenic tests	Gram stain/ culture of CSF	Culture on chocolate agar	Cold enrichment, rapid methods	Negative staining, biochemical tests, DNA probes	Identification of spherules, cultivation on Sabouraud's agar	Initially, absence of bacteria/fungi/ protozoa, followed by viral culture or antigen tests
Prevention	Conjugated vaccine; rifampin or tetracycline used to protect contacts	Two vaccines: Prevnar (children), and Pneumovax (adults)	Hib vaccine	Cooking food, avoiding unpasteurized dairy products	–	Avoiding airborne spores	–
Treatment	Penicillin G or cefotaxime	Cefotaxime; check for resistance (add vancomycin in that case)	Cefotaxime	Ampicillin, trimethoprim-sulfamethoxazole	Amphotericin B and fluconazole	Amphotericin B or oral or IV itraconazole	Usually none (unless specific virus identified and specific antiviral exists)
Distinctive Features	Petechiae, meningo-coccemia	Serious, acute, most common meningitis in adults	Serious, acute, less common since vaccine became available	Asymptomatic in healthy adults; meningitis in neonates, elderly, and immuno-compromised	Acute or chronic, most common in AIDS patients	Almost exclusively in endemic regions	Generally milder than bacterial or fungal

quently) during passage through the birth canal (although **Insight 19.1** describes a troubling exception to this trend). As more premature babies survive, the rates of neonatal meningitis increase, because the condition is favored in patients with immature immune systems. In the United States the two most common causes are *Streptococcus agalactiae* and *Escherichia coli*. *Listeria monocytogenes* is also found frequently in neonates. It has already been covered here but is included in **Disease Table 19.2** as a reminder that it can cause neonatal cases as well. In the developing world, neonatal meningitis is more commonly caused by other organisms.

Streptococcus agalactiae

This species of *Streptococcus* belongs to group B of the streptococci. It colonizes 10% to 30% of female genital tracts and is the most frequent cause of neonatal meningitis (for details about this condition in women, see chapter 23). The treatment for neonatal disease is penicillin G, sometimes supplemented with an aminoglycoside.

INSIGHT 19.1 Baby Food and Meningitis

It will come as no surprise to you that there are potentially dangerous bacteria in a wide variety of foods we consume. Cases of *E. coli* O157:H7 disease associated with hamburgers or hepatitis contracted by customers of a Mexican restaurant chain get a lot of media attention. It may surprise you to learn that pathogenic bacteria are found in dried infant formula and dried baby food, as well.

In 2001, an outbreak of meningitis in a neonatal intensive care unit in Tennessee was traced to a batch of powdered formula. The manufacturer recalled the product after the Centers for Disease Control and Prevention issued a warning. In 2004, scientists in England investigated 110 different types of baby foods. Ten percent of the powdered formula samples and 25% of the dried infant foods contained intestinal bacteria. In many of the samples, they found a bacterium called *Enterobacter sakazakii*, an intestinal bacterium that has been linked to several fatal outbreaks of meningitis in children's hospitals. The outbreaks have continued, with cases reported in at least 17 states.

The disease is rare but almost always associated with infant foods and has a 33% fatality rate, with up to 80% of infants suffering permanent neurological damage. So what is to be done? In this case, it is "consumer beware." Manufacturers have never claimed that their formulas and foods are sterile. The scientists who conducted the infant food study also investigated ideal conditions for preparing and storing the products. They noted that the bacterial doubling time in prepared formula is 10 hours when refrigerated, and 30 minutes at room temperature. This means that leaving prepared formula in your diaper bag or on the kitchen counter for even a few hours could lead to high levels of bacteria in the bottle.

Powdered formula is made by manufacturing the nutritious liquid and then freeze-drying it. It is sterile as a liquid but bacteria can be introduced during the freeze-drying and packaging phases. Since the outbreaks, the FDA has recommended that the powder be reconstituted with boiling water. The CDC has not supported this recommendation because of many problems with it including the risk of destroying important nutrients and the lack of data that boiling it would be sufficient to kill *E. sakazakii*. Hospitals are advised to use ready-to-feed or concentrated liquid formulas.

Escherichia coli

The K1 strain of *Escherichia coli* is the second most common cause of neonatal meningitis. Most babies who suffer from this infection are premature, and their prognosis is poor. Twenty percent of them die, even with aggressive antibiotic treatment, and those who survive often have brain damage.

The bacterium is usually transmitted from the mother's birth canal. It causes no disease in the mothers but can infect the vulnerable tissues of a neonate. It seems to have a predilection for the tissues of the central nervous system. Cefotaxime is usually administered intravenously, in combination with aminoglycosides (see Disease Table 19.2).

Disease Table 19.2 Neonatal Meningitis

Causative Organism(s)	*Streptococcus agalactiae*	*Escherichia coli*, strain K1	*Listeria monocytogenes*
Most Common Modes of Transmission	Vertical (during birth)	Vertical (during birth)	Vertical
Virulence Factors	Capsule	–	Intracellular growth
Culture/Diagnosis	Culture mother's genital tract on blood agar; CSF culture of neonate	CSF Gram stain/culture	Cold enrichment, rapid methods
Prevention	Culture and treatment of mother	–	Cooking food, avoiding unpasteurized dairy products
Treatment	Penicillin G plus aminoglycosides	Cefotaxime plus aminoglycoside	Ampicillin, trimethoprim-sulfamethoxazole
Distinctive Features	Most common; positive culture of mother confirms diagnosis	Suspected if infant is premature	–

Meningoencephalitis

Up to this point, we have described microorganisms causing meningitis (inflammation of the meninges). Next we discuss microorganisms that cause **encephalitis,** inflammation of the brain. Because the brain and the spinal cord (and the meninges) are so closely connected, infections of one of these structures may also involve the other.

But two microorganisms cause a distinct disease called *meningoencephalitis,* and they are both amoebas. *Naegleria fowleri* and *Acanthamoeba* are accidental parasites that invade the body only under unusual circumstances.

Naegleria fowleri

The trophozoite of *Naegleria* is a small, flask-shaped amoeba that moves by means of a single, broad pseudopod. It forms a rounded, thick-walled, uninucleate cyst that is resistant to temperature extremes and mild chlorination.

Most cases of *Naegleria* infection reported worldwide occur in people who have been swimming in warm, natural bodies of fresh water. Infection can begin when amoebas are forced into human nasal passages as a result of swimming, diving, or other aquatic activities. Once the amoeba is inoculated into the favorable habitat of the nasal mucosa, it burrows in, multiplies, and subsequently migrates into the brain and surrounding structures. The result is primary amoebic meningoencephalitis (PAM), a rapid, massive destruction of brain and spinal tissue that causes hemorrhage and coma and invariably ends in death within a week or so **(figure 19.11)**. We should note that this organism is very common—children often carry the amoeba as harmless biota, especially during the summer months, and the series of events leading to disease is exceedingly rare.

Unfortunately, *Naegleria* meningoencephalitis advances so rapidly that treatment usually proves futile. Studies have indicated that early therapy with amphotericin B, sulfadiazine, or tetracycline in some combination can be of some benefit. Because of the wide distribution of the amoeba and its hardiness, no general means of control exists. Public swimming pools and baths must be adequately chlorinated and checked periodically for the amoeba.

Acanthamoeba

This protozoan has a large, amoeboid trophozoite with spiny pseudopods and a double-walled cyst. It differs from *Naegleria* in its portal of entry; it invades broken skin, the conjunctiva, and occasionally the lungs and urogenital epithelia. Although it causes a meningoencephalitis somewhat similar to that of *Naegleria,* the course of infection is lengthier. The disease is called granulomatous amoebic meningoencephalitis (GAM). At special risk for infection are people with traumatic eye injuries, contact lens wearers, and AIDS patients exposed to contaminated water. We discussed ocular infections in chapter 18. Cutaneous and CNS infections with this organism are occasional complications in AIDS **(Disease Table 19.3).**

Pathologic changes in brain · *Naegleria*

Figure 19.11 *Naegleria fowleri* **in the brain.** The trophozoite form invades brain tissue, destroying it.

Disease Table 19.3 Meningoencephalitis

	Primary Amoebic Meningoencephalitis	Granulomatous Amoebic Meningoencephalitis
Causative Organism(s)	*Naegleria fowleri*	*Acanthamoeba*
Most Common Modes of Transmission	Vehicle (exposure while swimming in water)	Direct contact
Virulence Factors	Invasiveness	Invasiveness
Culture/Diagnosis	Examination of CSF; brain imaging, biopsy	Examination of CSF; brain imaging, biopsy
Prevention	Avoid warm fresh water	–
Treatment	Amphotericin B; mostly ineffective	Surgical excision of granulomas; ketoconazole may help

Acute Encephalitis

Encephalitis can present as acute or **subacute.** It is always a serious condition, as the tissues of the brain are extremely sensitive to damage by inflammatory processes. Acute encephalitis is almost always caused by viral infection. One category of viral encephalitis is caused by viruses borne by insects (arboviruses), including West Nile virus. Alternatively, other viruses, such as members of the herpes family, are causative agents. Bacteria such as those covered under meningitis can also cause encephalitis, but the symptoms are almost always more pronounced in the meninges than in the brain.

The signs and symptoms of encephalitis vary, but they may include behavior changes or confusion because of inflammation. Decreased consciousness and seizures frequently occur. Symptoms of meningitis are often also present. Few of these agents have specific treatments, but because swift initiation of acyclovir therapy can save the life of a patient suffering from herpesvirus encephalitis, most physicians will begin empiric therapy with acyclovir in all seriously ill neonates and most other patients showing evidence of encephalitis. Treatment will, in any case, do no harm in patients who are infected with other agents.

Arboviruses

Wherever there are arthropods, there are also arboviruses so, collectively, their distribution is worldwide. The vectors and viruses tend to be clustered in the tropics and subtropics, but many temperate zones report periodic epidemics. A given arbovirus type may have very restricted distribution, even to a single isolated region, but some types range over several continents, and others can spread along with their vectors **(figure 19.12).**

Most arthropods that serve as infectious disease vectors feed on the blood of hosts, a process that infects them for varying time periods. Infections show a peak incidence when the arthropod is actively feeding and reproducing, usually from late spring through early fall. Warm-blooded vertebrates also maintain the virus during the cold and dry seasons. Humans can serve as dead-end, accidental hosts, as in equine encephalitis, or they can be a maintenance reservoir, as in yellow fever (discussed in chapter 20).

Arboviral diseases have a great impact on humans. Although exact statistics are unavailable, it is believed that millions of people acquire infections each year and thousands of them die. One common outcome of arboviral infection is an acute fever, often accompanied by rash. Viruses that primarily cause these symptoms are covered in chapter 20.

The arboviruses discussed in this chapter can cause encephalitis, and we consider them as a group because the symptoms and management are similar. The transmission and epidemiology of individual viruses are different, however, and are discussed for each virus. **Insight 19.2** discusses West Nile virus, an arbovirus that has spread across North America in recent years.

▶ Pathogenesis and Virulence Factors

Arboviral encephalitis begins with an arthropod bite, the release of the virus into tissues, and its replication in nearby lymphatic tissues. Prolonged viremia establishes the virus in the brain, where inflammation can cause swelling and damage to the brain, nerves, and meninges. Symptoms are extremely variable and can include coma, convulsions, paralysis, tremor, loss of coordination, memory deficits, changes in speech and personality, and heart disorders. In some cases, survivors experience some degree of permanent brain damage. Young children and the elderly are most sensitive to injury by arboviral encephalitis.

The virulence of these viruses is not well understood, but much research has focused on proteins that the virus uses to attach to host tissues or to induce fusion with host cell membranes. Both of these functions facilitate invasion of the virus.

Figure 19.12 Worldwide distribution of major arboviral encephalitides.

INSIGHT 19.2 | **A Long Way from Egypt: West Nile Virus in the United States**

In 1999, the first cases of West Nile encephalitis were seen in several northeastern states. Over the next few years, West Nile virus spread westward across the country, resulting in at least 1 million infections and over 664 deaths by mid-2005. In the summer of 2003, the Centers for Disease Control and Prevention reported that they had detected the virus in 600 blood donors in the United States. Government officials were made aware of the need to test for the virus after 23 patients acquired West Nile from blood transfusions in 2002.

The arrival of a deadly new disease, especially at a time of public nervousness concerning potential biological warfare, led to a great deal of media attention concerning West Nile virus, much of it sensational, even if not entirely accurate.

West Nile virus is an arbovirus commonly found in Africa, the Middle East, and parts of Asia, but until mid-1999 had not been detected in the Americas. The virus is known to infect a host of mammals (including humans), as well as birds and mosquitoes. We now know that its spread across the United States was facilitated by a mutation in an envelope protein that allowed it to replicate at higher rates in birds, leading to higher transmission rates than had previously been seen with West Nile virus. Mosquitoes generally become infected when they feed on birds

infected with the virus, and they can then bite and transmit the virus to humans. If infection results, the illness is generally characterized by flulike symptoms that last just a few days and have no long-term consequences. Less than 1% of infected persons will suffer the potentially lethal inflammation of the brain known as West Nile encephalitis.

Because transmission of the virus depends on the presence of mosquitoes to act as vectors, viral control is synonymous with vector control. Insect repellant, long-sleeved shirts and long pants, and control of mosquito breeding grounds (primarily stagnant water) all decrease the spread of the virus. During the home foreclosure crisis that began in 2008, many municipalities were stepping up their monitoring of abandoned swimming pools in order to prevent outbreaks of this disease. Because the virus is bloodborne, person-to-person transmission is unlikely. There has been at least one confirmed case, however, in which the virus was transmitted from mother to fetus, as well as another case in which an infected organ donor passed on the virus to four organ recipients.

Epidemiologists are also closely monitoring the magnitude of the disease in animals. So far, the virus has been isolated in nearly 200 bird species as well as cats, dogs, rodents, horses, and even alligators.

▶ Culture and Diagnosis

Except during epidemics, detecting arboviral infections can be difficult. The patient's history of travel to endemic areas or contact with vectors, along with serum analysis, is highly supportive of a diagnosis. Rapid serological tests are available for some of the viruses.

▶ Prevention and Treatment

No satisfactory treatment exists for any of the arboviral encephalitides (plural of *encephalitis*). As mentioned earlier, empiric acyclovir treatment may be begun in case the infection is actually caused by either herpes simplex virus or varicella zoster. Treatment of the other infections relies entirely on support measures to control fever, convulsions, dehydration, shock, and edema.

Most of the control safeguards for arbovirus disease are aimed at the arthropod vectors. Mosquito abatement by eliminating breeding sites and by broadcasting insecticides has been highly effective in restricted urban settings. Birds play a role as reservoirs of the virus, but direct transmission between birds and humans does not occur.

Live attenuated vaccines are available for Western equine encephalitis and Eastern equine encephalitis and are administered to laboratory workers, veterinarians, ranchers, and horses.

Western Equine Encephalitis (WEE) This disease occurs sporadically in the western United States and Canada, appearing first in horses and later in humans. The mosquito that carries the virus emerges in the early summer when irri-

gation begins in rural areas and breeding sites are abundant. The disease is extremely dangerous to infants and small children, with a case fatality rate of 3% to 7%.

Eastern Equine Encephalitis (EEE) EEE is endemic to an area along the eastern coast of North America and Canada. The usual pattern is sporadic, but occasional epidemics can occur in humans and horses. High periods of rainfall in the late summer increase the chance of an outbreak, and disease usually appears first in horses and caged birds. The case fatality rate can be very high (70%).

California Encephalitis This condition may be caused by two different viral strains. The California strain occurs occasionally in the western United States and has little impact on humans. The LaCrosse strain is widely distributed in the eastern United States and Canada and is a prevalent cause of viral encephalitis in North America. Children living in rural areas are the primary target group, and most of them exhibit mild, transient symptoms. Fatalities are rare.

St. Louis Encephalitis (SLE) St. Louis encephalitis may be the most common of all American viral encephalitides. Cases appear throughout North and South America, but epidemics in the United States occur most often in the Midwest and South. Inapparent infection is very common, and the total number of cases is probably thousands of times greater than the 50 to 100 reported each year. The seasons of peak activity are spring and summer, depending on the region and species of mosquito.

West Nile Encephalitis

West Nile Encephalitis   The West Nile virus is a close relative of the SLE virus. It emerged in the United States in 1999, and by 2008 the CDC was reporting that 1% of people in the United States—or approximately 3 million people—had evidence of past or present infection. See Insight 19.2 for details.

Herpes Simplex Virus

Herpes simplex type 1 and 2 viruses can cause encephalitis in newborns born to HSV-positive mothers. In this case, the virus is disseminated and the prognosis is poor. Older children and young adults (ages 5 to 30), as well as older adults (over 50 years old), are also susceptible to herpes simplex encephalitis caused most commonly by HSV-1. In these cases, the HSV encephalitis represents a reactivation of dormant HSV from the trigeminal ganglion.

It should be noted the varicella-zoster virus (see chapter 18) can also reactivate from the dormant state, and it is responsible for rare cases of encephalitis.

JC Virus

The **JC virus (JCV)** gets its name from the initials of the patient in whom it was first diagnosed as the cause of illness. Serological studies indicate that infection with this polyoma virus is commonplace. In patients with immune dysfunction, especially in those with AIDS, it can cause a condition called **progressive multifocal leukoencephalopathy** (loo"-koh-en-sef"uh-lop'-uh-thee) **(PML).** This uncommon but generally fatal infection is a result of JC virus attack of accessory brain cells. The infection demyelinizes certain parts of the cerebrum. This virus should be considered when encephalitis symptoms are observed in AIDS patients. Recently a few deaths from this condition have been prevented with high doses of zidovudine.

Other Virus-Associated Encephalitides

Infection with measles and other childhood rash diseases can result 1 to 2 weeks later in an inappropriate immune response with consequences in the CNS. The condition is called post-infection encephalitis (PIE), and it is thought to be a result of immune system action and not of direct viral invasion of neural tissue. Very rarely PIE can occur after immunization with live attenuated vaccines against viral infections. Note that PIE is distinct from another possible sequela of measles virus infection called SSPE (discussed later in this chapter) **(Disease Table 19.4).**

Subacute Encephalitis

When encephalitis symptoms take longer to show up and when the symptoms are less striking, the condition is termed subacute encephalitis. The most common cause of subacute encephalitis is the protozoan *Toxoplasma*. Another form of subacute encephalitis can be caused by persistent measles virus as

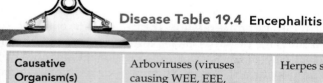

Disease Table 19.4 Encephalitis

Causative Organism(s)	Arboviruses (viruses causing WEE, EEE, California encephalitis, SLE, West Nile encephalitis)	Herpes simplex 1 or 2	JC virus	Immunologic reaction to other viral infections
Most Common Modes of Transmission	Vector (arthropod bites)	Vertical or reactivation of latent infection	? Ubiquitous	Sequelae of measles, other viral infections, and occasionally, vaccination
Virulence Factors	Attachment, fusion, invasion capabilities	–	–	–
Culture/Diagnosis	History, rapid serological tests	Clinical presentation, PCR, Ab tests, growth of virus in cell culture	PCR of cerebrospinal fluid	History of viral infection or vaccination
Prevention	Insect control; vaccines for WEE and EEE available	Maternal screening for HSV	None	–
Treatment	None	Acyclovir	Zidovudine or other antivirals	Steroids, anti-inflammatory agents
Distinctive Features	History of exposure to insect important	In infants, disseminated disease present; rare between 30 and 50 years	In severely immunocompromised, especially AIDS	History of virus/vaccine exposure critical

many as 7 to 15 years after the initial infection. Finally, a class of infectious agents known as prions can cause a condition called spongiform encephalopathy.

Toxoplasma gondii

Toxoplasma gondii is a flagellated parasite with such extensive cosmopolitan distribution that some experts estimate it affects the majority of the world's population at some time in their lives. Infection in the fetus and in immunodeficient people, especially those with AIDS, is severe and often fatal. Although infection in otherwise healthy people is generally unnoticed, recent data tells us it can have profound effects on their brain, and the responses it controls **(Insight 19.3).** People with a history of *Toxoplasma* infection are more likely to display thrill-seeking behaviors. Also, people with infection histories seem to have slower reaction times.

    T. gondii is a very successful parasite with so little host specificity that it can attack at least 200 species of birds and mammals. However, its primary reservoir and hosts are members of the feline family, both domestic and wild.

▶ Signs and Symptoms

As just mentioned, most cases of toxoplasmosis are asymptomatic or marked by mild symptoms such as sore throat, lymph node enlargement, and low-grade fever. In patients whose immunity is suppressed by infection, cancer, or drugs, the outlook may be grim. The infection causes a more chronic or subacute form of encephalitis than do most viruses, often producing extensive brain lesions and fatal disruptions of the heart and lungs. A pregnant woman with toxoplasmosis has a 33% chance of transmitting the infection to her fetus. Congenital infection occurring in the first or second trimester is associated with stillbirth and severe abnormalities such as liver and spleen enlargement, liver failure, hydrocephalus, convulsions, and damage to the retina that can result in blindness.

▶ Pathogenesis and Virulence Factors

Toxoplasma is an obligate intracellular parasite, making its ability to invade host cells an important factor for virulence.

▶ Transmission and Epidemiology

To follow the transmission of toxoplasmosis, we must first look at the general stages of the *Toxoplasma* life cycle in the cat **(figure 19.13a).** The parasite undergoes a sexual phase in the intestine and is then released in feces, where it becomes an infective *oocyst* that survives in moist soil for several months. Ingested oocysts release an invasive asexual tissue phase called a *tachyzoite* that infects many different tissues and often causes disease in the cat. These forms eventually enter an asexual cyst state in tissues, called a *pseudocyst.* Most of the time, the parasite does not cycle in cats alone and is spread by oocysts to intermediate hosts, usually rodents and birds. The cycle returns to cats when they eat these infected prey animals.

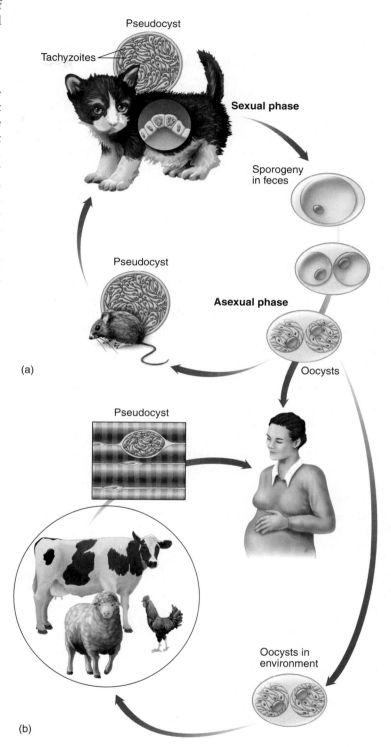

Figure 19.13 The life cycle and morphological forms of *Toxoplasma gondii.* **(a)** The cycle in cats and their prey. **(b)** The cycle in other animal hosts. The zoonosis has a large animal reservoir (domestic and wild) that becomes infected through contact with oocysts in the soil. Humans can be infected through contact with cats or ingestion of pseudocysts in animal flesh. Infection in pregnant women is a serious complication because of the potential damage to the fetus.

INSIGHT 19.3 Toxoplasmosis Leads to More Car Accidents?

If you are infected with *Toxoplasma* (and are Rh⁻) you may be 2.5 times more likely to crash your car. What?! Let's back up. It has long been recognized that the chain of transmission for *Toxoplasma* is facilitated by a change in infected rodents' brains that makes them lose their inhibitions, so that they are no longer afraid of cats, which can then eat them and become infected. As you read in the text, the rate of infection (which is lifelong) is very high, as high as 90% in some populations. Recently scientists found that the parasite can affect the brain of infected humans, also, causing some to have more thrill-seeking personalities and also to have slower reaction times. The final piece of the puzzle is that these effects only seem to be prominent in people with Rh⁻ blood. As you recall, Rh⁻ blood cells are missing a particular protein on their membranes. It is not yet clear whether this provides protection from invasion by the parasite or whether there is some other explanation. But in 2009 a group of Czech scientists studied 3,980 military drivers for a year and a half. The drivers who were *Toxoplasma*-positive and Rh⁻ were 2.5 times as likely to be in a car accident over the 18-month period than uninfected drivers. The astounding extrapolation from this study is that it suggests that between 400,000 and 1 million deaths worldwide from car crashes might be due to *Toxoplasma* infection. Could it be that someday airline pilots and truck drivers will have to be screened for infection?

In 2007, scientists at Stanford University found that the protozoan crowds into a part of the rat brain that usually directs the rat to avoid the smell of cat urine (a natural defense against a domestic rat's major predator). When *Toxoplasma* infects rat brains, the rats lose their fear of cats. Infected rats are then easily eaten by cats, ensuring the continuing *Toxoplasma* life cycle. All other neurological functions in the rat are left intact.

Other vertebrates become a part of this transmission cycle **(figure 19.13*b*).** Herbivorous animals such as cattle and sheep ingest oocysts that persist in the soil of grazing areas and then develop pseudocysts in their muscles and other organs. Carnivores such as canines are infected by eating pseudocysts in the tissues of carrier animals.

Humans appear to be constantly exposed to the pathogen. The rate of prior infections, as detected through serological tests, can be as high as 90% in some populations. Many cases are caused by ingesting pseudocysts in contaminated meats. A common source is raw or undercooked meat. The grooming habits of cats spread fecal oocysts on their body surfaces, and unhygienic handling of them presents an opportunity to ingest oocysts. Infection can also occur when oocysts are inhaled in air or dust contaminated with cat droppings and when tachyzoites cross the placenta to the fetus.

▶ Culture and Diagnosis

This infection can be differentiated from viral encephalitides by means of serological tests that detect antitoxoplasma antibodies, especially those for IgM, which appears early in infection. Disease can also be diagnosed by culture and histological analysis.

▶ Prevention and Treatment

The most effective drugs are pyrimethamine and leucovorin and sulfadiazine alone or in combination. Because these drugs do not destroy the cyst stage, they must be given for long periods to prevent recurrent infection.

In view of the fact that the oocysts are so widespread and resistant, hygiene is of paramount importance in controlling toxoplasmosis. There is no such thing as a safe form of raw meat, even salted or spiced. Adequate cooking or freezing below −20°C destroys both oocysts and tissue cysts. Oocysts can also be avoided by washing the hands after handling cats or soil possibly contaminated with cat feces, especially sandboxes and litter boxes. Pregnant women should be especially attentive to these rules and should never clean the cat's litter box.

Measles Virus: Subacute Sclerosing Panencephalitis

Subacute sclerosing panencephalitis (SSPE) is sometimes called a "slow virus infection." It occurs years after an initial measles episode and is different from immune-mediated postinfectious encephalitis, described earlier. SSPE seems to be caused by direct viral invasion of neural tissue. It is not clear what factors lead to persistence of the virus in some people. See chapter 18 for more details. SSPE's important features are listed in **Disease Table 19.5.**

Prions

As you read in chapter 6, prions are **proteinaceous infectious particles** containing, apparently, no genetic material. They are known to cause diseases called **transmissible spongiform encephalopathies (TSEs),** neurodegenerative diseases with long incubation periods but rapid progressions once they begin. The human TSEs are **Creutzfeldt-Jakob disease (CJD),** Gerstmann-Strussler-Scheinker disease, and fatal familial insomnia. TSEs are also found in animals and include a disease called scrapie in sheep and goats, transmissible mink encephalopathy, and bovine spongiform encephalopathy (BSE). This last disease is commonly known as mad cow disease and has been in the headlines in recent years due to its apparent link to a variant form of CJD human disease in Great Britain.

▶ Signs and Symptoms of CJD

Symptoms of CJD include altered behavior, dementia, memory loss, impaired senses, delirium, and premature senility. Uncontrollable muscle contractions continue until death, which usually occurs within 1 year of diagnosis.

Disease Table 19.5 Subacute Encephalitis

Causative Organism(s)	*Toxoplasma gondii*	Subacute sclerosing panencephalitis	Prions
Most Common Modes of Transmission	Vehicle (meat) or fecal-oral	Persistence of measles virus	CJD = direct/parenteral contact with infected tissue; or inherited vCJD = vehicle (meat, parenteral)
Virulence Factors	Intracellular growth	Cell fusion, evasion of immune system	Avoidance of host immune response
Culture/Diagnosis	Serological detection of IgM, culture, histology	EEGs, MRI, serology (Ab versus measles virus)	Biopsy, image of brain
Prevention	Personal hygiene, food hygiene	None	Avoiding tissue
Treatment	Pyrimethamine and/or leucovorin and/or sulfadiazine	None	None
Distinctive Features	Subacute, slower development of disease	History of measles	Long incubation period; fast progression once it begins

▶ Causative Agent of CJD

The transmissible agent in CJD is a prion. In some forms of the disease, it involved the transformation of a normal host protein (called PrP), a protein that is supposed to function to help the brain develop normally, and that has recently been found to protect against Alzheimer's disease. vCJD involves a mutation that alters the structure of this protein. Once this happens, the abnormal PrP itself becomes catalytic and able to spontaneously convert other normal human PrP proteins into the abnormal form. This becomes a self-propagating chain reaction that creates a massive accumulation of altered PrP, leading to plaques, spongiform damage (that is, holes in the brain), and severe loss of brain function.

Using the term **transmissible agent** may be a bit misleading, however, as some cases of CJD arise through genetic mutation of the *PrP* gene, which can be a heritable trait. So it seems that although one can acquire a defective PrP protein via transmission, one can also have an altered *PrP* gene passed on through heredity. It is thought that 10% to 15% of CJD cases are inherited in this way. They are termed familial CJD. Another form of CJD is termed sporadic CJD, which is the most mysterious and the most common. Up to 85% of CJD cases are of this type.

Prions are incredibly hardy "pathogens." They are highly resistant to chemicals, radiation, and heat. They can withstand prolonged autoclaving.

▶ Pathogenesis and Virulence Factors

Autopsies of the brain of CJD patients reveal spongiform lesions as well as tangled protein fibers (neurofibrillary tangles) and enlarged astroglial cells (**figure 19.14**). These changes affect the gray matter of the CNS and seem to be caused by the massive accumulation of altered PrP, which may be toxic to neurons. The altered PrPs apparently stimulate no host immune response.

(a)

(b)

Figure 19.14 The microscopic effects of spongiform encephalopathy.   (a) Normal cerebral cortex section, showing neurons and glial cells. (b) Sectioned cortex in CJD patient shows numerous round holes, producing a "spongy" appearance. This destroys brain architecture and causes massive loss of neurons and glial cells.

▶ Transmission and Epidemiology

Direct or indirect contact with infected brain tissue or cerebrospinal fluid has been thought to be necessary for prion transmission. Familial CJD and sporadic CJD are most common in elderly people.

In the late 1990s, it became apparent that humans were contracting a variant form of CJD (vCJD) after ingesting meat from cattle that had been afflicted by bovine spongiform encephalopathy. Presumably meat products had been contaminated with fluid or tissues infected with the prion. Cases of this disease have centered around Great Britain, where many cows were found to have BSE. As of late 2009, a total of 217 people worldwide have contracted the disease, 170 of them in the United Kingdom. There have been 3 cases in the United States, two of which are thought to have been picked up during travel to the United Kingdom. The median age at death of patients with vCJD is 28 years. In contrast, the median age at death of patients with other forms of CJD is 68 years.

Health care professionals should be aware of the possibility of CJD in patients, especially when surgical procedures are performed, as cases have been reported of transmission of CJD via contaminated surgical instruments. Due to the heat and chemical resistance of prions, normal disinfection and sterilization procedures are usually not sufficient to eliminate them from instruments and surfaces. The latest CDC guidelines for handling of CJD patients in a health care environment should be consulted. CJD has also been transmitted through corneal grafts and administration of contaminated human growth hormone. In 2003, a British patient died of CJD after receiving a blood transfusion in 1996 from a donor who had CJD. Experiments suggest that vCJD seems to be more transmissible through blood than classic CJD. For that reason, blood donation programs screen for possible exposure to BSE by asking about travel and residence history.

▶ Culture and Diagnosis

It is very difficult to diagnose CJD. Definitive diagnosis requires examination of biopsied brain or nervous tissue, and this procedure is usually considered too risky because of both the trauma induced in the patient and the undesirability of contaminating surgical instruments and operating rooms. Electroencephalograms and magnetic resonance imaging can provide important clues. A new test to distinguish abnormally folded proteins from correctly folded proteins may yield improved diagnostics for cattle very soon and within a few years for humans. The tests can only be performed after death, however.

▶ Prevention and/or Treatment

Prevention of this disease relies on avoiding infected tissues. Avoiding vCJD entails not ingesting tainted meats. No known treatment exists for either form of CJD, and patients inevitably die. Medical intervention focuses on easing symptoms and making the patient as comfortable as possible (see Disease Table 19.5).

Rabies

Rabies is a slow, progressive zoonotic disease characterized by a fatal encephalitis. It is so distinctive in its pathogenesis and its symptoms that we discuss it separately from the other encephalitides. It is distributed nearly worldwide, except for perhaps two dozen countries that have remained rabies-free by practicing rigorous animal control.

▶ Signs and Symptoms

The average incubation period of rabies is 1 to 2 months or more, depending on the wound site, its severity, and the inoculation dose. The incubation period is shorter in facial, scalp, or neck wounds because of closer proximity to the brain. The prodromal phase begins with fever, nausea, vomiting, headache, fatigue, and other nonspecific symptoms.

In the form of rabies termed *"furious,"* the first acute signs of neurological involvement are periods of agitation, disorientation, seizures, and twitching. Spasms in the neck and pharyngeal muscles lead to severe pain upon swallowing, leading to a symptom known as **hydrophobia** (fear of water). Throughout this phase, the patient is fully coherent and alert. With the *"dumb"* form of rabies, a patient is not hyperactive but is paralyzed, disoriented, and stuporous. Ultimately, both forms progress to the coma phase, resulting in death from cardiac or respiratory arrest. Until recently, humans were never known to survive rabies. But a handful of patients have recovered in recent years after receiving intensive, long-term treatment.

▶ Causative Agent

The rabies virus is in the family Rhabdoviridae, genus *Lyssavirus.* The particles of this virus have a distinctive bulletlike appearance, round on one end and flat on the other. Additional features are a helical nucleocapsid and spikes that protrude through the envelope **(figure 19.15).** The family con-

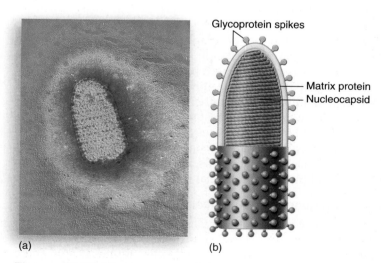

(a)   (b)

Figure 19.15 The structure of the rabies virus. **(a)** Color-enhanced virion shows internal serrations, which represent the tightly coiled nucleocapsid. **(b)** A schematic model of the virus, showing its major features.

tains about 60 different viruses, but only the rabies *Lyssavirus* infects humans.

▶ Pathogenesis and Virulence Factors

Infection with rabies virus typically begins when an infected animal's saliva enters a puncture site. The virus occasionally is inhaled or inoculated through the membranes of the eye. The rabies virus remains up to a week at the trauma site, where it multiplies. The virus then gradually enters nerve endings and advances toward the ganglia, spinal cord, and brain. Viral multiplication throughout the brain is eventually followed by migration to such diverse sites as the eye, heart, skin, and oral cavity. The infection cycle is completed when the virus replicates in the salivary gland and is shed into the saliva. Clinical rabies proceeds through several distinct stages that almost inevitably end in death, unless vaccination is performed before symptoms begin.

Scientists have discovered that virulence is associated with an envelope glycoprotein that seems to give the virus its ability to spread in the CNS and to invade certain types of neural cells.

▶ Transmission and Epidemiology

The primary reservoirs of the virus are wild mammals such as canines, skunks, raccoons, badgers, cats, and bats that can spread the infection to domestic dogs and cats. Both wild and domestic mammals can spread the disease to humans through bites, scratches, and inhalation of droplets. The annual worldwide total for human rabies is estimated at about 55,000 cases, but only a tiny number of these cases occur in the United States. Most U.S. cases of rabies occur in wild animals (about 6,000 to 7,000 cases per year), while dog rabies has declined **(figure 19.16)**.

The epidemiology of animal rabies in the United States varies. The most common wild animal reservoir host has changed from foxes to skunks to raccoons. Regional differences in the dominant reservoir also occur. Rats, skunks, and bobcats are the most common carriers of rabies in California, raccoons are the predominant carriers in the East, and coyotes dominate in Texas.

In 2004, the first cases of rabies in recipients of donated organs occurred. The lungs, kidneys, and liver of a man were donated to four patients; three of them died of rabies (the fourth died of surgical complications). The virus has previously been transmitted through cornea transplants.

▶ Culture and Diagnosis

When symptoms appear after an attack by a rabid animal, the disease is readily diagnosed. But the diagnosis can be obscured when contact with an infected animal is not clearly defined or when symptoms are absent or delayed. Anxiety, agitation, and depression can pose as a psychoneurosis; muscle spasms resemble tetanus; and encephalitis with convulsions and paralysis mimics a number of other viral infections. Often the disease is diagnosed only at autopsy. The direct fluorescent antibody test is the standard for post-mortem identification.

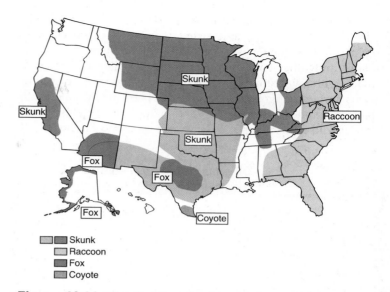

Figure 19.16 Distribution of rabies in the United States. Rabies is found in 10 distinct geographic areas. In each area, a particular animal is the reservoir as illustrated by four different colors. Not shown is the occurrence of insectivorous bats that cause sporadic cases of rabies in wild animals throughout the country.

Diagnosis before death requires multiple tests. Reverse transcription PCR is used with saliva samples but must be accompanied by detection of antibodies to the virus in serum or spinal fluid. Skin biopsies are also used.

▶ Prevention and Treatment

A bite from a wild or stray animal demands assessment of the animal, meticulous care of the wound, and a specific treatment regimen. A wild mammal, especially a skunk, raccoon, fox, or coyote that bites without provocation, is presumed to be rabid, and therapy is immediately begun. If the animal is captured, brain samples and other tissue are examined for verification of rabies. Healthy domestic animals are observed closely for signs of disease and sometimes quarantined. Preventive therapy is initiated if any signs of rabies appear.

Rabies is one of the few infectious diseases for which a combination of passive and active postexposure immunization is indicated (and successful). Initially the wound is infused with human rabies immune globulin (HRIG) to impede the spread of the virus, and globulin is also injected intramuscularly to provide immediate systemic protection. A full course of vaccination is started simultaneously. The current vaccine of choice is the **human diploid cell vaccine (HDCV).** This potent inactivated vaccine is cultured in human embryonic fibroblasts. The routine postexposure vaccination entails intramuscular or intradermal injection on the 1st, 3rd, 7th, 14th, 28th, and 60th days, with two additional boosters. Sometimes putting a patient, in whom disease has already manifested, in a drug-induced coma and on ventilator support can save his or her life. High-risk groups such as veterinarians, animal handlers, laboratory personnel, and travelers should receive three doses to protect against possible exposure. A DNA vaccine for rabies is in development.

Control measures such as vaccination of domestic animals, elimination of strays, and strict quarantine practices have helped reduce the virus reservoir. In recent years, the United States and other countries have utilized a live oral vaccine made with a vaccinia virus that carries the gene for the rabies virus surface antigen. The vaccine has been incorporated into bait (sometimes peanut butter sandwiches!) placed in the habitats of wild reservoir species such as skunks and raccoons.

Disease Table 19.6 Rabies

Causative Organism(s)	Rabies virus
Most Common Modes of Transmission	Parenteral (bite trauma), droplet contact
Virulence Factors	Envelope glycoprotein
Culture/Diagnosis	RT-PCR of saliva; Ab detection of serum or CSF; skin biopsy
Prevention	HDCV—inactivated vaccine
Treatment	Postexposure passive and active immunization; induced coma and ventilator support

Poliomyelitis

Poliomyelitis (poh"-lee-oh'my"-eh'ly'tis) (polio) is an acute enteroviral infection of the spinal cord that can cause neuromuscular paralysis. Because it often affects small children, in the past it was called infantile paralysis **(Insight 19.4).** No civilization or culture has escaped the devastation of polio. The efforts of a WHO campaign have significantly reduced the global incidence of polio. It was the campaign's goal to eradicate all of the remaining wild polioviruses by 2000, and then by 2005. It didn't happen. Eventually billionaire Bill Gates got involved and contributed $700 million to help eradicate the disease. During the course of 2009 it rippled through many countries that had previously been declared polio-free.

▶ Signs and Symptoms

Most infections are contained as short-term, mild viremia. Some persons develop mild nonspecific symptoms of fever, headache, nausea, sore throat, and myalgia. If the viremia persists, viruses can be carried to the central nervous system through its blood supply. The virus then spreads along specific pathways in the spinal cord and brain. Being **neurotropic,** the virus infiltrates the motor neurons of the anterior horn of the spinal cord, although it can also attack spinal ganglia, cranial nerves, and motor nuclei. Nonparalytic disease involves the invasion but not the destruction of nervous tissue. It gives rise to muscle pain and spasm, meningeal inflammation, and vague hypersensitivity.

In paralytic disease, invasion of motor neurons causes various degrees of flaccid paralysis over a period of a few hours to several days. Depending on the level of damage to motor neurons, paralysis of the muscles of the legs, abdomen, back, intercostals, diaphragm, pectoral girdle, and bladder can result. In rare cases of **bulbar poliomyelitis,** the brain stem, medulla, or even cranial nerves are affected. This situation leads to loss of control of cardiorespiratory regulatory centers, requiring mechanical respirators. In time, the unused muscles begin to atrophy, growth is slowed, and severe deformities of the trunk and limbs develop. Common sites of deformities are the spine, shoulder, hips, knees, and feet. Because motor function but not sensation is compromised, the crippled limbs are often very painful.

In recent times, a condition called post-polio syndrome (PPS) has been diagnosed in long-term survivors of childhood infection. PPS manifests as a progressive muscle deterioration that develops in about 25% to 50% of patients several decades after their original polio attack.

▶ Causative Agent

The poliovirus is in the family Picornaviridae, genus *Enterovirus*—named for its small **(pico)** size and its RNA core **(figure 19.17).** It is nonenveloped and nonsegmented. The naked capsid of the virus confers chemical stability and resistance to acid, bile, and detergents. By this means, the virus survives

Capsid

RNA core

(a)

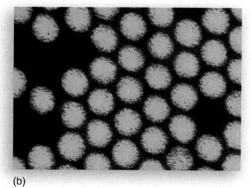

(b)

Figure 19.17 Typical structure of a picornavirus.
(a) A poliovirus, a type of picornavirus that is one of the simplest and smallest viruses (30 nm). It consists of an icosahedral capsid shell around a molecule of RNA. **(b)** A crystalline mass of stacked poliovirus particles in an infected host cell (300,000×).

the gastric environment and other harsh conditions, which contributes to its ease of transmission.

▶ Pathogenesis and Virulence Factors

After being ingested, polioviruses adsorb to receptors of mucosal cells in the oropharynx and intestine **(figure 19.18)**. Here, they multiply in the mucosal epithelia and lymphoid tissue. Multiplication results in large numbers of viruses being shed into the throat and feces, and some of them leak into the blood. The sequence of events just described then ensues. Depending on the number of viruses in the blood and their duration of stay there, an individual may exhibit no symptoms, mild nonspecific symptoms such as fever or short-term muscle pain, or devastating paralysis **(figure 19.19)**. Scientists studying poliovirus virulence focus on components of the virus that allow attachment and penetration of host cells.

▶ Transmission and Epidemiology

Sporadic cases of polio can break out at any time of the year, but its incidence is more pronounced during the summer and

Figure 19.19 Possible outcomes of poliovirus infection. The vast majority of poliovirus infections are asymptomatic; only a very small percentage cause paralytic polio.

fall. The virus is passed within the population through food, water, hands, objects contaminated with feces, and mechanical vectors. Although the 20th century saw a very large rise in paralytic polio cases, it was also the century during which effective vaccines were developed. The infection was eliminated from the Western Hemisphere in the late 20th century. Sadly, it is proving extremely difficulty to eradicate it from the developing world.

▶ Culture and Diagnosis

Poliovirus can usually be isolated by inoculating cell cultures with stool or throat washings in the early part of the disease. Viruses are sometimes then subjected to RNA fingerprinting to determine if they are wild strains or vaccine strains. The stage of the patient's infection can also be demonstrated by testing serum samples for the type and amount of antibody.

▶ Prevention and Treatment

Treatment of polio rests largely on alleviating pain and suffering. During the acute phase, muscle spasm, headache, and associated discomfort can be alleviated by pain-relieving drugs. Respiratory failure may require artificial ventilation maintenance. Prompt physical therapy to diminish crippling deformities and to retrain muscles is recommended after the acute febrile phase subsides.

The mainstay of polio prevention is vaccination as early in life as possible, usually in four doses starting at about 2 months of age. Adult candidates for immunization are travelers and members of the armed forces. The two forms of vaccine currently in use are inactivated poliovirus vaccine (IPV), developed by Jonas Salk in 1954, and oral poliovirus vaccine (OPV), developed by Albert Sabin in the 1960s. Both are prepared from animal cell cultures and are trivalent (combinations of the three serotypes of the poliovirus). Both vaccines are effective, but one may be favored over the other under certain circumstances.

For many years, the oral vaccine was used in the United States because it is easily administered by mouth, but it is not free of medical complications. It contains an attenuated virus that can multiply in vaccinated people and be spread to others. In very rare instances, the attenuated virus reverts to a neurovirulent strain that causes disease rather than protects against it. For this reason, IPV is the only vaccine used in the United States.

Figure 19.18 The stages of infection and pathogenesis of poliomyelitis. **(a)** First, the virus is ingested and carried to the throat and intestinal mucosa. **(b)** The virus then multiplies in the tonsils. Small numbers of viruses escape to the regional lymph nodes and blood. **(c)** The viruses are further amplified and cross into certain nerve cells of the spinal column and central nervous system. **(d)** Last, the intestine actively sheds viruses.

INSIGHT 19.4   Polio

Polio is a disease that in some ways defined the 20th century. Large epidemics of paralytic poliomyelitis started appearing around 1916 in the United States. Waves of epidemics continued throughout the first half of the 1900s. The disease seemed to strike in summer and early fall, and during those times children were cautioned not to drink from public water fountains and were not allowed to have slumber parties, because their parents feared polio so much. It was many years before scientists understood how the virus was transmitted, how it traveled in the body, and why it started causing a devastating form of paralysis in the early 1900s, because it had clearly been around for hundreds, if not thousands, of years.

Scientists eventually discovered that the rise in paralytic cases—dubbed **infantile paralysis** because it affected mainly small children—was probably due to *increased* public sanitation and hygiene. The poliovirus is spread through contaminated vehicles and through the fecal-oral route. During earlier times of poor sanitation, nearly everyone was exposed to the virus at a very early age—before the age of 6 months. Because babies still enjoy passive protection from maternal antibodies during this period, the poliovirus was kept in check. Most cases were confined to the gastrointestinal tract or limited to mild viremias. When these children were later exposed, they were protected by their naturally acquired active immunity.

Once water sources became more pure and the importance of personal hygiene and hand washing was understood, babies often escaped exposure for months or years. When they did encounter the virus, they had to battle it on their own; maternal antibodies were long gone. Many of these infections progressed into the paralytic form of the disease memorialized by so many photographs of children in iron lungs and with leg braces and crutches.

In 1921, a young adult became ill with a disease that was assumed to be polio—and his condition would change the history of the disease forever. The young man was Franklin Delano Roosevelt, and he would go on to become president of the United States in 1932. In 1938, he founded an organization called the National Foundation for Infantile Paralysis, putting his former law partner Basil O'Connor in charge. Every year, the Foundation held lavish fund-raising events on FDR's birthday, called "The Birthday Balls." Another fund-raising event was called the March of Dimes, which began with a nationwide call to send dimes to the president. Later it evolved into an event organized by mothers. On a single night, mothers would "march" through their neighborhoods, going door to door collecting donations from homes who

signaled their willingness to contribute by leaving their porch lights on. Hundreds of thousands of dollars were raised this way. The money went toward treatment and support of victims of polio, as well as toward research into a vaccine.

In 1954, massive field trials of an experimental killed virus vaccine developed by Jonas Salk were conducted. When it was deemed to be effective, nationwide vaccination was begun. By 1962, the Salk vaccine had been replaced by Albert Sabin's live attenuated vaccine, which was administered orally. And by 1964 the annual case rate had fallen from a high of 58,000 in 1952 to only 121. The last case of polio in the United States occurred in 1979; the World Health Organization is still trying to eradicate polio from the rest of the world.

Ironically, some modern scientists have suggested that FDR did not in fact have polio but was a victim of Guillain-Barré syndrome (GBS), a neuromuscular syndrome that can be brought on by viral or bacterial infection or by vaccination. Diagnosing either disease was very difficult in the 1920s (indeed, the existence of GBS as a distinct syndrome was still being debated in the 1920s), and FDR's paralysis was attributed to the poliovirus. But for thousands of polio victims who benefited from the president's commitment to their cause—and for a world that benefited from the vaccines—it hardly matters whether it was truly polio or not.

Disease Table 19.7   Poliomyelitis

Causative Organism(s)	Poliovirus
Most Common Modes of Transmission	Fecal-oral, vehicle
Virulence Factors	Attachment mechanisms
Culture/Diagnosis	Viral culture, serology
Prevention	Live attenuated (developing world) or inactivated vaccine (developed world)
Treatment	None, palliative, supportive

Figure 19.21 Neonatal tetanus. Baby with neonatal tetanus, showing spastic paralysis of the paravertebral muscles, which locks the back into a rigid, arched position. Also note the abnormal flexion of the arms and legs.

Figure 19.20 *Clostridium tetani.* Its typical tennis racket morphology is created by terminal spores that swell the end of the cell (170×).

Tetanus

Tetanus is a neuromuscular disease whose alternate name, lockjaw, refers to an early effect of the disease on the jaw muscle. The etiologic agent, *Clostridium tetani,* is a common resident of cultivated soil and the gastrointestinal tracts of animals. It is a gram-positive, spore-forming rod. The endospores it produces often swell the vegetative cell **(figure 19.20).** Spores are produced only under anaerobic conditions.

▶ Signs and Symptoms

C. tetani releases a powerful neurotoxin, **tetanospasmin**, that binds to target sites on peripheral motor neurons, spinal cord and brain, and in the sympathetic nervous system. The toxin acts by blocking the inhibition of muscle contraction. Without inhibition of contraction, the muscles contract uncontrollably, resulting in spastic paralysis. The first symptoms are clenching of the jaw, followed in succession by extreme arching of the back, flexion of the arms, and extension of the legs **(figure 19.21).** Lockjaw confers the bizarre appearance of *risus sardonicus* (sardonic grin), which looks eerily as though the person is smiling **(figure 19.22).** Death most often occurs due to paralysis of the respiratory muscles and respiratory arrest.

(a) (b) (c)

Figure 19.22 The events in tetanus. **(a)** After traumatic injury, bacteria infecting the local tissues secrete tetanospasmin, which is absorbed by the peripheral axons and is carried to the target neurons in the spinal column. **(b)** In the spinal cord, the toxin attaches to the junctions of regulatory neurons that inhibit inappropriate contraction. Released from inhibition, the muscles, even opposing members of a muscle group, receive constant stimuli and contract uncontrollably. **(c)** Muscles contract spasmodically, without regard to regulatory mechanisms or conscious control. Note the clenched jaw typical of *risus sardonicus.*

▶ Pathogenesis and Virulence Factors

The mere presence of spores in a wound is not sufficient to initiate infection because the bacterium is unable to invade damaged tissues readily. It is also a strict anaerobe, and the spores cannot become established unless tissues at the site of the wound are necrotic and poorly supplied with blood, conditions that favor germination.

As the vegetative cells grow, various metabolic products are released into the infection site, including the tetanospasmin toxin. The toxin spreads to nearby motor nerve endings in the injured tissue, binds to them, and travels via axons to the ventral horns of the spinal cord (see figure 19.22). The toxin blocks the release of neurotransmitter, and only a small amount is required to initiate the symptoms. The incubation period varies from 4 to 10 days, and shorter incubation periods signify a more serious condition.

The muscle contractions are intermittent and extremely painful, and they may be forceful enough to break bones, especially the vertebrae. The fatality rate, ranging from 10% to 70%, is highest in cases involving delayed medical attention, a short incubation time, or head wounds. Full recovery requires a few weeks, and no permanent damage to the muscles usually remains.

▶ Transmission and Epidemiology

Spores usually enter the body through accidental puncture wounds, burns, umbilical stumps, frostbite, and crushed body parts. The incidence of tetanus is low in North America. Most cases occur among geriatric patients and intravenous drug abusers. The incidence of neonatal tetanus—predominantly the result of an infected umbilical stump or circumcision—is higher in cultures that apply dung, ashes, or mud to these sites to arrest bleeding or as a customary ritual. The disease accounts for several hundred thousand infant deaths a year worldwide.

Prevention and Treatment

Tetanus treatment is aimed at deterring the degree of toxemia and infection and maintaining patient homeostasis. A patient with a clinical appearance suggestive of tetanus should immediately receive antitoxin therapy with human tetanus immune globulin (TIG). Although the antitoxin inactivates circulating toxin, it will not counteract the effect of toxin already bound to neurons. Other methods include thoroughly cleansing and removing the afflicted tissue, controlling infection with penicillin or tetracycline, and administering muscle relaxants. The patient may require the assistance of a respirator, and a **tracheotomy**[1] is sometimes performed to prevent respiratory complications such as aspiration pneumonia or lung collapse.

Tetanus is one of the world's most preventable diseases, chiefly because of an effective vaccine containing tetanus toxoid. The recommended vaccination series for 1- to 3-month-old babies consists of three injections given 2 months apart,

1. The surgical formation of an air passage by perforation of the trachea.

followed by booster doses about 1 and 4 years later. Children thus immunized probably have protection for 10 years. Additional protection against neonatal tetanus may be achieved by vaccinating pregnant women, whose antibodies will be passed to the fetus. Toxoid should also be given to injured persons who have never been immunized, have not completed the series, or whose last booster was received more than 10 years previously. The vaccine can be given simultaneously with passive TIG immunization to achieve immediate as well as long-term protection.

Disease Table 19.8 Tetanus

Causative Organism(s)	*Clostridium tetani*
Most Common Modes of Transmission	Parenteral, direct contact
Virulence Factors	Tetanospasm exotoxin
Culture/Diagnosis	Symptomatic
Prevention	Tetanus toxoid immunization
Treatment	Combination of passive antitoxin and tetanus toxoid active immunization, supportive

Botulism

Botulism is an **intoxication** (that is, caused by an exotoxin) associated with eating poorly preserved foods, although it can also occur as a true infection. Until recent times, it was relatively common and frequently fatal, but modern techniques of food preservation and medical treatment have reduced both its incidence and its fatality rate. However, botulism is a common cause of death in livestock that have grazed on contaminated food and in aquatic birds that have eaten decayed vegetation. In the United States, there are between 10 and 30 outbreaks of human botulism a year.

▶ Signs and Symptoms

There are three major forms of botulism, distinguished by their means of transmission and the population they affect. These are *food-borne botulism* (in children and adults), *infant botulism*, and *wound botulism*. Food-borne botulism in children and adults is an intoxication resulting from the ingestion of preformed toxin; the other two types of botulism are infections that are followed by the entrance of an exotoxin called **botulinum toxin** into the bloodstream (that is, toxemia). The symptoms are largely the same in all three forms, however. From the circulatory system, the toxin travels to its principal site of action, the neuromuscular junctions of skeletal muscles **(figure 19.23)**. The effect of botulinum is to prevent the release of the neurotransmitter substance, acetylcholine, that initiates the signal for muscle contraction. The usual time

Motor neuron end plate

Muscle cell membrane

Synapse

(a)

Vacuole

Acetylcholine

(b)

Presynaptic membrane

Botulin

(c)

Figure 19.23 The physiological effects of botulism toxin (botulinum). **(a)** The relationship between the motor neuron and the muscle at the neuromuscular junction. **(b)** In the normal state, acetylcholine released at the synapse crosses to the muscle and creates an impulse that stimulates muscle contraction. **(c)** In botulism, the toxin enters the motor end plate and attaches to the presynaptic membrane, where it blocks release of the chemical. This prevents impulse transmission and keeps the muscle from contracting. This causes flaccid paralysis.

before onset of symptoms is 12 to 72 hours, depending on the size of the dose. Neuromuscular symptoms first affect the muscles of the head and include double vision, difficulty in swallowing, and dizziness, but there is no sensory or mental lapse. Although nausea and vomiting can occur at an early stage, they are not common. Later symptoms are descending muscular paralysis and respiratory compromise. In the past, death resulted from respiratory arrest, but mechanical respirators have reduced the fatality rate to about 10%.

▶ **Causative Agent**

Clostridium botulinum, like *Clostridium tetani,* is a spore-forming anaerobe that does its damage through the release of an exotoxin. *C. botulinum* commonly inhabits soil and water and occasionally the intestinal tract of animals. It is distributed worldwide but occurs most often in the Northern

Hemisphere. The species has eight distinctly different types (designated A, B, C_α, C_β, D, E, F, and G) that vary in distribution among animals, regions of the world, and types of exotoxin. Human disease is usually associated with types A, B, E, and F, and animal disease with types A, B, C, D, and E.

Both *C. tetani* and *C. botulinum* produce neurotoxins; but tetanospasmin, the toxin made by *C. tetani,* results in spastic paralysis (uncontrolled muscle contraction). In contrast, botulinum, the *C. botulinum* neurotoxin, results in flaccid paralysis, a loss of ability to contract the muscles.

▶ **Pathogenesis and Virulence Factors**

As just described, the symptoms are caused entirely by the exotoxin botulinum.

▶ **Transmission and Epidemiology of Food-Borne Botulism in Children and Adults**

In the United States, the disease is often associated with low-acid vegetables (green beans, corn); fruits; and occasionally meats, fish, and dairy products. Many botulism outbreaks occur in home-processed foods, including canned vegetables, smoked meats, and cheese spreads. The demand for prepackaged convenience foods, such as vacuum-packed cooked vegetables and meats, has created a new source of risk, but most commercially canned foods are held to very high standards of preservation and are only rarely a source of botulism.

Several factors in food processing can lead to botulism. Spores are present on the vegetables or meat at the time of gathering and are difficult to remove completely. When contaminated food is put in jars and steamed in a pressure cooker that does not reach reliable pressure and temperature, some spores survive (botulinum spores are highly heat-resistant). At the same time, the pressure is sufficient to evacuate the air and create anaerobic conditions. Storage of the jars at room temperature favors spore germination and vegetative growth, and one of the products of the cell's metabolism is botulinum, the most potent microbial toxin known.

Bacterial growth may not be evident in the appearance of the jar or can or in the food's taste or texture, and only minute amounts of toxin may be present. Botulism is never transmitted person-to-person.

▶ **Transmission and Epidemiology of Infant Botulism**

Infant botulism was first described in the late 1970s in children between the ages of 2 weeks and 6 months who had ingested spores. It is currently the most common type of botulism in the United States, with approximately 75 cases reported annually. The exact food source is not always known, although raw honey has been implicated in some cases, and the spores are common in dust and soil. Apparently, the immature state of the neonatal intestine and microbial biota allows the spores to gain a foothold, germinate, and give off neurotoxin. As in adults, babies exhibit flaccid paralysis, usually manifested as a weak sucking response, generalized loss of tone (the "floppy baby syndrome"), and respiratory complications. Although adults can also ingest botulinum spores

INSIGHT 19.5   Botox: Anti-Wrinkles, Anti-Cancer

Every year, millions of people pay good money (and lots of it) to have one of the most potent toxins on earth injected into their faces. The toxin, of course, is Botox, short for botulinum toxin, and the story of how these injections came to be the most popular cosmetic procedure in the United States is a fascinating one.

Scientists have long known that death from *Clostridium botulinum* infection results from paralysis of the respiratory muscles. In fact, researchers had even determined that botulinum toxin causes death by interfering with the release of acetylcholine, a neurotransmitter that causes the contraction of skeletal muscles. The trick was finding a practical application for this knowledge.

In 1989 Botox was first approved to treat cross-eyes and uncontrollable blinking, two conditions resulting from the inappropriate contracting of muscles around the eye. Success in this first arena led to Botox treatment for a variety of neurological disorders that cause painful contraction of neck and shoulder muscles. A much wider use of Botox occurred in so-called "off label" uses, as doctors found that injecting facial muscles with the toxin inhibited contraction of these muscles and consequent wrinkling of the overlying skin. The "lunch-hour facelift" went over exactly as most people would imagine, becoming the most popular cosmetic procedure even before

winning official FDA approval (which it did in 2002). In a surprise twist, patients undergoing Botox treatment for wrinkles reported fewer headaches, especially migraines. Clinical trials have shown this result to be widespread and reproducible, but the exact mechanism by which Botox works to prevent headaches is unknown.

There are, of course, potential drawbacks to cosmetic use of Botox. The most common problem arising from Botox treatment is excessive paralysis of facial muscles, resulting from poorly targeted injections. Depending on the site of the injection, results such as drooping eyelids, facial paralysis, slurred speech, and drooling are possible. Even if the treatment works perfectly, the wrinkle-free visage is a result of muscle paralysis, meaning that patients are often unable to move their eyebrows or in some cases to frown or squint.

Now Botox seems to be getting back to its roots as a therapeutic tool (though the use of cosmetic Botox shows no signs of abating). New therapeutic uses for the toxin are being discovered frequently. Most recently scientists found a way to engineer the toxin so that it would target epithelial cells instead of neural cells. This form of Botox is able to shut down the production of excessive mucus in asthma, and the production of cytokines that can lead to cancer.

Case File 19   *Continuing the Case*

The cases of botulism diagnosed in the Indiana couple and the Texas children were the food-borne variety. This type of botulism is most often associated with home-processed foods. In an anaerobic environment with low acidity (pH > 4.6) and a temperature greater than 3.9°C (39.0°F), the endospores may germinate and produce botulin.

Commercially processed foods, such as the chili sauce implicated in this case file, are typically processed in a retort, a large chamber where the food is subjected to a combination of steam and high pressure that reliably kills endospores. Put into practice in the 1920s, retort canning has nearly eliminated the risk of acquiring botulism by consuming commercially processed food. Nevertheless, a well-rinsed can of Castleberry's Hot Dog Chili Sauce recovered from the recycling bin of the Indiana couple and the unopened can of chili sauce taken from the Texas house contained production codes indicating that they had been processed at the same facility within a few hours of one another. The knowledge that both cans came from the same location indicated a common source epidemic, in which each occurrence of an illness can be traced to the same source. An investigation of the processing plant was in order.

in contaminated vegetables and other foods, the adult intestinal tract normally inhibits this sort of infection.

▶ Transmission and Epidemiology of Wound Botulism

Perhaps three or four cases of wound botulism occur each year in the United States. In this form of the disease, spores enter a wound or puncture, much as in tetanus, but the symptoms are similar to those of food-borne botulism. Increased cases of this form of botulism are being reported in intravenous drug users as a result of needle puncture.

▶ Culture and Diagnosis

Diagnostic standards are slightly different for the three different presentations of botulism. In food-borne botulism, some laboratories attempt to identify the toxin in the offending food. Alternatively, if multiple patients present with the same symptoms after ingesting the same food, a presumptive diagnosis can be made. The cultivation of *C. botulinum* in feces is considered confirmation of the diagnosis since the carrier rate is very low.

In infant botulism, finding the toxin or the organism in the feces confirms the diagnosis. In wound botulism, the toxin should be demonstrated in the serum, or the organism should be grown from the wound. Because minute amounts of the toxin are highly dangerous, laboratory testing should only be performed by experienced personnel. A suspected case of botulism should trigger a phone call to the state health department or the CDC before proceeding with diagnosis or treatment.

▶ Prevention and Treatment

The CDC maintains a supply of type A, B, and E trivalent horse antitoxin, which, when administered early, can prevent the worst outcomes of the disease. Patients are also managed with respiratory and cardiac support systems. In all cases, hospitalization is required and recovery takes weeks. There is an overall 5% mortality rate.

Disease Table 19.9 Botulism

Causative Organism(s)	*Clostridium botulinum*
Most Common Modes of Transmission	Vehicle (food-borne toxin, airborne organism); direct contact (wound); parenteral (injection)
Virulence Factors	Botulinum exotoxin
Culture/Diagnosis	Culture of organism; demonstration of toxin
Prevention	Food hygiene; toxoid immunization available for laboratory professionals
Treatment	Antitoxin, supportive care

African Sleeping Sickness

This condition is caused by *Trypanosoma brucei,* a member of the protozoan group known as hemoflagellates because of their propensity to live in the blood and tissues of the human host. The disease, also called trypanosomiasis, has greatly affected the living conditions of Africans since ancient times. Today at least 50 million people are at risk, and 50,000 to 70,000 new cases occur each year. It imposes an additional hardship when it attacks domestic and wild mammals.

▶ Signs and Symptoms

Trypanosomiasis affects the lymphatics and areas surrounding blood vessels. Usually a long asymptomatic period precedes onset of symptoms. Symptoms include intermittent fever, enlarged spleen, swollen lymph nodes, and joint pain. There are two variants of the disease, caused by two different subspecies of the protozoan. In both forms, the central nervous system is affected, the initial signs being personality and behavioral changes that progress to lassitude and sleep disturbances. The disease is commonly called **sleeping sickness,** but in fact, uncontrollable sleepiness occurs primarily in the day and is followed by sleeplessness at night. Signs of advancing neurological deterioration are muscular tremors, shuffling gait, slurred speech, seizures, and local paralysis. Death results from coma, secondary infections, or heart damage.

▶ Causative Agent

Trypanosoma brucei is a flagellated protozoan, an obligate parasite that is spread by a blood-sucking insect called the tsetse fly, which serves as its intermediate host. It shares a complicated life cycle with other hemoflagellates. In chapter 5, we first described the trypanosome life cycle using the example of *T. cruzi,* the agent that causes Chagas disease.

▶ Transmission and Epidemiology

The cycle begins when a tsetse fly becomes infected after feeding on an infected reservoir host, such as a wild animal (antelope, pig, lion, hyena), domestic animal (cow, goat), or human **(figure 19.24).** In the fly's gut, the trypanosome multiplies,

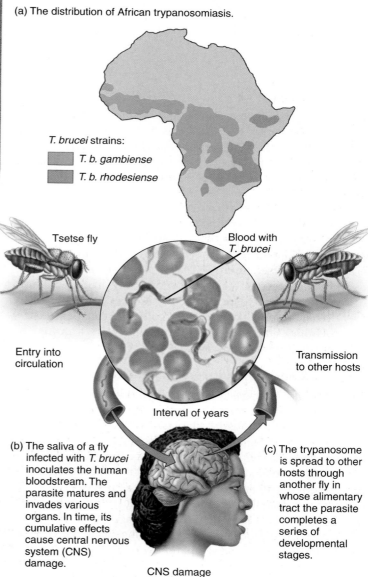

(a) The distribution of African trypanosomiasis.

T. brucei strains:
- T. b. gambiense
- T. b. rhodesiense

Tsetse fly

Blood with T. brucei

Entry into circulation

Transmission to other hosts

Interval of years

(b) The saliva of a fly infected with *T. brucei* inoculates the human bloodstream. The parasite matures and invades various organs. In time, its cumulative effects cause central nervous system (CNS) damage.

CNS damage

(c) The trypanosome is spread to other hosts through another fly in whose alimentary tract the parasite completes a series of developmental stages.

Figure 19.24 The generalized cycle between humans and the tsetse fly vector.

Case File 19 *Wrap-Up*

The U.S. Food and Drug Administration (FDA) initiated an investigation of Castleberry's Food Company on July 17, 2008, after finding that both cans of chili sauce had been manufactured in the same plant and in the same set of retorts. Tests of the facility's canning equipment revealed problems in two of the 100 retort cookers in the plant, such that either the temperature or the pressure was not high enough to destroy endospores. Examination of swollen cans in the plant revealed botulin in 16 out of 17 cans.

Based on the inspection results, a recall was issued not only for chili sauce processed at the plant, but also for 90 other products, including chili, meat, chicken, and dog food, that had been processed in the same set of retorts. Castleberry repaired the damaged cookers, installed backup valves to prevent a recurrence, and trained employees to recognize potential problems in the canning process.

See: CDC. 2009. *MMWR* 56:76769.

migrates to the salivary glands, and develops into the infectious stage. When the fly bites a new host, it releases the large, fully formed stage of the parasite into the wound. At this site, the trypanosome multiplies and produces a sore called the **primary chancre.** From there, the pathogen moves into the lymphatics and the blood (see figure 19.24). The trypanosome can also cross the placenta and damage a developing fetus.

Two variants of sleeping sickness are the Gambian (West African) strain, caused by the subspecies *Trypanosoma brucei gambiense,* and the Rhodesian (East African) strain, caused by *T. b. rhodesiense* (see figure 19.24).

African sleeping sickness occurs only in Sub-Saharan Africa. Tsetse flies exist elsewhere, and it is not known why they do not support *Trypanosoma* in other regions. Cases seen in the United States are only those that were acquired by travelers or emigres from Africa.

▶ Pathogenesis and Virulence Factors

The protozoan manages to flourish in the blood even though it stimulates a strong immune response. The immune response is counteracted by an unusual adaptation of the trypanosome. As soon as the host begins manufacturing IgM antibodies to the trypanosome, surviving organisms change the structure of their surface glycoprotein antigens. This change in specificity (sometimes referred to as an **antigenic shift**) renders the existing IgM ineffective, so that the parasite eludes control and multiplies in the blood. The host responds by producing IgM of a new specificity, but the protozoan changes its antigens again. The host eventually becomes exhausted and overwhelmed by repeated efforts to catch up with this trypanosome masquerade.

▶ Culture and Diagnosis

Trypanosomes are readily demonstrated in blood smears, as well as in spinal fluid or lymph nodes.

▶ Prevention and Treatment

Control of trypanosomiasis in western Africa, where humans are the main reservoir hosts, involves eliminating tsetse flies by applying insecticides, trapping flies, or destroying the shelter and breeding sites. In eastern regions, where cattle herds and large wildlife populations are reservoir hosts, control is less practical because large mammals are the hosts, and flies are less concentrated in specific sites. The antigenic shifting practiced by the trypanosome makes the development of a vaccine very difficult.

Chemotherapy is most successful if administered prior to nervous system involvement. Two drugs are available for the early stages of the disease. Suramin works against *T. b. rhodesiense,* and pentamidine is used for *T. b. gambiense.* Brain infection must be treated with drugs that can cross the blood-brain barrier. One of these is a highly toxic arsenic-based drug called melarsoprol. Another is called eflornithine.

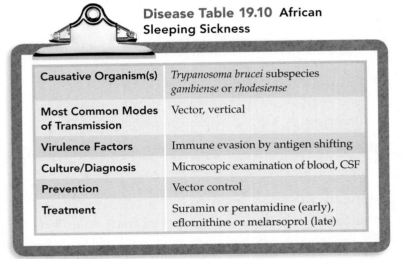

Disease Table 19.10 African Sleeping Sickness

Causative Organism(s)	*Trypanosoma brucei* subspecies *gambiense* or *rhodesiense*
Most Common Modes of Transmission	Vector, vertical
Virulence Factors	Immune evasion by antigen shifting
Culture/Diagnosis	Microscopic examination of blood, CSF
Prevention	Vector control
Treatment	Suramin or pentamidine (early), eflornithine or melarsoprol (late)

19.3 Learning Outcomes—Can You ...

4. ... list the possible causative agents, modes of transmission, virulence factors, diagnostic techniques, and prevention/treatment for meningitis and also for neonatal meningitis?

5. ... identify the most common and also the most deadly of the multiple possible causes of meningitis?

6. ... list the possible causative agents, modes of transmission, virulence factors, diagnostic techniques, and prevention/treatment for diseases most directly involving the brain? These are: meningoencephalitis, encephalitis, and subacute encephalitis.

7. ... identify which encephalitis-causing viruses you should be aware of in your geographical area?

8. ... list the possible causative agents, modes of transmission, virulence factors, diagnostic techniques, and prevention/treatment for other diseases in the nervous system? These are: rabies, poliomyelitis, tetanus, botulism, and African sleeping sickness.

9. ... explain the difference between the oral polio vaccine and the inactivated polio vaccine and under which circumstances each is appropriate?

▶ **Summing Up**

Taxonomic Organization **Microorganisms Causing Disease in the Nervous System**

Microorganism	Disease	Chapter Location
Gram-positive endospore-forming bacteria		
Clostridium botulinum	Botulism	Botulism, p. 574
Clostridium tetani	Tetanus	Tetanus, p. 573
Gram-positive bacteria		
Streptococcus agalactiae	Neonatal meningitis	Neonatal meningitis, p. 559
Streptococcus pneumoniae	Meningitis	Meningitis, p. 554
Listeria monocytogenes	Meningitis, neonatal meningitis	Meningitis, p. 555
		Neonatal meningitis, p. 558
Gram-negative bacteria		
Escherichia coli	Neonatal meningitis	Neonatal meningitis, p. 560
Haemophilus influenzae	Meningitis	Meningitis, p. 555
Neisseria meningitidis	Meningococcal meningitis	Meningitis, p. 553
DNA viruses		
Herpes simplex virus 1 and 2	Encephalitis	Encephalitis, p. 564
JC virus	Progressive multifocal leukoencephalopathy	Encephalitis, p. 564
RNA viruses		
Arboviruses	Encephalitis	Encephalitis, p. 562
Western equine encephalitis virus, Eastern equine encephalitis virus, California encephalitis virus (California and LaCrosse strains), St. Louis encephalitis virus, West Nile virus		
Measles virus	Subacute sclerosing panencephalitis	Subacute encephalitis, p. 566
Poliovirus	Poliomyelitis	Poliomyelitis, p. 570
Rabies virus	Rabies	Rabies, p. 568
Fungi		
Cryptococcus neoformans	Meningitis	Meningitis, p. 556
Coccidioides immitis	Meningitis	Meningitis, p. 557
Prions		
Creutzfeldt-Jakob prion	Creutzfeldt-Jakob disease	Subacute encephalitis, p. 566
Protozoa		
Acanthamoeba	Meningoencephalitis	Meningoencephalitis, p. 561
Naegleria fowleri	Meningoencephalitis	Meningoencephalitis, p. 561
Toxoplasma gondii	Subacute encephalitis	Subacute encephalitis, p. 565
Trypanosoma brucei subspecies *gambiense* and *rhodesiense*	African sleeping sickness	African sleeping sickness, p. 577

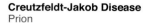

INFECTIOUS DISEASES AFFECTING
The Nervous System

Encephalitis
Arboviruses
Herpes simplex virus 1 or 2
JC virus

Subacute Encephalitis
Toxoplasma gondii
Measles virus
Prions

Rabies
Rabies virus

Tetanus
Clostridium tetani

African Sleeping Sickness
Trypanosoma brucei

Creutzfeldt-Jakob Disease
Prion

Meningoencephalitis
Naegleria fowleri
Acanthamoeba

Meningitis
Neisseria meningitidis
Streptococcus pneumoniae
Haemophilus influenzae
Listeria monocytogenes
Cryptococcus neoformans
Coccidioides immitis
Various viruses

Neonatal Meningitis
Streptococcus agalactiae
Escherichia coli
Listeria monocytogenes

Polio
Poliovirus

Botulism
Clostridium botulinum

Bacteria
Viruses
Protozoa
Fungi
Prions

System Summary Figure 19.25

Chapter Summary

19.1 The Nervous System and Its Defenses

- The nervous system has two parts: the central nervous system (the brain and spinal cord), and the peripheral nervous system (spinal and cranial nerves).
- The soft tissue of the brain and spinal cord is encased within tough casing of three membranes called the *meninges*. The subarachnoid space is filled with a clear serumlike fluid called cerebrospinal fluid (CSF).
- The nervous system is protected by the *blood-brain barrier*, which limits the passage of substances from the bloodstream to the brain.

19.2 Normal Biota of the Nervous System

- At the present time we believe there is no normal biota in either the CNS or PNS.

19.3 Nervous System Diseases Caused by Microorganisms

- **Meningitis:** Inflammation of the meninges. The more serious forms caused by bacteria, often facilitated by coinfection or previous infection with respiratory viruses.
  - *Neisseria meningitidis:* Gram-negative diplococcus, commonly known as the meningococcus; causes most serious form of acute meningitis.
  - *Streptococcus pneumoniae:* Gram-positive coccus; known as the pneumococcus; most frequent cause of community-acquired pneumococcal meningitis.
  - *Haemophilus influenzae:* Cases declined sharply because of vaccination.
  - *Listeria monocytogenes:* Most cases associated with ingesting contaminated dairy products, poultry, and meat.
  - *Cryptococcus neoformans:* Fungus; causes more chronic form of meningitis with more gradual onset of symptoms.
  - *Coccidioides immitis:* True systemic fungal infection; begins with pulmonary infection but can disseminate quickly throughout the body; highest incidence occurs in southwestern United States, Mexico, and parts of Central and South America.
  - Viruses: Viral meningitis very common, particularly in children; 90% are caused by enteroviruses.
- **Neonatal Meningitis:** Usually transmitted by mother in utero or during passage through birth canal. Primary causes in this country are *Streptococcus agalactiae, Escherichia coli,* and *Listeria monocytogenes.*
- **Meningoencephalitis:** Caused mainly by two amoebas, *Naegleria fowleri* and *Acanthamoeba.*
- **Acute Encephalitis:** Usually caused by viral infection. Arboviruses carried by arthropods often responsible. Arboviral encephalitis begins with arthropod bite, release of virus into tissues, and replication in nearby lymphatic tissues.
  - Western Equine Encephalitis (WEE): Occurs sporadically in western United States and Canada; carried by mosquito.
  - Eastern Equine Encephalitis (EEE): Endemic to eastern coast of North America and Canada.

- California Encephalitis: Caused by two different viral strains, the California strain and the LaCrosse strain.
- St. Louis Encephalitis (SLE): May be most common of American viral encephalitides. Appears throughout North, South America; epidemics occur most often in Midwest and South.
- West Nile Encephalitis: West Nile virus is close relative of SLE virus. Emerged in United States in 1999.
- Herpes simplex virus: Herpes simplex type 1 and 2 cause encephalitis in newborns born to HSV-positive mothers, older children and young adults (ages 5 to 30), older adults (over 50 years old).
- JC Virus: Can cause progressive multifocal leukoencephalopathy (PML), particularly in immunocompromised individuals. Fatal infection.
- **Subacute Encephalitis:** Refers to a disease when symptoms take longer to manifest.
  - *Toxoplasma gondii:* Protozoan, causes toxoplasmosis, most common form of subacute encephalitis. Relatively asymptomatic in the healthy; can be severe in immunodeficient people and fetuses.
  - Measles Virus: Can produce subacute sclerosing panencephalitis (SSPE) years after initial measles infection.
  - Prions: Proteinaceous infectious particles containing no genetic material. Cause transmissible spongiform encephalopathies (TSEs), neurodegenerative diseases with long incubation periods but rapid progressions once they begin. Human TSEs are Creutzfeldt-Jakob disease (CJD), Gerstmann-Strussler-Scheinker disease, and fatal familial insomnia.
- **Rabies:** Slow, progressive zoonotic disease characterized by fatal encephalitis. Rabies virus is in the family Rhabdoviridae.
- **Poliomyelitis:** Acute enterovirus infection of spinal cord; can cause neuromuscular paralysis. Two effective vaccines exist: Inactivated Salk poliovirus vaccine (IPV) is the only one used now in the United States; attenuated oral Sabin poliovirus vaccine (OPV) still being used in the developing world.
- **Tetanus:** Neuromuscular disease, also called lockjaw; caused by *Clostridium tetani,* gram-positive, spore-forming rod. *C. tetani* releases powerful neurotoxin, *tetanospasmin,* which binds target sites on spinal neurons, blocks inhibition of muscle contraction.
- **Botulism:** Caused by exotoxin of *C. botulinum;* associated with eating poorly preserved foods; can also occur as true infection. Three major forms of botulism: food-borne botulism (in children and adults), infant botulism, and wound botulism.
- **African Sleeping Sickness:** Caused by protozoan, *Trypanosoma brucei.* Affects central nervous system, leading to neurological deterioration: muscular tremors, shuffling gait, slurred speech, seizures, and local paralysis.

Multiple-Choice and True-False Questions   Knowledge and Comprehension

Multiple-Choice Questions. Select the correct answer from the answers provided.

1. Which of the following organisms does *not* cause meningitis?
   a. *Haemophilus influenzae*
   b. *Streptococcus pneumoniae*
   c. *Neisseria meningitidis*
   d. *Clostridium tetani*

2. The first choice antibiotic for bacterial meningitis is the broad-spectrum
   a. cephalosporin.   c. ampicillin.
   b. penicillin.   d. vancomycin.

3. Meningococcal meningitis is caused by
   a. *Haemophilus influenzae.*
   b. *Streptococcus pneumoniae.*
   c. *Neisseria meningitidis.*
   d. *Listeria monocytogenes.*

4. Which of the following neurological diseases is not caused by a prion?
   a. Creutzfeldt-Jakob disease
   b. scrapie
   c. mad cow disease
   d. St. Louis encephalitis

5. *Cryptococcus neoformans* is primarily transmitted by
   a. direct contact.   c. fomites.
   b. bird droppings.   d. sexual activity.

6. Which of the following is *not* caused by an arbovirus?
   a. St. Louis encephalitis
   b. Eastern equine encephalitis
   c. West Nile encephalitis
   d. PAM

7. CJD is caused by a(n)
   a. arbovirus.   c. protozoan.
   b. prion.   d. bacterium.

8. What food should you avoid feeding a child under 1 year old because of potential botulism?
   a. honey   c. apple juice
   b. milk   d. applesauce

9. *Naegleria fowleri* meningoencephalitis is commonly acquired by
   a. bird droppings.
   b. swimming in ponds and streams.
   c. mosquito bites.
   d. chickens.

10. Which organism is responsible for progressive multifocal leukoencephalopathy?
    a. JC virus   c. *E. coli*
    b. herpesvirus   d. *Haemophilus influenzae*

True-False Questions. If the statement is true, leave as is. If it is false, correct it by rewriting the sentence.

11. *Toxoplasma gondii* is a bacterium.

12. Penicillin G is the first line of treatment for coccidioido-mycosis.

13. A diagnosis of bacterial meningitis can be made by analyzing cerebral spinal fluid (CSF).

14. In the United States, dogs are a common reservoir for rabies.

15. The protein PrP is beneficial before it is transformed into an abnormal protein.

Critical Thinking Questions   Application and Analysis

These questions are suggested as a *writing-to-learn* experience. For each question, compose a one- or two-paragraph answer that includes the factual information needed to completely address the question.

1. Describe the components of the human nervous system.

2. a. What is meningitis?
   b. Describe the symptoms of this condition.
   c. Name the clinical symptom that can distinguish between this organism and the agent of meningococcal meningitis.

3. What is the common mode(s) of transmission in neonatal meningitis?

4. What is the difference between meningitis and encephalitis?

5. What sterilization methods are most effective against prions?

6. Discuss the transmission of CJD.

7. Name the infectious viral disease for which postexposure passive and active immunization is indicated. Describe the procedure.

8. In the section on meningococcal meningitis, the following sentence appears: "If no samples were obtained prior to antibiotic treatment, a PCR test is the best bet for identifying the pathogen." Why?

9. Why is there no normal biota associated with the nervous system?

10. Why is the Sabin oral polio vaccine no longer recommended in the United States for childhood vaccinations?

Concept Mapping   Synthesis

Appendix D provides guidance for working with concept maps.

1. Construct your own concept map using the following words as the *concepts*. Supply the linking words between each pair of concepts. Add other concepts if needed.

bacteria	vaccines
viruses	meningitis
fungi	colonization
droplets	transmission
vehicles	vaccination

2. Use 6 to 10 words from the Chapter Summary to create a concept map. Finish it by providing linking words.

Visual Connections   Synthesis

These questions use visual images or previous content to make connections to this chapter's concepts.

1. **From chapter 3, figure 3.21.** Without looking back to the figure in chapter 3, speculate on which meningitis-causing organism you are seeing here. How could your presumptive diagnosis be confirmed?

2. **From chapter 15, figure 15.18.** A vaccine used to immunize individuals against meningococcal meningitis is described as containing "meningococcal capsular polysaccharide antigens." Which of the vaccine production strategies shown in this illustration could be used to produce this vaccine? Explain your answer. (Flip back to page 448 to see the figure in more detail.)

www.connect.microbiology.com

Enhance your study of this chapter with study tools and practice tests. Also ask your instructor about the resources available through ConnectPlus, including the media-rich eBook, interactive learning tools, and animations.

20

Infectious Diseases Affecting the Cardiovascular and Lymphatic Systems

Case File 20

A 35-year-old male presented to a London hospital complaining of difficulty breathing. His symptoms progressed quickly, and he was transferred to the hospital's intensive treatment unit suffering from respiratory failure, which soon progressed to multiple organ failure. A blood culture revealed gram-positive, encapsulated, nonmotile rods preliminarily identified as *Bacillus anthracis*. This is the bacterium that causes the disease anthrax, and it has the ability to survive for long periods of time without water or nutrition. The presence of *B. anthracis* was later confirmed by the Novel and Dangerous Pathogens Division of Britain's Health Protection Agency.

- What characteristic of *B. anthracis* allows the bacterium to survive without water or nutrition?
- Where is *B. anthracis* found?

Continuing the Case appears on page 607.

Outline and Learning Outcomes

20.1 The Cardiovascular and Lymphatic Systems and Their Defenses

1. Describe the important anatomical features of the cardiovascular system.
2. List the natural defenses present in the cardiovascular system.

20.2 Normal Biota of the Cardiovascular and Lymphatic Systems

3. Discuss the "what" and the "why" of the normal biota of the cardiovascular system.

20.3 Cardiovascular and Lymphatic System Diseases Caused by Microorganisms

4. List the possible causative agents, modes of transmission, virulence factors, diagnostic techniques, and prevention/treatment for the two forms of endocarditis.
5. Discuss what series of events may lead to septicemia and how it should be prevented and treated.

6. List the possible causative agents, modes of transmission, virulence factors, diagnostic techniques, and prevention/treatment for cardiovascular system infections that have only one infectious cause. These are: plague, tularemia, Lyme disease, and infectious mononucleosis.
7. Discuss factors that distinguish hemorrhagic and nonhemorrhagic fever diseases.
8. List the possible causative agents, modes of transmission, virulence factors, diagnostic techniques, and prevention/treatment for hemorrhagic fever diseases.
9. List the possible causative agents, modes of transmission, virulence factors, diagnostic techniques, and prevention/treatment for nonhemorrhagic fever diseases.
10. Discuss all aspects of malaria, with special emphasis on epidemiology.
11. Describe what makes anthrax a good agent for bioterrorism and list the important presenting signs to look for in patients.
12. Discuss how the epidemiology of HIV infection in the United States has changed over time and why.
13. Discuss the epidemiology of HIV infection in the developing world.

20.1   The Cardiovascular and Lymphatic Systems and Their Defenses

The Cardiovascular System

The cardiovascular system is the pipeline of the body. It is composed of the blood vessels, which carry blood to and from all regions of the body, and the heart, which pumps the blood. This system moves the blood in a closed circuit, and it is therefore known as the *circulatory system*. The cardiovascular system provides tissues with oxygen and nutrients and carries away carbon dioxide and waste products, delivering them to the appropriate organs for removal. A closely related but largely separate system, the **lymphatic system** is a major source of immune cells and fluids, and it serves as a one-way passage, returning fluid from the tissues to the cardiovascular system.

The heart is a fist-size muscular organ that pumps blood through the body. It is divided into two halves, each of which is divided into an upper and lower chamber **(figure 20.1).**

Figure 20.1 The heart.

Right lung
Left lung
Diaphragm
Superior vena cava
Right auricle
Right atrium
Right ventricle
Aorta
Left auricle
Fibrous pericardium
Cut edge of parietal pericardium
Heart (covered by visceral pericardium)
Left ventricle
Pericardial cavity

The upper chambers are called atria (singular, atrium), and the lower are ventricles. The entire organ is encased in a fibrous covering, the pericardium, which is an occasional site of infection. The actual wall of the heart has three layers: from outer to inner, they are the epicardium, the myocardium, and the endocardium. The endocardium also covers the valves of the heart, and it is a relatively common target of microbial infection.

The atria receive blood coming from the body. This blood, which is low in oxygen and high in carbon dioxide, enters the right atrium and passes through to the right ventricle. From there it is pumped to the pulmonary arteries in the lung, where it becomes oxygenated and reenters the heart through the left atrium. Finally, the blood moves into the left ventricle and is pumped into the aorta and the rest of the body. The movement of blood into and out of the chambers of the heart is controlled by valves.

The blood vessels consist of *arteries, veins,* and *capillaries.* Arteries carry oxygenated blood away from the heart under relatively high pressure. They branch into smaller vessels called arterioles. Veins actually begin as smaller venules in the periphery of the body and coalesce into veins. The smallest blood vessels, the capillaries, connect arterioles to venules. Both arteries and veins have walls made of three layers of tissue. The innermost layer is composed of a smooth epithelium called endothelium. Its smooth surface encourages the smooth flow of cells and platelets through the system. The next layer is composed of connective tissue and muscle fibers. The outside layer is a thin layer of connective tissue. Capillaries, the smallest vessels, have walls made of only one layer of endothelium. **Figure 20.2** illustrates the complete cardiovascular system.

The Lymphatic System

Chapter 14 provided a detailed description of the lymphatic system; you may wish to review page 402 and figure 14.7 before continuing. In short, the lymphatic system consists mainly of the lymph vessels, which roughly parallel the blood vessels; lymph nodes, which cluster at body sites such as the groin, neck, armpit, and intestines; and the spleen. It serves to collect fluid that has left the blood vessels and entered tissues, filter it of impurities and infectious agents, and return it to the blood.

Defenses of the Cardiovascular and Lymphatic Systems

The cardiovascular system is highly protected from microbial infection. Microbes that successfully invade the system, how-

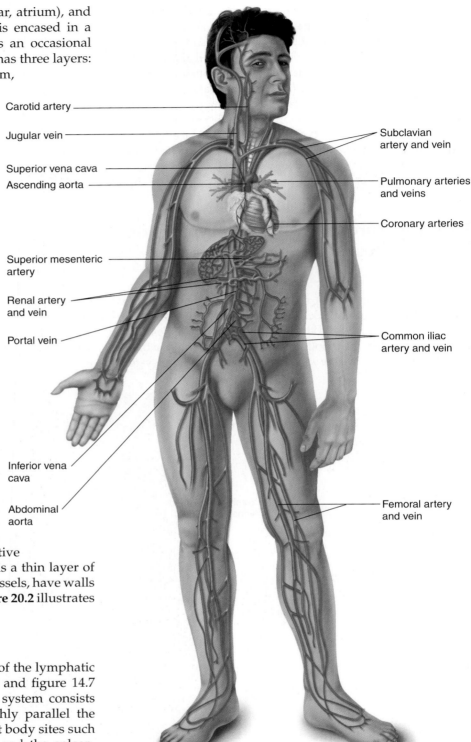

Carotid artery

Jugular vein

Superior vena cava

Ascending aorta

Subclavian artery and vein

Pulmonary arteries and veins

Coronary arteries

Superior mesenteric artery

Renal artery and vein

Portal vein

Common iliac artery and vein

Inferior vena cava

Abdominal aorta

Femoral artery and vein

Figure 20.2 The anatomy of the cardiovascular system.

ever, gain access to every part of the body, and every system may potentially be affected. For this reason, bloodstream infections are called **systemic** infections.

Multiple defenses against infection reside in the bloodstream. The blood is full of leukocytes, with approximately

5,000 to 10,000 white blood cells per milliliter of blood. The various types of white blood cells include the lymphocytes, responsible for specific immunity, and the phagocytes, which are so critical to nonspecific as well as specific immune responses. Very few microbes can survive in the blood with so many defensive elements. That said, a handful of infectious agents have nonetheless evolved exquisite mechanisms for avoiding blood-borne defenses.

Medical conditions involving the blood often have the suffix -emia. For instance, viruses that cause meningitis can travel to the nervous system via the bloodstream. Their presence in the blood is called **viremia.** When fungi are in the blood, the condition is termed **fungemia,** and bacterial presence is called **bacteremia,** a general term denoting only their *presence.* Although the blood contains no normal biota (see next section), bacteria frequently are introduced into the bloodstream during the course of daily living. Brushing your teeth or tearing a hangnail can introduce bacteria from the mouth or skin into the bloodstream; this situation is usually temporary. But when bacteria flourish and grow in the bloodstream, the condition is termed **septicemia.** Septicemia can very quickly lead to cascading immune responses, resulting in decreased systemic blood pressure, which can lead to **septic shock,** a life-threatening condition.

20.1 Learning Outcomes—Can You . . .

1. . . . describe the important anatomical features of the cardiovascular system?
2. . . . list the natural defenses present in the cardiovascular system?

INSIGHT 20.1 Floss for Your Heart?

Atherosclerosis is a condition you may not associate with infection. In atherosclerosis, plaques form on the inner endothelium of the arteries, decreasing the flexibility of the arterial walls and possibly leading to obstruction. The well-established cause of plaque formation seems to be an elevation in low-density lipoproteins (LDLs) in the plasma (originating in the diet) accompanied by chronic endothelial injury events. Injury to the endothelium results in adhesion of platelets to the surface, accumulation of other blood components, and release of growth factors that cause the proliferation of smooth muscle cells. This begs the question: What causes the chronic endothelial injury? The answer is complex and can include such things as nicotine in the bloodstream from cigarette smoke or high blood levels of insulin as seen in diabetics. But recent findings suggest that another of the causes may be chronic bloodstream infection with the bacterium *Chlamydophila pneumoniae,* other bacteria, or even various viruses. Lipopolysaccharide from *C. pneumoniae* has been found in arterial disease, though no causative relationship has yet been established.

A 2009 study reported that a wide variety of oral bacteria were detected via PCR in plaques in coronary arteries. Remember, though, that PCR detects genomic sequences and not live bacteria. But researchers in Florida did find live cells of *Porphyromonas gingivalis* and *Aggregatibacter actinomycetemcomitans,* two clear pathogens of periodontal disease, in atherosclerotic tissue. Evidence seems to be increasing that allowing our oral health to slide can have deeper consequences than once thought.

20.2 Normal Biota of the Cardiovascular and Lymphatic Systems

Like the nervous system, the cardiovascular and lymphatic systems are "closed" systems with no normal access to the external environment. Therefore current science believes they possess no normal biota. In the absence of disease, microorganisms may be transiently present in either system as just described. The lymphatic system serves to filter microbes and their products out of tissues. Thus, in the healthy state,

no microorganisms *colonize* either the lymphatic or cardiovascular systems. Of course, this is biology, and it is never quite that simple. Recent studies have suggested that the bloodstream is not completely sterile, even during periods of apparent health. It is tempting to speculate that these low-level microbial "infections" may contribute to diseases for which no etiology has previously been found or for conditions currently thought to be noninfectious **(Insight 20.1).**

20.2 Learning Outcomes—Can You . . .

3. . . . discuss the "what" and the "why" of the normal biota of the cardiovascular system?

20.3 Cardiovascular and Lymphatic System Diseases Caused by Microorganisms

Categorizing cardiovascular and lymphatic infections according to clinical presentation is somewhat difficult because most of these conditions are systemic, with effects on

Cardiovascular and Lymphatic Systems Defenses and Normal Biota

	Defenses	Normal Biota
Cardiovascular System	Blood-borne components of nonspecific and specific immunity—including phagocytosis, specific immunity	None
Lymphatic System	Numerous immune defenses reside here.	None

multiple organ systems. We begin with infections involving the heart and the blood in general and then discuss conditions with more specific causes.

Endocarditis

Endocarditis is an inflammation of the endocardium, or inner lining of the heart. Most of the time, endocarditis refers to an infection of the valves of the heart, often the mitral or aortic valve **(figure 20.3).** Two variations of infectious endocarditis have been described: acute and subacute. Each has distinct groups of possible causative agents. Rarely, endocarditis can also be caused by vascular trauma or by circulating immune complexes in the absence of infectious agents.

The surgical innovation of prosthetic valves presents a new hazard for development of endocarditis. Patients with prosthetic valves can acquire acute endocarditis if bacteria are introduced during the surgical procedure; alternatively, the prosthetic valves can serve as infection sites for the subacute form of endocarditis long after the surgical procedure. Because the symptoms and the diagnostic procedures are similar for both forms of endocarditis, they are discussed first; then the specific aspects of acute and subacute endocarditis are addressed.

▶ Signs and Symptoms

The signs and symptoms are similar for both types of endocarditis, except that in the subacute condition they develop more slowly and are less pronounced than with the acute disease. Symptoms include fever, anemia, abnormal heartbeat, and sometimes symptoms similar to myocardial infarction (heart attack). Abdominal or side pain is sometimes reported. The patient may look very ill and may have petechiae (small red-to-purple discolorations) over the upper half of the body and under the fingernails. In subacute cases, an enlarged spleen may have developed over time; cases of extremely long duration can lead to clubbed fingers and toes.

▶ Culture and Diagnosis

The diagnostic procedures for the two forms of endocarditis are essentially the same. One of the most important diagnostic

tools is a high index of suspicion. A history of risk factors, or behaviors, such as abnormal valves, intravenous drug use, recent surgery, or bloodstream infections, should lead one to consider endocarditis when the symptoms just described are observed. Blood cultures, if positive, are the gold standard for diagnosis, but negative blood cultures do not rule out endocarditis. If it is possible to obtain the agent, it is very important to determine its antimicrobial susceptibilities.

In acute endocarditis, the symptoms may be magnified. The patient may also display central nervous system symptoms suggestive of meningitis, such as stiff neck or headache.

Acute Endocarditis

Acute endocarditis is most often the result of an overwhelming bloodstream challenge with bacteria. Certain of these bacteria seem to have the ability to colonize normal heart valves. Accumulations of bacteria on the valves (vegetations) hamper their function and can lead directly to cardiac malfunction and death. Alternatively, pieces of the bacterial vegetation can break off and create emboli (blockages) in vital organs. The bacterial colonies can also provide a constant source of blood-borne bacteria, with the accompanying systemic inflammatory response and shock. Bacteria that are attached to surfaces bathed by blood (such as heart valves) quickly become covered with a mesh of fibrin and platelets that protects them from the immune components in the blood.

▶ Causative Agents

The acute form of endocarditis is most often caused by *Staphylococcus aureus*. Other agents that cause it are *Streptococcus pyogenes*, *Streptococcus pneumoniae*, and *Neisseria gonorrhoeae*, as well as a host of other bacteria. Each of these bacteria is described elsewhere in this book; all are pathogenic.

▶ Transmission and Epidemiology

The most common route of transmission for acute endocarditis is parenteral—that is, via direct entry into the body. Intravenous or subcutaneous drug users have been a growing risk group for the condition. Traumatic injuries and surgical procedures can also introduce the large number of bacteria required for the acute form of endocarditis.

▶ Prevention and Treatment

Prevention is based on avoiding the introduction of bacteria into the bloodstream during surgical procedures or injections. Untreated, this condition is invariably fatal. Recommended antibiotics are nafcillin or oxacillin with or without gentamicin. Alternatively, vancomycin + gentamicin can be used. High, continuous blood levels of antibiotics are required to resolve the infection because the bacteria exist in biofilm vegetations. In addition to the decreased access of antibiotics to bacteria deep in the biofilm, these bacteria often express a phenotype of lower susceptibility to antibiotics. Surgical debridement of the valves, accompanied by antibiotic therapy, is sometimes required **(Disease Table 20.1).**

Healthy valve

Infected valve

Vegetations

Figure 20.3 Endocarditis.   Infected valves don't work as well as healthy ones.

Subacute Endocarditis

Subacute forms of this condition are almost always preceded by some form of damage to the heart valves or by congenital malformation. Irregularities in the valves encourage the attachment of bacteria, which then form biofilms and impede normal function, as well as provide an ongoing source of bacteria to the bloodstream. People who have suffered rheumatic fever and the accompanying damage to heart valves are particularly susceptible to this condition (see chapter 21 for a complete discussion of rheumatic fever).

▶ Causative Agents

Most commonly, subacute endocarditis is caused by bacteria of low pathogenicity, often originating in the oral cavity. Alpha-hemolytic streptococci, such as *Streptococcus sanguis*, *S. oralis*, and *S. mutans*, are most often responsible, although normal biota from the skin and other bacteria can also colonize abnormal valves and lead to this condition.

▶ Transmission and Epidemiology

Minor disruptions in the skin or mucous membranes, such as those induced by vigorous toothbrushing, dental procedures, or relatively minor cuts and lacerations, can introduce bacteria into the bloodstream and lead to valve colonization. The bacteria are not, therefore, transmitted from other people or from the environment. The average age of onset for subacute endocarditis has increased in recent decades from the mid-20s to the mid-50s. Males are slightly more likely to experience it than females.

▶ Prevention and Treatment

The practice of prophylactic antibiotic therapy in advance of surgical and dental procedures on patients with underlying valve irregularities has decreased the incidence of this infection. When it occurs, treatment is similar to treatment for the acute form of the disease, described earlier **(Disease Table 20.1).**

Septicemias

Septicemia occurs when organisms are actively multiplying in the blood. Many different bacteria (and a few fungi) can cause this condition. Patients suffering from these infections are sometimes described as "septic." One infection that should be considered in cases of aggressive septicemia, especially if respiratory symptoms are also present, is anthrax.

▶ Signs and Symptoms

Fever is a prominent feature of septicemia. The patient appears very ill and may have an altered mental state, shaking chills, and gastrointestinal symptoms. Often an increased breathing rate is exhibited, accompanied by respiratory alkalosis (increased tissue pH due to breathing disorder). Low blood pressure is a hallmark of this condition and is caused by the inflammatory response to infectious agents in the bloodstream, which leads to a loss of fluid from the vasculature. This condition is the most dangerous feature of the disease, often culminating in death.

▶ Causative Agents

The vast majority of septicemias are caused by bacteria, and they are approximately evenly divided between gram-positives and gram-negatives. Perhaps 10% are caused by fungal infections. Polymicrobial bloodstream infections increasingly are being identified in which more than one microorganism is causing the infection.

▶ Pathogenesis and Virulence Factors

Gram-negative bacteria multiplying in the blood release large amounts of endotoxin into the bloodstream, stimulating a massive inflammatory response mediated by a host of cytokines. This response invariably leads to a drastic drop in blood pressure, a condition called **endotoxic shock.** Gram-positive bacteria can instigate a similar cascade of events when fragments of their cell walls are released into the blood.

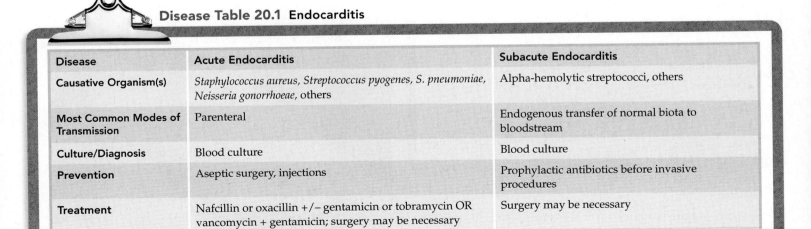

Disease Table 20.1 Endocarditis

Disease	Acute Endocarditis	Subacute Endocarditis
Causative Organism(s)	*Staphylococcus aureus, Streptococcus pyogenes, S. pneumoniae, Neisseria gonorrhoeae,* others	Alpha-hemolytic streptococci, others
Most Common Modes of Transmission	Parenteral	Endogenous transfer of normal biota to bloodstream
Culture/Diagnosis	Blood culture	Blood culture
Prevention	Aseptic surgery, injections	Prophylactic antibiotics before invasive procedures
Treatment	Nafcillin or oxacillin +/− gentamicin or tobramycin OR vancomycin + gentamicin; surgery may be necessary	Surgery may be necessary
Distinctive Features	Acute onset, high fatality rate	Slower onset

▶ Transmission and Epidemiology

In many cases, septicemias can be traced to parenteral introduction of the microorganisms via intravenous lines or surgical procedures. Other infections may arise from serious urinary tract infections or from renal, prostatic, pancreatic, or gallbladder abscesses. Patients with underlying spleen malfunction may be predisposed to multiplication of microbes in the bloodstream. Meningeal infections or pneumonia occasionally can lead to sepsis. Approximately half a million cases occur each year in the United States, resulting in more than 100,000 deaths.

▶ Culture and Diagnosis

Because the infection is in the bloodstream, a blood culture is the obvious route to diagnosis. A full regimen of media should be inoculated to ensure isolation of the causative microorganism. Antibiotic susceptibilities should be assessed. Empiric therapy should be started immediately before culture and susceptibility results are available. The choice of antimicrobial agent should be informed by knowledge of any suspected source of the infection, such as an intravenous catheter (in which case, skin biota should be considered), urinary tract infections (in which case, gram-negatives and *Streptococci* should be considered), and so forth.

▶ Prevention and Treatment

Empiric therapy, which is begun immediately after blood cultures are taken, often begins with a broad-spectrum antibiotic. Once the organism is identified and its antibiotic susceptibility is known, treatment can be adjusted accordingly.

Disease Table 20.2 Septicemia

Causative Organism(s)	Bacteria or fungi
Most Common Modes of Transmission	Parenteral, endogenous transfer
Virulence Factors	Cell wall or membrane components
Culture/Diagnosis	Blood culture
Prevention	–
Treatment	Broad-spectrum antibiotic until identification and susceptibilities tested

Plague

The word **plague** conjures up visions of death and morbidity unlike any other infectious disease. Although pandemics of plague have probably occurred since antiquity, the first one that was reliably chronicled killed an estimated 100 million people in the 6th century AD. The last great pandemic occurred in the late 1800s and was transmitted around the world, primarily by rat-infested ships. The disease was brought to the United States through the port of San Francisco around 1906. Infected rats eventually mingled with native populations of rodents and gradually spread the disease throughout the West and Midwest.

▶ Signs and Symptoms

Three possible manifestations of infection occur with the bacterium causing plague. **Pneumonic plague** is a respiratory disease, described in chapter 21. In **bubonic plague,** the bacterium, which is injected by the bite of a flea, enters the lymph and is filtered by a local lymph node. Infection causes inflammation and necrosis of the node, resulting in a swollen lesion called a **bubo,** usually in the groin or axilla **(figure 20.4).** The incubation period lasts 2 to 8 days, ending abruptly with the onset of fever, chills, headache, nausea, weakness, and tenderness of the bubo. Mortality rates, even with treatment, are greater than 15%.

These cases often progress to massive bacterial growth in the blood termed **septicemic plague.** The presence of the bacteria in the blood results in disseminated intravascular coagulation, subcutaneous hemorrhage, and purpura that may degenerate into necrosis and gangrene. Mortality rates, once the disease has progressed to this point, are 30% to 50% with treatment and 100% without treatment. Because of the visible darkening of the skin, the plague has often been called the "black death."

▶ Causative Agent

The cause of this dreadful disease is a tiny, harmless-looking gram-negative rod, *Yersinia pestis,* a member of the Family Enterobacteriaceae. Other species members are *Y. enterocolitica* and *Y. pseudotuberculosis.* These species cause gastrointestinal tract diseases in humans. *Y. pestis* displays unusual bipolar staining that makes it look like a safety pin **(figure 20.5).**

Figure 20.4 A classic inguinal bubo of bubonic plague.
This hard nodule is very painful and can rupture onto the surface.

Figure 20.5 *Yersinia pestis.* Note the more darkly stained poles of the bacterium, lending it a "safety pin" appearance.

▶ Pathogenesis and Virulence Factors

The number of bacteria required to initiate a plague infection is small—perhaps only 3 to 50 cells. Much research has been conducted on the differences between the two *Yersinia* species that cause GI tract disease and this *Yersinia,* because it has such different effects on the host. Scientists have discovered that *Y. pestis* carries additional genes that help it to cause disease in mice and to survive in the flea vector. Examples of these genes include a gene for capsule formation and a gene for plasminogen activation (similar to the streptokinase expressed by *S. pyogenes*) (see chapter 18). Plasminogen activation leads to clotting, which helps the microbe resist phagocytosis.

▶ Transmission and Epidemiology

The principal agents in the transmission of the plague bacterium are fleas. These tiny, bloodsucking insects have a special relationship with the bacterium. After a flea ingests a blood meal from an infected animal, the bacteria multiply in its gut. In fleas that effectively transmit the bacterium, the esophagus becomes blocked due to coagulation factors produced by

the pathogen. Being unable to feed properly, the ravenous flea jumps from animal to animal in a futile attempt to get nourishment. During this process, regurgitated infectious material is inoculated into the bite wound.

The plague bacterium exists naturally in many animal hosts, and its distribution is extensive. Although the incidence of disease has been reduced in the developed world, it has actually been increasing in Africa and other parts of the world. Plague still exists endemically in large areas of Africa, South America, the Mideast, Asia, and the former Soviet Union, and it sometimes erupts into epidemics such as the outbreak in India in the 1990s that infected hundreds of residents. This new surge of cases was attributed to increased populations of rats following the monsoon floods. In the United States, sporadic cases (usually less than 10 per year) occur as a result of contact with wild and domestic animals. This disease is considered endemic in U.S. western and southwestern states. Persons most at risk for developing plague are veterinarians and people living and working near woodlands and forests. Dogs and cats can be infected with the plague, often from contact with infected wild animals such as prairie dogs. Human cases have been traced to a chain of events involving a flea from a prairie dog moving to a domestic cat, and then a flea from the cat moving to a human.

The epidemiology of plague is among the most complex of all diseases. It involves several different types of vertebrate hosts and flea vectors, and its exact cycle varies from one region to another. A general scheme of the cycle is presented in **figure 20.6.** Humans can develop plague through contact with the fleas of wild or domestic or semidomestic animals. Contact with infected body fluids can also spread the disease. If a person has breaks in the skin on his or her hands, handling infected animals or animal skins is a possible means of transmission. (Persons with the pneumonic form of the disease can spread *Y. pestis* through respiratory droplets.)

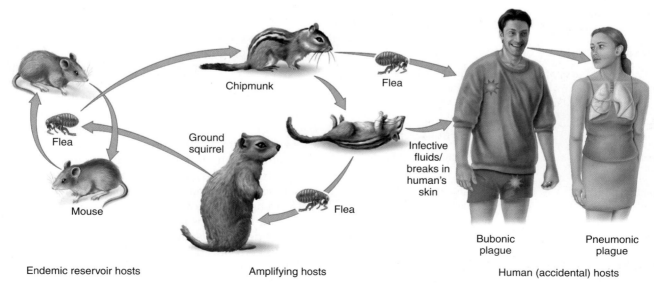

Endemic reservoir hosts   Amplifying hosts   Human (accidental) hosts

Figure 20.6 The infection cycle of *Yersinia pestis.*

The Animal Reservoirs The plague bacillus occurs in 200 different species of mammals. The primary long-term *endemic reservoirs* are various rodents, such as mice and voles, that harbor the organism but do not develop the disease. These hosts spread the disease to other mammals called *amplifying hosts* that become infected with the bacterium and experience massive die-offs during epidemics. These hosts, including rats, ground squirrels, chipmunks, and rabbits, are the usual sources of human plague. The particular mammal that is most important in this process depends on the area of the world. Other mammals (camels, sheep, coyotes, deer, dogs, and cats) can also be involved in the transmission cycle.

▶ Culture and Diagnosis

Because death can occur as quickly as 2 to 4 days after the appearance of symptoms, prompt diagnosis and treatment of plague are imperative. The patient's history, including recent travel to endemic regions, can help establish a diagnosis. Culture of the organism is the definitive method of diagnosis, although a Gram stain of aspirate from buboes often reveals the presence of the safety-pin-shaped bacteria.

▶ Prevention and Treatment

Plague is one of a handful of internationally quarantinable diseases (others are cholera and yellow fever). In addition to quarantine during epidemics, plague is controlled by trapping rodents and by poisoning their burrows with insecticide to kill fleas. These methods, however, cannot begin to control the reservoir hosts, so the potential for plague will always be present in endemic areas, especially as humans encroach into rodent habitats. A vaccine for plague is no longer available in the United States. Streptomycin or gentamicin are the drugs of choice.

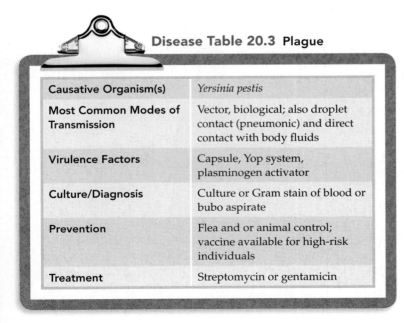

Disease Table 20.3 Plague

Causative Organism(s)	*Yersinia pestis*
Most Common Modes of Transmission	Vector, biological; also droplet contact (pneumonic) and direct contact with body fluids
Virulence Factors	Capsule, Yop system, plasminogen activator
Culture/Diagnosis	Culture or Gram stain of blood or bubo aspirate
Prevention	Flea and or animal control; vaccine available for high-risk individuals
Treatment	Streptomycin or gentamicin

Tularemia

▶ Signs and Symptoms

After an incubation period ranging from a few days to 3 weeks, acute symptoms of headache, backache, fever, chills, malaise, and weakness appear. Further clinical manifestations are tied to the portal of entry. They include ulcerative skin lesions, swollen lymph glands, conjunctival inflammation, sore throat, intestinal disruption, and pulmonary involvement. The death rate in the most serious forms of disease is 30%, but proper treatment with gentamicin or streptomycin reduces mortality to almost zero.

▶ Causative Agent

The causative agent of tularemia is a facultative intracellular gram-negative bacterium called *Francisella tularensis*. It has several characteristics in common with *Yersinia pestis*, and the two species were previously often included in a single genus called *Pasteurella*. It is a zoonotic disease of assorted mammals endemic to the Northern Hemisphere. Because it has been associated with outbreaks of disease in wild rabbits, it is sometimes called rabbit fever. It is currently listed as a pathogen of concern on the lists of bioterrorism agents (see Insight 21.3 for details).

▶ Transmission and Epidemiology

Tularemia is abundantly distributed through numerous animal reservoirs and vectors in northern Europe, Asia, and North America but not in the tropics. This disease is noteworthy for its complex epidemiology and spectrum of symptoms. Although rabbits and rodents (muskrats and ground squirrels) are the chief reservoirs, other wild animals (skunks, beavers, foxes, opossums) and some domestic animals are implicated as well. The chief route of transmission in the past had been through the activity of skinning rabbits, but with the decline of rabbit hunting, transmission via tick bites is more common. Ticks are the most frequent arthropod vector, followed by biting flies, mites, and mosquitoes.

Tularemia is strikingly varied in its portals of entry and disease manifestations. Although bites by a vector are the most common source of infection, in many cases infection results when the skin or eye is inoculated through contact with infected animals, animal products, contaminated water, and dust. Pulmonary forms of the infection can result from aerosolized soils or animal fluids and also from spread of the bacterium in the bloodstream. The disease is not communicated from human to human. With an estimated infective dose of between 10 and 50 organisms, *F. tularensis* is often considered one of the most infectious of all bacteria. The term "lawnmower" tularemia refers to tularemia acquired while performing grass-mowing or brush-cutting chores. Cases of tularemia have appeared in people who have accidentally run over dead rabbits while lawn mowing, presumably from inhaling aerosolized bacteria. In 2009, two different people in Alaska acquired tularemia after wresting infected rabbits from their dogs' mouths. In that same year two people in Oregon became infected after being bitten by cats and a third after removing an infected squirrel from her cat's clenched teeth.

▶ Prevention and Treatment

Because the intracellular persistence of *F. tularensis* can lead to relapses, antimicrobial therapy must not be discontinued prematurely. Protection is available in the form of a live attenuated vaccine. Laboratory workers and other occupationally exposed personnel must wear gloves, masks, and eyewear.

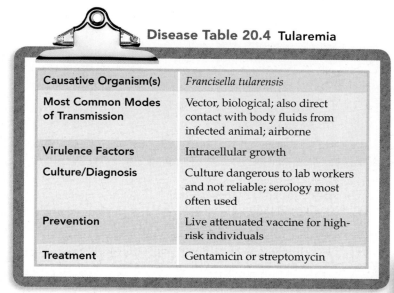

Disease Table 20.4 Tularemia

Causative Organism(s)	*Francisella tularensis*
Most Common Modes of Transmission	Vector, biological; also direct contact with body fluids from infected animal; airborne
Virulence Factors	Intracellular growth
Culture/Diagnosis	Culture dangerous to lab workers and not reliable; serology most often used
Prevention	Live attenuated vaccine for high-risk individuals
Treatment	Gentamicin or streptomycin

Lyme Disease

In the 1970s, an enigmatic cluster of arthritis cases appeared in the town of Old Lyme, Connecticut. The phenomenon caught the attention of nonprofessionals and professionals alike, whose persistence and detective work ultimately disclosed the unusual nature and epidemiology of Lyme disease. The process of discovery began in the home of Polly Murray, who, along with her family, was beset for years by recurrent bouts of stiff neck, swollen joints, malaise, and fatigue that seemed vaguely to follow a rash from tick bites. When Mrs. Murray's son was diagnosed as having juvenile rheumatoid arthritis, she became skeptical. Conducting her own literature research, she began to discover inconsistencies. Rheumatoid arthritis was described as a rare, noninfectious disease, yet over an 8-year period, she found that 30 of her neighbors had experienced similar illnesses. Ultimately, this cluster of cases and others were reported to state health authorities. Eventually Lyme disease was shown to be caused by *Borrelia burgdorferi*. It is now recognized that Lyme disease has been around for centuries.

▶ Signs and Symptoms

Lyme disease is nonfatal, but it often evolves into a slowly progressive syndrome that mimics neuromuscular and rheumatoid conditions. An early symptom in 70% of cases is a rash at the site of a tick bite. The lesion, called *erythema migrans*, looks something like a bull's-eye, with a raised erythematous (reddish) ring that gradually spreads outward and a pale central region **(figure 20.7)**. Other early symptoms are fever, headache, stiff neck, and dizziness. If not treated or if treated too late, the disease can advance to the second stage, during which cardiac and neurological symptoms, such as facial palsy, can develop. After several weeks or months, a crippling polyarthritis can attack joints. Some people acquire chronic neurological complications that are severely disabling.

▶ Causative Agent

Borrelia burgdorferi was discovered in 1981 by Dr. Willy Burgdorfer, although he did not realize at that time its connection with disease. Borrelia are spirochetes, but they are morphologically distinct from other pathogenic spirochetes. They are comparatively larger, ranging from 0.2 to 0.5 micrometer in width and from 10 to 20 micrometers in length, and they contain 3 to 10 irregularly spaced and loose coils **(figure 20.8)**. The nutritional requirements of *Borrelia* are so complex that the bacterium can be grown in artificial media only with difficulty.

Figure 20.7 Lesions of Lyme disease on the lower leg. Note the flat, reddened rings in the form of a bull's-eye.

Figure 20.8 *Borrelia* has 3 to 10 loose, irregular coils.

INSIGHT 20.2   The Arthropod Vectors of Infectious Disease

Many bacterial pathogens have evolved with and made complex adaptations to the bodies of arthropods, particularly insects and arachnids. In their role as biological vectors, they are an important source of zoonotic infections in humans. In this chapter alone, you learn about the flea transmitting plague; lice transmitting trench fever; and the very busy tick transmitting tularemia, Lyme disease, and ehrlichioses to humans, while playing a part in keeping Q fever cycling among animal species. Here we describe some main groups implicated in disease.

Ticks

There are over 810 species of ticks throughout the world. About 100 of them are vectors of infectious disease. Ticks are arachnids, as compared with fleas and lice, which are insects.

Hard (ixodid) ticks have adapted to a wide-ranging lifestyle, hitchhiking along as their hosts wander through forest, savanna, or desert regions. Depending on the species, ticks feed during larval, nymph, and adult metamorphic stages. The longevity of ticks is formidable; metamorphosis can extend for 2 years, and adults can survive for 4 years away from a host without feeding. The tiny unengorged ticks humans pick up from vegetation crawl on the body, embed their mouthparts in the skin, and fill with blood, expanding to hundreds of times in size. Ixodid ticks are implicated in Rocky Mountain spotted fever and Q fever, as well as the ehrlichioses.

Fleas

Fleas are laterally flattened, wingless insects with well-developed jumping legs and a prominent proboscis for piercing the skin of warm-blooded animals. They are known for their extreme longevity and resistance, and many are notorious in their nonspecificity, passing with ease from wild or domesticated mammals to humans. In response to mechanical stimulation and warmth, fleas jump onto their targets and crawl about, feeding as they go. A well-known example is the oriental rat flea that transmits *Rickettsia typhi,* the cause of murine typhus. The flea harbors the

Arthropod vectors. **(a)** Hard (ixodid) tick. **(b)** An engorged soft tick. **(c)** The body louse. **(d)** Cat flea.

pathogen in its gut and periodically contaminates the environment with virulent bacteria by defecating. This same flea is involved in the transmission of plague.

Lice

Lice (singular, louse) are small, flat insects equipped with biting or sucking mouthparts. The lice of humans usually occupy head and body hair or pubic, chest, and axillary hair. They feed by gently piercing the skin and sucking blood and tissue fluid. Infection develops when the louse (or its feces) is inadvertently squashed and rubbed into wounds, skin, eyes, or mucous membranes. See the discussion on trench fever to read about a disease transmitted by lice.

▶ Pathogenesis and Virulence Factors

The bacterium is a master of immune evasion. It changes its surface antigens while it is in the tick and again after it has been transmitted to a mammalian host. It provokes a strong humoral and cellular immune response, but this response is mainly ineffective, perhaps because of the bacterium's ability to switch its antigens. Indeed, it is possible that the immune response contributes to the pathology of the infection.

B. burgdorferi also has multiple proteins for attachment to host cells; these are considered virulence factors as well.

▶ Transmission and Epidemiology

B. burgdorferi is transmitted primarily by hard ticks of the genus *Ixodes.* (See **Insight 20.2** for a discussion of ticks and other arthropod vectors of diseases.) In the northeastern

part of the United States, *Ixodes scapularis* (the black-legged deer tick, **figure 20.9**) passes through a complex 2-year cycle that involves two principal hosts. As a larva or nymph, it feeds on either the white-footed mouse or birds or raccoons, where it picks up the infectious agent. The nymph is relatively nonspecific and will try to feed on nearly any type of vertebrate—thus, it is the form most likely to bite humans. The adult tick reproductive phase of the cycle is completed on deer. In California, the transmission cycle involves *Ixodes pacificus,* another black-legged tick, and the dusky-footed woodrat as reservoir.

The incidence of Lyme disease showed a gradual upward trend from about 10,000 cases per year in 1991 to 27,000 in 2007. This increase may be partly due to improved diagnosis, but it also reflects changes in the numbers of hosts and vec-

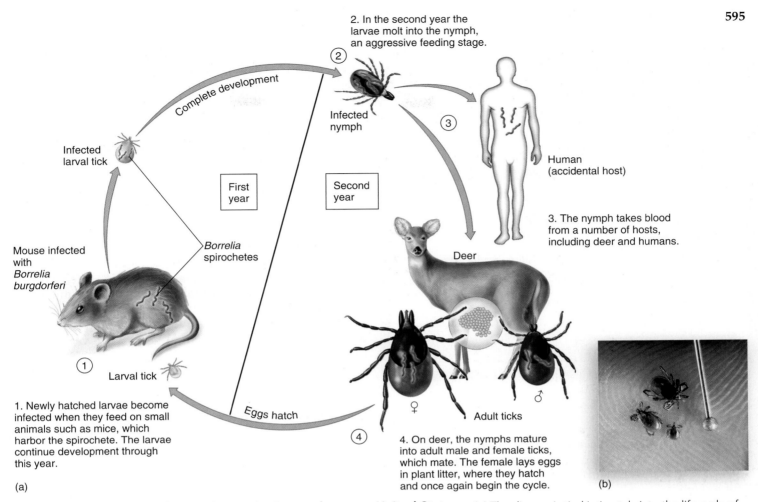

2. In the second year the larvae molt into the nymph, an aggressive feeding stage.

②

Complete development

Infected nymph

③

Infected larval tick

First year

Second year

Borrelia spirochetes

Human (accidental host)

3. The nymph takes blood from a number of hosts, including deer and humans.

Mouse infected with *Borrelia burgdorferi*

Deer

①

Larval tick

♀

♂

Adult ticks

1. Newly hatched larvae become infected when they feed on small animals such as mice, which harbor the spirochete. The larvae continue development through this year.

Eggs hatch

④

4. On deer, the nymphs mature into adult male and female ticks, which mate. The female lays eggs in plant litter, where they hatch and once again begin the cycle.

(a)

(b)

Figure 20.9 The cycle of Lyme disease in the northeastern United States. (a) The disease is tied intimately into the life cycle of a tick vector, which generally is completed over a 2-year period. The exact hosts and species of tick vary from region to region but still display this basic pattern. (b) Photograph gives an idea of the actual size and proportion of the nymph and adult black-legged deer ticks displayed on a human finger. Many people may not realize how very small and difficult to detect the feeding nymph can be.

tors. The greatest concentrations of Lyme disease are found in areas having high deer populations **(figure 20.10).** Most of the cases have occurred in New York, Pennsylvania, Connecticut, New Jersey, Rhode Island, and Maryland, but the numbers in the Midwest and West are growing. Highest risk groups include hikers, backpackers, and people living in newly developed communities near woodlands and forests.

▶ Culture and Diagnosis

Diagnosis of Lyme disease can be difficult because of the range of symptoms it presents. Most suggestive are the ring-shaped lesions, isolation of spirochetes from the patient, and serological testing with an ELISA method that tracks a rising antibody titer. Tests for spirochetal DNA in specimens is especially helpful for late-stage diagnosis.

▶ Prevention and Treatment

A vaccine for Lyme disease was available for a brief period of time, but it was withdrawn from the market in early 2002. Other vaccines are in development. Because dogs can also acquire the disease, there is a vaccine for them. Anyone involved in outdoor activities should wear protective clothing, boots, leggings, and insect repellant containing DEET.[1] Individuals exposed to heavy infestation should routinely inspect their bodies for ticks and remove ticks gently without crushing, preferably with

Areas of predicted Lyme disease transmission
■ High risk
▨ Moderate risk
▦ Low risk
□ Minimal or no risk

Figure 20.10 A map indicating risk of Lyme disease in the United States.

1. N,N-Diethyl-M-toluamide—the active ingredient in OFF! and Cutter brand insect repellants.

forceps or fingers protected with gloves, because it is possible to become infected by tick feces or body fluids.

Early, prolonged (3 to 4 weeks) treatment with doxycycline and amoxicillin is effective, and other antibiotics such as ceftriaxone and penicillin are used in late Lyme disease therapy.

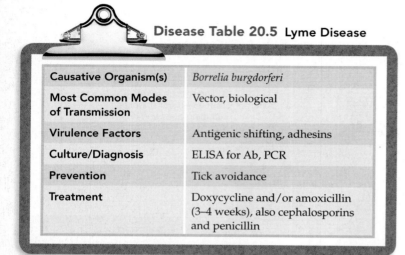

Disease Table 20.5 Lyme Disease

Causative Organism(s)	*Borrelia burgdorferi*
Most Common Modes of Transmission	Vector, biological
Virulence Factors	Antigenic shifting, adhesins
Culture/Diagnosis	ELISA for Ab, PCR
Prevention	Tick avoidance
Treatment	Doxycycline and/or amoxicillin (3–4 weeks), also cephalosporins and penicillin

Infectious Mononucleosis

This lymphatic system disease, which is often simply called "mono" or the "kissing disease," can be caused by a number of bacteria or viruses, but the vast majority of cases are caused by the **Epstein-Barr virus (EBV)**, a member of the herpes family.

▶ Signs and Symptoms

The symptoms of mononucleosis are sore throat, high fever, and cervical lymphadenopathy, which develop after a long incubation period (30 to 50 days). Many patients also have a gray-white exudate in the throat, a skin rash, and enlarged spleen and liver. A notable sign of mononucleosis is sudden leukocytosis, consisting initially of infected B cells and later T cells. Fatigue is a hallmark of the disease. Patients remain fatigued for a period of weeks. During that time, they are advised not to engage in strenuous activity due to the possibility of injuring their enlarged spleen (or liver).

Eventually, the strong, cell-mediated immune response is decisive in controlling the infection and preventing complications. But after recovery, people usually remain chronically infected with EBV.

Epstein-Barr Virus

Although "mono" was first described more than a century ago, its most frequent cause was finally discovered through a series of accidental events starting in 1958, when Michael Burkitt discovered an unusual malignant tumor in African children (Burkitt's lymphoma) that appeared to be infectious. Later, Michael Epstein and Yvonne Barr cultured a virus from tumors that showed typical herpesvirus morphology. Evidence that the two diseases had a common cause was provided when a laboratory technician accidentally acquired mononucleosis while working with the Burkitt's lymphoma virus. The Epstein-Barr virus shares morphological and antigenic features with other herpesviruses; and in addition, it contains a circular form of DNA that is readily spliced into the host cell DNA.

Scientists have long suspected a link between chronic EBV infection and other illnesses, especially Hodgkin's lymphoma, but the connection is still controversial. Research in 2010 found the virus in 40% of Hodgkin's lymphoma cases.

▶ Pathogenesis and Virulence Factors

The latency of the virus and its ability to splice its DNA into host cell DNA make it an extremely versatile virus that can avoid the host's immune response.

Disease Table 20.6 Infectious Mononucleosis

Causative Organism(s)	Epstein-Barr virus (EBV)	Cytomegalovirus (CMV)
Most Common Modes of Transmission	Direct, indirect contact; parenteral	Direct, indirect contact; parenteral; vertical
Virulence Factors	Latency, ability to incorporate into host DNA	Latency, ability to fuse cells
Culture/Diagnosis	Differential blood count, Monospot test for heterophile antibody, specific ELISA	Virus isolation and growth, ELISA or PCR tests
Prevention	–	Vaccine in trials
Treatment	Supportive	Only for immunosuppressed patients, not usually for mononucleosis
Distinctive Features	Most common in teens	More common in adults, dangerous to fetus

Lymphocyte   Red blood cell

Lymphocyte   Red blood cell

(a)

(b)

Figure 20.11 Histology of lymphocytes infected with Epstein-Barr virus (1,000×). (a) Blood smear of a normal lymphocyte, with round nucleus. (b) Blood smear of patient with infectious mononucleosis. Note a large atypical lymphocyte with irregular nucleus and indented border (arrows).

▶ Transmission and Epidemiology

More than 90% of the world's population is infected with EBV. In general, the virus causes no noticeable symptoms, but the time of life when the virus is first encountered seems to matter. In the case of EBV, infection during the teen years seems to result in disease, whereas infection before or after this period is usually asymptomatic.

Direct oral contact and contamination with saliva are the principal modes of transmission, although transfer through blood transfusions, sexual contact, and organ transplants is possible.

▶ Culture and Diagnosis

A differential blood count that shows excess lymphocytes, reduced neutrophils, and large, atypical lymphocytes with lobulated nuclei and vacuolated cytoplasm is suggestive of EBV infection **(figure 20.11)**. A test called the "Monospot test" detects *heterophile antibodies*—which are antibodies that are not directed against EBV but are seen when a person has an EBV infection. This test is not reliable in children younger than age 4, in which case a specific EBV antigen/antibody test is conducted.

▶ Prevention and Treatment

The usual treatments for infectious mononucleosis are directed at symptomatic relief of fever and sore throat. Hospitalization is rarely needed. Occasionally, rupture of the spleen necessitates immediate surgery to remove it **(Disease Table 20.6)**.

Hemorrhagic Fever Diseases

A number of agents that infect the blood and lymphatics cause extreme fevers, some of which are accompanied by internal hemorrhaging. The diseases are grouped into the category of "hemorrhagic fevers" and are covered in this section. The following section deals with diseases in which the main symptom is fever—without the hemorrhagic part.

All hemorrhagic fever diseases described here are caused by viruses in one of three families: Arenaviridae, Filoviridae, and Flaviviridae. Bunyaviridae is a fourth family with members that cause hemorrhagic fevers, but we do not discuss examples of these here. All of these viruses are RNA enveloped viruses, the distribution of which is restricted to their natural host's distribution.

Yellow Fever

This disease is caused by an arbovirus, a single-stranded RNA flavivirus that is generally called the yellow fever virus. It currently occurs only in parts of Africa and South America. Two patterns of transmission are seen in nature. One is an urban cycle between humans and the mosquito *Aedes aegypti*, which reproduces in standing water in cities. The other is a sylvan (forest) cycle, maintained between forest monkeys and mosquitoes.

The presence of the virus in the bloodstream causes capillary fragility and disrupts the blood-clotting system, which can lead to localized bleeding and shock. Infection begins acutely with fever, headache, and muscle pain. In some patients, the disease progresses to oral hemorrhage, nosebleed, vomiting, jaundice, and liver and kidney damage with significant mortality rates. Most cases occur during the rainy season.

Dengue Fever

Dengue fever is caused by a single-stranded RNA flavivirus that is also carried by *Aedes* mosquitoes. Although mild infection is the usual pattern, a form called dengue hemorrhagic shock syndrome can be lethal. Dengue fever is also called "breakbone fever" because of the severe pain it induces in muscles and joints (it does not actually cause fractures). The illness is endemic to Southeast Asia and India, and several epidemics have occurred in South America and Central America, the Caribbean, and Mexico. The Pan American

Health Organization has reported an ongoing epidemic of dengue fever in the Americas that increased from 390,000 cases in 1984 to more than 1 million cases in 2008. In Mexico, cases have increased 600% since 2001.

Researchers in Thailand, where dengue fever is one of the leading causes of child mortality, have developed a live attenuated vaccine, which is being tested in clinical trials. A low-tech approach has led to big successes in Vietnam. There, health officials urged local citizens to round up tiny crustaceans that are common in natural water sources and to put them in water tanks and wells. The crustaceans, which are not harmful to humans, eat the mosquitoes that carry dengue. Officials reported a complete elimination of the disease in communities where the strategy was used.

Chikungunya

The Chikungunya virus was discovered in 1955 and has caused sporadic outbreaks of disease since then. The name comes from an African phrase meaning "that which bends up," a reference to the arthritic stance people infected with this virus often assume. It is an alphavirus that is transmitted by *Aedes* mosquitoes, just like dengue fever. Symptoms are similar to dengue fever with the additional complication of severe joint pain, sometimes lasting for years. There is growing concern about this virus, since it has established itself in mosquitoes in Western Europe—the first time one of these hemorrhagic viruses has done so.

Ebola and Marburg

Unlike the two viruses causing yellow fever and dengue fever, the Ebola and Marburg viruses are filoviruses (Family Filoviridae). The two viruses are related and cause similar symptoms, although Ebola has received the greatest share of media attention. Its gruesome symptoms are extreme manifestations of the same kind of hemorrhagic events described for yellow fever and dengue fever. The virus in the bloodstream leads to extensive capillary fragility and disruption of clotting. Patients bleed from their orifices, even from their mucous membranes, and experience massive internal and external hemorrhage. Very often they manifest a rash on their trunk in early stages of the disease. The mortality rate is between 25% and 100%, and there is no effective treatment.

It is not known how humans acquire these viruses. They are both indigenous to Africa. In August of 2007 researchers found the virus in a cave-dwelling fruit bat. It is thought that bats are the natural reservoir of these viruses. Direct contact with an infected person or with their body fluids will transmit the virus. Hospital workers caring for Ebola patients are at high risk of becoming infected.

Two major outbreaks of Ebola occurred in Kikwit, Zaire, in 1995 and in Gulu, Uganda, in 2000.

Outbreaks with Marburg virus are also rare, but individuals have been infected sporadically since it was first recognized in 1967. In 2005, the largest Marburg outbreak in history occurred in and around a hospital in Angola.

Disease Table 20.7 Hemorrhagic Fevers

Disease	Yellow Fever	Dengue Fever	Chikungunya	Ebola and/or Marburg	Lassa Fever
Causative Organism(s)	Yellow fever virus	Dengue fever virus	Chikungunya virus	Ebola virus, Marburg virus	Lassa fever virus
Most Common Modes of Transmission	Biological vector	Biological vector	Biological vector	Direct contact, body fluids	Droplet contact (aerosolized rodent excretions), direct contact with infected fluids
Virulence Factors	Disruption of clotting factors	Disruption of clotting factors	Disruption of clotting factors	Disruption of clotting factors	Disruption of clotting factors
Culture/ Diagnosis	ELISA, PCR	Rise in IgM titers	PCR	PCR, viral culture (conducted at CDC)	ELISA
Prevention	Live attenuated vaccine available	Live attenuated vaccine being tested	–	–	Avoiding rats, safe food storage
Treatment	Supportive	Supportive	Supportive	Supportive	Ribavirin
Distinctive Features	Accompanied by jaundice	"Breakbone fever"— so named due to severe pain	Arthritic symptoms	Massive hemorrhage; rash sometimes present	Chest pain, deafness as long-term sequelae

Sixty-three people died during the 5-month outbreak. Symptoms are similar to Ebola virus infection.

There is no treatment and no vaccine for Ebola or Marburg, though some promising research is being conducted.

Lassa Fever

The Lassa fever virus is an arenavirus. Several related arenaviruses cause the diseases Argentine hemorrhagic fever, Bolivian hemorrhagic fever, and lymphocytic choriomeningitis (an infection of the brain and meninges). Lassa fever virus is found in West Africa. In most cases infection with this virus is asymptomatic, but in 20% of the cases a severe hemorrhagic syndrome develops. The syndrome includes chest pain, hemorrhaging, sore throat, back pain, vomiting, diarrhea, and sometimes encephalitis. Patients who recover suffer from deafness at a significant rate.

The reservoir of the virus is a rodent found in Africa called the multimammate rat. It is spread to humans through aerosolization of rat droppings, urine, hair, and so forth. Eating food contaminated by rat excretions also transmits the virus. Infected persons can spread it to other people through their own secretions. Vertical transmission also occurs, and the disease leads to spontaneous abortions in 95% of infected pregnant women.

This hemorrhagic fever has been shown to respond to the antiviral agent ribavirin, especially if administered in the early stages of infection. There is no vaccine **(Disease Table 20.7)**.

Nonhemorrhagic Fever Diseases

In this section, we examine some infectious diseases that result in a syndrome characterized by high fever but without the capillary fragility that leads to hemorrhagic symptoms. All of the diseases in this section are caused by bacteria.

Brucellosis

This disease goes by several different names (besides brucellosis): Malta fever, undulant fever, and Bang's disease.[2] It is on the CDC list of possible bioterror agents, though it is not designated as being "of highest concern."

▶ Signs and Symptoms

The *Brucella* bacteria responsible for this disease live in phagocytic cells. These cells carry the bacteria into the bloodstream, creating focal lesions in the liver, spleen, bone marrow, and kidney. The cardinal manifestation of human brucellosis is a fluctuating pattern of fever, which is the origin of the common name *undulant fever* **(figure 20.12)**. It is also accompanied by chills, profuse sweating, headache, muscle pain and weakness, and weight loss. Fatalities are not common, although the syndrome can last for a few weeks to a year, even with treatment.

2. After B. L. Bang, a Danish physician.

Figure 20.12 The temperature cycle in classic brucellosis. Body temperature undulates between day and night and between fever, normal, and subnormal.
Source: A. Smith, *Principles of Microbiology*, 10th ed., 1985.

▶ Causative Agent

The bacterial genus *Brucella* contains tiny, aerobic gram-negative coccobacilli. Two species can cause this disease in humans: *B. abortus* (common in cattle) and *B. suis* (from pigs). Humans can become infected with either of these bacteria and experience severe disease. Even though a principal manifestation of the disease in animals is an infection of the placenta and fetus, human placentas do not become infected.

▶ Pathogenesis and Virulence Factors

Brucella enters through damaged skin or via mucous membranes of the digestive tract, conjunctiva, and respiratory tract. From there it is taken up by phagocytic cells. Because it is able to avoid destruction in the phagocytes, the bacterium is transported easily through the bloodstream and to various organs, such as the liver, kidney, breast tissue, or joints. Scientists suspect that the up-and-down nature of the fever is related to unusual properties of the bacterial lipopolysaccharide.

▶ Transmission and Epidemiology

Brucellosis occurs worldwide, with concentrations in Europe, Africa, India, and Latin America. It is associated predominantly with occupational contact in slaughterhouses, livestock handling, and the veterinary profession. Infection takes place through contact with blood, urine, placentas, and through consumption of raw milk and cheese. Human-to-human transmission is rare. Needlesticks are one of the more common modes of transmission in the United States. In 2007, a researcher in a university lab that studied possible bioweapons agents contracted brucellosis while cleaning a chamber used to infect mice.

Brucellosis is also a common disease of wild herds of bison and elk. Cattle that share grazing land with these wild herds often suffer severe outbreaks of the placental infections (called Bang's disease).

▶ Culture and Diagnosis

The patient's history can be very helpful in diagnosis, as are serological tests of the patient's blood and blood culture of the pathogen. In areas where *Brucella* is endemic, serology is of limited use because significant proportions of the population already display antibodies to the bacterium. Blood culture is positive in less than 40% of cases; Gram staining of biopsy material from lymph nodes or bone marrow (from the sternum) is considered more reliable.

▶ Prevention and Treatment

Prevention is effectively achieved by testing and elimination of infected animals, quarantine of imported animals, and pasteurization of milk. Although several types of animal vaccines are available, those developed so far for humans are ineffective or unsafe. The status of this pathogen as a potential germ warfare agent makes a reliable vaccine even more urgent.

A combination of doxycycline and gentamicin or streptomycin taken for 3 to 6 weeks is usually effective in controlling infection.

Q Fever

The name of this disease arose from the frustration created by not being able to identify its cause. The Q stands for "query." Its cause, a bacterium called *Coxiella burnetii*, was finally identified in the mid-1900s. The clinical manifestations of acute Q fever are abrupt onset of fever, chills, head and muscle ache, and, occasionally, a rash. The disease is sometimes complicated by pneumonitis (30% of cases), hepatitis, and endocarditis. About a quarter of the cases are chronic rather than acute and result in vascular damage and endocarditis-like symptoms.

C. burnetii is a very small pleomorphic gram-negative bacterium, and for a time it was considered a rickettsia. It is an intracellular parasite, but it is much more resistant to environmental pressures because it produces an unusual type of endospore-like structure **(figure 20.13)**. *C. burnetii* is apparently harbored by a wide assortment of vertebrates and arthropods, especially ticks, which play an essential role in transmission between wild and domestic animals. Ticks do not transmit the disease to humans, however. Humans acquire infection largely by means of environmental contamination and airborne spread. Birth products, such as placentas, of infected domestic animals contain large numbers of bacteria. Other sources of infectious material include urine, feces, milk, and airborne particles from infected animals. The primary portals of entry are the lungs, skin, conjunctiva, and gastrointestinal tract.

C. burnetii has been isolated from most regions of the world. California and Texas have the highest case rates in the United States, although most cases probably go undetected. People at highest risk are farm workers, meat cutters, veterinarians, laboratory technicians, and consumers of raw milk products.

Mild or subclinical cases resolve spontaneously, and more severe cases respond to doxycycline therapy. A vaccine is available in many parts of the world, but not in the United States. Q fever is of potential concern as a bioterror agent because it is very resistant to heat and drying, it can

Endospore   Vegetative cell

Figure 20.13 The agent of Q fever.   The vegetative cells of *Coxiella burnetii* produce unique endospore-like structures that are released when the cell disintegrates. Free spores survive outside the host and are important in transmission.

be inhaled, and even a single bacterium is enough to cause disease. It is an organism that the U.S. military worked with during the period when potential biowarfare agents were being developed in this country (the 1950s and 1960s).

Cat-Scratch Disease

This disease is one of a group of diseases caused by different species of the small gram-negative rod *Bartonella*. *Bartonella* species are considered to be emerging pathogens. They are fastidious but not obligate intracellular parasites, so they will grow on blood agar. In addition to cat-scratch disease and trench fever, discussed next, a new species of *Bartonella* that causes high fever and life-threatening anemia was identified in 2007.

Bartonella henselae is the agent of cat-scratch disease (CSD), an infection connected with being clawed or bitten by a cat. The pathogen is present in over 40% of cats, especially kittens. There are approximately 25,000 cases per year in the United States, 80% of them in children 2 to 14 years old. The symp-

Figure 20.14 Cat-scratch disease.   A primary nodule appears at the site of the scratch in about 21 days. In time, large quantities of pus collect and the regional lymph nodes swell.

toms start after 1 to 2 weeks, with a cluster of small papules at the site of inoculation **(figure 20.14).** In a few weeks, the lymph nodes along the lymphatic drainage swell and can become pus-filled. Only about one-third of patients experience high fever. It is a particular problem in AIDS patients. Most infections remain localized and resolve in a few weeks, but drugs such as azithromycin, erythromycin, and rifampin can be effective therapies. The disease can be prevented by thorough antiseptic cleansing of a cat bite or scratch.

Trench Fever

This disease has a long history. Trench fever was once a common condition of soldiers in battle. The causative agent, *Bartonella quintana,* is carried by lice. Most cases occur in endemic regions of Europe, Africa, and Asia, although the disease is beginning to show up in poverty-stricken areas of large cities in the developed world. This version of the disease is called "urban trench fever." Highly variable symptoms can include a 5- to 6-day fever (the species epithet, *quintana,* refers to a 5-day fever). Symptoms also include leg pains, especially in the tibial region (the disease is sometimes called "shin-bone fever"), headache, chills, and muscle aches. A macular rash can also occur. (See Insight 18.3 for definitions of skin lesions.) Endocarditis can develop, especially in the urban version of the disease. The microbe can persist in the blood long after convalescence and is responsible for later relapses.

Trench fever may be treated with doxycycline or erythromycin.

New *Bartonella* Disease

In 2007, a woman who had been traveling in Peru came down with severe anemia, a long-lasting fever, and an enlarged spleen. It was later found to have been caused by a previously unknown bacterium, named *Bartonella rochalimae.* Since there have not been further cases we do not include it in Disease Table 20.8.

HGA and HME

There are two similar tick-borne, fever-producing diseases caused by members of the genera *Ehrlichia* and *Anaplasma.* The causative organisms for the two diseases were thought to be in the single species *Ehrlichia* until 2005, when a reclassification identified the two different genera.

Members of the two genera are small intracellular bacteria, and they share many characteristics with rickettsia, including a strict parasitic existence and association with ticks. *Ehrlichia chaffeensis* causes human monocytic ehrlichiosis (HME). *Anaplasma phagocytophilum* causes human granulocytic anaplasmosis (HGA). Another species, *Ehrlichia ewingii,* can cause either syndrome. The diseases are sometimes referred to as "spotless" Rocky Mountain spotted fever.

Both bacteria spend part of their life cycle in ticks in the genus *Ixodes.* The species of tick varies with the various regions of the United States and Europe. Serology samples taken from residents of endemic areas suggest that between 15% and 36%

of them have been infected with *A. phagocytophilum,* mostly without symptoms. Both HME and HGA are showing increased incidence, probably due to improved diagnosis.

The signs and symptoms of HGA and HME are similar: an acute febrile state manifesting headache, muscle pain, and rigors. Most patients recover rapidly with no lasting effects, but around 5% of older, chronically ill patients die from disseminated infection. Rapid diagnosis is enabled by PCR tests and indirect fluorescent antibody tests. It can be critical to differentiate or detect coinfection with Lyme disease *Borrelia,* which is carried by the same tick. Doxycycline will clear up most infections within 7 to 10 days.

Rocky Mountain Spotted Fever (RMSF)

This disease is named for the region in which it was first detected in the United States—the Rocky Mountains of Montana and Idaho. In spite of its name, the disease occurs infrequently in the western United States. The majority of cases are concentrated in the Southeast and eastern seaboard regions. It also occurs in Canada and Central and South America. Infections occur most frequently in the spring and summer, when the tick vector is most active. The yearly rate of RMSF is 20 to 40 cases per 10,000 population, with fluctuations coinciding with weather and tick infestations.

RMSF is caused by a bacterium called *Rickettsia rickettsii* transmitted by hard ticks such as the wood tick (*Dermacentor andersoni*), the American dog tick (*D. variabilis,* among others), and the Lone Star tick (*Amblyomma americanum*). The dog tick is probably most responsible for transmission to humans because it is the major vector in the southeastern United States.

After 2 to 4 days of incubation, the first symptoms are sustained fever, chills, headache, and muscular pain. A distinctive spotted rash usually comes on within 2 to 4 days after the prodrome **(figure 20.15).** Early lesions are slightly mottled like measles, but later ones are macular, maculopapular, and even petechial. In the most severe untreated cases, the enlarged lesions merge and can become necrotic, predisposing to gangrene of the toes or fingertips.

Figure 20.15 The appearance of the rash in RMSF. This case occurred in a child several days after the onset of fever.

Although the spots are the most obvious symptom of the disease, the most grave manifestations are cardiovascular disruption, including hypotension, thrombosis, and hemorrhage. Conditions of restlessness, delirium, convulsions, tremor, and coma are signs of the often overwhelming effects on the central nervous system. Fatalities occur in an average of 20% of untreated cases and 5% to 10% of treated cases.

Suspected cases of RMSF require immediate treatment even before laboratory confirmation. A recent aid to early diagnosis is a method for staining rickettsias directly in a tissue biopsy using fluorescent antibodies. Isolating rickettsias from the patient's blood or tissues is desirable, but it is expensive and requires specially qualified lab personnel and lab facilities. Specimens taken from the rash lesions are suitable for PCR assay, which is very specific and sensitive and can circumvent the need for culture.

The drug of choice for suspected and known cases is doxycycline administered for 1 week. Other preventive measures parallel those for Lyme disease: wearing protective clothing, using insect sprays, and fastidiously removing ticks **(Disease Table 20.8)**.

Malaria

Throughout human history, including prehistoric times, malaria has been one of the greatest afflictions, in the same rank as bubonic plague, influenza, and tuberculosis. Even now, as the dominant protozoan disease, it threatens 40% of the world's population every year. The origin of the name is from the Italian words *mal*, bad, and *aria*, air. The superstitions of the Middle Ages alleged that evil spirits or mists and vapors arising from swamps caused malaria, because many victims came down with the disease after this sort of exposure. We now know that a swamp was mainly involved as a habitat for the mosquito vector.

▶ Signs and Symptoms

After a 10- to 16-day incubation period, the first symptoms are malaise, fatigue, vague aches, and nausea with or without diarrhea, followed by bouts of chills, fever, and sweating. These symptoms occur at 48- or 72-hour intervals, as a result of the synchronous rupturing of red blood cells. The interval, length, and regularity of symptoms reflect the type of

Disease Table 20.8 Nonhemorrhagic Fever Diseases

Disease	Brucellosis	Q fever	Cat-Scratch Disease	Trench Fever	Ehrlichioses	Rocky Mountain Spotted Fever
Causative Organism(s)	*Brucella abortus* or *B. suis*	*Coxiella burnetii*	*Bartonella henselae*	*Bartonella quintana*	*Ehrlichia* species	*Rickettsia rickettsii*
Most Common Modes of Transmission	Direct contact, airborne, parenteral (needlesticks)	Airborne, direct contact, food-borne	Parenteral (cat scratch or bite)	Biological vector (lice)	Biological vector (tick)	Biological vector (tick)
Virulence Factors	Intracellular growth; avoidance of destruction by phagocytes	Endospore-like structure	Endotoxin	Endotoxin	–	Induces apoptosis in cells lining blood vessels
Culture/Diagnosis	Gram stain of biopsy material	Serological tests for antibody	Biopsy of lymph nodes plus Gram staining; ELISA (performed by CDC)	ELISA (performed by CDC)	PCR, indirect antibody test	Fluorescent antibody, PCR
Prevention	Animal control, pasteurization of milk	Vaccine for high-risk population	Clean wound sites	Avoid lice	Avoid ticks	Avoid ticks
Treatment	Doxycycline plus gentamicin or streptomycin	Doxycycline	Azithromycin	Doxycycline or erythromycin	Doxycycline	Doxycycline
Distinctive Features	Undulating fever, muscle aches	Airborne route of transmission, variable disease presentation	History of cat bite or scratch; fever not always present	Endocarditis common, 5-day fever	Seasonal occurrence (April–Oct.)	Most common in east and southeast United States

malaria (described next). Patients with falciparum malaria, the most virulent type, often manifest persistent fever, cough, and weakness for weeks without relief. Complications of malaria are hemolytic anemia from lysed blood cells and organ enlargement and rupture due to cellular debris that accumulates in the spleen, liver, and kidneys. One of the most serious complications of falciparum malaria is termed *cerebral malaria.* In this condition, small blood vessels in the brain become obstructed due to the increased ability of red blood cells (RBCs) to adhere to vessel walls (a condition called *cytoadherence* induced by the infecting protozoan). The resulting decrease in oxygen in brain tissue can result in coma and death. In general, malaria has the highest death rate in the acute phase, especially in children. Certain kinds of malaria are subject to relapses because some infected liver cells harbor dormant protozoans for up to 5 years.

▶ Causative Agent

Plasmodium species are protozoans in the sporozoan group. They are **apicomplexans,** which live in animal hosts and lack locomotor organelles in the mature state (chapter 5 describes protozoan classification). Apicomplexans alternate between sexual and asexual phases, often in different animal hosts. The genus *Plasmodium* contains four species: *P. malariae, P. vivax, P. falciparum,* and *P. ovale.* Humans are the primary vertebrate hosts for most of the species. The four species show variations in the pattern and severity of disease.

Development of the malarial parasite is divided into two distinct phases: the asexual phase, carried out in the human, and the sexual phase, carried out in the mosquito **(figure 20.16).** The *asexual phase* (and infection) begins when an infected female *Anopheles* mosquito injects saliva containing anticoagulant into a capillary in preparation for taking a blood meal. In the process, she inoculates the blood with motile, spindle-shaped asexual cells called **sporozoites** (Gr. *sporo,* seed, and *zoon,* animal). The sporozoites circulate through the body and migrate to the liver in a short time. Within liver cells, the sporozoites undergo asexual division called *schizogony* (Gr. *schizo,* to divide, and *gone,* seed), which generates numerous daughter parasites, or *merozoites.* This phase of *pre-erythrocytic development* lasts from 5 to 16 days, depending upon the species of *Plasmodium.* Its end is marked by eruption of the liver cell, which releases from 2,000 to 40,000 mature merozoites into the circulation.

During the *erythrocytic phase,* merozoites attach to special receptors on RBCs and invade them, converting in a short time to circular (ring-shaped) trophozoites **(figure 20.17).** This stage feeds upon hemoglobin, grows, and undergoes multiple divisions to produce a cell called a *schizont,* which is filled with more merozoites.

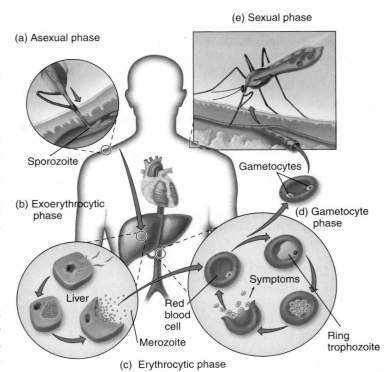

Figure 20.16   The life and transmission cycle of *Plasmodium,* the cause of malaria.   **(a)** In the asexual phase in humans, sporozoites enter a capillary through the saliva of a feeding mosquito. **(b)** Exoerythrocytic (liver) phase. Sporozoites invade the liver cells and develop into large numbers of merozoites. **(c)** Erythrocytic phase. Merozoites released into the circulation enter red blood cells. Initial infection is marked by a ring trophozoite; schizogony of the ringed form produces additional merozoites that burst out and infect other red blood cells. **(d)** Gametocytes that develop in certain infected red blood cells are ingested by another mosquito. **(e)** The sexual phase of fertilization and sporozoite formation occurs in the mosquito.

Figure 20.17   The ring trophozoite stage in a *Plasmodium falciparum* infection.   A smear of peripheral blood shows ring forms in red blood cells. Some RBCs have multiple trophozoites.

Bursting RBCs liberate merozoites to infect more red cells. Eventually, certain merozoites differentiate into two types of specialized gametes called *macrogametocytes* (female) and *microgametoctyes* (male). Because the human does not provide a suitable environment for the next phase of development, this is the end of the cycle in humans.

The *sexual phase* (sporogony) occurs when a mosquito draws infected red blood cells into her stomach. In the stomach, the microgametocyte releases spermlike gametes that fertilize the larger macrogametocytes. The resultant diploid cell (ookinete) implants into the stomach wall of the mosquito, becoming an oocyst, which undergoes multiple mitotic divisions, ultimately releasing sporozoites that migrate to the salivary glands and lodge there. This event completes the sexual cycle and makes the sporozoites available for infecting the next victim.

▶ Pathogenesis and Virulence Factors

The invasion of the merozoites into RBCs leads to the release of fever-inducing chemicals into the bloodstream. Chills and fevers often occur in a cyclic pattern. *Plasmodium* also metabolizes glucose at a very high rate, leading to hypoglycemia in the human host. The damage to RBCs results in anemia. The accumulation of malarial products in the liver and the immune stimulation in the spleen can lead to enlargement of these organs. The inducement of RBC adhesion to blood vessels in the brain (cytoadherence) adds to its virulence. A surface protein called GPI (glycosyl-phosphatidyl inositol) is thought to be responsible for the fever seen in malaria.

P. vivax and *P. ovale* have a propensity to persist in the liver; and without sufficient treatment, they can reemerge over the course of several years to cause recurrent bouts of malarial symptoms.

The fact that the protozoan has several different life stages within a host helps it escape immune responses mounted against any single life stage.

▶ Transmission and Epidemiology

All forms of malaria are spread primarily by the female *Anopheles* mosquito and occasionally by shared hypodermic needles and blood transfusions. Although malaria was once distributed throughout most of the world, the control of mosquitoes in temperate areas has successfully restricted it mostly to a belt extending around the equator **(figure 20.18)**. Despite this achievement, approximately 300 million to 500 million new cases are still reported each year, about 90% of them in Africa. The most frequent victims are children and young adults, of whom at least 2 million die annually. A particular form of the malarial protozoan causes damage to the placenta in pregnant women, leading to excess mortality among fetuses and newborns. The total case rate in the United States is about 1,000 to 2,000 new cases a year, most of which occur in immigrants.

▶ Culture and Diagnosis

Malaria can be diagnosed definitively by the discovery of a typical stage of *Plasmodium* in stained blood smears (see

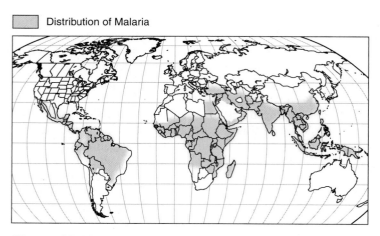

Distribution of Malaria

Figure 20.18 The malaria belt.   Darkened zones outline the major regions that harbor malaria. The malaria belt corresponds to a band around the equator.

figure 20.17). Newer serological procedures have made diagnosis more accurate while requiring less skill to perform. Other indications are knowledge of the patient's residence or travel in endemic areas and symptoms such as recurring chills, fever, and sweating.

▶ Prevention

World health officials have tried for decades to eradicate malaria. The most recent attempt is by the United Nations–backed Global Malaria Action Plan, which hopes to cut malaria by 75% between 2000 and 2015, and to reduce the number of malaria deaths to zero. Their final goal is to eradicate malaria altogether.

Malaria prevention is attempted through long-term mosquito abatement and human chemoprophylaxis. Abatement includes elimination of standing water that could serve as a breeding site and spraying of insecticides to reduce populations of adult mosquitoes, especially in and near human dwellings. Scientists have also tried introducing sterile male mosquitoes into endemic areas in an attempt to decrease mosquito populations. Humans can reduce their risk of infection considerably by using netting, screens, and repellants; by remaining indoors at night; and by taking weekly doses of prophylactic drugs. (Western travelers to endemic areas are often prescribed antimalarials for the duration of their trips.) People with a recent history of malaria must be excluded from blood donations. The WHO and other international organizations focus on efforts to distribute bed nets and to teach people how to dip the nets twice a year into an insecticide **(figure 20.19)**. The use of bed nets has been estimated to reduce childhood mortality from malaria by 20%. Here is an area where we can report some success: Bed-net use has tripled in 16 of 20 sub-Saharan African countries since 2000. Even with massive efforts undertaken by the WHO, the prevalence of malaria in endemic areas is still high.

The best protection would come from a malaria vaccine, and scientists have struggled for decades to develop one. A successful malaria vaccine must be capable of striking a

Figure 20.19 A public demonstration of impregnating bed nets with insecticide. Part of the events on Africa Malaria Day 2002 in Benin.

diverse and rapidly changing target. Scientists estimate that the parasite has 5,300 different antigens. Despite these odds, one vaccine has reached human trials. It is called RTS,S and contains a molecule expressed by the parasite as it enters the human in mosquito saliva. Another vaccine in the human trial stage targets the liver form of the parasite. Eventu-

ally the two may be combined to provide good protection against the disease. As with other mosquito-borne diseases, scientists are also constantly investigating mosquito control measures, which can have unintended consequences **(Insight 20.3).** Another potentially powerful strategy is the use of interfering RNAs in the mosquitoes to render them resistant to *Plasmodium* infection.

▶ Treatment

Quinine has long been a mainstay of malaria treatment. It is a compound originally found in the bark of the cinchona tree, which grows in the Andes, but is now synthesized in various forms. Quinine is an ingredient in tonic water; for that reason tonic water was popularized among 19th-century British colonists in India who believed that the tonic water could protect them from malaria. (In reality, the concentration of quinine is too low to be of medicinal use.) Chloroquine, the least toxic type, is used in nonresistant forms of the disease. In areas of the world where resistant strains of *P. falciparum* and *P. vivax* predominate, a course of mefloquine or pyrimethamine plus sulfadoxine (Fansidar) may be indicated, but more commonly artemisinin, another plant compound, has been most effective. Predictably,

---

INSIGHT 20.3   **Fewer Mosquitoes—Not So Fast**

In Insight 19.4 you learned that the rise of paralytic polio in the early 1900s—clearly, a bad thing—was probably due to a *good* thing that happened in public health—the sanitation of our water supplies, which resulted in children not being exposed to the virus until they were too old to be protected by maternal immunity. Well, the 21st century may see a repeat of such an upside-down outcome, in this case, in the epidemiology of dengue fever. For decades scientists have taken the approach of eliminating mosquitoes in order to control the multiple devastating infectious diseases they carry, such as yellow fever, malaria, and dengue fever. These efforts harken back to the days of widespread spraying of the pesticide DDT (which was banned in the United States in 1972) and today includes sophisticated efforts to engineer mosquitoes not to reproduce. It's hard to imagine that fewer mosquitoes could be a bad thing, and in most cases this is probably true.

But at least with respect to dengue fever, a group of scientists in London begs to differ. Here's the way dengue works: There are four different serotypes of the virus. The first time you are infected you generally get garden-variety dengue fever, with the severe limb pain and high fever, but it is rarely fatal. If you are infected a second time with another serotype, the antibodies you made previously will bind to the virus and infected cells, but won't destroy them. Instead, those antibodies and the new ones produced to new antigens cause an extreme overreaction, leading to the hemorrhagic form of the disease, and often death. However, if you are infected with that second serotype in quick order after the first infection, your immune response is effective at clearing the second invader, and you do not get a second episode. (Can you see this coming?) The British scien-

Workers spraying DDT in Madagascar in the 1990s.

tists hypothesized that if you decrease the mosquito population below a threshold level, second infections will not follow as quickly, and the incidence of the hemorrhagic form of the disease will increase. They tested their hypothesis using retrospective analysis of dengue and estimates of mosquito infestation rates. They found that if fewer than 30% of homes were infested with mosquitoes, all dengue cases decreased. But above 30% infestation rates, as infestation increased, dengue hemorrhagic fever cases decreased.

These results are controversial, as you can imagine, since so many other diseases could be curtailed by mosquito control. But it is an important illustration of the uncertainties in even the most well-accepted theories about disease and biology.

artemisinin resistance has been found in Cambodia. The World Health Organization now recommends only administering artemisinin in combination with other antimalarials, in order to prevent resistance development.

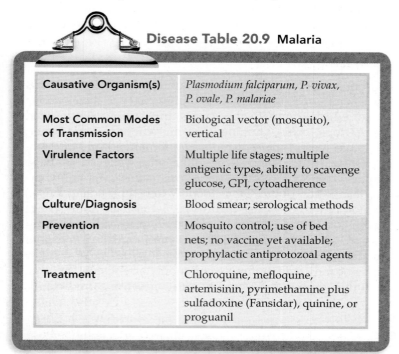

Disease Table 20.9 Malaria

Causative Organism(s)	*Plasmodium falciparum, P. vivax, P. ovale, P. malariae*
Most Common Modes of Transmission	Biological vector (mosquito), vertical
Virulence Factors	Multiple life stages; multiple antigenic types, ability to scavenge glucose, GPI, cytoadherence
Culture/Diagnosis	Blood smear; serological methods
Prevention	Mosquito control; use of bed nets; no vaccine yet available; prophylactic antiprotozoal agents
Treatment	Chloroquine, mefloquine, artemisinin, pyrimethamine plus sulfadoxine (Fansidar), quinine, or proguanil

Anthrax

Anthrax is discussed in other chapters as well as this one (for example, Insight 21.3 examines pulmonary anthrax). And because one of the possible sites of anthrax infection is the skin, cutaneous anthrax is described in chapter 18. We discuss anthrax in this chapter because it multiplies in large numbers in the blood and because septicemic anthrax is a possible outcome of all forms of anthrax.

For centuries, anthrax has been known as a zoonotic disease of herbivorous livestock (sheep, cattle, and goats). It has an important place in the history of medical microbiology because Robert Koch used anthrax as a model for developing his postulates in 1877 and, later, Louis Pasteur used the disease to prove the usefulness of vaccination.

▶ Signs and Symptoms

As just noted, anthrax infection can exhibit its primary symptoms in various locations of the body: on the skin (cutaneous anthrax), in the lungs (pulmonary anthrax), in the gastrointestinal tract (acquired through ingestion of contaminated foods), and in the central nervous system (anthrax meningitis). The cutaneous and pulmonary forms of the disease are the most common. In all of these forms, the anthrax bacterium gains access to the bloodstream, and death, if it occurs, is usually a result of an overwhelming septicemia. Pulmonary anthrax—and the accompanying pulmonary edema and hemorrhagic lung symptoms—can sometimes be the primary cause of death, although it is dif-

ficult to separate the effects of septicemia from the effects of pulmonary infection.

In addition to symptoms specific to the site of infection, septicemic anthrax results in headache, fever, and malaise. Bleeding in the intestine and from mucous membranes and orifices may occur in late stages of septicemia.

▶ Causative Agent

Bacillus anthracis is a gram-positive endospore-forming rod that is among the largest of all bacterial pathogens. It is composed of block-shaped, angular rods 3 to 5 micrometers long and 1 to 1.2 micrometers wide. Central spores develop under all growth conditions except in the living body of the host **(figure 20.20)**. The genus *Bacillus* is aerobic and catalase-positive, and none of the species are fastidious. *Bacillus* as a group is noted for its versatility in degrading complex macromolecules, and it is also a common source of antibiotics. Because the primary habitat of many species, including *B. anthracis*, is the soil, spores are continuously dispersed by means of dust into water and onto the bodies of plants and animals.

▶ Pathogenesis and Virulence Factors

The main virulence factors of *B. anthracis* are its polypeptide capsule and what is referred to as a "tripartite" toxin—an exotoxin "complex" composed of three separate proteins. One of the proteins is called *edema factor,* an enzyme that acts as an adenylyl cyclase, interfering with cellular metabolism by causing the production of high levels of cyclic AMP. Excess cyclic AMP leads to excess cellular secretion and other pathologic effects. Another part of the toxin is *protective antigen,* so named because it is a good target for vaccination, not because it protects the bacterium or the host directly. It helps the edema factor get to its target site. The third exotoxin is called *lethal factor.* It also uses enzymatic action to inhibit important cellular processes. The end result of lethal factor action is massive inflammation and initiation of shock.

Figure 20.20 *Bacillus anthracis.*   Note the centrally placed endospores and streptobacillus arrangement (600✕).

The *B. anthracis* exotoxin complex is like other bacterial "A-B toxins," which are described in detail in chapter 21. Most A-B toxins have two components: a "B" component that binds to host cells and an "A," or active, component that enters the cell and exerts some toxic effect. *B. anthracis* is a bit different; its protective antigen is the B component, and both lethal factor and edema factor are A components. The bacteria that cause cholera, shigellosis, pertussis, and diphtheria all use A-B exotoxins.

Additional virulence factors for *B. anthracis* include hemolysins and other enzymes that damage host membranes.

▶ Transmission and Epidemiology

The anthrax bacillus is a facultative parasite that undergoes its cycle of vegetative growth and sporulation in the soil. Animals become infected while grazing on grass contaminated with spores. When the pathogen is returned to the soil in animal excrement or carcasses, it can sporulate and become a long-term reservoir of infection for the animal population. The majority of natural anthrax cases are reported in livestock from Africa, Asia, and the Middle East. Most recent (natural) cases in the United States have occurred in textile workers handling imported animal hair or hide or products made from them. Because of effective control procedures, the number of cases in the United States is extremely low (fewer than 10 per year).

As a result of the terrorist attacks of 2001, anthrax has dominated the public consciousness as never before. The anthrax attack aimed at two senators and several media outlets focused a great deal of attention on the threat of bioterrorism. During that attack, 22 people acquired anthrax and 5 people died.

▶ Culture and Diagnosis

Diagnosis requires a high index of suspicion. This means that anthrax must be present as a possibility in the clinician's mind or it is likely not to be diagnosed, because it is such a rare disease in the developed world and because, in all of its manifestations, it can mimic other infections that are not so rare. (A very astute public health clinician in Florida first suspected anthrax in the attacks of 2001 and called for the proper tests.) First-level (presumptive) diagnosis begins with culturing the bacterium on blood agar and performing a Gram stain. Further tests can be performed to provide evidence regarding presence of *B. anthracis* as opposed to other *Bacillus* species. These tests include motility (*B. anthracis* is nonmotile) and a lack of hemolysis on blood agar. Ultimately, samples should be handled by the Centers for Disease Control and Prevention, which will perform confirmatory tests, usually involving direct fluorescent antibody testing and phage lysis tests.

▶ Prevention and Treatment

A vaccine containing live spores and a toxoid prepared from a special strain of *B. anthracis* are used to protect livestock in areas of the world where anthrax is endemic. Humans should be vaccinated with the purified toxoid if they have occupational contact with livestock or products such as hides and bone or if they are members of the military. Effective vaccination requires six inoculations given over 1.5 years, with yearly boosters. The cumbersome nature of vaccination has spurred research and development of more manageable vaccines. Persons who are suspected of being exposed to the bacterium are given prophylactic antibiotics, which seem to be effective at preventing disease even after exposure.

Carcasses of animals that have died from anthrax must be burned or chemically decontaminated before burial to prevent establishing the microbe in the soil. Imported items containing animal hides, hair, and bone should be gas sterilized.

The recommended treatment for anthrax is penicillin, doxycycline, or ciprofloxacin. During the attacks in 2001, initial treatment of exposed and sick persons was with ciprofloxacin because of fear that the *B. anthracis* strains used in the attacks could have been penicillin-resistant, either through intentional genetic engineering or due to the natural presence of beta-lactamase genes in the bacterium. Ciprofloxacin treatment continued for the course of the 2001 incident. The CDC is now recommending the use of doxycycline instead of ciprofloxacin, because ciprofloxacin is often used for empirical treatment of all types of infections of unknown etiology. More frequent use of ciprofloxacin could lead to higher levels of antibiotic resistance in bacteria in the U.S. population, which would render ciprofloxacin less effective as an empirical agent.

Case File 20 · *Continuing the Case*

The patient with apparent anthrax was a drum maker by trade, handcrafting traditional African drums from dried animal hides. This process required him to soak the hides in water for an hour and then scrape the hair off with a razor, thereby releasing large quantities of dust into his studio. Most of the animal skins were goat hides imported from Gambia.

Investigators from the Health Protection Agency examined the drum maker's property for the presence of the anthrax bacterium. In his studio they found endospores of *B. anthracis* on one of five drums and on a few animal skins. No other traces of the bacterium were found at the property. Although rare in the United Kingdom—and in the United States, for that matter—*B. anthracis* is found throughout much of the world. Its ability to form endospores and survive harsh environmental conditions (years of heat, cold, and ultraviolet radiation, along with a complete lack of water or nutrients) ensures that many endospores are found in soil. As animals graze, lie, or roll on the ground, some of the endospores are transferred onto their bodies. Livestock in Africa, Asia, and the Middle East account for the majority of anthrax cases seen worldwide.

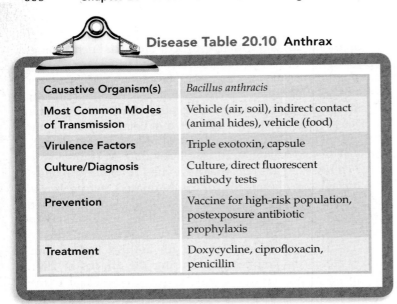

Disease Table 20.10 Anthrax

Causative Organism(s)	*Bacillus anthracis*
Most Common Modes of Transmission	Vehicle (air, soil), indirect contact (animal hides), vehicle (food)
Virulence Factors	Triple exotoxin, capsule
Culture/Diagnosis	Culture, direct fluorescent antibody tests
Prevention	Vaccine for high-risk population, postexposure antibiotic prophylaxis
Treatment	Doxycycline, ciprofloxacin, penicillin

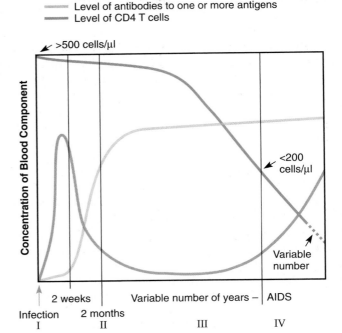

Virus levels are high during the initial acute infection and decrease until the later phases of HIV disease and AIDS. Antibody levels gradually rise and remain relatively high throughout phases III and IV. T-cell numbers remain relatively normal until the later phases of HIV disease and full-blown AIDS.

Figure 20.21 Dynamics of virus antigen, antibody, and T cells in circulation. The figure depicts a generalized curve. Specifics vary in actual infections.

HIV Infection and AIDS

The sudden emergence of AIDS in the early 1980s focused an enormous amount of public attention, research studies, and financial resources on the virus and its disease.

The first cases of AIDS were seen by physicians in Los Angeles, San Francisco, and New York City. They observed clusters of young male patients with one or more of a complex of symptoms: severe pneumonia caused by *Pneumocystis jiroveci* (ordinarily a harmless fungus), a rare vascular cancer called Kaposi's sarcoma, sudden weight loss, swollen lymph nodes, and general loss of immune function. Another common feature was that all of these young men were homosexuals. Early hypotheses attempted to explain the disease as a consequence of a "homosexual lifestyle" or as a result of immune suppression by chronic drug abuse or infections. Soon, however, cases were reported in nonhomosexual patients who had been transfused with blood or blood products. Eventually, virologists at the Pasteur Institute in France isolated a novel retrovirus, later named the **human immunodeficiency virus (HIV).** This cluster of symptoms was therefore clearly a communicable infectious disease, and the medical community termed it **acquired immunodeficiency syndrome,** or **AIDS.**

▶ Signs and Symptoms

A spectrum of clinical disease is associated with HIV infection. To understand the progression, follow **figure 20.21** closely. Symptoms in HIV infection are directly tied to two things: the level of virus in the blood and the level of T cells in the blood. (The figure shows two different lines that correspond to virus and T cells.) Note also that the figure depicts the course of HIV infection in the absence of medical intervention or chemotherapy.

Initial infection is often attended by vague, mononucleosis-like symptoms that soon disappear. This phase corresponds to the initial high levels of virus (the green line in the figure), and the subsequent drop in virus load. Within days of infection, about 50% of the T helper cells with memory for the virus are destroyed. Note that antibody levels (the orange line) rise at the same time that virus load is dropping; the immune response is responsible for the decreasing numbers of virus in the blood. This initial state is followed by a period of (mostly) asymptomatic infection that varies in length from 2 to 15 years (the average is 10). The lymphadenopathy that attended the initial infection usually persists throughout the entire infection. Note that during the mid- to late-asymptomatic periods, the number of T cells in the blood is steadily decreasing (purple line). Once the T cells reach low enough levels, symptoms of AIDS ensue.

Initial symptoms may be fatigue, diarrhea, weight loss, and neurological changes, but most patients first notice this phase of infection because of one or more opportunistic infections or neoplasms. These are detailed in **Insight 20.4.** Other disease-related symptoms appear to accompany severe immune deregulation, hormone imbalances, and metabolic disturbances. Pronounced wasting of body mass is a consequence of weight loss, diarrhea, and poor nutrient absorption. Recent data suggest that the virus is particularly hard on the GI tract. Protracted fever, fatigue, sore throat, and night sweats are significant and debilitating. Both a rash and generalized lymphadenopathy in several chains of lymph nodes are presenting symptoms in many AIDS patients.

INSIGHT 20.4 AIDS-Defining Illnesses (ADIs)

In AIDS patients who do not receive or do not comply with anti-retroviral therapy (and even in some who do), the slow destruction of the immune system results in a wide variety of infectious and noninfectious conditions called AIDS-associated illnesses or AIDS-defining illnesses (ADIs). It is almost always one or more of these conditions that cause death in AIDS patients.

Because the virus eventually collapses the immune system like a house of cards, it is not surprising that the body is beset by normally harmless microorganisms, many of which have been living in or on the host for decades without causing disease. The spectrum of AIDS-associated illnesses also provides insight into how vital the immune system is in controlling or mitigating cancerous changes in our cells. AIDS patients are at increased risk for Burkitt's lymphoma, Kaposi's sarcoma (KS), and invasive cervical carcinomas, all of which are associated with viral infections.

Since the beginning of the AIDS epidemic in the early 1980s, the CDC has maintained a list of conditions that are part of the case definition. The list has been modified periodically over the two decades of its existence. One of the ways that people currently meet the case definition for AIDS is if they are positive for the virus *and* experience one or more of these ADIs. The ADIs are listed in **table 20.A.** The diseases are listed according to the organ system where the presenting symptoms might be

Kaposi's sarcoma lesions on the arm. The flat, purple tumors occur in almost any tissue and are frequently multiple.

found. (Some of the conditions may be listed in more than one column.) You can see that most of them—or at least, the way they occur in AIDS patients—are very rare in the otherwise healthy population.

Table 20.A AIDS-Defining Illnesses

Skin and/or Mucous Membranes (includes eyes)	Nervous System	Cardiovascular and Lymphatic System or Multiple Organ Systems	Respiratory Tract	Gastrointestinal Tract	Genitourinary and/or Reproductive Tract
Cytomegalovirus retinitis (with loss of vision) Herpes simplex chronic ulcers (>1 month duration) Kaposi's sarcoma	Cryptococcosis, extrapulmonary HIV encephalopathy Lymphoma primarily in brain Progressive multifocal leukoencephalopathy Toxoplasmosis of the brain	Coccidioidomycosis, disseminated or extrapulmonary Cytomegalovirus (other than liver, spleen, nodes) Histoplasmosis cephalopathy Burkitt's lymphoma Immunoblastic lymphoma *Mycobacterium kansasii,* disseminated or extrapulmonary *Mycobacterium tuberculosis,* disseminated or extrapulmonary *Salmonella* septicemia, recurrent Wasting syndrome	Candidiasis of trachea, bronchi, or lungs Herpes simplex bronchitis or pneumonitis *Mycobacterium avium* complex Tuberculosis (*Mycobacterium tuberculosis*) *Pneumocystis jiroveci* pneumonia Pneumonia, recurrent	Candidiasis of esophagus, GI tract Herpes simplex chronic ulcers (>1 month duration) or esophagitis Isosporiasis, intestinal Cryptosporidiosis, chronic intestinal (>1 month duration)	Invasive cervical carcinoma (HPV) Herpes simplex chronic ulcers (>1 month duration)

Some of the most virulent complications are neurological. Lesions occur in the brain, meninges, spinal column, and peripheral nerves. Patients with nervous system involvement show some degree of withdrawal, persistent memory loss, spasticity, sensory loss, and progressive AIDS dementia.

▶ Causative Agent

HIV is a retrovirus, in the genus lentivirus. Many retroviruses have the potential to cause cancer and produce dire, often fatal diseases and are capable of altering the host's DNA in profound ways. They are named "retroviruses" because they reverse the usual order of transcription. They contain an unusual enzyme called **reverse transcriptase (RT)** that catalyzes the replication of double-stranded DNA from single-stranded RNA. The association of retroviruses with their hosts can be so intimate that viral genes are permanently integrated into the host genome. In fact, as you have read in earlier chapters, it has become increasingly evident that retroviral sequences are integral parts of host chromosomes. Not only can this retroviral DNA be incorporated into the host genome as a provirus that can be passed on to progeny cells, but some retroviruses also transform cells and regulate certain host genes.

The most prominent human retroviruses are the T-cell lymphotropic viruses I and II (HTLV-I and HTLV-II) and HTLV-III. Type I is associated with leukemia (discussed in a later section) and lymphoma; type III is now called HIV. There are two major types of HIV, namely HIV-1, which is the dominant form in most of the world, and HIV-2.

HIV and other retroviruses display structural features typical of enveloped RNA viruses **(figure 20.22a).** The outermost component is a lipid envelope with transmembrane glycoprotein spikes and knobs that mediate viral adsorption to the host cell. HIV can only infect host cells that present the required receptors, which is a combination receptor consisting of the CD4 marker plus a coreceptor. The virus uses these receptors to gain entrance to several types of leukocytes and tissue cells **(figure 20.22b).**

▶ Pathogenesis and Virulence Factors

As summarized in **figure 20.23,** HIV enters a mucous membrane or the skin and travels to dendritic cells, a type of phagocyte living beneath the epithelium. In the dendritic cell, the virus grows and is shed from the cell without killing it. The virus is amplified by macrophages in the skin, lymph organs, bone marrow, and blood. One of the great ironies of HIV is that it infects and destroys many of the very cells needed to combat it, including the helper (T4 or CD4) class of lymphocytes, monocytes, macrophages, and even B lymphocytes. The virus is adapted to docking onto its host cell's surface receptors (see figure 20.22). It then induces viral fusion with the cell membrane and creates syncytia.

Once the virus is inside the cell, its reverse transcriptase makes its RNA into DNA. Although initially it can produce a lytic infection, in many cells it enters a latent period in

the nucleus of the host cell and integrates its DNA into host DNA (see figure 20.23). This latency accounts for the lengthy course of the disease. Despite being described as a "latent" stage, research suggests that new viruses are constantly being produced and new T cells are constantly being manufactured, in an ongoing race that ultimately the host cells lose (in the absence of treatment).

The primary effects of HIV infection—those directly due to viral action—are harm to T cells and the central nervous system. The death of T cells and other white blood cells results

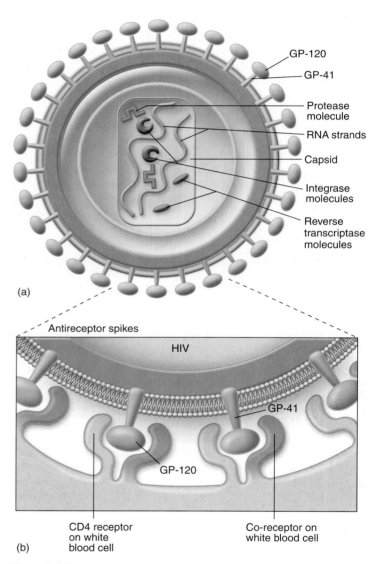

Figure 20.22 The general structure of HIV. **(a)** The envelope contains two types of glycoprotein (GP) spikes, two identical RNA strands, and several molecules of reverse transcriptase, protease, and integrase encased in a protein capsid. **(b)** The snug attachment of HIV glycoprotein molecules (GP-41 and GP-120) to their specific receptors on a human cell membrane. These receptors are CD4 and a co-receptor called CCR-5 (fusin) that permit docking with the host cell and fusion with the cell membrane.

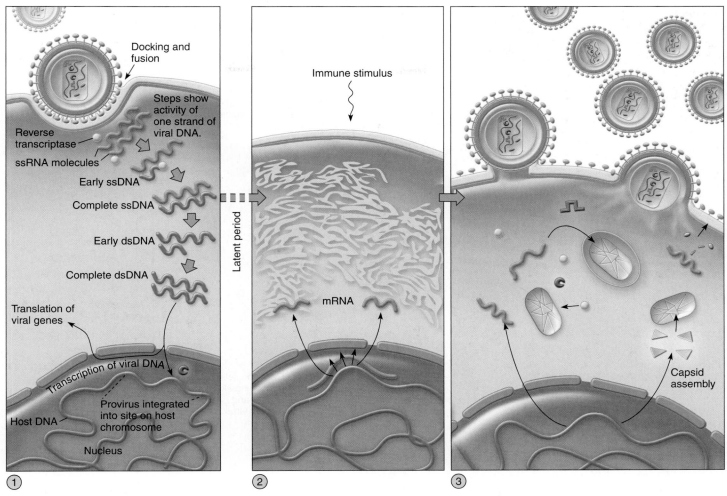

The virus is adsorbed and endocytosed, and the twin RNAs are uncoated. Reverse transcriptase catalyzes the synthesis of a single complementary strand of DNA (ssDNA). This single strand serves as a template for synthesis of a double strand (ds) of DNA. In latency, dsDNA is inserted into the host chromosome as a provirus.

After a latent period, various immune activators stimulate the infected cell, causing reactivation of the provirus genes and production of viral mRNA.

HIV mRNA is translated by the cell's synthetic machinery into virus components (capsid, reverse transcriptase, spikes), and the viruses are assembled. Budding of mature viruses lyses the infected cell.

Process Figure 20.23 **The general multiplication cycle of HIV.**

in extreme **leukopenia** and loss of essential T4 memory clones and stem cells. The viruses also cause formation of giant T cells and other syncytia, which allow the spread of viruses directly from cell to cell, followed by mass destruction of the syncytia. The destruction of T4 lymphocytes paves the way for invasion by opportunistic agents and malignant cells. The central nervous system is affected when infected macrophages cross the blood-brain barrier and release viruses, which then invade nervous tissue. Studies have indicated that some of the viral envelope proteins can have a direct toxic effect on the brain's glial cells and other cells.

The secondary effects of HIV infection are the opportunistic infections and malignancies that occur as the immune system becomes progressively crippled by viral attack. These are summarized in Insight 20.4.

▶ Transmission

HIV transmission occurs mainly through two forms of contact: sexual intercourse and transfer of blood or blood products **(figure 20.24)**. Babies can also be infected before or during birth, as well as through breast feeding. The mode of transmission is similar to that of hepatitis B virus, except that the AIDS virus does not survive for as long outside the host and it is far more sensitive to heat and disinfectants. And HIV is not transmitted through saliva, as hepatitis B can be.

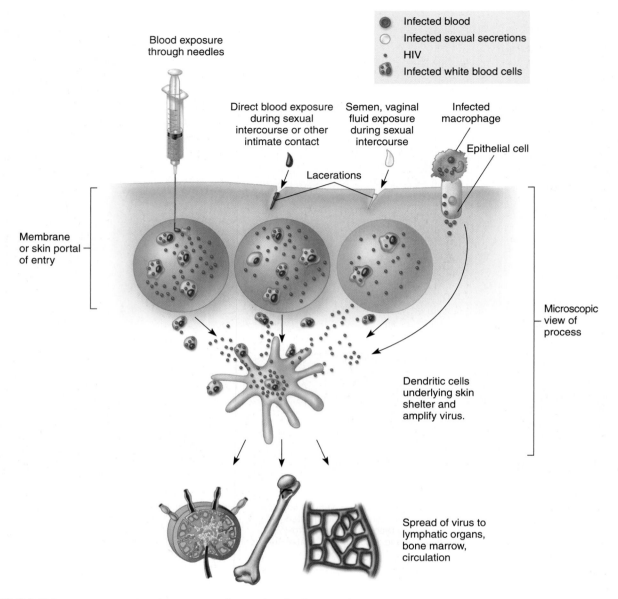

Figure 20.24 Primary sources and suggested routes of infection by HIV.

In general, HIV is spread only by direct and rather specific routes. Because the blood of HIV-infected people harbors high levels of free virus in both very early and very late stages of infection and high levels of infected leukocytes throughout infection, any form of intimate contact involving transfer of blood (trauma, needle sharing) can be a potential source of infection. Semen and vaginal secretions also harbor free virus and infected white blood cells, and thus they are significant factors in sexual transmission. The virus can be isolated from urine, tears, sweat, and saliva but in such small numbers that these fluids are not considered sources of infection. Because breast milk contains significant numbers of leukocytes, neonates who have escaped infection prior to and during birth can still become infected through nursing.

▶ Epidemiology

Since the beginning of the AIDS epidemic in the early 1980s, 25 million people have died worldwide. The best global estimate of the number of individuals currently infected with HIV (in 2007) is 33 million, with approximately 733,000 in the United States. A large number of these people have not yet begun to show symptoms. Due to efforts of many global AIDS initiatives, many more people in the developing world are receiving lifesaving treatments. But the number of new infections is still growing faster than access to drugs: For every two people receiving treatment, five new people are diagnosed.

AIDS first became a notifiable disease at the national level in 1984, and it has continued in an epidemic pattern, although the number of new AIDS cases occurring each year in the United States has decreased since 1994. Even in the United States, despite treatment advances, HIV infection/AIDS is the sixth most common cause of death among people ages 25 to 44, although it has fallen out of the top 150 list for causes of death overall.

Table 20.1 spells out some shifts in the behaviors that result in HIV infection in the United States. Throughout the course of the epidemic, close to half (47%) of all cases can be traced to male-to-male sexual contact. The big changes are in the percentage of cases being transmitted by heterosexual contact (31% in 2007 vs. 11% culumlatively through 2000). In large metropolitan areas especially, as many as 60% of intravenous drug users (IDUs) can be HIV carriers. Infection from contaminated needles is growing more rapidly than any other mode of transmission, and it is another significant factor in the spread of HIV to the heterosexual population.

In most parts of the world, heterosexual intercourse is the primary mode of transmission. In the industrialized world, the overall rate of heterosexual infection has increased dramatically in the past several years, especially in adolescent and young adult women. In the United States, about 31% of HIV infections arise from unprotected sexual intercourse with an infected partner of the opposite sex.

Now that donated blood is routinely tested for antibodies to the AIDS virus, transfusions are no longer considered a serious risk. Because there can be a lag period of a few weeks to several months before antibodies appear in an infected person, it is remotely possible to be infected through donated blood. Rarely, organ transplants can carry HIV, so they too should be tested. Other blood products (serum, coagulation factors) were once implicated in AIDS. Thousands of hemophiliacs died from the disease in the 1980s and 1990s. It is now standard practice to heat-treat any therapeutic blood products to destroy all viruses.

A small percentage of AIDS cases occur in people without apparent risk factors. This does not mean that some other unknown route of spread exists. Factors such as patient denial, unavailability of history, death, or uncooperativeness make it impossible to explain every case.

We should note that not everyone who becomes infected or is antibody-positive develops AIDS. About 1% of people who are antibody-positive remain free of disease, indicating that functioning immunity to the virus can develop. Any person who remains healthy despite HIV infection is termed a *nonprogressor*. These people are the object of intense scientific study. Some have been found to lack the cytokine receptors that HIV requires. Others are infected by a weakened virus mutant.

Treatment of HIV-infected mothers with a simple anti-HIV drug has dramatically decreased the rate of maternal-to-infant transmission of HIV during pregnancy. Current treatment regimens result in a transmission rate of approximately 11%, with some studies of multidrug regimens claiming rates as low as 5%. Evidence suggests that giving mothers protease inhibitors can reduce the transmission rate to around 1%. (Untreated mothers pass the virus to their babies at the rate of 33%.) The cost of perinatal prevention strategies (approximately $1,000 per pregnancy) and the scarcity of medical counseling in underserved areas has led to an increase in maternal transmission of HIV in developing parts of the world, at the same time that the developed world has seen a marked decrease.

Medical and dental personnel are not considered a high-risk group, although several hundred medical and dental workers are known to have acquired HIV or become antibody-positive as a result of clinical accidents. A health care worker involved in an accident in which gross inoculation with contaminated blood occurs (as in the case of a needlestick) has a less than 1 in 1,000 chance of becoming infected. We should emphasize that transmission of HIV will not occur through casual contact or routine patient care procedures and that universal precautions for infection control (see chapter 13) were designed to give full protection for both worker and patient.

▶ Culture and Diagnosis

First, let's define some terms. A person is diagnosed as having HIV infection if he or she has tested positive for the human immunodeficiency virus. This diagnosis is not the same as having AIDS.

In late 2006, the CDC issued new recommendations that HIV testing become much more routine. The guidelines call for testing all patients accessing health care facilities and for HIV testing to be included in the routine panel of prenatal screening for pregnant women. In both cases, patients can opt out of the test, although no separate consent will be solicited besides the general consent for medical care.

Most viral testing is based on detection of antibodies specific to the virus in serum or other fluids, which allows for the rapid, inexpensive screening of large numbers of samples.

Table 20.1	AIDS Cases in the United States by Exposure Category**	
Exposure Category	**Cumulative Percentage of New AIDS Cases Through 2000**	**Percentage of New AIDS Cases in 2007**
Male-to-male sexual contact	46	47
Injection drug use	25	17
Male-to-male sexual contact and injection drug use	6	5
Heterosexual contact	11	31
Other*	11	11

*Includes hemophilia, blood transfusion, perinatal, and risk not reported or identified.

**Data from the Centers for Disease Control and Prevention.

Testing usually proceeds at two levels. The initial screening tests include the older ELISA and newer latex agglutination and rapid antibody tests.

Although these tests are largely accurate, around 1% of results are false positives, and they always require follow-up with a more specific test called *Western blot* analysis (see p. 502). This test detects several different anti-HIV antibodies and can usually rule out false positive results.

Another inaccuracy can be false negative results that occur when testing is performed before the onset of detectable antibody production. To rule out this possibility, persons who test negative but feel they may have been exposed should be tested a second time 3 to 6 months later.

Blood and blood products are sometimes tested for HIV antigens (rather than for HIV antibodies) to close the window of time between infection and detectable levels of antibodies during which contamination could be missed by antibody tests.

In the United States, people are diagnosed with AIDS if they meet the following criteria: (1) they are positive for the virus, *and* (2) they fulfill one of these additional criteria:

- They have a CD4 (helper T cell) count of fewer than 200 cells per microliter of blood.
- Their CD4 cells account for fewer than 14% of all lymphocytes.
- They experience one or more of a CDC-provided list of AIDS-defining illnesses (ADIs).

The list of ADIs is long and includes opportunistic infections such as *Pneumocystis jiroveci* pneumonia and *Cryptosporidium* diarrhea; neoplasms such as Kaposi's sarcoma and invasive cervical cancer; and other conditions such as wasting syndrome (see Insight 20.4).

▶ **Prevention**

Avoidance of sexual contact with infected persons is a cornerstone of HIV prevention. Abstaining from sex is an obvious prevention method, although those who are sexually active can also take steps to decrease their risk. Epidemiologists cannot overemphasize the need to screen prospective sex partners and to follow a monogamous sexual lifestyle. And monogamous or not, a sexually active person should consider every partner to be infected unless proven otherwise. This may sound harsh, but it is the only sure way to avoid infection during sexual encounters. Barrier protection (condoms) should be used when having sex with anyone whose HIV status is not known with certainty to be negative. Although avoiding intravenous drugs is an obvious deterrent, many drug addicts do not, or cannot, choose this option. In such cases, risk can be decreased by not sharing syringes or needles or by cleaning needles with bleach and then rinsing before another use.

From the very first years of the AIDS epidemic, the potential for creating a vaccine has been regarded as slim, because the virus presents many seemingly insurmountable problems. Among them, HIV becomes latent in cells; its cell surface antigens mutate rapidly; and although it does elicit immune responses, it is apparently not completely controlled by them. In view of the great need for a vaccine, however, none of those facts has stopped the medical community from moving ahead.

Currently, multiple potential HIV vaccines are in clinical trials. Two very promising vaccines have failed to protect humans in clinical trials—the latest one tested in 2007 actually increased the chance of getting HIV in certain people. One of the problems seems to be that these vaccines are developed and then tested in primates, which is a problem since primates have not been successfully infected with HIV, but only with simian immunodeficiency virus, or SIV. It is closely related to HIV but apparently different enough that it gives misleading results with medicines meant for humans. That obstacle may have been overcome, as in late 2009 scientists announced that they had found a hybrid virus that can infect some types of primates and act like HIV. The next time a vaccine goes to human trials it may be that those results will more closely mirror the positive results in the animal model.

A growing group of scientists is arguing for a completely different, and deceptively simple, preventive approach. The news of their strategy often has headlines like "We Can Wipe Out HIV Completely." It sounds outrageous, but it is theoretically true. Their approach is to test everyone possible in all populations, and when you find all the people who are HIV-positive, treat them aggressively. We know that if we treat people with the drugs described in the next section, we can make them noninfectious. HIV would no longer be transmitted. It would be a massive effort—and cost a lot of money—but once we did it in a comprehensive way and everyone who was HIV-positive eventually died, HIV would be eliminated from the human population. Stay tuned to see how the world authorities who would have to come together for such an effort will respond to such an idea.

▶ **Treatment**

It must be clearly stated: There is no cure for HIV. None of the therapies do more than prolong life or diminish symptoms.

Clear-cut guidelines exist for treating people who test HIV-positive. These guidelines are updated regularly. The most recent update involves beginning treatment much earlier than previously. Until now, recommendations called for beginning aggressive antiviral chemotherapy after AIDS manifested itself. The newer recommendations call for treatment to begin soon after HIV diagnosis. In addition to antiviral chemotherapy, HIV-positive persons should receive a wide array of drugs to prevent or treat a variety of opportunistic infections and other ADIs such as wasting disease. These treatment regimens vary according to each patient's profile and needs.

The first effective drugs developed were the synthetic nucleoside analogs (reverse transcriptase inhibitors) azidothymidine (AZT), didanosine (ddI), lamivudine (Epivir) (3TC), and stavudine (d4T). They interrupt the HIV multiplication cycle by mimicking the structure of actual nucleosides and being added to viral DNA by reverse transcriptase. Because these drugs lack all of the correct binding sites for further DNA synthesis, viral replication and the viral cycle are terminated **(figure 20.25a)**. Other reverse transcriptase inhibitors that are not nucleosides are nevirapine and efavirenz (Sustiva), both of which bind to the enzyme and restructure it. Another important class of drugs is the protease inhibitors **(figure 20.25c),** which block the action of the HIV enzyme (protease) involved in the final assembly and maturation of the virus. Examples of these drugs include indinavir (Crixivan), ritonavir (Norvir), and amprenavir (Agenerase). Another class of drugs called integrase inhibitors provide a means to stop virus multiplication **(figure 20.25d).**

One of the latest additions to the arsenal is enfuvirtide (Fuzeon), a drug classified as a fusion inhibitor. It prevents the virus from fusing with the membrane of target cells, thereby stopping infection altogether **(figure 20.25b).**

A regimen that has proved to be extremely effective in controlling AIDS and inevitable drug resistance is **HAART,** short for *highly active antiretroviral therapy*. By combining two reverse transcriptase inhibitors and one protease inhibitor in a "cocktail," the virus is interrupted in two different phases of its cycle. This therapy has been successful in reducing viral load to undetectable levels and facilitating the improvement of immune function. It has also reduced the incidence of viral drug resistance, because the virus would have to undergo three separate mutations simultaneously, at nearly impossible odds. Patients who are HIV-positive but asymptomatic can remain healthy with this therapy as well. The primary drawbacks are high cost, toxic side effects, drug failure due to patient noncompliance, and an inability to completely eradicate the virus.

Although we opened this section by stating "There is no cure for HIV," there have been some promising advances. In 2007, an HIV-positive man received a bone marrow transplant from a person who was known to possess two copies of a gene that prevents HIV from invading lymphocytes. The gene from the donor continued a mutation that eliminated the T-cell co-receptor for HIV on T cells. As late as 2009 the recipient was still free of virus. That strategy is not likely to be an answer for worldwide HIV treatment, as bone marrow transplants would be too drastic to treat the millions of HIV-positive people in

(a) and (b) **Fusion inhibitors** prevent docking of the virus to host cells. A prominent group of drugs (AZT, ddl, 3TC) are **nucleoside analogs that inhibit reverse transcriptase.** They are inserted in place of the natural nucleotide by reverse transcriptase but block further action of the enzyme and synthesis of viral DNA. Non-nucleoside RT inhibitors are also in use.

(c) **Protease inhibitors** plug into the active sites on HIV protease. This enzyme is necessary to cut elongate HIV protein strands and produce functioning smaller protein units. Because the enzyme is blocked, the proteins remain uncut, and abnormal defective viruses are formed.

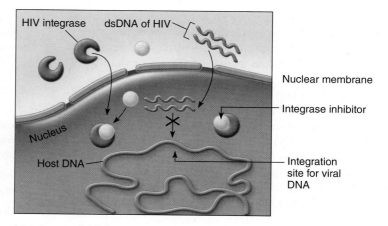

(d) **Integrase inhibitors** are a class of experimental drugs that attach to the enzyme required to splice the dsDNA from HIV into the host genome. This will prevent formation of the provirus and block future virus multiplication in that cell.

Figure 20.25 Mechanisms of action of anti-HIV drugs.

the world, and the donor genotype (two copies of the relevant gene) is very rare. But research continues into ways to exploit the knowledge gained in this hallmark experiment. One researcher is pursuing a gene therapy approach to redesign the T cells of infected patients so that they no longer have this receptor, hoping to eliminate the infection.

Disease Table 20.11 HIV Infection and AIDS

Causative Organism(s)	Human immunodeficiency virus 1 or 2
Most Common Modes of Transmission	Direct contact (sexual), parenteral (blood-borne), vertical (perinatal and via breast milk)
Virulence Factors	Attachment, syncytia formation, reverse transcriptase, high mutation rate
Culture/Diagnosis	Initial screening for antibody followed by Western blot confirmation of antibody
Prevention	Avoidance of contact with infected sex partner, contaminated blood, breast milk
Treatment	HAART (reverse transcriptase inhibitors plus protease inhibitors), Fuzeon, nonnucleoside RT inhibitors

Adult T-Cell Leukemia

Leukemia is the general name for at least four different malignant diseases of the white blood cell–forming elements originating in the bone marrow. Some forms of leukemia are acute and others are chronic. Leukemias have many causes, only two of which are thought to be viral. The retrovirus HTLV-I is associated with a form of leukemia called adult T-cell leukemia.

The signs and symptoms of all leukemias are similar and include easy bruising or bleeding, paleness, fatigue, and recurring minor infections. These symptoms are associated with the underlying pathologies of anemia, platelet deficiency, and immune dysfunction brought about by the disturbed lymphocyte ratio and function. In some cases of adult T-cell leukemia, cutaneous T-cell lymphoma is the prime clinical manifestation, accompanied by dermatitis, with thickened, scaly, ulcerative, or tumorous skin lesions. Other complications are lymphadenopathy and dissemination of the tumors to the lung, spleen, and liver.

The possible mechanisms by which retroviruses stimulate cancer are not entirely clear. One hypothesis is that the virus carries an oncogene that, when spliced into a host's chromosome and triggered by various carcinogens, can

immortalize the cell and deregulate the cell division cycle. One of HTLV's genetic targets seems to be the gene and receptor for interleukin-2, a potent stimulator of T cells.

Adult T-cell leukemia was first described by physicians working with a cluster of patients in southern Japan. Later, a similar clinical disease was described in Caribbean immigrants. In time, it was shown that these two diseases were the same. Although more common in Japan, Europe, and the Caribbean, a small number of cases occur in the United States. The disease is not highly transmissible; studies among families show that repeated close or intimate contact is required. Because the virus is thought to be transferred in infected blood cells, blood transfusions and blood products are potential agents of transmission. Intravenous drug users could spread it through needle sharing.

Treatment may include a number of antineoplastic drugs, radiation therapy, and transplants. Alpha-interferon has been used with some effectiveness.

Disease Table 20.12 Adult T-Cell Leukemia

Disease	Adult T-cell leukemia
Causative Organism(s)	HTLV-I
Most Common Modes of Transmission	Unclear—blood-borne transmission implicated
Virulence Factors	Induction of malignant state
Culture/Diagnosis	Differential blood count followed by histological examination of excised lymph node tissue
Prevention	–
Treatment	Antineoplastic drugs, interferon alpha

20.3 Learning Outcomes—Can You ...

4. ... list the possible causative agents, modes of transmission, virulence factors, diagnostic techniques, and prevention/treatment for the two forms of endocarditis?

5. ... discuss what series of events may lead to septicemia and how it should be prevented and treated?

6. ... list the possible causative agents, modes of transmission, virulence factors, diagnostic techniques, and prevention/treatment for cardiovascular system infections that have only one infectious cause? These are: plague, tularemia, Lyme disease, and infectious mononucleosis.

7. ... discuss factors that distinguish hemorrhagic and nonhemorrhagic fever diseases?

8. ... list the possible causative agents, modes of transmission, virulence factors, diagnostic techniques, and prevention/treatment for hemorrhagic fever diseases?

9. ... list the possible causative agents, modes of transmission, virulence factors, diagnostic techniques, and prevention/treatment for nonhemorrhagic fever diseases?

10. ... discuss all aspects of malaria, with special emphasis on epidemiology?

11. ... describe what makes anthrax a good agent for bioterrorism and list the important presenting signs to look for in patients?

12. ... discuss how the epidemiology of HIV infection in the United States has changed over time and why?

13. ... discuss the epidemiology of HIV infection in the developing world?

▶ Summing Up

Taxonomic Organization Summing up Microorganisms Causing Disease in the Cardiovascular and Lymphatic System

Microorganism	Disease	Chapter Location
Gram-positive endospore-forming bacteria		
Bacillus anthracis	Anthrax	Anthrax, p. 606
Gram-positive bacteria		
Staphylococcus aureus	Acute endocarditis	Endocarditis, p. 588
Streptococcus pyogenes	Acute endocarditis	Endocarditis, p. 588
Streptococcus pneumoniae	Acute endocarditis	Endocarditis, p. 588
Gram-negative bacteria		
Yersinia pestis	Plague	Plague, p. 590
Francisella tularensis	Tularemia	Tularemia, p. 592
Borrelia burgdorferi	Lyme disease	Lyme disease, p. 593
Brucella abortus, B. suis	Brucellosis	Nonhemorrhagic fever diseases, p. 599
Coxiella burnetii	Q fever	Nonhemorrhagic fever diseases, p. 600
Bartonella henselae	Cat-scratch disease	Nonhemorrhagic fever diseases, p. 600
Bartonella quintana	Trench fever	Nonhemorrhagic fever diseases, p. 601
Ehrlichia chaffeensis, E. phagocytophila, E. ewingii	Ehrlichiosis	Nonhemorrhagic fever diseases, p. 601
Neisseria gonorrhoeae	Acute endocarditis	Endocarditis, p. 588
Rickettsia rickettsii	Rocky Mountain spotted fever	Nonhemorrhagic fever diseases, p. 601
DNA viruses		
Epstein-Barr virus	Infectious mononucleosis	Infectious mononucleosis, p. 596
RNA viruses		
Yellow fever virus	Yellow fever	Hemorrhagic fevers, p. 597
Dengue fever virus	Dengue fever	Hemorrhagic fevers, p. 597
Ebola and Marburg viruses	Ebola and Marburg hemorrhagic fevers	Hemorrhagic fevers, p. 598
Lassa fever virus	Lassa fever	Hemorrhagic fevers, p. 599
Chikungunya virus	Hemorrhagic fever	Hemorrhagic fevers, p. 598
Retroviruses		
Human immunodeficiency virus 1 and 2	HIV infection and AIDS	HIV infection and AIDS, p. 608
Human T-cell lymphotropic virus I	Adult T-cell leukemia	Leukemias, p. 616
Protozoa		
Plasmodium falciparum, P. vivax, P. ovale, P. malariae	Malaria	Malaria, p. 602

INFECTIOUS DISEASES AFFECTING
The Cardiovascular and Lymphatic Systems

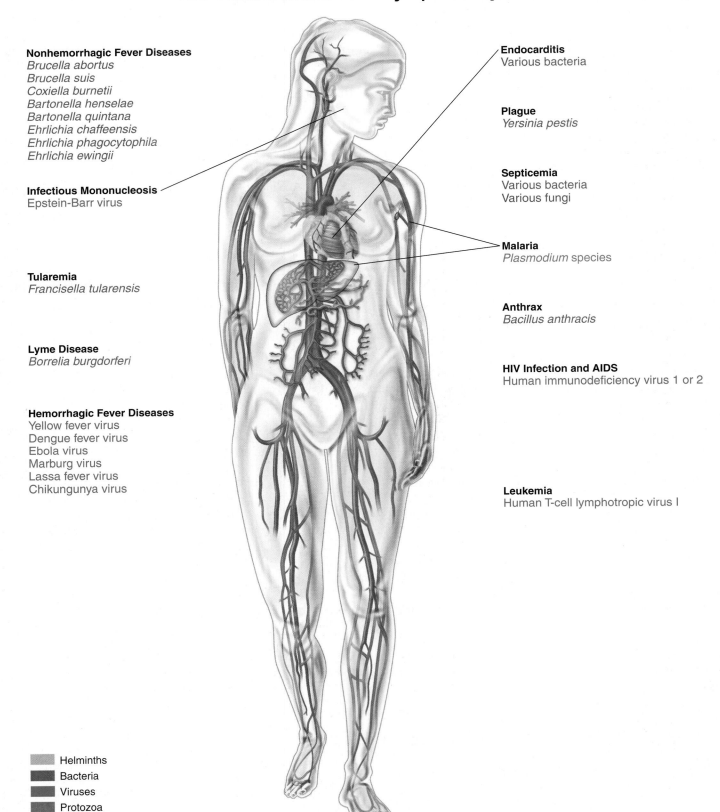

Nonhemorrhagic Fever Diseases
Brucella abortus
Brucella suis
Coxiella burnetii
Bartonella henselae
Bartonella quintana
Ehrlichia chaffeensis
Ehrlichia phagocytophila
Ehrlichia ewingii

Infectious Mononucleosis
Epstein-Barr virus

Tularemia
Francisella tularensis

Lyme Disease
Borrelia burgdorferi

Hemorrhagic Fever Diseases
Yellow fever virus
Dengue fever virus
Ebola virus
Marburg virus
Lassa fever virus
Chikungunya virus

Endocarditis
Various bacteria

Plague
Yersinia pestis

Septicemia
Various bacteria
Various fungi

Malaria
Plasmodium species

Anthrax
Bacillus anthracis

HIV Infection and AIDS
Human immunodeficiency virus 1 or 2

Leukemia
Human T-cell lymphotropic virus I

- Helminths
- Bacteria
- Viruses
- Protozoa
- Fungi

System Summary Figure 20.26

618

Chapter Summary

20.1 The Cardiovascular and Lymphatic Systems and Their Defenses

- The cardiovascular system is composed of the blood vessels and the heart. It provides tissues with oxygen and nutrients and carries away carbon dioxide and waste products.
- The lymphatic system is a one-way passage, returning fluid from the tissues to the cardiovascular system. The cardiovascular system is highly protected from microbial infection, as it is not an open body system and it contains many components of the host's immune system.

20.2 Normal Biota of the Cardiovascular and Lymphatic Systems

- At the present time we believe that the cardiovascular and lymphatic systems contain no normal biota.

20.3 Cardiovascular and Lymphatic System Diseases Caused by Microorganisms

- **Endocarditis:** An inflammation of the endocardium, usually due to an infection of the valves of the heart.
- **Acute Endocarditis:** Most often caused by *Staphylococcus aureus*, group A streptococci, *Streptococcus pneumoniae*, and *Neisseria gonorrhoeae*.
- **Subacute Forms of Endocarditis:** Almost always preceded by some form of damage to the heart valves or by congenital malformation. Alpha-hemolytic streptococci, such as *Streptococcus sanguis, S. oralis*, and *S. mutans*, are most often responsible; normal biota can also colonize abnormal valves.
- **Septicemias:** Occur when organisms are actively multiplying in the blood. Most caused by bacteria, to a lesser extent by fungi.
- **Plague:** Can manifest in three different ways: *Pneumonic plague* is a respiratory disease; *bubonic plague* causes inflammation and necrosis of the lymph nodes; *septicemic plague* is the result of multiplication of bacteria in the blood. *Yersinia pestis* is the causative organism. Fleas are principal agents in transmission of the bacterium.
- **Tularemia:** Causative agent is a facultative intracellular gram-negative bacterium called *Francisella tularensis*. Disease is often called rabbit fever.
- **Lyme Disease:** Caused by *Borrelia burgdorferi*. Syndrome mimics neuromuscular and rheumatoid conditions. *B. burgdorferi* is a unique spirochete transmitted primarily by *Ixodes* ticks.
- **Infectious Mononucleosis:** Vast majority of cases are caused by the herpesvirus *Epstein-Barr virus (EBV)*. Cell-mediated immunity can control the infection, but people usually remain chronically infected.
- **Hemorrhagic Fever Diseases:** Extreme fevers often accompanied by internal hemorrhaging. Hemorrhagic fever diseases described here are caused by RNA enveloped viruses in one of three families: Arenaviridae, Filoviridae, and Flaviviridae.
  - Yellow Fever: Caused by an arbovirus, a single-stranded RNA flavivirus transmitted by the mosquito *Aedes aegypti*.
  - Dengue Fever: Caused by a single-stranded RNA flavivirus, also carried by Aedes mosquitoes. Mild infection is most common; a form called dengue hemorrhagic shock syndrome can be lethal.
  - Ebola and Marburg viruses are filoviruses (Family Filoviridae) endemic to Central Africa. Virus in the bloodstream leads to extensive capillary fragility and disruption of clotting.
  - The Lassa Fever virus is an arenavirus found in West Africa. Reservoir of the virus is a rodent found in Africa called the multimammate rat.
- **Nonhemorrhagic Fever Diseases:** Characterized by high fever without the capillary fragility that leads to hemorrhagic symptoms.
  - Brucellosis: Also called Malta fever, undulant fever, Bang's disease. Genus *Brucella* contains tiny, aerobic gram-negative coccobacilli. Two species cause this disease in humans: *B. abortus* (in cattle) and *B. suis* (in pigs).
  - Q Fever: Caused by *Coxiella burnetii*, a very small pleomorphic gram-negative bacterium and intracellular parasite. *C. burnetii* harbored by wide assortment of vertebrates and arthropods, especially ticks. However, humans acquire infection mainly by environmental contamination and airborne transmission.
  - Cat-Scratch Disease: *Bartonella henselae* is causative agent. Infection connected with being clawed or bitten by a cat.
  - Trench Fever: Causative agent, *Bartonella quintana*, is carried by lice. Highly variable symptoms can include a 5- to 6-day fever, leg pains, headache, chills, and muscle aches.
- **Ehrlichioses:** There are four tick-borne, fever-producing diseases caused by members of the genus *Ehrlichia*.
- **Rocky Mountain Spotted Fever:** Another tick-borne disease; causes a distinctive rash. Caused by *Rickettsia rickettsii*.
- **Malaria:** Symptoms are malaise, fatigue, vague aches, and nausea, followed by bouts of chills, fever, and sweating. Symptoms occur at 48- or 72-hour intervals, as a result of synchronous rupturing of red blood cells. Causative organisms are *Plasmodium* species: *P. malariae, P. vivax, P. falciparum*, and *P. ovale*. Carried by *Anopheles* mosquito.
- **Anthrax:** Exhibits primary symptoms in various locations: skin (cutaneous anthrax), lungs (pulmonary anthrax), gastrointestinal tract, central nervous system (anthrax meningitis). Caused by *Bacillus anthracis*, gram-positive endospore-forming rod found in soil.
- **HIV Infection and AIDS:** Symptoms directly tied to the level of virus in the blood vs. the level of T cells in the blood.
  - HIV is a retrovirus (genus lentivirus). Contains *reverse transcriptase*, which catalyzes the replication of double-stranded DNA from single-stranded RNA. Retroviral DNA incorporated into the host genome as provirus that can be passed on to progeny cells in latent state.

- Destruction of T4 lymphocytes paves way for invasion by opportunistic agents and malignant cells.
- HIV transmission occurs mainly through sexual intercourse and transfer of blood or blood products.

- **Adult T-Cell Leukemia:** Leukemia is general name for at least four different malignant diseases of the white blood cell-forming elements of the bone marrow. Retrovirus HTLV-I is associated with one form of leukemia called adult T-cell leukemia.

Multiple-Choice and True-False   Knowledge and Comprehension

Multiple-Choice Questions. Select the correct answer from the answers provided.

1. When bacteria flourish and grow in the bloodstream, this is referred to as
   a. viremia.
   b. bacteremia.
   c. septicemia.
   d. fungemia.

2. Which of the following diseases is caused by a retrovirus?
   a. Lassa fever
   b. cat-scratch disease
   c. anthrax
   d. adult T-cell leukemia

3. The plague bacterium, *Yersinia pestis,* is transmitted mainly by
   a. mosquitoes.
   b. fleas.
   c. dogs.
   d. birds.

4. Rabbit fever is caused by
   a. *Yersinia pestis.*
   b. *Francisella tularensis.*
   c. *Borrelia burgdorferi.*
   d. *Chlamydia bunnyensis.*

5. A distinctive bull's-eye rash results from a tick bite transmitting
   a. Lyme disease.
   b. tularemia.
   c. Q fever.
   d. Rocky Mountain spotted fever.

6. Cat-scratch disease is caused by
   a. *Coxiella burnetii.*
   b. *Bartonella henselae.*
   c. *Bartonella quintana.*
   d. *Brucella abortus.*

7. The bite of the Lone Star tick, *Ixodes scapularis,* can cause
   a. ehrlichioses.
   b. Lyme disease.
   c. trench fever.
   d. both a and b.
   e. both b and c.

8. Cat-scratch disease is effectively treated with
   a. rifampin.
   b. penicillin.
   c. amoxicillin.
   d. acyclovir.

9. Wool-sorter's disease is caused by
   a. *Brucella abortus.*
   b. *Bacillus anthracis.*
   c. *Coxiella burnetii.*
   d. rabies virus.

10. Which of the following is *not* a hemorrhagic fever?
    a. Lassa fever
    b. Marburg fever
    c. Ebola fever
    d. trench fever

True-False Questions. If the statement is true, leave as is. If it is false, correct it by rewriting the sentence.

11. Brucellosis can be transmitted to humans by drinking contaminated milk.

12. Respiratory tract infection with *Bartonella henselae* is considered an AIDS-defining condition.

13. Lyme disease is caused by *Rickettsia rickettsii.*

14. Yellow fever is caused by a protozoan transmitted by fleas.

15. HIV in the United States is mainly transmitted via male homosexual sex.

Critical Thinking Questions   Application and Analysis

These questions are suggested as a *writing-to-learn* experience. For each question, compose a one- or two-paragraph answer that includes the factual information needed to completely address the question.

1. What is endotoxic shock?

2. Explain how eradicating mosquitoes could make dengue fever worse.

3. Describe the infectious cycle of HIV.

4. Describe the life cycle of the malarial parasite, including the significant events of sexual and asexual reproduction.

5. What criteria are used in the United States to diagnose a person with AIDS?

6. a. What are retroviruses? Where does the name come from?
   b. Name some retroviruses implicated in human diseases.

7. a. What are the different locations in the human body that anthrax infection can be exhibited?
   b. Which of these are the most common forms of the disease?
   c. What organism(s) cause this disease?

8. Use the terms *prevalence* and *incidence* (chapter 13) to explain how better treatment options have led to a higher prevalence of AIDS in the world.

9. Provide some possible scientific explanations about why there are people who are HIV-positive but remain healthy and never develop AIDS—so-called nonprogressors?

10. What characteristics make tularemia a potential bioweapon?

Concept Mapping   Synthesis

Appendix D provides guidance for working with concept maps.

1. Provide the missing concepts in this map.

Visual Connections   Synthesis

These questions use visual images or previous content to make connections to this chapter's concepts.

1. a. **From chapter 14, figure 14.15.** Imagine that the WBCs shown in this illustration are unable to control the microorganisms. Could the change that has occurred in the vessel wall help the organism spread to other locations? If so, how?

   b. If the organisms are able to survive phagocytosis, how could that impact the progress of this disease? Explain your answer.

(a)　　　　(b)

www.connect.microbiology.com

Enhance your study of this chapter with study tools and practice tests. Also ask your instructor about the resources available through ConnectPlus, including the media-rich eBook, interactive learning tools, and animations.

21

Infectious Diseases Affecting the Respiratory System

Case File 21

Have you even been on a mission trip with your church or youth group? Each year, thousands of Americans travel to other countries, or to disaster areas within their own country (such as New Orleans after Hurricane Katrina), where they pitch in to perform all kinds of ordinary, but important, manual tasks, such as simple construction, renovation, or flood cleanup.

For one such mission trip, a group of church volunteers from Pennsylvania and Virginia traveled to a church in Nueva San Salvador. A total of 35 volunteers went to El Salvador, traveling in three groups between January 3 and February 20, 2008. El Salvador didn't turn out very well. Twenty of the volunteers came down with a serious respiratory disease resembling acute influenza within 3 to 25 days of arriving in El Salvador.

To try to diagnose the disease and figure out how the patients had acquired it, public health officials began investigating the activities of all the volunteers, those affected by the illness as well as those unaffected. The volunteers had helped clean indoor and outdoor renovation sites, install electrical and plumbing components, build additional rooms onto the church, replace the roof, and excavate the septic tank. In addition, each of the mission groups had taken one day off during their stay to visit a local beach or lake.

- What diseases might be included in the differential diagnosis for this condition?
- When considering possible diseases, would the geographical location have any influence on your choices?

Continuing the Case appears on page 648.

Outline and Learning Outcomes

21.1 The Respiratory Tract and Its Defenses
1. Draw or describe the anatomical features of the respiratory tract.
2. List the natural defenses present in the respiratory tract.

21.2 Normal Biota of the Respiratory Tract
3. List the types of normal biota presently known to occupy the respiratory tract.

21.3 Upper Respiratory Tract Diseases Caused by Microorganisms

4. List the possible causative agents, modes of transmission, virulence factors, diagnostic techniques, and prevention/treatment for each of the diseases of the upper respiratory tract. These are: rhinitis, sinusitis, otitis media, pharyngitis, and diphtheria.

5. Identify which disease is often caused by a mixture of microorganisms.

6. Identify two bacteria that can cause dangerous pharyngitis cases.

21.4 Diseases Caused by Microorganisms Affecting Both the Upper and Lower Respiratory Tracts

7. List the possible causative agents, modes of transmission, virulence factors, diagnostic techniques, and prevention/treatment for each of the diseases infecting both the upper and lower respiratory tracts. These are: pertussis, RSV disease, and influenza.

8. Compare and contrast antigenic drift and antigenic shift in influenza viruses.

21.5 Lower Respiratory Tract Diseases Caused by Microorganisms

9. List the possible causative agents, modes of transmission, virulence factors, diagnostic techniques, and prevention/treatment for each of the diseases infecting the lower respiratory tract. These are: tuberculosis, community-acquired pneumonia, and nosocomial pneumonia.

10. Discuss the problems associated with MDR-TB and XDR-TB.

11. Demonstrate an in-depth understanding of the epidemiology of tuberculosis infection.

12. Describe the importance of the recent phenomenon of cold viruses causing pneumonia.

13. List the distinguishing characteristics of nosocomial versus community-acquired pneumonia.

21.1 The Respiratory Tract and Its Defenses

The respiratory tract is the most common place for infectious agents to gain access to the body. We breathe 24 hours a day, and anything in the air we breathe passes at least temporarily into this organ system.

The structure of the system is illustrated in **figure 21.1a.** Most clinicians divide the system into two parts, the *upper* and

(b) Ciliary defense of the tracheal mucosa (5,000×)

Cilia   Microvilli

Nasal cavity
Nostril
Oral cavity
Pharynx
Epiglottis
Larynx
Trachea
Bronchus
Bronchioles

(a)   Right lung   Left lung

(c)

Frontal sinus
Ethmoid sinus
Maxillary sinus
Sphenoid sinus

Figure 21.1 The respiratory tract. **(a)** Important structures in the upper and lower respiratory tracts. **(b)** Ciliary defense of the respiratory tract. **(c)** The four pairs of sinuses in the face and skull.

lower respiratory tracts. The upper respiratory tract includes the mouth, the nose, the nasal cavity and sinuses above it, the throat or pharynx, and the epiglottis and larynx. The lower respiratory tract begins with the trachea, which feeds into the bronchi and bronchioles in the lungs. Attached to the bronchioles are small balloonlike structures called alveoli, which inflate and deflate with inhalation and exhalation. These are the site of oxygen exchange in the lungs.

Several anatomical features of the respiratory system protect it from infection. As described in chapter 14, nasal hair serves to trap particles. Cilia **(figure 21.1b)** on the epithelium of the trachea and bronchi (the ciliary escalator) propel particles upward and out of the respiratory tract. Mucus on the surface of the mucous membranes lining the respiratory tract is a natural trap for invading microorganisms. Once the microorganisms are trapped, involuntary responses such as coughing, sneezing, and swallowing can move them out of sensitive areas. These are first-line defenses.

The second and third lines of defense also help protect the respiratory tract. Macrophages inhabit the alveoli of the lungs and the clusters of lymphoid tissue (tonsils) in the throat. Secretory IgA against specific pathogens can be found in the mucus secretions as well.

21.1 Learning Outcomes—Can You ...

1. ... draw or describe the anatomical features of the respiratory tract?
2. ... list the natural defenses present in the respiratory tract?

21.2 Normal Biota of the Respiratory Tract

Because of its constant contact with the external environment, the respiratory system harbors a large number of commensal microorganisms. The normal biota is generally limited to the upper respiratory tract, and gram-positive bacteria such as streptococci and staphylococci are very common. Note that some bacteria that can cause serious disease are frequently present in the upper respiratory tract as "normal" biota; these include *Streptococcus pyogenes*, *Haemophilus influenzae*, *Streptococcus pneumoniae*, *Neisseria meningitidis*, and *Staphylococcus aureus*. These bacteria can potentially cause disease if

their host becomes immunocompromised for some reason, and they can cause disease in other hosts when they are innocently transferred to them. Other normal biota bacteria include nonhemolytic and alpha-hemolytic streptococci, *Moraxella* species, and *Corynebacterium* species (often called diphtheroids). Yeasts, especially *Candida albicans*, also colonize the mucosal surfaces of the mouth.

In the respiratory system, as in some other organ systems, the normal biota performs the important function of microbial antagonism (see chapter 13). This reduces the chances of pathogens establishing themselves in the same area by competing with them for resources and space. As is the case with the other body sites harboring normal biota, the microbes reported here are those we have been able to culture in the laboratory. More microbes will come to light as scientists catalog the genetic sequences in the Human Microbiome Project.

21.2 Learning Outcome—Can You ...

3. ... list the types of normal biota presently known to occupy the respiratory tract?

21.3 Upper Respiratory Tract Diseases Caused by Microorganisms

Rhinitis, or the Common Cold

In the course of a year, people in the United States suffer from about 1 billion colds, called rhinitis because *rhin-* means nose and *-itis* means inflammation. Many people have several episodes a year. Economists estimate that this fairly innocuous infection costs the United States $40 billion a year in trips to the doctors, medications, and lost work time.

▶ Signs and Symptoms

Everyone is familiar with the symptoms of rhinitis: sneezing, scratchy throat, and runny nose (rhinorrhea), which usually begin 2 or 3 days after infection. An uncomplicated cold generally is not accompanied by fever, although children can experience low fevers (less than 102°F). The incubation period is usually 2 to 5 days. Note that people with asthma and other underlying respiratory conditions, such as chronic

Respiratory Tract Defenses and Normal Biota		
	Defenses	**Normal Biota**
Upper Respiratory Tract	Nasal hair, ciliary escalator, mucus, involuntary responses such as coughing and sneezing, secretory IgA	*Moraxella*, nonhemolytic and alpha-hemolytic streptococci, *Corynebacterium* and other diphtheroids, *Candida albicans* Note: *Streptococcus pyogenes*, *Streptococcus pneumoniae*, *Haemophilus influenzae*, *Neisseria meningitidis*, and *Staphylococcus aureus* often present as "normal" biota.
Lower Respiratory Tract	Mucus, alveolar macrophages, secretory IgA	None

obstructive pulmonary disease (COPD) often suffer severe symptoms triggered by the common cold.

▶ Causative Agents

The common cold is caused by one of over 200 different kinds of viruses. The particular virus is almost never identified, and the symptoms and handling of the infection are the same no matter which of the viruses is responsible.

The most common type of virus leading to rhinitis is the group called rhinoviruses, of which there are 99 serotypes. Coronaviruses and adenoviruses are also major causes. Most viruses causing the common cold never lead to any serious consequences, but some of them can be serious for some patients. Starting in 2007, an apparently mutated strain of adenovirus started making the news: It had become highly virulent, and more common. We will cover it in the section about pneumonias, since that is what this adenovirus often results in. Also, the respiratory syncytial virus (RSV) causes colds in most people, but in some, especially children, they can lead to more serious respiratory tract symptoms. (RSV is discussed later in the chapter.) In this section, we consider all cold-causing viruses together as a group because they are treated similarly.

Viral infection of the upper respiratory tract can predispose a patient to secondary infections by other microorganisms, such as bacteria. Secondary infections may explain why some people report that their colds improved when they were given antibiotics. The cold was caused by viruses; bacterial infection may have followed.

▶ Pathogenesis and Virulence Factors

Viruses that induce rhinitis do not have many virulence mechanisms. They must penetrate the mucus that coats the respiratory tract and then find firm attachment points. Once they are attached, they use host cells to produce more copies of themselves (see chapter 6). The symptoms we experience as the common cold are mainly the result of our body fighting back against the viral invaders. Virus-infected cells in the upper respiratory tract release chemicals that attract certain types of white blood cells to the site, and these cells release cytokines and other inflammatory mediators, as described earlier in chapters 14 and 16. These mediators generate a localized inflammatory reaction, characterized by swelling and inflammation of the nasal mucosa, leakage of fluid from capillaries and lymph vessels, and increased production of mucus. The similarity of these symptoms to those of inhalant allergies illustrates that the same immune reactions are involved in both conditions.

▶ Transmission and Epidemiology

Cold viruses are transmitted by droplet contact, but indirect transmission may be more common, such as when a healthy person touches a fomite and then touches one of his or her own vulnerable surfaces, such as the mouth, nose, or an eye. In some cases, the viruses can remain air-borne in droplet nuclei and aerosols and can be transmitted in that way.

The epidemiology of the common cold is fairly simple: Practically everybody gets them, and fairly frequently. Children have more frequent infections than adults, probably because nearly every virus they encounter is a new one and they have no secondary immunity to it. People can acquire some degree of immunity to a cold virus that they have encountered before, but because there are more than 200 viruses, this immunity doesn't provide much overall protection.

▶ Prevention

There is no vaccine for rhinitis. A traditional vaccine would need to contain antigens from about 200 viruses to provide complete protection. Researchers are studying novel types of immunization strategies, however. Because most of the viruses causing rhinitis use only a few different chemicals on host epithelium for their attachment site, some scientists have proposed developing a vaccine that would stimulate antibody to the docking site on the host. Other approaches include inducing antibody to the sites of action for the inflammatory mediators. But for now, the best prevention is to stop the transmission between hosts. The best way to prevent transmission is frequent hand washing, followed closely by stopping droplets from traveling away from the mouth and nose by covering them when sneezing or coughing. It is better to do this by covering the face with the crook of the arm rather than the hand, because subsequent contact with surfaces is less likely.

▶ Treatment

No chemotherapeutic agents cure the common cold. A wide variety of over-the-counter agents, such as antihistamines and decongestants, improve symptoms by blocking inflammatory mediators and their action. The use of these agents may also cut down on transmission to new hosts, because fewer virus-loaded secretions are produced.

Disease Table 21.1 Rhinitis

Causative Organism(s)	Approximately 200 viruses
Most Common Modes of Transmission	Indirect contact, droplet contact
Virulence Factors	Attachment proteins; most symptoms induced by host response
Culture/Diagnosis	Not necessary
Prevention	Hygiene practices
Treatment	For symptoms only

Sinusitis

Commonly called a *sinus infection,* this inflammatory condition of any of the four pairs of sinuses in the skull **(figure 21.1c)** can actually be caused by allergy (most common), infections, or simply by structural problems such as narrow passageways or a deviated nasal septum. The infectious agents that may be responsible for the condition commonly include a variety of viruses or bacteria and, less commonly, fungi. Infections of the sinuses often follow a bout with the common cold. The inflammatory symptoms of a cold produce a large amount of fluid and mucus and when trapped in the sinuses, these secretions provide an excellent growth medium for bacteria or fungi. So viral rhinitis is frequently followed by sinusitis caused by bacteria or fungi.

▶ Signs and Symptoms

A person suffering from any form of sinusitis experiences nasal congestion, pressure above the nose or in the forehead, and sometimes the feeling of a headache or a toothache. Facial swelling and tenderness are common. Discharge from the nose and mouth appears opaque and has a green or yellow color in the case of bacterial infections. Discharge caused by an allergy is usually clear, and the symptoms may be accompanied by itchy, watery eyes.

▶ Causative Agents

Bacteria Any number of bacteria that are normal biota in the upper respiratory tract may cause sinus infections. Many cases are caused by *Streptococcus pneumoniae, Streptococcus pyogenes, Staphylococcus aureus,* and *Haemophilus influenzae.* The causative organism is usually not identified, but treatment is begun empirically, based on the symptoms.

The bacteria that cause these infections are most often normal biota in the host and don't have an arsenal of virulence factors that lead to their ability to cause disease. The pathogenesis of this condition is brought about by the confluence of several factors: predisposition to infection because of underlying (often viral) infection; buildup of fluids, providing a rich environment for bacterial multiplication; and sometimes the anatomy of the sinuses, which can contribute to entrapment of mucus and bacterial growth.

Bacterial sinusitis is not a communicable disease. Of course, the virus originally causing rhinitis is transmissible, but the host takes it from there by creating the conditions favorable for respiratory tract microorganisms to multiply in the sinus spaces, which normally do not harbor microorganisms to any significant extent.

Sinusitis is extremely common, resulting in approximately 11.5 million office visits a year in the United States. A large proportion of these cases are allergic sinusitis episodes, but approximately 30% of them are caused by bacterial overgrowth in the sinuses. Women and residents of the southern United States have slightly higher rates. As with many upper respiratory tract infections, smokers have higher rates of infection than nonsmokers. Children who are exposed to large amounts of secondhand smoke are also more susceptible.

Broad-spectrum antibiotics may be prescribed when the physician feels that the sinusitis is bacterial in origin (that is, when allergic sinusitis and fungal sinusitis are ruled out).

Fungi Fungal sinusitis is rare, but it is often recognized when antibacterial drugs fail to alleviate symptoms. Simple fungal infections may normally be found in the maxillary sinuses and are noninvasive in nature. These colonies are generally not treated with antifungal agents but instead are simply mechanically removed by a physician. *Aspergillus fumigatus* is a common fungus involved in this type of infection. The growth of fungi in this type of sinusitis may be encouraged by trauma to the area.

More serious invasive fungal infections of the sinuses may be found in severely immunocompromised patients. Fungi such as *Aspergillus* and *Mucor* species may invade the bony structures in the sinuses and even travel to the brain or eye. These infections are treated aggressively with a combination of surgical removal of the fungus and intravenous antifungal therapy **(Disease Table 21.2).**

Disease Table 21.2 Sinusitis

Causative Organism(s)	Various bacteria, often mixed infection	Various fungi
Most Common Modes of Transmission	Endogenous (opportunism)	Introduction by trauma or opportunistic overgrowth
Virulence Factors	–	–
Culture/Diagnosis	Culture not usually performed; diagnosis based on clinical presentation, occasionally X rays or other imaging technique used	Same
Prevention	–	–
Treatment	Broad-spectrum antibiotics	Physical removal of fungus; in severe cases antifungals used
Distinctive Features	Much more common than fungal	Suspect in immunocompromised patients

Acute Otitis Media (Ear Infection)

This condition is another common sequela of rhinitis, or the common cold, and for reasons similar to the ones described for sinusitis. Viral infections of the upper respiratory tract lead to inflammation of the eustachian tubes and the buildup of fluid in the middle ear, which can lead to bacterial multiplication in those fluids. Although the middle ear normally has no biota, bacteria can migrate along the eustachian tube from the upper respiratory tract **(figure 21.2)**. When bacteria encounter mucus and fluid buildup in the middle ear, they multiply rapidly. Their presence increases the inflammatory response, leading to pus production and continued fluid secretion. This fluid is referred to as *effusion.*

Another condition, known as chronic otitis media, occurs when fluid remains in the middle ear for indefinite periods of time. Until recently, physicians considered it to be the result of a noninfectious immune reaction because they could not culture bacteria from the site and because antibiotics were not effective. New data suggest that this form of otitis media is caused by a mixed biofilm of bacteria that are attached to the membrane of the inner ear. Biofilm bacteria generally are less susceptible to antibiotics (as discussed in chapter 4), and their presence in biofilm form would explain the inability to culture them from ear fluids.

▶ Signs and Symptoms

Otitis media may be accompanied by a sensation of fullness or pain in the ear and loss of hearing. Younger children may exhibit irritability, fussiness, and difficulty in sleeping, eating, or hearing. Severe or untreated infections can lead to

rupture of the eardrum because of pressure of pus buildup, or to internal breakthrough of these infected fluids, which can lead to more serious conditions such as mastoiditis, meningitis, or intracranial abscess.

▶ Causative Agents

Many different viruses and bacteria can cause acute otitis media, but the most common cause is *Streptococcus pneumoniae* (also discussed in the section on pneumonia later in this chapter). *Haemophilus influenzae* is another common cause of this condition; however, the incidence of all types of infections with this bacterium was significantly reduced with the introduction of a childhood vaccine against it in the 1980s. Scientists have now found that the majority of otitis media cases are mixed infections with viruses and bacteria acting together.

Streptococcus pneumoniae appears as pairs of elongated, gram-positive cocci joined end to end. It is often called by the familiar name *pneumococcus,* and diseases caused by it are termed *pneumococcal.*

▶ Transmission and Epidemiology

Otitis media is a sequela of upper respiratory tract infection and is not communicable, although the upper respiratory infection preceding it is. Children are particularly susceptible, and boys have a slightly higher incidence than do girls.

▶ Prevention

A vaccine against *S. pneumoniae* has been a part of the recommended childhood vaccination schedule since 2000. The vaccine (Prevnar) is a seven-valent conjugated vaccine (see chapter 15). It contains polysaccharide capsular material from seven different strains of the bacterium complexed with a chemical that makes it more antigenic. It is distinct from another vaccine for the same bacterium (Pneumovax), which is primarily targeted to the older population to prevent pneumococcal pneumonia.

▶ Treatment

Until the late 1990s, broad-spectrum antibiotics were routinely prescribed for otitis media. When it became clear that frequently treating children with these drugs was producing a bacterial biota with high rates of antibiotic resistance, the treatment regimen was reexamined.

The current recommendation for uncomplicated acute otitis media with a fever below 104°F is "watchful waiting" for 72 hours to allow the body to clear the infection, avoiding the use of antibiotics. When antibiotics are used, antibiotic resistance must be considered. Children who experience frequent recurrences of ear infections sometimes have small tubes placed through the tympanic membranes into their middle ears to provide a means of keeping fluid out of the site when inflammation occurs **(Disease Table 21.3).**

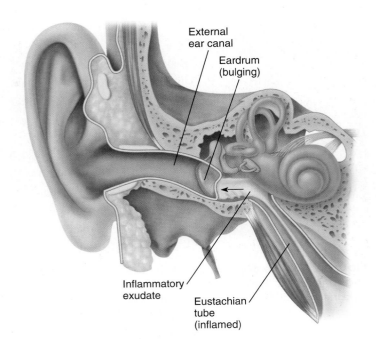

External ear canal

Eardrum (bulging)

Inflammatory exudate

Eustachian tube (inflamed)

Figure 21.2 An infected middle ear.

Disease Table 21.3 Otitis Media

Causative Organism(s)*	*Streptococcus pneumoniae*	*Haemophilus influenzae*	Other bacteria
Most Common Modes of Transmission	Endogenous (may follow upper respiratory tract infection by *S. pneumoniae* or other microorganisms)	Endogenous (follows upper respiratory tract infection)	Endogenous
Virulence Factors	Capsule, hemolysin	Capsule, fimbriae	–
Culture/Diagnosis	Usually relies on clinical symptoms and failure to resolve within 72 hours	Same	Same
Prevention	Pneumococcal conjugate vaccine (heptavalent)	Hib vaccine	None
Treatment	Wait for resolution; if needed, amoxicillin (are high rates of resistance) or amoxicillin + clavulanate or cefuroxime	Same as for *S. pneumoniae*	Wait for resolution; if needed, a broad-spectrum antibiotic (azithromycin) might be used in absence of etiologic diagnosis
Distinctive Features	–	–	Suspect if fully vaccinated against other two

*Keep in mind that many bacterial cases of otitis media are complicated with viral coinfections.

Pharyngitis

▶ Signs and Symptoms

The name says it all—this is an inflammation of the throat, which the host experiences as pain and swelling. The severity of pain can range from moderate to severe, depending on the causative agent. Viral sore throats are generally mild and sometimes lead to hoarseness. Sore throats caused by group A streptococci are generally more painful than those caused by viruses, and they are more likely to be accompanied by fever, headache, and nausea.

Clinical signs of a sore throat are reddened mucosa, swollen tonsils, and sometimes white packets of inflammatory products visible on the walls of the throat, especially in streptococcal disease **(figure 21.3)**. The mucous membranes may be swollen, affecting speech and swallowing. Often pharyngitis results in foul-smelling breath. The incubation period for most sore throats is generally 2 to 5 days.

▶ Causative Agents

A sore throat is most commonly caused by the same viruses causing the common cold. It can also accompany other diseases, such as infectious mononucleosis (described in chapter 20). Pharyngitis may simply be the result of mechanical irritation from prolonged shouting or from drainage of an infected sinus cavity. The most serious cause of pharyngitis is *Streptococcus pyogenes*. We will address this infection in depth, after a brief digression about an emerging cause of pharyngitis.

Fusobacterium necrophorum

Recently cases of severe sore throats caused by a bacterium called *Fusobacterium necrophorum* have cropped up in adolescents and young adults around the country. Some studies suggest it is as common as *S. pyogenes* in this age group. It can cause serious infections of the bloodstream and other organs, a condition called Lemierre's syndrome. Doctors speculate that this disease was previously rarely seen since most sore throats were empirically treated with

Figure 21.3 The appearance of the throat in pharyngitis and tonsillitis. The pharynx and tonsils become bright red and suppurative. Whitish pus nodules may also appear on the tonsils.

broad-spectrum antibiotics, a treatment that generally kills *F. necrophorum*. Now that physicians are being much more judicious with antibiotic treatment, and generally not treating at all if strep tests are negative, this bacterium has a doorway to cause disease. This bacterium is sensitive to penicillin and related drugs, which are the first-line drugs for *S. pyogenes* as well. It does make the use of second-line drugs for strep throats less desirable as some of them, such as azithromycin, have no effect on this bacterium. There are currently no rapid diagnostic tests for *F. necrophorum*.

Streptococcus pyogenes

S. pyogenes is a gram-positive coccus that grows in chains. It does not form spores, is nonmotile, and forms capsules and slime layers. *S. pyogenes* is a facultative anaerobe that ferments a variety of sugars. It does not form catalase, but it does have a peroxidase system for inactivating hydrogen peroxide, which allows its survival in the presence of oxygen.

▶ Pathogenesis

Untreated streptococcal throat infections occasionally can result in serious complications, either right away or days to weeks after the throat symptoms subside. These complications include scarlet fever, rheumatic fever, and glomerulonephritis. More rarely, invasive and deadly conditions such as necrotizing fasciitis can result from infection by *S. pyogenes*. These invasive conditions are described in chapter 18.

Scarlet Fever   Scarlet fever is the result of infection with an *S. pyogenes* strain that is itself infected with a bacteriophage. This lysogenic virus confers on the streptococcus the ability to produce erythrogenic toxin, described in the section on virulence. Scarlet fever is characterized by a sandpaper-like rash, most often on the neck, chest, elbows, and inner surfaces of the thighs. High fever accompanies the rash. It most often affects school-age children, and was a source of great suffering in the United States in the early part of the 20th century. In epidemic form, the disease can have a fatality rate of up to 95%. Most cases seen today are mild. They are easily recognizable and amenable to antibiotic therapy. Because of the fear elicited by the name "scarlet fever," the disease is often called scarlatina in North America.

Rheumatic Fever   Rheumatic fever is thought to be due to an immunologic cross-reaction between the streptococcal M protein and heart muscle. It tends to occur approximately 3 weeks after pharyngitis has subsided. It can result in permanent damage to heart valves **(figure 21.4)**. Other symptoms include arthritis in multiple joints and the appearance of nodules over bony surfaces just under the skin. Rheumatic fever is completely preventable if the original streptococcal infection is treated with antibiotics. Nevertheless, it is still a serious problem today in many parts of the world.

(a)

(b)   Mitral valve

Figure 21.4 The cardiac complications of rheumatic fever.   Pathologic processes of group A streptococcal infection can extend to the heart. In this example, it is believed that cross-reactions between streptococcal-induced antibodies and heart proteins have a gradual destructive effect on the atrioventricular valves (especially the mitral valve) or semilunar valves. Scarring and deformation change the capacity of the valves to close and shunt the blood properly. **(a)** A normal valve, viewed from above. **(b)** A scarred mitral valve. The color difference in the two views is artificial.

Glomerulonephritis   Glomerulonephritis is thought to be the result of streptococcal proteins participating in the formation of antigen-antibody complexes, which then are deposited in the basement membrane of the glomeruli of the kidney. It is characterized by **nephritis** (appearing as swelling in the hands and feet and low urine output), blood in the urine, increased blood pressure, and occasionally heart failure. It can result in permanent kidney damage. The incidence of poststreptococcal glomerulonephritis has been declining in the United States, but it is still common in Africa, the Caribbean, and South America.

Toxic shock syndrome and necrotizing fasciitis are other, less frequent consequences of streptococcal infections, and are discussed in chapter 18.

▶ **Virulence Factors**

The virulence of *S. pyogenes* is partly due to the substantial array of surface antigens, toxins, and enzymes it can generate.

Streptococci display numerous surface antigens **(figure 21.5)**. Specialized polysaccharides on the surface of the cell wall help to protect the bacterium from being dissolved by the lysozyme of the host. Lipoteichoic acid (LTA) contributes to the adherence of *S. pyogenes* to epithelial cells in the pharynx. A spiky surface projection called *M protein* contributes to virulence by resisting phagocytosis and possibly by contributing to adherence. A capsule made of hyaluronic acid (HA) is formed by most *S. pyogenes* strains. It probably contributes to the bacterium's adhesiveness. Because this HA is chemically indistinguishable from HA found in human tissues, it does not provoke an immune response from the host.

Extracellular Toxins   Group A streptococci owe some of their virulence to the effects of hemolysins called streptolysins. The two types are streptolysin O (SLO) and streptolysin S (SLS).[1] Both types cause beta-hemolysis of sheep blood agar (see "Culture and Diagnosis"). Both hemolysins rapidly injure many cells and tissues, including leukocytes and liver and heart muscle (in other forms of streptococcal disease).

A key toxin in the development of scarlet fever is **erythrogenic** (eh-rith″-roh-jen′-ik) **toxin.** This toxin is responsible for the bright red rash typical of this disease, and it also induces fever by acting upon the temperature regulatory center in the brain. Only lysogenic strains of *S. pyogenes* that contain genes from a temperate bacteriophage can synthesize this toxin. (For a review of the concept of lysogeny, see chapter 6.)

Some of the streptococcal toxins (erythrogenic toxin and streptolysin O) contribute to increased tissue injury

by acting as *superantigens*. These toxins elicit excessively strong reactions from monocytes and T lymphocytes. When activated, these cells proliferate and produce *tumor necrosis factor* (*TNF*), which leads to a cascade of immune responses resulting in vascular injury. This is the likely mechanism for the severe pathology of toxic shock syndrome and necrotizing fasciitis.

▶ **Transmission and Epidemiology**

Physicians estimate that 30% of sore throats may be caused by *S. pyogenes,* adding up to several million cases each year. Most transmission of *S. pyogenes* is via respiratory droplets or direct contact with mucus secretions. This bacterium is carried as "normal" biota by 15% of the population, but transmission from this reservoir is less likely than from a person who is experiencing active disease from the infection because of the higher number of bacteria present in the disease condition. It is less common but possible to transmit this infection via fomites. Humans are the only significant reservoir of *S. pyogenes.*

More than 80 serotypes of *S. pyogenes* exist, and thus people can experience multiple infections throughout their lives because immunity is serotype-specific. Even so, only a minority of encounters with the bacterium result in disease. An immunocompromised host is more likely to suffer from strep pharyngitis as well as serious sequelae of the throat infection.

Although most sore throats caused by *S. pyogenes* can resolve on their own, they should be treated with antibiotics because serious sequelae are a possibility.

▶ **Culture and Diagnosis**

The failure to recognize group A streptococcal infections can have devastating effects. Rapid cultivation and diagnostic techniques to ensure proper treatment and prevention measures are essential. Several different rapid diagnostic test kits are used in clinics and doctors' offices to detect group A streptococci from pharyngeal swab samples. These tests are based on antibodies that react with the outer carbohydrates of group A streptococci **(figure 21.6*a*)**. Because the rapid tests have a significant possibility of returning a false-negative result, guidelines call for confirming the negative finding with a culture, which can be read the following day.

A culture is generally taken at the same time as the rapid swab and is plated on sheep blood agar. *S. pyogenes* displays a beta-hemolytic pattern due to its streptolysins (and hemolysins) **(figure 21.6*b*)**. If the pharyngitis is caused by a virus, the blood agar dish will show a variety of colony types, representing the normal bacterial biota. Active infection with *S. pyogenes* will yield a plate with a majority of beta-hemolytic colonies. Group A streptococci are by far the most common beta-hemolytic isolates in human diseases, but lately an increased number of infections by group B streptococci (also beta-hemolytic), as well as the existence of beta-hemolytic enterococci, have made it important to use differentiation tests. A positive bacitracin disc test (figure 21.6*b*) provides additional evidence for group A.

---

1. In SLO, O stands for oxygen because the substance is inactivated by oxygen. In SLS, S stands for serum because the substance has an affinity for serum proteins. SLS is oxygen-stable.

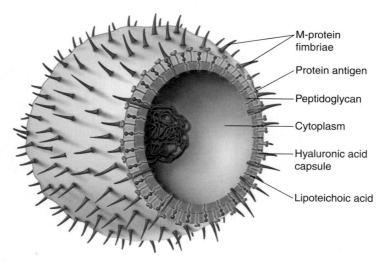

M-protein fimbriae

Protein antigen

Peptidoglycan

Cytoplasm

Hyaluronic acid capsule

Lipoteichoic acid

Figure 21.5 Cutaway view of group A streptococcus.

Figure 21.6 Streptococcal tests. **(a)** A rapid, direct test kit for diagnosis of group A infections. With this method, a patient's throat swab is introduced into a system composed of latex beads and monoclonal antibodies. *(Left)* In a positive reaction, the C-carbohydrate on group A streptococci produces visible clumps. *(Right)* A smooth, milky reaction is negative. **(b)** Bacitracin disc test. With very few exceptions, only *Streptococcus pyogenes* is sensitive to a minute concentration (0.02 µg) of bacitracin. Any zone of inhibition around the B disc is interpreted as a presumptive indication of this species. (Note: Group A streptococci are negative for sulfamethoxazole-trimethoprim [SXT] sensitivity and the CAMP test.)

(a)   Positive reaction   Negative reaction

Bacitracin disc   SXT disc

(−) CAMP test

(b)

▶ Prevention

No vaccine exists for group A streptococci, although many researchers are working on the problem. A vaccine against this bacterium would also be a vaccine against rheumatic fever, and thus it is in great demand. In the meantime, infection can be prevented by good hand washing, especially after coughing and sneezing and before preparing foods or eating.

▶ Treatment

The antibiotic of choice for *S. pyogenes* is penicillin; many group A streptococci have become resistant to erythromycin, a macrolide antibiotic. In patients with penicillin allergies, a first-generation cephalosporin, such as cephalexin, is prescribed **(Disease Table 21.4).**

Disease Table 21.4 Pharyngitis

Causative Organism(s)	*Fusobacterium necrophorum*	*Streptococcus pyogenes*	Viruses
Most Common Modes of Transmission	Opportunistic	Droplet or direct contact	All forms of contact
Virulence Factors	Endotoxin, leukotoxin	LTA, M protein, hyaluronic acid capsule, SLS and SLO, superantigens	–
Culture/Diagnosis	Growth on anaerobic agar	Beta-hemolytic on blood agar, sensitive to bacitracin, rapid antigen tests	Goal is to rule out *S. pyogenes*, further diagnosis usually not performed
Prevention	Hygiene practices	Hygiene practices	Hygiene practices
Treatment	Penicillin, cefuroxime	Penicillin, cephalexin in penicillin-allergic	Symptom relief only
Distinctive Features	Common in adolescents and young adults, infections spread to cardiovascular system or deeper tissues	Generally more severe than viral pharyngitis	Hoarseness frequently accompanies viral pharyngitis

Diphtheria

For hundreds of years, diphtheria was a significant cause of morbidity and mortality, but in the last 50 years, both the number of cases and the fatality rate have steadily declined throughout the world. In the United States in recent years, only one or two cases have been reported each year. But when healthy people are screened for the presence of the bacterium, it is found in a significant percentage of them, indicating that the lack of cases is due to the protection afforded by immunization with the diphtheria toxoid, which is part of the childhood immunization series.

Indeed, during the 1990s, a diphtheria epidemic occurred in the former Soviet Union in which 157,000 people became ill with diphtheria and 5,000 people died. This upsurge of cases was attributed to a breakdown in immunization practices and production of vaccine, which followed the breakup of the Soviet Union. These examples emphasize the importance of maintaining vaccination, even for diseases that have long been kept under control.

▶ Signs, Symptoms, and Causative Organism

The disease is caused by *Corynebacterium diphtheriae*, a non-spore-forming, gram-positive club-shaped bacterium **(figure 21.7)**. The symptoms of diphtheria are experienced initially in the upper respiratory tract. At first the patient experiences a sore throat, lack of appetite, and low-grade fever. A characteristic membrane, usually referred to as a pseudomembrane, forms on the tonsils or pharynx **(figure 21.8)**. The membrane is formed by the bacteria and consists of bacterial cells, fibrin, lymphocytes, and dead tissue cells; and it may be quite extensive. It adheres to tissues and cannot easily be removed. It may eventually completely block respiration. The patient may recover after this crisis. Alternatively, exotoxin manufactured by the bacterium may penetrate the bloodstream and travel throughout the body.

▶ Pathogenesis and Virulence Factors

The exotoxin is encoded by a bacteriophage of *C. diphtheriae*. Strains of the bacterium that are not lysogenized by this phage do not cause serious disease. The exotoxin is of a type called **A-B toxin**. It is illustrated in **figure 21.9** and explained briefly here. A-B toxins are so named because they consist of two parts, an A (active) component and a B (binding) component. The B component binds to a receptor molecule on the surface of the host cell. The next step is for the A component to be moved across the host cell membrane. The A components of most A-B toxins then catalyze a reaction by which they remove a sugar derivative called the ADP-ribosyl group from the coenzyme NAD and attach it to one host cell protein or another. This process is called *ADP-ribosylation*. This process disrupts the normal function of that host protein, resulting in some type of symptom for the patient.

The release of diphtheria toxin in the blood leads to complications in distant organs, especially myocarditis and neuritis. Myocarditis can cause abnormal cardiac rhythms and in the worst cases can lead to heart failure. Neuritis affects motor nerves and may result in temporary paralysis of limbs, the soft palate, and even the diaphragm, a condition that can predispose a patient to other lower respiratory tract infections.

▶ Prevention and Treatment

Diphtheria can easily be prevented by a series of vaccinations with toxoid, usually given as part of a mixed vaccine against tetanus and pertussis as well, called the *DTaP* (for diphtheria, tetanus, and acellular pertussis). If a patient has diphtheria, and it has progressed to the bloodstream, the adverse effects

Figure 21.8 Diagnosing diphtheria. The clinical appearance in diphtheria infection includes gross inflammation of the pharynx and tonsils marked by grayish patches (a pseudomembrane) and swelling over the entire area.

Figure 21.7 *Corynebacterium diphtheriae.*

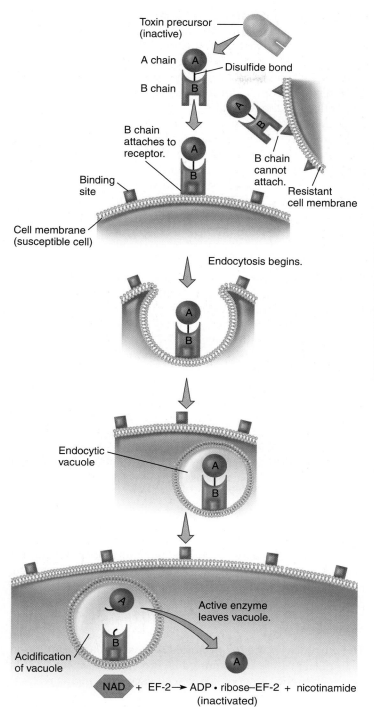

Figure 21.9 A-B toxin of *Corynebacterium diphtheriae.*   The B chain attaches to host cell membrane, then the toxin enters the cell. The two chains separate and the A chain enters the cytoplasm as an active enzyme that ADP-ribosylates a protein (EF-2) needed for protein synthesis. Cell death follows.

of toxemia are treated with diphtheria antitoxin derived from horses. Prior to injection, the patient must be tested for allergy to horse serum and be desensitized if necessary. The infection itself may be treated with antibiotics from the penicillin or erythromycin family. Bed rest, heart medication,

and tracheostomy or bronchoscopy to remove the membrane (sometimes called a pseudomembrane) may be indicated. Adults and adolescents should receive a DTaP booster.

Disease Table 21.5 Diphtheria

Causative Organism(s)	*Corynebacterium diphtheriae*
Most Common Modes of Transmission	Droplet contact, direct contact or indirect contact with contaminated fomites
Virulence Factors	Exotoxin: diphtheria toxin
Culture/Diagnosis	Tellurite medium—gray/black colonies, club-shaped morphology on Gram stain; treatment begun before definitive identification
Prevention	Diphtheria toxoid vaccine (part of DTaP)
Treatment	Antitoxin plus penicillin or erythromycin

21.3 Learning Outcomes—Can You . . .

4. . . . list the possible causative agents, modes of transmission, virulence factors, diagnostic techniques, and prevention/treatment for each of the diseases of the upper respiratory tract? These are: rhinitis, sinusitis, otitis media, pharyngitis, and diphtheria.
5. . . . identify which disease is often caused by a mixture of microorganisms?
6. . . . identify two bacteria that can cause dangerous pharyngitis cases?

21.4 Diseases Caused by Microorganisms Affecting Both the Upper and Lower Respiratory Tracts

A number of infectious agents affect both the upper and lower respiratory tract regions. We discuss the more well-known diseases in this section; specifically, they are whooping cough, respiratory syncytial virus (RSV), and influenza.

Whooping Cough

Whooping cough is also known as *pertussis* (the suffix *-tussis* is Latin for cough). A vaccine for this potentially serious infection has been available since 1926. The disease is still troubling to the public health community because its incidence has increased every year since the 1980s in the United

States, despite improvements in the vaccine. In addition, in the recent past there has been concern over the vaccine among the general public. For these reasons, it is an important disease for health care professionals to understand.

▶ Signs and Symptoms

The disease has two distinct symptom phases called the catarrhal and paroxysmal stages, which are followed by a long recovery (or convalescent) phase, during which a patient is particularly susceptible to other respiratory infections. After an incubation period of from 3 to 21 days, the **catarrhal** stage begins when bacteria present in the respiratory tract cause what appear to be cold symptoms, most notably a runny nose. This stage lasts 1 to 2 weeks. The disease worsens in the second **(paroxysmal)** stage, which is characterized by severe and uncontrollable coughing (a *paroxysm* can be thought of as a convulsive attack). The common name for the disease comes from the whooping sound a patient makes as he or she tries to grab a breath between uncontrollable bouts of coughing. The violent coughing spasms can result in burst blood vessels in the eyes or even vomiting. In the worst cases, seizures result from small hemorrhages in the brain.

As in any disease, the **convalescent phase** is the time when numbers of bacteria are decreasing and no longer cause ongoing symptoms. But the active stages of the disease damage the cilia on respiratory tract epithelial cells, and complete recovery of these surfaces requires weeks or even months. During this time, other microorganisms can more easily colonize and cause secondary infection.

▶ Causative Agent

Bordetella pertussis is a very small gram-negative rod. Sometimes it looks like a coccobacillus. It is strictly aerobic and fastidious, having specific nutritional requirements for successful culture.

▶ Pathogenesis and Virulence Factors

The progress of this disease can be clearly traced to the virulence mechanisms of the bacterium. It is absolutely essential for the bacterium to attach firmly to the epithelial cells of the mouth and throat, and it does so using specific adhesive molecular structures on its surface. One of these structures is called *filamentous hemagglutinin* (FHA). It is a fibrous structure that surrounds the bacterium like a capsule and is also secreted in soluble form. In that form, it can act as a bridge between the bacterium and the epithelial cell.

Once the bacteria are attached in large numbers, production of mucus increases and localized inflammation ensues, resulting in the early stages of the disease. Then the real damage begins: The bacteria release multiple exotoxins that damage ciliated respiratory epithelial cells and cripple other components of the host defense, including phagocytic cells.

The two most important exotoxins are *pertussis toxin* and *tracheal cytotoxin*. Pertussis toxin is a classic A-B toxin, like the

diphtheria toxin illustrated in figure 21.9. In the case of pertussis toxin, the host protein affected by the process of ADP-ribosylation is one that normally limits the production of cyclic AMP. Cyclic AMP is a critical molecule that regulates numerous functions inside host cells. The excessive amounts of cyclic AMP result in copious production of mucus and a variety of other effects in the respiratory tract and the immune system.

Tracheal cytotoxin results in more direct destruction of ciliated cells. The cells are no longer capable of clearing mucus and secretions, leading to the extraordinary coughing required to get relief. Another important contributor to the pathology of the disease is *B. pertussis* endotoxin. As always with endotoxins, its release leads to the production of a host of cytokines that have direct and indirect effects on physiological processes and on the host response.

▶ Transmission and Epidemiology

B. pertussis is transmitted via respiratory droplets. It is highly contagious during both the catarrhal and paroxysmal stages. The disease manifestations are most serious in infants. Twenty-five percent of infections occur in older children and adults, who generally have milder symptoms. The disease results in 300,000 to 500,000 deaths annually worldwide.

Pertussis outbreaks continue to occur in the United States and elsewhere. Even though it is estimated that approximately 85% of U.S. children are vaccinated against pertussis, it continues to be spread, perhaps by adults whose own immunity has dwindled. These adults may experience mild, unrecognized disease and unwittingly pass it to others. It has also been found that fully vaccinated children can experience the disease, possibly due to antigenic changes in the bacterium.

▶ Culture and Diagnosis

This disease is often diagnosed based solely on its symptoms because they are so distinctive. When culture confirmation is desired, nasopharyngeal swabs can be inoculated on specific media—Bordet-Gengou (B-G) medium, charcoal agar, or potato-glycerol agar.

▶ Prevention

The current vaccine for pertussis is an acellular formulation of important *B. pertussis* antigens. It results in far fewer side effects than the previous whole-cell vaccine, which was used until the mid-1990s. It is generally given in the form of the DTaP vaccine. Booster shots after the age of 11 are especially important for this disease.

A second prevention strategy is the administration of antibiotics to contacts of people who have been diagnosed with the disease. Erythromycin or trimethoprim-sulfamethoxazole is given for 14 days to prevent disease in those who may have been infected.

▶ Treatment

Treating someone who is already ill with pertussis is focused on supportive care; antibiotics may or may not shorten the course of the disease, which is often the case when major symptoms of a condition are the result of exotoxin secretion. Antibiotics (erythromycin) are sometimes administered because they do decrease the contagiousness of the patient.

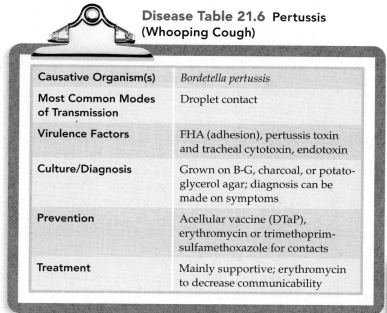

Disease Table 21.6 Pertussis (Whooping Cough)

Causative Organism(s)	*Bordetella pertussis*
Most Common Modes of Transmission	Droplet contact
Virulence Factors	FHA (adhesion), pertussis toxin and tracheal cytotoxin, endotoxin
Culture/Diagnosis	Grown on B-G, charcoal, or potato-glycerol agar; diagnosis can be made on symptoms
Prevention	Acellular vaccine (DTaP), erythromycin or trimethoprim-sulfamethoxazole for contacts
Treatment	Mainly supportive; erythromycin to decrease communicability

Respiratory Syncytial Virus Infection

As its name indicates, respiratory syncytial virus (RSV) infects the respiratory tract and produces giant multinucleated cells (syncytia). It is a member of the paramyxovirus family and contains single-stranded negative-sense RNA. It is an enveloped virus. Outbreaks of droplet-spread RSV disease occur regularly throughout the world, with peak incidence in the winter and early spring. Children 6 months of age or younger, as well as premature babies, are especially susceptible to serious disease caused by this virus. RSV is the most prevalent cause of respiratory infection in the newborn age group, and nearly all children have experienced it by age 2. An estimated 100,000 children are hospitalized with RSV infection each year in the United States. The mortality rate is highest for children with complications such as prematurity, congenital disease, and immunodeficiency. Infection in older children and adults usually manifests as a cold.

The first symptoms are fever that lasts for approximately 3 days, rhinitis, pharyngitis, and otitis. More serious infections progress to the bronchial tree and lung parenchyma, giving rise to symptoms of croup, which include acute bouts of coughing, wheezing, difficulty in breathing (called **dyspnea**), and abnormal breathing sounds (called rales). (Note: This condition is often called croup, and also bronchiolitis; be aware that both of these terms are clinical descriptions of diseases caused by a variety of viruses [in addition to RSV] and sometimes by bacteria.)

The virus is highly contagious and is transmitted through droplet contact but also through fomite contamination. Diagnosis of RSV infection is more critical in babies than in older children or adults. The afflicted child is conspicuously ill, with signs typical of pneumonia and bronchitis. The best diagnostic procedures are those that demonstrate the viral antigen directly from specimens (direct and indirect fluorescent staining, ELISA, and DNA probes).

There is no RSV vaccine available yet, but an effective passive antibody preparation is used as prevention in high-risk children and babies born prematurely. It is very expensive (about $6,000 for a five-dose treatment) and therefore insurance companies will only reimburse for it when children meet stringent criteria. But doctors say they're not sure it has much a benefit, anyway. Of course, when parents of high-risk children learn of it, they want it. Ribavirin, an antiviral drug, can be administered as an inhaled aerosol to very sick children, although the clinical benefit is uncertain.

Disease Table 21.7 RSV Disease

Causative Organism(s)	Respiratory syncytial virus (RSV)
Most Common Modes of Transmission	Droplet and indirect contact
Virulence Factors	Syncytia formation
Culture/Diagnosis	Direct antigen testing
Prevention	Passive antibody (humanized monoclonal) in high-risk children
Treatment	Ribavirin in severe cases

Influenza

The "flu" is a very important disease to study for several reasons. First of all, everyone is familiar with the cyclical increase of influenza infections occurring during the winter months in the United States. Second, many conditions are erroneously termed the "flu," while in fact only diseases caused by influenza viruses are actually the flu. Third, the way that influenza viruses behave provides an excellent illustration of the way other viruses can, and do, change to cause more serious diseases than they did previously.

Influenzas that occur every year are called "seasonal" flus. Often these are the only flus that circulate each year. Occasionally another flu strain appears, one that is new and may cause worldwide pandemics. In some years, such as in 2009, both of these flus were issues. They had different symptoms, affected different age groups, and had separate vaccine protocols.

▶ Signs and Symptoms

Seasonal influenza begins in the upper respiratory tract but in serious cases may also affect the lower respiratory tract. There is a 1- to 4-day incubation period, after which symptoms begin very quickly. These include headache, chills, dry cough, body aches, fever, stuffy nose, and sore throat. Even the sum of all these symptoms can't describe how a person actually feels: lousy. The flu is known to "knock you off your feet." Extreme fatigue can last for a few days or even a few weeks. An infection with influenza can leave patients vulnerable to secondary infections, often bacterial. Influenza infection alone occasionally leads to a pneumonia that can cause rapid death, even in young healthy adults.

Patients with emphysema or cardiopulmonary disease, along with very young, elderly, or pregnant patients, are more susceptible to serious complications.

The pandemic virus, H1N1, or the swine flu of 2009, had similar symptoms but with a couple of differences. Not all patients had a fever (very unusual for influenza), and many patients had gastrointestinal distress.

▶ Causative Agent

All influenza is caused by one of three influenza viruses: A, B, or C. They belong to the Family Orthomyxoviridae. They are spherical particles with an average diameter of 80 to 120 nanometers. Each virion is covered with a lipoprotein envelope that is studded with glycoprotein spikes acquired during viral maturation **(figure 21.10)**. Also note that the envelope contains proteins that form a channel for ions into the virus. The two glycoproteins that make up the spikes of the envelope and contribute to virulence are called hemagglutinin (H) and neuraminidase (N). The name hemagglutinin is derived from this glycoprotein's agglutinating action on red blood cells, which is the basis for viral assays used to identify the viruses. Hemagglutinin contributes to infectivity by binding to host cell receptors of the respiratory mucosa, a process that facilitates viral penetration. Neuraminidase breaks down the protective mucous coating of the respiratory tract, assists in viral budding and release, keeps viruses from sticking together, and participates in host cell fusion.

The ssRNA genome of the influenza virus is known for its extreme variability. It is subject to constant genetic changes that alter the structure of its envelope glycoproteins. Research has shown that genetic changes are very frequent in the area of the glycoproteins recognized by the host immune response but very rare in the areas of the glycoproteins used for attachment to the host cell **(figure 21.11)**. In this way, the virus can continue to attach to host cells while managing to decrease the effectiveness of the host response to its presence. This constant mutation of the glycoproteins is called **antigenic drift**—the antigens gradually change their amino acid composition, resulting in decreased ability of host memory cells to recognize them.

An even more serious phenomenon is known as **antigenic shift.** The genome of the virus consists of just 10 genes, encoded on eight separate RNA strands. Antigenic shift is the swapping out of one of those genes or strands with a gene or strand from a different influenza virus. Some explanation is in order. First, we know that certain influenza viruses infect both humans and swine. Other influenza viruses infect birds (or ducks) and swine. All of these viruses have 10 genes coding for the same important influenza proteins (including H and N)—but the actual sequence of the genes is different in the different types of viruses. Second, when the two viruses just described infect a single swine host, with both virus types infecting the same host cell, the viral packaging step can accidentally produce a human influenza virus that contains seven human influenza virus RNA strands plus a single duck influenza virus RNA strand **(figure 21.12)**. When that virus infects a human, no immunologic recognition of the protein that came from the duck virus occurs. Experts have traced the flu pandemics of 1918, 1957, 1968, 1977, and 2009 to strains of a virus that came from pigs (swine flu). Influenza A viruses are named according to the different types of H and N spikes they

Figure 21.11 Schematic drawing of hemagglutinin (HA) of influenza virus.   Blue boxes depict site used to attach virus to host cells; green circles depict sites for anti-influenza antibody binding.

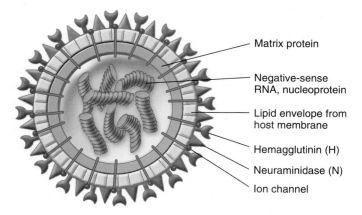

Figure 21.10 Schematic drawing of influenza virus.

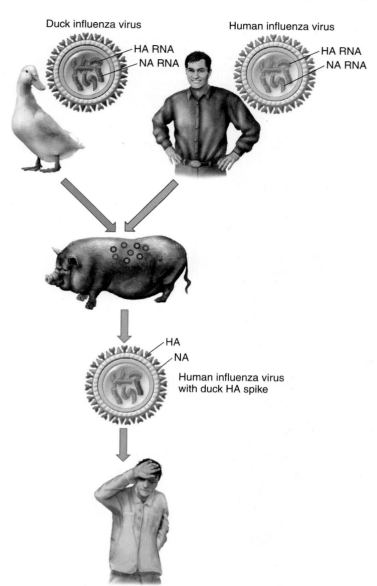

Figure 21.12 Antigenic shift event. Where ducks and swine and humans live close together, the swine can serve as a melting pot for creating "hybrid" influenza viruses that are not recognized by the human immune system.

display on their surfaces. For instance, in 2004 the most common circulating subtypes of influenza A viruses were H1N1 and H3N2. Influenza B viruses are not divided into subtypes because they are thought only to undergo antigenic drift and not antigenic shift. Influenza C viruses are thought to cause only minor respiratory disease and are probably not involved in epidemics.

Scientists have also recently found that antigenic drift and shift are not even required to make an influenza virus deadly. It appears that a minor genetic alteration in another influenza virus gene, one that seems to produce an enzyme used to manufacture new viruses in the host cell, can make the difference between a somewhat pathogenic influenza virus and a lethal one. It is still not clear exactly how many of these minor changes can lead to pandemic levels of infection and a catastrophe for the public health.

Insight 21.1 gives a breakdown of some of the important developments in the history of influenza.

▶ Pathogenesis and Virulence Factors

The influenza virus binds primarily to ciliated cells of the respiratory mucosa. Infection causes the rapid shedding of these cells along with a load of viruses. Stripping the respiratory epithelium to the basal layer eliminates protective ciliary clearance. Combine that with what is often called a "cytokine storm" caused by the viral stimulus and the lungs experience severe inflammation and irritation. The illness is further aggravated by fever, headache, and the other symptoms just described. The viruses tend to remain in the respiratory tract rather than spread to the bloodstream. As the normal ciliated epithelium is restored in a week or two, the symptoms subside.

As just noted, the glycoproteins and their structure are important virulence determinants. First of all, they mediate the adhesion of the virus to host cells. Second, they change gradually and sometimes suddenly, evading immune recognition. One feature of the 2009 H1N1 virus is that it bound to cells lower in the respiratory tract, and at a much higher rate, leading to massive damage, and often death, in the worst-affected patients. There were a total of around 12,000 deaths worldwide in the 2009 pandemic.

▶ Transmission and Epidemiology

Inhalation of virus-laden aerosols and droplets constitutes the major route of influenza infection, although fomites can play a secondary role. Transmission is greatly facilitated by crowding and poor ventilation in classrooms, barracks, nursing homes, dormitories, and military installations in the late fall and winter. The drier air of winter facilitates the spread of the virus, as the moist particles expelled by sneezes and coughs become dry very quickly, helping the virus remain airborne for longer periods of time. In addition, the dry cold air makes respiratory tract mucous membranes more brittle, with microscopic cracks that facilitate invasion by viruses. Influenza is highly contagious and affects people of all ages. Annually, there are approximately 36,000 U.S. deaths from seasonal influenza and its complications, mainly among the very young and the very old.

The 2009 H1N1 virus took a particularly heavy toll on young people. Previously healthy children and teenagers formed a small but important risk group, with quite a few becoming ill within hours and dying within days.

▶ Culture and Diagnosis

Very often, physicians will diagnose influenza based on symptoms alone. But there is a wide variety of culture-based and nonculture-based methods to diagnose the

INSIGHT 21.1   Flu Over the Years

Every year seasonal flu causes fairly predictable illness and death in the United States and in the world. As noted in this chapter, approximately 36,000 people die of seasonal flu every year. But when antigenic shifts occur in circulating flu viruses, pandemic flu can occur. The process by which this happens can be hard to follow. Here is an abbreviated summary of antigenic shift and pandemic events during the last 120 years.

Influenza Event	Historical Event
1889 — H2 strain replaces H1 for first time. One million die. People born before 1889 retain some immunity to H1, which will be helpful in 1918.	Johnstown flood
1918 — An H1N1 virus evolved from a bird virus into a human virus. 50 million worldwide die. Those born before 1889 (approximately 30 years old and above) have some immunity. Seasonal flu outbreaks from 1919 to 1957 are caused by H1 viruses.	1918 pandemic; WWI
1931 — Swine flu (H1N1) first isolated from U.S. pig.	Al Capone indicted
1957 — H1 human virus replaced by H2N2 causes Asian flu pandemic, which kills 1.5 million. People born after this date will have less immunity to the 2009 H1N1.	American Bandstand's first show
1968 — H3N2 virus causes Hong Kong flu; kills 1 million.	Martin Luther King Jr. assassinated
1976 — H1N1 pig virus kills 1 human. Forty-eight million people are vaccinated against this new virus, leading to 532 people suffering from Guillain-Barré syndrome.	Jimmy Carter elected president
1998 — H1N1 swine flu emerges in livestock; it is human/bird/swine and dominates U.S. pigs.	War rages in Kosovo
2004–6 — H5N1 bird flu hits. It is deadly to humans but does not spread between humans. It is also found in pigs.	Indian Ocean tsunami
2007–8 — Panic increases about H5N1 bird flu, but it does not mutate to be transmissible between humans.	Major worldwide recession
2009 — The WHO declares a pandemic with H1N1 swine flu. The pandemic began in Mexico, spread worldwide. There were fewer than 100,000 deaths.	Swine flu pandemic

infection. Rapid influenza tests (such as PCR, ELISA-type assays, or immunofluorescence) provide results within 24 hours; viral culture provides results in 3 to 10 days. Cultures are not typically performed at the point of care; they must be sent to diagnostic laboratories, and they require up to 10 days for results. Despite these disadvantages, culture can be useful to identify which subtype of influenza is causing infections, which is important for public health authorities to know. In 2009, officials did not often test for H1N1 but tested for influenza A or B; assuming if it was A that it was H1N1, since the circulating seasonal virus was influenza B. When specimens were tested, 100% of the influenza A isolates were in fact the H1N1. As the epidemic progressed, all flu cases that were identified were influenza A, indicating that it had replaced the seasonal virus.

▶ **Prevention**

Preventing influenza infections and epidemics is one of the top priorities for public health officials. The standard vaccine for seasonal flu contains inactivated dead viruses that were grown in embryonated eggs. It has an overall effectiveness of 70% to 90%. The vaccine consists of three different influenza viruses (usually two influenza A and one influenza B) that have been judged to most resemble the virus variants likely to cause infections in the coming flu season. Because of the changing nature of the antigens on the viral surface, annual vaccination is considered the best way to avoid infection. Anyone over the age of 6 months can take the vaccine, and it is recommended for anyone in a high-risk group or for people who have a high degree of contact with the public. Because research in monkeys shows that fetuses exposed to influenza in utero have a much higher risk of developing brain disorders resembling schizophrenia, vaccination of would-be mothers is also advised.

A vaccine called FluMist is a nasal mist vaccine consisting of the three strains of influenza virus in live attenuated form. It is designed to stimulate secretory immunity in the upper respiratory tract. Its safety and efficacy have so far been demonstrated only for persons between the ages of 5 and 49. It is not advised for immunocompromised individuals, and it is significantly more expensive than the injected vaccine.

During the 2009 H1N1 pandemic, new vaccine containing the pandemic strain was quickly prepared. Officials noted that if the strain had been noticed just a few weeks earlier it could have been included in the normal, seasonal vaccine. As it was, the existence of two vaccines added to the complexity of preventing the flu that year.

One of the most promising new vaccine prospects is a vaccine that would protect against *all* flu viruses and not need to be given every year. This vaccine, in testing stages, would target the ion-channel proteins that are present on the envelope of influenza viruses. Apparently these proteins are the same on all flu viruses, and they do not mutate readily.

This discovery has the possibility of revolutionizing influenza prevention.

▶ **Treatment**

Influenza is one of the first viral diseases for which effective antiviral drugs became available. The drugs must be taken early in the infection, preferably by the second day. This requirement is an inherent difficulty because most people do not realize until later that they may have the flu. Amantadine and rimantadine can be used to treat and prevent some influenza type A infections, but they do not work against influenza type B viruses.

Relenza (zanamivir) is an inhaled drug that works against influenza A and B. Tamiflu (oseltamivir) is available in capsules or as a powdered mix to be made into a drink. It can also be used for prevention of influenza A and B. Over the period of 2007–2009 different influenza viruses began to show resistance to one or more of these drugs, which called into question the practice of using the drugs preventively in epidemics. As we know with all antimicrobials, the more we use them, the more quickly we lose them (the more quickly they lose their effectiveness).

Disease Table 21.8 Influenza

Causative Organism(s)	Influenza A, B, and C viruses
Most Common Modes of Transmission	Droplet contact, direct contact or indirect contact
Virulence Factors	Glycoprotein spikes, overall ability to change genetically
Culture/Diagnosis	Viral culture (3–10 days) or rapid antigen-based or PCR tests
Prevention	Killed injected vaccine or inhaled live attenuated vaccine—taken annually
Treatment	Amantadine, rimantadine, zanamivir, or oseltamivir

21.4 Learning Outcomes—Can You ...

7. ... list the possible causative agents, modes of transmission, virulence factors, diagnostic techniques, and prevention/treatment for each of the diseases infecting both the upper and lower respiratory tracts? These are: pertussis, RSV disease, and influenza.

8. ... compare and contrast antigenic drift and antigenic shift in influenza viruses?

21.5 Lower Respiratory Tract Diseases Caused by Microorganisms

In this section, we consider microbial diseases that affect the lower respiratory tract primarily—namely, the bronchi, bronchioles, and lungs, with minimal involvement of the upper respiratory tract. Our discussion focuses on tuberculosis and pneumonia.

Tuberculosis

Mummies from the Stone Age, ancient Egypt, and Peru provide unmistakable evidence that tuberculosis (TB) is an ancient human disease. In fact, historically it has been such a prevalent cause of death that it was called "Captain of the Men of Death" and "White Plague." After the discovery of streptomycin in 1943, the rates of tuberculosis in the developed world declined rapidly. But since the mid-1980s, it has reemerged as a serious threat. Worldwide, 2 billion people are currently infected. Two billion—that is one-third of the world's population! The cause of tuberculosis is primarily the bacterial species *Mycobacterium tuberculosis,* informally called the tubercle bacillus.

▶ Signs and Symptoms

A clear-cut distinction can be made between infection with the TB bacterium and the disease it causes. In general, humans are rather easily infected with the bacterium but are resistant to the disease. Estimates project that only about 5% of infected people actually develop a clinical case of tuberculosis. Untreated tuberculosis progresses slowly, and people with the disease may have a normal life span, with periods of health alternating with episodes of morbidity. The majority (85%) of TB cases are contained in the lungs, even though disseminated TB bacteria can give rise to tuberculosis in any organ of the body. Clinical tuberculosis is divided into primary tuberculosis, secondary (reactivation or reinfection) tuberculosis, and disseminated or extrapulmonary tuberculosis.

Primary Tuberculosis The minimum infectious dose for lung infection is around 10 bacterial cells. Alveolar macrophages phagocytose these cells, but they are not killed and continue to multiply inside the macrophages. This period of hidden infection is asymptomatic or is accompanied by mild fever. Some bacteria escape from the lungs into the blood and lymphatics. After 3 to 4 weeks, the immune system mounts a complex, cell-mediated assault against the bacteria. The large influx of mononuclear cells into the lungs plays a part in the formation of specific infection sites called tubercles. Tubercles are granulomas that consist of a central core containing TB bacteria in enlarged macrophages and an outer wall made of fibroblasts, lymphocytes, and macrophages **(figure 21.13).** Although this response further checks spread of infection and helps prevent the disease, it also carries a potential for damage. Frequently, as neutrophils come on the scene and release their enzymes, the centers of tubercles break down into necrotic caseous

Granuloma cells

Caseous necrosis

Epithelioid cells

Giant cell

Figure 21.13 Tubercle formation. Photomicrograph of a tubercle (16×). The massive granuloma infiltrate has obliterated the alveoli and set up a dense collar of fibroblasts, lymphocytes (granuloma cells), and epithelioid cells. The core of this tubercle is a caseous (cheesy) material containing the bacilli.

(kay'-see-us) lesions that gradually heal by calcification—normal lung tissue is replaced by calcium deposits. The response of T cells to *M. tuberculosis* proteins also causes a cell-mediated immune response evident in the skin test called the tuberculin reaction, a valuable diagnostic and epidemiological tool **(figure 21.14).**

Secondary (Reactivation) Tuberculosis Although the majority of adequately treated TB patients recover more or less completely from the primary episode of infection, live bacteria can remain dormant and become reactivated weeks, months, or years later, especially in people with weakened immunity. In chronic tuberculosis, tubercles filled with masses of bacteria expand, cause cavities in the lungs, and drain into the bronchial tubes and upper respiratory tract. The patient gradually experiences more severe symptoms, including violent coughing, greenish or bloody sputum, low-grade fever, anorexia, weight loss, extreme fatigue, night sweats, and chest pain. It is the gradual wasting of the body that

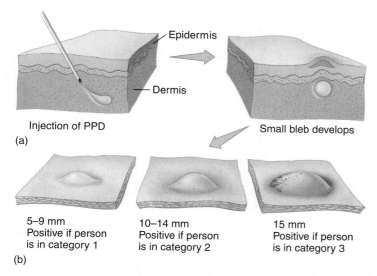

Injection of PPD
(a)

Epidermis

Dermis

Small bleb develops

(b)

5–9 mm
Positive if person
is in category 1

10–14 mm
Positive if person
is in category 2

15 mm
Positive if person
is in category 3

Figure 21.14 Skin testing for tuberculosis. (a, b) The Mantoux test. Tuberculin is injected into the dermis. A small bleb from the injected fluid develops but will be absorbed in a short time. After 48 to 72 hours, the skin reaction is rated by the degree (or size) of the raised area. The surrounding red area is not counted in the measurement. A reaction of less than 5 mm is negative in all cases. See also figure 16.14.

accounts for an older name for tuberculosis—*consumption.* Untreated secondary disease has nearly a 60% mortality rate.

Extrapulmonary Tuberculosis TB infection outside of the lungs is more common in immunosuppressed patients and young children. Organs most commonly involved in **extrapulmonary TB** are the regional lymph nodes, kidneys, long bones, genital tract, brain, and meninges. Because of the debilitation of the patient and the high load of TB bacteria, these complications are usually grave. Renal tuberculosis results in necrosis and scarring of the kidney and the pelvis, ureters, and bladder. This damage is accompanied by painful urination, fever, and the presence of blood and the TB bacterium in urine. Genital tuberculosis in males damages the prostate gland, epididymis, seminal vesicle, and testes; and in females, the fallopian tubes, ovaries, and uterus. Tuberculosis of the bones and joints is a common complication. The spine is a frequent site of infection, although the hip, knee, wrist, and elbow can also be involved. Advanced infiltration of the vertebral column produces degenerative changes that collapse the vertebrae, resulting in abnormal curvature of the thoracic region (humpback) or of the lumbar region (swayback). Neurological damage stemming from compression on nerves can cause extensive paralysis and sensory loss.

Tubercular meningitis is the result of an active brain lesion seeding bacteria into the meninges. Over a period of several weeks, the infection of the cranial compartments can create mental deterioration, permanent retardation, blindness, and deafness. Untreated tubercular meningitis is invariably fatal, and even treated cases can have a 30% to 50% mortality rate.

► Causative Agents

M. tuberculosis is the cause of tuberculosis in most patients. It is an acid-fast rod, long and thin. It is a strict aerobe, and technically speaking, there is still debate about whether it is a gram-positive or a gram-negative organism. It is rarely called gram anything, however, because its acid-fast nature is much more relevant in a clinical setting **(figure 21.15)**. It grows very slowly. With a generation time of 15 to 20 hours, a period of up to 6 weeks is required for colonies to appear in culture. (Note: The prefix *Myco-* might make you think of fungi, but this is a bacterium. The prefix in the name came from the mistaken impression that colonies growing on agar **[figure 21.16]** resembled fungal colonies. And be sure to differentiate this bacterium from *Mycoplasma*—they are unrelated.)

Figure 21.15 A fluorescent acid-fast stain of *Mycobacterium tuberculosis* from sputum. Smears are evaluated in terms of the number of AFB (acid-fast bacteria) seen per field. This quantity is then applied to a scale ranging from 0 to 4+, 0 being no AFB observed and 4+ being more than 9 AFB per field.

Figure 21.16 Cultural appearance of *Mycobacterium tuberculosis*. Colonies with a typical granular, waxy pattern of growth.

Robert Koch identified that *M. tuberculosis* often forms serpentine cords while growing, and he called the unknown substance causing this style of growth *cord factor.* Cord factor appears to be associated with virulent strains, and it is a lipid component of the mycobacterial cell wall. All mycobacterial species have walls that have a very high content of complex lipids, including mycolic acid and waxes. This chemical characteristic makes them relatively impermeable to stains and difficult to decolorize (acid-fast) once they are stained. The lipid wall of the bacterium also influences its virulence and makes it resistant to drying and disinfectants.

In recent decades, tuberculosis-like conditions caused by *Mycobacterium avium* and related mycobacterial species (sometimes referred to as the *M. avium* complex, or MAC) have been found in AIDS patients and other immunocompromised people. In this section, we consider only *M. tuberculosis,* although *M. avium* is discussed briefly near the conclusion.

Before routine pasteurization of milk, humans acquired bovine TB, caused by a species called *Mycobacterium bovis,* from the milk they drank. It is very rare today, but in 2004, six people in a nightclub acquired bovine TB from a fellow reveler. One person died from her infection.

▶ Pathogenesis and Virulence Factors

The course of the infection—and all of its possible variations—was previously described under "Signs and Symptoms." Important characteristics of the bacterium that contribute to its virulence are its waxy surface (contributing both to its survival in the environment and its survival within macrophages) and its ability to stimulate a strong cell-mediated immune response that contributes to the pathology of the disease.

▶ Transmission and Epidemiology

The agent of tuberculosis is transmitted almost exclusively by fine droplets of respiratory mucus suspended in the air. The TB bacterium is highly resistant and can survive for 8 months in fine aerosol particles. Although larger particles become trapped in mucus and are expelled, tinier ones can be inhaled into the bronchioles and alveoli. This effect is especially pronounced among people sharing small closed rooms with limited access to sunlight and fresh air.

The epidemiological patterns of *M. tuberculosis* infection vary with the living conditions in a community or an area of the world. Factors that significantly affect people's susceptibility to tuberculosis are inadequate nutrition, debilitation of the immune system, poor access to medical care, lung damage, and their own genetics. Put simply, TB is an infection of poverty. People in developing countries are often infected as infants and harbor the microbe for many years until the disease is reactivated in young adulthood. 1.8 million people died from TB in 2008, the equivalent of 4,500 a day.

Case rates have begun to drop in the United States, from a high in 2004. About 60% of cases in the United States are in foreign-born persons. This is important to know as a health care provider so you can be alert for TB in certain populations. The top five countries of origin of people in the United States with TB in 2009 were Mexico, Philippines, Vietnam, India, and China.

▶ Culture and Diagnosis

You are probably familiar with several methods of detecting tuberculosis in humans. Clinical diagnosis of tuberculosis relies on four techniques: (1) tuberculin testing, (2) chest X rays, (3) direct identification of acid-fast bacilli (AFB) in sputum or other specimens, and (4) cultural isolation and antimicrobial susceptibility testing.

Tuberculin Sensitivity and Testing   Because infection with the TB bacillus can lead to delayed hypersensitivity to tuberculoproteins, testing for hypersensitivity has been an important way to screen populations for tuberculosis infection and disease. Although there are newer methods available, the most widely used test is still the tuberculin skin test, called the **Mantoux test.** It involves local injection of purified protein derivative (PPD), a standardized solution taken from culture fluids of *M. tuberculosis.* The injection is done intradermally into the forearm to produce an immediate small bleb. After 48 and 72 hours, the site is observed for a red wheal called an **induration,** which is measured and interpreted as positive or negative according to size (see figure 21.14).

The accepted practices for tuberculin testing are currently limited to selected groups known to have higher risk for tuberculosis infection. It is no longer used as a routine screening method among populations of children or adults who are not within the target groups. The reasoning behind this change is to allow more focused screening and to reduce expensive and unnecessary follow-up tests and treatments. Guidelines for test groups and methods of interpreting tests are listed in the following summary.[2]

Category 1. Induration (skin reaction) that is equal to or greater than *5 millimeters* is classified as positive in persons:

- Who have had contact with actively infected TB patients
- Who are HIV-positive or have risk factors for HIV infection
- With past history of tuberculosis as determined through chest X rays

Category 2. Induration that is equal to or greater than *10 millimeters* is classified as positive in persons who are not in category 1 but who fit the following high-risk groups:

- HIV-negative intravenous drug users
- Persons with medical conditions that put them at risk for progressing from latent TB infection to active TB
- Persons who live or work in high-risk residences such as nursing homes, jails, or homeless shelters
- New immigrants from countries with high rates of TB
- Low-income populations lacking access to adequate medical care

---

2. See the entire guidelines at www.thoracic.org

- High-risk adults from ethnic minority populations as determined by local public health departments
- Children who have contact with members of high-risk adult populations

Category 3. Induration that is equal to or greater than *15 millimeters* is classified as positive in persons who do not meet criteria in categories 1 or 2.

A positive reaction in a person from one of the risk groups is fairly reliable evidence of recent infection or reactivation of a prior latent infection. Because the test is not 100% specific, false positive reactions will occasionally occur in patients who have recently been vaccinated with the BCG vaccine. Because BCG vaccination can also stimulate delayed hypersensitivity, clinicians must weigh a patient's vaccine history, especially among individuals who have immigrated from countries where the vaccine is routinely given. Another cause of a false positive reaction is the presence of an infection with a closely related species of *Mycobacterium*.

A negative skin test usually indicates that ongoing TB infection is not present. In some cases, it may be a false negative, meaning that the person is infected but is not yet reactive. One cause of a false negative test may be that it is administered too early in the infection, requiring retesting at a later time. Subgroups with severely compromised immune systems, such as those with AIDS, advanced age, and chronic disease, may be unable to mount a reaction even though they are infected. Skin testing may not be a reliable diagnostic indicator in these populations.

X Rays Chest X rays can help verify TB when other tests have given indeterminate results, and they are generally used after a positive test for further verification. X-ray films reveal abnormal radiopaque patches, the appearance and location of which can be very indicative. Primary tubercular infection presents the appearance of fine areas of infiltration and enlarged lymph nodes in the lower and central areas of the lungs **(figure 21.17)**. Secondary tuberculosis films show more extensive infiltration in the upper lungs and bronchi and marked tubercles. Scars from older infections often show up on X rays and can furnish a basis for comparison when trying to identify newly active disease.

Acid-Fast Staining The diagnosis of tuberculosis in people with positive skin tests or X rays can be backed up by acid-fast staining of sputum or other specimens. Several variations on the acid-fast stain are currently in use. The Ziehl-Neelsen stain produces bright red acid-fast bacilli (AFB) against a blue background **(figure 21.18)**. Fluorescence staining shows luminescent yellow-green bacteria against a dark background (see figure 21.15).

Diagnosis that differentiates between *M. tuberculosis* and other mycobacteria must be accomplished as rapidly as possible so that appropriate treatment and isolation precautions can be instituted. The newer fast-identification techniques such as fluorescent staining (see figure 21.15), high-performance

Figure 21.17 Primary tuberculosis.

Figure 21.18 Ziehl-Neelsen staining of *Mycobacterium tuberculosis* in sputum.

liquid chromatography (HPLC) analysis of mycolic acids, and PCR diagnosis can and should be used to identify isolates as *Mycobacterium*. Even though newer cultivation schemes exist that shorten the incubation period from 6 weeks to several days, this delay is unacceptable for beginning treatment or isolation precautions. But culture still must be performed because growing colonies are required to determine antibiotic sensitivities.

Because the specimens are often contaminated with rapid-growing bacteria that will interfere with the isolation of *M. tuberculosis*, they are pretreated with chemicals to remove contaminants and are plated onto selective medium (such as Lowenstein-Jensen medium). *M. tuberculosis* colonies are depicted in figure 21.16.

▶ Prevention

Preventing TB in the United States is accomplished by limiting exposure to infectious airborne particles. Extensive precautions, such as isolation in negative-pressure rooms, are used in health care settings when a person with active TB is identified. Vaccine is generally not used in the United States, although an attenuated vaccine, called BCG, is used in many countries. BCG stands for Bacille Calmette-Guerin, named for two French scientists who created the vaccine in the early 1900s. It is a live strain of a bovine tuberculosis bacterium that has been made avirulent by long passage through artificial media. In 2007 scientists made the observation that the BCG vaccine currently used is fairly ineffective and that original BCG strains from a much earlier time induce stronger immunity in patients. There is talk of reviving the older BCG strains and perhaps using this new-old BCG vaccine more widely, in the face of treatment failures and the huge infection rates. Remember that persons vaccinated with BCG may respond positively to a tuberculin skin test.

In the past, prevention in the context of tuberculosis referred to preventing a person with latent TB from experiencing reactivation. This strategy is more accurately referred to as treatment of latent infection and is considered in the next section.

▶ Treatment

Treatment of latent TB infection is effective in preventing full-blown disease in persons who have positive tuberculin skin tests and who are at risk for reactivated TB. Treatment with isoniazid for 9 months or with a combination of rifampin plus an additional antibiotic called pyrazinamide for 2 months is recommended.

Treatment of active TB infection when the microorganism has been found to have no antibiotic resistance consists of 9 months of treatment with isoniazid plus rifampin, with pyrazinamide also taken for the first 2 months. If there is evidence of extrapulmonary tubercular disease, the treatment should be extended to 12 months.

When the bacterium is resistant to one or more of the preceding agents, at least three additional antibiotics must be added to the treatment regimen and the duration of treatment should be extended.

One of the biggest problems with TB therapy is noncompliance on the part of the patient. It is very difficult, even under the best of circumstances, to keep to a regimen of multiple antibiotics daily for months. And most TB patients are not living under the best of circumstances. But failure to adhere to the antibiotic regimen leads to antibiotic resistance in the slow-growing microorganism, and in fact many *M. tuberculosis* isolates are now found to be **MDR-TB,** or multidrug-resistant TB. For

A Note About Directly Observed Therapy

Although it is highly labor intensive, directly observed therapy (DOT) seems to be the most effective means of curbing infections and preventing further development of antibiotic resistance. The WHO estimates that 8 million deaths have been prevented by DOT over the last 15 years. Patients are referred for DOT if a physician suspects they will have trouble adhering to the very rigorous and lengthy antibiotic schedule. At that point a public health worker is assigned to visit them at their home and/or workplace to watch them take their medicines. One innovative program to alleviate the labor-intensiveness of such an approach has been developed at the Massachusetts Institute of Technology. Patients receive a container of filter paper that dispenses a filter paper at timed intervals. They dip the paper in their urine and if the antibiotic is present in their urine the filter paper reveals a code that the patient texts to a central database. If they miss fewer than five pills a month they receive free minutes for their cell phones.

this reason, it is recommended that all patients with TB be treated by directly observed therapy (DOT), in which ingestion of medications is observed by a responsible person (see Note). The threat to public health is so great when patients do not adhere to treatment regimens that the United States and other countries have occasionally incarcerated people—and isolated them—when they don't follow their treatment schedules. In 2006, a new strain of *M. tuberculosis* was identified in Africa. It is particularly lethal for HIV-infected people and has been named **XDR-TB** (extensively drug-resistant TB). XDR-TB is defined as resistance to isoniazid and rifampin plus resistance to any fluoroquinolone and at least one of three injectable second-line anti-TB drugs. Since 2006 XDR-TB has spread around the world, and the CDC estimates that 500,000 new cases are seen every year. In the United States, a handful of cases of XDR-TB occur each year.

Mycobacterium avium Complex (MAC)

Before the introduction of effective HIV treatments, described in chapter 20, disseminated tuberculosis infection with MAC was one of the biggest killers of AIDS patients. It mainly affects patients with CD4 counts below 50 cells per milliliter of blood. Antibiotics to prevent this condition should be given to all patients with AIDS.

In 2009 scientists discovered that *M. avium* is a frequent inhabitant of showerheads that are served by city water systems, and can be an important source of infection for people with a variety of underlying respiratory conditions **(Disease Table 21.9).**

Disease Table 21.9 Tuberculosis

Causative Organism(s)	*Mycobacterium tuberculosis*	*Mycobacterium avium* complex
Most Common Modes of Transmission	Vehicle (airborne)	Vehicle (airborne)
Virulence Factors	Lipids in wall, ability to stimulate strong cell-mediated immunity (CMI)	–
Culture/Diagnosis	Rapid methods plus culture; initial tests are skin testing	Positive blood culture and chest X ray
Prevention	Avoiding airborne *M. tuberculosis*, BCG vaccine in other countries	Rifabutin or azithromycin given to AIDS patients at risk
Treatment	Isoniazid, rifampin, and pyrazinamide + ethambutol or streptomycin for varying lengths of time (always lengthy); if resistant, two other drugs added to regimen	Azithromycin or clarithromycin plus one additional antibiotic
Distinctive Features	Responsible for nearly all TB except for some HIV-positive patients	Suspect this in HIV-positive patients

Pneumonia

Pneumonia is a classic example of an *anatomical diagnosis*. It is defined as an inflammatory condition of the lung in which fluid fills the alveoli. The set of symptoms that we call pneumonia can be caused by a wide variety of different microorganisms. In a sense, the microorganisms need only to have appropriate characteristics to allow them to circumvent the host's defenses and to penetrate and survive in the lower respiratory tract. In particular, the microorganisms must avoid being phagocytosed by alveolar macrophages, or at least avoid being killed once inside the macrophage. Bacteria and a wide variety of viruses can cause pneumonias. Viral pneumonias are usually, but not always, milder than those caused by bacteria. At the same time, some bacterial pneumonias are very serious and others are not. In addition, fungi such as *Histoplasma* can also cause pneumonia. Overall, U.S. residents experience 2 to 3 million cases of pneumonia and more than 45,000 deaths due to this condition every year. It is much more common in the winter.

Physicians distinguish between community-acquired pneumonias and nosocomial pneumonias, because different bacteria are more likely to be causing the two types. Community-acquired pneumonias are those experienced by persons in the general population. Nosocomial pneumonias are those acquired by patients in hospitals and other health care residential facilities. All pneumonias have similar symptoms, which we describe next, followed by separate sections for each type of pneumonia.

▶ Signs and Symptoms

Pneumonias of all types usually begin with upper respiratory tract symptoms, including runny nose and congestion. Headache is common. Fever is often present, and the onset of lung symptoms follows. These symptoms are chest pain, fever, cough, and the production of discolored sputum. Because of the pain and difficulty of breathing, the patient appears pale and presents an overall sickly appearance.

The severity and speed of onset of the symptoms varies according to the etiologic agent.

▶ Causative Agents of Community-Acquired Pneumonia

Streptococcus pneumoniae (often called pneumococcus) accounts for about two-thirds of community-acquired bacterial pneumonia cases. It causes more lethal pneumonia cases than any other microorganism. *Legionella* is a less common but serious cause of the disease. *Haemophilus influenzae* had been a major cause of community-acquired pneumonia, but the introduction of the Hib vaccine in 1988 has reduced its incidence. A number of bacteria cause a milder form of pneumonia that is often referred to as "walking pneumonia." Two of these are *Mycoplasma pneumoniae* and *Chlamydophila pneumoniae* (formerly known as *Chlamydia pneumoniae*).[3] *Histoplasma capsulatum* is a fungus that infects many people but causes a pneumonia-like disease in relatively few. One virus causes a type of pneumonia that can be very serious: hantavirus, which emerged in 1993 in the United States. Pneumonia may be a secondary effect of influenza disease. Some physicians treat pneumonia empirically, meaning they do not determine the etiologic agent.

The rest of this section covers pneumonias caused by *S. pneumoniae, Legionella, Mycoplasma,* the hantavirus, and the fungi *Histoplasma* and *Pneumocystis* in more detail.

---

3. The genus formerly known as *Chlamydia* contains two important human pathogens, *Chlamydia pneumoniae* and *Chlamydia trachomatis*. The latter remains "Chlamydia," but the respiratory pathogen is now *Chlamydophila pneumoniae*.

Figure 21.19 *Streptococcus pneumoniae.* **(a)** Gram stain of sputum. **(b)** Alpha-hemolysis of *S. pneumoniae* on blood agar.

Streptococcus pneumoniae

This bacterium, which is often simply called the pneumococcus, is a small, gram-positive flattened coccus that often appears in pairs, lined up end to end **(figure 21.19a)**. It is alpha-hemolytic on blood agar **(figure 21.19b)**. *S. pneumoniae* is normal biota in the upper respiratory tract of from 5% to 50% of healthy people. Infection can occur when the bacterium is inhaled into deep areas of the lung or by transfer of the bacterium between two people via respiratory droplets. *S. pneumoniae* is very delicate and does not survive long out of its habitat. Factors that favor the ability of the pneumococcus to cause disease are old age, the season (rate of infection is highest in the winter), underlying viral respiratory disease, diabetes, and chronic abuse of alcohol or narcotics. Healthy people commonly inhale this and other microorganisms into the respiratory tract without serious consequences because of the host defenses present there.

Pneumonia is likely to occur when mucus containing a load of bacterial cells passes into the bronchi and alveoli. The pneumococci multiply and induce an overwhelming inflammatory response. The polysaccharide capsule of the bacterium prevents efficient phagocytosis, with the result that edematous fluids are continuously released into the lungs. In one form of pneumococcal pneumonia, termed **lobar pneumonia,** in which the infection is focused in and eventually totally fills an entire lobe of the lung, this fluid accumulates in the alveoli along with red and white blood cells. As the infection and inflammation spread rapidly through the lung, the patient can actually "drown" in his or her own secretions. If this mixture of exudates, cells, and bacteria solidifies in the air spaces, a condition known as *consolidation* **(figure 21.20)** occurs.

In infants and the elderly, the areas of infection are usually spottier and centered more in the bronchi than in the alveoli (bronchial pneumonia). Systemic complications of pneumonia are pleuritis and endocarditis, but pneumococcal bacteremia and meningitis are the greatest danger to the patient.

Because the pneumococcus is such a frequent cause of pneumonia in older adults, this population is encouraged to seek immunization with the older pneumococcal polysaccharide vaccine, which stimulates immunity to the capsular polysaccharides of 23 different strains of the bacterium. Active disease is treated with antibiotics, but the choice of antibiotic is often difficult. Many isolates of *S. pneumoniae* are resistant to penicillin and its derivatives, as well as to the macrolides, so often cephalosporins are now prescribed. Treatment also varies based on whether the patient is outpatient or inpatient, and whether they are in ICU or not. This bacterium is clearly capable of rapid development of resistance, and effective treatment requires that the practitioner be familiar with local resistance trends.

Legionella pneumophila

Legionella is a weakly gram-negative bacterium that has a range of shapes, from coccus to filaments. Several species or subtypes have been characterized, but *L. pneumophila* (lung-loving) is the one most frequently isolated from infections.

Although the organisms were originally described in the late 1940s, they were not clearly associated with human disease until 1976. The incident that brought them to the attention of medical microbiologists was a sudden and mysterious epidemic of pneumonia that afflicted 200 American Legion members attending a convention in Philadelphia and killed 29 of them. After 6 months of painstaking analysis, epidemiologists isolated the pathogen and traced its source to contaminated air-conditioning vents in the Legionnaires' hotel.

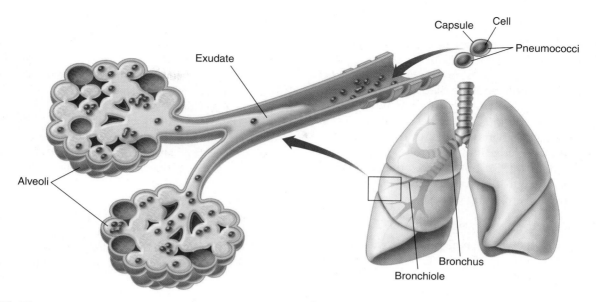

Figure 21.20 The course of bacterial pneumonia. As the pneumococcus traces a pathway down the respiratory tree, it provokes intense inflammation and exudate formation. The blocking of the bronchioles and alveoli by consolidation of inflammatory cells and products is evident.

Legionella's ability to survive and persist in natural habitats has been something of a mystery, yet it appears to be widely distributed in aqueous habitats as diverse as tap water, cooling towers, spas, ponds, and other fresh waters. It is resistant to chlorine. The bacteria can live in close association with free-living amoebas **(figure 21.21)**. It is released during aerosol formation and can be carried for long distances. Cases have been traced to supermarket vegetable sprayers,

hotel fountains, and even the fallout from the Mount St. Helens volcano eruption in 1980.

Although this bacterium can cause another disease called Pontiac fever, pneumonia is the more serious disease, with a fatality rate of 3% to 30%. *Legionella* pneumonia is thought of as an opportunistic disease, usually affecting elderly people and rarely being seen in children and healthy adults. It is difficult to diagnose, even with specific antibody tests. It is not transmitted person to person.

Mycoplasma pneumoniae

Mycoplasmas, as you learned in chapter 4, are among the smallest known self-replicating microorganisms. They naturally lack a cell wall and are therefore irregularly shaped. They may resemble cocci, filaments, doughnuts, clubs, or helices. They are free-living but fastidious, requiring complex medium to grow in the lab. (This genus should not be confused with *Mycobacterium*.)

Pneumonias caused by *Mycoplasma* (as well as those caused by *Chlamydia* and some other microorganisms) are often called atypical pneumonia—atypical in the sense that the symptoms do not resemble those of pneumococcal or other severe pneumonias. *Mycoplasma* pneumonia is transmitted by aerosol droplets among people confined in close living quarters, especially families, students, and the military.

Lack of acute illness in most patients has given rise to the name "walking pneumonia." For some reason, there is an increase in *Mycoplasma* pneumonias every 3 to 6 years in the United States.

Diagnosis of *Mycoplasma* may begin with ruling out other bacteria or viral agents. Serological or PCR tests confirm the diagnosis. These bacteria do not stain with Gram's stain and are not visible in direct smears of sputum.

Figure 21.21 *Legionella* living intracellularly in the amoeba *Hartmannella*. Amoebas inhabiting natural waters appear to be the reservoir for this pathogen and a means for it to survive in rather hostile environments. The pathogenesis of *Legionella* in humans is likewise dependent on its uptake by and survival in phagocytes.

Hantavirus

In 1993, hantavirus suddenly burst into the American consciousness. A cluster of unusual cases of severe lung edema among healthy young adults arose in the Four Corners area of New Mexico. Most of the patients died within a few days. They were later found to have been infected with hantavirus, an agent that had previously only been known to cause severe kidney disease and hemorrhagic fevers in other parts of the world. The new condition was named hantavirus pulmonary syndrome (HPS). Since 1993, the disease has occurred sporadically, but it has a mortality rate of at least 33%. It is considered an emerging disease.

▶ Symptoms, Pathogenesis, and Virulence Factors

Common features of the prodromal phase of this infection include fever, chills, myalgias (muscle aches), headache, nausea, vomiting, and diarrhea or a combination of these symptoms. A cough is common but is not a prominent early feature. Initial symptoms resemble those of other common viral infections. Soon a severe pulmonary edema occurs and causes acute respiratory distress (ARDS, or acute respiratory distress syndrome, has many microbial and nonmicrobial causes; this is but one of them).

The acute lung symptoms appear to be due to the presence of large amounts of hantavirus antigen, which becomes disseminated throughout the bloodstream (including the capillaries surrounding the alveoli of the lung). Massive amounts of fluid leave the blood vessels and flood the alveolar spaces in response to the inflammatory stimulus, causing severe breathing difficulties and a drop in blood pressure. The propensity to cause a massive inflammatory response could be considered a virulence factor for this organism.

▶ Transmission and Epidemiology

Very soon after the initial cases in 1993, it became clear that the virus was associated with the presence of mice in close proximity to the victims. Investigators eventually determined that the virus, an enveloped virus of the bunyavirus family, is transmitted via airborne dust contaminated with the urine, feces, or saliva of infected rodents. Deer mice **(figure 21.22)** and other rodents can carry the virus with

Figure 21.22 The deer mouse, a major carrier of hantavirus.

Case File 21   Continuing the Case

The church volunteers in El Salvador were doing heavy cleaning both indoors and outdoors, as well as working with soil (cleaning renovation sites, excavating the septic tank). Those activities point to the possible presence of two less common respiratory microorganisms: hantavirus and *Histoplasma*. Hantavirus is commonly found in places contaminated by mouse droppings, and the fungus *Histoplasma* often grows with the aid of bat and bird excrement in the places where it is endemic. Both microbes can become airborne when sweeping, digging, or vacuuming stirs up dust or dirt.

■ Can you do some quick research to see whether hantavirus or *Histoplasma* is endemic to El Salvador?

few apparent symptoms. Small outbreaks of the disease are usually correlated with increases in the local rodent population. Epidemiologists suspect that rodents have been infected with this pathogen for centuries. It has no doubt been the cause of sporadic cases of unexplained pneumonia in humans for decades, but the incidence seems to be increasing, especially in areas of the United States west of the Mississippi River.

▶ Treatment and Prevention

The diagnosis is established by detection of IgM to hantavirus in the patient's blood or by using PCR techniques to find hantavirus genetic material in clinical specimens. Treatment consists mainly of supportive care. Mechanical ventilation is often required.

There is no specific treatment other than supportive care.

Histoplasma capsulatum

Pulmonary infections with this dimorphic fungus have probably afflicted humans since antiquity, but it was not described until 1905 by Dr. Samuel Darling. Through the years, it has been known by various names: Darling's disease, Ohio Valley fever, and spelunker's disease. Certain aspects of its current distribution and epidemiology suggest that it has been an important disease for as long as humans have practiced agriculture. (See **Insight 21.2** for other important fungal lung pathogens.)

▶ Pathogenesis and Virulence Factors

Histoplasmosis presents a formidable array of manifestations. It can be benign or severe, acute or chronic, and it can show pulmonary, systemic, or cutaneous lesions. Inhaling a small dose of microconidia into the deep recesses of the lung establishes a primary pulmonary infection that is usually asymptomatic. Its primary location of growth is in the cytoplasm of phagocytes such as macrophages. It flourishes within these cells and is carried to other sites. Some people

INSIGHT 21.2 Fungal Lung Diseases

Increasingly, the microorganisms that cause pulmonary infections are fungi. Although still much rarer than bacterial lung infections, fungal pneumonias have shown a remarkable rise in incidence. One hospital in the Midwest reported an overall 20-fold increase in fungal infections (of all types) in the 10 years between the late 1970s and the late 1980s. And a great many of those infections occur in the lungs. As you read in chapter 5, two broad categories of fungi cause human infections: those considered to be *primary pathogens,* which readily cause disease even in healthy hosts, and *opportunists,* which cause disease primarily in hosts that are weakened due to underlying illness, advanced age, immune deficiency, or chemotherapy of some sort.

The primary pathogens usually have restricted geographic distributions. **Table 21.A** describes major characteristics of these fungi. As you can imagine, when primary pathogens invade people with weakened immune systems, the results can be disastrous.

In contrast to the primary pathogens, the opportunists are more likely to be ubiquitous and can affect weakened patients indiscriminately. **Table 21.B** lists some of the most common opportunistic fungal infections of the lungs. These opportunistic fungal infections are the ones increasing at a steady rate in the modern era, for several reasons:

- Fungi and their spores are everywhere. They constantly enter our respiratory tracts. They live in our GI tracts and on our skin.
- Antibiotic use decreases the bacterial count in our bodies, leaving fungi unhindered and able to flourish.
- More invasive procedures are being employed in hospitals and for outpatient procedures, opening pathways for fungi to access "sterile" areas of the body.
- The number of patients who are immunosuppressed (or otherwise "weakened") is constantly increasing.

For these reasons, health care professionals should be particularly vigilant for symptoms of fungal diseases in patients who are hospitalized, are HIV-positive, or have other underlying health problems. Invasive fungal infections are extremely difficult to treat effectively; there is a significant mortality rate for patients suffering from opportunistic fungal infections in the lungs.

Table 21.A Primary Fungal Pathogens of the Lungs

Pathogen	Geographic Distribution	Disease and Symptoms
Histoplasma capsulatum	All continents except Australia; highest rates in U.S. Ohio Valley	Histoplasmosis; aches, pains, and coughing; more severe symptoms include fever, night sweats, and weight loss
Blastomyces dermatitidis	Forest soils, areas of decaying wood and organic matter; worldwide distribution, in United States most common on East Coast and in Midwest	Blastomycosis—cough, chest pain, hoarseness, fever; severe cases involve skin and other organs; lung abscesses resemble malignant tumors; skin nodules, bone infections, involvement of central nervous system possible
Coccidioides immitis	Semiarid, hot climates; Mexico, Central and South America; southwest U.S., especially California and southern Arizona	Coccidioidomycosis—fever, chest pain, headaches, malaise, chronic infection can lead to pulmonary nodular growths and cavity formation in lungs
Paracoccidioides brasiliensis	Tropical and semitropical regions of South and Central America	Paracoccidioidomycosis—infections of lung and skin; in severe cases, fungus can invade lungs, skin, and lymphatic organs

Table 21.B Opportunistic Fungi in the Lungs

Pathogen	Geographic Distribution
Pneumocystis (carinii) jiroveci	"PCP" pneumonia (see p. 651); cough, fever, shallow respiration, and cyanosis
Aspergillus spp.	Aspergillosis; fungus balls form in the lungs and other tissues, necrotic pneumonia, dissemination to the brain, heart, skin
Geotrichum candidum	Geotrichosis; secondary infections in tuberculosis or very ill patients
*Cryptococcus neoformans**	Cryptococcosis; lung infections followed often by brain and meninges involvement
Candida albicans	Candidal lung infections; in HIV-positive and lung transplant patients

Cryptococcus could fit in either category—primary or opportunistic pathogen—but its array of virulence factors are (individually) less potent than most of those expressed by primary pathogens. However, it often causes disease in otherwise healthy patients.

INSIGHT 21.3 Bioterror in the Lungs

After the terrorist attacks of September 11, 2001, and the anthrax attacks via the U.S. Postal Service that occurred later that fall, the U.S. government renewed its interest in preparing for bioterror or biowarfare attacks of all kinds. The U.S. Public Health Service designated six infectious diseases as "Category A," meaning that they have the highest priority in research and funding. Category A agents have the following characteristics:

1. They can be easily disseminated or transmitted from person to person.
2. They result in high mortality rates and have the potential for major public health impact.
3. They have the ability to cause public panic and social disruption.
4. They require special action for public health preparedness.

X ray showing the widened mediastinum in inhalation anthrax.

Of the six diseases, three of them can have their primary effects in the respiratory tract: pulmonary anthrax, pneumonic plague, and tularemia. The other three diseases on the A list are botulism, smallpox, and viral hemorrhagic fevers.

One of the most important components of a successful bioterror prevention strategy is early detection of infected persons. Because most of the conditions on the A list are rarely seen in the United States, clinicians' index of suspicion may be low. Here are the symptoms of the three agents that cause overt respiratory symptoms.

Pulmonary Anthrax (or Inhalation Anthrax)

This disease is the result of lung infection with *Bacillus anthracis* (see chapter 20). It should be considered when there is lung congestion accompanied by fever, malaise, and headache. Chest X rays are very useful because a widened mediastinum (the interpleural space that appears as the dark divider in the center of most chest X rays) is **pathognomic** (path-oh-nōm-ik) for this disease. Typical bronchopneumonia does not occur. In about half of patients, a hemorrhagic meningitis accompanies the pneumonitis. It is not transmitted from person to person, but because the bacterium forms endospores, these are easily disseminated through a variety of methods.

The most useful test for this disease is blood culture, because the organism is abundant in blood. Treatment is with penicillin, doxycycline, or ciprofloxacin. People presumed to have been exposed to the agent are also treated with one of these antibiotics for 30 to 60 days, because the endospores may persist in the respiratory tract for several weeks before germinating and becoming susceptible to antibiotics.

A vaccine for anthrax is currently administered only to military personnel and to some with occupational exposure to livestock.

---

experience mild symptoms such as aches, pains, and coughing; but a few develop more severe symptoms, including fever, night sweats, and weight loss.

The most serious systemic forms of histoplasmosis occur in patients with defective cell-mediated immunity such as AIDS patients. In these cases, the infection can lead to lesions in the brain, intestines, heart, liver, spleen, bone marrow, and skin. Persistent colonization of patients with emphysema and bronchitis causes *chronic pulmonary histoplasmosis,* a complication that has signs and symptoms similar to those of tuberculosis.

▶ Transmission and Epidemiology

The organism is endemically distributed on all continents except Australia. Its highest rates of incidence occur in the eastern and central regions of the United States, especially in the Ohio Valley. This fungus appears to grow most abundantly in moist soils high in nitrogen content, especially those supplemented by bird and bat droppings **(figure 21.23).**

A useful tool for determining the distribution of *H. capsulatum* is to inject a fungal extract into the skin and monitor for

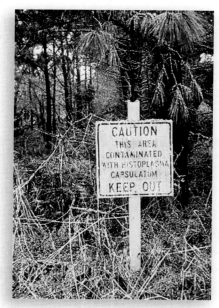

Figure 21.23 Sign in wooded area in Kentucky. The sign is covered in bird droppings. Up to 90% of the population in the Ohio Valley show evidence of past infection with *Histoplasma.*

Pneumonic Plague

This pneumonia illness is caused by *Yersinia pestis*, the same agent responsible for bubonic plague (chapter 20). The first signs of the pneumonic form are fever, headache, weakness, and rapidly developing pneumonia. Sometimes sputum is bloody or watery. Within 2 to 4 days, respiratory failure and shock can ensue. The incidence of plague in the United States is low and generally of the bubonic type, which is transmitted by fleas from a small mammal host. *Y. pestis* used as a bioterror

Wright-Giemsa stain of *Yersinia pestis* from peripheral blood.

agent would likely be disseminated as an aerosol, leading to large numbers of pneumonic cases. Gram staining of sputum, blood, or lymph node aspirates would reveal gram-negative rods, and additional staining with Wright or Giemsa stain would result in rods with characteristic bipolar staining.

Without treatment, patients die within 2 to 6 days; but swift antibiotic therapy with streptomycin, gentamicin, tetracyclines, or sulfonamides can save lives. A vaccine exists, but it does not protect against the pneumonic form of the disease and is no longer available in the United States.

Tularemia

This infection, caused by *Francisella tularensis*, is not widely known in the United States (see chapter 20). It can cause skin and bloodstream infections, lung disease, and severe ocular infections. The infectious dose is extremely low; as few as 10 bacteria can initiate serious dis-

ease. As a bioterror weapon, it would most probably be disseminated via the aerosol route and most of the infections would no doubt be of the respiratory variety. The abrupt appearance of large numbers of people with acute pneumonitis that progresses rapidly to sepsis would be the first sign that a tularemia bioterror incident has occurred. Because *F. tularensis* does not seem to be transmitted person to person, it would be unusual to find large numbers of infected people over a short period of time, which would raise the possibility that there was an intentional release.

Tularemia is difficult to diagnose, and the first steps in a suspected bioterror incident would be to rule out plague or anthrax pneumonic disease. The bacterium is extremely dangerous to laboratory workers, so caution must be used if *Francisella* is suspected. Antibiotics such as tetracycline and gentamicin can prevent death in most cases. An investigational vaccine has been developed, but its use is not approved.

As you can see, one of the greatest difficulties associated with managing a bioterror incident is that initial symptoms in patients are nonspecific. The time it takes for public health officials to begin to suspect one of these unusual etiologic agents (as opposed to common community-acquired respiratory infections) may make the difference between life and death for large numbers of people. We already have one advantage, however. Since the fall of 2001, U.S. health practitioners are much more alert to the possibility of intentional dissemination of infectious agents.

---

allergic reactions (much like the TB skin test). Application of this test has verified the extremely widespread distribution of the fungus. In high-prevalence areas such as southern Ohio, Illinois, Missouri, Kentucky, Tennessee, Michigan, Georgia, and Arkansas, 80% to 90% of the population shows signs of prior infection. Histoplasmosis prevalence in the United States is estimated at about 500,000 cases per year, with several thousand of them requiring hospitalization and a small number resulting in death.

People of both sexes and all ages incur infection, but adult males experience the majority of symptomatic cases. The oldest and youngest members of a population are most likely to develop serious disease.

▶ Culture and Diagnosis

Discovering *Histoplasma* in clinical specimens is a substantial diagnostic indicator. Usually it appears as spherical, "fisheye" yeasts intracellularly in macrophages and occasionally as free yeasts in samples of sputum and cerebrospinal fluid. Complement fixation and immunodiffusion serological tests can support a diagnosis by showing a rising antibody titer. (Because a positive histoplasmin [skin] test does not indicate

a new infection, this test is not useful in diagnosis.) Fluorescent antibody to the fungus is also a useful diagnostic tool.

▶ Prevention and Treatment

Avoiding the fungus is the only way to prevent this infection, and in many parts of the country this is impossible. Luckily, undetected or mild cases of histoplasmosis resolve without medical management. Chronic or disseminated disease calls for systemic antifungal chemotherapy. Amphotericin B and itraconazole are considered the drugs of choice and are usually administered in daily intravenous doses for up to several weeks. Surgery to remove affected masses in the lungs or other organs is sometimes also useful.

Pneumocystis (carinii) jiroveci

Although *Pneumocystis jiroveci* (formerly called *P. carinii*) was discovered in 1909, it remained relatively obscure until it was suddenly propelled into clinical prominence as the agent of *Pneumocystis* pneumonia (called PCP because of the old name of the fungus). PCP is the most frequent opportunistic infection in AIDS patients, most of whom will develop one or more episodes during their lifetimes.

▶ Symptoms, Pathogenesis, and Virulence Factors

In people with intact immune defenses, *P. jiroveci* is usually held in check by lung phagocytes and lymphocytes; but in those with deficient immune systems, it multiplies intracellularly and extracellularly. The massive numbers of fungi adhere tenaciously to the lung pneumocytes and cause an inflammatory condition. The lung epithelial cells slough off, and a foamy exudate builds up. Symptoms are nonspecific and include cough, fever, shallow respiration, and cyanosis (sī-ə-nō -sis).

▶ Transmission and Epidemiology

Unlike most of the human fungal pathogens, little is known about the life cycle or epidemiology of *Pneumocystis*. It is probably spread in droplet form between humans. Contact with the agent is so widespread that in some populations a majority of people show serological evidence of infection by the age of 3 or 4. Until the AIDS epidemic, symptomatic infections by this organism were very rare, occurring only among elderly people, premature infants, or patients that were severely debilitated or malnourished.

▶ Culture and Diagnosis

Although conventional microscopy performed on sputum or lavage fluids is often used, immunofluorescence using monoclonal antibodies against the organism has a higher sensitivity.

▶ Prevention and Treatment

Traditional antifungal drugs are ineffective against *Pneumocystis* pneumonia because the chemical makeup of the organism's cell wall differs from that of most fungi. The primary treatment is trimethoprim-sulfamethoxazole. This combination should be administered even if disease appears mild or is only suspected. It is sometimes given to patients with low T-cell counts to prevent the disease. The airways of patients in the active stage of infection often must be suctioned to reduce the symptoms **(Disease Table 21.10).**

Causative Agents of Nosocomial Pneumonia

About 1% of hospitalized or institutionalized people experience the complication of pneumonia. It is the second most common nosocomial infection, behind urinary tract infections. The mortality rate is quite high, between 30% and 50%. Although *Streptococcus pneumoniae* is frequently responsible, in addition it is very common to find a gram-negative bacterium called *Klebsiella pneumoniae* as well as anaerobic bacteria or even coliform bacteria in nosocomial pneumonia. Further complicating matters, many nosocomial pneumonias appear to be polymicrobial in origin—meaning that there are multiple microorganisms multiplying in the alveolar spaces.

In nosocomial infections, bacteria gain access to the lower respiratory tract through abnormal breathing and aspiration of the normal upper respiratory tract biota (and occasionally the stomach) into the lungs. Stroke victims have high rates of nosocomial pneumonia. Mechanical ventilation is another route of entry for microbes. Once there, the organisms take advantage of the usual lowered immune response in a hospitalized patient and cause pneumonia symptoms.

▶ Culture and Diagnosis

Culture of sputum or of tracheal swabs is not very useful in diagnosing nosocomial pneumonia, because the condition is usually caused by normal biota. Obtaining cultures of fluids obtained through endotracheal tubes or from bronchoalveolar

Disease Table 21.10 Pneumonia

Causative Organism(s)	*Streptococcus pneumoniae*	*Legionella* species	*Mycoplasma pneumoniae*	
Most Common Modes of Transmission	Droplet contact or endogenous transfer	Vehicle (water droplets)	Droplet contact	
Virulence Factors	Capsule	–	Adhesins	
Culture/Diagnosis	Gram stain often diagnostic, alpha-hemolytic on blood agar	Requires selective charcoal yeast extract agar; serology unreliable	Rule out other etiologic agents	
Prevention	Pneumococcal polysaccharide vaccine (23-valent)	–	No vaccine, no permanent immunity	
Treatment	Cefotaxime, ceftriaxone, much resistance	Fluoroquinolone, azithromycin, clarithromycin	Recommended not to treat in most cases, doxycycline or macrolides may be used if necessary	
Distinctive Features	Patient usually severely ill	Mild pneumonias in healthy people; can be severe in elderly or immunocompromised	Usually mild; "walking pneumonia"	

A Note About Emerging Pneumonias

In 2003 a virus from a family previously known only to cause cold-like symptoms burst onto the world stage as it started to cause pneumonias and death in Hong Kong. The SARS epidemic ended nearly as quickly as it started and since 2004 new cases of SARS have not been detected anywhere on the planet. Similarly, in 2007, a rare serotype of an adenovirus, which had previously only been known to cause mild respiratory disease, caused two U.S. outbreaks of severe pneumonia. We will highlight these two viruses briefly here. We do not include them in the main community-acquired pneumonia section and table since they are not well-established (in the case of the adenovirus) or currently active (in the case of SARS). But they are important illustrations of how changeable viruses can be, and how they can suddenly cause important outbreaks and epidemics.

Severe Acute Respiratory Syndrome–Associated Coronavirus

In the winter of 2002, reports of an acute respiratory illness, originally termed an *atypical pneumonia*, began to filter in from Asia. In March of 2003, the World Health Organization issued a global health alert about the new illness. By mid-April, scientists had sequenced the entire genome of the causative virus, making the creation of diagnostic tests possible and paving the way for intensive research on the virus. The epidemic was contained by the end of July 2003, but in less than a year it had sickened more than 8,000 people. About 9% of those died. The disease was given the name **SARS**, for **severe acute respiratory syndrome**. It was concentrated in China and Southeast Asia, although sev-eral dozen countries, from Australia and Canada to the United States, have reported cases. Most of the cases seem to have originated in people who had traveled to Asia or who had close contact with people from that region. Close contact (direct or droplet) seems to be required for its transmission. The virus is a previously unknown strain of coronavirus (family Coronaviridae).

Symptoms begin with a fever of above 38°C (100.4°F) and progress to body aches and an overall feeling of malaise. Early in the infection, there seems to be little virus in the patient and a low probability of transmission. Within a week, viral numbers surge and transmissibility is very high. After 3 weeks, if the patient survives, viral levels decrease significantly and symptoms subside. Patients may or may not experience classic respiratory symptoms. They may develop breathing problems. Severe cases of the illness can result in respiratory distress and death.

Adenovirus 14

Adenoviruses generally cause mild disease. But in 2007 two separate outbreaks of severe pneumonia were caused by one serotype, adenovirus 14. The two outbreaks occurred simultaneously but showed no apparent link—one was on an Air Force base in Texas and the other was a community outbreak in Oregon. The infections were severe; in Oregon more than 75% of those infected were hospitalized and 33% required intubation. Eighteen percent of the patients in Oregon died. Retrospective examination of samples stored from 1993 to 2007 in Oregon found that this virus only started showing up after 2005. Cases continued to occur through mid-2008, but the epidemic had subsided.

Hantavirus	*Histoplasma capsulatum*	*Pneumocystis jiroveci*
Vehicle—airborne virus emitted from rodents	Vehicle—inhalation of contaminated soil	Droplet contact
Ability to induce inflammatory response	Survival in phagocytes	–
Serology (IgM), PCR identification of antigen in tissue	Usually serological (rising Ab titers)	Immunofluorescence
Avoid mouse habitats and droppings	Avoid contaminated soil/ bat, bird droppings	Antibiotics given to AIDS patients to prevent this
Supportive	Amphotericin B and/or itraconazole	Trimethoprim-sulfamethoxazole
Rapid onset; high mortality rate	Many infections asymptomatic	Vast majority occur in AIDS patients

lavage provide better information but are fairly intrusive. It is also important to remember that if the patient has already received antibiotics, culture results will be affected.

▶ Prevention and Treatment

Because most nosocomial pneumonias are caused by microorganisms aspirated from the upper respiratory tract, measures that discourage the transfer of microbes into the lungs are very useful for preventing the condition. Elevating patients' heads to a 45-degree angle helps reduce aspiration of secretions. Good preoperative education of patients about the importance of deep breathing and frequent coughing can reduce postoperative infection rates. Proper care of mechanical ventilation and respiratory therapy equipment is essential as well.

Studies have shown that delaying antibiotic treatment of suspected nosocomial pneumonia leads to a greater likelihood of death. Even in this era of conservative antibiotic use, empiric therapy should be started as soon as nosocomial pneumonia is suspected, using multiple antibiotics that cover both gram-negative and gram-positive organisms.

Disease Table 21.11 Nosocomial Pneumonia

Causative Organism(s)	Gram-negative and gram-positive bacteria from upper respiratory tract or stomach
Most Common Modes of Transmission	Endogenous (aspiration)
Virulence Factors	–
Culture/Diagnosis	Culture of lung fluids
Prevention	Elevating patient's head, preoperative education, care of respiratory equipment
Treatment	Broad-spectrum antibiotics

Case File 21   *Wrap-Up*

The first time one of the church volunteers in El Salvador reported respiratory problems, a physician performed a chest X-ray. Although there are no specific radiographic signs that point definitively to histoplasmosis, this patient exhibited clear signs of inflammation, and the physician suspected *Histoplasma* because it is endemic to Central and South America as well as to eastern Asia, Australia, and the midwestern United States. The diagnosis was confirmed in all 20 patients by conducting ELISA tests of urine or serum.

■ Interestingly, histoplasmosis is highly prevalent in the Ohio River Valley of the United States. The majority of people living in this area are thought to have antibodies to the fungus, even though they may never have shown symptoms of the disease. Such persons may have been protected from the infection if they had taken a similar mission trip!

See: 2009. *JAMA* 301(5):478–80.

21.5 Learning Outcomes—Can You ...

9. ... list the possible causative agents, modes of transmission, virulence factors, diagnostic techniques, and prevention/treatment for each of the diseases infecting the lower respiratory tract? These are: tuberculosis, community-acquired pneumonia, and nosocomial pneumonia.
10. ... discuss the problems associated with MDR-TB and XDR-TB?
11. ... demonstrate an in-depth understanding of the epidemiology of tuberculosis infection?
12. ... describe the importance of the recent phenomenon of cold viruses causing pneumonia?
13. ... list the distinguishing characteristics of nosocomial versus community-acquired pneumonia?

▶ **Summing Up**

Taxonomic Organization Microorganisms Causing Disease in the Respiratory Tract

Microorganism	Disease	Chapter Location
Gram-positive bacteria		
Streptococcus pneumoniae	Otitis media, pneumonia	Otitis media, p. 627
		Pneumonia, p. 645
S. pyogenes	Pharyngitis	Pharyngitis, p. 628
Corynebacterium diphtheriae	Diphtheria	Diphtheria, p. 632
Gram-negative bacteria		
Haemophilus influenzae	Otitis media	Otitis media, p. 627
Fusobacterium necrophorum	Pharyngitis	Pharyngitis, p. 628
Bordetella pertussis	Whooping cough	Whooping cough, p. 633
*Mycobacterium tuberculosis,** M. avium* complex	Tuberculosis	Tuberculosis, p. 640
Legionella spp.	Pneumonia	Pneumonia, p. 646
Other bacteria		
Mycoplasma pneumoniae	Pneumonia	Pneumonia, p. 647
RNA viruses		
Respiratory syncytial virus	RSV disease	RSV disease, p. 635
Influenza virus A, B, and C	Influenza	Influenza, p. 635
Hantavirus	Hantavirus pulmonary syndrome	Pneumonia, p. 648
Fungi		
Pneumocystis jiroveci	*Pneumocystis* pneumonia	Pneumonia, p. 651
Histoplasma capsulatum	Histoplasmosis	Pneumonia, p. 648

*There is some debate about the gram status of the genus *Mycobacterium;* it is generally not considered gram-positive or gram-negative.

INFECTIOUS DISEASES AFFECTING
The Respiratory System

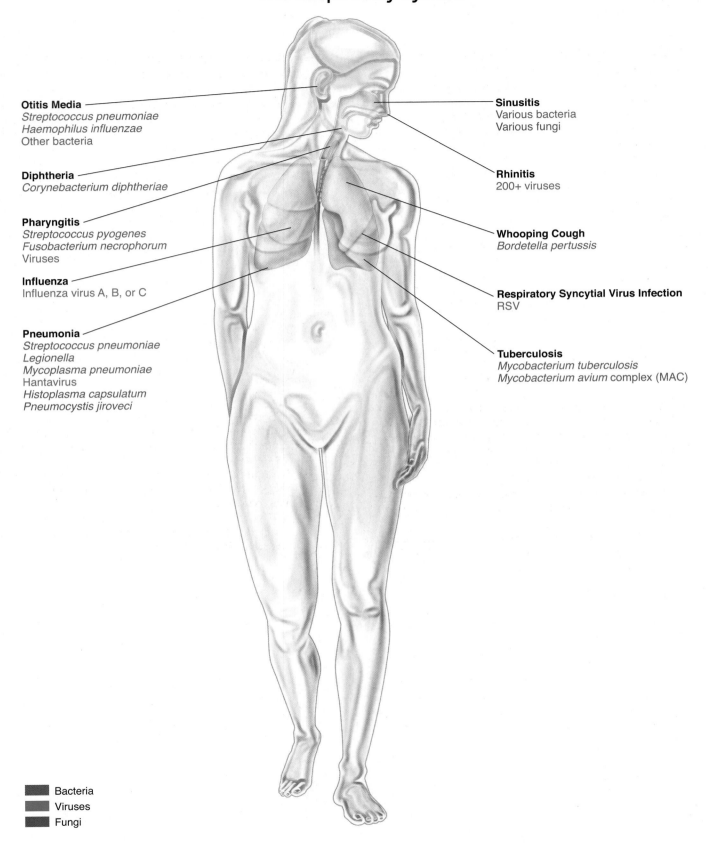

Otitis Media
Streptococcus pneumoniae
Haemophilus influenzae
Other bacteria

Diphtheria
Corynebacterium diphtheriae

Pharyngitis
Streptococcus pyogenes
Fusobacterium necrophorum
Viruses

Influenza
Influenza virus A, B, or C

Pneumonia
Streptococcus pneumoniae
Legionella
Mycoplasma pneumoniae
Hantavirus
Histoplasma capsulatum
Pneumocystis jiroveci

Sinusitis
Various bacteria
Various fungi

Rhinitis
200+ viruses

Whooping Cough
Bordetella pertussis

Respiratory Syncytial Virus Infection
RSV

Tuberculosis
Mycobacterium tuberculosis
Mycobacterium avium complex (MAC)

■ Bacteria
■ Viruses
■ Fungi

System Summary Figure 21.24

Chapter Summary

21.1 The Respiratory Tract and Its Defenses

- The upper respiratory tract includes the mouth, nose, nasal cavity and sinuses, throat (pharynx), and epiglottis and larynx.
- The lower respiratory tract begins with the trachea, which feeds into the bronchi and bronchioles in the lungs. Alveoli, the site of oxygen exchange in the lungs, are attached to the bronchioles.
- The ciliary escalator propels particles upward and out of the respiratory tract. Mucus on the surface of the mucous membranes traps microorganisms, and involuntary responses such as coughing, sneezing, and swallowing move them out of sensitive areas. Macrophages inhabit the alveoli of the lungs and the clusters of lymphoid tissue (tonsils) in the throat. Secretory IgA against specific pathogens can be found in the mucus secretions as well.

21.2 Normal Biota of the Respiratory Tract

- Normal biota include *Streptococccus pyogenes, Haemophilus influenzae, Streptococcus pneumoniae, Neisseria meningitidis, Staphylococcus aureus, Moraxella* and *Corynebacterium* species, and *Candida albicans.*

21.3 Upper Respiratory Tract Diseases Caused by Microorganisms

- **Rhinitis, or the Common Cold:** Caused by one of over 200 different kinds of viruses, most commonly the rhinoviruses, followed by the coronaviruses. Respiratory syncytial virus (RSV) causes colds in many people, but in some, especially children, can lead to more serious respiratory tract symptoms.
- **Sinusitis:** Inflammatory condition most commonly caused by allergy or by a variety of viruses or bacteria and, less commonly, fungi.
- **Acute Otitis Media (Ear Infection):** Viral infections of upper respiratory tract lead to inflammation of eustachian tubes and buildup of fluid in the middle ear, leading to bacterial multiplication in those fluids. Most common cause is *Streptococcus pneumoniae.*
- **Pharyngitis:** The same viruses causing the common cold commonly cause inflammation of the throat. However, two potentially serious causes of pharyngitis are *Streptococcus pyogenes* and *Fusobacterium necrophorum.* Untreated streptococcal throat infections can result in scarlet fever, rheumatic fever, glomerulonephritis, and necrotizing fasciitis. Untreated *F. necrophorum* infections can lead to Lemierre's syndrome.
- **Diphtheria:** Caused by *Corynebacterium diphtheriae,* a non-spore-forming, gram-positive club-shaped bacterium. Employs exotoxin encoded by a bacteriophage of *C. diphtheriae.*

21.4 Diseases Caused by Microorganisms Affecting Both the Upper and Lower Respiratory Tracts

- **Whooping Cough:** Caused by *Bordetella pertussis.* Releases exotoxins—*pertussis toxin* and *tracheal cytotoxin*—that damage ciliated respiratory epithelial cells and cripple other components of host defense, including phagocytic cells.
- **Respiratory Syncytial Virus (RSV):** Produces giant multinucleated cells (syncytia). RSV is most prevalent cause of respiratory infection in newborn age group.
- **Influenza:** Caused by one of three influenza viruses: A, B, or C. The ssRNA genome is subject to constant genetic changes that alter the structure of its envelope glycoprotein. This is called antigenic drift—resulting in decreased ability of host memory cells to recognize the virus. Antigenic shift, where one or more of eight RNA strands are swapped with gene or strand from a different influenza virus, is even more serious.

21.5 Lower Respiratory Tract Diseases Caused by Microorganisms

- **Tuberculosis:** The cause is primarily the bacterium *Mycobacterium tuberculosis.* Vaccine generally not used in the United States, although an attenuated vaccine, called BCG, is used in many countries.
  - *Mycobacterium avium complex:* Before introduction of effective HIV treatments, disseminated tuberculosis infection with MAC was one of biggest killers of AIDS patients.
- **Pneumonia:** An inflammatory condition of the lung in which fluid fills the alveoli; caused by wide variety of microorganisms.
  - *Streptococcus pneumoniae:* Main agent for community-acquired bacterial pneumonia cases. *Legionella* is a less common but serious cause of the disease. *Haemophilus influenzae* used to be a major cause, but use of the Hib vaccine has reduced its incidence.
  - Other bacterial causes are *Mycoplasma pneumoniae* and *Chlamydophila pneumoniae. Histoplasma capsulatum,* a fungus, causes a pneumonia-like disease. Hantavirus causes a pneumonia-like condition named hantavirus pulmonary syndrome (HPS).
  - Pneumonia may be a secondary effect of influenza disease. Physicians may treat pneumonia empirically, meaning they do not determine the etiologic agent.
  - *Streptococcus pneumoniae* and gram-negative *Klebsiella pneumoniae* are commonly responsible for nosocomial pneumonias. Furthermore, many nosocomial pneumonias appear to be polymicrobial in origin.

Multiple-Choice and True-False Questions   Knowledge and Comprehension

Multiple-Choice Questions. Select the correct answer from the answers provided.

1. The two most common groups of virus associated with the common cold are
   a. rhinoviruses.   d. both a and b.
   b. coronaviruses.   e. both a and c.
   c. influenza viruses.

2. Which of the following conditions are associated with *Streptococcus pyogenes*?
   a. pharyngitis   c. rheumatic fever
   b. scarlet fever   d. all of the above

3. Which is not a characteristic of *Streptococcus pyogenes*?
   a. group A streptococcus   c. sensitive to bacitracin
   b. alpha-hemolytic   d. gram-positive

4. The common stain used to identify *Mycobacterium* species is
   a. Gram stain.   c. negative stain.
   b. acid-fast stain.   d. spore stain.

5. Which of the following techniques is used to diagnose tuberculosis?
   a. tuberculin testing
   b. chest X rays
   c. cultural isolation and antimicrobial testing
   d. all of the above

6. The DTaP vaccine provides protection against the following diseases, *except*
   a. diphtheria.   c. pneumonia.
   b. pertussis.   d. tetanus.

7. Which of the following infections often has a polymicrobial cause?
   a. otitis media   c. sinusitis
   b. nosocomial pneumonia   d. all of the above

8. The vast majority of pneumonias caused by this organism occur in AIDS patients.
   a. hantavirus   c. *Pneumocystis jiroveci*
   b. *Histoplasma capsulatum* d. *Mycoplasma pneumoniae*

9. The beta-hemolysis of blood agar observed with *Streptococcus pyogenes* is due to the presence of
   a. streptolysin.   c. hyaluronic acid.
   b. M protein.   d. catalase.

10. An estimated ____ of the world population is infected with *Mycobacterium tuberculosis*.
    a. 1/2   c. 1/3
    b. 1/4   d. 3/4

True-False Questions. If the statement is true, leave as is. If it is false, correct it by rewriting the sentence.

11. *Bordetella pertussis* is the causative agent for whooping cough.

12. *Mycoplasma pneumoniae* causes "atypical" pneumonia and is diagnosed by sputum culture.

13. BCG vaccine is used in other countries to prevent Legionnaires' disease.

14. Respiratory syncytial virus (RSV) is a respiratory infection associated with elderly people.

15. The "flu shot" can cause the flu in immunocompromised people.

Critical Thinking Questions   Application and Analysis

These questions are suggested as a *writing-to-learn* experience. For each question, compose a one- or two-paragraph answer that includes the factual information needed to completely address the question.

1. What two vaccines are available for treating *Streptococcus pneumoniae,* and what are their target populations?

2. What parts of the body are affected by extrapulmonary tuberculosis?

3. a. What type of vaccine is used against *Corynebacterium diphtheriae?*
   b. What is the characteristic toxin produced by this microorganism?
   c. What treatment is suggested for a diphtheria infection?

4. a. Name the organisms responsible for the flu.
   b. To what family do these viruses belong?
   c. Describe the genome of this virus.

5. What are some of the likely explanations if you are not responding to antibiotic treatment for sinusitis?

6. Describe how you might design a vaccine against the common cold.

7. A 5-year-old boy is diagnosed with otitis media. He has severe pain in his left ear and a fever of 101°F. Inspection of the eardrum reveals that both membranes are red but intact. His history reveals that he seldom has ear infections. How would you treat this patient?

8. A graduate student from Namibia tests positive in the tuberculin skin test. Upon reading the patient history, the doctor determines that the test is a false positive and does not pursue further treatment. What is the possible explanation for the false positive skin test?

9. Why is noncompliance during TB therapy such a big concern?

10. Why do we need to take the flu vaccine every year? Why does it not confer long-term immunity to the flu like other vaccines?

Concept Mapping   Synthesis

Appendix D provides guidance for working with concept maps.

1. Construct your own concept map using the following words as the *concepts*. Supply the linking words between each pair of concepts.

FHA

coughing

multiplication

pertussis toxin

tracheal cytotoxin

endotoxin

cilia

mucus

Bordetella pertussis

Visual Connections   Synthesis

These questions use visual images or previous content to make connections to this chapter's concepts.

1. **Figure 21.2.** Some doctors suggest that gently forcing one's ears to "pop" is an effective way to treat or even prevent ear infection. Use the following illustration to explain how this could work.

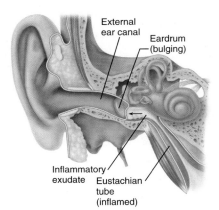

External ear canal

Eardrum (bulging)

Inflammatory exudate

Eustachian tube (inflamed)

2. **From chapter 3, figure 3.21.** Although there are many different organisms present in the respiratory tract, an acid-fast stain of sputum like the one shown here along with patient symptoms can establish a presumptive diagnosis of tuberculosis. Explain why.

Acid-fast stain
Red cells are acid-fast.
Blue cells are non-acid-fast.

 connect (plus+) **www.connect.microbiology.com**

|MICROBIOLOGY

Enhance your study of this chapter with study tools and practice tests. Also ask your instructor about the resources available through ConnectPlus, including the media-rich eBook, interactive learning tools, and animations.

22

Infectious Diseases Affecting the Gastrointestinal Tract

Case File 22

Following Hurricane Katrina in August 2005, relief agencies provided food and shelter to an estimated 240,000 of the region's residents in a variety of locations. Approximately 24,000 evacuees were temporarily housed in the Reliant Park Sports and Convention Center in Houston, Texas, which was renamed Reliant City for the time being. A medical clinic was set up to serve the immediate needs of the residents. Over the next several weeks, 1,169 individuals visited the clinic exhibiting symptoms of acute gastroenteritis, specifically diarrhea, vomiting, or both.

- What are the organisms most commonly associated with acute gastroenteritis?
- How did this outbreak likely begin? How did it probably spread?

Continuing the Case appears on page 682.

Outline and Learning Outcomes

22.1 The Gastrointestinal Tract and Its Defenses
1. Draw or describe the anatomical features of the gastrointestinal tract.
2. List the natural defenses present in the gastrointestinal tract.

22.2 Normal Biota of the Gastrointestinal Tract
3. List the types of normal biota presently known to occupy the gastrointestinal tract.
4. Describe how our view has changed of normal biota present in the stomach.

22.3 Gastrointestinal Tract Diseases Caused by Microorganisms (Nonhelminthic)
5. List the possible causative agents, modes of transmission, virulence factors, diagnostic techniques, and prevention/treatment for each of the kinds of oral diseases.
6. Discuss current theories about the connection between oral bacteria and cardiovascular disease.

7. List the possible causative agents, modes of transmission, virulence factors, diagnostic techniques, and prevention/treatment for mumps, gastritis, and gastric ulcers.

8. List the possible causative agents, modes of transmission, virulence factors, diagnostic techniques, and prevention/treatment for acute and chronic diarrhea, and also for acute diarrhea with vomiting.

9. Differentiate among the main types of hepatitis and discuss each causative agent, mode of transmission, diagnostic techniques, prevention, and treatment of each.

22.4 Gastrointestinal Tract Diseases Caused by Helminths

10. Describe some distinguishing characteristics and commonalities seen in helminthic infections.

11. List four helminths that cause primarily intestinal symptoms, and identify which life cycle they follow and one unique fact about each one.

12. List four helminths that cause intestinal symptoms that may be accompanied by migratory symptoms, and identify which life cycle they follow and one unique fact about each one.

13. List the modes of transmission, virulence factors, diagnostic techniques, and prevention/treatment for each of the helminth infections resulting in liver and intestinal symptoms. These are infections caused by *Opisthorchis sinensis*, *Clonorchis sinensis*, and *Fasciola hepatica*.

14. Describe the type of disease caused by *Trichinella* species.

15. Diagram the life cycle of *Schistosoma mansoni* and *S. japonicum*, discuss how it differs from the life cycle of the *Schistosoma* involved in urinary disease, and describe the importance of all three organisms in world health.

22.1 The Gastrointestinal Tract and Its Defenses

The gastrointestinal (GI) tract can be thought of as a long tube, extending from mouth to anus. It is a very sophisticated delivery system for nutrients, composed of *eight* main sections and augmented by *four* accessory organs. The eight sections are the mouth, pharynx, esophagus, stomach, small intestine, large intestine, rectum, and anus. Along the way, the salivary glands, liver, gallbladder, and pancreas add digestive fluids and enzymes to assist in digesting and processing the food we take in **(figure 22.1).** The GI tract is often called the *digestive tract* or the *alimentary tract*.

Anything inside the GI tract is in some ways not "inside" the body; it is passing through an internal tube, called a **lumen,** and only those chemicals that are absorbed through the walls of the GI tract actually gain entrance to the internal portions of the body. Food begins to be broken down into absorbable subunits as soon as it enters the mouth, where the teeth begin to mechanically break down solid particles and where enzymes in saliva break the food down chemically. The swallowed food travels through the pharynx and into the esophagus, emptying into the stomach. Here the food is mixed with gastric juice, which has a very low pH and contains the important gastric enzyme pepsin, which breaks down proteins (peptides). From here the food travels to the small intestine, a long, tightly coiled portion of the lumen where most nutrient absorption takes place. The small intestine is divided into the duodenum (leading directly out of the stomach), the jejunum (most of the coiled part), and the ileum (connecting the coils to the large intestine). The pancreas secretes a variety of digestive enzymes into the small intestine, and the liver and the gallbladder work together to add bile.

Once food leaves the small intestine, it enters the large intestine, which is divided into the cecum, the colon, the rectum, and the anus. In the large intestine, water and electrolytes are absorbed from any undigested food. What is left combines with mucus and bacteria from the large intestine, becoming fecal material. Forty to sixty percent of the mass of fecal material is composed of bacteria.

The GI tract has a very heavy load of microorganisms, and it encounters millions of new ones every day. Because of this, defenses against infection are extremely important. All intestinal surfaces are coated with a layer of mucus, which confers mechanical protection. Secretory IgA can also be found on most intestinal surfaces. The muscular walls of the GI tract keep food (and microorganisms) moving through the system through the action of peristalsis. Various fluids in the GI tract have antimicrobial properties. Saliva contains the antimicrobial proteins lysozyme and lactoferrin. The stomach fluid is antimicrobial by virtue of its extremely high acidity. Bile is also antimicrobial.

The entire system is outfitted with cells of the immune system, collectively called gut-associated lymphoid tissue (GALT). The tonsils and adenoids in the oral cavity and pharynx, small areas of lymphoid tissue in the esophagus, Peyer's patches in the small intestine, and the appendix are all packets of lymphoid tissue consisting of T and B cells as well as cells of nonspecific immunity. One of their jobs is to produce IgA, but they perform a variety of other immune functions. Perhaps because of the great density of immune players

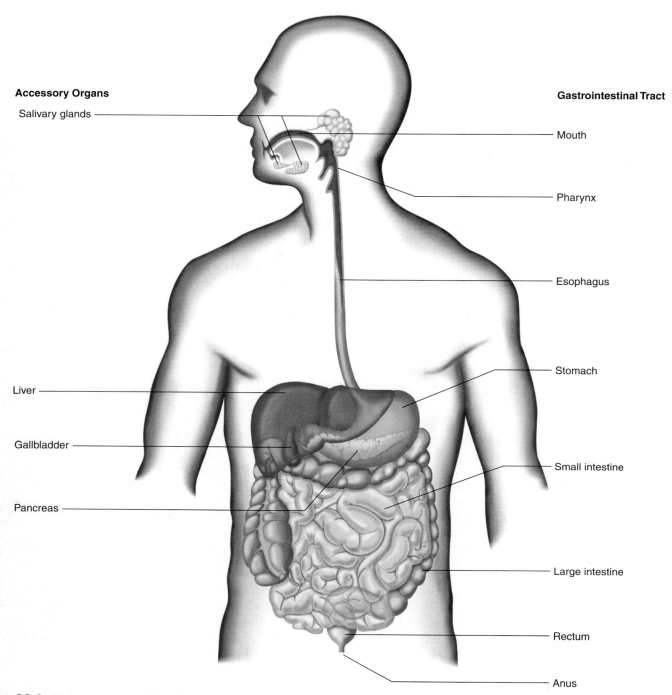

Figure 22.1 Major organs of the digestive system.

in the intestines, they experience disease that is caused, or aggravated, by inflammatory processes **(Insight 22.1).**

A huge population of commensal organisms lives in this system, especially in the large intestine. They provide the protection of microbial antagonism and avoid immune destruction through various mechanisms, including cloaking themselves with host sugars they find on the intestinal walls.

22.1 Learning Outcomes—Can You ...

1. ... draw or describe the anatomical features of the gastrointestinal tract?

2. ... list the natural defenses present in the gastrointestinal tract?

INSIGHT 22.1   Is Crohn's an Infection That We Get from Cows?

There are two gastrointestinal conditions that cause massive suffering, yet are not covered in this chapter. Ulcerative colitis and Crohn's disease are both considered inflammatory bowel diseases (IBDs), and as the name indicates, have long been thought to be the result of overactive and inappropriate immune reactions in the small and large intestines.

Now it looks like one of those conditions may, in fact, have a microbial cause. Or, better said, a microbe might be one of the factors that contributes to the damage in the disease. Crohn's disease has been the subject of intense scrutiny since it was noticed that cattle have a similar condition, characterized by chronic diarrhea, weight loss, neuropathy, and periods of remission. In cattle this is called Johne's disease and is unambiguously caused by *Mycobacterium avium* subspecies *paratuberculosis*, known as MAP. A whopping 68% of U.S. dairy cows are infected with this bacterium, and it can easily be transmitted to humans through the food chain (beef and milk).

As it happens, seven of eight Crohn's patients have MAP bacteria in their tissues. And when they are treated with antimycobacterial drugs, many of them experience relief. Of course, this is biology and nothing is neat. For one thing, not every patient with Crohn's is helped with antibiotic treatment. This could be explained by the difficulty of treating *Mycobacterium*, which we studied in the case of tuberculosis. Another puzzler is that one out of eight patients has no MAP. Some scientists

suspect a particular type of *E. coli* can also induce the inflammatory symptoms characteristic of Crohn's.

Supporting evidence for the role of MAP includes the fact that some patients treated with the traditional therapy, steroids to decrease the inflammation, actually do worse. It is tempting to speculate that this is because dampening the immune system would allow bacteria to flourish. Maybe it's time for the gold standard of infectious disease causation to be employed: Koch's postulates. Can you articulate a hypothesis and an experiment to prove that MAP causes Crohn's?

22.2 Normal Biota of the Gastrointestinal Tract

As just mentioned, the GI tract is home to a large variety of normal biota. The oral cavity alone is populated by more than 550 known species of microorganisms, including *Streptococcus, Neisseria, Veillonella, Staphylococcus, Fusobacterium, Lactobacillus, Corynebacterium, Actinomyces,* and *Treponema* species. Fungi such as *Candida albicans* are also numerous. A few protozoa (*Trichomonas tenax, Entamoeba gingivalis*) also call the mouth "home." Bacteria live on the teeth as well as the soft structures in the mouth. Numerous species of normal biota bacteria live on the teeth in large accretions called dental plaque, which is a kind of biofilm (see chapter 4). Bacteria are held in the biofilm by specific recognition molecules. Alpha-hemolytic streptococci are generally the first colonizers of the tooth surface after it has been cleaned. The streptococci attach specifically to proteins in the **pellicle,** a mucinous glycoprotein covering on the tooth. Then other species attach specifically to proteins or sugars on the surface of the streptococci, and so on.

The pharynx contains a variety of microorganisms, which were described in chapter 21. Although the stomach was previously thought to be sterile, researchers in 2008 found the molecular signatures of 128 different species of microorganisms in the stomach. These must have mechanisms for overcoming the extreme acidity of the stomach fluid and can survive there. The large intestine has always

been known to be a haven for billions of microorganisms (10^{11} per gram of contents), including the bacteria *Bacteroides, Fusobacterium, Bifidobacterium, Clostridium, Streptococcus, Peptostreptococcus, Lactobacillus, Escherichia,* and *Enterobacter;* the fungus *Candida;* and several protozoa as well. Researchers have also found archaea species there.

The normal biota in the gut provide a protective function, but they also perform other jobs as well. Some of them help with digestion. Some provide nutrients that we can't produce ourselves. *E. coli,* for instance, synthesizes vitamin K. Its mere presence in the large intestine seems to be important for the proper formation of epithelial cell structure. And the normal biota in the gut plays an important role in "teaching" our immune system to react to microbial antigens. Some scientists believe that the mix of microbiota in the healthy gut can influence a host's chances for obesity or autoimmune diseases.

The accessory organs (salivary glands, gallbladder, liver, and pancreas) are free of microorganisms, just as all internal organs are.

22.2 Learning Outcomes—Can You ...

3. ... list the types of normal biota presently known to occupy the gastrointestinal tract?
4. ... describe how our view has changed of normal biota present in the stomach?

22.3 Gastrointestinal Tract Diseases Caused by Microorganisms (Nonhelminthic)

Tooth and Gum Infections

It is difficult to pinpoint exactly when the "normal biota biofilm" just described becomes a "pathogenic biofilm." If left undisturbed, the biofilm structure eventually contains anaerobic bacteria that can damage the soft tissues and bones (referred to as the periodontium) surrounding the teeth. Also, the introduction of carbohydrates to the oral cavity can result in breakdown of hard tooth structure (the dentition) due to the production of acid by certain oral streptococci in the biofilm. These two separate circumstances are discussed here.

Dental Caries (Tooth Decay)

Dental caries is the most common infectious disease of human beings. The process involves the dissolution of solid tooth surface due to the metabolic action of bacteria. (**Figure 22.2** depicts the structure of a tooth.) The symptoms are often not noticeable but range from minor disruption in the outer (enamel) surface of the tooth to complete destruction of the enamel and then destruction of deeper layers (**figure 22.3**). Deeper lesions can result in infection to the soft tissue inside the tooth, called

the pulp, which contains blood vessels and nerves. These deeper infections lead to pain, referred to as a "toothache."

▶ Causative Agent

Two representatives of oral alpha-hemolytic streptococci, *Streptococcus mutans* and *Streptococcus sobrinus*, seem to be the main causes of dental caries, although a mixed species consortium, consisting of other *Streptococcus* species and some lactobacilli, is probably the best route to caries. Note that in the absence of dietary carbohydrates bacteria do not cause decay.

▶ Pathogenesis and Virulence Factors

In the presence of sucrose and, to a lesser extent, other carbohydrates, *S. sobrinus* and *S. mutans* produce sticky polymers of glucose called fructans and glucans. These adhesives help bind them to the smooth enamel surfaces and contribute to the sticky bulk of the plaque biofilm (**figure 22.4**). If mature plaque is not removed from sites that readily trap food, it can result in a carious lesion. This is due to the action of the streptococci and other bacteria that produce acid as they ferment the carbohydrates. If the acid is immediately flushed from the plaque and diluted in the mouth, it has little effect. However, in the denser regions of plaque, the acid can accumulate in direct contact with the enamel surface and lower the pH to below 5, which is acidic enough to begin to dissolve (decalcify) the calcium phosphate of the enamel in that spot. This initial lesion can remain localized in the enamel and can be repaired with various inert materials (fillings). Once the deterioration has reached the level of the dentin, tooth destruction speeds up and the tooth can be rapidly destroyed. Exposure of the pulp leads to severe tenderness and toothache, and the chance of saving the tooth is diminished.

Teeth become vulnerable to caries as soon as they appear in the mouth at around 6 months of age. Early childhood caries, defined as caries in a child between birth and 6 years of age, can extensively damage a child's primary teeth and affect the proper eruption of the permanent teeth. The practice of putting a baby down to nap with a bottle of fruit juice or formula can lead to rampant dental caries in the vulnerable primary dentition. This condition is called *nursing bottle caries*.

▶ Transmission and Epidemiology

The bacteria that cause dental caries are transmitted to babies and children by their close contacts, especially the mother or closest caregiver. There is evidence for transfer of oral bacteria between children in day care centers, as well. Although it was previously believed that humans don't acquire *S. mutans* or *S. sobrinus* until the eruption of teeth in the mouth, it now seems likely that both of these species may survive in the infant's oral cavity prior to appearance of the first teeth.

Dental caries has a worldwide distribution. Its incidence varies according to many factors, including amount of carbohydrate consumption, hygiene practices, and host genetic factors. Susceptibility to caries generally decreases with age, possibly due to the fact that grooves and fissures—common sites of dental caries—tend to become more shallow as teeth

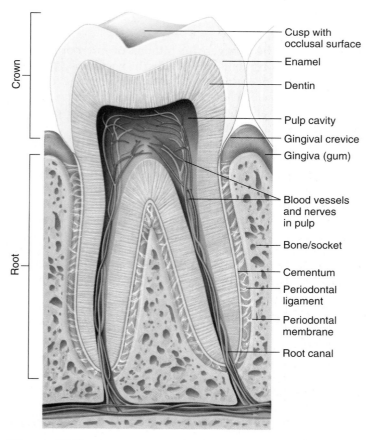

Figure 22.2 The anatomy of a tooth.

Cusp with occlusal surface
Enamel
Dentin
Pulp cavity
Gingival crevice
Gingiva (gum)
Blood vessels and nerves in pulp
Bone/socket
Cementum
Periodontal ligament
Periodontal membrane
Root canal

Crown

Root

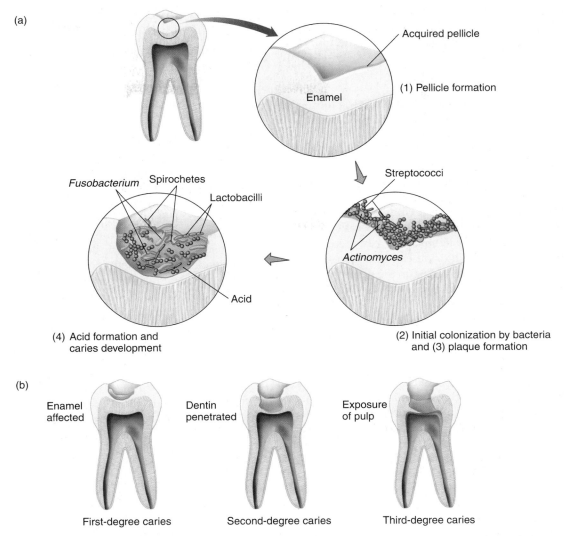

(a)

Acquired pellicle

Enamel

(1) Pellicle formation

Streptococci

Actinomyces

(2) Initial colonization by bacteria and (3) plaque formation

Fusobacterium Spirochetes

Lactobacilli

Acid

(4) Acid formation and caries development

(b)

Enamel affected

Dentin penetrated

Exposure of pulp

First-degree caries

Second-degree caries

Third-degree caries

Figure 22.3 Stages in plaque development and cariogenesis. **(a)** A microscopic view of pellicle and plaque formation, acidification, and destruction of tooth enamel. **(b)** Progress and degrees of cariogenesis.

(a)

(b)

Figure 22.4 The macroscopic and microscopic appearance of plaque. **(a)** Disclosing tablets containing vegetable dye stain heavy plaque accumulations at the junction of the tooth and gingiva. **(b)** Scanning electron micrograph of the plaque biofilm with long filamentous forms and "corn cobs" that are mixed bacterial aggregates.

are worn down. As the population ages, and natural teeth are retained for longer periods, the caries rate may well increase in the elderly, because receding gums expose the more susceptible root surfaces.

▶ Culture and Diagnosis

Dental professionals diagnose caries based on the tooth condition. Culture of the lesion is not routinely performed.

▶ Prevention and Treatment

The best way to prevent dental caries is through dietary restriction of sucrose and other refined carbohydrates. Regular brushing and flossing to remove plaque are also important. Most municipal communities in the United States add trace amounts of fluoride to their drinking water, because fluoride, when incorporated into the tooth structure, can increase tooth (as well as bone) hardness. Fluoride can also encourage the remineralization of teeth that have begun the demineralization process. These and other proposed actions of fluoride could make teeth less susceptible to decay. Fluoride is also added to toothpastes and mouth rinses and can be applied in gel form. Many European countries do not fluoridate their water due to concerns over additives in drinking water.

There are several vaccines being tested to prevent dental caries. Some utilize the proteins that bacteria use for initial attachment; others consist of the enzyme streptococci use to produce glucans. One of the more promising experimental approaches is the oral application of IgA antibody directed to bacterial attachment proteins (that is, passive immunization).

Treatment of a carious lesion involves removal of the affected part of the tooth (or the whole tooth in the case of advanced caries), followed by restoration of the tooth structure with an artificial material. An experimental treatment with great promise is the use of an antimicrobial peptide linked to a protein that attaches only to *S. mutans*, killing it and leaving the important normal biota intact.

Disease Table 22.1 Dental Caries

Causative Organism(s)	*Streptococcus mutans, Streptococcus sobrinus,* others
Most Common Modes of Transmission	Direct contact
Virulence Factors	Adhesion, acid production
Culture/Diagnosis	–
Prevention	Oral hygiene, fluoride supplementation
Treatment	Removal of diseased tooth material

Periodontal Diseases

Periodontal disease is so common that 97% to 100% of the population has some manifestation of it by age 45. Most kinds are due to bacterial colonization and varying degrees of inflammation that occur in response to gingival damage.

Periodontitis

▶ Signs and Symptoms

The initial stage of periodontal disease is **gingivitis,** the signs of which are swelling, loss of normal contour, patches of redness, and increased bleeding of the gingiva. Spaces or pockets of varying depth also develop between the tooth and the gingiva. If this condition persists, a more serious disease called periodontitis results. This is the natural extension of the disease into the periodontal membrane and cementum. The deeper involvement increases the size of the pockets and can cause bone resorption severe enough to loosen the tooth in its socket. If the condition is allowed to progress, the tooth can be lost **(figure 22.5).**

▶ Causative Agent

Dental scientists stop short of stating that particular bacteria cause periodontal disease, because not all of the criteria for establishing causation have been satisfied. In fact, dental diseases (in particular, periodontal disease) provide an excellent model of disease mediated by communities of microorganisms rather than single organisms. When the polymicrobial biofilms consist of the right combination of bacteria, such as the anaerobes *Tannerella forsythia* (formerly *Bacteroides forsythus*), *Aggregatibacter actinomycetemcomitans, Porphyromonas gingivalis,* and perhaps *Fusobacterium* and spirochete species, the periodontal destruction process begins. Evidence indicates that the presence of archaeal species in the gingival crevice is an important contributor to disease. If this is true, it will be the first link found between archaea and human disease. Scientists even suspect that aggressive versus chronic forms of periodontitis are mediated by communities that have different members or even different orders of succession. (Succession refers to the order in which microbes become part of the biofilm.) Other factors are also important in the development of periodontal disease, such as behavioral and genetic influences, as well as tooth position. The most common predisposing condition occurs when the plaque becomes mineralized (calcified) with calcium and phosphate crystals. This process produces a hard, porous substance called **calculus** above and below the gingival margin (edge) that can induce varying degrees of periodontal damage **(figure 22.6).** The presence of calculus leads to a series of inflammatory events that probably allow the bacteria to cause disease.

▶ Pathogenesis and Virulence Factors

Calculus and plaque accumulating in the gingival sulcus cause abrasions in the delicate gingival membrane, and the

(a) Normal, nondiseased state of tooth, gingiva, and bone

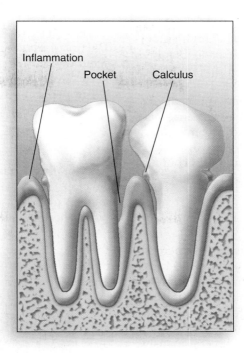

(b) Calculus buildup and early gingivitis

(c) Late-stage periodontitis, with tissue destruction, deep pocket formation, loosening of teeth, and bone loss

Figure 22.5 **Stages in soft-tissue infection, gingivitis, and periodontitis.**

Figure 22.6 **The nature of calculus.**   Radiograph of mandibular premolar and molar, showing calculus on the top and a caries lesion on the right. Bony defects caused by periodontitis affect both teeth.

chronic trauma causes a pronounced inflammatory reaction. The damaged tissues become a portal of entry for a variety of bacterial residents. The bacteria have an arsenal of enzymes, such as proteases, that destroy soft oral tissues. In response to the mixed infection, the damaged area becomes infiltrated by neutrophils and macrophages and, later, by lymphocytes, which cause further inflammation and tissue damage. There is now a great deal of evidence that people with high numbers of the bacteria associated with periodontitis also have thicker carotid arteries, and increased rates of cardiovascular disease.

▶ Transmission and Epidemiology

As with caries, the resident oral bacteria, acquired from close oral contact, are responsible for periodontal disease. Dentists refer to a wide range of risk factors associated with periodontal disease, especially deficient oral hygiene. But because it is so common in the population, it is evident that most of us could use some improvement in our oral hygiene.

▶ Culture and Diagnosis

Like caries, periodontitis is generally diagnosed by the appearance of the oral tissues.

▶ Prevention and Treatment

Regular brushing and flossing to remove plaque automatically reduce both caries and calculus production. Mouthwashes are relatively ineffective in controlling plaque formation because of the high bacterial content of saliva and the relatively short-acting time of the mouthwash. Once calculus has formed on teeth, it cannot be removed by brushing but can be dislodged only by special mechanical procedures (scaling) in the dental office.

Most periodontal disease is treated by removal of calculus and plaque and maintenance of good oral hygiene. Often, surgery to reduce the depth of periodontal pockets is required. Antibiotic therapy, either systemic or applied in periodontal packings, may also be utilized. There is some evidence that exposing the periodontium to blue light (similar to that used to whiten teeth) can selectively kill disease-causing anaerobes while leaving normal biota intact. It is also becoming clear that controlling the inflammation (through topical or systemic steroids) can have benefit, both for the periodontitis but also for focal disease such as in the cardiovascular system.

Necrotizing Ulcerative Gingivitis and Periodontitis

The most destructive periodontal diseases are necrotizing ulcerative gingivitis (NUG) and necrotizing ulcerative periodontitis (NUP). The two diseases were formerly lumped under one name, acute necrotizing ulcerative gingivitis, or ANUG. These diseases are synergistic infections involving *Treponema vincentii*, *Prevotella intermedia*, and *Fusobacterium* species. These pathogens together produce several invasive factors that cause rapid advancement into the periodontal tissues. The condition is associated with severe pain, bleeding, pseudomembrane formation, and necrosis. Scientists believe that NUP may be an extension of NUG, but the conditions can be distinguished by the advanced bone destruction that results from NUP. Both diseases seem to result from poor oral hygiene, altered host defenses, or prior gum disease rather than being communicable. The diseases are common in AIDS patients and other immunocompromised populations. Diabetes and cigarette smoking can predispose people to these conditions. NUG and NUP usually respond well to broad-spectrum antibiotics, after debridement of damaged periodontal tissue **(Disease Table 22.2).**

Mumps

The word *mumps* is Old English for lump or bump. The symptoms of this viral disease are so distinctive that Hippocrates clearly characterized it in the fifth century BC as a self-limited, mildly epidemic illness associated with painful swelling at the angle of the jaw **(figure 22.7).**

▶ Signs and Symptoms

After an average incubation period of 2 to 3 weeks, symptoms of fever, nasal discharge, muscle pain, and malaise develop. These may be followed by inflammation of the salivary glands (especially the parotids), producing the classic gopherlike swelling of the cheeks on one or both sides

Figure 22.7 The external appearance of swollen parotid glands in mumps (parotitis).

Disease Table 22.2 **Periodontal Diseases**

Disease	Periodontitis	Necrotizing Ulcerative Gingivitis and Periodontitis
Causative Organism(s)	Polymicrobial community including some or all of: *Tannerella forsythia*, *Aggregatibacter actinomycetemcomitans*, *Porphyromonas gingivalis*, others?	Polymicrobial community (*Treponema vincentii*, *Prevotella intermedia*, *Fusobacterium* species)
Most Common Modes of Transmission	–	–
Virulence Factors	Induction of inflammation, enzymatic destruction of tissues	Inflammation, invasiveness
Culture/Diagnosis	–	–
Prevention	Oral hygiene	Oral hygiene
Treatment	Removal of plaque and calculus, gum reconstruction, tetracycline, possibly anti-inflammatory treatments	Debridement of damaged tissue, metronidazole, clindamycin

(see figure 22.7). Swelling of the gland is called parotitis, and it can cause considerable discomfort. Viral multiplication in salivary glands is followed by invasion of other organs, especially the testes, ovaries, thyroid gland, pancreas, meninges, heart, and kidney. Despite the invasion of multiple organs, the prognosis of most infections is complete, uncomplicated recovery with permanent immunity.

Complications in Mumps   In 20% to 30% of young adult males, mumps infection localizes in the epididymis and testis, usually on one side only. The resultant syndrome of orchitis and epididymitis may be rather painful, but no permanent damage usually occurs. The popular belief that mumps readily causes sterilization of adult males is still held, despite medical evidence to the contrary. Perhaps this notion has been reinforced by the tenderness that continues long after infection and by the partial atrophy of one testis that occurs in about half the cases. Permanent sterility due to mumps is very rare.

In mumps pancreatitis, the virus replicates in beta cells and pancreatic epithelial cells. Viral meningitis, characterized by fever, headache, and stiff neck, appears 2 to 10 days after the onset of parotitis, lasts for 3 to 5 days, and then dissipates, leaving few or no adverse side effects. Another rare event is infection of the inner ear that can lead to deafness.

▶ Causative Agent

Mumps is caused by an enveloped single-stranded RNA virus (mumps virus) from the genus *Paramyxovirus*, which is part of the family Paramyxoviridae. Other members of this family that infect humans are *Morbillivirus* (measles virus) and the respiratory syncytial virus. The envelopes of paramyxoviruses possess spikes that have specific functions.

▶ Pathogenesis and Virulence Factors

A virus-infected cell is modified by the insertion of proteins called HN spikes into its cell membrane. The HN spikes immediately bind an uninfected neighboring cell, and in the presence of another type of spike called F spikes, the two cells permanently fuse. A chain reaction of multiple cell fusions then produces a *syncytium* (sin-sish'-yum) with cytoplasmic inclusion bodies, which is a diagnostically useful cytopathic effect **(figure 22.8)**. The ability to induce the formation of syncytia is characteristic of the family Paramyxoviridae.

▶ Transmission and Epidemiology of Mumps Virus

Humans are the exclusive natural hosts for the mumps virus. It is communicated primarily through salivary and respiratory secretions. Infection occurs worldwide, with increases in the late winter and early spring in temperate climates.

Figure 22.8 The effects of paramyxoviruses.   (a) When they infect a host cell, paramyxoviruses induce the cell membranes of adjacent cells to fuse into large multinucleate giant cells, or syncytia. (b) This fusion allows direct passage of viruses from an infected cell to uninfected cells by communicating membranes. Through this means, the virus evades antibodies.

High rates of infection arise among crowded populations or communities with poor herd immunity. Most cases occur in children under the age of 15, and as many as 40% are subclinical. Because lasting immunity follows any form of mumps infection, no long-term carrier reservoir exists in the population. The incidence of mumps had been reduced in the United States to around 300 cases per year. The incidence has become more unpredictable since 2006, though. In that year there were about 2,600 cases. The next 3 years saw cases in the low hundreds again, but then in 2010 there were more than 1,500 cases. The recommendation is to be sure to get two doses of MMR vaccine.

▶ Culture and Diagnosis

Diagnosis is usually based on the clinical sign of swollen parotid glands and known exposure 2 or 3 weeks previously. Because parotitis is not always present, and the incubation period can range from 7 to 23 days, a practical diagnostic alternative is to perform a direct fluorescent test for viral antigen or an ELISA test on a patient's serum.

▶ Prevention and Treatment

The general pathology of mumps is mild enough that symptomatic treatment to relieve fever, dehydration, and pain is usually adequate. The new vaccine recommendations call for a dose of MMR at 12 to 15 months and a second dose at 4 to 6 years. Health care workers and college students who haven't already had both doses are advised to do so.

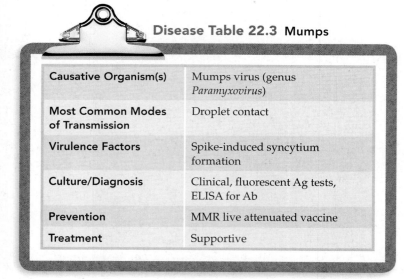

Disease Table 22.3 Mumps

Causative Organism(s)	Mumps virus (genus *Paramyxovirus*)
Most Common Modes of Transmission	Droplet contact
Virulence Factors	Spike-induced syncytium formation
Culture/Diagnosis	Clinical, fluorescent Ag tests, ELISA for Ab
Prevention	MMR live attenuated vaccine
Treatment	Supportive

Gastritis and Gastric Ulcers

The curved cells of *Helicobacter* were first detected by J. Robin Warren in 1979 in stomach biopsies from ulcer patients. He and an assistant, Barry J. Marshall, isolated the microbe in culture and even served as guinea pigs by swallowing a large inoculum to test its effects. Both developed transient gastritis.

▶ Signs and Symptoms

Gastritis is experienced as sharp or burning pain emanating from the abdomen. Gastric ulcers are actual lesions in the mucosa of the stomach (gastric ulcers) or in the uppermost portion of the small intestine (duodenal ulcers). Both of these conditions are also called *peptic ulcers*. Severe ulcers can be accompanied by bloody stools, vomiting, or both. The symptoms are often worse at night, after eating, or under conditions of psychological stress.

The second most common cancer in the world is stomach cancer (although it has been declining in the United States), and ample evidence suggests that long-term infection with *H. pylori* is a major contributing factor.

▶ Causative Agent

Helicobacter pylori is a curved gram-negative rod, closely related to *Campylobacter*, which we study later in this chapter.

▶ Pathogenesis and Virulence Factors

Once the bacterium passes into the gastrointestinal tract, it bores through the outermost mucous layer that lines the stomach epithelial tissue. Then it attaches to specific binding sites on the cells and entrenches itself. One receptor specific for *Helicobacter* is the same molecule on human cells that confers the O blood type. This finding accounts for the higher rate of ulcers in people with this blood type. Another protective adaptation of the bacterium is the formation of urease, an enzyme that converts urea into ammonium and bicarbonate, both alkaline compounds that can neutralize stomach acid. As the immune system recognizes and attacks the pathogen, infiltrating white blood cells damage the epithelium to some degree, leading to chronic active gastritis. In some people, these lesions lead to deeper erosions and ulcers that can lay the groundwork for cancer to develop.

Before the bacterium was discovered, spicy foods, high-sugar diets (which increase acid levels in the stomach), and psychological stress were considered to be the cause of gastritis and ulcers. Now it appears that these factors merely aggravate the underlying infection.

▶ Transmission and Epidemiology

The mode of transmission of this bacterium remains a mystery. Studies have revealed that the pathogen is present in a large proportion of the human population. It occurs in the stomachs of 25% of healthy middle-age adults and in more than 60% of adults over 60 years of age. *H. pylori* is probably transmitted from person to person by the oral-oral or fecal-oral route. It seems to be acquired early in life and carried asymptomatically until its activities begin to damage the digestive mucosa. Because other animals are also susceptible to *H. pylori* and even develop chronic gastritis, it has been proposed that the disease is a zoonosis transmitted from an animal reservoir. The bacterium has also been found in water sources.

Approximately two-thirds of the world's population are infected with *H. pylori*. It is not known what causes some people to experience symptoms, although it is most likely that those with the right combination of aggravating factors are those who experience disease.

▶ Culture and Diagnosis

Diagnosis has typically been accomplished with endoscopy, a procedure in which a long flexible tube **(figure 22.9)** is inserted through the throat into the stomach to visualize any lesions there. The urea breath test is sometimes used. In this test, patients ingest urea that has a radioactive tag on its carbon molecule. If *Helicobacter* is present in a patient's stomach, the bacterium's urease breaks down the urea and the patient exhales radioactively labeled carbon dioxide. In the absence of urease, the intact urea molecule passes through the digestive system. Patients whose breath is positive for the radioactive carbon are considered positive for *Helicobacter*.

A stool test is also available. The HpSA (*H. pylori* stool antigen test) is an ELISA format test.

▶ Prevention and Treatment

The only preventive approaches available currently are those that diminish some of the aggravating factors just mentioned. Many over-the-counter remedies offer symptom relief; most of them act to neutralize stomach acid. The best treatment is a course of antibiotics augmented by acid suppressors. The antibiotics most prescribed are clarithromycin or metronidazole. Bismuth subsalicylate (Pepto-Bismol) or the prescription medication omeprazole is the most frequently administered acid suppressor.

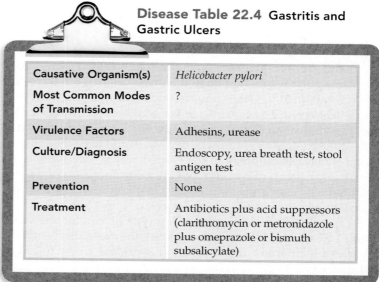

Disease Table 22.4 **Gastritis and Gastric Ulcers**

Causative Organism(s)	*Helicobacter pylori*
Most Common Modes of Transmission	?
Virulence Factors	Adhesins, urease
Culture/Diagnosis	Endoscopy, urea breath test, stool antigen test
Prevention	None
Treatment	Antibiotics plus acid suppressors (clarithromycin or metronidazole plus omeprazole or bismuth subsalicylate)

(a)

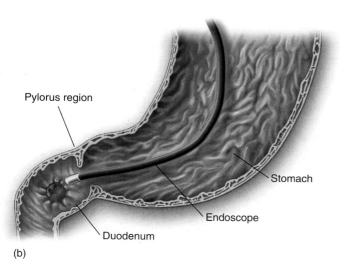

(b)

Figure 22.9 Endoscopy. **(a)** A flexible tube is inserted through the mouth into the stomach, **(b)** acting as a camera to visualize the stomach surface.

Light source

Eyepiece and controls

Viewing end

Pylorus region

Stomach

Endoscope

Duodenum

Acute Diarrhea

Diarrhea needs little explanation. In recent years, on average, citizens of the United States experienced 1.2 to 1.9 cases of diarrhea per person per year, and among children that number is twice as high. The incidence of diarrhea is even higher among children attending day care centers. In tropical countries, children may experience more than 10 episodes of diarrhea a year. In fact, more than 3 million children a year, mostly in developing countries, die from a diarrheal disease (see Insight 22.2). In developing countries, the high mortality rate is not the only issue. Children who survive dozens of bouts with diarrhea during their developmental years are likely to have permanent physical and cognitive effects. The effect on the overall well-being of these children is hard to estimate, but it is very significant.

In the United States, up to a third of all acute diarrhea is transmitted by contaminated food (a case of diarrhea is usually defined as three or more loose stools in a 24-hour period). In recent years, consumers have become much more aware of the possibility of *E. coli*–contaminated hamburgers or *Salmonella*-contaminated ice cream. New food safety measures are being implemented all the time, but it is still necessary for the consumer to be aware and to practice good food handling.

Although most diarrhea episodes are self-limiting and therefore do not require treatment, others (such as *E. coli* O157:H7) can have devastating effects. In most diarrheal illnesses, antimicrobial treatment is contraindicated (inadvisable), but some, such as shigellosis, call for quick treatment with antibiotics. For public health reasons, it is important to know which agents are causing diarrhea in the community, but in most cases identification of the agent is not performed.

In this section, we describe acute diarrhea having infectious agents as the cause. In the sections following this one, we discuss acute diarrhea and vomiting caused by toxins, commonly known as food poisoning, and chronic diarrhea and its causes.

Salmonella

A decade ago, one of every three chickens destined for human consumption was contaminated with *Salmonella*, but the rate is now about 10%. Other poultry, such as ducks and turkeys, is also affected. Eggs are infected as well because the bacteria may actually enter the egg while the shell is being formed in the chicken. In 2007, peanut butter was found to be the source of a *Salmonella* outbreak in the United States. *Salmonella* is a very large genus of bacteria, but only one species is of interest to us: *S. enterica* is divided into many variants, based on variation in the major surface antigens.

As mentioned in chapter 4, serotype or variant analysis aids in bacterial identification. Many gram-negative enteric bacteria are named and designated according to the following antigens: H, the flagellar antigen; K, the capsular antigen; and O, the cell wall antigen. Not all enteric bacteria carry the H and K antigens, but all have O, the polysaccharide portion of the lipopolysaccharide implicated in endotoxic shock (see chapter 20). Most species of gram-negative enterics exhibit a variety of subspecies, variant, or serotypes caused by slight variations in the chemical structure of the HKO antigens. Some bacteria in this chapter (for example, *E. coli* O157:H7) are named according to their surface antigens; however, we will use Latin variant names for *Salmonella*.

Salmonellae are motile; they ferment glucose with acid and sometimes gas; and most of them produce hydrogen sulfide (H_2S) but not urease. They grow readily on most laboratory media and can survive outside the host in inhospitable environments such as fresh water and freezing temperatures. These pathogens are resistant to chemicals such as bile and dyes, which are the basis for isolation on selective media.

▶ Signs and Symptoms

The genus *Salmonella* causes a variety of illnesses in the GI tract and beyond. Until fairly recently, its most severe manifestation was typhoid fever, which is discussed shortly. Since the mid-1900s, a milder disease usually called salmonellosis has been much more common **(figure 22.10)**. Sometimes the condition is also called enteric fever or gastroenteritis. Whereas typhoid fever is caused by the *typhi* variant, gastro-

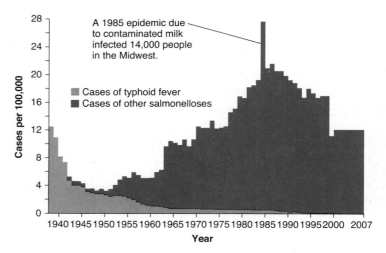

Figure 22.10 Data on the prevalence of typhoid fever and other salmonelloses from 1940 to 2007. Nontyphoidal salmonelloses did occur before 1940, but the statistics are not available.

enteritises are generally caused by the variant known as *paratyphi*, *hirschfeldii*, and *typhimurium*. Another variant, which is sometimes called *Arizona hinshawii* (even though it is still a *Salmonella*), is a pathogen found in the intestines of reptiles. Most of these strains come from animals, unlike the *typhi* strain, which infects humans exclusively. *Salmonella* bacteria are normal intestinal biota in cattle, poultry, rodents, and reptiles.

Salmonellosis can be relatively severe, with an elevated body temperature and septicemia as more prominent features than GI tract disturbance. But it can also be fairly mild, with gastroenteritis—vomiting, diarrhea, and mucosal irritation—as its major feature. Blood can appear in the stool. In otherwise healthy adults, symptoms spontaneously subside after 2 to 5 days; death is infrequent except in debilitated persons.

Typhoid fever is so named because it bears a superficial resemblance to typhus, a rickettsial disease, even though the two diseases are otherwise very different. In the United States, the incidence of typhoid fever has remained at a steady rate for the last 30 years, appearing sporadically (see figure 22.10). Of the 50 to 100 cases reported annually, roughly half are imported from endemic regions. In other parts of the world, typhoid fever is still a serious health problem, responsible for 25,000 deaths each year and probably millions of cases.

Typhoid fever, caused by the *typhi* variant of *S. enterica*, is characterized by a progressive, invasive infection that leads eventually to septicemia. Symptoms are fever, diarrhea, and abdominal pain. The bacterium infiltrates the mesenteric lymph nodes and the phagocytes of the liver and spleen. In some people, the small intestine develops areas of ulceration that are vulnerable to hemorrhage, perforation, and peritonitis. Its presence in the circulatory system may lead to nodules or abscesses in the liver or urinary tract.

Because it is so rare compared with the less severe salmonellosis, the rest of this section refers mainly to salmonellosis and not to typhoid fever.

▶ Pathogenesis and Virulence Factors

The ability of *Salmonella* to cause disease seems to be highly dependent on its ability to adhere effectively to the gut mucosa. Recent research has uncovered an "island" of genes in *Salmonella* that seems to confer virulence on the bacterium. There are other pathogenicity islands, but this one is directly related to attachment. It is also believed that endotoxin is an important virulence factor for *Salmonella.*

▶ Transmission and Epidemiology

Animal products such as meat and milk can be readily contaminated with *Salmonella* during slaughter, collection, and processing. Inherent risks are involved in eating poorly cooked beef or unpasteurized fresh or dried milk, ice cream, and cheese. A 2001 U.S. outbreak was traced to green grapes. A particular concern is the contamination of foods by rodent feces. Several outbreaks of infection have been traced to unclean food storage or to food-processing plants infested with rats and mice.

Most cases are traceable to a common food source such as milk or eggs. Some cases may be due to poor sanitation. In one outbreak, about 60 people became infected after visiting the Komodo dragon exhibit at the Denver zoo. They picked up the infection by handling the rails and fence of the dragon's cage. In 2002, two people apparently acquired salmonellosis from a blood transfusion, and one of them died. The blood donor, who had an asymptomatic infection with *Salmonella,* had contracted the infection from his pet snake.

▶ Prevention and Treatment

The only prevention for salmonellosis is avoiding contact with the bacterium. In 1998, a vaccine was approved for use in poultry, making it the first "food safety" vaccine. A vaccine for humans is undergoing testing as well.

Uncomplicated cases of salmonellosis are treated with fluid and electrolyte replacement; if the patient has underlying immunocompromise or if the disease is severe, trimethoprim-sulfamethoxazole is recommended.

Typhoid fever, by contrast, is always treated with antibiotics, in part to clear the patient of the *typhi* strain, which has a tendency to be shed for weeks after recovery. A small number of people chronically carry the bacterium for longer periods in the gallbladder; from this site, the bacteria are constantly released into the intestine and feces. In some people, gallbladder removal is necessary to stop the shedding. Two vaccines are available for the *typhi* strain and are recommended for people traveling to endemic areas.

Shigella

The *Shigella* bacteria are gram-negative straight rods, nonmotile and non-spore-forming. They do not produce urease or hydrogen sulfide, traits that help in their identification. They are primarily human parasites, though they can infect apes. All produce a similar disease that can vary in intensity. These bacteria resemble some types of pathogenic *E. coli* very closely. Diagnosis is complicated by the fact that several alternative candidates can cause bloody diarrhea, such as *E. coli* and others. Isolation and identification follow the usual protocols for enterics. Stool culture is still the gold standard for identification in the case of *Shigella* infections.

Although *Shigella dysenteriae* causes the most severe form of dysentery, it is uncommon in the United States and occurs primarily in the Eastern Hemisphere. In the past decade, the prevalent agents in the United States have been *Shigella sonnei* and *Shigella flexneri,* which cause approximately 20,000 to 25,000 cases each year, half of them in children.

▶ Signs and Symptoms

The symptoms of shigellosis include frequent, watery stools, as well as fever, and often intense abdominal pain. Nausea and vomiting are common. Stools often contain obvious blood and even more often are found to have occult (not visible to the naked eye) blood. Diarrhea containing blood is also called **dysentery.** Mucus from the GI tract will also be present in the stools.

▶ Pathogenesis and Virulence Factors

Shigellosis is different from many GI tract infections in that *Shigella* invades the villus cells of the large intestine rather than the small intestine. In addition, it is not as invasive as *Salmonella* and does not perforate the intestine or invade the blood. It enters the intestinal mucosa by means of lymphoid cells in Peyer's patches. Once in the mucosa, *Shigella* instigates an inflammatory response that causes extensive tissue destruction. The release of endotoxin causes fever. **Enterotoxin,** an exotoxin that affects the enteric (or GI) tract, damages the mucosa and villi. Local areas of erosion give rise to bleeding and heavy secretion of mucus **(figure 22.11).** *Shigella dysenteriae* (and perhaps some of the other species) produces a heat-labile exotoxin called **shiga toxin,** which seems to be responsible for the more serious damage to the intestine as well as any systemic effects, including injury to nerve cells. It is an A-B toxin (see figure 21.9). To review, the B portion of the toxin attaches to host cells, and the whole toxin is internalized. Once inside, the A portion of the toxin exerts its effect. In the case of the shiga toxin, the A portion of the toxin binds to ribosomes, interrupting protein synthesis and leading to the damage just described. You'll encounter shiga toxin again when we discuss *E. coli* O157:H7.

Figure 22.11 The appearance of the large intestinal mucosa in *Shigella* dysentery.   Note the patches of blood and mucus, the erosion of the lining, and the absence of perforation.

▶ Transmission and Epidemiology

In addition to the usual oral route, shigellosis is also acquired through direct person-to-person contact, largely because of the small infectious dose required (from 10 to 200 bacteria). The disease is mostly associated with lax sanitation, malnutrition, and crowding; and it is spread epidemically in day care centers, prisons, mental institutions, nursing homes, and military camps. As in other enteric infections, *Shigella* can establish a chronic carrier condition in some people that lasts several months.

▶ Prevention and Treatment

The only prevention of this and most other diarrheal diseases is good hygiene and avoiding contact with infected persons. Although some experts say that bloody diarrhea in this country should not be treated with antibiotics (which is generally accepted for *E. coli* O157:H7 infections), most physicians recommend prompt treatment of shigellosis with trimethoprim-sulfamethoxazole (TMP-SMZ).

E. coli O157:H7 (EHEC)

In January of 1993, this awkwardly named bacterium burst into the public's consciousness when three children died after eating undercooked hamburgers at a fast-food restaurant in Washington State. The cause of their illness was determined to be this particular strain of *E. coli,* which had actually been recognized since the 1980s. Since then, it has led to approximately 73,000 illnesses and about 50 deaths each year in the United States. It is considered an emerging pathogen.

Dozens of different strains of *E. coli* exist, many of which cause no disease at all. A handful of them cause various degrees of intestinal symptoms as described in this and the following section. Some of them cause urinary tract infections (see chapter 23). *E. coli* O157:H7 and its close relatives are the most virulent of them all. The group of *E. coli* of which this strain is the most famous representative is generally referred to as **enterohemorrhagic *E. coli*, or EHEC.**

▶ Signs and Symptoms

E. coli O157:H7 is the agent of a spectrum of conditions, ranging from mild gastroenteritis with fever to bloody diarrhea. About 10% of patients develop **hemolytic uremic syndrome (HUS),** a severe hemolytic anemia that can cause kidney damage and failure. Neurological symptoms such as blindness, seizure, and stroke (and long-term debilitation) are also possible. These serious manifestations are most likely to occur in children younger than 5 and in elderly people.

▶ Pathogenesis and Virulence Factors

This bacterium owes much of its virulence to shiga toxins (so named because they are identical to the shiga exotoxin secreted by virulent *Shigella* species). Sometimes this *E. coli* is referred to as STEC (shiga-toxin-producing *E. coli*). For simplicity, EHEC is used here. The shiga toxin genes are present on bacteriophage in *E. coli* but are on the chromosome of *Shigella dysenteriae,* suggesting that the *E. coli* acquired the virulence factor through phage-mediated transfer. As described earlier for *Shigella,* the shiga toxin interrupts protein synthesis in its target cells. It seems to be responsible especially for the systemic effects of this infection.

Another important virulence determinant for EHEC is the ability to efface (rub out or destroy) enterocytes, which are gut epithelial cells.

The net effect is a lesion in the gut (effacement), usually in the large intestine. The microvilli are lost from the gut epithelium, and the lesions produce bloody diarrhea.

▶ Transmission and Epidemiology

The most common mode of transmission for EHEC is the ingestion of contaminated and undercooked beef, although other foods and beverages can be contaminated as well **(figure 22.12).** Ground beef is more dangerous than steaks or other cuts of meat, for several reasons. Consider the way that the beef becomes contaminated in the first place. The bacterium is a natural inhabitant of the GI tracts of cattle. Contamination occurs when intestinal contents contact the animal carcass, so bacteria are confined to the surface of meats. Because high heat destroys this bacterium, even a brief trip under the broiler is usually sufficient to kill *E. coli* on the surface of steaks or roasts. But in ground beef, the "surface" of meat is mixed and ground up throughout a batch, meaning any bacteria are mixed in also. This mixing explains why hamburgers should be cooked all the way through. Hamburger is also a common vehicle because meat processing plants tend to grind meats from several cattle sources together, thereby contaminating large amounts of hamburger with meat from one animal carrier.

Other farm products may also become contaminated by cattle feces. Products that are eaten raw, such as lettuce, vegetables, and apples used in unpasteurized cider, are particularly problematic. In 2006, a major nationwide outbreak stemming from contaminated spinach held the headlines

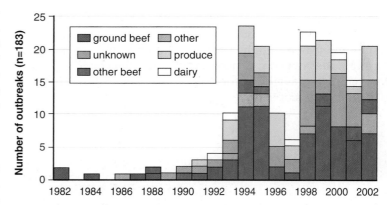

Figure 22.12 **The emergence of *E. coli* O157:H7** Note how ground beef is much more often a source than other (muscle) meats.

for weeks. The disease can also be spread via the fecal-oral route of transmission, especially among young children in group situations. Even touching surfaces contaminated with cattle feces can cause disease, since ingesting as few as 10 organisms has been found to be sufficient to initiate this disease.

▶ Culture and Diagnosis

Infection with this type of *E. coli* should be confirmed with stool culture or with ELISA or PCR.

▶ Prevention and Treatment

The best prevention for this disease is never to eat raw or even rare hamburger. The shiga toxin is heat-labile and the *E. coli* is killed by heat as well. If you are thinking "I used to be able to eat rare hamburgers," you are correct, but things have changed (see figure 22.12). The emergence of this pathogen in the early 1980s, probably resulting from a regular *E. coli* picking up the shiga toxin from *Shigella*, has changed the rules.

No vaccine exists for *E. coli* O157:H7. A great deal of research is directed at vaccinating livestock to break the chain of transmission to humans.

Antibiotics are contraindicated for this infection. Even with severe disease manifestations, antibiotics have been found to be of no help, and they may increase the pathology. Supportive therapy is the only option.

Other *E. coli*

At least four other categories of *E. coli* can cause diarrheal diseases. Scientists call these **enterotoxigenic** *E. coli,* **enteroinvasive** *E. coli,* **enteropathogenic** *E. coli,* and **enteroaggregative** *E. coli.* In clinical practice, most physicians are interested in differentiating shiga-toxin-producing *E. coli* (EHEC) from all the others. Each of these is considered separately and briefly here; in **Disease Table 22.5**, the non-shiga-toxin-producing *E. coli* are grouped together in one column.

Enterotoxigenic *E. coli* (ETEC) The presentation varies depending on which type of *E. coli* is causing the disease. Traveler's diarrhea, characterized by watery diarrhea, low-grade fever, nausea, and vomiting, is usually caused by enterotoxigenic *E. coli* (ETEC). These strains also cause a great deal of illness in infants in developing countries.

The bacterium is transmitted through the fecal-oral route or via contaminated vehicles or even fomites (such as a dirty glass). Travelers are susceptible to these strains because they are likely to be new to their immune systems. People living in endemic areas probably encounter the bacteria as infants. As the name suggests, the virulence of the bacterium derives from its ability to secrete two types of exotoxins that act on the enteric tract (enterotoxin). One toxin is a heat-labile A-B toxin, and it acts like the cholera toxin, described later. Another toxin, actually a group of toxins, is heat-stable. These toxins are very small proteins that alter host cell func-

tion in order to cause large amounts of fluid secretion into the intestinal tract. The bacterium mainly affects the small intestine.

Most infections with ETEC are self-limiting, however miserable they make you feel. They are treated only with fluid replacement. In infants, ETEC can be life-threatening, and fluid replacement is vital to survival.

Enteroinvasive *E. coli* (EIEC) These strains cause a disease that is very similar to *Shigella* dysentery. The bacteria invade gut mucosa and cause widespread destruction. Blood and pus will be found in the stool. Significant fever is often present. EIEC does not produce the heat-labile or heat-stable exotoxins just described and does not have a shiga toxin, despite the clinical similarity to *Shigella* disease. EIEC does seem to have a protein that is expressed inside host cells, which leads to its destruction.

Disease caused by this bacterium is more common in developing countries. It is transmitted primarily through contaminated food and water. Treatment is supportive (including rehydration).

Enteropathogenic *E. coli* (EPEC) These strains result in a profuse, watery diarrhea. Fever and vomiting are also common. The EPEC bacteria are very similar to the EHEC *E. coli* described earlier—they produce effacement of gut surfaces. The important difference between EPEC and EHEC is that EPEC does not produce a shiga toxin and, therefore, does not produce the systemic symptoms characteristic of those bacteria.

EPEC has been known to cause outbreaks in hospital nurseries in this country but is more notorious for causing diarrhea in infants in developing countries.

Most disease is self-limiting. As with any other diarrhea, however, it can be life-threatening in young babies. Rehydration is the main treatment.

Enteroaggregative *E. coli* (EAEC) These bacteria are most notable for their ability to cause chronic diarrhea in young children and in AIDS patients. EAEC is considered in the section on chronic diarrhea.

Campylobacter

Although you may never have heard of *Campylobacter*, it is considered to be the most common bacterial cause of diarrhea in the United States. It probably causes more diarrhea than *Salmonella* and *Shigella* combined, with 2 million cases of diarrhea credited to it per year.

The symptoms of campylobacteriosis are frequent watery stools, fever, vomiting, headaches, and severe abdominal pain. The symptoms may last longer than most acute diarrheal episodes, sometimes extending beyond 2 weeks. They may subside and then recur over a period of weeks.

Campylobacter jejuni is the most common cause, although there are other *Campylobacter* species. Campylobacters are slender, curved or spiral gram-negative bacteria propelled by polar flagella at one or both poles, often appearing in S-shaped or gull-winged pairs (**figure 22.13**). These bacteria tend to be microaerophilic inhabitants of the intestinal tract, genitourinary tract, and oral cavity of humans and animals. A close relative, *Helicobacter pylori,* is the causative agent of most stomach ulcers (described earlier). Transmission of this pathogen takes place via the ingestion of contaminated beverages and food, especially water, milk, meat, and chicken.

Once ingested, *C. jejuni* cells reach the mucosa at the last segment of the small intestine (ileum) near its junction with the colon; they adhere, burrow through the mucus, and multiply. Symptoms commence after an incubation period of 1 to 7 days. The mechanisms of pathology appear to involve a heat-labile enterotoxin that stimulates a secretory diarrhea like that of cholera. In a small number of cases, infection with this bacterium can lead to a serious neuromuscular paralysis called Guillain-Barré syndrome.

Guillain-Barré syndrome (GBS) is the leading cause of acute paralysis in the United States since the eradication of polio there. The good news is that many patients recover completely from this paralysis. The condition is still mysterious in many ways, but it seems to be an autoimmune reaction that can be brought on by infection with viruses and bacteria, by vaccination in rare cases, and even by surgery. The single most common precipitating event for the onset of GBS is *Campylobacter* infection. Twenty to forty percent of GBS cases are preceded by infection with *Campylobacter*. The reasons for this are not clear. (Note that even though 20% to 40% of GBS cases are preceded by *Campylobacter* infection, only about 1 in 1,000 cases of *Campylobacter* infection results in GBS.)

Diagnosis of *C. jejuni* enteritis requires isolation of the bacterium from stool samples and occasionally from blood samples. More rapid presumptive diagnosis can be obtained from direct examination of feces with a dark-field microscope, which accentuates the characteristic curved rods and darting motility. This procedure is difficult to perform and not often used except in specialized labs. Resolution of infection occurs in most instances with simple, nonspecific rehydration and electrolyte balance therapy. In more severely affected patients, it may be necessary to administer erythromycin. Antibiotic resistance is growing in these bacteria. Because vaccines are yet to be developed, prevention depends on rigid sanitary control of water and milk supplies and care in food preparation.

Yersinia Species

Yersinia is a genus of gram-negative bacteria that includes the infamous plague bacterium, *Yersinia pestis* (discussed in chapter 20). There are two species that cause GI tract disease: *Y. enterocolitica* and *Y. pseudotuberculosis.* The infections are most notable for the high degree of abdominal pain they cause. This symptom is accompanied by fever. Often the symptoms are mistaken for appendicitis.

The disease is uncommon in the United States, but outbreaks do occasionally occur. Food and beverages can become contaminated with these bacteria, which inhabit the intestines of farm animals, pets, and wild animals. Transmission also occurs when people handle raw food and then touch fomites such as toys or baby bottles without washing their hands.

The bacteria invade the small intestinal mucosa, and some enter the lymphatics and are harbored intracellularly in phagocytes. Inflammation of the ileum and mesenteric lymph nodes gives rise to severe abdominal pain. The infection occasionally spreads to the bloodstream, but systemic effects are rare. Two to three percent of patients experience joint pain a month following the diarrhea episode. This symptom resolves spontaneously within a few months. Infections with *Y. pseudotuberculosis* tend to be milder than those with *Y. enterocolitica* and center on lymph node inflammation rather than mucosal involvement.

Simple rules of food hygiene are usually sufficient to prevent the spread of this infection. Antibiotics are not usually prescribed for this disease, unless bacteremia is documented. In that case, doxycycline, gentamicin, or TMP-SMZ is used.

Clostridium difficile

Clostridium difficile is a gram-positive endospore-forming rod found as normal biota in the intestine. It was once considered relatively harmless but now is known to cause a condition called pseudomembranous colitis. It is also sometimes called antibiotic-associated colitis. In most cases, this infection seems to be precipitated by therapy with broad-spectrum antibiotics such as ampicillin, clindamycin, or cephalosporins. It is a major cause of diarrhea in hospitals, although community-acquired infections have been on the rise in the last few years. Also, new studies suggest that the use of gastric acid inhibitors for the treatment of heartburn can predispose patients to this infection. Although *C. difficile* is relatively noninvasive, it is able to superinfect the large intestine when drugs have disrupted the normal biota. It produces two enterotoxins, toxins A and B, that cause areas of necrosis in the wall of the intestine. The predomi-

Figure 22.13 Scanning micrograph of *Campylobacter jejuni*, showing comma, S, and spiral forms.

S   Comma   Spiral

nant symptom is diarrhea commencing late in therapy or even after therapy has stopped. More severe cases exhibit abdominal cramps, fever, and leukocytosis. The colon is inflamed and gradually sloughs off loose, membranelike patches called pseudomembranes consisting of fibrin and cells **(figure 22.14)**. If the condition is not stopped, perforation of the cecum and death can result.

Mild, uncomplicated cases respond to withdrawal of antibiotics and replacement therapy for lost fluids and electrolytes. More severe infections are treated with oral vancomycin or metronidazole for several weeks until the intestinal biota returns to normal. Because infected persons often shed large numbers of spores in their stools, increased precautions are necessary to prevent spread of the agent to other patients who may be on antimicrobial therapy. Some new techniques on the horizon are vaccination with *C. difficile* toxoid and restoration of normal biota by ingestion of a mixed culture of lactobacilli and yeasts.

Vibrio cholerae

Cholera has been a devastating disease for centuries. It is not an exaggeration to say that the disease has shaped a good deal of human history in Asia and Latin America, where it has been endemic. These days we have come to expect outbreaks of cholera to occur after natural disasters, war, or large refugee movements, especially in underdeveloped parts of the world.

Vibrios are comma-shaped rods with a single polar flagellum. They belong to the family Vibrionaceae. A freshly isolated specimen of *Vibrio cholerae* reveals quick, darting cells that slightly resemble a cooked hot dog or a comma **(figure 22.15)**. *Vibrio* shares many cultural and physiological characteristics with members of the Enterobacteriaceae, a closely related family. Vibrios are fermentative and grow on ordinary or selective media containing bile at 37°C. They possess unique O and H antigens and membrane receptor antigens that provide some basis for classifying members of the family. There are two major biotypes, called classic and *El Tor*.

Figure 22.15 *Vibrio cholerae.* Note the characteristic curved shape and single polar flagellum.

▶ Signs and Symptoms

After an incubation period of a few hours to a few days, symptoms begin abruptly with vomiting, followed by copious watery feces called secretory diarrhea. The intestinal contents are lost very quickly, leaving only secreted fluids. This voided fluid contains flecks of mucus, hence the description "rice-water stool." Fluid losses of nearly 1 liter per hour have been reported in severe cases, and an untreated patient can lose up to 50% of body weight during the course of this disease. The diarrhea causes loss of blood volume, acidosis from bicarbonate loss, and potassium depletion, which manifest in muscle cramps, severe thirst, flaccid skin, sunken eyes, and in young children, coma and convulsions. Secondary circulatory consequences can include hypotension, tachycardia, cyanosis, and collapse from shock within 18 to

(a)   (b)   (c)

Figure 22.14 Antibiotic-associated colitis. **(a)** Normal colon. **(b)** A mild form of colitis with diffuse, inflammatory patches. **(c)** Heavy yellow plaques, or pseudomembranes, typical of more severe cases. Photographs were made by a sigmoidoscope, an instrument capable of photographing the interior of the colon.

24 hours. If cholera is left untreated, death can occur in less than 48 hours, and the mortality rate approaches 55%.

▶ Pathogenesis and Virulence Factors

After being ingested with food or water, *V. cholerae* encounters the potentially destructive acidity of the stomach. This hostile environment influences the size of the infectious dose (10^8 cells), although certain types of food shelter the pathogen more readily than others. At the junction of the duodenum and jejunum, the vibrios penetrate the mucus barrier using their flagella, adhere to the microvilli of the epithelial cells, and multiply there. The bacteria never enter the host cells or invade the mucosa. The virulence of *V. cholerae* is due entirely to an enterotoxin called cholera toxin (CT), which disrupts the normal physiology of intestinal cells. It is a typical A-B type toxin as previously described for *Shigella*. When this toxin binds to specific intestinal receptors, a secondary signaling system is activated. Under the influence of this system, the cells shed large amounts of electrolytes into the intestine, an event accompanied by profuse water loss.

▶ Transmission and Epidemiology

Although the human intestinal tract was once thought to be the primary reservoir, it is now known that the parasite lives in certain endemic regions. The pattern of cholera transmission and the onset of epidemics are greatly influenced by the season of the year and the climate. Cold, acidic, dry environments inhibit the migration and survival of *Vibrio*, whereas warm, monsoon, alkaline, and saline conditions favor them. The bacteria survive in water sources for long periods of time. Recent outbreaks in several parts of the world have been traced to giant cargo ships that pick up ballast water in one port and empty it in another elsewhere in the world. Cholera ranks among the top seven causes of morbidity and mortality, affecting several million people in endemic regions of Asia and Africa.

In nonendemic areas such as the United States, the microbe is spread by water and food contaminated by asymptomatic carriers, but it is relatively uncommon. Sporadic outbreaks occur along the Gulf of Mexico, and *V. cholerae* is sometimes isolated from shellfish in that region.

▶ Culture and Diagnosis

During epidemics of this disease, clinical evidence is usually sufficient to diagnose cholera. But confirmation of the disease is often required for epidemiological studies and detection of sporadic cases. *V. cholerae* can be readily isolated and identified in the laboratory from stool samples. Direct dark-field microscopic observation reveals characteristic curved cells with brisk, darting motility as confirmatory evidence. Immobilization or fluorescent staining of feces with group-specific antisera is supportive as well. Difficult cases can be traced by detecting a rising antitoxin titer in the serum.

▶ Prevention and Treatment

Effective prevention is contingent on proper sewage treatment and water purification. Detecting and treating carri-

ers with mild or asymptomatic cholera are serious goals, but they are difficult to accomplish because of inadequate medical provisions in those countries where cholera is endemic. Vaccines are available for travelers and people living in endemic regions. One vaccine contains killed *V. cholerae* but protects for only 6 months or less. An oral vaccine containing live, attenuated bacteria was developed to be a more effective alternative, but evidence suggests it also confers only short-term immunity. It is not available in the United States.

The key to cholera therapy is prompt replacement of water and electrolytes, because their loss accounts for the severe morbidity and mortality. This therapy can be accomplished by various rehydration techniques that replace the lost fluid and electrolytes. One of these, oral rehydration therapy (ORT), is described in **Insight 22.2.**

Cases in which the patient is unconscious or has complications from severe dehydration require intravenous replenishment as well. Oral antibiotics such as tetracycline and drugs such as trimethoprim-sulfamethoxazole can terminate the diarrhea in 48 hours. They also diminish the period of vibrio excretion.

Cryptosporidium

Cryptosporidium is an intestinal protozoan of the apicomplexan type (see chapter 5) that infects a variety of mammals, birds, and reptiles. For many years, cryptosporidiosis was considered an intestinal ailment exclusive to calves, pigs, chickens, and other poultry, but it is clearly a zoonosis as well. The organism's life cycle includes a hardy intestinal oocyst as well as a tissue phase. Humans accidentally ingest the oocysts with water or food that has been contaminated by feces from infected animals. The oocyst "excysts" once it reaches the intestines and releases sporozoites that attach to the epithelium of the small intestine **(figure 22.16).**

Figure 22.16 Scanning electron micrograph of *Cryptosporidium* attached to the intestinal epithelium.

INSIGHT 22.2   A Little Water, Some Sugar, and Salt Save Millions of Lives

In 1970, a clinical trial was conducted on a very low-tech solution to the devastating problem of death from diarrhea, especially among children in the developing world. Until that time, the treatment, if a child could access it, was rehydration through an IV drip. This treatment usually required traveling to the nearest clinic, often miles or days away. Most children received no treatment at all, and 3 million of them died every year. Then scientists tested a simple sugar-salt solution that patients could drink. They tested it first in India, where cholera was rampant, and found that mortality rates were greatly decreased. After more testing in Bangladesh, Turkey, the Philippines, and the United States, oral-rehydration therapy (ORT) became the treatment of choice for diarrhea from all causes. The World Health Organization (WHO) and UNICEF began providing packages of the sugar and salt mixture and instructions for mixing it with boiled water to dozens of countries. They also oversaw training of individuals who could in turn teach townspeople and villagers about ORT.

Volunteers in front of an Oral Rehydration Clinic in the Philippines. ORT clinics are commonplace in developing countries.

The relatively simple solution, developed by the WHO, consists of a mixture of the electrolytes sodium chloride, sodium bicarbonate, potassium chloride, and glucose or sucrose dissolved in water. When administered early in amounts ranging from 100 to 400 milliliters per hour, the solution can restore patients in 4 hours, often bringing them literally back from the brink of death. Infants and small children who once would have died now survive so often that the mortality rate for treated cases of cholera is near zero. This therapy has several advantages, especially for countries with

few resources. It does not require medical facilities, high-technology equipment, or complex medication protocols. It also eliminates the need for clean needles, which is a pressing issue in many parts of the world.

In 1978, the British Medical journal *The Lancet* called ORT "potentially the most important medical advance this century." With estimates of at least a million lives saved every year since its introduction, this statement seems to have been proven correct.

The organism penetrates the intestinal cells and lives intracellularly in them. It undergoes asexual and sexual reproduction in the gut and produces more oocysts, which are excreted from the host and after a short time become infective again. The oocysts are highly infectious and extremely resistant to treatment with chlorine and other disinfectants.

The prominent symptoms mimic other types of gastroenteritis, with headache, sweating, vomiting, severe abdominal cramps, and diarrhea. AIDS patients may experience chronic persistent cryptosporidial diarrhea that can be used as a criterion to help diagnose AIDS. The agent can be detected in fecal samples or in biopsies (**figure 22.17**) using ELISA or acid-fast

Human intestinal cell

Cryptosporidium merozoites

(a)

Oocysts

(b)

Figure 22.17 (a) An electron micrograph of a *Cryptosporidium* merozoite that has penetrated the intestinal mucosa. (b) *Isospora belli*, showing oocysts in two stages of maturation.

staining. Stool cultures should be performed to rule out other (bacterial) causes of infection.

Cryptosporidiosis has a cosmopolitan distribution. Its highest prevalence is in areas with unreliable water and food sanitation. The carrier state occurs in 3% to 30% of the population in developing countries. The susceptibility of the general public to this pathogen has been amply demonstrated by several large-scale epidemics. In 1993, 370,000 people developed *Cryptosporidium* gastroenteritis from the municipal water supply in Milwaukee, Wisconsin. Other mass outbreaks of this sort have been traced to contamination of the local water reservoir by livestock wastes. Half of the outbreaks of diarrhea associated with swimming pools are caused by *Cryptosporidium*. Because chlorination is not entirely successful in eradicating the cysts, most treatment plants use filtration to remove them, but even this method can fail.

Treatment is not usually required for otherwise healthy patients. Antidiarrheal agents (antimotility drugs) may be used. Although no curative antimicrobial agent exists for *Cryptosporidium*, physicians will often try paromomycin, an aminoglycoside that can be effective against protozoa.

Rotavirus

Rotavirus is a member of the *Reovirus* group, which consists of an unusual double-stranded RNA genome with both an inner and an outer capsid. Globally, rotavirus is the primary viral cause of morbidity and mortality resulting from diarrhea, accounting for nearly 50% of all cases. It is estimated that there are 1 million cases of rotavirus infection in the United States every year, leading to 70,000 hospitalizations. Peak occurrences of this infection are seasonal; in the U.S. Southwest, the peak is often in the late fall, and in the Northeast the peak comes in the spring.

Diagnosis of rotavirus infections is usually not performed, as it is treated symptomatically. Nevertheless,

Disease Table 22.5   Acute Diarrhea

	Bacterial Causes				
Causative Organism(s)	*Salmonella*	*Shigella*	Shiga-toxin-producing *E. coli* O157:H7 (EHEC)	Other *E. coli* (non-shiga-toxin producing)	*Campylobacter*
Most Common Modes of Transmission	Vehicle (food, beverage), fecal-oral	Fecal-oral, direct contact	Vehicle (food, beverage), fecal-oral	Vehicle, fecal-oral	Vehicle (food, water), fecal-oral
Virulence Factors	Adhesins, endotoxin	Endotoxin, enterotoxin, shiga toxins in some strains	Shiga toxins; proteins for attachment, secretion, effacement	Various: proteins for attachment, secretion, effacement; heat-labile and/or heat-stable exotoxins; invasiveness	Adhesins, exotoxin, induction of autoimmunity
Culture/Diagnosis	Stool culture, not usually necessary	Stool culture; antigen testing for shiga toxin	Stool culture, antigen testing for shiga toxin	Stool culture not usually necessary; in absence of blood, fever	Stool culture not usually necessary; dark-field microscopy
Prevention	Food hygiene and personal hygiene	Food hygiene and personal hygiene	Avoid live *E. coli* (cook meat and clean vegetables)	Food and personal hygiene	Food and personal hygiene
Treatment	Rehydration; no antibiotic for uncomplicated disease	TMP-SMZ, rehydration	Antibiotics contraindicated, supportive measures	Rehydration, antimotility agent	Rehydration, erythromycin in severe cases (antibiotic resistance rising)
Fever Present	Usually	Often	Often	Sometimes	Usually
Blood in Stool	Sometimes	Often	Usually	Sometimes	No
Distinctive Features	Often associated with chickens, reptiles	Very low ID$_{50}$	Hemolytic uremic syndrome	EIEC, ETEC, EPEC	Guillain-Barré syndrome

studies are often conducted so that public health officials can maintain surveillance of how prevalent the infection is. Stool samples from infected persons contain large amounts of virus, which is readily visible using an electron microscope **(figure 22.18).** The virus gets its name from its physical appearance, which is said to resemble a "spoked wheel." An ELISA test is also available.

The virus is transmitted by the fecal-oral route, including through contaminated food, water, and fomites. For this reason, disease is most prevalent in areas of the world with poor sanitation. In the United States, rotavirus infection is relatively common, but its course is generally mild.

The effects of infection vary with the age, nutritional state, general health, and living conditions of the patient. Babies from 6 to 24 months of age lacking maternal antibodies have the greatest risk for fatal disease. These children present symptoms of watery diarrhea, fever, vomiting, dehydration, and shock. The intestinal mucosa can be damaged in

Figure 22.18 Rotavirus visible in a sample of feces from a child with gastroenteritis. Note the unique "spoked-wheel" morphology of the virus.

			Nonbacterial Causes		
Yersinia	*Clostridium difficile*	*Vibrio cholerae*	*Cryptosporidium*	Rotavirus	Other viruses
Vehicle (food, water), fecal-oral, indirect contact	Endogenous (normal biota)	Vehicle (water and some foods), fecal-oral	Vehicle (water, food), fecal-oral	Fecal-oral, vehicle, fomite	Fecal-oral, vehicle
Intracellular growth	Enterotoxins A and B	Cholera toxin (CT)	Intracellular growth	–	–
Cold-enrichment stool culture	Stool culture, PCR, ELISA demonstration of toxins in stool	Clinical diagnosis, microscopic techniques, serological detection of antitoxin	Acid-fast staining, ruling out bacteria	Usually not performed	Usually not performed
Food and personal hygiene	–	Water hygiene	Water treatment, proper food handling	Oral live virus vaccine	Hygiene
None in most cases, doxycycline, gentamicin or TMP-SMZ for bacteremia	Withdrawal of antibiotic, in severe cases metronidazole or vancomycin	Rehydration, in severe cases tetracycline, TMP-SMZ	None, paromomycin used sometimes	Rehydration	Rehydration
Usually	Sometimes	No	Often	Often	Sometimes
Occasionally	Not usually; mucus prominent	No	Not usually	No	No
Severe abdominal pain	Antibiotic-associated diarrhea	Rice-water stools	Resistant to chlorine disinfection	Severe in babies	–

a way that chronically compromises nutrition, and long-term or repeated infections can retard growth. Newborns seem to be protected by maternal antibodies. Adults can also acquire this infection, but it is generally mild and self-limiting.

Children are treated with oral replacement fluid and electrolytes. A vaccine was introduced in 1998 but was withdrawn 9 months later because of a side effect called intussusception, a form of intestinal blockage that seemed to be associated with immunization. A new oral live virus vaccine has been available since 2006.

Other Viruses

A bewildering array of viruses can cause gastroenteritis, including adenoviruses, noroviruses (sometimes known as Norwalk viruses), and astroviruses. They are extremely common in the United States and around the world. They are usually "diagnosed" when no other agent (such as those just described) is identified.

Transmission is fecal-oral or via contamination of food and water. Viruses generally cause a profuse, watery diarrhea of 3 to 5 days duration. Vomiting may accompany the disease, especially in the early phases. Mild fever is often seen.

In 2002, a series of gastroenteritis outbreaks occurred on cruise ships, most of which were ascribed to viruses other than rotavirus.

Treatment of these infections always focuses on rehydration **(Disease Table 22.5).**

Case File 22   *Continuing the Case*

Besides providing shelter to the evacuees displaced by Hurricane Katrina, Reliant City housed numerous staff members and volunteers who also required cots, bedding, food, water, toilets, and shower facilities. Soon these workers, along with police officers and others having direct contact with the shelter residents, were reporting gastrointestinal symptoms similar to those of the patients who had presented at the clinic. This secondary spread, presumably by person-to-person contact or fomite transmission, indicated a causative agent with a very low infectious dose (ID). Initial laboratory testing for bacterial species most commonly suspected in cases of acute gastroenteritis—*Salmonella, Shigella, E. coli,* and *Campylobacter*—was negative. Similarly, none of the most common parasitic enteropathogens—*Cryptosporidium,* rotavirus, and adenovirus—were found. However, testing of stool samples or rectal swabs from 44 of the symptomatic patients identified norovirus in 22 of these samples.

- Norovirus often strikes passengers on luxurious cruise ships, an environment seemingly far removed from that of Reliant City. What similarities might these two environments share that would increase the risk of a norovirus outbreak?

Acute Diarrhea with Vomiting (Food Poisoning)

If a patient presents with severe nausea and frequent vomiting accompanied by diarrhea, and reports that companions with whom he or she shared a recent meal (within the last 1 to 6 hours) are suffering the same fate, food poisoning should be suspected. **Food poisoning** refers to symptoms in the gut that are caused by a preformed toxin of some sort. In many cases, the toxin comes from *Staphylococcus aureus.* In others, the source of the toxin is *Bacillus cereus* or *Clostridium perfringens.* The toxin occasionally comes from nonmicrobial sources such as fish, shellfish, or mushrooms. In any case, if the symptoms are violent and the incubation period is very short, *intoxication* (the effects of a toxin) rather than *infection* should be considered. (**Insight 22.3** has information about outbreak investigations in general.)

Staphylococcus aureus Exotoxin

This illness is associated with eating foods such as custards, sauces, cream pastries, processed meats, chicken salad, or ham that have been contaminated by handling and then left unrefrigerated for a few hours. Because of the high salt tolerance of *S. aureus,* even foods containing salt as a preservative are not exempt. The toxins produced by the multiplying bacteria do not noticeably alter the food's taste or smell. The exotoxin (which is an enterotoxin) is heat-stable; inactivation requires 100°C for at least 30 minutes. Thus, heating the food after toxin production may not prevent disease. The ingested toxin acts upon the gastrointestinal epithelium and stimulates nerves, with acute symptoms of cramping, nausea, vomiting, and diarrhea. Recovery is also rapid, usually within 24 hours. The disease is not transmissible person to person. Often, a single source will contaminate several people, leading to a mini-outbreak.

The illness is caused by the toxin and does not require *S. aureus* to be present or alive in the contaminated food. If the bacterium is allowed to multiply in the food, it produces its exotoxin. Even if the bacteria are subsequently destroyed by heating, the preformed toxin will act quickly once it is ingested.

As you learned earlier, many diarrheal diseases have symptoms caused by bacterial exotoxins. In most cases, the bacteria take up temporary residence in the gut and then start producing exotoxin, so the incubation period is longer than the 1 to 6 hours seen with *S. aureus* food poisoning. Because this toxin is heat-stable, mishandling of food, such as allowing bacteria to multiply and then heating or reheating, can provide the perfect conditions for food poisoning to occur.

This condition is almost always self-limiting, and antibiotics are definitely not warranted.

Bacillus cereus Exotoxin

Bacillus cereus is a sporulating gram-positive bacterium that is naturally present in soil. As a result, it is a common resident on vegetables and other products in close contact with soil. It produces two exotoxins, one of which causes a diarrheal-type disease, the other of which causes an **emetic** (ee-met'-ik) or

INSIGHT 22.3 Microbes Have Fingerprints, Too

Until recently, epidemiological investigations of outbreaks of disease relied primarily on careful examination of oral case histories and reports from the patients themselves, which might provide clues about the source of exposure. If organisms could be isolated and identified in the laboratory, they could provide evidence to support or negate a hypothetical exposure, but usually they could not provide definitive proof.

When more sophisticated molecular methods for identifying microbial strains became available, the situation changed. A wide variety of techniques, including PCR, Southern blot analysis, and ribotyping, enabled the identification of bacteria below the species level and allowed the movement of a particular microbe to be traced through various hosts and environments. The most useful of these techniques for public health purposes seems to be the process called pulsed-field gel electrophoresis, or PFGE.

PFGE is a technique for macrorestriction analysis. Pathogens are isolated from a patient, and their DNA is harvested. The DNA is then cut up with restriction enzymes specifically chosen so that they find only a few places to cut into the organism's genome. The result is just a few very large pieces of DNA rather than the many small ones obtained with older methods of restriction analysis. The DNA fragments are then separated using the pulsed-field method of gel electrophoresis. This method involves constantly changing the direction of (pulsing) the electrical field during electrophoresis. You can think of it as teasing out the DNA pieces from one another

in the gel matrix. This method allows effective separation of the large pieces. Once the electrophoresis is finished, the fragments of different lengths can be seen as dark bands after the gel is immersed in a special stain. The lengths of the fragments and, thus, the pattern revealed by each microbe will be different—even for different strains of the same microbial species—because the enzymes are cut in different places on the genome where small DNA changes exist, corresponding to different strain types. This pattern is also called a DNA fingerprint, much like that used in forensic studies.

In 1993, the CDC used PFGE for the first time to trace an outbreak of food-borne illness in the United States. They determined that the strain of *E. coli* O157:H7 found in patients had the same PFGE pattern as the strain found in the suspected hamburger patties that had been served at a fast-food restaurant. The use of the technique led to the creation of a national database called PulseNet, which contains the PFGE patterns of common food-borne pathogens that have been implicated in outbreaks. Participating PulseNet laboratories all around the country can compare PFGE patterns they obtain from patients or suspected foods to patterns in the centralized database. In this way, outbreaks that are geographically dispersed (for instance, those caused by contaminated meat that may have been distributed nationally) can be identified quickly. When new patterns come in, they are also archived so that other laboratories submitting the same patterns will quickly realize that the cases are related.

A pulsed-field gel electrophoresis "fingerprint." The identity of the microbe is revealed in this pattern.

---

vomiting disease. The type of disease that takes place is influenced by the type of food that is contaminated by the bacterium. The emetic form is most frequently linked to fried rice, especially when it has been cooked and kept warm for long periods of time. These conditions are apparently ideal for the expression of the low-molecular-weight, heat-stable exotoxin having an emetic effect. The diarrheal form of the disease is usually associated with cooked meats or vegetables that are held at a warm temperature for long periods of time. These conditions apparently favor the production of the high-molecular-weight, heat-labile exotoxin. The symptom in these cases is a watery, profuse diarrhea that lasts only for about 24 hours.

Diagnosis of the emetic form of the disease is accomplished by finding the bacterium in the implicated food source. Microscopic examination of stool samples is used to diagnose the diarrheal form of the disease. Of course, in everyday practice, neither diagnosis nor treatment is performed because of the short duration of the disease.

In both cases, the only prevention is the proper handling of food.

Clostridium perfringens Exotoxin

Another sporulating gram-positive bacterium that causes intestinal symptoms is *Clostridium perfringens*. You first read about this bacterium as the causative agent of gas gangrene in chapter 18. Endospores from *C. perfringens* can also contaminate many kinds of foods. Those most frequently implicated in disease are animal flesh (meat, fish) and vegetables such as beans that have not been cooked thoroughly enough to destroy endospores. When these foods are cooled, spores germinate, and the germinated cells multiply, especially if the food is left unrefrigerated. If the food is eaten without adequate reheating, live *C. perfringens* cells enter the small intestine and release exotoxin. The toxin, acting upon epithelial cells, initiates acute abdominal pain, diarrhea, and nausea in 8 to 16 hours. Recovery is rapid, and deaths are extremely rare.

C. perfringens also causes an enterocolitis infection similar to that caused by *C. difficile*. This infectious type of diarrhea is acquired from contaminated food, or it may be transmissible by inanimate objects **(Disease Table 22.6).**

Disease Table 22.6 Acute Diarrhea with Vomiting (Food Poisoning)

Causative Organism(s)	*Staphylococcus aureus* exotoxin	*Bacillus cereus*	*Clostridium perfringens*
Most Common Modes of Transmission	Vehicle (food)	Vehicle (food)	Vehicle (food)
Virulence Factors	Heat-stable exotoxin	Heat-stable toxin, heat-labile toxin	Heat-labile toxin
Culture/Diagnosis	Usually based on epidemiological evidence	Microscopic analysis of food or stool	Detection of toxin in stool
Prevention	Proper food handling	Proper food handling	Proper food handling
Treatment	Supportive	Supportive	Supportive
Fever Present	Not usually	Not usually	Not usually
Blood in Stool	No	No	No
Distinctive Features	Suspect in foods with high salt or sugar content	Two forms: emetic and diarrheal	Acute abdominal pain

Chronic Diarrhea

Chronic diarrhea is defined as lasting longer than 14 days. It can have infectious causes or can reflect noninfectious conditions. Most of us are familiar with diseases that present a constellation of bowel syndromes, such as irritable bowel syndrome and ulcerative colitis, neither of which is directly caused by a microorganism as far as we know. (Crohn's disease may well have a microbial cause, Insight 22.1.) The other two conditions may indeed represent an overreaction to the presence of an infectious agent or another irritant, but the host response seems to be responsible for the pathology. When the presence of an infectious agent is ruled out by a negative stool culture or other tests, these conditions are suspected.

People suffering from AIDS almost universally suffer from chronic diarrhea. Most of the patients who are not taking antiretroviral drugs have diarrhea caused by a variety of opportunistic microorganisms, including *Cryptosporidium, Mycobacterium avium,* and so forth. Recently, investigators have found that patients who are aggressively treating their HIV infection with the cocktail of drugs known as HAART (see chapter 20) still suffer from chronic diarrhea at a high rate. The causes for this diarrhea are not completely understood. A patient's HIV status should be considered if he or she presents with chronic diarrhea.

Next we examine a few of the microbes that can be responsible for chronic diarrhea in otherwise healthy people. Keep in mind that practically any disease of the intestinal tract has a sexual mode of transmission in addition to the ones that are commonly stated. For example, any kind of oral-anal sexual contact efficiently transfers pathogens to the "oral" partner. This mode is more commonly seen in cases of chronic illness than it is in patients experiencing acute diarrhea, for obvious reasons.

Enteroaggregative *E. coli* (EAEC)

In the section on acute diarrhea, you read about the various categories of *E. coli* that can cause disease in the gut. One type, the enteroaggregative *E. coli* (EAEC), is particularly associated with chronic disease, especially in children. This bacterium was first recognized in 1987. It secretes neither the heat-stable nor heat-labile exotoxins previously described for enterotoxigenic *E. coli* (ETEC). It is distinguished by its ability to adhere to human cells in aggregates rather than as single cells **(figure 22.19).** Its presence appears to stimulate secretion of large amounts of mucus in the gut, which may be part of its role in causing chronic diarrhea. The bacterium also seems capable of exerting toxic effects on the gut epithelium, although the mechanisms are not well understood.

Transmission of the bacterium is through contaminated food and water. It is difficult to diagnose in a clinical lab because EAEC is not easy to distinguish from other *E. coli,* including normal biota. And the designation EAEC is not

Nucleus of epithelial cell

Figure 22.19 Enteroaggregative *E. coli* adhering to epithelial cells.

actually a serotype but is functionally defined as an *E. coli* that adheres in an aggregative pattern.

This bacterium seems to be associated with chronic diarrhea in people who are malnourished. It is not exactly clear whether the malnutrition predisposes patients to this infection or whether this infection contributes to malnutrition. Probably both possibilities are operating in patients, who are usually children in developing countries. More recently, the bacterium has been associated with acute diarrhea in industrialized countries, perhaps providing a clue to this question. It may be that in well-nourished hosts the bacterium produces acute, self-limiting disease.

Cyclospora

Cyclospora cayetanensis is an emerging protozoan pathogen. Since the first occurrence in 1979, hundreds of outbreaks have been reported in the United States and Canada. Its mode of transmission is fecal-oral, and most cases have been associated with consumption of fresh produce and water presumably contaminated with feces. This disease occurs worldwide, and although primarily of human origin, it is not spread directly from person to person. Outbreaks have been traced to imported raspberries, salad made with fresh greens, and drinking water. A major outbreak of this organism occurred on a cruise ship in April of 2009, where 135 of 1,318 passengers, and 25 crew members, became ill with *Cyclospora*.

The organism is 8 to 10 micrometers in diameter and stains variably in an acid-fast stain. Diagnosis can be complicated by the lack of recognizable oocysts in the feces. Techniques that improve identification of the parasite are examination of fresh preparations under a fluorescent microscope and an acid-fast stain of a processed stool specimen **(figure 22.20).** A PCR-based test can also be used to identify *Cyclospora* and differentiate it from other parasites. This form of analysis is more sensitive and can detect protozoan genetic material even in the absence of actual cysts.

The disease begins when oocysts enter the small intestine and release invasive sporozoites that invade the mucosa. After an incubation period of about 1 week, symptoms of watery diarrhea, stomach cramps, bloating, fever, and muscle aches appear. Patients with prolonged diarrheal illness experience anorexia and weight loss.

Most cases of infection have been effectively controlled with trimethoprim-sulfamethoxazole lasting 1 week. Traditional antiprotozoan drugs are not effective. Some cases of disease may be prevented by cooking or freezing food to kill the oocysts.

Giardia

Giardia lamblia is a pathogenic flagellated protozoan first observed by Antonie van Leeuwenhoek in his own feces. For 200 years, it was considered a harmless or weak intestinal pathogen; and only since the 1950s has its prominence as a cause of diarrhea been recognized. In fact, it is the most common flagellate isolated in clinical specimens. Observed straight on, the trophozoite has a unique symmetrical heart shape with organelles positioned in such a way that it resembles a face **(figure 22.21).** Four pairs of flagella emerge from

(a)

Trophozoite　　　　**Cyst**

(b)

Figure 22.21 *Giardia lamblia* trophozoite. **(a)** Schematic drawing. **(b)** Scanning electron micrograph of intestinal surface, revealing (on the left) the lesion left behind by adhesive disk of a *Giardia* that has detached. The trophozoite on the right is lying on its "back" and is revealing its adhesive disk.

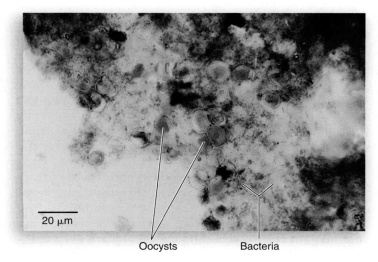

20 μm

Oocysts　　　　Bacteria

Figure 22.20 An acid-fast stain of *Cyclospora* in a human fecal sample. The large (8–10 μm) cysts stain pink to red and have a wrinkled outer wall. Bacteria stain blue.

the ventral surface, which is concave and acts like a suction cup for attachment to a substrate. *Giardia* cysts are small, compact, and contain four nuclei.

▶ Signs and Symptoms

Typical symptoms include diarrhea of long duration, abdominal pain, and flatulence. Stools have a greasy, malodorous quality to them. Fever is usually not present.

▶ Pathogenesis and Virulence Factors

Ingested *Giardia* cysts enter the duodenum, germinate, and travel to the jejunum to feed and multiply. Some trophozoites remain on the surface, while others invade the deeper crypts to varying degrees. Superficial invasion by trophozoites causes damage to the epithelial cells, edema, and infiltration by white blood cells, but these effects are reversible. The presence of the protozoan leads to maladsorption (especially of fat) in the digestive tract and can cause significant weight loss.

▶ Transmission and Epidemiology of Giardiasis

Giardiasis has a complex epidemiological pattern. The protozoan has been isolated from the intestines of beavers, cattle, coyotes, cats, and human carriers, but the precise reservoir is unclear at this time. Although both trophozoites and cysts escape in the stool, the cysts play a greater role in transmission. Unlike other pathogenic flagellates, *Giardia* cysts can survive for 2 months in the environment. Cysts are usually ingested with water and food or swallowed after close contact with infected people or contaminated objects. Infection can occur with a dose of only 10 to 100 cysts.

Outbreaks of giardiasis point to a spectrum of possible modes of transmission. Community water supplies in areas throughout the United States have been implicated as common vehicles of infection. *Giardia* epidemics have been traced to water from fresh mountain streams as well as chlorinated municipal water supplies in several states. Infections are not uncommon in hikers and campers who used what they thought was clean water from ponds, lakes, and streams in remote mountain areas. Because wild mammals such as muskrats and beavers are intestinal carriers, they could account for cases associated with drinking water from these sources. Checking water for purity by its appearance obviously is unreliable, because the cysts are too small to be detected.

Cases of fecal-oral transmission have been documented in day care centers; food contaminated by infected persons has also transmitted the disease.

▶ Culture and Diagnosis

Diagnosis of giardiasis can be difficult because the organism is shed in feces only intermittently. Sometimes ELISA tests are used to screen fecal samples for *Giardia* antigens, and PCR tests are available, although they are mainly used for detection of the protozoan in environmental samples.

▶ Prevention and Treatment

There is a vaccine against *Giardia* that can be given to animals, including dogs. No human vaccine is available. Avoiding drinking from freshwater sources is the major preventive measure that can be taken. Even municipal water is at some risk; water agencies have had to rethink their policies on water maintenance and testing. The agent is killed by boiling, ozone, and iodine; but unfortunately, the amount of chlorine used in municipal water supplies does not destroy the cysts.

Treatment is with tinidazole or metronidazole.

Entamoeba

Amoebas are widely distributed in aqueous habitats and are frequent parasites of animals, but only a small number of them have the necessary virulence to invade tissues and cause serious pathology. One of the most significant pathogenic amoebas is *Entamoeba histolytica* (en"-tah-mee'-bah his"-toh-lit'-ih-kuh). The relatively simple life cycle of this parasite alternates between a large trophozoite that is motile by means of pseudopods and a smaller, compact, nonmotile cyst **(figure 22.22a–c)**. The trophozoite lacks most of the organelles of other eukaryotes, and it has a large single nucleus that contains a prominent nucleolus called a *karyosome*. Amoebas from fresh specimens are often packed with food vacuoles containing host cells and bacteria. The mature cyst is encased in a thin yet tough wall and contains four nuclei as well as distinctive cigar-shaped bodies called *chromatoidal bodies*, which are actually dense clusters of ribosomes.

▶ Signs and Symptoms

As hinted by its species name, tissue damage is one of the formidable characteristics of untreated *E. histolytica* infection. Clinical amoebiasis exists in intestinal and extraintestinal forms. The initial targets of intestinal amoebiasis are the cecum, appendix, colon, and rectum. The amoeba secretes enzymes that dissolve tissues, and it actively penetrates deeper layers of the mucosa, leaving erosive ulcerations **(figure 22.22d)**. This phase is marked by dysentery (bloody, mucus-filled stools), abdominal pain, fever, diarrhea, and weight loss. The most life-threatening manifestations of intestinal infection are hemorrhage, perforation, appendicitis, and tumorlike growths called amoebomas. Lesions in the mucosa of the colon have a characteristic flask-like shape.

Extraintestinal infection occurs when amoebas invade the viscera of the peritoneal cavity. The most common site of invasion is the liver. Here, abscesses containing necrotic tissue and trophozoites develop and cause amoebic hepatitis. Another rarer complication is pulmonary amoebiasis. Other infrequent targets of infection are the spleen, adrenals, kidney, skin, and brain. Severe forms of the disease result in about a 10% fatality rate.

Figure 22.22 *Entamoeba histolytica.* **(a)** A trophozoite containing a single nucleus, a karyosome, and red blood cells. **(b)** A mature cyst with four nuclei and two blocky chromatoidals. **(c)** Stages in excystment. Divisions in the cyst create four separate cells, or metacysts, that differentiate into trophozoites and are released. **(d)** Intestinal amoebiasis and dysentery of the cecum. Red patches are sites of amoebic damage to the intestinal mucosa. **(e)** Trophozoite of *Entamoeba histolytica.* Note the fringe of very fine pseudopods it uses to invade and feed on tissue.

▶ Pathogenesis and Virulence Factors

Amoebiasis begins when viable cysts are swallowed and arrive in the small intestine, where the alkaline pH and digestive juices of this environment stimulate excystment. Each cyst releases four trophozoites, which are swept into the cecum and large intestine. There, the trophozoites attach by fine pseudopods **(figure 22.22e),** multiply, actively move about, and feed. In about 90% of patients, infection is asymptomatic or very mild, and the trophozoites do not invade beyond the most superficial layer. The severity of the infection can vary with the strain of the parasite, inoculum size, diet, and host resistance.

The secretion of lytic enzymes by the amoeba seems to induce apoptosis of host cells. This means that the host is contributing to the process by destroying its own tissues on cue from the protozoan. The invasiveness of the amoeba is also a clear contributor to its pathogenicity.

▶ Transmission and Epidemiology of Amoebiasis

Entamoeba is harbored by chronic carriers whose intestines favor the encystment stage of the life cycle. Cyst formation cannot occur in active dysentery because the feces are so rapidly flushed from the body; but after recuperation, cysts are continuously shed in feces.

Humans are the primary hosts of *E. histolytica.* Infection is usually acquired by ingesting food or drink contaminated with cysts released by an asymptomatic carrier. The amoeba is thought to be carried in the intestines of one-tenth of the world's population, and it kills up to 100,000 people a year. Its geographic distribution is partly due to local sewage disposal and fertilization practices. Occurrence is highest in tropical regions (Africa, Asia, and Latin America), where night soil (human excrement) or untreated sewage is used to fertilize crops, and sanitation of water and food can be substandard. Although the prevalence of the disease is lower in the United States, as many as 10 million people could harbor the agent.

Epidemics of amoebiasis are infrequent but have been documented in prisons, hospitals, juvenile care institutions, and communities where water supplies are polluted. Amoebic infections can also be transmitted by anal-oral sexual contact.

▶ Culture and Diagnosis

Diagnosis of this protozoal infection relies on a combination of tests, including microscopic examination of stool for the characteristic cysts or trophozoites, ELISA tests of stool for *E. histolytica* antigens, and serological testing for the presence of antibodies to the pathogen. PCR testing is currently being

Disease Table 22.7 Chronic Diarrhea

Causative Organism(s)	Enteroaggregative *E. coli* (EAEC)	*Cyclospora cayetanensis*	*Giardia lamblia*	*Entamoeba histolytica*
Most Common Modes of Transmission	Vehicle (food, water), fecal-oral	Fecal-oral, vehicle	Vehicle, fecal-oral, direct and indirect contact	Vehicle, fecal-oral
Virulence Factors	?	Invasiveness	Attachment to intestines alters mucosa	Lytic enzymes, induction of apoptosis, invasiveness
Culture/Diagnosis	Difficult to distinguish from other *E. coli*	Stool examination, PCR	Stool examination, ELISA	Stool examination, ELISA, serology
Prevention	?	Washing, cooking food, personal hygiene	Water hygiene, personal hygiene	Water hygiene, personal hygiene
Treatment	None, or ciprofloxacin	TMP-SMZ	Tinidazole, metronidazole	Metronidazole or tinidazole, followed by iodoquinol or paromomycin
Fever Present	No	Usually	Not usually	Yes
Blood in Stool	Sometimes, mucus also	No	No, mucus present (greasy and malodorous)	Yes
Distinctive Features	Chronic in the malnourished	–	Frequently occurs in backpackers, campers	–

refined. It is important to differentiate *E. histolytica* from the similar *Entamoeba coli* and *Entamoeba dispar*, which occur as normal biota.

▶ Prevention and Treatment

No vaccine yet exists for *E. histolytica*, although several are in development. Prevention of the disease therefore relies on purification of water. Because regular chlorination of water supplies does not kill cysts, more rigorous methods such as boiling or iodine are required.

Effective treatment usually involves the use of drugs such as iodoquinol, which acts in the feces, and metronidazole (Flagyl) or chloroquine, which work in the tissues. Dehydroemetine is used to control symptoms, but it will not cure the disease. Other drugs are given to relieve diarrhea and cramps, while lost fluid and electrolytes are replaced by oral or intravenous therapy. Infection with *E. histolytica* provokes antibody formation against several antigens, but permanent immunity is unlikely and reinfection can occur **(Disease Table 22.7).**

Hepatitis

When certain viruses in fect the liver, they cause **hepatitis,** an inflammatory disease marked by necrosis of hepatocytes and a mononuclear response that swells and disrupts the liver architecture. This pathologic change interferes with the liver's excretion of bile pigments such as bilirubin into the intestine. When bilirubin, a greenish-yellow pigment, accumulates in the blood and tissues, it causes **jaundice,** a yellow tinge in the skin and eyes. The condition can be caused by a variety of different viruses. They are all named hepatitis viruses but only because they all can cause this inflammatory condition in the liver.

Note that noninfectious conditions can also cause inflammation and disease in the liver, including some autoimmune conditions, drugs, and alcohol overuse.

Hepatitis A Virus

Hepatitis A virus (HAV) is a nonenveloped, single-stranded RNA enterovirus. It belongs to the family Picornaviridae. In general, HAV disease is far milder and shorter term than the other forms.

▶ Signs and Symptoms

Most infections by this virus are either subclinical or accompanied by vague, flulike symptoms. In more overt cases, the presenting symptoms may include jaundice and swollen liver. Darkened urine is often seen in this and other hepatitises. Jaundice is present in only about 10% of the cases. Hepatitis A occasionally occurs as a fulminating disease and causes liver damage, but this manifestation is quite rare.

The virus is not oncogenic (cancer causing), and complete uncomplicated recovery results.

▶ Pathogenesis and Virulence Factors

The hepatitis A virus is generally of low virulence. Most of the pathogenic effects are thought to be the result of host response to the presence of virus in the liver.

▶ Transmission and Epidemiology

There is an important distinction between this virus and hepatitis B and C viruses: Hepatitis A virus is spread through the fecal-oral route (and is sometimes known as infectious hepatitis). In general, the disease is associated with deficient personal hygiene and lack of public health measures. In countries with inadequate sewage control, most outbreaks are associated with fecally contaminated water and food. Rates of infection in the United States have fallen from 12 per 100,000 persons/yr in 1995 to 1 per 100,000 in 2007. Most of these result from close institutional contact, unhygienic food handling, eating shellfish, sexual transmission, or travel to other countries. In 2003, the largest single hepatitis A outbreak to date in the United States was traced to contaminated green onions used in salsa dips at a Mexican restaurant. At least 600 people who had eaten at the restaurant fell ill with hepatitis A.

Hepatitis A occasionally can be spread by blood or blood products, but this is the exception rather than the rule. In developing countries, children are the most common victims, because exposure to the virus tends to occur early in life, whereas in North America and Europe, more cases appear in adults. Because the virus is not carried chronically, the principal reservoirs are asymptomatic, short-term carriers (often children) or people with clinical disease.

▶ Culture and Diagnosis

Diagnosis of the disease is aided by detection of anti-HAV IgM antibodies produced early in the infection and by tests to identify HA antigen or virus directly in stool samples.

▶ Prevention and Treatment

Prevention of hepatitis A is based primarily on immunization. An inactivated viral vaccine (Havrix) has been in use since the mid-1990s. Short-term protection can be conferred by passive immune globulin. This treatment is useful for people who have come in contact with HAV-infected individuals, or who have eaten at a restaurant that was the source of a recent outbreak. It has also recently been discovered that administering Havrix after exposure can prevent symptoms. In the 2003 green onion outbreak, 9,000 patrons of the Mexican restaurant received passive immunization as a precaution. A combined hepatitis A/hepatitis B vaccine, called Twinrix, is recommended for people who may be at risk for both diseases, such as people with chronic liver dysfunction, intravenous drug users, and men who have sex with men. Travelers to areas with high rates of both diseases should obtain vaccine coverage as well.

A Note About Hepatitis E

Another RNA virus, called hepatitis E, causes a type of hepatitis very similar to that caused by hepatitis A. It is transmitted by the fecal-oral route, although it does not seem to be transmitted person to person. It is usually self-limiting, except in the case of pregnant women for whom the fatality rate is 15% to 25%. It is more common in developing countries, and almost all of the cases reported in the United States occur in people who have traveled to these regions. There is currently no vaccine.

No specific medicine is available for hepatitis A once the symptoms begin. Drinking lots of fluids and avoiding liver irritants such as aspirin or alcohol will speed recovery. Patients who receive immune globulin early in the disease usually experience milder symptoms than patients who do not receive it.

Hepatitis B Virus

Hepatitis B virus (HBV) is an enveloped DNA virus in the family Hepadnaviridae. Intact viruses are often called Dane particles. An antigen of clinical and immunologic significance is the surface (or S) antigen. The genome is partly double-stranded and partly single-stranded.

▶ Signs and Symptoms

In addition to the direct damage to liver cells just outlined, the spectrum of hepatitis disease may include fever, chills, malaise, anorexia, abdominal discomfort, diarrhea, and nausea. Rashes may appear and arthritis may occur. Hepatitis B infection can be very serious, even life-threatening. A small number of patients develop glomerulonephritis and arterial inflammation. Complete liver regeneration and restored function occur in most patients; however, a small number of patients develop chronic liver disease in the form of necrosis or cirrhosis (permanent liver scarring and loss of tissue). In some cases, chronic HBV infection can lead to a malignant condition.

Patients who become infected as children have significantly higher risks of long-term infection and disease. In fact, 90% of neonates infected at birth develop chronic infection, as do 30% of children infected between the ages of 1 and 5, but only 6% of persons infected after the age of 5. This finding is one of the major justifications for the routine vaccination of children. Also, infection becomes chronic more often in men than in women. The mortality rate is 15% to 25% for people with chronic infection.

HBV is known to be a cause of **hepatocellular carcinoma.** Investigators have found that mass vaccination against HBV in Taiwan, begun 18 years ago, has resulted in a significant decrease in liver cancer in that country. (Taiwan previously had one of the highest rates of this cancer.) It is speculated that cancer is probably a result of infection early in life and the long-term carrier state.

Some patients infected with hepatitis B are coinfected with a particle called the delta agent, sometimes also called a hepatitis D virus. This agent seems to be a defective RNA virus that cannot produce infection unless a cell is also infected with HBV. Hepatitis D virus invades host cells by "borrowing" the outer receptors of HBV. When HBV infection is accompanied by the delta agent, the disease becomes more severe and is more likely to progress to permanent liver damage.

▶ Pathogenesis and Virulence Factors

The hepatitis B virus enters the body through a break in the skin or mucous membrane or by injection into the bloodstream. Eventually, it reaches the liver cells (hepatocytes) where it multiplies and releases viruses into the blood during an incubation period of 4 to 24 weeks (7 weeks average). Surprisingly, the majority of those infected exhibit few overt symptoms and eventually develop an immunity to HBV, but some people experience the symptoms described earlier. The precise mechanisms of virulence are not clear. The ability of HBV to remain latent in some patients contributes to its pathogenesis. Strangely, hepatitis B infection seems to be able to influence the gender of offspring. If one parent is a carrier, the child is more likely to be male than female.

▶ Transmission and Epidemiology

An important factor in the transmission pattern of hepatitis B virus is that it multiplies exclusively in the liver, which continuously seeds the blood with viruses. Electron microscopic studies have revealed up to 10^7 virions per milliliter of infected blood. Even a minute amount of blood (a *millionth* of a milliliter) can transmit infection. The abundance of circulating virions is so high and the minimal dose so low that such simple practices as sharing a toothbrush or a razor can transmit the infection. Over the past 10 years, HBV has also been detected in semen and vaginal secretions, and it can be transmitted by these fluids. Spread of the virus by means of close contact in families or institutions is also well documented. Vertical transmission is possible, and it predisposes the child to development of the carrier state and increased risk of liver cancer. It is sometimes known as *serum hepatitis.*

Hepatitis B is an ancient disease that has been found in all populations, although the incidence and risk are highest among people living under crowded conditions, drug addicts, the sexually promiscuous, and those in certain occupations, including people who conduct medical procedures involving blood or blood products.

This virus is one of the major infectious concerns for health care workers. Needle sticks can easily transmit the virus, and therefore most workers are required to have the full series of HBV vaccinations. Unlike the more notorious HIV, HBV remains infective for days in dried blood, for months when stored in serum at room temperature, and for decades if frozen. Although it is not inactivated after 4 hours of exposure to 60°C, boiling for the same period can destroy it. Disinfectants containing chlorine, iodine, and glutaraldehyde show potent anti–hepatitis B activity.

Cosmetic manipulation such as tattooing and ear or body piercing can expose a person to infection if the instruments are not properly sterilized. The only reliable method for destroying HBV on reusable instruments is autoclaving.

▶ Culture and Diagnosis

Serological tests can detect either virus antigen or antibodies. Radioimmunoassay and ELISA testing permit detection of the important surface antigen of HBV very early in infection. These same tests are essential for screening blood destined for transfusions, semen in sperm banks, and organs intended for transplant. Antibody tests are most valuable in patients who are negative for the antigen.

▶ Prevention and Treatment

Since 1981, the primary prevention for HBV infection is vaccination. The most widely used vaccines are recombinant, containing the pure surface antigen cloned in yeast cells. Vaccines are given in three doses over 18 months, with occasional boosters. Vaccination is a must for medical and dental workers and students, patients receiving multiple transfusions, immunodeficient persons, and cancer patients. The vaccine is also now strongly recommended for all newborns as part of a routine immunization schedule. As just mentioned, a combined vaccine for HAV/HBV may be appropriate for certain people.

Passive immunization with hepatitis B immune globulin (HBIG) gives significant immediate protection to people who have been exposed to the virus through needle puncture, broken blood containers, or skin and mucosal contact with blood. Another group for whom passive immunization is highly recommended is neonates born to infected mothers.

Mild cases of hepatitis B are managed by symptomatic treatment and supportive care. Chronic infection can be controlled with recombinant human interferon, adefovir dipivoxil, lamivudine (another nucleotide analog best known for its use in HIV patients), or a newly approved drug called entecavir (Baraclude). All of these can help to stop virus multiplication and prevent liver damage in many but not all patients. None of the drugs are considered curative.

Hepatitis C Virus

Hepatitis C is sometimes referred to as the "silent epidemic" because more than 4 million Americans are infected with the virus, but it takes many years to cause noticeable symptoms. In the United States, its incidence fell between 1992 and 2003, but no further decreases have been seen since then. Liver failure from hepatitis C is one of the most common reasons for liver transplants in this country. Hepatitis C is an RNA virus in the Flaviviridae family. It used to be known as "non-A non-B" virus. It is usually diagnosed with a blood test for antibodies to the virus.

▶ Signs and Symptoms

People have widely varying experiences with this infection. It shares many characteristics of hepatitis B disease, but it is much more likely to become chronic. Of those infected, 75% to 85% will remain infected indefinitely. (In contrast, only about 6% of persons who acquire hepatitis B after the age of 5 will be chronically infected.) With HCV infection, it is possible to have severe symptoms without permanent liver damage, but it is more common to have chronic liver disease even if there are no overt symptoms. Cancer may also result from chronic HCV infection. Worldwide, HBV infection is the most common cause of liver cancer, but in the United States it is more likely to be caused by HCV.

▶ Pathogenesis and Virulence Factors

The virus is so adept at establishing chronic infections that researchers are studying the ways that it evades immunologic detection and destruction. The virus's core protein seems to play a role in the suppression of cell-mediated immunity as well as in the production of various cytokines.

▶ Transmission and Epidemiology

This virus is acquired in similar ways to HBV. It is more commonly transmitted through blood contact (both "sanctioned," such as in blood transfusions, and "unsanctioned," such as needle sharing by injecting drug users) than through transfer of other body fluids. Vertical transmission is also possible.

Before a test was available to test blood products for this virus, it seems to have been frequently transmitted through blood transfusions. Hemophiliacs who were treated with clotting factor prior to 1985 were infected with HCV at a high rate. Once blood began to be tested for HIV (in 1985) and screened for so-called "non-A non-B" hepatitis, the risk of contracting HCV from blood was greatly reduced. The cur-rent risk for transfusion-associated HCV is thought to be 1 in 100,000 units transfused.

Because HCV was not recognized sooner, a relatively large percentage of the population is infected. Eighty percent of the 4 million affected in this country are suspected to have no symptoms. It has a very high prevalence in parts of South America, Central Africa, and in China.

▶ Prevention and Treatment

There is currently no vaccine for hepatitis C. Various treatment regimens have been attempted; most include the use of therapeutic interferon and a more effective derivative of interferon called pegylated interferon. Some clinicians also prescribe ribavirin to try to suppress viral multiplication. The treatments are not curative, but they may prevent or lessen damage to the liver **(Disease Table 22.8).**

22.3 Learning Outcomes—Can You . . .

5. . . . list the possible causative agents, modes of transmission, virulence factors, diagnostic techniques, and prevention/treatment for each of the kinds of oral diseases?
6. . . . discuss current theories about the connection between oral bacteria and cardiovascular disease?
7. . . . list the possible causative agents, modes of transmission, virulence factors, diagnostic techniques, and prevention/treatment for mumps, gastritis, and gastric ulcers?
8. . . . list the possible causative agents, modes of transmission, virulence factors, diagnostic techniques, and prevention/treatment for acute and chronic diarrhea, and also for acute diarrhea with vomiting?
9. . . . differentiate among the main types of hepatitis and discuss the causative agent, mode of transmission, diagnostic techniques, prevention, and treatment of each?

Disease Table 22.8 Hepatitis

Causative Organism(s)	Hepatitis A or E virus	Hepatitis B virus	Hepatitis C virus
Most Common Modes of Transmission	Fecal-oral, vehicle	Parenteral (blood contact), direct contact (especially sexual), vertical	Parenteral (blood contact), vertical
Virulence Factors	–	Latency	Core protein suppresses immune function?
Culture/Diagnosis	IgM serology	Serology (ELISA, radioimmunoassay)	Serology
Prevention	Hepatitis A vaccine or combined HAV/HBV vaccine	HBV recombinant vaccine	–
Treatment	Hep A: hepatitis A vaccine or immune globulin; Hep E: immune globulin	Interferon, nucleoside analogs	(Pegylated) interferon, with or without ribavirin
Distinctive Features	2–7 weeks	1–6 months	2–8 weeks

22.4 Gastrointestinal Tract Diseases Caused by Helminths

Helminths that parasitize humans are amazingly diverse, ranging from barely visible roundworms (0.3 mm) to huge tapeworms (25 m long). In the introduction to these organisms in chapter 5, we grouped them into three categories: nematodes (roundworms), trematodes (flukes), and cestodes (tapeworms), and we discussed basic characteristics of each group. You may wish to review those sections before continuing. In this section, we examine the intestinal diseases caused by helminths. Although they can cause symptoms that might be mistaken for some of the diseases discussed elsewhere in this chapter, helminthic diseases are usually accompanied by an additional set of symptoms that arise from the host response to helminths. Worm infection usually provokes an increase in granular leukocytes called eosinophils, which have a specialized capacity to destroy worms. This increase, termed **eosinophilia,** is a hallmark of helminthic infection and is detectable in blood counts. If the following symptoms occur coupled with eosinophilia, helminthic infection should be suspected.

Helminthic infections may be acquired through the fecal-oral route or through penetration of the skin, but most of them spend part of their lives in the intestinal tract. (**Figure 22.23** depicts the four different types of life cycles of the helminths.) While the worms are in the intestines, they can produce a gamut of intestinal symptoms. Some of them also produce symptoms outside of the intestines; they are considered in separate categories.

General Clinical Considerations

Because the diseases in this book are always arranged in the same way, based on how the disease appears in terms of signs and symptoms (how the patient appears upon presentation to the health care provider), this section on helminthic diseases adopts a bit of a different approach. We talk about diagnosis, pathogenesis and prevention, and treatment of the helminths as a group in the next subsections. Each type of infection is then described in the sections that follow.

▶ Pathogenesis and Virulence Factors in General

In most cases, helminths that infect humans do not have sophisticated virulence factors. They do have numerous adaptations that allow them to survive in their hosts. They have specialized mouthparts for attaching to tissues and for feeding, enzymes with which they liquefy and penetrate tissues, and a cuticle or other covering to protect them from host defenses. In addition, their organ systems are usually reduced to the essentials: getting food and processing it, moving, and reproducing. The damage they cause in the host is very often the result of the host's response to the presence of the invader.

Many helminths have more than one host during their lifetimes. If this is the case, the host in which the adult worm is found is called the **definitive host** (usually a vertebrate).

Sometimes the actual definitive host is not the host usually used by the parasite but an accidental bystander. Humans often become the accidental definitive hosts for helminths whose normal definitive host is a cow, pig, or fish. Larval stages of helminths are found in intermediate hosts. Humans can serve as intermediate hosts, too. Helminths may require no intermediate host at all or may need one or more intermediate hosts for their entire life cycle.

▶ Diagnosis in General

Diagnosis of almost all helminthic infections follows a similar series of steps. A differential blood count showing eosinophilia and serological tests indicating sensitivity to helminthic antigens all provide indirect evidence of worm infection. A history of travel to the tropics or immigration from those regions is also helpful, even if it occurred years ago, because some flukes and nematodes persist for decades. The most definitive evidence, however, is the discovery of eggs, larvae, or adult worms in stools or other tissues. The worms are sufficiently distinct in morphology that positive identification can be based on any stage, including eggs. That said, not all of these diseases result in eggs or larval stages that can easily be found in stool.

▶ Prevention and Treatment in General

Preventive measures are aimed at minimizing human contact with the parasite or interrupting its life cycle. In areas where the worm is transmitted by fecally contaminated soil and water, disease rates are significantly reduced through proper sewage disposal, using sanitary latrines, avoiding human feces as fertilizer, and disinfection of the water supply. In cases where the larvae invade through the skin, people should avoid direct contact with infested water and soil. Food-borne disease can be avoided by thoroughly washing and cooking vegetables and meats. Also, because adult worms, larvae, and eggs are sensitive to cold, freezing foods is a highly satisfactory preventive measure. These methods work best if humans are the sole host of the parasite; if they are not, control of reservoirs or vector populations may be necessary.

Although several useful antihelminthic medications exist, the cellular physiology of the eukaryotic parasites resembles that of humans, and drugs toxic to them can also

Table 22.1	Antihelminthic Therapeutic Agents and Their Effects
Drug	**Effect**
Piperazine	Paralyzes worm so it can be expelled in feces
Pyrantel	Paralyzes worm so it can be expelled in feces
Mebendazole	Blocks key step in worm metabolism
Thiabendazole	Blocks key step in worm metabolism
Praziquantel	Interferes with worm metabolism

Cycle A

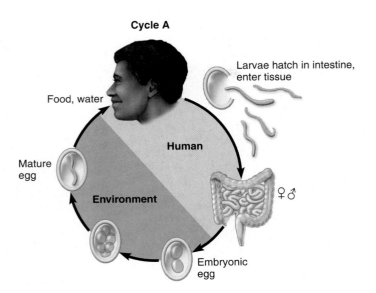

In cycle A, the worm develops in intestine; egg is released with feces into environment; eggs are ingested by new host and hatch in intestine (examples: *Ascaris, Trichuris*).

Cycle B

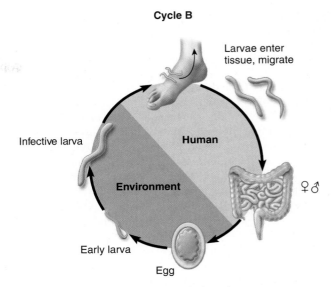

In cycle B, the worms mature in intestine; eggs are released with feces; larvae hatch and develop in environment; infection occurs through skin penetration by larvae (example: hookworms).

Cycle C

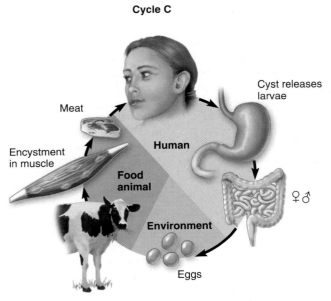

In cycle C, the adult matures in human intestine; eggs are released into environment; eggs are eaten by grazing animals; larval forms encyst in tissue; humans eating animal flesh are infected (example: *Taenia*).

Cycle D

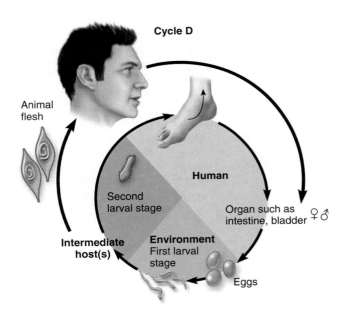

In cycle D, eggs are released from human; humans are infected through ingestion or direct penetration by larval phase (examples: *Opisthorchis* and *Schistosoma*).

Figure 22.23 Four basic helminth life and transmission cycles.

be toxic to us. Some antihelminthic drugs suppress a metabolic process that is more important to the worm than to the human. Others inhibit the worm's movement and prevent it from maintaining its position in a certain organ. Therapy is also based on a drug's greater toxicity to the more vulnerable helminths or on the local effects of oral drugs in the intestine.

Antihelminthic drugs of choice and their effects are given in **table 22.1.** Note that some helminths have developed resistance to the drugs used to treat them. In some cases, surgery may be necessary to remove worms or larvae, although this procedure can be difficult if the parasite load is high or is not confined to one area.

INSIGHT 22.4   Treating Inflammatory Bowel Disease with Worms?

Probably every one of us knows someone who suffers from an inflammatory bowel condition such as Crohn's disease or ulcerative colitis. Even though it seems that *Mycobacterium* species are responsible for Crohn's, no such microbial cause has been found for ulcerative colitis (see Insight 22.1). The work described here suggests that the inflammation that accompanies the infection (in Crohn's) and the entire syndrome (in ulcerative colitis) can be because the immune system is, well, bored.

Many recent epidemiological investigations have revealed that inflammatory bowel disease (IBD) is most common in Western industrialized countries and is very rare in developing countries. More specifically, the prevalence of IBD in any given country is inversely proportional to the prevalence of helminthic infections in that country. Looking at the picture in this country, the incidence of helminthic infections decreased dramatically between the 1930s and the 1950s; the incidence of IBD began its continuous rise in the 1950s. Scientists suspect a connection here: that the *absence* of exposure to helminthic infection predisposes a person to IBD.

These researchers have developed a hypothesis that the parts of the immune system that are activated during helminthic infection begin to "malfunction" when left idle, eventually resulting in damage to host tissue. Researchers wondered whether they could "treat" IBD by exposing patients to an intestinal helminthic infection. The first studies were conducted in mice, and the results looked promising. Then researchers at the University of Iowa conducted studies in human volunteers. They selected eight patients with either Crohn's disease or ulcerative colitis and administered to them Gatorade containing 2,500 eggs of the pig whipworm *Trichuris suis*. They chose this worm because it colonizes the intestines for a few weeks and then is completely eliminated without treatment. It does not invade tissues, and the eggs that are shed in the stools are not infective.

The researchers found marked improvement in the inflammatory bowel conditions in all of the patients. They determined that the effects were of short duration and asked several of the patients to continue in the study, receiving fresh doses of *T. suis* every 3 weeks. All of these patients experienced significant and long-lasting remission of their IBD symptoms. What's more, they indicated that they would be willing to continue the treatments indefinitely. There is also evidence that this approach could work for other autoimmune disorders, such as multiple sclerosis. And scientists in England have now determined that controlled infections with hookworms can ease the respiratory allergy symptoms of allergy sufferers. It seems that occasional contact with helminths keeps the complicated network of immunoregulatory mechanisms in good working order. This story serves to remind us about the intimate association between humans and their parasites.

Disease: Intestinal Distress as the Primary Symptom

Both tapeworms and roundworms can infect the intestinal tract in such a way as to cause primary symptoms there. The pork tapeworm (*Taenia solium*) and the fish tapeworm (*Diphyllobothrium latum*) are highlighted, as well as two nematodes (roundworms): the whipworm *Trichuris trichiura* and the pinworm *Enterobius vermicularis*. Both of the roundworms are deposited in the small intestine and migrate to the large intestine. We start with these.

Trichuris trichiura

The common name for this nematode—whipworm—refers to its likeness to a miniature buggy whip. Its life cycle and transmission is of the cycle A type (see figure 22.23). Humans are the sole host. Trichuriasis has its highest incidence in areas of the tropics and subtropics that have poor sanitation. Embryonic eggs deposited in the soil are not immediately infective and continue development for 3 to 6 weeks in this habitat. Ingested eggs hatch in the small intestine, where the larvae attach, penetrate the outer wall, and go through several molts. The mature adults move to the large intestine and gain a hold with their long, thin heads, while the thicker tail dangles free in the intestinal lumen. Following sexual maturation and fertilization, the females eventually lay 3,000 to 5,000 eggs daily into the bowel. The entire cycle requires about 90 days, and untreated infection can last up to 2 years.

Symptoms of this infection may include localized hemorrhage of the bowel caused by worms burrowing and piercing intestinal mucosa. This can also provide a portal of entry for secondary bacterial infection. Heavier infections can cause dysentery, loss of muscle tone, and rectal prolapse, which can prove fatal in children.

Enterobius vermicularis

This nematode is often called the pinworm, or seatworm. It is the most common worm disease of children in temperate zones. Some estimates put the prevalence of this infection in the United States at 5% to 15%, although most experts feel that this has declined in recent years. The transmission of this roundworm is of the cycle A type. Freshly deposited eggs have a sticky coating that causes them to lodge beneath the fingernails and to adhere to fomites. Upon drying, the eggs become airborne and settle in house dust. Worms are ingested from contaminated food or drink and from self-inoculation from one's own fingers. Eggs hatch in the small intestine and release larvae that migrate to the large intestine. There the larvae mature into adult worms and mate.

The symptoms of this condition are pronounced anal itching when the mature female emerges from the anus and lays eggs. Although infection is not fatal and most cases are asymptomatic, the afflicted child can suffer from disrupted sleep and sometimes nausea, abdominal discomfort, and diarrhea. A simple rapid test can be performed by pressing a piece of transparent adhesive tape against the anal skin and then applying it to a slide for microscopic examination. When one member of the family is diagnosed, the entire family should be tested and/or treated because it is likely that multiple members are infected.

Taenia solium

In contrast to the last two helminths, this one is a tapeworm. Adult worms are usually around 5 meters long and have a scolex with hooklets and suckers to attach to the intestine **(figure 22.24)**. Disease caused by *T. solium* (the pig tapeworm) is distributed worldwide but is mainly concentrated in areas where humans live in close proximity with pigs or eat undercooked pork. In pigs, the eggs hatch in the small intestine and the released larvae migrate throughout the organs. Ultimately, they encyst in the muscles, becoming *cysticerci,* young tapeworms that are the infective stage for humans. When humans ingest a live cysticercus in pork, the coat is digested and the organism is flushed into the intestine, where it firmly attaches by the scolex and develops into an adult tapeworm. Infection with *T. solium* can take another form when humans ingest the tapeworm eggs rather than cysticerci. Although humans are not the usual intermediate hosts, the eggs can still hatch in the intestine, releasing tapeworm larvae that migrate to all tissues. They form bladderlike sacs throughout the body that can cause serious damage. This transmission and life cycle are shown in cycle C in figure 22.23. The pork tapeworm is not the same as the more commonly known pork helminthic infection, *trichinosis.* It is discussed in a later section.

For such a large organism, it is remarkable how few symptoms a tapeworm causes. Occasionally, a patient discovers proglottids in his or her stool, and some patients complain of vague abdominal pain and nausea.

Other tapeworms of the genus *Taenia* infect humans. One of them is the beef tapeworm, *Taenia saginata.* It usually causes similar general symptoms of helminthic infection. But humans are not known to acquire *T. saginata* infection by ingesting the eggs.

Diphyllobothrium latum

This tapeworm has an intermediate host in fish. It is common in the Great Lakes, Alaska, and Canada. Humans are its definitive host. It develops in the intestine and can cause long-term symptoms. It can be transmitted in raw food such as sushi and sashimi made from salmon. (Reputable sushi restaurants employ authentic sushi chefs who are trained to carefully examine fish for larvae and other signs of infection.)

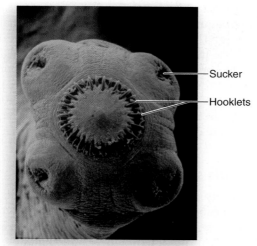

(a) Tapeworm scolex showing sucker and hooklets.

Sucker
Hooklets

(b) Adult *Taenia saginata*. The arrow points to the scolex; the remainder of the tape, called the strobila, has a total length of 5 meters.

Figure 22.24 Tapeworm characteristics.

As is the case with most tapeworms, symptoms are minor and usually vague and include possible abdominal discomfort or nausea. The tapeworm seems to have the ability to absorb and use the vitamin B$_{12}$, making it unavailable to its human host. Anemia is therefore sometimes reported with this infection. You should be aware that certain people of Scandinavian descent have a genetic predisposition for not adsorbing B$_{12}$. In these patients, *Diphyllobothrium latum* infection can be quite dangerous.

Hymenolepis species

These relatively small tapeworms are the most common tapeworm infections in the world. There are two species: *Hymenolepis nana,* known as the dwarf tapeworm because it is only 15 to 40 mm in length, and *H. diminuta*, the rat tapeworm, which is usually 20 to 60 cm in length as an adult.

The life cycle of these tapeworms often involves insects as well as the definitive host, which may be a rodent or a human. When eggs are passed in the feces of a rodent or human, they can be ingested by various insects, which are in turn accidentally ingested by humans (in cereals or other foods). Alternatively, eggs in the environment can be directly ingested by humans. Tapeworms become established in the small intestine, and eggs can be released after proglottids break off from the attached worms.

Symptoms are mild, and the treatment of choice is praziquantel **(Disease Table 22.9)**.

Disease: Intestinal Distress Accompanied by Migratory Symptoms

A diverse group of helminths enter the body as larvae or eggs, mature to the worm stage in the intestine, and then migrate into the circulatory and lymphatic systems, after which they travel to the heart and lungs, migrate up the respiratory tree to the throat, and are swallowed. This journey returns the mature worms to the intestinal tract where they then take up residence. All of these conditions, in addition to causing symptoms in the digestive tract, may induce inflammatory reactions along their migratory routes, resulting in eosinophilia and, during their lung stage, pneumonia. Three different examples of this type of infection follow.

Ascaris lumbricoides

Ascaris lumbricoides is a giant intestinal roundworm (up to 300 mm—a foot or more—long) that probably accounts for the greatest number of worm infections (estimated at 1 billion cases worldwide). Most reported cases in the United States occur in the southeastern states. *Ascaris* spends its larval and adult stages in humans and releases embryonic eggs in feces, which are then spread to other humans through food, drink, or contaminated objects placed in the mouth. The eggs thrive in warm, moist soils and resist cold and chemical disinfectants, but they are sensitive to sunlight, high temperatures, and drying. After ingested eggs hatch in

Disease Table 22.9 Intestinal Distress

Causative Organism(s)	*Trichuris trichiura* (whipworm)	*Enterobius vermicularis* (pinworm)	*Taenia solium* (pork tapeworm)	*Diphyllobothrium latum* (fish tapeworm)	*Hymenolepis nana* and *H. diminuta*
Most Common Modes of Transmission	Cycle A: vehicle (soil)—also fecal-oral	Cycle A: vehicle (food, water), fomites, self-inoculation	Cycle C: vehicle (pork)—also fecal-oral	Cycle C: vehicle (seafood)	Cycle C: vehicle (ingesting insects)—also fecal-oral
Virulence Factors	Burrowing and invasiveness	–	–	Vitamin B$_{12}$ usage	–
Culture/Diagnosis	Blood count, serology, egg or worm detection	Adhesive tape	Blood count, serology, egg or worm detection	Blood count, serology, egg or worm detection	Blood count, serology, egg or worm detection
Prevention	Hygiene, sanitation	Hygiene	Cook meat, avoid pig feces	Cook meat	Hygienic environment
Treatment	Mebendazole	Mebendazole, piperazine	Praziquantel	Praziquantel	Praziquantel
Distinctive Features	Humans sole host	Common in United States	Tapeworm; intermediate host is pigs	Large tapeworm; anemia	Most common tapeworm infection

Figure 22.25 **A mass of *Ascaris lumbricoides* worms.** These worms had been passed by a child in Kenya in 2007.

the human intestine, the larvae embark upon an odyssey in the tissues. First, they penetrate the intestinal wall and enter the lymphatic and circulatory systems. They are swept into the heart and eventually arrive at the capillaries of the lungs. From this point, the larvae migrate up the respiratory tree to the glottis. Worms entering the throat are swallowed and returned to the small intestine, where they reach adulthood and reproduce, producing up to 200,000 fertilized eggs a day.

Even as adults, male and female worms are not attached to the intestine and retain some of their exploratory ways. They are known to invade the biliary channels of the liver and gallbladder, and on occasion the worms emerge from the nose and mouth. Severe inflammatory reactions mark the migratory route; and allergic reactions such as bronchospasm, asthma, or skin rash can occur. Heavy worm loads can retard the physical and mental development of children **(figure 22.25)**. One possibility with intestinal worm infections is self-reinoculation due to poor personal hygiene.

Necator americanus and *Ancylostoma duodenale*

These two different nematodes are called by the common name hookworm. *Necator americanus* (nee-kay′-tor ah-mer″-ih-cah′-nus) is endemic to the New World, and *Ancylostoma duodenale* (an′-kih-los′-toh-mah doo-oh-den-ah′-lee) is endemic to the Old World, although the two species overlap in parts of Latin America. Otherwise, with respect to transmission, life cycle, and pathology, they are usually lumped together. The *hook* refers to the adult's oral cutting plates on its curved anterior end, by which it anchors to the intestinal villi **(figure 22.26)**.

Unlike other intestinal worms, hookworm larvae hatch outside the body and infect by penetrating the skin. Hookworm transmission is described by cycle B (see figure 22.23).

Ordinarily, the parasite is present in soil contaminated with human feces. It enters sites on bare feet such as hair follicles, abrasions, or the soft skin between the toes, but cases have occurred via mud that was splattered on the ankles of people wearing shoes. Infection has even been reported in people handling soiled laundry.

On contact, the hookworm larvae actively burrow into the skin. After several hours, they reach the lymphatic or blood circulation and are immediately carried into the heart and lungs. The larvae proceed up the bronchi and trachea to the throat. Most of the larvae are swallowed with sputum and arrive in the small intestine, where they anchor, feed on blood, and mature. Eggs first appear in the stool about 6 weeks after the time of entry, and the untreated infection can last about 5 years.

Symptoms from these infections follow the progress of the worm in the body. A localized dermatitis called *ground itch* may be caused by the initial penetration of larvae. The transit of the larvae to the lungs is ordinarily brief, but it can cause symptoms of pneumonia and eosinophilia. The potential for injury is greatest during the intestinal phase, when heavy worm burdens can cause nausea, vomiting, cramps, and bloody diarrhea. Because blood loss is significant, iron-deficient anemia develops, and infants are especially susceptible to hemorrhagic shock. Chronic fatigue, listlessness, apathy, and anemia worsen with chronic and repeated infections.

Hookworm infections are treated with antihelminthic drugs, but frequent reinfection is a problem. In 2000, the Bill and Melinda Gates Foundation, recognizing the impact of worldwide hookworm infections, contributed $18 million to the development of a hookworm vaccine, and in 2006 they increased that contribution.

(a)   (b)

Figure 22.26 **Cutting teeth on the mouths of** **(a)** *Necator americanus* and **(b)** *Ancylostoma duodenale.*

Strongyloides stercoralis

The agent of strongyloidiasis, or threadworm infection, is *Strongyloides stercoralis* (stron'-jih-loy-deez ster"-kor-ah'-lis). This nematode is exceptional because of its minute size and its capacity to complete its life cycle either within the human body or outside in moist soil. It shares a similar distribution and life cycle to hookworms and afflicts an estimated 100 to 200 million people worldwide. Infection occurs when soil larvae penetrate the skin (cycle B in figure 22.23). The worm then enters the circulation, is carried to the respiratory tract and swallowed, and then enters the small intestine to complete development. Although an adult *S. stercoralis* lays eggs in the gut just as hookworms do, the eggs hatch into larvae in the colon and can remain entirely in the host's body to complete the cycle. The larval form of the organism can likewise exit with feces and go through an environmental cycle. These numerous alternative life cycles greatly increase the chance of transmission and the likelihood for chronic infection.

The first symptom of threadworm infection is usually a red, intensely itchy skin rash at the site of entry. Mild migratory activity in an otherwise normal person can escape notice, but heavy worm loads can cause symptoms of pneumonitis and eosinophilia. The nematode activities in the intestine produce bloody diarrhea, liver enlargement, and malabsorption. In immunocompromised patients, there is a risk of disseminated infection involving numerous organs **(figure 22.27)**. Hardest hit are AIDS patients, transplant patients on immunosuppressant drugs, and cancer patients receiving irradiation therapy, who can die if not treated promptly **(Disease Table 22.10)**.

Figure 22.27 A patient with disseminated *Strongyloides* infection. Trails under the skin indicate the migration tracks of the worms.

Liver and Intestinal Disease

One group of worms that lands in the intestines has a particular affinity for the liver. Two of these worms are trematodes (flatworms), and they are categorized as liver flukes.

Opisthorchis sinensis and Clonorchis sinensis

Opisthorchis sinensis and *Clonorchis sinensis* are two worms known as Chinese liver flukes. They complete their sexual development in mammals such as humans, cats, dogs, and swine. Their intermediate development occurs in snail and fish hosts. Humans ingest metacercariae in inadequately

Disease Table 22.10 Intestinal Distress plus Migratory Symptoms

Causative Organism(s)	*Ascaris lumbricoides* (intestinal roundworm)	*Necator americanus* and *Ancylostoma duodenale* (hookworms)	*Strongyloides stercoralis* (threadworm)
Most Common Modes of Transmission	Cycle A: vehicle (soil/fecal-oral), fomites, self-inoculation	Cycle B: vehicle (soil), fomite	Cycle B: vehicle (soil), fomite
Virulence Factors	Induction of hypersensitivity, adult worm migration, and abdominal obstruction	Induction of hypersensitivity, adult worm migration, and abdominal obstruction	Induction of hypersensitivity, adult worm migration, and abdominal obstruction
Culture/Diagnosis	Blood count, serology, egg or worm detection	Blood count, serology, egg or worm detection	Blood count, serology, egg or worm detection
Prevention	Hygiene	Sanitation	Sanitation
Treatment	Albendazole	Albendazole	Ivermectin or thiabendazole
Distinctive Features	Roundworm; 1 billion persons infected	Penetrates skin, serious intestinal symptoms	Penetrates skin, severe for immunocompromised

cooked or raw freshwater fish (see cycle D in figure 22.23). Larvae hatch and crawl into the bile duct, where they mature and shed eggs into the intestinal tract. Feces containing eggs are passed into standing water that harbors the intermediate snail host. The cycle is complete when infected snails release cercariae that invade fish living in the same water.

Symptoms of *Opisthorchis* and *Clonorchis* infection are slow to develop but include thickening of the lining of the bile duct and possible granuloma formation in areas of the liver if eggs enter the stroma of the liver. If the infection is heavy, the bile duct could be blocked.

Fasciola hepatica

This liver fluke is a common parasite in sheep, cattle, goats, and other mammals and is occasionally transmitted to humans **(figure 22.28)**. Periodic outbreaks in temperate regions of Europe and South America are associated with eating wild watercress. The life cycle is very complex, involving the mammal as the definitive host, the release of eggs in the feces, the hatching of eggs in the water into *miracidia*, invasion of freshwater snails, development and release of cercariae, encystment of metacercariae on a water plant, and ingestion of the cyst by a mammalian host eating the plant. The cysts release young flukes into the intestine that wander to the liver, lodge in the gallbladder, and develop into adults. Humans develop symptoms of vomiting, diarrhea, hepatomegaly, and bile obstruction only if they are chronically infected by a large number of flukes.

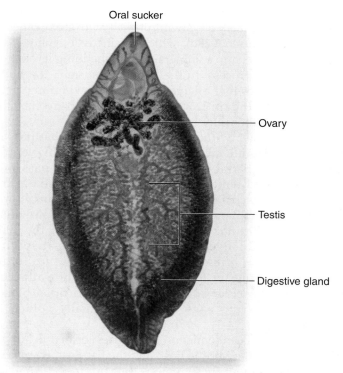

Figure 22.28 *Fasciola hepatica*, the sheep liver fluke (2×).

Labels: Oral sucker, Ovary, Testis, Digestive gland

Disease Table 22.11 Liver and Intestinal Disease

	Opisthorchis sinensis, Clonorchis sinensis	Fasciola hepatica
Causative Organism(s)		
Most Common Modes of Transmission	Cycle D: vehicle (fish or crustaceans)	Cycle D: vehicle (water and water plants)
Virulence Factors	–	–
Culture/ Diagnosis	Blood count, serology, egg or worm detection	Blood count, serology, egg or worm detection
Prevention	Cook food, sanitation of water	Sanitation of water
Treatment	Praziquantel	Triclabendazole
Distinctive Features	Live in liver	Live in liver and gallbladder

Disease: Muscle and Neurological Symptoms

Trichinosis is an infection transmitted by eating pork (and sometimes other wildlife) that have the cysts of *Trichinella* species embedded in the meat. The life cycle of this nematode is spent entirely within the body of a mammalian host such as a pig, bear, cat, dog, or rat. In nature, the parasite is maintained in an encapsulated (encysted) larval form in the muscles of these animal reservoirs and is transmitted when other animals prey upon them. The disease cannot be transmitted from one human to another except in the case of cannibalism.

Because all wild and domesticated mammals appear to be susceptible to *Trichinella* species, one might expect human trichinosis to be common worldwide. But in reality, it is more common in the United States and in Europe than in the rest of the world. This distribution appears to be related to regional or ethnic customs of eating raw or rare pork dishes or wild animal meats. Bear meat is the source of up to one-third of the cases in the United States. Home or small-scale butchering enterprises that do not carefully inspect pork can spread the parasite, although commercial pork can also be a source. Practices such as tasting raw homemade pork sausage or serving rare pork or pork-beef mixtures have been responsible for sporadic outbreaks.

The cyst envelope is digested in the stomach and small intestine, which liberates the larvae. After burrowing into the intestinal mucosa, the larvae reach adulthood and mate. The larvae that result from this union penetrate the intestine and enter the lymphatic channels and blood. All tissues are at risk for invasion, but final development occurs when the coiled larvae are encysted in the skeletal muscle. At maturity, the cyst is about 1 mm long and can be observed by careful inspection of meat. Although larvae can deteriorate over time, they have also been known to survive for years.

Symptoms may be unnoticeable or they could be life-threatening, depending on how many larvae were ingested in the tainted meat. The first symptoms, when present, mimic influenza or viral fevers, with diarrhea, nausea, abdominal pains, fever, and sweating. The second phase, brought on by the mass migration of larvae and their entrance into muscle, produces puffiness around the eyes, intense muscle and joint pain, shortness of breath, and pronounced eosinophilia. The most serious life-threatening manifestations are heart and brain involvement. Although the symptoms eventually subside, a cure is not available once the larvae have encysted in muscles.

The most effective preventive measures for trichinosis are to adequately store and cook pork and wild meats.

Disease Table 22.12 Muscle and Neurological Symptoms

Causative Organism(s)	*Trichinella* species
Most Common Modes of Transmission	Vehicle (food)
Virulence Factors	–
Culture/Diagnosis	Serology combined with clinical picture; muscle biopsy
Prevention	Cook meat
Treatment	Mebendazole, steroids
Distinctive Features	Brain and heart involvement can be fatal

Liver Disease

When liver swelling or malfunction is accompanied by eosinophilia, **schistosomiasis** should be suspected. Schistosomiasis has afflicted humans for thousands of years. The disease is caused by the blood flukes *Schistosoma mansoni* or *S. japonicum*, species that are morphologically and geographically distinct but share similar life cycles, transmission methods, and general disease manifestations. It is one of the few infectious agents that can invade intact skin.

▶ Signs and Symptoms

The first symptoms of infection are itchiness in the area where the worm enters the body, followed by fever, chills, diarrhea, and cough. The most severe consequences, associated with chronic infection, are hepatomegaly and liver disease and splenomegaly. Other serious conditions caused by a different schistosome occur in the urinary tract—bladder obstruction

and blood in the urine. This condition is discussed in chapter 23 (genitourinary tract diseases). Occasionally, eggs from the worms are carried into the central nervous system and heart and create a severe granulomatous response. Adult flukes can live for many years and, by eluding the immune defenses, cause a chronic affliction.

▶ Causative Agent

Schistosomes are trematodes, or flukes (see chapter 5), but they are more cylindrical than flat **(figure 22.29)**. They are often called blood flukes. Flukes have digestive, excretory, neuromuscular, and reproductive systems, but they lack circulatory and respiratory systems. Humans are the definitive hosts for the blood fluke, and snails are the intermediate host.

▶ Pathogenesis and Virulence Factors

This parasite is clever indeed. Once inside the host, it coats its outer surface with proteins from the host's bloodstream, basically "cloaking" itself from the host defense system. This coat reduces its surface antigenicity and allows it to remain in the host indefinitely.

Other virulence attributes are the organism's ability to invade intact skin and attach to vascular endothelium, to sequester iron from the bloodstream, and to induce a granulomatous response.

▶ Transmission and Epidemiology

The life cycle of the schistosome is of the "D" type, and is very complex (see figure 22.29). The cycle begins when infected humans release eggs into irrigated fields or ponds, either by deliberate fertilization with excreta or by defecating or urinating directly into the water. The egg hatches in the water and gives off an actively swimming ciliated larva called a **miracidium (figure 22.29a)**, which instinctively swims to a snail and burrows into a vulnerable site, shedding its ciliated covering in the process. In the body of the snail, the miracidium multiplies into a larger, fork-tailed swimming larva called a **cercaria (figure 22.29b)**. Cercariae are given off by the thousands into the water by infected snails.

Upon contact with a human wading or bathing in water, cercariae attach themselves to the skin by ventral suckers and penetrate into hair follicles. They pass into small blood and lymphatic vessels and are carried to the liver. Here, the schistosomes achieve sexual maturity, and the male and female worms remain permanently entwined to facilitate mating **(figure 22.29c)**. In time, the pair migrates to and lodges in small blood vessels at specific sites. *Schistosoma mansoni* and *S. japonicum* end up in the mesenteric venules of the small intestine. While attached to these intravascular sites, the worms feed upon blood, and the female lays eggs that are eventually voided in feces or urine.

The disease is endemic to 74 countries located in Africa, South America, the Middle East, and the Far East. *S. mansoni* is found throughout these regions, but not in the Far East.

(a) The miracidium phase, which infects the snail (300×).

(b) The cercaria phase, which is released by snails and burrows into the human host (5,000×).

(c) An electron micrograph of normal mating position of adult worms. The larger male worm holds the female in a groove on his ventral surface (2,000×).

Figure 22.29 Stages in the life cycle of *Schistosoma*.

S. japonicum has a much smaller geographical distribution than *S. mansoni,* only being found in the Far East. Schistosomiasis (including the urinary tract form) is the second most prominent parasitic disease after malaria, probably affecting 200 million people at any one time worldwide. Recent increases in its occurrence in Africa have been attributed to new dams on the Nile River, which have provided additional habitat for snail hosts.

▶ **Culture and Diagnosis**

Diagnosis depends on identifying the eggs in urine or feces. The clinical pictures of hepatomegaly, splenomegaly, or both also contribute to the diagnosis.

▶ **Prevention and Treatment**

The cycle of infection cannot be broken as long as people are exposed to untreated sewage in their environment. It is quite common for people to be cured and then to be reinfected because their village has no sewage treatment. A vaccine would provide widespread control of the disease, but so far none is licensed. More than one vaccine is in development, however.

Praziquantel is the drug treatment of choice. It works by crippling the worms, making them more antigenic and thereby allowing the host immune response to eliminate them. Clinicians use an "egg hatching test" to determine whether an infection is current and whether treatment is actually killing the eggs. Urine or feces containing eggs is placed in room temperature water, and if miracidia emerge, the infection is still "active."

Case File 22   *Wrap-Up*

Norovirus, the agent identified in many of the Reliant City patients, is a frequent cause of gastroenteritis outbreaks in the United States. Norovirus is highly contagious (ID less than 100 organisms) and is easily spread from person to person and by contact with contaminated materials. The typical incubation period is 24 to 48 hours, and the resulting symptoms persist for 12 to 60 hours. Such outbreaks are frequently caused by contaminated food or water and can also be associated with crowded living conditions, such as those at Reliant City.

It is likely that one or more individuals were infected with the norovirus when they arrived at the shelter. Although the source of the initial infection is unknown, contact with contaminated floodwaters is a definite possibility. The infection spread quickly due to the crowded living conditions and shared facilities. Infection control measures, including isolating symptomatic individuals, distributing gel hand sanitizer, and educating staff and evacuees, quickly brought the outbreak under control.

See: CDC. 2005. *MMWR* 54(40):1016–18

Disease Table 22.13 Liver Disease

Causative Organism(s)	*Schistosoma mansoni, S. japonicum*
Most Common Modes of Transmission	Cycle D: vehicle (contaminated water)
Virulence Factors	Antigenic "cloaking"
Culture/Diagnosis	Identification of eggs in feces, scarring of intestines detected by endoscopy
Prevention	Avoiding contaminated vehicles
Treatment	Praziquantel
Distinctive Features	Penetrates skin, lodges in blood vessels of intestine, damages liver

22.4 Learning Outcomes—Can You . . .

10. . . . describe some distinguishing characteristics and commonalities seen in helminthic infections?
11. . . . list four helminths that cause primarily intestinal symptoms, and identify which life cycle they follow and one unique fact about each one?
12. . . . list four helminths that cause intestinal symptoms that may be accompanied by migratory symptoms, and identify which life cycle they follow and one unique fact about each one?
13. . . . list the modes of transmission, virulence factors, diagnostic techniques, and prevention/treatment for each of the helminth infections resulting in liver and intestinal symptoms? These are infections caused by *Opisthorchis sinensis, Clonorchis sinensis,* and *Fasciola hepatica.*
14. . . . describe the type of disease caused by *Trichinella* species?
15. . . . diagram the life cycle of *Schistosoma mansoni* and *S. japonicum,* discuss how it differs from the life cycle of the *Schistosoma* involved in urinary disease, and describe the importance of all three organisms in world health.

▶ Summing Up

Taxonomic Organization **Microorganisms Causing Disease in the GI Tract**

Microorganism	Disease	Chapter Location
Gram-positive endospore-forming bacteria		
Clostridium difficile	Antibiotic-associated diarrhea	Acute diarrhea, p. 676
Clostridium perfringens	Food poisoning	Acute diarrhea and/or vomiting, p. 683
Bacillus cereus	Food poisoning	Acute diarrhea and/or vomiting, p. 682
Gram-positive bacteria		
Streptococcus mutans	Dental caries	Dental caries, p. 664
Streptococcus sobrinus	Dental caries	Dental caries, p. 664
Staphylococcus aureus	Food poisoning	Acute diarrhea and/or vomiting, p. 682
Gram-negative bacteria		
Campylobacter jejuni	Acute diarrhea	Acute diarrhea, p. 675
Helicobacter pylori	Gastritis/gastric ulcers	Gastritis/gastric ulcers, p. 670
Escherichia coli O157:H7	Acute diarrhea plus hemolytic syndrome	Acute diarrhea, p. 674
Other *E. coli*	Acute or chronic diarrhea	Acute diarrhea, p. 675
		Chronic diarrhea, p. 684
Salmonella	Acute diarrhea or typhoid fever	Acute diarrhea, p. 672
Shigella	Acute diarrhea and dysentery	Acute diarrhea, p. 673
Vibrio cholerae	Cholera	Acute diarrhea, p. 677
Yersinia enterocolitica and *Y. pseudotuberculosis*	Acute diarrhea	Acute diarrhea, p. 676
Tannerella forsythia, Aggregatibacter actinomycetemcomitans, Porphyromonas gingivalis, Treponema vincentii, Prevotella intermedia, Fusobacterium	Periodontal disease	Periodontal disease, p. 666
DNA viruses		
Hepatitis B virus	"Serum" hepatitis	Hepatitis, p. 689
RNA viruses		
Hepatitis A virus	"Infectious" hepatitis	Hepatitis, p. 688
Hepatitis C virus	"Serum" hepatitis	Hepatitis, p. 690
Hepatitis E virus	"Infectious" hepatitis	Hepatitis, p. 689
Mumps virus	Mumps	Mumps, p. 668
Rotavirus	Acute diarrhea	Acute diarrhea, p. 680
Protozoa		
Entamoeba histolytica	Chronic diarrhea	Chronic diarrhea, p. 686
Cryptosporidium	Acute diarrhea	Acute diarrhea, p. 678
Cyclospora	Chronic diarrhea	Chronic diarrhea, p. 685
Giardia lamblia	Chronic diarrhea	Chronic diarrhea, p. 685
Helminths—nematodes		
Ascaris lumbricoides	Intestinal distress plus migratory symptoms	Intestinal distress plus migratory symptoms, p. 696
Enterobius vermicularis	Intestinal distress	Intestinal distress, p. 695
Trichuris trichiura	Intestinal distress	Intestinal distress, p. 694
Necator americanus and *Ancylostoma duodenale*	Intestinal distress plus migratory symptoms	Intestinal distress plus migratory symptoms, p. 697
Strongyloides stercoralis	Intestinal distress plus migratory symptoms	Intestinal distress plus migratory symptoms, p. 698
Trichinella spp.	Muscle and neurological symptoms	Muscle and neurological symptoms, p. 699
Helminths—cestodes		
Hymenolepis	Intestinal distress	Intestinal distress, p. 696
Taenia solium	Intestinal distress	Intestinal distress, p. 695
Diphyllobothrium latum	Intestinal distress	Intestinal distress, p. 695
Opisthorchis sinensis and *Clonorchis sinensis*	Liver and intestinal disease	Liver and intestinal disease, p. 698
Fasciola hepatica	Liver and intestinal disease	Liver and intestinal disease, p. 699
Helminths—trematodes		
Schistosoma mansoni, S. japonicum	Schistosomiasis	Helminthic liver disease, p. 700

INFECTIOUS DISEASES AFFECTING
The Gastrointestinal Tract

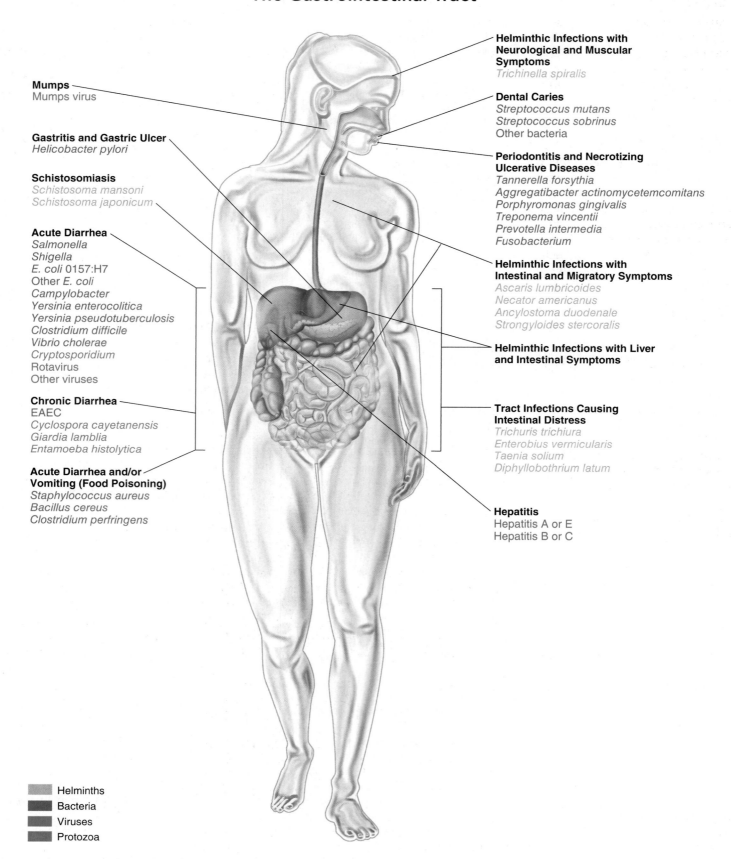

Helminthic Infections with Neurological and Muscular Symptoms
Trichinella spiralis

Mumps
Mumps virus

Dental Caries
Streptococcus mutans
Streptococcus sobrinus
Other bacteria

Gastritis and Gastric Ulcer
Helicobacter pylori

Periodontitis and Necrotizing Ulcerative Diseases
Tannerella forsythia
Aggregatibacter actinomycetemcomitans
Porphyromonas gingivalis
Treponema vincentii
Prevotella intermedia
Fusobacterium

Schistosomiasis
Schistosoma mansoni
Schistosoma japonicum

Acute Diarrhea
Salmonella
Shigella
E. coli 0157:H7
Other *E. coli*
Campylobacter
Yersinia enterocolitica
Yersinia pseudotuberculosis
Clostridium difficile
Vibrio cholerae
Cryptosporidium
Rotavirus
Other viruses

Helminthic Infections with Intestinal and Migratory Symptoms
Ascaris lumbricoides
Necator americanus
Ancylostoma duodenale
Strongyloides stercoralis

Helminthic Infections with Liver and Intestinal Symptoms

Chronic Diarrhea
EAEC
Cyclospora cayetanensis
Giardia lamblia
Entamoeba histolytica

Tract Infections Causing Intestinal Distress
Trichuris trichiura
Enterobius vermicularis
Taenia solium
Diphyllobothrium latum

Acute Diarrhea and/or Vomiting (Food Poisoning)
Staphylococcus aureus
Bacillus cereus
Clostridium perfringens

Hepatitis
Hepatitis A or E
Hepatitis B or C

Helminths
Bacteria
Viruses
Protozoa

System Summary Figure 22.30

Chapter Summary

22.1 The Gastrointestinal Tract and Its Defenses

- The gastrointestinal (GI) tract is composed of *eight* main sections—the mouth, pharynx, esophagus, stomach, small intestine, large intestine, rectum, and anus, and *four* accessory organs—the salivary glands, liver, gallbladder, and pancreas.
- The GI tract has a very heavy load of microorganisms, and it encounters millions of new ones every day. There are significant mechanical, chemical, and antimicrobial defenses to combat microbial invasion.

22.2 Normal Biota of the Gastrointestinal Tract

- Bacteria abound in all of the eight main sections of the gastrointestinal tract. Even the highly acidic stomach is heavily colonized.

22.3 Gastrointestinal Tract Diseases Caused by Microorganisms (Nonhelminthic)

- **Tooth and Gum Infections:** Alpha-hemolytic *Streptococcus mutans* and *Streptococcus sobrinus* are main causes of dental caries. Periodontitis: The anaerobic bacteria *Tannerella forsythia* (formerly *Bacteroides forsythus*), *Aggregatibacter actinomycetemcomitans*, *Porphyromonas*, *Fusobacterium*, and spirochete species are causative agents.
- **Necrotizing Ulcerative Gingivitis and Periodontitis:** Necrotizing ulcerative gingivitis (NUG) and necrotizing ulcerative periodontitis (NUP) are synergistic infections involving *Treponema vincentii*, *Prevotella intermedia*, and *Fusobacterium* species.
- **Mumps:** Swelling of the salivary gland—a condition called parotitis. Mumps is caused by an enveloped, single-stranded RNA virus (mumps virus) from the genus *Paramyxovirus*.
- **Gastritis and Gastric Ulcers:** Gastritis: sharp or burning pain emanating from the abdomen. Gastric ulcers: actual lesions in the mucosa of the stomach (gastric ulcers) or in the uppermost portion of the small intestine (duodenal ulcer). *Helicobacter pylori*, a curved gram-negative rod, is causative agent.
- **Acute Infectious Diarrhea:** In United States, a third of all acute diarrhea is transmitted by contaminated food.
  - *Salmonella:* *Salmonella enteritidis* is divided into many serotypes, based on major surface antigens. Animal and dairy products are often contaminated with the bacterium. Typhoid fever, caused by *S. enteritidis* variant *typhi*, is a progressive, invasive infection that can lead to septicemia.
  - *Shigella* species give symptoms of frequent, watery, bloody stools, fever, and often intense abdominal pain. Diarrhea containing blood and mucus is also called dysentery. The bacterium *Shigella dysenteriae* produces a heat-labile exotoxin called shiga toxin.
  - Dozens of different strains of *E. coli* exist: *E. coli* O157:H7 and its close relatives are most virulent. This group of *E. coli* is referred to as enterohemorrhagic *E. coli*, or EHEC. *E. coli* O157:H7 is the agent of a spectrum of conditions, ranging from mild gastroenteritis with fever to bloody diarrhea. About 10% of patients develop hemolytic uremic syndrome (HUS), a severe hemolytic anemia that can

cause kidney damage and failure. Virulence is due to shiga toxins (often called STEC—shiga-toxin-producing *E. coli*).
  - Other *E. coli:* At least four other categories of *E. coli* cause diarrheal diseases. These are enterotoxigenic *E. coli* (traveler's diarrhea), enteroinvasive *E. coli*, enteropathogenic *E. coli*, and enteroaggregative *E. coli*.
  - *Campylobacter:* Symptoms are frequent watery stools, fever, vomiting, headaches, and severe abdominal pain. Infrequently, infection can lead to serious neuromuscular paralysis called *Guillain-Barré syndrome*.
  - *Yersinia enterocolitica* and *Y. pseudotuberculosis* are both agents of GI disease via food and beverage contamination.
  - *Clostridium difficile* causes a condition called pseudomembranous colitis (antibiotic-associated colitis), precipitated by therapy with broad-spectrum antibiotics.
  - *Vibrio cholerae:* Symptoms of secretory diarrhea and severe fluid loss can lead to death in less than 48 hours. Produces enterotoxin called cholera toxin (CT), which disrupts the normal physiology of intestinal cells.
  - *Cryptosporidium:* Intestinal waterborne protozoan that infects mammals, birds, and reptiles.
  - Rotavirus: Primary viral cause of morbidity and mortality resulting from diarrhea, accounting for 50% of all cases.
- **Acute Diarrhea with Vomiting:** Food poisoning refers to symptoms in the gut that are caused by a preformed toxin.
  - *Staphylococcus aureus* exotoxin: Heat-stable enterotoxin requires 100°C for 30 minutes for inactivation. Ingested toxin acts on gastrointestinal epithelium and stimulates nerves; acute symptoms of cramping, nausea, vomiting, and diarrhea.
  - *Bacillus cereus* exotoxin: *B. cereus* is common resident on vegetables and soil. Produces two exotoxins; one causes a diarrheal-type disease, the other causes an emetic disease.
  - *Clostridium perfringens* exotoxin: The toxin initiates acute abdominal pain, diarrhea, and nausea in 8 to 16 hours.
- **Chronic Diarrhea**
  - Enteroaggregative *E. coli* (EAEC) is particularly associated with chronic disease, especially in children. Transmission is through contaminated food and water.
  - *Cyclospora cayetanensis:* Protozoan transmitted via the fecal-oral route; associated with fresh produce and water.
  - *Giardia lamblia:* Protozoan that can cause diarrhea of long duration, abdominal pain, and flatulence. Freshwater is common vehicle of infection.
  - *Entamoeba histolytica:* Freshwater protozoan that causes intestinal amoebiasis, targeting the cecum, appendix, colon, and rectum, leading to dysentery, abdominal pain, fever, diarrhea, and weight loss.
- **Hepatitis:** Inflammatory disease marked by necrosis of hepatocytes and a mononuclear response that swells and disrupts the liver, causing jaundice. Can be caused by a variety of different viruses.
  - Hepatitis A virus (HAV): A nonenveloped, single-stranded RNA enterovirus of low virulence. Spread through fecal-oral route. Inactivated vaccine available.

- Hepatitis B virus (HBV): Enveloped DNA virus in the family *Hepadnaviridae*. Can be very serious, even life-threatening; some patients develop chronic liver disease in the form of necrosis or cirrhosis. Also associated with hepatocellular carcinoma. Some patients infected with hepatitis B are coinfected with the delta agent, sometimes also called hepatitis D virus. HBV transmitted by blood and other bodily fluids. Virus is major infectious concern for health care workers.
- Hepatitis C virus: RNA virus in *Flaviviridae* family. Shares characteristics of hepatitis B disease, but is much more likely to become chronic. More commonly transmitted through blood contact than through other body fluids.

22.4 Gastrointestinal Tract Diseases Caused by Helminths

- **Helminthic Intestinal Infections: Intestinal distress as the primary symptom.** Both tapeworms and roundworms can infect intestinal tract in such a way as to cause primary symptoms there.
  - *Trichuris trichiura:* Symptoms may include localized hemorrhage of the bowel, caused by worms burrowing and piercing intestinal mucosa.
  - *Enterobius vermicularis:* "Pinworm"; most common worm disease of children in temperate zones. Not fatal, and most cases are asymptomatic.
  - *Taenia solium:* This tapeworm transmitted to humans by raw or undercooked pork. Other tapeworms of the genus *Taenia*, such as the beef tapeworm *Taenia saginata*, infect humans.

- *Diphyllobothrium latum:* The intermediate host is fish; can be transmitted in raw food such as sushi and sashimi made from salmon.
- **Helminthic Intestinal Infections: Intestinal distress accompanied by migratory symptoms.**
  - *Ascaris lumbricoides:* Intestinal roundworm that releases eggs in feces; eggs then spread to other humans through fecal-oral routes.
  - *Necator americanus* and *Ancylostoma duodenale:* Both called by the common name "hookworm." Hookworm larvae hatch outside the body in soil contaminated with feces and infect by penetrating skin.
  - *Strongyloides stercoralis:* Infection occurs when soil larvae penetrate skin, similar to hookworm infestations. Most susceptible are AIDS patients and immunocompromised patients.
- **Liver and Intestinal Disease:** One group of worms has a particular affinity for the liver—liver flukes.
  - *Opisthorchis sinensis* and *Clonorchis sinensis:* Humans infected by eating inadequately cooked or raw freshwater fish and crustaceans.
  - *Fasciola hepatica:* Common parasite in sheep, cattle, goats, and other mammals. Humans develop symptoms only if chronically infected by a large number of flukes.
- **Muscle and Neurological Symptoms**
  - Trichinosis: Transmitted by eating undercooked pork that has cysts of *Trichinella* embedded in the meat.
  - Schistosomiasis in intestines is caused by blood flukes *Schistosoma mansoni* and *S. japonicum*. Symptoms include fever, chills, diarrhea, liver and spleen disease.

Multiple-Choice and True-False Questions   Knowledge and Comprehension

Multiple-Choice Questions. Select the correct answer from the answers provided.

1. Food moves down the GI tract through the action of
   a. cilia.
   b. peristalsis.
   c. gravity.
   d. microorganisms.

2. The microorganism(s) most associated with acute necrotizing ulcerative periodontitis (ANUP) is (are)
   a. *Treponema vincentii.*
   b. *Prevotella intermedia.*
   c. *Fusobacterium.*
   d. all of the above.

3. Gastric ulcers are caused by
   a. *Treponema vincentii.*
   b. *Prevotella intermedia.*
   c. *Helicobacter pylori.*
   d. all of the above.

4. Virus family Paramyxoviridae contains viruses that cause which of the following diseases?
   a. measles
   b. mumps
   c. influenza
   d. both a and b
   e. both b and c

5. Which of these microorganisms is considered the most common cause of diarrhea in the United States?
   a. *E. coli*
   b. *Salmonella*
   c. *Campylobacter*
   d. *Shigella*

6. Which of these microorganisms is associated with Guillain-Barré syndrome?
   a. *E. coli*
   b. *Salmonella*
   c. *Campylobacter*
   d. *Shigella*

7. This microorganism is commonly associated with fried rice and produces an emetic (vomiting) toxin.
   a. *Bacillus cereus*
   b. *Clostridium perfringens*
   c. *Shigella*
   d. *Staphylococcus aureus*

8. This sporeformer contaminates meats as well as vegetables and is also the causative agent of gas gangrene.
   a. *Bacillus cereus*
   b. *Clostridium perfringens*
   c. *Shigella*
   d. *Staphylococcus aureus*

9. This hepatitis virus is an enveloped DNA virus.
   a. hepatitis A virus
   b. hepatitis B virus
   c. hepatitis C virus
   d. hepatitis E virus

10. In which helminth life cycle is a grazing animal involved?
    a. A   b. B   c. C   d. D

True-False Questions. If the statement is true, leave as is. If it is false, correct it by rewriting the sentence.

11. Mumps is a disease that affects humans and several other species.

12. *Giardia lamblia* is a water-borne, flagellated protozoan often associated with chronic diarrhea.

13. Pseudomembranous colitis (or antibiotic-associated colitis) is caused by *Clostridium difficile*.

14. Poor oral health has been associated with heart disease.

15. *Enterobius vermicularis*, commonly known as the pinworm, is a common cause of anal itching in young children in the United States.

Critical Thinking Questions Application and Analysis

These questions are suggested as a *writing-to-learn* experience. For each question, compose a one- or two-paragraph answer that includes the factual information needed to completely address the question.

1. a. Which microorganism(s) is (are) the major culprit(s) associated with tooth decay?
   b. How do these microorganisms facilitate tooth decay?

2. a. What is food poisoning?
   b. What are some likely microbial culprits associated with food poisoning?
   c. List some nonmicrobial sources of toxins involved in food poisoning.

3. *Entamoeba histolytica* can cause three different forms of amoebiasis. Discuss them.

4. How can hepatitis A infections be prevented?

5. a. What are the most common means of transmission of the hepatitis C virus?
   b. What is the current treatment for hepatitis C?

6. Describe how to definitively diagnose most helminthic infections.

7. Compare the methods of transmission of hepatitis A and hepatitis B.

8. Why is a hamburger a greater risk for *E. coli* contamination than a steak?

9. Describe your strategy for treating a cholera patient.

10. Why is heating food contaminated with *Staphylococcus aureus* no guarantee that the associated food poisoning will be prevented?

Concept Mapping Synthesis

Appendix D provides guidance for working with concept maps.

1. Use 6 to 10 words from the Chapter Summary to create a concept map. Finish it by providing linking words.

Visual Connections Synthesis

These questions use visual images or previous content to make connections to this chapter's concepts.

1. **From chapter 13, figure 13.6b.** Imagine for a minute that the organism in this illustration is *E. coli* O157:H7. What would be one reason not to treat a patient having this infection with powerful antibiotics?

2. **From chapter 12, figure 12.14.** Assume the growth on the first plate represents normal intestinal microbiota. How could you use these illustrations to explain the development of *C. difficile*–associated colitis?

McGraw Hill **connect** plus+ | MICROBIOLOGY

www.connect.microbiology.com

Enhance your study of this chapter with study tools and practice tests. Also ask your instructor about the resources available through ConnectPlus, including the media-rich eBook, interactive learning tools, and animations.

23

Infectious Diseases Affecting the Genitourinary System

Case File 23

Sometimes dedication to your job can get you in trouble. In 2004, a 56-year-old genetics professor at the University of Hawaii in Oahu was determined to continue working in his lab even though a local stream had overflowed and the campus was flooded. For 4 days, he slogged through standing water in his lab to keep his research going.

Some time afterward, the professor developed blisters on his feet. A few days later, he started having flulike symptoms: fever and chills, followed by nausea and vomiting. He began to feel better, but then developed another phase of illness that featured tremors, impaired balance, and illusions of color before his eyes.

■ Do you know of any diseases that a person can acquire simply by walking through standing water?

Continuing the Case appears on page 714.

Outline and Learning Outcomes

23.1 The Genitourinary Tract and Its Defenses
1. Draw or describe the anatomical features of the genitourinary tracts of both genders.
2. List the natural defenses present in the genitourinary tracts.

23.2 Normal Biota of the Genitourinary Tract
3. List the types of normal biota presently known to occupy the genitourinary tracts of both genders.

23.3 Urinary Tract Diseases Caused by Microorganisms
4. List the possible causative agents, modes of transmission, virulence factors, diagnostic techniques, and prevention/treatment for each type of urinary tract infection (including leptospirosis and schistosomiasis).

23.4 Reproductive Tract Diseases Caused by Microorganisms
5. Distinguish between vaginitis and vaginosis.
6. Discuss prostatitis.
7. List the possible causative agents, modes of transmission, virulence factors, and prevention/treatment for gonorrhea and *Chlamydia* infection.
8. Name three diseases that result in genital ulcers and discuss their important features.
9. Differentiate between the two diseases causing warts in the reproductive tract.
10. Provide some detail about the first "cancer vaccine" and how it works.
11. Identify the most important risk group for group B *Streptococcus* infection and why.

23.1 The Genitourinary Tract and Its Defenses

As suggested by the name, the structures considered in this chapter are really two distinct organ systems. The *urinary tract* has the job of removing substances from the blood, regulating certain body processes, and forming urine and transporting it out of the body. The *genital system* has reproduction as its major function. It is also called the *reproductive system*.

The urinary tract includes the kidneys, ureters, bladder, and the urethra (**figure 23.1**). The kidneys remove metabolic wastes from the blood, acting as a sophisticated filtration system. Ureters are tubular organs extending from each kidney to the bladder. The bladder is a collapsible organ that stores urine and empties it into the urethra, which is the conduit of urine to the exterior of the body. In males, the urethra is also the terminal organ of the reproductive tract, but in females the urethra is separate from the vagina, which is the outermost organ of the reproductive tract.

Several defenses are present in the urinary system that help to prevent infection when microorganisms are introduced. The most obvious defensive mechanism is the flushing action of the urine flowing out of the system. The flow of urine also encourages the **desquamation** (shedding) of the epithelial cells lining the urinary tract. For example, each time a person urinates, he or she loses hundreds of thousands of epithelial cells! Any microorganisms attached to them are also shed, of course. Probably the most common microbial threat to the urinary tract is the group of microorganisms that comprise the normal biota in the gastrointestinal tract, because the two organ systems are in close proximity. But the cells of the epithelial lining of the urinary tract have different chemicals on their surfaces than do those lining the GI tract. For that reason, most bacteria that are adapted to adhere to the chemical structures in the GI tract cannot gain a foothold in the urinary tract.

Urine, in addition to being acidic, also contains two antibacterial proteins, lysozyme and lactoferrin. You may recall that lysozyme is an enzyme that breaks down peptidoglycan. Lactoferrin is an iron-binding protein that inhibits bacterial

growth. Finally, secretory IgA specific for previously encountered microorganisms can be found in the urine.

The male reproductive system produces, maintains, and transports sperm cells and is the source of male sex hormones. It consists of the *testes*, which produce sperm cells and hormones, and the *epididymides*, which are coiled tubes leading out of the testes. Each epididymis terminates in a *vas deferens*, which combines with the seminal vesicle and

Figure 23.1 The urinary system.

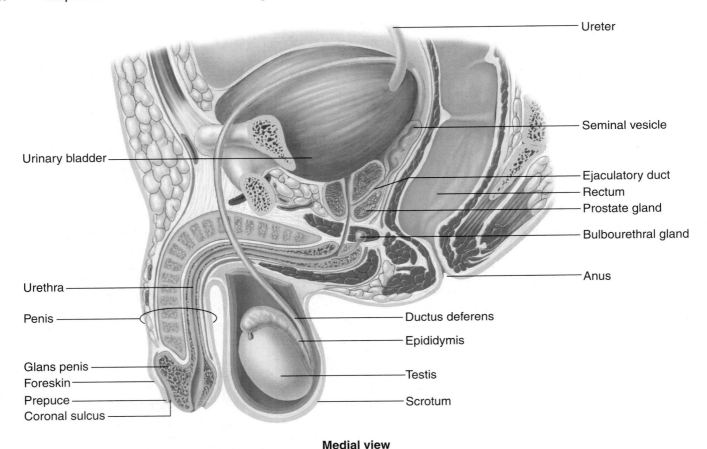

Medial view

Figure 23.2 The male reproductive system.

terminates in the ejaculatory duct **(figure 23.2)**. The contents of the ejaculatory duct empty into the urethra during ejaculation. The *prostate gland* is a walnut-shaped structure at the base of the urethra. It also contributes to the released fluid (semen). The external organs are the scrotum, containing the testes, and the *penis,* a cylindrical organ that houses the urethra. As for its innate defenses, the male reproductive system also benefits from the flushing action of the urine, which helps move microorganisms out of the system.

The female reproductive system consists of the *uterus,* the *fallopian tubes* (also called uterine tubes), *ovaries,* and *vagina* **(figure 23.3)**. During childbearing years, an egg is released from one of the ovaries approximately every 28 days. It enters the fallopian tubes, where fertilization by sperm may take place if sperm are present. The fertilized egg moves through the fallopian tubes to the uterus, where it is implanted in the uterine lining. If fertilization does not occur, the lining of the uterus degenerates and sloughs off; this is the process of menstruation. The terminal portion of the female reproductive tract is the vagina, which is a tube about 9 cm long. The vagina is the exit tube for fluids from the uterus, the channel for childbirth, and the receptive chamber for the penis during sexual intercourse. One very important tissue of the female reproductive tract is the *cervix,* which is the lower one-third of the uterus and the part that connects to the vagina. The opening of the uterus is part of the cervix.

The cervix is a common site of infection in the female reproductive tract.

The natural defenses of the female reproductive tract vary over the lifetime of the woman. The vagina is lined with mucous membranes and, thus, has the protective covering of secreted mucus. During childhood and after menopause, this mucus is the major nonspecific defense of this system. Secretory IgA antibodies specific for any previously encountered infections would be present on these surfaces. During a woman's reproductive years, a major portion of the defense is provided by changes in the pH of the vagina brought about by the release of estrogen. This hormone stimulates the vaginal mucosa to secrete glycogen, which certain bacteria can ferment into acid, lowering the pH of the vagina to about 4.5. Before puberty, a girl produces little estrogen and little glycogen and has a vaginal pH of about 7. The change in pH beginning in adolescence results in a vastly different normal biota in the vagina, described later. The biota of women in their childbearing years is thought to prevent the establishment and invasion of microbes that might have the potential to harm a developing fetus.

23.1 Learning Outcomes—Can You ...

1. ... draw or describe the anatomical features of the genitourinary tracts of both genders?
2. ... list the natural defenses present in the genitourinary tracts?

Medial view

Figure 23.3 The female reproductive system.

23.2 Normal Biota of the Genitourinary Tract

In both genders, the outer region of the urethra harbors some normal biota. The kidney, ureters, bladder, and upper urethra are presumably kept sterile by urine flow and regular bladder emptying (urinating). The principal known residents of the urethra are the nonhemolytic streptococci, staphylococci, corynebacteria, and some lactobacilli. Because the urethra in women is so short (about 3.5 cm long) and is in such close proximity to the anus, it can act as a pipeline for bacteria from the GI tract to the bladder, resulting in urinary tract infections. It should be noted that the outer surface of the penis is colonized by *Pseudomonas* and *Staphylococcus* species—aerobic bacteria. In an uncircumcised penis, the area under the foreskin is colonized by anaerobic gram-negatives. These

Genitourinary Tract Defenses and Normal Biota		
	Defenses	**Normal Biota**
Urinary Tract (both genders)	Flushing action of urine; specific attachment sites not recognized by most nonnormal biota; shedding of urinary tract epithelial cells, secretory IgA, lysozyme, and lactoferrin in urine	Nonhemolytic *Streptococcus*, *Staphylococcus*, *Corynebacterium*, *Lactobacillus*
Female Genital Tract (childhood and postmenopause)	Mucus secretions, secretory IgA	Same as for urinary tract
Female Genital Tract (childbearing years)	Acidic pH, mucus secretions, secretory IgA	Predominantly *Lactobacillus* but also *Candida*
Male Genital Tract	Same as for urinary tract	Urethra: Same as for urinary tract; outer surface of penis: *Pseudomonas* and *Staphylococcus*; sulcus of uncircumcised penis: anaerobic gram-negatives

bacteria tend to draw elements of the immune system closer to the skin surface and may make these men more susceptible to infections, especially by HIV, which infects immune cells.

Normal Biota of the Male Genital Tract

Because the terminal "tube" of the male genital tract is the urethra, the normal biota of the male genital tract (that is, in the urethra) is comprised of the same residents just described.

Normal Biota of the Female Genital Tract

In the female genital tract, only the vagina harbors a normal population of microbes. Starting at the cervix and for all organs above it, there is no normal biota. As just mentioned, before puberty and after menopause, the pH of the vagina is close to neutral and the vagina harbors a biota that is similar to that found in the urethra. After the onset of puberty, estrogen production leads to glycogen release in the vagina, resulting in an acidic pH. *Lactobacillus* species thrive in the acidic environment and contribute to it, converting sugars to acid. Their predominance in the vagina, combined with the acidic environment, discourages the growth of many microorganisms. The estrogen-glycogen effect continues, with minor disruptions, throughout the childbearing years until menopause, when the biota gradually returns to a mixed population similar to that of prepuberty. Note that the very common fungus *Candida albicans* is also present at low levels in the healthy female reproductive tract.

23.2 Learning Outcomes—Can You ...

3. ... list the types of normal biota presently known to occupy the genitourinary tracts of both genders?

23.3 Urinary Tract Diseases Caused by Microorganisms

We consider two types of diseases in this section. **Urinary tract infections (UTIs)** result from invasion of the urinary system by bacteria or other microorganisms. **Leptospirosis,** by contrast, is a spirochete-caused disease transmitted by contact of broken skin or mucous membranes with contaminated animal urine.

Urinary Tract Infections (UTIs)

Even though the flushing action of urine helps to keep infections to a minimum in the urinary tract, urine itself is a good growth medium for many microorganisms. When urine flow is reduced or bacteria are accidentally introduced into the bladder, an infection of that organ (known as *cystitis*) can occur. Occasionally, the infection can also affect the kidneys, in which case it is called *pyelonephritis*. If an infection is limited to the urethra, it is called *urethritis*. In practice,

urethritis is not a very useful term when referring to urinary tract infections; females often don't notice urinary tract infections if they are limited to the urethra. And a male experiencing urethritis could be suffering from a sexually transmitted infection (covered later in the chapter).

▶ Signs and Symptoms

Cystitis is a disease of sudden onset. Symptoms include pain in the pubic area, frequent urges to urinate even when the bladder is empty, and burning pain accompanying urination (called *dysuria*). The urine can be cloudy due to the presence of bacteria and white blood cells. It may have an orange tinge from the presence of red blood cells (*hematuria*). Fever and nausea are frequently present. If back pain is present, it is an indication that the kidneys may also be involved (pyelonephritis). Inadequately treated pyelonephritis may result in septicemia, especially in the immunocompromised. If only the bladder is involved, the condition is sometimes called acute uncomplicated UTI.

▶ Causative Agents

In 95% of cystitis and pyelonephritis cases, the cause is bacteria that are normal biota in the gastrointestinal tract. *Escherichia coli* is by far the most common of these. *Staphylococcus saprophyticus* and *Proteus mirabilis* are also common culprits. These last two are only referenced in **Disease Table 23.1** following the discussion of *E. coli*.

The *E. coli* species that cause UTIs are ones that exist as normal biota in the gastrointestinal tract. They are not the ones that cause diarrhea and other digestive tract diseases.

▶ Pathogenesis and Virulence Factors

E. coli secure themselves in the gastrointestinal tract using specific adhesins on the ends of long fimbriae. They can also use these adhesins to attach to slightly different chemicals present on the epithelial lining of the urinary tract. Many *E. coli* that cause disease in the urinary tract also have different fimbriae with adhesins that recognize chemicals only present on cells lining the ureters and kidney. These *E. coli* exhibit a motility that allows them to travel along mucosal surfaces, so they seem to be specially adapted to ascending the urinary system. Their presence in these normally sterile areas induces an inflammatory response that we experience as symptoms and that may lead to scarring in the ureters and kidneys.

▶ Transmission and Epidemiology

Community-acquired UTIs are nearly always "transmitted" *not* from one person to another but from one organ system to another, namely from the GI tract to the urinary system. They are much more common in women than in men because of the shorter length of the female urethra and because of the nearness of the female urethral opening to the anus (see figure 23.3). Many women experience what have been referred to as "recurrent urinary tract infections," although it is now known that some *E. coli* can invade the deeper tissue of the urinary tract and therefore avoid being destroyed by antibiotics. They can emerge later to cause symptoms again. It is not clear how many "recurrent" infections are actually infections that reactivate in this way.

Note that urinary tract infections are also the most common of nosocomial infections. Patients of both sexes who have urinary catheters are susceptible to infections with a variety of microorganisms, not just the three mentioned here.

▶ Prevention

There are currently two vaccines in clinical trials for this infection. But for now, prevention of all UTIs relies on more basic practices, such as emptying the bladder frequently and (for females) wiping from front to back after a bowel movement. People who are predisposed to UTIs often drink cranberry juice to prevent the disease. Scientists have found that there are multiple compounds in the juice that help to discourage the attachment of *E. coli* to urinary epithelium.

▶ Treatment

Ampicillin, amoxicillin, or sulfa drugs such as trimethoprim-sulfamethoxazole are most often used for UTIs of various etiologies. Often another nonantibiotic drug called phenazopyridine (Pyridium) is administered simultaneously. This drug relieves the very uncomfortable symptoms of burning and urgency. A large percentage of *E. coli* strains is resistant to penicillin derivatives, so these should be avoided. Also, a new strain of *E. coli* (ST131) has arisen which is highly virulent, and more troubling, resistant to multiple antibiotics. Medical professionals are ringing alarm bells about this strain saying that if it acquires resistance to one more class of antibiotics it will become virtually untreatable **(Disease Table 23.1).**

Leptospirosis

This infection is a zoonosis associated with wild animals and domesticated animals. It can affect the kidneys, liver, brain, and eyes. It is considered in this section because it can have its major effects on the kidneys and because its presence in animal urinary tracts causes it to be shed into the environment through animal urine.

▶ Signs and Symptoms

Leptospirosis has two phases. During the early, or leptospiremic, phase, the pathogen appears in the blood and cerebrospinal fluid. Symptoms are sudden high fever, chills, headache, muscle aches, conjunctivitis, and vomiting. During the second phase (called the immune phase), the blood infection is cleared by natural defenses. This period is marked by milder fever; headache due to leptospiral meningitis; and *Weil's syndrome*, a cluster of symptoms characterized by kidney invasion, hepatic disease, jaundice, anemia, and neurological disturbances. Long-term disability and even death can result from damage to the kidneys and liver, but they occur primarily with the most virulent strains and in elderly persons.

Disease Table 23.1 Urinary Tract Infections (Cystitis, Pyelonephritis)

	Escherichia coli	*Staphylococcus saprophyticus*	*Proteus mirabilis*
Causative Organism(s)			
Most Common Modes of Transmission	Endogenous transfer from GI tract (opportunism)	Opportunism	Opportunism
Virulence Factors	Adhesins, motility	–	Urease enzyme, leads to kidney stone formation
Culture/Diagnosis	Often "bacterial infection" diagnosed on basis of increased white cells in urinalysis; if culture performed, bacteria may or may not be identified to species level	Often "bacterial infection" diagnosed on basis of increased white cells in urinalysis; if culture performed, bacteria may or may not be identified to species level	Often "bacterial infection" diagnosed on basis of increased white cells in urinalysis; if culture performed, bacteria may or may not be identified to species level
Prevention	Vaccine may be available soon; hygiene practices	Hygiene practices	Hygiene practices
Treatment	Cephalosporins: check for resistance	Ampicillin, amoxicillin, trimethoprim-sulfamethoxazole	Ampicillin or cephalosporins
Distinctive Features	–	–	Kidney stones and severe pain may ensue

The dedicated genetics professor was diagnosed with leptospirosis, which, as you know, is usually transmitted by direct or indirect contact with animal urine. It is considered the most common zoonosis in the United States. Animals most commonly infected are cows, sheep, deer, and pigs.

The bacterium is a spirochete that probably enters the bloodstream through minute breaks in the skin.

- People in certain occupations are more likely than others to come in contact with *Leptospira*. What occupations might these be?

- The diagnostic test considered definitive for leptospirosis is the IgM ELISA. Why IgM and not IgG?

▶ Causative Agent

Leptospires are typical spirochete bacteria marked by tight, regular, individual coils with a bend or hook at one or both ends **(figure 23.4)**. *Leptospira interrogans* (lep"-toh-spy'-rah in-terr'-oh-ganz) is the species that causes leptospirosis in humans and animals. There are nearly 200 different serotypes of this species distributed among various animal groups, which accounts for extreme variations in the disease manifestations in humans.

▶ Pathogenesis and Virulence Factors

In 2003, Chinese scientists sequenced the entire genome of this bacterium and found a series of genes that code for virulence factors such as adhesins and invasion proteins. Because it appears that the bacterium evolved from its close relatives, which are free-living and cause no disease, finding out how the bacterium acquired these genes will be useful in understanding its pathogenesis.

▶ Transmission and Epidemiology

Leptospirosis is a zoonosis, affecting wild animals such as rodents, skunks, raccoons, and foxes and some domesticated animals, particularly horses, dogs, cattle, and pigs. It is found throughout the world, although it is more common in the tropics. It is an occupational hazard of people who work with animals or in the outdoors. Leptospires shed in the urine of an infected animal can survive for several months in neutral or alkaline soil or water. Infection occurs almost entirely through contact of skin abrasions or mucous membranes with animal urine or some environmental source containing urine. In 1998, dozens of athletes competing in the swimming phase of a triathlon in Illinois contracted leptospirosis from the water. In late 2009, the Philippines experienced a major outbreak after a series of typhoons flooded the country. At one point, 350 new cases a day were diagnosed. The disease is not transmissible person to person.

▶ Prevention

The new DNA sequence data should reveal new targets for vaccines that will be more broadly useful. For now, the best prevention is to wear protective footwear and clothing and to avoid swimming and wading in natural water sources that are frequented by livestock.

▶ Treatment

Early treatment with amoxicillin or doxycycline rapidly reduces symptoms and shortens the course of disease, but delayed therapy is less effective. Other spirochete diseases, such as syphilis (described later), exhibit this same pattern of being susceptible to antibiotics early in the infection but less so later.

Disease Table 23.2 Leptospirosis

Causative Organism(s)	*Leptospira interrogans*
Most Common Modes of Transmission	Vehicle—contaminated soil or water
Virulence Factors	Adhesins? Invasion proteins?
Culture/Diagnosis	Slide agglutination test of patient's blood for antibodies
Prevention	Avoiding contaminated vehicles
Treatment	Doxycycline, amoxicillin

Figure 23.4 *Leptospira interrogans*, **the agent of leptospirosis.**   Note the curved hook at the ends of the spirochete.

Hook

Urinary Schistosomiasis

In chapter 22, we talked about schistosomiasis, because one of its two distinct disease manifestations occurs in the liver and spleen, both parts of the digestive system. One particular species of the trematode (helminth) lodges in the blood vessels of the bladder. This may or may not result in symptoms. Alternatively, blood in the urine and, eventually, bladder obstruction can occur.

▶ Signs and Symptoms

As with the other forms of schistosomiasis, the first symptoms of infestation are itchiness in the area where the worm enters the body, followed by fever, chills, diarrhea, and cough. Urinary tract symptoms occur at a later date. Remember that adult flukes can live for many years and, by eluding the immune defenses, cause chronic infection.

▶ Causative Agent

The urinary manifestations occur if a host is infected with a particular species of schistosome, *Schistosoma haematobium*. It is found throughout Africa, the Caribbean, and the Middle East. (*S. mansoni* and *S. japonicum* are the species responsible for liver manifestations.) *Schistosomes* are trematodes, or flukes (illustrated in figure 22.29). Humans are the definitive hosts for schistosomes, and snails are the intermediate hosts.

▶ Pathogenesis and Virulence Factors

Like the other species, *S. haematobium* is able to invade intact skin and attach to vascular endothelium. It engages in the same antigenic cloaking behavior as the other two species. The disease manifestations occur when the eggs in the bladder induce a massive granulomatous response that leads to leakage in the blood vessels and blood in the urine. Significant portions of the bladder eventually can be filled with granulomatous tissue and scar tissue. Function of the bladder is decreased or halted altogether. Chronic infection with *S. haematobium* can also lead to bladder cancer.

▶ Transmission and Epidemiology

The life cycle of the schistosome is described completely in chapter 22. After the worms pass into small blood and lymphatic vessels, they are carried to the liver. Eventually *S. haematobium* enters the venous plexus of the bladder. While attached to these intravascular sites, the worms feed upon blood, and the female lays eggs that are eventually voided in urine. The appropriate snail vector does not exist in the United States, so cases found there are virtually all imported.

▶ Culture and Diagnosis

Diagnosis depends on identifying the eggs in urine.

▶ Prevention and Treatment

The cycle of infection cannot be broken as long as people are exposed to untreated sewage in their environment. It is quite common for people to be cured and then to be reinfected because their village has no sewage treatment. A vaccine would provide widespread control of the disease, but so far none is licensed. More than one vaccine is in development, however.

Praziquantel is the drug treatment of choice and is quite effective at eliminating the worms.

Disease Table 23.3 Urinary Schistosomiasis

Causative Organism(s)	*Schistosoma haematobium*
Most Common Modes of Transmission	Vehicle (contaminated water)
Virulence Factors	Antigenic "cloaking," induction of granulomatous response
Culture/Diagnosis	Identification of eggs in urine
Prevention	Avoiding contaminated vehicles
Treatment	Praziquantel

23.3 Learning Outcomes—Can You ...

4. ... list the possible causative agents, modes of transmission, virulence factors, diagnostic techniques, and prevention/treatment for each type of urinary tract infection (including leptospirosis and schistosomiasis)?

23.4 Reproductive Tract Diseases Caused by Microorganisms

We saw earlier that reproductive tract diseases in men almost always involve the urinary tract as well, and this is sometimes but not always the case with women. Note that although many of the infectious diseases of the reproductive tract are transmitted through sexual contact, not all of them are.

We begin this section with a discussion of infections that are symptomatic primarily in women: *vaginitis* and *vaginosis*. Men may also harbor these infections with or without symptoms. We next consider three broad categories of **sexually transmitted diseases (STDs):** *discharge diseases* in which increased fluid is released in male and female reproductive tracts; *ulcer diseases* in which microbes cause distinct open lesions; and the *wart diseases*. The section concludes with a neonatal disease caused by group B *Streptococcus* colonization.

Vaginitis and Vaginosis

▶ Signs and Symptoms

Vaginitis, an inflammation of the vagina, is a condition characterized by some degree of vaginal itching, depending on the etiologic agent. Symptoms may also include burning, and sometimes a discharge, which may take different forms as well. From the name, it is obvious that vaginitis only affects women, but most of the agents can also colonize the male reproductive tract.

▶ Causative Agents

The most common cause of vaginitis is *Candida albicans*. The vaginal condition caused by this fungus is known as a *yeast infection*. Most women experience this condition one or multiple times during their lives. Other causes can be bacterial, as in the case of *Gardnerella,* or even protozoal, as in the case of *Trichomonas.* We describe each of these agents here.

Candida albicans

C. albicans is a dimorphic fungus that is normal biota in from 50% to 100% of humans, living in low numbers on many mucosal surfaces such as the mouth, gastrointestinal tract, vagina, and so on. The vaginal condition it causes is often called vulvovaginal candidiasis. The yeast is easily detectable on a wet prep or a Gram stain of material obtained during a pelvic exam **(figure 23.5).** The presence of pseudohyphae in the smear is a clear indication that the yeast is growing rapidly and causing a yeast infection.

▶ Pathogenesis and Virulence Factors

The fungus grows in thick curdlike colonies on the walls of the vagina. The colony debris contributes to a white vaginal discharge. In otherwise healthy people, the fungus is not invasive and limits itself to this surface infection. Please note, however, that *Candida* infections of the bloodstream do occur and they have high mortality rates. They do not normally stem from vaginal infections with the fungus, however, but are seen most frequently in hospitalized patients.

▶ Transmission and Epidemiology

Vaginal infections with this organism are nearly always opportunistic. Disruptions of the normal bacterial biota or even minor damage to the mucosal epithelium in the vagina can lead to overgrowth by this fungus. Disruptions may be mechanical, such as wearing very tight pants, or they may be chemical, as when broad-spectrum antibiotics taken for some other purpose temporarily diminish the vaginal bacterial population. Diabetics and pregnant women are also predisposed to vaginal yeast overgrowths. Some women are prone to this condition during menstruation.

Figure 23.5 Gram stain of *Candida albicans* in a vaginal smear.

It is possible to transmit this yeast through sexual contact, especially if a woman is experiencing an overgrowth of it. The recipient's immune system may well subdue the yeast so that it acts as normal biota in them. But the yeast may be passed back to the original partner during further sexual contact after treatment. By that time, the circumstances that led to it becoming dominant in the vagina may have returned to normal and its growth would be limited by the normal bacterial biota. So the sexual route of transmission is difficult to assess. Nevertheless, it is recommended that a patient's sexual partner also be treated to short-circuit the possibility of retransmission. The important thing to remember is that *Candida* is an opportunistic fungus.

Women with HIV infection experience frequently recurring yeast infections. Also, a small percentage of women with no underlying immune disease experience chronic or recurrent vaginal infection with *Candida* for reasons that are not clear.

▶ Prevention and Treatment

No vaccine is available for *C. albicans.* Topical and oral azole drugs are used to treat vaginal candidiasis, and some of them are now available over the counter. If infections recur frequently or fail to resolve, it is important to see a physician for evaluation.

Gardnerella Species

The bacterium *Gardnerella* is associated with a particularly common condition in women in their childbearing years. This condition is usually called vaginosis rather than vaginitis because it doesn't appear to induce inflammation in the vagina. It is also known as BV, or bacterial vaginosis. Despite the absence of an inflammatory response, a vaginal discharge is associated with the condition, which is said to have a very fishy odor, especially after sex. Itching is common. But it is also true that many women have this condition with no noticeable symptoms.

Vaginosis is most likely a result of a shift from a predominance of "good bacteria" (lactobacilli) in the vagina to a predominance of "bad bacteria," and one of those is *Gardnerella vaginalis.* This genus of bacteria is aerotolerant and gram-positive, although in a Gram stain it usually appears gram-negative. Probably a mixed infection leads to the condition, however. Anaerobic streptococci and other bacteria, particularly a genus known as *Mobiluncus,* that are normally found in low numbers in a healthy vagina can also often be found in high numbers in this condition. The often-mentioned fishy odor comes from the metabolic by-products of anaerobic metabolism by these bacteria.

▶ Pathogenesis and Virulence Factors

The mechanism of damage in this disease is not well understood. But some of the outcomes are. Besides the symptoms just mentioned, vaginosis can lead to complications such as pelvic inflammatory disease (PID; to be discussed later in the chapter), infertility, and more rarely, ectopic pregnancies. Babies born to some mothers with vaginosis have low birth weights.

▶ Transmission and Epidemiology

This mixed infection is not considered to be sexually transmitted, although women who have never had sex rarely develop the condition. It is very common in sexually active women. It may be that the condition is associated with sex but not transmitted by it. This situation could occur if the act of penetration or the presence of semen (or saliva) causes changes in the vaginal epithelium, or in the vaginal biota. We do not know exactly what causes the increased numbers of *Gardnerella* and other normally rare biota. The low pH typical of the vagina is usually higher in vaginosis. It is not clear whether this causes or is caused by the change in bacterial biota.

▶ Culture and Diagnosis

The condition can be diagnosed by a variety of methods. Sometimes a simple stain of vaginal secretions is used to examine sloughed vaginal epithelial cells. In vaginosis, some cells will appear to be nearly covered with adherent bacteria. In normal times, vaginal epithelial cells are sparsely covered with bacteria. These cells are called clue cells and are a helpful diagnostic indicator **(figure 23.6)**. They can also be found on Pap smears.

▶ Prevention and Treatment

No known prevention exists. Asymptomatic cases are generally not treated. Women who find the condition uncomfortable or who are planning on becoming pregnant should be treated. Women who use intrauterine devices (IUDs) for contraception should also be treated because IUDs can provide a passageway for the bacteria to gain access to the upper reproductive tract. The usual treatment is oral or topical metronidazole or clindamycin.

Trichomonas vaginalis

Trichomonads are small, pear-shaped protozoa with four anterior flagella and an undulating membrane **(figure 23.7)**. *Trichomonas vaginalis* seems to cause asymptomatic infections in approximately 50% of females and males, despite its species name. Trichomonads are considered asymptomatic infectious agents rather than normal biota because of evidence that some people experience long-term negative effects. Even though *Trichomonas* is a protozoan, it has no cyst form and it does not survive long out of the host.

▶ Pathogenesis and Virulence Factors

Many cases are asymptomatic, and men seldom have symptoms. Women often have vaginitis symptoms, which can include a white to green frothy discharge. Chronic infection can make a person more susceptible to other infections, including HIV. Also, women who become infected during pregnancy are predisposed to premature labor and low-birth-weight infants. Chronic infection may also lead to infertility.

▶ Transmission and Epidemiology

Because *Trichomonas* is common biota in so many people, it is easily transmitted through sexual contact. It has been called the most common nonviral sexually transmitted infection. It does not appear to undergo opportunistic shifts within its host (that is, to become symptomatic under certain conditions), but rather, the protozoan causes symptoms when transmitted to a noncarrier. Some debate exists over whether the protozoan can be transmitted through communal bathing, public facilities, and from mother to child, but if this type of transmission happens, it is only rarely.

Figure 23.6 Clue cell in bacterial vaginosis.
These epithelial cells came from a pelvic exam. The cell in the middle has a large number of bacteria attached to it.

Figure 23.7 *Trichomonas vaginalis.*

Disease Table 23.4 Vaginitis/Vaginosis

Causative Organism(s)	*Candida albicans*	Mixed infection, usually including *Gardnerella*	*Trichomonas vaginalis*
Most Common Modes of Transmission	Opportunism	Opportunism?	Direct contact (STD)
Virulence Factors	–	–	–
Culture/Diagnosis	Wet prep or Gram stain	Visual exam of vagina, or clue cells seen in Pap smear or other smear	Protozoa seen on Pap smear or Gram stain
Prevention	–	–	Barrier use during intercourse
Treatment	Topical or oral azole drugs, some over-the-counter drugs	Metronidazole or clindamycin	Metronidazole, tinidazole
Distinctive Features	White curdlike discharge	Discharge may have fishy smell	Discharge may be greenish

▶ **Prevention and Treatment**

There is no vaccine for *Trichomonas*. The antiprotozoal drug metronidazole is the drug of choice, although some isolates are resistant to it **(Disease Table 23.4).**

Prostatitis

Prostatitis is an inflammation of the prostate gland (see figure 23.2). It can be acute or chronic. Acute prostatitis is virtually always caused by bacterial infection. The bacteria are usually normal biota from the intestinal tract or may have caused a previous urinary tract infection. Chronic prostatitis is also often caused by bacteria. Researchers have found that chronic prostatitis, often unresponsive to antibiotic treatment, can be caused by mixed biofilms of bacteria in the prostate. Some forms of chronic prostatitis have no known microbial cause, though many infectious disease specialists feel that one or more bacteria are involved, but they are simply not culturable with current techniques.

The symptoms of prostatitis are pain in the pelvic area, lower back, or genital area; frequent urge to urinate; blood in the urine; and/or painful ejaculation. Acute prostatitis is accompanied by fever and chills and flulike symptoms. Patients appear to be quite ill with the acute form of the disease.

Treatment involves antibiotics when bacteria are indicated. Also, muscle relaxers or drugs called alpha blockers, which relax the neck of the bladder, may be prescribed. Prostatitis is distinct from prostate cancer, a condition that may be associated with viral infection, according to recent research.

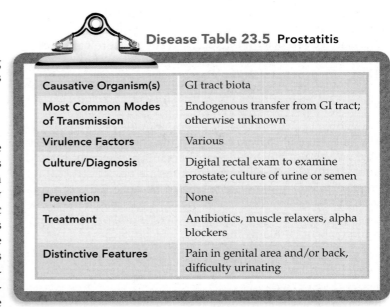

Disease Table 23.5 Prostatitis

Causative Organism(s)	GI tract biota
Most Common Modes of Transmission	Endogenous transfer from GI tract; otherwise unknown
Virulence Factors	Various
Culture/Diagnosis	Digital rectal exam to examine prostate; culture of urine or semen
Prevention	None
Treatment	Antibiotics, muscle relaxers, alpha blockers
Distinctive Features	Pain in genital area and/or back, difficulty urinating

Discharge Diseases with Major Manifestation in the Genitourinary Tract

Discharge diseases are those in which the infectious agent causes an increase in fluid discharge in the male and female reproductive tracts. Examples are trichomoniasis, gonorrhea, and *Chlamydia* infection. The causative agents are transferred to new hosts when the fluids in which they live contact the mucosal surfaces of the receiving partner. Trichomoniasis has been described in the preceding section because its disease manifestations are considered to be a vaginitis. In this section, we cover the other two major discharge diseases: gonorrhea and *Chlamydia* infection.

A Note About HIV and Hepatitis B and C

This chapter is about diseases *whose major (presenting) symptoms occur in the genitourinary tract.* But some sexually transmitted diseases do not have their major symptoms in this system. HIV and hepatitis B and C can all be transmitted in several ways, one of them being through sexual contact. HIV is considered in chapter 20 because its major symptoms occur in the cardiovascular and lymphatic systems. Because the major disease manifestations of hepatitis B and C occur in the gastrointestinal tract, these diseases are discussed in chapter 22. Anyone diagnosed with any sexually transmitted disease should also be tested for HIV.

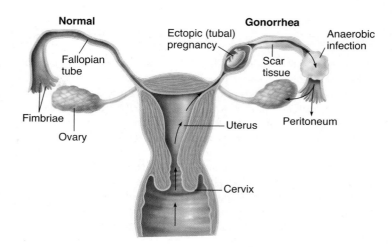

Figure 23.8 Invasive gonorrhea in women. *(Left)* Normal state. *(Right)* In ascending gonorrhea, the gonococcus is carried from the cervical opening up through the uterus and into the fallopian tubes. Pelvic inflammatory disease (PID) is a serious complication that can lead to scarring in the fallopian tubes, ectopic pregnancies, and mixed anaerobic infections.

Gonorrhea

Gonorrhea has been known as a sexually transmitted disease since ancient times. Its name originated with the Greek physician Claudius Galen, who thought that it was caused by an excess flow of semen. For a fairly long period in history, gonorrhea was confused with syphilis. Later, microbiologists went on to cultivate *N. gonorrhoeae,* also known as the **gonococcus,** and to prove conclusively that it alone was the etiologic agent of gonorrhea.

▶ Signs and Symptoms

In the male, infection of the urethra elicits urethritis, painful urination and a yellowish discharge, although a relatively large number of cases are asymptomatic. In most cases, infection is limited to the distal urogenital tract, but it can occasionally spread from the urethra to the prostate gland and epididymis (refer to figure 23.2). Scar tissue formed in the spermatic ducts during healing of an invasive infection can render a man infertile. This outcome is becoming increasingly rare with improved diagnosis and treatment regimens.

In the female, it is likely that both the urinary and genital tracts will be infected during sexual intercourse. A mucopurulent (containing mucus and pus) or bloody vaginal discharge occurs in about half of the cases, along with painful urination if the urethra is affected. Major complications occur when the infection ascends from the vagina and cervix to higher reproductive structures such as the uterus and fallopian tubes **(figure 23.8).** One disease resulting from this progression is **salpingitis** (sal"-pin-jy'-tis). This inflammation of the fallopian tubes may be isolated, or it may also include inflammation of other parts of the upper reproductive tract, termed pelvic inflammatory disease (PID). It is not unusual for the microbe that initiates PID to become involved in mixed infections with anaerobic bacteria. The buildup of scar tissue from PID can block the fallopian tubes, causing sterility or ectopic pregnancies **(Insight 23.1).**

Serious consequences of gonorrhea can occur outside of the reproductive tract. In a small number of cases, the gonococcus enters the bloodstream and is disseminated to the joints and skin. Involvement of the wrist and ankle can lead to chronic arthritis and a painful, sporadic, papular rash on the limbs. Rare complications of gonococcal bacteremia are meningitis and endocarditis.

Children born to gonococcus carriers are also in danger of being infected as they pass through the birth canal. Because of the potential harm to the fetus, physicians usually screen pregnant mothers for its presence. Gonococcal eye infections are very serious and often result in keratitis, ophthalmia neonatorum, and even blindness **(figure 23.9).** A universal precaution to prevent such complications is the

Figure 23.9 Gonococcal ophthalmia neonatorum in a week-old infant. The infection is marked by intense inflammation and edema; if allowed to progress, it causes damage that can lead to blindness. Fortunately, this infection is completely preventable and treatable.

INSIGHT 23.1   Pelvic Inflammatory Disease and Infertility

The National Center for Health Statistics estimates that more than 6 million women in the United States have impaired fertility. There are many different reasons for infertility, but the leading cause is pelvic inflammatory disease, or PID. PID is caused by infection of the upper reproductive structures in women, namely the uterus, fallopian tubes, and ovaries. These organs have no normal biota, and when bacteria from the vagina are transported higher in the tract, they start a chain of inflammatory events that may or may not be noticeable to the patient. The inflammation can be acute, resulting in pain, abnormal vaginal discharge, fever, and nausea, or it can be chronic, with less noticeable symptoms. In acute cases, women usually seek care; in some ways, these can be considered the lucky ones. If the inflammation is curbed at an early stage by using antibiotics to kill the bacteria, chances are better that the long-term sequelae of PID can be avoided.

The most notable long-term consequence is tubal infertility, caused by the repair step of inflammation. Inflammatory repair processes, especially in the fallopian tubes, can lead to the deposition of scar tissue that narrows the lumen in the tubes, in some cases closing them off completely. But if the lumen is only narrowed, fertilization may occur. A fertilized egg could then be unable to travel through the tube and implant in the uterine wall. In some cases, fertilized eggs implant in the tube walls or even leave the fallopian tubes and implant elsewhere in the abdominal cavity. Both of these situations are known as ectopic pregnancies. Women with a history of PID have a seven- to ten-fold greater chance of experiencing an ectopic pregnancy than other women. Ectopic pregnancy is a life-threatening situation. An embryo growing in the tube usually causes the tube to rupture in about 12 weeks, and an embryo in the abdominal cavity can cause the same complication as a tumor. Surgical intervention is usually required in either case to eliminate the embryo and save the woman's life.

Chlamydia infection is the leading cause of PID, followed closely by *N. gonorrhoeae* infection. But other bacteria, perhaps also including normal biota of the reproductive tract, can also cause PID if they are traumatically introduced into the uterus. Intercourse, tampon usage, the use of an intrauterine contraceptive device, and even douching can encourage the transmission of bacteria into the upper genital tract. (In addition to being a risk factor for PID, douching can also temporarily ease the symptoms of a reproductive tract infection, which could result in dangerous delays in seeking treatment.)

With the relatively high rates of infertility in the developed world, the message needs to be loud and clear: PID is a preventable condition. Women who suspect for any reason that they may have a reproductive tract infection should always seek diagnosis and treatment from health care professionals.

---

use of antibiotic eyedrops for newborn babies. The pathogen may also infect the pharynx and respiratory tract of neonates. Finding gonorrhea in children other than neonates is strong evidence of sexual abuse by infected adults, and it calls for child welfare consultation along with thorough bacteriologic analysis.

► Causative Agent

N. gonorrhoeae is a pyogenic gram-negative diplococcus. It appears as pairs of kidney bean–shaped bacteria, with their flat sides touching (figure 23.10).

► Pathogenesis and Virulence Factors

Successful attachment is key to the organism's ability to cause disease. Gonococci use specific chemicals on the tips of fimbriae to anchor themselves to mucosal epithelial cells. They only attach to nonciliated cells of the urethra and the cervix, for example. Once the bacterium attaches, it invades the cells and multiplies on the basement membrane.

The fimbriae may also play a role in slowing down effective immunity. The fimbrial proteins are controlled by genes that can be turned on or off, depending on the bacterium's situation. This phenotypic change is called phase variation. In addition, the genes can rearrange themselves to put together fimbriae of different configurations. This antigenic variation confuses the body's immune system. Antibodies that previously recognized fimbrial proteins may not recognize them once they are rearranged.

The gonococcus also possesses an enzyme called IgA protease, which can cleave IgA molecules stationed on mucosal surfaces. In addition, it pinches off pieces of its outer membrane. These "blebs," containing endotoxin, probably play a role in pathogenesis because they can stimulate portions of the nonspecific defense response, resulting in localized damage.

Figure 23.10 Gram stain of urethral pus from a male patient with gonorrhea (1,000×).   Note the intracellular (phagocytosed) gram-negative diplococci (arranged side-to-side) in polymorphonuclear leukocytes (neutrophils).

▶ Transmission and Epidemiology

N. gonorrhoeae does not survive more than 1 or 2 hours on fomites and is most infectious when transferred to a suitable mucous membrane. Except for neonatal infections, the gonococcus spreads through some form of sexual contact. The pathogen requires an appropriate portal of entry that is genital or extragenital (rectum, eye, or throat).

Gonorrhea is a strictly human infection that occurs worldwide and ranks among the most common sexually transmitted diseases. Although about 350,000 cases are reported in the United States each year, it is estimated that the actual incidence is much higher—in the millions if one counts asymptomatic infections. Please refer to **figure 23.11** and also the Note About STD Statistics on this page.

It is important to consider the reservoir of asymptomatic males and females when discussing the transmission of the infection. Because approximately 10% of infected males and 50% of infected females experience no symptoms, it is often spread unknowingly.

▶ Culture and Diagnosis

In males, it is easy to diagnose this disease; a Gram stain of urethral discharge is diagnostic. The normal biota of the male urethra is so sparse that it is easy to see the diplococcus inside of neutrophils (see figure 23.10). In females, other methods, such as ELISA or PCR tests, are called for. Alternatively, the bacterium can be cultured on Thayer-Martin agar, a rich chocolate agar base with added antibiotics that inhibit competing bacteria.

N. gonorrhoeae grows best in an atmosphere containing increased CO_2. Because *Neisseria* is so fragile, it is best to inoculate it onto media directly from the patient rather than using a transport tube. Gonococci produce catalase, enzymes for fermenting various carbohydrates, and the enzyme cytochrome oxidase that can be used for identification as well. Gonorrhea is a reportable disease.

▶ Prevention

Currently, no vaccine is available for gonorrhea, although finding one is a priority for government health agencies. The development of a vaccine is hampered by the fact that no good animal model exists for the disease. Using condoms is an effective way to avoid transmission of this and other discharge diseases.

▶ Treatment

The CDC runs a program called the Gonococcal Isolate Surveillance Project (GISP) to monitor the occurrence of antibiotic resistance in *N. gonorrhoeae*. Penicillin was traditionally the drug of choice, but a large percentage of isolates now are able to produce penicillinase. Others are tetracycline resistant. As alternatives, practitioners have been using quinolones (like ciprofloxacin) or cephalosporins. But there is constantly rising resistance to quinolones, as well. This development highlights the need for practitioners to be aware of local resistance patterns before prescribing antibiotics for gonorrhea. The GISP provides this local data. Every month in 28 local STD clinics around the country, *N. gonorrhoeae* isolates from the first 25 males diagnosed with the infection are sent to regional testing labs and their antibiotic sensitivities are determined and the data are provided to the GISP program at the CDC.

Chlamydia

Genital chlamydial infection is the most common reportable infectious disease in the United States. Annually, more than 1 million cases are reported but the actual infection rate may be 5 to 7 times that number. The overall prevalence among young adults in the United States is 4%. It is at least two to three times as common as gonorrhea. The vast majority of cases are asymptomatic. When we consider the serious consequences that may follow *Chlamydia* infection, those facts are very disturbing.

▶ Signs and Symptoms

In males who experience *Chlamydia* symptoms, the bacterium causes an inflammation of the urethra (a condition formerly called *nongonococcal urethritis*). The symptoms

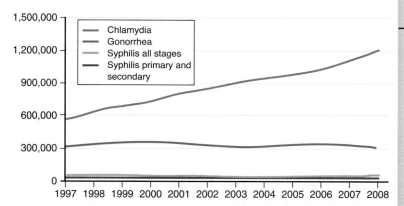

Figure 23.11 Cases of STDs reported by state health departments: United States, 1997–2008.

A Note About STD Statistics

It is difficult to compare the incidence of different STDs to one another, for several reasons. The first is that many, many infections are "silent," and therefore infected people don't access the health care system, and don't get counted. Of course, we know that many silent infections are actually causing damage that won't be noticed for years, and when it is, the original causative organism is almost never sought out. The second reason is that only some STDs are officially reportable to health authorities. *Chlamydia* infection and gonorrhea are, for example, but herpes and HPV are not (see table 13.10). In each section we will try to present accurate estimates of the prevalence and/or incidence of the diseases as we know them.

mimic gonorrhea, namely discharge and painful urination. Untreated infections may lead to epididymitis. Females who experience symptoms have cervicitis, a discharge, and often salpingitis. Pelvic inflammatory disease is a frequent sequela of female chlamydial infection. A woman is even more likely to experience PID as a result of a *Chlamydia* infection than as a result of gonorrhea. (The photo in figure 23.12 depicts *Chlamydia* bacteria adhering inside a fallopian tube.) Up to 75% of *Chlamydia* infections are asymptomatic, which puts women at risk for developing PID because they don't seek treatment for initial infections. The PID itself may be acute and painful, or it may be relatively asymptomatic, allowing damage to the upper reproductive tract to continue unchecked.

Certain strains of *C. trachomatis* can invade the lymphatic tissues, resulting in another condition called lymphogranuloma venereum. This condition is accompanied by headache, fever, and muscle aches. The lymph nodes near the lesion begin to fill with granuloma cells and become enlarged and tender. These "nodes" can cause long-term lymphatic obstruction that leads to chronic, deforming edema of the genitalia or anus. The disease is endemic to South America, Africa, and Asia but occasionally occurs in other parts of the world. Its incidence in the United States is about 500 cases per year.

Babies born to mothers with *Chlamydia* infections can develop eye infections and also pneumonia if they become infected during passage through the birth canal. Infant conjunctivitis caused by contact with maternal *Chlamydia* infection is the most prevalent form of conjunctivitis in the United States (100,000 cases per year). Antibiotic drops or ointment applied to newborns' eyes are chosen to eliminate both *Chlamydia* and *N. gonorrhoeae*.

▶ Causative Agent

C. trachomatis is a very small gram-negative bacterium. It lives inside host cells as an obligate intracellular parasite. All *Chlamydia* species alternate between two distinct stages: (1) a small, metabolically inactive infectious form called the elementary body, which is released by the infected host cell; and (2) a larger, noninfectious, actively dividing form called the reticulate body, which grows within the host cell vacuoles **(figure 23.12)**. Elementary bodies are tiny, dense spheres shielded by a rigid, impervious envelope that ensures survival outside the eukaryotic host cell. Studies of reticulate bodies indicate that they are "energy parasites," entirely lacking enzyme systems for synthesizing ATP, although they do possess ribosomes and mechanisms for synthesizing proteins, DNA, and RNA. Reticulate bodies ultimately become elementary bodies during their life cycle.

▶ Pathogenesis and Virulence Factors

Chlamydia's ability to grow intracellularly contributes to its virulence because it escapes certain aspects of the host's immune response. Also, the bacterium has a unique cell wall that apparently prevents the phagosome from fusing with the lysosome inside phagocytes. The presence of the bacteria inside cells causes the release of cytokines that provoke

Process Figure 23.12 The life cycle of *Chlamydia*.   ① The infectious stage, or elementary body (EB), is taken into phagocytic vesicles by the host cell. ② In the phagosome, each elementary body develops into a reticulate body (RB). ③ Reticulate bodies multiply by regular binary fission. ④ and ⑤ Mature RBs become reorganized into EBs. ⑥ Completed EBs are released from the host cell. Inset features a micrograph of *C. trachomatis* adhering to a fallopian tube (1,750×).

intense inflammation. This defensive response leads to most of the actual tissue damage in *Chlamydia* infection. Of course, the last step of inflammation is repair, which often results in scarring, as described in Insight 23.1. This can have disastrous effects on a narrow tube like the fallopian tube.

▶ Transmission and Epidemiology

The reservoir of pathogenic strains of *C. trachomatis* is the human body. The microbe shows an astoundingly broad distribution within the population. Adolescent women are more likely than older women to harbor the bacterium because it prefers to infect cells that are particularly prevalent on the adolescent cervix. It is transmitted through sexual contact and also vertically. Fifty percent of babies born to infected mothers will acquire conjunctivitis (more common) or pneumonia (less common).

▶ Culture and Diagnosis

Infection with this microorganism is usually detected initially using a rapid technique such as PCR or ELISA. Direct fluorescent antibody detection is also used. Serology is not always reliable. In addition, antibody to *Chlamydia* is very common in adults and often indicates past, not present, infection. Isolating the bacterium and growing it in cell culture is the best method for detecting this bacterium, but because it is time-consuming and expensive, it is performed only in cases where 100% accuracy is required—such as in rape or child abuse cases. A urine test is available, which has definite advantages for widespread screening, but it is slightly less accurate for females than males.

▶ Prevention

As yet, no vaccine exists for *Chlamydia.* Researchers have developed several types of experimental vaccines, including a DNA vaccine, but none has been approved for use to date. Avoiding contact with infected tissues and secretions through abstinence or barrier protection (condoms) is the only means of prevention.

▶ Treatment

Treatment for this infection relies on being aware of it, so part of the guidelines issued by the CDC is a recommendation for annual screening of young women for presence of the bacterium. It is also recommended that older women with some risk factor (new sexual partner, for instance) also be screened. If infection is found, treatment is usually with azithromycin, a macrolide antibiotic. Note that according to public health officials, many patients become reinfected soon after treatment; therefore, the recommendation is that patients be rechecked for *Chlamydia* infection 3 to 4 months after treatment. Repeated infections with *Chlamydia* increase the likelihood of PID and other serious sequelae **(Disease Table 23.6).**

Genital Ulcer Diseases

Three common infectious conditions can result in lesions on a person's genitals: syphilis, chancroid, and genital herpes. In this section, we consider each of these. One very important fact to remember about the ulcer diseases is that having one of them increases the chances of infection with HIV because of the open lesions.

Disease Table 23.6 Genital "Discharge" Diseases (in Addition to Vaginitis/Vaginosis)

	Gonorrhea	Chlamydia
Causative Organism(s)	*Neisseria gonorrhoeae*	*Chlamydia trachomatis*
Most Common Modes of Transmission	Direct contact (STD), also vertical	Direct contact (STD), vertical
Virulence Factors	Fimbrial adhesins, antigenic variation, IgA protease, membrane blebs/endotoxin	Intracellular growth resulting in avoiding immune system and cytokine release, unusual cell wall preventing phagolysosome fusion
Culture/Diagnosis	Gram stain in males, rapid tests (PCR, ELISA) for females, culture on Thayer-Martin agar	PCR or ELISA, can be followed by cell culture
Prevention	Avoid contact; condom use	Avoid contact; condom use
Treatment	Many strains resistant to various antibiotics; local and current guidelines must be consulted	Azithromycin, doxycycline, and follow-up to check for reinfection
Distinctive Features	Rare complications include arthritis, meningitis, endocarditis	More commonly asymptomatic than gonorrhea
Effects on Fetus	Eye infections, blindness	Eye infections, pneumonia

Syphilis

The origin of **syphilis**[1] is an obscure yet intriguing topic of speculation. The disease was first recognized at the close of the 15th century in Europe, a period coinciding with the return of Columbus from the West Indies. From this, some medical scholars have concluded that syphilis was introduced to Europe from the New World. However, a more probable explanation contends that the spirochete that causes the disease evolved from a related subspecies, perhaps an endemic bacterium already present in the Mediterranean basin. The combination of the immunologically naive population of Europe, the European wars, and sexual promiscuity set the stage for worldwide transmission of syphilis that continues to this day.

A disturbing chapter of syphilis history in the United States is worth noting here. Beginning in 1932, the U.S. government conducted a study called the Tuskegee Study of Untreated Syphilis in the Negro Male, which eventually involved 399 indigent African-American men living in the South. Infected men were recruited into the study, which sought to document the natural progression of the disease. These men were never told that they had syphilis and were never treated for it, even after penicillin was shown to be an effective cure. The study ended in 1972 after it became public. In 1997, President Bill Clinton issued a public apology on behalf of the U.S. government, and the government has paid millions of dollars in compensation to the victims and their heirs.

▶ Signs and Symptoms

Untreated syphilis is marked by distinct clinical stages designated as *primary, secondary,* and *tertiary syphilis.* The disease also has latent periods of varying duration during which it is quiescent. The spirochete appears in the lesions and blood during the primary and secondary stages and, thus, is transmissible at these times. During the early latency period between secondary and tertiary syphilis, it is also transmissible. Syphilis is largely nontransmissible during the "late latent" and tertiary stages. Symptoms of each of these stages and congenital syphilis are briefly described here.

▶ Primary Syphilis

The earliest indication of syphilis infection is the appearance of a hard **chancre** (shang'-ker) at the site of entry of the pathogen (see Disease Table 23.7 for photos of all three types of genital lesions). A chancre appears after an incubation period that varies from 9 days to 3 months. The chancre begins as a small, red, hard bump that enlarges and breaks down, leaving a shallow crater with firm margins. The base of the chancre beneath the encrusted surface swarms with spirochetes. Most chancres appear on the internal and external genitalia, but about 20% occur on the lips, oral cavity, nipples, fingers, or around the anus. Because these ulcers tend to be painless, they may escape notice, especially when they are on internal surfaces. Lymph nodes draining the affected region become

enlarged and firm, but systemic symptoms are absent at this point. The chancre heals spontaneously without scarring in 3 to 6 weeks, but the healing is deceptive because the spirochete has escaped into the circulation and is entering a period of tremendous activity.

▶ Secondary Syphilis

About 3 weeks to 6 months after the chancre heals, the secondary stage appears. By then, many systems of the body have been invaded and the signs and symptoms are more profuse and intense. Initial symptoms are fever, headache, and sore throat, followed by lymphadenopathy and a peculiar red or brown rash that breaks out on all skin surfaces, including the palms of the hands and the soles of the feet **(figure 23.13)**. A person's hair often falls out. Like the

(a)

(b)

Figure 23.13 Symptom of secondary syphilis. The skin rash in secondary syphilis can form on the trunk, arms, and even palms and soles (this latter location is particularly diagnostic). The rash does not hurt or itch and can persist for months.

---

1. The term *syphilis* first appeared in a poem entitled "Syphilis sive Morbus Gallicus" by Fracastorius (1530), about a mythical shepherd whose name eventually became synonymous with the disease from which he suffered.

chancre, the lesions contain viable spirochetes and disappear spontaneously in a few weeks. The major complications of this stage, occurring in the bones, hair follicles, joints, liver, eyes, and brain, can linger for months and years.

▶ Latency and Tertiary Syphilis

After resolution of secondary syphilis, about 30% of infections enter a highly varied latent period that can last for 20 years or longer. During latency, although antibodies to the bacterium are readily detected, the bacterium itself is not. The final stage of the disease, tertiary syphilis, is relatively rare today because of widespread use of antibiotics. But it is so damaging that it is important to recognize. By the time a patient reaches this phase, numerous pathologic complications occur in susceptible tissues and organs. Cardiovascular syphilis results from damage to the small arteries in the aortic wall. As the fibers in the wall weaken, the aorta is subject to distension and fatal rupture. The same pathologic process can damage the aortic valves, resulting in insufficiency and heart failure.

In one form of tertiary syphilis, painful swollen syphilitic tumors called **gummas** (goo-mahz′) develop in tissues such as the liver, skin, bone, and cartilage **(figure 23.14).** Gummas are usually benign and only occasionally lead to death, but they can impair function. Neurosyphilis can involve any part of the nervous system, but it shows particular affinity for the blood vessels in the brain, cranial nerves, and dorsal roots of the spinal cord. The diverse results include severe headaches, convulsions, atrophy of the optic nerve, blindness, dementia, and a sign called the Argyll-Robertson pupil—a condition caused by adhesions along the inner edge of the iris that fix the pupil's position into a small irregular circle.

▶ Congenital Syphilis

The syphilis bacterium can pass from a pregnant woman's circulation into the placenta and can be carried throughout the fetal tissues. An infection leading to congenital syphilis can occur in any of the three trimesters, but it is most common in the second and third. The pathogen inhibits fetal growth and disrupts critical periods of development with varied consequences, ranging from mild to the extremes of spontaneous miscarriage or stillbirth. Early congenital syphilis encompasses the period from birth to 2 years of age and is usually first detected 3 to 8 weeks after birth. Infants often demonstrate such signs as profuse nasal discharge **(figure 23.15a)**, skin eruptions, bone deformation, and nervous system abnormalities. The late form gives rise to an unusual assortment of problems in the bones, eyes, inner ear, and joints and causes the formation of Hutchinson's teeth **(figure 23.15b)**. The number of congenital syphilis cases is closely tied to the incidence in adults.

▶ Causative Agent

Treponema pallidum, a spirochete, is a thin, regularly coiled cell with a gram-negative cell wall. It is a strict parasite with complex growth requirements that necessitate cultivating it in living host cells. Most spirochete bacteria are nonpathogenic; *Treponema* and *Leptospira*, described earlier, are among the pathogens of this group.

Syphilis is a complicated disease to diagnose. Not only do the stages each mimic other diseases, but their appearance can

(a)

(b)

Figure 23.15 Congenital syphilis. **(a)** An early sign is snuffles, a profuse nasal discharge that obstructs breathing. **(b)** A common characteristic of late congenital syphilis is notched, barrel-shaped incisors (Hutchinson's teeth).

Figure 23.14 The pathology of late, or tertiary, syphilis. An ulcerating syphilis tumor, or gumma, appears on the nose of this patient. Other gummas can be internal.

also be so separated in time as to seem unrelated. The chancre and secondary lesions must be differentiated from bacterial, fungal, and parasitic infections; tumors; and even allergic reactions. Overlapping symptoms of sexually transmitted infections that the patient is concurrently experiencing, such as gonorrhea or *Chlamydia*, can further complicate diagnosis. The disease can be diagnosed using two different strategies: either by detecting the bacterium in patient lesions or by looking for antibodies in the patient's blood.

▶ Pathogenesis and Virulence Factors

Brought into direct contact with mucous membranes or abraded skin, *T. pallidum* binds avidly by its hooked tip to the epithelium **(figure 23.16)**. At the binding site, the spirochete multiplies and penetrates the capillaries nearby. Within a short time, it moves into the circulation, and the body is literally transformed into a large receptacle for incubating the pathogen. Virtually any tissue is a potential target.

The specific factor that accounts for the virulence of the syphilis spirochete appears to be outer membrane lipoproteins. These molecules appear to stimulate a strong inflammatory response, which is helpful in clearing the organism but can produce damage as well. *T. pallidum* produces no toxins and does not appear to kill cells directly. Studies have shown that, although phagocytes seem to act against it and several types of antitreponemal antibodies are formed, immune responses are unable to contain it. The primary lesion occurs when the spirochetes invade the spaces around arteries and stimulate an inflammatory response. Organs are damaged when granulomas form at these sites and block circulation.

▶ Transmission and Epidemiology

Humans are evidently the sole natural hosts and source of *T. pallidum*. The bacterium is extremely fastidious and sensitive and cannot survive for long outside the host, being rapidly destroyed by heat, drying, disinfectants, soap, high

oxygen tension, and pH changes. It survives a few minutes to hours when protected by body secretions and about 36 hours in stored blood. Research with human subjects has demonstrated that the risk of infection from an infected sexual partner is 12% to 30% per encounter. The bacterium can also be transmitted to the fetus in utero. Syphilis infection through blood transfusion or exposure to fomites is rare.

For centuries, syphilis was a common and devastating disease in the United States, so much so that major medical centers had "Departments of Syphilology." Its effect on social life was enormous. This effect diminished quickly when antibiotics were discovered. In the 20th and 21st centuries, syphilis, like other STDs, has experienced periodic increases during times of social disruption. Most cases tend to be concentrated in larger metropolitan areas among prostitutes, their contacts, and crack cocaine users. If you examine figure 23.11, you won't see much change in syphilis incidence. But since 2003, the rates have been increasing again in the United States. And syphilis continues to be a serious problem worldwide, especially in Africa and Asia. As mentioned previously, persons with syphilis often suffer concurrent infections with other STDs. Coinfection with the AIDS virus can be an especially deadly combination with a rapidly fatal course.

▶ Culture and Diagnosis

Syphilis can be detected in patients most rapidly by using dark-field microscopy of a suspected lesion. The lesions are gently squeezed or scraped to extract clear fluid. A wet mount is then observed for the characteristic size, shape, and motility of *T. pallidum* **(figure 23.17)**. A single negative test is

Figure 23.16 Electron micrograph of the syphilis spirochete attached to cells.

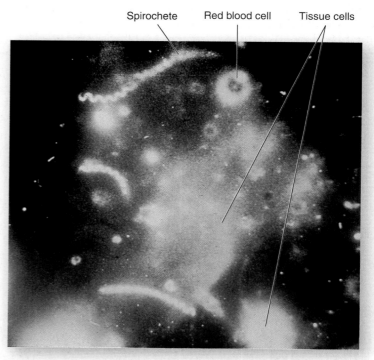

Figure 23.17 *Treponema pallidum* **from a syphilitic chancre, viewed with dark-field illumination.** Its tight spirals are highlighted next to human cells and tissue debris.

not enough to exclude syphilis because the patient may have removed the organisms by washing, so follow-up tests are recommended. Another microscopic test for discerning the spirochete directly in samples is direct immunofluorescence staining with monoclonal antibodies.

Very commonly, blood tests are used for this diagnosis. These tests are based on detection of antibody formed in response to *T. pallidum* infection. Two kinds of antibodies are formed: those that specifically react with treponemal antigens and, perhaps surprisingly, those that are formed against nontreponemal antigens. After infection with *T. pallidum*, the body abnormally produces antibodies to a natural constituent of human cells called *cardiolipin,* and the presence of these cardiolipin antibodies is also indicative of *T. pallidum* infection. Several different tests detect these antibodies, such as rapid plasma reagin (RPR), VDRL, Kolmer, and the Wasserman test.

More specific tests are available when considered necessary. One of these is the indirect immunofluorescent method called the FTA-ABS (fluorescent treponemal antibody absorbance) test. The test serum is first allowed to react with treponemal cells and then reacted with antihuman globulin antibody labeled with fluorescent dyes. If antibodies to the treponeme are present, the fluorescently labeled antibody will bind to the human antibody bound to the treponemal cells. The result is highly visible with a fluorescence microscope. A PCR test is available for syphilis, but its accuracy is dependent on the type of tissue being tested.

▶ Prevention

The core of an effective prevention program depends on detection and treatment of the sexual contacts of syphilitic patients. Public health departments and physicians are charged with the task of questioning patients and tracing their contacts. All individuals identified as being at risk, even if they show no signs of infection, are given immediate prophylactic penicillin in a single long-acting dose.

The barrier effect of a condom provides excellent protection during the primary phase. Protective immunity apparently does arise in humans, allowing the prospect of an effective immunization program in the future, although no vaccine exists currently.

▶ Treatment

Throughout most of history, the treatment for syphilis was a dose of mercury or even a "mercurial rub" applied to external lesions. In 1906, Paul Ehrlich discovered that a derivative of arsenic called salvarsan could be very effective. The fact that toxic compounds like mercury and arsenic were used to treat syphilis gives some indication of how dreaded the disease was and to what lengths people would go to rid themselves of it. In 1918, Paul A. O'Leary formalized the practice of infecting syphilis patients with malaria as a therapeutic approach. The patients were allowed to have a dozen or so episodes of high fever and then were cured of the malaria with quinine. This procedure proved to be effective in curing syphilis. ("Malaria therapy" has also been

investigated in recent years as an alternative treatment for HIV infection.)

Once penicillin became available, it replaced all other treatments, and penicillin G retains its status as a wonder drug in the treatment of all stages and forms of syphilis. It is given parenterally in large doses with benzathine or procaine. The goal is to maintain a blood level lethal to the spirochete for at least 7 days. Alternative drugs (tetracycline and erythromycin) are less effective, and they are indicated only if penicillin allergy has been documented. It is important that patients be monitored for successful clearance of the spirochete.

Chancroid

This ulcerative disease usually begins as a soft papule, or bump, at the point of contact. It develops into a "soft chancre" (in contrast to the hard syphilis chancre), which is very painful in men, but may be unnoticed in women (see Disease Table 23.7). Inguinal lymph nodes can become very swollen and tender.

Chancroid is caused by a **pleomorphic** gram-negative rod called *Haemophilus ducreyi.* Recent research indicates that a hemolysin (exotoxin) is important in the pathogenesis of chancroid disease. It is very common in the tropics and subtropics and is becoming more common in the United States. Chancroid is transmitted exclusively through direct contact, especially sexually. This disease is associated with prostitutes and poor hygiene; uncircumcised men seem to be more commonly infected than those who have been circumcised. People may carry this bacterium asymptomatically.

No vaccine exists. Prevention of chancroid is the same as for other sexually transmitted diseases: Avoid contact with infected tissues, either by abstaining from sexual contact or by proper use of barrier protection.

Antibiotics such as azithromycin and ceftriaxone are effective, but patients should be reexamined after a course of treatment to ensure that the bacterium has been eliminated.

Genital Herpes

Virtually everyone becomes infected with a herpesvirus at some time, because this large family of viruses can infect a wide range of host tissues. (We studied three herpesviruses in chapter 21 alone.) Genital herpes is caused by herpes simplex viruses (HSVs). Two types of HSV have been identified, HSV-1 and HSV-2. Other members of the herpes family are herpes zoster (causing chickenpox and shingles), cytomegalovirus (associated with congenital disease and also with HIV-associated disease), Epstein-Barr virus (causing infection of the lymphoid tissue as in infectious mononucleosis), and more recently identified viruses (herpesvirus-6, -7, and -8).

Genital herpes is much more common than most people think.

▶ Signs and Symptoms

Genital herpes infection has multiple presentations. After initial infection, a person may notice no symptoms.

Alternatively, herpes could cause the appearance of single or multiple vesicles on the genitalia, perineum, thigh, and buttocks. The vesicles are small and are filled with a clear fluid **(see Disease Table 23.7).** They are intensely painful to the touch. The appearance of lesions the first time you get them can be accompanied by malaise, anorexia, fever, and bilateral swelling and tenderness in the groin. Occasionally central nervous system symptoms such as meningitis or encephalitis can develop. Thus, we see that initial infection can either be completely asymptomatic or be serious enough to require hospitalization.

After recovery from initial infection, a person may have recurrent episodes of lesions. They are generally less severe than the original symptoms, although the whole gamut of possible severity is seen here as well. Some people never have recurrent lesions. Others have nearly constant outbreaks with little recovery time between them. On average, the number of recurrences is four or five a year. Their frequency tends to decrease over the course of years.

In most cases, patients remain asymptomatic or experience recurrent "surface" infections indefinitely. Very rarely, complications can occur. Every year, one or two persons per million with chronic herpes infections develop encephalitis. The virus disseminates along nerve pathways to the brain (although it can also infect the spinal cord). The effects on the central nervous system begin with headache and stiff neck and can progress to mental disturbances and coma. The fatality rate in untreated encephalitis cases is 70%, although treatment with acyclovir is effective. Patients with underlying immunodeficiency are more prone to severe, disseminated herpes infection than are immunocompetent patients. Of greatest concern are patients receiving organ grafts, cancer patients on immunosuppressive therapy, those with congenital immunodeficiencies, and AIDS patients. Recent data suggest that people with HSV-1 are more prone to Alzheimer's disease, particularly if they carry a particular variant of a particular gene. This is quite sobering when you think that approximately 80% of elderly people are HSV-1-positive, and up to 30% of them carry the gene variant. However, there is hope: Anti-herpes drugs may make a difference in Alzheimer's in these people.

▶ Herpes of the Newborn

Although HSV infections in healthy adults are annoying and unpleasant, only rarely are they life-threatening. However, in the neonate and the fetus **(figure 23.18),** HSV infections are very destructive and can be fatal. Most cases occur when infants are contaminated by the mother's reproductive tract immediately before or during birth, but they have also been traced to hand transmission from the mother's lesions to the baby. Because HSV-2 is more often associated with genital infections, it is more frequently involved; however, HSV-1 infection has similar complications. In infants whose disease is confined to the mouth, skin, or eyes, the mortality rate is 30%, but disease affecting the central nervous system has a 50% to 80% mortality rate.

Because of the danger of herpes to fetuses and newborns and also because of the increase in the number of cases of genital herpes, it is now standard procedure to screen preg-

Figure 23.18 Neonatal herpes simplex. This premature infant was born with the classic "cigarette burn" pattern of HSV infection. Babies can be born with the lesions or develop them 1 to 2 weeks after birth.

nant women for the herpesvirus early in their prenatal care. (Don't forget that most women who are infected do not even know it.) Pregnant women with a history of recurrent infections must be constantly monitored for any signs of viral shedding, especially in the last 4 weeks of pregnancy. If no evidence of recurrence is seen, vaginal birth is indicated, but any evidence of an outbreak at the time of delivery necessitates a cesarean section.

▶ Causative Agent

Both HSV-1 and HSV-2 can cause genital herpes if the virus contacts the genital epithelium, although HSV-1 is thought of as a virus that infects the oral mucosa, resulting in "cold sores" or "fever blisters" **(figure 23.19),** and HSV-2 is thought of as the genital virus. In reality, either virus can infect either region, depending on the type of contact.

HSV-1 and HSV-2 are DNA viruses with icosahedral capsids and envelopes containing glycoprotein spikes. Like other enveloped viruses, herpesviruses are prone to deactivation by organic solvents or detergents and are unstable outside the host's body.

Figure 23.19 Oral herpes infection. Tender itchy papules erupt around the mouth and progress to vesicles that burst, drain, and scab over. These sores and fluid are highly infectious and should not be touched.

▶ Pathogenesis and Virulence Factors

Herpesviruses have a tendency to become latent. The molecular basis of latency is not entirely clear. During latency, some type of signal causes most of the HSV genome not to be transcribed. This allows the virus to be maintained within cells of the nervous system between episodes. Recent research has found that microRNAs are responsible for the latency of HSV-1. It is further suggested that in some peripheral cells, viral replication takes place at a constant, slow rate, resulting in constant low-level shedding of the virus without lesion production.

HSV-2 (or HSV-1, if it has infected the genital region) usually becomes latent in the ganglion of the lumbosacral spinal nerve trunk **(figure 23.20)**. Reactivation of the virus can be triggered by a variety of stimuli, including stress, UV radiation (sunlight), injury, menstruation, or another microbial infection. At that point, the virus begins manufacturing large numbers of entire virions, which cause new lesions on the surface of the body served by the neuron, usually in the same site as previous lesions.

HSV-1 (or HSV-2 if it is in the oral region) behaves in a similar way, but it becomes latent in the trigeminal nerve, which has extensive innervations in the oral region.

▶ Transmission and Epidemiology

Herpes simplex infection occurs globally in all seasons and among all age groups. Because these viruses are relatively sensitive to the environment, transmission is primarily through direct exposure to secretions containing the virus. People with active lesions are the most significant source of infection, but studies indicate that genital herpes can be transmitted even when no lesions are present (due to the constant shedding just referred to).

As with all sexually transmitted diseases, many different figures are cited as to its prevalence in society. As you saw in the Note About STD Statistics in this chapter, the terminology associated with STDs can be confusing. Earlier in this chapter, you read that *Chlamydia* infection is the most common *reported* infectious disease in the United States. Elsewhere you might hear that gonorrhea is one of the most common reportable *STDs* in the United States. Both statements are true. It is also true that genital herpes is much more common than either of these diseases. Herpes, however, is not an officially *reportable* disease.

It is estimated that about 20% of American adults have genital herpes. That estimate would put the number of infected people in this country at more than 42 million. Two-thirds of people who are infected don't even know it, either because they have rare symptoms that they fail to recognize or because they have no symptoms at all.

▶ Culture and Diagnosis

These two viruses are sometimes diagnosed based on the characteristic lesions alone. PCR tests are available to test for these viruses directly from lesions. Alternatively, antibody to either of the viruses can be detected from blood samples. Detecting antibody to either HSV-1 or HSV-2 in blood does not necessarily indicate whether the infection is oral or genital or whether the infection is new or preexisting.

Herpes-infected mucosal cells display notable characteristics in a Pap smear **(figure 23.21)**. Laboratory culture and specific tests are essential for diagnosing severe or complicated herpes infections. They are also used when screening pregnant women for the presence of virus on the vaginal mucosa. A specimen of tissue or fluid is inoculated into a primary cell culture line and is then observed for cytopathic effects, which are characteristic for specific viruses.

▶ Prevention

No vaccine is currently licensed for HSV, but more than one is being tested in clinical trials, meaning that vaccines may

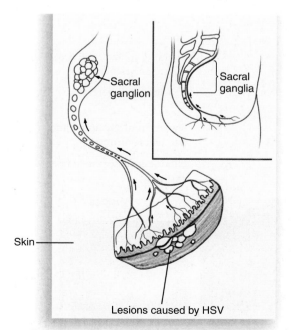

Figure 23.20 HSV latent in lumbosacral ganglion. The ganglion is the nerve root near the base of the spine. When the virus is reactivated, it travels down the neuron to the body's surface.

Figure 23.21 The appearance of herpesvirus infection in a Pap smear. A Pap smear of a cervical scraping shows enlarged (multinucleate giant) cells and intranuclear inclusions typical of herpes simplex, type 2. This appearance is not specific for HSV, but most other herpesviruses do not infect the reproductive mucosa.

Figure 23.22 The female condom.   The condom has a closed ring that fits over the cervix and an open ring that rests on the external genitalia.

Disease Table 23.7 Genital Ulcer Diseases

	Syphilis	Chancroid	Herpes
Causative Organism(s)	*Treponema pallidum*	*Haemophilus ducreyi*	Herpes simplex 1 and 2
Most Common Modes of Transmission	Direct contact and vertical	Direct contact (vertical transmission *not* documented)	Direct contact, vertical
Virulence Factors	Lipoproteins	Hemolysin (exotoxin)	Latency
Culture/Diagnosis	Direct tests (immunofluorescence, dark-field microscopy), blood tests for treponemal and nontreponemal antibodies, PCR	Culture from lesion	Clinical presentation, PCR, Ab tests, growth of virus in cell culture
Prevention	Antibiotic treatment of all possible contacts, avoiding contact	Avoiding contact	Avoiding contact, antivirals can reduce recurrences
Treatment	Penicillin G	Azithromycin, ceftriaxone, ciprofloxacin	Acyclovir and derivatives
Distinctive Features	Three stages of disease plus latent period, possibly fatal	No systemic effects	Ranges from asymptomatic to frequent recurrences
Effects on Fetus	Congenital syphilis	None	Blindness, disseminated herpes infection
Appearance of Lesions			Vesicles

become available very soon. In the meantime, avoiding contact with infected body surfaces is the only way to avoid HSV. Condoms provide good protection when they actually cover the site where the lesion is, but lesions can occur outside of the area covered by a condom. Women with herpes are sometimes counseled to use the female condom **(figure 23.22)** because these cover a substantial portion of the female external genitalia. In general, people experiencing active lesions should avoid sex. Because the virus can be shed when no lesions are present, barrier protection should be practiced at all times by persons infected with HSV.

Mothers with cold sores should be careful in handling their newborns; they should never kiss their infants on the mouth. Hospital attendants with active oral herpes infection should be barred from the newborn nursery.

Some of the drugs used to "treat" genital herpes really function to prevent recurrences of lesions. In this way, they serve as prevention for potential partners of people with herpes.

▶ Treatment

Several agents are available for treatment. These agents often result in reduced viral shedding and a decrease in the frequency of lesion occurrence. They are not curative. Acyclovir and its derivatives (Zovirax, Valtrex) are very effective. Topical formulations can be applied directly to lesions, and pills are available as well. Sometimes medicines are prescribed on an ongoing basis to decrease the frequency of recurrences, and sometimes they are prescribed to be taken at the beginning of a recurrence to shorten it **(Disease Table 23.7).**

Wart Diseases

In this section, we describe two viral STDs that cause wartlike growths. The more serious disease is caused by the *human papillomavirus (HPV)*; the other condition, called *molluscum contagiosum*, apparently has no serious effects outside of the growths themselves.

Human Papillomaviruses

These viruses are the causative agents of genital warts. But an individual can be infected with these viruses without having any warts, while still risking serious consequences.

▶ Signs and Symptoms

Symptoms, if present, may manifest as warts—outgrowths of tissue on the genitals **(Disease Table 23.8).** In females, these growths can occur on the vulva and in and around the vagina. In males, the warts can occur in or on the penis and

Disease Table 23.8 Wart Diseases

	HPV	Molluscum Contagiosum
Causative Organism(s)	Human papillomaviruses	Poxvirus, sometimes called the molluscum contagiosum virus (MCV)
Most Common Modes of Transmission	Direct contact (STD)—also autoinoculation, indirect contact	Direct contact (STD), also indirect and autoinoculation
Virulence Factors	Oncogenes (in the case of malignant types of HPV)	–
Culture/Diagnosis	PCR tests for certain HPV types, clinical diagnosis	Clinical diagnosis, also histology, PCR
Prevention	Vaccine available; avoid direct contact; prevent cancer by screening cervix	Avoid direct contact
Treatment	Warts or precancerous tissue can be removed; virus not treatable	Warts can be removed; virus not treatable
Distinguishing Features	Infection may or may not result in warts; infection may result in malignancy	Wartlike growths are only known consequence of infection
Effects on Fetus	May cause laryngeal warts	–
Appearance of Lesions		

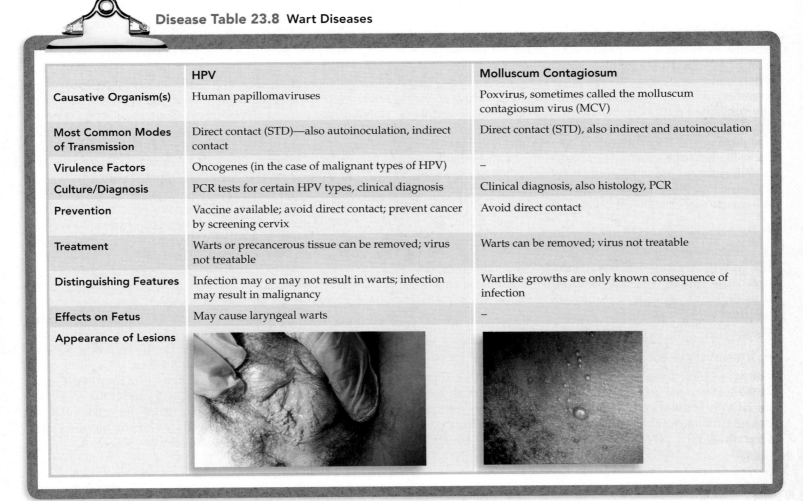

the scrotum. In both sexes, the warts can appear in or on the anus and even on the skin around the groin, such as the area between the thigh and the pelvis. The warts themselves range from tiny, flat, inconspicuous bumps to extensively branching, cauliflower-like masses called **condyloma acuminata.** The warts are unsightly and can be obstructive, but they don't generally lead to more serious symptoms.

Other types of HPV can lead to more subtle symptoms. Certain types of the virus infect cells on the female cervix. This infection may be "silent," or it may lead to abnormal cell changes in the cervix. Some of these cell changes can eventually result in malignancies of the cervix. The vast majority of cervical cancers are caused by HPV infection. (It is possible that chronic infections with other microorganisms cause a very small percentage of cervical malignancies.) Approximately 4,000 women die each year in the United States from cervical cancer. Also, data released in 2007 indicate a link between having had more than five oral sex partners and a greatly increased risk of throat cancer, presumably due to HPV.

Males can also get cancer from infection with these viruses. The sites most often affected are the penis and the anus. These cases are much less common than cervical cancer.

▶ Causative Agent

The human papillomaviruses are a group of nonenveloped DNA viruses belonging to the Papovaviridae family. There are more than 100 different types of HPV. Some types are specific for the mucous membranes; others invade the skin. Some of these viruses are the cause of plantar warts, which often occur on the soles of the feet. Other HPVs cause the common or "seed" warts and flat warts. In this chapter, we are concerned only with the HPVs that colonize the genital tract.

Among the HPVs that infect the genital tract, some are more likely to cause the appearance of warts. Others that have a preference for growing on the cervix can lead to cancerous changes. Five types in particular, HPV-16, -18, -31, -33, and -35, are closely associated with development of cervical cancer.

▶ Pathogenesis and Virulence Factors

Scientists are working hard to understand how viruses cause the growths we know as warts and also how some of them can cause cancer. The major virulence factors for cancer-causing HPVs are **oncogenes,** which code for proteins that interfere with normal host cell function, resulting in uncontrolled growth.

▶ Transmission and Epidemiology

Young women have the highest rate of HPV infections; 25–46% of women under the age of 25 are infected with genital HPV. It is estimated that 14% of female college students become infected with this incurable condition each year. Overall, about 15% of people between 15 and 49 are HPV-

positive. It is difficult to know whether genital herpes or HPV is more common, but it is probably safe to assume that any unprotected sex carries a good chance of encountering either HSV or HPV.

The mode of transmission is direct contact. Autoinoculation is also possible—meaning that the virus can be spread to other parts of the body by touching warts. Indirect transmission occurs but is more common for nongenital warts caused by HPV.

▶ Culture and Diagnosis

PCR-based screening tests can be used to test samples from a pelvic exam for the presence of dangerous HPV types. These tests are now recommended for women over the age of 30.

▶ Prevention

When discussing HPV prevention, we must consider two possibilities. One of these is infection with the viruses, which is prevented the same way other sexually transmitted infections are prevented—by avoiding direct, unprotected contact, but also by a vaccine approved in 2006 called Gardasil. The vaccine prevents infection by four types of HPV and is recommended in girls as young as age 9. Despite the fears of some parents, being vaccinated against the virus does not encourage girls to become sexually active, but instead causes them to realize the dangers of sex, according to a study conducted in 2009 among 553 teenage girls in Britain.

The second issue is the prevention of cervical cancer. Even though women now have access to the vaccine, cancer can still result from HPV types not included in the vaccine. The good news is that cervical cancer is slow in developing, so that even if a woman is infected with a malignant HPV type, regular screening of the cervix can detect abnormal changes early. The standardized screen for cervical cell changes is the Pap smear **(Insight 23.2).** Precancerous changes show up very early, and the development process can be stopped by removal of the affected tissue. Women should have their first Pap smear by age 21 or within 3 years of their first sexual activity, whichever comes first. New Pap smear technologies have been developed; and depending on which one your physician uses, it is now possible that you need to be screened only once every 2 or 3 years. But you should base your screening practices on the sound advice of a physician.

▶ Treatment

Infection with any HPV is incurable. Genital warts can be removed through a variety of methods, some of which can be used at home. But the virus causing them will most likely remain with you. It is possible for the viral infection to resolve itself, but this is very unpredictable.

Treatment of cancerous cell changes is an important part of HPV therapy, and it can only be instituted if the changes are detected through Pap smears. Again, the *results* of the infection are treated (cancerous cells removed), but the viral infection is not amenable to treatment.

INSIGHT 23.2 The Pap Smear

In the early part of the 20th century, a Greek-born physician named George Papanicolaou, who taught at Cornell University and collaborated with hospital physicians there, became interested in the cytological changes that take place in precancerous and cancerous tissue of the female reproductive tract. He developed a technique for evaluating "vaginal smears" for precancerous changes and in 1943 published a paper that would change women's lives forever. The title was "Diagnosis of Uterine Cancer by the Vaginal Smear." The test came to be known as the Pap smear.

The Pap smear is still the single best screening procedure available for cervical cancer, a disease that claims the lives of over 4,000 women every year in the United States. This incidence has decreased 74% since 1955, almost entirely due to the increased use of the Pap smear. The procedure is simple and painless: During a pelvic exam, a sample of cells is taken from the cervix using a wooden spatula or a small cervical brush. Then the sample is "smeared" onto a glass microscope slide and preserved with a fixative. In a newer method, the brush or spatula is rinsed with preservative fluid, the fluid is saved, and later it is automatically applied in a thin layer to a microscope slide. Whether the slide was made as a "smear" or as a "thin prep," it is then viewed microscopically by a technician or, in newer methods, by a computer so that abnormal cells can be detected.

A variety of "abnormal" results can be found and reported to the patient after a Pap smear. Here are some words that may appear on the Pap report:

- Dysplasia—abnormal cells found, not cancer but with a slight potential for developing into very early cancer of the cervix, depending on the degree of dysplasia (mild, moderate, severe, or the most severe form called carcinoma in situ).
- Squamous intraepithelial lesion (SIL)—a term that refers to the type of cells (squamous) that form the outer surface of the cervix. The "intraepithelial" designation refers to the observation that abnormal cells are only present on the surface of the cervix and not in the deeper tissue.
- Cervical intraepithelial neoplasia (CIN)—another term referring to abnormal cells. "Neoplasia" means an abnor-

Normal cells are the small ones with small nuclei. The ones grouped together with large nuclei in them are abnormal.

mal growth of cells. There will often be a number after the CIN (that is, CIN-1 or CIN-3). The photo in this insight represents a smear diagnosed to be CIN-2. The number corresponds with how far the abnormal cells extend into the cervix.
- Atypical squamous cells—cells appear abnormal, but the nature and degree of abnormality are unclear.

Cervical cancer is nearly always caused by infection with human papillomavirus, as detailed in the section on HPV in this chapter. Because some types of HPV are shown to be more strongly associated with cervical cancer, a physician may perform a PCR test on cervical material to look for the presence of these HPV types. A negative HPV test can provide reassurance that the abnormalities detected on a Pap smear do not point to a cancerous or precancerous condition.

Nearly all cervical cancer can be prevented if women get Pap smears on the recommended schedule.

Thanks to the relatively simple Pap smear, countless women have avoided not only early deaths from cancer but also hysterectomies, which later stages of cervical cancer require.

Molluscum Contagiosum

An unclassified virus in the pox family can cause a condition called molluscum contagiosum. This disease can take the form of skin lesions, and it can also be transmitted sexually. The wartlike growths that result from this infection can be found on the mucous membranes or the skin of the genital area (see Disease Table 23.8). Few problems are associated with these growths beyond the warts themselves. In severely immunocompromised people, the disease can be more serious.

The virus causing these growths can also be transmitted through fomites such as clothing or towels and through autoinoculation. For a more detailed description of this condition, see chapter 18 **(Disease Table 23.8).**

Group B *Streptococcus* "Colonization"— Neonatal Disease

Ten to forty percent of women in the United States are colonized, asymptomatically, by a beta-hemolytic *Streptococcus*

Case File 23   *Wrap-Up*

Once the professor had been definitively diagnosed with leptospirosis, health officials issued an Internet survey on campus to try to determine if any of the hundreds of students and staff who had helped with flood cleanup had been affected. In the end, they diagnosed only one other case, although 90 people did report experiencing a febrile illness within 30 days of the flood.

One problem with leptospirosis is that the early signs are no different from those of other flulike illnesses, so affected people do not necessarily present to the health care system. Certain occupations predispose people to this disease, namely ones that put people in touch with animal urine. This includes veterinarians, meat packers, and farmers. IgM is considered a more useful diagnostic tool than IgG since if it is elevated, it indicates a recent infection.

In this case, 48 of the 90 suspected cases were eventually tested, but other than the one additional case, no other ELISA test results were positive.

See: 2007. *Am. J. Trop. Med. Hyg.* 76(5):882–85.

In 2002, the CDC recommended that all pregnant women be screened for group B *Streptococcus* colonization at 35 to 37 weeks of pregnancy. Women positive for the bacterium should be treated with penicillin or ampicillin unless the bacterium is found to be resistant to these and unless allergy to penicillin is present.

Disease Table 23.9 Group B *Streptococcus* Colonization

Causative Organism(s)	Group B *Streptococcus*
Most Common Modes of Transmission	Vertical
Virulence Factors	–
Culture/Diagnosis	Culture of mother's genital tract
Prevention/Treatment	Treat mother with penicillin/ ampicillin

in Lancefield group B. Nonpregnant women experience no ill effects from this colonization. But when these women become pregnant and give birth, about half of their infants become colonized by the bacterium during passage through the birth canal or by ascension of the bacteria through ruptured membranes; thus, this colonization is considered a reproductive tract disease.

A small percentage of infected infants experience life-threatening bloodstream infections, meningitis, or pneumonia. If they recover from these acute conditions, they may have permanent disabilities such as developmental disabilities, hearing loss, or impaired vision. In some cases, the mothers also experience disease, such as amniotic infection or subsequent stillbirths.

23.4 Learning Outcomes—Can You ...

5. ... distinguish between vaginitis and vaginosis?
6. ... discuss prostatitis?
7. ... list the possible causative agents, modes of transmission, virulence factors, and prevention/treatment for gonorrhea and *Chlamydia* infection?
8. ... name three diseases that result in genital ulcers and discuss their important features?
9. ... differentiate between the two diseases causing warts in the reproductive tract?
10. ... provide some detail about the first "cancer vaccine" and how it works?
11. ... identify the most important risk group for group B *Streptococcus* infection and why?

▶ **Summing Up**

Taxonomic Organization Microorganisms Causing Disease in the Genitourinary Tract

Microorganism	Disease	Chapter Location
Gram-positive bacteria		
Staphylococcus saprophyticus	Urinary tract infection	UTI, p. 712
Gardnerella (note: stains gram-negative)	Vaginosis	Vaginitis or vaginosis, p. 716
Group B *Streptococcus*	Neonatal disease	Group B strep neonatal disease, p. 733
Gram-negative bacteria		
Escherichia coli	Urinary tract infection	UTI, p. 712
Leptospira interrogans (spirochete)	Leptospirosis	Leptospirosis, p. 713
Proteus mirabilis	Urinary tract infection plus kidney stones	UTI, p. 712
Neisseria gonorrhoeae	Gonorrhea	Discharge diseases, p. 719
Chlamydia trachomatis	"Chlamydia"	Discharge diseases, p. 721
Treponema pallidum (spirochete)	Syphilis	Genital ulcer diseases, p. 724
Haemophilus ducreyi	Chancroid	Genital ulcer diseases, p. 727
DNA viruses		
Herpes simplex viruses 1 and 2	Genital herpes	Genital ulcer diseases, p. 727
Human papillomaviruses	Genital warts, cervical carcinoma	Wart diseases, p. 731
Poxviruses	Molluscum contagiosum	Wart diseases, p. 733
Fungi		
Candida albicans	Vaginitis	Vaginitis or vaginosis, p. 715
Protozoa		
Trichomonas vaginalis	Trichomoniasis (vaginitis)	Vaginitis or vaginosis, p. 717
Helminth—trematode		
Schistosoma haematobium	Urinary schistosomiasis	Urinary schistosomiasis, p. 714

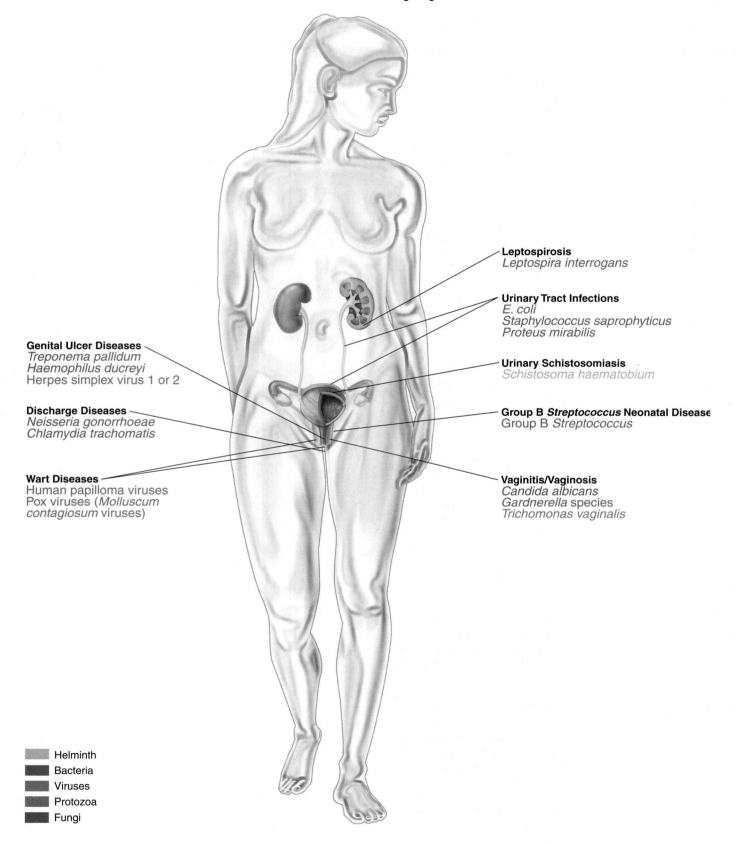

INFECTIOUS DISEASES AFFECTING
The Genitourinary System

Leptospirosis
Leptospira interrogans

Urinary Tract Infections
E. coli
Staphylococcus saprophyticus
Proteus mirabilis

Urinary Schistosomiasis
Schistosoma haematobium

Group B *Streptococcus* Neonatal Disease
Group B *Streptococcus*

Vaginitis/Vaginosis
Candida albicans
Gardnerella species
Trichomonas vaginalis

Genital Ulcer Diseases
Treponema pallidum
Haemophilus ducreyi
Herpes simplex virus 1 or 2

Discharge Diseases
Neisseria gonorrhoeae
Chlamydia trachomatis

Wart Diseases
Human papilloma viruses
Pox viruses (*Molluscum*
contagiosum viruses)

Helminth
Bacteria
Viruses
Protozoa
Fungi

System Summary Figure 23.23

INFECTIOUS DISEASES AFFECTING
The Genitourinary System

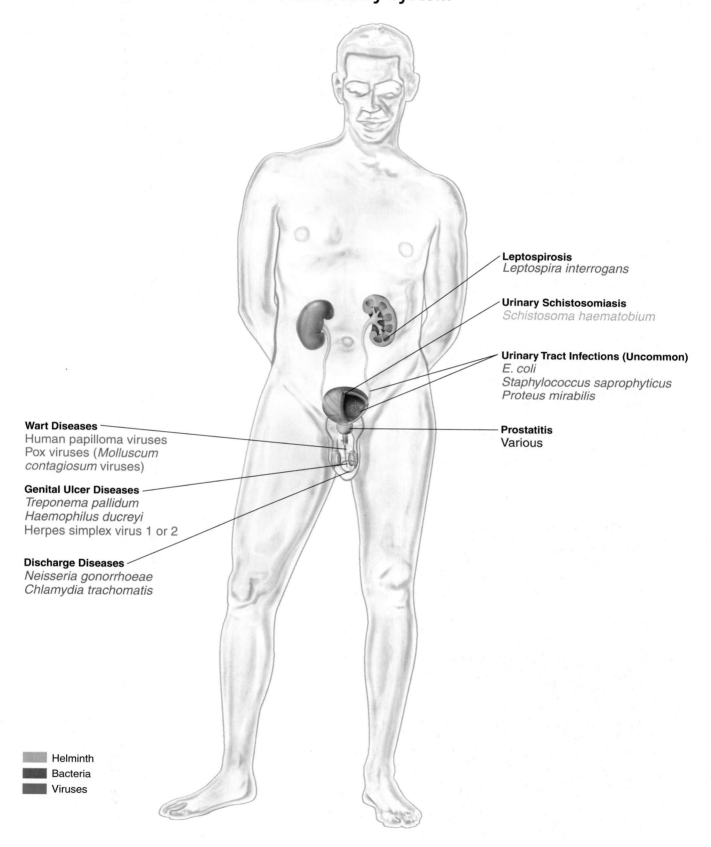

Leptospirosis
Leptospira interrogans

Urinary Schistosomiasis
Schistosoma haematobium

Urinary Tract Infections (Uncommon)
E. coli
Staphylococcus saprophyticus
Proteus mirabilis

Prostatitis
Various

Wart Diseases
Human papilloma viruses
Pox viruses (*Molluscum contagiosum* viruses)

Genital Ulcer Diseases
Treponema pallidum
Haemophilus ducreyi
Herpes simplex virus 1 or 2

Discharge Diseases
Neisseria gonorrhoeae
Chlamydia trachomatis

Helminth
Bacteria
Viruses

System Summary Figure 23.23

Chapter Summary

23.1 The Genitourinary Tract and Its Defenses

- The reproductive tract in males and females is composed of structures and substances that allow for sexual intercourse and the creation of a new fetus; protected by normal mucosal defenses and specialized features (such as low pH of the adult female reproductive tract).
- The urinary system allows the excretion of fluid and wastes from the body. It has mechanical, chemical defense mechanisms.

23.2 Normal Biota of the Genitourinary Tract

- Current knowledge is that the genital and the urinary systems have normal biota only in most distal regions. Normal biota in the male reproductive and urinary systems are in the distal part of the urethra and resemble skin biota. Same is generally true for the female urinary system. The normal biota in the female reproductive tract changes over the course of her lifetime.

23.3 Urinary Tract Diseases Caused by Microorganisms

- **Urinary Tract Infections (UTIs):** Can occur at a number of sites; the bladder (*cystitis*), the kidneys (*pyelonephritis*), and the urethra (*urethritis*). Most common causes are *Escherichia coli, Staphylococcus saprophyticus,* and *Proteus mirabilis.* Community-acquired UTIs are most often transmitted from GI tract to urinary system. UTIs are most common of nosocomial infections.
- **Leptospirosis:** Zoonosis associated with wild animals that affects kidneys, liver, brain, and eyes. Causative agent is *Leptospira interrogans*, a spirochete.
- **Urinary Schistosomiasis:** This form of schistosomiasis is caused by *S. haematobium.* Bladder is damaged by trematode eggs and the granulomatous response they induce.

23.4 Reproductive Tract Diseases Caused by Microorganisms

- **Vaginitis and Vaginosis**
  - Vaginitis most commonly caused by *Candida albicans.* Nearly always an opportunistic infection.
  - *Gardnerella* is associated with vaginosis that has a discharge but no inflammation in the vagina. Vaginosis could lead to complications such as pelvic inflammatory disease (PID).
  - *Trichomonas vaginalis* causes mostly asymptomatic infections in females and males. *Trichomonas*, a flagellated protozoan, is easily transmitted through sexual contact.
- **Prostatitis:** Inflammation of the prostate; can be acute or chronic. Not all cases established to have microbial cause, but most are.
- **Discharge Diseases with Major Manifestation in the Genitourinary Tract:** Diseases in which there is increase in fluid discharge in the male and female reproductive tracts.
  - Gonorrhea can elicit urethritis in males, but many cases are asymptomatic. In females, both the urinary and genital tracts may be infected during sexual intercourse. Major complications occur when infection reaches uterus and fallopian tubes.

One disease resulting from this is salpingitis, which can lead to pelvic inflammatory disease (PID). Causative agent, *Neisseria gonorrhoeae,* is a gram-negative diplococcus.
  - Chlamydia: Genital chlamydia is most common reportable infectious disease in the United States. In males: an inflammation of the urethra (NGU). Females: cervicitis, discharge, salpingitis, and frequently PID.

    Certain strains of *Chlamydia trachomatis* can invade lymphatic tissues, resulting in condition called lymphogranuloma venereum.
- **Genital Ulcer Diseases**
  - Syphilis: Caused by spirochete *Treponema pallidum,* a thin, regularly coiled cell with a gram-negative cell wall. Three distinct clinical stages: *primary, secondary,* and *tertiary syphilis,* with a latent period between secondary and tertiary. Spirochete appears in lesions and blood during primary and secondary stages; is transmissible at these times. Also transmissible during early latency period. Largely nontransmissible during "late latent" and tertiary stages.

    The syphilis bacterium can lead to congenital syphilis, inhibiting fetal growth and disrupting critical periods of development. This can lead to spontaneous miscarriage or stillbirth.
  - Chancroid: Caused by *Haemophilus ducreyi*, a pleomorphic gram-negative rod. Transmitted exclusively through direct—mainly sexual—contact.
  - Genital herpes is caused by herpes simplex viruses (HSVs). Two types: HSV-1 and HSV-2. May be no symptoms, or may be fluid-filled, painful vesicles on genitalia, perineum, thigh, and buttocks. In severe cases, meningitis or encephalitis can develop. Patients remain asymptomatic or experience recurrent "surface" infections indefinitely. Infections in neonate and fetus can be fatal.

    HSV-1 and HSV-2 are DNA viruses with icosahedral capsids and envelopes containing glycoprotein spikes. Herpesviruses can become latent, via the incorporation of viral nucleic acid into the host genome in nerve cells.
- **Wart Diseases**
  - *Human papillomaviruses:* Causative agents of genital warts. Certain types infect cells on female cervix that eventually result in malignancies of the cervix. Males can also get cancer from these viral types.
    - Human papillomaviruses are a group of nonenveloped DNA viruses belonging to the *Papovaviridae* family. At least five types are associated with cervical cancer.
    - Infection with any HPV is incurable. Genital warts can be removed, but virus will remain. Treatment of cancerous cell changes is an

important part of HPV therapy, and it can only be instituted if the changes are detected through Pap smears. Vaccine for several types of HPV is now available.

- A pox family virus causes a condition called molluscum contagiosum. Can take the form of wartlike growths in the membranes of the genitalia, and it can also be transmitted sexually.

- **Group B** *Streptococcus* **"Colonization"—Neonatal Disease:** Asymptomatic colonization of women by a beta-hemolytic *Streptococcus* in Lancefield group B is very common. When these women give birth, about half of their infants become colonized by the bacterium during passage through the birth canal or by ascension of the bacteria through ruptured membranes; some infected infants experience life-threatening bloodstream infections, meningitis, or pneumonia.

Multiple-Choice and True-False Questions   Knowledge and Comprehension

Multiple-Choice Questions. Select the correct answer from the answers provided.

1. Cystitis is an infection of the
   a. bladder.
   b. urethra.
   c. kidney.
   d. vagina.

2. Nongonococcal urethritis (NGU) is caused by
   a. *Neisseria gonorrhoeae*.
   b. *Chlamydia trachomatis*.
   c. *Treponema pallidum*.
   d. *Trichomonas vaginalis*.

3. Leptospirosis is transmitted to humans by
   a. person to person.
   b. fomites.
   c. mosquitoes.
   d. contaminated soil or water.

4. Syphilis is caused by
   a. *Treponema pallidum*.
   b. *Neisseria gonorrhoeae*.
   c. *Trichomonas vaginalis*.
   d. *Haemophilus ducreyi*.

5. Bacterial vaginosis is commonly associated with the following organism:
   a. *Candida albicans*
   b. *Gardnerella*
   c. *Trichomonas*
   d. all of the above
   e. none of the above

6. This dimorphic fungus is a common cause of vaginitis.
   a. *Candida albicans*
   b. *Gardnerella*
   c. *Trichomonas*
   d. all of the above

7. There are estimates that approximately _____ % of adult Americans have genital herpes.
   a. 2
   b. 10
   c. 20
   d. 50

8. Genital herpes transmission can be reduced or prevented by all of the following except
   a. a condom.
   b. abstinence.
   c. the contraceptive pill.
   d. a female condom.

9. This protozoan can be treated with the drug Flagyl.
   a. *Neisseria gonorrhoeae*
   b. *Chlamydia trachomatis*
   c. *Treponema pallidum*
   d. *Trichomonas vaginalis*

10. Which group has the highest rate of HPV infection?
    a. female college students
    b. male college students
    c. college professors of either gender
    d. baby-boomers

True-False Questions. If the statement is true, leave as is. If it is false, correct it by rewriting the sentence.

11. Genital herpes can be treated with acyclovir.

12. Chancroid is caused by a fungus.

13. The majority of cervical cancers are caused by human papillomavirus.

14. *Chlamydia* infection is the most common STD in the United States.

15. Group B *Streptococcus* infection is generally silent in adult females.

Critical Thinking Questions   Application and Analysis

These questions are suggested as a *writing-to-learn* experience. For each question, compose a one- or two-paragraph answer that includes the factual information needed to completely address the question.

1. Describe the symptoms of Weil's syndrome.

2. Describe the common treatments for gonorrhea.

3. a. What is PID?
   b. What are the two most common microorganisms associated with this disease?
   c. Describe the long-term consequences of untreated PID.

4. Describe the life cycle of *Chlamydia*.

5. What are some of the stimuli that can trigger reactivation of a latent herpesvirus infection? Speculate on why.

6. What are the clinical stages of syphilis?

7. In the photo in Insight 23.2, the abnormal cells have extraordinarily large nuclei. Speculate on why this is the case.

8. Why do you suppose a urine screening test for *Chlamydia* is more accurate for males than for females?

9. It has been stated that the actual number of people in the United States who have genital herpes may be a lot higher than official statistics depict. What are some possible reasons for this discrepancy?

10. Why are urinary tract infections such common nosocomial infections?

Concept Mapping   Application and Analysis

Appendix D provides guidance for working with concept maps.

1. Construct your own concept map using the following words as the *concepts*. Supply the linking words between each pair of concepts.

genital warts

discharge

herpes

chancroid

bacterium

molluscum contagiosum

virus

curable

ulcers

warts

syphilis

incurable

cancer

Visual Connections   Synthesis

These questions use visual images or previous content to make connections to this chapter's concepts.

1. a. **From chapters 20 and 23, figures 20.15 and 23.13a.**
   Compare these two rashes. What kind of information would help you determine the diagnosis in both cases?

   b. Now compare both of these to the rashes summarized in **Disease Table 18.7** (p. 533). Which of the diseases in Disease Table 18.7 most resembles the rashes in the preceding question, and how would you distinguish among the three?

Environmental Microbiology

Case File 24

On March 24, 1989, the oil tanker *Exxon Valdez* ran aground on Bligh Reef in Prince William Sound, Alaska. Almost 41 million liters of crude oil spilled into the beautiful, pristine wilderness of the Sound. At this time (before the 2010 spill in the Gulf of Mexico), this was the largest oil spill in U.S. history. Americans watched in horror as about 2,000 kilometers of some of the most spectacular shores in the country were reduced to oil-covered graves for indigenous flora and fauna.

As anyone who has washed clothes knows, oil stains can be difficult to remove. Extracting spilled oil from the natural environment is far more arduous and complex than removing oil stains from laundry. But just as in cleaning heavily stained clothes, the cleanup response team used hot water—specifically, steam under high pressure—to remove oil from the shores. At first this technique seemed to work. The shores superficially appeared as they had been before the oil spill; however, closer examination revealed that oil remained. The high-pressure steam cleaning had forced much of the oil deeper into the rocky shores of the Sound. Clearly, an additional solution was needed.

- Do you think steam cleaning was beneficial to the cleanup process?
- Can you think of some approaches environmental microbiologists might have used to speed up bioremediation in Prince William Sound?

Continuing the Case appears on page 744.

Outline and Learning Outcomes

24.1 Ecology: The Interconnecting Web of Life
1. Define microbial ecology.
2. Summarize why our view of the abundance of microbes on earth has changed in recent years.
3. Discuss the terms ecosystem and community in relation to one another.
4. Differentiate between habitat and niche.
5. Draw an example of an energy pyramid, labeling producers and consumers.
6. Define bioremediation.

This chapter emphasizes microbial activities that help maintain, sustain, and control the life support systems on the earth. This subject is explored from the standpoint of the natural roles of microorganisms in the environment and their contributions to the ecological balance, including soil, water, and mineral cycles.

24.1 Ecology: The Interconnecting Web of Life

The study of microbes in their natural habitats is known as **microbial ecology;** the study of the practical uses of microbes in food processing, industrial production, and biotechnology is known as industrial or **applied microbiology** (see chapter 25). The two areas actually overlap to a considerable degree—largely because most natural habitats have been altered by human activities. Human intervention in natural settings has changed the earth's warming and cooling cycles, increased wastes in soil, polluted water, and altered some of the basic relationships between microbial, plant, and animal life. We know one thing for certain: Microbes—the most vast and powerful resource of all—will be silently working in nature.

In chapter 7, we first touched upon the widespread distribution of microorganisms and their adaptations to most habitats of the world, from extreme to temperate. Although we have known for a long time that geological features on the earth, including coal and limestone, are formed in small or large part by microbes, it is only recently that we have come to understand the sheer mass of microbial life present on our planet. Remember that the vast majority of microbial life has not yet been cultured. With the development of genomic techniques that do not rely on cultivating bacteria, we have discovered abundant microbial life all over—and within and around—our planet **(figure 24.1).** We are learning about the planet-shaping effects of bacteria deep in the earth's core

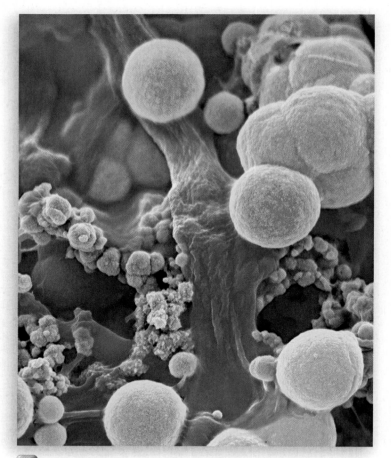

Figure 24.1 A sample of water from a deep cavern as imaged by scanning electron microscopy.   This view shows a bacterial biofilm that actively forms mineral deposits of zinc and sulfate (light green and yellow). This single image brings focus to several themes of this chapter: (1) Microbes work together in mixed communities, (2) microbes can alter the chemistry of the nonliving environment, and (3) microbes can be used to control undesirable wastes created by humans.

and deep in glaciers. The sheer abundance of viral life in the oceans has been a huge surprise. In fact, half of the earth's biomass is probably made up of microbes.

Regardless of their exact location or type of adaptation, microorganisms necessarily are exposed to and interact with their environment in complex and extraordinary ways. Microbial ecology studies interactions between microbes and their environment and the effects of those interactions on the earth. Unlike studies that deal with the activities of a single organism or its individual characteristics in the laboratory, ecological studies are aimed at the interactions taking place between organisms and their environment at many levels at any given moment. Therefore, ecology is a broad-based science that merges many subsciences of biology as well as geology, physics, and chemistry.

Ecological studies deal with both the biotic and the abiotic components of an organism's environment. **Biotic** factors are defined as any living or dead organisms[1] that occupy an organism's habitat. **Abiotic** factors include nonliving components such as atmospheric gases, minerals, water, temperature, and light. You may recall these from chapters 7 and 11 as factors that affect microbial growth. A collection of organisms together with its surrounding physical and chemical factors is defined as an **ecosystem.**

The Organization of Ecosystems

The earth initially may seem like a random, chaotic place, but it is actually an incredibly organized, fine-tuned machine. Ecological relationships exist at several levels, ranging from the entire earth all the way down to a single organism **(figure 24.2).** The most all-encompassing of these levels, the **biosphere,** contains all physical locations on earth that support life, including the thin envelope of life that surrounds the earth's surface and extending several miles below. This global ecosystem comprises the **hydrosphere** (water), the **lithosphere** (a few miles into the soil), and the **atmosphere** (a few miles into the air). The biosphere maintains or creates the conditions of temperature, light, gases, moisture, and minerals required for life processes. The biosphere can be naturally subdivided into terrestrial and aquatic realms. The terrestrial realm is usually distributed into particular climatic regions called **biomes** (by'-ohmz), each of which is characterized by a dominant plant form, altitude, and latitude. Particular biomes include grassland, desert, mountain, and tropical rain forest. The aquatic biosphere is generally divisible into freshwater and marine realms. We have also recently learned that the earth's crust also supports a vast and diverse number of life forms, estimated to be equal to or even greater than life as we know it in aquatic and terrestrial realms.

Biomes and aquatic ecosystems are generally composed of mixed assemblages of organisms that live together at the same place and time and that usually exhibit well-defined nutritional

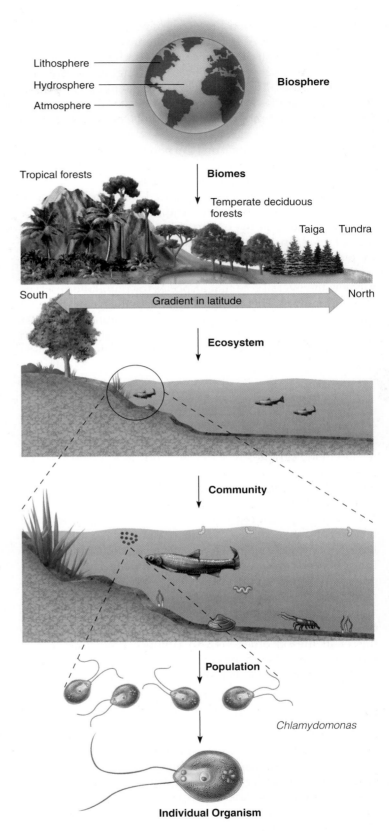

Figure 24.2 Levels of organization in an ecosystem, ranging from the biosphere to the individual organism.

---

1. Biologists make a distinction between nonliving and dead. A nonliving thing has never been alive, whereas a dead thing was once alive but no longer is.

or behavioral interrelationships. These clustered associations are called **communities.** Although most communities are identified by their easily visualized dominant plants and animals, they also contain a complex assortment of bacteria, fungi, algae, protozoa, and even viruses. The basic units of community structure are **populations,** groups of organisms of the same kind. For organisms with sexual reproduction, this level is the species. In contrast, prokaryotes are classified using taxonomic units such as "strain." The organizational unit of a population is the individual organism, and each multicellular organism, in turn, has its own levels of organization (organs, tissues, cells).

Ecosystems are generally balanced, with each organism existing in its particular habitat and niche. The **habitat** is the physical location in the environment to which an organism has adapted. In the case of microorganisms, the habitat is frequently a *microenvironment,* where particular qualities of oxygen, light, or nutrient content are somewhat stable. The **niche** is the overall role that a species (or population) serves in a community. This includes such activities as nutritional intake (what it eats), position in the community structure (what is eating it), and rate of population growth. A niche can be broad (such as scavengers that feed on nearly any organic food source) or narrow (microbes that decompose cellulose in forest litter or that fix nitrogen).

Note that microbes exist as communities in and on plants and animals as well, including humans. Pure cultures are seldom found anywhere in nature. One exception to this rule is particularly noteworthy. In 2008, researchers found a bacterium living completely alone, with no other life forms in its ecosystem. It was found in a South African gold mine, in fluid collected in cracks in the rock 2 miles below the surface. Obviously, there is no light there, and there are also no photosynthetic organisms (such as plants) to offer the indirect benefits of photosynthesis for the bacterium to use. The bacterium, named *Desulforudis audaxviator,* has to extract everything it needs from an abiotic environment. Apparently it garners energy from the radioactive decay of uranium in the rocks, and it possesses genes that enable it to leach carbon and nitrogen from the environment. The interesting spin on this discovery is that it now makes the possibility of finding microbial life on other—mostly abiotic—planets suddenly more plausible. As one researcher said of *Desulforudis:* "This is just the kind of organism that could survive on Mars."

Energy and Nutritional Flow in Ecosystems

All living things must obtain nutrients and a usable form of energy from their abiotic and biotic environments. The energy and nutritional relationships in ecosystems can be described in a number of convenient ways. A **food chain,** or **energy pyramid,** provides a simple summary of the general trophic (feeding) levels, designated as producers, consumers, and decomposers, and traces the flow and quantity of available energy from one level to another **(figure 24.3).** It is worth noting that microorganisms are the only living beings that exist at all three major trophic levels. The nutritional roles of microorganisms in ecosystems are summarized in **table 24.1.**

Case File 24 *Continuing the Case*

Steam cleaning the shores of Prince William Sound was beneficial in that it quickly removed large quantities of oil and improved the shoreline's aesthetic appearance. But that cleaning method may have killed many of the bacteria that could have facilitated more rapid cleanup of the oil. Soon the cleanup crews had to employ an additional approach, one that relied on microorganisms to remove the oil.

Many microorganisms—even those inhabiting the rocks on the shores of the Sound—have the capacity to utilize oil as a source of carbon and energy, simultaneously transforming it into harmless water and carbon dioxide. This process is called bioremediation. Crude oil is composed of hydrocarbons, which are rich sources of carbon for microorganisms; however, microorganisms require nutrients in addition to carbon. In fact, without additional nutrients, bacterial metabolism and bioremediation often do not proceed very quickly. Rapid cleanup of the Sound was imperative to minimize further negative impacts of the spill on this once-pristine environment.

- What needed to happen to rapidly increase the numbers of oil-degrading microbes on the shore?

Figure 24.3 A trophic and energy pyramid. The relative size of the blocks indicates the number of individuals that exist at a given trophic level. The orange arrow on the right indicates the amount of usable energy from producers to top consumers. Both the number of organisms and the amount of usable energy decrease with each trophic level. Decomposers are an exception to this pattern but only because they can feed from all trophic levels (gray arrows). Blocks shown on the left indicate the general nutritional types and levels that correspond with the pyramid.

Table 24.1 The Major Roles of Microorganisms in Ecosystems

Role	Description of Activity	Examples of Microorganisms Involved
Primary producers	Photosynthesis	Algae, bacteria, sulfur bacteria
	Chemosynthesis	Chemolithotrophic bacteria in thermal vents
Consumers	Predation	Free-living protozoa that feed on algae and bacteria; some fungi that prey upon nematodes
Decomposers	Degradation of plant and animal matter and wastes	Soil saprobes (primarily bacteria and fungi) that degrade cellulose, lignin, and other complex macromolecules
	Mineralization of organic nutrients	Soil bacteria that reduce organic compounds to inorganic compounds such as CO_2 and minerals
Cycling agents for biogeochemical cycles	Recycling compounds containing carbon, nitrogen, phosphorus, sulfur	Specialized bacteria that transform elements into different chemical compounds to keep them cycling from the biotic to the abiotic and back to the biotic phases of the biosphere
Parasites	Living and feeding on hosts	Viruses, bacteria, protozoa, fungi, and worms that play a role in population control

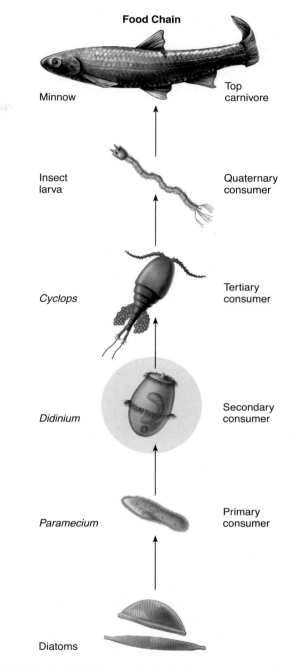

Food Chain

Minnow — Top carnivore

Insect larva — Quaternary consumer

Cyclops — Tertiary consumer

Didinium — Secondary consumer

Paramecium — Primary consumer

Diatoms

Figure 24.4 Food chain. A food chain is the simplest way to present specific feeding relationships among organisms, but it may not reflect the total nutritional interactions in a community (figure not to scale).

Life would not be possible without **producers,** because they provide the fundamental energy source that drives the trophic pyramid. Producers are the only organisms in an ecosystem that can produce organic carbon compounds such as glucose by assimilating (fixing) inorganic carbon (CO_2) from the atmosphere. If CO_2 is the sole source from which they can obtain carbon for growth, these organisms are called **autotrophs.** Most producers are photosynthetic organisms, such as plants and bacteria, that convert the sun's energy into chemical bond energy. Photosynthesis was covered in chapter 8. A smaller but not less important amount of CO_2 assimilation is brought about by bacteria called lithotrophs. These organisms derive energy from simple inorganic compounds such as ammonia, sulfides, and hydrogen by using redox reactions. In certain ecosystems (see thermal vents, Insight 7.3), lithotrophs are the sole supporters of the energy pyramid as primary producers.

Consumers feed on other living organisms and obtain energy from bonds present in the organic substrates they contain. The category includes animals, protozoa, and a few bacteria and fungi. A pyramid usually has several levels of consumers, ranging from *primary consumers* (grazers or herbivores), which consume producers; to *secondary consumers*

(carnivores), which feed on primary consumers; to *tertiary consumers,* which feed on secondary consumers; and up to *quaternary consumers* (usually the last level), which feed on tertiary consumers. **Figures 24.4** and **24.5** show specific organisms at these levels.

Decomposers, primarily microbes inhabiting soil and water, break down and absorb the organic matter of dead organisms, including plants, animals, and other microorganisms. Because of their biological function, decomposers are active at all levels of the food pyramid. Without this

Figure 24.5 Food web. More complex trophic patterns are accurately depicted by a food web, which traces the multiple feeding options that exist for most organisms. Note: Arrows point toward the consumers. Compare this pattern of feeding with the chain in figure 24.4 (organisms not to scale).

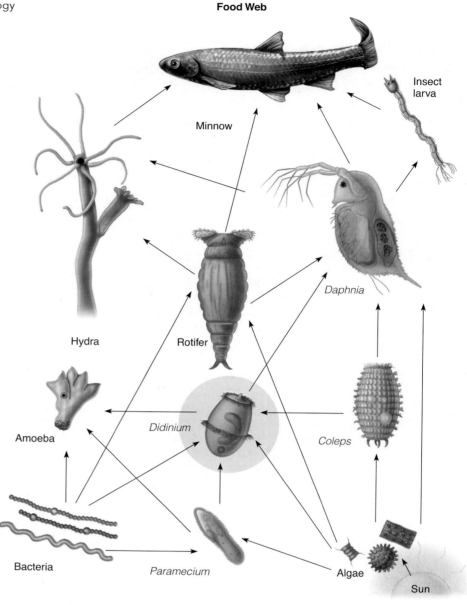

Food Web

Minnow

Insect larva

Daphnia

Hydra   Rotifer

Amoeba   *Didinium*   *Coleps*

Bacteria   *Paramecium*   Algae

Sun

important nutritional class of saprobes, the biosphere would stagnate and die. The work of decomposers is to reduce organic matter into inorganic minerals and gases that can be cycled back into the ecosystem, especially for the use of primary producers. This process, also termed **mineralization,** is so efficient that almost all biological compounds can be reduced by some type of decomposer. Numerous microorganisms decompose cellulose and lignin, polysaccharides from plant cell walls that account for the vast bulk of detritus in soil and water. Surprisingly, decomposers can also break down most man-made compounds that are not naturally found on earth. This process is referred to as **bioremediation.** Often, bioremediation involves more than one kind of microbe, and the collection of participating microbes in this process is known as a **consortium.**

The pyramid in figure 24.3 illustrates several limitations of ecosystems with regard to energy. Unlike nutrients, which can be passed among trophic levels, recycled, and reused, energy does not cycle. Maintenance of complex interdependent trophic relationships such as those shown in figures 24.4 and

24.5 requires a constant input of energy at the producer level. As energy is transferred to the next level, a large proportion (as high as 90%) of the energy will be lost in a form (primarily heat) that cannot be fed back into the system. Thus, the amount of energy available decreases at each successive trophic level. This energy loss also decreases the actual number of individuals that can be supported at each successive level.

24.1 Learning Outcomes—Can You …

1. … define microbial ecology?
2. … summarize why our view of the abundance of microbes on earth has changed in recent years?
3. … discuss the terms ecosystem and community in relation to one another?
4. … differentiate between habitat and niche?
5. … draw an example of an energy pyramid, labeling producers and consumers?
6. … define bioremediation?

24.2 The Natural Recycling of Bioelements

Because of the finite supply of life's building blocks, the long-term sustenance of the biosphere requires continuous **recycling** of elements and nutrients. Essential elements such as carbon, nitrogen, sulfur, phosphorus, oxygen, and iron are cycled through biological, geologic, and chemical mechanisms called **biogeochemical cycles.** Although these cycles vary in certain specific characteristics, they share several general qualities, as summarized in the following list:

- All elements ultimately originate from a nonliving, long-term reservoir in the atmosphere, the lithosphere, or the hydrosphere. They cycle in pure form (N_2) or as compounds (PO_4). Their cycling is facilitated by redox reactions.
- Elements make the rounds between the abiotic environment and the biotic environment.
- Recycling maintains a necessary balance of nutrients in the biosphere so that they do not build up or become unavailable.
- Cycles are complex systems that rely on the interplay of producers, consumers, and decomposers. Often the waste products of one organism become a source of energy or building material for another.
- All organisms participate directly in recycling, but only certain categories of microorganisms have the metabolic pathways for converting inorganic compounds from one nutritional form to another.

For billions of years, microbes have played prominent roles in the formation and maintenance of the earth's crust, the development of rocks and minerals, and the formation of fossil fuels. This revolution in understanding the biological involvement in geologic processes has given rise to a new field called *geomicrobiology.* A logical extension of this discipline is **astromicrobiology,** also known as exobiology—which is the study of life on planets and bodies other than earth.

In the next several sections, we examine how, jointly and over a period of time, the varied microbial activities affect and are themselves affected by the abiotic environment.

Atmospheric Cycles

The Carbon Cycle

Because carbon is the fundamental atom in all biomolecules and accounts for at least one-half of the dry weight of biomass, the **carbon cycle** is more intimately associated with the energy transfers and trophic patterns in the biosphere than are other elements. Carbon exists predominantly in the mineral state and as an organic reservoir in the bodies of organisms. A much smaller amount of carbon also exists in the gaseous state as carbon dioxide (CO_2), carbon monoxide (CO), and methane (CH_4). In general, carbon is recycled through ecosystems via carbon fixation, respiration, or fermentation of organic molecules, limestone decomposition,

and methane production. A convenient starting point from which to trace the movement of carbon is with carbon dioxide, which occupies a central position in the cycle and represents a large common pool that diffuses into all parts of the ecosystem **(figure 24.6).** As a general rule, the cycles of oxygen and hydrogen are closely allied to the carbon cycle.

The principal users of the atmospheric carbon dioxide pool are photosynthetic autotrophs (photoautotrophs) such as plants, algae, and bacteria. An estimated 165 billion tons of organic material per year are produced by terrestrial and aquatic photosynthesis. Although we don't yet know exactly how many autotrophs exist in the earth's crust, a small amount of CO_2 is used by these bacteria (chemolithoautotrophs) that derive their energy from bonds in inorganic chemicals. A review of the general equation for photosynthesis in figure 8.26 reveals that phototrophs use energy from the sun to fix CO_2 into organic compounds such as glucose that can be used in synthesis. Photosynthesis is also the primary means by which the atmospheric supply of O_2 is regenerated.

Just as photosynthesis removes CO_2 from the atmosphere, other modes of generating energy, such as respiration and fermentation, can be used to return it. As you may recall from the discussion of aerobic respiration in chapter 8, in the presence of O_2, organic compounds such as glucose are degraded completely to CO_2, with the release of energy

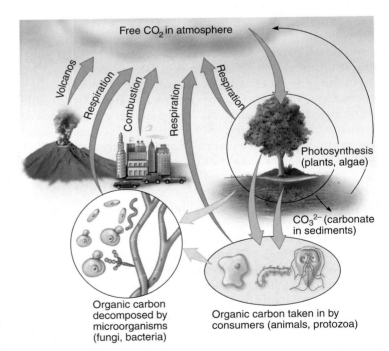

Figure 24.6 The carbon cycle. This cycle traces carbon from the CO_2 pool in the atmosphere to the primary producers (green) where it is fixed into protoplasm. Organic carbon compounds are taken in by consumers (blue) and decomposers (yellow) that produce CO_2 through respiration and return it to the atmosphere (pink). Combustion of fossil fuels and volcanic eruptions also add to the CO_2 pool. Some of the CO_2 is carried into inorganic sediments by organisms that synthesize carbonate (CO_3) skeletons. In time, natural processes acting on exposed carbonate skeletons can liberate CO_2.

and the formation of H_2O. Carbon dioxide is also released by anaerobic respiration and by certain types of fermentation reactions.

A small but important phase of the carbon cycle involves certain limestone deposits composed primarily of calcium carbonate ($CaCO_3$). Limestone is produced when marine organisms such as mollusks, corals, protozoa, and algae form hardened shells by combining carbon dioxide and calcium ions from the surrounding water. When these organisms die, the durable skeletal components accumulate in marine deposits. As these immense deposits are gradually exposed by geologic upheavals or receding ocean levels, various decomposing agents liberate CO_2 and return it to the CO_2 pool of the water and atmosphere.

The complementary actions of photosynthesis and respiration, along with other natural CO_2-releasing processes such as limestone erosion and volcanic activity, have maintained a relatively stable atmospheric pool of carbon dioxide. Recent figures show that this balance is being disturbed as humans burn *fossil fuels* and other organic carbon sources. Fossil fuels, including coal, oil, and natural gas, were formed through millions of years of natural biological and geologic activities. Humans are so dependent upon this energy source that, within the past 25 years, the proportion of CO_2 in the atmosphere has steadily increased from 32 to 36 ppm. Although this increase may seem slight and insignificant, most scientists now feel it has begun to disrupt the delicate temperature balance of the biosphere **(Insight 24.1).**

Compared with carbon dioxide, methane gas (CH_4) plays a secondary part in the carbon cycle, though it can be a significant product in anaerobic ecosystems dominated by **methanogens** (methane producers). In general, when methanogens reduce CO_2 by means of various oxidizable substrates, they give off CH_4. The practical applications of methanogens are covered in chapter 25 in a section on sewage treatment, and their contribution to the greenhouse effect is also discussed in Insight 24.1.

The Nitrogen Cycle

Nitrogen (N_2) gas is the most abundant component of the atmosphere, accounting for nearly 79% of air volume. As we will see, this extensive reservoir in the air is largely unavailable to most organisms. Only about 0.03% of the earth's nitrogen is combined (or fixed) in some other form such as nitrates (NO_3), nitrites (NO_2), ammonium ion (NH_4^+), and organic nitrogen compounds (proteins, nucleic acids).

The **nitrogen cycle** is relatively more intricate than other cycles because it involves such a diversity of specialized microbes to maintain the flow of the cycle. In many ways, it is actually more of a nitrogen "web" because of the array of adaptations that occur. Higher plants can utilize NO_3^- and NH_4^+; animals must receive nitrogen in organic form from plants or other animals; however, microorganisms can use all forms of nitrogen: NO_2^-, NO_3^-, NH_4^+, N_2, and organic nitrogen. The cycle includes four basic types of reactions: nitrogen fixation, ammonification, nitrification, and denitrification **(figure 24.7).**

Process Figure 24.7 A simplified view of events in the nitrogen cycle.   (1) In nitrogen fixation, gaseous nitrogen (N_2) is acted on by nitrogen-fixing bacteria, which give off ammonia (NH_3). (2) Ammonia is converted to nitrite (NO_2^-) and nitrate (NO_3^-) by nitrifying bacteria in nitrification. (3) Plants, algae, and bacteria use nitrates to synthesize nitrogenous organic compounds (proteins, amino acids, nucleic acids). (4) Organic nitrogen compounds are used by animals and other consumers. (5) In ammonification, nitrogenous macromolecules from wastes and dead organisms are converted to NH_4^+ by ammonifying bacteria. NH_4^+ can be either directly recycled into nitrates or (6) returned to the atmospheric N_2 form by denitrifying bacteria (denitrification).

Root Nodules: Natural Fertilizer Factories   A significant symbiotic association occurs between **rhizobia** (ry-zoh'-bee-uh) (bacteria in genera such as *Rhizobium, Bradyrhizobium,* and *Azorhizobium*) and **legumes** (plants such as soybeans, peas, alfalfa, and clover that characteristically produce seeds in pods). The infection of legume roots by these gram-negative, motile, rod-shaped bacteria causes the formation of special nitrogen-fixing organs called **root nodules (figure 24.8).** Nodulation begins when rhizobia colonize specific sites on root hairs. From there, the bacteria invade deeper root cells and induce the cells to form tumorlike masses. The bacterium's enzyme system supplies a constant source of reduced nitrogen to the plant, and the plant furnishes nutrients and energy for the activities of the bacterium. The legume uses the NH_4^+ to aminate (add an amino group to) various carbohydrate intermediates and thereby synthesize amino acids and other nitrogenous compounds that are used in plant and animal synthesis.

Plant–bacteria associations have great practical importance in agriculture, because an available source of nitrogen is often a limiting factor in the growth of crops. The self-fertilizing nature of legumes makes them valuable food plants in areas with poor soils and in countries with limited resources. It has been shown that crop health and yields can be improved by inoculating legume seeds with pure cultures of rhizobia, because the soil is often deficient in the proper strain of bacteria for forming nodules **(figure 24.9).**

Ammonification, Nitrification, and Denitrification In another part of the nitrogen cycle, nitrogen-containing organic matter is decomposed by various bacteria (*Clostridium, Proteus,* for example) that live in the soil and water. Organic detritus consists of large amounts of protein and nucleic acids from dead organisms and nitrogenous animal wastes such as urea and uric acid. The decomposition of

Figure 24.9 Inoculating legume seeds with *Rhizobium* bacteria increases the plant's access to nitrogen. The legumes in **(a)** were inoculated and are healthy. The poor growth and yellowish color of the uninoculated legumes in **(b)** indicate a lack of nitrogen.

these substances splits off amino groups and produces NH_4^+. This process is thus known as **ammonification.** The ammonium released can be reused by certain plants or converted to other nitrogen compounds, as discussed next.

The oxidation of NH_4^+ to NO_2^- and NO_3^- is a process called **nitrification.** It is an essential conversion process for generating the most oxidized form of nitrogen (NO_3). This reaction occurs in two phases and involves two different kinds of lithotrophic bacteria in soil and water. In the first phase, certain gram-negative genera such as *Nitrosomonas, Nitrosospira,* and *Nitrosococcus* oxidize NH_3 to NO_2^- as a means of generating energy. Nitrite is rapidly acted upon by a second group of nitrifiers, including *Nitrobacter, Nitrosospira,* and *Nitrococcus,* which perform the **final** oxidation of NO_2^- to NO_3^-. Nitrates can be assimilated through several routes by a variety of organisms (plants, fungi, and bacteria). Nitrate and nitrite are also important in anaerobic respiration where they serve as terminal electron acceptors; some bacteria use them as a source of oxygen as well.

The nitrogen cycle is complete when nitrogen compounds are returned to the reservoir in the air by a reaction series that converts NO_3^- through intermediate steps to atmospheric nitrogen. The first step, which involves the reduction of nitrate to nitrite, is so common that hundreds of different bacterial species can do it. Several genera such as *Bacillus, Pseudomonas, Spirillum,* and *Thiobacillus* can carry out this **denitrification** process to completion as follows:

$$NO_3^- \rightarrow NO_2^- \rightarrow NO \rightarrow N_2O \rightarrow N_2 \text{ (gas)}$$

This process illustrates that incomplete denitrification is the main source of the greenhouse gas nitrous oxide (N_2O).

Sedimentary Cycles

The Sulfur Cycle

The sulfur cycle resembles the carbon cycle more than the nitrogen cycle in that sulfur is mostly in solid form and originates from natural sedimentary deposits in rocks, oceans, lakes, and swamps rather than from the atmosphere. Sulfur

Figure 24.8 Nitrogen fixation through symbiosis.
(a) Events leading to formation of root nodules. Cells of the bacterium *Rhizobium* attach to a legume root hair and cause it to curl. Invasion of the legume root proper by *Rhizobium* initiates the formation of an infection thread that spreads into numerous adjacent cells. The presence of bacteria in cells causes nodule formation. **(b)** Mature nodules that have developed in a sweet clover plant.

INSIGHT 24.1   Greenhouse Gases, Fossil Fuels, Cows, Termites, and Global Warming

The sun's radiant energy does more than drive photosynthesis; it also helps maintain the stability of the earth's temperature and climatic conditions. As radiation impinges on the earth's surface, much of it is absorbed, but a large amount of the infrared (heat) radiation bounces back into the upper levels of the atmosphere. For billions of years, the atmosphere has been insulated by a layer of gases (primarily CO_2; CH_4; water vapor; and nitrous oxide, N_2O) formed by natural processes such as respiration and decomposition, which are part of biogeochemical cycles. This layer traps a certain amount of the reflected heat, yet also allows some of it to escape into space. As long as the amounts of heat entering and leaving are balanced, the mean temperature of the earth will not rise or fall in an erratic or life-threatening way. Although this phenomenon, called the **greenhouse effect**, is popularly viewed in a negative light, it must be emphasized that its function for eons has been primarily to foster life.

The greenhouse effect has become a matter of concern because *greenhouse gases* appear to be increasing at a rate that could disrupt the temperature balance. In effect, a denser insulation layer will trap more heat energy and gradually heat the earth. The amount of CO_2 released collectively by respiration, anaerobic microbial activity, fuel combustion, and volcanic activity has increased more than 30% since the beginning of the industrial era. By far the greatest increase in CO_2 production results from human activities such as combustion of fossil fuels, burning forests to clear agricultural land, and manufacturing.

Deforestation has the added impact of removing large areas of photosynthesizing plants that would otherwise consume some of the CO_2.

Originally, experts on the greenhouse effect were concerned primarily about increasing CO_2 levels, but it now appears that the other greenhouse gases combined may have a greater contribution than CO_2, and they, too, are increasing. One of these gases, methane (CH_4) released from the gastrointestinal tract of ruminant animals such as cattle, goats, and sheep, has doubled over the past century. A single cow is estimated to release 200–400 pounds of methane a year through its belching and flatulence. The gut of termites also harbors wood-digesting bacteria and methanogenic archaea. Even the human intestinal tract can support methanogens. Methane traps 21 times more heat than does carbon dioxide. Other greenhouse gases such as nitrous oxide and sulfur dioxide (SO_2) are also increasing through automobile and industrial pollution.

There is not yet complete agreement as to the extent and effects of global warming. It has been documented that the mean temperature of the earth has increased by $\pm 1.0°C$ since 1860. If the rate of increase continues, by 2050 a rise in the average temperature of 4°C to 5°C will begin to melt the polar ice caps and raise the levels of the ocean 2 to 3 feet. Some experts predict more serious effects, including massive flooding of coastal regions, changes in rainfall patterns, expansion of deserts, and long-term climatic disruptions.

Global Mean Temperature over Land & Ocean

exists in the elemental form (S) and as hydrogen sulfide gas (H_2S), sulfate (SO_4), and thiosulfate (S_2O_3). Most of the oxidations and reductions that convert one form of inorganic sulfur to another are accomplished by bacteria. Plants and many microorganisms can assimilate only SO_4, and animals must have an organic source. Organic sulfur occurs in the amino acids cystine, cysteine, and methionine, which contain sulfhydryl (—SH) groups and form disulfide (S—S) bonds that contribute to the stability and configuration of proteins.

One of the most remarkable contributors to the cycling of sulfur in the biosphere are the thiobacilli. These gram-negative, motile rods flourish in mud, sewage, bogs, mining drainage, and brackish springs that can be inhospitable to organisms that require complex organic nutrients. But the metabolism of these specialized lithotrophic bacteria is adapted to extracting energy by oxidizing elemental sulfur, sulfides, and thiosulfate. One species, *T. thiooxidans*, is so efficient at this process that it secretes large amounts of sulfuric acid into its environment, as shown by the following equation:

$$Na_2S_2O_3 + H_2O + O_2 \rightarrow$$
$$Na_2SO_4 + H_2SO_4 \text{ (sulfuric acid)} + 4S$$

The marvel of this bacterium is its ability to create and survive in the most acidic habitats on the earth. It also plays an essential part in the phosphorus cycle, and its relative, *T. ferrooxidans,* participates in the cycling of iron. Other bacteria that can oxidize sulfur to sulfates are the photosynthetic sulfur bacteria mentioned in the section on photosynthesis.

The sulfates formed from oxidation of sulfurous compounds are assimilated into biomass by a wide variety of organisms. The sulfur cycle reaches completion when inorganic and organic sulfur compounds are reduced. Bacteria in the genera *Desulfovibrio* and *Desulfuromonas* anaerobically reduce sulfates to hydrogen sulfide or metal sulfide as the final step in electron transport. Sites in ocean sediments and mud where these bacteria live usually emanate a strong, rotten-egg stench from H_2S and may be blackened by the iron they contain.

The Phosphorus Cycle

Phosphorus is an integral component of DNA, RNA, and ATP, and all life depends upon a constant supply of it. It cycles between the abiotic and biotic environments almost exclusively as inorganic phosphate (PO_4) rather than its elemental form **(figure 24.10).** The chief inorganic reservoir is phosphate rock, which contains the insoluble compound fluorapatite, $Ca_5(PO_4)_3F$. Before it can enter biological systems, this mineral must be *phosphatized*—converted into more soluble PO_4^{3-} by the action of acid. Phosphate is released naturally when the sulfuric acid produced by *Thiobacillus* dissolves phosphate rock. Soluble phosphate in the soil and water is the principal source for autotrophs, which fix it onto organic molecules and pass it on to heterotrophs in this form. Organic phosphate is returned to the pool of soluble phosphate by decomposers, and it is finally cycled back to the mineral reservoir by slow geologic processes such as sedimentation. Because the low phosphate content of many soils can limit productivity, phosphate is added to soil to increase agricultural yields. The excess runoff of fertilizer into the hydrosphere is often responsible for overgrowth of aquatic pests (see eutrophication in a subsequent section on aquatic habitats).

Other Forms of Cycling

The involvement of microbes in cycling elements and compounds can be escalated by the introduction of toxic substances into the environment. Such toxic elements as arsenic, chromium, lead, and mercury as well as hundreds of thousands of synthetic chemicals introduced into the environment over the past hundred years are readily caught up in cycles by microbial actions. Some of these chemicals

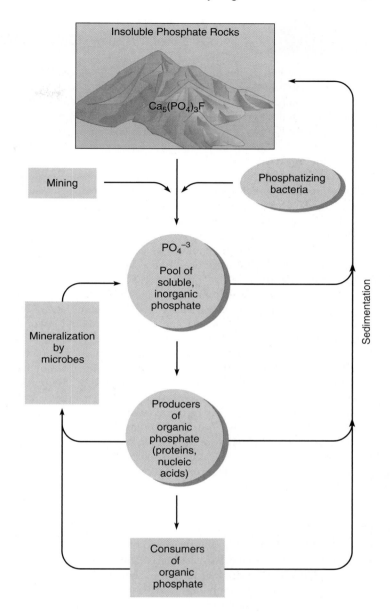

Figure 24.10 The phosphorus cycle. The pool of phosphate existing in sedimentary rocks is released into the ecosystem either naturally by erosion and microbial action or artificially by mining and the use of phosphate fertilizers. Soluble phosphate (PO_4^{3-}) is cycled through producers, consumers, and decomposers back into the soluble pool of phosphate, or it is returned to sediment in the aquatic biosphere.

will be converted into less harmful substances, but others, such as PCB and heavy metals, persist and flow along with nutrients into all levels of the biosphere. If such a pollutant accumulates in living tissue and is not excreted, it can be accumulated by living things through the natural trophic flow of the ecosystem. This process is known as bioaccumulation. Microscopic producers such as bacteria and algae begin the accumulation process. With each new level of the food chain, the consumers gather an increasing amount

INSIGHT 24.2   Cute Killer Whale—Or Swimming Waste Dump?

In the early 1990s, Keiko the killer whale stole hearts as the star of the movie *Free Willy*. Eleven years later, Keiko died of pneumonia in a fjord in Norway, never having fully adjusted to being back in the wild. Even though whales that die close to shore are usually towed out to sea, Keiko was buried on the beach where he was found, probably because of the close connection humans felt with him. That was not the end of the story, however. Environmental groups in Norway raised concerns about burying the animal onshore due to the high probability that his tissues contained high amounts of PCBs. It was nothing personal against Keiko; whales all over the world have been found to have bioaccumulated this toxic chemical.

PCBs (polychlorinated biphenyls) are very stable manufactured compounds that were heavily used in industrial settings from the 1930s to the 1970s. They found widespread use as insulating fluids in electrical applications. They are highly soluble in lipid compounds, and for that reason they bioaccumulate in the fat tissues of animals. The bioaccumulation seems to be worst near the poles of the earth, where many higher animals (including humans) use contaminated fish as a major part of their diets. Complicating this fact is the concentration of volatile PCBs in the atmosphere. Atmospheric circulation carries PCBs to the poles, and the cold temperatures cause the pollutants to condense and fall to the surface, where they further contaminate the food chain. In 1998, a group of polar bears in Norway was found to have bizarre developmental deformities. Seven bears of a group of 450 surveyed (approximately 2%) possessed both male and female reproductive organs—a bizarre mutation that was attributed to PCB accumulation in the bears' bodies.

PCB contamination of wildlife is not limited to the poles, however. In Belgium in 1994, four sperm whales were stranded and died in coastal waters. All were found to have 30 parts per million (ppm) PCBs in their kidneys and blubber. Beluga whales in the Gulf of St. Lawrence in eastern Canada have been found to have 3,200 ppm PCBs in their tissues—a level 1,600 times higher than the level of contamination that triggers EPA regulations requiring the incineration of any materials found to have that concentration of PCB. A bottlenose dolphin in Cape Cod was recently found to have 6,800 ppm PCBs. "This animal was, by definition, a swimming toxic waste dump," says Roger Payne, author of *Among Whales*.

And that brings us back to Keiko. For weeks after he was buried in a quiet ceremony, local schoolchildren came to place rocks on his grave in a Viking tradition of respect. The stark contrast between that loving act and the fact that many people feel he should have been dug up and incinerated highlights the conflicted relationship we have with nature. We love it, but are we ignoring the damage we inflict upon it?

Keiko was buried on the shore of the Taknes Bay in Norway, December 15, 2003.

---

of the chemical, until the top consumers can contain toxic levels **(Insight 24.2)**.

One example of this is mercury compounds used in household antiseptics and disinfectants, agriculture, and industry. Elemental mercury precipitates proteins by attaching to functional groups and is most toxic in the ethyl or methyl mercury form. Recent studies have disclosed increased mercury content in fish taken from oceans and freshwater lakes in North America and even in canned tuna, adding to the risk in consumption of these products.

24.2 Learning Outcomes—Can You . . .

7. . . . list five important elements of biogeochemical cycles?
8. . . . diagram a carbon cycle?
9. . . . point out where methanogens influence the carbon cycle?
10. . . . list the four reactions involved in the nitrogen cycle?
11. . . . describe the process of nitrogen fixation, and provide some examples of organisms that perform it?
12. . . . give brief summaries of the sulfur and phosphorus cycles?

24.3 Microbes on Land and in Water

As you have heard several times already in this book, until fairly recently, our understanding of which microbes inhabited a place, whether it was the human gut or your backyard pond, relied on culturing them. Just as there is a Human Microbiome Project, scientists have been busy using these techniques to identify the microbes living in the environment, which includes land, water, and air. The field of environmental genomics has revealed many surprising things, such as bacteria living in glaciers and deep under the seafloor.

Environmental Sampling in the Genomic Era

The methods for identifying bacteria and genes in the environment are evolving rapidly. As you know, when the genes of all microbes in a habitat are sampled, it is called metagenomics. We'll discuss the basic principles here. The process always begins with an environmental sample, such as a gallon of seawater or a gram of soil. Techniques are available to extract the DNA from such samples. Fragments can then be cloned into plasmid vectors in the same way that we described in chapter 10. A library of DNA fragments can then be preserved and amplified. If specific gene sequences

are sought (and known in advance) PCR can be used directly on the environmental sample to fish the "needle out of the haystack." This is commonly performed when seeking 16s rRNA molecules. Novel sequences are still found in this way as the "fishing" is done with conserved sequences found on the different molecules. Once the DNA pieces are retrieved using either method, they can be sequenced, and it can be determined whether they match known sequences or are new to us. The DNA sequences can also be cloned into expression vectors, which can then be screened for their functions, or their products. These processes are summarized in **figure 24.11.**

Soil Microbiology: The Composition of the Lithosphere

At the microscopic level, soil is a dynamic ecosystem that supports complex interactions between numerous geologic, chemical, and biological factors. This rich region, called the lithosphere, teems with microbes, serves a dynamic role in biogeochemical cycles, and is an important repository for organic detritus and dead terrestrial organisms.

Rock decomposition releases various-size particles, ranging from rocks, pebbles, and sand grains to microscopic

Figure 24.11 Construction and screening of genomic libraries directly from the environment.   DNA has been extracted directly from **(a)** bacterial mats at Yellowstone National Park, **(b)** soil samples from Alaska, **(c)** cabbage white butterfly larvae, and **(d)** tube worms from hydrothermal vents. The DNA is cloned into suitable vectors and transformed into a bacterial host. Sequences or gene products can then be analyzed.

morsels that lie in a loose aggregate **(figure 24.12).** The porous structure of soil creates various-size pockets or spaces that provide numerous microhabitats. Some spaces trap moisture and form a liquid phase in which mineral ions and other nutrients are dissolved. Other spaces trap air that will provide gases to soil microbes, plants, and animals. Because both water and air compete for these pockets, the water content of soil is directly related to its oxygen content. Water-saturated soils contain less oxygen, and dry soils have more. Gas tensions in soil can also vary vertically. In general, the concentration of O_2 decreases and that of CO_2 increases with the depth of soil. Aerobic and facultative organisms tend to occupy looser, drier soils, whereas anaerobes are adapted to waterlogged, poorly aerated soils.

Within the superstructure of the soil are varying amounts of humus, the slowly decaying organic litter from plant and animal tissues. This soft, crumbly mixture holds water like a sponge. It is also an important habitat for microbes that decompose the complex litter and gradually recycle nutrients. The humus content varies with climate, temperature, moisture and mineral content, and microbial action. Warm, tropical soils have a high rate of humus production and microbial decomposition. Because nutrients in these soils are swiftly released and used up, they do not accumulate. Fertilized agricultural soils in temperate climates build up humus at a high rate and are rich in nutrients. Humans can artificially increase the amount of humus by mixing plant refuse and animal wastes with soil and allowing natural decomposition to occur, a process called *composting.* Composting is a very active metabolic process that generates a great deal of heat. The temperature inside a well-maintained compost can reach 80°C to 100°C.

Living Activities in Soil

The rich culture medium of the soil supports a fantastic array of microorganisms (bacteria, fungi, algae, protozoa, and viruses). A gram of moist loam soil with high humus content can have a microbe count as high as 10 billion, each competing for its own niche and microhabitat. Some of the most distinctive biological interactions occur in the **rhizosphere,** the zone of soil surrounding the roots of plants, which contains associated bacteria, fungi, and protozoa (see figure 24.12). Plants interact with soil microbes in a truly synergistic fashion. Studies have shown that a rich microbial community grows in a biofilm around the root hairs and other exposed surfaces. Their presence stimulates the plant to exude growth factors such as carbon dioxide, sugars, amino acids, and vitamins. These nutrients are released into fluid spaces, where they can be readily captured by microbes. Bacteria and fungi likewise contribute to plant survival by releasing hormone-like growth factors and protective substances. They are also important in converting minerals into forms usable by plants. We saw numerous examples in the nitrogen, sulfur, and phosphorus cycles.

We previously observed that plants can form close symbiotic associations with microbes to fix nitrogen. Other mutualistic partnerships between plant roots and microbes

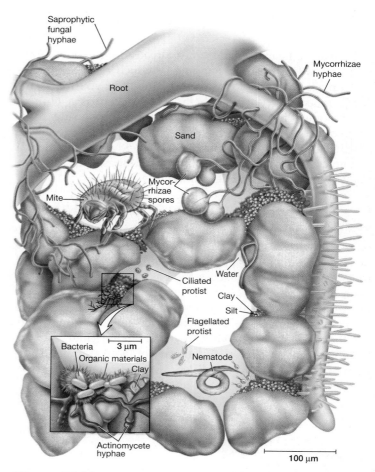

Figure 24.12 The soil habitat. A typical soil habitat contains a mixture of clay, silt, and sand along with soil organic matter. Roots and animals (e.g., nematodes and mites), as well as protozoa and bacteria, consume oxygen, which rapidly diffuses into the soil pores where the microbes live. Note that two types of fungi are present: mycorrhizal fungi, which derive their organic carbon from plant roots; and saprophytic fungi, which help degrade organic material.

are **mycorrhizae** (my″-koh-ry′-zee). These associations occur when various species of basidiomycetes, ascomycetes, or zygomycetes attach themselves to the roots of vascular plants **(figure 24.13).** The plant feeds the fungus through photosynthesis, and the fungus sustains the relationship in several ways. By extending its mycelium into the rhizosphere, it helps anchor the plant and increases the surface area for capturing water from dry soils and minerals from poor soils. Plants with mycorrhizae can inhabit severe habitats more successfully than plants without them.

The topsoil, which extends a few inches to a few feet from the surface, supports a host of burrowing animals such as nematodes, termites, and earthworms. Many of these animals are decomposer-reducer organisms that break down organic nutrients through digestion and also mechanically reduce or fragment the size of particles so that they are more readily mineralized by microbes. Aerobic bacteria initiate the digestion of organic matter into carbon dioxide and

Figure 24.13 Mycorrhizae. These symbiotic associations between fungi and plant roots favor the absorption of water and minerals from the soil.

water and generate minerals such as sulfate, phosphate, and nitrate, which can be further degraded by anaerobic bacteria. Fungal enzymes increase the efficiency of soil decomposition by hydrolyzing complex natural substances such as cellulose, keratin, lignin, chitin, and paraffin.

The soil is also a repository for agricultural, industrial, and domestic wastes such as insecticides, herbicides, fungicides, manufacturing wastes, and household chemicals. Applied microbiologists, using expertise from engineering, biotechnology, and ecology, work to explore the feasibility of harnessing indigenous soil microbes to break down undesirable hydrocarbons and pesticides (see chapter 25).

Deep Subsurface Microbiology

For the past 30 years, scientists have been sampling the deep subsurface—2 miles and more below the surface. From the very beginning of these studies, the results have been astounding. With the advent of genomic sampling, the discoveries are piling up. For instance, bacteria deep beneath the surface metabolize petroleum to CO_2 at a rate a million times slower than that of surface microbes, suggesting that the microbes may be anywhere from 100 years old to 100,000 years old. Many of these bacteria exist solely in biofilms on rock surfaces. Scientists are pondering how bacteria survive in very nearly abiotic environments, and are discovering new metabolic capabilities that may turn out to provide clues to the very origin of life.

Aquatic Microbiology

Water occupies nearly three-fourths of the earth's surface. The **hydrologic cycle (figure 24.14)** begins when surface water (lakes, oceans, rivers) exposed to the sun and wind evaporates and enters the vapor phase of the atmosphere. Living beings contribute to this reservoir by various activities. Plants lose moisture through transpiration (evapora-

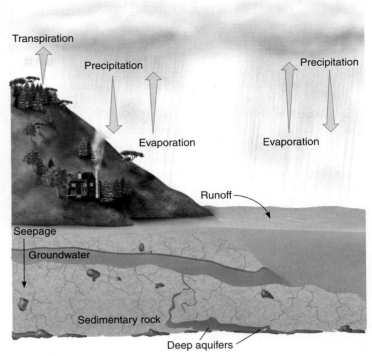

Figure 24.14 The hydrologic cycle. The largest proportion of water cycles through evaporation, transpiration, and precipitation between the hydrosphere and the atmosphere. Other reservoirs of water exist in the groundwater or deep storage aquifers in sedimentary rocks. Plants add to this cycle by releasing water through transpiration, and heterotrophs release it through respiration.

tion through leaves), and all aerobic organisms give off water during respiration. Airborne moisture accumulates in the atmosphere, most conspicuously as clouds.

Water is returned to the earth through condensation or precipitation (rain, snow), a process influenced by bacteria **(Insight 24.3)**. The largest proportion of precipitation falls back into surface waters, where it circulates rapidly between running water and standing water. Only about 2% of water seeps into the earth or is bound in ice, but these are very important reservoirs. **Table 24.2** shows how water

Table 24.2 Distribution of Water on Earth's Surface

Water Source	Water Volume, in Cubic Miles	Percentage of Total Water
Oceans	317,000,000	97.2269
Icecaps, glaciers	7,000,000	2.14
Groundwater	2,000,000	0.61
Freshwater lakes	30,000	0.009
Inland seas	25,000	0.008
Soil moisture	16,000	0.005
Atmosphere	3,100	0.001
Rivers	300	0.0001
		100.0000

Source: U.S. Geological Survey.

INSIGHT 24.3 | It's Raining Bacteria

Is precipitation just a clever mechanism bacteria use to disperse themselves in the environment? It seems that's at least one reason it rains. Meteorologists have known for a long time that clouds release rain and snow when particles of water become too large for the fine mist of a cloud to support. Tiny particles that cause the water to coalesce, termed *nucleators*, encourage the formation of raindrops or snowflakes. Traditionally, dust particles are thought to be the most important nucleators, though researchers have known since the 1970s that bacteria can serve this role as well. They just didn't appreciate how frequently they do it. In 2008, a scientist from Louisiana State University analyzed snows around the world and found that bacteria served as nucleators in almost all of them. In other words: Bacteria were causing the precipitation. The news that bacteria were causing it to rain reverberated through the climate change community. The process of nucleation, and therefore, precipitation, seemed unpredictable when it only involved dust particles. The discovery that bacteria are largely responsible opens brand new avenues for predicting, and possibly controlling, the global climate. As just one thought experiment: Imagine the implications for drought-stricken areas of the world.

is distributed in the various surface compartments. Surface water collects in extensive subterranean pockets produced by the underlying layers of rock, gravel, and sand. This process forms a deep groundwater source called an **aquifer.** The water in aquifers circulates very slowly and is an important replenishing source for surface water. It can resurface through springs, geysers, and hot vents, and it is also tapped as the primary supply for one-fourth of all water used by humans.

Although the total amount of water in the hydrologic cycle has not changed over millions of years, its distribution and quality have been greatly altered by human activities. Two serious problems have arisen with aquifers. First, as a result of increased well drilling, land development, and persistent local droughts, the aquifers in many areas have not been replenished as rapidly as they have been depleted. As these reserves are used up, humans will have to rely on other delivery sys-

tems such as pipelines, dams, and reservoirs, which can further disrupt the cycling of water. Second, because water picks up materials when falling through air or percolating through the ground, aquifers are also important collection points for pollutants. As we will see, the proper management of water resources is one of the greatest challenges of this century.

Marine Environments

The ocean exhibits extreme variations in salinity, depth, temperature, hydrostatic pressure, and mixing. Even so, it supports a great abundance of bacteria and viruses, the extent of which has only been appreciated in very recent years. In the opening to chapter 1, you read that in 2004, J. Craig Venter (the same Venter from the Human Genome Project, chapter 10) set sail on a 100-ft yacht to the Sargasso Sea to get the DNA profile of an entire ecosystem. The Sargasso Sea was thought to be relatively sparsely populated by life forms, as it was nutrient-poor. His team found a rich variety of life and discovered 1,800 new species and more than 1.2 million new genes. His group widened the search over the next 2 years and sailed around the world, collecting ocean samples all along the way. They eventually discovered 6 million new genes and thousands of new proteins—essentially doubling the number of known proteins. Proteins, of course, are responsible for nearly all of the activities of cells. The capabilities of microbes have been greatly underappreciated, in other words, because we have not been able to cultivate the vast majority of them in the laboratory.

In another startling study, green sulfur photosynthetic bacteria were found growing in deep-sea vents, a place where the sun's light cannot penetrate. These bacteria cannot live without light. It appears that the light they use to photosynthesize comes from chemical reactions, the breaking of mineral crystals, or from bubble formation. If these results hold up over time, this will be the first organism found to photosynthesize with anything other than sunlight.

Oceans contain several million viruses per milliliter. Most of these viruses are bacteriophages and therefore pose no danger to humans, but as parasites of bacteria, they appear to be a natural control mechanism for these populations. Plus, their lysis of bacteria plays an important role in the turnover of nutrients in the ocean. An important discovery is that bacteriophages of cyanobacteria contain genes responsible for photosynthesis. It has been estimated that bacteriophages may be responsible for 5% of the planet's photosynthesis (with marine cyanobacteria responsible for 40% or more).

Aquatic Communities

The freshwater environment is a site of tremendous microbiological activity. Microbial distribution is associated with sunlight, temperature, oxygen levels, and nutrient availability. The uppermost portion is the most productive self-sustaining region because it contains large numbers of **plankton,** a floating microbial community that drifts with wave action and currents. A major member of this assemblage is the phytoplankton, containing a variety of photosynthetic algae and cyanobacteria. The phytoplankton provide nutrition for **zooplankton,** microscopic consumers such as protozoa and invertebrates that filter, feed, prey, or scavenge. The plankton supports numerous other trophic levels such as larger invertebrates and fish. With its high nutrient content, the deeper regions also support an extensive variety and concentration of organisms, including aquatic plants, aerobic bacteria, and anaerobic bacteria actively involved in recycling organic detritus.

Larger bodies of standing water develop gradients in temperature or thermal stratification, especially during the summer **(figure 24.15).** The upper region, called the *epilimnion,* is warmest, and the deeper *hypolimnion* is cooler. Between these is a buffer zone, the **thermocline,** that ordinarily prevents the mixing of the two. Twice a year, during the warming cycle of spring and the cooling cycle of fall, temperature changes in the water column break down the thermocline and cause the water from the two strata to mix. Mixing disrupts the stratification and creates currents that bring nutrients up from the sediments. This process, called *upwelling,* is associated with increased activity by certain groups of microbes and is one explanation for the periodic emergence of *red tides* in oceans **(figure 24.16)** caused

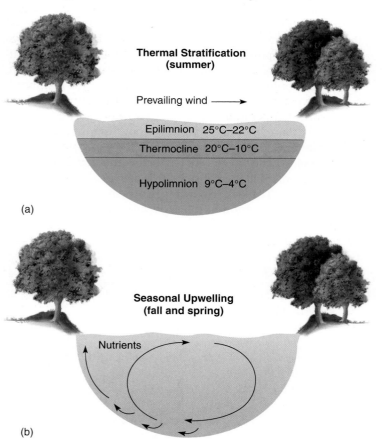

Thermal Stratification (summer)

Prevailing wind ⟶

Epilimnion   25°C–22°C
Thermocline   20°C–10°C
Hypolimnion   9°C–4°C

(a)

Seasonal Upwelling (fall and spring)

Nutrients

(b)

Figure 24.15 Profiles of a lake. **(a)** During summer, a lake becomes stabilized into three major temperature strata. **(b)** During fall and spring, cooling or heating of the water disrupts the temperature strata and causes upwelling of nutrients from the bottom sediments.

(a)

(b)

(c)

Figure 24.16 Red tides. **(a)** Single-celled red algae called dinoflagellates (*Gymnodinium* shown here) bloom in high-nutrient, warm seawater and impart a noticeable red color to it, as shown in (b). **(b)** An aerial view of California coastline in the midst of a massive red tide. **(c)** Fish washed ashore during a red tide bloom.

Case File 24   *Wrap-Up*

Bioremediation, as discussed at the beginning of this chapter and also in the next chapter, relies on microorganisms to mineralize pollutants, such as oil spilled from an oil tanker. As with all microorganisms, those involved in bioremediation require nutrients. Oil is rich in carbon that microorganisms can utilize, but it lacks other essential nutrients, such as nitrogen and phosphorus. For this reason, environmental microbiologists attempted to accelerate bioremediation of the *Exxon Valdez* oil spill by applying fertilizers containing nitrogen and phosphorus. Approximately 50,000 kg of nitrogen and 5,000 kg of phosphorus were applied between 1989 and 1992. Overall, these enormous applications appeared to have the desired effect: Bacteria from fertilized beaches mineralized the components of oil up to 18 times faster than bacteria from beaches that did not receive fertilizer. While today the shoreline has still not completely recovered, the actions of the bacteria—with a little push from humans—set Prince William Sound's shore on the right path.

The cleanup in the Gulf of Mexico is a different story. The oil is dispersed across hundreds of miles of ocean water, and is much less concentrated than in the Alaska spill. Still, some believe that newly identified bacteria are sopping up the oil there as well.

See: 1994. *Nature.* 368:413–418.

Figure 24.17 Heavy surface growth of algae and cyanobacteria in a eutrophic pond.

by toxin-producing dinoflagellates. A recent outbreak of fish and human disease on the eastern seaboard has been attributed to the overgrowth of certain species of these algae in polluted water. These algae produce a potent muscle toxin that can be concentrated by shellfish through filtration feeding. When humans eat clams, mussels, or oysters that contain the toxin, they develop paralytic shellfish poisoning. People living in coastal areas are cautioned not to eat shellfish during those months of the year associated with red tides (varies from one area to another).

Because oxygen is not very soluble in water and is rapidly used up by the plankton, its concentration forms a gradient, from highest in the epilimnion to lowest at the bottom. In general, the amount of oxygen that can be dissolved is dependent on temperature. Warmer strata on the surface tend to carry lower levels of this gas. But of all the characteristics of water, the greatest range occurs in nutrient levels. Nutrient-deficient aquatic ecosystems are called **oligotrophic** (ahl"-ih-goh-trof'-ik). Species that can make a living on such starvation rations are *Hyphomicrobium* and *Caulobacter*. These bacteria have special stalks that capture even minuscule amounts of hydrocarbons present in oligotrophic habitats. At one time, it

was thought that viruses were present only in very low levels in aquatic habitats, but researchers have now discovered that there are anywhere from 2 to 10 times as many viruses as bacteria in marine and freshwater communities. The addition of excess quantities of nutrients to aquatic ecosystems, termed **eutrophication,** often wreaks havoc on the communities involved. The sudden influx of abundant nutrients along with warm temperatures encourages a heavy surface growth of cyanobacteria and algae called a bloom **(figure 24.17).** This heavy mat of biomass effectively shuts off the oxygen supply to the lake below. The oxygen content below the surface is further depleted by aerobic heterotrophs that actively decompose the organic matter. The lack of oxygen greatly disturbs the ecological balance of the community. It causes massive die-offs of strict aerobes (fish, invertebrates), and only anaerobic or facultative microbes will survive.

24.3 Learning Outcomes—Can You ...

13. ... outline the basic process used to perform metagenomic analysis of the environment?
14. ... list two important partnerships that occur in the soil?
15. ... diagram the hydrologic cycle?
16. ... discuss what metagenomic sampling of oceans has revealed?
17. ... name the regions, top to bottom, of large bodies of standing water?
18. ... define eutrophication and discuss its consequences?

Chapter Summary

24.1 Ecology: The Interconnecting Web of Life

- The study of ecology includes both living (biotic) and nonliving (abiotic) components of the earth.
- Ecosystems are organizations of living populations in specific habitats. Environmental ecosystems require a continuous outside source of energy for survival and a nonliving habitat consisting of soil, water, and air.
- A living community is composed of populations that show a pattern of energy and nutritional relationships called a food web. Microorganisms are essential producers and decomposers in any ecosystem.

24.2 The Natural Recycling of Bioelements

- Nutrients and minerals necessary to communities and ecosystems must be continuously recycled. These biogeochemical cycles involve transformation of elements from inorganic to organic forms and back again. Specific types of microorganisms are needed to convert many nutrients from one form to another.
- Elements of critical importance to all ecosystems that cycle through various forms are carbon, nitrogen, sulfur, phosphorus, and water. Carbon and nitrogen are part of the atmospheric cycle. Sulfur and phosphorus are part of the sedimentary cycling of nutrients.

24.3 Microbes on Land and in Water

- The earth's land, water, and air are colonized by more microbes than we ever imagined. We have discovered the magnitude of their numbers through metagenomics, the sampling of the environment for DNA sequences.
- The lithosphere, or soil, is an ecosystem in which mineral-rich rocks are decomposed to organic humus, the base for the soil community. Soil ecosystems vary according to the kinds of rocks and amount of water, air, and nutrients present.
- The deep subsurface, below land and sea, is colonized by a rich array of microbes that have a wide variety of metabolic capabilities.
- The food web of the aquatic community is built on phytoplankton and zooplankton. The nature of the aquatic community varies with the temperature, depth, minerals, and amount of light present in each zone.
- The ocean is populated by millions of microorganisms per milliliter. Photosynthetic bacteriophages are abundant.
- Eutrophication of freshwater and marine systems is caused by the addition of excess nutrients. It causes major disruptions in the ecology of these systems.

Multiple-Choice and True-False Questions   Knowledge and Comprehension

Multiple-Choice Questions. Select the correct answer from the answers provided.

1. Which of the following is *not* a major subdivision of the biosphere?
   - a. hydrosphere
   - b. lithosphere
   - c. stratosphere
   - d. atmosphere

2. A/an ____ is defined as a collection of populations sharing a given habitat.
   - a. biosphere
   - b. community
   - c. biome
   - d. ecosystem

3. The quantity of available nutrients ____ from the lower levels of the energy pyramid to the higher ones.
   - a. increases
   - b. decreases
   - c. remains stable
   - d. cycles

4. Which of the following is considered a greenhouse gas?
   - a. CO_2
   - b. CH_4
   - c. N_2O
   - d. all of these

5. Root nodules contain ____, which can ____.
   - a. *Azotobacter*, fix N_2
   - b. *Nitrosomonas*, nitrify NH_3^-
   - c. rhizobia, fix N_2
   - d. *Bacillus*, denitrify NO_3^-

6. Which element(s) has/have an inorganic reservoir that exists primarily in sedimentary deposits?
   - a. nitrogen
   - b. phosphorus
   - c. sulfur
   - d. both b and c

7. What percentage of the earth's biomass is made of microbes?
   - a. a small fraction
   - b. at least half of it
   - c. all of it
   - d. all of the above

8. Genomic analysis of the land, sea, and air has shown us that
   - a. there are many more animals than we expected.
   - b. there were much fewer microbes than we expected.
   - c. seawater is much more sterile than we expected.
   - d. microbes colonize places we never imagined.

9. Microbes in the environment are likely to be
   - a. living in biofilms on surfaces.
   - b. living solitary and planktonic lives.
   - c. nonculturable in the lab.
   - d. two of the above.

10. Recent studies reveal that
    - a. 100% of photosynthesis is accomplished by plants.
    - b. viruses may well be responsible for some photosynthesis.
    - c. the sun is the only source of energy for photosynthesis.
    - d. none of the above

True-False Questions. If the statement is true, leave as is. If it is false, correct it by rewriting the sentence.

11. Pure cultures are very common in the biosphere.

12. Bioremediation usually involves more than one type of microorganism.

13. The production of all nitrogenous compounds begins with the process called nitrogen fixation.

14. The high mercury content found in some fish is the result of a process called bioaccumulation.

15. As far as we know, all microorganisms exist in multiple-species communities.

Critical Thinking Questions   Application and Analysis

These questions are suggested as a *writing-to-learn* experience. For each question, compose a one- or two-paragraph answer that includes the factual information needed to completely address the question.

1. Compare the concepts of habitat and niche using *Chlamydomonas* (figure 24.2) as an example.

2. a. Outline the general characteristics of a biogeochemical cycle.
   b. What are the major sources of carbon, nitrogen, phosphorus, and sulfur?

3. a. In what major forms is carbon found? Name three ways carbon is returned to the atmosphere.
   b. Name a way it is fixed into organic compounds.
   c. What form is the least available for the majority of living things?

4. a. Describe nitrogen fixation, ammonification, nitrification, and denitrification.
   b. What form of nitrogen is required by plants? By animals?

5. a. Describe the structure of the soil and the rhizosphere.
   b. What is humus?
   c. Compare and contrast root nodules with mycorrhizae.

6. a. Outline the modes of cycling water through the lithosphere, hydrosphere, and atmosphere.
   b. What are the roles of precipitation, condensation, respiration, transpiration, surface water, and aquifers?

7. a. What causes the formation of the epilimnion, hypolimnion, and thermocline?
   b. What is upwelling?
   c. In what ways are red tides and eutrophic algal blooms similar and different?

8. What makes the bacterium found living alone in the South African gold mine the type of microbe that could survive on Mars?

9. a. What factors cause energy to decrease with each trophic level?
   b. How is it possible for energy to be lost and the ecosystem to still run efficiently?
   c. Are the nutrients on the earth a renewable resource? Why, or why not?

10. What eventually happens to the nutrients that run off into the ocean with sewage and other effluents?

Concept Mapping   Synthesis

Appendix D provides guidance for working with concept maps.

1. Supply your own linking words or phrases in this concept map, and provide the missing concepts in the empty boxes.

Visual Connections   Synthesis

These questions use visual images or previous content to make connections to this chapter's concepts.

1. **From chapter 6, figure 6.19.** We suggested that bacteriophages in the ocean have two important functions, photosynthesis and the turnover of nutrients. Which of these two activities is more likely to be accomplished when the bacteriophage is in the lysogenic state?

2. **From chapter 8, figure 8.26.** What process does this represent? How does it link to the biogeochemical cycles from this chapter?

www.connect.microbiology.com

Enhance your study of this chapter with study tools and practice tests. Also ask your instructor about the resources available through ConnectPlus, including the media-rich eBook, interactive learning tools, and animations.

25

Applied Microbiology and Food and Water Safety

Case File 25

There are bacteria adapted to survive in every kind of habitat. There are marine bacteria and freshwater bacteria—and even some that thrive only in brackish waters, which are part marine and part fresh. Lately, bacteria that live in brackish waters have been causing serious wound infections, and even some deaths, in humans.

In 2006, a mortgage broker in his 30s fell into a harbor in Hawaii 6 days after a sewage pipe failure had allowed 48 million gallons of sewage to flow into the harbor water. The man was admitted to the hospital, and within days he died from massive organ failure caused by septicemia with *Vibrio vulnificus*. You may be familiar with *Vibrio cholerae*, the diarrhea agent. Its relative, *V. vulnificus*, tends to invade breaks in the skin and then proliferate in the bloodstream, often causing massive infections necessitating amputation, and sometimes even leading to death.

- Once the man was admitted to the hospital, what steps would you take to determine what was making him ill?

- If you were a public official in charge of Hawaii's recreational waters, how would you determine when the waters were safe again?

Continuing the Case appears on page 769.

Outline and Learning Outcomes

25.1 Applied Microbiology and Biotechnology

1. Define biotechnology.
2. Compose a sentence about the history of applied microbiology.

25.1 Applied Microbiology and Biotechnology

This chapter emphasizes the artificial applications of microbes in communal waste remediation, water treatment, and the manufacture of food, medical, biochemical, drug, and agricultural products. Key to the application of microbes is understanding their ecology (see chapters 7, 8, and 24) and the structure of their natural environments. Microbes have evolved by responding to functional pressures, as when nutrients are limited or unevenly available, or when other organisms are competing for the nutrients. Applied and industrial microbiologists have learned from microbes' own survival mechanisms and have devised ways to manipulate them for use by people.

The profound and sweeping involvement of microbes in the natural world is inescapable. Although our daily encounters with them usually go unnoticed, human and microbial life are clearly intertwined on many levels. It is no wonder that long ago humans realized the power of microbes and harnessed them for specific metabolic tasks. The practical applications of microorganisms in manufacturing products or carrying out a particular decomposition process belong to the large and diverse area of **biotechnology.** Biotechnology has an ancient history, dating back nearly 6,000 years to those first observant humans who discovered that grape juice left to sit resulted in wine or that bread dough properly infused with a starter would rise. Today, biotechnology has become a fertile ground for hundreds of applications in industry, medicine, agriculture, food sciences, and environmental protec-

tion, and it has even come to include the genetic alterations of microbes and other organisms.

Most biotechnological systems involve the actions of bacteria, yeasts, molds, and algae that have been selected or altered to synthesize a certain food, drug, organic acid, alcohol, or vitamin. Many such food and industrial end products are obtained through **fermentation,** a general term used here to refer to the mass, controlled culture of microbes to produce desired organic compounds. It also includes the use of microbes in sewage control, pollution control, metal mining, and bioremediation, which was introduced in chapter 24 **(Insight 25.1).**

25.1 Learning Outcomes—Can You ...
1. ... define biotechnology?
2. ... compose a sentence about the history of applied microbiology?

25.2 Microorganisms in Water and Wastewater Treatment

Most drinking water comes from rivers, aquifers, and springs. Only in remote, undeveloped, or high mountain areas is this water used in its natural form. In most cities, it must be treated before it is supplied to consumers. Water supplies such as deep wells that are relatively clean and free of contaminants require less treatment than those from surface sources laden with wastes. The stepwise process in water purification as carried

INSIGHT 25.1	Bioremediation: The Pollution Solution?

The soil and water of the earth have long been considered convenient repositories for solid and liquid wastes. Humans have been burying solid wastes for thousands of years, but the process has escalated in the past 50 years. Every year, about 300 metric tons of pollutants, industrial wastes, and garbage are deposited into the natural environment. Often, this dumping is done with the mistaken idea that naturally occurring microbes will eventually biodegrade (break down) waste material.

Landfills currently serve as a final resting place for hundreds of castoffs from an affluent society, including yard wastes, paper, glass, plastics, wood, textiles, rubber, metal, paints, and solvents. This conglomeration is dumped into holes and is covered with soil. Although it is true that many substances are readily biodegradable, materials such as plastics and glass are not. Successful biodegradation also requires a compost containing specific types of microorganisms, adequate moisture, and oxygen. The environment surrounding buried trash provides none of these conditions. Large, dry, anaerobic masses of plant materials, paper, and other organic materials will not be successfully attacked by the aerobic microorganisms that dominate in biodegradation. As we continue to fill up hillsides with waste, the future of these landfills is a prime concern. One of the most serious of these concerns is that they will be a source of toxic compounds that seep into the ground and water.

In a search for solutions, waste management has turned to **bioremediation**—using microbes to break down or remove toxic wastes in water and soil. Some of these waste-eating microbes are natural soil and water residents with a surprising capacity to decompose even artificial substances. Because the natural, unaided process occurs too slowly, most cleanups are accomplished by commercial bioremediation services that treat the contaminated soil with oxygen, nutrients, and water to increase the rate of microbial action. Through these actions, levels of pesticides such as 2,4-D can be reduced to 96% of their original levels, and solvents can be reduced from 1 million parts per billion (ppb) to 10 ppb or less. Bacteria are also being used to help break up and digest oil from spills and refineries.

Among the most important bioremedial microbes are species of *Pseudomonas*, *Geobacter*, and *Bacillus* and various toxin-eating fungi.

So far, about 35 recombinant microbes have been created for bioremediation. Species of *Rhodococcus* and *Burkholderia* have been engineered to decompose PCBs, and certain forms of *Pseudomonas* now contain genes for detoxifying heavy metals, carbon tetrachloride, and naphthalene. With over 3,000 toxic waste sites in the United States alone, the need for effective bioremediation is a top priority.

Source: 2006. *Proceedings of the National Academy of Science* 103:15280–15287.

This marsh had been used to dump oil refinery waste. The level of certain pollutants was over 130,000 ppm.

After bioremediation with nutrients and microbes, the levels were reduced to less than 300 ppm in 4 months. This area has been bioremediated to the point that the land may be used for growing plants.

out by most cities is shown in **figure 25.1.** Treatment begins with the impoundment of water in a large reservoir such as a dam or catch basin that serves the dual purpose of storage and sedimentation. The access to reservoirs is controlled to avoid contamination by animals, wastes, and runoff water. In addition, overgrowth of cyanobacteria and algae that add undesirable qualities to the water is prevented by pretreatment with copper sulfate (0.3 ppm). Sedimentation to remove large particulate matter is also encouraged during this storage period.

Next, the water is pumped to holding ponds or tanks, where it undergoes further settling, aeration, and filtration.

The water is filtered first through sand beds or pulverized diatomaceous earth to remove residual bacteria, viruses, and protozoa and then through activated charcoal to remove undesirable organic contaminants. Pipes coming from the filtration beds collect the water in storage tanks. The final step in treatment is chemical disinfection by bubbling chlorine gas through the tank until it reaches a concentration of 1 to 2 ppm (some municipal plants use chloramines for this purpose) (see chapter 11). A few pilot plants in the United States are using ozone or peroxide for final disinfection, but these methods are expensive and cannot sustain an antimicrobial

Figure 25.2 Water: one source, many uses.

but a large quantity is still being emptied raw (untreated) into the aquatic environment primarily because heavily contaminated waters require far more stringent and costly methods of treatment than are currently available to most cities.

Sewage contains large amounts of solid wastes, dissolved organic matter, and toxic chemicals that pose a health risk. To remove all potential health hazards, treatment typically requires three phases: The primary stage separates out large matter; the secondary stage reduces remaining matter and can remove some toxic substances; and the tertiary stage completes the purification of the water **(figure 25.3)**. Microbial activity is an integral part of the overall process. The systems for sewage treatment are massive engineering marvels.

In the **primary phase** of treatment, floating bulkier materials such as paper, plastic waste, and bottles are skimmed

Figure 25.1 The major steps in water purification as carried out by a modern municipal treatment plant.

effect over long storage times. The final quality varies, but most tap water has a slight odor or taste from disinfection.

In many parts of the world, the same water that serves as a source of drinking water is also used as a dump for solid and liquid wastes **(figure 25.2)**. Continued pressure on the finite water resources may require reclaiming and recycling of contaminated water such as sewage. Sewage is the used wastewater draining out of homes and industries that contains a wide variety of chemicals, debris, and microorganisms. The dangers of typhoid, cholera, and dysentery linked to the unsanitary mixing of household water and sewage have been a threat for centuries. In current practice, some sewage is treated to reduce its microbial load before release,

Figure 25.3 The primary, secondary, and tertiary stages in sewage treatment.

off. The remaining smaller, suspended particulates are allowed to settle. Sedimentation in settling tanks usually takes 2 to 10 hours and leaves a mixture rich in organic matter. This aqueous residue is carried into a **secondary phase** of active microbial decomposition, or biodegradation. In this phase, a diverse community of natural bioremediators (bacteria, algae, and protozoa) aerobically decomposes the remaining particles of wood, paper, fabrics, petroleum, and organic molecules inside a large digester tank **(figure 25.4).** This forms a suspension of material called *sludge* that tends to settle out and slow the process. To hasten aerobic decomposition of the sludge, most processing plants have systems to *activate* it by injecting air, mechanically stirring it, and recirculating it. A large amount of organic matter is mineralized into sulfates, nitrates, phosphates, carbon dioxide, and water. Certain volatile gases such as hydrogen sulfide, ammonia, nitrogen, and methane may also be released. Water from this process is siphoned off and carried to the tertiary

phase, which involves further filtering and chlorinating prior to discharge. Such reclaimed sewage water is usually used to water golf courses and parks rather than for drinking, or it is gradually released into large bodies of water.

In some cases, the solid waste that remains after aerobic decomposition is harvested and reused. Its rich content of nitrogen, potassium, and phosphorus makes it a useful fertilizer. It is estimated that 63 percent of the 5.6 million tons of sludge made in the United States annually is recycled and applied to land. This has been viewed as a "green" alternative to burying or burning the sludge. But scientists are now raising concerns that hundreds of thousands of pounds of potent antimicrobial substances such as triclosan are also being spread on the ground, since these chemicals accumulate in the sludge and are not degraded by the typical process of wastewater treatment. Surprisingly, the levels of these substances in reused sludge are not regulated by the Environmental Protection Agency. The EPA does set acceptable levels for metals and for certain pathogenic bacteria.

Recently, scientists found a way to harness the bacteria found in sewage to construct a microbial fuel cell to produce usable energy. In these experiments, wastewater bacteria form biofilms on special rods inserted in the sewage that is being treated. These biofilms generate electrons that are transferred via copper wires to cathodes, producing electricity. Considering the mounting waste disposal and energy shortage problems, these technologies should gain momentum.

Water Monitoring to Prevent Disease

Microbiology of Drinking Water Supplies

We do not have to look far for overwhelming reminders of the importance of safe water. Worldwide epidemics of cholera have killed thousands of people, and an outbreak of *Cryptosporidium* in Wisconsin in the 1990s affecting 370,000 people was traced to a contaminated municipal water supply. In a large segment of the world's population, the lack of sanitary water is responsible for billions of cases of diarrheal illness that kill 3 million children each year (see chapter 22). In the United States, nearly 1 million people develop water-borne illness every year.

Good health is dependent on a clean, potable (drinkable) water supply. This means the water must be free of pathogens; dissolved toxins; and disagreeable turbidity, odor, color, and taste. As we shall see, water of high quality does not come easily, and we must look to microbes as part of the problem and part of the solution.

Through ordinary exposure to air, soil, and effluents, surface waters usually acquire harmless, saprobic microorganisms. But along its course, water can also pick up pathogenic contaminants. Among the most prominent water-borne pathogens of recent times are the protozoa *Giardia* and *Cryptosporidium*; the bacteria *Campylobacter, Salmonella, Shigella, Vibrio,* and *Mycobacterium*; and hepatitis A and Norwalk viruses. Some of these agents (especially encysted protozoa) can survive in natural waters for long periods without a human host, whereas others are present only transiently and are rapidly lost. The microbial content of drinking water must be continuously monitored to ensure that the water is free of infectious agents.

(a)

(b)

Figure 25.4 Treatment of sewage and wastewater.
(a) Digester tanks used in the primary phase of treatment; each tank can process several million gallons of raw sewage a day. **(b)** View inside the secondary reactor shows the large stirring paddle that mixes the sludge to aerate it to encourage microbial decomposition.

Attempting to survey water for specific pathogens can be very difficult and time-consuming, so most assays of water purity are more focused on detecting fecal contamination. High fecal levels can mean the water contains pathogens and is consequently unsafe to drink. Thus, wells, reservoirs, and other water sources can be analyzed for the presence of various **indicator bacteria.** These species are intestinal residents of birds and mammals, and they are readily identified using routine lab procedures.

Enteric bacteria most useful in the routine monitoring of microbial pollution are gram-negative rods called *coliforms* and enteric *streptococci,* which survive in natural waters but do not multiply there. Finding them in high numbers thus implicates recent or high levels of fecal contamination. Environmental Protection Agency standards for water sanitation are based primarily on the levels of coliforms, which are described as gram-negative, lactose-fermenting, gas-producing bacteria such as *Escherichia coli, Enterobacter,* and *Citrobacter.* Fecal contamination of marine waters that poses a risk for gastrointestinal disease is more readily correlated with gram-positive cocci, primarily in the genus *Enterococcus.* Occasionally, coliform bacteriophages and reoviruses (the Norwalk virus) are good indicators of fecal pollution, but their detection is more difficult and more technically demanding.

Water Quality Assays A rapid method for testing the total bacterial levels in water is the standard plate count. In this technique, a small sample of water is spread over the surface of a solid medium. The numbers of colonies that develop provide an estimate of the total viable population without differentiating coliforms from other species. This information is particularly helpful in evaluating the effectiveness of various water purification stages. Another general indicator of water quality is the level of dissolved oxygen it contains. It is established that water containing high levels of organic matter and bacteria will have a lower oxygen content because of consumption by aerobic respiration.

Coliform Enumeration Water quality departments employ some standard assays for routine detection and quantification of coliforms. The techniques available are:

- simple tests, such as presence-absence broth, that detect coliform activity but do not quantify it;
- rapid tests that isolate coliform colonies and provide quantities of coliforms present; and
- rapid tests that identify specific coliforms and determine numbers.

In many circumstances (drinking water, for example), it is important to *differentiate* between facultative coliforms (*Enterobacter*) that are often found in other habitats (soil, water) *and* true **fecal coliforms** that live mainly in human and animal intestines. Microbiologists are calling for the discontinuation of the use of coliforms as an indicator of fecal contamination **(Insight 25.2).** But this method is still widespread, so we cover its principles here.

INSIGHT 25.2   The Waning Days of a Classic Test?

Keeping water and the seafood we harvest from it free from fecal contamination is absolutely imperative in making it safe to ingest. In the late 1800s, it was suggested that a good way to determine if water or its products had been exposed to feces was to test for *E. coli.* Although most *E. coli* strains are not pathogenic, they almost always come from a mammal's intestinal tract so their presence in a sample is a clear indicator of fecal contamination.

Because at the time it was too difficult to differentiate *E. coli* from the closely related species of *Citrobacter, Klebsiella,* and *Enterobacter,* laboratories instead simply reported whether a sample contained one of these isolates. (All of these bacteria ferment lactose and are phenotypically similar.) The terminology adopted was "coliform-" (*E. coli–*like) positive or negative. In other words, one of these bacteria was present in the sample but it was not necessarily *E. coli.*

The use of this coliform assay has been the standard procedure since 1914, and it is still in widespread use. Pick up a newspaper in the summer, and you will likely find a report about a swimming pool or a river with a high coliform count. Coliform counts are also used to regulate food production and to trace the causes of food-borne outbreaks. Recently, microbiologists have noted serious problems with the use of coliforms to indicate fecal contamination. The main issue is that the three other bacterial species already mentioned, among others, are commonly found growing in nonfecal environments such as fresh water and plants that eventually become food. In other words, if you're not looking specifically for *E. coli,* you can't be sure you're looking for feces.

In 1995, there was a minor panic when media outlets reported that iced tea from restaurants contained significant numbers of "fecal coliforms." The public was outraged. One headline read, "Iced Tea Worse Than River Water." Restaurants were named, and their reputations were damaged. When scientists did more detailed testing, they found that the predominant species found were *Klebsiella* and *Enterobacter,* both of which are normal colonizers of plants, such as tea leaves. Furthermore, despite the reports of widespread contamination with large numbers of "fecal coliforms," no one ever became sick from drinking iced tea.

Microbiologists are now advocating that *E. coli* alone—not the outdated grouping of coliforms—be used as an indicator of fecal contamination. Newer identification techniques make this as simple, if not simpler, than the standard coliform tests. But old habits die hard, and regulatory and public laboratories are proving slow to convert to the *E. coli* standard. An additional wrinkle has been added by the discovery by a research group in 2008 that *E. coli* can be present in biofilms on surfaces that the water is exposed to, without being detected by methods that only sample the water phase.

The membrane filter method is a widely used rapid method that can be used in the field or lab to process and test larger quantities of water. This method is more suitable for dilute fluids, such as drinking water, that are relatively free of particulate matter, and it is less suitable for water containing heavy microbial growth or debris. This technique is related to the method described in chapter 11 for sterilizing fluids by filtering out microbial contaminants, except that in this system, the filter containing the trapped microbes is the desired end product. The steps in membrane filtration are diagrammed in **figure 25.5a,b.** After filtration, the membrane filter is placed in a Petri dish containing selective broth. After incubation, both nonfecal and fecal coliform colonies can be counted and often presumptively identified by their distinctive characteristics on these media **(figure 25.5c,d).**

Another more time-consuming but useful technique is the **most probable number (MPN)** procedure, which detects coliforms by a series of *presumptive, confirmatory,* and *completed* tests. The presumptive test involves three subsets of fermentation tubes, each containing different amounts of lactose or lauryl tryptose broth. The three subsets are inoculated with various-size water samples. After 24 hours of incubation, the tubes are evaluated for gas production. A positive test for gas formation is presumptive evidence of coliforms; negative for gas means no coliforms. The number of positive tubes in each subset is tallied, and this set of numbers is applied to a statistical table to estimate the most likely or probable concentration of coliforms.

It does not specifically detect fecal coliforms. When a test is negative for coliforms, the water is considered generally fit for human consumption. But even slight coliform levels are allowable under some circumstances. For example, municipal waters can have a maximum of 4 coliforms per 100 ml; private wells can have an even higher count. There is no acceptable level for fecal coliforms, enterococci, viruses, or pathogenic protozoa in drinking water. Waters that will not be consumed but are used for fishing or swimming are permitted to have counts of 70 to 200 coliforms per 100 ml. If the coliform level of recreational water reaches 1,000 coliforms per 100 ml, health departments usually bar its usage.

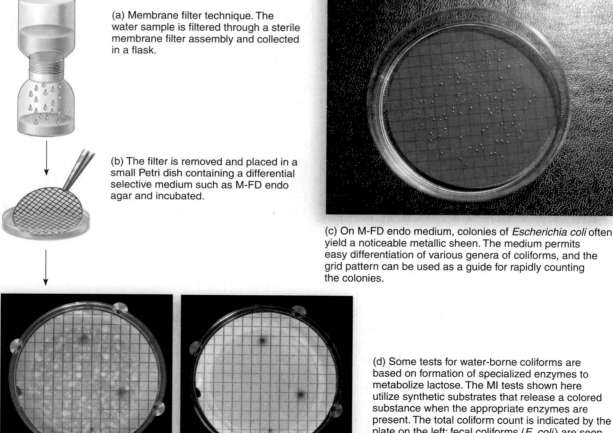

(a) Membrane filter technique. The water sample is filtered through a sterile membrane filter assembly and collected in a flask.

(b) The filter is removed and placed in a small Petri dish containing a differential selective medium such as M-FD endo agar and incubated.

(c) On M-FD endo medium, colonies of *Escherichia coli* often yield a noticeable metallic sheen. The medium permits easy differentiation of various genera of coliforms, and the grid pattern can be used as a guide for rapidly counting the colonies.

(d) Some tests for water-borne coliforms are based on formation of specialized enzymes to metabolize lactose. The MI tests shown here utilize synthetic substrates that release a colored substance when the appropriate enzymes are present. The total coliform count is indicated by the plate on the left; fecal coliforms (*E. coli*) are seen in the plate on the right. This test is especially accurate with surface or groundwater samples.

Total coliforms fluoresce under a black light.

E. coli colonies are blue under natural light.

Figure 25.5 Rapid methods of water analysis for coliform contamination.

25.2 Learning Outcomes—Can You . . .

3. . . . outline the steps in water purification?

4. . . . differentiate water purification from sewage treatment?

5. . . . describe the primary and secondary phases of sewage treatment?

6. . . . list five important pathogens of drinking water?

7. . . . explain why indicator bacteria are used as surrogates for pathogenic bacteria in examination of water safety?

8. . . . discuss the relevance of fecal coliforms?

25.3 Microorganisms Making Food and Spoiling Food

All human food—from vegetables to caviar to cheese—comes from some other organism, and rarely is it obtained in a sterile, uncontaminated state. Food is but a brief stopover in the overall scheme of biogeochemical cycling. This means that microbes and humans are in direct competition for the nutrients in food, and we must be constantly aware that microbes' fast growth rates give them the winning edge. Somewhere along the route of procurement, processing, or preparation, food becomes contaminated with microbes from the soil, the bodies of plants and animals, water, air, food handlers, or utensils. The final effects depend on the types and numbers of microbes and whether the food is cooked or preserved. In some cases, specific microbes can even be added to food to obtain a desired effect. The effects of microorganisms on food can be classified as beneficial, detrimental, or neutral to humans, as summarized by the following outline:

Beneficial Effects
Food is fermented or otherwise chemically changed by the addition of microbes or microbial products to alter or improve flavor, taste, or texture.
Microbes can serve as food.

Detrimental Effects
Microbes cause food poisoning or food-borne illness.
Microbes spoil food.
Growth of microbes makes food unfit for consumption; adds undesirable flavors, appearance, and smell; destroys food value.

Neutral Effects
The presence or growth of certain microbes does not cause disease or change the nature of the food.

As long as food contains no harmful substances or organisms, its suitability for consumption is largely a matter of taste. But what tastes like rich flavor to some may seem like decay to others. The test of whether certain foods are edible is guided by culture, experience, and preference. The flavors, colors, textures, and aromas of many cultural delicacies are supplied by bacteria and fungi. Poi, pickled cabbage, Norwegian fermented fish, and Limburger cheese are notable examples. If you examine the foods of most cultures, you will find some foods that derive their delicious flavor from microbes.

Microbial Fermentations in Food Products from Plants

In contrast to methods that destroy or keep out unwanted microbes, many culinary procedures deliberately add microorganisms and encourage them to grow. Common substances such as bread, cheese, beer, wine, yogurt, and pickles are the result of **food fermentations.** These reactions actively encourage biochemical activities that impart a particular taste, smell, or appearance to food. The microbe or microbes can occur naturally on the food substrate, as in sauerkraut, or they can be added as pure or mixed samples of known bacteria, molds, or yeasts called **starter cultures.** Many food fermentations are synergistic, with a series of microbes acting in concert to convert a starting substrate to the desired end product. Because large-scale production of fermented milk, cheese, bread, alcoholic brews, and vinegar depends upon inoculation with starter cultures, considerable effort is spent selecting, maintaining, and preparing these cultures and excluding contaminants that can spoil the fermentation. Most starting raw materials are of plant origin (grains, vegetables, beans) and, to a lesser extent, of animal origin (milk, meat).

Bread

Microorganisms accomplish three functions in bread making:

1. leavening the flour-based dough,
2. imparting flavor and odor, and
3. conditioning the dough to make it workable.

Leavening is achieved primarily through the release of gas to produce a porous and spongy product. Without leavening, bread dough remains dense, flat, and hard. Although various microbes and leavening agents can be used, the most common ones are various strains of the baker's yeast *Saccharomyces cerevisiae*. Other gas-forming microbes such as coliform bacteria, certain *Clostridium* species, heterofermentative lactic acid bacteria, and wild yeasts can be employed, depending on the type of bread desired.

Yeast metabolism requires a source of fermentable sugar such as maltose or glucose. Because the yeast respires aerobically in bread dough, the chief products of maltose fermentation are carbon dioxide and water rather than alcohol (the main product in beer and wine). Other contributions to bread texture come from kneading, which incorporates air into the dough, and from microbial enzymes, which break down flour proteins (gluten) and give the dough elasticity.

Besides carbon dioxide production, bread fermentation generates other volatile organic acids and alcohols that impart delicate flavors and aromas. These are especially well developed in handmade bread, which is leavened more slowly than commercial bread. Yeasts and bacteria can also impart unique flavors, depending upon the culture mixture and baking techniques used. The pungent flavor of rye bread, for example, comes in part from starter cultures of lactic acid bacteria such as *Lactobacillus plantarum*, *L. brevis*, *L. bulgaricus*, *Leuconostoc mesenteroides*, and *Streptococcus thermophilus*. Sourdough bread gets its unique tang from *Lactobacillus sanfrancisco*.

Beer

The production of alcoholic beverages takes advantage of another useful property of yeasts. By fermenting carbohydrates in fruits or grains anaerobically, they produce ethyl alcohol, as shown by this equation:

$$C_6H_{12}O_6 \rightarrow 2C_2H_5OH + 2CO_2$$
$$\text{(Yeast + Sugar = Ethanol + Carbon dioxide)}$$

Depending on the starting materials and the processing method, alcoholic beverages vary in alcohol content and flavor. The principal types of fermented beverages are beers, wines, and spirit liquors.

The earliest evidence of beer brewing appears in ancient tablets by the Sumerians and Babylonians around 6000 BC. The starting ingredients for both ancient and present-day versions of beer, ale, stout, porter, and other variations are water, malt (barley grain), hops, and special strains of yeasts. The steps in brewing include malting, mashing, adding hops, fermenting, aging, and finishing.

For brewer's yeast to convert the carbohydrates in grain into ethyl alcohol, the barley must first be sprouted and softened to make its complex nutrients available to yeasts. This process, called **malting,** releases amylases that convert starch to dextrins and maltose, and proteases that digest proteins. Other sugar and starch supplements added in some forms of beer are corn, rice, wheat, soybeans, potatoes, and sorghum. After the sprouts have been separated, the remaining malt grain is dried and stored in preparation for mashing.

The malt grain is soaked in warm water and ground up to prepare a **mash.** Sugar and starch supplements are then introduced to the mash mixture, which is heated to a temperature of about 65°C to 70°C. During this step, the starch is hydrolyzed by amylase and simple sugars are released. Heating this mixture to 75°C stops the activity of the enzymes. Solid particles are next removed by settling and filtering. **Wort,** the clear fluid that comes off, is rich in dissolved carbohydrates. It is boiled for about 2.5 hours with **hops,** the dried scales of the female flower of *Humulus lupulus* **(figure 25.6),** to extract the bitter acids and resins that give aroma and flavor to the finished product. Boiling also caramelizes the sugar and imparts a golden or brown color, destroys any bacterial contaminants that can destroy flavor, and concentrates the mixture. The filtered and cooled supernatant is then ready for the addition of yeasts and fermentation.

Fermentation begins when wort is inoculated with a species of *Saccharomyces* that has been specially developed for beer making. Top yeasts such as *Saccharomyces cerevisiae* function at the surface and are used to produce the higher alcohol content of *ales*. Bottom yeasts such as *S. uvarum* (*carlsbergensis*) function deep in the fermentation vat and are used to make other beers. In both cases, the initial inoculum of yeast starter is aerated briefly to promote rapid growth and increase the load of yeast cells. Shortly thereafter, an insulating blanket of foam and carbon dioxide develops on the surface of the vat and promotes anaerobic conditions **(figure 25.7).** During 8 to 14 days of fermentation, the wort sugar is converted chiefly to ethanol and carbon dioxide. The diversity of flavors in the finished product is partly due to the release of small amounts of glycerol, acetic acid, and esters. Fermentation is self-limited, and it essentially ceases when a concentration of 3% to 6% ethyl alcohol is reached.

Freshly fermented, or "green," beer is **lagered,** meaning it is held for several weeks to months in vats near 0°C. Dur-

Figure 25.6 Hops.   Female flowers of hops, the herb that gives beer some of its flavor and aroma.

**Figure 25.7
Anaerobic conditions
in homemade beer
production.** A layer
of carbon dioxide foam
keeps oxygen out.

ing this maturation period, yeast, proteins, resin, and other materials settle, leaving behind a clear, mellow fluid. Lager beer is subjected to a final filtration step to remove any residual yeasts that could spoil it. Finally, it is carbonated with carbon dioxide collected during fermentation and packaged in kegs, bottles, or cans.

Wine and Liquors

Wine is traditionally considered any alcoholic beverage arising from the fermentation of grape juice, but practically any fruit can be rendered into wine. The essential starting point is the preparation of **must,** the juice given off by crushed fruit that is used as a substrate for fermentation. In general, grape wines are either white or red. The color comes from the skins of the grapes, so white wine is prepared either from white-skinned grapes or from red-skinned grapes that have had the skin removed. Red wine comes from the red- or purple-skinned varieties. Major steps in making wine include must preparation (crushing), fermentation, storage, and aging **(figure 25.8).**

Processing Step		Outcome
Grape pressing		Formation of must with fruit sugars
Heat sterilization		Elimination of contaminants
Yeast inoculation		Addition of desired organisms
Fermentation of must	Tank	Alcohol production from sugars
Storage in barrels to age	Barrel	Development of final wine bouquet
Filtration and collection		Removal of yeast and particles
Bottling		

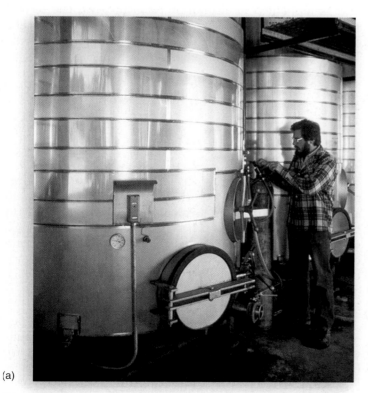

(a)

(b)

Figure 25.8 Wine making. **(a)** Wine fermentation vats in a large commercial winery. **(b)** General steps in wine making.

For proper fermentation, must should contain 12% to 25% glucose or fructose, so the art of wine making begins in the vineyard. Grapes are harvested when their sugar content reaches 15% to 25%, depending on the type of wine to be made. Grapes from the field carry a mixed biofilm on their surface called the *bloom* that can serve as a source of wild yeasts. Some wine makers allow these natural yeasts to dominate, but many wineries inoculate the must with a special strain of *Saccharomyces cerevisiae*, variety *ellipsoideus*. To discourage yeast and bacterial spoilage agents, wine makers sometimes treat grapes with sulfur dioxide or potassium metabisulfite. The inoculated must is thoroughly aerated and mixed to promote rapid aerobic growth of yeasts, but when the desired level of yeast growth is achieved, anaerobic alcoholic fermentation is begun.

The temperature of the vat during fermentation must be carefully controlled to facilitate alcohol production. The length of fermentation varies from 3 to 5 days in red wines and from 7 to 14 days in white wines. The initial fermentation yields ethanol concentrations reaching 7% to 15% by volume, depending on the type of yeast, the source of the juice, and ambient conditions. The fermented juice (raw wine) is decanted and transferred to large vats to settle and clarify. Before the final aging process, it is flash-pasteurized to kill microorganisms and filtered to remove any remaining yeasts and sediments. Wine is aged in wooden casks for varying time periods (months to years), after which it is bottled and stored for further aging. During aging, nonmicrobial changes produce aromas and flavors (the bouquet) characteristic of a particular wine.

The fermentation processes discussed thus far can only achieve a maximum alcoholic content of 17%, because concentrations above this level inhibit the metabolism of the yeast. The fermentation product must be distilled to obtain higher concentrations such as those found in liquors. During distillation, heating the liquor separates the more volatile alcohol from the less volatile aqueous phase. The alcohol is then condensed and collected. The alcohol content of distilled liquors is rated by *proof*, a measurement that is usually two times the alcohol content. Thus, 80 proof vodka contains 40% ethyl alcohol.

Distilled liquors originate through a process similar to wine making, although the starting substrates can be extremely diverse. In addition to distillation, liquors can be subjected to special treatments such as aging to provide unique flavor or color. Vodka, a colorless liquor, is usually prepared from fermented potatoes, and rum is distilled from fermented sugarcane. Assorted whiskeys are derived from fermented grain mashes; rye whiskey is produced from rye mash, and bourbon from corn mash. Brandy is distilled grape, peach, or apricot wine.

Other Fermented Plant Products

Fermentation provides an effective way of preserving vegetables, as well as enhancing flavor with lactic acid and salt. During pickling fermentations, vegetables are immersed in an anaerobic salty solution (brine) to extract sugar and nutrient-laden juices. The salt also disperses bacterial clumps, and its high osmotic pressure inhibits proteolytic bacteria and sporeformers that can spoil the product.

Sauerkraut is the fermentation product of cabbage. Cabbage is washed, wilted, shredded, salted, and packed tightly into a fermentation vat. Weights cover the cabbage mass and squeeze out its juices. The fermentation is achieved by natural cabbage microbiota or by an added culture. The initial agent of fermentation is *Leuconostoc mesenteroides*, which grows rapidly in the brine and produces lactic acid. It is followed by *Lactobacillus plantarum*, which continues to raise the acid content to as high as 2% (pH 3.5) by the end of fermentation. The high acid content restricts the growth of spoilage microbes.

Fermented cucumber pickles come chiefly in salt and dill varieties. Salt pickles are prepared by washing immature cucumbers, placing them in barrels of brine, and allowing them to ferment for 6 to 9 weeks. The brine can be inoculated with *Pediococcus cerevisiae* and *Lactobacillus plantarum* to avoid unfavorable qualities caused by natural microbiota and to achieve a more consistent product. Fermented dill pickles are prepared in a somewhat more elaborate fashion, with the addition of dill herb, spices, garlic, onion, and vinegar.

Natural vinegar is produced when the alcohol in fermented plant juice is oxidized to acetic acid, which is responsible for the pungent odor and sour taste. Although a reasonable facsimile of vinegar could be made by mixing about 4% acetic acid and a dash of sugar in water, this preparation would lack the traces of various esters, alcohol, glycerin, and volatile oils that give natural vinegar its pleasant character. Vinegar is actually produced in two stages. The first stage is similar to wine or beer making, in which a plant juice is fermented to alcohol by *Saccharomyces*. The second stage involves an aerobic fermentation carried out by acetic acid bacteria in the genera *Acetobacter* and *Gluconobacter*. These bacteria oxidize the ethanol in a two-step process, as shown here:

$$2C_2H_5OH + \tfrac{1}{2}O_2 \rightarrow CH_3CHO + H_2O$$
$$\text{Ethanol} \qquad\qquad \text{Acetaldehyde}$$

$$CH_3CHO + \tfrac{1}{2}O_2 \rightarrow CH_3COOH$$
$$\text{Acetaldehyde} \qquad\quad \text{Acetic acid}$$

The abundance of oxygen necessary in commercial vinegar making is furnished by exposing inoculated raw material to air by arranging it in thin layers in open trays, allowing it to trickle over loosely packed beechwood twigs and shavings, or aerating it in a large vat. Different types of vinegar are derived from substrates such as apple cider (cider vinegar), malted grains (malt vinegar), and grape juice (wine vinegar).

Microbes in Milk and Dairy Products

Milk has a highly nutritious composition. It contains an abundance of water and is rich in minerals, protein (chiefly casein), butterfat, sugar (especially lactose), and vitamins. It starts its journey in the udder of a mammal as a sterile substance, but as it passes out of the teat, it is inoculated by the animal's normal biota. Other microbes can be introduced by milking utensils. Because milk is a nearly perfect culture medium, it is highly susceptible to microbial growth. When raw milk is left at room temperature, a series of bacteria ferment the lactose, produce acid, and alter the milk's content and texture **(figure 25.9)**. This progression can occur naturally, or it can be induced, as in the production of cheese and yogurt.

In the initial stages of milk fermentation, lactose is rapidly attacked by *Streptococcus lactis* and *Lactobacillus* species. The resultant lactic acid accumulation and lowered pH cause the milk proteins to coagulate into a solid mass called the **curd.** Curdling also causes the separation of a watery liquid called **whey** on the surface. Curd can be produced by microbial action or by an enzyme, **rennin** (casein coagulase), which is isolated from the stomach of unweaned calves.

Cheese

Since 5000 BC, various forms of cheese have been produced by spontaneous fermentation of cow, goat, or sheep milk. Present-day, large-scale cheese production is carefully controlled and uses only freeze-dried samples of pure cultures. These are first inoculated into a small quantity of pasteurized milk to form an active starter culture. This amplified culture is subsequently inoculated into a large vat of milk, where rapid curd development takes place. Such rapid growth is desired because it promotes the overgrowth of the desired inoculum and prevents the activities of undesirable contaminants. Rennin is usually added to increase the rate of curd formation.

After its separation from whey, the curd is rendered to produce one of the 20 major types of soft, semisoft, or hard cheese **(figure 25.10)**. The composition of cheese is varied by adjusting water, fat, acid, and salt content. Cottage and cream cheese are examples of the soft, more perishable variety. After light salting and the optional addition of cream, they are ready for consumption without further processing. Other cheeses acquire their character from "ripening," a complex curing process involving bacterial, mold, and enzyme reactions that develop the final flavor, aroma, and other features characteristic of particular cheeses.

The distinctive traits of soft cheeses such as Limburger, Camembert, and Liederkranz are acquired by ripening with a reddish-brown mucoid coating of yeasts, micrococci, and molds. The microbial enzymes permeate the curd and ferment lipids, proteins, carbohydrates, and other substrates. This process leaves assorted acids and other by-products that give the finished cheese powerful aromas and delicate flavors. Semisoft varieties of cheese such as Roquefort, bleu, or Gorgonzola are infused and aged with a strain of *Penicillium roqueforti* mold. Hard cheeses such as Swiss, cheddar, and Parmesan develop a sharper flavor by aging with selected bacteria. The pockets in Swiss cheese come from entrapped carbon dioxide formed by *Propionibacterium*, which is also responsible for its bittersweet taste.

Other Fermented Milk Products

Yogurt is formed by the fermentation of milk by *Lactobacillus bulgaricus* and *Streptococcus thermophilus*. These organisms produce organic acids and other flavor components and can grow in such numbers that a gram of yogurt regularly contains 100 million bacteria. Live cultures of *Lactobacillus acidophilus* are an important additive to acidophilus milk, which is said to benefit digestion and to help maintain the normal biota of the intestine. Fermented milks such as kefir, koumiss, and buttermilk are a basic food source in many cultures.

Figure 25.9 Microbes at work in milk products. Litmus milk is a medium used to indicate pH and consistency changes in milk resulting from microbial action. The first tube is an uninoculated, unchanged control. The second tube has a white, decolorized zone indicative of litmus reduction. The third tube has become acidified (pink), and its proteins have formed a loose curd. In the fourth tube, digestion of milk proteins has caused complete clarification or peptonization of the milk. The fifth tube shows a well-developed solid curd overlaid by a clear fluid, the whey.

Figure 25.10 Cheese making. The curd-cutting stage in the making of cheddar cheese.

Microorganisms as Food

At first, the thought of eating bacteria, molds, algae, and yeasts may seem odd or even unappetizing. We do eat their macroscopic relatives, such as mushrooms, truffles, and seaweed, but we are used to thinking of the microscopic forms as agents of decay and disease or, at most, as food flavorings. The consumption of microorganisms is not a new concept. In Germany during World War II, it became necessary to supplement the diets of undernourished citizens by adding yeasts and molds to foods. Several countries now commercially mass-produce food yeasts, bacteria, and in a few cases, algae. Although eating microbes has yet to win total public acceptance, their use as feed supplements for livestock is increasing. A technology that shows some promise in increasing world food productivity is single-cell protein (SCP). This material is produced from waste materials such as molasses from sugar refining, petroleum by-products, and agricultural wastes. In England, an animal feed called Pruteen is produced by mass culture of the bacterium *Methylophilus methylotrophus*. Mycoprotein, a product made from the fungus *Fusarium graminearum*, is also sold there. The filamentous texture of this product makes it a likely candidate for producing meat substitutes for human consumption.

Health food stores carry bottles of dark green pellets or powder that are a culture of a spiral-shaped cyanobacterium called *Spirulina*. This microbe is harvested from the surface of lakes and ponds, where it grows in great mats. In some parts of Africa and Mexico, *Spirulina* has become a viable alternative to green plants as a primary nutrient source. It can be eaten in its natural form or added to other foods and beverages.

Microbial Involvement in Food-Borne Diseases

The CDC estimates that several million people suffer each year from some form of food infection (see chapter 22). Until very recently, reports of food poisoning were escalating rapidly in the United States and worldwide. Outbreaks attributed to common pathogens (*Salmonella, E. coli, Vibrio,* hepatitis A, *Listeria, Campylobacter,* and various protozoa) had doubled in the past 20 years. A major factor in the escalation was the mass production and distribution of processed food such as raw vegetables, fruits, and meats. Improper handling can lead to gross contamination of these products with soil or animal wastes.

Growing concerns about food safety led to a new approach to regulating the food industry. The system is called Hazard Analysis and Critical Control Point, or HACCP, and it is adapted from procedures crafted for the space program in the 1970s. It involves principles that are more systematic and scientific than previous random-sampling quality procedures. The program focuses on the identification, evaluation, control, and prevention of hazards at all stages of the food production process. Since 1998, HACCP has been phased in by the U.S. Department of Agriculture for meat and poultry processing plants and by the Food and Drug Administration for seafood

and juice plants. HACCP projects are taking place in facilities that process cheese, breakfast cereals, salad dressings, and bread. **Figure 25.11** shows the changes that have taken place in the last decade in the incidences of specific confirmed food-borne diseases. You see that illness caused by most of the food-borne organisms has significantly decreased (this is the case when both the data point and the bars representing the confidence intervals are below the "no change" bar). *Salmonella* and *Campylobacter* show no significant change over the decade. The only food-borne illness showing a significant increase is that caused by *Vibrio* species. Keep in mind that many reported food poisoning outbreaks occur where contaminated food has been served to large groups of people,[1] but most cases probably occur in the home and are not reported.

Prevention Measures for Food Poisoning and Spoilage

It will never be possible to avoid all types of food-borne illness because of the ubiquity of microbes in air, water, food, and the human body. But most types of food poisoning require the growth of microbes in the food. In the case of food infections, an infectious dose (sufficient cells to initiate infection) must be present, and in food intoxication, enough cells to produce the toxin must be present. Thus, food poisoning or spoilage can be prevented by proper food handling, preparation, and storage. The methods shown in **figure 25.12**

---

1. One-third of all reported cases result from eating restaurant food.

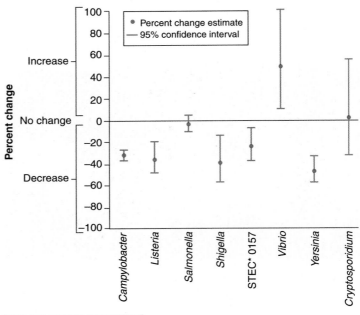

*Shiga-toxin-producing *Escherichia coli*

Figure 25.11 Percentage change in incidence of food-borne illnesses in 2008 in United States compared with 1996–1998. Data are from the Foodborne Diseases Active Surveillance Network, and include only laboratory-confirmed cases of bacterial and parasitic illness.

Care in Harvesting, Preparation

Destruction of Microbes

Heat

Canning	Pasteurization	Cooking

Radiation

Filtration

Prevention of Growth

Maintenance temperature

Hot — Cold freezing

Preservative additives

Gas — Salt — Sugar — Nitrogen salts

Figure 25.12 The primary methods of preventing food poisoning and food spoilage.

are aimed at preventing the incorporation of microbes into food, removing or destroying microbes in food, and keeping microbes from multiplying.

Preventing the Incorporation of Microbes into Food

Most agricultural products such as fruits, vegetables, grains, meats, eggs, and milk are naturally exposed to microbes. Vigorous washing reduces the levels of contaminants in fruits and vegetables, whereas meat, eggs, and milk must be taken from their animal source as aseptically as possible. Aseptic techniques are also essential in the kitchen. Contamination of foods by fingers can be easily remedied by hand washing and proper hygiene, and contamination by flies or other insects can be stopped by covering foods or eliminating pests from the kitchen. Care and common sense also apply in managing utensils. It is important to avoid cross-contaminating food by, for example, using the same cutting board for meat and vegetables without disinfecting it between uses. The subject of cutting board safety is discussed in **Insight 25.3.**

Preventing the Survival or Multiplication of Microbes in Food

Because it is not possible to eliminate all microbes from certain types of food by clean techniques alone, a more efficient approach is to preserve the food by physical or chemical methods. Hygienically preserving foods is especially important for large commercial companies that process and sell bulk foods and must ensure that products are free from harmful contaminants. Regulations and standards for food processing are administered by two federal agencies: the Food and Drug Administration (FDA) and the U.S. Department of Agriculture (USDA).

Temperature and Food Preservation

Heat is a common way to destroy microbial contaminants or to reduce the load of microorganisms. Commercial canneries preserve food in hermetically sealed containers that have been exposed to high temperatures over a specified time period. The temperature used depends on the type of food, and it can range from 60°C to 121°C, with exposure times ranging from 20 minutes to 115 minutes. The food is usually processed at a thermal death time (TDT; see chapter 11) that will destroy the main spoilage organisms and pathogens but will not alter the nutrient value or flavor of the food. For example, tomato juice must be heated to between 121°C and 132°C for 20 minutes to ensure destruction of the spoilage agent *Bacillus coagulans*. Most canning methods are rigorous enough to sterilize the food completely, but some only render the food "commercially sterile," which means it contains live bacteria that are unable to grow under normal conditions of storage.

Another use of heat is **pasteurization,** usually defined as the application of heat below 100°C to destroy nonresistant

INSIGHT 25.3   Wood or Plastic: On the Cutting Edge of Cutting Boards

Inquiring cooks have long been curious for the final word on which type of cutting board is the better choice for food safety. When the USDA recommended plastic cutting boards, it seemed the logical, reasonable choice. After all, plastic is nonabsorbent and easy to clean, presumably making it less likely to harbor bacteria and other microorganisms on its surface than wood is. But this recommendation was never based on evidence from scientific tests. Recently, two separate research groups turned their attention to this important kitchen question. What emerged from these studies came as rather a surprise—the two groups reached exactly opposite conclusions.

First came the study by a team of microbiologists from the University of Wisconsin. They experimented with hardwood chopping blocks and acrylic plastic boards inoculated with pathogens such as *Salmonella, Escherichia coli,* and *Listeria monocytogenes.* One of the most unexpected results was that the wooden boards actually killed 99.9% of the bacteria within a few minutes. The team concluded from the lack of viable cells that wood must contain some antibacterial substances, although they were unable to isolate them. The plastic boards did not similarly reduce the numbers of pathogens and they failed to live up to expectations in other ways. For instance, they continued to harbor bacteria if left unwashed for a given time period. If they were scored by knives from extensive use, even after scrubbing with soap and water, they still held live bacteria. In contrast, even heavily used wooden boards did not grow microorganisms and had a far lower bacterial count. The Wisconsin researchers concluded that the grounds for advocating plastic are questionable and that wood is as safe as plastic, if not superior to it.

In the other study, researchers from the Food and Drug Administration performed an electron microscope study of wood. They found that pathogens such as *E. coli* O157:H7 and *Campylobacter* became trapped in the porous spaces of wooden boards and were able to survive for 2 hours to several days, depending on the moisture content of the wood. They continue to recommend the use of plastic because bacteria trapped in wood would be difficult to remove and could be released during use.

What is a chef to do? Although these contradictory studies seem not to provide a definitive answer, they can serve to emphasize an important point. The solution still exists in simple, commonsense guidelines that are the crux of good kitchen practices. It is apparent that both boards can be safe if properly

(a)

(b)

Double-sided plates of blood agar (top) and MacConkey agar (bottom) after swabbing with samples from cutting boards. The boards were equally contaminated with a fresh chicken carcass, and the samples were taken 10 minutes later. Results appear in **(a)** for the wooden board and in **(b)** for the plastic board. Note that, in this case, the wooden board yielded significantly fewer colonies on both types of media.

handled and their limitations are taken into account. All boards should be scrubbed with soap and hot water and disinfected between uses, especially if meats, poultry, or fish have been cut on them. Boards should be replaced if their surface has become too roughened with use, and wooden boards must not be left moist for any period of time.

---

bacteria and yeasts in liquids such as milk, wine, and fruit juices. The heat is applied in the form of steam, hot water, or even electrical current. The most prevalent technology is the *high-temperature short-time (HTST),* or flash method, using extensive networks of tubes that expose the liquid to 72°C for 15 seconds **(figure 25.13).** An alternative method, ultra-high-temperature (UHT) pasteurization, steams the product until it reaches a temperature of 134°C for at least 1 second. Although milk processed this way is not actually sterile, it is

often marketed as sterile, with a shelf life of up to 3 months. Older methods involve large bulk tanks that hold the fluid at a lower temperature for a longer time, usually 62.3°C for 30 minutes.

Cooking temperatures used to boil, roast, or fry foods can render them free or relatively free of living microbes if carried out for sufficient time to destroy any potential pathogens. A quick warming of chicken or an egg is inadequate to kill microbes such as *Salmonella.* In fact, any meat is a potential

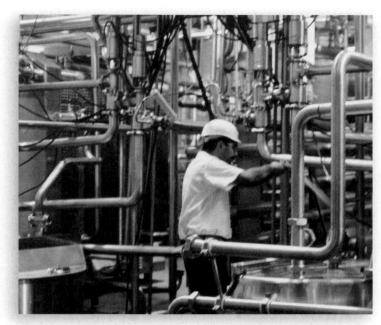

Figure 25.13 A modern flash pasteurizer, a system used in dairies for high-temperature short-time (HTST) pasteurization.
Source: Photo taken at Alta Dena Dairy, City of Industry, California.

*Under ideal conditions, bacteria can divide every 20 minutes. At this rate, bacterial numbers could increase from 1 to 2,097,152 within 7 hours.

Figure 25.14 Temperatures favoring and inhibiting the growth of microbes in food. Most microbial agents of disease or spoilage grow in the temperature range of 15°C to 40°C. Preventing unwanted growth in foods in long-term storage is best achieved by refrigeration or freezing (4°C or lower). Preventing microbial growth in foods intended to be consumed warm in a few minutes or hours requires maintaining the foods above 60°C.
Source: From Ronald Atlas, *Microbiology: Fundamentals and Applications*, 2nd ed., © 1998, p. 475. Reprinted by permission of Prentice Hall, Upper Saddle River, New Jersey.

source of infectious agents and should be adequately cooked. Because most meat-associated food poisoning is caused by nonsporulating bacteria, heating the center of meat to at least 80°C and holding it there for 30 minutes is usually sufficient to kill pathogens. Roasting or frying food at temperatures of at least 200°C or boiling it will achieve a satisfactory degree of disinfection.

Any perishable raw or cooked food that could serve as a growth medium must be stored to prevent the multiplication of bacteria that have survived during processing or handling. Because most food-borne bacteria and molds that are agents of spoilage or infection can multiply at room temperature, manipulation of the holding temperature is a useful preservation method **(figure 25.14).** A good general directive is to store foods at temperatures below 4°C or above 60°C.

Regular refrigeration reduces the growth rate of most mesophilic bacteria by 10 times, although some psychrotrophic microbes can continue to grow at a rate that causes spoilage. This factor limits the shelf life of milk, because even at 7°C, a population could go from a few cells to a billion in 10 days. Pathogens such as *Listeria monocytogenes* and *Salmonella* can also continue to grow in refrigerated foods. Freezing is a longer-term method for cold preservation. Foods can be either slow-frozen for 3 to 72 hours at −15°C to −23°C or rapidly frozen for 30 minutes at −17°C to −34°C. Because freezing cannot be counted upon to kill microbes, rancid, spoiled, or infectious foods will still be unfit to eat after freezing and defrosting. *Salmonella* is known to survive several months in frozen chicken and ice cream, and *Vibrio parahaemolyticus*

can survive in frozen shellfish. For this reason, frozen foods should be defrosted rapidly and immediately cooked or reheated. However, even this practice will not prevent staphylococcal intoxication if the toxin is already present in the food before it is heated.

Foods such as soups, stews, gravies, meats, and vegetables that are generally eaten hot should not be maintained at warm or room temperatures, especially in settings such as cafeterias, banquets, and picnics. The use of a hot plate, chafing dish, or hot water bath will maintain foods above 60°C, well above the incubation temperature of food-poisoning agents.

As a final note about methods to prevent food poisoning, remember the simple axiom: "When in doubt, throw it out."

Radiation

Ultraviolet (nonionizing) lamps are commonly used to destroy microbes on the surfaces of foods or utensils, but they do not penetrate far enough to sterilize bulky foods or food in packages. Food preparation areas are often equipped with UV radiation devices that are used to destroy spores on the surfaces of cheese, breads, and cakes and to disinfect packaging machines and storage areas.

Food itself is usually sterilized by gamma or cathode radiation because these ionizing rays can penetrate denser materials. It must also be emphasized that this method does not cause the targets of irradiation to become radioactive.

Concerns have been raised about the possible secondary effects of radiation that could alter the safety and edibility of foods. Experiments over the past 30 years have demonstrated some side reactions that affect flavor, odor, and vitamin content, but it is currently thought that irradiated foods are relatively free of toxic by-products. The government has currently approved the use of radiation in sterilizing beef, pork, poultry, fish, spices, grain, and some fruits and vegetables. Radiation also increases the shelf life of perishable foods, thus lowering their cost.

Other Forms of Preservation

The addition of chemical preservatives to many foods can prevent the growth of microorganisms that could cause spoilage or disease. Preservatives include natural chemicals such as salt (NaCl) or table sugar and artificial substances such as ethylene oxide. The main classes of preservatives are organic acids, nitrogen salts, sulfur compounds, oxides, salt, and sugar.

Organic acids, including lactic, benzoic, and propionic acids, are among the most widely used preservatives. They are added to baked goods, cheeses, pickles, carbonated beverages, jams, jellies, and dried fruits to reduce spoilage from molds and some bacteria. Nitrites and nitrates are used primarily to maintain the red color of cured meats (hams, bacon, and sausage). By inhibiting the germination of *Clostridium botulinum* spores, they also prevent botulism intoxication, but their effects against other microorganisms are limited. Sulfite prevents the growth of undesirable molds in dried fruits, juices, and wines and retards discoloration in various foodstuffs. Ethylene and propylene oxide gases disinfect various dried foodstuffs. Their use is restricted to fruit, cereals, spices, nuts, and cocoa.

The high osmotic pressure contributed by hypertonic levels of salt plasmolyzes bacteria and fungi and removes moisture from food, thereby inhibiting microbial growth. Salt is commonly added to brines, pickled foods, meats, and fish. However, it does not retard the growth of pathogenic halophiles such as *Staphylococcus aureus*, which grows readily even in 7.5% salt solutions. The high sugar concentrations of candies, jellies, and canned fruits also exert an osmotic preservative effect. Other chemical additives that function in preservation are alcohols and antibiotics. Alcohol is added to flavoring extracts, and antibiotics are approved for treating the carcasses of chickens, fish, and shrimp.

Food can also be preserved by **desiccation,** a process that removes moisture needed by microbes for growth by exposing the food to dry, warm air. Solar drying was traditionally used for fruits and vegetables, but modern commercial dehydration is carried out in rapid-evaporation mechanical devices. Drying is not a reliable microbicidal method, however. Numerous resistant microbes such as micrococci, coliforms, staphylococci, salmonellae, and fungi survive in dried milk and eggs, which can subsequently serve as agents of spoilage and infections.

In 2006, the Food and Drug Administration approved the spraying of bacteriophages onto ready-to-eat meat products. The bacteriophages are specific for *Listeria* and will act to kill the bacteria that would not otherwise be killed because the cold cuts and poultry are usually not cooked before consumption.

25.3 Learning Outcomes—Can You ...

9. ... name five foods and/or beverages that benefit from microbial fermentation?
10. ... explain what microbial actions lead to leavening in bread?
11. ... write the equation for turning yeast and sugar into alcoholic beverages?
12. ... discuss why microorganisms themselves might be useful as food products?
13. ... provide some background about HACCP procedures?
14. ... report 10-year trends in food-borne illness?
15. ... outline basic principles of using temperature to preserve food?
16. ... list mechanisms other than temperature that are used to preserve food?

25.4 Using Microorganisms to Make Things We Need

Virtually any large-scale commercial enterprise that enlists microorganisms to manufacture consumable materials is part of the realm of industrial microbiology. Here the term pertains primarily to bulk production of organic compounds such as antibiotics, hormones, vitamins, acids, solvents **(table 25.1),** and enzymes **(table 25.2).** Many of the processing steps involve fermentations similar to those described in food technology, but industrial processes usually occur on a much larger scale, produce a specific compound, and involve numerous complex stages. The aim of industrial microbiology is to produce chemicals that can be purified and packaged for sale or for use in other commercial processes. Thousands of tons of organic chemicals worth several billion dollars are produced by this industry every year. To create just one of these products, an industry must determine which microbes, starting compounds, and growth conditions work best. The research and development involved usually require an investment of 10 to 15 years and billions of dollars.

Table 25.1 Industrial Products of Microorganisms

Chemical	Microbial Source	Substrate	Applications
Pharmaceuticals			
Cephalosporins	*Cephalosporium*	Glucose	Antibacterial antibiotics, broad spectrum
Penicillins	*Penicillium chrysogenum*	Lactose	Antibacterial antibiotics, broad and narrow spectrum
Vitamin B_{12}	*Pseudomonas*	Molasses	Dietary supplement
Steroids (hydrocortisone)	*Rhizopus, Cunninghamella*	Deoxycholic acid, stigmasterol	Treatment of inflammation, allergy; hormone replacement therapy
Food additives and amino acids			
Citric acid	*Aspergillus, Candida*	Molasses	Acidifier in soft drinks; used to set jam; candy additive; fish preservative; retards discoloration of crabmeat; delays browning of sliced peaches
Xanthan	*Xanthomonas*	Glucose medium	Food stabilizer; not digested by humans
Acetic acid	*Acetobacter*	Any ethylene source, ethanol	Food acidifier; used in industrial processes
Miscellaneous			
Ethanol	*Saccharomyces*	Beet, cane, grains, wood, wastes	Additive to gasoline (gasohol)
Acetone	*Clostridium*	Molasses, starch	Solvent for lacquers, resins, rubber, fat, oil
Glycerol	Yeast	By-product of alcohol fermentation	Explosive (nitroglycerine)
Dextran	*Klebsiella, Acetobacter, Leuconostoc*	Glucose, molasses, sucrose	Polymer of glucose used as adsorbents, blood expanders, and in burn treatment; a plasma extender; used to stabilize ice cream, sugary syrup, candies

Table 25.2 Industrial Enzymes and Their Uses

Enzyme	Source	Application
Amylase	*Aspergillus, Bacillus, Rhizopus*	Flour supplement, desizing textiles, mash preparation, syrup manufacture, digestive aid, precooked foods, spot remover in dry cleaning
Cellulase	*Aspergillus, Trichoderma*	Denim finishing ("stone-washing"), digestive aid, increase digestibility of animal feed, degradation of wood or wood by-products
Hyaluronidase	Various bacteria	Medical use in wound cleansing, preventing surgical adhesions
Keratinase	*Streptomyces*	Hair removal from hides in leather preparation
Pectinase	*Aspergillus, Sclerotina*	Clarifies wine, vinegar, syrups, and fruit juices by degrading pectin, a gelatinous substance; used in concentrating coffee
Proteases	*Aspergillus, Bacillus, Streptomyces*	To clear and flavor rice wines, process animal feed, remove gelatin from photographic film, recover silver, tenderize meat, unravel silkworm cocoon, remove spots
Rennet	*Mucor*	To curdle milk in cheese making
Streptokinase	*Streptococcus*	Medical use in clot digestion, as a blood thinner

One of the most active areas of research in industrial microbiology is the use of algal species to produce biofuels. The fuels would replace gasoline and jet fuel. You may recall that original attempts to produce biofuels involved plants such as corn and soybeans. This proved to be unpopular since the plants and acreage used to grow it could have—and should have—been used for food. Quickly scientists realized that algae could be grown more easily and could produce vast quantities of oil in a controlled manner. The oil produced would also be easily biodegradable. The algae produce oil when exposed to sunlight

(figure 25.15). They use photosynthesis to manufacture O_2 and biomass—namely, lipids or oils. Many government and private industries around the world are investing in massive research projects to bring this technology to a scale that will replace significant amounts of fossil fuels.

Very often the microbes used by biotechnology and fermentation industries are mutant strains of fungi or bacteria that selectively synthesize large amounts of various metabolic intermediates, or **metabolites.** Two basic kinds of metabolic products are harvested by industrial processes: (1) *Primary metabolites* are produced during the major metabolic pathways and are essential to the microbe's function. (2) *Secondary metabolites* are by-products of metabolism that may not be critical to the microbe's function **(figure 25.16).**

In general, primary products are compounds such as amino acids and organic acids synthesized during the logarithmic phase of microbial growth, and secondary products are compounds such as vitamins, antibiotics, and steroids synthesized during the stationary phase (see chapter 7). Most strains of industrial microorganisms have been chosen for their high production of a particular primary or secondary metabolite. Certain mutated strains of yeasts and bacteria can produce 20,000 times more metabolite than a wild strain of that same microbe.

Industrial microbiologists have several tricks to increase the amount of the chosen end product. First, they can manipulate the growth environment to increase the synthesis of a metabolite. For instance, adding lactose instead of glucose as the fermentation substrate increases the production of penicillin by *Penicillium.* Another strategy is to select microbial strains that genetically lack a feedback system to regulate the formation of end products, thus encouraging mass accumulation of this product. Many syntheses occur in sequential fashion, wherein the waste products of one organism become the building blocks of the next. During these *biotransformations,* the substrate undergoes a series of slight modifications, each of which gives off a different by-product. The production of an antibiotic such as tetracycline requires several microorganisms and 72 separate metabolic steps.

From Microbial Factories to Industrial Factories

Industrial fermentations begin with microbial cells acting as living factories. When exposed to optimum conditions, they multiply in massive numbers and synthesize large volumes of a desired product. Producing appropriate levels of growth and fermentation requires cultivation of the microbes in a carefully controlled environment **(figure 25.17).** This process is basically similar to culturing bacteria in a test tube of nutri-

Figure 25.15. Algal bioreactor. The photobioreactor contains algae, water, and trace elements.

Figure 25.16 The origins of primary and secondary microbial metabolites harvested by industrial processes.

Figure 25.17 A cell culture vessel used to mass-produce pharmaceuticals. Such elaborate systems require the highest levels of sterility and clean techniques.

ent broth. It requires a sterile medium containing appropriate nutrients, protection from contamination, provisions for introduction of sterile air or total exclusion of air, and a suitable temperature and pH.

Many commercial fermentation processes have been worked out on a small scale in a lab and then *scaled up* to a large commercial venture. An essential component for scaling up is a **fermentor,** a device in which mass cultures are grown, reactions take place, and product develops. Some fermentors are large tubes, flasks, or vats, but most industrial types are metal cylinders with built-in mechanisms for stirring, cooling, monitoring, and harvesting product **(figure 25.18).** Fermentors are made of materials that can withstand pressure and are rust-proof, nontoxic, and leakproof. They range in holding capacity from small, 5-gallon systems used in research labs to larger, 5,000- to 100,000-gallon vessels and, in some industries, to tanks of 250 million to 500 million gallons.

For optimum yield, a fermentor must duplicate the actions occurring in a tiny volume (a test tube) on a massive scale. Most microbes performing fermentations have an aerobic metabolism, and the large volumes make it difficult to provide adequate oxygen. Fermentors have a built-in device called a *sparger* that aerates the medium to promote aerobic growth. Paddles (*impellers*) located in the central part of the fermentor increase the contact between the microbe and the nutrients by vigorously stirring the fermentation mixture. Their action also maintains its uniformity.

Substance Production

The general steps in mass production of organic substances in a fermentor are illustrated in **figure 25.19.** These can be summarized as:

1. introduction of microbes and sterile media into the reaction chamber;
2. fermentation;
3. *downstream processing* (recovery, purification, and packaging of product); and
4. removal of waste.

Figure 25.18 A schematic diagram of an industrial fermentor for mass culture of microorganisms.
Such instruments are equipped to add nutrients and cultures; to remove product under sterile or aseptic conditions; and to aerate, stir, and cool the mixture automatically.

Figure 25.19 The general layout of a fermentation plant.
These general steps are followed for industrial production of drugs, enzymes, fuels, vitamins, and amino acids.

INSIGHT 25.4   Microbes Degrade—and Repair—Ancient Works of Art

It has long been understood that microorganisms cause the deterioration of old books, statues, and paintings. The process of **biodegradation,** deterioration by living organisms (microbes or insects), is responsible for the crumbling of stone monuments and buildings all over the world, such as the Mayan temple depicted in the photo. Both bacteria and fungi are notorious for colonizing old books, paintings, stone, mortar, and concrete. This happens because microbes release chemicals that damage stone, and they can use cellulose (paper), glues (book binding), and other organic chemicals (paints, pigments) as nutrients. Watercolor and oil paintings are particularly vulnerable to microbial attack.

A newer and more encouraging finding is that microbes can actually be used to *restore* works of art. In 2004, a group of Italian scientists managed to uncover a painting that had been obscured by a technique that earlier curators had used to "preserve" the fresco when it was no longer prudent for it to hang in its building in Pisa, Italy. When the 14th-century painting *The Conversion of Saint Efisio and Battle* by Spinello Aretino was damaged in a bomb that fell during World War II, technicians used an animal-based glue to apply gauze to the front of it and lifted it off of the wall onto the gauze matrix. They then applied a canvas to the back of the painting, attached it to a supporting sheet, and stored it. Illustration (a) depicts the painting covered by gauze.

The idea behind that strategy in the 1940s was that the gauze on the front of the painting could later be removed by using solvents that would dissolve the glue. But over time, the glue formed complexes with other chemicals in the painting and became resistant to all known solvents. After these failed attempts, the scientists determined the chemical structure of the glue. Luckily, the glue was purely organic, and the paints used by the artist were purely inorganic. The scientists decided to apply a paste of whole bacteria that contained a mix of enzymes that they predicted would dissolve the glue but not the paint. Cultures of *Pseudomonas stutzeri* (b) were applied to the painting on saturated cotton wool. The scientists also added an extra protease, which served to "clean up" the organic residues that were left after the cleanup process. It was successful! The glue dissolved and the gauze was removed, revealing the painting underneath (c).

Finally, after centuries of only damaging precious artworks, microbes, with a little help from humans, are repairing them.

(a)

(b)

(c)

All phases of production must be carried out aseptically and monitored (usually by computer) for rate of flow and quality of product. The starting raw substrates include crude plant residues, molasses, sugars, fish and meat meals, and whey. Additional chemicals can be added to control pH or to increase the yield. In *batch fermentation,* the substrate is added to the system all at once and taken through a limited run until product is harvested. In *continuous feed systems,* nutrients are continuously fed into the reactor and the product is siphoned off throughout the run.

Table 25.1 itemizes some of the major pharmaceutical substances, food additives, and solvents produced by microorganisms. Some newer technologies employ extremophiles and their enzymes to run the processes at high or low temperatures or in high-salt conditions. Hyperthermophiles have been adapted for high-temperature detergent and enzyme production. Psychrophiles are used for cold processing of reagents for molecular biology and medical tests. Halophiles are effective for processing of salted foods and dietary supplements.

Pharmaceutical Products

Health care products derived from microbial biosynthesis are antibiotics, hormones, vitamins, and vaccines. The first mass-produced antimicrobic was penicillin, which came from *Penicillium chrysogenum,* a mold first isolated from a cantaloupe in Wisconsin. The current strain of this species has gone through decades of selective mutation and screening to increase its yield. (The original wild *P. chrysogenum* synthesized 60 mg/ml of medium, and the latest isolate yields 85,000 mg/ml.) The semisynthetic penicillin derivatives are produced by introducing the assorted side-chain precursors to the fermentation vessel during the most appropriate phase of growth. These experiences with penicillin have provided an important model for the manufacture of other antibiotics.

Several steroid hormones used in therapy are produced industrially. Corticosteroids of the adrenal cortex, cortisone and cortisol (hydrocortisone), are invaluable for treating inflammatory and allergic disorders, and female hormones such as progesterone or estrogens are the active ingredients in birth control pills. For years, the production of these hormones was tedious and expensive because it involved purifying them from slaughterhouse animal glands or chemical syntheses. In time, it was shown that, through biotransformation, various molds could convert a precursor compound called diogenin into cortisone. By the same means, stigmasterol from soybean oil could be transformed into progesterone.

Miscellaneous Products

An exciting innovation has been the development and industrial production of natural *biopesticides* using *Bacillus thuringiensis.* During sporulation, these bacteria produce intracellular crystals that can be toxic to certain insects. When the insect ingests this endotoxin, its digestive tract breaks down and it dies, but the material is relatively nontoxic to other organisms. Commercial dusts are now on the market to suppress caterpillars, moths, and worms on various agricultural crops and trees. A strain of this bacterium is also being considered to control the mosquito vector of malaria (chapter 20) and the black fly vector of onchocerciasis (river blindness; chapter 18).

Enzymes are critical to chemical manufacturing, the agriculture and food industries, textile and paper processing, and even laundry and dry cleaning. The advantage of enzymes is that they are very specific in their activity and are readily produced and released by microbes. Microbes and their enzymes are even proving to be useful in preserving our cultural heritage **(Insight 25.4).** Mass quantities of proteases, amylases, lipases, oxidases, and cellulases are produced by fermentation technology (see table 25.2). The wave of the future appears to be custom designing enzymes to perform a specific task by altering their amino acid content. Other compounds of interest that can be mass-produced by microorganisms are amino acids, organic acids, solvents, and natural flavor compounds to be used in air fresheners and foods.

25.4 Learning Outcomes—Can You ...

17. ... state the general aim(s) of industrial microbiology?
18. ... distinguish between primary and secondary metabolites?
19. ... list the four steps of industrial product production from microbes?
20. ... list five different types of substances produced from industrial microbiology, and their applications?

Case File 25   *Wrap-Up*

Climate change seems to be causing the overgrowth of *V. vulnificus,* as well as other bacteria, in waters that previously were less supportive of their growth. (We saw this also in the case file for chapter 7.) At the same time, the bacteria also continue to grow in southern waters. The result has been a 51% increase in *Vibrio*-caused wound infections in a recent 6-year period. In fact, more people die annually from *Vibrio* wound infections than from shark attacks.

It seems that a new definition for microbiologically "safe" water may need to be devised.

See: 2006. *The Honolulu Advertiser,* online version, June 10.

Chapter Summary

25.1 Applied Microbiology and Biotechnology
- The use of microorganisms for practical purposes to benefit humans is called biotechnology.

25.2 Microorganisms in Water and Wastewater Treatment
- Wastewater or sewage is treated in three stages to remove organic material, microorganisms, and chemical pollutants. The primary phase removes physical objects from the wastewater. The secondary phase removes the organic matter by biodegradation. The tertiary phase disinfects the water and removes chemical pollutants.
- Significant water-borne pathogens include protozoa, bacteria, and viruses.
- Water quality assays screen for coliforms as indicator organisms, or may assess the most probable number of microorganisms. As these results may be misleading, more emphasis is being placed on identifying the actual pathogens.

25.3 Microorganisms Making Food and Spoiling Food
- Microorganisms can compete with humans for the nutrients in food. Their presence in food can be beneficial, detrimental, or of neutral consequence to human consumers.
- Food fermentation processes utilize bacteria or yeast to produce desired components such as alcohols and organic acids in foods and beverages. Beer, wine, yogurt, and cheeses are examples of such processes.
- Some microorganisms are used as a source of protein. Examples are single-cell protein, mycoprotein, and *Spirulina*. Microbial protein could replace meat as a major protein source.
- Food-borne disease can be an intoxication caused by microbial toxins produced as by-products of microbial decomposition of food. Or it can be a food infection when pathogenic microorganisms in the food attack the human host after being consumed.
- Heat, radiation, chemicals, and drying are methods used to limit numbers of microorganisms in food. The type of method used depends on the nature of the food and the type of pathogens or spoilage agents it contains.

25.4 Using Microorganisms to Make Things We Need
- Industrial microbiology refers to the bulk production of any organic compound derived from microorganisms.
- It is likely that algal biofuels will soon replace large portions of fossil fuels currently being produced.
- Industrial processes now produce antibiotics, hormones, vitamins, acids, solvents, vaccines, and enzymes from microbes.

Multiple-Choice and True-False Questions   Knowledge and Comprehension

Multiple-Choice Questions. Select the correct answer from the answers provided.

1. Drinking water utilities monitor their production system for the occurrence of
   a. methanogens.
   b. coliform bacteria.
   c. nematodes.
   d. yeasts.

2. Milk is usually pasteurized by
   a. the high-temperature short-time method.
   b. ultrapasteurization.
   c. the batch method.
   d. electrical currents.

3. During sewage treatment, microbial action on a large scale first takes place in the
   a. primary phase.
   b. secondary phase.
   c. Microbial action is not a part of sewage treatment.
   d. Microbial action takes place after the secondary phase.

4. Which of the following is unlikely to be a waterborne pathogen?
   a. *Giardia lamblia*
   b. *Salmonella*
   c. *Vibrio*
   d. *Staphylococcus*

5. The "bloom" in wine making refers to
   a. the flowering of the grape plant.
   b. the biofilm on the skin of the grapes.
   c. the fermentation taking place in vats.
   d. none of the above.

6. When algae produce biofuels, what is the other significant by-product of photosynthesis?
   a. CO_2
   b. energy
   c. waste
   d. O_2

7. Secondary metabolites of microbes are formed during the _____ phase of growth.
   a. exponential
   b. stationary
   c. trophophase
   d. idiophase

8. In industrial fermentation, which step precedes *downstream processing*?
   a. removal of waste
   b. introduction of microbes into chamber
   c. packaging of product
   d. fermentation

9. Which of the following are currently being produced through biotechnology?
   a. glycerol
   b. vitamins
   c. steroids
   d. all of the above

10. In biotechnology, fermentation refers to
    a. the anaerobic metabolism of microorganisms.
    b. the creation of alcoholic beverages.
    c. the mass culturing of microorganisms to yield large quantities of products.
    d. all of the above.

True-False Questions. If the statement is true, leave as is. If it is false, correct it by rewriting the sentence.

11. Raw sewage is still being dumped into the aquatic environment in many places around the world.

12. Food products should always be kept completely free of microorganisms.

13. Alcoholic beverages are produced by the fermentation of sugar to ethanol and carbon dioxide.

14. The incidence of many food-borne illnesses has been declining for some years now.

15. Refrigerating food prevents the growth of all bacteria.

Critical Thinking Questions   Application and Analysis

These questions are suggested as a *writing-to-learn* experience. For each question, compose a one- or two-paragraph answer that includes the factual information needed to completely address the question.

1. a. Draw a diagram of the flow of water in a water utility plant.
   b. Describe the three phases of sewage treatment.
   c. What is activated sludge?

2. Describe five types of fermentations.

3. When are microbes on food harmless?

4. Which microbes are used as starter cultures in bread, beer, wine, cheeses, and sauerkraut?

5. What are curds and whey, and what causes them?

6. Every year, supposedly safe municipal water supplies cause outbreaks of enteric illness.
   a. How in the course of water analysis and treatment might these pathogens be missed?
   b. What kinds of microbes are they most likely to be?

   c. Why is there less tolerance for a fecal coliform in drinking or recreational water than other bacteria?

7. If fermentation of sugars to produce alcohol in wine is anaerobic, why do winemakers make sure that the early phase of yeast growth is aerobic?

8. Predict the differences in the outcome if raw milk is incubated for 48 hours versus pasteurized milk being incubated for the same length of time.

9. Explain the ways that co-metabolism and biotransformations of microorganisms are harnessed in industrial microbiology.

10. Review chapter 10 and describe several ways that recombinant DNA technology can be used in biotechnology processes.

Concept Mapping   Synthesis

Appendix D provides guidance for working with concept maps.

1. Construct your own concept map using the following words as the *concepts*. Supply the linking words between each pair of concepts. You may add additional concepts if desired.

primary metabolites	microbes	pH
secondary metabolites	downstream processing	biotransformations
fermentation	substrate	

Visual Connections   Synthesis

These questions use visual images or previous content to make connections to this chapter's concepts.

1. **From chapter 3, figure 3.9b.** If this MacConkey agar plate was inoculated with well water, would you report that coliforms were present in the water?

2. **From Insight 25.3, illustration (a).** This is a plate with blood agar on the top and MacConkey agar on the bottom. It has been inoculated with samples from a wooden cutting board that had been exposed to a raw chicken carcass. Knowing what you know about the properties of these two agars, say as much as you can about the bacteria growing on them.

www.connect.microbiology.com

|MICROBIOLOGY

Enhance your study of this chapter with study tools and practice tests. Also ask your instructor about the resources available through ConnectPlus, including the media-rich eBook, interactive learning tools, and animations.

Exponents

Dealing with concepts such as microbial growth often requires working with numbers in the billions, trillions, and even greater. A mathematical shorthand for expressing such numbers is with exponents. The exponent of a number indicates how many times (designated by a superscript) that number is multiplied by itself. These exponents are also called common *logarithms*, or logs. The following chart, based on multiples of 10, summarizes this system.

Exponential Notation for Base 10				
Number	**Quantity**	**Exponential Notation***	**Number Arrived at By:**	**One Followed By:**
1	One	10^0	Numbers raised to zero power are equal to one	No zeros
10	Ten	10^{1**}	10×1	One zero
100	Hundred	10^2	10×10	Two zeros
1,000	Thousand	10^3	$10 \times 10 \times 10$	Three zeros
10,000	Ten thousand	10^4	$10 \times 10 \times 10 \times 10$	Four zeros
100,000	Hundred thousand	10^5	$10 \times 10 \times 10 \times 10 \times 10$	Five zeros
1,000,000	Million	10^6	10 times itself 6 times	Six zeros
1,000,000,000	Billion	10^9	10 times itself 9 times	Nine zeros
1,000,000,000,000	Trillion	10^{12}	10 times itself 12 times	Twelve zeros
1,000,000,000,000,000	Quadrillion	10^{15}	10 times itself 15 times	Fifteen zeros
1,000,000,000,000,000,000	Quintillion	10^{18}	10 times itself 18 times	Eighteen zeros

Other large numbers are sextillion (10^{21}), septillion (10^{24}), and octillion (10^{27}).

*The proper way to say the numbers in this column is 10 raised to the nth power, where n is the exponent. The numbers in this column can also be represented as 1×10^n, but for brevity, the $1 \times$ can be omitted.

**The exponent 1 is usually omitted.

Converting Numbers to Exponent Form

As the chart shows, using exponents to express numbers can be very economical. When simple multiples of 10 are used, the exponent is always equal to the number of zeros that follow the 1, but this rule will not work with numbers that are more varied. Other large whole numbers can be converted to exponent form by the following operation: First, move the decimal (which we assume to be at the end of the number) to the left until it sits just behind the first number in the series (example: 3568. = 3.568). Then count the number of spaces (digits) the decimal has moved; that number will be the exponent. (The decimal has moved from 8. to 3., or 3 spaces.) In final notation, the converted number is multiplied by 10 with its appropriate exponent: 3568 is now 3.568×10^3.

Rounding Off Numbers

The notation in the previous example has not actually been shortened, but it can be reduced further by rounding off the decimal fraction to the nearest thousandth (three digits), hundredth (two digits), or tenth (one digit). To round off a number, drop its last digit and either increase the one next to it or leave it as it is. If the number dropped is 5, 6, 7, 8, or 9, the subsequent digit is increased by one (rounded up); if it is 0, 1, 2, 3, or 4, the subsequent digit remains as is. Using the example of 3.528, removing the 8 rounds off the 2 to a 3 and produces 3.53 (two digits). If further rounding is desired, the same rule of thumb applies, and the number becomes 3.5 (one digit). Other examples of exponential conversions follow.

Number	Is the Same As	Rounded Off, Placed in Exponent Form
16,825.	$1.6825 \times 10 \times 10 \times 10 \times 10$	1.7×10^4
957,654.	$9.57654 \times 10 \times 10 \times 10 \times 10 \times 10$	9.58×10^5
2,855,000.	$2.855000 \times 10 \times 10 \times 10 \times 10 \times 10 \times 10$	2.86×10^6

Negative Exponents

The numbers we have been using so far are greater than 1 and are represented by positive exponents. But the correct notation for numbers less than 1 involves negative exponents (10 raised to a negative power, or 10^{-n}). A negative exponent says that the number has been divided by a certain power of 10 (10, 100, 1,000). This usage is handy when working with concepts such as pH that are based on very small numbers otherwise needing to be represented by large decimal fractions—for example, 0.003528. Converting this and other such numbers to exponential notation is basically similar to converting positive numbers, except that you work from left to right and the exponent is negative. Using the example of 0.003528, first convert the number to a whole integer followed by a decimal fraction and keep track of the number of spaces the decimal point moves (example: 0.003528 = 3.528). The decimal has moved three spaces from its original position, so the finished product is 3.528×10^{-3}. Other examples follow.

Number	Is the Same As	Rounded Off, Expressed with Exponents
0.0005923	$\dfrac{5.923}{10 \times 10 \times 10 \times 10}$	5.92×10^{-4}
0.00007295	$\dfrac{7.295}{10 \times 10 \times 10 \times 10 \times 10}$	7.3×10^{-5}

Significant Events in Microbiology

Date	Discovery/People Involved
1546	Italian physician Girolamo Fracastoro suggests that invisible organisms may be involved in disease.
1660	Englishman Robert Hooke explores various living and nonliving matter with a compound microscope that uses reflected light.
1668	Francesco Redi, an Italian naturalist, conducts experiments that demonstrate the fallacies in the spontaneous generation theory.
1676	Antonie van Leeuwenhoek, a Dutch linen merchant, uses a simple microscope of his own design to observe bacteria and protozoa.
1796	English surgeon Edward Jenner introduces a vaccination for smallpox.
1838	Phillipe Ricord, a French physician, inoculates 2,500 human subjects to demonstrate that syphilis and gonorrhea are two separate diseases.
1847–1850	The Hungarian physician Ignaz Semmelweis substantiates his theory that childbed fever is a contagious disease transmitted to women by their physicians during childbirth.
1853–1854	John Snow, a London physician, demonstrates the epidemic spread of cholera through a water supply contaminated with human sewage.
1857	French bacteriologist Louis Pasteur shows that fermentations are due to microorganisms and originates the process now known as pasteurization.
1861	Louis Pasteur completes the definitive experiments that finally lay to rest the theory of spontaneous generation.
1867	The English surgeon Joseph Lister publishes the first work on antiseptic surgery, beginning the trend toward modern aseptic techniques in medicine.
1876–1877	German bacteriologist Robert Koch* studies anthrax in cattle and implicates the bacterium *Bacillus anthracis* as its causative agent.
1881	Pasteur develops a vaccine for anthrax in animals.
	Koch introduces the use of pure culture techniques for handling bacteria in the laboratory.
1882	Koch identifies the causative agent of tuberculosis.
1884	Koch outlines his postulates.
	Elie Metchnikoff,* a Russian zoologist, lays groundwork for the science of immunology by discovering phagocytic cells.
	The Danish physician Hans Christian Gram devises the Gram stain technique for differentiating bacteria.
1885	Pasteur develops a special vaccine for rabies.
1892	A Russian, D. Ivanovski, is the first to isolate a virus (the tobacco mosaic virus) and show that it could be transmitted in a cell-free filtrate.
1898	R. Ross* and G. Grassi demonstrate that malaria is transmitted by the bite of female mosquitoes.
1899	Dutch microbiologist Martinus Beijerinck further elucidates the viral agent of tobacco mosaic disease and postulates that viruses have many of the properties of living cells and that they reproduce within cells.
1903	American pathologist James Wright and others demonstrate the presence of antibodies in the blood of immunized animals.
1905	Syphilis is shown to be caused by *Treponema pallidum,* through the work of German bacteriologists Fritz Schaudinn and E. Hoffman.

Date	Discovery/People Involved
1908	The German Paul Ehrlich* becomes the pioneer of modern chemotherapy by developing salvarsan to treat syphilis.
1910	An American pathologist, Francis Rous,* discovers viruses that can induce cancer.
1928	Frederick Griffith lays the foundation for modern molecular genetics by his discovery of transformation in bacteria.
1929	A Scottish bacteriologist, Alexander Fleming,* discovers and describes the properties of the first antibiotic, penicillin.
1933–1938	Germans Ernst Ruska* and B. von Borries develop the first electron microscope.
1935	Gerhard Domagk,* a German physician, discovers the first sulfa drug and paves the way for the era of antimicrobic chemotherapy.
1941	Australian Howard Florey* and Englishman Ernst Chain* develop commercial methods for producing penicillin; this first antibiotic is tested and put into widespread use.
1944	Oswald Avery, Colin MacLeod, and Maclyn McCarty show that DNA is the genetic material.
	Joshua Lederberg* and E. L. Tatum* discover conjugation in bacteria.
	The Russian Selman Waksman* and his colleagues discover the antibiotic streptomycin.
1953	James Watson,* Francis Crick,* Rosalind Franklin, and Maurice Wilkins* determine the structure of DNA.
1954	Jonas Salk develops the first polio vaccine.
1959–1960	Gerald Edelman* and Rodney Porter* determine the structure of antibodies.
1972	Paul Berg* develops the first recombinant DNA in a test tube.
1973	Herb Boyer and Stanley Cohen clone the first DNA using plasmids.
1982	Development of first hepatitis B vaccine using virus isolated from human blood.
1983	Isolation and characterization of human immunodeficiency virus (HIV) by Luc Montagnier* and Francoise Barre'-Sinoussi* of France and Robert Gallo of the United States.
	The polymerase chain reaction is invented by Kary Mullis.*
	First release of recombinant strain of *Pseudomonas* to prevent frost formation on strawberry plants.
1989	Cancer-causing genes called oncogenes are characterized by J. Michael Bishop, Robert Huber, Hartmut Michel, and Harold Varmus.
1990	First clinical trials in gene therapy testing.
	Vaccine for *Haemophilus influenzae,* a cause of meningitis, is introduced.
1994	Human breast cancer gene isolated.
1995	First bacterial genome fully sequenced, for *Haemophilus influenzae.*
2000	A rough version of the human genome is mapped.
2001	Mailed anthrax spores cause major bioterrorism event.
2003	New roles for small nuclear RNAs discovered.
2006	New vaccine for a persistent microbe, human papillomavirus (HPV), is introduced. In 2008 Harald zur Hausen* was awarded the Nobel Prize for his discovery that human papilloma viruses cause cervical cancer.

*These scientists were awarded Nobel prizes for their contributions to the field.

Answers to Multiple-Choice and True-False and Matching Questions

Chapter 1
1. d
2. d
3. d
4. a
5. c
6. c
7. c
8. d
9. 1st col:
   3, 7, 4, 2
   2nd col:
   8, 5, 6, 1
10. c
11. F: Organisms in the same family are more closely related than those in the same order.
12. F: Eukaryotes and prokaryotes emerged independently.
13. T
14. T
15. T

Chapter 2
1. c
2. c
3. b
4. d
5. c
6. a
7. b
8. c
9. a
10. b
11. T
12. F: Covalent bonds are those formed when two elements share electrons.
13. F: A compound is called "organic" if it contains both carbon and hydrogen bonded

together in various combinations.
14. T
15. F: Membranes are mainly composed of macro-molecules called phospholipids.

Chapter 3
1. b
2. c
3. b
4. b
5. c
6. c
7. a
8. b
9. abf, df, abf, ef, af, bef, ac, bef
10. c or d
11. F: Agar is not easily decomposed by micro-organisms (gelatin can be).
12. T
13. F: The factor that most limits the clarity of an image in a microscope is the *resolution*.
14. F: Living specimens can be examined with phase-contrast or differential interference microscopy.
15. F: The best stain to use to visualize a microorganism with a large capsule is a negative stain.

Chapter 4
1. d
2. c
3. a
4. c
5. b
6. d
7. b
8. d
9. b
10. c
11. F: One major difference in the envelope structure between gram-positive bacteria and gram-negative bacteria is the presence or absence of an outer membrane.
12. F: A research microbiologist looking at evolutionary relatedness between two bacterial species is more likely to use *Bergey's Manual of Systematic Bacteriology.*
13. T
14. T
15. T

Chapter 5
1. b
2. d or e
3. d
4. b
5. b
6. d
7. d
8. b
9. c
10. a
11. T
12. T
13. F: Both the trophozoite

and the cyst stages of protozoans can be infective.
14. F: In humans, fungi can infect skin, mucous membranes, lungs, and other areas.
15. F: Fungi generally derive nutrients by digesting organic substrates.

Chapter 6
1. c
2. d
3. d
4. a
5. a
6. b
7. d
8. a
9. Herpesvirus
10. rabies, cold sores, genital warts, mumps, rubella
11. T
12. F: A viral capsid is composed of subunits called capsomeres.
13. F: The envelope of an animal virus is derived from the cell membrane of its host's cell.
14. F: The nucleic acid of animal viruses enters the cell through a process called penetration.
15. T

Chapter 7
1. a
2. a
3. c
4. b
5. a
6. a
7. b
8. c
9. c
10. b
11. F: Active transport of a substance across a membrane requires energy.
12. T
13. F: Some biofilms consist of multiple species of bacteria.
14. F: An obligate halophile is an organism that requires high salt concentration.
15. F: A facultative anaerobe can grow with or without oxygen.

Chapter 8
1. a
2. d
3. d
4. b
5. b
6. b
7. a
8. b
9. c
10. c
11. T
12. T
13. F: One cycle of fermentation yields much less energy than one cycle

of aerobic respiration.
14. T
15. F: Exoenzymes are produced inside a cell then released to the outside.

Chapter 9
1. b
2. b
3. b
4. c
5. b
6. a
7. b
8. d
9. b
10. c
11. F: The DNA base pairs are held together primarily by hydrogen bonds.
12. T
13. T
14. F: Messenger RNA is formed by transcription of a gene on the DNA template strand.
15. T

Chapter 10
1. c
2. d
3. a
4. b
5. c
6. c
7. c
8. d
9. a
10. d
11. F: The synthetic unit of the polymerase chain reaction is the amplicon.

12. T
13. F: A DNA fragment with 450 bp will migrate farther toward the positive pole (away from the origin) than one with 2,500 bp.
14. T
15. F: Plasmids and bacteriophages are commonly used as cloning vectors.

Chapter 11
1. c
2. a
3. c
4. b
5. d
6. b
7. d
8. d
9. a
10. b
11. T
12. F: The acceptable temperature-pressure combination for an autoclave is 121°C and 15 psi.
13. F: Ionizing radiation dislodges electrons from atoms.
14. T
15. F: Prions are highly resistant to denaturation by heat.

Chapter 12
1. b
2. c
3. b
4. d
5. b
6. d
7. a or b
8. c
9. c
10. b
11. F: Most antiviral agents work by blocking an essential viral activity.
12. F: Sulfonamide drugs work by disrupting folic acid synthesis.
13. T
14. T
15. F: Drug resistance can occur when a bacterium stops being susceptible to an antibiotic.

Chapter 13
1. a
2. b
3. d
4. c
5. d
6. b
7. c
8. d
9. a
10. a
11. F: The presence of a few bacteria in the blood is called bacteremia.
12. T
13. F: A nosocomial infection is one that is acquired in a hospital or medical facility.
14. F: The general term that describes a decrease in the number of white blood cells is leukopenia.
15. T

Chapter 14
1. b
2. b
3. d
4. b
5. b
6. c
7. d
8. a
9. d
10. c
11. F: The liquid component of unclotted blood is called plasma.
12. F: Pyrogenic bacteria are commonly associated with fever.
13. T
14. T
15. F: The immune system uses markers on the surface of cells to distinguish self from nonself.

Chapter 15
1. a
2. c
3. a
4. c
5. c
6. a
7. e
8. c
9. d
10. d
11. T
12. F: Antibodies are secreted by plasma cells.
13. F: Vaccination is artificial active immunity.
14. F: IgA antibodies are found in body secretions.
15. F: The process of reducing the virulence of microbes so they can be used in vaccines is called attenuation.

Chapter 16
1. d
2. d
3. c
4. c
5. b
6. a
7. d
8. d
9. d
10. d
11. T
12. F: A positive tuberculin skin test is an example of delayed hypersensitivity.
13. F: Contact dermatitis can be caused by chemicals absorbed through the skin.
14. T
15. T

Chapter 17
1. b
2. a
3. b
4. c
5. c
6. b
7. c
8. a
9. a
10. d
11. F: The tuberculin skin test is an example of an *in vivo* serological test.
12. T
13. T
14. T
15. F: Microorganisms that are grown from clinical samples should be evaluated to determine their clinical significance.

Chapter 18
1. b
2. a
3. d
4. e
5. c
6. b
7. d
8. d
9. b
10. c
11. F: The enzyme coagulase is associated with pathogenic strains of *Staphylococcus aureus*.
12. F: Fifth disease has no vaccine and no treatment.
13. T
14. F: The blistering and peeling of the skin in SSS are due to the ability of *S. aureus* to produce exfoliative toxins.
15. F: *Pseudomonas* and *Janthinobacterium* dominate the normal skin biota.

Chapter 19
1. d
2. a
3. c
4. d
5. b
6. d
7. b
8. a
9. b
10. a
11. F: *Toxoplasma gondii* is a protozoan.
12. F: Amphotericin or itraconazole are the first-line treatments for coccidioidomycosis.
13. T
14. F: In the United States, wild animals are a common reservoir for rabies.
15. T

Chapter 20
1. c
2. d
3. b
4. b
5. a
6. b
7. d
8. a
9. b
10. d
11. T
12. F: Respiratory tract infection with *Pneumocystis jiroveci* is an ADI.
13. F: Lyme disease is caused by *Borrelia burgdorferi*.
14. F: Yellow fever is caused by a virus transmitted by mosquitoes.
15. T

Chapter 21
1. d
2. d
3. b
4. b
5. d
6. c
7. d
8. c
9. a
10. c
11. T
12. T

Chapter 22
1. b
2. d
3. c
4. d
5. c
6. c
7. a
8. b
9. b
10. c
11. F: Humans are the only natural host for the mumps virus.
12. T
13. T
14. T
15. T

Chapter 23
1. a
2. b
3. d
4. a
5. b
6. a
7. c
8. c
9. d
10. a
11. T
12. F: Chancroid is caused by a bacterium.
13. T
14. Chamydia is the most common reportable STD in the U.S.
15. T

Chapter 24
1. c
2. b
3. b
4. d
5. c
6. d
7. b
8. d
9. d
10. b
11. F: Pure cultures are very rare in the biosphere.
12. T
13. T
14. T
15. F: One microbe has been found to live in a single-organism community.

Chapter 25
1. b
2. a
3. b
4. d
5. b
6. d
7. b
8. d
9. d
10. c
11. T
12. F: Food products will usually be colonized by harmless microorganisms.
13. T
14. T
15. F: Refrigerating food prevents the growth of many bacteria, but some pathogens, such as *Listeria* and *Salmonella*, can continue to grow at low temperatures.

Chapter 22 (BCG)
13. F: BCG vaccine is used in other countries to prevent TB.
14. F: RSV is a respiratory infection associated with infants.
15. F: The "flu shot" is an inactivated virus and cannot cause influenza.

An Introduction to Concept Mapping

Concept maps are visual tools for presenting and organizing what you have learned. They can take the place of an outline, though for most people they contain much more meaning and can illustrate connections and interconnections in ways that ordinary outlines cannot. They are also very flexible. If you are creating a concept map, there is a nearly infinite number of ways that they can be put together and still be "correct." Concept maps are also a way to incorporate and exploit your own creative impulses, so that you are not stuck inside a rigid framework but can express your understanding of concepts and their connections in ways that make sense to you.

This is an example of a relatively large concept map:

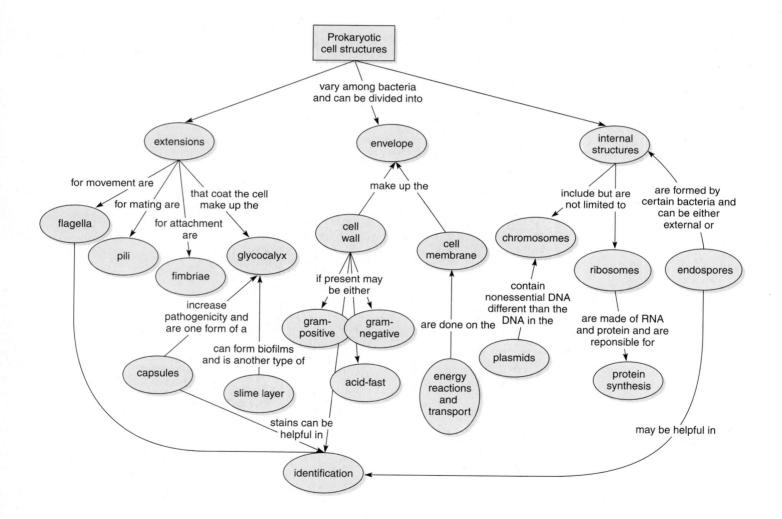

There is a wide variety of different ways to work with concept maps, such as using them as an introductory overview of material or using them as an evaluation tool. There are even software programs that enable concept mappers to create elaborate maps, complete with sound bytes and photos. Some of these will even convert an outline into a concept map for you. In the end-of-chapter materials in this book, we use only three different methods, all of them fairly simple. These three are explained and illustrated here.

All concept maps are made of two basic components:

1. Boxes or circles, each containing a single *concept*, which is most often a noun. The boxes are arranged on the page in vertical, horizontal, or diagonal rows or arrangements. They may also be arranged in a more free-form manner.
2. Connecting lines that join each concept box to at least one other box. Each connecting line has a word or a phrase associated with it—a linking word. These words/phrases are almost never nouns—but are verbs (like "requires") or adjectives or adverbs (like "underneath").

In the end, a picture is created that maps what you know about a subject. It illustrates which concepts are bigger and which are details. It illustrates that multiple concepts may be connected. Experts say that concept maps almost always lead us to conclude that all concepts in a subject can be connected in some way. This is true! And nowhere is it truer than in biology. The trick is to get used to finding the right connecting word to show how two concepts are, indeed, related. When you succeed, you will know the material in a deeper way than is possible by simply answering a single question or even a series of questions.

The first kind of concept map used in this book is the "fill-in-the-blank" version. In these concept maps, you are provided with all the boxes and most of the concepts in the boxes. Some boxes may be blank for you to fill in with the appropriate concept. You will do this by looking at the concepts close to the box and examining the connecting word. In these maps, you will also encounter blanks for linking words/phrases. Sometimes all the blanks will be filled in, but there will be no connecting lines or phrases and you will have to supply these. In a few of these maps, you may be asked to draw the linking lines themselves.

This is an exercise most like answering a simple question. In the example below, for instance, say to yourself, "Enzymes are _____ by pH and temperature." You might ask yourself, "What relation do pH and temperature have with

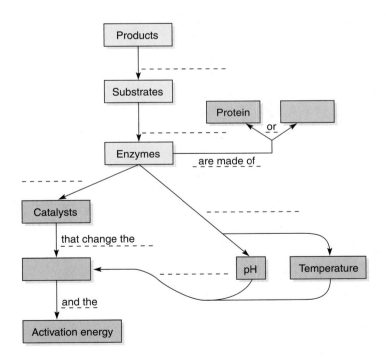

Acknowledgment: Pat Johnson, Palm Beach Community College, supplied information and a concept map for this Appendix.

enzymes?" Either way, you would probably end up with a linking phrase like *are affected by* or *can be regulated by*. There is some variation in what is a correct answer, but not wide variation.

The second kind of concept map you will see is one in which you will be provided a list of words to be used as concepts. You will be asked to draw the boxes and put the words in them in some way that makes sense. Here, there will be a lot of variability based on your view of how the concepts might relate to each other. After you put the concepts in your own boxes, you will need to add linking words/phrases. By the time you have drawn your boxes and added the concepts, you will have many ideas about what kind of linkers you want.

The last type of concept map in this book is the "freestyle" version. You will simply be asked to choose 6 to 10 key words from the chapter and create a map—complete with linking words.

Many students report that their first experiences with concept mapping can be frustrating. But when they have invested some time in their first few concept maps, many of them find they can never "go back" to organizing information in linear ways. Maps can make the time fly when you're studying. And creating concept maps with a partner or a group is also a great way to review material in a meaningful way. Give concept maps a try. Let your creative side show!

Glossary

A

A-B toxin   A class of bacterial exotoxin consisting of two components: a binding (B) component and an active (A) or enzymatic component.

abiogenesis   The belief in spontaneous generation as a source of life.

abiotic   Nonliving factors such as soil, water, temperature, and light that are studied when looking at an ecosystem.

ABO blood group system   Developed by Karl Landsteiner in 1904; the identification of different blood groups based on differing isoantigen markers characteristic of each blood type.

abscess   An inflamed, fibrous lesion enclosing a core of pus.

abyssal zone   The deepest region of the ocean; a sunless, high-pressure, cold, anaerobic habitat.

acellular vaccine   A vaccine preparation that contains specific antigens such as the capsule or toxin from a pathogen and not the whole microbe. Acellular (without a cell).

acid-fast   A term referring to the property of mycobacteria to retain carbol fuchsin even in the presence of acid alcohol. The staining procedure is used to diagnose tuberculosis.

acid-fast stain   a solution containing carbol-fuchsin which, when bound to lipids in the envelopes of *Mycobacterium* species, cannot be removed with an acid wash.

acidic   A solution with a pH value below 7 on the pH scale.

acidic fermentation   An anaerobic degradation of pyruvic acid that results in organic acid production.

acquired immunodeficiency syndrome   See *AIDS.*

actin   protein component of long filaments of protein arranged under the cell membrane of bacteria; contribute to cell shape and division.

actin cytoskeleton   A scaffoldlike structure made of protein that lies under the cytoplasmic membrane of some bacteria.

actinomycetes   A group of filamentous, funguslike bacteria.

active immunity   Immunity acquired through direct stimulation of the immune system by antigen.

active site   The specific region on an apoenzyme that binds substrate. The site for reaction catalysis.

active transport   Nutrient transport method that requires carrier proteins in the membranes of the living cells and the expenditure of energy.

acute   Characterized by rapid onset and short duration.

acyclovir   A synthetic purine analog that blocks DNA synthesis in certain viruses, particularly the herpes simplex viruses.

adenine (A)   One of the nitrogen bases found in DNA and RNA, with a purine form.

adenosine deaminase (ADA) deficiency   An immunodeficiency disorder and one type of SCIDS that is caused by an inborn error in the metabolism of adenine. The accumulation of adenine destroys both B and T lymphocytes.

adenosine triphosphate (ATP)   A nucleotide that is the primary source of energy to cells.

adhesion   The process by which microbes gain a more stable foothold at the portal of entry; often involves a specific interaction between the molecules on the microbial surface and the receptors on the host cell.

adjuvant   In immunology, a chemical vehicle that enhances antigenicity, presumably by prolonging antigen retention at the injection site.

adsorption   A process of adhering one molecule onto the surface of another molecule.

aerobe   A microorganism that lives and grows in the presence of free gaseous oxygen (O_2).

aerobic respiration   Respiration in which the final electron acceptor in the electron transport chain is oxygen (O_2).

aerosols   Suspensions of fine dust or moisture particles in the air that contain live pathogens.

aerotolerant   The state of not utilizing oxygen but not being harmed by it.

aflatoxin   From *Aspergillus flavus* toxin, a mycotoxin that typically poisons moldy animal feed and can cause liver cancer in humans and other animals.

agammaglobulinemia   Also called hypogammaglobulinemia. The absence of or severely reduced levels of antibodies in serum.

agar   A polysaccharide found in seaweed and commonly used to prepare solid culture media.

agglutination   The aggregation by antibodies of suspended cells or similar-size particles (agglutinogens) into clumps that settle.

agranulocyte   One form of leukocyte (white blood cell) having globular, nonlobed nuclei and lacking prominent cytoplasmic granules.

AIDS   Acquired immunodeficiency syndrome. The complex of signs and symptoms characteristic of the late phase of human immunodeficiency virus (HIV) infection.

alcoholic fermentation   An anaerobic degradation of pyruvic acid that results in alcohol production.

algae   Photosynthetic, plantlike organisms that generally lack the complex structure of plants; they may be single-celled or multicellular and inhabit diverse habitats such as marine and freshwater environments, glaciers, and hot springs.

allele   A gene that occupies the same location as other alternative (allelic) genes on paired chromosomes.

allergen   A substance that provokes an allergic response.

allergy   The altered, usually exaggerated, immune response to an allergen. Also called hypersensitivity.

alloantigen   An antigen that is present in some but not all members of the same species.

allograft   Relatively compatible tissue exchange between nonidentical members of the same species. Also called homograft.

allosteric   Pertaining to the altered activity of an enzyme due to the binding of a molecule to a region other than the enzyme's active site.

alternative splicing   The ability of eukaryotic organisms to create variant mRNAs from a single genetic sequence by cutting it in different places.

amantadine   Antiviral agent used to treat influenza; prevents fusion and uncoating of virus.

Ames test   A method for detecting mutagenic and potentially carcinogenic agents based upon the genetic alteration of nutritionally defective bacteria.

amination   The addition of an amine ($-NH_2$) group to a molecule.

amino acids   The building blocks of protein. Amino acids exist in 20 naturally occurring forms that impart different characteristics to the various proteins they compose.

aminoglycoside   A complex group of drugs derived from soil actinomycetes that impairs ribosome function and has antibiotic potential. Example: streptomycin.

ammonification   Phase of the nitrogen cycle in which ammonia is released from decomposing organic material.

amphibolism   Pertaining to the metabolic pathways that serve multiple functions in the breakdown, synthesis, and conversion of metabolites.

amphipathic   Relating to a compound that has contrasting characteristics, such as hydrophilic-hydrophobic or acid-base.

amphitrichous   Having a single flagellum or a tuft of flagella at opposite poles of a microbial cell.

amplicon   DNA strand that has been primed for replication during polymerase chain reaction.

anabolism   The energy-consuming process of incorporating nutrients into protoplasm through biosynthesis.

anaerobe   A microorganism that grows best, or exclusively, in the absence of oxygen.

anaerobic digesters   Closed chambers used in a microbial process that converts organic sludge from waste treatment plants into useful fuels such as methane and hydrogen gases. Also called bioreactors.

anaerobic respiration   Respiration in which the final electron acceptor in the electron transport chain is an inorganic molecule containing sulfate, nitrate, nitrite, carbonate, and so on.

analog   In chemistry, a compound that closely resembles another in structure.

anamnestic response   In immunology, an augmented response or memory related to a prior stimulation of the immune system by antigen. It boosts the levels of immune substances.

anaphylaxis   The unusual or exaggerated allergic reaction to antigen that leads to severe respiratory and cardiac complications.

anion   A negatively charged ion.

anoxygenic   Non-oxygen-producing.

annotating   In the context of genome sequencing, it is the process of assigning biological function to genetic sequence.

antagonism   Relationship in which microorganisms compete for survival in a common environment by taking actions that inhibit or destroy another organism.

antibiotic   A chemical substance from one microorganism that can inhibit or kill another microbe even in minute amounts.

antibody   A large protein molecule evoked in response to an antigen that interacts specifically with that antigen.

antibody-mediated immunity   specific protection from disease provided by the products of B cells.

anticodon   The trinucleotide sequence of transfer RNA that is complementary to the trinucleotide sequence of messenger RNA (the codon).

antigen   Any cell, particle, or chemical that induces a specific immune response by B cells or T cells and can stimulate resistance to an infection or a toxin. See *immunogen.*

antigen binding site   Specific region at the ends of the antibody molecule that recognize specific antigens. These sites have numerous shapes to fit a wide variety of antigens.

antigenic drift   Minor antigenic changes in the influenza A virus due to mutations in the spikes' genes.

antigenic shift   Major changes in the influenza A virus due to recombination of viral strains from two different host species.

antigenicity   The property of a substance to stimulate a specific immune response such as antibody formation.

antigen-presenting cell (APC)   A macrophage or dendritic cell that ingests and degrades an antigen and subsequently places the antigenic determinant molecules on its surface for recognition by CD4 T lymphocytes.

antigen-presenting cells   Cells of the immune system that digest foreign cells and particles and place pieces of them on their own surfaces in such a way that other cells of the immune system recognize them.

antihistamine   A drug that counters the action of histamine and is useful in allergy treatment.

antimetabolite   A substance such as a drug that competes with, substitutes for, or interferes with a normal metabolite.

antimicrobial   A special class of compounds capable of destroying or inhibiting microorganisms.

antimicrobial peptides   Short protein molecules found in epithelial cells; have the ability to kill bacteria.

antisense DNA   A DNA oligonucleotide that binds to a specific piece of RNA, thereby inhibiting translation; used in gene therapy.

antisense RNA   An RNA oligonucleotide that binds to a specific piece of RNA, thereby inhibiting translation; used in gene therapy.

antisepsis   Chemical treatments to kill or inhibit the growth of all vegetative microorganisms on body surfaces.

antiseptic   A growth-inhibiting agent used on tissues to prevent infection.

antiserum   Antibody-rich serum derived from the blood of animals (deliberately immunized against infectious or toxic antigen) or from people who have recovered from specific infections.

antitoxin   Globulin fraction of serum that neutralizes a specific toxin. Also refers to the specific antitoxin antibody itself.

apicomplexans   A group of protozoans that lack locomotion in the mature state.

apoenzyme   The protein part of an enzyme, as opposed to the nonprotein or inorganic cofactors.

apoptosis   The genetically programmed death of cells that is both a natural process of development and the body's means of destroying abnormal or infected cells.

appendages   Accessory structures that sprout from the surface of bacteria. They can be divided into two major groups: those that provide motility and those that enable adhesion.

applied microbiology   The study of the practical uses of microorganisms.

aquifer   A subterranean water-bearing stratum of permeable rock, sand, or gravel.

archaea   Prokaryotic single-celled organisms of primitive origin that have unusual anatomy, physiology, and genetics and live in harsh habitats; when capitalized **(Archaea),** the term refers to one of the three domains of living organisms as proposed by Woese.

arthroconidia   Reproductive body of *Coccidioides immitis,* also *arthrospore.*

Arthus reaction   An immune complex phenomenon that develops after repeat injection. This localized inflammation results from aggregates of antigen and antibody that bind, complement, and attract neutrophils.

artificial immunity   Immunity that is induced as a medical intervention, either by exposing an individual to an antigen or administering immune substances to him or her.

ascospore   A spore formed within a saclike cell (ascus) of Ascomycota following nuclear fusion and meiosis.

ascus   Special fungal sac in which haploid spores are created.

asepsis   A condition free of viable pathogenic microorganisms.

aseptic technique   Methods of handling microbial cultures, patient specimens, and other sources of microbes in a way that prevents infection of the handler and others who may be exposed.

assay medium   Microbiological medium used to test the effects of specific treatments to bacteria, such as antibiotic or disinfectant treatment.

assembly (viral)   The step in viral multiplication in which capsids and genetic material are packaged into virions.

astromicrobiology   A branch of microbiology that studies the potential for and the possible role of microorganisms in space and on other planets.

asymptomatic   An infection that produces no noticeable symptoms even though the microbe is active in the host tissue.

asymptomatic carrier   A person with an inapparent infection who shows no symptoms of being infected yet is able to pass the disease agent on to others.

atmosphere   That part of the biosphere that includes the gaseous envelope up to 14 miles above the earth's surface. It contains gases such as carbon dioxide, nitrogen, and oxygen.

atom   The smallest particle of an element to retain all the properties of that element.

atomic number (AN)   A measurement that reflects the number of protons in an atom of a particular element.

atomic weight   The average of the mass numbers of all the isotopic forms for a particular element.

atopy   Allergic reaction classified as type I, with a strong familial relationship; caused by allergens such as pollen, insect venom, food, and dander; involves IgE antibody; includes symptoms of hay fever, asthma, and skin rash.

ATP synthase   A unique enzyme located in the mitochondrial cristae and chloroplast grana that harnesses the flux of hydrogen ions to the synthesis of ATP.

attenuate   To reduce the virulence of a pathogenic bacterium or virus by passing it through a non-native host or by long-term subculture.

AUG (start codon)   The codon that signals the point at which translation of a messenger RNA molecule is to begin.

autoantibody   An "anti-self" antibody having an affinity for tissue antigens of the subject in which it is formed.

autoclave   A sterilization chamber that allows the use of steam under pressure to sterilize materials. The most common temperature/ pressure combination for an autoclave is 121°C and 15 psi.

autograft   Tissue or organ surgically transplanted to another site on the same subject.

autoimmune disease   The pathologic condition arising from the production of antibodies against autoantigens. Example: rheumatoid arthritis. Also called autoimmunity.

autoimmune regulator (AIRE)   A protein that regulates the transcription of self antigens in the thymus; defects in AIRE can lead to inappropriate responses to self antigens.

autotroph   A microorganism that requires only inorganic nutrients and whose sole source of carbon is carbon dioxide.

axenic   A sterile state such as a pure culture. An axenic animal is born and raised in a germ-free environment. See *gnotobiotic.*

axial filament   A type of flagellum (called an endoflagellum) that lies in the periplasmic space of spirochetes and is responsible for locomotion. Also called periplasmic flagellum.

azole   Five-membered heterocyclic compounds typical of histidine, which are used in antifungal therapy.

B

B lymphocyte (B cell)   A white blood cell that gives rise to plasma cells and antibodies.

bacillus   Bacterial cell shape that is cylindrical (longer than it is wide).

bacitracin   Antibiotic that targets the bacterial cell wall; component of over-the-counter topical antimicrobial ointments.

back-mutation   A mutation that counteracts an earlier mutation, resulting in the restoration of the original DNA sequence.

bacteremia   The presence of viable bacteria in circulating blood.

bacteremic   Bacteria present in the bloodstream.

Bacteria   When capitalized can refer to one of the three domains of living organisms proposed by Woese, containing all nonarchaea prokaryotes.

bacteria   (plural of bacterium) Category of prokaryotes with peptidoglycan in their cell walls and circular chromosome(s). This group of small cells is widely distributed in the earth's habitats.

bacterial chromosome   A circular body in bacteria that contains the primary genetic material. Also called nucleoid.

bactericide   An agent that kills bacteria.

bacteriocin   Proteins produced by certain bacteria that are lethal against closely related bacteria and are narrow spectrum compared with antibiotics; these proteins are coded and transferred in plasmids.

bacteriophage   A virus that specifically infects bacteria.

bacteristatic   Any process or agent that inhibits bacterial growth.

bacterium   A tiny unicellular prokaryotic organism that usually reproduces by binary fission and usually has a peptidoglycan cell wall, has various shapes, and can be found in virtually any environment.

barophile   A microorganism that thrives under high (usually hydrostatic) pressure.

basement membrane   A thin layer (1–6 μm) of protein and polysaccharide found at the base of epithelial tissues.

basic   A solution with a pH value above 7 on the pH scale.

basidiospore   A sexual spore that arises from a basidium. Found in basidiomycota fungi.

basidium   A reproductive cell created when the swollen terminal cell of a hypha develops filaments (sterigmata) that form spores.

basophil   A motile polymorphonuclear leukocyte that binds IgE. The basophilic cytoplasmic granules contain mediators of anaphylaxis and atopy.

beta oxidation   The degradation of long-chain fatty acids. Two-carbon fragments are formed as a result of enzymatic attack directed against the second or beta carbon of the hydrocarbon chain. Aided by coenzyme A, the fragments enter the Krebs cycle and are processed for ATP synthesis.

beta-lactamase   An enzyme secreted by certain bacteria that cleaves the beta-lactam ring of penicillin and cephalosporin and thus provides for resistance against the antibiotic. See *penicillinase.*

binary fission   The formation of two new cells of approximately equal size as the result of parent cell division.

binomial system   Scientific method of assigning names to organisms that employs two names to identify every organism— genus name plus species name.

biochemistry   The study of organic compounds produced by (or components of) living things. The four main categories of biochemicals are carbohydrates, lipids, proteins, and nucleic acids.

biodegradation   The breaking down of materials through the action of microbes or insects.

bioenergetics   The study of the production and use of energy by cells.

bioethics   The study of biological issues and how they relate to human conduct and moral judgment.

biofilm   A complex association that arises from a mixture of microorganisms growing together on the surface of a habitat.

biogenesis   Belief that living things can only arise from others of the same kind.

biogeochemical cycle   A process by which matter is converted from organic to inorganic form and returned to various nonliving reservoirs on earth (air, rocks, and water) where it becomes available for reuse by living things. Elements such as carbon, nitrogen, and phosphorus are constantly cycled in this manner.

biological vector   An animal that not only transports an infectious agent but plays a role in the life cycle of the pathogen, serving as a site in which it can multiply or complete its life cycle. It is usually an alternate host to the pathogen.

biomes   Particular climate regions in a terrestrial realm.

bioremediation   Decomposition of harmful chemicals by microbes or consortia of microbes.

biosensor   A device used to detect microbes or trace amounts of compounds through PCR, genome techniques, or electrochemical signaling.

biosphere   Habitable regions comprising the aquatic (hydrospheric), soil-rock (lithospheric), and air (atmospheric) environments.

biota   Beneficial or harmless resident bacteria commonly found on and/or in the human body.

biotechnology   The use of microbes or their products in the commercial or industrial realm.

biotic   Living factors such as parasites, food substrates, or other living or once-living organisms that are studied when looking at an ecosystem.

blast cell   An immature precursor cell of B and T lymphocytes. Also called a lymphoblast.

blocking antibody   The IgG class of immunoglobulins that competes with IgE antibody for allergens, thus blocking the degranulation of basophils and mast cells.

blood cells   Cellular components of the blood consisting of red blood cells, primarily responsible for the transport of oxygen and carbon dioxide, and white blood cells, primarily responsible for host defense and immune reactions.

blood-brain barrier   Decreased permeability of the walls of blood vessels in the brain, restricting access to that compartment.

botulinum   *Clostridium botulinum* toxin. Ingestion of this potent exotoxin leads to flaccid paralysis.

bradykinin   An active polypeptide that is a potent vasodilator released from IgE-coated mast cells during anaphylaxis.

broad spectrum   Denotes drugs that have an effect on a wide variety of microorganisms.

Brownian movement   The passive, erratic, nondirectional motion exhibited by microscopic particles. The jostling comes from being randomly bumped by submicroscopic particles, usually water molecules, in which the visible particles are suspended.

brucellosis   A zoonosis transmitted to humans from infected animals or animal products; causes a fluctuating pattern of severe fever in humans as well as muscle pain, weakness, headache, weight loss, and profuse sweating. Also called undulant fever.

bubo   The swelling of one or more lymph nodes due to inflammation.

bubonic plague   The form of plague in which bacterial growth is primarily restricted to the lymph and is characterized by the appearance of a swollen lymph node referred to as a bubo.

budding   See *exocytosis.*

bulbar poliomyelitis   Complication of polio infection in which the brain stem, medulla, or cranial nerves are affected. Leads to loss of respiratory control and paralysis of the trunk and limbs.

bullous   Consisting of fluid-filled blisters.

C

calculus   Dental deposit formed when plaque becomes mineralized with calcium and phosphate crystals. Also called tartar.

Calvin cycle   A series of reactions in the second phase of photosynthesis that generates glucose.

cancer   Any malignant neoplasm that invades surrounding tissue and can metastasize to other locations. A carcinoma is derived from epithelial tissue, and a sarcoma arises from proliferating mesodermal cells of connective tissue.

capsid   The protein covering of a virus's nucleic acid core. Capsids exhibit symmetry due to the regular arrangement of subunits called capsomers. See *icosahedron.*

capsomer   A subunit of the virus capsid shaped as a triangle or disc.

capsular staining   Any staining method which highlights the outermost polysaccharide and/or protein structure on a bacterial, fungal or protozoal cell.

capsule   In bacteria, the loose, gel-like covering or slime made chiefly of polysaccharides. This layer is protective and can be associated with virulence.

carbohydrate   A compound containing primarily carbon, hydrogen, and oxygen in a 1:2:1 ratio.

carbohydrate fermentation medium   A growth medium that contains sugars that are converted to acids through fermentation. Usually contains a pH indicator to detect acid protection.

carbon cycle   That pathway taken by carbon from its abiotic source to its use by producers to form organic compounds (biotic), followed by the breakdown of biotic compounds and their release to a nonliving reservoir in the environment (mostly carbon dioxide in the atmosphere).

carbon fixation   Reactions in photosynthesis that incorporate inorganic carbon dioxide into organic compounds such as sugars. This occurs during the Calvin cycle and uses energy generated by the light reactions. This process is the source of all production on earth.

carbuncle   A deep staphylococcal abscess joining several neighboring hair follicles.

carotenoid   Yellow, orange, or red photosynthetic pigments.

carrier   A person who harbors infections and inconspicuously spreads them to others. Also, a chemical agent that can accept an atom, chemical radical, or subatomic particle from one compound and pass it on to another.

caseous lesion   Necrotic area of lung tubercle superficially resembling cheese. Typical of tuberculosis.

catabolism   The chemical breakdown of complex compounds into simpler units to be used in cell metabolism.

catalyst   A substance that alters the rate of a reaction without being consumed or permanently changed by it. In cells, enzymes are catalysts.

catalytic site   The niche in an enzyme where the substrate is converted to the product (also active site).

catarrhal   A term referring to the secretion of mucus or fluids; term for the first stage of pertussis.

cation   A positively charged ion.

cell   An individual membrane-bound living entity; the smallest unit capable of an independent existence.

cell wall   In bacteria, a rigid structure made of peptidoglycan that lies just outside the cytoplasmic membrane; eukaryotes also have a cell wall but may be composed of a variety of materials.

cell-mediated immunity   The type of immune responses brought about by T cells, such as cytotoxic and helper effects.

cellulitis   The spread of bacteria within necrotic tissue.

cellulose   A long, fibrous polymer composed of β-glucose; one of the most common substances on earth.

cephalosporins   A group of broad-spectrum antibiotics isolated from the fungus *Cephalosporium.*

cercaria   The free-swimming larva of the schistosome trematode that emerges from the snail host and can penetrate human skin, causing schistosomiasis.

cestode   The common name for tapeworms that parasitize humans and domestic animals.

chancre   The primary sore of syphilis that forms at the site of penetration by *Treponema pallidum*. It begins as a hard, dull red, painless papule that erodes from the center.

chancroid   A lesion that resembles a chancre but is soft and is caused by *Haemophilus ducreyi.*

chemical bond   A link formed between molecules when two or more atoms share, donate, or accept electrons.

chemical mediators   Small molecules that are released during inflammation and specific immune reactions that allow communication between the cells of the immune system and facilitate surveillance, recognition, and attack.

chemiosmosis   The generation of a concentration gradient of hydrogen ions (called the proton motive force) by the pumping of hydrogen ions to the outer side of the membrane during electron transport.

chemoautotroph   An organism that relies upon inorganic chemicals for its energy and carbon dioxide for its carbon. Also called a chemolithotroph.

chemoheterotroph   Microorganisms that derive their nutritional needs from organic compounds.

chemokine   Chemical mediators (cytokines) that stimulate the movement and migration of white blood cells.

chemostat   A growth chamber with an outflow that is equal to the continuous inflow of nutrient media. This steady-state growth device is used to study such events as cell division, mutation rates, and enzyme regulation.

chemotactic factors   Chemical mediators that stimulate the movement of white blood cells. See *chemokines.*

chemotaxis   The tendency of organisms to move in response to a chemical gradient (toward an attractant or to avoid adverse stimuli).

chemotherapy   The use of chemical substances or drugs to treat or prevent disease.

chemotroph   Organism that oxidizes compounds to feed on nutrients.

chitin   A polysaccharide similar to cellulose in chemical structure. This polymer makes up the horny substance of the exoskeletons of arthropods and certain fungi.

chloramphenicol   Antibiotic that inhibits protein synthesis by binding to the 50S subunit of the ribosome.

chlorophyll   A group of mostly green pigments that are used by photosynthetic eukaryotic organisms and cyanobacteria to trap light energy to use in making chemical bonds.

chloroplast   An organelle containing chlorophyll that is found in photosynthetic eukaryotes.

cholesterol Best-known member of a group of lipids called steroids. Cholesterol is commonly found in cell membranes and animal hormones.

chromatin The genetic material of the nucleus. Chromatin is made up of nucleic acid and stains readily with certain dyes.

chromosome The tightly coiled bodies in cells that are the primary sites of genes.

chronic Any process or disease that persists over a long duration.

cilium (plural: *cilia*) Eukaryotic structure similar to a flagellum that propels a protozoan through the environment.

class In the levels of classification, the division of organisms that follows phylum.

classical pathway Pathway of complement activation initiated by a specific antigen-antibody interaction.

clonal selection theory A conceptual explanation for the development of lymphocyte specificity and variety during immune maturation.

clone A colony of cells (or group of organisms) derived from a single cell (or single organism) by asexual reproduction. All units share identical characteristics. Also used as a verb to refer to the process of producing a genetically identical population of cells or genes.

cloning host An organism such as a bacterium or a yeast that receives and replicates a foreign piece of DNA inserted during a genetic engineering experiment.

coagulase A plasma-clotting enzyme secreted by *Staphylococcus aureus*. It contributes to virulence and is involved in forming a fibrin wall that surrounds staphylococcal lesions.

coccobacillus An elongated coccus; a short, thick, oval-shaped bacterial rod.

coccus A spherical-shaped bacterial cell.

codon A specific sequence of three nucleotides in mRNA (or the sense strand of DNA) that constitutes the genetic code for a particular amino acid.

coenzyme A complex organic molecule, several of which are derived from vitamins (e.g., nicotinamide, riboflavin). A coenzyme operates in conjunction with an enzyme. Coenzymes serve as transient carriers of specific atoms or functional groups during metabolic reactions.

coevolution A biological process whereby a change in the genetic composition in one organism leads to a change in the genetics of another organism.

cofactor An enzyme accessory. It can be organic, such as coenzymes, or inorganic, such as Fe^{2+}, Mn^{2+}, or Zn^{2+} ions.

cold sterilization The use of nonheating methods such as radiation or filtration to sterilize materials.

coliform A collective term that includes normal enteric bacteria that are gram-negative and lactose-fermenting.

colony A macroscopic cluster of cells appearing on a solid medium, each arising from the multiplication of a single cell.

colostrum The clear yellow early product of breast milk that is very high in secretory antibodies. Provides passive intestinal protection.

commensalism An unequal relationship in which one species derives benefit without harming the other.

common source epidemic An outbreak of disease in which all affected individuals were exposed to a single source of the pathogen, even if they were exposed at different times.

communicable infection Capable of being transmitted from one individual to another.

community The interacting mixture of populations in a given habitat.

competitive inhibition Control process that relies on the ability of metabolic analogs to control microbial growth by successfully competing with a necessary enzyme to halt the growth of bacterial cells.

complement In immunology, serum protein components that act in a definite sequence when set in motion either by an antigen-antibody complex or by factors of the alternative (properdin) pathway.

complementary DNA (cDNA) DNA created by using reverse transcriptase to synthesize DNA from RNA templates.

compounds Molecules that are a combination of two or more different elements.

concentration The expression of the amount of a solute dissolved in a certain amount of solvent. It may be defined by weight, volume, or percentage.

condyloma acuminata Extensive, branched masses of genital warts caused by infection with human papillomavirus.

congenital Transmission of an infection from mother to fetus.

congenital rubella Transmission of the rubella virus to a fetus in utero. Injury to the fetus is generally much more serious than it is to the mother.

congenital syphilis A syphilis infection of the fetus or newborn acquired from maternal infection in utero.

conidia Asexual fungal spores shed as free units from the tips of fertile hyphae.

conidiospore A type of asexual spore in fungi; not enclosed in a sac.

conjugation In bacteria, the contact between donor and recipient cells associated with the transfer of genetic material such as plasmids. Can involve special (sex) pili. Also a form of sexual recombination in ciliated protozoans.

conjunctiva The thin fluid-secreting tissue that covers the eye and lines the eyelid.

consortium A group of microbes that includes more than one species.

constitutive enzyme An enzyme present in bacterial cells in constant amounts, regardless of the presence of substrate.

Enzymes of the central catabolic pathways are typical examples.

consumer An organism that feeds on producers or other consumers. It gets all nutrients and energy from other organisms (also called heterotroph). May exist at several levels, such as primary (feeds on producers) and secondary (feeds on primary consumers).

contagious Communicable; transmissible by direct contact with infected people and their fresh secretions or excretions.

contaminant An impurity; any undesirable material or organism.

contaminated culture A medium that once held a pure (single or mixed) culture but now contains unwanted microorganisms.

convalescence Recovery; the period between the end of a disease and the complete restoration of health in a patient.

corepressor A molecule that combines with inactive repressor to form active repressor, which attaches to the operator gene site and inhibits the activity of structural genes subordinate to the operator.

covalent A type of chemical bond that involves the sharing of electrons between two atoms.

covalent bond A chemical bond formed by the sharing of electrons between two atoms.

Creutzfeldt-Jakob disease (CJD) A spongiform encephalopathy caused by infection with a prion. The disease is marked by dementia, impaired senses, and uncontrollable muscle contractions.

crista The infolded inner membrane of a mitochondrion that is the site of the respiratory chain and oxidative phosphorylation.

cryptosporidiosis A gastrointestinal disease caused by *Cryptosporidium parvum*, a protozoan.

culture The visible accumulation of microorganisms in or on a nutrient medium. Also, the propagation of microorganisms with various media.

curd The coagulated milk protein used in cheese making.

cutaneous Second level of skin, including the stratum corneum and occasionally the upper dermis.

cyanosis Blue discoloration of the skin or mucous membranes indicative of decreased oxygen concentration in blood.

cyst The resistant, dormant but infectious form of protozoans. Can be important in spread of infectious agents such as *Entamoeba histolytica* and *Giardia lamblia*.

cystine An amino acid, HOOC—CH(NH$_2$)—CH$_2$—S—S—CH$_2$—CH(NH$_2$)COOH. An oxidation product of two cysteine molecules in which the OSH (sulfhydryl) groups form a disulfide union. Also called dicysteine.

cytochrome A group of heme protein compounds whose chief role is in electron and/or hydrogen transport occurring in the last phase of aerobic respiration.

cytokine   A chemical substance produced by white blood cells and tissue cells that regulates development, inflammation, and immunity.

cytopathic effect   The degenerative changes in cells associated with virus infection. Examples: the formation of multinucleate giant cells (Negri bodies), the prominent cytoplasmic inclusions of nerve cells infected by rabies virus.

cytoplasm   Dense fluid encased by the cell membrane; the site of many of the cell's biochemical and synthetic activities.

cytoplasmic membrane   Lipid bilayer that encloses the cytoplasm of bacterial cells.

cytosine (C)   One of the nitrogen bases found in DNA and RNA, with a pyrimidine form.

cytotoxicity   The ability to kill cells; in immunology, certain T cells are called cytotoxic T cells because they kill other cells.

D

daptomycin   A lipopeptide antibiotic that disrupts the cytoplasmic membrane.

deamination   The removal of an amino group from an amino acid.

death phase   End of the cell growth due to lack of nutrition, depletion of environment, and accumulation of wastes. Population of cells begins to die.

debridement   Trimming away devitalized tissue and foreign matter from a wound.

decomposer   A consumer that feeds on organic matter from the bodies of dead organisms. These microorganisms feed from all levels of the food pyramid and are responsible for recycling elements (also called saprobes).

decomposition   The breakdown of dead matter and wastes into simple compounds that can be directed back into the natural cycle of living things.

decontamination   The removal or neutralization of an infectious, poisonous, or injurious agent from a site.

deduction   Problem-solving process in which an individual constructs a hypothesis, tests its validity by outlining particular events that are predicted by the hypothesis, and then performs experiments to test for those events.

deductive approach   Method of investigation that uses **deduction**. See *deduction*.

definitive host   The organism in which a parasite develops into its adult or sexually mature stage. Also called the final host.

degerm   To physically remove surface oils, debris, and soil from skin to reduce the microbial load.

degranulation   The release of cytoplasmic granules, as when cytokines are secreted from mast cell granules.

dehydration synthesis   During the formation of a carbohydrate bond, the step in which one carbon molecule gives up its OH group and the other loses the H from its OH group, thereby producing a water molecule. This process is common to all polymerization reactions.

denaturation   The loss of normal characteristics resulting from some molecular alteration. Usually in reference to the action of heat or chemicals on proteins whose function depends upon an unaltered tertiary structure.

dendritic cell   A large, antigen-processing cell characterized by long, branchlike extensions of the cell membrane.

denitrification   The end of the nitrogen cycle when nitrogen compounds are returned to the reservoir in the air.

dental caries   A mixed infection of the tooth surface that gradually destroys the enamel and may lead to destruction of the deeper tissue.

deoxyribonucleic acid (DNA)   The nucleic acid often referred to as the "double helix." DNA carries the master plan for an organism's heredity.

deoxyribose   A 5-carbon sugar that is an important component of DNA.

dermatophytes   A group of fungi that cause infections of the skin and other integument components. They survive by metabolizing keratin.

dermolytic   Capable of damaging the skin.

desensitization   See *hyposensitization.*

desiccation   To dry thoroughly. To preserve by drying.

desquamate   To shed the cuticle in scales; to peel off the outer layer of a surface.

diabetes mellitus   A disease involving compromise in insulin function. In one form, the pancreatic cells that produce insulin are destroyed by autoantibodies, and in another, the pancreas does not produce sufficient insulin.

diapedesis   The migration of intact blood cells between endothelial cells of a blood vessel such as a venule.

dichotomous keys   Flow charts that offer two choices or pathways at each level.

differential medium   A single substrate that discriminates between groups of microorganisms on the basis of differences in their appearance due to different chemical reactions.

differential stain   A technique that utilizes two dyes to distinguish between different microbial groups or cell parts by color reaction.

diffusion   The dispersal of molecules, ions, or microscopic particles propelled down a concentration gradient by spontaneous random motion to achieve a uniform distribution.

DiGeorge syndrome   A birth defect usually caused by a missing or incomplete thymus gland that results in abnormally low or absent T cells and other developmental abnormalities.

dimorphic   In mycology, the tendency of some pathogens to alter their growth form from mold to yeast in response to rising temperature.

diplococci   Spherical or oval-shaped bacteria, typically found in pairs.

direct or total cell count   1. Counting total numbers of individual cells being viewed with magnification. 2. Counting isolated colonies of organisms growing on a plate of media as a way to determine population size.

disaccharide   A sugar containing two monosaccharides. Example: sucrose (fructose + glucose).

disease   Any deviation from health, as when the effects of microbial infection damage or disrupt tissues and organs.

disinfection   The destruction of pathogenic nonsporulating microbes or their toxins, usually on inanimate surfaces.

division   In the levels of classification, an alternate term for phylum.

DNA   See *deoxyribonucleic acid.*

DNA polymerase   Enzyme responsible for the replication of DNA. Several versions of the enzyme exist, each completing a unique portion of the replication process.

DNA profiling   A pattern of restriction enzyme fragments that is unique for an individual organism.

DNA sequencing   Determining the exact order of nucleotides in a fragment of DNA. Most commonly done using the Sanger dideoxy sequencing method.

DNA vaccine   A newer vaccine preparation based on inserting DNA from pathogens into host cells to encourage them to express the foreign protein and stimulate immunity.

domain   In the levels of classification, the broadest general category to which an organism is assigned. Members of a domain share only one or a few general characteristics.

doubling time   Time required for a complete fission cycle—from parent cell to two new daughter cells. Also called generation time.

droplet nuclei   The dried residue of fine droplets produced by mucus and saliva sprayed while sneezing and coughing. Droplet nuclei are less than 5 μm in diameter (large enough to bear a single bacterium and small enough to remain airborne for a long time) and can be carried by air currents. Droplet nuclei are drawn deep into the air passages.

drug resistance   An adaptive response in which microorganisms begin to tolerate an amount of drug that would ordinarily be inhibitory.

dysentery   Diarrheal illness in which stools contain blood and/or mucus.

dyspnea   Difficulty in breathing.

E

echinocandins   antifungal drugs that inhibit the manufacture of fungal cell walls.

ecosystem   A collection of organisms together with its surrounding physical and chemical factors.

ectoplasm   The outer, more viscous region of the cytoplasm of a phagocytic cell such as an amoeba. It contains microtubules, but not granules or organelles.

eczema   An acute or chronic allergy of the skin associated with itching and burning sensations. Typically, red, edematous, vesicular lesions erupt, leaving the skin scaly and sometimes hyperpigmented.

edema   The accumulation of excess fluid in cells, tissues, or serous cavities. Also called swelling.

electrolyte   Any compound that ionizes in solution and conducts current in an electrical field.

electron   A negatively charged subatomic particle that is distributed around the nucleus in an atom.

electrophoresis   The separation of molecules by size and charge through exposure to an electrical current.

electrostatic   Relating to the attraction of opposite charges and the repulsion of like charges. Electrical charge remains stationary as opposed to electrical flow or current.

element   A substance comprising only one kind of atom that cannot be degraded into two or more substances without losing its chemical characteristics.

ELISA   Abbreviation for **e**nzyme-linked **i**mmuno**s**orbent **a**ssay, a very sensitive serological test used to detect antibodies in diseases such as AIDS.

emerging disease   Newly identified diseases that are becoming more prominent.

emetic   Inducing to vomit.

encephalitis   An inflammation of the brain, usually caused by infection.

endemic disease   A native disease that prevails continuously in a geographic region.

endergonic reaction   A chemical reaction that occurs with the absorption and storage of surrounding energy. Antonym: exergonic.

endocytosis   The process whereby solid and liquid materials are taken into the cell through membrane invagination and engulfment into a vesicle.

endoenzyme   An intracellular enzyme, as opposed to enzymes that are secreted.

endogenous   Originating or produced within an organism or one of its parts.

endoplasmic reticulum (ER)   An intracellular network of flattened sacs or tubules with or without ribosomes on their surfaces.

endospore   A small, dormant, resistant derivative of a bacterial cell that germinates under favorable growth conditions into a vegetative cell. The bacterial genera *Bacillus* and *Clostridium* are typical sporeformers.

endosymbiosis   Relationship in which a microorganism resides within a host cell and provides a benefit to the host cell.

endotoxic shock   A massive drop in blood pressure caused by the release of endotoxin from gram-negative bacteria multiplying in the bloodstream.

endotoxin   A bacterial toxin that is not ordinarily released (as is exotoxin). Endotoxin is composed of a phospholipid-polysaccharide complex that is an integral part of gram-negative bacterial cell walls. Endotoxins can cause severe shock and fever.

energy of activation   The minimum energy input necessary for reactants to form products in a chemical reaction.

energy pyramid   An ecological model that shows the energy flow among the organisms in a community. It is structured like the food pyramid but shows how energy is reduced from one trophic level to another.

enriched medium   A nutrient medium supplemented with blood, serum, or some growth factor to promote the multiplication of fastidious microorganisms.

enteric   Pertaining to the intestine.

enteroaggregative   The term used to describe certain types of intestinal bacteria that tend to stick to each other in large clumps.

enterohemorrhagic *E. coli* (EHEC)   A group of *E. coli* species that induce bleeding in the intestines and also in other organs; *E. coli* O157:H7 belongs to this group.

enteroinvasive   Predisposed to invade the intestinal tissues.

enteropathogenic   Pathogenic to the alimentary canal.

enterotoxigenic   Having the capacity to produce toxins that act on the intestinal tract.

enterotoxin   A bacterial toxin that specifically targets intestinal mucous membrane cells. Enterotoxigenic strains of *Escherichia coli* and *Staphylococcus aureus* are typical sources.

enumeration medium   Microbiological medium that does not encourage growth and allows for the counting of microbes in food, water or environmental samples.

enveloped virus   A virus whose nucleocapsid is enclosed by a membrane derived in part from the host cell. It usually contains exposed glycoprotein spikes specific for the virus.

enzyme   A protein biocatalyst that facilitates metabolic reactions.

enzyme induction   One of the controls on enzyme synthesis. This occurs when enzymes appear only when suitable substrates are present.

enzyme repression   The inhibition of enzyme synthesis by the end product of a catabolic pathway.

eosinophil   A leukocyte whose cytoplasmic granules readily stain with red eosin dye.

eosinophilia   An increase in eosinophil concentration in the bloodstream, often in response to helminth infection.

epidemic   A sudden and simultaneous outbreak or increase in the number of cases of disease in a community.

epidemiology   The study of the factors affecting the prevalence and spread of disease within a community.

epitope   The precise molecular group of an antigen that defines its specificity and triggers the immune response.

Epstein-Barr virus (EBV)   Herpesvirus linked to infectious mononucleosis, Burkitt's lymphoma, and nasopharyngeal carcinoma.

erysipelas   An acute, sharply defined inflammatory disease specifically caused by hemolytic *Streptococcus*. The eruption is limited to the skin but can be complicated by serious systemic symptoms.

erythroblastosis fetalis   Hemolytic anemia of the newborn. The anemia comes from hemolysis of Rh-positive fetal erythrocytes by anti-Rh maternal antibodies. Erythroblasts are immature red blood cells prematurely released from the bone marrow.

erythrocytes (red blood cells)   Blood cells involved in the transport of oxygen and carbon dioxide.

erythrogenic toxin   An exotoxin produced by lysogenized group A strains of β-hemolytic streptococci that is responsible for the severe fever and rash of scarlet fever in the nonimmune individual. Also called a pyrogenic toxin.

eschar   A dark, sloughing scab that is the lesion of anthrax and certain rickettsioses.

essential nutrient   Any ingredient such as a certain amino acid, fatty acid, vitamin, or mineral that cannot be formed by an organism and must be supplied in the diet. A growth factor.

ester bond   A covalent bond formed by reacting carboxylic acid with an OH group:

$$R - \overset{\overset{\textstyle O}{\|}}{C} - O - R9$$

Olive and corn oils, lard, and butter fat are examples of triacylglycerols—esters formed between glycerol and three fatty acids.

ethylene oxide   A potent, highly water-soluble gas invaluable for gaseous sterilization of heat-sensitive objects such as plastics, surgical and diagnostic appliances, and spices.

etiologic agent   The microbial cause of disease; the pathogen.

eubacteria   Term used for nonarchaea prokaryotes, means "true bacteria."

Eukarya   One of the three domains (sometimes called superkingdoms) of living organisms, as proposed by Woese; contains all eukaryotic organisms.

eukaryotic cell   A cell that differs from a prokaryotic cell chiefly by having a nuclear membrane (a well-defined nucleus), membrane-bounded subcellular organelles, and mitotic cell division.

eutrophication   The process whereby dissolved nutrients resulting from natural seasonal enrichment or industrial pollution of water cause overgrowth of algae and cyanobacteria to the detriment of fish and other large aquatic inhabitants.

evolution   Scientific principle that states that living things change gradually through hundreds of millions of years, and these changes are expressed in structural and functional adaptations in each organism. Evolution presumes that those traits that favor survival are preserved and passed on to following generations, and those traits that do not favor survival are lost.

exanthem An eruption or rash of the skin.

exergonic A chemical reaction associated with the release of energy to the surroundings. Antonym: endergonic.

exfoliative toxin A poisonous substance that causes superficial cells of an epithelium to detach and be shed. Example: staphylococcal exfoliatin. Also called an epidermolytic toxin.

exocytosis The process that releases enveloped viruses from the membrane of the host's cytoplasm.

exoenzyme An extracellular enzyme chiefly for hydrolysis of nutrient macromolecules that are otherwise impervious to the cell membrane. It functions in saprobic decomposition of organic debris and can be a factor in invasiveness of pathogens.

exogenous Originating outside the body.

exon A stretch of eukaryotic DNA coding for a corresponding portion of mRNA that is translated into peptides. Intervening stretches of DNA that are not expressed are called introns. During transcription, exons are separated from introns and are spliced together into a continuous mRNA transcript.

exotoxin A toxin (usually protein) that is secreted and acts upon a specific cellular target. Examples: botulin, tetanospasmin, diphtheria toxin, and erythrogenic toxin.

exponential Pertaining to the use of exponents, numbers that are typically written as a superscript to indicate how many times a factor is to be multiplied. Exponents are used in scientific notation to render large, cumbersome numbers into small workable quantities.

exponential growth phase The period of maximum growth rate in a growth curve. Cell population increases logarithmically.

extrapulmonary tuberculosis A condition in which tuberculosis bacilli have spread to organs other than the lungs.

extremophiles Organisms capable of living in harsh environments, such as extreme heat or cold.

F

facilitated diffusion The passive movement of a substance across a plasma membrane from an area of higher concentration to an area of lower concentration utilizing specialized carrier proteins.

facultative Pertaining to the capacity of microbes to adapt or adjust to variations; not obligate. Example: the presence of oxygen is not obligatory for a facultative anaerobe to grow. See *obligate.*

family In the levels of classification, a midlevel division of organisms that groups more closely related organisms than previous levels. An order is divided into families.

fastidious Requiring special nutritional or environmental conditions for growth. Said of bacteria.

fecal coliforms Any species of gram-negative lactose-positive bacteria (primarily *Escherichia coli*) that live primarily in the intestinal tract and not the environment. Finding evidence of these bacteria in a water or food sample is substantial evidence of fecal contamination and potential for infection (see *coliform*).

feedback inhibition Temporary end to enzyme action caused by an end product molecule binding to the regulatory site and preventing the enzyme's active site from binding to its substrate.

fermentation The extraction of energy through anaerobic degradation of substrates into simpler, reduced metabolites. In large industrial processes, fermentation can mean any use of microbial metabolism to manufacture organic chemicals or other products.

fermentor A large tank used in industrial microbiology to grow mass quantities of microbes that can synthesize desired products. These devices are equipped with means to stir, monitor, and harvest products such as drugs, enzymes, and proteins in very large quantities.

fertility (F') factor Donor plasmid that allows synthesis of a pilus in bacterial conjugation. Presence of the factor is indicated by F^+, and lack of the factor is indicated by F^-.

filament A helical structure composed of proteins that is part of bacterial flagella.

fimbria A short, numerous-surface appendage on some bacteria that provides adhesion but not locomotion.

Firmicutes Taxonomic category of bacteria that have gram-positive cell envelopes.

flagellar staining A staining method which highlights the flagellum of a bacterium.

flagellum A structure that is used to propel the organism through a fluid environment.

fluid mosaic model A conceptualization of the molecular architecture of cellular membranes as a bilipid layer containing proteins. Membrane proteins are embedded to some degree in this bilayer, where they float freely about.

fluorescence The property possessed by certain minerals and dyes to emit visible light when excited by ultraviolet radiation. A fluorescent dye combined with specific antibody provides a sensitive test for the presence of antigen.

fluoroquinolones Synthetic antimicrobial drugs chemically related to quinine. They are broad spectrum and easily adsorbed from the intestine.

focal infection Occurs when an infectious agent breaks loose from a localized infection and is carried by the circulation to other tissues.

folliculitis An inflammatory reaction involving the formation of papules or pustules in clusters of hair follicles.

fomite Virtually any inanimate object an infected individual has contact with that can serve as a vehicle for the spread of disease.

food chain A simple straight-line feeding sequence among organisms in a community.

food fermentations Addition to and growth of known cultures of microorganisms in foods to produce desirable flavors, smells, or textures. Includes cheeses, breads, alcoholic beverages, and pickles.

food poisoning Symptoms in the intestines (which may include vomiting) induced by preformed exotoxin from bacteria.

food web A complex network that traces all feeding interactions among organisms in a community (see *food chain*). This is considered to be a more accurate picture of food relationships in a community than a food chain.

formalin A 37% aqueous solution of formaldehyde gas; a potent chemical fixative and microbicide.

fosfomycin trimethamine Antibiotic that inhibits an enzyme necessary for cell wall synthesis.

frameshift mutation An insertion or deletion mutation that changes the codon reading frame from the point of the mutation to the final codon. Almost always leads to a nonfunctional protein.

free energy energy in a chemical system that can be used to do work.

fructose One of the carbohydrates commonly referred to as sugars. Fructose is commonly fruit sugars.

functional group In chemistry, a particular molecular combination that reacts in predictable ways and confers particular properties on a compound. Examples: — COOH, —OH, —CHO.

fungemia The condition of fungi multiplying in the bloodstream.

fungi Macroscopic and microscopic heterotrophic eukaryotic organisms that can be uni- or multicellular.

fungus Heterotrophic unicellular or multicellular eukaryotic organism that may take the form of a larger macroscopic organism, as in the case of mushrooms, or a smaller microscopic organism, as in the case of yeasts and molds.

furuncle A boil; a localized pyogenic infection arising from a hair follicle.

fuzeon Anti-HIV drug that inhibits viral attachment to host cells.

G

Gaia Theory The concept that biotic and abiotic factors sustain suitable conditions for one another simply by their interactions. Named after the mythical Greek goddess of earth.

gamma globulin The fraction of plasma proteins high in immunoglobulins (antibodies). Preparations from pooled human plasma containing normal antibodies make useful passive immunizing agents against pertussis, polio, measles, and several other diseases.

gas gangrene   Disease caused by a clostridial infection of soft tissue or wound. The name refers to the gas produced by the bacteria growing in the tissue. Unless treated early, it is fatal. Also called myonecrosis.

gastritis   Pain and/or nausea, usually experienced after eating; result of inflammation of the lining of the stomach.

gel electrophoresis   A laboratory technique for separating DNA fragments according to length by employing electricity to force the DNA through a gel-like matrix typically made of agarose. Smaller DNA fragments move more quickly through the gel, thereby moving farther than larger fragments during the same period of time.

gene   A site on a chromosome that provides information for a certain cell function. A specific segment of DNA that contains the necessary code to make a protein or RNA molecule.

gene probe   Short strands of single-stranded nucleic acid that hybridize specifically with complementary stretches of nucleotides on test samples and thereby serve as a tagging and identification device.

gene therapy   The introduction of normal functional genes into people with genetic diseases such as sickle cell anemia and cystic fibrosis. This is usually accomplished by a virus vector.

generation time   Time required for a complete fission cycle—from parent cell to two new daughter cells. Also called doubling time.

genetic engineering   A field involving deliberate alterations (recombinations) of the genomes of microbes, plants, and animals through special technological processes.

genetics   The science of heredity.

genital warts   A prevalent STD linked to some forms of cancer of the reproductive organs. Caused by infection with human papillomavirus.

genome   The complete set of chromosomes and genes in an organism.

genomics   The systematic study of an organism's genes and their functions.

genotype   The genetic makeup of an organism. The genotype is ultimately responsible for an organism's phenotype, or expressed characteristics.

genus   In the levels of classification, the second most specific level. A family is divided into several genera.

geomicrobiology   A branch of microbiology that studies the role of microorganisms in the earth's crust.

germ free   See *axenic*.

germ theory of disease   A theory first originating in the 1800s that proposed that microorganisms can be the cause of diseases. The concept is actually so well established in the present time that it is considered a fact.

germicide   An agent lethal to non-endospore-forming pathogens.

giardiasis   Infection by the *Giardia* flagellate. Most common mode of transmission is contaminated food and water. Symptoms include diarrhea, abdominal pain, and flatulence.

gingivitis   Inflammation of the gum tissue in contact with the roots of the teeth.

gluconeogenesis   The formation of glucose (or glycogen) from noncarbohydrate sources such as protein or fat. Also called glyconeogenesis.

glucose   One of the carbohydrates commonly referred to as sugars. Glucose is characterized by its 6-carbon structure.

glycerol   A 3-carbon alcohol, with three OH groups that serve as binding sites.

glycocalyx   A filamentous network of carbohydrate-rich molecules that coats cells.

glycogen   A glucose polymer stored by cells.

glycolysis   The energy-yielding breakdown (fermentation) of glucose to pyruvic or lactic acid. It is often called anaerobic glycolysis because no molecular oxygen is consumed in the degradation.

glycosidic bond   A bond that joins monosaccharides to form disaccharides and polymers.

gnotobiotic   Referring to experiments performed on germ-free animals.

Golgi apparatus   An organelle of eukaryotes that participates in packaging and secretion of molecules.

gonococcus   Common name for *Neisseria gonorrhoeae*, the agent of gonorrhea.

Gracilicutes   Taxonomic category of bacteria that have gram-negative envelopes.

graft   Live tissue taken from a donor and transplanted into a recipient to replace damaged or missing tissues such as skin, bone, blood vessels.

graft versus host disease (GVHD)   A condition associated with a bone marrow transplant in which T cells in the transplanted tissue mount an immune response against the recipient's (host) normal tissues.

Gram stain   A differential stain for bacteria useful in identification and taxonomy. Gram-positive organisms appear purple from crystal violet mordant retention, whereas gram-negative organisms appear red after loss of crystal violet and absorbance of the safranin counterstain.

gram-negative   A category of bacterial cells that describes bacteria with an outer membrane, a cytoplasmic membrane, and a thin cell wall.

gram-positive   A category of bacterial cells that describes bacteria with a thick cell wall and no outer membrane.

grana   Discrete stacks of chlorophyll-containing thylakoids within chloroplasts.

granulocyte   A mature leukocyte that contains noticeable granules in a Wright stain. Examples: neutrophils, eosinophils, and basophils.

granuloma   A solid mass or nodule of inflammatory tissue containing modified macrophages and lymphocytes. Usually a chronic pathologic process of diseases such as tuberculosis or syphilis.

granzymes   Enzymes secreted by cytotoxic T cells that damage proteins of target cells.

Graves' disease   A malfunction of the thyroid gland in which autoantibodies directed at thyroid cells stimulate an overproduction of thyroid hormone (hyperthyroidism).

greenhouse effect   The capacity to retain solar energy by a blanket of atmospheric gases that redirects heat waves back toward the earth.

group translocation   A form of active transport in which the substance being transported is altered during transfer across a plasma membrane.

growth curve   A graphical representation of the change in population size over time. This graph has four periods known as lag phase, exponential or log phase, stationary phase, and death phase.

growth factor   An organic compound such as a vitamin or amino acid that must be provided in the diet to facilitate growth. An essential nutrient.

guanine (G)   One of the nitrogen bases found in DNA and RNA in the purine form.

Guillain-Barré syndrome   A neurological complication of infection or vaccination.

gumma   A nodular, infectious granuloma characteristic of tertiary syphilis.

gut-associated lymphoid tissue (GALT)   A collection of lymphoid tissue in the gastrointestinal tract that includes the appendix, the lacteals, and Peyer's patches.

gyrase   The enzyme responsible for supercoiling DNA into tight bundles; a type of topoisomerase.

H

HAART   Highly active antiretroviral therapy; three-antiviral treatment for HIV infection.

habitat   The environment to which an organism is adapted.

halogens   A group of related chemicals with antimicrobial applications. The halogens most often used in disinfectants and antiseptics are chlorine and iodine.

halophile   A microbe whose growth is either stimulated by salt or requires a high concentration of salt for growth.

Hansen's disease   A chronic, progressive disease of the skin and nerves caused by infection by a mycobacterium that is a slow-growing, strict parasite. Hansen's disease is the preferred name for leprosy.

hapten   An incomplete or partial antigen. Although it constitutes the determinative group and can bind antigen, hapten cannot stimulate a full immune response without being carried by a larger protein molecule.

Hashimoto's thyroiditis   An autoimmune disease of the thyroid gland that damages the thyroid follicle cells and results in decreased production of thyroid hormone (hypothyroidism).

hay fever   A form of atopic allergy marked by seasonal acute inflammation of the conjunctiva and mucous membranes of the respiratory passages. Symptoms are irritative itching and rhinitis.

helical   Having a spiral or coiled shape. Said of certain virus capsids and bacteria.

helminth   A term that designates all parasitic worms.

helper T cell   A class of thymus-stimulated lymphocytes that facilitate various immune activities such as assisting B cells and macrophages. Also called a T helper cell.

hemagglutinin   A molecule that causes red blood cells to clump or agglutinate. Often found on the surfaces of viruses.

hematopoiesis   The process by which the various types of blood cells are formed, such as in the bone marrow.

hemoglobin   A protein in red blood cells that carries iron.

hemolysin   Any biological agent that is capable of destroying red blood cells and causing the release of hemoglobin. Many bacterial pathogens produce exotoxins that act as hemolysins.

hemolytic disease   Incompatible Rh factor between mother and fetus causes maternal antibodies to attack the fetus and trigger complement-mediated lysis in the fetus.

hemolytic uremic syndrome (HUS)   Severe hemolytic anemia leading to kidney damage or failure; can accompany *E. coli* O157:H7 intestinal infection.

hemolyze   When red blood cells burst and release hemoglobin pigment.

hepatitis   Inflammation and necrosis of the liver, often the result of viral infection.

hepatitis A virus (HAV)   Enterovirus spread by contaminated food responsible for short-term (infectious) hepatitis.

hepatitis B virus (HBV)   DNA virus that is the causative agent of serum hepatitis.

hepatocellular carcinoma   A liver cancer associated with infection with hepatitis B virus.

herd immunity   The status of collective acquired immunity in a population that reduces the likelihood that nonimmune individuals will contract and spread infection. One aim of vaccination is to induce herd immunity.

heredity   Genetic inheritance.

hermaphroditic   Containing the sex organs for both male and female in one individual.

herpes zoster   A recurrent infection caused by latent chickenpox virus. Its manifestation on the skin tends to correspond to dermatomes and to occur in patches that "girdle" the trunk. Also called shingles.

heterotroph   An organism that relies upon organic compounds for its carbon and energy needs.

hexose   A 6-carbon sugar such as glucose and fructose.

hierarchies   Levels of power. Arrangement in order of rank.

histamine   A cytokine released when mast cells and basophils release their granules. An important mediator of allergy, its effects include smooth muscle contraction, increased vascular permeability, and increased mucus secretion.

histiocyte   Another term for macrophage.

histone   Proteins associated with eukaryotic DNA. These simple proteins serve as winding spools to compact and condense the chromosomes.

HLA   An abbreviation for **h**uman **l**eukocyte **a**ntigens. This closely linked cluster of genes programs for cell surface glycoproteins that control immune interactions between cells and is involved in rejection of allografts. Also called the major histocompatibility complex (MHC).

holoenzyme   An enzyme complete with its apoenzyme and cofactors.

hops   The ripe, dried fruits of the hop vine (*Humulus lupulus*) that are added to beer wort for flavoring.

horizontal gene transfer   transmission of genetic material from one cell to another through non-reproductive mechanisms; i.e., from one organism to another living in the same habitat.

host   Organism in which smaller organisms or viruses live, feed, and reproduce.

host range   The limitation imposed by the characteristics of the host cell on the type of virus that can successfully invade it.

human diploid cell vaccine (HDCV)   A vaccine made using cell culture that is currently the vaccine of choice for preventing infection by rabies virus.

human immunodeficiency virus (HIV)   A retrovirus that causes acquired immunodeficiency syndrome (AIDS).

Human Microbiome Project   a project of the National Institutes of Health to identify microbial inhabitants of the human body and their role in health and disease; uses metagenomic techniques instead of culturing.

human papillomavirus (HPV)   A group of DNA viruses whose members are responsible for common, plantar, and genital warts.

humoral immunity   Protective molecules (mostly B lymphocytes) carried in the fluids of the body.

hybridization   A process that matches complementary strands of nucleic acid (DNA-DNA, RNA-DNA, RNA-RNA). Used for locating specific sites or types of nucleic acids.

hybridoma   An artificial cell line that produces monoclonal antibodies. It is formed by fusing (hybridizing) a normal antibody-producing cell with a cancer cell, and it can produce pure antibody indefinitely.

hydration   The addition of water as in the coating of ions with water molecules as ions enter into aqueous solution.

hydrogen bond   A weak chemical bond formed by the attraction of forces between molecules or atoms—in this case, hydrogen and either oxygen or nitrogen. In this type of bond, electrons are not shared, lost, or gained.

hydrologic cycle   The continual circulation of water between hydrosphere, atmosphere, and lithosphere.

hydrolysis   A process in which water is used to break bonds in molecules. Usually occurs in conjunction with an enzyme.

hydrophilic   The property of attracting water. Molecules that attract water to their surface are called hydrophilic.

hydrophobic   The property of repelling water. Molecules that repel water are called hydrophobic.

hydrosphere   That part of the biosphere that encompasses water-containing environments such as oceans, lakes, rivers.

hypertonic   Having a greater osmotic pressure than a reference solution.

hyphae   The tubular threads that make up filamentous fungi (molds). This web of branched and intertwining fibers is called a mycelium.

hypogammaglobulinemia   An inborn disease in which the gamma globulin (antibody) fraction of serum is greatly reduced. The condition is associated with a high susceptibility to pyogenic infections.

hyposensitization   A therapeutic exposure to known allergens designed to build tolerance and eventually prevent allergic reaction.

hypothesis   A tentative explanation of what has been observed or measured.

hypotonic   Having a lower osmotic pressure than a reference solution.

I

icosahedron   A regular geometric figure having 20 surfaces that meet to form 12 corners. Some virions have capsids that resemble icosahedral crystals.

immune complex reaction   Type III hypersensitivity of the immune system. It is characterized by the reaction of soluble antigen with antibody, and the deposition of the resulting complexes in basement membranes of epithelial tissue.

immunity   An acquired resistance to an infectious agent due to prior contact with that agent.

immunoassays   Extremely sensitive tests that permit rapid and accurate measurement of trace antigen or antibody.

immunocompetence   The ability of the body to recognize and react with multiple foreign substances.

immunodeficiency   Immune function is incompletely developed, suppressed, or destroyed.

immunodeficiency disease   A form of immunopathology in which white blood cells are unable to mount a complete, effective immune response, which results in recurrent infections. Examples would be AIDS and agammaglobulinemia.

immunogen Any substance that induces a state of sensitivity or resistance after processing by the immune system of the body.

immunoglobulin (Ig) The chemical class of proteins to which antibodies belong.

immunology The study of the system of body defenses that protect against infection.

immunopathology The study of disease states associated with overreactivity or underreactivity of the immune response.

immunotherapy Preventing or treating infectious diseases by administering substances that produce artificial immunity. May be active or passive.

in utero Literally means "in the uterus"; pertains to events or developments occurring before birth.

in vitro Literally means "in glass," signifying a process or reaction occurring in an artificial environment, as in a test tube or culture medium.

in vivo Literally means "in a living being," signifying a process or reaction occurring in a living thing.

incidence In epidemiology, the number of new cases of a disease occurring during a period.

incineration Destruction of microbes by subjecting them to extremes of dry heat. Microbes are reduced to ashes and gas by this process.

inclusion A relatively inert body in the cytoplasm such as storage granules, glycogen, fat, or some other aggregated metabolic product.

inclusion body One of a variety of different storage compartments in bacterial cells.

incubate To isolate a sample culture in a temperature-controlled environment to encourage growth.

incubation period The period from the initial contact with an infectious agent to the appearance of the first symptoms.

index case The first case of a disease identified in an outbreak or epidemic.

indicator bacteria In water analysis, any easily cultured bacteria that may be found in the intestine and can be used as an index of fecal contamination. The category includes coliforms and enterococci. Discovery of these bacteria in a sample means that pathogens may also be present.

induced mutation Any alteration in DNA that occurs as a consequence of exposure to chemical or physical mutagens.

inducible enzyme An enzyme that increases in amount in direct proportion to the amount of substrate present.

inducible operon An operon that under normal circumstances is not transcribed. The presence of a specific inducer molecule can cause transcription of the operon to begin.

induction The process whereby a bacteriophage in the prophage state is activated and begins replication and enters the lytic cycle.

induration Area of hardened, reddened tissue associated with the tuberculin test.

infection The entry, establishment, and multiplication of pathogenic organisms within a host.

infectious disease The state of damage or toxicity in the body caused by an infectious agent.

inflammation A natural, nonspecific response to tissue injury that protects the host from further damage. It stimulates immune reactivity and blocks the spread of an infectious agent.

inoculation The implantation of microorganisms into or upon culture media.

inorganic chemicals Molecules that lack the basic framework of the elements of carbon and hydrogen.

integument The outer surfaces of the body: skin, hair, nails, sweat glands, and oil glands.

interferon (IFN) Natural human chemical that inhibits viral replication; used therapeutically to combat viral infections and cancer.

interferon gamma A protein produced by a virally infected cell that induces production of antiviral substances in neighboring cells. This defense prevents the production and maturation of viruses and thus terminates the viral infection.

interleukins A class of chemicals released from host cells that have potent effects on immunity.

intermediate filament proteinaceous fibers in eukaryotic cells that help provide support to the cells and their organelles.

intoxication Poisoning that results from the introduction of a toxin into body tissues through ingestion or injection.

intron The segments on split genes of eukaryotes that do not code for polypeptide. They can have regulatory functions. See *exon.*

iodophor A combination of iodine and an organic carrier that is a moderate-level disinfectant and antiseptic.

ion An unattached, charged particle.

ionic bond A chemical bond in which electrons are transferred and not shared between atoms.

ionization The aqueous dissociation of an electrolyte into ions.

ionizing radiation Radiant energy consisting of short-wave electromagnetic rays (X ray) or high-speed electrons that cause dislodgment of electrons on target molecules and create ions.

irradiation The application of radiant energy for diagnosis, therapy, disinfection, or sterilization.

irritability Capacity of cells to respond to chemical, mechanical, or light stimuli. This property helps cells adapt to the environment and obtain nutrients.

isograft Transplanted tissue from one monozygotic twin to the other; transplants between highly inbred animals that are genetically identical.

isolation The separation of microbial cells by serial dilution or mechanical dispersion on solid media to create discrete colonies.

isoniazid Older drug that targets the bacterial cell wall; used against *M. tuberculosis.*

isotonic Two solutions having the same osmotic pressure such that, when separated by a semipermeable membrane, there is no net movement of solvent in either direction.

isotope A version of an element that is virtually identical in all chemical properties to another version except that their atoms have slightly different atomic masses.

J

jaundice The yellowish pigmentation of skin, mucous membranes, sclera, deeper tissues, and excretions due to abnormal deposition of bile pigments. Jaundice is associated with liver infection, as with hepatitis B virus and leptospirosis.

JC virus (JCV) Causes a form of encephalitis (progressive multifocal leukoencephalopathy), especially in AIDS patients.

K

Kaposi sarcoma A malignant or benign neoplasm that appears as multiple hemorrhagic sites on the skin, lymph nodes, and viscera and apparently involves the metastasis of abnormal blood vessel cells. It is a clinical feature of AIDS.

keratin Protein produced by outermost skin cells that provide protection from trauma and moisture.

killed or inactivated vaccine A whole cell or intact virus preparation in which the microbes are dead or preserved and cannot multiply but are still capable of conferring immunity.

killer T cells A T lymphocyte programmed to directly affix cells and kill them. See *cytotoxicity.*

kingdom In the levels of classification, the second division from more general to more specific. Each domain is divided into kingdoms.

Koch's postulates A procedure to establish the specific cause of disease. In all cases of infection: (1) The agent must be found; (2) inoculations of a pure culture must reproduce the same disease in animals; (3) the agent must again be present in the experimental animal; and (4) a pure culture must again be obtained.

Koplik's spots Tiny red blisters with central white specks on the mucosal lining of the cheeks. Symptomatic of measles.

Krebs cycle or tricarboxylic acid cycle (TCA) The second pathway of the three pathways that complete the process of primary catabolism. Also called the citric acid cycle.

L

L form   a stage in the lives of some bacteria in which they have no peptidoglycan.

labile   In chemistry, molecules, or compounds that are chemically unstable in the presence of environmental changes.

lactoferrin   A protein in mucosal secretions, tears and milk that contains iron molecules and has antimicrobial activity.

lactose   One of the carbohydrates commonly referred to as sugars. Lactose is commonly found in milk.

lactose (*lac*) operon   Control system that manages the regulation of lactose metabolism. It is composed of three DNA segments, including a regulator, a control locus, and a structural locus.

lag phase   The early phase of population growth during which no signs of growth occur.

lager   The maturation process of beer, which is allowed to take place in large vats at a reduced temperature.

lagging strand   The newly forming 5′ DNA strand that is discontinuously replicated in segments (Okazaki fragments).

lantibiotics   Short peptides produced by bacteria that inhibit the growth of other bacteria.

latency   The state of being inactive. Example: a latent virus or latent infection.

leading strand   The newly forming 3′DNA strand that is replicated in a continuous fashion without segments.

leaven   To lighten food material by entrapping gas generated within it. Example: the rising of bread from the CO_2 produced by yeast or baking powder.

Legionnaire's disease   Infection by *Legionella* bacterium. Weakly gram-negative rods are able to survive in aquatic habitats. Some forms may be fatal.

legumes   Plants that produce seeds in pods. Examples include soybeans and peas.

lepromas   Skin nodules seen on the face of persons suffering from lepromatous leprosy. The skin folds and thickenings are caused by the overgrowth of *Mycobacterium leprae.*

lepromatous leprosy   Severe, disfiguring leprosy characterized by widespread dissemination of the leprosy bacillus in deeper lesions.

leprosy   See *Hansen's disease.*

lesion   A wound, injury, or some other pathologic change in tissues.

leukocidin   A heat-labile substance formed by some pyogenic cocci that impairs and sometimes lyses leukocytes.

leukocytes   White blood cells. The primary infection-fighting blood cells.

leukocytosis   An abnormally large number of leukocytes in the blood, which can be indicative of acute infection.

leukopenia   A lower-than-normal leukocyte count in the blood that can be indicative of blood infection or disease.

leukotriene   An unsaturated fatty acid derivative of arachidonic acid. Leukotriene functions in chemotactic activity, smooth muscle contractility, mucus secretion, and capillary permeability.

ligase   An enzyme required to seal the sticky ends of DNA pieces after splicing.

light-dependent reactions   The series of reactions in photosynthesis that are driven by the light energy (photons) absorbed by chlorophyll. They involve splitting of water into hydrogens and oxygen, transport of electrons by NADP, and ATP synthesis.

light-independent reactions   The series of reactions in photosynthesis that can proceed with or without light. It is a cyclic system that uses ATP from the light reactions to incorporate or fix carbon dioxide into organic compounds, leading to the production of glucose and other carbohydrates (also called the Calvin cycle).

lipase   A fat-splitting enzyme. Example: triacylglycerol lipase separates the fatty acid chains from the glycerol backbone of triglycerides.

lipid   A term used to describe a variety of substances that are not soluble in polar solvents such as water but will dissolve in nonpolar solvents such as benzene and chloroform. Lipids include triglycerides, phospholipids, steroids, and waxes.

lipopolysaccharide   A molecular complex of lipid and carbohydrate found in the bacterial cell wall. The lipopolysaccharide (LPS) of gram-negative bacteria is an endotoxin with generalized pathologic effects such as fever.

lipoteichoic acid   Anionic polymers containing glycerol that are anchored in the cytoplasmic membranes of gram-positive bacteria.

liquid media   growth-supporting substance in fluid form.

lithoautotroph   Bacteria that rely on inorganic minerals to supply their nutritional needs. Sometimes referred to as chemoautotrophs.

lithosphere   That part of the biosphere that encompasses the earth's crust, including rocks and minerals.

lithotroph   An autotrophic microbe that derives energy from reduced inorganic compounds such as N_2S.

lobar pneumonia   Infection involving whole segments (lobes) of the lungs, which may lead to consolidation and plugging of the alveoli and extreme difficulty in breathing.

localized infection   Occurs when a microbe enters a specific tissue, infects it, and remains confined there.

locus   A site on a chromosome occupied by a gene. Plural: loci.

log phase   Maximum rate of cell division during which growth is geometric in its rate of increase. Also called exponential growth phase.

lophotrichous   Describing bacteria having a tuft of flagella at one or both poles.

lumen   The cavity within a tubular organ.

lymphadenitis   Inflammation of one or more lymph nodes. Also called lymphadenopathy.

lymphatic system   A system of vessels and organs that serve as sites for development of immune cells and immune reactions. It includes the spleen, thymus, lymph nodes, and GALT.

lymphocyte   The second most common form of white blood cells.

lyophilization   A method for preserving microorganisms (and other substances) by freezing and then drying them directly from the frozen state.

lyse   To burst.

lysin   A complement-fixing antibody that destroys specific targeted cells. Examples: hemolysin and bacteriolysin.

lysis   The physical rupture or deterioration of a cell.

lysogenic conversion   A bacterium acquires a new genetic trait due to the presence of genetic material from an infecting phage.

lysogeny   The indefinite persistence of bacteriophage DNA in a host without bringing about the production of virions.

lysosome   A cytoplasmic organelle containing lysozyme and other hydrolytic enzymes.

lysozyme   An enzyme found in sweat, tears, and saliva that breaks down bacterial peptidoglycan.

M

macromolecules   Large, molecular compounds assembled from smaller subunits, most notably biochemicals.

macronutrient   A chemical substance required in large quantities (phosphate, for example).

macrophage   A white blood cell derived from a monocyte that leaves the circulation and enters tissues. These cells are important in nonspecific phagocytosis and in regulating, stimulating, and cleaning up after immune responses.

macroscopic   Visible to the naked eye.

major histocompatibility complex   A set of genes in mammals that produces molecules on surfaces of cells that differentiate among different individuals in the species.

malt   The grain, usually barley, that is sprouted to obtain digestive enzymes and dried for making beer.

maltose   One of the carbohydrates referred to as sugars. A fermentable sugar formed from starch.

Mantoux test   An intradermal screening test for tuberculin hypersensitivity. A red, firm patch of skin at the injection site greater than 10 mm in diameter after 48 hours is a positive result that indicates current or prior exposure to the TB bacillus.

mapping   Determining the location of loci and other qualities of genomic DNA.

marine microbiology   A branch of microbiology that studies the role of microorganisms in the oceans.

marker   Any trait or factor of a cell, virus, or molecule that makes it distinct and recognizable. Example: a genetic marker.

mash In making beer, the malt grain is steeped in warm water, ground up, and fortified with carbohydrates to form mash.

mass number (MN) Measurement that reflects the number of protons and neutrons in an atom of a particular element.

mast cell A nonmotile connective tissue cell implanted along capillaries, especially in the lungs, skin, gastrointestinal tract, and genitourinary tract. Like a basophil, its granules store mediators of allergy.

matrix The dense ground substance between the cristae of a mitochondrion that serves as a site for metabolic reactions.

matter All tangible materials that occupy space and have mass.

maximum temperature The highest temperature at which an organism will grow.

MDRTB Multidrug-resistant tuberculosis.

mechanical vector An animal that transports an infectious agent but is not infected by it, such as houseflies whose feet become contaminated with feces.

medium (plural, *media*) A nutrient used to grow organisms outside of their natural habitats.

meiosis The type of cell division necessary for producing gametes in diploid organisms. Two nuclear divisions in rapid succession produce four gametocytes, each containing a haploid number of chromosomes.

membrane In a single cell, a thin double-layered sheet composed of lipids such as phospholipids and sterols and proteins.

memory (immunologic memory) The capacity of the immune system to recognize and act against an antigen upon second and subsequent encounters.

memory cell The long-lived progeny of a sensitized lymphocyte that remains in circulation and is genetically programmed to react rapidly with its antigen.

Mendosicutes Taxonomic category of bacteria that have unusual cell walls; archaea.

meninges The tough tri-layer membrane covering the brain and spinal cord. Consists of the dura mater, arachnoid mater, and pia mater.

meningitis An inflammation of the membranes (meninges) that surround and protect the brain. It is often caused by bacteria such as *Neisseria meningitidis* (the meningococcus) and *Haemophilus influenzae*.

merozoite The motile, infective stage of an apicomplexan parasite that comes from a liver or red blood cell undergoing multiple fission.

mesophile Microorganisms that grow at intermediate temperatures.

messenger RNA (mRNA) A single-stranded transcript that is a copy of the DNA template that corresponds to a gene.

metabolic analog Enzyme that mimics the natural substrate of an enzyme and vies for its active site.

metabolism A general term for the totality of chemical and physical processes occurring in a cell.

metabolites Small organic molecules that are intermediates in the stepwise biosynthesis or breakdown of macromolecules.

metabolomics The study of the complete complement of small chemicals present in a cell at any given time.

metachromatic Exhibiting a color other than that of the dye used to stain it.

metachromatic granules A type of inclusion in storage compartments of some bacteria that stain a contrasting color when treated with colored dyes.

metagenomics The study of all the genomes in a particular ecological niche, as opposed to individual genomes from single species.

methanogens Methane producers.

MHC Major histocompatibility complex. See *HLA.*

MIC Abbreviation for **m**inimum **i**nhibitory **c**oncentration. The lowest concentration of antibiotic needed to inhibit bacterial growth in a test system.

microaerophile An aerobic bacterium that requires oxygen at a concentration less than that in the atmosphere.

microbe See *microorganism.*

microbial antagonism Relationship in which microorganisms compete for survival in a common environment by taking actions that inhibit or destroy another organism.

microbial ecology The study of microbes in their natural habitats.

microbicides Chemicals that kill microorganisms.

microbiology A specialized area of biology that deals with living things ordinarily too small to be seen without magnification, including bacteria, archaea, fungi, protozoa, and viruses.

microbistatic the quality of inhibiting the growth of microbes.

microfilaments Cellular cytoskeletal element formed by thin protein strands that attach to cell membrane and form a network through the cytoplasm. Responsible for movement of cytoplasm.

micronutrient A chemical substance required in small quantities (trace metals, for example).

microorganism A living thing ordinarily too small to be seen without magnification; an organism of microscopic size.

microscopic Invisible to the naked eye.

microscopy Science that studies structure, magnification, lenses, and techniques related to use of a microscope.

microtubules Long hollow tubes in eukaryotic cells; maintain the shape of the cell and transport substances from one part of cell to another; involved in separating chromosomes in mitosis.

miliary tuberculosis Rapidly fatal tuberculosis due to dissemination of mycobacteria in the blood and formation of tiny granules in various organs and tissues. The term *miliary* means resembling a millet seed.

mineralization The process by which decomposers (bacteria and fungi) convert organic debris into inorganic and elemental form. It is part of the recycling process.

minimum inhibitory concentration (MIC) The smallest concentration of drug needed to visibly control microbial growth.

minimum temperature The lowest temperature at which an organism will grow.

miracidium The ciliated first-stage larva of a trematode. This form is infective for a corresponding intermediate host snail.

missense mutation A mutation in which a change in the DNA sequence results in a different amino acid being incorporated into a protein, with varying results.

mitochondrion A double-membrane organelle of eukaryotes that is the main site for aerobic respiration.

mitosis Somatic cell division that preserves the somatic chromosome number.

mixed acid fermentation An anaerobic degradation of pyruvic acid that results in more than one organic acid being produced (e.g., acetic acid, lactic acid, succinic acid).

mixed culture A container growing two or more different, known species of microbes.

mixed infection Occurs when several different pathogens interact simultaneously to produce an infection. Also called a synergistic infection.

molecule A distinct chemical substance that results from the combination of two or more atoms.

molluscum contagiosum Poxvirus-caused disease that manifests itself by the appearance of small lesions on the face, trunk, and limbs. Can be associated with sexual transmission.

monoclonal antibodies (MAbs) Antibodies that have a single specificity for a single antigen and are produced in the laboratory from a single clone of B cells.

monocyte A large mononuclear leukocyte normally found in the lymph nodes, spleen, bone marrow, and loose connective tissue. This type of cell makes up 3% to 7% of circulating leukocytes.

monomer A simple molecule that can be linked by chemical bonds to form larger molecules.

mononuclear phagocyte system A collection of monocytes and macrophages scattered throughout the extracellular spaces that function to engulf and degrade foreign molecules.

monosaccharide A simple sugar such as glucose that is a basic building block for more complex carbohydrates.

monotrichous Describing a microorganism that bears a single flagellum.

morbidity A diseased condition.

morbidity rate The number of persons afflicted with an illness under question or with illness in general, expressed as a numerator, with the denominator being some unit of population (as in $x/100,000$).

mordant   A chemical that fixes a dye in or on cells by forming an insoluble compound and thereby promoting retention of that dye. Example: Gram's iodine in the Gram stain.

morphology   The study of organismic structure.

mortality rate   The number of persons who have died as the result of a particular cause or due to all causes, expressed as a numerator, with the denominator being some unit of population (as in $x/100,000$).

most probable number (MPN)   Test used to detect the concentration of contaminants in water and other fluids.

motility   Self-propulsion.

mumps   Viral disease characterized by inflammation of the parotid glands.

must   Juices expressed from crushed fruits that are used in fermentation for wine.

mutagen   Any agent that induces genetic mutation. Examples: certain chemical substances, ultraviolet light, radioactivity.

mutant strain   A subspecies of microorganism that has undergone a mutation, causing expression of a trait that differs from other members of that species.

mutation   A permanent inheritable alteration in the DNA sequence or content of a cell.

mutualism   Organisms living in an obligatory but mutually beneficial relationship.

mycelium   The filamentous mass that makes up a mold. Composed of hyphae.

mycoplasma   A genus of bacteria; contain no peptidoglycan/cell wall, but the cytoplasmic membrane is stabilized by sterols.

mycorrhizae   Various species of fungi adapted in an intimate, mutualistic relationship to plant roots.

mycosis   Any disease caused by a fungus.

myonecrosis   Death of muscle tissue.

N

NAD/NADH   Abbreviations for the oxidized/reduced forms of nicotinamide adenine dinucleotide, an electron carrier. Also known as the vitamin niacin.

nanobacteria (also *nanobes*)   Bacteria that are up to 100 times smaller than average bacteria.

nanobes   Cell-like particles found in sediments and other geologic deposits that some scientists speculate are the smallest bacteria. Short for nanobacteria.

narrow spectrum   Denotes drugs that are selective and limited in their effects. For example, they inhibit either gram-negative or gram-positive bacteria but not both.

natural immunity   Any immunity that arises naturally in an organism via previous experience with the antigen.

natural selection   A process in which the environment places pressure on organisms to adapt and survive changing conditions. Only the survivors will be around to continue the life cycle and contribute their genes to future generations. This is considered a major factor in evolution of species.

necrosis   A pathologic process in which cells and tissues die and disintegrate.

negative stain   A staining technique that renders the background opaque or colored and leaves the object unstained so that it is outlined as a colorless area.

nematode   A common name for helminths called roundworms.

nephritis   Inflammation of the kidney.

neurotropic   Having an affinity for the nervous system. Most likely to affect the spinal cord.

neutralization   The process of combining an acid and a base until they reach a balanced proportion, with a pH value close to 7.

neutron   An electrically neutral particle in the nuclei of all atoms except hydrogen.

neutrophil   A mature granulocyte present in peripheral circulation, exhibiting a multilobular nucleus and numerous cytoplasmic granules that retain a neutral stain. The neutrophil is an active phagocytic cell in bacterial infection.

niche   In ecology, an organism's biological role in or contribution to its community.

nitrification   Phase of the nitrogen cycle in which ammonium is oxidized.

nitrogen base   A ringed compound of which pyrimidines and purines are types.

nitrogen cycle   The pathway followed by the element nitrogen as it circulates from inorganic sources in the nonliving environment to living things and back to the nonliving environment. The longtime reservoir is nitrogen gas in the atmosphere.

nitrogen fixation   A process occurring in certain bacteria in which atmospheric N_2 gas is converted to a form (NH_4) usable by plants.

nitrogenous base   A nitrogen-containing molecule found in DNA and RNA that provides the basis for the genetic code. Adenine, guanine, and cytosine are found in both DNA and RNA while thymine is found exclusively in DNA and uracil is found exclusively in RNA.

nomenclature   A set system for scientifically naming organisms, enzymes, anatomical structures, and so on.

noncommunicable   An infectious disease that does not arrive through transmission of an infectious agent from host to host.

noncompetitive inhibition   Form of enzyme inhibition that involves binding of a regulatory molecule to a site other than the active site.

nonionizing radiation   Method of microbial control, best exemplified by ultraviolet light, that causes the formation of abnormal bonds within the DNA of microbes, increasing the rate of mutation. The primary limitation of nonionizing radiation is its inability to penetrate beyond the surface of an object.

nonpolar   A term used to describe an electrically neutral molecule formed by covalent bonds between atoms that have the same or similar electronegativity.

nonself   Molecules recognized by the immune system as containing foreign markers, indicating a need for immune response.

nonsense codon   A triplet of mRNA bases that does not specify an amino acid but signals the end of a polypeptide chain.

nonsense mutation   A mutation that changes an amino-acid-producing codon into a stop codon, leading to premature termination of a protein.

normal biota   The native microbial forms that an individual harbors.

nosocomial infection   An infection not present upon admission to a hospital but incurred while being treated there.

nucleocapsid   In viruses, the close physical combination of the nucleic acid with its protective covering.

nucleoid   The basophilic nuclear region or nuclear body that contains the bacterial chromosome.

nucleolus   A granular mass containing RNA that is contained within the nucleus of a eukaryotic cell.

nucleosome   Structure in the packaging of DNA. Formed by the DNA strands wrapping around the histone protein to form nucleus bodies arranged like beads on a chain.

nucleotide   The basic structural unit of DNA and RNA; each nucleotide consists of a phosphate, a sugar (ribose in RNA, deoxyribose in DNA), and a nitrogenous base such as adenine, guanine, cytosine, thymine (DNA only), or uracil (RNA only).

numerical aperture   In microscopy, the amount of light passing from the object and into the object in order to maximize optical clarity and resolution.

nutrient   Any chemical substance that must be provided to a cell for normal metabolism and growth. Macronutrients are required in large amounts, and micronutrients in small amounts.

nutrition   The acquisition of chemical substances by a cell or organism for use as an energy source or as building blocks of cellular structures.

O

obligate   Without alternative; restricted to a particular characteristic. Example: an obligate parasite survives and grows only in a host; an obligate aerobe must have oxygen to grow; an obligate anaerobe is destroyed by oxygen.

Okazaki fragment   In replication of DNA, a segment formed on the lagging strand in which biosynthesis is conducted in a discontinuous manner dictated by the $5' \rightarrow 3'$ DNA polymerase orientation.

oligodynamic action   A chemical having antimicrobial activity in minuscule amounts. Example: certain heavy metals are effective in a few parts per billion.

oligonucleotides Short pieces of DNA or RNA that are easier to handle than long segments.

oligotrophic Nutrient-deficient ecosystem.

oncogene A naturally occurring type of gene that when activated can transform a normal cell into a cancer cell.

oncovirus Mammalian virus capable of causing malignant tumors.

oocyst The encysted form of a fertilized macrogamete or zygote; typical in the life cycles of apicomplexan parasites.

operator In an operon sequence, the DNA segment where transcription of structural genes is initiated.

operon A genetic operational unit that regulates metabolism by controlling mRNA production. In sequence, the unit consists of a regulatory gene, inducer or repressor control sites, and structural genes.

opportunistic In infection, ordinarily nonpathogenic or weakly pathogenic microbes that cause disease primarily in an immunologically compromised host.

opsonization The process of stimulating phagocytosis by affixing molecules (opsonins such as antibodies and complement) to the surfaces of foreign cells or particles.

optimum temperature The temperature at which a species shows the most rapid growth rate.

orbitals The pathways of electrons as they rotate around the nucleus of an atom.

order In the levels of classification, the division of organisms that follows class. Increasing similarity may be noticed among organisms assigned to the same order.

organelle A small component of eukaryotic cells that is bounded by a membrane and specialized in function.

organic chemicals Molecules that contain the basic framework of the elements carbon and hydrogen.

osmophile A microorganism that thrives in a medium having high osmotic pressure.

osmosis The diffusion of water across a selectively permeable membrane in the direction of lower water concentration.

osteomyelitis A focal infection of the internal structures of long bones, leading to pain and inflammation. Often caused by *Staphylococcus aureus.*

outer membrane An additional membrane possessed by gram-negative bacteria; a lipid bilayer containing specialized proteins and polysaccharides. It lies outside of the cell wall.

oxidation In chemical reactions, the loss of electrons by one reactant.

oxidation-reduction Redox reactions, in which paired sets of molecules participate in electron transfers.

oxidative phosphorylation The synthesis of ATP using energy given off during the electron transport phase of respiration.

oxidizing agent An atom or a compound that can receive electrons from another in a chemical reaction.

oxygenic Any reaction that gives off oxygen; usually in reference to the result of photosynthesis in eukaryotes and cyanobacteria.

P

palindrome A word, verse, number, or sentence that reads the same forward or backward. Palindromes of nitrogen bases in DNA have genetic significance as transposable elements, as regulatory protein targets, and in DNA splicing.

palisades The characteristic arrangement of *Corynebacterium* cells resembling a row of fence posts and created by snapping.

PAMPs Pathogen-associated molecular patterns. Chemical signatures present on many different microorganisms but not on host which are recognized by host as foreign.

pandemic A disease afflicting an increased proportion of the population over a wide geographic area (often worldwide).

papilloma Benign, squamous epithelial growth commonly referred to as a wart.

parasite An organism that lives on or within another organism (the host), from which it obtains nutrients and enjoys protection. The parasite produces some degree of harm in the host.

parasitism A relationship between two organisms in which the host is harmed in some way while the colonizer benefits.

parenteral Administering a substance into a body compartment other than through the gastrointestinal tract, such as via intravenous, subcutaneous, intramuscular, or intramedullary injection.

paroxysmal Events characterized by sharp spasms or convulsions; sudden onset of a symptom such as fever and chills.

passive carrier Persons who mechanically transfer a pathogen without ever being infected by it. For example, a health care worker who doesn't wash his/her hands adequately between patients.

passive immunity Specific resistance that is acquired indirectly by donation of preformed immune substances (antibodies) produced in the body of another individual.

passive transport Nutrient transport method that follows basic physical laws and does not require direct energy input from the cell.

pasteurization Heat treatment of perishable fluids such as milk, fruit juices, or wine to destroy heat-sensitive vegetative cells, followed by rapid chilling to inhibit growth of survivors and germination of spores. It prevents infection and spoilage.

pathogen Any agent (usually a virus, bacterium, fungus, protozoan, or helminth) that causes disease.

pathogen-associated molecular patterns molecules on the surfaces of many types of microbes that are not present on host cells that mark the microbes as foreign; PAMPs.

pathogenicity The capacity of microbes to cause disease.

pathogenicity islands areas of the genome containing multiple genes which contribute to a new trait for the organism that increases its ability to cause disease.

pathognomic Distinctive and particular to a single disease, suggestive of a diagnosis.

pathologic Capable of inducing physical damage on the host.

pathology The structural and physiological effects of disease on the body.

pattern recognition receptors molecules on the surface of host defense cells that recognize pathogen-associated molecular patterns on microbes; PRRs.

pellicle A membranous cover; a thin skin, film, or scum on a liquid surface; a thin film of salivary glycoproteins that forms over newly cleaned tooth enamel when exposed to saliva.

pelvic inflammatory disease (PID) An infection of the uterus and fallopian tubes that has ascended from the lower reproductive tract. Caused by gonococci and chlamydias.

penetration (viral) The step in viral multiplication in which virus enters the host cell.

penicillinase An enzyme that hydrolyzes penicillin; found in penicillin-resistant strains of bacteria.

penicillins A large group of naturally occurring and synthetic antibiotics produced by *Penicillium* mold and active against the cell wall of bacteria.

pentose A monosaccharide with five carbon atoms per molecule. Examples: arabinose, ribose, xylose.

peptide Molecule composed of short chains of amino acids, such as a dipeptide (two amino acids), a tripeptide (three), and a tetrapeptide (four).

peptide bond The covalent union between two amino acids that forms between the amine group of one and the carboxyl group of the other. The basic bond of proteins.

peptidoglycan A network of polysaccharide chains cross-linked by short peptides that forms the rigid part of bacterial cell walls. Gram-negative bacteria have a smaller amount of this rigid structure than do gram-positive bacteria.

perforin Proteins released by cytotoxic T cells that produce pores in target cells.

perinatal In childbirth, occurring before, during, or after delivery.

period of invasion The period during a clinical infection when the infectious agent multiplies at high levels, exhibits its greatest toxicity, and becomes well established in the target tissues.

periodontal Involving the structures that surround the tooth.

periplasmic space The region between the cell wall and cell membrane of the cell envelopes of gram-negative bacteria.

peritrichous In bacterial morphology, having flagella distributed over the entire cell.

petechiae Minute hemorrhagic spots in the skin that range from pinpoint- to pinhead-size.

Peyer's patches Oblong lymphoid aggregates of the gut located chiefly in the wall of the terminal and small intestine. Along with the tonsils and appendix, Peyer's patches make up the gut-associated lymphoid tissue that responds to local invasion by infectious agents.

pH The symbol for the negative logarithm of the H ion concentration; p (power) or $[H^+]_{10}$. A system for rating acidity and alkalinity.

phage A bacteriophage; a virus that specifically parasitizes bacteria.

phagocyte A class of white blood cells capable of engulfing other cells and particles.

phagocytosis A type of endocytosis in which the cell membrane actively engulfs large particles or cells into vesicles.

phagolysosome A body formed in a phagocyte, consisting of a union between a vesicle containing the ingested particle (the phagosome) and a vacuole of hydrolytic enzymes (the lysosome).

phase variation The process of bacteria turning on or off a group of genes that changes its phenotype in a heritable manner.

phenotype The observable characteristics of an organism produced by the interaction between its genetic potential (genotype) and the environment.

phosphate An acidic salt containing phosphorus and oxygen that is an essential inorganic component of DNA, RNA, and ATP.

phospholipid A class of lipids that compose a major structural component of cell membranes.

phosphorylation Process in which inorganic phosphate is added to a compound.

photoactivation (light repair) A mechanism for repairing DNA with ultraviolet-light-induced mutations using an enzyme (photolyase) that is activated by visible light.

photoautotroph An organism that utilizes light for its energy and carbon dioxide chiefly for its carbon needs.

photolysis The splitting of water into hydrogen and oxygen during photosynthesis.

photon A subatomic particle released by electromagnetic sources such as radiant energy (sunlight). Photons are the ultimate source of energy for photosynthesis.

photophosphorylation The process of electron transport during photosynthesis that results in the synthesis of ATP from ADP.

photosynthesis A process occurring in plants, algae, and some bacteria that traps the sun's energy and converts it to ATP in the cell. This energy is used to fix CO_2 into organic compounds.

phototrophs Microbes that use photosynthesis to feed.

phycobilin Red or blue-green pigments that absorb light during photosynthesis.

phylum In the levels of classification, the third level of classification from general to more specific. Each kingdom is divided into numerous phyla. Sometimes referred to as a division.

physiology The study of the function of an organism.

phytoplankton The collection of photosynthetic microorganisms (mainly algae and cyanobacteria) that float in the upper layers of aquatic habitats where sun penetrates. These microbes are the basis of aquatic food pyramids and, together with zooplankton, make up the plankton.

pili Small, stiff filamentous appendages in gram-negative bacteria that function in DNA exchange during bacterial conjugation.

pilus A hollow appendage used to bring two bacterial cells together to transfer DNA.

pinocytosis The engulfment, or endocytosis, of liquids by extensions of the cell membrane.

plague Zoonotic disease caused by infection with *Yersinia pestis.* The pathogen is spread by flea vectors and harbored by various rodents.

plankton Minute animals (zooplankton) or plants (phytoplankton) that float and drift in the limnetic zone of bodies of water.

plantar warts Deep, painful warts on the soles of the feet as a result of infection by human papillomavirus.

plaque In virus propagation methods, the clear zone of lysed cells in tissue culture or chick embryo membrane that corresponds to the area containing viruses. In dental application, the filamentous mass of microbes that adheres tenaciously to the tooth and predisposes to caries, calculus, or inflammation.

plasma The carrier fluid element of blood.

plasma cell A progeny of an activated B cell that actively produces and secretes antibodies.

plasmids Extrachromosomal genetic units characterized by several features. A plasmid is a double-stranded DNA that is smaller than and replicates independently of the cell chromosome; it bears genes that are not essential for cell growth; it can bear genes that code for adaptive traits; and it is transmissible to other bacteria.

platelet-activating factor A substance released from basophils that causes release of allergic mediators and the aggregation of platelets.

platelets Formed elements in the blood that develop when megakaryocytes disintegrate. Platelets are involved in hemostasis and blood clotting.

pleomorphism Normal variability of cell shapes in a single species.

pluripotential Stem cells having the developmental plasticity to give rise to more than one type. Example: undifferentiated blood cells in the bone marrow.

pneumococcus Common name for *Streptococcus pneumoniae,* the major cause of bacterial pneumonia.

pneumonia An inflammation of the lung leading to accumulation of fluid and respiratory compromise.

pneumonic plague The acute, frequently fatal form of pneumonia caused by *Yersinia pestis*.

point mutation A change that involves the loss, substitution, or addition of one or a few nucleotides.

point source epidemic An outbreak of disease in which all affected individuals were exposed to a single source of the pathogen at a single point in time.

polar Term to describe a molecule with an asymmetrical distribution of charges. Such a molecule has a negative pole and a positive pole.

poliomyelitis An acute enteroviral infection of the spinal cord that can cause neuromuscular paralysis.

polyclonal In reference to a collection of antibodies with mixed specificities that arose from more than one clone of B cells.

polyclonal antibodies A mixture of antibodies that were stimulated by a complex antigen with more than one antigenic determinant.

polymer A macromolecule made up of a chain of repeating units. Examples: starch, protein, DNA.

polymerase An enzyme that produces polymers through catalyzing bond formation between building blocks (polymerization).

polymerase chain reaction (PCR) A technique that amplifies segments of DNA for testing. Using denaturation, primers, and heat-resistant DNA polymerase, the number can be increased several-million-fold.

polymicrobial Involving multiple distinct microorganisms.

polymorphonuclear leukocytes (PMNLs) White blood cells with variously shaped nuclei. Although this term commonly denotes all granulocytes, it is used especially for the neutrophils.

polymyxin A mixture of antibiotic polypeptides from *Bacillus polymyxa* that are particularly effective against gram-negative bacteria.

polypeptide A relatively large chain of amino acids linked by peptide bonds.

polyribosomal complex An assembly line for mass production of proteins composed of a chain of ribosomes involved in mRNA transcription.

polysaccharide A carbohydrate that can be hydrolyzed into a number of monosaccharides. Examples: cellulose, starch, glycogen.

population A group of organisms of the same species living simultaneously in the same habitat. A group of different populations living together constitutes the community level.

porin Transmembrane proteins of the outer membrane of gram-negative cells that permit transport of small molecules into the periplasmic space but bar the penetration of larger molecules.

portal of entry Route of entry for an infectious agent; typically a cutaneous or membranous route.

portal of exit Route through which a pathogen departs from the host organism.

positive stain A method for coloring microbial specimens that involves a chemical that sticks to the specimen to give it color.

potable Describing water that is relatively clear, odor-free, and safe to drink.

PPNG Penicillinase-producing *Neisseria gonorrhoeae*.

prebiotics Nutrients used to stimulate the growth of favorable biota in the intestine.

prevalence The total number of cases of a disease in a certain area and time period.

primary infection An initial infection in a previously healthy individual that is later complicated by an additional (secondary) infection.

primary response The first response of the immune system when exposed to an antigen.

primary structure Initial protein organization described by type, number, and order of amino acids in the chain. The primary structure varies extensively from protein to protein.

primers Synthetic oligonucleotides of known sequence that serve as landmarks to indicate where DNA amplification will begin.

prion A concocted word to denote "proteinaceous infectious agent"; a cytopathic protein associated with the slow-virus spongiform encephalopathies of humans and animals.

probes Small fragments of single-stranded DNA (RNA) that are known to be complementary to the specific sequence of DNA being studied.

probiotics Preparations of live microbes used as a preventive or therapeutic measure to displace or compete with potential pathogens.

prodromal stage A short period of mild symptoms occurring at the end of the period of incubation. It indicates the onset of disease.

producer An organism that synthesizes complex organic compounds from simple inorganic molecules. Examples would be photosynthetic microbes and plants. These organisms are solely responsible for originating food pyramids and are the basis for life on earth (also called autotroph).

product(s) In a chemical reaction, the substance(s) that is(are) left after a reaction is completed.

proglottid The egg-generating segment of a tapeworm that contains both male and female organs.

progressive multifocal leukoencephalopathy (PML) An uncommon, fatal complication of infection with JC virus (polyoma virus).

prokaryotic cells Small cells, lacking special structures such as a nucleus and organelles. All prokaryotes are microorganisms.

promastigote A morphological variation of the trypanosome parasite responsible for leishmaniasis.

promoter Part of an operon sequence. The DNA segment that is recognized by RNA polymerase as the starting site for transcription.

promoter region The site composed of a short signaling DNA sequence that RNA polymerase recognizes and binds to commence transcription.

propagated epidemic An outbreak of disease in which the causative agent is passed from affected persons to new persons over the course of time.

prophage A lysogenized bacteriophage; a phage that is latently incorporated into the host chromosome instead of undergoing viral replication and lysis.

prophylactic Any device, method, or substance used to prevent disease.

prostaglandin A hormonelike substance that regulates many body functions. Prostaglandin comes from a family of organic acids containing 5-carbon rings that are essential to the human diet.

protease Enzymes that act on proteins, breaking them down into component parts.

protease inhibitors Drugs that act to prevent the assembly of functioning viral particles.

protein Predominant organic molecule in cells, formed by long chains of amino acids.

proteomics The study of an organism's complement of proteins (its *proteome*) and functions mediated by the proteins.

proton An elementary particle that carries a positive charge. It is identical to the nucleus of the hydrogen atom.

protoplast A bacterial cell whose cell wall is completely lacking and that is vulnerable to osmotic lysis.

protozoa A group of single-celled, eukaryotic organisms.

provirus The genome of a virus when it is integrated into a host cell's DNA.

PRRs Pattern recognition receptors. Molecules on the surface of host cells that recognize pathogen-associated molecular patterns (PAMPs) on microbial cells.

pseudohypha A chain of easily separated, spherical to sausage-shaped yeast cells partitioned by constrictions rather than by septa.

pseudomembrane A tenacious, noncellular mucous exudate containing cellular debris that tightly blankets the mucosal surface in infections such as diphtheria and pseudomembranous enterocolitis.

pseudopodium A temporary extension of the protoplasm of an amoeboid cell. It serves both in amoeboid motion and for food gathering (phagocytosis).

pseudopods Protozoan appendage responsible for motility. Also called "false feet."

psychrophile A microorganism that thrives at low temperature (0°C–20°C), with a temperature optimum of 0°C–15°C.

pulmonary Occurring in the lungs. Examples include pulmonary anthrax and pulmonary nocardiosis.

pure culture A container growing a single species of microbe whose identity is known.

purine A nitrogen base that is an important encoding component of DNA and RNA. The two most common purines are adenine and guanine.

pus The viscous, opaque, usually yellowish matter formed by an inflammatory infection. It consists of serum exudate, tissue debris, leukocytes, and microorganisms.

pyogenic Pertains to pus formers, especially the pyogenic cocci: pneumococci, streptococci, staphylococci, and neisseriae.

pyrimidine Nitrogen bases that help form the genetic code on DNA and RNA. Uracil, thymine, and cytosine are the most important pyrimidines.

pyrimidine dimer The union of two adjacent pyrimidines on the same DNA strand, brought about by exposure to ultraviolet light. It is a form of mutation.

pyrogen A substance that causes a rise in body temperature. It can come from pyrogenic microorganisms or from polymorphonuclear leukocytes (endogenous pyrogens).

Q

quaternary structure Most complex protein structure characterized by the formation of large, multiunit proteins by more than one of the polypeptides. This structure is typical of antibodies and some enzymes that act in cell synthesis.

quats A word that pertains to a family of surfactants called quaternary ammonium compounds. These detergents are only weakly microbicidal and are used as sanitizers and preservatives.

quinine A substance derived from cinchona trees that was used as an antimalarial treatment; has been replaced by synthetic derivatives.

quinolone A class of synthetic antimicrobic drugs with broad-spectrum effects.

quorum sensing The ability of bacteria to regulate their gene expression in response to sensing bacterial density.

R

rabies   The only rhabdovirus that infects humans. Zoonotic disease characterized by fatal meningoencephalitis.

radiation   Electromagnetic waves or rays, such as those of light given off from an energy source.

radioactive isotopes   Unstable isotopes whose nuclei emit particles of radiation. This emission is called radioactivity or radioactive decay. Three naturally occurring emissions are alpha, beta, and gamma radiation.

rales   Sounds in the lung, ranging from clicking to rattling; indicate respiratory illness.

reactants   Molecules entering or starting a chemical reaction.

real image   An image formed at the focal plane of a convex lens. In the compound light microscope, it is the image created by the objective lens.

receptor   Cell surface molecules involved in recognition, binding, and intracellular signaling.

recombinant   An organism that contains genes that originated in another organism, whether through deliberate laboratory manipulation or natural processes.

recombinant DNA technology   A technology, also known as genetic engineering, that deliberately modifies the genetic structure of an organism to create novel products, microbes, animals, plants, and viruses.

recombination   A type of genetic transfer in which DNA from one organism is donated to another.

recycling   A process that converts unusable organic matter from dead organisms back into their essential inorganic elements and returns them to their nonliving reservoirs to make them available again for living organisms. This is a common term that means the same as mineralization and decomposition.

redox   Denoting an oxidation-reduction reaction.

reducing agent   An atom or a compound that can donate electrons in a chemical reaction.

reducing medium   A growth medium that absorbs oxygen and allows anaerobic bacteria to grow.

reduction   In chemistry, the gain of electrons.

redundancy   The property of the genetic code that allows an amino acid to be specified by several different codons.

refraction   In optics, the bending of light as it passes from one medium to another with a different index of refraction.

regulated enzymes   Enzymes whose extent of transcription or translation is influenced by changes in the environment.

regulator   DNA segment that codes for a protein capable of repressing an operon.

regulatory B cells (B$_{reg}$ cells)   a type of activated B cell that controls the immune response.

regulatory site   The location on an enzyme where a certain substance can bind and block the enzyme's activity.

rennin   The enzyme casein coagulase, which is used to produce curd in the processing of milk and cheese.

replication   In DNA synthesis, the semiconservative mechanisms that ensure precise duplication of the parent DNA strands.

replication fork   The Y-shaped point on a replicating DNA molecule where the DNA polymerase is synthesizing new strands of DNA.

reportable disease   Those diseases that must be reported to health authorities by law.

repressible operon   An operon that under normal circumstances is transcribed. The buildup of the operon's amino acid product causes transcription of the operon to stop.

repressor   The protein product of a repressor gene that combines with the operator and arrests the transcription and translation of structural genes.

reservoir   In disease communication, the natural host or habitat of a pathogen.

resident biota   The deeper, more stable microbiota that inhabit the skin and exposed mucous membranes, as opposed to the superficial, variable, transient population.

resistance (R) factor   Plasmids, typically shared among bacteria by conjugation, that provide resistance to the effects of antibiotics.

resolving power   The capacity of a microscope lens system to accurately distinguish between two separate entities that lie close to each other. Also called resolution.

respiratory chain   A series of enzymes that transfer electrons from one to another, resulting in the formation of ATP. It is also known as the electron transport chain. The chain is located in the cell membrane of bacteria and in the inner mitochondrial membrane of eukaryotes.

respiratory syncytial virus (RSV)   An RNA virus that infects the respiratory tract. RSV is the most prevalent cause of respiratory infection in newborns.

restriction endonuclease   An enzyme present naturally in cells that cleaves specific locations on DNA. It is an important means of inactivating viral genomes, and it is also used to splice genes in genetic engineering.

reticuloendothelial system   Also known as the mononuclear phagocyte system, it pertains to a network of fibers and phagocytic cells (macrophages) that permeates the tissues of all organs. Examples: Kupffer cells in liver sinusoids, alveolar phagocytes in the lung, microglia in nervous tissue.

retrovirus   A group of RNA viruses (including HIV) that have the mechanisms for converting their genome into a double strand of DNA that can be inserted on a host's chromosome.

reverse transcriptase (RT)   The enzyme possessed by retroviruses that carries out the reversion of RNA to DNA—a form of reverse transcription.

Reye's syndrome   A sudden, usually fatal neurological condition that occurs in children after a viral infection. Autopsy shows cerebral edema and marked fatty change in the liver and renal tubules.

Rh factor   An isoantigen that can trigger hemolytic disease in newborns due to incompatibility between maternal and infant blood factors.

rhizobia   Bacteria that live in plant roots and supply supplemental nitrogen that boosts plant growth.

rhizosphere   The zone of soil, complete with microbial inhabitants, in the immediate vicinity of plant roots.

ribonucleic acid (RNA)   The nucleic acid responsible for carrying out the hereditary program transmitted by an organism's DNA.

ribose   A 5-carbon monosaccharide found in RNA.

ribosomal RNA (rRNA)   A single-stranded transcript that is a copy of part of the DNA template.

ribosome   A bilobed macromolecular complex of ribonucleoprotein that coordinates the codons of mRNA with tRNA anticodons and, in so doing, constitutes the peptide assembly site.

ribozyme   A part of an RNA-containing enzyme in eukaryotes that removes intervening sequences of RNA called introns and splices together the true coding sequences (exons) to form a mature messenger RNA.

rickettsias   Medically important family of bacteria, commonly carried by ticks, lice, and fleas. Significant cause of important emerging diseases.

ringworm   A superficial mycosis caused by various dermatophytic fungi. This common name is actually a misnomer.

RNA editing   The alteration of RNA molecules before translation, found only in eukaryotes.

RNA polymerase   Enzyme process that translates the code of DNA to RNA.

rolling circle   An intermediate stage in viral replication of circular DNA into linear DNA.

root nodules   Small growths on the roots of legume plants that arise from a symbiotic association between the plant tissues and bacteria (Rhizobia). This association allows fixation of nitrogen gas from the air into a usable nitrogen source for the plant.

rosette formation   A technique for distinguishing surface receptors on T cells by reacting them with sensitized indicator sheep red blood cells. The cluster of red cells around the central white blood cell resembles a little rose blossom and is indicative of the type of receptor.

rough endoplasmic reticulum (RER) Microscopic series of tunnels that originates in the outer membrane of the nuclear envelope and is used in transport and storage. Large numbers of ribosomes, partly attached to the membrane, give the rough appearance.

rubeola (red measles) Acute disease caused by infection with Morbillivirus.

S

saccharide Scientific term for sugar. Refers to a simple carbohydrate with a sweet taste.

salpingitis Inflammation of the fallopian tubes.

sanitize To clean inanimate objects using soap and degerming agents so that they are safe and free of high levels of microorganisms.

saprobe A microbe that decomposes organic remains from dead organisms. Also known as a saprophyte or saprotroph.

sarcina A cubical packet of 8, 16, or more cells; the cellular arrangement of the genus *Sarcina* in the family Micrococcaceae.

satellitism A commensal interaction between two microbes in which one can grow in the vicinity of the other due to nutrients or protective factors released by that microbe.

saturation The complete occupation of the active site of a carrier protein or enzyme by the substrate.

schistosomiasis Infection by blood fluke, often as a result of contact with contaminated water in rivers and streams. Symptoms appear in liver, spleen, or urinary system depending on species of *Schistosoma*. Infection may be chronic.

schizogony A process of multiple fission whereby first the nucleus divides several times, and subsequently the cytoplasm is subdivided for each new nucleus during cell division.

scientific method Principles and procedures for the systematic pursuit of knowledge, involving the recognition and formulation of a problem, the collection of data through observation and experimentation, and the formulation and testing of a hypothesis.

scolex The anterior end of a tapeworm characterized by hooks and/or suckers for attachment to the host.

sebaceous glands The sebum- (oily, fatty) secreting glands of the skin.

sebum Low pH, oil-based secretion of the sebaceous glands.

secondary infection An infection that compounds a preexisting one.

secondary response The rapid rise in antibody titer following a repeat exposure to an antigen that has been recognized from a previous exposure. This response is brought about by memory cells produced as a result of the primary exposure.

secondary structure Protein structure that occurs when the functional groups on the outer surface of the molecule interact by forming hydrogen bonds. These bonds cause the amino acid chain to either twist, forming a helix, or to pleat into an accordion pattern called a β-pleated sheet.

secretory antibody The immunoglobulin (IgA) that is found in secretions of mucous membranes and serves as a local immediate protection against infection.

selective media Nutrient media designed to favor the growth of certain microbes and to inhibit undesirable competitors.

selectively toxic Property of an antimicrobial agent to be highly toxic against its target microbe while being far less toxic to other cells, particularly those of the host organism.

self Natural markers of the body that are recognized by the immune system.

self-limited Applies to an infection that runs its course without disease or residual effects.

semiconservative replication In DNA replication, the synthesis of paired daughter strands, each retaining a parent strand template.

semisolid media Nutrient media with a firmness midway between that of a broth (a liquid medium) and an ordinary solid medium; motility media.

semisynthetic Drugs that, after being naturally produced by bacteria, fungi, or other living sources, are chemically modified in the laboratory.

sensitizing dose The initial effective exposure to an antigen or an allergen that stimulates an immune response. Often applies to allergies.

sepsis The state of putrefaction; the presence of pathogenic organisms or their toxins in tissue or blood.

septic shock Blood infection resulting in a pathological state of low blood pressure accompanied by a reduced amount of blood circulating to vital organs. Endotoxins of all gram-negative bacteria can cause shock, but most clinical cases are due to gram-negative enteric rods.

septicemia Systemic infection associated with microorganisms multiplying in circulating blood.

septicemic plague A form of infection with *Yersinia pestis* occurring mainly in the bloodstream and leading to high mortality rates.

septum A partition or cellular cross wall, as in certain fungal hyphae.

sequela A morbid complication that follows a disease.

sequencing Determining the actual order and types of bases in a segment of DNA.

serology The branch of immunology that deals with *in vitro* diagnostic testing of serum.

seropositive Showing the presence of specific antibody in a serological test. Indicates ongoing infection.

serotonin A vasoconstrictor that inhibits gastric secretion and stimulates smooth muscle.

serotyping The subdivision of a species or subspecies into an immunologic type, based upon antigenic characteristics.

serum The clear fluid expressed from clotted blood that contains dissolved nutrients, antibodies, and hormones but not cells or clotting factors.

serum sickness A type of immune complex disease in which immune complexes enter circulation, are carried throughout the body, and are deposited in the blood vessels of the kidney, heart, skin, and joints. The condition may become chronic.

severe acute respiratory syndrome (SARS) A severe respiratory disease caused by infection with a newly described coronavirus.

severe combined immunodeficiencies A collection of syndromes occurring in newborns caused by a genetic defect that knocks out both B- and T-cell types of immunity. There are several versions of this disease, termed SCIDS for short.

sex pilus A conjugative pilus.

sexually transmitted disease (STD) Infections resulting from pathogens that enter the body via sexual intercourse or intimate, direct contact.

shiga toxin Heat-labile exotoxin released by some *Shigella* species and by *E. coli* O157:H7; responsible for worst symptoms of these infections.

shingles Lesions produced by reactivated human herpesvirus 3 (chickenpox) infection; also known as herpes zoster.

siderophores Low-molecular-weight molecules produced by many microorganisms that can bind iron very tightly.

sign Any abnormality uncovered upon physical diagnosis that indicates the presence of disease. A sign is an objective assessment of disease, as opposed to a symptom, which is the subjective assessment perceived by the patient.

silent mutation A mutation that, because of the degeneracy of the genetic code, results in a nucleotide change in both the DNA and mRNA but not the resultant amino acid and thus, not the protein.

simple stain Type of positive staining technique that uses a single dye to add color to cells so that they are easier to see. This technique tends to color all cells the same color.

slime layer A diffuse, unorganized layer of polysaccharides and/or proteins on the outside of some bacteria.

smooth endoplasmic reticulum (SER) A microscopic series of tunnels lacking ribosomes that functions in the nutrient processing function of a cell.

solute A substance that is uniformly dispersed in a dissolving medium or solvent.

solution A mixture of one or more substances (solutes) that cannot be separated by filtration or ordinary settling.

solvent   A dissolving medium.

somatic (O or cell wall antigen)   One of the three major antigens commonly used to differentiate gram-negative enteric bacteria.

source   The person or item from which an infection is directly acquired. See *reservoir*.

Southern blot   A technique that separates fragments of DNA using electrophoresis and identifies them by hybridization.

species   In the levels of classification, the most specific level of organization.

specificity   In immunity, the concept that some parts of the immune system only react with antigens that originally activated them.

spheroplast   A gram-negative cell whose peptidoglycan, when digested by lysozyme, remains intact but is osmotically vulnerable.

spike   A receptor on the surface of certain enveloped viruses that facilitates specific attachment to the host cell.

spirillum   A type of bacterial cell with a rigid spiral shape and external flagella.

spirochete   A coiled, spiral-shaped bacterium that has endoflagella and flexes as it moves.

spontaneous generation   Early belief that living things arose from vital forces present in nonliving, or decomposing, matter.

spontaneous mutation   A mutation in DNA caused by random mistakes in replication and not known to be influenced by any mutagenic agent. These mutations give rise to an organism's natural, or background, rate of mutation.

sporadic   Description of a disease that exhibits new cases at irregular intervals in unpredictable geographic locales.

sporangiospore   A form of asexual spore in fungi; enclosed in a sac.

sporangium   A fungal cell in which asexual spores are formed by multiple cell cleavage.

spore   A differentiated, specialized cell form that can be used for dissemination, for survival in times of adverse conditions, and/or for reproduction. Spores are usually unicellular and may develop into gametes or vegetative organisms.

sporicide   A chemical agent capable of destroying bacterial endospores.

sporozoite   One of many minute elongated bodies generated by multiple division of the oocyst. It is the infectious form of the malarial parasite that is harbored in the salivary gland of the mosquito and inoculated into the victim during feeding.

sporulation   The process of spore formation.

start codon   The nucleotide triplet AUG that codes for the first amino acid in protein sequences.

starter culture   The sizable inoculation of pure bacterial, mold, or yeast sample for bulk processing, as in the preparation of fermented foods, beverages, and pharmaceuticals.

stasis   A state of rest or inactivity; applied to nongrowing microbial cultures. Also called microbistasis.

stationary growth phase   Survival mode in which cells either stop growing or grow very slowly.

stem cells   Pluripotent, undifferentiated cells.

sterile   Completely free of all life forms, including spores and viruses.

sterilization   Any process that completely removes or destroys all viable microorganisms, including viruses, from an object or habitat. Material so treated is sterile.

STORCH   Acronym for common infections of the fetus and neonate. Storch stands for **s**yphilis, **t**oxoplasmosis, **o**ther diseases (hepatitis B, AIDS, and chlamydiosis), **r**ubella, **c**ytomegalovirus, and **h**erpes simplex virus.

strain   In microbiology, a set of descendants cloned from a common ancestor that retain the original characteristics. Any deviation from the original is a different strain.

streptolysin   A hemolysin produced by streptococci.

strict or obligate anaerobe   An organism that does not use oxygen gas in metabolism and cannot survive in oxygen's presence.

stroma   The matrix of the chloroplast that is the site of the dark reactions.

structural gene   A gene that codes for the amino acid sequence (peptide structure) of a protein.

subacute   Indicates an intermediate status between acute and chronic disease.

subacute sclerosing panencephalitis (SSPE)   A complication of measles infection in which progressive neurological degeneration of the cerebral cortex invariably leads to coma and death.

subcellular vaccine   A vaccine preparation that contains specific antigens such as the capsule or toxin from a pathogen and not the whole microbe.

subclinical   A period of inapparent manifestations that occurs before symptoms and signs of disease appear.

subculture   To make a second-generation culture from a well-established colony of organisms.

subcutaneous   The deepest level of the skin structure.

substrate   The specific molecule upon which an enzyme acts.

subunit vaccine   A vaccine preparation that contains only antigenic fragments such as surface receptors from the microbe. Usually in reference to virus vaccines.

sucrose   One of the carbohydrates commonly referred to as sugars. Common table or cane sugar.

sulfonamide   Antimicrobial drugs that interfere with the essential metabolic process of bacteria and some fungi.

superantigens   Bacterial toxins that are potent stimuli for T cells and can be a factor in diseases such as toxic shock.

superficial mycosis   A fungal infection located in hair, nails, and the epidermis of the skin.

superinfection   An infection occurring during antimicrobial therapy that is caused by an overgrowth of drug-resistant microorganisms.

superoxide   A toxic derivative of oxygen; (O_2^-).

surfactant   A surface-active agent that forms a water-soluble interface. Examples: detergents, wetting agents, dispersing agents, and surface tension depressants.

sylvatic   Denotes the natural presence of disease among wild animal populations. Examples: sylvatic (sylvan) plague, rabies.

symbiosis   An intimate association between individuals from two species; used as a synonym for mutualism.

symptom   The subjective evidence of infection and disease as perceived by the patient.

syncytium   A multinucleated protoplasmic mass formed by consolidation of individual cells.

syndrome   The collection of signs and symptoms that, taken together, paint a portrait of the disease.

synergism   The coordinated or correlated action by two or more drugs or microbes that results in a heightened response or greater activity.

syngamy   Conjugation of the gametes in fertilization.

synthesis (viral)   The step in viral multiplication in which viral genetic material and proteins are made through replication and transcription/translation.

synthetic biology   The use of known genes to produce new applications.

syntrophy   The productive use of waste products from the metabolism of one organism by a second organism.

syphilis   A sexually transmitted bacterial disease caused by the spirochete *Treponema pallidum*.

systemic   Occurring throughout the body; said of infections that invade many compartments and organs via the circulation.

T

T lymphocyte (T cell)   A white blood cell that is processed in the thymus gland and is involved in cell-mediated immunity.

Taq polymerase   DNA polymerase from the thermophilic bacterium *Thermus aquaticus* that enables high-temperature replication of DNA required for the polymerase chain reaction.

tartar   See *calculus*.

taxa   Taxonomic categories.

taxonomy   The formal system for organizing, classifying, and naming living things.

teichoic acid   Anionic polymers containing glycerol that appear in the walls of gram-positive bacteria.

temperate phage   A bacteriophage that enters into a less virulent state by becoming incorporated into the host genome as a prophage instead of in the vegetative or lytic form that eventually destroys the cell.

template The strand in a double-stranded DNA molecule that is used as a model to synthesize a complementary strand of DNA or RNA during replication or transcription.

Tenericutes Taxonomic category of bacteria that lack cell walls.

teratogenic Causing abnormal fetal development.

tertiary structure Protein structure that results from additional bonds forming between functional groups in a secondary structure, creating a three-dimensional mass.

tetanospasmin The neurotoxin of *Clostridium tetani,* the agent of tetanus. Its chief action is directed upon the inhibitory synapses of the anterior horn motor neurons.

tetracyclines A group of broad-spectrum antibiotics with a complex 4-ring structure.

tetrads Groups of four.

theory A collection of statements, propositions, or concepts that explains or accounts for a natural event.

theory of evolution the evidence cited to explain how evolution occurs.

therapeutic index The ratio of the toxic dose to the effective therapeutic dose that is used to assess the safety and reliability of the drug.

thermal death point The lowest temperature that achieves sterilization in a given quantity of broth culture upon a 10-minute exposure. Examples: 55°C for *Escherichia coli,* 60°C for *Mycobacterium tuberculosis,* and 120°C for spores.

thermal death time The least time required to kill all cells of a culture at a specified temperature.

thermocline A temperature buffer zone in a large body of water that separates the warmer water (the epilimnion) from the colder water (the hypolimnion).

thermoduric Resistant to the harmful effects of high temperature.

thermophile A microorganism that thrives at a temperature of 50°C or higher.

thrush *Candida albicans* infection of the oral cavity.

thylakoid Vesicles of a chloroplast formed by elaborate folding of the inner membrane to form "discs." Solar energy trapped in the thylakoids is used in photosynthesis.

thymine (T) One of the nitrogen bases found in DNA but not in RNA. Thymine is in a pyrimidine form.

thymus Butterfly-shaped organ near the tip of the sternum that is the site of T-cell maturation.

tincture A medicinal substance dissolved in an alcoholic solvent.

tinea Ringworm; a fungal infection of the hair, skin, or nails.

tinea versicolor A condition of the skin appearing as mottled and discolored skin pigmentation as a result of infection by the yeast *Malassezia furfur.*

titer In immunochemistry, a measure of antibody level in a patient, determined by agglutination methods.

toll-like receptors (TLRs) a category of pattern recognition receptors that binds to pathogen-associated molecular patterns on microbes.

tonsils A ring of lymphoid tissue in the pharynx that acts as a repository for lymphocytes.

topoisomerases Enzymes that can add or remove DNA twists and thus regulate the degree of supercoiling.

toxemia Condition in which a toxin (microbial or otherwise) is spread throughout the bloodstream.

toxigenicity The tendency for a pathogen to produce toxins. It is an important factor in bacterial virulence.

toxin A specific chemical product of microbes, plants, and some animals that is poisonous to other organisms.

toxinosis Disease whose adverse effects are primarily due to the production and release of toxins.

toxoid A toxin that has been rendered nontoxic but is still capable of eliciting the formation of protective antitoxin antibodies; used in vaccines.

trace elements Micronutrients (zinc, nickel, and manganese) that occur in small amounts and are involved in enzyme function and maintenance of protein structure.

transamination The transfer of an amino group from an amino acid to a carbohydrate fragment.

transcript A newly transcribed RNA molecule.

transcription mRNA synthesis; the process by which a strand of RNA is produced against a DNA template.

transduction The transfer of genetic material from one bacterium to another by means of a bacteriophage vector.

transferrin A protein in the plasma fraction of blood that transports iron.

transfer RNA (tRNA) A transcript of DNA that specializes in converting RNA language into protein language.

transformation In microbial genetics, the transfer of genetic material contained in "naked" DNA fragments from a donor cell to a competent recipient cell.

transfusion Infusion of whole blood, red blood cells, or platelets directly into a patient's circulation.

translation Protein synthesis; the process of decoding the messenger RNA code into a polypeptide.

transposon A DNA segment with an insertion sequence at each end, enabling it to migrate to another plasmid, to the bacterial chromosome, or to a bacteriophage.

transport medium Microbiological medium that is used to transport specimens.

traveler's diarrhea A type of gastroenteritis typically caused by infection with enterotoxigenic strains of *E. coli* that are ingested through contaminated food and water.

trematode A category of helminth; also known as flatworm or fluke.

trichinosis Infection by the *Trichinella spiralis* parasite, usually caused by eating the meat of an infected animal. Early symptoms include fever, diarrhea, nausea, and abdominal pain that progress to intense muscle and joint pain and shortness of breath. In the final stages, heart and brain function are at risk, and death is possible.

trichomoniasis Sexually transmitted disease caused by infection by the trichomonads, a group of protozoa. Symptoms include urinary pain and frequency and foul-smelling vaginal discharge in females or recurring urethritis, with a thin milky discharge, in males.

triglyceride A type of lipid composed of a glycerol molecule bound to three fatty acids.

triplet See *codon.*

trophozoite A vegetative protozoan (feeding form) as opposed to a resting (cyst) form.

true pathogen A microbe capable of causing infection and disease in healthy persons with normal immune defenses.

trypomastigote The infective morphological stage transmitted by the tsetse fly or the reduviid bug in African trypanosomiasis and Chagas disease.

tubercle In tuberculosis, the granulomatous well-defined lung lesion that can serve as a focus for latent infection.

tuberculin A glycerinated broth culture of *Mycobacterium tuberculosis* that is evaporated and filtered. Formerly used to treat tuberculosis, tuberculin is now used chiefly for diagnostic tests.

tuberculin reaction A diagnostic test in which PPD, or purified protein derivative (of *M. tuberculosis*), is injected superficially under the skin and the area of reaction measured; also called the Mantoux test.

tuberculoid leprosy A superficial form of leprosy characterized by asymmetrical, shallow skin lesions containing few bacterial cells.

tubulin protein component of long filaments of protein arranged under the cell membrane of bacteria; contribute to cell shape and division.

turbid Cloudy appearance of nutrient solution in a test tube due to growth of microbe population.

tyndallization Fractional (discontinuous, intermittent) sterilization designed to destroy spores indirectly. A preparation is exposed to flowing steam for an hour, and then the mineral is allowed to incubate to permit spore germination. The resultant vegetative cells are destroyed by repeated steaming and incubation.

typhoid fever Form of salmonellosis. It is highly contagious. Primary symptoms include fever, diarrhea, and abdominal pain. Typhoid fever can be fatal if untreated.

U

ubiquitous   Present everywhere at the same time.

ultraviolet (UV) radiation   Radiation with an effective wavelength from 240 nm to 260 nm. UV radiation induces mutations readily but has very poor penetrating power.

uncoating   The process of removal of the viral coat and release of the viral genome by its newly invaded host cell.

undulant fever   See *brucellosis.*

universal donor   In blood grouping and transfusion, a group O individual whose erythrocytes bear neither agglutinogen A nor B.

universal precautions (UPs)   Centers for Disease Control and Prevention guidelines for health care workers regarding the prevention of disease transmission when handling patients and body substances.

uracil (U)   One of the nitrogen bases in RNA but not in DNA. Uracil is in a pyrimidine form.

urinary tract infection (UTI)   Invasion and infection of the urethra and bladder by bacterial residents, most often *E. coli.*

V

vaccination   Exposing a person to the antigenic components of a microbe without its pathogenic effects for the purpose of inducing a future protective response.

vaccine   Originally used in reference to inoculation with the cowpox or vaccinia virus to protect against smallpox. In general, the term now pertains to injection of whole microbes (killed or attenuated), toxoids, or parts of microbes as a prevention or cure for disease.

vacuoles   In the cell, membrane-bounded sacs containing fluids or solid particles to be digested, excreted, or stored.

valence   The combining power of an atom based upon the number of electrons it can either take on or give up.

van der Waals forces   Weak attractive interactions between molecules of low polarity.

vancomycin   Antibiotic that targets the bacterial cell wall; used often in antibiotic-resistant infections.

variable region   The antigen binding fragment of an immunoglobulin molecule, consisting of a combination of heavy and light chains whose molecular conformation is specific for the antigen.

varicella   Informal name for virus responsible for chickenpox as well as shingles; also known as human herpesvirus 3 (HHV-3).

variolation   A hazardous, outmoded process of deliberately introducing smallpox material scraped from a victim into the nonimmune subject in the hope of inducing resistance.

vector   An animal that transmits infectious agents from one host to another, usually a biting or piercing arthropod like the tick, mosquito, or fly. Infectious agents can be conveyed mechanically by simple contact or biologically whereby the parasite develops in the vector. A genetic element such as a plasmid or a bacteriophage used to introduce genetic material into a cloning host during recombinant DNA experiments.

vegetative   In describing microbial developmental stages, a metabolically active feeding and dividing form, as opposed to a dormant, seemingly inert, nondividing form. Examples: a bacterial cell versus its spore; a protozoan trophozoite versus its cyst.

vehicle   An inanimate material (solid object, liquid, or air) that serves as a transmission agent for pathogens.

vesicle   A blister characterized by a thin-skinned, elevated, superficial pocket filled with serum.

viable nonculturable (VNC)   Describes microbes that cannot be cultivated in the laboratory but that maintain metabolic activity (i.e., are alive).

vibrio   A curved, rod-shaped bacterial cell.

viremia   The presence of viruses in the bloodstream.

virion   An elementary virus particle in its complete morphological and thus infectious form. A virion consists of the nucleic acid core surrounded by a capsid, which can be enclosed in an envelope.

viroid   An infectious agent that, unlike a virion, lacks a capsid and consists of a closed circular RNA molecule. Although known viroids are all plant pathogens, it is conceivable that animal versions exist.

virtual image   In optics, an image formed by diverging light rays; in the compound light microscope, the second, magnified visual impression formed by the ocular from the real image formed by the objective.

virucide   A chemical agent that inactivates viruses, especially on living tissue.

virulence   In infection, the relative capacity of a pathogen to invade and harm host cells.

virulence factors   A microbe's structures or capabilities that allow it to establish itself in a host and cause damage.

virus   Microscopic, acellular agent composed of nucleic acid surrounded by a protein coat.

virus particle   A more specific name for a virus when it is outside of its host cells.

vitamins   A component of coenzymes critical to nutrition and the metabolic function of coenzyme complexes.

W

wart   An epidermal tumor caused by papillomaviruses. Also called a verruca.

Western blot test   A procedure for separating and identifying antigen or antibody mixtures by two-dimensional electrophoresis in polyacrylamide gel, followed by immune labeling.

wheal   A welt; a marked, slightly red, usually itchy area of the skin that changes in size and shape as it extends to adjacent area. The reaction is triggered by cutaneous contact or intradermal injection of allergens in sensitive individuals.

whey   The residual fluid from milk coagulation that separates from the solidified curd.

whitlow   A deep inflammation of the finger or toe, especially near the tip or around the nail. Whitlow is a painful herpes simplex virus infection that can last several weeks and is most common among health care personnel who come in contact with the virus in patients.

whole blood   A liquid connective tissue consisting of blood cells suspended in plasma.

Widal test   An agglutination test for diagnosing typhoid.

wild type   The natural, nonmutated form of a genetic trait.

wort   The clear fluid derived from soaked mash that is fermented for beer.

X

XDRTB   Extensively drug-resistant tuberculosis (worse than multidrug-resistant tuberculosis).

xenograft   The transfer of a tissue or an organ from an animal of one species to a recipient of another species.

Z

zoonosis   An infectious disease indigenous to animals that humans can acquire through direct or indirect contact with infected animals.

zooplankton   The collection of nonphotosynthetic microorganisms (protozoa, tiny animals) that float in the upper regions of aquatic habitat and together with phytoplankton comprise the plankton.

zygospore   A thick-walled sexual spore produced by the zygomycete fungi. It develops from the union of two hyphae, each bearing nuclei of opposite mating types.

Photographs

Chapter 1

Opener: © Jim Kidd/Alamy; **Table1.1A:** James Gathany/Centers for Disease Control; **Table1.1B:** Centers for Disease Control, Division of Vector Borne Infectious Diseases; **Table1.1C:** © James King-Holmes/Photo Researchers; **Table1.1D:** Photo by Keith Weller/USDA, ARS, IS Photo Unit; **Table1.1E:** Photo by Scott Baue/USDA, ARS, IS Photo Unit; **Table1.1F:** © Christopher Berkey/epa/Corbis; **1.2a:** © Doug Sokell/Tom Stack & Associates; **1.2b:** © Michel & Christine Denis-Huot/Photolibrary; **1.3a:** © Corale L. Brierley/Visuals Unlimited; **1.3b:** © Bloomberg via Getty Images; **1.3c:** NOAA; **Insight 1.1 (left):** National Institutes of Health (NIH)/U.S. National Library of Medicine; **Insight 1.1 (right):** © Ron Edmonds/AP Photo; **1.6 (Taenia solium):** Centers for Disease Control; **1.6 (Syncephalastrum):** © Dr. Arthur Siegelman/Visuals Unlimited; **1.6 (Vorticella):** © Carolina Biological Supply/Phototake; **1.6 (E. coli):** Janice Carr/Public Health Image Library; **1.6 (Herpes):** Centers for Disease Control; **1.7a:** © Biophoto Associates/Photo Researchers; **1.7b:** Centers for Disease Control/Dr. Lucille K. Georg; **1.8a ((both)):** © Kathy Park Talaro/Visuals Unlimited; **1.8b:** © Science VU/Visuals Unlimited; **1.9:** © Steve Gschmeissner/Photo Researchers; **1.10 (left):** © Tom Grill/Corbis RF; **p. 423 (left):** © Koester Axel/Corbis; **p. 423 (middle):** © Milton P. Gordon, Department of Biochemistry, University of Washington; **p. 423 (right):** Courtesy of Richard Shade, Purdue University; **1.10 (right):** © Tom Grill/Corbis RF; **1.11:** © AKG/Photo Researchers; **Insight 1.3 (left):** David McKay/NASA; **Insight 1.3 (right):** Courtesy of Renno et al., J. Geophys. Res. (2009).

Chapter 2

Opener "b": © Vo Trung Dung/Look at Sciences/SPL/Photo Researchers; **Insight 2.1 (left):** © Joe Donohue; **Insight 2.1 (top):** © PJ Stewart, 2007, translated into digital form by Carl Wenczek of Born Digital Ltd.; **Insight 2.1 (bottom):** © 2010 periodictable.com; **2.7d:** © Kathy Park Talaro; **2.11a-c:** © John W. Hole; **Insight 2.3a:** © Donald Fawcett/Visuals Unlimited.

Chapter 3

Opener: © AP Photo/Steve Pope; **3.3b, d, f:** © Kathy Park Talaro; **Insight 3.1:** Courtesy of Charles River Lab; **3.4b:** © Kathy Park Talaro; **3.5a:** © Fundamental Photographs; **3.5b, 3.6b, 3.7a-b, 3.9a-b, 3.10a-b:** © Kathy Park Talaro; **3.11:** © Harold J. Benson; **3.12a-c:** © Kathy Park Talaro; **3.14:** © Kathy Park Talaro/Visuals Unlimited; **3.15:** Courtesy of Leica Microsystems Inc.; **Table3.5a:** © Carolina Biological Supply, Co/Visuals Unlimited; **Table3.5b-d:** © Michael Abbey/Visuals Unlimited; **Table3.5e:** © Molecular Probes, Inc.; **Table3.5f:** Courtesy of Dr. Jeremy Allen/University of Salford, Biosciences Research Institute; **Table3.5g:** © Billy Curran, Department of Veterinary Science, Queen's University Belfast; **Table3.5h:** © Science Photo Library RF/Getty Images; **Table3.5i:** Courtesy of Dr Valerie Sim; **Table3.5j:** "Electronic structure of single DNA molecules resolved by transverse scanning tunneling spectroscopy," *Nature Materials* 7, 68–74 (2008) Published online: 25 November 2007. Errez Shapir, Hezy Cohen, Arrigo Calzolari, Carlo Cavazzoni, Dmitry A. Ryndyk, Gianaurelio Cuniberti, Alexander Kotlyar, Rosa Di Felice & Danny Porath; **3.21a (top):** © Kathy Park Talaro; **3.21a (bottom):** © Harold J. Benson; **3.21b (top & middle):** © Jack Bostrack/Visuals Unlimited; **3.21b (bottom):** © Manfred Kage/Peter Arnold/Photolibrary; **3.21c (top):** © A.M. Siegelman/Visuals Unlimited; **3.21c (bottom):** © David Frankhauser; **Insight 3.2a:** Courtesy of IBM Research/Almaden Research Center; **Insight 3.2b:** Courtesy of Dr. Karl-Heinz Rieder, Institut für Experimentalphysik, Berlin; **p. 79, 1b:** © Kathy Park Talaro; **p. 79, 2 (top left):** Janice Carr/Public Health Image Library; **p. 79, 2 (top right):** © Dr. Arthur Siegelman/Visuals Unlimited; **p. 79, 2 (bottom left):** Centers for Disease Control; **p. 79, 2 (bottom right):** © Carolina Biological Supply/Phototake.

Chapter 4

Opener: Dr. David Phillips/Visuals Unlimited; **4.2b:** *Journal of Molecular Biology*, Volume 235, Issue 4, 27 January 1994, Pages 1261-1270. "Isolation, Characterization and Structure of Bacterial Flagellar Motors Containing the Switch Complex," Noreen R. Francis, Gina E. Sosinsky, Dennis Thomas and David J. DeRosier; **4.3a:** Courtesy of Dr. Jeffrey C. Burnham; **4.3b:** Reichelt and Baumann, "Taxonomy of the marine, luminous bacteria," ARCHIVES OF MICROBIOLOGY Vol 94, No 4, 283-330; fig 19. © Springer-Verlag 1973. With kind permission of Springer Science and Business Media; **4.3c:** From Noel R. Krieg in Bacteriological Reviews, March 1976, Vol. 40(1):87 fig 7; **4.3d:** From Preer et al., Bacteriological Review, June 1974, 38(2);121, fig 7. © ASM; **4.6c:** Stanley F. Hayes, Rocky Mountain Laboratories, NIAID, NIH; **4.7a:** © Eye of Science/Photo Researchers; **4.7b:** Dr. S. Knutton from D.R. Lloyd and S. Knurron, Infection and Immunity, January 1987, p 86-92. © ASM; **4.8:** © L. Caro/SPL/Photo Researchers; **Insight 4.1 (all):** Courtesy of D.G. Allison and I.W. Sutherland; **4.10a:** © John D. Cunningham/Visuals Unlimited; **4.10b1-2:** Courtesy of Graham C. Walker; **4.11:** © Science VU-Charles W. Stratton/Visuals Unlimited; **4.12a:** © S.C Holt/Biological Photo Service; **4.12b:** © T. J. Beveridge/Biological Photo Service; **4.15:** © David M. Phillips/Visuals Unlimited; **4.17:** © E.S. Anderson/Photo Researchers; **4.19a:** © Paul W. Johnson/Biological Photo Service; **4.19b:** © D. Balkwill and D. Maratea; **4.20:** © Rut Carballido-Lopez/I.N.R.A. Jouy-en-Josas, Laboratoire de Génétique Microbienne; **4.21-22:** © George Chapman/Visuals Unlimited; **Insight 4.3:** © Max Planck Institute for Marine Microbiology, Germany; **4.23a:** © J.T. Staley, M.P. Bryant, N. Pfennining and J.G. Holt, Bergey Manual of Systematic Bacteriology, Vol 3 © 1989 Williams and Wilkins Co. Baltimore; **4.23b:** Courtesy of Jeff Broadbent; **4.23c:** From Jacob S. Teppema, "In Vivo Adherence and Colonization of Vibro Cholerae Strains that differ in Hemagglutinating Activity and Motility" *Journal of Infection and Immunity*, 55(9): 2093-2102, Sept. 1987. Reprinted by permission of American Society for Microbiology.; **4.23d:** Photo by De Wood. Digital colorization by Chris Pooley; **4.23e:** © VEM/Photo Researchers; **4.23f:** Centers for Disease Control/Dr. David Berd; **4.24:** Centers for Disease Control/Dr. William Kaplan; **4.25a:** © Wayne P. Armstrong, Palomar College; **4.25b:** Dr. Mike Dyall-Smith, University of Melbourne; **p. 107:** © Kathy Park Talaro.

Chapter 5

Opener "a": © D. Trozzo/Alamy; **5.1a-b:** © Andrew Knoll; **Insight 5.1:** Courtesy of Lynn Margulis; **5.3a:** © Scientifica/RMF/Visuals Unlimited, Inc.; **5.3b:** © RMF/FDF/Visuals Unlimited; **5.5a:** © John J. Cardamone, Jr./Biological Photo Service. All rights reserved.; **5.6:** © Donald Fawcett/Visuals Unlimited; **5.7b:** © Science VU/Visuals Unlimited; **5.12b:** © Donald Fawcett/Visuals Unlimited; **5.14b:** © Albert Tousson/PhotoTake; **5.15a-b:** Courtesy of Dr. Judy A. Murphy, San Joaquin Delta College, Department of Microscopy, Stocton, CA; **5.16b:** © David M. Phillips/Visuals Unlimited; **5.17a:** © Kathy Park Talaro; **5.17b:** © Everett S. Beneke/Visuals Unlimited; **5.18d:** © Dr. George L. Barron; **Insight 5.2a:** © Dennis Kunkel Microscopy, Inc./Visuals Unlimited; **Insight 5.2b:** Kelly Cheng Travel Photography/Getty Images; **5.20a:** © Kathy Park Talaro; **5.20b:** © William Marin, Jr./The Image Works; **5.21a:** © A.M. Siegelman/Visuals Unlimited; **5.21b:** © John D. Cunningham/Visuals Unlimited; **5.21c:** Courtesy of Neil Carlson, Department of Environmental Health and Safety; **5.22a:** © David M. Phillips/Visuals Unlimited; **5.22b:** © Stephen Durr; **5.22c:** © BioMEDIA ASSOCIATES; **5.22d:** © Yuuji Tsukii, Protist Information Server, http://protist.i.hosei.ac.jp/protist_menuE.html; **5.25b:** © Carol Geake/Animals Animals; **5.25d:** © Arthur Siegelman/Visuals Unlimited; **p. 138:** © Wayne P. Armstrong, Palomar College.

Chapter 6

Opener: © WoodyStock/Alamy; **Insight 6.1:** © Science VU/Wayside/Visuals Unlimited; **6.2a:** © K.G. Murti/Visuals Unlimited; **6.2b:** © Centers for Disease Control/Phototake; **6.2c:** © A.B. Dowsette/SPL/Photo Researchers; **6.3:** © Omnikron/Photo Researchers; **6.6b:** © Dennis Kunkel/CNRI/Phototake; **6.6d:** © K.G. Murti/Visuals Unlimited; **6.7d:** © Dr. Linda M. Stannard, University of Cape Town/Photo Researchers; **6.8a (top):** Fred P. Williams, Jr./EPA; **6.8a (bottom):** © Dr Linda Stannard, Uct/Photo Researchers; **6.8b:** © Eye of Science/Photo Researchers; **6.9a:** © Harold Fisher; **6.10a:** © Lennart Nilsson-Scanpix; **6.10b:** © Kathy Park Talaro; **6.15:** © K.G. Murti/Visuals Unlimited; **6.16b:** © Chris Bjornberg/Photo Researchers; **6.17a:** © Patricia Barber/Custom Medical Stock; **6.17b:** Courtesy of Massimo Battaglia, INeMM CNR, Rome Italy; **6.21:** © K.G. Murti/Visuals Unlimited; **6.23a:** Courtesy of Ted Heald, State of Iowa Hygienic Laboratory; **6.24a-b:** Centers for Disease Control; **6.24c:** © Visuals Unlimited; **Insight 6.2:** © Dr. Dennis Kunkel/Visuals Unlimited.

Chapter 7

Opener: © Hiroya Minakuchi/Minden Pictures; **7.1a:** © Ralph Robinson/Visuals Unlimited; **7.1b:** Jack Jones/EPA; **Insight 7.1a:** Courtesy of E.E. Adams, Montana

State University/National Science Foundation, Office of Polar Programs; **Insight 7.1b:** © Ralph Robinson/Visuals Unlimited; **7.9a:** © Pat Armstrong/Visuals Unlimited; **7.9b:** Image courtesy Nozomu Takeuchi; **Insight 7.2:** © Michael Milstein; **7.10a:** © Hank Morgan/SPL/Photo Researchers; **7.11:** © Terese M. Barta, Ph.D.; **Insight 7.3a:** © Dr. Ken MacDonald/SPL/Photo Researchers; **Insight 7.3b:** © Mike Abbey/Visuals Unlimited; **7.12:** © Science VU-Fred Marsik/Visuals Unlimited; **7.13a:** Courtesy of Ellen Swogger and Garth James, Center for Biofilm Engineering, Montana State University; **7.17a:** © Kathy Park Talaro/Visuals Unlimited.

Chapter 8

Opener: © Gordon M. Grant/Alamy; **Insight 8.4:** © David Tietz/Editorial Image, LLC.

Chapter 9

Opener: © AP Photo/Jacob Silberberg; **9.1:** © PhotoDisc VO6, Nature, Wildlife and the Environment; **9.3:** © K.G. Murti/Visuals Unlimited; **Insight 9.1 (left):** © A. Barrington Brown/Photo Researchers; **Insight 9.1 (right):** © Lawrence Livermore Laboratory/SPL/Custom Medical Stock Photo; **9.12b:** © Center for Molecular Biology of RNA, UC-Santa Cruz; **9.16c:** Courtesy of Steven McKnight and Oscar L Miller, Department of Biology, University of Virginia; **Insight 9.3:** © Getty Images; **p. 267:** © Eye of Science/Photo Researchers.

Chapter 10

Opener: © AFP/Getty Images; **10.3b:** © Kathy Park Talaro; **Insight 10.1:** © Stephen Jaffe/AFP/Getty Images; **10.8 (left):** © Koester Axel/Corbis; **10.8 (middle):** © Milton P. Gordon, Department of Biochemistry, University of Washington; **10.8 (right):** © Andrew Brookes/Corbis; **Insight 10.2:** © Marilyn Humphries; **Insight 10.3:** © AP Photo/Noah Berger; **Table 10.3 (top):** Courtesy of David M. Stalker; **Table10.3 (middle):** Courtesy of Richard Shade, Purdue University; **Table 10.3 (bottom):** Courtesy of Peter Beyer, UNI-Freiburg; **10.15:** Courtesy of Dr. Michael Baird.

Chapter 11

Opener: © Douglas R. Clifford/Times/Newscom; **Insight 11.1:** © Bettmann/Corbis; **Insight 11.2:** © Stephen Jaffe/AFP/Getty Images; **11.5a:** © Science VU/Visuals Unlimited; **11.6:** © Raymond B. Otero/Visuals Unlimited; **11.8:** Photo courtesy of Dr. Brendan A. Niemira/U.S. Department of Agriculture; **11.10:** © Tom Pantages; **11.11:** © Fred Hossler/Visuals Unlimited; **Insight 11.3:** © Plush Studios/Bill Reitzel/Getty Images RF; **11.13:** STERIS Corporation. System 1 ® is a registered trademark of STERIS Corporation; **Insight 11.4a:** © David M. Phillips/Visuals Unlimited; **Insight 11.4b:** © Kathy Park Talaro; **11.16:** © Kathy Park Talaro/Visuals Unlimited; **p. 326:** © George Chapman/Visuals Unlimited.

Chapter 12

Opener: © Konrad Wothe/Minden Pictures; **Insight 12.1:** © Bettmann/Corbis; **12.2 (top):** © David Scharf/Peter Arnold/Photolibrary; **12.2 (bottom):** © CNRI/Photo Researchers; **Insight 12.2:** © Kathy Park Talaro/Visuals Unlimited; **12.9:** © Cabisco/Visuals Unlimited; **12.15:** © Kathy Park Talaro; **12.16:** © Kenneth E. Greer/Visuals Unlimited; **12.18b:** © Kathy Park Talaro; **12.19:** Etest® is a registered trademark belonging to AB BIODISK, Sweden, and the product and underlying technologies are patented by AB BIODISK in all major markets; **12.20:** Image courtesy David Ellis.

Chapter 13

Opener: © AFP/Getty Images; **Insight 13.1:** © Eurelios/Phototake; **Insight 13.2:** Centers for Disease Control; **13.13:** Marshall W. Jennison, Massachusetts Institute of Technology, 1940; **p. 396 (left):** © Kathy Park Talaro; **p. 396 (right):** © Science VU-Charles W. Stratton/Visuals Unlimited.

Chapter 14

Opener: © John Moore/Getty Images; **14.3b:** © Ellen R. Dirksen/Visuals Unlimited; **14.10d:** © Gunilla Elam/Photo Researchers; **14.12a:** © David M. Phillips/Visuals Unlimited; **14.15b:** Courtesy of Steve Kunkel; **14.17:** © Dennis Kunkel/Phototake; **14.20:** © 1966 Rockefeller University Press. *The Journal of Experimental Medicine,* June 1966, Vol 123, p. 969-984.

Chapter 15

Opener: © Watney Collection/Phototake; **15.11b:** U.S. National Library of Medicine; **15.16:** © Lennart Nilsson, "The Body Victorious"/Scanpix; **15.17 (all):** © Photodisc/Getty RF; **15.17 (right):** © Creatas/PictureQuest RF; **Insight 15.2:** James Gillray (English, 1757-1815), *The Cow-Pock*, Gift of Thomas F. Furness in memory of William McCallin McKee, 1928.1407, The Art Institute of Chicago. Photography © The Art Institute of Chicago. **Insight 15.3:** © Brand X Pictures/PunchStock RF.

Chapter 16

Opener: © Keith Brofsky/Getty Images RF; **16.2b:** © SPL/Photo Researchers; **16.2c:** © David M. Phillips/Visuals Unlimited; **16.5a:** © Kenneth E. Greer/Visuals Unlimited; **16.5b:** © Kathy Park Talaro; **16.6a:** © STU/Custom Medical Stock; **16.10a-b:** © Stuart I. Fox; **16.14:** © Kathy Park Talaro; **16.15b:** © Kenneth E. Greer/Visuals Unlimited; **Insight 16.3 (left):** © Renee Lynn/Photo Researchers; **Insight 16.3 (middle):** © Walter H. Hodge/Peter Arnold/Photolibrary; **Insight 16.3 (right):** © Runk/Schoenberger/Grant Heilman Photography; **16.16a:** © Diepgen TL, Yihume G et al. *Dermatology Online Atlas* published online at: www.dermis.net. Reprinted with permission.; **16.16b:** © SIU/Visuals Unlimited; **16.19:** Reprinted from R. Kretchmer et. al, "Congenital Aplasia of the Thymus Gland (DiGeorge's Syndrome)," *New England Journal Of Medicine,* 279:1295, Dec. 12, 1968 Massachusetts Medical Society. All rights reserved.; **Insight 16.5:** Courtesy of Baylor College of Medicine, Public Affairs.

Chapter 17

Opener: © By Ian Miles-Flashpoint Pictures/Alamy; **Insight 17.1:** NIH Roadmap for Medical Research website—Source: http://nihroadmap.nih.gov/; **17.4b:** © Fred Marsik/Visuals Unlimited; **17.5:** © LeBeau/Custom Medical Stock Photo; **17.7:** Image provided by AdvanDx, Inc.; **17.11:** © Joel Gordon; **17.12:** Genelabs Diagnostics Pte Ltd; **17.14c:** CHEMICON® International, Inc; **17.15b:** © Hank Morgan/Science Source/Photo Researchers; **17.16a:** © Carroll H. Weiss/Camera M.D. Studios; **17.16b1:** © A.M. Siegelman/Visuals Unlimited; **17.16b2:** © Science VU/CDC/Visuals Unlimited; **17.16c1:** © K.G. Murti/Visuals Unlimited; **17.16c2:** © Dr. Linda M. Stannard, University of Cape Town/Photo Researchers; **17.16d:** Rigurat; **p. 511 (left):** © Kathy Park Talaro; **p. 511 (right):** © Kenneth E. Greer/Visuals Unlimited.

Chapter 18

Opener: © Brand X Pictures/PunchStock RF; **18.3:** © Dr. Ken Greer/Visuals Unlimited; **18.4a:** © David M. Phillips/Visuals Unlimited; **18.4b:** © Kathy Park Talaro/Visuals Unlimited; **Insight 18.1(left & second):** © Carroll H. Weiss/Camera M.D. Studios; **Insight 18.1(third):** © ISM/Phototake; **Insight 18.1(right):** © Biomedical Communications/Custom Medical Stock Photo; **18.6:** Analytab Products, a division of Sherwood Medical; **18.8a:** National Institute Slide Bank/The Welcome Centre for Medical Sciences; **18.8b:** © Dr. Ken Greer/Visuals Unlimited; **18.9:** © John Watney/Photo Researchers; **18.10:** © Biophoto Associates/Photo Researchers; **18.11a-b:** Centers for Disease Control; **18.12b:** © Logical Images, Inc. All rights reserved; **Insight 18.2:** © AP Photo/Damian Dovarganes; **Table18.6 (left):** © Phil Degginger; **Table 18.6 (right):** © World Health Org./Peter Arnold/Photolibrary; **18.13:** © Kenneth E. Greer/Visuals Unlimited; **18.14:** © James Stevenson/Photo Researchers; **Table 18.7 (measles):** © Lennart Nilsson/Scanpix; **Table 18.7 (rubella):** Centers for Disease Control; **Table 18.7 (fifth disease):** © Jack Ballard/Visuals Unlimited; **Table 18.7 (roseola):** © Scott Camazine/Phototake; **Table 18.7 (scarlet fever):** © Mediscan/Corbis; **Table18.8 (left):** © Kenneth E. Greer/Visuals Unlimited; **Table18.8 (right):** © Charles Stoer/Camera M.D. Studios; **Table 18.9 (left):** Centers for Disease Control; **Table18.9 (right):** © Science VU-Charles W. Stratton/Visuals Unlimited; **18.15:** © Everett S. Beneke/Visuals Unlimited; **18.16, 18.17a:** © Kenneth E. Greer/Visuals Unlimited; **18.17b:** Reprinted from J. Walter Wilson, Fungous Diseases of Man, Plate 42 (middle right), © 1965, The Regents of the University of California; **18.18a, c:** From Elmer W. Koneman and Roberts, Practical Laboratory Mycology, 1985, pages 133, 134 © Williams and Wilkins Co., Baltimore, MD; **18.18b:** © A.M. Siegelman/Visuals Unlimited; **18.19:** © Carroll H. Weiss/Camera M.D. Studios; **18.22:** © Science VU-Bascom Palmer Institute/Visuals Unlimited; **18.23:** Armed Forces Institute of Pathology; **18.24:** © ISM/Phototake.

Chapter 19

Opener: © Matt Bowman/Getty Images; **19.3:** © Kwangshin Kim/Photo Researchers; **19.5:** © Kathy Park Talaro/Visuals Unlimited; **19.6:** © Dr. Gary Gaugler/Visuals Unlimited; **19.7 (both):** © Gordon Love, M.D. VA, North CA Healthcare System, Martinez, CA; **19.8:** Reprinted from J. Walter Wilson, Fungous Diseases of Man, Plate 21, © 1965, The Regents of the University of California; **19.9a:** Centers for Disease Control/Dr. Hardin; **19.9b:** Centers for Disease Control/Mercy Hosp Toledo OH; Brian J. Harrington; **Insight 19.1:** © Royalty-Free/Corbis/Vol. 124; **19.11:** Centers for Disease Control; **19.14a:** © M. Abbey/Photo Researchers; **19.14b:** © Pr. J.J. Hauw/ISM/Phototake; **19.15a:** © Tektoff RM/CNRI/SPL/Custom Medical Stock Photo; **19.17b:** © Science VU-CDC/Visuals Unlimited; **Insight 19.4:** © AP Photo/Chet Magnuson; **19.20:** © John D. Cunningham/Visuals Unlimited; **19.21:** Courtesy of Dr. T. F. Sellers, Jr.; **19.24:** © Biophoto Associates/Photo Researchers; **p. 583:** Centers for Disease Control/Dr. Leanor Haley.

Chapter 20

Opener: © Nigel Hicks/Getty Images; **20.4:** Centers for Disease Control; **20.5:** © JAMA; **20.7:** © CDC/Peter Arnold/Photolibrary; **20.8:** © Science VU-Charles W. Stratton/Visuals Unlimited; **Insight 20.2a:** © Dwight Kuhn; **Insight 20.2b:** © Science VU/Visuals Unlimited; **Insight 20.2c:** © A.M. Siegelman/Visuals Unlimited; **Insight 20.2d:** © George D. Lepp/Corbis; **20.9b:** © Scott Camazine/Photo Researchers; **20.11a:** © Dr. John Cunningham/Visuals Unlimited; **20.11b:** Research originally published in *Blood.* Peter Maslak and Susan McKenzie, "Infectious Mononucleosis" *Blood.* 2002; © American Society of Hematology; **20.13:** McCaul and Williams, "Development Cycle of C. Burnetii," *Journal of Bacteriology,* 147:1063, 1981. Reprinted with permission of American Society for Microbiology; **20.14:** © Kenneth E. Greer/Visuals Unlimited; **20.15:**

Centers for Disease Control; **20.17:** Courtesy of Stephen B. Aley, PhD., University of Texas at El Paso; **20.19:** © Roll Back Malaria Partnership; **20.20:** © A.M. Siegelman/Visuals Unlimited; **Insight 20.3:** © Thierry Berrod, Mona Lisa Production/Photo Researchers; **Insight 20.4:** © SPL/Photo Researchers; **p. 621:** Courtesy of Steve Kunkel.

Chapter 21

Opener: © Ariel Skelley/Corbis; **21.1b:** © Ellen R. Dirksen/Visuals Unlimited; **21.3:** © Pulse Picture Library/CMP Images/PhotoTake; **21.4a:** Multimedia Library, Congenital Heart Disease, Children's Hospital, Boston. Editor: Robert Geggel, MD. www.childrenshospital.org/mml/cvp; **21.4b:** © Dr. E. Walker/Photo Researchers; **21.6a (both):** Diagnostic Products Corporation; **21.6b:** © Dr. David Schlaes/John D. Cunningham/Visuals Unlimited; **21.7:** Federal Agriculture Research Centre; **21.8:** Centers for Disease Control; **Insight 21.1 (Johnstown):** © Library of Congress Prints & Photographs Division [LC-USZ62-60959]; **Insight 21.1 (1918 flu):** © Corbis; **Insight 21.1 (WWI troops):** U.S. Army Signal Corps/Library of Congress; **Insight 21.1 (Capone, MLK Jr., Kosovo):** Getty Images; **Insight 21.1 (AB):** © ABC via Getty Images; **Insight 21.1 (Carter):** Trikosko, Marion S., photographer/Library of Congress; **Insight 21.1 (Tsunami, swine flu):** © AFP/Getty Images; **Insight 21.1 (stock market):** © Getty Images; **21.13:** © John D. Cunningham/Visuals Unlimited; **21.15:** © Elmer Koneman/Visuals Unlimited; **21.16:** © CDC/PhotoTake; **21.17:** © SIU Bio Med/Custom Medical Stock Photo; **21.18:** © Dr. Leonid Heifets, National Jewish Medical Research Center; **21.19a:** From Nester et al. Microbiology: A Human Perspective, 4th ed. © Evans Roberts; **21.19b:** © L.M. Pope and D.R. Grote/Biological Photo Service; **21.21:** Centers for Disease Control; **21.22:** © NPS photo by John Good; **Insight 21.3 (left):** Centers for Disease Control; **Insight 21.3 (right):** © JAMA; **21.23:** © Tom Volk; **p. 659:** © Jack Bostrack/Visuals Unlimited.

Chapter 22

Opener: FEMA Photo/Andrea Booher; **Insight 22.1:** © AP Photo/Damian Dovarganes; **22.4a:** © R. Gottsegen/Peter Arnold/Photolibrary; **22.4b:** © Stanley Flegler/Visuals Unlimited; **22.6:** © Science VU-Max A. Listgarten/Visuals Unlimited; **22.7:** Centers for Disease Control; **22.8a:** Exeen M. Morgan and Fred Rapp, "Measles Virus and Its Associates Disease," *Bacteriological Reviews*, 41(3):636-666, 1977. Reprinted by permission of American Society for Microbiology; **22.9a:** © PhotoTake; **22.13:** R.R. Colwell and D.M. Rollins, "Viable but Nonculturable Stage of Campylobacter jejuni and its Role in Survival in the Natural Aquatic Environment," *Applied and Environmental Microbiology*, 52(3): 531-538, 1986. Reprinted with permission of American Society for Microbiology; **22.14a:** © David Musher/Photo Researchers; **22.14b:** Courtesy of Fred Pittman; **22.14c:** Farrar and Lambert: Pocket Guide for Nurses: Infectious Diseases. © 1984, Williams and Wilkins, Baltimore, MD; **22.15:** Centers for Disease Control; **22.16:** © Moredun Animal Health Ltd./Photo Researchers; **Insight 22.2:** © Kathleen Jagger; **22.17a:** © Custom Medical Stock Photo; **22.18:** © K.G. Murti/Visuals Unlimited; **Insight 22.3:** © Tom Pantages; **22.19:** © Iruka Okeke; **22.20:** © Ynes R. Ortega; **22.21:** Centers for Disease Control/Dr. Stan Erlandsen; **22.22d:** © Science VU-Charles W. Stratton/Visuals Unlimited; **22.22e:** © Eye of Science/Photo Researchers; **Insight 22.4:** © Sinclair Stammers/Photo Researchers; **22.24a:** © Stanley Flegler/Visuals Unlimited; **22.24b:** Katz et al., "Parasitic Diseases," 1982 © Springer-Verlag. With

kind permission of Springer Science and Business Media; **22.25:** Centers for Disease Control/Henry Bishop; **22.26a:** © R. Calentine/Visuals Unlimited; **22.26b:** © Science VU-Fred Marsik/Visuals Unlimited; **22.27:** © Carroll H. Weiss/Camera M.D. Studios; **22.28:** © A.M. Siegelman/Visuals Unlimited; **22.29a:** © Cabisco/Visuals Unlimited; **22.29b:** Courtesy of Harvey Blankespoor; **22.29c:** © Science VU/Visuals Unlimited.

Chapter 23

Opener: © AP Photo/Honolulu Star-Bulletin, Richard Walker; **23.4:** © Science VU/Fred Marsik/Visuals Unlimited; **23.5:** Courtesy Danny L. Wiedbrauk; **23.6:** © Custom Medical Stock Photo; **23.7:** © David M. Phillips/The Population Council/Photo Researchers; **23.9:** James Bingham, *Pocket Guide for Clinical Medicine: Sexually Transmitted Diseases.* © 1984 Williams and Wilkins Co., Baltimore, MD; **23.10:** © George J. Wilder/Visuals Unlimited; **23.12:** Courtesy Morris D. Cooper, Ph.D., Professor of Medical Microbiology, Southern Illinois University School of Medicine, Springfield, IL; **23.13a:** © Science VU/Visuals Unlimited; **23.13b:** © Martin M. Rotke/Photo Researchers; **23.14:** Centers for Disease Control/J. Pledger; **23.15a-b:** © Science VU/CDC/Visuals Unlimited; **23.16:** © Custom Medical Stock Photo, Inc; **23.17:** © Science VU/CDC/Visuals Unlimited; **23.18:** © Kenneth E. Greer/Visuals Unlimited; **23.19:** © Carroll H. Weiss/Camera M.D. Studios; **23.21:** © Dr. Walker/Photo Researchers; **23.22:** © Chor Sokunthea/Reuters/Corbis; **Table 23.7 (all):** © Carroll H. Weiss/Camera M.D. Studios; **Table 23.8 (left):** © Kenneth E. Greer/Visuals Unlimited; **Table 23.8 (right):** © Charles Stoer/Camera M.D. Studios; **Insight 23.2:** © Martin Rotker/Phototake; **p. 740 (left):** Department of Health and Human Resources, Courtesy of Dr. W. Burgdorfer; **p. 740 (right):** © Science VU/Visuals Unlimited.

Chapter 24

Opener: © Vanessa Vick/Photo Researchers; **24.1:** Reprinted Cover image from December 1, 2000 Science with permission from Jillian Banfield, Vol 290, 12/1/2000. © 2000 American Association for the Advancement of Science; Image courtesy of Jillian Banfield; **24.8b:** © John D. Cunningham/Visuals Unlimited; **24.9a-b:** © Sylvan Wittwer/Visuals Unlimited; **Insight 24.2 (top):** © Gorm Kallestad/AP Photo; **Insight 24.2 (bottom):** © Kevin Schafer/Peter Arnold/Photolibrary; **24.11a-d:** Jo Handelsman, "Metagenomics: Application of Genomics to Uncultured Microorganisms," Microbiology and Molecular Biology Reviews, December 2004, p. 669-685, Vol. 68, fig 3 page 674; **24.13:** © John D. Cunningham/Visuals Unlimited; **Insight 24.3:** © Mark Lewis/Getty Images; **24.16a:** © Dr. David Phillips/Visuals Unlimited/Getty Images; **24.16b:** © Carleton Ray/Photo Researchers; **24.16c:** © Phillip Slattery/Visuals Unlimited; **24.17:** © John D. Cunningham/Visuals Unlimited.

Chapter 25

Opener: © Bruce Chambers, The Orange County Register/Newscom; **Insight 25.1 (both):** © Carl Oppenheimer; **25.2:** © Getty Images; **25.4a-b:** Courtesy of Sanitation Districts of Los Angeles County; **25.5c:** © Kathy Park Talaro; **Insight 25.2:** © Renee Comet/National Cancer Institute; **25.5d (both):** Reprinted from EPA Method 1604 (EPA-821-R-02-024) courtesy of Dr. Kristen Brenner from the Microbial Exposure Research Branch, Microbiological and Chemical Exposure Assessment Research Division, National Exposure Research Laboratory, Office of Research and Development, U.S Environmental Protection Agency;

25.6: © John D. Cunningham/Visuals Unlimited; **25.7:** © Ryan Hatch; **25.8a:** © Kevin Schafer/Peter Arnold/Photolibrary; **25.9:** © Kathy Park Talaro/Visuals Unlimited; **25.10:** © Joe Munroe/Photo Researchers; **Insight 25.3a-b, 25.13:** © Kathy Park Talaro; **25.15:** © Volker Steger/SPL/Photo Researchers; **25.17:** © J.T. MacMillan; **Insight 25.4 (top):** © R H Productions/Robert Harding World Imagery/Getty Images; Insight 25.4a: Giancarlo Ranalli et. al, "Biotechnology applied to cultural heritage: biorestoration of frescoes using viable bacterial cells and enzymes," *Journal of Applied Microbiology*, Volume 98, Issue 1, pages 73–83, January 2005; **Insight 25.4b-c:** © Giancarlo Ranalli/*Journal of Applied Microbiology*; **p. 785 (both):** © Kathy Park Talaro.

Line Art

Chapter 1

Table 1.2: Data from latest "World Health Report"

Chapter 6

Figure 6.9: Detailed Structure of Complex Viruses, from Westwood, et al., Journal of Microbiology, 34:67. Reprinted with permission of the Society of General Microbiology.

Chapter 8

Figure 8.18: The reactions of a single turn of the Krebs cycle, adapted from *Life: The Science of Biology*, 7/e, by Purfes, Sadava, Orions, & Heller. © Sinauer Associates, Inc. Reprinted with permission.

Chapter 10

Figure 10.16: © *New Scientist Magazine*. Reprinted by permission

Chapter 11

Figure 11.05b: From Perkins, *Principles and Methods of Sterilization in Health Science*, 2nd ed. Courtesy of Charles C. Thomas Publisher, Ltd., Springfield, Illinois; **Figure 11.15:** From Nolte, et al., *Oral Microbiology*, 4e. © 1982 Mosby

Chapter 13

Continuing the Case File: Graph is a screenshot from Google Flu Trends. Reprinted by permission

Chapter 15

Figure 15.14: From Joseph A. Bellanti, MD. *Immunology III*. (Philadelphia, PA: W.B. Saunders, 1985). Reprinted by permission; **Insight Box 15.4:** Data from the Organisation for Economic Co-operation and Development; OECD Health Statistics Online Database, 2008

Chapter 22

Figure 22.12: From *American Scientist*, 95:6, 2007; "Safer Salads" by Fonseca and Ravishankar. Reprinted by permission

Chapter 23

Figure 23.11: Data from AVERT organization; **Figure 23.20:** From www.infectiousdiseasenews.com/200007alexander1aCREAM.gif. Reprinted by permission

Inside Back Cover

Figures 1–4: from abstract by Nicole P. Lindsey, MS, J. Erin Staples, MD, PhD, Jennifer A. Lehman, and Marc Fischer, MD; Division of Vector-Borne Infectious Diseases, National Center for Emerging and Zoonotic Infectious Diseases, CDC

Index

Note: In this index, page numbers followed by a t refer to tables, page numbers followed by an f refer to figures, page numbers set in **boldface** refer to boxed material, and page numbers set in *italics* refer to definitions or introductory discussions.

Displaying Disease Statistics

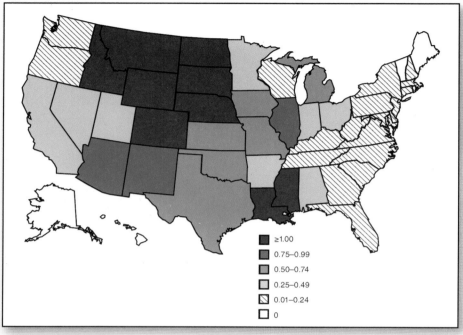

Infectious disease specialists use a number of different methods to visually represent the numbers of disease cases or deaths.

Legend:
- ≥1.00
- 0.75–0.99
- 0.50–0.74
- 0.25–0.49
- 0.01–0.24
- 0

Average annual incidence* per 100,000 population of West Nile virus neuroinvasive disease (n = 11,822), by state of residence—United States, 1999–2008
*Calculated using U.S. Census Bureau population estimates for July 1, 2004.

Some methods emphasize the geographical distribution of disease.

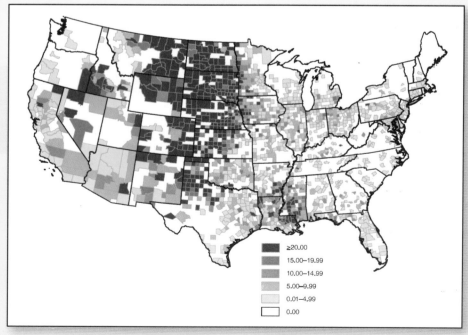

Legend:
- ≥20.00
- 15.00–19.99
- 10.00–14.99
- 5.00–9.99
- 0.01–4.99
- 0.00

Average annual incidence* per 100,000 population of West Nile virus neuroinvasive disease (n = 11,822), by county of residence—United States, 1999–2008
*Calculated using U.S. Census Bureau population estimates for July 1, 2004.